KEN ADAM AND THE ART OF PRODUCTION DESIGN

Ken Adam

and the art of production design

CHRISTOPHER FRAYLING

ff

faber and faber

First published in 2005
by Faber and Faber Limited
3 Queen Square London WC1N 3AU

Published in the United States by Faber and Faber Inc.
an affiliate of Farrar, Straus and Giroux LLC, New York

Typeset by Faber and Faber Limited
Printed in England by TJ International, Padstow, Cornwall

A CIP record for this book is available from the British Library

ISBN 0–571–23109–8 (hardback)
ISBN 0–571–22057–6 (paperback)

10 9 8 7 6 5 4 3 2 1

Contents

Prologue

INT. *The front room of a late Georgian town house in Knightsbridge, late afternoon . . .*

The bright and airy room is also a studio, with a drawing board, a jar of felt pens with flat nibs and twin anglepoise lamps. On one wall is a bookcase, containing histories of art, design and architecture, studies of cinema, volumes about the Second World War – especially the war in the air – and a couple of reference works rescued from Berlin in 1934. The entrance hall has a curving partition instead of a straight wall, which gives that part of the room a 1920s feel even though the partition was in fact designed in the early 1960s. There are plan chests, filing cabinets and a model of a Hawker Typhoon aircraft. Through the window, parked on the street outside, can just be seen a 1959 ivory-coloured Rolls-Royce Silver Cloud 1 convertible.

It is summer 2003. A distinguished-looking man with silver hair, dark penetrating eyes behind horn-rimmed spectacles and a white shirt with the sleeves rolled up, is reminiscing in a slight German accent about his career spanning over fifty years in the film business. He does not waste or mince words – choosing them with great care – and occasionally he takes a puff on a huge Cuban cigar. His memory for names and places is prodigious, and he seems a lot younger than his eighty-two and a half years. He is talking to a man with fair curly hair and a moustache, deep-set eyes and also horn-rimmed spectacles, who is dressed in a smart suit because he has just arrived hotfoot from some committee meeting or speech or other. Beside this man is a green Harrods carrier bag containing papers, notes, Xeroxes, stills and books; a tape recorder plus microphone are perched precariously on a narrow wooden stool between these two men.

The elderly man is KEN ADAM, who has recently become Sir Ken and is widely considered to be the world's greatest living production designer. The other man is CHRISTOPHER FRAYLING, in his mid-fifties and a long-standing admirer of Adam's work as well as a writer and broadcaster on art, design and cinema. They are together preparing this book.

On a wall opposite them are certificates for Academy Awards and BAFTAs; on the wall beside them is a romantic portrait on board of the young Letizia Adam, Ken's wife since 1952. Resting on the plan chest are two Oscar statuettes and more certificates, including an OBE and an honorary doctorate from the Royal College of Art.

I first encountered Ken Adam's work as a film designer – although of course it would be many years before I became aware of his precise role – in 1956 when I was taken as an end-of-holiday treat to see *Around the World in Eighty Days* on the huge 70mm screen in London's Astoria Theatre. It seemed to me the most spectacular film I had ever seen, the most spectacular *anything*. Even the credit titles were animated. To this day, I have to hide my disappointment that London clubs such as the Reform Club are not as huge, as leathery and as velvety as the one in this film – from which the Victorian gentleman Phileas Fogg sets out on his journey and to which he returns from it. Then, a few years later, I watched *Gideon's Day* several times in the cinema of a Greek Line cruise ship called *Lakonia*, which sank soon afterwards, presumably with the colour print of this John Ford film still on board. It was one of only two films on offer, for a two-week cruise, and the cinema was among the few attractions. At least this enabled me to get beyond the story and concentrate on the details. *Sodom and Gomorrah* and *Dr No* were guilty pleasures – in the case of *Sodom and Gomorrah* not quite guilty enough I felt even then – in the sidestreets of Derby, playing hookey for the afternoon from Repton School – a boarding establishment – instead of pretending to be athletic. When the lights came up at the end of *Sodom and Gomorrah*, shortly after Lot's wife, played by Pier Angeli, had turned into a pillar of salt thanks to a so-so special effect, I discovered that by coincidence the Scripture master had been sitting three rows in front of me. He looked startled – for the perfectly innocent reason that it might seem as though he was preparing his lessons on the Old Testament by watching low-grade epics – and said he wouldn't report me for being 'out of bounds' if I didn't spread it around that he'd been seen watching a film called *Sodom and Gomorrah* – a film, by the way, which opens with the immortal line 'Beware of Sodomite patrols.' In an all-boys school, his interest could perhaps be misconstrued. It was a deal. I've kept my word until this day. I have also retained in my mind the sandy, mud-built Moroccan settings of the film itself – so much more persuasive than the grandiose Victorian illustrations in my school Bible. *Dr Strangelove*, seen at the Odeon Kensington a week after it opened, was treated by all my schoolfriends as 'just another Peter Sellers film' but, unusually, one with big American actors in it as well. Even at the age of sixteen I was vaguely aware that the 'look' of the film had played an important part in its impact: and, to judge by the reviews (which I did in those days), the 'look' attracted about as much critical notoriety as Stanley Kubrick's decision to play nuclear politics as a black comedy. In the context of Aldermaston, the Bay of Pigs and Kennedy's assassination *Dr Strangelove* packed much more of a direct punch then than it does now, and I remember that there wasn't much laughter among the capacity audience. At a talk back at school, in the 'Civics' series, by someone who had been personally involved in nuclear tests in the South Seas, I asked a question about what the islanders thought about their homeland being used as a testing ground, and their wildlife as guinea pigs. The reply was that the tests had to happen *somewhere* – before they were banned – if Britain was to keep up in the nuclear race, and the South Seas were as remote as they could legally get. *Dr Strangelove*'s black comedy seemed even less of a comedy after that. But where Ken Adam's contribution was concerned, it was *Goldfinger* that finally did it for me. I saw the film at the Odeon Leicester Square the day it opened, and joined in the general applause when the Korean hitman Oddjob was electrocuted thanks to the metal rim of his bowler hat becoming stuck between the bars of the gold vault of Fort Knox. It was the intrepid James Bond (Sean Connery) who was being applauded – OK, the pay-off was far-fetched and aware of it, but that was part of the fun – but it was also the extraordinarily elaborate set. Before the Second World War, in the theatre the designs of Oliver Messel – the most prestigious stage designer of his day – would often be applauded by West End audiences as the curtain rose. But in the *cinema* this was – for me anyway – something quite new. James Bond's Aston Martin DB5 – with all its lethal accessories, explained in painstaking detail by latter-day boffin Q so we all got the message – was a turning point as well. A history master at school, when I went back the following term, showed me a copy of the magazine *Sight and Sound* for winter 1964, which featured an article on 'Three Designers' – the first of whom was Ken Adam – with reproduced preliminary sketches from *Dr Strangelove* and *Goldfinger*. After that, I began to make a mental note of his name on credit titles and to notice his distinctive contribution. I even went to the local library in Wimbledon to ask for a book – any book – about film design. There was just Edward Carrick's *Designing for Films* and that seemed to me a pedestrian 'who does what' information guide. Even today, you could count the significant film design books – as distinct from catalogues – on the fingers of one hand and still have a digit or two to spare. After *Goldfinger*, I saw every one of the fourteen films designed by Ken Adam, between 1964 and 1979 – the year of *Moonraker* – on their first runs. And talked about his work with my friends studying architecture: it was, at that time, well beneath their visual threshold. Later, when they relaxed and started *Learning from Las Vegas*, they changed their tune. Puritanism, Classicism and Modernism were out; *joie de vivre*, eclecticism and postmodernism were in (even after *Las Vegas*, 'isms' persisted). I found myself sometimes comparing Ken Adam's *Führerbunkers* with Giovanni Piranesi's fantasy *Carceri* and the overpowering proportions of Etienne-Louis Boullée's concept for *Newton's Cenotaph* (1784) – prisons on the one hand and utopias on the other, just like the dual functions of the twentieth-century Adam style in the movies. I was researching 'Art and the French Revolution' at the time. Meanwhile, I was able to view the back numbers – notably *Captain Horatio Hornblower RN*, *The Crimson Pirate*, *Night of the Demon* and *The Trials of Oscar Wilde* – on television. There was something very special about Ken Adam's work – not just the James Bond creations – something which drew attention to the increasingly important role of the production designer, which encouraged me to concentrate on films as a visual – rather than literary – experience (even though everyone else was encouraging me to concentrate on the literary) and which took me into secret places which, even if they don't really look like that, ought to. And with the Bonds there was a definite *progression* in his design work from *Dr No* right through to *Moonraker*, something unique in modern cinema. There was no doubt in my mind. This was the most gifted, innovative and masterly designer working in – not only British films, but in films anywhere. I wasn't sure what a production designer actually *did* – and how this might differ from the art director's role – but I knew that some films had a visual coherence, while others most certainly didn't.

INT. *Royal Albert Hall, Kensington Gore, midday*
It is the Convocation ceremony of the Royal College of Art, at the beginning of July 1995, and Ken Adam is receiving an honorary doctorate. The Public Orator – Christopher Frayling – is delivering the citation from a wooden lectern on stage right of the hall. Behind him are four hundred art and design graduands. In the audience, among the many hundreds of parents and partners and brothers and sisters and friends are Letizia Adam and Nigel Hawthorne, who has recently appeared as George III in *The Madness of King George*. Ken Adam is standing slightly uncomfortably in the middle of the stage, wearing his scarlet-and-burgundy robes.

'I don't know about you, but the things I remember most about films are not so much the lines of dialogue as the visual images. The lines of dialogue which tend to be immortalised in history books – "Play it again, Sam"; "Come up and see me sometime" – are actually tricks of the memory: they were never said by anyone. But the images stay in the mind, in focus, for ever. Images such as the monochrome Lloyd's of

London with the "names" all dressed in black and white, and the waiters in scarlet, in the otherwise full-colour *Around the World in 80 Days* (1957); the antique and modern villain's headquarters – with the Goya Wellington propped up on an armchair – in *Dr No* (1962); the huge triangular Pentagon War Room with its giant poker table and light ring in *Dr Strangelove* (1963); the Aston Martin DB5 – complete with such essential accessories as an ejector seat, an oil-slick squirter and a wheel scythe – in *Goldfinger* (1964); the London warehouse which looks like an East European prison in *The Ipcress File* (1965); the missile launcher hidden beneath a lake and inside a Japanese volcano – the largest set ever constructed in Europe – in *You Only Live Twice* (1967); the English baronial hall full of tricks, mechanical dolls and automata in *Sleuth* (1972), which many thought was a real National Trust country-house interior; the astonishing candle-lit eighteenth-century rooms – all from *real* country houses this time – in *Barry Lyndon* (1975); the mammoth supertanker which digests into a single compartment three nuclear submarines in *The Spy Who Loved Me* (1977); the 1930s city of the night, inspired by painters and photographers of the period, in *Pennies from Heaven* (1981); the weird gingerbread-gothic interiors belonging to Morticia and Gomez in *Addams Family Values* (1993) – no relation, I am assured – a lasting homage, in three dimensions, to the celebrated *New Yorker* cartoons; and the mixture of the historical and the stylised in *The Madness of King George*, a film which was originally entitled *The Madness of George III*, but whose title was changed for fear people might think they'd somehow missed the first two parts *George One* and *George Two*. Hidden within this astonishing list of some of the grandest illusions in the history of cinema are two Oscars (one this year), three Oscar nominations, two British Academy Awards and five further nominations; and standing before you, stirred – no doubt – but we hope not shaken, is the man responsible for designing every single one of them - a mere selection from the sixty-five films with which he's been involved. For it is Ken Adam who supplies for us today the answer to the age-old question: "When Adam delved, and other span, who was then the gentleman?" He was, and that is why we are honouring him today. Nothing, it seems, is beyond our Ken. As a favourite industry one-liner put it: "Adam created James Bond seven times over; Bond did not make Adam." Another, in reply to the question: "Who is the real star of James Bond – Connery, Lazenby or Moore?" was: "The real star is Ken Adam." Quite right. The fruit of his tree of knowledge has been ripe, and very tasty, for nearly fifty years.

'Born in Berlin, where he must surely have seen *The Cabinet of Dr Caligari* at an impressionable age, he moved to his adopted home in

England in 1934, studied architecture at the Bartlett, served as a fighter pilot in the RAF's 609 Squadron, and entered the film industry as a draughtsman just after the Second World War. Since then, he has – in the words of one critic – "contributed more to the success of British post-war cinema than anyone else, with a list of credits as a draughtsman, designer and artistic director on feature films which is hardly credible". And he's even found time to design – outside the cinema – everything from espresso bars (with names like "The Gondola" and "The Harlequin") in the 1950s, to an historic and still revived production of Puccini's *Girl of the Golden West* at Covent Garden in the late 1970s, which attracted a well-deserved fistful of accolades. The Cabinet of Dr Adam – Dr Adam, after today – is, indeed, incredibly full. The man himself is far too modest and sensible to admit it, but he is a key contributor to twentieth-century visual culture and a very influential one. His trademark as a designer has always been a form of architectural stylisation which has been called "theatrical realism" or "hyper-reality by design". He has even been called "the Frank Lloyd Wright of *décor noir*".

'The work of the art director and production designer is often undervalued in writings about film, in favour of the director, the writer or the star. But today – in this year of the centenary of cinema – we state categorically, in a misremembered quotation from *Gone With the Wind* – the first film incidentally to feature a production designer on the credits – we state: "Frankly, my dear, we do give Adam." And we give him an honorary doctorate of the Royal College of Art.'

At that same convocation, immediately afterwards, the distinguished art critic David Sylvester received a senior fellowship. He later wrote that my 'oration in Ken Adam's honour brought home to [him] that no one had been more important for the popular arts in Britain in our time'. So over lunch, the idea for an exhibition at the Serpentine Gallery, curated by David – the first ever exhibition to be devoted to the work of a production designer in a major art gallery in the UK – was hatched. And so, indirectly, was this book.

CREDITS: Ken Adam and the Art of Production Design *is based on over thirty hours of tape-recorded conversations, which took place in Knightsbridge between June and November 2003. These have been supplemented where necessary by various taped question-and-answer sessions – including a two-and-a-half hour marathon at the RCA in Spring 1995 on my 'Grand Illusions' course, during which Ken Adam was quizzed to exhaustion by a lecture theatre full of eager industrial designers, architects, interior designers, fashion designers, graphic designers, illustrators, interaction designers and engineers. I am deeply grateful to the subject of this book for his generosity, patience, good humour and for his argumentativeness; also to Letizia Adam for her constant encouragement and support. Over the past nine years, I have dined in style – at the Adams' table – with several of the film directors who feature in Ken Adam's reminiscences. Thanks, too, to Philip French, with whom I have had many stimulating discussions over the years about the 'Adam style'; and to successive generations of postgraduate art and design students who have constantly re-evaluated Ken Adam's designs from their own individual perspectives and have often proved to be 'the ones, the ones with the Midas touch'. End of song, beginning of story . . .*

All the pictures in this book are from Ken Adam's personal archive unless otherwise credited.
*Stills courtesy of BFI Posters, Stills and Design. Copyright for the stills are held by the following: Warner Bros. (*Helen of Troy, Barry Lyndon*);*
*United Artists (*Around the World in Eighty Days*).*
James Bond materials courtesy of Eon Productions, copyright United Artists.
Special thanks to the Serpentine Gallery.
Opening image of Ken Adam and Christopher Frayling © Ute Langkafel

1 Growing Up in Berlin and London

Berlin

CHRISTOPHER FRAYLING: *I want to start by reading you a quotation about your work written by Donald Albrecht, who is exhibitions curator at the Cooper Hewitt Museum of Design in New York: 'While perfecting his craft as a production designer, Ken Adam conjured a celluloid universe where he exorcised the evil spirits of his youth.' And then he talks about how your work is, in some way, getting your youth out of your system; the emphasis on Expressionism, the emphasis on* Führerbunkers *where masterminds live. Is there any truth in that?*

KEN ADAM: Well, I must say, Expressionism definitely influenced me since I saw *The Cabinet of Dr Caligari*. And early architectural studies in London when I was very interested in the architect Erich Mendelsohn. My second boss at the architectural firm where I worked had been an assistant of Mendelsohn's, and we talked a lot about it. That certainly influenced me. But consciously, that was the only influence, really. I loved the way *Caligari* was designed and, you have to remember, I was never sure, in my early days, whether I wanted to be a stage or film designer. To me *Caligari* was exaggerated, but it really showed me what one day I was hoping to achieve in film design. In other words, a theatricalisation; using film to create a reality that in effect was not.

Ken Adam in front of his ruined family home, Berlin 1958

So it was both real and theatrical at the same time.
Yes. That idea – without any doubt – influenced me.

You've designed so many places where the villains intent on world domination live in these bunkers; what Albrecht is suggesting is that in some way you're getting the Nazi period out of your system. You don't feel that consciously?
Well, no, I didn't feel that consciously because I always treated it tongue-in-cheek, with a sense of humour, going bigger and more dramatic. But I don't think it was a result of any persecution. Sure, the world was traumatised by Hitler, and this had an effect. Particularly in the Bond films, where we always had a villain who wanted to conquer the world or even space. But I think it was an instinctive thing. The only time I took it seriously was on a film like *Dr Strangelove*. With hindsight, I think my design of the War Room was successful because it expressed so well the dramatic concept of the script. It was probably the best design I ever did.

Grandparents' apartment, with Lilli
Adam holding her firstborn son Peter,
Berlin 1914

We'll get to that, and to a bizarre link between Dr Strangelove *and your childhood. Let's start then with your birth on 5 February 1921 in Berlin, the Tiergarten Strasse, number 8. Evoke for us the place you lived in; it was a large, elegant apartment . . .*

In Berlin itself you very rarely had houses. The only big villas were in the Grunewald. But my family had one of these enormous Berlin apartments where the rooms were sixteen foot high. The Tiergarten Strasse was at that time the most prestigious area in Berlin where most of the embassies were situated, and it was known as the Old West. The Kurfürsten Damm area was known as the New West. My family were unfortunately rather snobby so if some of my school friends were living in the New West I was not allowed to visit them.

Was this like 'old money' and 'new money'?

Yes, I think it was. Also, I don't know why, but I think the Jewish community in Berlin were terribly snobby and were only exceeded – which I found out only recently – by the Hamburg Jewish community! We were brought up quite strictly. My mother was very frugal and she didn't like to spoil us in any way, whereas my father was much more easygoing and tried to give us anything we wanted. I was never conscious of being brought up in a beautiful apartment.

Can you remember the décor? I have this vision of panelled rooms with antique furniture.

Yes, but a lot of it was phoney antique too. There was a great feeling of

2

'Herrenzimmer' in the Berlin apartment

Italian Renaissance furniture. The table upstairs is part of that. It's very beautiful. It's supposed to be from the Palazzo Davanzati in Florence but it's obviously a copy. There was neo-Renaissance furniture and neo-Gothic writing desks and low-hanging chandeliers. The apartment had a large dining room that could fit thirty-six people, and we had a circular table which could pull out. My mother had silver for every type of party, and glasses; my father was a wine connoisseur and we had a big wine cellar. I remember, when those big parties were given, the thing that impressed me most were these golden chairs that were hired for the guests to sit on!

The cultural theorist Walter Benjamin came from the same quarter but from an earlier generation. In one of his essays he wrote about the décor of these apartments as a cocoon in which a particular class protected itself from the world; does that ring true?
Yes, that rings absolutely true. You had a big dining room and then you had a salon. Our salon was very beautiful because it had a gigantic Aubusson carpet and beautiful crystal chandeliers and some very nice eighteenth-century furniture; it was very elegant. The dining room was designed by a firm of interior decorators who at that time were *le dernier cri*. The bedroom of my parents was designed by the same people. The dining room was ivory coloured with this faded rose damask panelling. It was very beautiful, and so was the salon. Then there was the *Herrenzimmer* – I don't know what you would call that in English. A room for gentlemen.

3

Dining room in the Berlin apartment

A retiring room?
Yes, a retiring room or a smoking room, which had my father's writing desk. It was rather bland. Rather heavy and dark-looking. Then there was a study for my father. All these rooms were facing the front. German apartments are built around a courtyard so you have the front section and then you have the two wings going round the courtyard. The entrance lobby was rather glum.

With a big staircase I imagine. Which floor were you on?
We were on the second floor.

So you'd have had grand staircases . . .
They weren't very grand, but they were very typical of Berlin; they're marble and they go round an elevator, which is normally wrought iron with glass doors. And that elevator goes through the whole building. But the staircase was not like some of the sweeping spiral staircases that I later designed.

That's what I'm driving at, because you have this total recall of the visual environment you grew up in and I'm exploring the connections.
But eventually – don't ask me why – I became fascinated by Georgian architecture and these sweeping staircases and so on. Maybe because of my time at the Bartlett School.

4

Some of the Modernists loved Georgian architecture because of all the geometry and classicism rather than ornament and decoration. But there weren't many white walls and straight lines in your apartment; Modernism was going on outside, not indoors.

Not in our apartment, no. But the funny thing is that in 1928 my father asked Mies Van Der Rohe to design a new store for him.

I was going to get to that, because your father Fritz inherited the family store S Adam, a very fashionable sports and fashion house at the corner of the Leipziger Strasse and the Friedrichstrasse, one of the busiest intersections in Berlin.

Yes, it was like Piccadilly Circus, only much more fashionable . . .

So for a lot of your early life you had connections with a fashion and sports house where there were famous explorers and movie stars, connections with the media of the day. In fact, I believe your father advised on some sporting movies such as Die Weisse Hölle am Piz Palü/'The White Hell of Piz Palu' *and Friedrich Wilhelm Murnau's* Schloss Vogelöd.

Yes, and on *Das Wunder des Schneesschuhs/'The Wonder of Ski'*, so he was very much aware of the publicity value of equipping films and expeditions. For example, he equipped Roald Amundsen's aerial expedition to the North Pole. I was introduced to Amundsen one day when he came to tea! Also, I remember noticing as a child that some of the window displays, particularly as it was Christmas time, were mechanical: mechanical skiers and so on. It was fascinating to see that. Even though the building was constructed in 1863. My father was really a very modern man.

As you say, there was this correspondence with the architect Mies Van Der Rohe in the late 1920s to knock down this 1863 building and presumably put up a glass-and-steel building in the Bauhaus style – the latest thing. But this never happened.

No, it didn't. It would have been a steel skeleton supporting huge glass panels – a tower of glass. And my father was a bit of an adventurer too. He was a very good family man and a good husband and he adored his children. He always liked to surprise us by arriving in a plane at our country place even though he didn't pilot it. But he was also interested in aeronautics because he was one of the very first passengers on the airship *Parsival* before the First World War.

And there was a famous reception in the 1920s for the German fliers that crossed the Atlantic.

The S. Adam store, around 1910

Mies van der Rohe design model
for the proposed new store, 1928

I remember that extremely well because all of us four children were present at the first reception in front of the store. I was the third child, born after Peter and Loni. Dieter followed me in 1924. We were all there at the store. Then there was the reception at the Kaiserhof – a famous hotel in Berlin – for the aviators, one of whom was a German aristocrat and another an Irish Major called Fitzmaurice. I remember meeting one of the daughters who had a big teddy bear, so I was fascinated by all that. My father did a lot of those events. He arranged one before that for Jackie Coogan.

When Chaplin's The Kid *opened?*
Yes. In December 1928, when Jackie Coogan visited Berlin, the store gave a reception in his honour at the Hotel Adlon.

6

You were photographed dressed up as 'the Kid' next to Coogan himself. You seem to have been touching the movie world very early on in life.
Yes, but I was not really aware of it. Also, we weren't allowed to go to the cinema; my mother Lilli insisted that we go to the theatre. One day I was allowed to see a nature film. I'll never forget it; it was called *Chang*. I remember a horrible scene in which a tiger fights with a python. But on the whole I could only see films such as Charlie Chaplin's at children's parties. My mother preferred me to watch plays by Schiller at the Deutsche Theatre or *White Horse Inn* at the Grosse Schauspielhaus.

It sounds as if most of your visual experiences as a child weren't really from the world of Modernism at all. The things we associate today with Berlin in the 1920s – did they touch you at the time?
No, not really. But growing up at that time, in a cultured family, and with an older brother, Berlin in the 1920s was the foundation of my future education – it must have been part of me: the Berlin of Max Reinhardt and Elizabeth Bergner, of the modern architects, of the painters Groz, Otto Dix, Klee and Kandinsky and so on. I remember one personal experience, though. There was one building not far from the Tiergarten apartment which was designed by the architect Emil Fahrenkamp, and that impressed me enormously. I was watching it going up and I always went past it to see the progress. It was the Shell House, designed in the new functional style. I knew something of the architecture of Gropius and Mendelsohn, but no, I can't say that consciously it had a big influence on me.

So you grew up as Klaus Hugo Adam in fashionable Berlin and also in a summer house in Bellin on the Baltic Sea, next to the Stettiner Haff, an inlet of the Baltic. When did you start drawing?
I started drawing at six or seven, and I was very good at copying. I could literally copy anything. I was afraid of expressing myself a little bit. When I did my first imaginary painting of a stag in a green field, I was very proud of it and I showed it to my uncle. He said it looked like spinach with egg, which completely destroyed me!

What sort of things did you copy; were they technical drawings?
No. They were portraits and paintings and drawings, but not technical stuff. My hobby was building things and making models.

Meccano and so on?
Yes, I did have a Meccano set as a child, but that didn't interest me so much. I preferred doing it right from scratch, like building models of ships and aeroplanes. In the Baltic the sea used to freeze over in winter

Jackie Coogan (centre) with Klaus Adam (front right) and his brother and sister in front of the S. Adam store, December 1928

Dressed as Jackie Coogan

Klaus Adam's sketch of his Typhoon
aircraft, April 1944

time and one of the sports was ice sailing so I built my own ice yacht. It
was very simple; a cross with a pair of skates on each extremity, and
then on the back, where I sat in a box, I connected string to a skate
which would swivel. And I put a mast where the cross intersected. You
could get up to speeds of seventy or eighty kilometres an hour.

Like a boxcar on ice.
Yes, and very dangerous because the ice had holes in it.

All this presumably happened in your Baltic summer house . . .
Yes. Apparently, according to my family, I had an incredible imagination
because I would swear I'd seen a tiger or a lion or something. Even
when I had a temperature I was inventing the most incredible things
that I saw in my mind; the curtain became organ pipes. I was absolutely
fearless in a way. At one time a troupe of gypsies came through with
dancing bears and so on, and I disappeared with them. My parents had
a heart attack trying to find me. But I loved that. So my father, bless his
soul, always thought: *This boy is not going to be an academic, and I'm
not sure if he's good enough to be an artist – in any case being an artist
might lead to a life of poverty – so he's going to inherit the country
estate.* He felt I was going to be a landowner, a farmer or something.
But he was never sure about me. I was also very difficult because I was
introverted. I didn't have the confidence to express my own imagination.

You went to school at the Französisches Gymnasium on the Reichtag-

Klaus Adam (at front) in his canoe,
Stettiner Haff 1929

sufer – which was unusual because the language they used was French for all the subjects except maths, so you were speaking French all the time – almost an aristocratic thing to do.

Yes, because all the ambassador's children were there. They had a few girls there too, but they must have been daughters of the military attaché or something like that. I think there were only two schools in the whole of Germany that sustained that standard of education, and they're still the same. One was the Französisches Gymnasium, which was founded by the Huguenots in the seventeenth century, and the other one is called Das Graue Kloster, which is still there today.

Also in Berlin?

Also in Berlin. They had a very high standard of education and some very famous people went there as a result. The Französisches Gymnasium really was the last one that resisted the Nazis. I was very lazy as a pupil, I must say, also because I had some of the most brilliant friends who I convinced to write or copy or whatever. When I eventually came to St Paul's in England I found I had to do these things myself!

But some of your fellow pupils – there's quite a roll call: Freud's three grandsons, Max Reinhart's son and, in a senior form, Wernher Von Braun. Which is the most astonishing historical irony; that he should be at the same school as you.

He was older though, and had recently left when I arrived.

And the son of a Prussian aristocrat, who was also Minister of Agriculture.

There were quite a number of Prussian aristocrats. My brother Peter was seven years older than me. When I started at the bottom of the school he was in the top form. They were a very famous form, all very brilliant, and strangely enough very liberal, left-inclined. Peter was certainly the most intelligent and most cultured child of the family, and he had constant battles with my father. My brother could see what was happening in Germany but my father could not. They were continuously at loggerheads. My mother could also see what was happening in Germany. Peter studied law in France so he was outside Germany in 1932. From a foreign country he had a much better perspective of what was happening in Germany. When he came back, because my parents had this gigantic bed, the whole family would have breakfast in bed on Sundays. And I'll never forget my brother saying, 'Well I think the time has come when the two kid brothers will have to go abroad to either France or England to carry on with their education.' My father was livid.

Apart from your visual interests, did you have a good art teacher at the Gymnasium?
Not really. I remember making a copy of Vincent Van Gogh's painting of the peasant dressed in blue in art class, and I became the centre of attention. But the art teaching wasn't up to much. I was able to draw rather well though.

What were your literary interests? Did you read much?
Yes, I read enormous amounts, according to my father. I found a letter which he wrote to the headmaster: 'I don't know what to make of Ken. He writes poetry and reads three books at a time.' But I think I was more interested in Karl May's novels of the Wild West than in serious literature.

Well, there are many volumes of those.
I read all the children's books: Karl May, Fenimore Cooper, Erich Kastner's *Emil and the Detectives*. And there was a famous cartoonist called Wilhelm Bush. I had seen all his books. My mother was more intellectual. She used to read to us at night. Then I read Grimm's fairy tales and Andersen's fairy tales and then some of the best-known works by Schiller, like *Maria-Stuart* and *Die Räuber*. My brother was much more cultured, but of course he was older.

So we're in the late 1920s now; can you remember the first time that the rise of the Third Reich impinged on you personally?
Yes, when somebody shouted 'Jew Boy' at me on my summer holidays. I was absolutely destroyed because I didn't know what was wrong with me. Unfortunately, or fortunately – depending on which way you look at it – I didn't have a Jewish upbringing. I did not understand what 'Jew Boy' meant. My parents had to explain it to me back home.

It was not a religious household?
Not at all religious. My parents were married at a Liberal Reformgemeinde and I was never bar mitzvahed or circumcised. Nor my younger brother, whereas my older brother was. It was always a strange thing. I had never even seen the interior of a synagogue. My family were assimilated and open-minded and we celebrated Christmas like everyone around us. So I didn't know what it meant to be 'Jewish'. For this to be used as a term of abuse hit me personally. And especially from village boys who I considered my friends.

That would be in the late 1920s? Maybe early '30s?
I would say early '30s.

There was another incident at the Potsdamer Platz . . .

Well the big thing at the Potsdamer Platz was the Christmas market. Again, we celebrated Christmas as only Christmas can be celebrated: with a gigantic tree which my father used to get into the apartment. Then the night before, 24 December, he entertained all the staff around the tree. We were never allowed to see the tree until Christmas Eve. I was going around the market at the Potsdamer Platz with my sister when someone grabbed hold of her head, pointing out that it was 'a typical Aryan skull'; she had blonde hair and grey eyes. I didn't have the slightest intention of changing his mind.

For a child to be exposed to that. And I suppose that by 1933 there were uniforms on the streets.
And uniforms also in the classroom. There was a boy who we thought was not quite normal – he was the worst pupil until he arrived in boots and Hitler Youth uniform. But we couldn't take him seriously. And then my maths teacher, Herr Winter – a ghastly man – came in wearing an SS uniform. He was a real sadist. He was not a nice man. Instead of rapping my knuckles with a ruler he twisted my cheek, running his ruler through it, which was very painful. But such people were few and far between at the school so I didn't take anti-Semitism that seriously at the time, though I hated what was happening. And also you kept seeing these open police trucks full of Nazis who would beat people up. It was quite traumatic.

And you saw the Reichstag burn down on the way to school one day.
When I saw it on the morning of 28 February 1923, it was just smoke and ruins. It had actually burnt down the night before.

Your brother Peter, who was interested in socialism, was saying, 'Watch out'; your father was saying, 'Just sit tight. It'll be OK'; while your mother was much more sensitive towards your changing circumstances.
Much more sensitive. She was unbelievably courageous because I used to go shopping with her to thc market – she loved to go shopping – and she used to make the loudest anti-Nazi remarks. I grew up very quickly and said to her, 'You mustn't do that. You'll get us all in trouble.' You didn't know who was going to give you away at any moment. Even your own staff. At dinner you had to go more and more into French or another foreign language so they wouldn't understand. A real case of 'Pas devant les domestiques . . .'

Was there a moment when the penny dropped? When the family realised this was serious?
Yes. That was Christmas 1933. What happened on Christmas Eve was that my father disappeared into another room with my mother's brothers

for a talk amongst the men. After their meeting he had tears in his eyes. It was the first time I ever saw my father cry. That was a terrifying shock because we were a close family. So we knew that this was really serious. Christmas was always our biggest celebration with most of the family present. And there was my father, with tears in his eyes.

The family business had hit hard times before. In 1932 there was inflation, depression, unemployment . . . Berlin was changing too.
I think my father made some financial mistakes. He had a lot of money invested in property, and in those days the whole property market collapsed, so he lost a fortune. And the strange thing was that my older brother was a brilliant businessman but he never invested in any property. He could have been a multi-millionaire just after the war, but he never put a penny in it.

So the family business collapsed . . .
The business had collapsed in 1932. My father, who was an unbelievable optimist, decided to launch a new store called Sport Adam in January 1933: a much more modern store, a block away on the Leipzigerstrasse. But then the boycott started and that completely destroyed him. The shop windows of boycotted Jewish stores were covered in vicious slogans. My father got arrested too.

That happened at the summer house?
In the country, yes. He was arrested by the local police, although there was no proof of any wrongdoing. They called it '*untersuchungshaft*': being on remand. The irony of it was that, through the intervention of a department head of the new store – who was in the SS and adored my father – he was released after forty-eight hours. There was no proof of anything, but that was the last straw, the writing on the wall. On Christmas Eve 1933 he realised that we had to leave Berlin.

London

Then, in April 1934, accompanied by your mother and your younger brother Dieter, you became a refugee at the age of thirteen. Had your older brother left earlier?
A year or so earlier. He went to France and found it very difficult to get the family to follow. Remember he was twenty years old or thereabouts, so he was a young man. Fortunately we had an English aunt called Constance Hoster who was quite well known in London; she was originally a suffragette and had opened the first secretarial college

in Grosvenor Place. The girls that were trained there were known as 'Mrs Hoster's girls'. They were normally diplomatic secretaries. She adored my older brother Peter and she helped us get to England and introduced my brother to the people at the Home Office, and so on because it was very difficult to get visas to organise our emigration to France or Holland. It was because of Aunt Connie that we went to England.

Wasn't there a refugee organisation in Woburn House that master-minded this?
The committee for Jewish refugees at Woburn House gave us some help. Peter obtained the visas and, with Aunt Connie, found suitable schools for us. A minor public school near Edinburgh accepted Dieter and myself. Aunt Connie paid for Loni's education. In April 1934 my mother, Dieter and I left Hamburg by steamer and, via Grimsby, arrived in Scotland, where my mother deposited us at this tiny little school. It was a pretty awful experience because we weren't used to the British habit of opening every window in mid-winter.

Plus you didn't speak a word of English.
Not a word. And my mother had left us there. She spoke very little English herself. We went to a terrible hotel in Edinburgh where you had to go outside to the loos. It was terrifying. So I was very worried about her, and once she'd dropped us off she had to go back to Germany. I was very worried about both my parents at this time. Very protective. Then being introduced to not the best type of public school system in Scotland, where a lot of quite terrifying things happened to me. I was not very popular, particularly with the prefects and seniors. I remember going swimming and they were ducking me under the water. I thought I was going to drown.

Aged 14 in front of 80 Greencroft Cardens

Like an initiation ritual?
An initiation ritual, yes. So I was very unhappy. Then my parents moved with my sister Loni to London in June 1934, and I felt I had to be near them to protect them. I developed a complete neurosis. My mother realised that she couldn't keep me in school there so she got me out, and my younger brother and I came to London.

So you went to another prep school called Vernon House. Was that in London?
It was in Willesden. That's where I learnt English. That's also where I met David Sylvester – later the art critic – who was in my form. He was a weed of a man and we didn't take him very seriously because he was collected by his parents to and from school, whereas I went on a

bicycle. He has a lot of interesting things to say in his autobiography about me, because apparently I was very popular in class. We had an excellent headmaster. The essential thing he taught me was always to look up when you're walking down the street or in the park because people miss so much: 'Always look up and get an overall view of things.'

Be observant?
Yes, be more observant. That's where I really learned English. It was a happy time. I was quite happy there.

And you sat the Common Entrance Exam there, to go to St Paul's in London?
That's right.

Why did they choose St Paul's do you think? Were they turning you into an English gentleman? You had to wear a uniform presumably in those days?
Yes, but so did the school in Scotland; they had to wear top hats on Sundays. St Paul's had a very good reputation, particularly if you didn't want to go to boarding school. There was Harrow, Eton and Winchester. I remember when I was fencing we challenged Eton to a match and the reply came, 'We know Harrow, we've heard of Winchester, but who are St Paul's?!' All this took a lot of getting used to.

I have an image of this young man in a bowler hat, black jacket, striped pants, umbrella – better at English than you used to be – being moulded in the image of an English gentleman.
Yes, particularly when you became a senior and wore a boater. We had wonderful teachers, unbelievably good teachers, so I found the standard of education was very similar to the Französisches Gymnasium. And some of my classmates from Berlin were at St Paul's too; I think the Freuds were there and quite a number of other people. I really took to the system of being taught to think for yourself in combination with sport, because in Germany that didn't exist. OK, you had gym classes in Germany, but games . . .

No team sport?
No team sport at all. You didn't play football, you didn't play rugby, you didn't play cricket. You didn't play any of those games. Whereas this became a very important part of my education.

What of your father, at this time?
It was a sad story. He found it difficult to adjust to the new circum-

stances of being a penniless immigrant. In Berlin, my father had always tried to protect my mother from unpleasantness. He did not want her to worry about anything. But in London it was she who helped us to survive in those years. The roles they played were reversed. He tried to make a living as a representative of some Czech sock and glove exporters – but he found it very difficult to start again from scratch. He was a broken man, Christopher. Because he had lost everything, including the money in Switzerland that, as a good German, he had taken back to Germany. So he lost that too.

Because the regime asked everyone to be a patriot.
Yes. And he could never re-adjust. Now it's a cliché, but he was a German through and through. He came out of the First World War much decorated, very respected in social circles in Germany. He had been a cavalry officer with the Furstenwalder Uhlans and was decorated several times on the Western Front. He was one of the few Jewish cavalry officers to be decorated with the Iron Cross. So, as he said, 'I remain a German and I think German.' But suddenly it was my mother's turn to be strong. She always was strong, but my father would not allow her to touch anything in Germany. He never got over the fact of being forced to leave. Once he was a respected member of Berlin society. Now he was an unsuccessful glove salesman.

Your mother ran an upmarket boarding house in Hampstead at this time . . .
Right. A boarding house in Greencroft Gardens, Hampstead. She knew from Berlin how to run a large household, and her guesthouse became a meeting place for immigrants to London. Meanwhile, my father was selling gloves from a suitcase. I used occasionally to go with him to a buyer. To see this great man at the mercy of these buyers: it killed me. And then he had a weak heart. I remember both of us running to catch a bus and he couldn't breathe when we got on it. All these things were really traumatic for me. So was his death because it needn't have happened. Today he would not have died. Two days before, my mother took him to our local doctor who said there was no need to worry about his heart. So when he had this bronchial attack we had no medication to give him. My mother said to me, 'Ring the doctor,' and it took an hour for the doctor to come. I was with my father when he died and I could see that he didn't want to die.

This was on 17 January 1936. He was fifty-six.
Yes.

The year of the Olympic Games, which in different circumstances he would have supplied. Meanwhile, at school, the art class provided something of a haven for you. You had a good art teacher and so for the first time your individual talent was encouraged in class.

Yes, he was wonderful. I think his name was Steers or something, and he encouraged me. I also think he thought that I had talent. So when it came to what in those days was the Oxford and Cambridge School Certificate, I got a distinction in Art. And that's how I got into London University.

Rather than going to the Slade or to an art school, you chose to go to an architecture school for evening class, aged seventeen.

Yes, as an external student. I tell you, I think it had something to do with Vincent Korda, who I met through a Hungarian painter staying at the boarding house. His name was Gabor Pogany and he later became a famous cameraman living in Italy. He was painting Hungarian restaurants and so on, and the Kordas said, 'Stop painting and work for us in films.' So he became an assistant focus-puller or something like that, and he introduced me to Vincent Korda at Denham Studios. When Vincent was told I would like to get into films eventually, he said to me, 'Well, even though I had a painting background, I think the best background for somebody who wants to become an art director in films is to study architecture. You don't have to qualify but you have to have an architectural background.' So that's why I went into architecture.

When you went to Denham, the Kordas were shooting Knight Without Armour *with Marlene Dietrich and Robert Donat. Did you meet Marlene?*

No.

Pity, because there's a rather good scene in a bath.

Yes, but I wasn't allowed to go near the actors!

Already at that age you were beginning to work out your career. It is interesting that in the golden age of Hollywood most of the art directors where architecture-trained. A lot of them were immigrants from Europe, from northern Europe, and they brought their native styles of architecture to the Hollywood studios. The director Ernst Lubitsch once observed of the inter-war era, 'There is Paramount Paris and MGM Paris and RKO Paris and Universal Paris and of course the real Paris. But Paramount Paris was the most Parisian of all!' One of the great lines about the days of the 'supervising art director'. But, as you say, Vincent Korda was unusual in that way because he was a painter. In fact, he sometimes arrived on the set in a Van Gogh straw hat, espadrilles and denims, looking like a painter. Van Gogh the craftsman.

That I didn't know.

It happened on Things to Come! *He was himself unusual but he was giving you very good advice, because the normal way in was through architecture.*

I would say that a good 70 to 75 per cent of the art directors I knew – British art directors – were either ARIBAs or FRIBAs; they had all come from architecture. And whether it was Carmen Dillon, or Ralph Brinton, or John Bryan, they all came from an architectural background. Whereas the stage designers didn't, like Oliver Messel or Roger Furse.

Or Hein Heckroth, Michael Powell's designer?
He was German.

But was he an architect or a painter?
A painter. He was a protégé of Alfred Junge. But I'm not sure if he came from an architectural background as well.

Were you still at St Paul's when you met Vincent Korda?
Yes, I was still at St Paul's. Vincent said he always felt, up until his death, that he was responsible for my career, which is not strictly true. But he was responsible as far as his advice was concerned. Get an architectural background – history of architecture, design, composition, draughting – all very useful. That's why I enrolled at the Bartlett, University College, London. It had been difficult because my father had long been dead and my mother had fought to get us into St Paul's, but now I was at university in the evenings and in the daytime I was articled with a firm of architects called C.W. Glover & Partners.

While you were doing the course? Was it a requirement?
Yes. I spent three years at university and with C. W. Glover & Partners, and both experiences were very important. In Glover & Partners I had a big firm of architects and civil engineers. He was a genius on acoustics.

Mr Glover?
Yes, Captain Glover. from the First World War. I had to illustrate a lot of his books about gas masks and air-raid shelters and all that sort of thing. His junior partner was a man called Quine-Lay, and he was the one who had been associated with Mendelsohn and was very much Bauhaus-orientated, very modern in his thinking. The progressive university in those days was the Architectural Association, whereas the Bartlett, which was run by Professor Richardson – we used to call him Dickie – was much more traditional, extremely traditional. But it was wonderful for me because being there from six-thirty in the evening to ten-thirty at night, five or six times a week, I managed to get all the big

professors to deal with me. I had the run of the place. And I think they were also a little fascinated by me because I was very rebellious in those days; Bauhaus-orientated. I almost had to laugh when for four weeks I did my testimony studies for the RIBA examination – the project was to design a country house – and Richardson came round to see my work one evening. I can't say it was a Bauhaus type of building but it was a reasonably modern project. After spending twenty minutes with me there wasn't a line left. He had gone through the whole lot with red pencil and then said, 'It's interesting, but if you want to pass your inter-RIBA I suggest you design in a style like Queen Anne or Georgian.' I was a little upset, obviously, after four weeks of work. But it was my other boss at Glovers, Quine-Lay, who kept pushing me. He said, 'Don't let them get you down.' He was the one who wrote a verse about me:

> Adam, so we are told,
> Suffered a bit from a cold.
> Now he has taken to wear
> Post-impressionist hair
> And a tie with a surrealist fold!

To some extent Glover was one of these fantastic English people who was very much aware of immigration and the misery of the immigrants and he was a do-gooder. When I was supposed to be interned on the Isle of Man – I suppose it was towards the end of 1940 – my mother said I couldn't be interned because I was working on wartime stuff – munitions factories, air-raid shelters and so on – which Glovers had to do. I rang Glover up and he said, 'They can't intern you. I'm going to ring up Scotland Yard.' When they came they collected my younger brother Dieter instead, who could hardly speak German, and locked him up on the Isle of Man. But I wasn't interned. Dieter was sixteen years old at the time. But I carried on with Glover. They had a job to provide the whole of the St Pancras area with air-raid shelters. It meant that some of their staff had to knock on every door and go in, and I think they could have one of three types of shelter: an Anderson shelter, a Trench shelter if they had a garden, or strengthening of the basement. My job was to decide what they were going to have, but my experience of St Pancras in 1940 was that people were very suspicious of my German accent. Glovers said they would pay me half a crown for every shelter I designed. Well, I made a lot of money and they finally decided I was making too much!

You made a Trench shelter for Greencroft Gardens, which you designed and made yourself.

That was a disaster. I had help from an ex-German cavalry officer from the First World War in riding boots, who was a boarder in my mother's boarding house. I must have underestimated the shoring up of the dug trench. Also, in Hampstead, where we were living, it was raining throughout that winter and I probably didn't put enough struts in, or something, because one night it collapsed. That was my first ever architectural job.

So there was a mixed bag of people staying with your mother in Hampstead?

Yes, from all over Europe: Austrian, German, Czech, Italian, Hungarian. In hindsight I think I probably learnt more during the period in my mother's boarding house than I did in a university or school. She was still able to bring all her furniture over from Berlin so we had a dining table at which every evening twenty-six people were sitting round, and they had to be there sharp at seven o'clock; my mother was very much a disciplinarian. And I was listening to the conversation of all these people. They were psychiatrists or famous lawyers or famous musicians or artists. I met a complete mixture of people, listening to their sometimes ghastly experiences, but I was learning so much about life, which I would never have done under normal circumstances. My mother's dining room was like a university to me.

I guess much of the discussion was about what was happening in Germany. Did any of your family stay behind?

Yes, a part of the family. They did not want to believe that in the land of Goethe, Schiller and Beethoven, anything bad could happen to them. None of them survived the war. Uncle Paul and Aunt Kaethe were deported to Riga concentration camp, and Aunt Emmi took poison in Theresienstadt when she discovered she was about to be deported to Auschwitz.

Meanwhile, in your spare time between your evening class and working in the day, you assisted one of the members of the MARS group. Was that connected to the boarding house?

Yes, that was Raldi Weinreich, a young architect who was a member of the Modern Architectural Research Group of refugees in London. He wasn't staying at the boarding house but he was a friend of somebody there, and I knew he had a studio in Hampstead. He asked me if I wanted to help him with his drawings over the weekends. He was a very good designer, and of course that interested me too.

I'm keen to delve deeper into the Bauhaus influence on you. One of the Glover partners had worked with Mendelsohn and was a great fan, you

worked with the MARS group, and you grew up in a city where Mies Van Der Rohe designed a shop for your father . . .
Yes, but I didn't realise that at the time.

Even in the 1930s, though, you were steeped in the Bauhaus but colliding with rather tweedy British architecture in the evenings. Did you study the Bauhaus at this time?
No.

Did you look at the architecture magazines or Mendelsohn's buildings?
I looked at Mendelsohn's buildings, but mainly when I came to this country, through Quine-Lay. There were also some Bauhaus architects building in Frognal, Hampstead. There was a modern building and I used to go and see it. So I was interested, yes, no doubt about it, but I learnt more about the Bauhaus when I was in England.

Do you think the Bauhaus philosophy influenced you? In one way the Bauhaus is a long way from your philosophy; everything very functional, straight lines, appropriate materials, fitness for purpose . . .
But Mendelsohn himself didn't always use straight lines!

He did many non-functional things. But I've always classed you as an Expressionist more than a Modernist.
Yes, but with me they went very much hand in hand. On one hand there was film and theatrical design, in which expressionism influenced me very much, and on the other there was modern architecture, in which I was influenced by the Bauhaus. So yes, expressionism influenced me. Because with films like *Dr Mabuse* and *Caligari* I could see that a group of artists had designed the backgrounds; they were completely unrealistic but were unbelievably dramatic. That fascinated me and excited me. I saw those films, and Lang's *Metropolis*, shortly after I arrived in England. They made a great impression. There was always this uncertainty within me. Do I want to be a designer in films, or do I want to be a designer in the theatre? Eventually, of course, I think I managed to get the best of both worlds because I tried wherever possible to treat film design with theatrical overtones, a stylisation of reality.

Certainly there's a Bauhaus influence; you like modern materials, you like using glass, steel and metal. And you think 'less is more'.
Yes.

And this combination of straight lines and decorative features that you get in the Bauhaus. But they were quite severe. There was a kind of Puritanism.
But Mendelsohn didn't care two hoots if he used tons of concrete to

make a shape, even though it didn't have a functional purpose.

I've never thought of you as a Puritan, Ken.
No, no.

'Ornament is a crime'? 'Over elaboration is suspect' . . .
It's interesting you should say that because the longer I am alive and meeting critics and people like that – and even now, working for some new media people – the more people think I'm a minimalist. I've never believed in over-decoration.

And everything is justified.
Everything is justified by just a few lines. It's not only me. My wife Letizia, quite independently though we are a unit, has always been a minimalist herself. Maybe when we got married and her trousseau was a lot of baroque Italian furniture and so on, I liked the squiggles, I liked the ornamentation. It quite appealed to me, but it didn't last very long. You find that in period films I always try to make a point with just a few typical items of the period. Whether they are decorative or dressing, I always try to make a point for the scene.

Your sets are never cluttered.
No.

You mentioned that at the Bartlett there was a big emphasis on Georgian architecture, and in the late 1930s the British emphasis on Georgian architecture was a kind of Modernism; very geometric, very classical, obeying the rules, big rooms with high ceilings and a few well-placed things. It's sparse compared with the Victorians and the Edwardians.
Absolutely.

It must have been a very interesting time in the mid to late '30s because Walter Gropius came over in 1934 and stayed a couple of years, and many of the Bauhaus refugees came to London and almost found a niche, but not quite. There was a moment when it looked as though they'd settled. But then they found there wasn't much interest in England. Their experience of fighting traditional architecture and not getting commissions demoralised them. So they went to New York and Chicago and the Bauhaus happened there. Did you feel any of that at the time?
Yes, because I remember the Bauhaus buildings that were put up in London were attacked unmercifully. And of course there was the contrast in my life between the Bartlett and the MARS Group.

In Old Church Street, Chelsea, there's one Mendelsohn and one Gropius. The press hated them at the time. In a way, I think the

Bauhaus ideas were confined to specialist magazines and intellectuals in Hampstead. Critics and the public were way behind.
Yes! The son of Sigmund Freud, who was a friend of my mother, was an architect. I used to see him quite a lot.

Sigmund Freud?
Yes.

In Hampstead?
Yes. So I did meet quite a number of architects. Also Pogany, who had introduced me to Vincent, came from a very famous family of Hungarian architects. His father had designed the League of Nations in Geneva. So I tended to mix in those circles.

Did you read all the latest architectural journals?
I didn't read that much.

It's terribly sad. Moholy Nagy, a great artist, filmmaker and sculptor, ended up doing window displays in Simpson's, Piccadilly.

I know.

And Lubetkin created the penguin pond at London Zoo.
But it was brilliantly done!

If they'd stayed it could have changed the course of British architecture, for better or worse.
You see it much more in Los Angeles and California. A lot of the Bauhaus architects created a niche for themselves there. The last house we had in Malibu was designed by Richard Neutra. They're priceless, those houses.

They're classics.
England was very far behind. I think the Architectural Association was more advanced, but of course the situation changed completely. In one way the war helped me because it prevented me from studying for more than three years. I might have become too rigid and too influenced by the practical applications of architecture.

2 609 Squadron
Pilot Training

Then, in October 1940, after the outbreak of the Second World War, you joined the Auxiliary Military Pioneer Corps, which was a branch specifically for exiles and refugees.

I think Britain was very clever, or perhaps it was Churchill, because they used only ex-diplomats or ex-career officers, retired, to become the staff officers of this organisation. Since I had Officer Training Corps (OTC) training at St Paul's they immediately gave me two stripes as a corporal and I was put on the training staff in Ilfracombe where the headquarters were of the AMPC. I remember Sir Gerald Boles, who used to be Governor of Bermuda, and ex-cavalry officer Major Stork. Lord Reading was First Commanding Officer. They were all of high intelligence. It was just as well because they had a mixture of twenty nationalities and some very famous people: opera singers and Coco the Clown and famous lawyers, painters and actors. I was very much aware of that because I was only eighteen years old. I had my two stripes and a lot of authority and these people used to come up to me and say, in very broken English, 'Corporal Adam, I knew your father back in Berlin. My family is in London. Can you use your good services to get me a weekend pass to London?' And so on. And I saw the irony in this. Another time I went to the recruiting officer and he was expecting fifty or sixty French Foreign Legionnaires who'd been evacuated from Narvik and needed English military training. So my first job was the responsibility of taking French Foreign Legion troops, some of whom had been at Verdun, you know, down to Ilfracombe.

You were just eighteen.

Yes, a snotty young corporal. The nine or ten months I spent at Ilfracombe were another education for me, because to meet all these different nationalities of varying backgrounds . . .

An education in how to manage people, when to hold back and when to intervene. That's a very hard lesson to learn and I guess you learnt very quickly.

Very quickly.

Particularly when to stand back.

Absolutely, I was wise enough. I was unwise, though, on one occasion when I flirted with the Colonel's daughter and was not discreet enough because I was walking with her on the promenade of Ilfracombe when

I was supposed to be training somebody, so I was arrested. Actually the Colonel was a lovely man. It was after Lord Reading had left, and he said he couldn't have me socialising with his daughter, especially since I was meant to be training some people. But he said he'd let it go if it never happened again. Then much to my surprise, and I'll never know if he was partly responsible, I got my transfer to the RAF. Mind you, I applied regularly and I was always turned down. I feel in the back of my mind that my Colonel had something to do with it.

A tactical retreat! To rewind, everyone says they can remember where they were when Kennedy was shot and the day that war was declared in September 1939; can you remember?
Yes, I was staying with my mother in Hampstead and we were listening to the radio. And then I remember there was an air-raid siren shortly after the declaration of war. That was one of the most frightening moments, having seen the Spanish Civil War and films like *Things to Come*. One immediately expected billions of planes bombing London.

What did it feel like as a German émigré in London, declaring war on your home country? Did it feel like that?
No, we were delighted because we hated the Nazis. Even in those early days we had news that a cousin of mine – his mother got a letter – was shot trying to escape a concentration camp. So one knew what was going on. Remember, my father had died in 1936 as a result of everything that had gone on in Germany. Also, we all had to pass a tribunal, and myself and my brother were passed as friendly aliens. Except after Dunkirk and all that disaster everybody panicked, and anyone who came from Germany was an enemy alien. Even Germans today often ask me did I feel any qualms when I attacked German soldiers during the war. I say, 'No, I didn't.' Apart from anything else, when you're flying in a single-seater fighter aircraft, you are not in contact with the death you create on the ground. You're very much in contact with the death of your friends who are shot down or crash in flames, but not with the people on the ground. By that, I mean the military. Obviously, we didn't attack any civilians. But, having said that, even if I had been eye to eye with it, I'd decided that we'd got to win the war and we'd got to get rid of Hitler and the Nazis. The first real shock I had, and my first encounter with mass death, was when my squadron – my flight in particular – were stationed on an airstrip in France. In those days we were probably the most powerful close-support weapon the army had, with our rockets and air-to-ground attack aircraft. We were continuously attacking the Germans who were trapped in the Falaise Gap and preventing the British and Canadian Army from getting out of the bridge-

With Volkswagen staff car captured at
Falaise, July 1944

head. So we had to destroy them. I was very much involved in those
attacks and they were annihilated. Churchill made the famous statement about the massacre we caused. Twenty-four hours later my commanding officer asked me if I would like to have a look at the
battlefield. I said yes.

We used to work one flight on, one flight off, twenty-four pilots, so
my twelve boys and myself started driving to the front in a truck, which
was horrific even then because the roads were blocked by armoured
cars and tanks and so on. We moved at a snail's pace and soon we were
engulfed in this ghastly sweet smell of death. The first things I saw were
the animals that were killed; horses and cows, their legs rigid in the air
with rigor mortis. The smell, Christopher. You have no idea. We all put
handkerchiefs in front of our faces. After about an hour and a half – it
was only around the corner really – we arrived in Falaise. All the dead
bodies were still there. They were all SS divisions, which I particularly
hated, but to see these bloated bodies and the smell was something I've
never forgotten. We found a Volkswagen and there were two SS men in
it. I had New Zealanders and Australians and Canadians with me who
were much tougher than I was, so they kicked the bodies out of the VW

and asked me to drive it back to base. Which I did. And I had it almost for the rest of the war, but I could never get rid of the sweet smell of death. We tried everything – disinfectant and so on. I've never forgotten that smell. So that was really the first and only time I confronted it directly.

It is extraordinary that early in 1941 you joined the RAF. You were under twenty-one, you had a German passport, your younger brother Dieter was interned on the Isle of Man; you had everything against you getting in. But you sailed into the RAF and stayed there from 1941 to 1945 as probably the only German fighter pilot. Until your brother Dieter eventually joined the RAF you were the only one who had a German passport. You really wanted to fly. Is that what was behind this?
Yes, fly. And also have the opportunity to do something active, not because I was particularly courageous but because we kept hearing about these thousands of Jews and displaced personnel being transported to concentration camps by train. And they were incapable of defending themselves. Also by this time I knew that some of my uncles and aunts had been taken to concentration camps. I said, 'This is my big chance to do something more active.' It was those two things, without a doubt. Already when I was at the Bartlett I tried to get into the university air squadron. I instinctively knew I was a good pilot. I was what they call a natural pilot, a born pilot. I proved that too.

How did you know that, because you hadn't even got a driving licence?
No, but I had a motorcycle!

I have this image of you in Berlin in the late 1920s in a store that specialises in sports goods. You're meeting all these great sports pioneers, aviators, all these people who loved speed. So that's in your blood. But how did you know you were a natural pilot?
I don't know. I think the only thing I was afraid of – because I remember some of the Channel crossings – was getting seasick. I said to myself, 'Oh my God, what if I get airsick?' But fortunately I never did because I was so fascinated. I loved aerobatics and all that, it was a further expression of myself because . . . It's difficult to explain because I don't think I would have made a good bomber pilot. Like I met people in trains who were submariners and they said, 'You're up 20,000 feet? You wouldn't get me up there.' And I said, 'Well, do you think you'd get me 800 feet under the water?!' The feeling of being in a single-seater fighter, that is hopefully a good machine, and being in complete control of every function – aerobatics, firing, throwing the thing around – is an incredible sensation. You are either natural with that or you are not. Remember that a lot of people failed. On my course in America they'd

just come into the war after Pearl Harbor and we were mixed up with the American cadets. We were over a thousand. Since I was an NCO I was placed in charge and a lot didn't make it. They didn't even become pilots. They became navigators or air-gunners or bomb aimers or they were eliminated from the course. Some committed suicide because they were so upset about that.

About not making the grade?
Yes.

You started your training in Scotland.
Right.

So you sign on with the RAF and they send you to Scotland for initial training?
No, they first sent you to an initial training wing at Scarborough, where you learned drill, a lot of PT and a certain amount of square-bashing and theoretical navigation, radio, Morse code. Once you passed that you went to 11EFTS in Scotland, where you had your first experience in flying a Tiger Moth. It was a terrible winter and we had skis fitted under the Tiger Moth to land. Again, I was very fortunate. I had an instructor who was a Battle of Britain pilot, a typical Battle of Britain pilot. I adored this man. He taught me everything he knew. Except they suddenly decided to post all of us to Canada because they didn't have any more training facilities in this country. So then we went to Canada.

England, then Scotland, then Canada . . .
Yes. I'll never forget crossing the Atlantic on an armed merchant cruiser. And there were a lot of us: eight hundred. We were very valuable cargo so we had two destroyers accompanying us all the way. The ship was called the *Letizia*, the name of my future wife.

How extraordinary.
It had one anti-aircraft gun and these destroyers gave you a lot of confidence – the way they were shepherding you around. But on its next trip the *Letizia* was sunk by German U-boats. In any case, we arrived safely in Halifax and from there we went to a place called Moncton. It was in June of 1942, and it was incredible because we could already smell the pine trees of Canada a hundred miles from the shore. The Canadians were wonderful to us. We had beautiful food which we hadn't seen in England.

No shortages, no air-raid shelters . . .
Nothing. Also I think I wangled my posting a little bit because I had a girlfriend in New York and I didn't particularly want to stay in Canada

In front of Stearman aircraft, Lakeland Florida, August 1942

With John Garfield (centre), Tampa Terrace Hotel Florida, August 1942

for my training. I knew there was an American training scheme called the Arnold's scheme that was training a number of British cadets to become pilots. So I wangled a posting there. It took me three days to get from Moncton to Lakeland, Florida, where I started my proper flying training.

A small group of English people and a large group of Americans?
Yes.

This would be in summer 1942?
Yes. In fact, before we went to Lakeland they sent us to Turner Field in Georgia. Because the heat was unbelievable and we had to get acclimatised.

Mainly American flyers?
Yes, and they all came from military academies at that time. They had a completely different background to us because there was very strict discipline there. When you had such a mix of ethnic people there, they had to have strict discipline.

You say 'a mix of ethnic people', but Florida and Georgia in 1942 can't have been exactly multi-racial. Were there any black pilots?
No, not at all.

So multi-ethnic means American, British, Italian, Irish, Hungarian ...
America was a melting pot. On the contrary, when I was in Alabama we were not allowed to go in the black quarters, and if we were found there we were immediately eliminated from the course. It was terribly racist on that level.

In Florida you apparently met John Garfield?
Yes.

He wasn't in the army; he was making a movie.
He was making a movie called *Airforce*. We had every second or third weekend off and we used to go to Tampa, Florida; there was a beautiful hotel, Tampa Terrace Hotel, which was a bit of luxury for us, even though it was very cheap. John was staying there for the filming of *Airforce*, so I got friendly with him. I was already interested in films so he took me under his wing and told me stories about filming and Hollywood and so on.

It must have seemed incredibly glamorous after three years of war.
Yes. And one of my instructors was an ex-English film star called Michael Rennie.

Good Lord!

Very good-looking. He was one of the RAF instructors. At Lakeland, Florida, most of them were civilian instructors because it was a civilian school. At basic, which was Cochrane Field in Georgia, they had military instructors. I'm not sure whether Michael Rennie was at Cochrane Field or at Lakeland.

In the fifties Michael Rennie appeared as The Third Man *on television after being an intelligent alien in* The Day the Earth Stood Still.
Yes.

He was older than I thought then.
But very good-looking.

He could never act but he looked good.
Never could act, no. We knew that even then!

So you learned the basics about aerial combat.
Yes, before you learned flying by the seat of your pants, as they say. I always passed above average and from Lakeland I went to Cochrane and from there we started flying monoplanes, BT13As. Then we started learning more: night, cross-country and instrument flying and so on. I hated that. The only advantage in the United States, because my navigation was never any good, was that if you got lost in the daytime all you had to do was go down to a water tower and you saw the name of the town written on it. So you never got lost. At night-time we flew along these light lines from town to town, but when I eventually came back to England I hadn't the faintest idea where I was. Because in England one town merges into another town. Thank God we had good controllers with good radio contact.

Can you remember any of the tricks of the trade they taught you? Did they simulate situations like how to cope with an aerial duel?
Yes, but they were obviously not as experienced as the RAF, who had all that experience from the Battle of Britain. The Americans had only just come into the war. They were very good pilots, because most of them had been pilots all their life, so they certainly knew everything about flying and aerobatics and forced landings – which we had to do. But aerial combat we learned more at advanced, which was in Alabama – Dothan and Elgin Field, Alabama. We started firing guns. We were flying Harvard AT6s and shooting at drones towed by towing planes. That's where you learned something about aerial combat. AT6s were almost like fighter planes.

There's this dual thing going on because you love the flying but you don't particularly like the authority. When you were training were you

always kicking against authority?
Yes.

*And I sense even in your description of it now, that you slightly resent-
ed being pushed around.*
It's funny how you notice, Christopher. I wasn't going to talk about it,
but on one occasion, when we were at elementary, we had a lieutenant
who was our physical-training instructor. He had bulging muscles
everywhere and he was a bit of a sadist. His name was Lieutenant
Albano. I'll never forget it. On the last day of elementary training he
wouldn't give us the day off to go into town because somebody had
done something wrong and he was punishing us. Myself, some American friends, and certainly two or three of my RAF friends, decided we
were all going out, but we all had to stick together. If we all got out and
all came back through the main gate, and didn't try to get over the
barbed wire, then we'd be OK. Everyone agreed. But what happened
was a lot of people got drunk and of course they tried to get through
the barbed wire, the electrified wire, and sheriffs started firing at them.
Thank God nobody was killed, although one person was hit in the foot.
I went through the gate and straight into the British barracks. Lieutenant Albano was too scared to come into the British barracks, but he
went into the American barracks and ordered everybody, at about two
in the morning, out on the concrete in bare feet and drilled them for
two hours. When I heard about that I said everybody should report
sick, as they did. Albano got into serious problems, but at the same
time they sent down an RAF Group Captain who said to the so-called
ring leaders, 'You can't do that sort of thing.' Lieutenant Albano was
really a nasty piece of work.

*It's so funny hearing you talk about it. Even now the resentment comes
through.*
Yes, God did I resent him! But I knew that if we all stuck together then
we'd get away with it. If you don't then you get court-martialled or you
get eliminated from the course. He did that fatal error of drilling four
hundred young American pilots in bare feet on the concrete. They all
had blisters and so on. Terrible. Every time we were posted to the next
airfield, the Commanding Officers would take us aside because they'd
heard about our reputation and tell us not to try anything like that
again. We were much better that time, very good, and we had a very
good relationship. It was just that first time. Although when I passed
the elementary training with flying honours – on Stearman PT17s I
think they were – I went solo after four hours and then did something I
shouldn't have done. There was a famous girls' college nearby which

Graduation photo Napier Field, Dothan Alabama, February 1943 (KA third from right)

was called Wesleyan, and on the last day I decided to shoot up the college, which meant doing aerobatics and coming down low. I was the first one; some of the others followed me. But by that time the headmistress got pissed off and started taking numbers. And, of course, everybody had their number taken except me. It was very tragic. But fortunately they never got my number!

Presumably things like this were on your file, so they must have followed you round. They might even have held you back?
Yes, I think they did. I was always above average. I was a cadet officer and I graduated with flying honours. Then I went to New York after graduation to visit my uncle who showed me off everywhere. I came back and I should have automatically become a pilot officer or a second lieutenant in the RAF, because first we got the American wings and then the RAF wings. But when I came back from leave, my Commanding Officer called me in and said they'd received a telex from British Air Staff Washington: 'Pending further investigations, aviation cadet K. H. Adam will revert to the rank of sergeant pilot and should be posted back to the United Kingdom.' Up to this present day I have never found out why. We all thought it may have had something to do with me being a German, or that my father had been in the German army in the First World War. But who knows?

When did you become Ken, rather than Klaus or K. H. Adam?

31

It's a very good question, and one that I cannot answer because nobody in the RAF – those that are still alive when I go to the reunions – knew me as Ken. I had changed my name for security reasons; if I was shot down I didn't want Klaus Hugo Adam so I had changed it to Keith Howard and I put an 's' on Adam. Keith Howard Adams. The Gestapo would have found out very quickly who I was. But not Ken. Ken must have started with the first or second film I worked on, because somebody decided it was too difficult to call me Klaus and started calling me Ken.

So it wasn't you? It wasn't a conscious decision?
I can't remember. Even at the last reunion three months ago my Commanding Officer heard about the knighthood and said, 'But what is your name now?' To us you are Klaus!' My nickname in the RAF was Heinie – the *Daily Sketch* in September 1944 called me 'Heinie the Tankbuster'. The people at the reunion said, 'Make up your mind'.

Cutting from *Daily Sketch*,
September 1944

Let's talk about your return. You'd had this good time in the States, so you were used to eating good food and not being under bombardment; it must have been difficult to adjust to austere British wartime conditions. Also you were being demoted. No commission.
Yes, it's amazing. If this hadn't happened I probably would have been an instructor in California or Arizona, which wouldn't have been bad

because I was already interested in films. But at the same time I did have that urge to do something active against the Nazis. So I was upset about being demoted. And we had a terrible crossing on the *Queen Elizabeth*. Fortunately the *QE* was fast – it took us six days to get to Scotland – but I had all my stuff stolen on the first night. So I went all around the ship trying to find somewhere to sleep. I found an empty room next to the captain's cabin and most of the time I stayed there! In any case I arrived in Scotland and was sent to Number 55 OTU in Annan, to do some further flying training on Masters and Hurricanes. That was when we really learned about aerial combat.

Were you interested in the design of the planes, or did you treat them as purely functional?
By now I was a plane buff. But funnily enough I was mainly interested in what the plane could do. I have a very good ear for the engine – if something's gone wrong or isn't quite right. I've never lost that, even though I never understood the mechanics. I had an Australian friend who was eventually killed, but he spent all his spare time when he wasn't flying Typhoons looking at this incredible 24-cylinder Napier Sabre engine. He knew every bit of it. I never did but I could hear when something was wrong. So that aspect of it, I was very lucky. I just made the plane do what I wanted it to do. I was in control of that plane. But when something goes wrong and you're not in control, you panic, you know.

Aerial Combat

What happened after OTU in Scotland?
Well, much to my surprise, on 1 October 1943 I was posted to the top-scoring single-seater fighter squadron in the RAF's 11 Group, the 609 West Riding Squadron. It's motto: 'Tally Ho!'

Flying Hawker Typhoons?
Yes, Typhoons.

Which were one of the most advanced flying machines of their day.
In those days they were. They were fantastic planes: very powerful. You could fly at 8,000 feet at over four hundred miles an hour. Typhoons were powered by a 24-cylinder liquid-cooled engine, around 2200hp. But the new pilots never had much of a chance to attack the few enemy planes that were around, so we were more often used on ranger operations where you had to fly across the English Channel at zero feet, hop across the radar, and then attack German trains, or whatever. The first

Climbing into a Typhoon cockpit before attacking tanks, July 1944

33

time I was on a weather recce there were two of us sitting in our planes at Manston at five in the morning. The sun started rising, we had a signal, and then we crossed the Channel and flew over the French coast. Of course I was shot at and I knew it had to be me – which wasn't a comfortable feeling. To be there and to know that everybody is shooting at you, it's rather like – I used to shoot pheasants and things like that – a pheasant shoot, only everybody on the ground is using *me* for target practice! It was an unpleasant feeling. That was the first time I ever came into contact with enemy fire.

As you say, you were more of a fighter type than a bomber type.
Yes, I would never have been a bomber pilot. Speed was second nature to me and I had split-second reactions. It's an unbelievable feeling. I was a good pilot and so to be in charge of a machine all on your own and make the thing do what you want it to do is to be the king of the air. You quickly learn – otherwise afterwards, of course . . . It was exciting to be a fighter pilot, whereas I don't think my psyche or my courage would have suited bombers. I'm someone who, on the spur of the moment, can be very courageous, but I have not got the temperament to face danger for hours. Strangely enough one of the first people to congratulate me on my knighthood was Ossy Morris, the well-known cameraman, who was a famous bomber pilot in the Second World War. I always used to talk to him about sitting for eight or nine hours in these big crates. I don't think I would have had the courage. But he said it's surprising because there was a crew of eight or nine people and you could talk to each other, but as the captain you had responsibility for them all. But I was alone, by myself. It was fantastic to join the top-scoring fighter squadron with all these aces around, but they were very protective. They gave me the oldest plane! It was very difficult to get on 'a show' because most fighter work was over by that time, and any chance to shoot down a German was always taken by a squadron commander or someone higher. If you want to talk about these experiences, Christopher, we can certainly talk!

It obviously relates to your later career in that you love speed, you love technology, and you liked living dangerously. And your wartime experiences were just as hair-raising as the adventures in the films you later designed. When you were with 609 Squadron it was 1944 so you were supporting the Allied troops. When was the first time you saw real action?
Well, I had seen action on escort duty for American medium-sized bombers and I was very keen in those days. I thought, here I have the best fighter in the world with four 20mm canons. I'm king. Then you

quickly wake up to the fact that you are not king. One of my first experiences was escorting American Marauders on a bombing raid to Abbeville in France. But after the briefing I was the last pilot to my plane and it didn't have long-range fuel tanks. I thought I would be all right. We were just going to fly there and back, a journey of an hour and twenty minutes. The first problem was that the American bombers couldn't find us at our rendezvous point twenty thousand feet over Beachy Head. When they did, we'd been circling for ten minutes and then finally we managed to go to the French coast, but as I was flying on main tanks my engine started cutting out. It's not funny because I had to switch over to reserve tanks, and what often happened is you got an airlock; you had a problem to start the engine again. You had to do all sorts of things to get the propeller turning. So I'm now on reserve tank and I call my commanding officer – who was a lovely man called Thornton Brown – and I said, 'I'm on reserve now, will I be OK?' And he said, 'You bloody fool, reduce your revs and get a homing on the radio. Try to glide as much as you can back to England.' So I had to turn around. Luckily I got a fantastic homing to Manston and, as I landed, my engine cut because I was out of petrol. I later found out that Thornton Brown and two other pilots were bounced by a high-level American escort – which we knew about but nobody took any notice of – who decided we were German Focke-Wulf 190s! The Americans had not seen Typhoons before so they did one dirty great dive. They shot down Thornton Brown, they shot down an American pilot we had in the squadron and they shot down another pilot.

'Friendly fire.'
Yes, friendly fire. But Thornton Brown was killed. I met his wife, or ex-wife, only about three years ago, which was a very emotional get-together. That was my first experience of action.

You still had a German passport. You weren't naturalised.
No, because I couldn't be before I was twenty-one.

One of your colleagues at that time – the squadron doctor – has written that as far as the other pilots were concerned, being taken prisoner by the Germans would simply have meant the end of the war. But for you, it would have been the start of a nightmare. What did that feel like? It's such a strange situation.
Well . . . It's a very good question you are asking me, and sometimes I think about it. But, remember, we were quite an international squadron. Obviously we didn't have any other Germans but there were Norwegians, Poles, Canadians, New Zealanders, Australians . . . That reminds me: I got a phone call yesterday from the only surviving

Australian pilot. He congratulated me on my knighthood, which was really very sweet of him. So, first of all, we were a team. That was, again, the British influence, no question about it, and that's what saved my life emotionally. Because I'm a pretty sensitive human being, but when you treat it all as a game of rugby or a sporting event . . .

It distances you.

It distances you. Eventually, when we got to the hard part, it was almost essential. But at this time it was still fun. They thought it was a big joke to have a German with them. The Belgians were not sure about me, but I only found that out recently because they told me at the reunions! I didn't realise at the time. We had mock combat in the air and if somebody managed to turn inside me he could say he shot down a Jerry! So it was a big game. I was not aware at that time of any bad feelings towards me, though there must have been some. So we did these few fighter escort things that were a piece of cake really, and I never got a chance to fire at a German plane. And then, for better or worse – very much for better actually – the air force decided that we would be the first squadron equipped with air-to-ground rockets. We were no longer Fighter Command 11 Group. We became 2nd Tactical Airforce. So although we were in England we had to sleep under canvas and became part of the army. We had an Intelligence set-up in which there were naval officers and army officers and liaison officers, and RAF all living like troops in camps. And we had to learn what to do with these damn rockets. They were 60lb warheads; each one had the explosive power of a 6-inch naval gun shell. We also had four 20mm Hispano cannons plus eight rockets and we were posted to Fairwood Common in Wales – to learn how to fire these damn rockets. And, remember, we didn't have any rocket gunsights so we had to use our reflector sights from the cannons to fire these rockets, allowing for the angle, the speed, the wind. Because the rocket leaves the aircraft at the same speed, it has no recoil. It then pulls away at a very much greater speed. It was fun. It wasn't such fun if you were on the ground because you would see the rockets diving down. And the noise was just frightening. But I thought – and we all did – this is fantastic. I think my average error – if you look at my logbook – was something like forty yards. So now we have our first opportunity to use them during an attack on a radar station near Le Havre in France. The idea was that the American medium bombers would bomb the hell out of that place and then two or three Typhoon squadrons would come in to finish off the radar station. A crazy idea to use rockets, especially because they were reinforced concrete bunkers and the radar towers were a web of steel mesh that the rockets would go straight through. Also our plan was to fly into inland France, go into echelon starboard, and then dive down and attack towards the sea on our way back to England. Well the first thing I noticed, because I was one of the last men in, was that planes were going down in flames before we'd even got over the French coast. I heard it over the radio and I thought, 'My God!' And then the next thing I found, when we were attacking, was that the German anti-aircraft guns were just aiming at the first plane because if they didn't hit it, they hit the one behind. So I slid out to one side and came in at an angle, which probably saved my life. We'd never had serious losses before. But suddenly, in one show, the first really important one, we lost three aircraft. To lose three people was traumatic for all of us. In fact, when we landed back in England there was general depression. There was one pilot who bailed out – Junior his name was – and since I was the last one to attack I saw him hit the water. I sent out a Mayday to scramble Air Sea Rescue and I circled round him until my petrol became too low and I had to leave. But they never found him. We were probably the most effective close-support weapon the army had, and our losses were horrendous, really horrendous. As a vague estimate, from the beginning of 1944 to November '44 we lost nearly twice the establishment of the squadron. Not all killed: some became prisoners, you know. But still a terrifying loss. Because, although we were incredibly effective, we were also unbelievably vulnerable. We were flying at 8,000 feet, and when we started attacking we built up enormous speeds. We were hit by flak from the Germans, which was very effective. Sometimes pilots pulled out too late; the Typhoon had a nasty habit of stalling at high speed. In other words, if you pulled out too quickly the plane flipped over and went straight into the ground. They had invented a system called 'Cab Rank', which was wonderful really. There were four of us at the end of an airstrip in France – airstrips were dangerous enough: people killed themselves trying to take off or land. I had a grid map on my knees and I had to climb up to 8,000 feet above the airstrip because the Germans were only four or five miles away. When I was at 8,000 feet a controller in a tank at the front line would take over and say 'Fly to grid reference so and so and in fifteen seconds there will be green, yellow or blue smoke for you to go down and attack.' So, from there you went down to attack, because from that height I could barely make out what I was attacking. Then I'd see German tanks or artillery and I'd scream down. As I took off, another section of Typhoons would take our place. So I attacked, came back, got re-armed, and sometimes did two or three shows a day. However, the Typhoon had that gigantic radiator scoop, and you only needed one revolver bullet in it and the engine would seize within twenty seconds.

It's strange but your first reaction when you saw your greatest friend go down in flames was always, 'Thank God it wasn't me.' But then once you landed the other reactions set in. In many ways it was a great experience for the survivors. We're having a meeting in July 2003 – the last one probably – at Duxford, because they're publishing a new book which they want us all to sign. My mates of that time remember me as Klaus or Heinie, and they tell me things about my past that I'd long forgotten. But most of them became station commanders or test pilots or whatever. They lived in the past. My life started anew, after the war.

It was their finest hour.
Yes. But the friendships which were created during wartime were really very special.

The shared adrenalin, the teamwork . . .
You'd never have it again.

It's amazing you've all kept in touch with each other.
The first people to congratulate me on my knighthood were from the other side of the world.

At the end of the war you went to Germany and were put in charge of German labour units constructing an airfield. That must have been strange, because up until then you'd been distanced in the air. Now you were on the ground. And you'd been commissioned.
I was commissioned in November 1944. By Anthony Eden, incidentally, then the Foreign Minister. Did you know that? My wing commander was a man called Scott, a New Zealander. At that time we could not get replacements, even though there was a pool of fighter pilots. Nobody wanted to volunteer because of the losses we had. So I said to him, 'Scottie, I've been with the squadron now for a year and my commission is always turned down. I'm getting pissed off with this. If I'm not going to get my commission I want you to post me to coastal command where I can fly on the Sunderland and get eggs and bacon for breakfast.' And he said, 'I couldn't agree more.' He mentioned it to Anthony Eden, his tennis partner, and I received my commission by special gazette.

About time.
So I was in charge of 10,000 ex-Luftwaffe prisoners of war in a place called Wunstorf in northern Germany, near Hanover. The RAF asked me to sign on for another year to form these prisoners of war into labour units to reconstruct the airfield – the airfield that in 1948 and 1949 became one of the principal bases for supplying Berlin. It was a strange experience, but the funny thing is I was very popular with them

even though they knew my background. I took the whole of the officer staff, still in uniforms, to Bergen-Belsen concentration camp two or three weeks after Belsen had been liberated, and it's something I'll never forget. The inmates, by this time, had been taken out of the camps and were living in the SS barracks, but they were almost proud to show us around, you know, proud of the horrors they'd lived through. I did not see one German who was not emotionally shattered by it. One tried to commit suicide two days later. It would have been easier to hate them, but I could not. Only if somebody had behaved arrogantly towards me would I have shot him dead. After that, they more or less administered themselves and they did some very good work.

A lot of books have been written about the squadron, and you feature in many of them.
There are so many stories. Flying at 400 m.p.h. at ground level and trying to avoid trees and high-tension cables and pylons and church steeples . . . We often came back with tree branches stuck in our radiators!

Were you ever hit?
Yes, I was hit. But I always managed to limp back. I had an elevator shot off on one occasion. But, Christopher, I was very lucky. Unbelievably lucky.

The mortality rate in your squadron was unusually high.
Terrifying. It was, I suppose, nearly as high as bomber command. On one operation I noticed one of our Canadian pilots, Piwi Williams, losing height and flying straight towards enemy lines. I called him on my radio and he replied that he was hit. His spine was injured and he must have been paralysed. And I can still remember his last words: 'Don't forget to order me a late tea.'

What's amazing is that you mention squadron reunions. We're in 2003, and a proportion of these men are still around, well into their eighties.
Not many.

The ones that survived.
It's amazing. I have more of a rapport – more of a relationship – with people I flew with sixty years ago, than most other people in my life.

It's interesting, the animated way you talk about it. Maybe because there was no financial relationship. You were all fighting for a common cause. You sound warmer and closer to these people than to anyone in the film business. Such strong bonds of friendship, loyalty, camaraderie .
Yes.

Because it's a different sort of relationship, in wartime . . .
Completely different. An amazing thing, Christopher. Obviously I spent fifty-six years working in film and that became my life, but all the people I used to fly with kept on flying. They became test pilots or station commanders. They were always involved with flying because that's all they knew. Very few did something else. So when I see them they remember everything of that period, things I'd completely forgotten because my life was a different life. But their life is still based on that.

After the war, when did you last fly?
I flew for about five years in the volunteer reserve.

From 1945 to 1950?
Yes, at Panshanger, near Hatfield. I also used to fly some wealthy people who had their own planes but were a bit scared of flying across the Channel. So they asked an ex-RAF pilot to fly them across for the weekend, which I did. The problem was getting back because those planes were not properly equipped for instrument flying. You have good weather in Belgium or France and suddenly you go halfway across the Channel and a blanket comes down. I nearly lost my life on one of those occasions. But apart from that, I didn't fly much. When you're working on films you can't afford to be two days late. The owners of the plane didn't mind about being late, but I had to get back.

3 Draughtsman to Art Director

Early Films

How did you start working in films? You could have stayed in the RAF as a career; many did.

Yes, but when I mentioned it to my older brother, he put me off. Because I'd also written a report for the Potsdam Conference which a wing commander submitted because in those days I was very interested in all those things. So I said to Peter, 'I think I'm going to apply for a permanent commission.' And he said, 'Don't be crazy.' He had been in Intelligence and was a major.

In the army?

In the army, but he'd been out of it for some time, even though they'd offered him a senior job in the control commission. He said, 'You are a twenty-five-year-old with a German accent, you're not naturalised British, you are in the RAF; even if you're the most capable person you might become a Group Captain in three or four years' time, which I doubt, because to the British you're always a foreigner. Get out. You have an artistic talent.' Though I had a fantastic time, though I was living in great luxury with cars and boats and so on, I decided to get out. But remember, as a fighter pilot during the war I had very good connections in the film world and theatre and they all promised that once I got out of it I could go and see them, but nothing worked out. I came to see all these people and they'd say, 'You have to be a member of the union.' So I said, 'All right, I'll become a member of the union.' 'But you can't be a member of the union until you've worked for six weeks.' It was a disaster and I was getting more and more desperate. I was really living it up on my allowance and everything. Then by chance my sister Loni was working in the American embassy in public relations and a buyer came in and said could she provide him with props for a film with an American setting and she said, 'Yes, I can do that, and maybe you can help my younger brother who's just recently come out of the RAF, who draws well and would love to work in films.'

So you started off as a junior draughtsman. But the books vary about which was your very first film. Some say it was a film called This Was a Woman, *directed by Tim Whelan, an American who had worked off and on in Britain in the 1930s. It was a stage adaptation.*
Yes.

So that was the first film, in 1947, and you were at Hammersmith.

Flying Officer Adam, 1945

Ken Adam with his mother Lilli, in 1946

41

That's right, Riverside Studio.

And subsequently Twickenham.
I was only at Hammersmith for a couple of weeks.

Doing renderings and drawings?
Working on details of windows or something like that, together with
Tony Masters; and John Box was there a few weeks before me, I think.
There were three studios: Riverside, Twickenham and Southall. They
all belonged to a company called the Alliance Group. They changed us
around so I was in Riverside for two weeks on *This Was a Woman* and
then was sent to Twickenham on *The Brass Monkey*.

*A 'B' picture with Carole Landis and Herbert Lom, which is also known
as* Lucky Mascot. *It had two titles: one in England, one in America. The
director was Thornton Freeland. Again you were a junior draughtsman.*
Yes. In those days the film industry was very much like a military
organisation and you had your art department, your assistant art director and your chief draughtsman and then the art director was in charge
of it all. The art director was a man called Wally Scott, and I'll never
forget him. He came in desperation one day into the art department
and said, 'I can't get through to the director and the producer' – the
producer was Nat Bronsten, the director Thornton Freeland – 'and they
don't seem to like my designs. Why don't you have a go at them?' And
I remember the design. It was a radio music hall and I did something
completely imaginary, but they liked it. So in one of my first films they
used my designs.

You didn't get a credit.
No, but it was a little peephole. The producer of course didn't know it
was me, but there was a construction manager at Twickenham called
Peter Dukelow, an Irish navvy who'd been kicked out of the States; a
wonderful man. He knew I'd done the drawings, and from that
moment on he became my biggest sponsor. He took me under his wing
and taught me what is and what is not possible in films. It is important
that a film designer understands construction problems. Up to his death
we were great friends. Peter was a rough diamond but I adored him. So
I was really lucky to get a break like that, especially to have somebody
like a construction manager backing me. Because they talk amongst
themselves and they get the word to the director and the producer. They
say there's a young guy who's just come out of the RAF and he can
draw and design. This is really what happened.

Then as an assistant designer on Thorold Dickinson's Queen of Spades,
an adaptation of Pushkin's novel. The designer was Oliver Messel, who

came from that tradition you were talking about earlier, very much a theatrical, high-culture tradition. Not the workman-like art director type at all. It's odd in some ways because you're joining the business when the Italian Neo-realists are beginning to shoot on the streets, on location, and everyone's saying the future of the film industry lies in location filming. Leon Barsaq, for example, in his book on film design, says that in the battle between the two traditions – the street (Neo-realism; Hollywood film noirs) and the studio – the moment real-life exteriors became fashionable and feasible 'the future of the film set was virtually decided'. But there you are on the tail-end of this prestige theatrical tradition of big studio sets and I think you still like working in studios better than on the streets because you have more control. Can you remember much about Queen of Spades *and working with Oliver Messel?*
Even though I was in a very junior capacity Oliver liked me and I liked him. He liked my freehand drawing.

He didn't like you too *much . . .?*
No, no! But he was a great talent and he taught me a lot about period design. In this case, early nineteenth-century Russia. Today you might feel it's a little over the top, very ornate, but he was a very good painter. The greatest difficulty was to interpret his paintings and make them work. But there was a wonderful chief draughtsman, Peter Glazier, who was brilliant at interpreting the paintings. Oliver liked me so he'd give me a lot of freehand work to do: engravings of the period and so on. I got on very well with the cameraman, who was Otto Heller. It was the first time I met Otto. And I don't know why, but I always had a relationship with the actors, with Anton Walbrook and Yvonne Mitchell, Edith Evans and so on. It was a great experience. I learned something about the diversity of a film designer's role.

St Petersburg in 1815 – an interesting design challenge.
Incredible.

It still works as a movie. It's very theatrical, as you say, but I think it still works. Martin Scorsese recently singled out the 'lighting and décor' for special praise, and at the time Dilys Powell wrote, 'Oliver Messel's settings and costumes are among the most beautiful I can remember seeing.' So it was a good start. Interesting too that you mention Otto Heller because another aspect of the British film industry at that time is the high number of refugees working in the business. There are all these people just after the Second World War contributing to the visual richness of the British film industry; Otto Heller was another émigré from Nazi Germany, Michael Powell owed everything to Hein Heckroth, for example . . .

It was Pressburger too.

I don't know whether you felt that at the time . . .
No, I didn't feel it. What felt so incredible, then and on subsequent work, was the support. You see, Teddy Carrick, who had a very cultural background, was supervising art director at Pinewood Studios, and he used to walk into my office in the evening – when I was there, because I worked impossible hours – and he used to help me and advise me. There was no jealousy, no envy at all. They were out to help me. At least I thought they were. Even Alfred Junge, who was a disciplinarian and the highest-paid designer in England at that time, went out of his way to give me advice. And John Bryan. It was great for me to be encouraged.

Edward Carrick wrote a couple of books – in 1941 and 1948 – about art direction, so he had a teacher streak in him. They are written very clearly, like Everyman's guides. So obviously you had a teacher there.
Yes, and it was helpful. Also, because we're talking about *Queen of Spades*, Anatole De Grunwald employed me on *World Premier* with Marlene Dietrich and Luise Rainer and Pierre Brasseur. The designer was George Wakhevitsch and it was at Teddington.

Another immigrant, this time from Russia.
And George was a brilliant artist; his paintings were fantastic. And he liked me, although I was just one of the assistants. One of the sets was Dante's Inferno – Hell – and he said, 'Ken, I wonder if you'd build a half-inch scale model for that?' I said, 'Come on, George, what do you want me to do?' He said, 'Do it in plaster.' He was brilliant. He had worked in plaster so he helped me do this model in plaster with the skeletons of rats to accentuate the morbid. I was influenced by George. Although he had designed films like *La Grande Illusion* for Renoir, he was better known for his work in opera and theatre. A stage designer has to create a self-sufficient universe within the proscenium arch and the dimensions of the stage. These limits mean that one can't simply reproduce reality; one is much more dependent on imagination. I began to think about how this approach might be applied to film. But unfortunately *World Premier* never got made. Another designer I met at that time was Paul Sheriff, who had been the White Russian Count Schouvaloff. He made beautiful paintings for his set designs, but they were sometimes difficult to interpret as designs. When I mentioned this to him he gave me this advice: 'Ken, you must never commit yourself in your design. Film people are snobs. If they do not understand a sketch, which obviously they don't want to admit, they will praise it!' This was advice I did *not* heed!

Paul Sheriff had designed the sets – from Globe Theatre to medieval history – for Laurence Olivier's Henry V. *Your first credit on screen was for* Obsession *or* Hidden Room, *directed by Edward Dmytryk. It was made at Pinewood Studios and it's about an obsessed doctor (Robert Newton) who locks his wife's lover in the cellar! The first of your concrete bunkers . . . Can you remember anything about that?*

Yes, I do remember one thing. Maybe it's unkind what I'm saying, but the art director was a man called Duncan Sutherland who – maybe you shouldn't quote me – was known as 'Drunken' Sutherland. He never did any proper sketches. He used to drink in the pub in the evening and scribble on the inside of his hand. It was the first time I really had a lot of responsibility. I designed the period set and found it fascinating that I could do it.

It wasn't a period movie, was it?

No, it was a present-day movie, fifty years ago or whenever it was, and it was set in Church Row by Hampstead Heath. I was always in love with the actress Sally Gray, who played the female lead. I was really crazy about her. This film gave me a lot of confidence because Duncan was a nice man but he left an enormous amount of work to me, and I didn't resent it. In a way it gave me the opportunity to learn more and do more, so I enjoyed it.

Have you seen it lately? It doesn't get shown.

No. It was a thriller.

Three Ships

Then we move on to your first major film made by Warner Brothers in Europe – Captain Horatio Hornblower RN, *directed by Raoul Walsh in 1950. By then you'd had a couple of credits (*Obsession *and* Your Witness) *but your new job as assistant art director was to deal with the ships of the Napoleonic period. Do you know why they chose you? Had you done any ships before?*

No! The man who ran Warner Brothers in England, a man called Gerry Blattner, felt that I was the only one he could think of that should get involved in this picture. So the first thing I did was find out about ships of the period. I spent a couple of weeks at the National Maritime Museum in Greenwich – which is fantastic – doing research. I also met some very interesting people, such as Colonel Wiley, a great expert on the period. Then we put out some feelers about whether one can still buy these ships somewhere, and the only place where there was a possibility

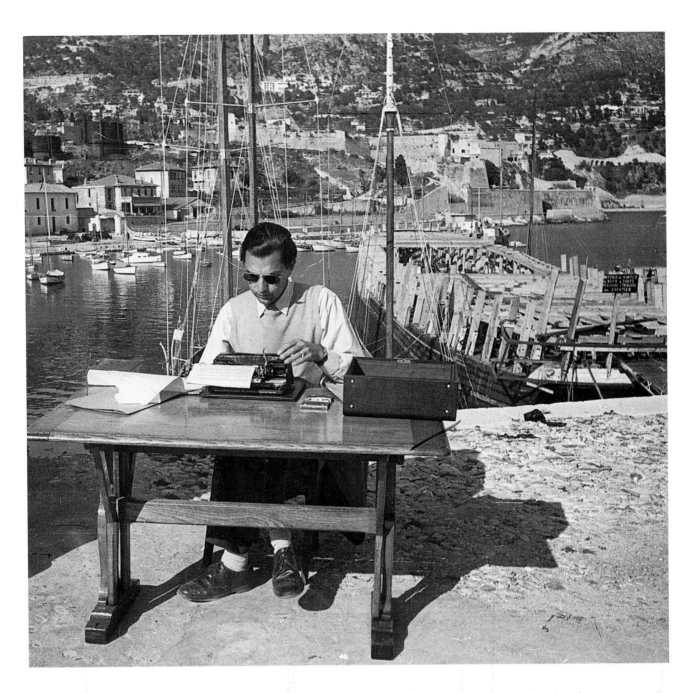

At Villefranche, with Hornblower's frigate under construction, September 1949

of finding them was the South of France or the North African coast. So I was sent down there. I'd never been to the Riviera before so it was a fantastic job for me. Before that I looked at a ship of the period still existing in this country – the *Implacable*. It was a 74-gun ship of the line, in Portsmouth, which had been taken as a prize from the French in the Battle of Trafalgar. So I looked at it and it had no rigging, nothing, but it was floating. It was unbelievable because it was built out of solid oak. It was beautiful. And there it was, floating, and nothing was being done about it. So I contacted Camper Nicholson through Colonel

46

Wiley and asked if they were prepared to rig it up again as it originally was. They were of course very keen, and although they asked for a lot of money, Warners didn't seem to be too concerned about that. But the next thing I knew the whole thing fell through. A question was raised in Parliament because apparently the British government or the Admiralty had problems with the French, who wanted the ship back in France! So the Admiralty decided to get rid of it. They towed it out to mid-Channel, filled the hold of the ship with dynamite, and blew it up. The irony of it was that the bottom fell out but the upper part of the ship remained floating, so they had to send two or three destroyers to finish it off with gunfire. Just so the French couldn't get it! So then I went to the South of France where I was looking all over the Riviera to the Spanish border. And I met some very shady characters – remember it was 1949 when I went there – who all had contacts in Algiers and North Africa. Shipbuilders contacted me of course, and I met a young shipbuilder called Bernard Voisin, who was two or three years older than me and knew a lot about this period, because it was his hobby. He understood my drawing and we immediately began a partnership. We went to the Spanish border where we found a three-masted schooner called *La France*. It had been used for cod fishing on the shores of Newfoundland – it smelled accordingly – and we bought it for five thousand pounds from a man who was a well-known café violinist. It had two old diesel engines which didn't work very well so we had to tow it to Villefranche, then ballasted the hold down with two hundred tons of concrete, and started building up from there. You saw the film – it looks fantastic, doesn't it? So that was really my main job: Hornblower's flagship.

You had to re-rig the ship . . .
Rigging, right. Sails and all that. And make sure those diesel engines worked so it didn't run aground during filming. It was a lot of fun, but I also happened to get an attack of very bad yellow jaundice. At that time – shortly after the war – I thought nothing could happen to me. But I was as yellow as a lemon and I got very depressed. I had to meet the American director, Raoul Walsh, at the airport when he flew over. I got out of bed and I wasn't feeling too well but Raoul said, 'I wouldn't worry, you are a little bit of an Oriental type.' I had a Russian doctor whose name was Rosanoff, and he said to me, 'Ken, if you don't take care of yourself you will be dead in two weeks.' So I had all my conferences in the hotel. Raoul was very understanding, although once or twice I had to show him some locations. I moved out of the hotel because I couldn't stand the smell, and I moved to a small hotel in Villefranche where I remember being in the room when the owner rang the

Raising the Mercedes, Villefranche 1949

doctor to see whether I was contagious or not! But I tried to have a good time as well. I went to nightclubs. Unfortunately I burned the candle at both ends – remember it was the first time I'd been away.

Just after the war.

Bernard Voisin lent me an old pre-war Mercedes to drive, and the first thing I did – coming back at about three in the morning – was fall asleep at the wheel. I wrote off about twenty deck chairs on the Promenades des Anglais. Fortunately there was nobody in them, but I didn't have any papers on me. I was arrested by the French police and they escorted me in two Jeeps, both mounted with machine guns, to where Bernard lived. At three in the morning Bernard opened a brandy bottle and the whole thing was forgotten! But a week later I unfortunately parked the car outside the dry dock. I had to start it on the crank because the battery was flat – it was one of those old cars with hand gas – and I'd forgotten that I'd left it in gear. The car started and headed straight for a twenty-foot drop. I jumped on the bonnet and myself and the car went sailing into the water! Then the famous cable came from Jack Warner who said, 'I will not accept responsibility for Ken Adam's madness.' It took Bernard three days to raise the car, even though he was a very good diver and he'd hired a crane from Nice. And no one could get in or out of the dock. So that was my immediate adventure on that film. Then of course we were learning all the time because nobody knew how to sail these things, so Bernard, who came from Brittany, brought a crew over who knew about square-rigged ships. We started trial runs but they were already wanting to shoot. Then the engines didn't go astern like they should, but fortunately we had tugs around which could pull us off the rocks. So there were disasters all the way through.

From a technical point of view, the full-sized ship was used for the long shots, but were models or mock-ups back in the studio used for the close-ups and on deck and for the battles?

Yes. We built a full-sized two-level set on hydraulic rockers back at Denham studios. But there was another disaster. Remember, this was the first time a major American production came to Europe so we were all shit-scared; it was important. We had somebody called Jim Hall who designed the rockers so that the ship would have lateral movement, and it seemed to work all right. But when Raoul Walsh came to the first rehearsal with fifty extras on deck, the ship made one movement and got stuck! They didn't know what to do. They said, 'Ken, what are we going to do?!' I said, 'Obviously the hydraulic rams are not man enough.' And I had a new set of stronger rams installed with help

48

from the Lockheed aircraft factory, and the problem was solved. So we had two full-sized decks, we had the biggest tank at Denham that was called City Square – don't ask me why – and we put up a sky backing seventy foot long and forty or fifty foot high. And we built one-sixth-full-sized models that were nearly thirty feet long. In each model we had a three-man crew: one to fire the guns, another to handle the sails, and a third man to navigate! And to create the wind we purchased four Rolls-Royce Merlin engines from some old wartime Mosquito fighter bombers. Then we had wave machines. That was a big operation. Reading one of the write-ups of it, they said the battle sequences were some of the best battle sequences ever.

I always think that one of the last major problems for special-effects people is the sea, because even if you have small models the waves remain full-sized. So in a lot of films of this period you get these funny large-scale waves on tiny ships. It's still the last of the big problems.
That's why we built the models so big and shot it in a tank. I'd learned that lesson. Much later, on *The Spy Who Loved Me*, we built an enormous-sized supertanker because we shot it in the Bahamas at sea. It had to be really big and that's why it always looked real. You're absolutely right – you have to use very big models or the scene looks phoney.

And you get these little crinkles . . .
Yes, but there are all sorts of different wave machines that one can use.

Any reminiscences of Raoul Walsh?
He was a blood-and-guts director.

Did he already have an eye patch in those days?
Yes. He was a great action director but had absolutely no regard for safety. I was a bit mad at the time too, I must say. I would dive off the ship when the anchor got caught up. He used to put stuntmen or extras over the side in bad weather conditions, and so on, and fortunately we never had a fatal accident. One of the funniest things was when we were setting up a beautiful shot of my frigate sailing across the Cap Ferrat, and at that moment the American Sixth Fleet came steaming into the shot! So Raoul blew his top and said, 'I know the Admiral in charge and I'm going to get hold of him.' And he did, and the fleet moved out!

A hard drinker of Jack Daniel's too, but always very professional.
He had an attractive young wife who was lovely. We all fell in love with her. Mind you, at that time the greatest hotel in the South of France was the Reserve in Beaulieu, so everybody was staying there and having a great time. Then I was very fortunate because we needed a second ship and somebody told me there were wrecks lying in Marseilles. So I drove

Filming *Hornblower* in the south of
France with Raoul Walsh (left) and Guy
Green (top), May 1950

there to the old port of Marseilles and found a ship called the *Marie
Annick*. It was a ketch that had been used for ferrying illegal immigrants to Palestine in those days, and it was rotting away. I bought it for
four hundred and fifty pounds, I think, and we rigged it up as a
schooner of the period.

*It's amazing that these sailing ships were just lying around in these har-
bours. Not so easy now.*
No.

*Mind you, they'd just paint them in digitally now. Gregory Peck once
told me a slightly rude story about Virginia Mayo – who played Lady
Barbara Wellesley – when I interviewed him for television a few years
ago. Originally it was to have been Margaret Leighton playing the part.
She did a screen test that went to Jack Warner, and his one comment
was, 'She's out, kid – no tits.' So they had Virginia Mayo instead. Margaret Leighton, this classical actress who spoke beautifully, was cast
into the outer darkness because her chest wasn't quite big enough – you
do need a bit of bosom for these bodice-ripping romances.*
But it was amazing, you see, because the Riviera in 1949 and 1950 was
full of Americans. Jack Warner had bought a villa, and one of his art

directors from Hollywood came to help with the decoration. The social life was unbelievable; we were surrounded by film stars and we had a fantastic time. Great nights, and weekends in Haut de Cagnes.

As a result of the success of Hornblower, *you became something of a specialist in ships, despite the fact it wasn't really your specialism. I think the next ship movie you were involved in as associate art director was* The Crimson Pirate, *released in 1952.*
It was made in '51.

Hornblower *is set during the Napoleonic war, but* The Crimson Pirate *is in a different period, some sixty years before.*
It was supposed to be like a pirate galleon. I was having such a good time designing ships because I was always interested in the sea. So I redid *La France*, which was the *Hornblower* ship in Marseilles, and was helped very much with the cannons and props by the Victorine studios in Nice. I did that and on the first sea trial I got up at four in the morning to go to Marseilles. Suddenly a sailor runs into the office and says, '*La France* is sinking!' At first we couldn't understand what had happened. The propeller had got caught on something which had pulled the axle out of the shaft and the ship was taking in water and sinking – really sinking! So we called the local fire brigade and they came with these ocean-going fire floats. They rammed my plasterwork and damaged it! But at least they pumped the ship out in no time at all. That nearly gave us a heart attack. It was a nightmare. I had learned a lot from *Hornblower*; I'd got the right sails, the right material. I had a naval advisor who was a film director himself, absolutely the personification of everything that's great in this country – Vernon Sewell. He's still around, I think. He must be in his nineties. I worked on one of Vernon Sewell's first films. He had one of the biggest steam yachts in Britain called the *Gellert*, and what he used to do was invite actors on it for a weekend, somewhere in the South of England, and go to France, shooting a film during the crossing! Vernon was a brilliant technician – he knew how to do sound and everything – and he shot the film in a weekend! He was that sort of character. I adored Vernon and he became my technical advisor on *The Crimson Pirate*. There was a lot of competition and rivalry between the crews on the two ships, *La France* and the *Marie Annick*. Jack Warner insisted we sail these two ships to Ischia, six hundred miles away. So Vernon said, 'We're not going on the big ship. We're going on the small one.' Because he had installed the engine. We had caviar, lobster and everything at the expense of Warner Brothers. One morning, when the sea was like a

Crimson Pirate galleon crossing from
Nice to Ischia, June 1951

mirror, we sailed the two ships to Ischia, where Burt Lancaster and
everybody was already waiting for these two essential props. And, as
always happens, I had to go on watch and I nearly fell asleep because
we'd been out the night before. And off Cap Corse we were hit by a
gale. The bigger ship, *La France*, was riding the gale pretty well but
the *Marie Annick* didn't have proper ballast, so when I woke up
below deck I could hear water swilling in the double hulls where
there were leaks and I thought, 'This is it . . .' I climbed on deck and
then the engine broke down. Vernon was a fantastic mechanic but

his head kept popping out of the engine room and eventually he said, with a stammer in his voice, 'The reduction gear has been stripped and I can't repair it.' Now we were in a terrible situation. The bigger ship was on the horizon, you see. We had no radio; our only form of communication was our Aldis lamp and some rockets. So we tried the lamp, but the batteries were flat. Fortunately Captain Olivier of *La France* saw the emergency rockets that we sent up, turned round and took us into tow. But the tow had to go through my beautiful plasterwork at the back of the big ship, so I said to Vernon, 'I'm going to steer this thing myself if it's the last thing I do because I'm not having the stern ripped off.' So we were towed by *La France* into Bastia, Corsica, and we left Vernon trying to fix the engine on the *Marie Annick* whilst I sailed with my drunken Breton sailors for another four or five days to Ischia. It was an incredible experience; with my imagination, as I paced the quarterdeck with its cannons, I felt like a pirate.

It must have been amazing in a three-master to observe Vesuvius on the horizon.
Unbelievable. We passed it in the Bay of Naples and, because these Breton sailors knew how to handle a square-rigged ship, we were doing nearly nine knots. Fantastic. Of course, I didn't wash or anything, so when we finally arrived in Ischia I must have looked like a pirate myself. That was certainly my future wife Letizia's impression of me! We were quarantined to start off with. Then, when I finally got off, I was burned almost black with my long hair in a bandanna. I think that influenced Letizia in some way.

That visit to Ischia must still have a warm place in your heart. How did you meet Letizia?
Well, she was without doubt the prettiest girl in Ischia, and you can imagine a period ship of this size arriving in port for the first time – the whole of Ischia came down to greet us. Paul Sheriff, the production designer, had been in Ischia before on a location scout, and because he knew of my interest in the opposite sex he said, 'There's a very, very beautiful girl with long blonde hair.' When I arrived in Ischia I saw this very beautiful girl with long blonde hair, and she discovered me too. I chased her for about two or three weeks before we met. Her name was Letizia Moauro. She had experienced the bombing of Naples but she was a sunny and completely unpretentious person. The Ischians never forgave me for robbing them of their sunshine.

The film is very interesting from the point of view of future developments because it's absolutely full of eighteenth-century gadgets. And

Letizia on a speedboat, Ischia 1952

there's a character played by James Hayter who's a sort of Q figure, a professor who designs these things. Were you involved in that side of the production?

Yes.

Preparing the complex balloon sequence in *The Crimson Pirate*

Someone decided to make this a spoof with these outlandish inventions. In some ways it's like what happened to Bond . . .

Like a sort of period Bond, yes. It was amazing. It was a combination of Burt Lancaster – remember, his company was co-producing the film – the writer Roland Kibbee, and the director Robert Siodmak, agreeing that it didn't work as a normal pirate story. So they decided they would make it as a spoof. Every night we used to meet and come up with ideas, like how funny it would be to have a submarine, or to bombard a fortress from a balloon. My problems were enormous because in those days it took two hours to get to the mainland by steamer. I had brought over a fantastic construction crew from Rome – about fifteen people – so it was not easy to deal with these requirements. Each one came up with a new idea, but the fun part of it was that the production designer, Paul Sheriff, who I was very fond of, was so very Russian in his ideas. He said, 'Ken, I'll leave it to you. But remember one thing: between one and four I'm going to have a snooze, and nobody is allowed to wake me.' So we had a pretty good relationship! The other thing was that Ischia was so primitive in those days. There were no

54

With Burt Lancaster, Nick Cravat and a barrel of fish, Ischia 1951

hotels, so people were staying in private villas that we rented. The film-making stories . . . I learned a lot. One of the things I learned: Jack Warner sent a cable to Burt Lancaster and Robert Siodmak, saying that he was going to pull the plug because the picture was not the picture he thought he was going to get, and unless we did what he wanted us to do, the picture would be cancelled. By this time we'd been shooting for several weeks and I was absolutely panicking, but Burt said to me, 'Don't worry about it. If they cancel the picture now, they've got half a picture and nothing else. They can't cancel it.' The other thing I learned was rather nerve-racking for the cameraman, who was Otto Heller, and it was his first film in Technicolor. Otto was sharing a villa with me so I knew what was going on; he had to take a shot of Burt and Nick Cravat in the rigging. He said, 'I can't light it at that height.' But he was told to 'just shoot it'. Of course in the dailies – which we didn't see – Burt's face was black, so Warner wanted to fire Otto. We were all up in arms because Otto was a brilliant cameraman and it wasn't his fault. They sent over Guy Green, who was already a very well-known colour cameraman, and Guy spent two days saying that everything Otto did

55

was fine. So Otto finished the picture – but he had a nervous breakdown.

The Crimson Pirate *stands up well because, unlike so many early fifties adventure films, it has this sense of irony; it is watching itself.*
That's what saved it. Plus the brilliant acrobatics of Burt Lancaster, who did most of the stunts himself.

He seems to be having a wonderful time.
Yes, but he didn't take any risks. He knew exactly what he was doing. We had to rig up a sort of field with equipment, and sandbags were used to practise the swing before he did the stunt. We also had a wonderful American special-effects man called Russ Shearman, and his team were so unbelievably professional. There was only one occasion when Burt used a stuntman, and that man nearly killed himself. We had this balloon that was running on a traveller between two towers about a hundred and twenty feet up, so it was mechanical. Burt was supposed to climb out of the gondola, into the rigging, and take over the ship. Now that's easier said than done because remember there are waves. The ship's mast is a hundred and twenty feet high; the slightest movement means the mast moves from one side to another, and the cable stretched between the two towers is rigid. So what happened was that even though we'd strung a lot of additional lines between the rigging, when the stuntman was supposed to climb out of the balloon's gondola, the ship was at an angle. So he had to get out. Fortunately he managed to get hold of some extra rigging that we'd strung up, and it saved his life.

It is an extraordinary scene. It begins with Burt Lancaster in drag, with the balloon in a wooden cage that falls down, and Lancaster clambering into it. The whole thing is a complete riot and yet it looks so effortless. Of course, as you describe it, it was a very complex series of shots.
Very complex, considering that Ischia was another part of the world with no equipment or anything; everything had to be moved from Rome down to Naples, and then to us. But we had very good people. I learnt a lot on that picture. By the way, a local fisherman called Augostino Lauro, who helped with the day-to-day running of the ships, is now the owner of one of the biggest shipping companies in all Italy!

The third of your ship pictures, shot in Palermo and released in 1953, was The Master of Ballantrae, *directed by William Keighley and art directed by Ralph Brinton.*
It was filmed in 1952.

With William Keighley in Palermo, 1952

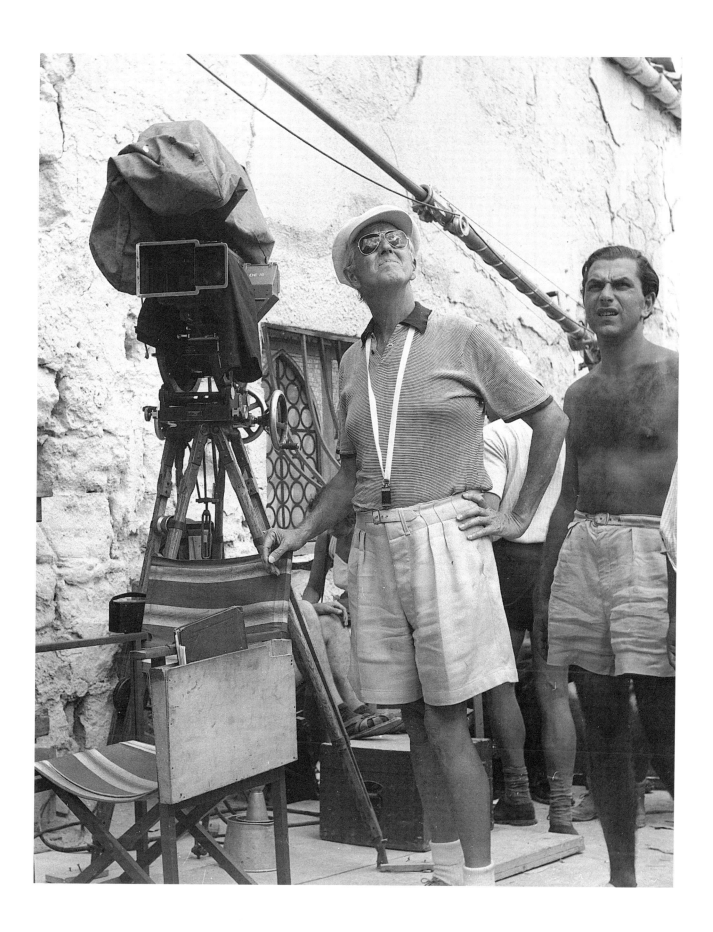

It was around the same time, and in the same part of the world . . .
The Crimson Pirate was shot in '51, so *The Master of Ballantrae* was made in the year I got married, 1952. I redesigned those ships again, in Ischia this time, and then sailed them to Palermo. In fact, Warners were very generous when I married Letizia: they gave me forty-eight hours leave and a first class cabin on the *City of Tunisia*, a big Italian cruise ship that went from Naples to Palermo. The trouble was, as I arrived in Naples, I was met by a Warners executive who said, 'I'm afraid we can't get you into the cabin because the ship is fully booked. I'm afraid you and Letizia will have to sleep on deck.' So we boarded the ship, which was overcrowded, and I said, 'I'm going to speak to the purser of the ship.' I said to him, 'I have a big problem. I'm supposed to have the state cabin.' And he said, 'What can I do?' I said, 'I just got married today to an Italian girl from Ischia.' Well, I got the state cabin! There are so many anecdotes: Letizia used to travel with a suitcase that had a tray inside it, but she'd forgotten the tray, so her father tried to catch up with us in a speedboat. We couldn't care less!

Do you remember much about working with Errol Flynn in his declining years?
Yes, he was already drinking quite a lot in those days, but I really adored him. He was very much a man's man. We were all staying at this fantastic old honeymoon hotel in Palermo, the Villa Igiea, so me and Letizia – who immediately started working on the picture as assistant costume designer – we used to eat almost every evening with Errol, and we got along really well. But it was amazing how some people used to provoke him because he was a big star, in the hope he would react badly.

What was the division of labour on The Master of Ballantrae?
Ralph Brinton, the art director, did the sets in England, whereas I did everything on the boat on location in Sicily. I adored Ralph too. His brother was an Oxford don and Ralph was very much like an Oxford don himself. He had an enormous sense of humour. In those days you didn't have taxis in Ischia; you had horse-drawn carriages. Ralph wanted to collect me from my villa so we could catch the boat to Palermo, but he was late. So I said, 'What happened?' He said, 'Well I was in the *carozza* and the horse kept sitting down!' In Palermo I was drawing a lot – on the boat and so on – and Ralph used to come in and see what I was doing. And he said a thing that I will never forget; he said, 'Ken, one day you'll be a very good production designer. And the one thing you have to promise me is that, on the film that you're going to do as production designer, I will be employed as your chief draughtsman.' I

said, 'Ralph, come on, you must be joking.' He said, 'I don't want the responsibility of all the politics. I love drawing.' He was a brilliant draughtsman. But it never came to that!

He was of the older generation too.
All qualified architects.

Then, a couple of years later, came Helen of Troy. *Having prepared one and a half ships for* Hornblower, *and subsequent pirate ships, this was the film that launched a thousand ships. Robert Wise was the main director, and Raoul Walsh directed the second unit – although he was uncredited – because they ran out of time. Did you do one ship and then paint the rest in for the Greek fleet?*
Yes, but I did a lot more than that. The art director, Edward Carrere, was a very talented man from Hollywood who had notably designed King Vidor's *The Fountainhead*, about a genius architect. He came to Rome and we couldn't find any film draughtsmen. The art directors in those days used to do a little elevation and plan, and the construction department would work from that. So Eddie, who was brought up in the Hollywood school, said, 'What are we going to do?' I had a friend called Francesco Borghese who was a qualified architect. I said to him, 'Francesco, would you like to help me out?' To cut a long story short, we formed an art department with seven or eight young Italian architects who learnt very quickly. I was in charge – not only of the ship, but also of the art department, of building the city of Troy and its forty-foot-high walls.

And the wooden horse.
And the wooden horse. Again, through Eddie, who was brilliant, we found out that instead of using fake marble floors on some of the settings we could use real marble floors – because it was cheaper! But we had a lot of problems. One big problem – and thank God we'd nearly finished shooting the siege of Troy – was that we had shot the Greeks as they scaled the city walls in their towers.

The siege towers.
Yes, the siege towers. We had organised the Rome fire brigade to stand by at lunchtime – because it was one of those hot Italian summers – and suddenly, while we're all having lunch, I hear that the set is on fire. It took them the best part of twenty-four hours to extinguish the flames.

Because it was all wood.
Wood and plaster. Luckily we'd shot most of the important action. But it was a big, big shock. Now, back to the ship: I found a place called Torre del Greco where there were still shipbuilders. So I took a whole

shipbuilding family to Fiumicino, which is the port in Rome, where they helped me to rebuild this ship. What I'd got was an old coal barge, so that I had a floating platform; I didn't have to build it from scratch. We could then build up from the coal barge because the Greek ships are all sweeping lines. This family – Giovanni was the grandfather – hand-made all the planking to fit this shape. They were unbelievable. And of course Giovanni refused to take part in the first trial because he was scared of the sea! So we got all these macho rowers from Rome Rowing Club and taught them how to row this gigantic boat. But again, as we were late and didn't have time, we had to shoot on the first day of the trial run. Our naval advisor was Commander Gibbons, and I was on the boat with Jacques Sernas, who played Paris, and one or two other stars. The sea was calm as we were heading out, but then Gibbons said, 'I'm afraid it's a rising sea.' I could see the waves coming up, and of course in those days we didn't have radios. We had an army unit with radio equipment on a gigantic pontoon, plus wardrobe, plus make-up, and we had to deal with all that because we didn't have room on that Greek galley. So we tried to turn back, only now there was a gale. As we approached Fiumicino we saw the boards were up. We couldn't enter the harbour, so we tried to reach Anzio. All of the macho rowers were seasick; they were lying across the deck. There was only myself, the naval advisor and one or two other people running the ship. We got to Anzio, but we were exhausted and we'd lost the pontoon. By this time Jack Warner had been informed in Hollywood, and apparently he said, 'Get a tug over to them. We can't afford to lose the stars.' So they sent out an ocean-going tug and they finally managed to rescue the pontoon, on which everybody looked dead because they were so seasick. The whole crew, the army, the wardrobe, make-up – they arrived in Anzio three hours later. Then of course the ocean-going tug crew tried to claim prize money for saving them. These were just some of the little problems!

It's interesting to watch that film today because a lot of those Hollywood epics were made to use up frozen US dollars that couldn't be spent outside Italy. So you had this incredibly elaborate production design and spectacle. But the script was never quite up to the same standard; there's that moment where Cedric Hardwicke looks out to sea and says, 'I see a hundred, five hundred ships, a thousand ships!' It's so corny. But the design and look of it is amazing. The wooden horse is . . .
Beautiful.

. . . and very credible because it's made out of deck boards. It's the kind of horse sailors might have made. In other films it's rounded and sculpted;

The wooden horse from *Helen of Troy*, 1954

you don't know how the hell they made it. But in this, the horse is cobbled together by sailors, and I thought that was very clever. Without going into too much detail, there was a rumour at the time that somebody set fire to the set; that there was a racket going on.
I don't think so. That's the first time I've heard that.

It's an extraordinary film, visually.
Well Roger Furse did all the costumes, quite brilliantly, I thought. And the number of props was enormous. Thousands of extras had to be costumed and armed with fibreglass weapons. On some days we had two units shooting with three thousand extras each: one at Anzio, and

another at Cinecittà. To service two units with all those props and costumes was a major job.

There seem to have been problems with time because Raoul Walsh was called in late to do more with the second unit than was originally planned. Something obviously went wrong with the schedule.
You have to remember that these were mammoth pictures. I was very lucky to be involved in them. There was a famous American production executive, Henry Hennickson, who smoked cigars. He was a great man. I think he had produced *Quo Vadis*. Hennickson wasn't involved with *Helen of Troy*, but he was around, scouting for MGM. He called me in afterwards to do all the practical structural calculations for the Circo Massimo on *Ben-Hur*.

You were involved in pre-production?
Oh yes, for about three or four months. Eddie Carfagno was the designer.

Were you involved with the sea battle in Ben-Hur?
No.

The Antioch Circus is amazing because the whole backlot of Cinecittà was taken over to build it. There's no digital painting there. It's all real.
Henry Hennickson was very clever because he introduced to Italy – a country that always used timber structures – imported tubular scaffolding. Eventually it became very Italian, and the whole of the Circo Massimo was supported by it.

Was there a moment when you might have become the art director and designed Ben-Hur?
No. Eddie Carfagno had been working on the picture in Hollywood for some time. I was more like a practical or technical advisor on it.

The difference in scale between the productions you worked on at this time must have been extraordinary. A lot of your early films were a sort of two-man band, but by the time you get to Helen of Troy *and* Ben-Hur, *you're responsible for an army.*
An army of people I had to train, particularly on *Helen of Troy*. But they all became great friends, and we had a lot of fun. One of my greatest architect friends eventually went into films and he designed all of Sergio Leone's films.

Carlo Simi.
Yes. He was my closest friend. Is he still around?

No. He died last year.

62

I'm sorry to hear that. Carlo was lovely.

I knew him a little, and I know his wife Elizabetta. They're setting up an architectural foundation in his name. Carlo worked on Helen of Troy?

Yes, it was the first film he did. He was my draughtsman. Carlo had an incredible sense of humour. My brother bought a boat in Sardinia, and on the weekends we used to fly out to use it. We didn't have a crew – I used to run it and Letizia used to cook – but Sardinia was tricky. One day I invited Carlo. We sailed out to sea and – the usual story – a gale came up. So we went back to the port. But during the night Carlo woke me up and said, 'There's something strange happening. I can see the most enormous shape!' A cargo ship had come in and anchored, and we were right underneath it. So I decided the best thing to do was go out to sea again. I'll never forget Carlo waking me up.

He was a very affable man and his contribution to the Leone films has never really been recognised; he did the costumes for the 'Dollars' films as well.

Did he? I didn't know.

We've skipped two films: The Intruder, *directed by Guy Hamilton in 1953; and* Star of India, *directed in 1954 by Arthur Lubin. Do you have any memories of those?*

We filmed *The Intruder* at Shepperton. It was an army story. The art director, a man called Joseph Bato, had been a pupil of Henri Matisse. Joseph was a painter really, and he was brought over by Korda, as they always were. Joseph was a delightful man, but by this time was already in his late sixties, and he was very worried. Thank God that Korda had great crews. Our scenic artist, Ferdy Bellan, was probably one of the greatest scenic artists I've ever known. Working at this fantastic studio you were surrounded by great artists; only the best. The sad thing – because unfortunately there are many sad stories – is that Joseph Bato had recently lost his wife, and so was living by himself somewhere in Holland Park. I had a great relationship with Joseph and I really loved him. Although he was not necessarily a great film designer, he was a great artist and we became good friends. Letizia was very fond of him too. But then he became blind. And you know, for someone who's worked with his eyes all his life, it was awful. It was very, very sad.

What about Star of India?

Star of India? I had a boat again! We had a Thames barge that I had to sail to Pebble Beach in Dorset.

It was set in early eighteenth-century France, and it had a colonial theme. It was a British/Italian co-production.

Yes. Cedric Dawe was the art director and he was a wonderful illustrator. And Arthur Lubin, the director, was very easy to work with. But I can't remember much else.

Lubin wasn't one of the top-liners; he'd made several Abbot and Costello comedies, and some very early Clint Eastwood movies, but they were uninspired 'nuts and bolts' productions. Let's talk about research. You mentioned earlier that you had used the National Maritime Museum in Greenwich for Hornblower. *But* Crimson Pirate *was set in the early eighteenth century and you'd prepared a Greek galley for* Helen of Troy. *Tell me something about the research process in those days.*

Well, I normally found an expert. For the Greek galley I found somebody in Italy who could get me painted vases with replica pictures of the Greek galleys, and so on. And I spent time doing research in museums. What was always so amazing was that the curators spent a lifetime in their museums, and I had maybe a couple of days in which I had to digest as much information as I could from them.

Mainly visual material I presume. In the 1930s – the days of the Hollywood studio system – they had what they called a 'bible' for each production, a visual bible that was a reference for everyone. Did you accumulate material like that?

No. Hornblower's 'bible' was the National Maritime Museum. Later, when I did *King David*, I used lots of books. You have to do research, but what I've always done is digested as much information and as many visual references as I can in a very short period of time. Then, what I normally do is put it aside. Because if I look at some image every two minutes I lose my spontaneity as a designer.

Also, your interest is completely different to the curators'. As historians, they are concerned with historical and contextual accuracy, whereas you are interested in how to make history work because you've got to think practically. Working out how *a Greek galley actually works is part of your job because it has to look convincing.*

It always amazes me – and it's funny you bring up the subject of research – that when I go to the experts they cannot understand that I, in a couple of days, have to digest sufficient material to design and *make it work*.

Do you ever get their reactions? I once gave a lecture in Bristol about maritime movies and there's always someone in the audience who knows a hell of a lot about rigging. Did you get any snide critics?

Yes, but I was very fortunate with the boats. I had a fantastic draughts-

man called Bill Holmes whose hobby was rigging boats; he knew everything about it.

*It's one of those subjects where you get extraordinary buffs, usually
retired naval buffs.*
Today you could probably learn a lot building models from scratch or
from computer imaging. But how can you take all that stuff in, including the rigging? It's so specialised. However, to be honest, I'm also a little superficial. If it looks good, it looks right.

Coffee Bars

*In the mid-1950s – in between films – you produced two interior
designs for coffee bars: one in Oxford called The Harlequin, and one
called The Cul-de-Sac in London. Can you tell me about those?*
The problem was, I had decided that I wanted to be an independent
designer and art director. But until you've made a reputation for yourself, there are periods when you are out of work. I had no money, so I
had to earn it another way. The first coffee bars had just come into
vogue, so I started off with The Harlequin in Oxford. It was way out.
My film construction manager Peter Dukelow built it for me at the
Wilberforce Hotel, and it became an enormous success. I treated it more
or less as a futuristic set with a very stylised Harlequin as a motif. It was
there for years. Then somebody asked me to design The Cul-de-Sac. It
was in a basement, so I came up with the idea of doing it like the exteri-
or of a French street, with cafés and so on. Again, I used some techniques like false perspective. In any case, it paid me for those periods
that I was out of work. I was asked to design a lot of coffee bars, but I
couldn't do them because I was back working in film again. I did design
one more in Richmond called The Gondola, which had a Venice motif.
It was an incredible period. The coffee bar was a completely new idea.

*You later wrote in a 1968 article on colour, 'I designed some of the first
new-style coffee bars in England and used various coloured walls. It
was the vogue and, I must admit, it appealed to me. So when we moved
into our own flat I decorated the entire place with various coloured
walls. I loved it at first. But after two weeks it almost drove me insane
and I redid the whole place in more restful tones. Ever since then, I have
been in favour of white walls . . .'*
Well it was the vogue at the time. No doubt we'll talk later about my
firm belief that on every tin of colour paint there should be printed the
words 'Danger – handle with care!'

In the mid-1950s we were just leaving behind the austerity of the Second World War, including rationing, and there was this sudden interest in coffee bars – partly European, partly American.

People used to sit there, meet and drink coffee. Also at this time, and later, Letizia worked in London as a fashion model for Yves Saint-Laurent, and she designed her own handbag collection.

Were you ever tempted to do more designing for the 'real world' during your career?

Not really. I was very fortunate, Christopher, because there were rarely periods when I was out of work. Even designing the opera for Covent Garden in 1976 or '77 was a major commitment for me. In fact, I remember working on one of the Bond films – forgive me if I can't remember – and I was doing designs at the studio and then going to Covent Garden to liaise . . .

Was it La Fanciulla del West?

Yes, the Puccini opera. I got that through some film people in Hollywood. It was amazing. The supervising art director at Universal Studios, Alex Golitzen, had dinner one night with Zubin Mehta and Lew Wasserman, *éminence grise* of Hollywood. Lew was a lovely man who had been very nice to me when I made my first picture in Hollywood. Zubin wanted to take a more filmic approach to *La Fanciulla*, so Lew Wasserman and Alex Golitzen said, 'We've got just the man for you; it's Ken Adam.' So John Tooley contacted me and asked if I would be interested in doing it.

It was film connections that got you this work?

Yes.

In more recent years you have been doing a lot of things outside the film world: exhibition design, the Millennium exhibition in Berlin . . . But they always seem to relate to film designs.

Yes, but remember one thing too: the last film I did in Hollywood was *The Out-of-Towners* in 1998, and it was a very unfortunate experience. I was called over by a friend of mine, Scott Rudin, who I admired as a producer, and he introduced me to a young director; we immediately hit it off. But, to cut a long story short, Scott Rudin threw the towel in. Then the director threw it in, and I was left holding the baby. Also, I wanted to leave but my agent said I had to carry on with the film to safeguard my good relations with Paramount and my reputation in Hollywood. So I stayed, and they brought in a new director who'd done one film. The *Out-of-Towners* was credited to Sam Weisman. Steve Martin and Goldie Hawn were in it; Goldie was a strong person and her company was involved with Paramount, and Steve was a friend – I adored him. I went way out on some designs but they never appeared on the screen. Like the penthouse: it's very important in the script, but you only see one corner of it in the film. So I was very disillusioned. Then a curator from Germany came over and asked me if I would be interested in designing the main section of the Martin-Gropius building for the Millennium exhibition in Berlin. It was a chance to do something new. I'd never done anything like it before.

We should have kept you here. You could have designed the Millennium Dome in Greenwich!
I wouldn't have minded it. Although I don't know if I have a strong enough personality to assert myself with all the people involved in it. Maybe I'm too superficial, but I think the problem with the Dome was . . . who designed it?

Richard Rogers.
I think the problem with the Dome was that he didn't know what was going inside it.

That's right. It was just an empty space.
It's like some museum designs. The designers – I shan't mention any names – do these brilliant designs, but the curators don't know how to use the space. So I learnt, right from my earliest time in architecture, that the exterior in some way has to reflect what you're going to put inside it.

Can you imagine Prince Albert saying, 'Let's have a wonderful Crystal Palace,' having it built, and only then asking, 'What are we going to do with it?' All the basic principles of architecture – that form follows function, and vice versa – were, I think, forgotten when the Millennium Dome was designed. And there are all these tent poles everywhere, so it's quite a difficult space. It should have been called 'The Millennium Tent'.
Yes!

Anyway, before we get to Around the World in Eighty Days, *let's talk about – and you'll remember this one –* Soho Incident. *It was directed by Vernon Sewell, and you were the art director.*
Oh yes, I forgot about that!

You mentioned that Vernon Sewell was a close friend, and that he worked very fast.
Yes, with Vernon I had fun. I really enjoyed doing that film. The stars were Faith Domergue and Lee Patterson. Faith Domergue was a fasci-

nating character because a) she was the only person that I allowed to drive my supercharged Mercedes car, and b) she had been a girlfriend of the incredible Howard Hughes, so I learnt a lot of fascinating things about this incredible character. That's all I remember about that film: my relationship with Faith and the stories she used to tell me.

And Child in the House, *directed by Cy Endfield? You were art director on that one too.*
Yes. That picture came through a producer called Benjamin Fisz, and we had a lot of fun on it. Cy Endfield was a very good director actually. Phyllis Calvert was in the cast, and Mandy Miller as well. I went way out again. We talked before about spiral staircases, Georgian architecture and so on. In those days Benny Fisz was very tight with his budget. He made what was known as a blanket deal with Walton-on-Thames Studios to do the film. A blanket deal is when they give a fixed amount of money for the sets, and that's it. So Wally Smith, the head of construction at Walton Studios, was tearing his hair out when I used to say, 'We've only done eleven sets, we've got one more set to go,' and so on. Wally used to say, 'You can't do this to me!' So one day Benny Fisz came up to me and said, 'Ken, do me a favour: design on a giant piece of cardboard the most baroque set you can think of with a double sweeping staircase.' Which I did, as a joke. Then we called everyone in, including Wally Smith. Poor Wally nearly had a heart attack. He took his hat off, threw it on the floor, and said, 'You can't do this to me. This is over the blanket deal!' I'll always remember it. Wally was not too happy about my big sets, especially as we always had 'one more to do' as part of the deal.

Cy Endfield was a very interesting character; he came to England because he was blacklisted and then made a successful film about lorry drivers called Hell Drivers. *He stayed in England for some time, but then went to South Africa to film* Sands of the Kalahari *and* Zulu, *both with Stanley Baker, who'd starred in* Child in the House *as a man on the run who hides out in a London dancing academy. All those 'Zulu' films were by Cy Endfield.*
He was a very good director. You know, there were a lot of Hollywood émigrés. We were talking earlier about Eddie Dmytryk; he had a similar background. He was one of the 'Hollywood Ten'. What drew me to Eddie was that he was building model aircraft. It was his hobby. There were also a lot of political Americans like Joe Losey. They all arrived around the same time.

So it was an exciting time creatively.
Yes, very.

Around the World in Eighty Days

We come now to Around the World in Eighty Days. *How did you become involved with this film?*

By this time I was popular with Columbia. I'd done one or two pictures, such as *Soho Incident*, for Mike Frankovich – 'Big Mike' we used to call him; he was an all-American football player – who was running Columbia in England. I'd also redesigned his offices in Wardour Street. I gave him a real tycoon's office with the biggest desk in history! So he felt I was the right person to work for this real tycoon, producer Mike Todd, originally known as Avram Goldenbogen. I was already sort of friendly with the man who was by then the director, Mickey Anderson, although we had never worked together. But Mike Todd was bigger-than-life in every possible way. He was very impressive, enormously possessive, and incredibly frightening. I'll never forget when I first met him. It was in the Oliver Messel suite in the Dorchester Hotel. As with so many of these American tycoons who came over, he just stepped out of the shower, half-nude, and sat on a throne-like chair, dictating to a Japanese secretary while being shaved. And Vincent Korda was standing in one corner giving him instructions on buying an Impressionist painting. Todd was acting like I imagine Napoleon would: quite vulgar, but with enormous power. At the same time, he was saying that this would be the biggest and best film of all time. I seem to be attracted – and always have been attracted – to these bigger-than-life people. Then I met his associate producer, William Cameron Menzies – the first real production designer – who was the most delightful man. But I think he had been an alcoholic, and he just couldn't cope with the pressure. He died either during or after filming. Letizia and I had been married for two or three years and we had this flat on Pont Street. I gutted it and then had the film construction people redo it for me. And Bill (William Cameron Menzies) used to come over almost every night, crying his eyes out and getting through a bottle of Scotch – which I couldn't afford really! Then there were these touches of genius which came out of him, but he was nearly having a nervous breakdown. Mike Todd made him so nervous! You never knew what Todd was going to do next. On bank holiday weekend he gave a press conference at the Dorchester Hotel. I later found out the details from a great friend called Tom Wiseman, who was a correspondent for the *Evening Standard*. Todd claimed that he'd thought of the satellite in space before Eisenhower or the Russians! The press were rather sceptical – they loved teasing him – and so asked to be shown proof of his design. Todd said, 'I haven't got it on me. But if you come back on Tuesday, I'll show you.' So he told Bill Menzies to find a design for a three-stage rocket and a satellite – and soon. Bill knew nothing about it – neither did I for that matter – and he came to me, shaking all over, and said, 'You've got to do something.' And I said, 'Well, I have no reference here, and it's bank holiday, and all the bookshops are closed.' But I went to W. H. Smith's on Victoria station, where they had quite a lot of science fiction, and I bought whatever I could lay my hands on. In those days I would use charcoal, so on a piece of card – I thought: 'The bigger, the better'; I think it was 5 foot by 3 foot – I designed an enormous three-stage rocket and satellite. Bill Menzies was in seventh heaven and Todd had his proof!

Around the World in Eighty Days *actually begins with a prologue about space travel by Ed Murrow. He explains that it's possible to go round the world in eighty minutes, and then we see these rockets and satellites . . .*
Money was of no importance, so Mike Todd got the best people. He got Saul Bass to do those incredible credits. It was actually the first time that credit-title design was itself a visual experience in a big-budget film.

Did you have the chance to talk to William Cameron Menzies about his own career? Because he went back to the 1920s when he designed for Douglas Fairbanks – The Thief of Baghdad *and other films.*
I knew those films, and *Things to Come* as well, which he'd directed in 1936. To be working with Menzies! I felt like I was in a trance! I admired him, especially for his contribution to *Gone With the Wind*, 99 per cent of which was filmed in the studio. That was why he won the first screen credit of 'Production designed by . . .' So yes, we talked, but not a great deal; we couldn't think about anything else but Mike Todd. Menzies *was* enormously helpful to me when we were talking about colour and design, and stylisation. He said, 'Don't be afraid of it. Do whatever comes into your mind.' He encouraged me in the stylisation of sets and the use of colours; he taught me not to be afraid to use colour in bold ways. And even though the designs in *Around the World* were not originated by me, I had to translate them into reality because he had storyboards and other things to do. So he encouraged me enormously. We had the idea of treating Lloyd's of London all in black and white. The backing outside the windows was black, the costumes were black – I even painted the mahogany library steps black – because we wanted to make a point about the waiters of Lloyd's, who wore these

bright scarlet-red robes in this enormous new system. I can't remember exactly, but the scene starts with everybody in black and white, and then you get these scarlet-robed waiters walking through the frame.

And the board with the betting odds written on it.
That's right.

You were responsible for the London and the French interiors?
And the exteriors.

So location hunting as well?
Yes. It also allowed me to come into contact with people like Noël Coward and John Gielgud, who were both in the film.

All the bigwigs in the Reform Club were played by stalwarts of the London stage because the Club, where Phileas Fogg's wager begins and ends, is the other big set in the film. It has a dark-leather and velvety-green feeling to it.
Mickey Anderson was very good because he encouraged collaboration. Anything was possible. I had ideas, Mickey had ideas, Mike had ideas

The Reform Club from *Around the World in Eighty Days*, 1955

. . . I remember the Reform Club. I said to Mickey Anderson, 'What if you had all these people sitting in enormous club chairs and everybody is hidden by newspapers and we track through them.' I can't remember it exactly, but it developed as the film went on.

I remember seeing it when it first opened at the Astoria on Charing Cross Road – one of the few cinemas equipped to project 70mm film – and it was one of the most spectacular experiences I'd ever had. Unless you sat quite far back you couldn't see the whole screen at once because it had a curve. Up to this point, you'd been mainly designing for standard-ratio movies. But with Around the World in Eighty Days *the camera's position,* vis-à-vis *the actors, was completely different.*

Completely. All the sets were designed with a different approach. In fact, I wrote an article for *Kinematograph Weekly* in May 1956 about Todd-AO and 70mm. Todd was unpredictable. We had an associate producer/production manager called Cecil Foster-Kemp who had good connections to the royal family, so Todd wanted to shoot at Buckingham Palace with the guards marching out. But we were turned down, so we used Wellington Barracks with their guards marching out instead.

On Birdcage Walk.

Yes. But setting up the cameras wasn't so easy. The cameraman had the camera in position ready and, as the guards started marching towards the gate, Todd suddenly ordered one of the cameramen to put the camera straight in the middle of the gate so that the guards had to march round it. It was unforgivable in a way.

Crazy.

But he did it. Foster had to send a crate of whisky to the guards because they weren't very happy! But Todd did things like that all the time. With me too.

There's a story about the Rue de Rivoli and Place Vendôme in Paris. You had to negotiate the removal of cars so that the balloon could take off . . .

There were so many stories. One day, while I was dressing a set at MGM in Elstree Studios – and, incidentally, talking about Alfred Junge, that was the first time I saw Alfred being human – he was watching every move I made and encouraging me to do more, which was of course wonderful; having someone like Alfred do that. Well, Mike Todd arrived. He said I had to go to Paris with him, because in those days I dressed my own set too. We would be taking his plane and flying back that night. So we went to Paris and back, but I had to fly out again to design the Rue de Rivoli and Place Vendôme, all in period. The problem was, nobody at the studio in Billancourt had been paid for about two weeks. So they all came to me and said, 'Ken, we love you dearly, and we'd love to do this picture, but unless we get the money tomorrow we're going to down tools.' The French can be very tough like that. So I rang up Todd and he said, 'Well find the money.' I said, 'Mike, I'm the production designer on this picture, not the accountant.' And he said – and it was the first time I'd heard it, it's a Jewish expression – 'Don't be a schmuck.' He told me to get hold of so-and-so, but I refused to get involved. So the next day he arrived, or one of his cronies arrived, with a suitcase full of cash to pay the crew. Todd was so completely ruthless – and, actually, it wasn't me who was responsible for it – but we had to shoot in the Rue de Rivoli and Place Vendôme, and we had organised with the police to clear all the cars because it was a period picture. Kevin McClory, an ex-sound boom operator who was then a bit of a fixer, was dealing with that problem. But when it came to shooting there were about five or six cars left, so the police towed them away. Unfortunately they turned out to be diplomatic cars. After that incident, no foreign productions were allowed to be shot in Paris for two years! And the Chief of Police resigned.

But they are great shots of Paris, so it certainly worked. After all that – it was your biggest production so far, and your second major Hollywood film, after Hornblower *– it must have been very galling to see your name misspelt in the credits.*
Adams. Ken Adams, London.

After all that, they couldn't even get your name right!
Yes. Todd was involved in so many things that he had to rely on other people to get things right. I had another funny story . . . You see, he was so vulgar but so powerful. I could never say 'no' to him for some reason.

I don't think anyone could. He persuaded all those actors to appear in the same movie; nobody could say 'no'. After all, he'd fired the original director, John Farrow, just as shooting began.
But it's also the money. He'd say, 'Don't talk about money. You'll get paid whatever you want.' That was his attitude. So the film was over, I was working on *John Paul Jones*, and suddenly I got a phone call from Todd saying, 'Get your ass over to the Dorchester.' Now my first reaction, when somebody says 'get your ass over', is not to go. But I went. He wanted me to design the first-night party for *Around the World in Eighty Days*, which the *Daily Telegraph* or someone was sponsoring. I

came up with a very Victorian concept for the invitation and the party, and at the *Telegraph* Lady Somebody-or-other liked it very much. Then Todd – who was by this time married to Liz Taylor and living in the South of France – said, 'I want to see those designs.' He asked me to fly over to Paris and see the film, which hadn't been shown yet. In Paris I was met by a United Artists representative who told me I would be staying in Mr Todd's suite at the Hôtel Meurice. I said, 'I can't stay in Mr Todd's suite. There must be some mistake.' But he said, 'We've had strict instructions that you're staying in his suite and you're seeing the film tonight.' So I watched the film, which wasn't very nice for me because it was in French, and then I had nothing with me and I stayed in one of the rooms in Todd's suite. The next morning, about seven-thirty or eight, much to my surprise, Mike was going apeshit, saying, 'What are you doing in my bed?!' I said, 'Don't blame me. It's got nothing to do with me. It's David Hannah' – I even remember his name – 'who put me in here.' So he went into the bathroom to shave. Liz Taylor had another room, you see. I was just waiting for the right moment to get out of bed because I didn't have any pyjamas on! To cut a long story short – we were then discussing how much I liked the film and I did like it enormously, but I had certain reservations. And he said, 'Ken Adam didn't like the film.' I said, 'I didn't say that.' Then he said, in the bathroom with all this going on, that he wanted to see my sketches. So I showed him and he said, 'That's so much shit.' and stomped out of the room. At this moment Liz came in and, I mean, she was the most beautiful woman I'd ever seen – I'd never seen violet eyes before – and she said, 'Well, I think they're absolutely divine.' Twenty minutes later I got a call from Mike who had just held a press conference down below and wanted to see me. So I went down. He said he'd reconsidered his opinion about the sketches and he now thought they were subtle!

He died soon after that in his private plane. It was called the Lucky Liz. *You'd clearly hit the big time, but you were still 'art director'. You weren't yet 'production designer'.*
No, because that term wasn't generally used.

Exactly.
Menzies was associate producer on that picture. I did one or two more pictures as art director but I never met James W. Sullivan, the art director who worked on the Hollywood studio sets and other locations for *Around the World in Eighty Days*. I really couldn't go wrong with Mike Todd; I was his blue-eyed boy. I was so pleased that he gave me that credit. I was at Columbia when I got the Oscar nomination for Art Direction (colour), and there were celebrations all round.

Then John Paul Jones. *You didn't actually design the film, but you did the preliminary work. Is that right?*

There was a Russian producer, Samuel Bronston, who made all those pictures in Spain, and his friend Boris Leven, another Russian, was one of the greatest production designers in Hollywood. He did Martin Scorsese's *New York, New York*. Boris was a lovely man, one of the best, and he became a close personal friend. Boris was trying to keep the peace with Sam Bronston, who was in New York at the time. Again, I had to deal with all the ships, so we went to Italy and I set up an art department there, which I knew of course from *Helen of Troy*. There was a famous sailing-ship expert, a man called Arthur Villiers.

Yes, he wrote numerous books about sailing and the sea.

That's right. So I took Arthur with me to Sicily and we bought two big wooden schooners in pretty good condition. I brought them to Fiumicino, near Rome, and set up the whole art department. I started designing the ships and we started building them – all the cannons and everything. I had hired a wonderful Bulgarian draughtsman in the art department, and one morning when we came in he saw a lizard on the wall and said, 'This is going to bring bad luck to everything.' The next thing I know, I've received a letter from my bank manager in London saying that my pay cheques have bounced because of insufficient funds. By this time Boris was back in Hollywood. I held the fort in Italy. The Italian staff were with the bank of Sicily and their money was still coming through, but I was constantly on the phone to New York saying, 'What's happening?' They said, 'Don't worry. We've decided to change the name of the company. While all this goes on, you'll have to excuse us. You will get your money.' Then these cheques started bouncing for everyone in Italy too. I got a call from Sam Bronston's right-hand man, Barney Glassman, saying, 'We're getting Admiral Nimitz and the Pierpoint Morgans coming to Rome and we would like Letizia and you to take them out' and I said, 'Wait a moment. I haven't got any money!' He said, 'Well Ken, you know you're going to get it.' So we had to do it because it was a big prestigious picture for the Americans about the first American naval hero.

Set in the American Revolution.

That's right. And the ships were being built by a cooperative – so all these people weren't being paid either – and we had these ships lying in Fiumicino. So I finally decided to get a lawyer and we closed shop. I auctioned all the art department equipment and props because we had to pay at least some of the Italian staff. I had – thank God – a return ticket to London for me and Letizia. It was disastrous. Back in London Boris Leven hadn't been paid either. I told the story to my friend Mike

Frankovich and he said, 'You've got to sue them. You can use my lawyer.' His name, which I'll never forget, was Gustav Jahr. The first thing he wanted was a retainer of approximately $220 to take on the case. I said to Mike it was like throwing good money after bad money and he said, 'It's your choice.' So I paid the retainer and a year passed. I then got two letters from Gustav that said he'd instigated a search but there was no money to be found. So by now I was doing a big job for John Ford, and I get a phone call from Samuel Bronston and Barney Glassman, saying they're at the Dorchester and they would like to have breakfast with me. I told John Ford the story and he said, 'You'd better go see them. But don't let them con you into anything.' So we had breakfast. They wanted to talk about my drawings that were in safe keeping with the lawyers in Italy, along with the boats. So I said, 'Sorry children, but I don't have them.' They said, 'We'll come with you to Rome and you'll see that we pay all your staff.' John Ford gave me two days off to make sure they paid everybody. And they did pay everybody, and they got the drawings and the ships and they made the picture about a year and a half later. Although my ship designs were used in the final version, Franz Bachelin was the only credited art director.

That's a terrible story. I think Samuel Bronston's financing was always wobbly when he made those huge films outside Madrid: El Cid, King of Kings, 55 Days at Peking, The Fall of the Roman Empire ...
Yes, but he was a typical Russian entrepreneur. He did some incredible pictures. The nice thing about doing *John Paul Jones*, for me, was that it started one of the closest friendships of my career with Boris Leven. When I came to Hollywood Boris advised me on everything. He told me where I could get the best assistants and so on. We became really, really close friends.

You obviously have a gift for making connections and establishing friendships and networks.
Well, maybe.

Because one thing always leads to another.
Yes, but with Boris it was different. He wasn't paid either, and Samuel Bronston was supposed to be one of his pals. He was a Russian too. We both suffered for a while so it established a common cause between us.

John Ford

Let's move on to 1957 and Gideon's Day, *a film about twenty-four hours in the life of a Scotland Yard Inspector. It was written by T. E. B.*

Clarke, who'd scripted The Blue Lamp. *There was one of the greats, John Ford, who had recently made a small film in Ireland called* The Rising of the Moon. *Ford's career was at a low point; he was not making big westerns with John Wayne in Monument Valley. Instead he was in London making this thriller. I gather you met John Ford in a state of undress as well.*

Yes. They had always 'just stepped out of the shower'. The producer was a lovely man called Michael Killanin.

Who produced The Rising of the Moon, *and helped with* The Quiet Man. *I believe he was trying to establish an Irish film industry.*

Yes, and he was involved in the Olympics at one time. John Ford considered himself to be completely Irish, like Killanin. When I met Ford for the first time he had a handkerchief that he used to chew and bite on, and the thing in the eye, you know. He was also just stepping out of the shower. The first thing he said to me – which I'll never forgot – was, 'I've heard a lot about you.' So I said, 'Mr Ford, I've heard a lot about *you*. I'm a great fan of yours.' He said, 'Yes, but if you think that I'm the sort of arty-crafty director who pokes the camera up the nostrils of the actors or between their legs, that's not me. I shoot a picture the way I see it, the way I feel the camera move. And if I don't like the script, I tear out the pages. If you understand that, I'm sure we'll get on fine.' So that was my first meeting. I had a near disaster on that picture. It wasn't a very interesting picture – Jack Hawkins plays the Chief Inspector and most of the action takes place in his office at old Scotland Yard – so I was desperately thinking about how to make it more visually interesting. We were shooting at MGM studios in Elstree, and I had a pretty good special-effects department, so I thought instead of having a painted backing outside the windows, we'd build Westminster Bridge in miniature, with all the traffic. I discussed this with the special-effects man and he said, 'Yes, we can do that.' John Ford arrived and it's fantastic – there's Westminster Bridge and a red bus is going over it. Ford staged the scene with Hawkins sitting in front of the window so that we could see the bridge with the traffic. I was standing next to Ford when suddenly I saw the buses jerking and coming to a halt. At first, Ford said nothing. Then he shouted, 'Cut!' He looked at me and asked, 'What went wrong?' I thought, this is me getting sacked! I said, 'I can't help you. I'll have to get the special-effects department to find out.' He said, 'Don't worry too much about it, but it has to work tomorrow.' What had happened was that the heat of the lamps had stretched the canvas on which the toy buses and cars were sewn, that went around a roller. So they redid the whole thing overnight with leather. Thank God leather wasn't affected by the heat.

They're still a bit jerky, I have to say.
Are they?!

The little red bus looks slightly improbable as it crosses the bridge. But it's very strange because in the early 1960s I went on a cruise ship with my family and the cinema on board was showing two movies, and one of them was Gideon's Day. *So I saw that film about eight times.*
Oh no!

Most British movies about the police at that time – and most Jack Hawkins movies – were black and white, so at least there's richness to the colour. But it's a bit 'tourist London', and for some reason it was released in the United States in black and white.

Night of the Demon

Then came Night of the Demon, *directed by Jacques Tourneur late in his career. He was the son of a great silent-film director and had made some terrific* noir *films in 1940s Hollywood. I'm a great fan of* Night of the Demon, *but the big question about the film is whether there should have been a demon or not. The writer, Charles Bennett, gave an interview in which he said there was no demon in his script; it was all suggested. It was footprints. It was in the corner of the retina. It was one of those ghost stories where you don't quite see what's there, like the original M. R. James story. But the producer, who also got a co-writer credit . . .*
Hal E. Chester.

Design of the Fire Demon, 1956

Who's still alive and lives in north London – he worked on the script and put in this bug-eyed monster. So Bennett blamed Chester for wrecking the concept and making it into a type of drive-in movie. I don't know where you stand on that?
I designed the monster, but under protest. I agreed completely with Tourneur. We both felt that it was completely wrong to show the monster because we felt the footsteps – when you see steam coming from the imprints – were enough. But they insisted, even though we were dead against it. Jacques Tourneur was a lovely man to work with, except when we had this big battle with Hal E. Chester!

In the US Night of the Demon *was cut into a much shorter film – about eighty minutes – and called* Curse of the Demon. *It was issued as part of a double bill at the drive-ins and did pretty well.*
It's amazing. You are not alone, Christopher; David Sylvester loved it

too. And yesterday these kids from Electronic Arts in Hollywood came here and Danny Bilson said to me, 'Why is everybody so crazy about *Night of the Demon*?' I said, 'Have you seen it?' He hadn't, but his producer Dave Davis had, and he loved it. It's become a cult movie.

It has. Most of the interiors are sets, but not all; you also shot in the British Museum Round Library with lots of readers in the background. There's an overhead shot of the Reading Room, and then the close-ups taken in another part of the library.
You don't think they cut to a set for the close-up stuff?

No, I'm pretty sure it's in the library!
Tourneur was very good and we had an excellent cast: Niall MacGinnis, Peggy Cummins . . . And I really went to town on the sets, designing these big country-house sets and so on. But, otherwise, I don't remember much about it.

It was around this time, in 1958, that Vernon Sewell directed Battle of the V-1, *or* Unseen Heroes, *as it was known in the US. You were production designer.*
I think that came before. Although I designed every set and location for *Battle of the V-1*, I asked Vernon Sewell to release me from the physical work on the picture because I was doing the John Ford picture.

You did the preliminary work?
Yes, I did all the designs. In fact, I've still got them all. I got the production design credit, but it was my assistant Bernard Sarron who did all the practical work, and he was credited as art director.

4 Production Designer

In August 1956 you wrote an article for Films & Filming *magazine called 'Designing Sets for Action', and it already contained your thesis that the point of production design is to create an idea of a place rather than a real place. 'When designing an apparently realistic background,' you say, 'I depart in some way or another from reality.' So realism is a style, a style that changes with the times. You also say that you prefer to work for directors who give you 'the opportunity to be creative and less reproductive'. The case-study in the article is Cy Endfield's* Child in the House, *where the director 'preferred to play his action in the foreground, in order to establish the set and depth behind the actors'. You responded by 'stylising slightly some of the sets'. What's interesting about the article is that your philosophy of film design was already well thought out. You like to heighten reality . . .*
I would love to read that article again. I must have it here somewhere. I've got the issue of *Sight and Sound* where they talked to me.

That was in winter 1964. This is even earlier. It has stills of two of your drawings to illustrate this 'heightening'.
Really?

In 1956, long before Bond and Dr Strangelove, *you already had a very coherent idea – hammered out between the late 1940s and mid-1950s – of what a production designer's role should be. It says a lot about your future career – that you do not conform to the school of 'shooting on the streets' like the Italian Neo-realists, or the Hollywood exposés with their subways and neon-lit exteriors, or the hyper-realists who created a detailed documentary effect in the studio, an 'illusion of life' to segue seamlessly into location footage. Or to the old-fashioned, theatrical 'cinema of quality', the painterly tradition that we've discussed. You are somewhere between all of them – ahead of all of them – because your work looks real, but there's always something magnified about it that creates an effect in the mind of the audience. You say you find it boring to copy reality so your job is to create a different kind of reality in the studio. The drawings from* Child in the House *are much more expressive than technical drawings too.*
Well, at this time I decided to liberate myself from my inhibitions and the rigidity of my architectural studies. I sketched more freely and in less detail with powerful strokes. As we've discussed, I had a good grounding in architecture, design and composition. Drawing with a

hard pencil and a T-square certainly appealed to my pedantic sense, and these beautiful drawings, my early drawings, were a kind of self-defence, really. I was playing safe. I was inhibited. I was afraid to let go and express myself. I would usually start by drawing plans and elevations for my set designs. The drawings were certainly precise but they lacked character and atmosphere. It was Letizia – I must give her credit for this – having seen me doing these large, laboured and rather lifeless perspective drawings, who kept fishing my first rough scribbles out of the waste-paper basket and saying, 'These are much more alive and exciting than those dead sketches.' So with the help of felt pens – which had recently been invented – I changed my drawing technique completely. My designs became much bolder and more expressive. I increasingly used a felt pen with a wedge-shaped tip instead of pencil, conté or pen and ink. A Flow-master, rather than a hard pencil. I used broader strokes and eliminated unnecessary details. As a result, my sketches became stronger, allowing me to experiment with light and shade as a guide for the cameraman when lighting the set. In order to heighten the 'chiaroscuro' effect, I did my sketches in black and white. And I now began with a sketch, rather than a technical drawing – which was important in helping me to visualise the eventual effect in three dimensions – however rough the sketch. It is something to do with the way my mind works.

Apart from Letizia, did anyone else encourage you in this direction during your 'art director' days?
I remember John Bryan once saying to me, 'Roughness of your sketch will bring it to life.' And Lotte Eisner, the director of the Cinémathèque in Paris, selected some of my first roughs for her collection. She much preferred them to my big projections.

I think your first credit as 'production designer' was around this time, too: in 1959. The original definition of 'production designer' famously came from David O. Selznick in a 1938 memo during pre-production on Gone With the Wind. *He wrote, 'I hope to have* Gone With the Wind *prepared almost down to the last camera angle before we start shooting.' And of William Cameron Menzies' role in this he added, 'His work in this picture, as I see it, will be a lot greater in scope than is normally associated with the term 'art direction'.' As you say, his credit in the end was 'This Production Designed by William Cameron Menzies'. As an independent producer, Selznick was able to make unilateral decisions like this. Ken, obviously the duties of a production designer vary according to the scale of the production and the size of the team, but how would* you *define the role in relation to the other craft skills within the art department'*

The first person to be referred to as production designer was, as you say, William Cameron Menzies. His function was to design almost every frame of *Gone with the Wind*. In other words, after first discussing the concept with a director, the function of a production designer is to establish a style and visual progression for the film, and then physically realise it. Ideally speaking, that means supervising everything that is visual: sets, locations, props, coordination of costumes with the settings . . . I personally like to be involved from a very early stage. In script discussions, if possible. In order to allow me more creative freedom, I always like to have an art director collaborating with me who, like a personal assistant, is responsible for the practical organisation and the budget. It is the production designer who assembles the art department. Then there is a set decorator who, based on the production designer's work, has to provide the furnishings and props for the film. His work is difficult; he must be experienced and have good taste. He has to assemble the right furniture, paintings, fabrics, lamps and so on, and dress the sets. More than anything he has to understand the parts played by the actors; the background of the various characters in the script. On top of that, he has to satisfy me, the production designer! Then there are the draughtsmen who translate the production designer's visual concepts into working drawings and models. And the construction department is supervised by the construction coordinator, also part of the team. As production designer, one always depends a great deal on the efficiency of the art department and its effectiveness as a team. If you are asking me how to succeed as a production designer, I always say there are three requirements. The first requirement is talent and imagination. Secondly, you need luck. And the third requirement is the ability to assess and cope with personalities such as the director's, the ability to communicate with people, and the courage of your convictions. I'd say those are the essential qualities.

So, in the ten years between 1948 and 1958 you graduated from architectural draughtsmen to dependable art director to fully fledged creative artist. By the late 1950s it was really beginning to happen for you.
Well, getting back to the heightened effect, where I really went to town for the first time – apart from *Around the World in Eighty Days* – was in 1960 on *The Trials of Oscar Wilde*. I completely stylised everything. It seems naïve now, but I had the idea that each set should make a definite colour statement. I discussed it long before with the cameraman, Ted Moore, and even went so far as to put colour gelatines on all my sketches to give him an idea of the mood for each set. It was a new idea in those days and Ted was wonderful; he kept to that. Stylisation of design and so on we can discuss later. By the way, I reverted to using

Watercolour design for the Marquess of
Queensberry's reception room

pen and ink and watercolour for my sketches here. I felt it was more
suitable for the film.

The famous set in The Trials of Oscar Wilde *is the Marquess of
Queensberry's reception room. The story goes that you had to do it for
almost nothing because the money had run out. Can you tell me about
that?*

Well, it was hard because a) the money had run out and b) I didn't have
time to do research about what Queensberry's castle in Scotland looked
like. So what I decided to do was a complete stylisation using all the
classical elements of the St James's Theatre and the Café Royal. The
only new design element was a very tall, slender French window with a
circular top at the end of the set. Then I used Georgian doors from the
St James's and I painted the whole floor like Siena marble. I had a very
good painter and it was beautifully done. Then I had the idea of treating the set in two colours only – terracotta for the walls, and everything
else in black – because it was after the funeral. I talked the director, Ken
Hughes, into dressing all the actors in black. And the whole set was
built in a forced perspective. It was the first time that I got recognition
for my work from the critics and others: Luchino Visconti was President of the Moscow Film Festival in 1961 and he gave me the first prize
for best design.

That was your first major award.
Yes, but I got the nomination for *Around the World in Eighty Days.*

*This time you actually won! It sounds like a mad situation, like waiting
for a bus and then three arrive, because there'd been no feature film*

about Oscar Wilde and then suddenly two are being made at the same time. You had to get yours finished first. The competition was Gregory Ratoff's Oscar Wilde *with Robert Morley.*

Ours was in colour and theirs was in black and white. It was crazy. Somebody should have withdrawn. But remember we had two executive producers on *The Trials of Oscar Wilde*: Cubby Broccoli and Irving Allen. But the power was with Allen. He was another monster in a way. He was an ex-editor so he started four cutting rooms, running at the same time. I think you will find that six or seven weeks after we started shooting at Associated British – who in those days were at Elstree – the film was released on the West End screens.

Unbelievable.
It *was* unbelievable.

You blew the other film out of the water.
Yes, but you see, Ken Hughes was a very good director, but neurotic. He got on with Cubby but not with Irving Allen. So one day, when Irving Allen appeared on set, Ken stopped shooting. Irving thought better of it and disappeared. It was a race, but Peter Finch was fantastic in the title role.

You only had a budget of £15,000 for all the sets and props, but this seemed to concentrate the mind creatively. The Queensberry set cost a mere £750.
Yes. The budget ruled out any attempt to create an authentic reconstruction of the past, even if I'd wanted to. And I stuck to this principle for over fifty years!

Robert Aldrich

In the late 1950s, around the same time as The Trials of Oscar Wilde, *you worked with the American director Robert Aldrich on three films:* Ten Seconds to Hell, The Angry Hills *and* Sodom and Gomorrah. *How did they come about?*
Well again, through Mike Frankovich of Columbia. Michael Carreras, who was then just a kid, had been set to produce this picture by his father who was head of the Variety Club or something, and they thought I was the right person to design it. So I met Bob Aldrich and it was another one of those meetings: he was just stepping out of the shower! Bob had the build of a football player. He was an all-American, I think from Virginia University. He came from the famous Aldrich family, cousins of the Rockefellers and the Vanderbilts. He was a rebel,

but he thought big. For him, having money was a means of making films, and his great ambition was to be the big boss of his own studio. He was highly intelligent and had enormous charm. I remember we didn't know where we were going to make this picture.

Was this Ten Seconds to Hell, *the first one – made for Hammer Films?*
Yes. We were driving in the car and – because I always say what I believe – I told Bob that I'd read the script and I thought it had two stories. So we argued about it and left it at that. About fifteen years later he asked me, 'Who was that snotty young production designer who had the chutzpah to tell me what he thought of the story?'

It was a post-Second World War drama set in 1945 Berlin.
It was about the German bomb-disposal police who were ex-soldiers of the German army. We shot it in Berlin in 1958 with American actors: Jeff Chandler, Jack Palance . . . And the French actress Martine Carol played the girl, Margot. It was an incredible experience. Berlin in 1958 was fantastic because it was like an island in no-man's land. Everyone in Berlin wanted to have a good time. We were working at UFA Studios in Tempelhof, and because the Berlin Wall didn't exist, my labourers came from both the East and West. Half the studio workers commuted from the East. I was very lucky to find an old villa in the Ballenstedter Strasse near the Kurfürsten Damm, and of course I gave big parties and we had a ball all the time! The more time I spent with Bob, the more I was attracted to him, and the more I learnt from him. He was an old American pro, who started as the combined first assistant director and production manager to Charlie Chaplin, Julien Duvivier, and many other great directors in Hollywood. So you couldn't pull the wool over his eyes; he knew everything. He caught me out a few times and said, 'You're full of shit.' Or, 'You're bluffing.' So I never attempted to tell him something that wasn't true because he would always find me out. Much later, in 1960, when we were doing *Sodom and Gomorrah* in Italy, he said, 'Ken, it's only a six-week job for an Italian company.' I can't remember the name . . .

Titanus. The producer was Goffredo Lombardo.
Yes. And to cut a *very* long story short, I actually worked on that picture for a year and a half! We were shooting in the Sahara. One bank holiday I took the star, Anouk Aimée, and her boyfriend to the famous Gazelle D'Or hotel.

In Morocco?
In Morocco. They put on a special dance for us. But I knew Anouk had to shoot the next morning so I kept putting pressure on her to leave.

With Jeff Chandler (left) and Robert Aldrich (right), Berlin 1958

85

Then she was given a live goat. I remember driving them back very late in a big American car and I asked them to fill it up but found out halfway home that they hadn't. And in the desert that's not funny. So we finally stopped at an outpost and I had to wake up the mayor of the community because he had a pump. Anyway, I finally arrived back with Anouk who, without any sleep, went immediately into make-up. We lost a day's shooting because she couldn't look into the sun. She was terrible. And Bob, who I told you I couldn't lie to, kept saying, 'What happened? You have to tell me.' I said, 'I just ran out of petrol.' About fifteen years later in LA, I told him the true story. After that, he wouldn't talk to me! That's the sort of person he was. Going back to *Ten Seconds to Hell*, it was a great experience for me. We always had fun. Bob used to put me in the film as an extra. We were burning the candle at both ends and there were the Americans, of course, and the German girls were beautiful and some of them were just going crazy. I'll never forget my birthday: I held a big party in the old tradition – rather like those in the days of my father – with a small orchestra. Some of the waiters had even worked at the Hotel Adlon before the war and had known my father, and there were a lot of these girls who were models showing in the spring collections. And Leon Uris, who had just published *Exodus*, appeared at the door and said, 'Ken, how can you, with your past, fraternise with German girls?' Well to cut a long story short, it was he who got very involved with one of them! Bob Aldrich got involved too. Tremendously involved; it broke up his marriage.

He really knew how to use a production designer.
Yes, absolutely. We had a relationship where he knew I was always honest with him, and he liked my sketches for the film. We had a ball. Letizia visited – she was working in London so she couldn't be there all the time – and she was very attracted to Bob. They became close friends. And what was so interesting, because he was a very good director, we always felt that there was old American money behind him. He was the first person to invite Letizia and I to Hollywood in 1961 or '62.

He seems to have been a strange character – very wealthy, the black sheep of the family, making some very interesting offbeat movies, like Kiss Me Deadly.
He was leftish-liberal and he was physically very tough.

And a lot of his movies were about violence, the beast in man.
Yes. And that was one thing that used to disturb me because at times he would drink a lot and we had Jack Palance, who played an anti-Nazi architect, who was an ex-boxer, and I was always trying to stop him

and Bob coming to blows in my bloody villa. So it was constantly tense when they were drinking. They were aggressive drunks.

Were you around during the shooting?
All the time. Remember, Christopher, this was the first occasion that I'd been to Berlin since the war. I knew that many of the UFA studio staff at Tempelhof must have worked under the Nazis. And as I say, Berlin was like an island in an uncertain sea; it had the atmosphere of a frontier city. Whilst I was working with Bob and having a ball, I didn't have time to dwell on unpleasant memories. However, I did see the burnt-out ruins of our Tiergarten apartment.

Did your mother Lilli join you at any time in 1958?
Yes, she visited and went to some of the shops and cafés she knew along the Kurfürsten Damm. She was not at all sentimental. To her, Berlin belonged to the past, not the present. She'd made a completely new life in London. Whereas for me, Berlin's atmosphere in the 1950s was like an extension of the late 1920s. Everyone wanted to have a good time because in that uncertain political climate, nobody knew how long it would last. Two years later the Wall was constructed and Berlin was turned from a swinging city into two provincial towns.

At least in Ten Seconds to Hell, *the film featured another bunker with a low ceiling – the engineers' operations room! Then in the same year you collaborated on* The Angry Hills *with Robert Aldrich.*
That came immediately afterwards. Bob had a theory which I think was the greatest theory of anyone I was ever connected with: 'I expect people to be professional and I am professional but what's the good if you don't have any laughs on the picture?' He had a great sense of humour and so although we were working extremely hard and under enormous pressure we always had a laugh.

Where was The Angry Hills *made?*
We made it at MGM in Elstree and in Greece around Athens with Gia Scala, Stanley Baker and Robert Mitchum. Mitchum was a lovely person. He and his wife spent a lot of time at the flat Letizia and I still had in Pont Street. But they were hard drinkers, alcoholics I would say. She broke our glass table once. One day at the studio Mitchum returned from a drink at the local pub with the boys, and he was staggering when he came onto the stage. Bob Aldrich saw him and said, 'We're not going to shoot this afternoon.' But Mitchum went into the portable dressing room near the stage and he came back out when we were ready to shoot. He had a big scene with Donald Wolfit, and Mitchum didn't fluff once. Later on, I talked to Mitchum about it. He admitted

that he'd had too much to drink and he knew that everybody, including Aldrich, thought filming would stop. But nobody knew that he had a photographic mind. So while everyone was waiting he was memorising his lines. In those days all the stars, certainly those I was involved with, were all drinking like hell.

Can you recall much about The Angry Hills? *It is set in Nazi-occupied Greece, and centres on the Robert Mitchum character's gradual discovery of commitment. According to Robert Aldrich, the shoot did not go well.*
I don't remember. It was another wartime picture and we used a lot of Greek locations. I don't know if I should tell you this story, but I'm going to: Letizia was in Italy and Gia Scala was Italian and we were all great friends. But one evening Gia had a terrible row with her father and asked me for help. So I drove her for more than an hour in my supercharged Mercedes until I nearly ran out of petrol and invited her into our Pont Street apartment for a drink. She had been drinking like hell and didn't want me to take her home and I didn't want a scandal, but of course I got a scandal! I took her downstairs, paid a taxi driver to take her home, and then went to bed. At about five in the morning I got a phone call from a police station asking me if I knew Gia Scala because they'd just stopped her from jumping off Waterloo Bridge!

Oh dear!
So, as usual in these situations, I rang Bob Aldrich. He always took a sleeping pill so he used to hate it when I woke him up, but I said, 'Bob, she's your star and she's got to shoot!' Of course, the press got wind of it and they started checking up. They were terrible. They found out that I had a row with Gia in Pont Street at three in the morning. So Letizia immediately phones me from Rome asking, 'What's happened?!' We had to put Gia in the back of my Mercedes, cover her up, and smuggle her into MGM to avoid the press. She was very unstable.

Gia Scala was a big star. She played the Greek resistance fighter Anna in The Guns of Navarone *in 1961. Unfortunately she succeeded in killing herself in 1972.*
Yes. She was a lovely person, and actually very friendly with Letizia. But very unstable. It was a strange situation. With Bob Aldrich's pictures, you always got involved. We were shooting *Sodom and Gomorrah* in Rome when I got a call at three in the morning telling me that somebody was trying to kill Anouk Aimée, and could I do something about it? I didn't like the sound of it; I knew her boyfriend Julio was six foot three inches tall. So I rang Bob Aldrich and said, 'I can't save her

by myself. I need some muscle!' And he said, 'I don't give a shit; I've taken my sleeping pill.' So I drove there on my own in my Mini – by the way, I'd had the engine hotted up, before the Cooper came out – and there she was in tears. I talked to Julio – who was very dangerous – so then he walked out with a little suitcase. I was left driving her around in the Mini for the rest of the night, until we saw Julio standing on a corner with his suitcase, trying to get a cab. We said, 'Let's pick him up.' So I did, and that was the end of the story!

You always seemed to carry the can.
Yes. I don't know why, but I always did. We worked very hard in Greece on *The Angry Hills*, then again there was a bank holiday and Bob Aldrich chartered a big yacht and invited me, Letizia, Gia Scala, Jane Stuart and all these people for forty-eight hours of sailing. Bob always believed in working hard and playing hard. Very classy. We soon met Stanley Kubrick, and the discussions between those two were fascinating. Everybody came to our flat in Pont Street too, and later to the house here in Knightsbridge. It was always interesting to watch great people like Stanley, Bob and Joe Mankiewicz talk. I just listened . . .

Let's talk about Sodom and Gomorrah *in 1960 to '61. It was an interesting design challenge; you'd created ancient designs for* Helen of Troy, *but when you came to* Sodom and Gomorrah, *there were only two verses in the Old Testament to work from. All you've got is a pillar of salt and the two cities of Sodom and Gomorrah. How did you start?*
I designed it in Rome and it was stylised: a bit Egyptian. But there were a lot of mechanical problems because we had to build the salt mine in the Moroccan desert.

It was Cinecittà in Rome and Morocco?
Yes, and we had one disaster after another. I went on a location recce by myself and a local Arab told me about an interesting village called Ait Ben Haddou. There was no road to it, but it was fantastic. It was later used for *The Man Who Would Be King*, and it's been used ever since. To me it was what I imagined biblical architecture would have looked like, because it's all this mud architecture. So I built an enormous gate and we shot a great deal there. I used Italian and Moroccan crews who built it all for real, so it's still standing!

From what I've read it wasn't a happy production; Sergio Leone was assistant director, but he was fired.
Yes, he directed the second unit. I had to prepare the runway for the cavalry outside Marrakech so I was with him in the morning when they were preparing to shoot. But the cavalry didn't turn up, and I didn't

Main gate and walls, Ait Ben Haddou,
Morocco 1960

know why. We found out they'd been sent to Mauritania to fight a war!
But the biggest problem, Christopher, was that Rossana Podestà, who
was also the star in *Helen of Troy*, suddenly got a heart problem in the
desert, like a heart attack, even though she was only a young girl. So the
doctor sent her back to Italy to recover. Bob Aldrich said to me, 'Can
we shoot around her for five or six weeks?' Well we did. Rossana came
back to an air-conditioned trailer, but after two or three days in that
terrible heat, she was ill again. So we packed up everything in Morocco and went back to Cinecittà in Italy where I had to rebuild a whole
section of Sodom and Gomorrah outside Cinecittà. Luckily I found
some sand dunes on the way to Fiumicino that looked like Morocco, so
we filmed the rest there. Everybody said, 'Why did we have to go to
Morocco in the first place?!' It shows you what can go wrong. Bob
Aldrich had read somewhere that a Spanish art director had collapsed
actual buildings on top of extras and actors without hurting them on
the set of Sergio Leone's *The Colossus of Rhodes*, so Bob told me to
find out what this guy used. He used foam blocks. So we built our collapsing buildings in the city of Sodom and Gomorrah out of foam as
well. But then began four weeks of rain, so we had to shoot inside the
studio. When the rain stopped, the first scene we shot outside was two
lovers kissing in a doorway. Then BANG! We collapsed the building.
Afterwards, we couldn't find the actors! It was terrible. Everybody was
digging through the foam. When we did find them, they were knocked
out cold. Fortunately they were only stunned, but I told Bob I wanted

90

to investigate. We found out from the construction manager that he had sub-contracted labourers who, instead of using mud to bind the foam blocks together, had used cement!

Big pieces of dried cement falling down . . .
They could have killed somebody. So we had to stop shooting and I had to revise every one of those collapsible buildings to make sure they were all right.

Rossana Podestà continued to work in films until the mid-1980s. In 1983 she played Hera, the wife of Zeus, in the Lou Ferrigno Hercules. One of the oddities of Sodom and Gomorrah *is that in the Bible there are two cities, whereas in this movie there is only one, even though they are called 'twin cities'. The other oddity is that nothing particularly sinful actually takes place. But there were some very interesting designs: strange implements of torture and so on.*
I loved that set.

There's a giant wheel with bodies on it, revolving like a rotisserie. And big prisons . . .
You have reminded me. I'd forgotten that big wheel. I remember Maurice Binder directing the credits. He wanted to direct the orgy and Bob let him do it. It should have taken one day, but he made it last three! He drove everybody crazy.

Isn't the orgy going on behind the credits?
Yes. But we had a lot of laughs filming it. And there was the famous time – one of the first of many – that Wally Veevers saved my life.

How was that?
Well, there's a scene in which a dam built by the Hebrews is destroyed in order to engulf the Helamite cavalry. I used an existing concrete dam in the desert by painting old stones and dressing it up with wooden uprights. But in the film the dam has to collapse. So I phoned Wally Veevers and he flew out to the desert – even though he wasn't well – and said that if I gave him some idea of how I imagined it, he'd have a solution by the next day. He built a gigantic model of this dam at Shepperton and just blew it up. How he got the water to gush out over the charging cavalry . . .

It's clever because the cavalry genuinely look as though they've been stopped in their tracks, and the water really does seem to engulf them. A few years ago there was an exhibition at the Museum of Modern Art in Paris about the art of storyboarding, and they had the drawings of that sequence, attributed to you.

Sodomite torture chamber at Cinecittà, 1960

Well, I did some of them, but I had a wonderful assistant who was a professor at the Rome Academy. He had problems but he adored me. He had a fantastic touch and he did the most beautiful sketches. So I used him for that. He was also one of my early assistants on *Helen of Troy*.

Sodom and Gomorrah *wasn't the success that Bob Aldrich wanted it to be.*
No. I think Joseph E. Levine was in trouble on that one.

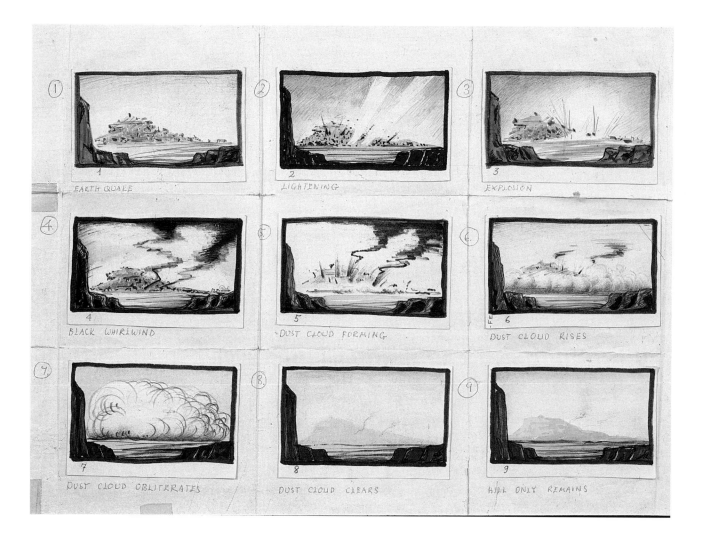

Storyboard showing destruction of
Sodom and Gomorrah, with mushroom
cloud

Dr No

In 1959, before you began working on Dr No, *you did some preparatory work for* The Long Ships, *a Viking movie.*
I was working for Irving Allen and Cubby Broccoli was at that time his partner.

Was that your first introduction to Cubby Broccoli?
Yes, through Irving Allen, and he was another very tough American producer. Very explosive and vulgar at times, but a good showman. I'll never forget when Maurice Binder and myself – having established a relationship with Cubby – met with Irving because we had our own project and asked for his help to set it up.

Was this for you to design?
No, it was to produce *and* design. But he said, 'I've got enough geniuses

around me. Who needs you two?!' And he threw us out of the office. Irving was always doing that. Cubby, who had an office across the way, used to collect the wreckage and urge you not to take Irving seriously. Anyway, Irving asked me to go on a location trip for *The Long Ships* with his Yugoslavian friend – I can't remember his name – who was supposed to help me. *The Long Ships* is meant to take place in Norway, Scandinavia, but Irving said, 'Nobody cares. Yugoslavia is cheap. Go and see what you can do.' Christopher, I was all over Yugoslavia for five weeks. It was one of the worst trips I've ever had. The roads didn't exist and my Yugoslav assistants were all macho men who loved to drink. I struggled to keep up with them. It was terrible. Awful. I found some beautiful locations but they had nothing to do with *The Long Ships*. So I finally ended up in Dubrovnik, a fabulous city. Do you know it?

I've never been.
It's like a little Venice. Beautiful. I took a lot of pictures and eventually came back to London. I said to Irving, 'There are palm trees all over the location.' And he said, 'Who cares? A tree's a tree!' I said, 'But you'd never get a palm tree in Norway!' They couldn't shoot the picture at that time, but fours year later they went back to Yugoslavia and Jack Cardiff directed it.

It's a spin-off from The Vikings.
Irving Allen was the sort of person who thought a house is a house and a tree is a tree. He had me doing preparatory work with my art department in Soho Square for *The Hellions*, the only Western I ever designed. I loved doing the Western street. We built a model of the whole thing. But again, the picture was iffy or something, and then suddenly Irving and Cubby – for Warwick films – decided to do *The Trials of Oscar Wilde* instead. I was immediately switched to that movie, which I also designed in Soho Square, and somebody else did *The Hellions*.

When The Hellions *was released in 1961 the production design was credited to William Constable. Ken Annakin directed it. Do you remember where it was filmed?*
South Africa.

It was set in 1860 and it felt very multinational. Richard Todd and the pop singer Marty Wilde were in it.
I don't think I ever saw it.

It was about juvenile delinquents in the Wild West, over-age juvenile delinquents if I recall. So then came Dr No. *You'd met Cubby Broccoli through* The Hellions, The Long Ships *and* The Trials of Oscar Wilde . . . And I'd worked on two other pictures for him: *Let's Get Married* in 1960, and *In the Nick* in 1959, both starring Anthony Newley. So I knew Cubby and I also knew Harry Saltzman; he had asked me to help him with a television series in Italy, which I turned down. So when Cubby and Harry were planning *Dr No*, the first person they approached was me. I was given the first hundred pages of the script in the reception area of the Carlton Towers Hotel. Letizia doesn't normally read scripts, but she read these pages – we'd just come back from Italy and I was sub-letting the house to my older brother – and she made the famous remark: 'You can't possibly do this! You would prostitute yourself!' And I must admit, when I read them I wasn't too impressed either. I remember being offered a profit participation deal. But because of my reservations about the script, I turned down the offer and opted for a fixed fee instead! *Dr No* was an opportunity to work with a director who I was very fond of, Terence Young, and he was very fond of me.

Was Terence Young slotted at an early stage?
Yes. That's why I decided to do it.

According to Cubby Broccoli's memoirs, the earliest draft of the script – which was co-written by Wolf Mankowitz – had mad things in it, like Dr No turning out to be a monkey! The villain goes around with a monkey on his shoulder, and the monkey is called Dr No. It was a forty-page draft.
I never read that version.

Did the version you read already envisage spectacular sets?
No, it was a small whodunit based on Ian Fleming's book. But Terence Young was a fan of mine, maybe because of *Oscar Wilde*, and he thought of himself as James Bond. He had been a tank commander in the Irish Guards during the war, and he was responsible for grooming Sean Connery for the role. So I thought we would have a lot of fun. I also felt that this chaotic secret-agent plot might enable me to experiment with a new form of design. We went on a location trip to Florida to look at marsh buggies, and then to Jamaica, but we didn't have a great deal of time because we had to start shooting. I had a young English-Jamaican assistant called Chris Blackwell who was interested in films and absolutely passionate about Jamaican music and jazz. I liked him. He's a billionaire now! Then Syd Cain, my art director, came out to join us. I supervised the main locations but went back to London to work on the sets. I tried to discuss concepts with Terence but all he said was, 'Ken, I leave it up to you.' All he wanted was a rough plan of

some of the sets so that he knew where the entrances and exits were. The design was my business. Nobody had a precise idea of what the sets should look like.

Presumably they had to match the shots in Jamaica – the pier, the arrival of the boat . . .

I wasn't worried about matching anything really. I wanted to design the sets at Shepperton because my previous experience of Pinewood hadn't been great. But I went to Pinewood anyway, called in all the heads of department – the construction manager, chief plasterer, chief painter – and said I wanted to play around with new materials, new technologies, new techniques, anything they could think of. And they were fantastic. They rose to the challenge. That stimulated my imagination and I just started scribbling. It gave me the chance to give vent to my imagination

Let's go through the sets that you designed at that time. There's Dr No's apartment, the escape route from his lair full of metal tubes and iron grilles, and the casino. The casino was a set, right?

Yes. That was loosely based on Les Ambassadeurs because I wanted a certain amount of luxury. The most difficult set for me was the nuclear water-reactor because I knew nothing about reactors. But Harry had a contact at Harwell in Oxfordshire, so two young scientists spent a couple of hours with me at Pinewood where they explained to me the principles of a nuclear water-reactor, and that was it. They helped me again with the laser in *Goldfinger*.

There are two aspects of Dr No *that suggest the shape of things to come. Firstly, a heightened sense of reality: the sets are one big step larger than life. And secondly, a contrast between the gleaming equipment and gantries of the high-tech laboratories on the one hand, and the baronial dwellings of the bad guys on the other. A Piranesi-like labyrinth of power, and an apartment under the sea in a very particular style. The apartment has many Ken Adam touches: interesting textures, a strange mixture of metal and wood. How did you achieve those effects?*

I used an American process that I had picked up from working on *Helen of Troy* in Italy. You can metalise any smooth surface by spraying a nitric acid solution on it. After four or five sprays, it's like a mirror finish. Then you can put a lacquer on top to make it look like brass, steel, copper or whatever the required colour. It was a Hollywood process – I can't remember the technical term for it – but I introduced it to Pinewood. I also wanted to get away from the old-fashioned method of using paper over hessian before the painters got to work because the labour was turning out to be expensive, since the painters had to over-grain on top of the wood paper to make it look real, so a lot of money was being wasted on labour. I tried to eliminate that. The underground apartment with the fish was, of course, a great thing for me to do. Except we didn't have enough money to film tropical fish at an aquarium. So we used stock footage, only to find out they were the size of goldfish. We used rear projection for the large plate-glass window and our fish were enlarged to ten times their actual size. Thank God somebody in the dialogue says . . .

Yes, both James Bond and Dr No make a point about the magnification. They look like sharks and barracudas. The villains' apartments always have antique, period detail mixed with a modern, contemporary sixties style. But the villains never seem to wear contemporary costume. At some point in the films every single villain wears an outfit that makes him look like a Renaissance prince. So the lair of the villain is adorned with antiques, large fireplaces, vast tables, paintings by the old masters . . .

You're absolutely right, Christopher. I always felt *Dr No* was the first time that I mixed contemporary – slightly ahead of contemporary – design and shapes with antique furniture. Very often I used props and furniture from our house, like lamps. It was very funny, especially if

Design for Dr. No's underwater apartment

97

you consider the risks one took at that time; I filled three or four stages at Pinewood with sets that Terence Young hadn't even seen yet.

The sets were built while they were shooting in Jamaica?
Yes. They came back on a Friday and we started shooting on the Monday. Luckily they liked my design. The first person to walk onto the stage – I'll never forget it – was Terence Young. He said, 'It's fantastic.' He loved it. And of course Cubby and Harry, who might have thought 'How much more money is he going to ask for the next movie?' agreed with him. When Cubby saw Dr No's underwater lair he said, 'It's like Leo Carrillo's ranch house!' When people say about my past and whether I was influenced by Hitler and megalomania and so on, I always tried to treat it tongue-in-cheek, always with a sense of humour, always a little bigger than life. That attitude was contagious. Suddenly everybody was coming up with obscure ideas and dreaming up funny situations and new scenes. The studio became a democratic debating society and remained that way throughout the later Bond films.

In Dr No *all the humour is in the sets because there aren't yet any quips and throwaway lines.*
Yes. One of the writers, a woman called Johanna Harwood, wrote extra scenes. She was there when everybody was shown the set, and I think it was she who said, 'Wouldn't it be funny if we discover that Dr No has some famous piece of art that's been stolen.' So that's how Goya's portrait of the Duke of Wellington was born.

It's a wonderful double-take because that painting had been stolen from the National Gallery the previous year. Did you paint it?
Yes. I projected a slide from the National Gallery and painted it over the weekend!

There's an interesting contrast between the villain's antique-meets-contemporary lair and the big Piranesi-like corridors where Bond escapes up a giant chimney.
I started with gunmetal and I stuck with gunmetal for the rest of my life! Actually, that's a very nice little expressionistic set with the grille before you get into the duct. Terence advised me on the duct. He said, 'You can't shoot in profile in a tube and you can't cut a tube in half because it's got to be elliptical.' So for all the side angles of Sean Connery we used an elliptical tube rather than a tube cut in half. That way you're covered: you can see the top and the bottom. We cast a lot of the tubing, and then I built perspective pieces which I put on the end of a twenty-foot run of tube to make it look like two hundred feet.

The original budget for the sets was only £14,000 out of a total of

£350,000. But you managed to beat them up to £20,000. One of the sets is Dr No's ante-room. It appears thirty-five minutes into the film. We don't see Dr No, but we hear his voice. He says, 'Sit down.' Then a shifty professor enters to pick up a tarantula in a box. There is a grille in the ceiling like a spider's web and it throws a distorted Caligari-type shadow across the room. It's only visible for a few moments, but it registers very strongly. It's a very distinctive Ken Adam set.

This was a complete afterthought. We'd all forgotten that we needed a room where Professor Dent talks to Dr No, and it was in the last week of shooting so I only had £450 left. So I came up with that idea. I built the set on a platform in forced perspective with that big circular grille, and Terence – again, he was unbelievable – said, 'If you want us to see the whole grille, you have to give me at least a six-foot extension to the ceiling piece.' So he was very art-minded. And Ted Moore did a brilliant job with the lighting. It's amazing to talk to Bond aficionados and critics, wherever they are in the world, because they always mention that set. They think it established a style. It was dressed with just one table, one chair and one tarantula, and it is my favourite scene in the film – an example of stylisation to achieve a desired effect.

Absolutely. In the mid-1920s Fritz Lang and also the architect Robert Mallet-Stevens wrote an article about screen design in which they argued that the best sets tell you about the characters who inhabit them before they appear on screen. You immediately know something about them before they've opened their mouth. Dr No's ante-room is a classic example. The spider, the expressionism, the curve of the wall; it's an extraordinarily economical way of introducing a super-villain. It's entirely visual. You gave tarantulas a bad name; they're not actually that poisonous.

No, but we had nurses standing by with serum.

It was just an excuse to show off Sean Connery's hairy chest.

We didn't actually shoot it with Sean. Terence had the idea of putting a sheet of glass over Sean and having the tarantula walk on that. So I had to turn the bedroom set on its side. We did shoot it but they didn't like the shot with the glass, so instead they filmed the tarantula crawling over the shoulder of the stuntman, Bob Simmons. That poor tarantula lost a leg when the prop man tried to get some action out of it.

Wouldn't it have been simpler to take its venom out?

No, it dies.

Oh. I always thought they could.

We thought that too.

The nuclear water-reactor provides a terrific climax, especially when the shining light rises out of the water. Spy stories on television were always gleaming and modern, but Dr No *has texture; it's not all futuristic and shiny. At the time, did anybody realise how important the sets were?*

Well I don't know it at the time. Nobody expected the explosion of success that *Dr No* had. I got fan mail from people all over the world who had seen the film. Ursula Andress wrote to us in July 1963: 'Dear Letizia, dear Ken. The compliments I have received for you are innumerable. Every time that somebody comes up to me they say, "Oh, I saw you in *Dr No* and the sets were fantastic."' It was because of *Dr No* that Stanley Kubrick offered me *Dr Strangelove*.

One of the great mysteries that Bond fans come to blows over is when Sean Connery and Ursula Andress are taken to Dr No's lair . . .
The shower.

Was Ursula wearing any clothes or not?
I don't know!

Did you design the buggy with dragon's teeth? The metal flame-thrower?
No, I don't think I did. I left that to Syd Cain to do. I don't have any sketches. I think I left Syd Cain to do that in Jamaica. We picked out a marsh buggy. Harry Saltzman was an unbelievable showman – he was brought up in the circus. Harry may have had nineteen bad ideas but one idea, number twenty, would be brilliant. He had hundreds of ideas. But some of them worked, some of them didn't.

Did you really have complete freedom when they were in Jamaica, or did Harry sign off your sketches? Did he even see them?
No, no.

Really? You were given complete control? They completely trusted you. Mind you, they had worked with you before.
After *Dr No* they wanted to see my sketches for *Goldfinger*. I showed them the Fort Knox concept but they weren't sure at all. They thought it looked like a prison. That was what I was trying to do: put the gold behind bars and keep the audience out. I remember Harry and Cubby having big arguments with the director, Guy Hamilton, who liked my idea and backed me up. Designing is not just about coming up with an idea, but selling the idea, and then having somebody who will accept the idea. *Goldfinger* was my second Bond film after *Dr No* and I think Harry and Cubby were more interested in the 'stud farm' and the rumpus room, so I really went to town on those.

The nuclear water-reactor in Dr No *is the first of your 'secret places'. Like Fort Knox, the War Room, and other Bond film sets, it looks fairly innocuous from the outside, but inside there are all sorts of strange things going on. It's an interesting design idea because you are creating the imagery of these secret places. Audiences only have a vague idea of what goes on behind locked doors, and even you don't know what these places really look like, but you create something believable. You are letting us into a secret place that you have invented. Was Fort Knox in any way based on fact?*

Well, not exactly. I saw Fort Knox from the outside so I reproduced the exterior design to scale. But they didn't let me inside. I'm glad they didn't because it would have been dull. It comes back to my feelings about stylisation. Being somewhat theatrical, I think I can create a reality that people accept, and people *have* accepted it. Fort Knox was completely impractical as a gold depository – I mean, where do you find gold forty feet high? But audiences believed it and it caused a big stir. When *Goldfinger* was released people were asking why a British film unit had been allowed to shoot inside Fort Knox when even the American President was not allowed in.

It's more real than real. It reminds me of a story about a scene in Butch Cassidy and the Sundance Kid. *They're in Bolivia and at the railway station there are some llamas. A seminar was held after the film came out and George Roy Hill, the director, was questioned by a Bolivian student who said, 'There aren't any llamas in Bolivia.' Hill paused for a minute and then said, 'Well, there are now!' In a way that's what you did: the reality is more prosaic, but in everyone's mind you created what it looks like. And you did it for the first time with Dr No's water-reactor. Just before Dr No you sold your beloved supercharged Mercedes. Was this because times were hard?*

No, although times *were* hard. I'd been working on *Sodom and Gomorrah* in Italy for a year and a half, and one week I came back with one of the producers, Maurice Lodifé. The Mercedes was in a garage on Sloane Avenue and I knew I'd have to spend a lot of money to get it back on the road again. I looked at the car, my garage bill was just unbelievable and I knew I had to spend about twelve hundred pounds to get it back on the road again. Edward Montague wanted it for the motor museum in Beaulieu . . .

Was it pre-war?
Late '30s. A supercharged two-seater Mercedes 540k Cabriolet. I came back for a weekend and sold it to a man called Major Frank Cox for £200.

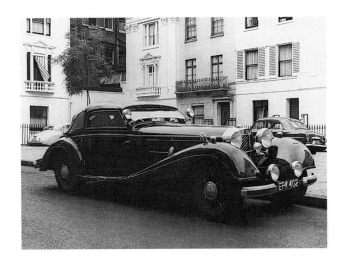 

Mercedes 540K in Victoria Square,
London 1955 (left)

With 'E' Type Jaguar, Montpelier Street,
London 1961

By then you'd moved from Pont Street to the house in Knightsbridge.
Yes, at the end of 1959.

Did you buy a new car as a result of Dr No? *You must have bought the
E-type Jaguar about then because you had it for* Dr Strangelove.
No, I had the Mini before that. I had it hotted up and was road-racing
it all over Italy during *Sodom and Gomorrah.* I bought the E-type when
I got back.

You've always had this thing about stylish fast cars.
Yes. I got that from flying. We did ranger operations where we flew out
across the Channel at sea level and just pulled up to get over the coast.
When you fly a Typhoon at over four hundred miles an hour you need
split-second reactions to avoid trees and high-tension wires and
steeples. Your life depends on it. So eventually I transferred that to very
fast sports cars.

*A lot of the characteristics that we associate with Bond – Q, the gad-
gets, the fast cars – are absent from* Dr No. *Even in* From Russia with
Love *there's only a glimpse of Bond's Bentley. I wonder if you had an
influence on future Bond movies . . .*
Of course.

5 Working with Stanley Kubrick

Dr Strangelove

How did you first meet Stanley Kubrick?
One day I got a phone call from Stanley. I think he was staying at the
Westbury Hotel. He said that he'd seen *Dr No*, he was very impressed
with the design of it, and would I be interested in doing a film for him?
'It's about the atomic destruction of the world,' he said; 'a sort of comedy.' So we met. He was very young and I was impressed by his enthu-
siasm. He had a naïveté about him, a curiosity that very often occurs in
the second generation of New York Jewish immigrants. He questioned
things. I was almost taken in initially and then you find out there's a
super brain working behind it. And it wasn't an artificiality. It was him.
He wasn't trying to make me feel at ease or anything. So he explained
a little the concept of the film that he was trying to make and we immediately had a chemistry that worked, which was amazing. I'm not sure
whether it was during the first or second meeting that we had, but I
started doodling whilst we talked – which I used to do in those days. He
looked at those doodles and he was thrilled. He said it was exactly
what he wanted and I thought, 'This is going to be easy.' He already
had a reputation at this time for being a difficult director, but I admired
his *Paths of Glory* enormously, as well as *Spartacus* and his earlier
smaller pictures. So we immediately hit it off; there was a chemistry.

I've been tracing the origins of Dr Strangelove *and it begins with a
novel titled* Two Hours to Doom *by an ex-RAF man called Peter
George, who had joined the Campaign for Nuclear Disarmament. Then
it was published in America as* Red Alert. *The novel is set mainly on a
B52 bomber that's been sent across the border to unload its bombs on
Russia. It cuts between the interior of the B52, the Pentagon and a military base where an insane general has given the order to attack. No
comedy: just a straightforward thriller. At some stage Kubrick decided
that he liked the story but he didn't want to tell it straight. Although the
script is credited to both the author Peter George and screenwriter
Terry Southern, the black comedy and satire was obviously brought in
by Terry. Can you remember what state the script was in when you first
met Kubrick?*
It's a good question, but frankly, I don't remember. It was already satirical, no question about that, and Terry Southern was obviously very
comedy-orientated and satirical. But I think what Stanley wanted was
an element of realism. At that stage, or sometime later, he decided that

Photo of Ken Adam by Stanley Kubrick,
in Kubrick's London flat 1962

Photo by Ken Adam of Stanley Kubrick
at his home (left)

Photo by Stanley Kubrick of Ken
Adam with Terry Southern in Kubrick's
dressing room, Shepperton 1962

the only way to successfully make a picture about a nuclear holocaust
and the end of the world was to make it as black satire. The more we
worked on it, the more this became apparent. And the fact that he cast
Peter Sellers convinces me – now that I think about it – that was Stanley's intention.

In those days Peter Sellers was playing four parts, not three.
Yes. Stanley and I had big arguments very shortly after we met because
he thought Peter was the greatest actor alive. I knew Peter very well
from earlier days and I knew that in many ways he was a genius, but he
had to base his performance on satirising somebody.

Mimicking somebody.
Yes, he had to mimic. He could not play a Laurence Olivier part. So I
argued with Stanley, but he said I was wrong. Later on I was proved
right because although Peter was quite brilliant as both the RAF Group
Captain and Dr Strangelove, Stanley had serious problems with him as
the American President. One day I came back from a location scout to
London airport and the whole stage was in tears of laughter. They had
all been sitting in the War Room when Peter had decided that he could-
n't play a President straight. So he asked the props to give him an asth-
ma inhaler and he played the part as though he had a terrible cold,
which was hilariously funny. Stanley must have shot the scene for one
or two days, and remember I was driving Stanley to and from the studio and we kept arguing about the scene. And I don't remember
whether it was I or Stanley who began to have doubts since the President of the United States is the only part that has to be somewhat
straight, otherwise all the others don't make sense. So he started re-
shooting the whole scene. Initially Peter had great difficulties playing
that part straight. Then of course, he began improvising like hell.

That's interesting because it suggests there was improvisation as you went along. I sense that Terry Southern was constantly adding ideas. Was he around at that stage?

Yes, he was around.

You can almost see George C. Scott and Peter Sellers thinking up ideas and business. But it must have been controlled . . .

A very strong element of improvisation, but that was Stanley. At that time, and later, it became an obsession that he tried to permutate an actor's performance in innumerable takes until he got the thing which was right. That started on *Strangelove*. Previous pictures had been much more controlled. So the picture was continuously improvised. I think Terry Southern had an overall satirical concept, but most of Peter's performance was improvised. It's funny when you see the film today and you see Strangelove and Peter Bull standing next to him as the Russian Ambassador and he couldn't keep a straight face; he started laughing. That was always a problem with anybody playing with Peter. My first experience of his improvisations was when Peter was playing the Group Captain. He was lying on the couch and he suddenly started talking about the 'string' in his leg which he got during wartime. Not scripted at all; that was Peter improvising. And of course the most difficult thing for the others was to keep a straight face while Peter was going crazy.

I think I've found the piece of film that Peter Sellers used to mimic Wernher Von Braun at the end. Walt Disney made a film for television in the mid-1950s called Man in Space *that stars Braun as the link man, and the turns of phrase and the accent are absolutely identical to Sellers in* Dr Strangelove. *He needed a model, as you say, to mimic. Ironically, you went to the same school as Wernher von Braun all those years before, and then you end up on a film set with an actor imitating Wernher as a crazy Nazi scientist. It's the most astonishing coincidence. So every day you drove Kubrick from London to Shepperton in your E-type Jaguar at no more than 30 m.p.h. because it made Kubrick nervous. You were trapped in the cockpit of that car for an hour to an hour and a half every day. I presume you talked a lot about the project as it evolved. Was he sharing his ideas with you?*

Yes, by this time he had a great admiration for me. Not necessarily as a designer at that stage, though I think that helped. But about my past and all the things that basically he would have liked to have done – be a fighter pilot. We talked for hours about the Second World War and whether I shot down any planes. Aerial combat and all this sort of thing, which was fascinating to him. It was like a form of escapism for him. He wanted to find out what made me tick. I kept him entertained with these experiences.

Did you run out of stories? I can scarcely imagine it!
Yes. In the end I had to invent stories because I just couldn't think of any more! But remember, we were on the film for probably five or six months and drove every day for roughly three hours. And Stanley is not the silent type. So we got to know each other extremely well, and I think it established a relationship which I've never had since with another director. It was also very beneficial for the film, because when Stanley came up with a new idea, I was the first one to know. We were always discussing it. I had to provide him with the sets and so on and very often it meant changing something that we'd already constructed. He had his famous theory in those days that the director had the right to change his mind up until the moment the cameras started turning. But *he* changed his mind *after* the cameras were rolling! For me, it was enormously demanding, because until then I was basically a pretty organised person. But I wasn't yet flexible enough to meet these some-times impossible demands that he came up with. So I was going through an anxiety crisis. But at the same time I knew that every time he changed his mind, he came up with a brilliant idea. So I knew I had to meet his demands in some way, even if it seemed impossible from a practical point of view.

So you never fought him? You never questioned him when he changed his mind?
No, never. Because I immediately, if reluctantly, grasped that his ideas were brilliant. Because Stanley never accepted from anybody – technician or actor – that something wasn't possible. I learnt that very quickly. The word 'impossible' did not exist in his vocabulary. And the moment somebody said it, they were in trouble, because in fact he was a brilliant technician. He was obviously limited in terms of designing – he was the first to admit that – but he had an incredible visual eye.

He started off as a stills photographer, a photo-journalist. His organisation of the image was unbeatable.
Stanley was a brilliant photographer and he could have taken over the editing, sound or any of the technical requirements. But he didn't know how to design. So I had to deal with those problems. He filmed Peter Sellers playing the bomber pilot, Major T. J. 'King' Kong, and realised, after two days of shooting, that Peter couldn't play the part. Fortunately Peter hurt his ankle and Stanley – who also had practical considerations – knew he could make an insurance claim.

Photo by Ken Adam of Stanley Kubrick in Montpelier Street, London

He had an 'out'.

He had an out, because Stanley was always very money-minded. Driving to the studios one morning he told me he'd come up with an idea. He'd asked this cowboy actor he met in California, Slim Pickens, to play Major Kong. It was one of the most brilliant ideas he had on that film, but it changed everything from my point of view because I'd already constructed the bomb bay and suspended it on one of the stages at Shepperton. It didn't have practical bomb doors – we didn't need them in the script at that time – and the set was almost ready to shoot. And Stanley said, 'We *need* practical bomb doors.' He wanted this Texan cowboy to ride the bomb like a bronco into the Russian missile site. I did some set-ups, sketches for the whole thing, and Stanley asked me when it would be ready. I said, 'If I work three crews twenty-four hours a day, you still won't have it for at least a week, and that's too late.' So now I arrive at Shepperton and I'm having kittens because I knew it was a fantastic idea but physically, mechanically, we couldn't get it done. So again it was Wally Veevers, our special-effects man, who saved the day, saying he'd sleep on it and come up with an idea. He always did that, even though he was having heart problems and wasn't well. Wally came back and said, 'We're going to take a ten-by-eight still of the bomb bay interior, cut out the bomb-door opening, and shoot the bomb coming down against blue backing.' And that's the way we did it.

Presumably you miniaturised the bomb as it fell.

Well, we suspended the bomb on the stage at Shepperton, and then we craned back and optically reduced the last bit.

So instead of falling, he's just getting smaller.

You know, there were all sorts of interesting things that happened on *Dr Strangelove*. I could talk for hours. But one of the things I will always remember is that I had a very good matte painter called Alan Maley. We were debating whether we should build a model of the Russian missile site, or do a matte painting, when Alan said he could do it. So he painted it, I would say eight feet by six feet, and at that time I believe Walt Disney visited the studio. He saw that painting and was so impressed that he gave Alan a contract in Hollywood. So a lot of other things happened through *Strangelove*.

Can we talk about the three sets? There's the Burpelson Air Base office where General Jack D. Ripper is going mad and launching this destruction, there's the War Room, and there's the interior of the B52 bomber. There are others, but these are the main three.

Like the hotel suite with George C. Scott as General Turgidson, and Tracy Reed as Miss Scott.

Let's talk about the War Room. It's probably the most famous set you ever designed. Steven Spielberg once called it the best set in the history of film. It's got so many different elements: the maps on the slanted wall, the lights that give you strategic information about the bombers, the shiny black floor and its reflections, the circular table covered in baize, the circular light ring above it that illuminates the actors within this vast, cavernous bunker. It's partly a poker game, partly a strategic centre, partly a nuclear bunker. Talk us through all that.

When I was doodling I came up first with an idea for a two-level set

Final concept drawing of the War Room

with a gallery around the top, and Stanley liked it very much. So I thought I was in business. I already had people in pre-pre-production working on the set when he suddenly asked, 'What am I going to do with the extra level?' I knew I was in trouble again; I was anxious. He was right, of course, because I never thought about what they'd do with a second level. I thought Stanley would come up with an idea. I remember arriving at Shepperton and walking in these beautiful gardens to calm down – they didn't have tranquillisers in those days – and when I got back to my office I started scribbling again! Stanley must have sensed that I was pretty demoralised. He came into my little office and was standing behind me while I was doodling some shapes. Again, whether I was influenced by German Expressionism or not, I don't know, but out of my scribbles came this leaning triangular shape with slanting walls. Stanley stopped me and said, 'Hold on. Isn't the triangle the strongest geometric form?' I said, 'I think so, yes.' He said, 'If we were going ahead with it, what would I build it out of?' I suggested reinforced concrete, and he said, 'Like a gigantic bomb shelter?' So that's how the idea was born. And you know, I always had this thing about having a circle somewhere. So I designed the circular table.

Like the circular 'tarantula' grille in Dr No. *Sloping walls – with no central perspective – and a circle somewhere in the middle. Very unnerving.*
Yes, it was an extension of that. You'll find a circle in all my designs somewhere. It was Stanley's idea that the War Room would be like a poker game and he was fascinated by the light ring. He thought we could light the whole scene with that light ring. It resulted in us spending hours in my Shepperton office or in his flat, experimenting at night-time. I've got photographs that he shot of me sitting in a chair whilst he held up the lights at a certain height, at a certain angle, to see what effect they had and to work out what strength of bulb to use. He lit everything in the War Room with that light ring. We had phoney light sources and beams from one wall, and maybe a little fill light here and there. But the main light source was the ring.

Did you design the lighting of the set as well?
I did lighting sketches. Any designer who sketches will put light into their sketches. You have to create an atmosphere, to give an idea of the mood you are trying to set.

What's very clever about the War Room is that it's a cavernous space, but the light ring makes it feel claustrophobic; it pushes the ceiling down and you feel cramped.
Yes. It's funny you should mention that, Christopher, because – and it's never happened to me before or since on any other set – that as I was constructing the set it was my idea to come up with this shiny black floor and these gigantic inclined maps. And I was feeling claustrophobic too! Which was the right element, because the actors felt that strange atmosphere. That's why I think it was my most successful set, because everybody became part of the set.

Reacted to it.
Exactly. But I was furious with Stanley because I always wanted my now famous sketch of the War Room to be an establishing shot. I

attacked Stanley, saying, 'When are we going to get the establishing shot?' He said, 'I don't know, but don't worry about it.' He didn't want the audience to know exactly where they were. He wanted to slowly reveal the set. And he was, of course, absolutely right.

How did you begin imagining a War Room? OK, it said 'Interior: War Room' in the script. But where did you start?

I had some stills of NORAD, the North American Air Defense, which is a control centre somewhere in the United States. Its motto was also 'Peace is Our Profession.' But it wasn't at all interesting. It was less interesting than space control, mission control. So I said it was no good. So I came up with these gigantic maps. The problem was how to create them. We drew them out on an imperial-sized drawing board and, because we had the technology for photographic enlargements, blew them up to this enormous size. The next problem I had – and Stanley was very much involved in all my problems – was how we were going to make these symbols of nuclear bombers approach Russia. I remember Stanley and I driving to Pinewood where they had a very famous rear projection man called Charlie Staffel who said he could do it with 16mm rear projectors. We calculated that we needed twenty-four projectors. As we were driving back Stanley said, 'That's going to be a disaster.' So we used actual light bulbs instead.

One light bulb for each of those symbols? Today you would do it digitally.

Yes. But I did make a mistake because I mounted the photo maps on plywood, built a light box behind it with hundred-watt bulbs, and then put perspex over the box: imagine a gigantic sheet of plywood, cut out a little square which is then covered with perspex, and put the photograph on top. What I didn't realise was that there was so much heat generated by all these bulbs – there were at least a thousand – that the photographic material was blistering away from the perspex. So we had to come up with various air-conditioning ventilation units to cool it down. There were a lot of problems, but somehow we always managed to overcome them. The overall effect of the War Room was so real that people in the highest places tried looking for it. I later learned from reliable sources that when Ronald Reagan moved to the White House he asked his Chief of Staff to show him the War Room.

Dr Strangelove *was made around the time of the Cuban Missile Crisis, so there was a high state of paranoia about nuclear weapons. But it was also being shot or edited when news broke of President Kennedy's assassination.*

I think it was in post-production.

Which I believe had two immediate effects on the film: firstly, if you read Slim Pickens' lips when he's checking the supplies in the B52, he clearly says, 'A man could have a really good weekend in Dallas on this.' But they replaced it with 'Vegas' instead.
Oh really?

But the second and more significant effect was that the ending changed. Tell us about that.
Well, the ending in the script was a gigantic custard-pie fight, which we filmed for well over a week. I had organised over three thousand custard pies to be used and it was the most fantastic pie fight that had ever been filmed. The actors all got into it. George C. Scott was swinging from the gigantic light ring and the whole War Room floor was covered in pies. It ended with the Russian Ambassador and the American President sitting on the floor and building sandcastles out of the pies like children. The first screening we had, I was there, the pie fight was in and Blake Edwards was so impressed that he used it in one of his films.

Yes, The Great Race. *A sequence takes place in a pie shop.*
Then Stanley decided not to use it because of the Kennedy assassination. So he cut it out. We all ganged up on him, as we always did. I mean we all did. I was probably as close to him as Kristiana or anyone of the family, but everybody said that he must keep it in. Stanley absolutely insisted that he should lose it. About three years ago a man came here to interview me about Stanley because he was writing a book about him. And he said that if I liked, because nobody ever saw the pie fight again, we could go into the vaults of the BFI and watch it. So we did. And we both came out knowing why he didn't want to use it, because stylistically – Stanley had used effects like slow motion – it didn't suit the picture.

I've seen an extract from the script. It mentions the pie fight and, by a terrible coincidence, there's a moment when the President doesn't get hit by any of the pies whizzing past, like Tony Curtis in The Great Race, *and then George C. Scott says, 'Ladies and Gentlemen, the President has been struck down in his prime.'*
Absolutely.

A terrible coincidence, and another reason why he didn't want to use it. It was too near the knuckle. It also meant that although Dr Strangelove *was previewed in November 1963, it wasn't released until 1964. It now has a very sudden ending.* Dr Strangelove *stands up, says, 'Mein Führer, I can walk,' and then BANG! The nuclear explosion. It's quite a shock, and it takes a moment to realise that it's all happening simultaneously, that all these bombs are going off while they're arguing in the War Room. It works, but there's something missing. Tell us about the B52, the second set. Is it a very detailed reconstruction of the interior, or fantasy?*

No, it wasn't fantasy; it was complete reconstruction. I don't want to take too much credit because I had a fantastic art director, Peter Murton, who was wonderful at getting all the bits from junkyards and so on. With Peter's help I reconstructed the B52 to its minutest detail, based on aeronautical magazines, because it was all a secret in those days. Stanley was like a Boy Scout because he adored switches and dials. And the Air Force jargon; he loved the way people talked with no emotion in their voices.

Like Kong's speech as he goes through the supplies.

He knew about the survival packs from me because I must have told him about the packs we used in the Second World War. We weren't allowed to open them. They were in perspex boxes with tape around them. But they had pills in there that were meant to give you enormous energy, so some of us did open them to take the pills. We couldn't sleep for three days! Stanley was fascinated by these things and it shows in the scenes with the B52. He would spend about half an hour just playing with switches and lights. He was absolutely fascinated. We decided that the whole scene should be as realistic as possible so we must have used thousands of black-and-white Polaroids to check the balance between the inside and the outside lighting before each shot. Stanley was a great believer in source lighting. There was a funny incident when American air force personnel were invited onto the set and they saw our CRM-114 or whatever it was called, a box of no return. We just came up with something because we had no idea what the real thing looked liked, but apparently it was very near to the mark. They went white when they saw all that classified information in the film. I got a memo from Stanley, who hoped I could justify all my research because we could be investigated by the CIA!

I watched Wolfgang Petersen's Das Boot *the other day and it has a very similar atmosphere to the B52 scenes; there's this very claustrophobic circular tube and they're all cramped in there as if they're on a life-sized craft. They didn't attempt to build a bigger set as would have happened in a Hollywood Second World War movie. It looks very cramped and very difficult to shoot in.*

Let me tell you something about *Das Boot*. I was called to Munich by Bavaria Films. They had, with typical German efficiency in those days, built an actual submarine out of steel, and not, as you say, increased the size. It was designed by the art director of *Cabaret*, and it was correct in every detail, except that it could be taken apart in sections. It even had a functioning engine room. They'd spent a fortune – the equivalent of a million dollars in 1976/77 – building a submarine, but they didn't any longer have a film to go with it. So it was just sitting on a stage. Nobody wanted it. But a few years later Wolfgang Petersen came up with the idea for *Das Boot*, and he used it for that. They were delighted. They built miniatures too.

It is a brilliant rendering of a confined space. There's no other movie that represents life in an enclosed area so effectively. And with such a variety of shots.
I was called over to advise, and I said to myself, 'I've just built three nuclear subs out of marine plywood for a great deal less money than this "real" submarine!' Hopefully I didn't say it to them.

It was an art director-led movie! Coming back to Dr Strangelove, *I presume Slim Pickens' cockpit was one set, and then the cabin with the guy looking at his special orders with a torch . . .*
It was a two-level set.

Real size or larger?
Real size, but we could float walls away. Except for the bomb bay, which was a different set. Stanley loved that sequence. He was, as I say, like a Boy Scout. I think we sent an actual camera crew to somewhere in the Arctic Circle to film the rear projection plates for the B52, and also for the models. We built several B52 models of various sizes, but where we went wrong, and we knew it, was building a very large one with rippling skin and wings that dropped down when the plane landed and rose when it took off. Everything worked beautifully. But it looked phoney the first day we started shooting it. I should have known better because I knew that on any painted backdrop outside the set, the more loosely it is painted, the better it looks. Because your eye is never focused. So then I built smaller models for the B52 scenes.

What where they made of?
The big one was made out of metal. I don't know about the smaller ones. I think they were built by a specialist model maker. Sometimes, to me, they don't quite look real.

By today's standards. The movie opens with a real shot of a B52 refuelling in the air to the strains of 'Try a Little Tenderness', which I love. But, having seen a real B52, it makes the models look fake. The third big set was Burpelson Air Base. You went to Heathrow airport to film

*part of the exterior. The style in which the battle at Burpelson is filmed
is very newsreel-like. It's completely different to the rest of the film.*
That's Stanley, because he shot that himself.

Was that on the edge of Heathrow?
No. I thought the establishing shot that has that big white building at
Heathrow would make a good Burpelson Air Base because we couldn't
shoot in the United States. But the actual battle was shot near Shepperton studios. Stanley decided to shoot it himself with a hand-held Arri-
flex to give it a documentary style.

*Dr Strangelove is a collision of styles: the War Room is expressionistic,
the B52 is like a documentary, and the siege of the Burpelson Air Base
is hand-held and newsreel-like. Three different styles for three different
sets.*
But it works.

*It certainly does. It shouldn't work, but it all holds together fantastical-
ly well. Did you realise at the time that Stanley Kubrick was really onto
something with this movie? That it was going to be something special?*
Yes, I think we did. It's funny how Stanley borrowed a lot of ideas from
personal experience. I was already smoking cigars, so Stanley started
smoking them too – the only film he had ever smoked cigars on. Then
he decided it would be great if Sterling Hayden smoked an enormous
cigar in the film. So everyday life somehow influenced the making of
this film. Stanley was very, very concerned. Even after he's passed away,
I'm still not going to use the word 'paranoia', because when I gave
interviews to the press after *Barry Lyndon* – which I only did because
he wouldn't face them – I used the 'p-word' and Stanley said I shouldn't
have. But he *was* the p-word! He was also very practical. He spent
hours poring over maps to decide where the safest place in the world
for us would be if the shit hit the fan. He decided it was Cork in the
West of Ireland. I still don't know how he ever arrived at that conclu-
sion. He told Letizia and I to take all our money out of the bank so we
were prepared to move at a moment's notice!

*Everyone else would be going to Australia and New Zealand, but you'd
be going to Cork.*
Yes! But we were all very concerned at that time. It's amazing how few
people realised the enormity of a possible nuclear war.

*Trying to imagine you making the movie is so strange. There you are
making a rip-roaring comedy about something that was unbelievably
serious at that time. It's like someone doing a song-and-dance about the*

war in Iraq. It's such an extraordinary thing to be taking the mickey out of it while tension rises on the international scene. Stanley Kubrick once said that he couldn't tell that film straight, that he had to distance himself by laughing at it because the whole situation was so absurd. The only way to play that thing was as a comedy otherwise he couldn't confront it. I'm sure he's right. It makes it bearable.
Did you see Failsafe?

Yes. In the original book of Strangelove *by Peter George the President has to decide if the bomber gets through and drops the bomb, whether or not he would be prepared to sacrifice an American city as a reprisal. So the President sits in the War Room and offers up New York for bombing if the B52 hits Russia. That doesn't appear in* Dr Strangelove, *but it does in* Failsafe, *so there was a lawsuit and a settlement. Columbia bought the film but held it from release because of* Strangelove. *So the movie wasn't seen for a year. I think* Failsafe *is a very distinguished film by Sidney Lumet, but by telling the story straight it's so melodramatic that it's difficult to stomach, and it shows exactly why Kubrick was right. You can see why Stanley took a step back.* Failsafe *is a good movie, and it's interesting that it had the same source, but yours blew it out of the water.*
Peter George was a pilot.

Yes. He also wrote under the name Peter Bryant. It's a good story but it ends on a very sentimental note with the President and the Premier on the phone saying, 'It must never happen again.' Because the bomber doesn't hit its target; it unloads in the sea. Did you like Failsafe?
I don't remember now, but I don't think I liked it much. I'll never forget Terry Southern's quirky sense of humour. When the War Room was almost finished construction he came on the set, looked around and said, 'It looks interesting, Ken, but will it dress?' You know, those sort of crazy things. We had some more technical problems by that time. I thought the black shiny floor would be easy to do, but when Stanley and I first walked onto the set it was half-covered with black shiny material and it looked like a seascape. So we had to rip it all out, use a much heavier board and straighten the sub-floor. I always wondered how they did it in Hollywood for the Fred Astaire movies.

Well exactly; the effect hadn't been used since Top Hat.
They had paper floors, lacquered in black and repainted after each take.

When it was all over and Stanley had decided to cut out the pie scene, did he seem pleased with the result? Did he ever say, 'This is fabulous'?

He didn't say that. He wasn't the type. But he was very pleased with it and we knew that we were doing something very special. We were very close. Our working relationship was almost like a marriage. One morning I opened the *Daily Express* and I read an interview with Stanley about how he had conceived the War Room. I was livid. When I collected him in the morning I said, 'Have you seen the *Express*? David Lewin has written about *your* concept for the War Room.' He denied saying it but I said, 'You can't deny it because David is a friend of mine and he wouldn't report it if you didn't say it.' I knew some of the critics at that time. Stanley said, 'Ken, don't be paranoid about this.' He offered to put an advertisement in the *Hollywood Reporter* and *Variety* saying 'Stanley Kubrick thanks Ken Adam for his great concept of the War Room', and we'd share the cost! I'll never forget that.

As you described earlier, you work and draw intuitively, usually in monochrome, and your designs then have to be interpreted. So you're an intuitive person who works from the gut. But your description of Stanley is the absolute opposite: someone who is completely rational, who understands the technicalities, who constantly asks 'why?' and takes things to pieces to see how they work. So on the face of it you're very different people – chalk and cheese – but the chemistry worked.
But it's very destructive because Stanley had that incredible brain – he was already in the master class of chess players when he was a teenager – and he reminded me of a computer. He had to permutate through every possible solution, and he had to find out what makes you tick.

And find out everything for himself.
Yes. We've talked about intuition, but Stanley would not accept that. He'd ask where it came from. He was questioning me all the time, and I can't justify every line I draw. It's like the War Room and the triangle . . .

His comment about the triangle was an odd thing to say, looking at your wonderful drawing.
Yes, he had to justify everything. It all had to have a realistic possibility, a potential for use.

At some deep intellectual level.
Yes.

I think the seeds of future conflict were already apparent. By the end of Dr Strangelove *you must have been completely worn out.*
I was, and I said, 'Never again.' I thought it was a fantastic picture and my relationship with Stanley was incredible, but I thought, 'Life is too short.' I couldn't go through another six months or more of the same questioning process with Stanley.

A few months later you said, 'We developed an extremely close working relationship, and as a result I had to live almost completely on tranquillisers.' So there were tranquillisers in those days, thank goodness! Then Stanley made 2001 – A Space Odyssey. *I gather he approached you to design that.*

Yes, but I turned him down, even though I would have liked to design that film. I went to his New York apartment where he had been working for nearly a year with some experts from NASA. One of them, Harry Lange, later worked for me. And Stanley knew as much about space as the experts. He certainly knew more than I did. And I thought to myself, 'I couldn't do that.' Because if I did it and Stanley knew more about it, every time I designed something that was intuitive, like my idea for a space station, he would say, 'It isn't what NASA says.'

So you turned him down. He really wanted you to do it?
Yes. I got letters from him on two occasions. One was handwritten and delivered to the house by hand. It said, 'The fact that you have become a star should not cause you to act like one. You should know that a rejected offer goes stale in minutes. Love, Stanley.'

He was upset.
I really felt that however much I liked to be in his company – he was, after all, a fascinating person – it was not worth going through that period, emotionally, on another film.

Apart from the beginning with the apes, and the ending, 2001 *is hyper-realist in its design. It's like a brochure for NASA. He was aiming for a documentary in space.*
That's what it was.

Having seen it, and knowing it was so influential, do you regret not doing it? Do you not feel a slight twinge?
No, I don't. I think it's a very good film.

Nobody remembers the designer's name, or talks about it.
Even when you say the actors, Stanley used to say he wished he didn't have to use actors!

He almost succeeded with 2001! *There's a very odd design decision at the end, which I still don't understand. He's whizzing through infinity and then he's in this room. I'm not sure whether it's meant to be Georgian or a bad hotel room?*
That was bad design. And Stanley didn't like it either. In fact he hated it.

You could have really gone to town with 2001. *I think they missed a few opportunities. But while you were shooting* Strangelove, Cubby *Broccoli and Harry Saltzman were filming* From Russia With Love. *In Cubby's memoirs he talks about how you met and worked on* The Trials of Oscar Wilde, *about your role on* Dr No, *and then moves on to* Goldfinger *without talking about the design of* From Russia With Love *at all. Were you worried that someone else might muscle in and take over the Bond franchise while you were away?*

No, not at all. *Strangelove* was an important film to me, and I knew that if they were making more Bond films, they would come back to me.

From Russia With Love *is constantly on the move. The big scene takes place on a train . . .*
It's a good picture.

But it lacks the Ken Adam touch; there's no larger-than-life villain's lair, which presumably was what attracted Kubrick to you. Whether they decided not to have one because they didn't have Ken Adam, or they just wanted to tell a different kind of story, I'm not sure. But it's the only Bond story of that period in which the baddie doesn't live in some sort of over-the-top den.

You see also, I don't want it to sound like I'm blowing my own trumpet but I always felt that I could contribute something that would add an interesting visual element; even if it meant a slight change in the script or the story, I used to do it. Syd Cain, who was my assistant on *Dr No*, is a very capable designer, but I think that's where it ends.

Did he design From Russia With Love? *It's slightly unimaginative.*
Yes, but it's a good picture.

The design is no longer a character in the story.
Right. But they were clever in casting someone like Lotte Lenya.

Barry Lyndon

After Dr Strangelove *you said you were never going to work with Stanley Kubrick again because he was a genius but too stressful and demanding. And yet on 1 January 1973 you started work on* Barry Lyndon. *How did that happen?*
It happened because he tracked me down in the South of France, where I was doing a film called *The Last of Sheila*, directed by Herbert Ross, and he was at his most charming self. He said he needed me to do this fantastic film but he couldn't pay my normal fee. He was always trying

Potsdam sequence of *Barry Lyndon*, filmed by the second unit

to get people to do something for next to nothing because of his status. I said I loved him dearly but I was afraid he would have to pay me. He threatened to get the next-best production designer, so I said, 'Go ahead.' Five or six weeks later I got another call from Stanley, the naïve little boy Stanley, who said, 'The second-best production designer doesn't seem to understand what I want, and your money is not really going to be a problem. In any case you're an old friend and you have to help me out.' He talked me into it, and when you know beforehand that you should not be making this film, it doesn't help. Stanley had a strange side to his character; he wanted to prove the norm wrong. He always wanted to do things differently. Right from the beginning he said, 'No studio.' I said I preferred, when it was right for the scene, to do a combination of studio and location. He said he was going to shoot everything in reality, which was the first contradiction. He wanted to shoot it like an accurate documentary of the eighteenth century. The film was a series of contradictions, and when you're faced with that kind of conflict or argument all the time with someone as close to you as Stanley was to me, it finally wears you out. He certainly could wear you out.

Presumably he'd already chosen the William Makepeace Thackeray novel, The Luck of Barry Lyndon, *the story of a penniless eighteenth-century Irish adventurer who wants to be a gentleman. Maybe Stanley was so very secretive because it was public domain and he didn't want anyone to know what he was doing.*

He thought that Thackeray was better than any screenwriter alive. I said, 'Come on, Stanley, film didn't exist at the time of Thackeray.' He was so secretive. Fortunately I had read the book, but he used to tear out pages which he had xeroxed for other people working on the film. And he didn't give a script to anyone. That was the first time he was proved wrong because he eventually found out that he couldn't shoot the book. So he had to write the screenplay himself. Although Stanley could write, he wasn't a great scriptwriter by any means, so he became completely exhausted and eventually had to borrow material from *Casanova* and other texts to make it work.

He borrowed from other eighteenth-century biographies and autobiographies?

Yes, to fill it out. So that was a contradiction. But you have to remember that he'd recently done *A Clockwork Orange*, and although it was, I think, the most commercially successful film he'd made, he'd also received life-threatening letters. And possibly because I was close to him and knew him well, I was the only person he showed the letters to, because he didn't want to upset his family. And they were horrendous really. We discussed how he would protect himself from someone trying to assassinate him. He was going to get firearms and so on. It was extreme. And he was getting more and more anxious. He didn't want to leave his house in Borehamwood. So I said, 'This is crazy. If you want to do a picture entirely on location, then we should be looking for locations.' He got all these books about buildings and he employed six young photographers, including a niece of mine, Nikki, who could all click a camera, and we set up a miniature War Room in the garage of his house. All the walls were covered with big Ordnance Survey maps and we worked within a radius of five to thirty miles around his house. They had to photograph literally every square inch. Every day they were sent out, not really knowing what they were shooting. I knew very well that the only stately home of any importance in the vicinity was Hatfield, but I didn't think it was right because I wasn't attracted to Jacobean architecture. So we spent months going through this process. We bought every art book about painters of the eighteenth century, and at night-time we projected these slides, and I felt rather like you would feel as a professor at the Royal College of Art. I could sense a voyeurism in Stanley; if there was an unmade bed or something in the interior of a building, he'd discover things that I would never notice. I knew it was really a complete waste of time, but I couldn't get him out on location. I don't know, he thought economically and realistically it was the only way to do this sort of documentary approach to the eighteenth century, but at the same time it was at odds with his own insecurity. We had terrible fights during these night-time sessions. He was initially attracted to the impurities of Victorian architecture; the sparseness of the eighteenth century didn't appeal to him. I would pick out things and he'd say, 'Prove to me why this is Victorian.' I'd say, 'Stanley, I know this is Victorian. How do you want me to prove a wallpaper is Victorian?' This was going on at the same time as I was fighting him on every issue. Then suddenly, practically overnight, he decided that we were going to shoot the film in Ireland. I left for Ireland a few days before him but it put enormous stress on me because I suddenly found myself chasing all over Ireland trying to find locations, looking for buildings from an earlier period than the eighteenth century, only to discover that most medieval, Tudor and Jacobean architecture had been destroyed by Oliver Cromwell! In the end we used Waterford and Kilkenny, then the interiors at Dublin Castle, Powerscourt, Caher Castle and Huntingdon. The Lyndon rural farmhouse wasn't difficult except that I had to rebuild it. For the interior of Barry's cousin's house, I used Caher Castle.

The exterior of that manor house was partly Ballinatrae and partly Huntingdon, combined with the interior at Caher. There's a scene where Ferdy Mayne is standing as the Prussian General with this castle in the background. That's Caher Castle too, near Tipperary.
Yes, it's all in Ireland. There's a long story attached to that. I was so happy to find Huntingdon because it was built in the early seventeenth century, and although the windows were wrong, the correct ones were made at Pinewood and then shipped out. But Stanley didn't like the people who owned Huntingdon because they were practising all sorts of strange rites and so he wouldn't allow his daughters anywhere near it; he felt very uncomfortable. I told him I wasn't going to find anything else so we at least had to shoot the establishing shot there. He left it to me and everything became a nightmare. Then he wanted to find the Prussian locations in Ireland. Fortunately I found Powerscourt – which later burned down – near Dublin, which I think was designed by a German architect. It had some baroque interiors and pine forests so we got away with a certain amount of it, but for a film made entirely on location I said to Stanley, 'You have to go to Potsdam, Germany. It's in the east, but it's still untouched.' He said no. We had to use Powerscourt and some rooms in Dublin Castle for most of the Potsdam interiors.

There's a story about that great scene where Hardy Kruger is on a horse riding along a ridge in the Comeragh Mountains and the sun bursts through the clouds. Tell me about that.
Stanley used to ask me what we were filming the next day when we were by ourselves watching the dailies at about ten-thirty in the evening. I was the only one seeing dailies. And I would have no idea. He said, 'You took some great stills of mountainscapes.' He thought they

were wonderful. So he said, 'Why don't we shoot that?' By this time Stanley decided he was going to imitate Rommel and the whole unit would be mobile in Volkswagen minibuses. I told him that if he took twenty to thirty vehicles up this mountain it would take hours to get to the top, and then hours to turn round and come back down. But he said, 'Who gives a shit?' It happened exactly as I said. When we got to the top we had to turn round, and we nearly lost a day's shooting. Then suddenly, on our way down, this fantastic sky opened up. So everybody halted. We got the horse out of the horsebox, Kruger got on it, and we shot the scene.

The light is fantastic.
Like a Goya.

It's such a risk shooting a big movie in Ireland. It's beautiful and green but movies have died because of the rain.
I was happy to get out of the house in Elstree. At least by this time I'd broken Stanley's fear of leaving his familiar surroundings, and I think he was quite enjoying being in Ireland. Every day we were completely unprepared; nobody had a complete script and we were trying to shoot all the night scenes by candlelight. Stanley was an innovator. He tried to come up with an innovation for every film he made. For the eighteenth-century scenes shot in candlelight, he had experts in Hollywood adapting a new lens used by NASA.

The ultra-fast 50mm Zeiss lens was apparently the lens used on the Apollo moon shot for photographing the moon. What Stanley did was customise the BNC-Mitchell camera to make this lens fit, which was a real innovation.
Yes, no question about it. He had this special lens adapted or built for the candlelight sequence.

In terms of production design at this stage, you're presumably dressing these sets and looking at how the colour works, how the whole design of the image works; the costumes relating to the colour of the room relating to the light. It's nothing like studio work.
I never did one single sketch. The only sketches were done by a brilliant assistant who could draw camera projections of various lenses, like how many soldiers you see in the front line of the British attack, because we were experimenting with paper costumes and even dummies in the second and third lines. In my opinion it was a dress rehearsal for *Napoleon*, which Stanley badly wanted to do. There's going to be an exhibition of Stanley's work in Frankfurt in 2004. They spent two weeks looking through his archive and found eighteen thou-

sand slides of pictorial reference on Napoleon. Because Stanley related to him. He was giving me examples of how Napoleon, from Paris, controlled battles in the Spanish Peninsular War.

So Stanley could be at home in Borehamwood and control campaigns in Ireland.
Yes! He used to send instructions to the second unit on *2001* in cipher so that nobody else could decode them.

In Barry Lyndon *the design of that battle in the Seven Years War is wonderful: the enemy in white coats and the Brits in red against a background of green. Visually, it's astonishing. Was that from drawings?*
Well, partly drawings. It was possibly the longest tracking shot I ever had to build. I think it was the best part of a kilometre. It was an enormous construction but it paid off.

How did you cope with the candlelight?
I ordered a lot of cheap candelabras from Italy and we experimented with different candles to see how much light they gave off. There were single-wick candles, double-wick candles, and even treble-wick candles. So even though we used period candelabras in the scene, we used these cheap ones to give us the fill light because Stanley refused to use electric light. But it created enormous problems for everyone. First of all, it was very difficult to hold focus between two people talking – like we're doing now – because the depth of focus was very different in those days. The other problem was that the candles started dripping, even though they were meant to be non-drip. And the heat given off by the candles in the interiors was terrifying. The owners or curators of the stately home didn't want their paintings to be ruined so I had to design big heat shields to protect them. We tried to make fun of it because we were talking in terms of how much candlepower we had! But I never had time to stand next to Stanley and look. I was too busy tearing around all over Ireland trying to find locations for scenes which he might have written the previous night, and then come back with photographs of the location. He'd like it, and then he'd go there and start shooting the scene. But then the scene wouldn't work and so I'd have to find a different location.

Were you involved in costume as well?
Yes. I had to supervise their designs as well because Stanley said, 'You are the fucking production designer.' We had this girl from Sweden who had done *The Immigrants* and both Stanley and I were very impressed by it. Her name was Ulla-Britt Søderlund and she made all the costumes for it herself. He also imagined a beautiful Swedish girl to arrive, you

know, and there was this little Swedish girl. She was very practical. A friend of Letizia, an Italian girl called Milena Canonero who had good taste and was madly keen, also wanted to work on this movie. I think she had also done *A Clockwork Orange*. We sent her to auctions to buy actual eighteenth-century costumes, but they were all too small for the artists.

People were smaller in the eighteenth century?
Yes, much smaller. Sometimes the artists could wear a waistcoat or something, but we had to start our own costume factory at Radlett with Ulla-Britt and a dressmaker friend of Letizia's who was working there. We had all these people making these costumes or opening up the eighteenth-century garments to make new ones in exactly the same patterns. But they needed a lot of supervision so I often found myself going to Radlett at six in the morning to see them. Milena was very useful. She had that natural Italian good taste so she was good at selecting fabrics. And we had Leonard to do the wigs, which were probably the best wigs ever made. It was an enormous amount of work and I must say, Stanley normally came with me too. So in addition to this crazy hunting for locations I had to deal with all the costumes as well. Stanley even made the artists wear their costumes before shooting began because he wanted them to feel completely at home in clothes of the eighteenth century, to wear them properly.

I hear that he banned the word 'costume'; he wanted Barry Lyndon *to be a documentary rather than a costume film. They were clothes, not costumes. When was the decision made to use English country houses?*
We knew we had to. When I first took Stanley out to look at locations in England, before we went to Ireland, I think I got him as far as Hatfield because I knew we needed a house of either the seventeenth or the sixteenth century. He had seen photos taken by our kid photographers of hundreds of stately homes. But he wanted to do the Irish and continental locations first, and then come back to England. One morning we were driving and he asked me what I thought would happen if he shut down the production for six weeks to gather our thoughts. I said, 'Stanley, anybody else but you would get fired, but you'll get away with it because of your relationship with Warner Brothers.' He closed down the production and everybody was fired. The pressure on me was even greater and eventually I cracked up.

You were closeted with him, batting around ideas about locations, structure, costumes . . . And only half of the film had been shot.
Not even that much.

It basically drove you to a nervous breakdown.

Yes, it did. One can never put the blame on someone else because you are your own person and you can make your own decisions. But I felt incapable. For the first time in my life I felt incapable of confronting the problems and demands of a film. I became so neurotic that I bore all of Stanley's crazy decisions on my own shoulders. I was always apologising to actors for something that had gone wrong. I felt responsible for every detail of Stanley's film, for all his mistakes and neuroses. *I was apologising to the actors for Stanley's unreasonable demands.*

You were the man in the middle, with a vengeance . . .

Yes. These things had nothing to do with me, but because of my relationship with Stanley, because we were so close, I felt like I was responsible and it became too much. Apart from being physically exhausted from driving to the location at six or seven o'clock every morning, I was not sleeping properly.

And wardrobe. You were going to the factory early because they arrived at five.

Yes, and the first person who noticed something was wrong was Letizia, of course, when she came out to Ireland. Stanley sent me back to England for a couple of weeks to rest, but of course it took much longer than that.

A personal question: once you were ill, did Stanley take an interest?

Oh yes, and that was one of the problems! Stanley would tell me in detail what he'd done almost every day. I was continuously involved and I wasn't in a mental state to be involved. I spent the spring of 1974 in medical care and then in the clinic of a famous Scottish psychiatrist. He told me that unless I cut the umbilical cord to Stanley, I would never get better. When I finally got out of the clinic and arrived home – it's amusing but it was actually serious – I got a phone call from Stanley who said how pleased he was that I was better and how he'd done everything that I'd asked. He'd sent a second unit to Potsdam to shoot a sequence and he wanted me to direct it! Well, that gave me such a shock that the next day I was back in the clinic!

Oh Ken!

By late spring of 1974 I was getting better. The problem – and I don't want to talk too much about it, Christopher – was that I lost every bit of confidence in myself. I thought I was a phoney and that everything I'd done was false. I had to relive and re-conquer again every single experience in my life, and after such a complete breakdown it was very difficult. I felt completely drained, as if all my skills and experiences had been wiped out. Each step was a new experience. But I was very fortunate to have a talented Italian director visit me, who understood what I'd been through and who asked me to design *Salon Kitty*.

Tinto Brass?
Yes, Tinto. And I got my confidence back again. Then I did *The Seven-Per-Cent Solution* and my confidence returned completely. I was over it. Eventually there was an explosion of creativity within myself and I went to town on films like *The Spy Who Loved Me*. But overall, it had not been a very happy period.

For the second half of Barry Lyndon *you went round various English stately homes. I gather that Lady Lyndon's house was shot in ten or twelve different locations. You created an imaginary house out of individual rooms from a selection of English houses, among them Wilton, Petworth, Longleat, Blenheim, Castle Howard and Corsham Court.*
Stanley became very selective and his only references were painters of the period, so we had the most incredible library. I always used to say to him that a painter or artist of the period wouldn't necessarily reproduce everything. He wouldn't accept that, you see.

No. They're imaginative, not photographers. Kubrick had a very literal interpretation of paintings.
But it was his only reference really.

I think that Barry Lyndon *is at its worst when it slowly pulls back into a tableau that resembles a painting. For example, in the scene at the London club where Barry is drinking we go in through the hall and there's a person slumped over, looking exactly like a picture by Hogarth.*
With the paintings at the top of the frame.

Exactly. Or the scene at the beginning with the duel. The camera pulls back and locks so that there's a tree on either end, and it's exactly like a Gainsborough landscape. When the film does that, it teeters on kitsch. It's reproducing the greatest hits of eighteenth-century painting. It's at its best when it lets rip a little. Apart from the battle, the best scene in the film is the duel between Barry Lyndon and Lord Bullingdon inside the disused church. The tension of it and the Handel music; it lets rip and gets away from historical tableaux.
That's Stanley. That's where his talent came out. Many times we discussed how one would react in a duel if faced with that situation, and to some extent Stanley projected himself in Bullingdon: the fear. So that was really the director functioning as he should.

It becomes a personal thing.

It becomes an emotional and dramatic thing rather than imitation. When we were discussing the merits of studio and location shooting, Stanley said to me, 'You cannot tell me you could do it better in a studio.' And I replied, 'Not better perhaps, but more dramatically.'

The list of painters that he imitates is amazing: English painters such as Gainsborough, Reynolds, Hogarth, Stubbs and Rowlandson; French painters like Watteau; Italians such as Zoffany; even the Polish artist Chodowiecki for the continental scenes. It's quite a galaxy. Historians of eighteenth-century painting love this film because they can spot all the references.

Stanley went even further because he wanted us to research whether they had condoms, what toothbrushes they used, the arsenic in the wigs, all the lice in their hair and God knows what else. He went through every detail but in fact we never made use of them.

No, there are no condoms! Unless I missed them! Did you go to Potsdam in the end?

No.

A second unit went. Stanley didn't go but he was alleged to have directed it partly in cipher, partly down the telephone.

He always did that.

It's the scene of the carriages crossing.

That's right, in front of the royal castle.

It's a wonderful shot, and that was all done by 'distance direction'.

It was. I told him he had to do it because I knew that street in Potsdam – which fortunately wasn't bombed very much – and it made a great shot of eighteenth-century Europe.

Is it true that Stanley wouldn't shoot in Germany? I read somewhere that the reason he shot the German sections in Ireland was because he refused to go there.

No, that's not true. On the contrary, his greatest success – *Paths of Glory* – was shot in Munich. He refused to go to Germany because he didn't want to travel anywhere.

Can I ask you about the music? When Sergio Leone made Once Upon a Time in the West *the music was recorded before they shot the film and then the film was structured around the music, which makes the relationship between music and image very interesting. Leone told me that he and Kubrick would phone each other at this time . . .*

Stanley phoned everybody.

. . . and Kubrick told him that the music for Barry Lyndon *was also chosen before the film was shot, and that he immersed himself in the music whilst filming.*

Absolutely. I remember driving with him when we were looking for locations and he was always playing cassettes of music.

So he had it in his head that he'd cut this film to music. In a way, if there's one structure to this film, it's the music; he timed the shots to the crescendos in the music and it's very direct at times. You could call it Once Upon a Time in Georgian England. *He must have had a music advisor because it is all eighteenth-century music, though not always of the precise period: Handel, Bach, Mozart, Vivaldi, Schubert, even a march by Frederick the Great. And some of it is little known.*

Yes, but Stanley was pretty knowledgeable about music. And also jazz.

So the Ireland section had been shot, Potsdam had been shot by the second unit, and the interiors and exteriors of all those British country houses had been filmed. How long was the shoot in total, including the six-week gap?

About a year and a half.

So, a very long-suffering crew and cast.

And changing too because he fired everybody during those six weeks. He got one or two back, but not all of them.

Were you involved in the editing?

No.

Do you know if it was difficult to edit? Did he overshoot a lot? I don't mean the number of takes, but sequences he cut out.

I would say yes, but remember at that time I wasn't involved. The only thing during post-production was that he asked me if I would do the press coverage for the film – having been ill! Because after *Strangelove* he never held any more press conferences; he was too frightened of them. So he only gave one or two individual interviews.

You were becoming his PR lackey.

I had to go to France and Italy to do all these press things.

Really, as it was released? The promotional things?

Yes. But he checked every word I said. One day I came back and, he asked me why I had used the word 'paranoid'. I said, 'Yes, I did use it. But the other words I used to describe you were 'genius' and 'talent' and so on.' But he wouldn't accept that.

Then, three years after shooting began on Barry Lyndon, *you won your*

first Academy Award – for 'Best Art Direction'.
Yes, and obviously I could not have been more pleased. But at the same time it was ironic that I should have received it for a film shot entirely on location! There's no doubt that the imagery of *Barry Lyndon* is exceptionally beautiful, but somehow I feel that my purely creative and imaginative contribution on other films might have been more deserving of the award.

'. . . to be more creative and less reproductive . . .' as you said in that article twenty years beforehand.
Yes.

I feel you should have won your Oscar for Dr Strangelove *or* James Bond, *but you got it for* Barry Lyndon. *I'm not saying it wasn't deserved, but the Academy does seem to be drawn to elegant period pictures.*
Particularly at that time: I was also nominated for *Around the World in Eighty Days*. And a beautiful-looking period picture like *Barry Lyndon* seemed to be an obvious choice. But Stanley never got an Academy Award for any of his pictures. There's no question about the irony. I wasn't even at the ceremony to accept mine; I was here.

You didn't collect it?
No, I think Charlotte Rampling accepted it for me.

It's as if production design is only recognised if it's set in the past. Somehow movies set in the present or recent past don't count as production design. It's a weird way of thinking for professionals, who should know better.
I don't think it's still the case. Also, in most cases the Academy presumes that the period has to be recreated or invented in a studio. But *Barry Lyndon* was a big picture shot entirely on location. It was a one-off.

Unique. Normally, even on a period film, one would have to build some interiors. How did you part with Stanley Kubrick at this stage? You'd been through this long and intense experience together. You'd won an Oscar, which he was presumably thrilled about. But what was the state of your relationship by the time you finished Barry Lyndon?
It was very good. Funnily enough, we became closer friends in a strange way. Although I knew I would never – ever – work with him again. Life is too short. After all, if you almost lose your life making a film, there's something wrong. Stanley was fascinated by my work on the Bond films and the way in which my career exploded after *Barry Lyndon*. He was also fascinated by the opera I designed at Covent Garden, *La Fan-*

ciulla del West. I took him to Covent Garden – you know he was such a shy person – and invited him backstage to see how things are done in the theatre, and he was fascinated by it.

You did in fact work with Stanley Kubrick one more time, but only – as far as I can tell – for one day. It was on The Spy Who Loved Me.
I always kept that secret.

Now, Ken, it can be told.
The first time I ever mentioned this was in a tribute to Stanley at the Director's Guild in Hollywood two years ago, and that's because he always felt that those gigantic Bond sets were never properly lit. You can't really blame the cameramen for that. Probably the most experienced cameraman I ever did a Bond film with was Freddie Young. Everybody said I was out of my mind, that there was no cameraman in the world who would know how to light the gigantic set I'd designed. But Freddie was so experienced and he did it. On *The Spy Who Loved Me* we had a brilliant cameraman called Claude Renoir, grandson of the painter Pierre-Auguste Renoir, but he was nervous because we had this so-called supertanker with three nuclear submarines inside. I knew he needed a great deal of help from what in films we call 'source lighting': in other words, the actual lamps in shot. So I rang Stanley and I said, 'I've got this gigantic set. We built a stage for it at Pinewood and I've got to help Claude as much as I can with lighting it. You're a friend and you owe me something so . . .' He said, 'Ken, come on. You can ask me anything. But can you imagine me arriving at Pinewood? Everybody would know.' He couldn't do it. So I said, 'We could do it on a Sunday when there's nobody about. I swear, nobody would ever know that you'd been here.' After a lot of talking and soul searching, he said he'd do it. He came to Pinewood with me on a Sunday morning and we crawled over the empty set for about four hours.

Was it helpful?
Yes, he was helpful. But Stanley said, 'This must remain our secret.'

That's wonderful; the last time you worked together was inside the James Bond supertanker. Which film did Freddie Young shoot?
You Only Live Twice. It was the interior of the Japanese volcano.

When was the last time you saw Stanley?
Seven years ago. He often used to come to dinner here because he preferred to entertain his American VIPs in our kitchen with Letizia's pasta. He would pay for the wine and so on. From 1979 onwards I spent a lot of time on and off in America – we had a house in Malibu –

so I was not here as much. I used to get a lot of phone calls from Stanley, but we didn't really see each other in the eighties or nineties.

The Madness of King George

Let's move on to 1994 and The Madness of King George, *for which you won a second Academy Award. It was an adaptation by Alan Bennett of his own play,* The Madness of George III. *Set in 1788 England, it could have been shot like* Barry Lyndon *in assorted royal palaces. But that's another mistake Stanley Kubrick made: location shooting proved to be more expensive, not less.*

Everything was right on *The Madness of King George* and everything was wrong on *Barry Lyndon* to start with. I was working on a picture in New York at the time when I got a phone call from somebody calling himself Nicholas Hytner, who said he wanted to interest me in a picture he was directing. I hadn't seen the play but I'd heard about its success at the National Theatre, so I said, 'Let's talk.' I was staying at the Essex House. Nick came over looking like a beatnik carrying a plastic bag and a copy of Alan Bennett's script, and we immediately hit it off. Afterwards I rang my agent and said, 'Even if I get paid nothing for this picture, I want to do it.' In fact, I accepted half my normal fee. Here's a director who's never directed a film before but who has a complete concept – because of his experience in theatre – of how he wants the film to look. He had a wonderful cameraman called Andrew Dunn and a very good costume designer called Mark Thompson, who also designed sets. And this incredible cast and a very low budget. We shot the whole picture in eight weeks for eight million dollars. I knew I would do it the way I knew how to do it. In other words, I built most of the royal apartments at Shepperton studios and they were all ready at the same time. It gave Nick time to visualise how he wanted to move around in them. And for some of the really big rooms I recommended the double-cube room at Wilton. So we used that.

You used Eton College for the Houses of Parliament.
Yes. Mind you, we did look round Westminster. But we couldn't shoot there; it was impossible. And Winchester. But Eton seemed just right. Stanley Kubrick had taught me a lot about photography and lenses and choosing the right lens before deciding on a location. I found that worked very well on my location scouting.

You also used the roof of Arundel Castle, which you dressed with extra-tall chimneys.

132

Yes, well, that's probably one of the best examples of production design. Windsor was out of the question, especially because a lot of it is so Victorian, so we chose Arundel. I knew it well because it's owned by a friend of mine. I was so impressed by the roof of Arundel Castle and its gigantic chimneys that I thought, *If I add half a dozen more chimneys, it's almost like a Greek temple.* We shot that whole scene, where the King goes mad and collects the children from the royal nursery, at Shepperton. But we found this unbelievable spiral staircase at St Paul's Cathedral for when he climbs to the roof. So we start at the studio in Shepperton, go to the staircase at St Paul's Cathedral, and end up on the roof at Arundel. I thought the whole scene was like a Greek tragedy. It's a great example of . . .

Creative production design. And it's heightened too; it's exaggerated. It's so far from being a documentary of the eighteenth century. It's the perfect setting for the dialogue between King and Queen: 'Something is happening. Something is not right.'
Exaggerated in simplicity, I like to think. We also used Thame Park, which was a derelict Georgian mansion that the Japanese had bought and wanted to turn into a hotel. I used that place as Kew Palace – which doesn't exist any more – where King George spent his time getting better with medical treatment. I decided to use a few key pieces of dressing to make my point. In the scene where he eats soup with the spoon for the first time, I think you'll find there are maybe three paintings on the walls – many are removed as part of the King's cure – the table and one chair where he eats, and a few other props, but nothing else in this rather nicely proportioned Georgian room. The set was reduced to its bare essentials. And that, to me, is production design. It's to help the dramatic theme.

In a subtle way it's a rather theatrical production. You've said this film is an example of how you like to design a picture. Sometimes less is more.
Yes.

The Madness of King George *was obviously a much happier experience than* Barry Lyndon. *You were in sync with the director for a start.*
With the director, the cameraman, and with the cast. We had a great working relationship. I always feel that when you have a good relationship with the key people working on a film, it turns out to be a good one. We came up with ideas all the time. The scene we shot at Arundel, where King George has to go to the loo, was beautifully done between Nick Hytner, the cameraman and myself. And also the scene where the King is being chased round the royal apartments and then we

Design of the Robing Room (Eton),
1994

crane up to see him sitting in this chair, and it's designed like an electric chair, like something from the French Revolution. That's the fun part of doing a picture like that. I was very protective of Nick Hytner because Hollywood was always getting involved and he was getting upset. But Nick is a very strong-willed person. I said to him, 'When they ask for a close-up, give it to them. But when they ask you to change the concept, tell them to go to hell!'

Did he have anyone at his side? An experienced film director to advise him?
No.

So he really did achieve this as a theatre director, as a first-timer to film?
Yes.

Orson Welles once said the great qualification for making a movie as a film director was to have no experience whatsoever. He'd done radio and theatre before Citizen Kane, *but he went straight in without knowing the rules, and so broke them all without realising it. He hadn't yet developed a formula.*
Nick consulted the cameraman a lot, who was wonderful and extremely helpful, as of course we all were. But he was completely at home with the cast.

You were awarded your second Oscar for The Madness of King George

134

in March 1995. Again, for 'Best Art Direction'. How did you feel about that?

Well, I didn't expect to get it, frankly.

Can you remember who the opposition was?

Yes. I thought that Dante Ferretti would get it; he did a brilliant set for *Interview With the Vampire*. So I wasn't prepared, particularly after *Barry Lyndon*. It came as a complete surprise.

You were at the ceremony this time. What did you say in your acceptance speech?

I repeated the word 'incredible' several times. I'm best when I don't prepare a speech. It was very funny because Letizia had to stand up – she was so excited – to let my set dresser come out. But knowing Letizia, I thought she was trying to come up to the stage with me, so I had to tell her to sit down. And you see all this in the coverage! Then I think I said, 'My thanks to the brilliant first-time director, Nick Hytner, Alan Bennett's script, and the cast.'

Did you have a big party afterwards?

Yes. But I've never liked these big parties for awards. And Letizia wouldn't let go of the Oscar!

The Oscar itself was designed by Cedric Gibbons.

I didn't know that. So it's art deco.

Yes, it's a real art deco piece: a classic 1928 design depicting a knight holding a crusader's sword and standing on a reel of film with five spokes – the original branches of the Academy. It should have been in the V. & A.'s exhibition. One of the great stories about Cedric Gibbons is that he was credited for thirty-two years as art director, by contract, on every MGM film from 1924. He only designed a handful of movies himself, but he ran the art department as the supervising art director. One of the things he did design, though, was the Oscar, which was awarded to him a few times for films he hadn't designed! One more question about The Madness of King George: *you'd seen the script and it was basically the adapted play. But besides that, you didn't have much preparation time. Why the rush? Was it being pushed through?*

Yes. We were shooting it in the summer and we had to do these snow sequences. Luckily my assistant found this incredible young man who had invented a way of making snow using a form of paper. So we snowed in the whole of Arundel. Although it was terribly hot, we almost felt cold because everything around us was white. This young man and a team of six helpers worked through the night to snow in all the chestnut trees around Thame Park, and when I arrived the next morning in my car – it was one of those misty, grey mornings – every-thing was white. Unbelievable. But the stressful part was getting rid of it all before the next day's shooting, when we shot the King Lear sequence in summer.

The film is called The Madness of King George, *whereas the original play is called* The Madness of George III. *Legend has it that the reason for changing the title was that if it had 'III' after it, some people would think they'd missed* The Madness of George I *or hadn't seen* The Mad-ness of George II.
That did happen.

I think that's so funny; an example of 'sequel-itis'. The craze for I, II and III had already started with The Godfather. *So they changed the King of England's name because it might look like a sequel!*
Yes!

6 Designing James Bond

Goldfinger

In Sight and Sound, *winter 1964, you reiterated that 'no design is worth doing if you just reproduce reality. I don't believe you can get a sense of reality by copying. I think you can get that better by not copying. But you must always be honest. You mustn't do things just to create chi-chi effects. You must have a reason . . .' This was in an article that began with the words, 'The work of the designer . . . is often overlooked, except where it is the greatest element in a film's success, as it is in* Goldfinger.' *And it included your rough sketches for the War Room in* Dr Strangelove *and the Rumpus Room in* Goldfinger. *With the Bond films between 1964 and 1979, you at last had the opportunity to stretch that design philosophy to its limits: not offending the audience's 'sense of reality', but pushing it further and further, with tongue in cheek as well. Realism was a shifting term – a style on the natural side of film conventions then in use. You also gave more prominence to the role of production designer than ever before. Can you remember the origins of your involvement in* Goldfinger?

Yes. I couldn't do *From Russia With Love* so Cubby Broccoli and Harry Saltzman were hoping that I could do *Goldfinger*. I'd done two or three films since *Dr No*. By this time, with the success of *From Russia With Love*, James Bond became much more important. I think *Goldfinger* was the last really complete script based on Ian Fleming's book and it gave me a great opportunity to go further as a designer. As we always do on Bond films, we researched. First we went to Kentucky to look at stud farms. Fort Knox was there, but we weren't allowed to look at it. And then to Florida for the Fountain Blue Hotel and Miami sequence.

But you were allowed to fly over Fort Knox.
Eventually I was allowed to fly over it. It was quite a frightening experience because the roof of Fort Knox was guarded with machine guns and anti-aircraft weapons. On the ground, when I walked around the perimeter, there were loudspeaker messages telling me not to go any further: 'You are now entering a restricted area.' And there was a big army base next to it.

Is it true that one of the reasons you got to fly over Fort Knox, which was a very unusual privilege, was because the Kennedys liked the James Bond books?

Yes. In the end, I think that was it. But we also had a liaison man: a friend of Cubby called Charlie Russhon, who was a retired ex-army colonel. He had a good relationship with the Kennedys and set things up for us. So we got permission to fly over. In a way, I was delighted that we didn't get permission to go inside Fort Knox, because that triggered my idea of having this rather innocuous 1920s art deco building and inventing a completely imaginary interior for it. I remember looking at the interiors of the gold vaults at the Bank of England and finding them most uninteresting. In reality they were very low – a series of tunnels really – because gold is never stacked very high; it is so heavy. So I decided to use stylisation. I would give the audience a different form of reality. I designed the set on one of the big stages at Pinewood with the actual vault about forty feet high. I designed it like a prison with gold stacked up behind the bars and on the floor so that the camera was moving through gold all the time.

It has the feel of a cathedral with bars; a golden cathedral built in steel and granite, with downlighting from a vaulted ceiling and full of stacks of gold which nobody could ever move or get to. Of course, the public wanted to see lots of gold in Fort Knox.
That's the whole idea. If you go to the biggest gold depository in the world you expect to see gold towering up to the heavens. In hindsight, I think *Goldfinger* was maybe the best example of a Bond film that I designed, where the settings accentuate the dramatic message of the film. I had a completely free hand.

But Goldfinger *is still a heightened version of Fleming's novel, rather than taking off into a fantastical world. Fort Knox is interesting because it's like the War Room: nobody has been there so we can only imagine what it looks like. It's one of those secret places, and the great magic of cinema is being able to give people a kind of privileged access. You seem to love imagining places for us and making them larger than life, giving away a secret even though it's fantasy.*
The fantasy is more acceptable and believable to the public than what Fort Knox probably looks like inside, based on my experiences at the Bank of England. I used a combination of stage and film design for the set. A stage designer has to create a reality that is limited by the stage, the audience and other factors, whereas a film designer designs mainly for the camera. But I felt I had to combine the theatricality of a stage design for film as well to create the reality which I thought and which, as it turned out, the film audience accepted in the War Room and in Fort Knox. When the film came out United Artists received three hundred letters – mostly irate – asking how a British film unit and a British

On the set of Fort Knox, Pinewood 1964

139

Design of the Laser Room

director were allowed to shoot in Fort Knox when even the American President is not allowed in. It was a great compliment.

It reminds me of another Cedric Gibbons story. When he was supervising art director at MGM he complained to his boss, Irving Thalberg, that he'd been asked to come up with 'a moonlit ocean in Paris'. Without a moment's hesitation Thalberg replied, 'Whatever you put there, they'll believe it!' In the case of Goldfinger, *that's what Fort Knox looks like, because it's the closest we're going to get. There's a point in the script where Oddjob, the Korean bodyguard, throws his steel-rimmed bowler hat and it gets stuck between the bars of your Fort Knox. I was wondering whether that fun idea with the hat came out of script conferences with you.*

I think that came out as we went along with the shooting. We'd already used the bowler hat at the golf game when Oddjob throws the hat and

140

it decapitates a statue, so I suppose Guy Hamilton, the director, must have thought, 'How can Sean deal with this superman?' He came up with the idea of electrifying the bars so that, when Oddjob tries to retrieve his bowler hat in the final confrontation, he gets electrocuted. I do not think that was in the initial script.

I went to the first afternoon screening of Goldfinger *at the Odeon in Leicester Square, and the audience erupted with applause – even at a matinée – when Oddjob got his comeuppance by being electrocuted, and when the timer on the bomb counts down 006 seconds, 5, 4, and so on. I'd never known a cinema audience spontaneously applaud like that. But there was something about the way in which that sequence worked; it satisfied everybody. It's interesting what you say about the film's relationship to the novel because I have a quote here from* Goldfinger *about the other great design in this film, the Aston Martin. If one reads the novel it's a pretty ordinary thing. Bond has just traded in his supercharged four-litre Bentley for the Aston Martin DB3: 'The DB3 had the advantage of an inconspicuous colour – battleship grey – and certain extras that might or might not come in handy. These included switches to alter the type and colour of the front and rear lights, reinforced steel bumpers, a Colt .45 in a trick compartment and a radio pick-up.' They are fairly ordinary gadgets, even at the time the novel was written, but in the process of transforming those words into the scene of a film, extraordinary things happened. The now famous scene in Goldfinger has Q explaining how the gadgets work, the sheer range of which is astounding. How did that happen? It's a key moment in the evolution of Bond.*

Certainly in terms of gadgetry. No question about it. I remember Cubby, Harry, Guy and myself debating what car we would give Bond because there were the E-type Jaguars, the Aston Martins and the Italian Ferraris and Alfa Romeos. We decided the Aston Martin, which was by far the most expensive British sports car, would be the right prop for Bond. So myself and the special-effects man, Johnny Stears, went to see David Brown at the plant in Newport Pagnell.

David Brown as in DB?

Yes. We tried to persuade him to give us two Aston Martins: one for driving and the other for all the gadgets. But they weren't keen at all. So Johnny and I came back to Pinewood and talked to Cubby and Harry. Eventually, reluctantly, Aston let us have the two DB5s. Aston weren't doing that well at the time, but after the success of *Goldfinger* their sales went up by about 47 per cent. We never had any problems getting cars for nothing after that!

It is said to be the first major example of product placement in a movie.
Yes, I think it was.

Because nobody thought about product placement at that time. They didn't know whether it was good or bad for a product's image – especially an upmarket product.
When you say product placement, do you mean merchandising?

Yes, but as well as that I mean using products in movies as part of a marketing campaign. Where merchandising is concerned, I can still remember seeing in 1964 Goldfinger négligées in a shop window with the slogan, 'Go to bed dressed to kill.' How could I forget! And of course, the Corgi toy Aston Martin in silver or gold. It all seems to begin with the DB5.
I was largely responsible for thinking up the gadgets for the Aston Martin; the machine gun, the scythe, the passenger ejector seat. Principally

because I was a sports-car freak. I had an E-type Jaguar and in those days it didn't have any forward bumper, so my car was continuously being damaged by other people. I got my own back with the DB5. It got rid of all my frustrations.

So you'd like to drive round Knightsbridge with a flame-thrower and wheel scythes?
Yes! It's very tongue-in-cheek. I was very fortunate to have Johnny Stears working with me because he was a brilliant engineer who, once I made a sketch, made it all happen. Of course, we couldn't have three machine guns. But we had one!

It looks as though all the gadgets worked . . .
Yes, they did. The ejector seat certainly worked; it was from a fighter plane. We needed a second car for that because the mechanics had to be hidden inside it to make the gadgets work. In those days Bob Simmons, an old friend of mine, was our main stunt double for Bond in all the tricky parts. He drove the Aston Martin in that famous chase that we filmed. I knew I only had one working car so I built a brick wall out of foam, but I realised that about twenty feet behind the foam was an actual concrete wall. So I warned Bob to start breaking early when he hit the phoney brick wall because I didn't want the car to be damaged, but of course he broke too late and hit the brick wall at the end. We had to work all-night and part of the next day trying to replace the parts of the car he damaged.

There were some gadgets in your drawings that didn't make it onto the Aston Martin in the movie. Twin flame-throwers mounted behind the fog lights, for example. But the ejector seat, the wheel scythe, the number plates that revolve and the homing device, they were all written into the script.
And the overrider that came out like a boxing glove.

That's the revenge of the bumper! The scriptwriter Tom Mankiewicz – who wrote a subsequent Bond film – said that from the moment Q explained the Aston Martin, Bond could never quite be serious again. It was a turning point in the series, plus of course the relationship between Q and Bond: the jokiness. You're introduced to each of these gadgets in reel two because in reel five you know they're going to be put through their paces. And because you know it's going to happen, it gives a jokey suspense to the audience. At that moment the films began to separate themselves from the books. Is that true do you think?
Yes, absolutely right.

Some of the gadgets you concocted for the James Bond films are now standard issue: the mobile phone, the radio transmitter watch, the satellite navigation system in the DB5 – which nowadays comes as standard in upmarket cars.

Yes, but we did that at the time by using a cut-out road map and a moving dot of light behind it!

Apparently the KGB took a very close look at your Bond weapons. They even produced a ballpoint pen that could shoot people! But the great thing about the Aston Martin is its Britishness. If you look at that scene closely you'll see in Q's workshop a Mini van in the background, a parking meter, an anglepoise lamp – all these classics of British design. And then there's the Aston Martin with its hand-stitched leather upholstery in the tradition of gentlemanly British design. Was that deliberate?

Yes, it was deliberate. It was also an expression of the period. I introduced typical items of that period into the dressing of Q's workshop.

It's a great moment for British design buffs. The greatest hits of industrial design culminate in the Aston Martin. The other thing about that car is that it's very like the whole strategy you adopt with the sets and gadgets. It has a very gentlemanly exterior with this beautiful silver birch hand-beaten aluminium body, but inside there are really horrible and nasty things going on. It's like those beautiful exotic places where – if you look more closely – there's something vicious behind the innocent façade, something that's not in the travel brochure. It's the same with the Aston Martin. Beautiful on the outside: weapons on the inside. That was already becoming part of the formula too.

I was not aware of that but you're not the first one who's said that to me. I tried to give the villains' lairs a menacing look to them, but always slightly tongue-in-cheek. People have criticised me for designing enormous places for Bond villains, but they were megalomaniacs. So I built them in reinforced concrete and then put priceless paintings and antique furniture in them. I mixed it all up, and tried to have a sense of humour. Maybe that was originated or accentuated by what you said about Q and the Aston Martin; they were funny scenes.

The Bond films begin to have their tongue firmly in their cheek. And the formula emerges: the gadgets, the throwaway lines, Q the schoolmaster and Bond the surly pupil, the villain's lair . . . The Goldfinger *lair is interesting. It relates to the atmosphere of the lair in* Dr No, *but also to your own taste in white walls and antiques. A modern interior with antique furniture and/or antique paintings to break it up. In* Goldfinger *the walls are made of stone and wood – it has a touch of Frank Lloyd Wright – and there's always a globe or map to epitomise the megalomania of the characters, rather like the War Room with its maps and arrows depicting nuclear bombers. For* Goldfinger *it's an ordinary table that transforms into a map of Fort Knox.*

Yes. It was a billiard table that turns into a model of Fort Knox. It wasn't easy because Goldfinger is the owner of a stud farm, which is why he lives in Kentucky and has a racetrack and all that. We called the set where he keeps the harnesses and tack the rumpus room. In some ways I was influenced by the War Room, but I knew this Rumpus Room had to convert into a gas chamber, so all the walls were designed to close. Even the big stainless steel fireplace came down so that no fresh air could get in. It was pretty horrifying actually. And at the same time the other moving objects, like the billiard table, had a practical purpose by turning round and becoming the briefing model of the raid on Fort Knox. The rotating bar was a little gratuitous, but once I'd started I thought, I might as well! So it turned from a rather harmless-looking, luxurious tack room into a combined War Room and gas chamber.

My theory about your command centres – which I mentioned earlier – is that maybe you're exorcising the demons of your past: Goldfinger is virtually a Nazi character with a gas chamber; Dr No is of German-Chinese parentage; there's Stromberg in a future Bond film. Very often the baddies are Nazis or neo-Nazis. Although the stories may be set in the Cold War, the characters are creations of the Second World War.

But remember it was the 1960s. The Second World War was still very much in everybody's minds.

I still think that at some level these megalomaniac interiors were Ken Adam getting the 1920s and '30s out of his system. But you seem to resist this idea.

It's difficult for me. Maybe I did it instinctively. I was conscious of what I was doing but I'm not sure whether it was a result of my childhood experiences.

We've talked about the innovations in Goldfinger, *but I think there are some aspects of it that are quite traditional. It appears that Sean Connery never went to America; the opening scenes in Miami are back-projected.*

I built part of the Fountain Blue Hotel exterior on the stage at Pinewood.

The main actors were not going to these places. Sometimes they went to Europe, but I sense there still wasn't a huge budget to play with. Do you agree?

Sean possibly came to Florida, but I'm not sure. Christopher, I've just remembered a rather amusing scene which is perfectly true: Harry

Saltzman had made a deal with Ford – who were much more generous than Aston Martin – to give us this Lincoln Continental. There's a scene in which Goldfinger sends one of his gangsters, driven by Oddjob, to a breaker's yard where the car is crushed into a three- or four-foot cube. This brand new Lincoln Continental arrived at the yard, we took out the engine, and then this terrible squeezing thing happened. First it became like a sausage, and then it was pushed the other way to become like a cube. And I suddenly thought that I hadn't considered the weight of this condensed car because we only had a tiny pick-up truck to carry the cube. So I whispered to Guy whether we could cut the scene. He asked why, and I told him that I didn't think the pick-up was going to support the weight of the cube. So we decided to split the scene, which gave me the opportunity to cut part of the car off – which was more difficult than I thought – once it had become a sausage, to reduce the weight. It took an hour or more. Even now, when you see the cube being loaded into the pick-up, the suspension goes down. To the unit hanging around it was like castration: this beautiful Lincoln being treated that way. There was no laughter.

It's interesting that Ford had a more relaxed attitude to product placement. They were maybe a little ahead of the British at that time. So Goldfinger *is a huge success. At the French première in Paris Sean Connery drove an Aston Martin down the Champs Elysées, accompanied by sixty gold-painted women. Bond suddenly becomes a real series. It's gained confidence and it's found its formula. But then you do another spy film that isn't a Bond:* The Ipcress File.

The Ipcress File

Directed by Sidney J. Furie, The Ipcress File *is in some ways the complete opposite to James Bond. Sergeant Harry Palmer is a soldier with a chip on his shoulder on secondment to the secret service. He's an anti-hero in a raincoat wandering around a rather dismal post-war London. Most of the film looks as though it was shot on location.*
Yes, about 90 per cent.

London looks pretty sordid in this film; it's grey and brown and gloomy. It's not glamorous or exotic at all. How did you switch from the glamour of Bond to the gloom of The Ipcress File?
Well Sid Furie and myself formed a team with a one-time producer called Charles Kasher, who was from New York and had never done a film before. He was a friend of Harry Saltzman, who gave him an

opportunity to produce his first film. Harry thought at the time he was doing a poor man's Bond, but we felt that was entirely wrong. We wanted to make an anti-hero, an anti-Bond. And Michael Caine seemed like the ideal choice. I will say this about Harry: he was incredible. I remember him arriving from Hollywood after trying to get some finance for the film. We all ganged up on him and said, 'If you think you're going to make a cheap Bond, it's the wrong choice. We feel it's got to be an anti-hero.' Harry, who was very volatile, exploded at first. But then he saw it, although he didn't quite understand it. I'll give you an example: I found an Edwardian interior in Grosvenor Street near Victoria that I thought would make a great headquarters for MI5; it had big rooms and tall windows. One of the rooms appealed to me as the office of M, played by Nigel Green. It had lovely proportions with two or three very tall windows. Harry said I could have anything I wanted in terms of computers or the latest gadgetry; I just had to let him know. But that night – one of my many sleepless nights – I started thinking about it. I thought, *Wouldn't it be interesting if this military character only has a trestle table in his office. He doesn't even have a chair for anybody to sit in. He has a camp bed so we know he spends nights there and maybe he has a bust of a famous warrior like Caesar or someone like that.* I thought it would be very dramatic but I hadn't discussed it with either Harry or Charlie or Sid. So in the morning I talked to Sid Furie about the idea. He said it was interesting, but wanted five minutes to think about it. He came back and said, 'You're absolutely right. Let's go ahead with it.' Dissolve: we start shooting and a couple of hours later Harry Saltzman arrives on this empty set and he just goes ape. I tried to explain to him why we did it that way but Harry accused me of trying to come between him and the director. He was screaming so loudly that the whole unit disappeared. Everyone remembers it. I went to Pinewood last Sunday for a rather sad occasion – it was a memorial for Peter Hunt – and people were talking about this incident, which everybody who was around still remembers. And Harry disappeared. But two hours later he came back as if nothing had happened and said, 'You're right.' When somebody lost control like that I felt more relaxed in a way; I couldn't take them seriously.

The office of Guy Doleman, the head of MI5 in The Ipcress File, *is an amazing location. It overlooks Trafalgar Square. You found a real apartment to shoot that from.*
Yes. The only studio in that film was what I call 'the Brainbox'.

The huge warehouse with a box inside it, where they try to brainwash Harry Palmer.

With the projectors. There may have been one or two other sets – the prison cell and the corridor – but everything else was shot on location. I had this wonderful cameraman with me too, Otto Heller, who I'd done several films with. He was a completely instinctive cameraman because he never looked at the light meter; he always had an assistant doing that. Otto did everything the way he felt. He was always coming up with ideas. He told me that he started his career with one of those hand-cranked cameras filming the funeral of the Emperor Franz Joseph in Vienna. Otto is a small man so he said he couldn't even see what he was filming! That's how he started and he became a famous cameraman. Again, I think *The Ipcress File* is an example of a film where everything seemed to click. We had a great relationship with Sid Furie, we had a wonderful cameraman . . .

There's a distinctive look to the film. It is almost monochrome at times.
Yes, we had a very good camera operator too, shooting through keyholes.

There's a terrific moment when Nigel Green enters St James's Park with a colleague and he's framed through the cymbals of a military band. It's the first intimation that something odd is going on.
I thought it was quite brilliantly conceived. And Michael Caine gave a fantastic performance too.

For years I tried to crack two eggs with one hand: remember, behind the credits, Caine does all that cookery? He has two eggs in his hand, cracks them both, and opens them into a bowl. It came from Len Deighton's newspaper cookery strips – The Action Cookbook: How to Seduce Through Cookery. *I read every one of them! After Bond, it must have been quite difficult for you to adjust to a low-budget film.*
But we were very excited about it, just to be doing the opposite of Bond. And it was the right concept for the film. Harry realised that eventually. The next year I was nominated twice by the British Film Academy for Best Art Direction on both *Goldfinger* and *The Ipcress File*. Harry Saltzman and Cubby Broccoli booked this big table for the ceremony, but when I won the award for *The Ipcress File* Cubby practically didn't talk to me for the rest of the evening!

I think you got one subsequent Oscar nomination for Bond: The Spy Who Loved Me. *But there's this snobbery about the whole series. There's something about Bond which is 'beneath' the view of the jury. It's silly because, in retrospect, it was one of your finest hours after* Dr Strangelove. *It's like the Academy has to swallow its pride before giving an award to a Bond film.*

Well also *The Ipcress File* was an anti-Bond picture, it was Michael Caine's second or third film, and it was full of ideas and concepts that seemed to work. That's why a cheap, simple location picture became an enormous success.

It also had a sense of humour, which was nice. There's one scene I remember, because it was filmed outside the Royal College of Art, where a bald-headed villain walks out onto the street. You assume he's going to murder somebody but he starts feeding the parking meter with money. There's also a shoot-out in an underground car park, which later became a visual cliché in the 1970s.

Thunderball

After The Ipcress File *you returned to James Bond with* Thunderball *in 1964/65. Directed by Terence Young this time rather than Guy Hamilton,* Thunderball *had a bigger budget than* Goldfinger. *Much of the challenge is that a lot of it is set underwater. For the first time in a Bond film – it subsequently happened quite often – there are underwater sequences with submarines, sunken Vulcan aeroplanes, nautical design, frogmen, sharks . . . It's a whole new design challenge. Until then you hadn't designed anything to be used underwater. But it became one of your trademarks.*

I remember the whole art department learning to dive in swimming pools with bottles and so on. Cubby and Harry covered us by hiring the Ivan Tors divers, who were a team of underwater experts making the *Flipper* television series in Florida, to advise us on underwater shooting. I came across a cameraman who looked like a whale himself, Lamar Boren. By that time he'd spent nearly five thousand hours underwater photographing sharks at the Great Barrier Reef. So we knew what we were letting ourselves in for. As a designer, it gave me another dimension to work in. And because I suppose I'm like a Boy Scout, I loved designing underwater bomb carriers and things. I was so amazed when I found people who could make my designs work. They were obviously not made by the studio because they were specialist props that had to work underwater, but I was fortunate to contact Jordan Klein in Miami who had built mini-submarines and other underwater craft. So I flew over and showed him my design. He said it would work, but he'd have to alter some of the design for balance and so on.

There were also the strange little flying saucers that people clung on to underwater.

THUNDERBALL

Design of underwater bomb carrier

Yes. I designed all those things and somebody made them work. Furthermore, I met a man called Jack Manson who worked for Allied Marine, a shipbuilding company in Miami. They built my design for the *Disco Volante*, the villain's super-fast yacht, which was based on a hydrofoil. We didn't know whether it was going to work because it had to be a craft that could travel at fifty knots or more while still looking like a normal luxury yacht. But apart from powerful racers there weren't any yachts that could go that fast in 1965. So I came up with the idea of using a hydrofoil and doubling its length to make it look like a large yacht. Harry Saltzman found an ad for an old hydrofoil in Puerto Rico. So we flew over and bought this thing that was lying on the dry for about $10,000, not realising that the Mercedes engine needed to be replaced. It worked out to be very expensive, especially as we had to bring it to Florida. I came up with the design for the two hulls, based on a catamaran principle. The first hydrofoil that I was shown was an enormous American hydrofoil called the Denison. We took it for trial runs in the Atlantic. With two aircraft jet engines it used to go at sixty or seventy knots, but the noise was unbearable and it was quite impractical for our purpose. So then we used this Rodriguez hydrofoil. Allied Marine were a little doubtful whether my designs would work, and all the naval experts said I couldn't put two hulls together like that because they would break in a bad sea, so we eventually came up with two one-inch slipbolts that held the two halves together on either side so that the catamaran and the hydrofoil could work independently. It worked like a dream. What I've found, particularly with Bond films, is that some of the most complicated things that take the most time and thought work beautifully on film. But the things you don't worry about too much, like the paint finish on a door behind the star of the film, you suddenly see in a close up and it looks terrible. Every detail counts on the screen. Fortunately the important things did work, thanks to a wonderful team of collaborators. I kept my art director, Peter Murton, in Florida for three months to supervise the construction of the *Disco Volante*.

You're not an engineer: you provide the concept, the sketch; then it is put into three-dimensions. The actual engineering is presumably up to somebody else.
Experts.

And even if it doesn't work, they make it look as though it does.
But you see, with Bond it did work. On those early Bond films we decided that we didn't want to fool the audience, so we used the minimum amount of effects and did it all for real. But we had to find people that could make it work. Today, two or three generations later, young cinema-goers – like my nephews – know the original Bonds did it for real, but they don't believe in modern films that use all these digital effects.

Surely the full-sized Vulcan bomber that gets hijacked and ends up on the ocean bed covered in nets was a mock-up. It must have been.
It was a mock-up; we built it in the Bahamas. It's full-sized, though. Not the whole plane, but certainly the cockpit, the nose cone and part of the wings. I took along my brilliant construction manager from Pinewood, Ronnie Udell, and his sidekick and we constructed it in the Bahamas because it had to be done in fibreglass. I also had incredible cooperation from the Chief of Fighter or Bomber Command – an Air Marshall – who allowed me to look at the Vulcan bomber, which was classified in those days. Then Johnny Steers built a big model of the bomber with a wingspan of about ten feet and we shot it ditching in the Bahamas with wires, and it's very believable. Then we nearly had a fatal accident. We sank my mock-up bomber in sixty feet of water in the Bahamas with one of Ivan Tors' experts doubling for the pilot in the cockpit. He had an alarm button in case something went wrong and something did go wrong but he didn't want to spoil the scene so he waited before pressing the button. By the time we got him out he was unconscious. He was in a very bad way and we rushed him to hospital. Fortunately he got away with his life, but people don't realise on the Bonds how many other accidents we had because of these big under-

water battles. The man who was directing the underwater sequences, Ricou Browning, was shot through his leg or thigh with a bolt from a harpoon gun; they were terribly dangerous. We also learnt to treat the sharks with a certain amount of respect. We had these sticks with shotgun cartridges on the end in case a shark attacked, but you never knew what could happen. A shark is like any wild animal. We would see a hundred sharks and they wouldn't do anything to you, but then one would turn on you. So it was quite a dangerous pastime. Anecdotally, Letizia and I, along with Sean, Diane Cilento, Luciana Paoluzzi and Anita Ekberg – who I think was married to one of the actors – all had bungalows at a place called Love Beach in the Bahamas. It was beautiful. Everybody swam in the clear water. I knew there were sharks in the Bahamas when I did my first scout, and you could see the buggers from the air, but nobody would admit it. Everybody said they were just basking sharks. I never trusted them too much. I found this incredible villa belonging to Mr and Mrs Sullivan, an American couple. They had a seawater pool and a normal swimming pool, so I thought it would be fun if we could get the sharks into their seawater pool. We rang up the Miami Seaquarium who went out on a boat and in one night caught about fifteen sharks, all off Love Beach. The biggest was about ten foot. Well, you can be sure we took more care swimming in the sea after that! We put them in the Sullivan's seawater pool but it was a problem to keep them alive, so the Ivan Tors boys were swimming them around to keep them moving. We also had to provide the pool with a permanent supply of oxygen. The smell was horrendous. Another problem was that – maybe I shouldn't say this, but I'll let you decide – Mrs Sullivan drank a lot and I was terribly worried that she might fall into the pool at night, so we had guards there too!

And Sean Connery had a problem with one of the sharks . . .
Yes. When we were about to shoot the scene in which Bond is suddenly confronted by a shark, I assured him that he had nothing to worry about because it was separated from him by a Plexiglas corridor I had constructed in the saltwater pool. What I hadn't told him was that I had been unable to purchase quite enough Plexiglas sheets in Nassau. There was one sheet missing, which left a four-foot gap at the end of the corridor. For safety, I stationed one of Ivan Tors' underwater boys down there to make sure that the shark didn't get through the gap. In any case, the sharks were pretty drugged by this time. I can't remember the exact sequence of events, whether the underwater guard was somewhere else, but the shark took one look at the gap and swam straight through it. We all saw it happen except Sean, who just thought it was one of the underwater guards. He wasn't worried until we all started

screaming at him to get out. You never saw him move so quickly out of the pool; he walked on water! I don't think the shark would have attacked him, but you can never be too sure. You never fool around with sharks.

You all needed danger money! The other thing about Thunderball *is that it has two interesting interiors; one is the combined command centre, and the other is the SPECTRE headquarters. Two famous Ken Adam designs. The command centre for top brass of the Admiralty is typical because it's a Georgian room with high-backed Vatican chairs, but behind the tapestries are all these modern strategic charts. Behind the art there is usually something sinister. On the other hand, there's the SPECTRE headquarters with these modernist chairs but no table . . .*
I was getting fed up with boardrooms and long tables. It was getting more and more difficult to come up with new concepts for conference rooms. So I decided they would just be sitting on armchairs with a little shelf attached for all the buttons and lamps: the control console. It was a pretty contemporary design. Of course, we never see the villain because I had the glass partly obscured. We didn't want to establish the villain at that time.

Do you see the cat?
Yes, you see him stroking the cat. Then Guy Hamilton or I came up with the idea – which I thought was rather funny – that the chair would disappear into the floor.

To fry somebody.
Yes, and would come back up empty. A button is pressed, the gangster who has betrayed the organisation disappears into the floor, and the chair comes up again minus the gangster.

It's the ultimate paranoid committee room . . . if you don't like what someone's saying!
Right!

The command centre is again very Adam. It's antique and Whitehall-y but with all these modernist charts behind them. This was the biggest room of its kind that you'd designed.
Yes. When we talk about the dimensions of the set, the tapestries were nearly forty feet in height and sixty feet wide. You can't find tapestries like that. I had probably the greatest scenic artist in film, Ferdie Bellan. He was Austrian and had been discovered by the Kordas and worked for them. He was a brilliant scenic painter. I found a tapestry which I wanted painted this enormous size so I called Ferdie and, unlike most scenic artists, he didn't even grid it out in squares. He just started painting

on one side of this enormous canvas. He was an absolute genius. I needed people like that to implement my ideas.

You said two things about this at the time. You said that you needed the confidence of your convictions, and the more outlandish your convictions, the more confident you'd better be, because somebody somewhere has got to do it; you come up with these incredible ideas and a technician has to implement them. The other thing you said was that, as you moved into this area of heightened reality, everything became 'to the power of two'; everything was getting bigger. You wanted the audience to be awestruck by what they saw.
Yes, and at the same time it creates the right mood for the audience when they're watching the film because it's also slightly tongue-in-cheek.

Taking the luxury yacht with the hydrofoil hiding inside it as an example, you seem to be obsessed with hiding things inside other things. I don't want to go into the psychology of this, but very often you design an innocuous exterior and something hidden inside it.
I like to fool the audience; I think that's true. There was a very practical reason behind the yacht. It was impossible to get a yacht that size which could travel that fast, so by combining the catamaran with the hydrofoil it at least looked like a big yacht. Then, when the hydrofoil came out like a bullet, there was a practical purpose behind it too. If I understand you correctly, what I like to do is design against the audience's first impression.

Some people have analysed the Bond films as the dark side of 1960s consumerism: international travel is available on a large scale for the first time but you're showing what really happens in the Bahamas; behind the glossiness or the models in their bikinis, there's probably someone trying to do you in with her stiletto.
We started that film in the Chateau D'Anêt in France with Bob Simmons dressed up as the widow! And then Charlie Russhon thought of this jetpack. He'd just heard from his pals at the Pentagon that somebody had invented a jetpack that enabled you to fly for a short time. But he didn't say how dangerous it was! Sean wouldn't touch it. Even the expert had to keep checking his stopwatch because the backpack only had a limited amount of fuel and there was no alarm to warn him it was running out. But that was all done for real.

The formula really settles in with Thunderball. *There's a very action-packed pre-credits sequence where you're almost exhausted by the time the titles arrive, even though it has only been a minute or two. Then we start the story proper. M establishes Bond's mission and Bond goes to the quartermaster's branch to get kitted out with some gadgets that we know will be used later on in the movie. Dissolve: Bond meets an Amazon woman who we think is working for the baddies but who we know will team up with Bond and end up in his arms in the final reel. Then Bond, like Theseus and the Minotaur, enters the maze of the villain's lair, gets captured, possibly tortured, manages to escape using the gadgets, blows up the villain's lair, saves the Western world and, with a final joke, gets together with the Amazon. That's basically the story of* Dr No, Goldfinger *and* Thunderball. *The variations are the girl, the gadgets, the locations, the villain, and the maze where the Minotaur lives – which becomes more and more elaborate and set in increasingly strange places. The interest in the story comes from the variations the design brings to it and the colourful performances. The story recedes and the design takes over.*

Right, yes.

And in this process the production designer becomes more and more important because that's how you differentiate the product. I think this was unique in the history of cinema up to that date. You get a whole cycle of films where you can see an individual's development as a designer across a palette of seven movies, but at the same time you also see the design values becoming increasingly important to the cinematic experience. I presume, because the design issue is a script issue, that you became part of the scriptwriting process from Thunderball *onwards?*

Yes. The design, the visuals – whether it was the settings, locations or gadgets – became more and more important, so my function became equally important. By that time the producers and the directors had confidence in me. Guy Hamilton, Terence Young, Lewis Gilbert; they were all professionals. Lewis had a great sense of humour – cockney humour – and a great deal of experience. I never had problems with the directors or the cameraman either. On a later picture, *You Only Live Twice*, when I designed the interior of the volcano, everyone in the film industry said I was crazy. They told me I'd never find a cameraman in this country or in America who is capable of lighting a set four hundred and sixty feet in diameter and one hundred and twenty feet high. I said, 'I think I will.' Freddie Young said he'd do it. In hindsight it took a lot of courage, or perhaps foolhardiness, but once I had an idea and I was convinced it was the right thing to do . . . I had to go ahead with it.

It's also scary because of the responsibility.

It's enormous.

You mentioned, when talking about Thunderball's *underwater sequences, the possibility of something going wrong; it must have been hard to sleep at night.*

Yes. Not only for me, but for the key people in my department too, like the construction manager. It was a challenge for everybody. By this time we worked as a team and they knew they had to come up with answers to my designs.

Critics writing in the 1960s – after Cahiers du Cinéma – *tended to say that you can only express yourself in low-budget B movies because the pressure of the studio and the big budget isn't on you. And if you want to find real film art you look at these small, low-budget films. But in your case it seems to be the opposite; you come into your own when these films get big.*

Yes, but you just mentioned *The Ipcress File*. That was a low-budget movie.

But where the Bond films are concerned, you thrive on the larger scale. You love big-budget mainstream cinema.

I did! At that time. I took up the challenge and wasn't neurotic about it because I felt I could deal with it. I also felt, as a designer, that I could design anything. I had a lot of confidence in myself. What also happened was that we were getting less input from the Fleming books and the producers relied more and more on the spectacle value of the films. Running out of Fleming stories made the designs that much more important. So they gave me a reasonably free hand and I exploited it.

From You Only Live Twice *onwards I imagine they'd send you an outline and then you'd go location hunting together, find new gadgets, new special effects, new spectacular sequences . . . And then the script would be redrafted around your design. Is that roughly what happened?*

Not entirely, but almost like that. The formula in my day was that I'd get an outline or the first draft of a script. Then it was a question of going round the world trying to find the most exotic locations. Once we found something which seemed to fit into the idea, then the script was adapted to suit what we found on location, or what I consequently came up with in my designs. But the location hunt came first, and that normally involved the producers – Harry Saltzman and Cubby Broccoli in those days – the director, myself, and sometimes a cameraman. We covered half the globe looking for exciting locations.

From the air, I guess.

Yes, starting from the air. We had quite a lot of adventures in South America and Guatemala and so on, but that's another story! Cubby was like a Boy Scout too, and even though I was the same; anything that was slightly dangerous and unique-looking, I wanted to see. Then Cubby would never let me go by myself. I'd say, 'Cubby, let me go on a small plane and find this jungle village.' But he would always want to come along and sometimes it became very dangerous. But that's maybe for another day!

We'll come back to some of those incidents later. After Thunderball *you did* Funeral in Berlin, *adapted from Len Deighton's novel. It was the first movie you'd done on location in Berlin since* Ten Seconds to Hell *in 1958. It was also the first in contemporary Berlin with the rubble of East Germany on one side of the Wall, and the modernisation of West Germany on the other. What do you remember about making the film?*
It was a strange situation. I spent about a week in Berlin looking for suitable locations with Guy Hamilton, the director, but Harry and Cubby thought it was more important for me to do *You Only Live Twice*, and that was in Japan. I think we had two or three location scouts for the main Berlin locations. So I handed over all my designs for *Funeral in Berlin* to Peter Murton, my top collaborator. Peter did most of the film because I was flying all over Japan preparing *You Only Live Twice*.

Do you remember how much studio work there was in Funeral in Berlin, *and how much location?*
There was a lot of location. Not as much as *The Ipcress File*, because there were some studio sets.

For me, the most memorable moment in Funeral in Berlin *is the opening sequence where someone escapes over the Wall from East Germany to West in a mechanical 'grab'. You can't have used the real Berlin . . .*
No, no. They built a piece of wall somewhere else.

The other great moment is when Harry Palmer walks into a bar in Berlin. The barman says, 'Bitte?' And Harry says, 'No, mild please.'
I'll have to look at the film again!

You Only Live Twice

In 1966 you fly to Japan to prepare for You Only Live Twice. *The budget is really big now and presumably you are location hunting for a castle with a poison garden, which was in the original novel. Instead you end up with a volcano and a missile base inside it.*
Well, it was a desperate situation. We had an American scriptwriter who initially came with us to Japan and we rented two helicopters and

Final concept drawing of volcano interior

started covering the main island of Japan and eventually the south island. In three weeks we covered nearly two-thirds of the country. We flew about seven hours every day in these damn helicopters and landed wherever was possible, but we didn't find a thing. We decided that Ian Fleming had either never been to Japan or had not spent too much time there because the castles were nothing like our Western idea of castles; they were very different. So everyone was getting desperate: I was in the helicopter with the director, Lewis Gilbert; Cubby Broccoli was in a helicopter with director of photography, Freddie Young; and Harry Saltzman was trying to organise things on the ground, looking for salt mines. Why he came up with that idea I don't know, because we never found them. There were a number of amusing incidents: Lewis Gilbert

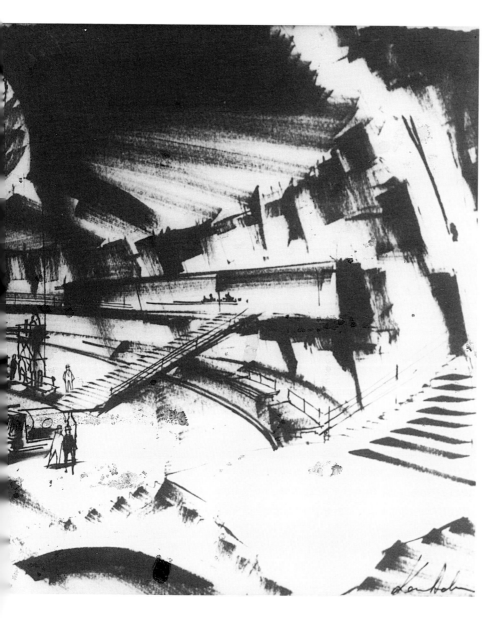

was absolutely paranoid about flying in the helicopter and on take-off he was so scared. And we had a Japanese pilot whose hands were always shaking. We later found out that he had been trained in the war as a kamikaze pilot!

Presumably he never saw action!
We had a sense of humour about it too. He was actually a very good pilot, but it didn't give us a great deal of confidence. The only good thing about it was that Cubby would radio ahead to wherever we were flying and order a massage for all of us, because after sitting in a bloody helicopter for hours we were pooped. That was our relaxation. But we still hadn't found anything, although we were fascinated by the Sumo wrestlers.

So they got written into the script?
Yes. And we heard about the 'Ninjas', a legendary commando unit, so we dedicated a sequence to them as well. And we'd all experienced a relaxing massage with beautiful Japanese ladies, so they became part of the story too.

It's an extraordinary way to construct a script.
You also have to remember, Christopher, that the producer – today it would give me a heart attack – had already signed a deal at United Artists with the distributors for the picture to open at four thousand cinemas in five months' time. And there was no script! Terrifying.

You added elements as you went along?
Absolutely. But we still hadn't found a really spectacular setting. I'll never forget Lewis and I flying in a helicopter over Kagoshima I think it was called – over the island of Kyushu. The heat was unbelievable; I've never known such humidity. And we flew over this incredible volcanic area in which there must have been six or seven extinct volcanoes next to each other. It looks like the surface of Mars or the Moon. So instinctively I thought it was interesting. After we landed and went back to the hotel we started talking, and I can't remember whether it was me or Cubby or Lewis, but somebody said, 'Wouldn't it be interesting if our villain has his headquarters underneath one of those craters?' That was the first major breakthrough. I thought it was an interesting idea but the crater was gigantic, even if we scaled it down. In the evening I did some thumbnail sketches which I showed to Cubby the next day, and he said, 'That's quite good. I wonder how much it's going to cost?' I said, 'I have no idea.' He said, 'If I give you a million dollars, will you do it?' And I said, 'I'll do it.'

That's much more than the entire budget of Dr No.
Yes, and that's where my worries started. I said I could do it – one of those bravado things – but I didn't know how. Anyway, the crater became the major find of the location hunt. Also, both producers decided that the writer we had up until that time wasn't right, so Roald Dahl was hired to start a new screenplay based on what we had seen in Japan. I had to fly back post-haste – in those days it was a long journey from Tokyo to London – to start designing and building this damn volcano. I broke the journey by stopping in Bangkok, where I phoned a friend who was a charming French diplomat and whose beautiful Thai wife was starring in Robert Wise's film, *The Sand Pebbles*. He collected me at the airport in his white Mercedes and took me to his palatial home, where we were served a dinner in grand style by numerous mem-

bers of his staff wearing white gloves. Since his wife was filming abroad, he had invited her best friend and a Japanese airhostess to keep us company. The rather formal dinner ended somewhat informally – in what can only be described as an orgy! He told me later that he and his wife kept a diary of their experiences. A few years later I discovered that his material was part of the extremely successful series of books and films *Emmanuelle*.

Then hastily back to London to start on the ambitious volcano designs. Yes. I wasn't irresponsible because a) I had a very good team with me, and b) we decided this was no longer a traditional film set because we couldn't find a big enough stage to put it in. We would have to build it on the lot and we'd need a firm of structural engineers to advise us what is, and what is not, feasible. So I went through the normal procedure. I did a more elaborate design with perspective and inclined surfaces and the art department made a model. Then we built a bigger model and gathered the producers, the director, the cameraman, the writer – everybody – around it to come up with ideas, like the monorail and the helicopter that goes into the crater. That nearly gave me a heart attack, because when we were shooting on location in Japan we saw that bloody helicopter disappear below the rim of the volcano and it didn't appear again for nearly five minutes. What had happened was that the pilot had encountered down currents and had a hell of a job to get out of them because the helicopter was so bloody light and underpowered. And then this damn helicopter had to fly into my set – which was basically an interior set – through a sixty-foot hole one hundred and twenty feet up. Nobody knew what kind of currents he was going to encounter once he got into an enclosed space. So I had a few kittens. I had to see a skin specialist because I developed eczema, and it was the first time I went on Valium.

I'm not surprised. Anyone would have kittens if they had to build – against the clock – a volcano forty metres high with a diameter of one hundred and thirty-five metres topped with a sliding artificial lake. Plus a mobile heliport and a thirty-three-metre space rocket. Somebody said about the set, 'Everyone believed the dimensions were in feet. But Ken thought in metres!' There were other reasons to have kittens. One of them was that in the climactic scene you needed about four hundred stuntmen to abseil into the crater on ropes, with lots of movement on different levels and this bloody great missile in the middle of it. So there was a lot to build on the back lot.
The main problem, which I mentioned earlier, was that all the experts said I'd never find a cameraman to light it. But I worked with Freddie

Young, one of the greatest cameramen in this country, already in his late sixties.

He'd done Lawrence of Arabia *in 1962, and* Dr Zhivago *shortly before* You Only Live Twice. *And he later said of your set, 'It was the size of two football fields; it would take practically every lamp in the studio to light it.'*

Yes. By this time I had quite a big model for him to look at. He said he could light it, and all the sceptics were silenced. But of course, there were other technical problems, even with help from engineering companies. This sixty-foot diameter artificial lake had to slide open, but I had designed it at a slant because I wanted them to see the full circle. So they had to calculate the stresses involved. They kept saying to me, 'We'd know how to deal with the Empire State Building. But this is a new experience for us too.' I'll never forget, Christopher, when we tried to open the lake for the first time before shooting. It was one of the most terrifying moments of my life, even considering my experiences in the Second World War. It was held by a winch down below with a steel cable. Suddenly, as we all stood around watching the lake open, there was a sound like a bomb exploding; an enormous cracking noise. I nearly fainted. We thought the whole thing was going to crash. By this time we had used seven hundred tonnes of structural steel, so you can imagine. We stopped. Nothing else happened besides the enormous exploding sound, but we had to investigate before we did anything else. Somebody had left a block and tackle on the rail, and the steel wheels of the lake had crushed it and made that horrendous noise. Fortunately it wasn't serious. But it could have been.

In the film there is a famous cut from real water to the glass water of your artificial lake. Was that shot in Japan or Pinewood?
Both.

So Bond and the girl look over the ridge of the volcano in Japan, and then the cut from real water to your artificial lake was shot in Pinewood?
Yes.

That's clever because it could have looked very hokey.
Yes, it's very well done. Also, I had to create a perspective mountain along the edge of the crater. Otherwise, when they tried to shoot from the set down below, there would have just been an opening and no background. It would have looked phoney. That all worked pretty well, and so did the heliport that I had travelling on rails. In fact, everything seemed to function all right because again it was a very expensive and

With Cubby Broccoli, during construction of the 007 stage at Pinewood for *The Spy Who Loved Me*.

important set. But the pressure of knowing that the film would be on release in five months' time was immense. I'm the designer, but they are the people who had to build it, working night and day. The plasterers had to work one hundred and twenty feet up on an incline to cover the structure with fibreglass. They had safety belts around them. At first the riggers and other workers said they wanted additional danger money, but then, as they saw the set grow, they became so enthusiastic about it that on a Sunday they brought their grandmothers and children and grandchildren to see it. Everybody got enthused by it. One freezing cold night Letizia and I were returning from some party here when I said to her, 'Those are my boys working up there. Let's get two bottles of port or brandy and drive out to Pinewood to keep them company at least.' Which we did. I remember having a problem – which I haven't got any longer, fortunately – with heights. I hated going on scaffolding.

You used to get vertigo?
I got vertigo, but it went as the set grew. So Letizia and myself, one hundred and twenty feet up, gave the plasterers some drink. They never forgot it. But working on that set was fraught with danger, even if you tried to protect everyone. I think we had one fatal accident; one of the riggers fell.

You really were performing without a net because there were no pre-existing models to work from. You had at least some reference points for the designs you'd done up to now, but this was new. It was the most expensive freestanding set in the recorded history of cinema.

Afterwards some people said we could have done it in model form. And yes, I suppose I could. But we could not have had four hundred stuntmen abseiling down a model. Today you would probably do everything digitally, but the fact that it was real added an enormous amount to the tension. Two hundred and fifty craftsmen worked twelve-hour shifts every day of the week from May until 28 October 1966. The next day a photograph of the volcano appeared in nearly every newspaper in the world.

Do you remember how many of the interiors were shot in Japan and England?

No. But there were very few. The Sumo wrestlers were shot in Japan, and the scene in which Bond meets his bride-to-be.

But you designed most of the Japanese interiors that were shot in England. The sliding doors, Tiger Tanaka's office . . .

Yes. I love Tanaka's office. Today you would call it a minimalist set. It somehow flowed right. I came up with these two copper bowls for television sets and an aluminium chute that Sean slides down into a chair.

It's really stripped down.

Yes. I came up with these ideas but I needed a director who would shoot it and an editor – Peter Hunt was brilliant at frame cutting – to make you see this incredible thing: Bond's going along that corridor, something opens, he falls into the chute and it goes on and on until he ends up in the chair in Tanaka's office. Those were all sets.

Characteristically, there isn't much colour in Tanaka's office.

Yes, I generally try to avoid painting walls in a variety of colours. As I've mentioned, every tin of colour paint should be printed with the words: 'Danger – Handle with Care'. Colour can be soothing, delightful, comforting and exciting. It can also be a monster. It can bring places to life, but it can also kill them. Tanaka's office was treated as reinforced concrete with leather furniture and television monitors in copper: a most colourful setting without really using colour at all.

The new gadget in You Only Live Twice *is Little Nellie, the mini gyrocopter, which has a couple of wonderful touches: it dismantles into pieces, and it's carried in a series of crocodile-leather suitcases.*

That was my idea. It came about because in the morning, when I was shaving, I listened to Jack de Manio on the radio . . .

On the BBC Today *programme.*

Yes. And he was interviewing this eccentric Wing Commander, Kenneth Wallace, who had invented this gyrocopter, as opposed to a helicopter – which in those days you could get for a thousand pounds if you wanted to. I was fascinated by it, so I rang up the BBC and they gave me the Wing Commander's telephone number. I asked him to come up to Pinewood and demonstrate this machine, and he did. It was incredible. The rotors didn't rotate mechanically – he had to get them spinning by hand to get airborne – but it had a propeller that moved it forward. That fascinated me. So I designed all the weaponry for it: rocket launchers, flame-throwers and so on. Then, because Letizia was designing Italian-made crocodile handbags, I thought, 'Wouldn't it be funny if the gyrocopter was a do-it-yourself set by Q and packed in four crocodile-leather suitcases with red-velour lining?' That, plus the incredible courage, or craziness, of Wing Commander Kenneth Wallace, who used to fly this thing up to eight or nine thousand feet above Japan. He was incredible. But again, we had an accident. In that famous helicopter battle – which, incidentally, was beautifully shot – you see the shadows of four helicopters attacking Little Nellie . . .

Much copied, as in Black Hawk Down.
Yes. We had a brilliant aerial cameraman, Johnny Jordan, and he was sitting in one of the helicopters with his legs on the skids. Suddenly one of the other rotors came too close and it chopped off his leg. That was terrible. We all felt terrible, particularly Cubby who donated a large amount of money to Johnny on top of the insurance claim. But a year later Johnny was flying again on a Mike Nichols picture.

Catch 22.
Catch 22. They'd taken the rear gun turret out of a Mitchell bomber, and when the pilot had to take some avoiding action by going over into a negative g, Johnny was sucked out the back of the plane. He had been careless; he should have been wearing a safety belt. His camera operator, who remained a friend of mine, didn't have a safety belt on either, but he managed to hold on to something. But he was in hospital for three months afterwards just for shock.

Chitty Chitty Bang Bang

After finishing You Only Live Twice, *which did open on time in those four thousand cinemas, you moved on to another Ian Fleming adaptation, but not a Bond. It was* Chitty Chitty Bang Bang. *Today everybody recognises it from the musical and the posters for it, but it all started of*

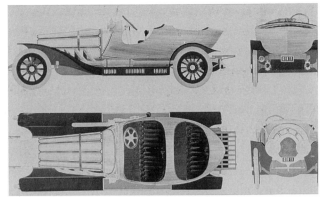

In Ken Adam's Pinewood office, designing the car for *Chitty Chitty Bang Bang*

Working drawing of the car

course with your design. Chitty Chitty Bang Bang *is a children's story set in Edwardian times, and it must have been quite a challenge because it's science fiction – a car that flies and drives through water – but in an Edwardian idiom.*

That's what made it much more difficult for me. It would have been second nature to me to design a modern car, but to come up and design a sexy-looking Edwardian vintage car, I found very difficult. It almost became my Waterloo. People who are still around remember me then because I built a full-sized mock-up at Pinewood. One of my carpenters called me when I was in Canada and said, 'You drove everybody crazy changing things.' I had so many problems on that film. Ken Hughes was the very talented if somewhat neurotic director, and Cubby Broccoli was the producer. There was some friction between Cubby and Harry Saltzman at this time because Harry wanted me to design *Battle of Britain*. But Cubby prevailed. There were these two choreographers from Hollywood, Dee Dee Wood and Marc Breaux, and the Sherman brothers who composed the songs for *Mary Poppins*. In fact, Cubby was trying to repeat the success of that film.

There was an element of that in the casting of Dick Van Dyke as Caractacus Potts.

I really let out all the stops on *Chitty Chitty Bang Bang*, if you think about it. But we nearly had more than one disaster. Boats I could cope with, but I had to design the airship for Baron Bomburst. I knew I was going to do it as a model and that the model was going to cost about £6,000. Then one day two famous balloonists – one of them became famous at the BBC – walked into my office and said, 'Ken, we can build this full size for you.' I thought they must be joking, but they said they could do it for about £8,000. I said, 'You can't build a hundred-and-twenty-foot airship for £8,000.' They told me they could put a VW engine in a gondola and the hull or envelope could be sewn together at the old airship hangars in Cardington. So I said, 'Let me talk to the

166

producers and United Artists and see what they think.' Both Cubby and United Artists agreed that if they could do it for £8,000 then it was worth the risk. The balloonists wanted to fill the airship with hydrogen but we insisted on helium, which was very expensive. Well, we had the worst September in England with constant gales. None of us had the experience to deal with a full-sized airship in any kind of weather, but it wasn't so much the full-sized airship as how to anchor it. And where we were shooting there was no hangar to put it in so the riggers had to build a huge structure to anchor it down. The first time the airship flew with the two balloonists in it was at Turville near Hambledon in the Thames Valley; a fabulous location. And we were set up with five cameras.

There's a windmill there.
Yes, an old windmill which I fitted with sails. It has an incredible view over the Chilterns. Anyway, we were set up with our five cameras when the airship suddenly dived at us and nearly didn't come out of it. Everyone scattered and I was furious because these so-called balloonists were not using the throttle properly. I thought, 'They've got an engine. Why don't they get out of it?' They later said they'd used the engine but something was unstable. So I contacted the last remaining Zeppelin experts in Germany and France – some were in their eighties – and asked them to come over and advise me. I offered to fly the airship myself but they said, 'Not on your life. We don't want you to.' Everybody was standing around and giving advice when a French expert came into my office and said, 'You based your design on a French airship called the *Labaudier?*' I said, 'That's correct.' He said, 'But the *Labaudier* never flew!' So one day the whole airship broke loose from the moorings because of these gales and crashed into some high power lines in Dorset, cutting off the electric supply to some irate farmers who were trying to milk their cows and so on. It was very dangerous in terms of being sued. But in the end we got the footage. Admittedly, I had to build a model as well, but the main footage was of the full-sized airship.

The car itself is interesting because it's partly a Rolls-Royce body with wonderful brass work and coach lamps, but the rounded radiator is like a Bugatti, and the strap around the bonnet like a vintage Mercedes.
Absolutely.

So it's a fascinating composite of classic cars from the early motoring days. It even has these strange angel wings on the side.
The Bugatti always fascinated me and I loved the ship body of the classic old Rolls-Royces, so I combined them. I found some wonderful people to build it. I did a mock-up at Pinewood but the actual car was built

by Alan Mann with a chassis and power units and other parts supplied by Ford. Alan Mann, who had a racing stable, had built the Ford GT that had won Le Mans the year before, so I couldn't believe it when I went to his workshop and saw all those racing cars with an engine here, a chassis there. I said, 'When are you racing that?' He said, 'Oh, tomorrow!' The speed with which they built these things was amazing. Then I had a shipbuilder construct the beautiful body.

In metal?
No, in wood. When the car arrived at Pinewood for the first time the whole studio stood still in admiration. It was really beautiful. You must remember that we had to build Chitty as a racing car as well as the other racing cars of the period. Then, to convert Chitty into a hovercraft was a big challenge. Fortunately, Bernard Voisin, my shipbuilder friend from Villefranche who had built the ships for *Hornblower* and *The Crimson Pirate*, came up with the idea of placing the body of the car and its skirt over a 'Christina', a British powerboat. This contraption made a convincing hovercraft.

So it has a full-size boat underneath it, hidden in its skirt?
Yes, it was all full size.

We are talking the day after the final flight of Concorde, and it reminds me of British technology in all those movies of the 1960s. I think there were two things going on: firstly, there was Q, the eccentric boffin character who produced all these gadgets out of the best of British designs; and secondly, there was a whole series of very nostalgic movies in the mid-1960s about how ingenious the Brits were in the past, like Magnificent Men in their Flying Machines *or the Jules Verne stories. America had taken over as the leading technological nation, and what we were left with was nostalgia for the good old days when the Brits built Rolls-Royces and other handcrafted things. In films of the mid-1960s there's often a boffin with long hair inventing these wonderfully ingenious examples of British engineering. In the case of* Chitty Chitty Bang Bang *it's Lionel Jeffries as Grandpa Potts tinkering in his potting shed. In other cases it's Peter Cushing, or Dr Who, or some other eccentric tweedy boffin. It is rather sad how Britain began to lose its technological influence globally and so looked to the past. You can't really believe that we're a force to be reckoned with in the space race or in technology any more; that's America.*
But remember, Christopher, that in the 1960s we had the most important recent renaissance in this country in terms of creative people: Britain was never a centre of feminine fashion, but Mary Quant invented

the miniskirt; the Beatles suddenly appeared; actors like Michael Caine emerged from working-class backgrounds. Suddenly all the barriers were thrown away and there was a revolution. In the most simplistic terms, British people decided that we were no longer an empire. Fuck the empire; that was something of the past. So we were also enormously inventive and innovative.

That's true. But we often took the mickey out of Victoriana as well. There's Sergeant Pepper *with its uniforms, and people were wearing old guardsman's uniforms in Carnaby Street. And* Chitty Chitty Bang Bang *fits that trend of giving the stuffy past a trendy new makeover. One of the very interesting designs in* Chitty Chitty Bang Bang *is the sweet factory where, rather like Lloyd's of London in* Around the World in Eighty Days, *it's entirely black and white and the only splash of colour is the sweets. It's quite an avant-garde technique in a mainstream film.*
I wasn't sure whether I'd gone too far. The choreographers Marc and Dee Dee particularly loved it because, again, everything was inclined. It was almost expressionistic. I thought it would be interesting to treat it as black and white and then let the sweets have the colour.

We talked earlier about white walls and handling colour 'with care'. In Ideal Home, *December 1968 – the month* Chitty *opened in London – you wrote an article entitled 'Adam on Colour': 'There is a world of difference in scale and purpose between film work and home decoration, but thoughts and rules about the use of colour and furnishings can be the same for both. One of my golden rules is to avoid the use of colour on walls as much as possible.' You then discuss in detail the set for the Edwardian sweet factory and the splashes of colour given to it by the trays of red, green, yellow and chocolate sweets. You finish with some household tips about white walls, the mixing of period and modern furniture. And you add to 'Danger – Handle with Care' three more words: 'Avoid if possible!' You are always sparing with colour, at home and on the set. It is very often for details rather than structures.*
That's probably because my background is not that of a painter. I think I have a very good sense of colour, but I try to use colour sparingly when making a point.

At the end of Chitty Chitty Bang Bang *the characters reach a Never Never Land where the Childcatcher is played by Robert Helpmann. In that scene the streets and costumes are all black and white as well. Quite frightening. Like steel engravings of the Brothers Grimm; there's that slightly chilling feel of the German children's story.*
Mind you, Neuschwanstein Castle in Germany was like a Disney castle. When you drive through that countryside you come across these

medieval villages that are very beautiful but quite frightening too, because they've got narrow streets and gabled roofs.

Like the cobbled streets of Holstenwall in Dr Caligari.
Yes, very *Caligari*. For that, I think Bobby Helpmann was brilliant in *Chitty*. And Benny Hill as the Toy Maker. Ken Hughes did the casting and it all worked.

To tread on slightly thin ice, the image of the car that you designed is on every poster of today's musical of Chitty Chitty Bang Bang. *It's even used by Ken Livingstone's London office to publicise the congestion charge. I have not seen the show, but apparently the design is very similar. Have you seen it?*
Yes, I went to the first night. I think they did an incredible job. How they used computers and electronics to virtually fly the car over the audience is a miracle; I think it is the star of the show. On a personal level I felt a little upset that nobody had asked for my permission. They owned the copyright of my design for the film.

Do you get royalty payments from the musical?
No.

So the whole thing was signed over to Cubby Broccoli and the people making the musical negotiated with his company?
They must have done.

It has been a huge hit and no doubt will be all over the world.
I got a nice mention in the programme!

Terrific! I'm so glad they mentioned you. The whole corporate image of the show is yours. It's your car; they haven't changed it.
I know. There's something wrong with the copyright laws. But I don't believe in taking legal action; I've been around too long for that kind of thing. Anyway, it's a compliment that they're using my stuff. I always thought the copyright was for the picture *Chitty Chitty Bang Bang*, but not for a musical thirty years later.

How could anybody have predicted it? At the time, all sorts of Chitty *toys were produced. And it is said about the James Bond merchandising bonanza that all you received was a cheque for sixty-four pounds!*
Yes, two cheques actually. One for sixty-four pounds and a second for forty-nine!

That is astonishing, because all the merchandising was a spin-off from your designs. Presumably Saltzman and Broccoli's contract sewed all that up.

The only time they gave me a percentage, Harry was furious when he found out that he had signed a contract giving me one. So he offered me between sixteen and twenty thousand pounds to buy me out, which was a lot of money in the 1960s. I asked my agent at the time, Laurie Evans, who was maybe the biggest agent of MCA, to sell. But he said no because his accountants had checked the previous merchandising receipts and my share was already three times that amount!

There's no justice in show business! You still never got the money. After that, in 1968, you briefly worked on pre-production for On Her Majesty's Secret Service, *but not on the movie itself. I believe you did some location hunting in Switzerland?*
That's right. I think we were Harry Saltzman's guests in Chamonix for Christmas. But at the same time he wanted me to scout locations for *On Her Majesty's Secret Service.* It was quite hair-raising because in addition to using Harry's station wagon on icy roads and sliding all over the place, I also flew in helicopters to see the mountain peaks. The way they fly is incredible. So I did a preliminary scout. But then the film was postponed and I did something else.

Peter Hunt was set to direct. I think his first promotion to director.
Yes. He'd directed the second unit on the hovercraft sequence of *Chitty Chitty Bang Bang.* I was with him in the South of France when he shot that and we sat around for days and days because of bad weather. Then he got his first big break.

Syd Cain, your ex-assistant, took over as production designer for On Her Majesty's Secret Service. *Again, were you worried that if you stepped off the Bond escalator they might not ask you back?*
No. I did some other pictures at the time: *Goodbye, Mr Chips* and *The Owl and the Pussycat.*

Are there any of your designs in On Her Majesty's Secret Service?
No.

Just your work on the locations then. It's quite ironic – in the light of future developments – that the story is about Bond pretending to have a knighthood and going to the College of Heralds in order to get into this château. He chooses as his motto, 'The world is not enough.' Now that you have a knighthood, it has come full circle!

Diamonds Are Forever

Then in 1971 you worked on the next Bond film, Diamonds Are Forever. *The big controversy surrounding this film was that everybody thought it was going to be made in America, and without Sean Connery. They even cast an actor called John Gavin, who later became – I think – the American Ambassador to Mexico for Ronald Reagan.*
John was very good-looking.

Yes, he'd appeared in Psycho *and* Spartacus. *But eventually a deal was struck with Sean Connery and the movie shifted back to England. That must have been quite nerve-racking.*
Yes, it was nerve-racking. It was also interesting in a way because it was my first experience of working in Hollywood, and because Harry Saltzman owned Technicolor at the time, which was part of Universal, we were VIP visitors at Universal Studios. It was still run like the old classic film studios: the art department had a pool of over a hundred assistants, like sketch artists, and the production designer wasn't allowed to do his own sketches; the illustrators did all that for him. They had the most professional staff who were under contract to Universal and had worked there for years and years, happy to be either an illustrator or draughtsman. The chief art director – the equivalent of Cedric Gibbons – was Alex Golitzen. I found myself in a tiny office without a window so I said to Alex, 'I'm sorry, but I can't work like this. I need a window.' He said they had twenty art directors working like this. But we had muscle, so Alex gave me the only office with a window. The block was called the Black Tower. In fact, it's still called that. I also got the best team from the art department to work for me. Boris Leven, who I was very friendly with, advised me who to use for the Bond movie. So it worked pretty well. Around this time Cubby, who was a friend of Howard Hughes, had the idea of doing a spoof in a way of the Howard Hughes persona. Then the disasters struck. The first was whilst Herbert Ross and Nora Kaye – great friends of ours and I'd done some pictures with them – were doing a film in Chicago, they lent Letizia and I their house in Beverly Hills and one morning at six o'clock we woke up and everything was rattling. Letizia said, '*Terremoto*,' which means 'Earthquake'. I'd never been in an earthquake before. Then suddenly everything started going wrong: books fell out of the shelves, the television fell over, the swimming pool overflowed like a saucer. And when we got outside, the palm trees were swaying dangerously. I got a phone call from my sister in London who'd heard on the BBC that an earthquake

in Los Angeles had been measured at 7.3 on the Richter scale. I was organising breakfast and trying to get the maid to clear up the mess when the doorbell rang, and there was Harry and Jackie Saltzman. They had been staying in the penthouse suite at the Beverly Wiltshire Hotel and she had grabbed her mink coat and jewels but not much else. Then Guy Hamilton arrived with his wife Kerima. They were staying in an apartment on La Cienaga on the twenty-sixth floor and the block was designed to sway eight or nine feet at that height; can you imagine?! I don't think Kerima ever fully recovered from the shock. And lastly there was an Italian screenwriter who arrived clutching a photograph of his mother! So we became like a refugee camp. That was the fun of it. And in my stupidity I thought, 'Well, an earthquake is an earthquake. It's over. There are no aftershocks.' So I drove to the studios – everybody said I was crazy – but there was nobody there. I got into my office and all my sketches had been blown all over the place. It was a very modern block; we used magnetic tape to attach our sketches to the steel walls, rather than drawing pins. But now the magnets didn't work. I couldn't get hold of anybody on the telephone. And some of the freeway had collapsed. So I decided to drive back. It was quite a traumatic experience, but I can see the funny side of it now. We carried on planning the film at Universal Studios and also in Las Vegas.

For the moon buggy?
Yes, the moon buggy. And a very important car chase for which Harry had discovered these French stunt drivers who were able to flip a car on its side and drive like that. I learnt a lot because Ford provided all the cars and they had to be properly ballasted to do this stuff. Basically we all had a very good time, but I remember Dave Chasman, who was pretty high up in the UA hierarchy, came to Universal one morning and said, 'You're crazy to do this film with John Gavin.' Dave knew we were paying Gavin nothing in comparison to the two million dollars that Sean Connery wanted, if I remember rightly, but he said we could recoup that money with EADY Money, which was a tax shelter in England.

In effect, a grant.
So, to cut a long story short, Sean got the film. We were going to shoot the scenes that we had already set up like the Las Vegas sequence, the oilrig in Santa Barbara, the car chase . . .

The moon buggy in a gypsum mine close to Las Vegas . . .
Yes. Shoot all that there and then film the interiors and other sets in Pinewood. This was decided late in the day. For me it was a gigantic logistical problem because I had nobody from the British Bond team

with me. So I rang Peter Lamont, who was fortunately available to fly out and liaise with the American art department, and then set up an art department in Pinewood for when I got back.

The moon buggy picked up on the real one we'd recently seen on television from the moon shot – as ever, reflecting things that were in the news and extending them.

That was not my idea. Guy Hamilton decided that it should look grotesque so I extended the mechanical arms. I copied the fibreglass conical wheels of the real moon buggy but they kept breaking at high speed on the rough terrain of the moonscape we based on NASA photographs, so eventually Sony gave me balloon tyres and we completed the sequence with them. It was nearly a disaster. But Las Vegas was a fascinating place.

There's a great shot in the film – that looks like a futuristic set but I think it's a real location – of Bond standing in an exterior glass elevator going up the side of a building. It seems almost science fiction.

It's partly on location. There was a hotel that no longer exists, The Sands maybe, and it was a bit like a tower with one of these exterior glass elevators. I wanted to show it to Cubby, so I went to the hotel with my 16mm camera and stepped into the elevator, but a security man told me I couldn't shoot there. I told Cubby and he made a call to Howard Hughes who was living in a penthouse. Hughes apparently said, 'Don't worry about it. Get your production designer back there and he'll get the VIP treatment.' So I went back there and everybody was bowing and scraping to me. At the time, half of Las Vegas belonged to Hughes and the other half to various syndicates. Cubby even got me permission to enter Hughes's ranch in Nevada, where the security guards looked at me and said, 'Are you Mr Hughes?' They had no idea what he looked like!

By this time I think Hughes had a long beard, long unwashed hair and very long fingernails.

It was amazing. Cubby was the only person who could get through to him. I was present when he spoke to Hughes on the phone, but I never met him. So Las Vegas was fascinating. The whole art department was staying with me at a hotel that belonged to one of those syndicates and it didn't cost us a cent. But the big problem was that nobody went to bed. At four in the morning I found my chief draughtsman – my assistant – in the casino. And there were so many beautiful women. There were ten women to each man.

The thing that's so strange about those hotels is that there are no clocks.

The owners want people to gamble twenty-four hours day and so you lose all sense of time. It's a twenty-four hour city: unnerving.

The climate was very good. It's a desert climate, and somehow we didn't feel tired. Cubby, who was a big gambler, decided he would play baccarat every evening. He said I was his lucky mascot and I had to sit next to him and play. For some reason he called me 'the U-boat commander'. I limited my gambling; if I lost five or six hundred dollars then that's it, I was out. But Cubby used to give me a thousand dollars to keep on playing. He made me play for the whole night. I was actually present one night when he must have won between two hundred and three hundred thousand dollars. Of course, the security was enormous. But a few days later Cubby lost more than that. These sums were just incomprehensible to somebody from England. Then I found out that the owners of the hotel had given instructions to the pit bosses that none of the film crew should lose more than a relatively small amount of money, because everybody was gambling.

Big Brother was watching you . . .

Big Brother, yes. I could tell you hair-raising stories about that. Another friend of Cubby, a famous lawyer, helped me get to Palm Springs because I was looking for a location for Bond's fight with the two women. I had breakfast at the bistro with this gentleman who rang up someone in Chicago and said, 'I've got this young production designer from England who's working on a Bond film and he wants to see some fantastic pads in Palms Springs.' So the next day a black limousine collected me from the airport. I didn't see Frank Sinatra's house but I did find a fantastic-looking house made of reinforced concrete. It was very futuristic and I thought, 'I couldn't have designed it better myself.' But the owner was a bit difficult. He said, 'Who gave you the authority to film and photograph here?' I said, 'Mr Broccoli. It's for a Bond film.' He wanted to know how much money was involved but I said, 'I don't know, I'm just a designer.' Within twenty minutes of getting back we had the permission. It's a famous building called the Arthur Elrod house. It looks incredible in the film.

Wheels within wheels.
And quite frightening.

A moment I remember very well is when one of the girls, who goes by the name of Plenty O'Toole, gets thrown out of the window. She shouts, 'I've got friends in this town,' and then falls about eighty storeys into a swimming pool. That's an extraordinary stunt. Nowadays, in films like Lethal Weapon, *they make a point of stunt people jumping out of windows to see how far they can fall. There's a famous continuity*

error in Diamonds Are Forever. *I hate to mention this, but the car on its side . . .*
Oh, it comes up the other way!

In one shot it's balancing on its right-hand wheels, and in the next shot it's on its left. Which is odd because presumably you weighted the car on one side, but for some reason it flips. Unless it was printed the wrong way round?
It may have been that. Or perhaps it was a cutting-room error. It was quite amazing what those French drivers did.

Was it the Remy Julienne team who did The Italian Job?
Maybe. They were the best, you know. We shot part of that sequence in downtown Las Vegas and another part in between the stages at Universal studios. Then we shot the oilrig off Santa Barbara.

And all the other interiors back at Pinewood. By the way, when you mention 'the syndicates', you really mean 'the Teamsters', don't you, Ken? You just don't want to say the word!
Yes!

How did you get the elevator shot, in the end?
We shot the main elevator sequence on location and then I built the elevator as a set at Pinewood. So we see Sean climbing up in there, firing that gadget, and then swinging across to the penthouse. It wasn't easy because I had Las Vegas in back projection. An amusing thing that Cubby always remembered was that Howard Hughes held many of his most important business conferences on his loo, so I designed the toilet that Sean comes across before he enters the penthouse.

An in-joke.
Yes. I think the Willard Whyte penthouse was a good set.

It's a classic Ken Adam design. But it was based on the idea of Howard Hughes, the idea of a recluse's apartment.
Yes, and I knew he had a penthouse. And since he was an inventor, adventurer and brilliant engineer, I built the model in the glass floor and incorporated every conceivable gadget and comfort. But much of it ended up on the cutting-room floor.

Fortunately the waterbed was spared.
Yes! In Sean's Vegas hotel suite.

I remember seeing that and I just couldn't believe my eyes. Waterbeds were just about heard of, but a huge waterbed with fishes in it?!
I think it was Cubby's idea.

How on earth did you engineer that? The fish are trapped inside this space with people lying on top of them.

We had the waterbed sent over from the United States but there was no way I could get tropical fish inside it, so I designed a series of circular perspex tanks around the bed. We had Sean Connery and Jill St John fornicating on the bed with the fish swimming in the foreground. The first problem was that the waterbed leaked onto my very expensive new carpet, so that leak had to be stopped. And then either the security man or the prop man at Pinewood switched off the heating unit for all these aquariums at night, and when we arrived the next morning most of the fish were dead. So we had to put the fish on ice because we couldn't get replacements; it was impossible. We then had, for the shot, frozen dead fish!

There were deceased fish floating in the tanks?
Not all of them.

But it seemed incredibly affluent, this waterbed with the fish, in a kitsch way. I wondered how the fish could breathe but presumably you had oxygen-producing pumps inside the aquariums. That was a classic over-the-top Bond concept.
I loved the waterbed idea but I never liked designing those kitschy Las Vegas sets. The Willard Whyte penthouse was loosely based on Howard Hughes, but it was less realistic, more operatic.

The colours – all the pinks – are very *non-Ken Adam!*

The Spy Who Loved Me

Then, between 1971 and 1976, both Live and Let Die *and* The Man With the Golden Gun *are made, the first two Bond films to star Roger Moore as 007. You weren't involved in either of these films, but you rejoined the Bond franchise in 1976 with* The Spy Who Loved Me. *The long break that you took after the strain of making* Barry Lyndon *obviously did you good because you came back fighting. Of your later Bond films,* The Spy Who Loved Me *is your masterpiece, and on a huge scale. Lewis Gilbert directed, as he had done on* You Only Live Twice, *and Christopher Wood and Richard Maibaum wrote the script, which was a significant departure from the novel. I think Ian Fleming had requested in his will that he didn't want the original book to be adapted for film.*
Oh, I didn't know that.

Design of Stromberg's living quarters
inside 'Atlantis' and (below) of the
'Atlantis' exterior

Because The Spy Who Loved Me *is a small-scale domestic love story set
in England and told from a woman's point of view. It's about how
Bond fell in love with her. So the scriptwriters had to discard the novel
and reinvent it from scratch. The main set is the famous supertanker,
part of the subterranean empire run by the villain, Stromberg. But this
supertanker, which holds three nuclear submarines inside its bowels,
was an incredibly grandiose concept. It's like* Thunderball *to the power
of ten. It's another one of your secret places, another 'something inside
something', but on a much greater scale. How did that set come about?*
Well, the supertanker came out of the screenplay, which was still being

written at the time. I knew I had to design the interior of that supertanker and that it would have to be huge to swallow up three nuclear
submarines, each of which are a few hundred feet long . . . and in any
case you couldn't have it in reality because the supertanker had compartments and so on. But I wasn't going to make the same mistakes I'd
made on *You Only Live Twice*. On that film we had a workable but
ultimately wasteful free-standing set. This time I was going to build a
structure that would stay put. So I designed the supertanker interior in
terms of what could remain for use after the film was finished. I
designed the set and the stage at the same time.

The famous James Bond soundstage at Pinewood.
The 007 stage. At the time, United Artists were worried about the cost
– $1.8 million in 1976 currency – but it paid off because a big stage is
always in use and the 007 stage has rarely been empty. I also said I was
going to make a feature of the structure of the supertanker, of the interior, as part of the set. So all the gantries . . .

The compartments and those big girders that hold it together . . .

That's right; they became part of the design. At the same time I felt it was about time to start experimenting with curved surfaces instead of my usual linear designs. That happened to some extent because I'd been looking for exteriors in Sardinia and I had found some incredible architecture by a French architect called Cuelle. He designed the most incredible private houses and other buildings – like the hotel Calla de Volpe, where we were staying – to fit rock formations in the landscape. So I experimented with curves and sculptural forms and that's how the underwater structure of 'Atlantis' was conceived. Cubby had also heard of an underwater structure that was built off the coast of Okinawa and supposedly rose out of the water.

The Floating City.
Yes, so we flew to Okinawa. But this Floating City didn't rise out of the water at all; it was permanently *on* the water. It looked like a giant oil-rig. So I came back to Pinewood and spent a week trying to make it work somehow because we'd spent so much time travelling there, but whatever I did didn't somehow work. So then I came up with this original structure . . .

It's extraordinary. It looks like a huge metal spider coming out of the water. And it incorporates a helicopter pad, shark pool, Stromberg's living quarters, and a control room.
But of course, the question was: how are we going to build the exterior? I knew we couldn't build it for real so we built a very large model. I called a brilliant visual-effects man over from Hollywood, Alan Maley. By that time he had been working at Disney, he was English and had worked for me on *Dr Strangelove*. He said, 'The model is no problem.' We shot the model in Sardinia and I built part of a full-sized leg in the actual sea off the Costa Smeralda, which covered just the shot of the speedboat arriving. Alan, who I called 'the Professor', invented the sequence where the helicopter takes off inside the dome. We shot it on an empty stage at Pinewood and Alan did the rest with a combination of painted mattes. I had a lot of fun with the interiors, like Stromberg's circular, two-level apartment. I didn't repeat the mistake of *Dr No*; this time we had the right footage of the fish from Okinawa. Again, I was experimenting. I used antique furniture and lamps for the lower part and the most modern lamps and settees available for the upstairs part. It was a difficult set for the plasterers to build at Pinewood because it was curve upon curve. To mould it all was very difficult. Then I decided for the first time to stick my neck out and design *against* the exterior, which was Stromberg's dining room. I treated it in a linear way as a very long sort of Renaissance . . .

Baronial hall, or ducal palace perhaps.
Yes, Italian: a palazzo. I designed this refectory table that was over sixty feet in length. It was beautifully done, but unfortunately after the film who can have a sixty-foot refectory table in their home? Because Ferdie was no longer with us, I had this wonderful girl Gill Noyes who I met at Covent Garden when I did the opera. She painted a number of tapestries based on Andrea Mantegna, Carpaccio, Piero della Francesca . . . And I had the *Birth of Venus* by Botticelli, behind which Stromberg watched a shark eat his secretary!

It's a classic Ken Adam design. There are bare walls and huge antique objects, but press a button and there's nastiness going on behind.
The idea of the tapestries was 'How am I going to show the audience that we're underwater?' So the idea was to have the tapestries rising up so you see you're underwater, and it works. I don't think people worried that it was a linear design rather than a curved design like the rest of the interior.

At one stage you were going to use a real supertanker.
Yes, Cubby had some friends who owned supertankers. Remember, it was more or less the period when gigantic oil tankers were first used. We thought it was completely impractical that anybody would give us a supertanker for nothing, until somebody came up and said, 'When the tanker's empty, you can have it.' But of course, then we found out that we couldn't use any of our effects; the explosions were too dangerous. Also, because the tanker was empty, it would have been too high out of the water to suit the visuals. So our special-effects man, Derek Meddings, built an eighty-foot model, which we shot in the Bahamas. You have to build a model that big in order to get the correct relationship between the height of the waves and the tanker, and it worked like a dream. It was one of the biggest models ever made.

How did you design the interior of the supertanker to accommodate three nuclear submarines?
My design for that was simple. Basically, it was like a floating dock in the bowels of the tanker. The real interior of a supertanker is split up into smaller compartments, which for films is uninteresting. I created three levels, which were serviced by two parallel exposed elevators. The top level was like a free suspension bridge in the shape of an X, and all levels were reached by exposed flights of stairs. As I say, for the first time I used the structural elements of the set for visual impact as part of the overall composition. The whole structure was treated as gunmetal with stainless-steel sheeting for the sides, and we had two magnetic induction craft travelling along both sides, to transport both the crew

and the nuclear weapons. Lewis Gilbert came up with the idea of extending the device to the bow of the tanker so as to propel Stromberg and his beautiful Russian prisoner to the safety of 'Atlantis'.

The Times Literary Supplement recently quoted Lord Foster – Norman Foster – to the effect that your set had inspired his London Underground station at Canary Wharf.
I read that too.

How did you know what nuclear submarines looked like?
I'd spent some time with the Navy in Scotland and they were unbelievably helpful. I don't think they had Polaris submarines but they had the 'nuclear hunter/killers', as they called them, and they were fascinating. We were allowed to go in the control room, and I found out – don't ask me how or why – that these submarines could travel below the water at something like forty knots. I don't know if this is correct, but it's an incredible speed. They would stay underwater for perhaps three months so they had this incredible lighting system – daytime is bright light, night-time is red light – to accustom the crew to daily routine because they never saw actual daylight. So the Navy were extremely helpful and that made it easier to design the submarines, which were relatively simple. I knew that full-size subs would be too big even for the 007 stage, but I thought I could get away with five-eighths full size, in relation to the size of a person. At over three hundred feet in length, they were still big. We built them out of marine ply and covered them with a skin of fibreglass. Then we built the stage over an existing tank and put rails on the bottom for the submarine to run along. That worked like a dream. But the irony of it all was that after principal photography, when we were through shooting on that stage, we still had to film a scene at sea in which Roger Moore and Barbara Bach drop into the conning tower of an actual submarine.

According to Charlie Russhon or whoever, we could borrow one from the American Navy, but they suddenly changed their minds. We couldn't have a nuclear submarine for a James Bond sequence. They would have liked to have helped, but couldn't. So we didn't get it. Then we tried the Royal Navy, but they said that if the Americans couldn't give one to us, neither could they. So I had to come up with another solution. What we did was take one of my plywood submarines off its rails, cut it into three sections, put it on low loaders, and towed it to a port near Chichester on the south coast. Then we assembled it, put it on big oil drums, and floated it out to sea. And you know, it looked fine. Sometimes one has to improvise in this way.

The other vehicle in The Spy Who Loved Me *was the Lotus Esprit,*

With Roger Moore and a jet ski, Sardinia 1977

which could be driven underwater. How on earth did you come up with that?

I had a Lotus at the time and I thought it was fantastic piece of engineering. The size of the engine and the speed were unbelievable. But it kept breaking down all the time; it was like a racing car. But the new Esprit had an incredible look, a streamlined body, and I thought it would be ideal to convert into a sub-aqua vehicle. I did my sketches and then I think it was Perry Submarine in the United States who actually built it for us. It was no problem at all. We shot a lot of stuff underwater with the full-size Lotus. We had to use oxygen tanks to breathe in the car, which was not pressurised, but otherwise it was travelling at about seven knots to a depth of fifteen metres. It was amazing! We also used a small model in the Bahamas with a model unit. It was funny to see my Pinewood riggers swimming underwater with bottles and tubes on their shoulders and communicating with hand signals in those days. It became second nature to everyone. We used underwater experts again to keep sharks at bay and to check that the oxygen bottles were filled up and we didn't have any accidents.

Did you go underwater?

Yes, of course. I went down to sixty feet, but after that I didn't like it because it gets very dark and I get very claustrophobic. As long as I can see light above me, I don't mind!

In The Spy Who Loved Me *everything seemed to come together: you were nominated for an Oscar – the one and only James Bond Oscar nomination; you're at your most flamboyant and confident; and the design of the film really holds together. Not just individual sets, but a production design progression. Even the locations are flamboyant; the pre-credits ski sequence was filmed in St Moritz and twenty miles north of the Polar Circle, and then to the pyramids and temples in Egypt.*
Yes, and it was Lewis Gilbert directing again.

You seem to have got on very well with him. The chemistry worked.
I think it was also – a psychiatrist might be able to explain it better – like an explosion after the breakdown I'd experienced just before. It was like releasing myself from all those inhibitions, and once I started letting myself go, I kept on letting myself go. And I think it helped the creative process. It was almost like I couldn't go wrong. The only problem I had was looking at this damn structure in Okinawa and trying to make it work as Atlantis. But as soon as I threw those sketches away and came up with an original design, I had no problems.

Watching The Spy Who Loved Me *today, one can have reservations about the story. But the design of it, among the late Bonds, was your finest hour.*
I think so.

On the Pyramid Control Room set

Moonraker

You worked on your final Bond film, Moonraker, *in 1978–9. The director was again Lewis Gilbert, but this time it was a French–British co-production. It was shot in France; why was that?*
The reasons are very simple. Three people – Lewis Gilbert, Cubby Broccoli and Roger Moore – had tax problems in Britain, where it was very high in those days. So they didn't want to shoot the picture in England. Cubby would have liked to have shot it in Hollywood, but Lewis was against it because he felt that Big Brother would be watching: MGM, UA, the studios; he didn't want that kind of supervision. But he had worked in France, and obviously I had made some pictures there too, so Lewis said, 'Why don't you see if we can do it in Paris?' And Cubby said, 'Provided you feel that we don't sacrifice any production value. If you recommend that we shoot it in Paris then we will go there.' So we took over the only three film studios in Paris, which were Billancourt, Boulogne and Epinay. But the French unions were very tough so

184

I was only allowed to take my first art director, a man called Charlie Bishop; Peter Lamont was kept in London to supervise the special effects unit, directed by Derek Meddings at Pinewood. Other than that, I had to use a completely new French team. My French art director was Max Douy, someone I knew before but who now became a great friend. He was also head of the union, and a communist, and he said to me, 'If you think you can get away with working us Saturdays or Sundays you've got another think coming.' Well, I proved them wrong because they did work overtime on some very interesting sets like the space station and the shuttle launch pad. They even brought their families along. The amazing thing I found, Christopher, is that you can work anywhere in the world in this film business and eventually you'll find someone who's brilliant. And I found some brilliant people in Paris. I found a little mechanic who built the rotating centrifuge that I designed. Derek Meddings was furious with me; he always stood behind me when I did the design and said, 'I could do that as a model,' but this time I said, 'I know, but wouldn't it be fantastic if we had it full size with Roger inside?' We had quite a battle. The little mechanic built it full size and it worked beautifully, but it couldn't reach the speed required. So Derek built a model after all!

Moonraker *must have been the most complex film you'd ever worked on.*

Yes, with those three studios in Paris, up to four separate units shooting all over the world at once, plus all the special effects! We shot combinations of real locations, full-scale mock-ups, partial mock-ups, and miniatures, and they all cut together quite well. But it was a logistical nightmare. Even with the three studios, there wasn't very much stage space for the interiors. So as soon as we'd finished with a set, it was taken down and a new one built in its place. This meant having to go on location a lot. In fact, on *Moonraker* we shot more location interiors than on any of the previous Bond films. From California to the Amazon jungle . . . to outer space!

Did you have your usual adventures while location hunting?
Well, I crossed the whole American continent in a Lear jet for some time. I flew from the jet propulsion laboratory in California to London, and then to Mexico and Guatemala to find – among other locations – a remote Indian village. Cubby and I discovered the village from the air. We hired a bush pilot, since it was the only way to get there. The so-called landing strip was, as it turned out, completely overgrown, and we almost nosed over on landing. But Cubby and I were OK and we set off in the direction of the Indian village. We thought it strange that not

Final concept drawing of the Pyramid
Control Room

a single Indian greeted us. We had the feeling that we were being constantly observed, so in the end we decided that caution was the lesser of two evils and turned back. Later, we discovered that our pilot had recently swindled the Indians in a barter deal and they had sworn revenge on him!

Hugo Drax's Californian domain must have been quite a challenge. It is a classic example of one of your villain's lairs: ultra-modern laboratory, baronial living quarters. Drax has a vast factory outside Los Angeles producing missiles, and next door to it is a Louis XIV château that he brought over from the Loire brick by brick! It doesn't look like a set. It wasn't. The Drax complex was partly the French palace of Vaux-le-Vicomte and partly the Pompidou Centre, including Holly Goodhead's office. We also shot locations in Venice, where we used various boats and the hovercraft gondola that I designed for the motorised chase

through Venice and along the canals. And I had to construct part of the Venetian Palazzo Carazzonico for Drax's secret laboratory.

I also designed a control room in the shape of a pyramid with an adjoining Great Hall in the Mayan style, both of which were to be concealed behind the Iguaçu Waterfalls on the Brazilian–Argentine border. So it was very, very complex. But the key to *Moonraker* was, of course, the space station.

It must have been quite a challenge to keep ahead with the space station: in the late 1960s 2001: A Space Odyssey *had turned some of those images into clichés, and* Star Wars *had recently been released.*
Star Wars, yes, because it won the Oscar instead of *The Spy Who Loved Me*!

And that brought with it a whole new set of clichés. It must have been

difficult to ring the changes. What were your thought processes on that?
Well, I spent a couple of days at NASA in California and they showed me some of their very futuristic conceptual designs, but the actual space stations – the designs that were effective – were a series of cylinders bolted together in space with solar panels to give them power, and they didn't look very interesting to me. Plus, I knew I had to introduce artificial gravity. So I came up with this idea of using more or less a system of tubes, a mobile-like rotating structure to simulate artificial gravity. Harry Lange, who had worked at NASA and been technical advisor on *2001*, helped me to achieve an authentic look.

Harry Lange worked as a youth doing technical drawings at Peenemunde under Wernher Von Braun's management! Your space station was indeed like a mobile: a completely irregular form.
Yes, and making it rotate gives you a different composition from whatever angle you look at it. So I gave it irregular arms and irregular things like that and it worked extremely effectively. Even NASA said, 'Why not?' They had designed the space shuttle so I thought we'd use that too.

So your space shuttle was actually quite close to the real thing?
Yes, that's right. I wanted to get away from the Kubrick concept of the giant rotating wheel – it always felt to me as though they were shooting inside a bicycle tyre – and this gave me much more freedom somehow. We built our space station at Epinay, and one of the disasters that happened there occurred on nearly the last day of shooting. We had to blow up the main set, as we always do, when Hugo Drax makes his famous Hitler-like speech as if he is at the Nuremberg Rally. Although it was a steel construction I had used a lot of plastic covering, so I told our practical-effects man that he shouldn't use any of the petrol jelly because it was potentially very dangerous. He said he wouldn't. Lewis Gilbert didn't want to be on the stage so he sat behind a monitor a hundred metres away. But I, like a stupid man, stood at the edge of the stage. When the explosion happened there was so much smoke from all the chemicals and then the whole thing started catching fire because the effects man must have used petrol jelly after all. We had six Parisian fire engines standing by but it still took them all night to put it out. Even the rafters of the stage were burning. Lewis was just pleased it was over.

You certainly left the Bond franchise with a bang! Did it look all right?
It looked all right! I remember an amusing incident, but it's rather nationalistic. When I worked in France on previous films like *Around the World in Eighty Days* or *The Last of Sheila*, they had superb plasterers. I was never worried about finding one. But when I returned in 1978 they had all gone, and I had a big set to plaster. So in desperation

I got permission to use my team of plasterers from Pinewood, who had worked with me on the most complicated designs. They were superb, and they trained young people. So one day they arrived by air – fifteen of them, I think – and they didn't even go to the hotel; they all changed into their white overalls either in the coach or at the airport and they arrived at Epinay studios ready to start work an hour after landing. All the French labourers were looking on, gaping; they couldn't believe it.

That's nice.
And they did a fantastic job, of course.

Why was it your last Bond film?
For a variety of reasons: I had a lot of difficulties because shooting the film in Paris proved expensive, and I suddenly got the blame for it. Cubby kept saying, 'Why do we need this? Why do we need that?' It was the first time that had happened to me and I was so upset because I knew I had kept – more or less – to my budget. I called a friend who was then president of United Artists in Hollywood, Dan Rissner, who was living in a house in Malibu. I said to him, 'I've got a problem.' He said, 'I've had a quadruple heart bypass operation, I've got a nurse sitting here, and you come to me with *your* problems? Fuck your problems!' So I didn't get a great deal of sympathy from him. But by then I also felt that, having gone into space, we'd gone as far as we could go. And the Bond team had changed; the old writers that I was used to had disappeared, like Dick Maibaum, and Lewis Gilbert wasn't going to direct another one.

He was quite a veteran by then.
Careful! Lewis is only a year older than I am! A lot of my team were no longer with me and the whole structure of making Bond movies had changed. I felt I wanted a rest from this.

Did they offer you future Bonds?
Not at that time. I went to Hollywood and spent nearly four or five years living in Los Angeles. Then I came back again.

So you just drifted apart.
Yes, we drifted apart.

There was a new regime.
Yes, a completely new regime. And however much I adore Barbara Broccoli – I knew Barbara shortly after she was born, and she also turned out to be very good – it became, as you say, a new regime. And I also felt, rightly or wrongly – probably wrongly – that the Bonds were a British expression of the 1960s and '70s which I could relate to. But I

189

find it very difficult to relate to Bond today, even though the films are successful.

*Also, maybe because you weren't working as part of the original team on the pre-production process, or maybe because they thought about the projects differently post-*Star Wars *and blockbusterism, the stories changed a lot. Critic Alexander Walker wrote about the 1960s and '70s James Bond films, 'Almost by accident, Saltzman, Broccoli, Adam and all the other contributors had discovered one of the era's great recipes for alternately stimulating and appeasing a captive audience.' There's no doubt that with your passion for fast cars, fast aircraft, the latest engineering, fancy hotels with excellent restaurants in exotic places – plus your passion for cinema itself – you personally had a huge influence on the evolution of the James Bond series. In the big sets – the sinister* Führerbunkers *belonging to Dr No or Auric Goldfinger or Emilio Largo or Ernst Blofeld or Stromberg or Hugo Drax – your sense of theatre and your expressionist imagination was able to run riot, partly because the producers trusted you to get on with them. I would argue that these command centres, run by Second World War villains, also relate to your experiences in the 1930s and 1940s . . . But instead of big sets, the post-*Moonraker *Bonds substitute explosions, chases, stunts and speed – an action climax every ten minutes – so that the visuals do not lodge in the memory. And the villains are constantly on the move.*

Also, the villains are not particularly villainous. It's funny: I've been working for a video game company, and what they found was that some of my designs looked rather menacing. But they've always been that way. It was you who said that even the tarantula room in *Dr No* was menacing. So it's a natural instinct of mine to design a villain's lair that, although super-luxurious or enormous, is always menacing. I feel that the Bond films lost those big settings. Maybe they had it on the latest picture, but certainly not on the others.

In the latest Bond film there was an ice palace. But this idea of the 'menacing setting' also comes from your formation as a designer, because in the 1920s there was this famous essay – which I have referred to before – written by the French architect and interior designer Robert Mallet-Stevens. He wrote that the classic film décors tell you much about the character before he's even entered. This became orthodoxy in the late silent era. That's what you were doing with these lairs, giving us information about the villain: the megalomania, the Napoleon complex. All with renaissance antiques, paintings, globes and maps. Everything magnified. We know so much about the villain before he even opens his mouth, which is something of a trademark of yours. There isn't much design like that in films these days . . .

But what I am finding more and more, strangely enough in television – shows like *CSI* and *Law and Order* – is that they have good designers using a minimalist style of design in realistic settings. Like white walls and maybe just a spot of colour. I think they get all their furnishings and scientific props from a scientific organisation. So the look of these shows on television is much better then it has been for a long time.

But in some ways post-CGI effects have had a reverse effect on audiences: they are less believable than they used to be. There's one more Bond set that we should talk about: Gogol's office in the The Spy Who Loved Me. *I mention it because it's another 1920s reference. It's like an* October *interior, but hugely magnified; Sergei Eisenstein through an enlarger. And not what you'd expect in today's Soviet Union . . .*

Well that's why I did it. I was very conscious of that. I knew that everyone in the audience would expect the head of the secret service in the Soviet Union to be working in a miserable office in a back room somewhere. So I said, 'No, I'm going to "go Eisenstein" and design an enormous crypt-like structure.'

It's like Kerensky in October *strutting up the stairs to all these grand interiors. It was wonderful for film buffs, but I don't know how many people appreciated it.*

That was very conscious, even in the pre-credit sequence where Barbara Bach was in bed with the Russian spy. It wasn't that well shot but it was like a palatial room in the Hermitage to play against the usual concept of Russia.

Like Catherine the Great rather than the secret service. Did the movie get shown in Russia?

I'm not sure. It might have been. They collaborated with us.

That's true in general. The Bond series started off in the Cold War era, but then gradually became Russians, Americans and Brits against gangsters rather than each other. So the Cold War aspect is out of date; it's international terrorism they're fighting now. But not fundamentalist terrorism – it's about money rather than a cause. The villains are always holding a piece of equipment for ransom or blackmailing someone or breaking the Bank of England or whatever. The punch line is money, not beliefs.

Yes, at that stage. But *Moonraker* was about world domination and replacing humans with a master-race created by Drax.

He was a French neo-Nazi.

Yes.

7 Hollywood

Herbert Ross

Some of your most interesting design work – outside the James Bond series – comes through working with two directors: Stanley Kubrick, who we've talked about, and Herbert J. Ross, with whom you made seven films from Goodbye, Mr Chips *in 1969 right through to* Boys on the Side *in 1994. They are smaller, much lower-key films than the Bonds, and Herbert Ross is not the kind of filmmaker they write books about, the way they do about Kubrick. So I must admit that I know much less about Ross. But I do know that he came through theatre and ballet to cinema, that his roots lay in theatre and choreography . . .*

Herb was not a major but a minor choreographer who started in ballet. He was never a great dancer but he was highly intelligent and fell in love with one of the principal ballerinas in New York – of the United States actually – Nora Kaye. She was a classical ballerina who danced in the 1950s. They had an incredible relationship and toured Europe, including Spoleto and so on. Herb then decided to direct films. He got his first break directing second unit on a Barbra Streisand picture, *Hello Dolly* or one of the others. It was the famous helicopter sequence which ended up on a tug in the Hudson river.

Funny Girl?

Funny Girl, yes, with a song going on all the time. It was very cleverly done. Herb also directed some second unit on *Dr Dolittle*, including choreography, and directed second unit on *Summer Holiday*, which was set in Greece. So he had a certain amount of experience. I met him in the 1960s at some party when he was up to direct *Goodbye, Mr Chips* as a musical with Peter O'Toole and Petula Clarke. Arthur Jacobs was the producer and they asked me to design it. Herbert Ross was an extremely difficult person to work with and you really had to establish yourself. He had to feel comfortable with you, and it took a little time before that happened. He could be vicious with people he didn't like, really very cruel, although he possibly didn't mean it. We had a good relationship on *Goodbye, Mr Chips*. We shot a lot of it at Sherborne, in Dorset, and it was my first experience of working out dance numbers, visually, for the boys at school. I had a brilliant assistant at the time, Ivor Beddoes, who was a ballet dancer himself and a great sketch artist. He used to sketch out every number; it was fantastic. We had a great time on the picture, filming in Positano and Pompeii and so on. I tricked Ossie Morris into shooting in Positano, which was completely insane and impractical. When the associate producer came to visit us he thought we'd all gone crazy because we had miles and miles of cabling from the top of Positano right to the bottom.

Not to mention getting there along those cliffside roads.
Yes. That was the first time Herb and I worked together and we established a very good relationship. I think the second picture was *The Owl and the Pussycat.*

But before that, in 1969, just after Goodbye, Mr Chips, *you worked together on* Peter Pan.
Ah, that's right.

A project that was slotted for Mia Farrow. People have enthused about the drawings they've seen of yours, particularly Captain Hook's pirate ship coming through the mist.
Herb was going to direct it and Mel Ferrer was producing it. I worked out of my office in Pinewood and here, at home. I designed the whole overall concept, but I also had two brilliant assistants: Ivor Beddoes, who sketched out flying sequences to Never Never Land, and a Polish illustrator, who worked on other conceptual paintings. But somehow the picture didn't materialise.

Would it have been a musical?
Yes, for Universal. I sent 90 per cent of that artwork to them and they got very excited about it. So when I finally went there in 1971 to do *Diamonds Are Forever* Alex Golitzen looked at me with a rather silly face and apologised. Then he said the artwork was so fantastic they'd used it anyway. I said, 'I didn't know you made *Peter Pan*?' They hadn't. They used it on some other film, which was unbelievable because a lot of the artwork was abstract.

I must try to track that one down. Your next production with Herb Ross was The Owl and the Pussycat *in 1970. Barbra Streisand played a prostitute in New York opposite George Segal. It was one of your few screen appearances too.*
It was. Herb didn't hit it off with the American production designer so I stepped in. I didn't even get production designer credit; I was 'design supervisor'. But I got on very well with Barbra Streisand. She reminded me of Stanley Kubrick: the female equivalent. I can justify that because they had similar Brooklyn-Jewish backgrounds and the same naïve curiosity. They both had the irritating habit of questioning everything. I'll give you an example: Barbra was a huge star at that time and she lived in New York because she felt more relaxed there than in Hollywood. So Letizia and an Italian friend of ours – a senior journalist; a

foreign correspondent – decided to make a pasta dinner for Barbra and invite some Italian friends round. I proposed it to Barbra but she was not sure. She said it was a good idea but she didn't speak any Italian. I said, 'Barbra, you don't have to speak Italian. Everybody there will speak English.' But she insisted on taking Italian lessons and so every morning she came onto the set with some new Italian expressions. That was Barbra. On the day of the actual dinner she got cold feet. I could sense it. Letizia said, 'Why don't you collect her from her apartment?' So I drove over to Barbra's place on the West Side where she offered me a drink and showed me her Victorian button collection; any excuse not to go. I said, 'I think we'd better go.' She said, 'I'll quickly cook you something here.' When I eventually got her out of the apartment she said, 'You'll never get a taxi at this hour.' I told her I didn't need one; I had a car. So we drove across the park to the East Side, arrived at the apartment, and just as we were going up in the elevator she said, 'I can't go through with it. I feel sick.' I got very tough with her then, and I made her go in. Of course, Barbra ate more pasta at that party than anybody else! But she's that sort of person. She was very shy and she took everything too seriously. I was talked into appearing in the film because an actor didn't turn up. He was supposed to play a middle-aged letch who picks up the hooker, Doris Wadsworth – played by Barbra – and makes love to her whilst George Segal watches them through the open window of his apartment if you follow me. So the producer, Ray Stark, said to me, 'You've *got* to do this part.' I thought they were playing another joke on me, but Ray was very serious. And desperate. I really couldn't get out of it. So I rang Letizia to warn her. I said to her, 'I have to go to bed with Barbra.' And she said, 'What underwear are you wearing?' It's absolutely true! We had to send somebody out to get the right underwear and more attractive socks. Then of course, I didn't have to undress completely, but Barbra did, and she was very nervous about it. Herb Ross said he only needed me for a couple of shots. I didn't mind doing the scene in the bedroom from George Segal's point of view, but picking Barbra up in a limousine meant the camera would be getting a close-up of me, and I said I wasn't prepared to do it. But in the end, we had a ball.

We shot for two nights – of course, it took much longer than expected – and it was so cold outside that the rain, provided by New York fire engines, started freezing, and Barbra was wearing one of those very cheap fur coats. I was smoking my cigar and Barbra used it in one of her comedy routines. When the film was finally screened, my stripping in that scene was limited to taking off my jacket! After the London première I received a letter from Ray Stark, written from the Dorchester

The one and only guest appearance: with Barbra Streisand in *The Owl and the Pussycat*, 1970

Hotel: 'September 28th 1970. Dear Ken, you came out brilliantly as an actor – but the sets are terrible. I think this may change your career, so that from now on whenever they need a dirty old man you will be cast, although it will mean you lose the job as dirty old Art Director. Best, Ray Stark.'

By all accounts, Barbra Streisand wasn't easy to work with.
But Herb Ross, and Nora Kaye in particular, adored her. Herb and Nora were more of a professional team than even Letizia and I. Letizia was in the background but Nora was very much in the foreground. Being such a famous ballerina, at the same time knowing about the stage and having a very healthy and humorous outlook on life, and she was quite tough too. Barbra, who had already been directed by Herb on *Funny Girl*, adored them both.

I think The Owl and the Pussycat *was one of his first non-musicals. At the time, I remember being quite surprised that he'd directed it.*
But it was a very funny script by Buck Henry. He played a small part in it too.

The next of your collaborations with Herbert Ross was in 1972 on The Last of Sheila. *It was made partly in La Victorine studios in Nice and partly on the Riviera, with Richard Benjamin and Dyan Cannon.*
We had six or seven stars and Warner Brothers decided they didn't really want a production designer of my calibre because the whole picture was going to be shot on a big yacht they'd chartered. So I said, 'That's

OK.' But then Herb Ross phoned me and said, 'I know you would like a holiday on your boat' – my brother's forty-foot cabin cruiser which could go very fast, about thirty-seven knots – 'If Warner Brothers pay all your fuel and running expenses, would you like to come down and just be technical advisor on what we intend to do, which doesn't seem to make a great deal of sense?' It was wonderful, going out there and staying on my boat. Except they were absolutely crazy. They had six stars: Raquel Welch, James Mason, Richard Benjamin, Dyan Cannon, James Coburn and Joan Hackett. I don't care how big the yacht is, shooting with six stars who have no experience of the sea at all is fatal. So they were arguing with me, asking why. I said a) people get seasick, and b) you can't hold a yacht still in one position. Then disaster struck. The yacht they were going to shoot had run aground on a Greek rock because the skipper was drunk or something. So, because I was pretty friendly with Sam Spiegel and I knew he had a big yacht but not quite as big as the other one, I said to Nora and Herb, 'I know Sam is in San Tropez. If we drive down there he might let us have the boat.' So the four of us drove down to San Tropez and I asked Sam if we could borrow his yacht for a week or something like that. He said he'd think about it. Then he decided to let us use it – I didn't realise at the time that it was owned by Columbia. It saved the picture to some extent. The first day out at sea was off St Honoré, Cannes. We had all the cast on the top deck and Herb said, 'Tell the captain to drop anchor.' I was sure he couldn't drop anchor there because it was too deep, and I told him so. He said, 'Can't you drop more chain to drop the anchor wherever you like?' I said, 'Of course not.' And so did the captain. So when we started shooting this dialogue scene the boat started turning. One moment St Honoré was in the background, and the next it wasn't. It was a disaster. Herb got very depressed. A few days later he rang me up from Cannes, where he and Nora were staying, and said, 'Can you come up here now?' It was about eleven o'clock at night. Suddenly Nora was on the phone saying, 'You'd better come straightaway because if you don't, I think Warners will cancel the picture, considering the mood that Herb is in.' So I drove over to Cannes and Herb rang up Warner Brothers. Nora kept telling to me to interrupt the call because of the way Herb was talking. She was sure they'd cancel the picture. I don't know whose idea it was, Warners or mine, but I talked to somebody on the phone about building part of the yacht as a set at the studios. I predicted it would take me about three or four weeks. So then they asked Herb if he could shoot around the boat because there was a lot of searching and detective work to film on land. It was a game-playing type of script, a whodunit, written by Tony Perkins and

196

Stephen Sondheim. We never really found out what happened . . . I think Herb Ross and possibly James Mason were the only two people who knew what on earth the story was about. So Herb agreed to shoot on location and I agreed to build the set, and four weeks later we started shooting in the studio.

Truffaut and Fellini

Whilst shooting The Last of Sheila *you met François Truffaut . . .*
That's right, Truffaut was filming *Day for Night*, and he came into my office one evening when I was working late. We were a mutual admiration society: I admired him for his films and he admired me for my designs. He said to me, 'I think my future films are all going to be in the studio, obviously with a good production designer.' At the time he had in mind Alexandre Trauner, a great designer. Truffaut said there was a magical quality about a studio in which you can create your own reality. It gave him more freedom to express himself. He really meant it, you know. The other person I talked to who also had that theory was Federico Fellini. When a director has a very strong concept – Truffaut and Fellini certainly had – and they have a good team and designer, they can create something magical in the studio that you wouldn't be able to in reality, even if the result is *Rex*, the phoney-looking Italian liner in Fellini's *Amarcord*.

Amarcord *is magical, though. Didn't you nearly work with Federico Fellini at one stage?*
Yes, a little while later. Letizia and I invited him to Malibu because he was going through a period of depression. By this time the popularity of Letizia's cooking had spread and every weekend we had these big spaghetti parties on the beach in Malibu. I thought, rather naïvely, that if we could get him away from his surroundings in Rome and Cinecittà, then he would not feel under this pressure. He sent me a lovely but rather depressing letter turning me down. He feared that in Hollywood he would be under too much pressure from the studios to immediately come up with a concept. On 3 August 1980, Fellini wrote: 'I am playing around with ideas for a new film, but I am feeling a little discouraged and disheartened. To make a film here in Italy is becoming more and more an unattainable dream. The dream of a poor madman who doesn't realise that things have changed; that everything is different and that the cinema was a pleasant, extravagant sweet folly of a bygone time, which will never return. You say I am too pessimistic? Hopefully you are right. But honestly, just the thought of setting up the framework for one

of my films, seems to me, nowadays, like planning the invasion of Normandy, or even the conquest of the moon; I mean exploits already achieved and which are no longer any use to anyone.' A rather depressing letter, Christopher. Earlier, at dinner with Letizia and I in Rome, he'd said, 'Try and find me a good story by Poe or Fitzgerald or one of the great American writers and I might film it.' There was considerable interest among my friends in Hollywood, but . . .

I'm not sure it would have worked. The trouble with Fellini is that he had such a strong vision of what he wanted that I doubt there would have been enough latitude for you . . .
You're absolutely right.

He was in love with the sound stages at Cinecittà. And in a way he was his own production designer, drawing his own sketches. In fact, I'm not quite sure what his production designers actually did.
When I first met Federico Fellini, Dante Ferretti was working for him, but he didn't get much latitude. So I was very flattered by the possibility of working with him, but I felt – exactly what you were saying – that I would be extremely limited. It would be fun, but . . .

Staying with Italy, there was another unrealised project just after Peter Pan *called* Lord L, *a joint project with the prolific screenwriter Ennio De Concini, who was a friend of yours. His name is on just about every other Italian film of the 1960s.*
Yes, he won the Oscar for *Divorce Italian Style*. Ennio is a unique being and I think one only finds them in Italy. He may not be the greatest writer but he is the greatest storyteller; he comes up with unbelievable ideas. We were great friends so we decided to form a company – I can't

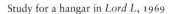
Study for a hangar in *Lord L*, 1969

remember what it was called. It was a partnership in which I would design and produce, and Ennio would write and direct. The problem with Ennio was that he spoke very little English. Although the major Hollywood studios expressed a lot of interest in our four, five, six incredible projects, including the very controversial *Lord L*, it became more and more difficult to set anything up because they didn't want Ennio directing. They wanted an English director or an American director. And that was basically the problem. It's a shame because he had fabulous ideas.

Some very strange ideas. The idea of Lord L *is that God comes back to Earth in the countercultural 1960s and is unimpressed with the way the world is going. Even Karl Marx and Sigmund Freud make guest appearances. It all sounds very odd. Do you think it could have worked?*

Oh yes, it was very controversial; very much anti-superstition and anti-organised religion. Sean Connery was willing to play a good man – not one of the hippies – who cycles around holding a transistor set to his ear, listening for a message. I think the script ends with Lord L floating up to space as a balloon that eventually bursts. It was very controversial, but Columbia in England were willing to do it on a very limited budget, on the condition that Ennio De Concini didn't direct it. I said I couldn't do that to Ennio.

Sleuth

Then in 1972, Sleuth, *directed by Joe Mankiewicz, a famous writer and director who had won four Oscars. His brother, Herman Mankiewicz, wrote most of* Citizen Kane. Sleuth *was to be Joe's last film.*

He had also worked as a journalist in Berlin, and his father had been a friend of Einstein. Joe was the *éminence grise* of the Hollywood intellectual scene.

He was Hollywood aristocracy, again with roots in the theatre.
Yes, intellectual aristocracy, and a brilliant raconteur.

I remember seeing Sleuth *on the stage in the late 1960s. It's a very clever play, a two-hander pretending to have a larger cast.*
By Anthony Shaffer.

It was set in the living room of a crime writer, Andrew Wyke. A hairdresser from a lower social class, Milo Tindle, has an affair with his wife, and the two men battle it out. It's snobbery with violence.

INT. CLOAK MANOR - GT. HALL   SLEUTH

Design of the Great Hall interior at
'Cloak Manor', 1972

Who played the hairdresser on the stage?

I saw it with Marius Goring as the crime writer and Anthony Valentine as the hairdresser, a young British actor who subsequently went on to do television. The part was also played by Keith Baxter. The stage actors looked more Italianate than Michael Caine. Sleuth *ran for eight years in the West End, so whether Marius Goring created the part I'm not sure, but it was a memorable experience, especially for crime-novel buffs.*

I saw it too.

It was a very theatrical idea, so it must have been a real challenge to turn it into a movie, to match the wit and cleverness of the text in the set and furnishings. How did the project develop as a movie?

Well, Joe Mankiewicz contacted me and we somehow hit it off. Letizia and I were invited to Bedford, New York – or maybe it was Connecticut; I'm not sure – to spend about ten days in Joe's country house, which was quite an experience. He had a little office set apart in the woods with his four Oscars on a mantelpiece, and every day at nine o'clock he would go there to smoke his pipe and read and write. But he was already rather bitter at that stage. In any case, apart from my experience with Stanley, it was a luxury to spend ten days in close proximity with a director, talking about concepts and the way he saw it through every detail. Right at the beginning he made a rather cynical statement. He said, 'Listen, Ken. For my films I try to surround myself with the best creative talents around. Then we sit down together and discuss how I see and feel about the film. Once that is clear I will leave the visual interpretation entirely to you. I'll give you a completely free hand. I intend to benefit from every idea and every bit of talent you have to offer. If the film is a success, as a director I will take all the credit. If you fuck up, I can always blame you!'

That put you in your place.
Yes. His idea was that we have these two players, the two actors, Laurence Olivier and Michael Caine, and that the audience would be the third player in the game. And in the film, the set and props and automated dolls would be the third actor. After talking to him and understanding his concept and the way he wanted to shoot it, I knew, and he knew, that it had to be a set. When I came back to London a man called Robin Feddon, who ran the National Trust, was kind enough to get me into every stately home from Devon and Cornwall to Dorset and the Midlands. But I found that medieval architecture was fine but it wouldn't fit the story, until I came to a place called Athelhampton . . .

Near Dorchester.
It was owned by an MP called Robert Cooke, and it had a big oriel window and grounds with topiary. I thought I could build the maze there. And the exterior would allow me to design whatever I wanted for the interior. It would be believable. So I showed Joe Mankiewicz photos of this location and then started designing the interior set. And if ever there was need for a film set, this was it, because Joe wanted to shoot it all in continuity. He wanted the opportunity to go from one room to the other without cutting. So I designed the main part of the set on the big stage at Pinewood, and built all the flats out of very light fibreglass on castors so we could move them. We built the cellar and one of the upstairs rooms separately, but the main set – study, billiard room, main hall – was all built in composite. I also built the main entrance and the oriel window in the studio to match the exterior of the house on location. The interesting thing was, when Joe came to England he said, 'You have to allow me forty-eight hours to live on your set, to spend as much time as I need. And I don't want you or Ossie Morris or anyone else around. You can give me a prop man in case I want to change some of your dressings, but otherwise I want to be left alone. Only then am I ready to shoot.' And that's exactly what he did. He spent forty-eight

hours on that set and, with the prop man, made one or two changes. I knew he wanted the set to reflect the 1930s with photos of Ivor Novello, Flo Desmond and Noël Coward. For the automated dolls I found a woman in Harrogate who had an incredible collection.

They're sitting everywhere; they almost become extra characters.
We built the sailor.

He's part of the plot.
Yes, but all the other automated dolls were rented. Also they had to be in perfect working order because Joe used them in tracking shots. We filmed for I don't know how many weeks. It was a big problem for Ossie Morris. To avoid losing any time he had to pre-light almost everything because of the continuous movement. It was fascinating.

It's an interesting design: a mixture of Gothic, with that grand staircase, and 1930s. It's a Gothic house but the crime writer still seems to be living in a cocoon of 1930s games and toys and automata. He hasn't adjusted to the modern world. The swinging sixties haven't reached him. And I think it works very well.
I thought it worked pretty well. What was the stage set like?

Very cluttered. There were stairs because they created a platform. At one point the crime writer, Andrew Wyke, stands on it and speaks. I remember the famous scene in which the hairdresser, Milo Tindle, appears to get shot and falls down the stairs. It turns out to be a blank cartridge, so Milo has just passed out from the shock. I remember that on stage. But it didn't have the coherence and it certainly didn't have the spookiness of your film, with these very creepy automata sitting in the background and these strange mechanical games. Laurence Olivier was an actor who famously loved props – false noses and so on. But he also liked fiddling with objects when he was acting, so presumably he familiarised himself with the set as well?
Yes, he loved it, and so did Michael Caine. I'd never worked with Laurence Olivier before. This was the first of two pictures I made with him; the second was *The Seven-Per-Cent Solution* in 1976. But I was fascinated by the way Larry would ask me if I minded changing an item of dressing on the fireplace or somewhere like that. Even with a director like Joe, once they rehearsed the scene and Larry had placed himself, he wouldn't move; that position was the right position. Once, he decided to play an entire scene from a position by the fireplace I'd designed. And when Larry decides to play the part, nobody is going to budge him. He shoved himself right in front of the mantelpiece with three bronzes the set dresser had put there. Well, as I watched Larry rehearse, my attention

was distracted by those three cheap props on the mantelpiece. So I sneaked up behind him and removed them. After we'd shot the scene he said to me, 'I'm so glad you did that. I knew they wouldn't fit in.' He'd noticed, you see. So we established a very good relationship. He didn't go to the Pinewood commissary for lunch because he ate in his dressing room, but once or twice he asked me to join him. He wanted to find out more about Michael Caine, who was a friend of mine. He knew that Michael was pulling out all the stops as an actor. It was really a duel.

A clash between two styles of acting: the theatrical and the filmic. In fact, Michael Caine fared slightly better. Laurence Olivier plays too big, whereas Michael knows when to hold back. It's fascinating to watch. The other design feature is the maze outside. At the time, there was a television documentary about the making of Sleuth, *and in it Joe Mankiewicz talked about his innovative crane with a camera suspended from it so he could shoot the maze from above. In those days digital technology wasn't available.*

It wasn't so much that, Christopher. You have to remember that these hedges, which we spent days building out of chicken wire – Peter Lamont found the green stuff – were about seven feet high. The only way to see what was happening in the maze was to shoot it from above. So we had to come up with some device. I don't know whether it was already the wescam, but we suspended the camera from a huge construction crane and controlled it from the ground. Of course, it later became common technology.

It's a clever effect. The maze was not in the play; it was an attempt to open the film out into the garden. Were the owners at Athelhampton tempted to leave the maze in the garden after filming was completed?
No.

Was it a commercially successful movie?
Yes. It was amazing. Even though you would never find an actual country house like that, the Academy and location scouts in this country wrote me letters asking where we had shot the interior. So they believed it.

Even though it was over the top, heightened perhaps for international audiences?
Yes, it was very extreme, but they believed it. Everybody thought it was shot in reality. I received a nomination from the British Film Academy, but not from the American Motion Picture Academy because they thought it was real.

Salon Kitty

We've talked about Federico Fellini and Ennio De Concini, but a third Italian filmmaker that you were associated with was Tinto Brass. I suspect that in 1975 Salon Kitty *was a surprisingly important film to you because it was your symbolic exit from* Barry Lyndon. *It came to your rescue just as you were finishing Stanley Kubrick's film.* Salon Kitty *wasn't seen much in this country. I suspect it was an underrated movie because of its sordid theme and the gusto, frankly, with which it was handled. There was a whole series of films around the mid-1970s that, using the Nazi period as a springboard, made statements about sexual politics and fetishism: Pasolini's* Salo, *Visconti's* Götterdämmerung/The Damned, The Night Porter, *numerous Cinecittà derivatives – and* Salon Kitty. *It was far enough away from the war to run with that idea without offending too many people. It started with arthouse films, then progressed to the popular mainstream. But* Salon Kitty *is in some ways the most extreme of the lot. It's about a brothel with specially trained German girls who are either going to test the loyalty of high ranking people in the Nazi regime, or be spies. The brothel in Berlin is run by the Gestapo.*
It's a true story.

But your design is astonishing: a sort of Nazi deco.
Well I used two styles. I did the first brothel in art nouveau, and then in order to accentuate the difference between them, the Nazi listening-device brothel was designed to be in art deco. It created a lot of problems for me.

Gustav Klimt for the first brothel, Grosz and Dix for the second. Was it shot at Cinecittà?
No, the 'Dear' studios in Rome. We had a very limited budget and Tinto Brass was wonderful. He'd got me on the rebound from *Barry Lyndon* and he realised I had gone through absolute purgatory, so he was very sensitive about it. My sketches were a bit small – I was afraid to do big ones – but Tinto loved them. In fact, he kept all the originals. I only have a few bad photocopies. He came up with all these brilliant ideas for shooting. He's an extraordinarily talented director, but he's got this sexual obsession which is really unfortunate in some ways.

He's become associated with soft porn. But he's actually a cultivated man. I've met him.
Very cultured.

But he pretends not to be. One of the most memorable sets in Salon Kitty *is the vast Nazi office, which is so large that the officer roller-skates the length and breadth of it. It has huge high ceilings, giant windows and swastikas everywhere. It's overpowering.*

Well I wanted to do it that way. And when you say roller-skating, in Italy it was cheaper to use real marble when we were doing a shiny floor than to do a mock-up, but of course nobody believed it at the time. I'd done it on *Helen of Troy* so I did it again for *Salon Kitty*. Tinto was fascinated by the actual marble floor so the officer skates along it in the scene. It was a brilliant idea.

There's an officer who sits at his desk and shouts all the time; he is a little man in a big job, and the office epitomises the vast megalomaniac environment with these rather small men working in it.

Helmut Berger played the lead.

Yes. He also appeared in Luchino Visconti's The Damned *in a very extreme uniform. He changes his uniform in a very stylish way in almost every shot.*

He's no longer around. We had a Swiss costume designer called Jost Jakob who was way out and who Tinto thought was the right man to design the costumes. His designs were kinky, and he came up with some incredible things.

You didn't feel at all squeamish with the theme, having had personal experience of the Nazis?

No.

Parts of the film were censored because they were so extreme: the naked tarts playing strange drunken games in the nightclub. It was accused of being exploitative by some who found it too strong.

Particularly at that time. But I don't think it would be today.

It certainly looks as if everyone had a wonderful time!

Yes, we did have a wonderful time. But I thought Tinto sometimes was going a little over the top again. He offered me *Caligula*, but after reading the script I said no. *Salon Kitty* was my introduction to soft porn, and it was enough.

Tinto Brass is very extreme. He made an Italian western called Yankee, *which is one of the most sadistic films I've ever seen. It was censored out of existence. He seems to lose his safety catch. He's got all these good ideas but each scene goes a lot further than it should. In terms of taste, Tinto crossed the line with* Yankee, *and to a certain extent with* Salon Kitty *too; had it been a little less steamy, it could have been a classic movie.*

But he is a little bit like that himself; he is a bon viveur. He comes from a cultured Venetian family and he's married to Carla Cipriani of the famous Cipriani family. They both love food. I introduced Tinto to cigars and now he smokes ten cigars a day, you know. He always has to do more. He's bigger than life in a way. But he is a wonderful friend and a great person to work with, if it wouldn't be that he goes over the top.

Of all your major movies, I think Salon Kitty *is the most neglected because it was never shown as much as it should have been.*
It was quite successful in Hollywood.

Was it? It was called Madam Kitty *in the States.*
Yes. When you brought it up with me before, Christopher, I'd forgotten about it. I've got the video and I showed it to a lot of my titled lady friends and they adored it! I hadn't seen it for years. I thought it's interesting design-wise, and the way it starts. The style is very *Cabaret.*

Yes, that's another film of that period. I think the most extreme moment in Salon Kitty *is when the member of the Nazi high command projects Leni Riefenstahl's* Triumph of the Will *onto a prostitute's naked body. It's the only way he can get sexually excited.*
Right! I remember her standing there.

That's gross. I recently noticed, whilst reading the credits, that Ennio De Concini contributed to the screenplay of Salon Kitty.
I'd forgotten about that.

You mentioned that pre-war brothels were very art nouveau – elaborate and ornate – whereas the Nazi period brothels were much more deco. So you get this contrast between the two. How did you research Salon Kitty? *Did you research the original Gestapo brothel in Berlin?*
Tinto and I went to Berlin and we did in fact find the original Pension Schmidt off the Kurfürsten Damm. It doesn't exist any more. The cellar was still the Gestapo cellar where they overheard all the conversations. They'd taken out the listening wax cylinders, but there were still traces of the eavesdropping devices. The decision to use the two styles – nouveau and deco – was my decision, and Tinto was fascinated by it. I said, 'We have to differentiate stylistically between the two periods.' The Nazis had completely redecorated the Pension Schmidt at the time – they had their own trained girls – so I decided to design the original brothel in art nouveau, which was very popular in Berlin during the 1920s. Then, to emphasise the change, I used art deco. Tinto loved it. As I say, he's got all my sketches. All I've got is a few lousy Xeroxes. I was still afraid to let myself go with big lines after my breakdown, so

all my sketches were fax size. They were rather delicate, but they were very pretty. I also had a very good assistant. I established a department of six people in Rome who did nothing but make art deco furniture and lamps. They were specialists, completely separate from the construction crew. One of the problems in those days was that if you did a brothel or a nightclub and you needed forty wall brackets of the same kind – or settees, coffee tables, lamps, carpets – you might find one or two, but you wouldn't find them anywhere in great numbers. Besides, they would have been too costly. So we had to build it all. It was lovely. Do you remember those art deco tables with the mirrored facets and the light wood veneer?

It was curved wood. And zigzags.
Yes, a lot of curved wood. A lot of art deco grilles. And the wavy lines and so on. It worked extremely well.

Some of the Nazi interiors, the big swastikas and big windows, are very Albert Speer . . .
Yes.

Salon Kitty *is undervalued from a design point of view. People, film buffs included, say to me, 'Did Ken Adam design that?!'*
I've got a book on it; Tinto gave me a book about the film. It's very interesting. Beautiful photographs.

The opening scene out-Cabaret's Cabaret . . . *There's this bizarre woman dancing with two painted sides to her.*
Ingrid Thulin.

There are two sides to her costume; she turns one way to look like a man, and the other to look like a woman. It makes Cabaret *look like child's play.*
I agree. I think *Salon Kitty* is an underrated film.

The Seven-Per-Cent Solution

In 1975, following Salon Kitty, *you worked on* The Seven-Per-Cent Solution. *It was directed by Herbert Ross, photography was by Ossie Morris, and Nicholas Meyer adapted the screenplay from his own novel. The film is a pastiche of Sherlock Holmes. When you think of Holmes, you either envisage Basil Rathbone in those B movies of the 1940s . . .*
Or the one Alexandre Trauner designed for Billy Wilder, *The Private Life of Sherlock Holmes.*

Yes, with his immaculate reconstruction of Baker Street. But this was a very different kind of project. Can you remember the thinking?

Well, first of all it was a very interesting story. Holmes is a cocaine or heroine addict and he encounters Sigmund Freud, who tries to cure both his habit and his fixation with Professor Moriarty, played by Larry Olivier. Having seen Alex Trauner's and Billy Wilder's film – Sherlock Holmes is a cult in this country – I decided, rightly or wrongly, to design Sherlock's home in Baker Street, showing the audience that this was a man living with drugs, seeing his living quarters through his eyes with inclined walls and other distortions. It's a device, maybe not very honest. I discussed it with Herb at great length and he said, 'Why not?' As long as I let him see how I was going about it. I got a little frightened because I really distorted everything in the settings. Ossie Morris backed me, but when I brought Herb in to have a look he said, 'Maybe it's going a bit too far.' So I wasn't sure any more. But we found a compromise and, although I didn't go as far as I wanted to, it certainly isn't the normally accepted design.

No. If you tamper with stories like Sherlock Holmes they tend to be treated like Holy Writ. You broke all the rules.

Yes.

Like the casting: Nicol Williamson is not everyone's idea of Sherlock Holmes. Holmes is not even the main character in The Seven-Per-Cent Solution. *It's much more to do with Freud and Watson.*

Watson was played by Robert Duvall. It was one of his earliest films. He was wonderful.

And then you went to Vienna for some exteriors.

I wanted to see Sigmund Freud's apartment. We were never going to shoot there, but I wanted to reproduce his apartment – as it was – completely as a set. But the funny thing was: the exterior was great. There were still cobblestones in the street. So I took some photos – I always take photographs of my locations – and showed them to everybody, and they were delighted. But when we arrived there two or three weeks later there was not a single cobblestone left! They'd taken all the cobblestones out! Everybody was in tears with laughter because I was absolutely destroyed, you know. I had to find a different location after that.

The interiors were back in England at Pinewood?

Yes.

You constructed there the Watsons' cosy London home, the distorted Baker Street and Freud's art nouveau consulting room where Holmes 'reads' the psychoanalyst by what he puts on his walls! Also the arena where Holmes and Freud are nearly trampled by the Lipizzaner horses. The riding academy had to be very stylised because I didn't have the money to build it as it exists. So I kept it very dark and claustrophobic; simple, but big. Then there was the train chase in the Severn Valley. We had a lot of fun with that. A group of enthusiasts still run steam trains there.

Do you think The Seven-Per-Cent Solution *was a success? I don't remember it making much of a splash. And obviously the Sherlock Holmes buffs felt offended by it.*
Yes, I'm sure they were. But I think it was quite successful.

Star Trek and Coppola

You were involved in pre-production on Star Trek – The Motion Picture *in 1977, with Gene Roddenberry as producer and Phil Kaufman as director. The television series had been created many years beforehand, but the memory of it was still strong. It must have been difficult to think beyond the TV concept.*
Right, especially because Gene Roddenberry was very conservative. The TV series was phenomenally successful – don't knock success – but it was very difficult to convince Gene of Phil's Kaufman's concept. Phil was a very talented director and he had written a new script that I found very exciting. I had been to his house in San Francisco, but at that time he had taken a house on the beach at Malibu, close to where Letizia and I were eventually going to live. In fact, it was my first introduction to Malibu, thinking back now. I spent more than a week there going through the whole idea with Phil, and then I came back here to start designing it with the help of one of my personal collaborators, Charlie Bishop. I also got Ralph McQuarrie from Hollywood, who was brilliant with spaceships and so on. *Star Trek* was set in AD 2400. That didn't worry me too much, except we had to come up with many concepts: a different planet environment, and even what the Earth might look like that far in the future. I spoke to Stanley Kubrick about the extra-terrestrials and he said, 'Don't even try it.' Because he had unsuccessfully tried to do the same thing in the preparation for *2001: A Space Odyssey* and in the end he had to give up. We did try, but it was never satisfactory. If you start sketching things out they always look ridiculous, with three eyes or one leg! I think the only way one could successfully do it is if one consults a scientist who can tell you what kind of biological development is possible at that time on the planet or any

Concept for the Super Brain, 1977

Study of the Starship *Enterprise*, 1977

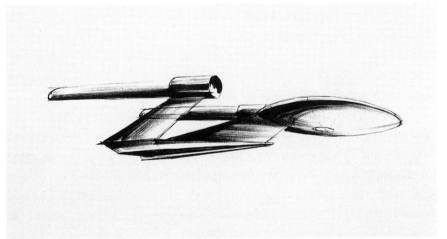

other planet, and from that start designing an extra-terrestrial, because it might be just a micro-organism or something. In any case, we never did that. Then I came up with this Super Brain and redesigned the Starship *Enterprise* and Phil was very pleased. Somehow the film, based on Kaufman's script and my designs, was never made. It was only made about two years later with Bob Wise directing it, based on a Nick Meyer script.

Yes, and it was a surprise hit. This thing of visualising aliens is interesting because since Close Encounters *the cliché has been this strange embryo-looking creature with no features and a stick-thin body.* Gollum in *The Lord of the Rings.*

*Yes, and anyone who claims to have had an alien abduction experience
claims that they all look like Steven Spielberg's. So that's what they now
look like. Even that is a silly idea; stick men with big eyes. Maybe it
originated in 2001's 'star child', the embryo in space. Whereas the hard-
ware is justifiable. You can work out how the engines work. There's
logic to it. But there's no logic to the extra-terrestrial. In the late 1970s
through to the early '80s you had a surprising number of unrealised
projects in Hollywood. You had one for John Frankenheimer called*
Destinies . . .
That was in summer 1979.

. . . which had a Cuban theme. Then a project called The Aquarius Mission, *also 1979, which was an underwater adventure, and* Dress Grey
for Herb Ross, about the West Point Military Academy . . .
A Gore Vidal script.

*. . . and one about the American Civil War for Francis Ford Coppola.
What happened?*
I was called to Los Angeles in late 1979 by John Frankenheimer to do
Destinies, a fantastic story about the Cuban exiles in Miami. I worked
out of Frankenheimer's office in Santa Monica and we actually flew to
Cuba with his wife, who was also one of the actresses in *Bonnie and
Clyde*. We were received like very important people by the Cubans until
John was asked to show them one of his films. He selected *The
Manchurian Candidate*, which didn't go down very well in 1979 Cuba.
So we became *persona non grata* after almost a week in Havana. I've
got a lot of amusing stories because things were very primitive. The one
big hotel was all booked up so they gave us these villas on the beach,
but there were no loo seats, no loo paper, no soap and no hot water, so
one had to wash in the sea: unbelievably primitive. But still. I also spent
a lot of time in Miami on the picture and then went to Mexico and
Guatemala to see if I could find similar locations to the ones we looked
at in Cuba, because the film was partly set there. When I came back
from an exhausting location trip, but a very successful one, I was suddenly told the picture was off. I've heard all sorts of theories about it,
but one of them was that John Frankenheimer was flirting with the girl-
friend or wife of someone financing the picture.

And he didn't like it too much!
But I don't know the real reason; I never found out. From that, I went
on to the Gore Vidal film, *Dress Grey*, which Herb Ross was going to
direct for Paramount. I was working at Paramount for three months
and I went to West Point and scouted that – I've got all my designs – but
then for some reason or another, Herb and Gore Vidal fell out and the

film wasn't made. It was a period with projects collapsing one after the other.

The third was The Aquarius Mission.
Well that was never really a 'go' picture. There was, if I remember rightly, a producer and she was part of the 'Patino' family – a famous Latin American family – who eloped with Jimmy Goldsmith years and years ago. She became a film producer, a rather attractive woman, and I met her in Hollywood and she came up with *The Aquarius Mission*. But I never really worked on that. I spent time at meetings with her, discussing concepts and so on, but the film was never made. It was to have been about an underwater civilisation.

You first met Francis Ford Coppola at the première of Apocalypse Now *in Cannes in 1979, and I gather he later asked you to design one of his projects. By then you and Letizia were renting a house in Malibu, overlooking the Pacific.*
Yes, after Christmas in 1979 we moved to Malibu. Frankenheimer was staying in Malibu so I met people there and we found this very pretty, unpretentious beach house on the Malibu road. We stayed there in that house for three years, actually. It was while I was working on *Destinies*.

So you'd met Coppola before moving to the States . . .
Yes, he wanted to show me his studio, Zoetrope. He knew I'd been using Zoetrope for research; he had a very good research library there, run by Lilian Michelson. He was so fascinated by the old Korda studios and the way he did *Lady Hamilton* or whatever it was, so Coppola wanted to build Zoetrope and base it on the Korda concept. He came up and said, 'I have an interesting picture for you.' He had an outline at the time – I don't think I ever saw a script – and it was basically the American Civil War sea battle between the *Merrimack* and the *Monitor*, these two iron-clad ships. It was the first naval battle in history – 9 March 1862 – to involve two ironclads. I don't think the film was ever made.

It wasn't. I did a TV interview with Coppola in 1980 and I remember seeing rows and rows of books on the Civil War in his editing suite at home in the Napa Valley.
You didn't go to the Silver Caravan?

No, we went to his home and adjoining editing rooms. A great Ken Adam project I would have thought – involving shipbuilding and new technology, 1862-style.
We became quite friendly actually because he came to several of Letizia's weekend spaghetti parties and he brought a lot of his own

wine from the Napa Valley. Francis was very much an Italian family man.

It used to retail at about $40 a bottle, so it was quite an upmarket label. I had lunch with him and Eleanor at his long table; a huge bowl of pasta, olives . . . It was wonderful. He would have been interesting to work for.

He had a production designer who was a great friend of mine and who I've lost touch with in the last two years, Dean Tavoularis. I don't think he lives in LA any longer; he lives in France somewhere. He's a very talented guy and very cultured. I was very friendly with Dean. But this project would have interested me. Francis was thinking about a million and one things at the time that didn't necessarily materialise.

He made One From the Heart *around this time, his attempt to make a studio musical.*
Yes, that was Las Vegas wasn't it? He scaled it all down.

Yes, with lots of neon. It didn't do too well but it was an interesting experiment – part of Coppola's love affair with Korda and Denham.

The Girl of the Golden West

Meanwhile, in 1977, before all this, you'd designed the opera La Fanciulla del West *for the Royal Opera House, Covent Garden, at the request of Zubin Mehta and the chief executive, John Tooley. This was the one that Stanley Kubrick visited, behind the scenes. You hadn't designed an opera before but, as you say, they 'wanted a more filmic approach' to La Fanciulla del West. When I went to see it with the critic and writer Philip French, we were both convinced it was your 'Spaghetti Western' project, because of the long coats and hats, the rickety bridge and the hill; a ramshackle Western town with planks of wood everywhere.*
Like Sergio Leone!

Exactly. But I remember you saying at the time that the design was based more on archive photos of mining towns – although Leone got many of his ideas from archive photos too, and the Italian Western 'look' was certainly in the ether at that time.
We had hundreds and hundreds of archive photos; it is a well-documented period. The director, Piero Faggioni, and I did a lot of research on that and I believe it's been one of the most successful operas at Covent Garden. Everybody talks about it.

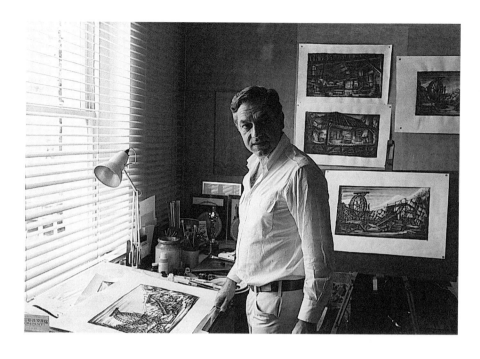

In Ken Adam's studio at home, designing the opera *La Fanciulla Del West*, 1977

I'd love to claim the design as 'Spaghetti Western', Ken, because in a way Puccini wrote the very first Italian Western and the first horse opera . . .

It was based on a play by David Belasco, and Puccini was fascinated by that period.

And it opened at the Met in New York at the end of 1910, with Caruso playing the lead.

I remember seeing Jeremy Isaacs there last year for something and he said, 'This is the man who built the biggest sets ever!'

They went from floor to ceiling, and they took a hell of a time to change. The intervals had to be record length.

Yes, I know. I think it took them forty minutes on the first night, and John Tooley went crazy. So did I. But it wasn't entirely my fault. Remember I used the art department at Covent Garden to draw out these sets so they should have advised me! But also the director Piero Faggioni was very demanding and wanted exact materials and so on. They had an industrial dispute at the time, the stagehands and the Covent Garden management. Helga Schmidt, an Austrian, was in charge. On the morning of the dress rehearsal I got a phone call from her and she said the stagehands were on strike. I didn't know what she wanted me to do, but she said, 'You'd better tell Zubin Mehta.' I said, 'It's not my job.' Zubin said that providing I gave him fifteen minutes of the first act, fifteen minutes of the second act, and thirty minutes of the final act so he could be through by one o'clock, he could do it. And

215

the stagehands agreed to that. But we never had a proper dress rehearsal, so it was all very much touch-and-go. And I'll never forget the first night because we also didn't have the full complement of stagehands and we had these very complicated sets. So John said I had to try and work with the stagehands in the interval, if they'd let me help. Afterwards I was introduced to Prince Charles and he said not to worry, everyone was very happy in the crush bar! I'm not sure whether this was a compliment! But I made sure that future scene changes took no longer than thirty minutes. Piero Faggioni rang me last week because they are bringing it out as a DVD and trying to revive the opera with the actual sets in a couple of years time, in 2005. The original sets look terrible – they are falling apart – but I tell you, with the new equipment and the new space they have, they can change in ten minutes.

There's a long wooden bridge in the gold mine set, and a high flight of stairs leading to it: a rickety stairway from the mine. It is said you made the walk along the bridge a bit too long for the solo, so by the time the singer had reached the bottom of the stairs, they'd run out of Puccini's music.

Yes! I keep reminding Zubin Mehta of that story because he said not to worry; he could always add a few bars. I was standing next to him at the dress rehearsal and I couldn't believe it. It was one of those things, as a film designer, you don't think about. But of course, the stars of opera are much more amenable than film stars. They love the big star entrances and exits and they wouldn't have me reduce one step. Now Zubin denies saying that!

Your design for the temporary mining town is terrific. I've seen photos of the original 1910 production at the Met where it was a much more traditional Wild West look, whereas you went for an exaggerated gold rush . . .

I was very much influenced by Piero, who had done the opera in La Scala or somewhere in Italy. It was really his concept. He wanted a more filmic approach too.

Pennies from Heaven

Which bring us to Pennies from Heaven. *Having had a few false starts at a time when Hollywood was restructuring, you were not just having bad luck. The whole structure of the industry was changing. Accountants were taking over and the film divisions were just one floor of a huge corporate building which dealt with insurance, car parks, oil; a tiny part of a huge multinational corporation. So the 'Hollywood' of the 1950s had virtually gone. It was a much less stable place than when you arrived. It was now run by agents and lawyers and graduates of Harvard Business School.*

Yes, and what everybody said in Hollywood was that the major executives didn't feel safe committing to anything. They would read scripts, they would discuss them, but once they committed to a project, their heads were on the block. That's why very few committed to major projects. They made a lot of promises but did not dare to make a decision. I don't know whether Herb Ross had seen the Dennis Potter TV version of *Pennies from Heaven*, but I certainly had, and we loved it here. Did you see it?

Yes, it was an eight-hour BBC serial screened in 1978 with Bob Hoskins and Cheryl Campbell. It had some very evocative 1930s records: cockney dreams in the Depression.

Letizia and I were so keen on it that if we were out and they were running it we came back specially in order to see it on television, because we thought it was quite brilliant. But when Herb interested Dennis Potter and MGM – it was still the old MGM at Culver City – to do this as an American film, Herb had many doubts and Nora and I tried to push him. I wanted to do a musical at MGM because to me the MGM studios were magic, going back to Fred Astaire and Gene Kelly and all those other films. And even though they'd got rid of their exterior lot, there were still the big MGM studios that had been there for years. Everybody had history. While I was doing the film there, there were seven or eight major productions being shot at the same time, and of course there were a lot of friends of mine: Billy Wilder was doing *Buddy Buddy*; not one of his better pictures, but I adored Billy. We would have lunch together and he would say, quite seriously, 'I am through filming at three o'clock in the afternoon but you are still filming at seven or eight o'clock in the evening. Why?' It was his way of working, as a director of the old school who wrote or co-wrote most of his scripts: 'One thinks through a scene until it works and then one just has to shoot it!'

Pennies from Heaven *is said to be the last big musical ever to be made at MGM.*

It wasn't really an MGM musical in the true sense of the word. It had a very sad and important message. It was Dennis Potter, of course, and the Depression era. The musical aspect was this new idea of lip-synching to old songs, either female or male; it didn't make any difference. Dennis Potter spent a lot of time with us in Malibu. He never stayed

On the set of the bank, MGM Soundstage 1980

with us, but he came for the weekend and he was a fascinating character. He drank a lot of red wine but he was brilliant, there's no question about it, though not necessarily cheering.

Sometimes gloomy and bitter?
Yes, gloomy and depressing, but brilliant. The major problem I had on the film was that we had real sequences and dream sequences, and somehow Herb could never make up his mind what was what. It was very confusing for me. So you'll find I did a lot of designs for reality, and then designs for a dream sequence, but in the end they all became one because we ran out of money to do it that way.

How about the transposition because the original series was about an unhappily married East End sheet-music salesman who runs away to the provinces, travelling round southern England with his naïve girl-friend. There were fantasies woven around these settings and you had to transpose them to Chicago in the same period. How did that work?
Well, we had big problems. I was very much involved in the discussions with Herb because in England it was simple: you had a cockney playing the part, like Hoskins, and the audience immediately knew his background – who he is, where he is, and so on. In America, we were talking about Brooklyn, and we finally came up with the Midwest, so I was sent to Chicago. I must say, I spent days in Chicago and found all the major locations that we were looking for. I got to know Chicago pretty well. Then on the final location scout, when Herb arrived with the cameraman Gordon Willis, I noticed right from the start that he was very temperamental and I thought he wasn't going to like anything. And it was a bit like that. It wasn't that he didn't like Chicago, but he had decided in his mind that it was easier – and apparently backed by MGM – to do the whole Chicago sequence in the studio. But by this time we were running seriously out of preparation time, so suddenly I was catapulted back from Chicago to MGM, which was busy also. I only managed to get a couple of stages so I had to use Goldwyn and another studio. I think we used three different studios in total. I built the Chicago street on a big stage at MGM.

The street was part of the Chicago 'el'. It's actually an intersection of two streets. There's an elevated railway up the middle of it, with a pool hall and a speakeasy and a whole row of shops, so it's quite a set. I gather that if you'd shot it on location you'd either need a wide-angle lens or you'd need to push the camera right back, so you must have altered the perspective to make it possible to shoot?
Yes, we did.

That was a very big set, wasn't it?
Yes, and in fact MGM kept it for three years after the film because they thought they could use it like the backlot at Warner Brothers: let other people use it. But I don't think it was a proper commercial proposition. It was really quite impressive. My problem was what to put in the street, and that's when I came up with the idea – I discussed it with Herb, and he agreed – of using painters like Edward Hopper and Reginald Marsh for some of the exteriors. So I used Hopper's *Nighthawks* on the corner.

With the artificial lighting of the person in the bar seen from outside?
That's right. And we shot the scene.

And also Hopper's New York Movie *and Marsh's* A Movie Theater.
The usherette. And the employment agency and the pawnshop came from the photographer Walker Evans. It became a jigsaw puzzle of various artists of the period. We attempted for the first time to bring the work of these artists to life.

There's a scene in Pennies from Heaven *in which they dance in front of a collage of Walker Evans photographs, which also has a Reginald Marsh feel to it. Like his paintings of Coney Island.*
But I used Reginald Marsh for a second-hand fur shop on the second floor, the second level of the street, because there's a famous painting by

Final concept drawing of the "El"
street intersection in Chicago, MGM
1980

Marsh of models modelling furs in an upper level. I used the painters
and then Walker Evans for the collage, which is an incredible sequence.
This fabulous dancer, Vernel Bagneris, a Latin American choreographer, steps out of the diner and dances to *Pennies from Heaven* in front
of that collage. It was about sixty feet long and forty feet high, so it was

big. It accentuated the depression to have Bagneris dancing as a tiny figure in front of it.

There's the speakeasy, the basement where Christopher Walken performs his dance for Bernadette Peters – which opens out – and the bank of course, which is an even bigger example of going from reality into fantasy. The whole physical structure of the set changes as you shift into the gear of dreams. For the bank, you were inspired by the exterior of the Board of Trade building in Chicago, but once you get inside there's this vast deco palace – 'a marble cathedral to the power of money', you've called it – which is very different to the English television version, where it's a small office in a provincial bank. You give it the full Fred Astaire treatment with this very expensive and glittering set.

Yes, very expensive and glittering, because the sets not only had to reflect the gloom of the 1930s, but also the dreams of money and wealth. Those banks in Chicago really were enormous palaces. And for me it was so exciting to see one hundred and fifty girls all dancing; you only saw that in the old musicals. We were very fortunate because Nora Kaye was a professional ballerina and the choreographer was a tap dancer of Italian origin. But we couldn't afford to pay all the dancers – that's why they don't make these musicals any more – for rehearsal time, so what Nora and the choreographer did was rehearse all the sequences with about four dancers and then only had one day's rehearsal with the whole lot. But for me this was magic. I remember Cary Grant coming in to watch the sequence. It cost a lot, but the industry needed uplift.

The other set was a facsimile of the Astaire/Rogers musical Follow the Fleet, *where they go and see the film in this Hopper-type cinema and then find themselves in the sequence itself: 'Let's Face the Music and Dance'.*

Well, it was unbelievable. I can't take any credit for it because I think it was the brilliance of Steve Martin, Herb Ross, Nora Kaye and the tap-dance choreographer. You must remember that Steve was not a dancer, but in five months he learned to tap-dance. Nora knew that for Steve to dance with Bernadette Peters in front of Fred Astaire and Ginger Rogers was just unbelievable. The way Herb shot it, he tried to help with the composition, et cetera. I helped with certain things, like all the sticks.

How do you mean?

We wanted to give the feeling that they're imprisoned, so the walking sticks of the men in tails suddenly grow until they end up like the bars of a prison. Basically the sequence starts off with an enlarged big-screen version of an Astaire and Rogers picture, so I had to build that set again. And do you think I could get any drawings from RKO or whoever it was who did that picture? No I could not. Nobody could find the drawings. I had one black-and-white eight by ten still and I built the set from that. One thing that I've come across again and again on pictures all over the world is how to get the shiny floors that they used in the old musicals. We've never been able to do it, and the people who made those floors are no longer alive. As I've said, they were paper floors and they repapered or relacquered them after each take. I thought I'd resolved it. I warned my construction manager and painter on *Pennies from Heaven* that we were going to have a problem because the stages were old. I said, 'We've got to build a sub-floor to level everything out.' Well, the same problem happened. Halfway through the completion of the set Herb and I found a wavy floor and this young construction manager who had consulted everybody – because they're very professional in Hollywood – well, he nearly shot himself. Then the next day he came up with a solution. He said the only way we'd get it smooth and shiny was by using terrazzo, because you pour terrazzo and it levels itself out. Then you polish it afterwards and it becomes like a mirror, which it did. The only thing is that it was very tough on the dancers. But it certainly worked visually.

It is typical that they didn't have the drawings, because they never worried about archives in the golden age of Hollywood.
Even more typical: after I finished *Pennies from Heaven* a friend of mine who was running MGM actually rang me up and asked me to leave all the drawings with them because they owned the copyright. So I let them have all my originals. Three years later I wanted to refer back to one or two of my sketches so I went to MGM and asked if I could have a look at them. They couldn't find them.

And it's the same with costumes. One aspect of Pennies from Heaven *is that it's subsequently been treated as a classic of period-film design. There was an exhibition of Edward Hopper in New York a few years ago where they had a section on the impact of Hopper on popular culture, and your* Nighthawks *was in there as a classic transcription of a 1930s painting into the medium of film. But you have an odd credit for the film: your credit is 'associate producer' on the one hand, and 'visual consultant' on the other, but not production designer.*
No. That's why I never got the nomination for the Academy Award. I didn't worry about it because I was very excited about doing the picture. It was a strange situation. To cut a very long story short, I had been a member of the New York union ever since Ray Stark forced me to play a part in the Streisand film, and what I forgot to tell you was that I blackmailed him into paying the two-thousand-dollar initiation fee of the New York union. So ever since 1970 I had been a member of the New York branch, who had a reciprocal agreement with the Hollywood union. There was no necessity for me to join the Hollywood

union because all you did was pay your dues to the local there when you were working in Hollywood. What happened on *Pennies from Heaven* was that the two unions had a big fight and they stopped this reciprocal agreement, so that anybody who was from New York couldn't work in Hollywood, and anybody from Hollywood couldn't work in New York. It was one of those ridiculous disputes.

Turf war.
Yes. The head of the Los Angeles union, Gene Allen, who by this time had become quite a friend of mine and who was Cecil Beaton's art director on *My Fair Lady* – Gene was typically Irish – told me I couldn't work on the film. I said, 'The head of MGM wants me to work on the film.' He said I could work on the film if I was a producer. I said I didn't want to be producer on the film. So he said, 'Why don't you take an associate producer credit on the main titles? Then you could be visual consultant.' I just wanted to do the picture whatever. I had two Hollywood art directors as my assistants, Fred Tuch and Bernie Cutler. Lovely people, and I still see them nowadays. When it came to the Oscar, what happened was that the Art Directors' Guild had final say on the eligibility of each film, and they decided that *Pennies from Heaven* was not eligible. Because if it won the Academy Award, then my two art directors would get it, and that would not be right because I did all the designs.

That's sad.
It is. I brought it up last year in March 2002 when the same Art Directors' Guild gave me its Lifetime Achievement Award.

You at last had the opportunity to say it?
I said, 'Well, twenty-five years ago there was this situation . . . But that's Hollywood.'

The movie wasn't a box-office success. It was the period in Hollywood of early George Lucas, early Spielberg, all the feel-good movies, uplifting movies. Everybody wanted to leave the cinema singing 'When You Wish Upon a Star'. But Pennies from Heaven *finishes with Steve Martin having the hood pulled over his head just before he's hanged, and singing the very poignant title song. It's downhill all the way. It's also a difficult mixture of sentimentality and self-parody. The scale and the glamour of the fantasy scenes are ironic. Was it also not marketed well?*
It was not marketed very well because they promoted it as a typical MGM musical, which it wasn't.

And a Steve Martin movie.
The public expected a comedy because of Steve, who had just had an

enormous success with *The Jerk*. They simply could not accept him as a loser. But today of course, it's a classic. Just ten months ago they had a reprint of it showing at the Academy, and Steve Martin actually got up to make a speech and said, 'We have to be so grateful to Ken Adam.' I only heard that later – because of my credit as associate producer and visual consultant.

That's nice.
Today it's seen as a classic. It's amazing how things change. You know, not to the same extent, but you were talking about *Night of the Demon* and how a lot of film buffs are watching it . . .

There's even a book coming out about it.
We were of course so disappointed about not being nominated for *Pennies from Heaven* because I'd been on the film on and off for about a year and a half. I took four weeks off before shooting because I was on the Cannes Film Festival jury in 1980, but the film lasted till 1981. I enjoyed working with Gordon Willis, who was a brilliant but strange cameraman, and all these dancers, including Steve Martin, in the old atmosphere of MGM. Of the seven films I've designed for Herbert Ross, I believe *Pennies from Heaven* was his best.

You worked again with Dennis Potter just after this, in 1981–82, on a mobile cinema for Twentieth Century Fox.
Oh yes!

Fox asked you to produce a cinema of the future, to try and bring back the magic of going to the pictures.
The magic of the old movie palace. That was not my idea and I don't think it was Fox's either. It was an idea partly by Herb Ross and Dan Melnick, who was a very successful film producer and a very flamboyant character. I think they gave the idea to Fox, who were very interested. It was to bring back, as you say, the magic of these movie temples and palaces of the 1920s and '30s, with more than one programme; they had the Wurlitzer organ and two films and even stage acts like vaudeville. To bring it up to date. There was no mention of a mobile cinema at that stage; the thought came to me later when I was thinking of new concepts for the cinema, like a pre-movie experience. I was working at Dan Melnick's office on the Fox lot and I had to park my car – my old Rolls-Royce I had in LA for two or three years – in front of the building because Danny felt it gave prestige to the project. I was really working very hard and I came up with a pre-movie experience that was like going through the interior of a space station. I couldn't think of anything else at the time. I was also being advised on space

225

technology by Caltech in Pasadena, and they were so excited to help me because they'd just sent out their probes and cameras and were getting eight by ten stills back every hour from millions of miles away. I said, 'Well, if you can make a camera that size to fit into a space probe, and we have these gigantic cameras, why don't you get together with the film industry?' They were very excited by the idea because they had problems justifying their space budget. After that I came up with the idea for an inflatable cinema . . .

And Dennis Potter wrote a script about a journey through space. Was it IMAX technology?
Yes, well that was the latest thing. I did a lot of research with the Canadians, who had invented the IMAX. It had a fantastic 70mm widescreen process, which impressed me so much that I designed it like an IMAX theatre. Then the whole thing somehow fitted like a dome shape and so I thought – remember in those days you had all these inflatable tennis courts – why don't we do it as an inflatable? So I asked some experts on inflatables if it would work and they said, 'Why not?' So you've got this structure which is one-tenth of the price of an actual cinema and the whole idea at the time was to start with twelve or fifteen cinemas near major cities in the United States, and the main requirement was to find an area which could be used as a parking lot. So to have a mobile inflatable cinema seemed like a good idea, and Fox went for it; they really went for it. Then I had more staff coming in to work on things and the man who at one time was in charge of production at MGM, Lew Rackmil, became my production executive. He was like a Boy Scout – another one – because he'd had a heart attack and was supposed to take it easy, but it was so exciting for him. We all thought we were going to be in the money! That we'd get a three- or four-year contract with Fox. It was the talking point of Los Angeles.

Dennis Potter's screenplay was about a spaceship full of a thousand embryos journeying into space. I think the destination was the Garden of Eden or somewhere . . .
No, it wasn't. The destination, we are told, was another planet. But during the trip the spaceship hits an asteroid or there is some electrical failure or something which affects some of the embryos, and after twenty years – I'm trying to remember – they land on a planet and they find it's the Garden of Eden on our Earth.

Good and evil.
That was the idea. The people who were affected by the electrical failure became evil and the others were good. I don't know how it went on but that was the idea, and I'd already started designing the movie. So

226

then we had a big presentation with Marvyn Davis, the head of Fox – he was a gigantic man; I had to get a special chair in for him – and twenty or thirty executives. It was beautifully laid out and everybody was very excited. We were like children afterwards. Two weeks passed and the project was off. And do you know why? Because Danny Melnick was crazy: he kept remodelling his office, so in the morning when I came in to talk to him he would tell me not to lean on the couch or the chair. Great design sense, great taste, but also crazy. He had an English secretary, Elizabeth, who I adored and who kept me informed about everything, and she said, 'You can't go into the office today because Danny's putting a new carpet down.' I saw it and said, 'It's the same colour that was there before.' 'No,' she said, 'it's a slightly different shade of charcoal grey' – to give you an idea. The whole place was recarpeted with a slightly different shade, and I couldn't see the difference. What happened was that Marvyn Davis found out Danny had spent a million or a million and a half dollars redecorating his office and they must have had a big row. The Fox Special Project was never mentioned again.

You could have beaten the Millennium Dome by twenty years.
Yes!

8   On the World Stage

New Hollywood

When you came to Hollywood in the 1970s – for example on Diamonds Are Forever – *you usually stayed for short periods as guests of friends in Beverly Hills. But from 1979 to 1983 you preferred to rent a house in Malibu 'miles away from the artificiality of Beverly Hills and Hollywood'. Letizia organised some legendary weekend pasta parties on the beach, and a number of British, Italian and American friends would visit you there. But in 1983 you came back home to England. Was that because Hollywood had run out of steam for you?*

Well, I'd had a bad experience on the Special Project at Fox, where we all thought we were going to have a three- or four-year contract because the demo had been successful. But just because of this row between Danny Melnick and Marvyn Davis, the whole thing was forgotten. At the same time I had a call from Bruce Beresford asking if I would be interested in doing *King David*. So that was one of the reasons too.

You worked on that in 1983–84?
Yes.

There were a couple more unrealised projects between Pennies from Heaven *and* King David. *One of them was* The Fantasticks, *which was going to be an adaptation of the off-Broadway show.*
Yes, the most successful off-Broadway show they ever had.

What went wrong with that? It looked gilt-edged.
It did. The young man who was producing was a friend of ours called Michael Braun. He was a social butterfly: when there was a party in England or New York, he was there. A compulsive partygoer. He was a friend of Getty.

The London Getty or the Malibu Getty?
The Malibu Getty, John Paul Getty Jr; he was living in Santa Monica. So Michael got the rights for *The Fantasticks* but he didn't have a director, and that was the problem really. For months and months he couldn't find a director. Whereas I was working out of the house in Malibu doing design after design based on the musical, but not based on a film script as such. It was very difficult for me. I could only do what I thought to stimulate discussion. I thought Michael was in seventh heaven, but then he disappeared. And then no more cheques arrived. I had a

Study of castle staircase for *The Fantasticks*, 1982

very good, tough agent, Roger Davis, who was actually the legal head of the William Morris Agency. And Roger said, when I was going back to England, to let him have all the drawings since I hadn't been paid. But Michael had disappeared.

Completely?
He was a close friend but he completely disappeared.

And no one ever saw him again?
Certainly not me. Then I heard recently – in the last few years – that he died from a heart attack.

The Fantasticks *was a zany, surreal show. So was it fun, fantasy design?*
Yes, but for some of it I went back to the early Errol Flynn pictures – fighting on battlements and staircases and so on, which I loved. In *The Fantasticks* there are two identical houses next to each other, but one is well kept and the other is completely neglected. It's about two families – like a *Romeo and Juliet* story almost – getting together. So I did it a little bit like Grandma Moses: very simple. Michael and Getty were just absolutely in seventh heaven.

The second unrealised project was Mermaid, *which would have been directed by Herbert Ross for Columbia in 1983. Apparently you researched many locations but there was bad medicine between producer Ray Stark and Herb Ross.*

229

Yes, and somebody else was also making a film about mermaids.

Splash, *probably.*
Yes, *Splash.* Ray Stark gave me a free hand and I wanted to look at the East Coast from Newport, Rhode Island. So I went all down the East Coast right to Miami, and it was funny in a way because it was so freezing cold that my camera froze. Letizia had to put it under her fur coat. But Newport was unbelievable. It had all these enormous villas. And I had the best connections there.

It's very Great Gatsby, *the whole thing. More 'old money' than 'new money'.*
Yes, old money. I had a great friend who I met on *Thunderball* called Buzzy Warburton, who was from that clique, and he had a beautiful yacht called the *Black Pearl*, which is in the background of *Thunderball* actually. It was unique. I met Buzzy again in Newport and his cousin was working for me on research. I had the idea – there was the America's Cup the following year – to film the America's Cup and weave it into the story. So I thought it was a brilliant idea and Buzzy, who was commodore of the yacht club, said I could have carte blanche. I rang up Ray Stark and said, 'I'm in Newport and I think I've got a good idea.' He said I should discuss it with him the next day at the studio, but I said it would take me at least six hours to fly back. He thought I was in Newport, California. I'd been talking to him for ten minutes before he realised! But it was a very interesting location scout.

Was there a script at that stage?
There was a script. Then Herb either got cold feet or he and Ray had a disagreement. They were so close they were always fighting. When I came back to my office at Columbia or wherever it was, the picture had been cancelled.

The films you were involved in over the next ten years or so were outside Hollywood: in Europe or Canada or China or India or non-Hollywood America. Looking back, do you think that 1980s Hollywood was becoming a place you didn't want to be, or was it going in a direction that didn't suit you?
I was very disappointed by the Special Project because we'd really done some useful work and it was interesting in terms of concept and so on. And getting CALTEC, who were happy to help out. So I was very disappointed. And yes, things were changing in Hollywood. I quite liked the old movie moguls. They might have been monsters, but I was always attracted to those sorts of people. Some of the great studio bosses were monsters – ruthless, intelligent and often vulgar – but I liked them.

They had only one purpose in life: to make films. When I first arrived in Hollywood it was still their era and I was excited to have the opportunity to meet some of them. I will never forget when Bob Aldrich, Letizia and I were on a flight from Europe and we were diverted from Los Angeles to San Francisco due to bad weather conditions. Bob was furious, and after landing threatened to buy the airline, TWA. The thing was, Christopher, he meant it! *Pennies from Heaven* was really the last major picture done at MGM, and this was happening all round. To be back in England, at Pinewood, preparing *King David* with Bruce Beresford, was a refreshing experience.

Also, the moguls had this flair for design because most of them originally came from the rag trade. They had an intuitive understanding of the look of film, whereas the new people seemed to equate it with special effects.
Provided they could discuss deals, these Harvard Business School people were happy.

Protecting their backs. One thing you can definitely say about Ken Adam movies is that they do require decisions!
Oh yes!

King David

So, King David, *directed by Bruce Beresford. Interiors at Pinewood, locations in Italy. An odd project in a way because in the mid-1980s the biblical epic and movies about ancient times were seriously out of fashion. This is long before* Gladiator *and long after* Spartacus. *But it is an interesting film visually because it doesn't seem to belong to that movie tradition at all.*
Well, who was the writer? He also wrote *The Lost Boys.*

Andrew Birkin.
I worked pretty closely with Andrew and with Bruce Beresford and we had a lot of fun. What I was trying to do . . . Well, I didn't want to make another *Sodom and Gomorrah.* So first of all I did a lot of research into Assyrian art history and 1000 BC and so on. I was fascinated by that. And I found this incredible location in southern Italy, which was purely because I'd seen a film by Pasolini . . .

The Gospel According to St Matthew.
Yes, in black and white. I was so impressed that I looked at this place in Southern Italy, Matera, which practically nobody in Italy knew

Before and after: design for the exterior
of David's Palace in Jerusalem, Matera
1984

about. It was a town built into a canyon. It's unbelievable because it is
probably the oldest habitation or small city in the world – over five
thousand years old – and you see all these various influences from cave
dwellings to medieval times. There is a modern city up on top, on the
other side, which you don't see and which is awful. But to give you an
example, I was going into caves and cave-like buildings and there were
these frescos going back to the eleventh or twelfth century, and you
could have just cut them out: there was nobody in charge. So I decided
to create Jerusalem in Matera: the walls, the tower, the entrance gate.
And I also found the desert nearby, which was a big mistake because
when I was there it looked like parts of the Sahara. No plants or anything. So I said, 'We don't have to go to Tunisia or Morocco. We can
shoot it all here.' And everybody was delighted. But then they had a terrible winter – it must have been the winter of 1983 to '84 – and everything got covered in snow. In fact, my assistants got stuck in a
snowdrift. And in spring, when we were supposed to shoot there, there

232

was just an explosion of fauna. There was every plant and flower you could imagine! So I had my painter with a big tanker truck spraying everything in that area with brown paint, spraying by the kilometre! That picture was nothing but disasters, even though we had a sense of humour about it. The same thing happened in Sardinia; I found this incredible plateau that you could hardly drive up to. It was easier to go by helicopter. And Paramount were getting very conscious of the budget. The producer was Marty Elfand, who was a delightful person but not very experienced in films. Finally we got the whole unit up to this plateau, and I must say, the Italians showed us up, because the British drivers refused to drive through this mountain road, but the Italians were all up there at six in the morning. How they ever got up there, don't ask me. But they did. It was so high that on that day the plateau was covered in cloud. I remember it was like fog; we couldn't shoot anything. I used it for David's birthplace. It was rocky and wild and you had clear views for about twenty miles on a good day. Marty Elfand became very nasty. Then in the afternoon there was a break in the clouds and we got a few shots, but we really didn't get what we wanted. But that happened all the time on that picture. It was the same in Campo Imperatore, where the Germans in the Second World War rescued the Italian dictator Benito Mussolini. It's a wild mountainscape in Abruzzi, and I wanted to know when the snow would melt there. The locals told me that by April we'd be absolutely safe. But when we were there in June – where I had constructed the Hebrew camp – to film the battle of David and Goliath, looking in one direction there was still snow. I thought we could get rid of the snow so I hired some enormous bulldozers, but they couldn't shift it because it was ice and it was ten feet deep. I knew I couldn't use water paint or anything like that. So I don't know whether it was my idea or not, but we sprayed the whole thing with cement! It was the only way we could mask the snow, by spraying grey cement on it. We got the shots, but a day or two day later I was nearly arrested!

I should think you were!
It was one of those films where everything went wrong.

King David *doesn't obey the conventions of epic films where there's spectacle and scale and glamour. Instead it has these little walled citadels and primitive communities. I don't know where you'd find out what biblical times looked like. There are no practical visual tools. You have to create them from scratch, like you did with* Sodom and Gomorrah.

I'd also done some research in Israel, Jerusalem, but of course they didn't have much going back to that time. One enormous stroke of luck was finding a disused quarry near Matera. I came up with the idea of using it as a city. I put up a few columns of the Minoan period and it looked really sensational, just like a city. But it was a quarry.

As we're talking now, the news has come through that Denis Quilley, who played the part of Samuel, has died. I think the film stands up because it doesn't try to be one of those 1960s epics.
It wasn't pretentious.

It was a great risk though, to back a movie about King David *in 1985 when such films were so out of fashion and at a time when the Bible was no longer read very much. At least in the 1950s and '60s Hollywood could assume the target audience had some knowledge of biblical stories.*
I thought Richard Gere made a valiant effort, but to play with a cast of British Shakespearean actors, I don't think it worked.

He looked good, if not entirely convincing! The film was made in 1983–84, so it was a long stint.
Yes, we were on that film a long time.

The Last Emperor

Then came The Last Emperor, *about the life of the last Emperor of China. It must have been another very complex production, this time for producer Jeremy Thomas and director Bernardo Bertolucci. You worked on it for quite some time.*
Nearly a year.

Can you talk us through that?
Well, again, I didn't know Jeremy beforehand, but I liked him and I liked Bernardo too.

You met in London, I presume?
We first met in London and then we went to China for four weeks, where we had an amazing experience. We were the first film unit to be allowed into the Forbidden City. To film there in those days – 1985 – was unheard of. The surviving brother of the ex-Emperor Pu-Yi was our technical advisor, and I'll never forget when we took him to the Forbidden City. It was the first time he'd been back there because he'd been in prison for many years . . .

Since he was a child.

Final concept drawing of the storage chamber in the 'Forbidden City', 1985

Yes, and you know the Chinese don't show a lot of emotion, but he did. It was an incredible experience. We also met a lot of interesting people because just at that time some of the Chinese artists were beginning to express themselves, some good, some not so good because they played safe. And everybody was hoping either to go to the Royal College in London or to study in America. So we spent a lot of evenings together with these people. And we witnessed the first signs of change to Western dress and transport, because when we arrived there the majority of people were on bicycles in their blue uniforms, but when I went to Shanghai it was the first time I had a bit of a feeling of European culture. The teenagers, the young, were beginning to wear Western clothes.

Leading up to the Tiananmen Square massacre . . .
Yes. So it was exciting. I had very good Chinese assistants too. Then we came back and I started designing the picture here.

Were the interiors to be in Rome or England?
In Rome.

235

Interiors in Rome: exteriors in China.

Yes. So Bernardo Bertolucci used to come up to the house and we spent a lot of time together. He was not an easy person to please but he really loved – with the exception of maybe two or three sketches – everything. But Jeremy Thomas had enormous financial problems, so I wasn't paid. And Bernardo wasn't really interested because he's a little bit like a medieval prince; he has his court around him. He said, 'I can't be bothered about your financial problems with Jeremy. People work for me because they want to work for me.' I said to Bernardo at the time, 'If I let you have all these sketches, this is my capital.' But to cut a long story short, he got copies of the sketches to discuss with his cameraman Vittorio Storaro, and I started an art department in Rome, working but not being properly paid – paid in dribs and drabs because Jeremy had a terrible problem and was travelling all over Europe trying to get money from people. At that time Bernardo was going back to Peking and he wanted me to organise the art department. I had a phone call from Dino De Laurentiis in New York asking if I could come and meet him for the weekend to talk to Bruce Beresford about one of their future projects, *Crimes of the Heart*. I rang Jeremy to see if there would be any conflicts of interest but he didn't think Bernardo would mind. He said, 'It doesn't mean you have to do the picture. Talk to them and when you get back hopefully I will have more money.' I was in New York for a day and a half and then back to Rome. When I arrived back in Rome there was a Telex from Bernardo saying he didn't want me any longer on the picture. I was furious because Jeremy was aware of what I'd been doing and I hadn't committed to anything and so on. I found out afterwards that by chance Bernardo had talked to CAA or some agents in New York – at that time Bernardo and Dino didn't talk to each other, although I notice from the Venice Film Festival that they are the greatest of friends again – and they said, 'Do you know that Ken Adam is negotiating with Dino?' And Bernardo was furious about it. I got a six-page letter of apology from Bernardo about a week or ten days later, written on a 747 flying back from Beijing, but at that time also I was a little bit of a prima donna and packed all my original sketches and left Rome for London. I knew I hadn't done anything wrong. 'Fuck you all,' you know, 'I've behaved honourably.' Then it became very nasty because agents were involved and everybody said I had to take legal action. I said I'd never taken legal action, or if I had it had been disastrous. My art department sympathised with me and wanted to resign in protest, but I begged them to stay on because they could not afford to be out of work. When it came to a legal settlement I said I didn't want credit as production designer but I would like some form of credit. But I was told that Bernardo hadn't used any of my designs, even though the art department, who kept working on the film, told me that he did use a lot of my designs. So Jeremy Thomas paid a small amount of the money he owed me and that was it. So we parted really rather bitterly. Bernardo and Jeremy recently came to an exhibition of my work at the Serpentine Gallery in London and they embraced and kissed me. They felt a little guilty about the whole thing.

So they should. They employed Ferdinando Scarfiotti instead. I wondered whether the big problem you had was that you weren't Italian, because Bertolucci likes working with Italians.
Yes, he likes to have his court around him. He's a star. In fact, I was also doing an opera at the time and I got a phone call from Bernardo and he was telling me off about something. I can't remember what. And I said, 'I know you're a big star but let me be a little star!'

One doesn't immediately associate your aesthetic with China: Chinese interiors have very elaborate traditional decorations. But The Last Emperor *is set at a transitional time – deco meets traditional . . .*
We went to Manchuria and Harbin, which nobody had been to. It was so primitive. And where the Japanese poison factory was and all that. It was unbelievably primitive but the Palace of Po-Yi was there and we used it in the film. You're very perceptive about this, Christopher, because I could never relate much to Chinese art. So again I tried this stylisation, using the elements that appealed to me and repeating them: the grilles and the circular openings. I was quite happy and certainly Bernardo was very happy.

Some of that appears in the finished movie, though I think it is less stylised. What did you feel when you saw the movie? Did you ever see it?
I did see it. I thought it was an interesting movie . . .

That's a diplomatic answer!
I wasn't too sure about some of the Manchurian stuff because I'd really gone for art deco and that didn't come out too much.

The most memorable moment was when the little boy Emperor comes out on the balcony and there's a huge canopy, and this tiny little child looking bewildered with this vast crowd bowing down before him. Did you design that?
No, I don't think that one . . . but the one in the Forbidden City when he visits the dying dowager empress . . .

Yes?

237

That one I designed, yes.

The Last Emperor is untypical of your career because there have been many unrealised projects but very few that went into production and then the relationships went wrong. I think it may even be the only one. It can't have done your nerves any good.
No, it didn't. I was very upset and I think Jeremy and Bernardo knew that. Maybe I didn't behave very rationally either by packing up everything and coming back here.

One final thing: ten days later Bertolucci writes his very nice letter of apology but already 'by this time it was too late'. Maybe Scarfiotti had been appointed already in those ten days. When I read about this sequence of events, I think maybe it could have been a palace revolution
As I've said, he liked to have his court around him. I knew Nando Scarfiotti very well, but unfortunately he died after that. He was a talented designer but it can't have been easy for him to use my designs. I had all my staff there, in Rome. They told me that Bernardo had copies of my designs bound in a beautiful leather folder.

Agnes of God

After that, maybe because you burnt your fingers on The Last Emperor, the next few projects you get involved in are on a smaller scale, a lot of them adaptations of stage plays. So the challenge for the designer is opening them out rather than creating big spectacles. Whether these projects came your way or whether you selected them, you seem to be pulling in your horns, with a more domestic, small-scale approach to design.
In fact, I think what I did after that was with Bruce Beresford again – we were really close because he also directed a new version of the opera *La Fanciulla del West* in Charleston, South Carolina and Spoleto, Italy. So we had a great personal relationship. And about seven or eight months later I did *Crimes of the Heart*.

Crimes of the Heart was in 1986. Before that you did Agnes of God in 1984–85, directed by Norman Jewison and based on a play set almost entirely in a Montreal convent. There was a challenge for the designer.
Yes, it was a disused school near Toronto. Norman Jewison is Canadian and I knew him for many years when he was over here. I built the cloisters and the bell tower and rebuilt the interiors of the school. It was demanding to use a lot of real locations, adapting locations, building on locations, and building sets at Kleinburg, near Toronto. Some exte-

riors were filmed in Montreal, as was the female psychiatrist's apartment. We were working with Jane Fonda, who I'd worked with years before, and Anne Bancroft, who I hadn't. Anne is a great actress and a lovely human being. And Meg Tilly, who played Sister Agnes, was a charming young actress. It was more like a family picture. It was amazing because there was a great atmosphere on the set. They were all playing nuns and Norman was very shrewd in the way he accentuated that. We had a Jesuit priest as our technical advisor but he knew nothing about Latin Mass and so on, so Letizia became the technical advisor and she got a mention in the end credits. So it was like a family. What was interesting was that after six or seven weeks of shooting everybody in nuns' clothing, the actresses almost believed that they *were* nuns, and we believed it too! We couldn't accept them in modern clothes and there was this strange atmosphere. The liturgical music and the Latin Mass became a part of us all.

It has a very wintry, bleak look, which I suppose had a lot to do with Sven Nykvist, the cinematographer.
You know, the interesting thing is that I had the idea of having the nuns in their habits skating on an ice rink, and so Norman said, 'Why don't you direct it?' So I went with the second unit to direct the sequence and I was up on a tower, sixty foot high. It was freezing cold and I didn't have proper clothes on; I thought I'd get pneumonia. But I wasn't going to get down again from that tower because I was too proud! It was an incredible shot because we made our own ice lake, and by not seeing the confines of the white ice, you just see the nuns skating. It looks surrealistic, like they are skating in space. Of course, when we showed the rushes everybody loved it. I thought it would never be in the picture but I think you'll find Norman used it for the credits. I haven't seen it for years but I know the shot is there.

Ken Adam, the director.
The only time I ever did it.

This was also a time when a lot of movies were relocating to Canada. It was getting difficult to shoot in New York – and expensive to shoot in America – so a lot of productions were being shot in Toronto and Montreal. Montreal often stands in for period New York, or Toronto for modern New York. Norman Jewison very often shot in Canada.
Yes, because he's Canadian and he's considered the greatest Canadian director. He's very conscious of doing things for Canada. It wasn't easy in those days because there were two A teams of Canadian technicians who were all right, but the others had no experience. It was very difficult to get a good team together because they didn't allow American

technicians to work in Canada, except very senior technicians.

Agnes of God has a bleak theme: a novice accused of murdering her baby, a Mother Superior who turns out to be a relation of the novice, an examining psychiatrist who is a divorced lapsed Catholic; it's a dark story. The film has been called a companion piece to Alfred Hitchcock's I Confess, *which is about a priest who hears a murder being confessed but who can't tell anyone because it was in the privilege of the confessional. It was filmed in Quebec. They make a fascinating double bill, both about guilt in enclosed communities.*
Stigmata too.

Meg Tilly gives a convincing performance as Sister Agnes.
Yes, she was wonderful.

What happened to her? She hasn't done much lately. I thought she was terrific.
She had, I think, an unhappy marriage.

It was the performance of her career.
Yes.

Crimes of the Heart

After Zorba, *a musical that was to have been directed by Robert Wise based on the 1964 film* Zorba the Greek *and the Broadway musical of the early 1980s but which never got off the ground, you designed another adapted play,* Crimes of the Heart. *Bruce Beresford was again director, and it was shot on location in North Carolina.*
It was interesting. It was for Dino de Laurentiis, who had built the studios in Wilmington, North Carolina. He brought the chef over from Italy and had the best food, even though we weren't shooting at the studio. I'd found a location, a place called Southport in North Carolina, where the American Civil War had actually started. It was half an hour's drive from Wilmington but we used to drive back for lunch because the food at the studio was so superb! The interesting challenge for me was that for the first time I rebuilt an existing derelict building, with turrets – a mixture of American Queen Anne and Eastlake style – and used it at the same time as an interior. So I did interior *and* exterior; we didn't use any studio at all. It was the first time I'd done that and it worked pretty well. In fact, it got enormous publicity in the *New York Architectural Digest*, all the interiors. Dino De Laurentiis was very much a businessman. He told me to make the bathrooms practical

and all that because then he could sell it on later. He sold it eventually and made more money than I ever spent on adapting it!

Because someone bought the house?
Yes, of course. So that was interesting: to redesign a derelict place as a folly and redesign the interiors at the same time. We shot all the interiors in that building and I designed a completely new staircase with an exposed top landing.

Crimes of the Heart *feels like a play, an adapted play, because it's really a three-hander between Diane Keaton, Jessica Lange and Sissy Spacek. I'm not sure it's a* movie *movie. Were the 'opening out' decisions made by the time the project reached you?*
No. I think Bruce was very much aware of that. We scouted for seven days, or even weeks, all over the Southern states to find interesting locations. We found one of those typical large colonial houses, I seem to remember, and these small townships – which still exist – with the railways going right through the centre of the main street. So we tried to capture that atmosphere.

It was claustrophobic, but I guess that was partly the point.

Conquering Horse

Another fascinating project at this time was the unrealised Conquering Horse *in 1987, a pre-Western about the North American Plains Indians before contact with the white man.*
Yes, it was what we call a feasibility study. I was contacted by Jake Eberts, who ran Goldcrest, and of course by the director, Michael Cimino. Cimino had put everything into this project. I think he'd written the script. It was very interesting, very way out, because the Indians lived in a different world. I mean, if it was a sunny day, they got up in the morning and thought it was a nice day to die. I think Michael got that in the screenplay, or the outline – I can't remember now – and he wanted me to find the most picturesque locations, so I scouted a lot on the other side of Montana and in Canada, which is very similar. I spent time on Indian reservations there; their burial grounds are still untouched. Did I tell you that anecdote about the two Indians? I had an ex-Mounted Policeman as my security guard because it wasn't very safe. At a filling station we saw these two Indians arguing because they wanted to get some gas but they didn't want to pay for it. So I said, 'Let's pay for it and maybe they'll take us onto their reservation.' Which they did. There was a gale blowing and the door of my Jeep was

blown off. I was leaning against the wind trying to take pictures and I fell flat on my face once the gust had passed. The resulting photos were unbelievably dramatic. Anyway, one of these Indians was more educated than the other one and he said my accent wasn't American but certainly not wholly English, so I said I was born in Germany. He said, 'You were brought up on Karl May!' I mean, on an Indian reservation in the sticks of Canada!

I love that! Winnetou the Warrior lives . . . And you also did some research in Germany, did you not?
That was most amazing. I went to Stanford University because they had a Sioux curator there – a woman – and I was trying to get some of the artefacts. Not the beads and the pearls and all that, but the porcupine quills. She brought one moccasin that she had and said, 'It'll be very difficult to find anything in North America, but there's a colleague of mine at the Smithsonian.' So I went to the Smithsonian. I spent four days there and they were fantastic to me. The Sioux curator wasn't very happy about a film being made about Indians because they think they're always portrayed badly. I said that was not the case with this film because it's pre-contact with whites and so on. So then she melted a little bit and said I ought to look at the photographic archives. They had ethnographic pictures dating back to 1845 or something when photography started, and they allowed me to photograph them. I think I took about a thousand shots. These pictures were very fragile but I could take them all out, and of course there were some horrific pictures of the atrocities that were committed against the Indians. Thousands of Indians died. Unfortunately I gave everything to Cimino when I'd finished. In any case, they had no early artefacts either, so I went to New York to see if the museum there had anything. They said, 'You're not going to find it here, but you'll find it in Germany and Switzerland.' So I went to Stuttgart, I think, and Berlin. I didn't go to Switzerland because I found these incredible collections of early Indian art in Germany. I've never seen anything like it. They exhibited some of their treasures, but in back corridors there were enormous cupboards full of thousands of porcupine art works, weapons, clothes, and so on. The curators were delighted because nobody had shown any interest in them before and suddenly here comes a production designer. They couldn't understand that I would spend maybe two days there and that was enough for me to get the feeling, whereas they spent all their lives researching North American Plains Indians. I found out there was a German prince – Maximilian, I think – who, with the help of the American Fur Company, went up the Missouri river in the 1830s and spent four years with the Plains Indians.

I recall he had a painter with him.
A Swiss painter.

Karl Bodmer.
Karl Bodmer, yes. Incredible pictures. He, in four years, collected all that stuff.

And the missionaries too, from Germany. I remember going to the Villa Shatterhand near Dresden, Karl May's house, and he had a vast collection of Apache artefacts that he'd purchased off missionaries who'd returned to Germany from the United States. Pre-contact, pre-small-pox; these cultures were intact when the Germans saw them. And then of course the cultures disintegrated. It is astonishing that Germany should be such a centre for American studies.
Well, because we were all brought up on Karl May, we knew that he'd been in prison and never actually visited these places.

But he still managed to buy these Apache artefacts from returning missionaries. Sadly, Conquering Horse *was never made. Did it become tangled up with* Heaven's Gate?
Yes, without a doubt. And unfortunately Michael Cimino never lived that down.

No, he started to make movies in Europe, for Dino De Laurentiis, I think.
He did one or two small films.

A version of Salvatore Giuliano with Christopher Lambert, called The Sicilian, *a Mafia movie with Joss Ackland in the Marlon Brando part. Terrible! Anyway, they didn't want Cimino to eat lunch in this town again.*

The Deceivers and *Dead Bang*

That same year you worked with Merchant–Ivory on The Deceivers. *Nicholas Meyer, who'd written* The Seven-Per-Cent Solution, *was the director. Largely filmed on location in India: a Raj story set in the nineteenth century.*
I took it as a challenge really because by this time I had the reputation of being one of the most expensive production designers, and so on. Ismail Merchant and James Ivory said it was a low budget and they couldn't afford a lot, so I said, 'Who said anything about affording?' I said, 'I am going to do the picture with three key people.' I used: an Italian art director who'd worked with me on a lot of films, Franco Fuma-

gali; a brilliant Italian prop man; and Giles Masters, the son of Tony Masters, as my personal assistant. They were the only staff I took with me to India, apart from Letizia. Unfortunately my Indian set dresser, a very beautiful girl, had serious domestic problems because her husband had died. I can't remember exactly. We also had a scene in our film which depicted 'sati', the cremation of a widow to join her deceased husband. It's now illegal, but widows are still not treated very well, and there had been a recent case in Rajasthan.

So we were filming a lot for about three months in Jaipur, Rajasthan, which we adored. Letizia really did a lot of the set dressing and also got eighteenth-century materials. She spent all her days in a little village where all fifty members of the same family did nothing but block-printing of textiles, so we got yards and yards of it. And we had to borrow, through Ismail, silver from some of the well-known Indian families. We had no money but it was an enormous adventure. Eventually we went to Madhya Pradesh where they have those famous pornographic sculptures. There are miles and miles of teak jungle with tigers and we found this old abandoned palace right in the middle of it. In fact they found a tigress there who had given birth to cubs and we had to move her on. I had to dress this white, empty palace with literally everything, but the palace was up five hundred steps. To climb up those steps every day was really strenuous. But we loved it.

Letizia in an abandoned palace, while filming *The Deceivers*, Madhya Pradesh

Ismail Merchant wrote an amusing book about the filming of The Deceivers, *called* Hullabaloo in Old Jeypore.

There's a chapter on me and Letizia, which is very complimentary because we all fell in love. But Ismail is a strange character because if he has problems with actors, he starts cooking; he's a wonderful cook! Again, it was a family picture.

In the book, Merchant also praises you for 'understanding instinctively what the film required – I was amazed at how his final concepts reflected, and were so in tune with, the country and its textures and moods'. The star, who played William Savage, was James Bond-to-be: Pierce Brosnan.

Yes, and he wanted to be Bond, even at that time.

Not the most subtle of actors, but he looks suitably dashing.

Yes, very good-looking.

Then in 1988 another Canadian film, directed by John Frankenheimer, called Dead Bang. *With Don Johnson and William Forsythe.*

Yes.

Interiors in warehouses at Calgary: locations in the Rockies.

244

We were based in Calgary. *Dead Bang* was a true story about neo-Nazis in North America, the story of an LA homicide detective, Jerry Beck – I've still got his card. It was interesting to me because I got an insight into the Los Angeles homicide department. I had one frightening experience because they already had computers everywhere and I said to Jerry, 'You can't tell me that you have records of everybody.' And he said, 'Do you want to see *your* record?' I said, 'You mean to say I have one?!' He switched on the computer and then he switched it off again; I never saw what it said! But really, it's Big Brother, all those files. And of course, Frankenheimer was actually a very good action director. It was very tough because we were shooting in the Rockies in the snow, and I had to build a whole camp for these neo-Nazis with swastika flags and anti-Semitic slogans and literature. And I didn't feel very comfortable about that, I must say. But otherwise, it was the sort of picture where we had a lot of laughs.

We were talking about Salon Kitty *earlier and how the Second World War was far enough away from people's memories – assuming most of the cinema audience is between sixteen and twenty-two – to play fast and loose with the imagery of the Nazis. The imagery means something very different to people who lived through the experience.*
I didn't feel uncomfortable with *Salon Kitty*, but I felt very uncomfortable with this neo-Nazi situation on *Dead Bang*. Also because they were really there. I remember, even in the woods surrounding the studio, they had what they called 'war games' every weekend.
Survivalists . . .
Yes.

. . . in the wilderness. People in combat fatigues and long beards: very right wing and very creepy.
Yes, very right wing. Quite frightening.

The Freshman

Immediately after that you designed The Freshman, *directed by Andrew Bergman. I'd read one of Bergman's novels before then – a thriller set in 1930s and '40s Hollywood – but I don't know if he'd ever directed a movie before?*
Maybe one.

He wrote as well as directed The Freshman, *and somehow managed to persuade Marlon Brando to star, which was a hell of a coup for a relatively modest movie. How did that happen?*

I think he and the producer, Mike Lobell, went to some island that Brando owned in the South Pacific.

Near Tahiti.

Yes, not far from there. And they talked Brando into it. I must say, Andy Bergman is a charmer: great sense of humour and highly intelligent. That must have appealed to Marlon. It was a very funny script, with Matthew Broderick starring too.

Broderick plays a naïve film student who finds himself in New York, arrives at Grand Central Station and has his luggage pinched, and then gets enmeshed in this small-time mafiosi world. On one level it's a parody of The Godfather, *with Brando playing at being Brando.*

I was fascinated with Brando; he was a great actor and a great personality too. Very professional. When we were shooting in New York he said, 'I'll be on the set at eight o'clock, but eight hours later I am going, come what may.' An eight-hour day: he insisted on that. But he was always punctual in the morning and eight hours later he left, and there was nothing anybody could do about it. Once we knew that, it worked very well. He was fascinated with props. We shot mainly in Toronto . . .

Including the railway station. I hadn't realised that the designer of Toronto station was the same designer as Grand Central, so you could use Toronto as Grand Central Station.

Yes, it's like a smaller version of Grand Central. The biggest fun I had was with the 'social club', but I didn't realise how dangerous it would be. We sent somebody to Little Italy in New York to take photographs of the social club's exteriors and his camera got smashed because they don't like anybody taking pictures. Then they got one of the bosses – I don't want to mention his name – and I couldn't believe it: this was real life. I had to meet with him in a car on the corner of a street because he wasn't allowed to go into the other part which was not his territory. One of the conditions for his trying to help us was that we would eat in one of his Italian restaurants, which was the worst cooking! We had to suffer bad spaghetti for days!

This was on the recce?

No, this was when we were shooting exteriors in New York. I wasn't allowed into any of the social clubs, but then this boss said I could just take a glance but not take photographs or anything. So I had a look, and that gave me enough atmosphere to do the set in Toronto, which again I designed in false perspective in order to build up Marlon Brando.

You seem to have taken the ceiling down and raised the floor so he seems almost squashed.

That was on purpose.

To parody his overpowering presence. And sometimes filming with an industrial window behind him, which is interesting because usually when you want to build up charisma, you have something solid as background, but you had a window.
Yes, because I wanted him more or less in silhouette you see. And the texture on the walls in that scene was really incredible. We papered the walls, repapered them, then painted them and peeled them off! There's a very amusing moment when Matthew Broderick comes in and he says, 'Isn't that a picture of Mussolini?' And Brando replies, 'It ain't Tony Bennett.' But Brando, like other actors I had come across before, came from the theatre and loved props. One day he asked me to get the prop man to get him some walnuts. We didn't know why he wanted them. Then in the scene with Matthew, in order to intimidate him, Brando takes the nuts and crushes them in his hand.

It wasn't in the script?
No, not at all.

Very sinister. A parody of sinister. Like someone crushing a beer can.
Yes, very sinister. And Marlon had these ideas.

Did he memorise his lines or was he using idiot boards? Because he's famous for reading rather than learning his lines.
No, he had a device – I don't know if I'm allowed to say this – in his ear, which was hardly visible. If you did a close up on his ear you'd probably only just see it. He had a girl sitting off set feeding him lines. You'd never have guessed it.

Apart from Brando's salary, presumably The Freshman *did not have a huge budget.*
No, no.

People say it's a parody of The Godfather, *but visually it's very different. Apart from the lighting, where they went for that Little Italy look . . .*
Who was the cameraman?

William Fraker. He directed one or two films but his forte is cinematography, which he taught. The lighting is very Godfather *at times, but the design isn't at all. It has a* Godfather *atmosphere without really resembling it.*
I went completely way out – talking about art deco – in that restaurant. Do you remember? It wasn't very well shot. We had to build everything because we couldn't find it. We had problems doing a shiny black floor again because the paint didn't dry properly. Brando loved that set and

at the end of the production he asked me – which was very sweet – if I would mind if he gave the end-of-production party in the set. I said, 'Don't ask. Of course I would be flattered.'

It has two huge suspended and angled lights – in the drawings anyway. I don't remember them in the movie . . .
Yes, it's funny, they were there. The whole thing was a parody in any case, with these Komodo dragons, and I thought it would be interesting if the kitchen had the feeling of an operating theatre. So I used two operating-theatre lamps.

With shiny surgical instruments. Because the dragon is an endangered species, one of the only survivors in the world, and this esoteric dining club wants to eat it. There's something macabre about the whole sequence.
The kitchen as an operating theatre. But again, I worked very closely with Andy Bergman because Andy has that Jewish type of humour which is so typical in New York, and we were constantly inventing as we were going along.

So a lot of this wasn't scripted? It came out of production conversations just before shooting?
Yes. 'Don't you think this would be a good idea?' and so on.

This project seems almost the polar opposite of the Bond films, where everything had to be prepared down to the last detail because of the logistics. Whereas The Freshman *is an adventurous but intimate movie. I'm not being disrespectful to Andrew Bergman's directing style, but in some ways it's like an apprentice film; you feel like anything is possible and he's experimenting, some of which works and some of which doesn't. The film feels like that, anyway.*
Yes, you are absolutely right. Andy is now rather bitter because he says you don't get those type of stories any more – those smallish ones.

As Steven Spielberg recently said, you get blockbusters and you get tiny films, but there's no longer any 'middle class' of films. HBO and television have maybe taken over that territory.

Company Business

After The Freshman *you went back to Berlin to make a Cold War thriller,* Company Business.
Yes, a disaster!

Directed by Nicholas Meyer, with interiors at CCC-Film Studios in Berlin, Company Business *was your first return since* Salon Kitty. *It must have been an astonishing time to be there.*
Yes, we started the film in October 1989. We hadn't started shooting yet but I had started preparing the sets at the studio and so on, and suddenly the Berlin Wall came down.

And it's a Cold War spy movie. Problem!
Yes. An ex-CIA man and an ex-KGB man: one was Mikhail Baryshnikov, the other one was Gene Hackman. The story no longer made sense so Nick was going crazy trying to rewrite and at the same time direct the picture. It wasn't a happy picture. Nick had problems with Gene Hackman, so the picture suffered. The story also suffered. Every day we were overtaken by new dramatic developments and in the end the story did not make any sense at all. Frankly, I was not overly concerned about this. What mattered to me most was that I was an eyewitness of the first months of a reunited Berlin.

Did Company Business *get much theatrical distribution?*
Yes. The beginning of the film is quite interesting, but then I think it falls to pieces.

But amazing for you to be back in Berlin as the Wall was coming down.
That was unbelievable.

And revisiting familiar places as the East–West division was breaking down.
Not really, because I had been there before, but it was one of the most dramatic experiences I've ever had, to see the Wall come down. For three miles there were television cameras, rostrums, platforms, caravans . . . Everybody was waiting for that moment, so it was a very dramatic moment. And you could always recognise the people coming from the East because they had received 100 Deutschmark at the crossing and they were all buying things. You could recognise them by their plastic bags which they were proudly showing off. There was euphoria. Today it's changed.

I'll never forget that night, the countdown and this cosmic moment of the end of an ideology, presented as a great historic moment. Then they interviewed this woman coming through and they said to her, 'What's the great advantage of coming to the West?' And she said, 'I can go shopping, at last.' But it made Cold War movies instantly out of date. Bond had the same problem: that everything to do with the Cold War was finito. So they had to look to the Middle East or international terrorism.

That's right. In my time the villain was always German because the Second World War was always fresh, but then they became Russian!

The Doctor

After that unfortunate filmmaking experience on Company Business, *you did an interesting project that, again, wasn't given enough attention:* The Doctor, *on which you worked in the United States from 1990–91.*

With Randa Haines, an extraordinarily talented American female director who had done *Children of a Lesser God*, which was a masterpiece in many ways. And I think the girl got the Oscar, I can't remember. Randa rang me from LA and we had what they call a conference call, which are sometimes the most dangerous things. But on the phone we hit it off because I understood her concept immediately: to make this egocentric surgeon like a sun god, a doctor in a hospital where he operates in the penthouse level and is always in sunlight, but as he gets throat cancer he goes into the bowels of the earth. So that idea appealed to me.

The surgeon gets 'a taste of his own medicine', which was in fact the title of the original book.

That's right.

Literally.

Yes, literally. And it almost destroys his family life. It was for Disney, who wanted me to find actual locations, so I spent four or five weeks looking at hospitals. But hospitals are working hospitals, and the others that were not working were old-fashioned. So I decided to build the whole hospital in an enormous disused warehouse that had just been completed in a place called Valencia, outside Los Angeles. It took me three hours to drive there and back each day, but it paid off. I could give Randa Haines the penthouse look that she wanted. I wanted everything white and shiny, stainless steel and shiny. We had a wonderful Australian cameraman, John Seale, and I asked him if he was worried about reflections, but he said he wasn't and agreed to do it. The camera crew were in white as though they were going skiing in the snow. Everything was white and shiny. That way I could show the change of going into the basement, the radiation room and all that. Randa was fantastic. By building the whole set we gave her enormous freedom, particularly as she wasn't the most experienced director at that time. She could shoot whichever way she wanted to go, and I think the film benefited from it. I had a very close relationship with Randa Haines on this film.

Again, The Doctor *has the feel of a small-ish-scale experimental movie, and you take quite a number of visual risks. The look is heightened in all sorts of ways. And a very gloomy theme again, not easy to handle.*
The operations were brilliantly done. It was the first time I heard them play music while doing a heart transplant.

What was it like to work with Disney? That was a new experience.
Yes. Difficult! Very budget-conscious. But then once they saw the setting, they became happier.

Presumably they had wanted you to shoot in a real hospital to save money, and were scared that you might run up bills.
Yes, but it would have been impossible to do.

You mention the shiny surfaces. The hospital of tomorrow is very inhuman; it feels glacial.
But you see, that was what Randa wanted. We went even further in their private home, which was actually an empty house that I found in Malibu, though not on the beach. It had glass partitions everywhere so that the surgeon – the William Hurt character, Jack MacKee – is always separated when he talks to his family; they were always on either side of the glass partition. Randa wanted that visual separation.

Talking of Malibu, Ken, you moved back to Los Angeles in November 1990, returning to the place where you had lived from 1979 to 1983, but not the same house. This time you rented the upper floor of a Malibu house that had a large deck overlooking the ocean, and you said at the time that living there gave you 'the sensation of living on a ship'. You must have felt there were enough projects happening in Los Angeles, that you were embedded in Hollywood sufficiently, to make this worthwhile . . .
We got a small penthouse apartment that I redesigned. We loved being by the beach – Letizia and I were both brought up by the sea – and Malibu is not Hollywood, you know. I think you'll find I went back to England and did something there . . .

But before that you did Undercover Blues *for Herb Ross,* Addams Family Values *for Barry Sonnenfeld, and then* Boys on the Side, *again for Herb Ross. Only then did you go back to England for* The Madness of King George, *and that was in 1994. So you were based in California for four years.*
Yes.

There was one unrealised project, a Harrison Ford one, which was to have been directed by Harold Becker for Paramount. It was called Night Ride Down, *and it was about the Pullman attendants' strike in the 1930s, which sounds extraordinarily complicated: a period movie on Pullman trains. It didn't come off.*

No. I worked for three months on it and we did some fantastic work designing train carriages of that period, but the difficulty was the cost. Just to get the steam engines going on railway lines was six million dollars, and then I had to build these stations too. We did a lot of location scouting and I did a lot of sketching, but then Paramount decided to pull Harrison Ford out. They never quite licked the ending. But it was a wonderful script.

Was it a comedy or period drama?
A period drama. They had another project for Harrison Ford: a political thriller. So they switched him to that and we were all very disillusioned.

I'm always fascinated when films use period locomotives. Do these collectors on branch lines all over the States steam them up and take them by rail, or do they move them on a flatbed truck?
I think they bring them on a flatbed truck.

I've seen photos of these huge locomotives being craned onto trucks. I presume they take them very slowly to the location.
But you also have to find the right railway line. As I said, it's incredibly expensive. I think that's why Paramount also got cold feet. You see, when you use steam trains, you should go to the East or to China or Russia, because in those countries you still find these incredible locomotives.

Then in 1992 you did another film directed by Herb Ross, Undercover Blues, *starring Kathleen Turner.*
It was a fun film because we shot a lot of it in New Orleans. It was nice to do a film there, but it wasn't a great picture.

Andrew Bergman produced, but he didn't write it. The script was by Ian Abrams. Herb Ross and Andrew Bergman were executive producers, and the production company was Lobell/Bergman.
Oh yes, that's right.

Addams Family Values

Also in 1992, Addams Family Values – Addams with two 'd's, based on the New Yorker cartoons by Charles Addams. An extraordinary piece of design because I guess over 90 per cent of it was shot in the studio. Very little was shot on location, although I gather you did find an interior of a house, so I've been trying to spot which bit of the movie is actually filmed in a real interior . . .

Oh yes, there was a house. It had to be kitsch supreme but luxurious, and the amazing thing was that I found it. The owners were so happy that it was going to be used that I briefed the crew to say it was the most beautiful house, because that was why they'd given it to us. The truth is, it was the most vile interior you can imagine! And it was just right for Fester.

Uncle Fester and the Nanny, played by Joan Cusack.

The whole picture was an enormous challenge for me because, as usual, Paramount called me to do the picture eight weeks before shooting and

Design of the Addams Family Mansion, Paramount 1992

it was, as you say, 95 per cent studio. So we had to find an art department big enough and capable enough to design the picture and build the settings in eight weeks. When I complained to the producers they said, 'Well why do you think we got you to do it?' So I had a big problem getting an art department, which today is much more difficult. Thirty years ago the studios had big art departments where you could get the best people, but nowadays they don't exist, so you have to assemble a team. Also I decided, because I was so attracted to the Charles Addams cartoons of the *New Yorker*, what I'd try to do was to translate his cartoons into actual three-dimensional settings. Which meant false perspective, true perspective, no straight walls. I felt a great affinity with the cartoons, perhaps because of their morbid sense of humour or their distorted perspectives, so I decided to bring them to life. Fortunately I had two or three very good people helping me. I had a young kid, the son of a production designer/art director, who was just starting out. Somebody told me he was very good at making very quick cardboard art department models. Since nothing in my sketches was straight – either the floor sloped up or the walls leaned in or something – it was very useful to have this eighteen-year-old standing almost behind me when I did the sketch and then building three-dimensional models for me with enormous speed. I could immediately see where things were distorted and that's why it had that character. It was so important because I didn't have enough stages at Paramount; I had to use Warner Brothers and Studio City. We were working hard to get all this stuff ready in eight weeks.

Is it true that when you went to see Barry Sonnenfeld in Los Angeles you found that the script had been radically altered, which was a disaster because you'd accepted on certain presuppositions?
Yes, I'd accepted it and they'd altered it.

Had they made it more complex?
I can't remember. They called me from London – I arrived in Los Angeles pretty tired – and I had to read the script by the following morning. I said, 'Give me a break.' But I read the script and I found it wasn't the same. So I rang up Barry Sonnenfeld, who was living in Santa Monica at the time, and I said, 'This is not the same.' He agreed that everything I was saying was true, but why didn't I talk with Scott Rudin? Scott Rudin was the most successful producer in the States at that time – he still is today – and he said I had to fly to New York. I'd just come from London, but the next day I was on my way back to New York. Scott was staying at a hotel in the city and we met for two days, and I must say, he was wonderful. He was very receptive. Sometimes I was right

and other times I was not right, but the script was altered. They changed a lot of things that I didn't like. And when I came back to LA, Barry was very happy because he had more or less agreed with me on everything.

It differs from the first Addams Family *film quite a lot. That was designed by Richard MacDonald, but your designs seem closer to the cartoons – only in three dimensions. My favourite set is the exterior of the family house with the cemetery in the garden; it's like the drawing has come to life. The gingerbread-Gothic house with its family vault. Whereas the first movie doesn't really have this cartoon quality. Was that a conscious decision – not to make it look like the first movie?*
Yes, I said I would only do it if it's not like a sequel. Richard MacDonald was a great friend of mine and I respected and admired him as a designer – he was a very good designer – but I felt that I wanted to get more Addams into it.

Again it has this monochrome feel, rather like the sweet factory in Chitty Chitty Bang Bang *and Lloyd's in* Around the World in Eighty Days. *There are splashes of colour like when they go to the summer camp and they act out the Pocahontas story. But generally it is like a black-and-white cartoon. Were you pleased with the result? You got an Academy Award nomination.*
I was very pleased.

It must have been the fastest time you'd ever prepared designs for a nomination.
Yes, but I lost it to the Spielberg picture, *Schindler's List.*

You said at the time: 'It was a fantastic undertaking only to be compared with some of the Bonds.' Was that because you were using so many sound stages simultaneously?
Yes, logistically it was a nightmare. Fortunately I had a fantastic construction crew. We had a short shooting schedule too which meant all the sets had to be ready at the same time, at Paramount, Warners and Studio City.

I think it is also the biggest-budget movie that you worked on at this time. If you compare it with The Doctor *and* The Freshman *and* The Madness of King George, *which are medium-budget movies,* Addams Family Values *had a blockbuster budget with the pressures and tensions that come with that. It can't have been an easy ride. It must have been very pressurised.*
Very pressurised, yes. The only fun or bit of relief we had was when we shot in the mountains for the camp.

255

And at last you got a chance to make a Red Indian movie! Pocahontas in the forest with this terrible child who never smiles . . .
Christina Ricci has become a big star now.

It's a wonderful moment when at last she smiles, because she has caused mayhem!

Boys, Bogus and Dr James Barry

Then, in 1994, Boys on the Side, *directed by Herb Ross and starring Whoopi Goldberg and Mary Louise Parker.*
I'm trying to think who the writer was.

Don Roos.
Oh yes. *Boys on the Side* was one of Herb's better films and it was fun working with Whoopi Goldberg. She was delightful. The film was really about the relationship between these three women, one of whom was dying of cancer, if I remember rightly. Design-wise it was nice. We were in Arizona for a lot of the time.

That's right, in Tucson, Arizona. Interiors at Studio City.
We had a few disasters because I remember being in Arizona when the fires and the earthquakes hit Malibu and LA, and I was worried because Letizia was by herself and she can't drive. So I was scouting locations and I rang Letizia – Herb had a mobile phone or whatever was the equivalent – and she said they may have to evacuate the place. I was really upset. But that's the wonderful thing about Malibu. It's like England or London during the Battle of Britain: everybody is very friendly. Some neighbours were already wetting down the roof of the house because these fires are the most frightening things in the world. They can travel at eighty miles an hour. Once it's spread across the Pacific Highway that's pretty much it. So I talked to Letizia all through the night, advising her what to do, ringing other people up to see that she had a car to get away from this place. But she could have only gone into the sea because both sides of the road were blocked. The earthquake destroyed – not completely, but damaged a lot of – the stages at Studio City, and again I must say in those sort of things I really take off my hat to the Americans because within a week they had everything repaired. Even the main bridge over the PCH to Malibu had collapsed and they were going to repair it – these were big bridges – in two months, but they actually did it in just over four weeks, working day and night. So I was frightened because I was in Arizona and Letizia was by herself in Malibu. We got a private plane to Santa Monica, and nor-

mally it takes me twenty minutes, sometimes quarter of a hour, to get from Santa Monica to Malibu. But it took me four and a half hours! The traffic jams were unbelievable and all the roads were kept open for the fire engines. These were some of the problems we had to cope with. But *Boys on the Side* was a nice picture. I loved Whoopi.

That was the first of two projects where you worked with her.
Yes. The next one I did with her, *Bogus*, was almost a disaster from the start.

Another Canadian film, produced and directed by Norman Jewison.
Yes. Norman is a wonderful director and he was working with a very famous writer, Alvin Sargent. But the part that Whoopi was eventually cast in was supposed to be played by a man! It was a story about this little boy who grows up in the show business of Las Vegas. I think his mother dies so he then has to stay with his uncle in New York. Then somehow – I don't know whether it was the actor or something else that didn't work – they decided to cast Whoopi; not only a woman, but a black woman. The story became completely different so Sargent and Norman were working day and night to lick the script, but I don't think they ever did. Norman was so concerned about the sort of picture he was making – whether it was for an adult audience or for children. Of course, we were all affected by that. You can't work properly that way. I made Norman look at the Cirque du Soleil, who were in Vegas at the time. We were so impressed by their imagination and the things they did. We had a dream sequence in the film and Norman wanted the Cirque du Soleil to do it and they were very keen. But there were the usual problems: the man who was responsible wanted to get a direc-tor's credit. They had a French-Canadian girl who was brilliant at dreaming up these grotesque costumes, so we used her. To cut a long story short, we shot for two weeks with the Cirque du Soleil in an old steel mill in Toronto, but in the end Norman cut it out, although I think there's a little bit over the credits. It was the dream sequence of the kid looking for his mother.

Some locations in New York City, but mainly in Toronto.
Yes.

Then, in 1996, following an unrealised project, you turned down The English Patient. *Anthony Minghella had asked you to design it. What went wrong there?*
Well, I liked Anthony Minghella and I think he liked me. He came here three times. I met him the first time when I was doing *The Doctor*, because he was a friend of Randa Haines, and he'd just done *Truly,*

Madly, Deeply. We discussed the concepts for *The English Patient* and had many good discussions about it but then – and I don't know if you can quote me – but I got a call from my agent in Hollywood, Larry Mirisch. He said that they had problems financing the film and that apparently John Seale, the cameraman, had agreed to work for half his fee because he had been told that I agreed to do the same, which I hadn't. It was not true. To commit to the film under those circumstances was not for me. I didn't approve of being used like that.

At your age, and with your status in the industry, you don't need that.
No, at my age one has to think carefully about which films one should be involved in.

It would have been an interesting project, with the variety of locations and sets, though they didn't have much money to play with.
No. Anthony was very upset and so was I. He said everybody on the crew was prepared to work for less, and if the picture became a success then they would all get their money. I said, 'Anthony, I adore you. But please, I think it's a very important picture, but I don't like to start a picture that way.' As far as I was concerned, it wasn't honest.

Did you see the movie?
Yes.

What did you think?
Well, I think parts of it were . . .

You're so diplomatic! The design doesn't stand out as particularly interesting.
No.

It's about performance.
It's also a bit of a tear jerker. I remember now: I thought the original Minghella script dealt with the past of the characters, whereas they lost that completely in the film. They were a group of people who, before the Second World War, were exploring the Sahara and so on. They had enormously close relationships. There were Germans and Italians and Brits. That relationship, if I remember rightly, was lost.

The back-story.
Yes, the back-story, which was crucial.

Then the unrealised film Dr James Barry, *which you worked on in 1995–96 with director Martha Coolidge. It's the true story of a woman posing as a man in the nineteenth-century British Army. You went to South Africa because the woman became the chief medical officer in*

South Africa.
I went two or three times.

What happened?
I don't know. It was in the hands of the producer, Aaron Spelling, and basically it was a big budget picture. I had come up with a very interesting concept, obviously using a certain amount of CGI. In fact, I wanted to use as little as possible because I came across all the problems that the CGI boys had with the ships. But I went to the island where Nelson Mandela was kept prisoner, Robben Island, and I found a deserted beach there that I wanted to use for the first landing of Dr James Barry in Cape Town, with the Table Mountain in the background, getting rid of the modern buildings. Do you know the story?

Yes. Holly Hunter was going to be James Barry, wasn't she? What was the particular take on the story?
Well, it was very strange because there are several biographies on her – on him – and if you go to the Castle Museum in Cape Town there are portraits of him. Nobody quite knows whose child she was, but she was well born, as they say, and some people even thought she was the daughter of the Prince Regent. She was brought up by a South America adventurer, a famous man who had the biggest library in London in those days. She was very interested in anatomy, but at the beginning of the nineteenth century it was impossible for a girl to study medicine. So he brought her up as a boy and taught her riding, shooting, fencing . . . All those manly arts. That's all factual. She was then admitted to Edinburgh University as a man, got a degree, and became assistant to one of the most famous surgeons of the time. Then she joined the British Army. How she got past the various inspections, I don't know. She must have had an accomplice high up who knew and protected her. She went to Cape Town after three months on a boat and became a protégé of Lord Somerset. You have to remember that the Governor of the Cape was like a king in his own right; an absolute power. But Barry was a very strong personality and she went over people superior to her. She hated the prison system, the corruption. She fought everybody and got away with it. She also cured Somerset's daughter. Whether Lord Somerset knew that she was a woman and kept shtum about it I don't know. She had a really fascinating life. In fact, when Napoleon was a prisoner of us on St Helena, Somerset sent for Barry to cure Napoleon. But by the time she arrived, he was dead. She also later met Florence Nightingale in the Crimea and they didn't get along at all. And she fought a duel in South Africa – which was very funny, because it shows the feminine side of her – with one of Somerset's aides, because she was

jealous of some woman he was involved with. She fought him because she felt he was insulting the Governor. Then eventually she got posted to the West Indies and continued to rise in rank. She was a very powerful personality and did an enormous amount of good work. I think she died in the 1870s as an old man/lady in relative poverty. At her postmortem they discovered that not only was she a woman but she'd also been pregnant and given birth, although they never established where the child was born. At one time she was posted to Mauritius and some of the biographies said that she may have had the child there. But who the child was, nobody knows.

A story with a lot of potential.
How she got away with it! She bound up her breasts and so on. And of course, when the press found out she was a woman – a general, the most senior medical officer in the Army, and in the Household Cavalry – people came up and claimed they knew she wasn't a man because she never shaved, and things like that. She became very ill in the West Indies where she nearly died, and she had two medical officers looking after her. In one of the biographies they said that she swore them to secrecy.

I'm amazed Holly Hunter was tall enough for the role, actually.
But neither was Barry.

What stopped the project?
Nobody knows. We thought we were in business. I had a great relationship with Martha Coolidge; when I got my Lifetime Achievement Award, she gave the speech. We had the cameraman, we had the final location scout with the production boys, the big boys, wanting to know the budget and so on. I took one of my assistants. We had it all mapped out, but they just didn't find the money.

Or scripting problems?
But the scripting problems were only at the end. Of course, for the American market they introduced a type of love relationship with an American adventurer who was in South Africa at the time. But it should have been made. I think somebody made a television programme about it in this country.

The theme of masquerade, or gender-bending, is a timely one.
Apparently there were no lesbian tendencies there at all. She danced beautifully as a man and she was a great sportsman or woman, riding and shooting and having a duel with guns.

Intriguing.
It is something that should be done.

In and Out

In 1996–97 – I don't know which order these came in – you did In and
Out, *which I enjoyed very much, and also* Wozzeck, *the opera by Alban
Berg.*
I didn't do the opera, but I did some sketches for it.

Was that before or after In and Out?
Before, with Billy Friedkin. He was going to direct it at the Maggio
Fiorentino in Florence, and I think he eventually did.

You did some preliminary work?
Yes, he was quite excited about it. And then somehow it didn't happen.
I've seen the sketches reproduced. They are very expressionistic – Cali-
gari-*like.*
Yes, I've still got them.

It's a pity your designs were never realised.
Then I was busy with *In and Out*. It was Scott Rudin again. He called
me in LA and I came to New York. It was a wonderful script, starring
Kevin Klein.

Paul Rudnick was the scriptwriter and Frank Oz the director.
Yes. It was a very amusing script and remember I was getting to the
stage where I was more interested in a good story or a good script. People saw *In and Out* and said, 'Well what was the challenge in that?' But
there was an enormous challenge that I didn't realise at the time I wanted to work on the film. When I arrived in New York I found out that
neither Scott Rudin nor Frank Oz nor Kevin Klein wanted to leave New
York, and that's the sort of thing that's happening today in the United
States: people like to stay with their family. So they said I had to do it
all in New York. But this was a story that was set entirely in the Midwest somewhere. In fact, Frank Oz and I took a plane to the Midwest
and he said, 'Nobody's going to shoot there. You've got to do it in New
York.' So I spent most of my time driving round the state of New York,
New Jersey, Connecticut, everywhere – it was like a jigsaw puzzle. I
found a church somewhere on the east coast with the sea on one side,
which we couldn't see. And I found the interior of the church somewhere else, New Jersey or somewhere. There's also a little scene in Viet-
nam that I shot in the Bronx in New York City. So it was interesting to
do this film using bits and pieces.

*It's an idyllic Midwest community, like a Frank Capra or Andy Hardy
kind of small-town community. And that's the whole fun of it because*

you have this very conventional tight-knit group and suddenly the schoolteacher comes out. A gentle comedy of small-town America.

And we never used a small town! It was a combination of several places. And then I had to recreate the Academy Awards – which was quite a lot of fun – because the Matt Dillon character won the Oscar. For the exterior of the Oscars I used the Lincoln Center and dressed it all up with the crowds around it. For the interior I found a college outside New York which had a big theatre, and I did a big Oscar setting. Glenn Close presented the Oscar and Scott loved the design I did for it. He was an amazing producer – difficult but amazing – and with a designer like me they never accept something that is maybe realistic but not special. But you can't always be special on a subject which is realistic, you know. But with the Oscars I could use imagination.

There's an amusing reference to Spartacus *in* In and Out, *when the schoolteacher comes out at a parent–teachers meeting and everybody stands up and says, 'I am gay.' Just like 'I am Spartacus.' And there's a very touching couple played by Debbie Reynolds and Wilford Brimley. But what a strange thing to do: piecing together Frank Capra-land from locations around the metropolitan New York area.*

Kevin didn't want to leave, Frank Oz was living in Connecticut and he didn't want to go, Scott certainly didn't want to go: it had to be New York.

Very often when we talk about your film projects you refer to the producers approaching you, rather than the director or the writer, as if the initial contact is always with the producer.

Well, Scott Rudin is a very important producer. I think he is one of the most creative producers in Hollywood. He is also very much involved in theatre. He's had several productions on Broadway. But I also met the writer, who I got on with, Paul Rudnick, who had a great sense of humour. And Frank Oz, who was maybe a little worried about a designer of my reputation. But I won him over. To me, the one who called the shots was Scott. Scott was so much involved with that picture that he was on the set every day and he was doing three or four other projects at the same time.

And you often talk with affection about these hard-nosed but creative, larger-than-life Hollywood characters. Obviously you're attracted to them. Even if they are difficult, you enjoy their company. Cubby Broccoli, I guess . . .

They're different because Scott is highly intelligent. He is also in many ways very insecure. You know, there are people who hate him in America, but Paramount never looked back since he's been producing for them. That's what got me into trouble with the next one.

That's The Out-of-Towners, *with Robert Evans as producer. You mentioned this earlier as 'a very unfortunate experience'.*

What happened was that Scott, again, called me. By this time I was back in London and he called me over to do *The Out-of-Towners.* He had a young director attached to it whose name escapes me, before Sam Weisman, and we got on like a house on fire. We were working at Paramount, and by this time Scott was getting bigger and bigger. He was doing a John Travolta picture somewhere else and so on. Goldie Hawn's company was involved too and this young director, who had a young crew of writers with him, said, 'You have to understand one thing. I know how to do these sort of comedies, but the way the script is at the moment, it doesn't work.' So he was working on rewrites. Then one day when I arrived at the studios he told me that he was off the picture. Scott had also left the film because he was too busy on other projects. I rang my agent, Larry Mirisch, for his advice, and was told that I should carry on with the film to safeguard my good relations with Paramount. So I was left holding the baby. As I said, they brought in this new director from television, Sam Weisman, who was very much under Goldie Hawn's influence, and we didn't see eye to eye. Some of my most important sets – a very pretty penthouse, the whole hotel where Scott used to stay in New York – were never properly exploited. It was not a happy experience. The remake of a successful comedy is always risky, especially if you leave the decisions to the main comedy actors, and I don't think it worked.

The original version, when the Neil Simon screenplay was fresh, was delightful. This one wasn't. Your last experience of new Hollywood – and star power – was not a happy one.

No.

9 Back to Berlin

Berlin Millennium Exhibition

In April 1998 you were approached by the curator of the Martin-Gropius Bau in Berlin . . .

Yes, Gereon Sievernich came to Los Angeles from out of nowhere and asked me if I would be interested in designing the core of the Millennium Exhibition there. I liked him – the question was charmingly put – and I thought, well, I'd never done this sort of thing before. It seemed exciting and a new experience, and I was really unhappy at that time. It was a change from film design. Also, I had the feeling it was a kind of honour to be asked. Letizia says that in forty-eight hours I had more or less designed the main concept of it, and the next time that Sievernich came to visit me – on behalf of the Berliner Festspiele – I presented my designs and he never altered them very much. They were influenced in some ways by my experiences on Bond and the War Room in *Dr Strangelove*. I was quite prepared for the organisers to consider them too ambitious, but Sievernich just said, 'We can do it.' It was exactly what Ron Udell, the construction manager at Pinewood, had always said, and it was exactly what I wanted to hear.

Unlike the Millennium Dome here in Greenwich, this had a theme and a subtitle: 'Seven Hills – images and signs of the twenty-first century'. A celebration of science, technology and invention . . .
Yes, of which I knew nothing!

From the photos that I've seen, the centrepiece of the glassed-over inner court of the Martin-Gropius building was to be a huge translucent globe of the Earth.
Absolutely. First of all, my problem was how to get the public interested; they probably know a great deal more about science and DNA than I do.

Because there's a twenty-metre-high double helix in stainless steel as well.
Yes, and there were neutrons and so on. So I decided I would treat it like I would design a film set, by accentuating certain aspects, like the neutrons and the DNA. They had two enormous antique globes about five metres in diameter in mind, and they were hoping to get them from the French government and bring them to Berlin. I didn't think they were right. What I wanted – and I don't think, to my knowledge, this has ever been done before – was to shoot the inside of the Earth. I did

a little bit of research and of course my curators were all scientists. I said, 'I would like to shoot the centre of the Earth as the biggest light source and then show the magma canals going to the surface of the Earth and the various volcanoes.' It was quite a problem because, if you think about it, you first of all have to create the various layers of the Earth. It's not like cutting an orange. The centre of the Earth had to be a sphere maybe six foot diameter and then another sphere and another sphere and another sphere over that. The globe was, I think, twenty foot in diameter. So we had to come up with a way of constructing these spheres. Then the centre of the Earth had to be the strongest light source, but we didn't want to burn everything around it! We did the magma canals with fibre-optics and I found some company in Berlin who had three people working on it.

It was huge.
Yes.

Could you walk through the structure? Or was it above you?
No, you couldn't walk through it, but you could walk around it. It had a diameter of about twenty feet and it was only supported on two struts and it rotated. The Earth rotates at twenty-four hours, but I did this one to rotate at one-eighth – three hours or a little less – so you could see it rotate very slowly, to give the audience an idea of the various continents. So that was my main design. Then I came up with this DNA structure, the double helix, which I thought would be interesting to do like a sculpture: sixty feet high in stainless steel. And believe me, that was also difficult, because you start off with metal tubes with a diameter of eighteen inches, and then these tubes had to wind up and be reduced to practically nothing. I found a young sculptor or blacksmith, who had some derelict place outside Berlin where he used to weld things together, and he did it for me. In fact, I think it's the only piece that's still exhibited somewhere because it's a beautiful sculpture and it is indeed about sixty foot high. Israel wanted the whole exhibition but they couldn't get the right venue. It was an unbelievably successful exhibition and I'll tell you what I think the secret was: the public saw these six or seven very important, exaggerated scientific things and it attracted them so they wanted to see more. And then Dr Beck, a curator who was in charge of that part of the exhibition, provided the brain of Descartes so the public could walk around and look at it and other objects. It was a homage to his 'Cogito, ergo sum.'

Historical references as well?
Yes, historical things.

Final concept drawing for the Millennium Exhibition, Martin Gropius Building, Berlin 2000

Photo by Ken Adam of the Millennium Exhibition from reverse angle

The globe – incorporating smaller spheres – and the DNA: were they your main contributions?

Well, there was also a simulated brain that a professor in Eastern Germany, Ernst Haeckel, had programmed to project thoughts. I never knew how it worked – it was all done on computers – but it was very effective and people knew what it was, even if I didn't! I designed a skull-like projection screen for it. The neurons and neutrons: one doesn't realise what is happening in this world unless you are in science. Then there was also the biggest particle accelerator in Switzerland. As my steelwork went up I thought to put this gigantic accelerator high up on one side, like a Gothic rosette.

Like a rose window?
Yes. Again, somebody else built it for me.

Apparently the overall shape of the exhibit was originally designed to look like a pyramid, but you decided to change the concept to a cathedral structure with giant sloping walls.
Yes, also remember that you have the inner court of the Gropius Bau – constructed in 1881 – which is seventy feet high and rather beautiful. And I wanted to optically increase the height of the court while preserving the look of the Victorian architecture. I didn't want to mask the court and lose the architecture.

You wanted visitors to see the existing architecture?
Yes, and so I came up with this steel structure. We had problems, as you can imagine, with a steel structure seventy feet high. How to transport all that stuff and so on. Gereon Sievernich and his very nice architect were very optimistic all the time, but I couldn't see how they would finish it. I spent the last six weeks in Berlin supervising everything myself, pushing like I would do on a film. Then, two weeks before the opening, I got cold feet and asked Julia to come over because she had experience.

Julia Peyton-Jones, Director of the Serpentine Gallery?
Yes, and she came over and it was awful! Nowhere near finished. I said, 'We have another ten days.' She said, 'And you say the President of Germany and the Mayor of Berlin are going to come?' 'Yes,' I said, 'but if they come it's going to be ready!' And it *was* ready. I was terrified because I treated it like a film set but then came up against all the building by-laws, which you would know about, but I certainly didn't.

Of course: planning restrictions.
I had a glass lift going up and down as a viewing platform for visitors and the relevant authorities came and said I couldn't have this and that. Then they wanted me not to do the structure in steel, and I said, 'But come on!' They said steel would melt in a fire – all these sorts of things.

It's amazing that you'd got through your entire professional life up till then without planning permission, and suddenly you're confronting it!
Yes! And I had designed this ring – a gangway – around the globe so that people could look at it close up, but it only had two supports and

a gigantic staircase going up to it. Then these engineers came in and asked me to strengthen it. So it was designed for about sixty or seventy people up there. But at the opening there were about three thousand people, and on the ring itself, people were packed like sardines. I was dying! If something had happened, I'd have ended up in jail – at my advanced age! But fortunately it all stood up.

It must have been solidly built.
It was very solidly built.

It's interesting because simultaneously I was working on the Millennium Dome in Greenwich – as you know: we met a lot at this time – where they had an amazing external structure but a lot of confusion about the interior, whereas with the Martin-Gropius Bau you had a great existing building and a strong idea about what would go inside it. It was the wrong way round with the Millennium Dome; there wasn't a narrative.
I am surprised in a way. You are asked to design the most gigantic dome ever and you don't know what goes on inside it? In architecture the one thing we've always learnt – perhaps it is out of date by now – is that when you design something, you know the function.

Form follows function.
Yes.

The original idea, which survived to some extent, was that there would be three main 'zones': the mind, the body and the spirit. I was overseeing 'the spirit zone', which at a late stage became 'the faith zone'.
So that's religions.

Yes, all the different faith communities. Where 'the mind zone' was concerned, in Berlin you had the open skull of the philosopher René Descartes, whereas in London we had at the heart of the zone a small brain wearing a fez and doing Tommy Cooper jokes! If that was thought to be the summit of civilisation, then we really are in trouble!
I think it was something that wasn't properly thought through.

The Frankfurter Allgemeine Zeitung, *16 May 2000, wrote that you transformed the central hall of the building 'into a futuristic cathedral of knowledge . . . Ken Adam the movie iconographer has made Earth the fiery lodestar of an imaginary postmodern cult. Standing at the bottom of the steps to this purloined altar to the Sun God, one feels something of the show's hidden religious core.' And the article was headed 'Sacrifice to the Gods of a New Religion' – the religion of science, technology and its wonders. So you certainly had a big theme. And you mentioned the Berlin curator, or co-curator: there was a single ringmaster. But there wasn't a ringmaster at the Dome when I came along, just a huge committee that spawned sub-committees and so on. If you don't have a ringmaster, it is like a film without a director.*

It rarely works. The reason why the new PotsdamerPlatz in Berlin was not really revolutionary, with some of the greatest architects from all over the world, was because the city of Berlin had a committee which was controlling the architects. It's not the best way. I remember the PotsdamerPlatz as a child, and I don't like the new one. There are one or two buildings of good design, but I think it is so impersonal and cold. I wouldn't want to live there!

Taking Sides

Just after you'd completed the Millennium Exhibition in Berlin, you started scouting locations there for Taking Sides, *a film about the conductor Wilhelm Furtwängler, to be directed by István Szabó from the play written by Ronald Harwood. It was set just after the last days of the Third Reich, which must have been particularly poignant for you, given the fact that in those days the Martin-Gropius building had been right next door to the Gestapo headquarters. How did* Taking Sides *come about?*

Well, the man who ran the Babelsberg studio was called Rainer Shaper, an ex-production designer himself. He had seen the Millennium Exhibition and so Rainer rang me up and said would I be interested in meeting with the director?

Had you seen Mephisto *and* Colonel Redl?

Yes. István Szabó is very talented, but very surreal. So I met with them in Potsdam-Babelsberg. I loved the script and had seen the play here, and I was friends with Ronald Harwood, so I said, 'It's a film I would like to do.' István is a very good director, Harvey Keitel is a wonderful actor, and Stellan Skarsgord too, and they were delighted because they'd got one of the old timers like me to work at the studio. Have you seen the studio?

No.

It's gigantic; a relic from the East. So they were delighted to have me design this picture, and I really enjoyed it. It was interesting because some of the people from the East were still working there. In the East, they had been getting the same amount of money whether they were an art director, a carpenter or electrician. They were very good craftsmen, but very set and rigid in their ideas. And do you know one thing when I am designing a film, it's got to be my way and not the way that some painter tells me. So I had several run-ins, which was good for the studio. So I had the plus side of getting some very good craftsmen and the negative in that I had to fight them all. Also, although much had been modernised, the stages – dating from the 1920s – had not yet been updated and were not properly soundproofed.

I visited Dresden art academy around this time.
We shot in Dresden.

There was a theatre design department dating from the old East German days and their craft skills were astonishing. But in month one they did baroque, in month two they did Gothic, month three was expressionist . . . They had all the vocabulary, but it was very formulaic and dull. I was wondering what these people would be like to work with because they were brilliant technically but they were not encouraged to be imaginative or flexible. They were learning the grammar of theatre design.
Yes. But what they did – which really impressed me, and I said so – was the thing that we have forgotten in this country and in France and in Hollywood too; that is, for the craftsmen to train young people to learn their craft from them.

A couple of years ago I went to Madam Tussaud's, the sculpture department, and most of the sculptors seemed to be from Eastern Europe. All these youngsters who could do brilliant figurative sculpture in wax.
To me, the plaster shop was a revelation. There were these girls of twenty, twenty-one, and young men too, all working brilliantly and learning their craft. But we never have that here. We had it years ago but we haven't got it any more. We've let it go.

Taking Sides *is the story of the conductor, Furtwängler, and the great conundrum of which side he was on during the Nazi period. Harvey Keitel plays a de-Nazification officer from the American Army and in a way it's a two-hander. But there are some tour-de-force settings. One of them is the wreckage of Berlin, a sequence where they walk through the street market and there are ruins everywhere, including the ruined Reichstag building. You can see the wreckage through the windows of the interrogation room. It's almost in monochrome.*
That was deliberate. They had these people who can now print out photographic backdrops of the ruins on gigantic rollers. But the moment they added colour, it didn't look right. So Lajos Koltai, the cameraman, wanted it treated as much as possible in black and white-because he could control it then.

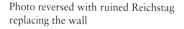

Graffiti wall next to bare wall in Berlin, with Letizia

Photo reversed with ruined Reichstag replacing the wall

So it's foreground in three dimensions, and the background as a back-drop?
Yes.

Reconstructing the devastation must have been like working on your autobiography.
Yes. Mind you, I had seen the city in 1945. I was in Berlin unofficially because my Wing Commander had said, 'I know you want to go there.' It was very dangerous: just a few months after Berlin had been conquered. He said I could take a Jeep. I spent two or three days there and I had a lot of very dangerous experiences actually, but it was fascinating. I also had an accident. I was hit by a Russian truck on the auto-

271

Sketch for interior of interrogator's office, Babelsberg 2000

bahn and the Commander of the Russian convoy and myself tried to understand each other. The roads were iced over and one of their trucks had lost control, gone over the centre divide, and hit me in my Jeep. Everything was all right until I asked the Commander to just give me a little bit of paper to confirm what had happened. Then he got very nasty and disappeared. So I was stuck in a snowstorm with a broken Jeep on the autobahn and there was nobody there because it was no-man's land. There were Russian deserters in the surrounding woods, and after about an hour the first lot of deserters came out with big smiles. I had jerry cans in the back and they wanted to get them. I put

up a brave face and they disappeared into the woods, but I thought it was ridiculous; if they came again, they were all armed. So I'd already made up my mind that I was going to abandon the Jeep, walk into the woods, go to the first German house I could find, get civilian clothes, and become a German. Fortunately a British Military Police patrol then came past. At first they wouldn't stop because I looked like a gangster. You remember how fighter pilots used to dress with the scarf and the black flying boots? I looked terrible. They weren't sure whether I was a British officer or what I was, so they stopped about two hundred yards down the road and I ran towards them. They wired base or somewhere and got a breakdown truck to load up the Jeep. In fact, they took me and the Jeep to Gatow, a British airbase in Berlin at the time, and I knew some of the air fitters there so they pinched bits from other Jeeps. In about three days they had my Jeep going again.

What an amazing story. All the more reason to identify with the ruins of Berlin.
Yes, it was funny because the few ruins left in Berlin nowadays are all

On the balcony of the office set, with backdrop of Berlin ruins

hippy places with graffiti everywhere, and when I went on a scout trying to find them I found a big empty space. I took Letizia and my driver and started taking pictures because I'd seen an incredible picture of the Reichstag as it was in 1945 in a book published by Nicolai. Then I asked the CGI boys working at the studio, 'Why can't we put the Reichstag from the book behind Letizia and the driver?' Because I had to convince István, who had very little studio experience and no CGI experience at all, that we could shoot a scene in front of the Reichstag, and that sold him eventually. István is a director who has to see things in front of him. Then the CGI people let me down because all these computer-generated images are done after principal photography. They're not going to pay a production designer to stick around while they do it. So all the preparation is done beforehand. You talk to these CGI people and leave it to them. Well, two months later I got a phone call from István, who was editing the film in Paris, saying that the tram going through the ruins, which was also CGI, they couldn't use. Nor

274

could they use the Reichstag. I said, 'I'd better fly to Berlin.' So I did. And we had the most incredible 16mm footage that George Stevens had shot in 1945. It was a moving shot through the ruins of Berlin, in colour. But the CGI boys said they couldn't use it because if you blow it up to 35mm it requires so much work that it's easier to build a computer model of it. I said, 'Well, you're the experts.' But they didn't use the George Stevens footage, and they did their own computer model and it looked terrible. I had to do three or four trips back to Berlin. I could see what was wrong, being a designer, and on a piece of paper I made a sketch and said, 'This is what it should be like. Why didn't you work to George Stevens' fantastic footage that looks real?' But they said it would take them ten days to correct. That's the problem, and I didn't realise that. So eventually they got it right, but they went about it in the wrong way in the first place.

The next striking setting is the partial ruin of the Berliner Dom, where Furtwängler conducts a concert. Instead of having the concert in an opera house, you have it in this semi-open dome.
Yes, and I must say that using the dome was my idea. The former Philharmonic in Berlin was destroyed and replaced with a modern building in the 1960s, so István said, 'Why don't you look at opera houses?' So I did, but they were all horseshoe-shaped, and the Philharmonic wasn't like that. And then by chance – I had a very good art director called Anja doing some research – I found a photograph of Furtwängler conducting in the dome in 1944. So I said to István, 'Why don't we shoot it there?' It had been restored and so on, but he wasn't sure. He thought it was too difficult to light. István had worked with Lajos Koltai on twenty projects or more – they spoke in Hungarian, which I didn't understand – and they were like a Mafia team; he tried to protect Lajos. He was a wonderful cameraman, but István thought to light this gigantic area would be too difficult. But then I talked him into it and we shot it there.

It's a great scene. There's also another concert, with the rain coming through the roof and they're very stoically sitting it out . . .
That was the one we shot in Dresden, in the ruins of a church; they wanted us to shoot in Dresden for financial reasons because Saxony put up two hundred thousand dollars on the condition we shot certain stuff there. I found that ruined church and I thought it would be brilliant. I had every rain machine in the country working on this. All the umbrellas go up and they're playing Schubert; Symphony No.5, I think.

Yes, it's a beautiful sequence. The third location, which is interesting – and in some ways brings us right back to square one – is the old Berlin

Design of living room set, Straube
apartment

apartment of the secretary's aristocratic mother, which seems to be
based on the apartment you grew up in. It is not a particularly impor-
tant scene, but I gather you took a great deal of trouble over it.
Yes, it's dressed that way and some of the furniture was based on my
childhood memories. Letizia was helping me and we had a very good
German set dresser. We had the biggest headache because you cannot
find that type of furniture in Berlin any longer, although there may be
one piece in some antique dealer's cellar. But the art nouveau stuff is so
ridiculous and we certainly didn't have it in our house, so the set dresser went to London, Vienna and Prague – or Budapest, I'm not sure –
and he found all the furnishings that no longer exist in Germany.
Remember, when we were immigrants to England in 1934 my mother
fortunately brought all the stuff with her. But what happened to the
stuff that was left behind in Berlin, I don't know. It doesn't exist anywhere. That became a nightmare.

Nice idea: to reconstruct the apartment of your childhood.
Yes, and the lampshades, their shape and colour, which I remembered
very well. We also had one of those circular tables that you could pull
out and sit sixteen people.

Taking Sides *finishes with this remarkable piece of archive footage of*

276

the famous concert that Furtwängler gave with Goebbels in the audience. He shakes hands with Goebbels and then brings a little handkerchief out of his pocket and wipes the palm of his hand. The camera goes in to watch this moment over and over again. Is he wiping his hands because he feels tainted by the Nazis, or is he simply nervous? Was he a collaborator or wasn't he?

That was a brilliant idea by István Szabó, who had looked at a lot of footage and discovered this detail in a long shot. And don't ask me how, but they managed to zoom in on the hand.

It's a powerful ending. Moments like that, and the street scene of bombed Berlin, and the concert in the rain, open it out from being a play to becoming a movie.

I thought it worked pretty well. István had this intellectual concept that all the characters in the film were really displaced persons. So he did not want the Harvey Keitel character to be in a lonely office; he wanted a big circular staircase. In our first meeting we discussed with thumbnail sketches whether he wanted fascist architecture – spare and rigid – or whether I should go more into baroque. He said he wanted baroque because it feels out of place.

Everything is out of scale too: little people in big rooms.

Yes. István really pushed me and I went with it because I was so fascinated by this concept. In fact, that gigantic staircase was not a set, because a year or two before I had found a derelict museum – the Bode Museum – which had this incredible neo-baroque double staircase. When we had our conference I asked to be excused for an hour to see if the museum was still there. We drove down and there were three derelict buildings, but it was still there.

That's an important part of your modus operandi, having a photographic memory, so that when the need arises you can choose the location without too much trouble.

Yes. That was very important, as it was the key for my set. The upper corridor and the office is where the action takes place, so I could design the office much more interestingly, much bigger. It had a gigantic fireplace on one side.

Huge windows, with a view of Berlin.

Yes.

Electronic Arts

*In the middle of 2003, you were approached by an American company
called Electronic Arts to help them design a computer game/video game
on the loose theme of James Bond.*
Right. *Goldeneye – rogue agent.*

*And the idea of the game is that Goldeneye is an ex-British agent who
has defected to the other side and now works for both Dr No and
Goldfinger . . .*
Yeah, sort of in between, and he's got a 'cybernetic eye' – whatever that
may mean. They approached me at the beginning of 2003 and they
came over here and at first I had no idea whether I could do it. So I told
my agent that I wanted a trial period to see if I could still come up with
ideas in sketch form. They also took all the sketches I'd ever done for
the Bond films, as a guide, and they were young people – I mean the
oldest one was forty, Danny Bilson, and they were terribly complimentary and enthusiastic which of course helped me! Then they took me to
their studios in Chertsey – which were designed by Lord Foster, like a
rather beautiful glass palace – where everybody was sitting together in
these cubicles with their computers and I said, 'This is not for me.' So
they said, 'Well, you can work out of your home.' And suddenly I
found that I had become a one-man band, whereas on all the films I
always had an art department. I suddenly found myself sitting in this
little room and designing ideas, then having the problem of how to
transmit them – first we used Fed Ex and I did big sketches, then I
decided to go down to fax size because my fax can also do photographic reproduction, although it takes for ever – and I had no research
back-up either – so I said, 'If you want something in Switzerland, get
me the background material; you want something in Vegas . . . I haven't
got time to go around researching.' So they agreed to all that and it was
at the end of July 2003 that I finally decided I would sign an agreement
with them. Also, they'd all met me at my exhibition at the Motion Picture Academy in Hollywood in April–May 2003.

Talking about the things that I learned from the experience: when
you design a film, apart from the fact that you have either an outline or
a script and you discuss it with the director, here you only had the
vaguest form of outline; in films you design for the camera and you
know the limits of your set – the limits of the frame and also what the
director requires, because he may say, 'I only want a three-wall set,' or
even, 'One wall is sufficient,' and so on. In video games it is complete-

ly different. It is always the point of view of the player or players so the scene is moving around all the time. The first experience I had with Fort Knox was when I said, 'But we've got a great ready-made set; you've got it all there.' 'Ah no, no,' they said, 'because we've got to go into the corridors, into the other rooms, and we've got to have places they can hide behind.' With my long experience of designing for films I had become, as you know, more minimalist in my work, but now I discovered that if I didn't add certain elements, somebody among the three hundred people of the Game Playing division would put in barriers or screens or something in order for the game to function. That was a basic, basic difference.

INITIAL CONCEPT BOARD ROOM FORT KNOX (REDUCED)

I've seen the drawings you sent, and the 'sets'. For the Goldfinger sequences: Fort Knox, the boardroom of Fort Knox – which wasn't, of course, in the original – the Midas Casino in Las Vegas, and a smelting centre where gold is melted down at Auric Enterprises in Switzerland – a huge mountainside complex, originally on stilts but eventually an arrow-shaped dome structure surrounded by the Alps, with another boardroom inside it . . .

Initial concept of Fort Knox boardroom for Electronic Arts, 2003

We've got the main interior of the dome, which had to have a big pool, Goldfinger's living quarters and I came up with this jungle setting too – all interior – because the idea was that his place is under ice or snow and then you come into this beautiful interior which is tropical and all

POSSIBLE
CABEL CAR.

Ken Adam Nov. 2003

MONO RAIL TO
SMELTING PLANT

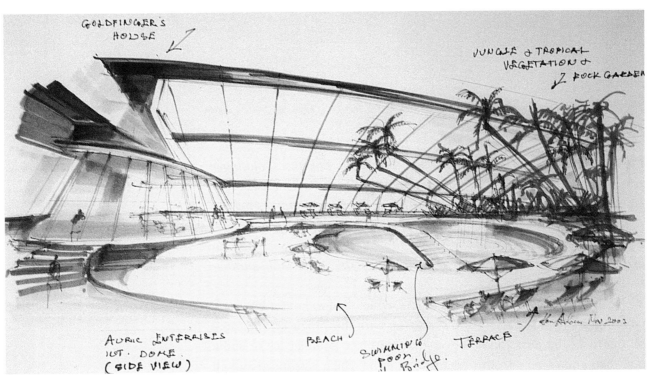

GOLDFINGER'S
HOUSE

JUNGLE & TROPICAL
VEGETATION &
ROCK GARDEN

Ken Adam Nov 2003

AURIC ENTERPRISES
INT. DOME.
(SIDE VIEW)

BEACH

SWIMMING
POOL
& Bridge.

TERRACE

280

these adventures happen. It created a continuous subject for discussion with the creative people because I said 'Well when we did it in the film, we tended to forget many of the details. We had a shot of some wooded slopes, then you go to some limited kind of factory and through some shutters you see the Rolls-Royce being melted down and taken to pieces as gold. But here you are giving so much more importance to the place, and so many more options.

Then for the Dr No sequences, you've got a fortress at Crab Key – a monolithic fortress in Jamaica – and his underwater resort called Octopus with shark pools and fish tanks. This seems like a development of the original Dr No *– from just having a jetty and a reactor room to this vast fortress complex. And then there is the volcano from* You Only Live Twice, *which has now turned into the SPECTRE headquarters and, underneath that, a shooting range . . .*

You see, they were very keen to use that volcano, but it worked in the film because the focal point of the design was that huge three-stage rocket targeted at space, obviously with the lake on top. I had to lose the rocket this time, and come up with something else, so I created another dome inside the volcano and then had to design what goes on underneath that dome which was the SPECTRE headquarters. I initially drew for the headquarters that famous boardroom where the chair goes through the floor, almost exactly like in *Thunderball*. But then for

Concept of Auric Enterprises exterior in Switzerland, 2003 (opposite top)

Interior of Auric Enterprises, 2003

Exterior of Dr No's fortress at Crab Key, 2004

the other rooms of the boardroom I didn't have enough information, so it was left in abeyance and I don't know what in the end they decided to do. One of the problems is that these organisations today are so enormous and there are so many different departments – animation, storyboard, design and all that – it was very difficult to get the right reaction out of the right person. And that became more difficult at the beginning of 2004 because every time I tried to talk to somebody, they said they were in a meeting. And I'm used, when somebody says, 'I'm in a meeting,' to treat it as an excuse that they won't talk to me. But when I went over there, I found out that they really *were* spending, I would say the best part of a day, in meetings, but meetings with some executive who I never met and who must have told them, 'We don't like this idea, we'd prefer you to go after this or that.' So they were exhausted from being at these meetings all the time. I don't know if I can compare it with films, but with films in the olden days when you had a big studio like Warner Brothers or MGM or Columbia or Fox or whoever, it was the chief executive like Jack Warner or Harry Cohn who told the various directors, 'You can only do this, or you mustn't do that.' The situation today is similar, but on a much, much bigger scale.

Completing our tour of the Goldeneye – rogue agent *'sets', in addition to the* Goldfinger *complex and the* Dr No *complex, there's MI6 – a 'virtual training centre', for the player to train – plus assorted flying machines such as the 'Ospreys', and a power boat.*
Well I didn't do the Ospreys, and the boat was all changed you see.

And a V2 rocket.
No, not a V2. They called it a V1 or something. It belongs to Goldfinger and he hides it in the bowels beneath Auric Enterprises in Switzerland.

The player becomes the James Bond figure fighting this Goldeneye character, who then rushes around all these different locations connected with Dr No and Goldfinger . . .
And Dr No fights Goldfinger as well. They are the two main characters in the story . . .

A battle of the giants. And there are eight sequences in all, or which you must have designed – with Las Vegas, Fort Knox, Switzerland, Jamaica, the underwater resort, MI6 – six of them. Or at least the starting point of six of them.
I didn't do – because I didn't want to do – Hong Kong and I didn't do the Hoover Dam, which from what I've seen, is actually rather good. But, Christopher, it's like not designing a single film but really like

designing eight films. You also have to remember that one of these video games goes on for twenty hours and let's say we have eight different sequences and each sequence has God knows how many sets, and here I'm sitting in my room – to do it really well and oversee everything, I'd have had to be constantly in Hollywood with the team. Even then, it became so chaotic there that they had to use an extra studio in Hollywood and finally yet another, a third studio in Montreal! Now if you think that each art department has about eighty people – well, if you have three studios you've got about three hundred people and the coordination, the liaison is incredibly difficult. Remember it is a young art, it's been going for only about twenty years and it has become unbelievably competitive because, whether it's Sony or Microsoft, everybody is coming up with new technologies. But the technology has limitations. I found this out on Fort Knox, which to me was second nature because I remembered what I did for *Goldfinger*; I wanted to see gold. But when they showed me the first computer-built models, I said, 'Where's all the gold?' They said, 'Well, we had to put it in crates.' I said, 'Why? Because the whole idea was to have gold piled high.' 'You see, we have problems with the colour gold and the reflections.' Like they also had problems with gunmetal and stainless steel – reflective surfaces which I always use a lot – there they had problems because surfaces like these make things so much more complicated for them. I didn't know these things. I thought they could do everything. They are so amazing with their animation and other things. But they can't do everything.

From your experience of designing video games, Ken, in one way it seems to be a liberation and in another way it seems the opposite. A liberation, in that you don't have to worry about the practicalities of building a set, so you can think up anything – it can be an impossible structure like a Piranesi prison or an Escher print. But a constraint, in that there's this lack of control which is very unusual for you; you are used to being in charge of your own set and here you are faxing a sketch over to Hollywood where three hundred people are going to have a crack at amending it, adding extra dimensions – and in that process anything can happen: it might completely lose the individuality you put into it. You have no way of knowing. It's like doing the initial design for a film, then moving on to another film, and not knowing what the hell the filmmakers are going to do with your initial work.

You are so right, Christopher. But even from their point of view, one department very often doesn't know what another department is doing. That is the incredible thing, because I had my equivalent – Jay Riddle, the art director – well, he became a nervous wreck, you know, and

ASER LAB. IN B/G.   SWIMMING POOL ABOVE ↓

when I spent March 2004 in Hollywood I got very close to him and he took me round the various computer stations – he could work the controls to enter every nook and cranny – and then he would say, 'Well, who on earth came up with that and why is this there?' To have overall control is a gigantic task.

Looking at your drawings, they are an anthology of some of the great-

TRAVELLING GANTRIES

Gold smelting plant of Auric Enterprises, 2004

est hits of Ken Adam's designs for James Bond – Crab Key from Dr No, *Fort Knox from* Goldfinger, *the volcano from* You Only Live Twice, *Atlantis from* The Spy Who Loved Me *which turns into the Octopus resort, Dr No's underwater resort . . .*

But my first version of the Octopus resort was thought to be 'too sinister' and I redesigned it!

Really? Today's game-players can't cope with expressionism! Overall, though, what was it like after all these years going back to some of your visual ideas?

Well, it's a very good question. I was concerned about it because I didn't know whether I still had the creative input to come up with something new. So first of all – knowing they had all my Bond designs from me – I had to go back to designs I did in the 1960s. So I said to myself, 'I don't really want to go back . . .', but I started off playing safe – for example, using some of the elements of the gambling room in the penthouse of the Midas Casino in Vegas, which I could have done like *Diamonds Are Forever*. But then I found that not very satisfying. And that's why I didn't want to commit myself, because I wanted to see how my work was developing. Then, eventually, I started to release myself more and even with the thumbnail sketches which I faxed, or had an assistant of mine to e-mail them, even with these I think some of the designs are now better and more original than they were, though they still have my stamp on them.

It's like revisiting your designs thirty, forty years after the fact, but extending them and taking them in new directions. They are still unmistakably Ken Adam. Variations on a theme.

But it was in one way so sweet and in another so naïve when I went over there and the various design teams were trying to imitate my style by inclining surfaces and so on – but what they did of course was to incline them the wrong way! It can't be that simple to copy a style, unless you are making fun of it.

Where 'doing a Ken Adam' is concerned, in one of the sets they even added a light-ring from Dr Strangelove *into the design . . .*
In the boardroom, yes.

Which was extremely cheeky of them. You sent it over as a boardroom and they put in a light-ring, as a Ken Adam reference.
Lately – from summer to autumn 2004 – there's been a lot of politics, and all the people I worked with seem to have disappeared or are now doing something else. Even a producer threw it in. Because the pressure is just unbelievable. And remember they are not part of IATSE or any trade unions.

They work twenty-five hours a day . . .
Yes, and they just get burned out after a time. There's obviously a lot of politics because there's so much money involved . . .

What is the budget?
I'm not sure but I would say this video game must have cost something

in the region of thirty or forty million dollars. But they do know that they can get back something like between two hundred and three hundred million dollars. The figures are just staggering.

10 Epilogue: Reflections

By this stage in your career, when you worked on Taking Sides, *you had been awarded all kinds of honours by the industry, professional bodies and others. In 1995 you were awarded an honorary doctorate by the Royal College of Art – we were the first, I'm glad to say. David Sylvester received a senior fellowship that same day, and over lunch the idea of what would become the exhibition at the Serpentine Gallery four years later – 'Moonraker, Strangelove and other celluloid dreams' – was hatched. The OBE and the Oscar for* The Madness of King George *were also awarded in 1995. A retrospective exhibition in Munich, Vienna, Wiesbaden, Mannheim and Dusseldorf –* Production Design: Ken Adam *– in 1994–95. Then your design for the Millennium Exhibition in Berlin, the Serpentine show, the honorary doctorate of Greenwich University in July 2000, and in 2003 an exhibition at the American Motion Picture Academy. Plus the Lifetime Achievement Award in 2002, and your participation in the tribute to Stanley Kubrick at the Directors' Guild in Hollywood. Culminating in your knighthood in 2003.*
Right.

All this is very unusual, because on the whole production designers are prophets without honour.
Back-room boys.

And if one looks along the shelves there are countless film books about directors, about stars, even about cinematographers, but very few about production designers. Just one or two picture books.
Particularly old-time production designers, whose work was of course much more important in those days because most pictures were made in film studios. It was not economical or practical to shoot big dialogue scenes between actors on location. They didn't yet have very fast lenses. So they had much more control in the studio, and that's why 90 per cent of the films were shot there. And that's how I started in films: the studio films. But the designers of those days either came from a theatrical, painting or architectural background. There were some great designers. There's a book called *Le Décor au Cinéma*, and it deals mainly with the German designers, the silent films of Fritz Lang and so on. You just knew that the designer was very much part of that team.

One problem is the survival of the material. You tend to get the same material written about in all these books because there happens to be an archive. There's a Metropolis *archive, a* Wizard of Oz *archive, a* King Kong *archive, a* Citizen Kane *archive . . . You can almost predict which films the books will cover because they know the material is around. That's worrying, because the history being written is patchy. It misses out whole swathes of films where no material happened to survive.*

You're absolutely right, and it's funny you should bring that up because I have been talking to Ellen Harrington, who runs the Special Events section at the Motion Picture Academy, and she said the biggest problem they have is finding the material. I have personal experience of that. The Bond people do look after my stuff, but the copyright situation at MGM meant I had to give all my designs to the studio. As I've said, I remember doing the Special Project three years after *Pennies from Heaven* and I wanted to refer back to something from the film. But when I went back to MGM, they didn't have it.

MGM is a classic case because there's the famous story that at the time of the MGM auctions in the 1960s they were selling off all the visual material and junking everything else. One of the matte artists went into the archives at MGM and saw all these glass paintings smashed on the floor. They'd just chucked them out. In those days they weren't interested in archives at all. It's scandalous that the major collective art form of the twentieth century had so little systematic archiving. That's the problem with writing about production design: you can only go on what survives.
Yes.

The other is working out exactly who did what, because in a studio there was a Head of Design, like Gibbons at MGM, who oversaw the look of a studio's products but didn't do much of the actual designing. It was a case of design management rather than design. Cedric Gibbons, for example, had a very strong aesthetic which was apparent in several people's designs: the big white brightly lit set.
Have you seen Cedric's house in Hollywood?

No.
We went to several parties there. It's very art deco. All white and very impressive. You're absolutely right: the studios were run like cities in those days. It was like a bureaucracy really. The chief designer got the credit for each film, but it was other designers who did the work.

As we've discussed, Gibbons' contract with MGM stated that his name should appear in big letters on every MGM film. Underneath it, in small

letters, was the word 'and' followed by the name of the person who probably did all the work.
Right.

All of which means that it's very difficult to attribute credit, and I think that has held back writing about production design. Apart from the fact that people don't notice it – that it's taken for granted – you've also got to do a lot of archaeology to find out who's responsible.
Today, the difficulty is that you get a very good designer like Stuart Craig, who does the *Harry Potter* films, but the design is so mixed up with visual effects. Also you lose control eventually because with all the computer-generated images that are usually done in post-production by companies all over the world, you don't know who did what.

And you're not around for the final cut.
Also, the problem today with these enormous spectacle films and computer-generated images is that the actors have to use a completely different technique because they don't have a set.

They're just standing against a backing, against a blue screen.
I don't know how Marlon Brando or Laurence Olivier or any of the great actors I had the privilege to work with would have done it. They'd be lost.

The actor becomes part of the design.
Yes.

While you were working on Taking Sides, *John Nelson, the man who did some of the computer-generated effects on* Gladiator, *came to visit you. He obviously had a great deal of respect for you and showed you his wares. The famous set in* Gladiator *is the Roman Colosseum. What did you think of that?*
I must tell you, this is a difficult thing for me to talk about. Firstly, I don't like Roman architecture. As much as I love Ancient Greek architecture, Roman architecture is really just a spin-off from Greek architecture. The Romans were fabulous engineers, but their architecture never really excites me. It looked so unreal to me, the Colosseum. And secondly, Ridley Scott is a very talented director, but those bird's-eye perspectives of the Colosseum make it look like the Miami Super Bowl. It's not natural to me. If you want to make a historical picture, then shoot it the way the people at that time would or might have seen it, not shot from a blimp or something like that. At the time of the Emperor Augustus, there were no airships or aerial views.

Interesting. Comment.

You see, what is so fascinating and exciting for directors is that everything is possible. But you have to treat it with a great deal of caution and not let the CGI boys take over, no matter how clever they are. What John Nelson has done certainly is very clever, but I think you lose some of the realism. Young people realise these are computer-generated images, and when we talk about the earlier Bonds, they know that we tried to be as realistic as possible.

It's like the special-effects work of Ray Harryhausen, which you know was done on his kitchen table, and that makes it much more satisfying because there's a feeling of a human being having done it. On a bigger and more sophisticated scale, I think knowing that your Bond sets were in three dimensions and that someone actually took the trouble to build them, adds to the magic.

Even with *Lord of the Rings*: I thought Peter Jackson did an incredible job, but he also fell in love with showing hundreds of thousands of people attacking walls and so on, and it doesn't look believable. So however clever they are – and they *are* – it still needs very careful supervision from a very good designer.

In one way it is the ultimate director's dream come true because it turns all filmmaking into animation – complete control, nothing accidental, everything designed like an animator. It's like Snow White *but with real people. But there is a price to pay for that: if you are not careful, it feels too controlled.*

When something is well done, it excites me, but not as a designer. I don't want to be involved in those types of films any longer because although it is a spectacle, although it is an art, to me the story is still the most important part of the film, and that will never age. You have to tell a story. The studios at one time had twenty to thirty writers under contract. Today they believe that visual spectacle alone can carry a film; I believe they are wrong. The screenplay is the most important element, because 3000 years ago they told stories and they will continue to do so in 3000 years to come.

In the last ten years you have become probably the most honoured art director in history.
Well, probably!

There's something about your career that has raised the profile of the production designer, of the importance of 'the look' of a film as well as its themes, and has drawn attention to your own achievements. You are the one who has become a celebrity. Do other production designers get jealous?

Yes, there's a lot of jealousy. It's silly, because if I get honoured as a production designer it should reflect on the whole profession, and anybody who's anybody should be ambitious enough to say, 'I will do what I can do and whether it gets honoured or not is beside the point.' To bring production design into the foreground for once means that, although we are the back-room boys – and always will be the back-room boys – somebody has decided this is worthwhile talking about.

It takes you from the tradesman's entrance to the front door . . .
But you see, in the theatre it was different. People like Roger Furse and Oliver Messel and so on got honoured. It's in films where you become marginalised.

Another thing that's changed – and you've mentioned this – is that there's no ready-made team at the studio any more. I sense that the role of the cameraman has changed. Maybe we haven't talked enough about your relationship with the cameraman, because that's a key relationship – between the person visualising and the person designing. I sense that with young, inexperienced directors the role of the cinematographer, particularly the veteran cinematographer, is becoming more important as an anchorage for a project. Is that true, do you think?
Absolutely. It's interesting that you've brought this up. In the 1960s, as a production designer, I was financially on the same level as Freddie Young; we were the top in our field. Today, the production designer gets one tenth of what the cameraman gets. It has happened for several reasons. One of them is that most pictures are shot on locations and the function of a production designer has changed. It's still important, but the function of the director of photography has become more so. When I did *Pennies from Heaven* I worked with Gordon Willis, who was considered to be one of the greatest American cinematographers at that time. We had many discussions about this. Gordon was getting enormous amounts of money and we talked about how things had changed. He said that the cameraman today not only lights the scene and location, but in many instances he also has to stage the action for the director and the camera, because there are many directors who get wonderful performances from an actor, but they don't know how to stage the camera movement. Gordon said directors of photography have to fulfil two functions: to light the setting or location, and to stage the action. For these two functions, they ought to be paid. And I agree.

But they save money on the directors! Ismail Merchant, in his book Hullabaloo in Old Jeypore, *says that when he first approached you to design* The Deceivers *people said to him, 'Ken Adam designed the Bond films, he smokes a big cigar, he's expensive, he likes big budgets – out of your league.' Merchant adds, 'I have never had very good relationships with art directors or production designers. I have always regarded them as a necessary evil, and my manner sooner or later conveys this to them ... I've always felt they are wasting the production's money.' He goes on to say that, having worked with you, he now admires you enormously 'both as an artist and as a person'. But the point is, do you think that your association with Bond held you back, because people were frightened to approach you?*

It didn't hold me back.

OK, but did it mean that some projects which might have been offered to you weren't, because they thought you were out of their league?

Yes. It still happens today, and it's a great pity. With that particular film – *The Deceivers* – I wanted to prove to Merchant–Ivory, who are very tight with their budgets, that I could do a picture for next to nothing.

It is an interesting point. Moonraker *was in 1979, so for the last twenty-four years you have been living under the shadow of Bond with the reputation of building missile launchers inside volcanoes and nuclear submarines inside supertankers. So a first- or second-time director with an adapted play or a little film is a bit scared of you.*

Yes, there's no question about it. They are hesitant for several reasons, for that and also because they might think I will overpower them. If you really want to analyse the cost of my films, apart from the later Bonds like *Moonraker*, I wasn't expensive, because I knew how to cut corners. But the producers gave me that reputation because it was good for their publicity. I told you about the volcano set that cost just over a million dollars. Well, I came on the set and there was Harry Saltzman and Cubby Broccoli telling all the European distributors there that the set cost four million dollars. I was livid that they lied, just for good publicity. So that reputation stuck with me. But on the other hand I proved many times . . .

On these smaller post-1980 movies we've been talking about . . .

Yes . . . that I knew how to cut corners. But I think it's almost the fear, particular in young directors, that I might have an overpowering personality, because I always like to be involved in the script. If the script is wonderful, then I'm most delighted. But if I think I can improve it through design or by putting a different accent on a scene or something, I will say so. I've always done that because it's a big part of your life to make a movie, and a great deal of stress. After *Barry Lyndon* I said, 'Never again . . .'

Exactly. Very often in our conversations you've talked about the stress of redesigning the War Room in Dr Strangelove, *or the responsibility of building the volcano in* You Only Live Twice – *times when you're on a high wire. You're obviously a very meticulous person and want to be absolutely certain that things are going to work well, but part of you is constantly thinking, 'Maybe this isn't going well.' There's a little part of you that's mistrustful of everything that's going on around you.*

Well, I don't know. I had a very good team on all of those pictures and I think that's so important. That cliché, 'You're only as good as your team' – it's partly true. You still have to come up with the ideas and guide the team, but then you need a very good team to realise it. I was very fortunate in that sense because I've nearly always had first-class people. You mentioned Ismail Merchant; there I hardly had any support at all, and it becomes very difficult because you have to deal with everything yourself. Whereas with good assistants you can allocate a lot of responsibility.

Pushing you on this, it has been written of you that you're a little mistrustful of the ground on which you stand. That you can't quite believe it's going to work. Maybe that means you're still the fighter pilot at heart and that in the end you've got to depend on yourself and only yourself.

I think I would put it differently. I think that, though I believe I am a very responsible person, there is a sort of bravado which could almost be called irresponsible. You come up with way-out ideas which need courage and bravado and hopefully you have the right back-up to make them work. I think the word 'mistrust' worries me.

It's actually from the German book The Worlds of Ken Adam. *An interesting quote.*
I hope I'd translate it differently!

You are certainly wary and you've been bitten a few times. Your antennae have to be quite sensitive.
Very sensitive, yes. That's what I keep telling people, that you also need a lot of courage to put over your ideas, and diplomacy to sell your ideas to the director and producer without upsetting their egos.

You must be brilliant at that because I think you're quite a thin-skinned person but you work with some very thick-skinned people and you get your own way with them. You must be excellent at diplomacy because you're not doing it by being a scrapper; you're not fighting all the time. You're not that sort of person. But you negotiate your solutions and win through with these very hard-nosed people.

You have to be. I always remember that time working with the production designer Ralph Brinton on the Errol Flynn picture *The Master of Ballantrae*. We were in Sicily and I was doing all the drafting for him too. Ralph came in one day – he was highly intelligent – and he said, 'You have to promise when you get a big film as production designer I will be your chief draughtsman. I'm very happy to just sit at my drawing board and draft out your designs without all the politics and the responsibility.' In the olden days, particularly in England, we had the most superb draughtsmen: Charlie Bishop, Reg Green at MGM, Ernie Archer . . . They were fabulous draughtsmen. You could give them anything. But they didn't have anything like the responsibility of the production designer.

Earlier, you suggested that the successful production designer requires various things: talent, imagination and training. We've talked a lot about those. We have also talked about luck, those moments when chance encounters or working relationships led to new challenges and projects. The effectiveness of the art department as a team. Also the courage of your convictions. But one thing that has come over very strongly is your final requirement: 'the ability to assess and cope with personalities such as the director's. The ability to communicate with people . . .' Over and over again in our conversations the 'politics and the responsibility' have loomed large. With Mike Todd, Stanley Kubrick, the later Bonds, Herb Ross on Pennies from Heaven – *all have tested your diplomatic skills to the full. One thing that we've skated over, though, is the agents you've been with. How long have you been with the Mirisch Agency, and who were you with before that?*
Oh my God. I've been with Mirisch for approximately eighteen years. Before Mirisch I was with William Morris and Phil Gersh during the 1970s and '80s.

And in the '50s and '60s?
I was with Dennis Van Thal and Dennis Selinger, both based in London. I started with Laurie Evans at MCA, which was one of the big agencies, and so I had a lot of agents. I frequently used to change them.

Can I ask why – whether it's them or you?!
Probably a combination of both. Something wasn't quite right.

Does it work like a literary agent, where someone approaches you informally about a project, you discuss it, you reach a point where you're going to try and get a deal, you hand it over to the agent to do the negotiation . . . Does it work like that?
Not really. First, you sign with an agent of your choice, who ultimately

is responsible for negotiating your deal. The producer should contact your agent first, and then the agent gets them to send you a script. Also, the agent should look out for suitable projects and generally advise you – a sort of father confessor. It's also protective.

LETIZIA ADAM [who joined us at this point]: Sometimes they try to contact Ken, and I tell them that he'd say, 'Contact the agent.'

It objectifies the relationship. They look for suitable projects and sometimes you get them.
Yes. A very good case was *The Madness of King George*, when I rang my agent and said if they don't want to pay much money, I'll do it all the same.

I've been adding up your filmography. I think it's eighty-nine projects, including the unrealised ones. Seventy-five actually realised. That's seventy-five movies between the late 1940s and the present day, including the seven Bonds. The amount of work and design energy that went into these films is the sort of energy that an architect would put into a building, only it is times seventy-five. Does it worry you that you don't have seventy-five buildings to show for it? That you don't have a permanent monument? Does it worry you that what you do have is these flickering images that we hope are being looked after and restored so that they will survive.
No. What worries me more, particularly now when I have exhibitions, is that I find designs for *Peter Pan* or *The Fantasticks*, and they are really good designs but the film has never been made. It's a great pity.

LA: You were destroyed really. When it was a good idea, like *Peter Pan*.

Yes, it was destructive. But when a film is well shot and my sets, designs and locations are shown the way I want, then I don't mind when my sets are destroyed.

LA: Once he's done it and seen it on the screen, then he's happy. When I say, 'Ken, they're going to destroy the War Room,' or whatever, he says, 'Darling, there is always the next one.' He's looking forward to the next one.

I start on something else. I have no sentimentality. People keep asking me if I would have liked to keep the War Room, but no.

Not even the models? Because you're meticulous about archiving your drawings.
No. Well, you haven't got the space for them. You'd need a big hangar to have all the models.

It means that exhibitions of production design tend to be all about flat work and not about the next stage, which is how these drawings are turned into three dimensions. They go straight from flat work to movie, missing all those stages in between. Which is a shame.

It's a big shame.

Because they're all links in the chain.

The beautiful models . . . whether they are little art-department models or whatever. Remember one thing, which we haven't really talked about: when I started films, the studios didn't expect you to do everything from scratch. They had these incredible scene docks with fireplaces, old baroque flats, everything. And they expected you to use those doors, windows, the whole lot. But it doesn't exist any more because they haven't got the space. It became too expensive.

The real estate. Their backlot became more valuable than the things that were on it.

Yes, that's right. Models take up a lot of room so they were always destroyed.

Ken, you've been absolutely meticulous about documenting your own career. Not many people have. It's a great thing to have accumulated.

I don't know how that happened. I think it happened partly because Lotte Eisner wanted my work for the Cinémathèque in Paris. She was the first one who really looked through my material and collected the stuff. She said Letizia was absolutely right about the thumbnail sketches having more life, impulsive things which are more intuitive. Not the cold technical drawings.

But in most cases you've kept the drawings. Did Eon take the Bonds?

Yes, the originals. They kept those. I had to hand them over.

The production designer, an invention of the twentieth century, is in a way the first virtual architect in history. Architects are often obsessed with leaving behind as many monuments as possible with their name on them, and to some extent engineers as well. But your work is entirely virtual. It's an experience.

Because it's a part of the film.

It's not an end in itself.

Yes. I think that's very important to realise, even though sometimes one has been accused of almost overpowering the actors and so on, in the Bonds maybe – though that was the nature of the Bonds – but not in others. I think the most satisfying design is when it really fits into the dramatic scene or structure.

And of course your sets can only work in that particular context, and from that perspective. If you can imagine pulling the camera back outside the frame, it's difficult to conceive what would happen then because the War Room works precisely in the frame, lit as it is. It's the same with Fort Knox and all those great sets: they fulfil the purpose they were built for. It's a kind of fitness for purpose.
They work for the scene.

You can't quite imagine what the rest of it might look like.
Yes. And that was Kubrick's idea. He never wanted to establish the complete architecture.

Although you extended it recently for the print and introductory image at the Serpentine Gallery.
Yes, I did! It was because I had to cover a whole wall of the Serpentine and it was of Cinemascope proportions, so I had to do the sketch much wider.

And there's always the thought that you might well have an influence on architecture in the real world. I've mentioned Foster and The Spy Who Loved Me . . .
Well, at the Serpentine exhibition there were a lot of architects that came to see my sketches. The compliment they paid me was that they felt my designs had influenced quite a lot of their architectural designs in the '60s and '70s. Then I got a letter from Julia, the director of the Serpentine Gallery, with the photograph of the interior of a pavilion designed by Daniel Libeskind, telling me it looks very much like a Ken Adam set! I am very impressed by his use of space, his lines, and his use of chiaroscuro . . . I have been approached to design people's houses but I have never taken it seriously because I would be bored by all the practical problems that one encounters. The point of my designs is that they are part of the film.

You once said, 'I always feel restless, probably because of my past.'
Yes, I think that is true. I have suffered all my life from anxieties and that certainly must go back to something. Obviously I wasn't that affected as a child by the Nazis, but when I saw the effect they had . . .
Yes, without a doubt. And the death of my father. Obviously I don't like to talk about it, Christopher, but it affected me seriously. And the war was not without anxiety. So all that took its toll.

And you do seem restless. Not easily satisfied. Constantly pushing for more. You've still got things to offer and you want to keep going.
I'm amazed I still have things to offer because that was my anxiety and my doubt – can I still draw or come up with a reasonably original idea?

That caused and causes a lot of anxiety. I'd rather go with Letizia to a beach somewhere, but once you start, that becomes an important part of your life.

LA: He's never satisfied . . . It's a bit of persecution . . .

Like a touch of persecution complex?
Yes, no question.

LA: I do feel that he does.

That's come through a few times in our conversations.
Of course, it was important for me to marry somebody who had none of this. The sad part of it is that all – or at least a great deal – of my anxieties have gone over to Letizia.

LA: No persecution to me.

No, but you've absorbed some of it. One of the leitmotifs of our conversations has been Letizia. Ever since we talked about The Crimson Pirate *she has appeared in the picture very strongly, whether as your assistant, dressing the set, testing ideas, giving you the confidence to draw expressively . . .*
More as a critic. And today, in particular when I'm dealing with somewhat new ideas, or even somewhat old ideas, I go to her. I don't want her to watch while I'm doodling something, but when I'm more or less there, I will show it to her.

Have you always done that?
I don't think I always did, no. I didn't have the opportunity when I was working . . .

LA: Working from the studio.

Yes, but you didn't come to the studio that often, darling, if you think of the number of sets I did.

LA: I know . . . Ah well, not everyone like you would do it here at home.

Ken, you still own a Rolls-Royce Silver Cloud I convertible, dating from 1959, so you still love well-designed cars and you say you're still 'a sports car fiend'. But you can't drive around in these low-slung sports cars any more . . .
I could. In fact, until recently I always had a second car. But it's a question of comfort. When you sit right on the floor it's a little bit more difficult to get out. I never in my wildest dreams thought that I would like a Rolls: it was not my image. Letizia knows that I've always had special

With Rolls Royce Silver Cloud I
Convertible in the south of France,
1972

cars, but mainly sports cars. Then I got used to this old monster and it's
very beautiful in its way. It – touch wood – is still like a part of the family,
even though it's enormous and makes parking difficult and all that . . .

LA: But he does drive it like a man of twenty.

Hopefully.

LA: The parking, I mean. I'm amazed.

How long have you had it?
Since 1969.

*The famous advertising line used to say – I think I've got this right –
that in a Silver Cloud, at sixty miles per hour the only thing you can
hear is the ticking of the clock? Is that true?*
Well, I wish it was! They are very silent, very simple. Except the clock
hasn't worked since I got the car!

LA: The only thing I hear in the morning is when he turns it on and it
makes a funny cracking noise.

That's because it's on the choke. But it doesn't make as much noise as
when I started the Mercedes and the supercharger was freewheeling
like a jet engine.

LA: That was a jet.

I was a speed freak like you are, Christopher. If you have a sports car,
you have to drive it like a sports car. The only problem is doing long distances: you're exhausted when you arrive because you have to concen-

300

trate and have split-second reactions and so on. Whereas in the Rolls, even when we drive all over Europe and even in the United States . . .

You shipped the car over?
Oh yes.

Of course . . . the Rolls that looked so prestigious parked outside Twentieth Century Fox. It must have caused a sensation in Malibu.

LA: That was lovely there. Here, they sometimes go, 'Hmm.' But there they say, 'Great car!'

A classic Rolls-Royce in Hollywood. That sounds like the perfect place to end.

Index

Camionetas Nissan Manual de Reparación

por Rik Paul, Ken Freund y John H Haynes

Miembro del Gremio de escritores del automovilismo

Arnaldo Sánchez Jr Editor técnico

Modelos cubiertos:

Las camionetas Nissan/Datsun **1980 al 1996**
Pathfinder **1987 al 1995**

No incluye información para los motores diesel

ABCDF
FGH

Grupo de Publicaciones Haynes
Sparkford Nr Yeovil
Somerset BA22 7JJ Inglaterra

Haynes de Norte América, Inc
861 Lawrence Drive
Newbury Park
California 91320 E.E.U.U.

Reconocimientos

Estamos agradecidos por la ayuda y cooperación de la Compañía Nissan, Ltd. por su ayuda con las informaciones técnicas, ciertas ilustraciones y fotografías del vehículo. Nissan también suministró el vehículo en la cubierta trasera.

Un libro de la serie de **Manuales Haynes para Reparaciones Automotrices**

Imprimido en U.S.A. (Estados Unidos de Norte América)

ISBN 1 56392 253 3

Biblioteca del Congreso Número de la Tarjeta del Catalogo 97-80261

Contenidos

Camioneta Nissan de cabina grande modelo D21

Acerca de este manual

El propósito

El propósito de este manual es ayudarlo a obtener el mejor valor de su vehículo. Usted puede hacer esto en varias maneras. Puede ayudarlo a decidir qué trabajo se debe hacer, aun cuando usted escoja que la reparación sea hecha por un departamento de servicio automotriz o un taller de reparaciones; provee informaciones y procedimientos para el mantenimiento de rutina y servicio; y ofrece diagnósticos y procedimientos de reparación para seguir cuando un problema ocurre.

Esperamos que use este manual para que usted haga el trabajo. Para muchos trabajos simples, haciendo el trabajo usted mismo pueda que sea más rápido de tener que hacer una cita para llevar el vehículo a un taller de reparación y hacer los viajes de llevarlo y recogerlo. Más importante, se puede ahorrar bastante dinero evitando los cargos que el taller le pasaría a usted para cubrir la labor y los sobrecargos de los costos. El beneficio adicional es la satisfacción de haber hecho el trabajo usted mismo.

Usando el manual

El manual está dividido en Capítulos. Cada Capítulo está dividido en Secciones con números, que se encabezan con letras grandes en líneas horizontales. Cada Sección consta de párrafos consecutivamente numerados.

Al principio de cada Sección numerada, usted será referido a cualquier ilustración que es aplicada a los procedimientos en esa Sección. El número de referencia usado en la ilustración apunta a la Sección indicada y los pasos con esa Sección. Esto sería, ilustración 3.2, significa que la ilustración se refiere a la Sección 3 y paso (o párrafo) 2 en esa Sección.

Los procedimientos, una vez descriptos en el texto, no se repetirán normalmente. Cuando sea necesario referirse a otro Capítulo, se dará como referencia el Capítulo y el número de la Sección. Cruces de referencias dados sin el uso de la palabra "Capítulo" se aplica a la Sección y/o párrafo en el Capítulo. Por ejemplo, "vea Sección 8" quiere decir que es el mismo Capítulo.

Referencias a la izquierda o al lado derecho del vehículo se supone que usted está sentado en el asiento del chofer, mirando hacia el frente.

Aunque mucho cuidado se tomó cuando se estaba preparando este manual, ni el publicador ni el autor pueden aceptar responsabilidad por cualquier error u omisión de la información que se ha dado.

NOTA

Una **Nota** provee información necesaria para completar apropiadamente un procedimiento o información, que hace los pasos para seguir más fácil de entender.

CAUCIÓN

Una **Caución** indica un procedimiento especial o pasos especiales que se deben de tomar en el curso de completar el procedimiento, en donde la **Caución** es encontrada, es necesario para evitar daño al ensamblaje que se esté trabajando.

PELIGRO

Un **Peligro** indica un procedimiento especial o paso especial que se debe de tomar en el curso de completar el procedimiento, en donde el **Peligro** es encontrado es necesario para evitar que la persona que está haciendo el procedimiento sufra una lesión.

Introducción a las camionetas Nissan/Datsun y Pathfinder

Las camionetas Nissan/Datsun y Pathfinder son de motores convencionales al frente y tracción trasera; y con tracción en las cuatro ruedas (4WD) en algunos modelos opcionales.

Motores de 4 cilindros y V6 han sido usados sobre el periodo de existencia de estos modelos, con inyección de combustible disponible en los modelos más modernos. La potencia del motor se transfiere a una transmisión manual o una transmisión automática, en los modelos de dos tracciones (2WD). En los modelos de cuatro tracciones (4WD), una caja de transferencia es usada para accionar las ruedas del frente a traves de un eje propulsor.

La suspensión delantera es independiente, con barras de torsión y con dirección hidráulica disponible en los modelos más modernos. Resortes de hojas son usados en la suspensión trasera.

Tienen frenos de discos al frente y frenos de tambor o de discos con ajuste automático en la parte trasera que son asistidos por un amplificador de vacío.

Números de identificación del vehículo

Las modificaciones son parte de un continuo y sin ser publicado proceso de la fabricación de los vehículos. Ya que las partes de respuestos y las listas son acopiladas en una base numérica, los números individuales de los vehículos son esenciales para poder identificar los componentes requeridos.

Número de identificación del vehículo (VIN)

Este número de identificación es muy importante, está localizado en un plato asegurado en la parte izquierda superior del tablero del vehículo, cerca del parabrisas

(vea ilustración). El VIN también aparece en el certificado del titulo del vehículo. Contiene información tal como donde y cuando el vehículo fue producido, el modelo del año y el estilo de la carrocería.

Plato de identificación del vehículo

Este plato de metal, conectado al lado derecho en el compartimiento del motor, contiene información importante incluyendo el tipo de vehículo, tipo de motor, desplazamiento y el máximo de caballos de fuerza tal como el número de serie del chasis.

Número de serie del chasis

El número de serie del chasis es hallado en la placa de identificación del vehículo y está también estampado en el carril derecho delantero del chasis, adyacente al motor.

Número de identificación del motor

El número de identificación del motor en los motores de cuatro cilindros hasta el 1990 está estampado en una almohadilla en el lado derecho del bloque (vea ilustraciones). En los 1991 y los motores de cuatro cilindros, el número está al lado izquierdo del bloque,

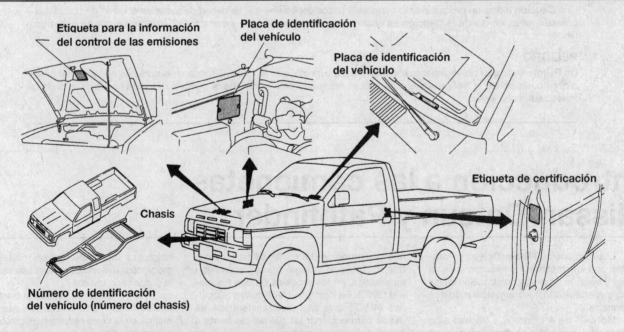

Etiqueta para la información del control de las emisiones

Placa de identificación del vehículo

Placa de identificación del vehículo

Etiqueta de certificación

Chasis

Número de identificación del vehículo (número del chasis)

El número VIN (Número de Identificación del Vehículo) y otros números importante están instalados en el vehículo en diferentes localidades

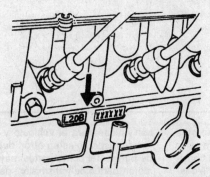

Ubicación de los números de identificación de los modelos más antiguos (con una sola bujía) con motor de cuatro cilindros

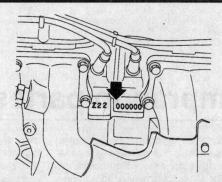

Ubicación de los números de identificación de los modelos más modernos (con dos bujías) con motor de cuatro cilindros

en la parte trasera. En los motores V6, el número de identificación está localizado en la parte trasera del bloque, debajo de la cabeza derecha para los cilindros **(vea ilustración)**.

Número de serie de la transmisión manual

El número de serie de la transmisión manual está localizado en una almohadilla al lado superior del albergue del embrague.

Número de serie de la transmisión automática

En los modelos 1990 y más antiguos, el número de serie de la transmisión automática está localizado en una etiqueta al lado derecho del albergue de la transmisión **(vea ilustración)**. En los modelos 1991 y más moder-

nos, el número está al lado derecho de la extensión.

Número de serie de la caja de transferencia (modelos de 4 tracciones)

El número de serie de la caja de transferencia está localizado al lado derecho del albergue, en la parte delantera o la parte superior del albergue **(vea ilustraciones)**.

Etiqueta de información para el control de las emisiones del vehículo

La etiqueta de información para el control de las emisiones del vehículo está puesta en la parte inferior del capó.

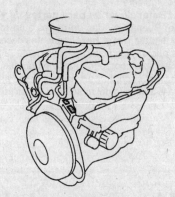

Ubicación de los números de identificación de los motores V6

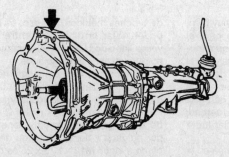

Ubicación de los números de identificación para las transmisiones manuales (flecha)

Ubicación de la etiqueta con los números de identificación para las transmisiones automática - modelos 1990 y mas antiguos (flecha)

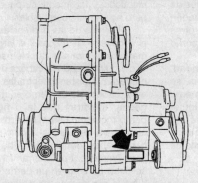

Ubicación de los números de identificación para las cajas de transferencia en los modelos más antiguos (flecha)

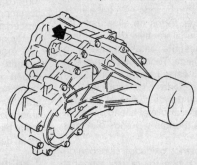

Ubicación de los números de identificación para las cajas de transferencia en los modelos más modernos (flecha)

Comprando partes

Las partes de remplazo son disponibles de muchas fuentes, que generalmente caen en una de dos categorías - distribuidor de partes para el vehículo autorizados (concesionarios de vehículos) y vendedores al menudeo independientes de partes de vehículo. Nuestro consejo acerca de estas partes es lo siguiente:

Refaccionarías para partes de vehículo: Buenas tiendas de partes auto-motrices tendrán partes muy frecuentes necesitadas que se desgastan relativamente rápido, por ejemplo componentes del embrague, sistema del escape, partes de frenos, partes para la afinación del motor, etc. Estas tiendas

muy frecuente pueden suministrar partes nuevas o reconstruidas en una base de cambio, que puede ahorrarle una cantidad considerable de dinero. Las refaccionarías de descuento muy frecuente son lugares muy buenos para comprar partes y materiales necesitados para el mantenimiento general del vehículo como aceite, grasa, filtros, bujías, bandas, pinturas, bombillas etc. También, muy frecuente venden herramientas y accesorios generales, tienen horarios convenientes, los precios son bajos y muy frecuente no están muy lejos del hogar.

Distribuidores de partes autorizados: Ésta es la mejor fuente para las partes que

son únicas para el vehículo y no generalmente disponibles en otros departamentos de partes (tal como partes mayores para el motor, partes de transmisión, partes para las molduras del interior, etc.).

Información de la garantía: ¡Si el vehículo todavía está bajo de garantía, esté seguro que cualquier parte que compre - sin importar donde la compró - no vaya a invalidar la garantía!.

Esté seguro de obtener las partes correctas, tenga el número del motor y del chasis disponible y, si es posible, lleve las partes viejas con usted para la identificación positiva.

Técnicas del mantenimiento, herramientas y facilidades de trabajo

Técnicas para el mantenimiento

Hay varias técnicas envueltas en el mantenimiento y reparación que van a ser referidas atravées de este manual. Aplicación de estas técnicas, ayudará al mecánico del hogar ser más eficaz, mejor organizado y capaz de ejecutar las varias tareas apropiadamente, que asegurará que el trabajo de la reparación sea completo y cabal.

Broches

Broches son tuercas, pernos, tornillos, espárragos, usados para aguantar dos o más partes juntas. Hay varias cosas que se deben de tener en la mente cuando esté trabajando con broches. Casi todos de ellos usan un tipo de cierre, o una arandela de seguridad, contratuerca, pestaña para bloquearla, o adhesivo en la tuerca. Todos los broches con roscas deben de estar limpios y rectos, sin tener las roscas dañadas o las esquinas en la cabeza hexagonal donde se instala la herramienta dañada. Desarrolle el hábito de reemplazar todas las tuercas y pernos dañados con nuevos.

Tuercas y pernos oxidados se deben de tratar con un fluido penetrante para ayudar el procedimiento de removerlos y prevenir de que se rompan. Unos mecánicos usan aceite

trementina en una lata que trabaja muy bien. Después de aplicar el penetrante para el óxido, permítale que trabaje por unos minutos antes de tratar de remover la tuerca o el tornillo. Broches que estén muy oxidados, pueda que tengan que ser removidos con un cincel o ser cortados o romperlos con una herramienta especial para romper tuercas, que se puede encontrar en cualquier lugar donde vendan herramientas.

Si un perno o espárrago se rompe en la asamblea, se puede hacer un hoyo con una barrena y removerlo con una herramienta especial para remover, disponible para este procedimiento. La mayoría de los talleres de torno/rectificación para vehículos pueden desempeñar esta tarea, también como otros procedimientos de reparación, tales como roscas que se hayan barrido.

Arandelas planas y de seguridad, cuando se remuevan de una asamblea, se deben reemplazar siempre exactamente como se removieron. Reemplace cualquier arandela dañada con nuevas. Nunca use una arandela de seguridad en una superficie de metal blanda (tal como aluminio), plancha de metal delgado o plástico.

Tamaños de los broches

Por varias razones, los fabricantes de vehículos están haciendo el uso más amplio

de broches métricos. Por eso, es importante poder notar la diferencia entre normal (a veces llamado U.S. o SAE) y métrico, ya que no pueden ser intercambiados.

Todos los pernos, sean normales o métricos, se clasifican según el tamaño del diámetro, ángulo de la rosca y la longitud. Por ejemplo, un perno normal 1/2 - 13 x 1 es de 1/2 pulgada de diámetro, tiene 13 roscas por pulgada y tiene 1 pulgada de largo. Un perno métrico M12 - 1.75 x 25 es de 12 (mm) en diámetro, el ángulo de las roscas es de 1.75 (mm) (la distancia entre las roscas) y es 25 (mm) de largo. Los dos pernos son casi idénticos, y fácilmente se pueden confundir, pero no son intercambiables.

Además de las diferencias en diámetro, el ángulo de las roscas y el largo, los pernos métricos y normales también se pueden distinguir examinando la cabeza del perno. Para empezar, la distancia entre las partes planas en la cabeza de un perno es medida en pulgadas, mientras que la dimensión en un perno métrico es en milímetros (lo mismo es cierto para las tuercas). Como resultado, una herramienta normal no se debe de usar en un perno métrico y una herramienta métrica no se debe de usar en un perno normal. También, la mayoría de los pernos normales tienen ranuras sobresalientes en la parte del centro de la cabeza del perno, que es una

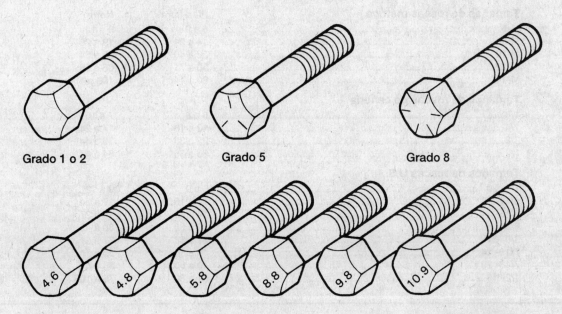

Grado 1 o 2   Grado 5   Grado 8

Marcas de la fuerza del perno (la parte de encima normales/SAE/USS; la parte de abajo métricos)

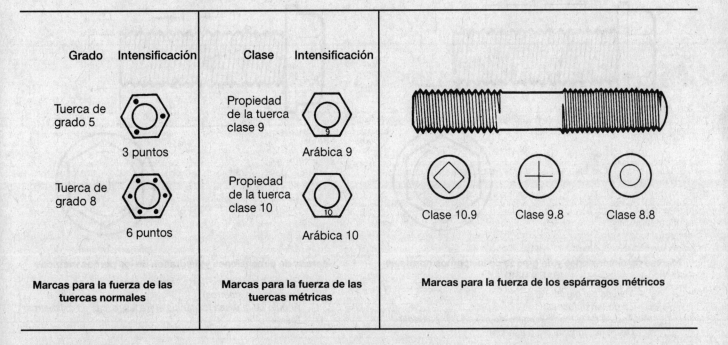

Grado	Intensificación	Clase	Intensificación	
Tuerca de grado 5	3 puntos	Propiedad de la tuerca clase 9	Arábica 9	
Tuerca de grado 8	6 puntos	Propiedad de la tuerca clase 10	Arábica 10	

Clase 10.9   Clase 9.8   Clase 8.8

Marcas para la fuerza de las tuercas normales   **Marcas para la fuerza de las tuercas métricas**   **Marcas para la fuerza de los espárragos métricos**

indicación de la cantidad de torsión que se le puede aplicar. La mayor cantidad de ranuras sobresalientes, lo más potente es el perno. Grado 0 al 5 son muy comúnmente usados en los vehículos. Pernos métricos tienen una clase de número de (grado), en vez de tener ranuras sobresalientes, moldeadas en la cabeza para poder indicar la resistencia que el perno puede resistir. En este caso, según más alto sea el número, lo más fuerte que es el perno. Números de clases apropiados 8.8, 9.8 y 10.9 son comúnmente usados en los vehículos.

Marcas de resistencia que pueden obtenerse también se pueden encontrar para distinguir las tuercas normales de las tuercas métricas. Muchas tuercas normales tienen puntos estampados en un lado, mientras de que las tuercas métricas están marcadas con un número. La mayor cantidad de puntos, o el número más alto, lo más resistente que es la tuerca.

Se marcan también en sus fines según su clase la propiedad de los espárragos de acuerdo al grado. Los espárragos más grandes están numerados (igual que los pernos métricos), mientras de que los espárragos más pequeños tienen un código geométrico para poder denotar el grado.

Se debe notar que muchos broches, sobre todo los de calidades de 0 al 2, no tienen ninguna marca de distinción en ellos. Cuando tal sea el caso, la manera única de determinar si es normal o métrico es de medir la rosca o compararla con otro broche del mismo tamaño.

Los broches normales a menudo se conocen como SAE, opuesto a los métricos. De cualquier modo, se debe notar que la referencia técnica SAE, se refiere a un broche que no sea métrico *de rosca fina solamente*. Broches de roscas gruesas que no sean métricos se les refieren como de tamaños USS.

Habiendo tantos broches del mismo

Tamaños de roscas métrica	Pies-libras	Nm/m
M-6	6 a 9	9 a 12
M-8	14 a 21	19 a 28
M-10	28 a 40	38 a 54
M-12	50 a 71	68 a 96
M-14	80 a 140	109 a·154

Tamaños de roscas de cañería		
1/8	5 a 8	7 a 10
1/4	12 a 18	17 a 24
3/8	22 a 33	30 a 44
1/2	25 a 35	34 a 47

Tamaños de roscas U.S.		
1/4- 20	6 a 9	9 a 12
5/16- 18	12 a 18	17 a 24
5/16- 24	14 a 20	19 a 27
3/8- 16	22 a 32	30 a 43
3/8- 24	27 a 38	37 a 51
7/16- 14	40 a 55	55 a 74
7/16- 20	40 a 60	55 a 81
1/2- 13	55 a 80	75 a 108

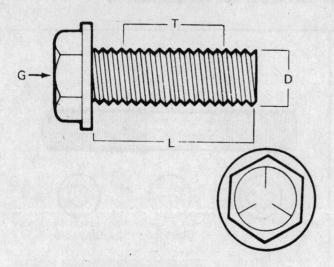

Marcas de dimensiones y de grados de los pernos normales (SAE y USS)

g   Marcas del grado
l   Largo (en pulgadas)
t   Ángulo de la rosca (número de roscas por pulgada)
d   Diámetro nominal (en pulgadas)

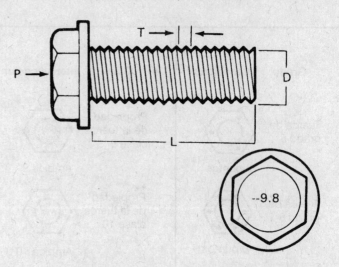

Marcas de dimensiones y de grados de los pernos métricos

p   Propiedad de clase (fortaleza del perno)
l   Largo (en milímetros)
t   Ángulo de la rosca (distancia entre las roscas en milímetros)
d   Diámetro

tamaño (ambos normales y métricos) pueden tener diferente medidas de resistencia, esté seguro de instalar cualquier perno, espárrago o tuerca que se haya removido del vehículo en su localidad original del vehículo. También, cuando esté reemplazando un broche con uno nuevo, esté seguro de que el nuevo tenga la misma resistencia o mayor que el original.

Sucesiones y procedimientos de apretar

La mayoría de los broches con roscas se deben de apretar a un par de torsión especificado (par de torsión es la resistencia de torcer aplicada a un componente con roscas, tal como un perno o una tuerca). Sobre apretar un broche puede debilitarlo y causar que se rompa, mientras dejándolo suelto/flojo puede causar que eventualmente se zafe. Pernos, tornillos y espárragos, depende del material de que se hacen y sus diámetro de las roscas, tienen valores específicos para el par de torsión, muchas de estas se pueden encontrar en las características técnicas al principio de cada Capítulo. Esté seguro de seguir las recomendaciones

para el par de torsión exactamente. Para broches que no tengan asignado un par de torsión específico, una guía general es presentada aquí como valor para el par de torsión. Estos valores del par de torsión son para broches secos (sin lubricar) para roscas en acero o acero forjado (no aluminio). Según se mencionó anteriormente, el tamaño y el grado de los broches determina la cantidad de torsión que se le puede aplicar sin riesgo. Las figuras listadas aquí son aproximadas para broches de grado 2 y grado 3. Grados más altos pueden tolerar valores de torsión más alto.

Broches puestos en un patrón en orden, tal como pernos para las cabezas de los cilindros, pernos para la cacerola del aceite, pernos para la tapa del diferencial, etc., se deben de aflojar o apretar en secuencia para prevenir de que los componentes se tuerzan. Normalmente se mostrará esta sucesión en el Capítulo apropiado. Si no se otorga un dibujo específico, los siguientes procedimientos se pueden seguir para prevenir que se doblen.

Inicialmente, los pernos y las tuercas se deben de instalar y apretar con los dedos solamente. Seguido, se deben de apretar una vuelta completa cada uno, en una sección en cruce o patrón diagonal. Después de que cada uno se a apretado una vuelta completa, regrese al primero y apriételo todos una media vuelta, siguiendo el mismo patrón. Finalmente, apriete cada uno de ellos un cuarto de vuelta a la vez hasta que cada broche se haya apretado al par de torsión apropiado. Para aflojar y remover los broches, el procedimiento es el reverso.

Desarme de los componentes

El desarme de los componentes se deben de hacer con precaución y propósito para asegurarse de que las partes se instalarán de regreso apropiadamente. Siempre guarde la sucesión en el orden que se removieron las partes. Tome nota de las características especiales o marcas en las partes que se puedan instalar más de una manera, tal como arandelas de torsión con ranuras en un eje. Es una buena idea poner las partes que se han desarmado afuera en una superficie limpia y en el orden que se removieron. También puede ayudar si se hacen diagramas o se toman fotografías instantáneas de los componentes antes de que se remuevan.

Cuando remueva los broches de un componente, guarde la trayectoria de sus localidades. A veces enroscando un perno en una parte, o instalando las arandelas y tuercas en un espárrago, puede prevenir confusiones más tarde. Si los pernos y tuercas no se pueden instalar de regreso en sus localidades originales, se deben guardar en una caja o una serie de cajas pequeñas. Una copa o vaso de papel es ideal para este propósito, debido a que cada cavidad puede retener los pernos y las tuercas de una área en particular (pernos de la cacerola del aceite, pernos para la cubierta de las válvulas, pernos del motor, etc.). Una cacerola de este tipo es especialmente útil cuando esté trabajando con partes muy pequeñas, tal como el carburador, alternador, tren de válvulas o partes interiores del tablero. Se pueden marcar las cavidades con pintura o cinta para identificar su contenido.

Cuando grupos de alambres, arnés eléctricos o conectores sean separados, es una buena idea de identificar las dos mitades con pedazos de cintas numeradas para que sean fácil de reinstalar.

Superficie para el sello de las juntas

En cualquier parte de un vehículo, se usan juntas para sellar las superficies de las dos partes que se unen y para retener lubricantes, fluidos, vacío o presión contenida en una asamblea.

Muchas veces estas juntas están cubiertas con un sellador de líquido o pasta antes de instalarse. Edad, calor y presión pueden causar a veces que las dos partes se peguen juntas, tan herméticamente que es muy difíciles separarlas. A menudo, el ensamblaje se puede aflojar golpeándolo con un martillo de cara blanda cerca de las partes que se unen. Se puede usar un martillo regular si se pone un bloque de madera entre el martillo y la parte que se va a golpear. No martille en partes fundidas o partes que se puedan dañar fácilmente. Con cualquier parte que esté muy difícil de remover, siempre verifique dos veces para estar seguro de que todos los pernos se han removido.

Evite usar un destornillador o una palanca para separar una asamblea, porque pueden arañar las superficies de las partes donde se instala la junta, quienes deben de estar muy lisas. Si es absoluto necesario usar una palanca, use el mango de una escoba vieja, pero mantenga en mente de que limpieza extra se necesitará si el mango de la escoba se hace astillas.

Después de que las partes se separen, la junta vieja se debe remover con mucho cuidado y limpiar las superficies para la junta. Juntas difíciles de remover se pueden remojar con penetrante para óxido o tratadas con un químico especial para aflojarlas para que sea más fácil de removerlas. Se puede fabricar un rascador de un pedazo de tubería cobre aplastando y dándole filo en una punta. Algunas juntas se pueden remover con un cepillo de alambre, pero sin importar que método se usa, las superficies que hacen contacto deben de estar muy limpias y lisas. Si por cualquier razón la superficie de la junta es rallada, entonces un sellador para juntas lo suficiente grueso para llenar los rayones se deberá de usar durante el ensamblaje de los componentes. Para la mayoría de las aplicaciones, un sellador que no se seque muy rápido o que se seque bastante despacio se debe usar.

Ayuda para remover las mangueras

Peligro: *Si el vehículo está equipado con aire acondicionado, no desconecte ninguna de las mangueras del A/C sin primero dejar de que una estación de servicio o un concesionario de vehículos remueva la presión al sistema del aire acondicionado primero.*

Precauciones para remover las mangueras son casi iguales a las precauciones para remover las juntas. Evite rayar o acanalar la superficie donde la manguera hace conexión o la conexión tendrá fugas/goteras. Esto es verdadero sobre todo con mangueras del radiador. A causa de reacciones químicas, la goma en las mangueras puede pegarse al metal donde se une la manguera. Para remover una manguera, primero afloje la abrazadera que aguanta la manguera. Entonces, con alicates especiales de puntas resbalosas, agarre la manguera en el punto donde está la abrazadera y gírela. Dele vueltas hacia adelante y hacia atrás y de lado a lado hasta que esté completamente libre, entonces remuévala. Silicona U otro lubricante ayudará a remover la manguera si se puede aplicar entre la parte de adentro de la manguera y la superficie donde hace contacto. Aplique el mismo lubrificante al interior de la manguera y el exterior donde hace contacto para simplificar la instalación.

Como último recurso (y si la manguera se va a reemplazar con una nueva de todos modo), la goma se puede cortar con un cuchillo y la manguera ser pelada de su superficie como una naranja. Si esto se debe de hacer, esté seguro de que la conexión de metal no se dañe.

Si una abrazadera de manguera está rota o dañada, no la use otra vez. Abrazaderas de tipo de alambre por lo general se aflojan con el tiempo, es una buena idea de reemplazarlas con las de tipo de tornillo, cuando se remueva una manguera.

Herramientas

Una selección de herramientas buenas es un requisito básico para cualquiera que tenga planes de mantener y reparar su propio vehículo. Para el dueño que tiene muy pocas herramientas, la inversión inicial puede parecer muy alta, pero cuando se compare con el costo alto de un taller de mantenimiento y reparaciones, es una buena inversión.

Para ayudar al dueño en decidir que tipo de herramienta es necesario para hacer el trabajo diseñado en este manual, la lista siguiente de herramienta es: *Mantenimiento y reparación menor, Reparación/completa y Especialidades.*

El novato a la mecánica debe de empezar con el juego de herramientas de mantenimiento y reparación menor, que es adecuado para los trabajos simples hechos en un vehículo. Después, según la confidencia y la experiencia crezca, el dueño puede hacer

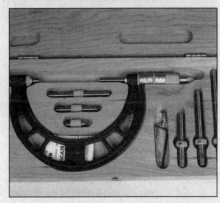

Juego de micrómetros

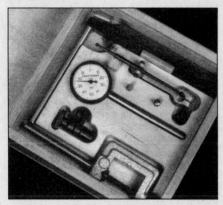

Indicador de tipo reloj

Calibrador de tipo reloj

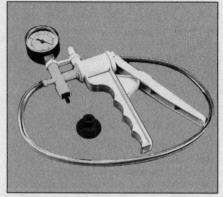

Bomba de vacío operada a mano

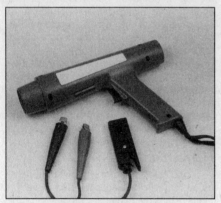

Luz para chequear el tiempo

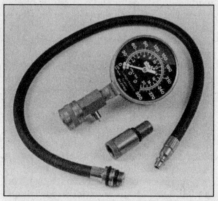

Manómetro para chequear la compresión con adaptador para el hoyo de la bujía

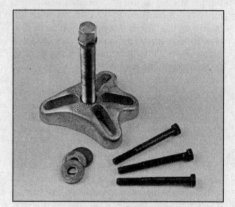

Extractor para volante y compensador armónico

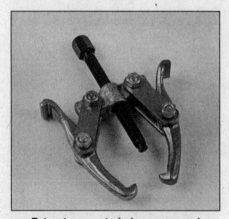

Extractor para trabajos en general

Herramienta para remover buzos hidráulicas

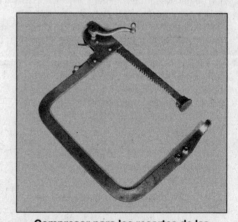

Compresor para los resortes de las válvulas de la cabeza

tareas más difíciles, comprando herramientas adicionales según se necesiten. Eventualmente el juego básico se extenderá dentro del juego de herramientas de reparación completa. Sobre el periodo de un tiempo, el mecánico de hogar recopilara un juego de herramientas lo suficiente mente completo para las mayores reparaciones menores y mayores y agregará herramientas de la categoría especial cuando se piense que el gasto es justificado por la frecuencia del uso.

Herramientas para el mantenimiento y reparaciones menores

Las herramientas en esta lista se deben de considerar lo mínimo requerido para poder desempeñar reparaciones rutinarias de mantenimiento, servicio y trabajo de reparaciones menores. Nosotros recomendamos que se obtengan herramientas de combinaciones (con un lado cerrado y el otro lado abierto que es una sola herramienta). Mientras que más caras que las herramientas abiertas, ofrecen la ventaja de un tipo de herramienta de dos tipos

Juego de herramientas de combinación (1/4 de pulgada a 1 pulgada o de 6 mm a 19 mm
Herramienta ajustable de 8 pulgadas
Herramienta de bujía con inserción de caucho

Compresor para los resortes de las válvulas de la cabeza

Removedor para la rebarba de los cilindros

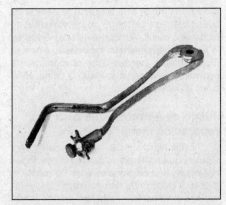

Herramienta para limpiar las ranuras de los pistones

Herramienta para instalar y remover los anillos del pistón

Compresor para los anillos del pistón

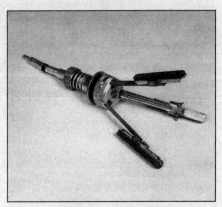

Pulidor para cilindros

Herramienta para los resortes de los frenos

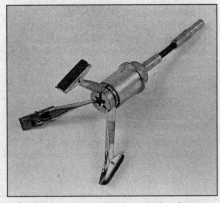

Pulidor para los cilindros de los frenos

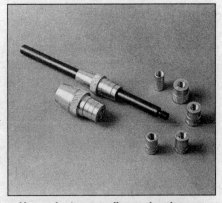

Herramienta para alinear el embrague

Herramienta para ajustar el agujero de la bujía
Juego de calibrador palpador
Herramienta para purgar los frenos
Destornillador normal (5/16 de pulgada x 6 pulgadas)
Destornillador Phillips/de cruces (No. 2 x 6 pulgadas)
Alicates de combinación - de 6 pulgadas
Un surtido de hojas de segueta
Calibrador para la presión de los neumáticos
Pistola de grasa

Lata de aceite
Tela de esmeril fina
Cepillo de alambre
Herramienta para limpiar los postes y los cables de la batería
Herramienta para remover el filtro de aceite
Embudo (de tamaño mediano)
Lentes para la seguridad de los ojos
Soportes (2)
Cacerola de desagüe

Nota: *Si afinación de motor básica va a ser parte del mantenimiento rutinario, seria nece-*

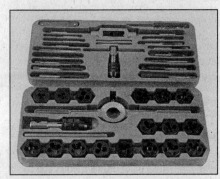

Juego de terrajas hembras y macho

sario de comprar una lampara de tiempo de buena calidad y un metro de combinación de tacómetro/dwell. Aunque estén cubiertos en la lista de herramientas especiales, es mencionado aquí porque son absolutamente necesarios para afinar la mayoría de los vehículos apropiadamente.

Juego de herramientas para reparación menor y mayor

Estas herramientas son esenciales para alguien quien piensa ejecutar reparaciones mayores y son adicionales a las de mantenimiento y el juego de herramientas para reparaciones menores. Incluyen un juego de dados compresivo que, aunque caro, son muy necesarios por su versatilidad, especialmente cuando varias extensiones y tamaños están disponibles. Nosotros recomendamos el juego de 1/2 pulgada sobre el de 3/8 de pulgada. Aunque el juego más grande es más voluminoso y más caro, tiene la capacidad de aceptar una variedad de dados más grande. Idealmente, el mecánico debe de tener un juego de 3/8 y uno de 1/2 pulgada.

Juego(s) de dado
Triquete/matraca reversible
Extensión de 10 pulgadas
Junta universal
Herramienta para el par de torsión (del mismo tamaño del juego de dados)
Martillo de bola de 8 onzas
Martillo de cara blanda (plástico/caucho)
Destornillador normal (1/4 de pulgada x 6 pulgadas)
Destornillador normal (grueso de 5/16 de pulgada)
Destornillador Phillips/cruz (No.3 x 8 pulgadas)
Destornillador Phillips/cruz (grueso No.2)
Alicates de presión
Alicates regulares
Alicates con nariz de punta
Alicates para anillos de presión (interior y exterior)
Cincel frío de 1/2 pulgada
Marcador
Rascador (hecho de tubería plana de cobre)
Punzón
Punzones de alfiler (1/16, 1/8, 3/16 de pulgada)
Regla de acero de 12 pulgadas
Juego de herramientas Allen (de 1/8 a 3/8 de pulgada o de 4 (mm) a 10 (mm)
Una selección de limas
Cepillo del alambre (grande)
Soportes para el vehículo (segundo juego)
Gato (de tipo tijeras o tipo hidráulico)

Nota: *Otra herramienta que es usada muy común es un taladro eléctrico con capacidad para barrenas de 3/8 de pulgada y un buen juego de brocas para el taladro.*

Herramientas especiales

Las herramientas en esta lista incluyen esas que no se usan regularmente, son caras de comprar, o las que se necesitan de acuerdo con las instrucciones de los fabricantes. A menos que estas herramientas se usen frecuentemente, no es muy económico comprar muchas de ellas. Una consideración sería, de dividir el costo entre usted y un amigo o amigos. Además, estas herramientas se puede obtener en un lugar donde rentan herramientas en una base temporaria.

Esta lista principalmente contiene sólo esas herramientas e instrumentos extensamente disponible al público, y no esas herramientas especiales producidas por el fabricante del vehículo para distribución a los concesionarios de vehículos. De vez en cuando, referencias a las herramientas especiales del fabricante son incluidas en el texto de este manual. Generalmente, un método alternativo de hacer el trabajo sin la herramienta especial es ofrecido. Donde no haya otra alternativa y la herramienta no se pueda comprar o pedir prestada, el trabajo debe de ser dirigido a un taller de servicio de un distribuidor de vehículos o a un taller de reparaciones de vehículos.

Compresor de los resortes de las válvulas
Herramienta para limpiar la ranura de los anillos en el pistón
Compresor para los anillos del pistón
Herramienta para instalar los anillos del pistón
Manómetro para chequear la compresión de los cilindros
Removedor de rebaba para los cilindros
Piedra para pulir los cilindros
Herramienta para verificar el diámetro de los cilindros
Micrómetros y/o calibradores de reloj
Herramienta para remover los buzos/levantador hidráulicos
Herramienta para remover las rotulas
Extractor de tipo universal
Destornillador de impacto
Juego de indicadores de reloj
Luz para verificar el tiempo del encendido (captador inductivo)
Bomba de vacío operada a mano
Metro de tacómetro/dwell
Multímetro universal eléctrico
Elevador por cable
Herramienta para remover e instalar los resortes de los frenos
Gato de piso

Compra de herramientas

Para el que va hacer el trabajo por si mismo y está empezando a envolverse en el mantenimiento y reparación del vehículo, hay un número de alternativas cuando se compren las herramientas. Si mantenimiento y reparaciones menores es la magnitud del trabajo que se va hacer, la compra de herramientas individuales es satisfactorio. Si, en cambio, se planea hacer trabajo extensivo, sería una buena idea comprar un juego de herramientas buenas en una sucursal de cadenas de tiendas mayores. Un juego por lo general se puede comprar a un ahorro considerable sobre la inversión de herramientas separadas, y por lo general vienen con una caja para las herramientas. Según herramien-

tas adicionales se vayan necesitando, juegos para agregar, herramientas individuales y una caja de herramientas más grande se puede comprar para extender la selección de las herramientas. Construyendo un juego de herramientas gradualmente le permite que el costo de las herramientas se extienda por un periodo de tiempo más largo y le da al mecánico la libertad de escoger solamente las herramientas que actualmente se usarán.

Tiendas de herramientas serán por lo general la única alternativa de obtener herramientas especiales que se necesiten, sin importar donde se compren las herramientas, trate de evitar las baratas, especialmente cuando esté comprando destornilladores y dados, porque no duran mucho. El gasto envuelto en reponer las herramientas baratas eventualmente será más grande que el costo inicial de herramientas de calidad.

Cuidado y mantenimiento de las herramientas

Herramientas buenas son caras, así que se deben de tratar con cuidado. Guárdelas limpias y en condición utilizable y guárdelas apropiadamente cuando no se estén usando. Siempre limpie cualquier suciedad, grasa o metal antes de guardarlas. Nunca deje herramientas alrededor del área de trabajo. Cuando termine un trabajo, siempre chequee cuidadosamente debajo del capó por herramientas que se hayan dejado olvidadas para que no se vallan a perder durante el tiempo que se prueba el vehículo en la carretera.

Algunas herramientas, tal como destornilladores, alicates y dados, se pueden colgar en un panel montado en el garaje o en la pared del cuarto de trabajo, mientras que las otras se pueden mantener en una caja de herramientas o una bandeja. Instrumentos de medir, relojes, metros, etc. se deben guardar cuidadosamente donde no puedan ser dañados por la interpedie o impacto de otra herramientas.

Cuando se usan las herramientas con cuidado y se guardan apropiadamente, durarán un tiempo muy largo. Hasta con el mejor de los cuidados, las herramientas se gastarán si se usa frecuentemente. Cuando se daña una herramienta o se gasta, se debe de reemplazar. Los trabajos subsecuentes serán más seguros y más agradables si usted hace esto.

Facilidades para trabajar

No se debe de pasar por alto cuando se discute de herramientas, es el taller. Si cualquier cosa más que mantenimiento rutinario se va a llevar a cabo, alguna área adecuada de trabajo es esencial.

Es entendido, y apreciado, que muchos mecánicos del hogar no tienen un taller bueno o garaje disponible, y en fin terminan removiendo un motor o asiendo reparaciones mayores a la interpedie. Es recomendable, que una reparación completa o reparación menor sea completada debajo de un techo.

Un banco de trabajo limpio y plano o una mesa de altura acomodable es una necesidad absoluta. El banco de trabajo debe de estar equipado con una prensa (tornillo de banco) que tenga una mandíbula de por lo menos cuatro pulgadas.

Como se mencionó previamente, se requieren algunos espacios limpios y secos para almacenar las herramientas, igual que los lubricantes, fluidos, solventes de limpieza, etc. que llegarán a ser necesario.

A veces aceite desechado y fluidos, drenado del motor o del sistema de enfriamiento durante mantenimiento normal o reparacio- nes, presentan un problema de disposición. Para evitar de drenarlos en la tierra o en el sistema de drenaje, vacíe los fluidos en recipientes grandes, séllelos con una tapa y llévelos a un lugar autorizado para ser desechado o un centro para ser reciclados. Envases de plástico, tales como recipientes de anticongelante viejos, son ideales para este propósito.

Siempre guarde un suministro de periódicos viejos y trapos limpios disponible. Toallas viejas son excelentes para trapear derramamientos. Muchos mecánicos usan rollos de toallas de papel para la mayoría de los trabajos, porque son disponibles y se pueden desechar. Para ayudar a mantener el área debajo del vehículo limpia, una caja de cartón grande se puede abrir y aplastarla para proteger el piso del área de trabajo.

Cuando esté trabajando sobre una superficie pintada, tal como cuando se recline a un guarda lodo para darle servicio a algo debajo del capo, siempre cúbralo con una colcha vieja o un sobre cama para proteger el terminado de la pintura. Cubiertas de vinilo, hechas especialmente para este propósito, están disponibles en los auto partes.

Arranque con paso/salto de corriente

Ciertas precauciones se deben de tomar cuando esté usando una batería para dar paso de corriente a un vehículo.

a) *Antes de que conecte los cables para dar el paso de corriente, esté seguro de que el interruptor de la ignición está en la posición apagado (OFF).*

b) *Apague las luces, calefacción y cualquier otro accesorio eléctrico.*

c) *Los ojos deben de estar cubiertos. Espejuelos de seguridad son una buena idea.*

d) *Asegúrese de que la batería amplificadora es del mismo voltaje de la batería que está muerta en el vehículo.*

e) *¡Los dos vehículos NO DEBEN TOCAR el uno con el otro!*

f) *Asegúrese de que la transmisión está en Neutral (manual) o Estacionamiento (automática).*

g) *Si la batería amplificadora no es de un tipo de mantenimiento libre, remueva las tapas de ventilación e instale una tela* encima de la abertura de los agujeros de ventilación.

Conecte el cable rojo a los términos positivos (+) de cada batería **(vea ilustración)**.

Conecte una terminal del cable negro al termino negativo (-) de la batería que va a proporcionar el paso de corriente. El otro terminal de este cable se debe de conectar a una buena tierra del vehículo que se va a poner en marcha, tal como un perno o un soporte del bloque del motor. Use caución para asegurarse de que el cable no se ponga en contacto con el abanico, las bandas o cualquier otra parte que se esté moviendo en el motor.

Ponga el motor en marcha usando la batería suministrada para dar el paso de corriente, después, con el motor en marcha mínima, desconecte los alambres para el paso de corriente en el orden de reversa de como se conectó.

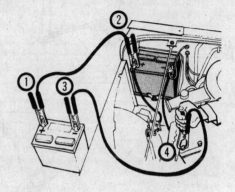

Conexiones para los cables de la batería auxiliar (note que el cable negativo no está adjunto al borne negativo de la batería muerta)

Alzar y remolquear

Alzar

El gato suministrado con el vehículo solamente se debe de usar para levantar el vehículo cuando esté cambiando una rueda o instalando soportes debajo del chasis. **Peligro:** *Nunca trabaje debajo del vehículo o ponga el motor en marcha mientras se está usando este gato como el único medio de soporte.*

El vehículo debe de estar en un piso nivelado con las ruedas bloqueadas y la transmisión en Estacionamiento (automática) o Reversa (manual). En los vehículos de 4WD (tracción en las cuatro ruedas), la caja de transferencia debe de estar en la posición 2H, 4H o 4L.

Si un neumático se tiene que cambiar, remueva la tapadera (si está equipado), afloje la tuerca media vuelta y déjela en su posición hasta que el neumático se levante del piso. Ponga el gato en la parte inferior del vehículo en la posición indicada **(vea ilustraciones).**

Opere el gato bien despacio y con cuidado hasta que los neumáticos se hayan levantado del piso. Termine removiendo las tuercas, entonces remueva el neumático e instale el de respuesto. Instale las tuercas y apriételas hasta que estén firme, pero espere hasta que la rueda esté en el piso para apretarlas con la herramienta. Baje el vehículo, remueva el gato y apriete las tuercas en un patrón de cruce. Gire la herramienta en dirección de las manecillas del reloj.

Remolque

Estos vehículos se pueden remolcar con las cuatro ruedas en el piso, proveyendo de que la velocidad no exceda 30 mph y la distancia no sea más de 40 millas, de otra forma puede resultar en daño a la transmisión. Si es necesario de remolcar el vehículo a una velocidad más alta y/o una distancia más larga, remueva el eje(s) de propulsión.

Equipo para remolque especialmente diseñado para este propósito se debe de usar y ser instalado a la estructura principal del miembro del vehículo, no a los para choques o los soportes.

Seguridad es el factor más importante cuando remolque y todas la leyes aplicables estatales y locales se deben de obedecer. Un sistema con cadena de seguridad se debe de usar para todos los remolques.

Mientras está remolcando, el freno de estacionamiento debe de estar libre y la transmisión en Neutral. En los modelos de cuatro tracción, la palanca de control debe de estar en Neutral y los cubos de las ruedas deben de estar en una posición libre. El volante debe de estar libre sin estar cerrado (interruptor de la ignición en la posición Apagado). ¡Recuerde de que la suspensión con asistencia y los frenos de poder no trabajarán con el motor apagado!

Frente (modelos de tracción en las dos ruedas traseras)

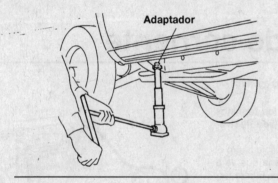

Frente (modelos de tracción en las cuatro ruedas)

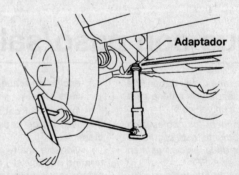

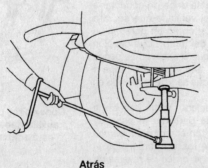

Detalles de como poner el gato en el vehículo de modelo D21

Atrás

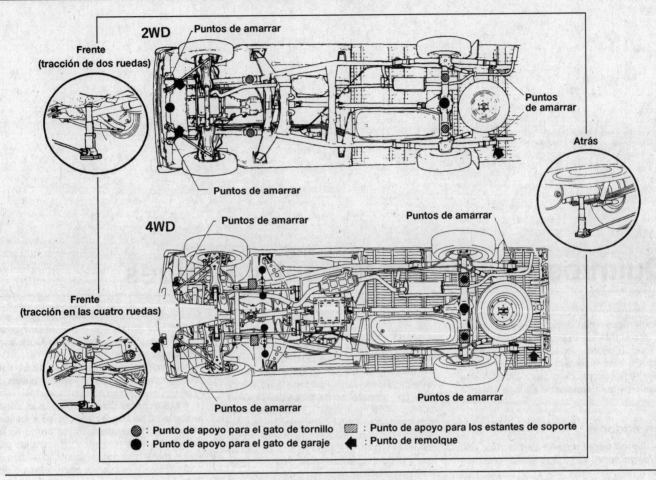

2WD

Frente
(tracción de dos ruedas)

Puntos de amarrar

Puntos de amarrar

Puntos de amarrar

Atrás

4WD

Frente
(tracción en las cuatro ruedas)

Puntos de amarrar

Puntos de amarrar

Puntos de amarrar

Puntos de amarrar

⬤ : Punto de apoyo para el gato de tornillo ▨ : Punto de apoyo para los estantes de soporte

⬤ : Punto de apoyo para el gato de garaje ◄ : Punto de remolque

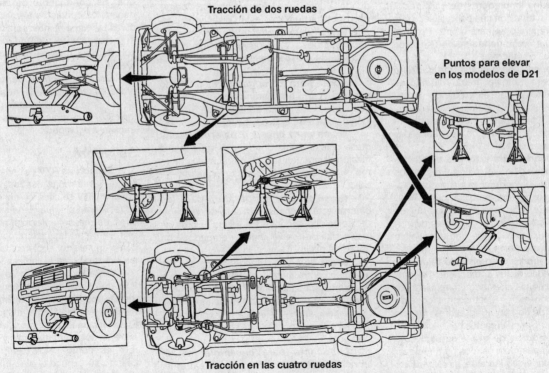

Tracción de dos ruedas

Puntos para elevar
en los modelos de D21

Tracción en las cuatro ruedas

Cuando esté elevando el vehículo o soportándolo sobre soportes, esté seguro de posicionar el equipo como se
muestra en este diagrama (modelo de vehículo 720)

Químicos y lubricantes automotrices

Un número de químicos y lubricantes automotrices están disponibles para usarse durante el mantenimiento y la reparación del vehículo. Ellos incluyen una variedad de productos que se extienden de solventes de limpiar y removedores de grasa a lubricantes y rociadores para proteger el caucho, plástico y vinilo.

Limpiadores

Limpiadores para el carburador y el estrangulador son unos solventes muy fuerte para remover barniz y carbón. La mayoría de los limpiadores de carburador dejan un lubricante con una película seca que no se endurecerá o se hará barniz. Por esta película, no es recomendable de usarlo en componentes eléctricos.

Limpiadores para el sistema de freno es usado para remover grasa y líquido de freno del sistema de freno, cuando superficies limpias son absolutamente necesarias. No deja ningún residuo y muy frecuente eliminan ruidos de los frenos causados por contaminantes.

Limpiadores para sistemas eléctricos remueven oxidación, corrosión y depósitos de carbón de los contactos eléctricos, restaurando el flujo de corriente completo. También se puede usar para limpiar las bujías, espreas del carburador, reguladores de voltajes y otras partes donde una super-ficie libre de aceite es deseada.

Removedores de humedad remueven agua y humedad de los componentes eléctricos tales como los alternadores, reguladores de voltaje, conectores eléctricos y bloque de fusibles. Estos no son conductores, no son corrosivos y no son flamantes.

Removedores de grasa son solvente para trabajos pesados, usados para remover grasa de la parte de afuera del motor y de los componentes del chasis. Estos se pueden atomizar o ser aplicados con una brocha y, dependiendo en el tipo, enjugados con agua o solvente.

Lubricantes

Aceite de motor es el lubrificante formulado para usarlo en los motores. Normalmente contiene una variedad amplia de aditivos para prevenir corrosión y reducir la espuma y desgaste. El aceite para motor viene en una variedad de pesos (valuaciones de viscosidad) de 0 al 50. El peso del aceite recomendado para el motor depende en la estación del año, temperatura y la demanda del motor. Aceite delgado se usa en climas fríos y donde la demanda del motor es baja. Aceites gruesos se usan en climas calientes y donde la demanda del motor es alta. Aceites de viscosidad múltiple están diseñados para que tengan características de los dos delgado y grueso y se pueden hallar en un número de pesos desde 5W - 20 hasta 20W - 50.

Aceite para los engranes es diseñado para ser usado en diferenciales, transmisiones manuales y otras áreas donde lubricación de alta temperatura es requerido.

Grasa para chasis y baleros es una grasa gruesa usada donde la carga y la alta fricción se encuentran, tal como en los baleros de las ruedas, rotulas y uniones universales.

Grasa de alta temperatura para los baleros está diseñada para sostener las temperaturas alta encontradas en los baleros de las ruedas de los vehículos equipados con frenos de disco.

Grasa blanca es una grasa gruesa para aplicación entre metal y metal donde el agua es un problema. La grasa blanca se mantiene suave durante temperaturas bajas y altas (por lo general de -100 hasta +190 grados F), y no se sale del metal o diluye en la presencia del agua.

Lubricante para ensamblar es un lubricante especial de presión extrema, comúnmente conteniendo moly, usado para lubricar partes de alta fricción/cargo (tal como cojinetes principales, de bielas y árbol de levas) para el arranque inicial de un motor.

El lubricante para ensamblar lubrica las partes sin ser exprimido hacia afuera o ser lavado hasta que el sistema de lubricación del motor esté funcionando.

Lubricantes de silicio se usan para proteger caucho, plástico, vinilo y partes de nilón.

Lubricantes de grafito se usan donde el aceite no se puede usar debido a los problemas de contaminación, tal como en las cerraduras. El grafito seco lubricará las partes de metal mientras se mantendrá fuera de contaminación del polvo, agua, aceite o ácidos. Es conductible de electricidad y no dañará los contactos eléctricos en las cerraduras tal como el interruptor de la ignición.

Penetrantes de tipo moly aflojan, lubrican pernos, tuercas oxidadas, corroídas y previenen corrosión y oxidación en el futuro.

Grasa de calor penetrante es una grasa eléctrica especial no conductiva, que se usa para montar módulos electrónicos de ignición, donde es esencial que el calor se transfiera del módulo.

Selladores

Selladores RTV es uno de los compuestos de juntas más usados. Hechos de silicona, el RTV se seca con el aire, sella, pega, es resistente al agua, llena superficies irregulares, se mantiene flexible, no se encoge, es relativamente fácil de remover, y es usado como un sellador suplemental con casi todas las juntas de baja y mediana temperatura.

Sellador anaerobio es muy parecido al RTV que se puede usar para sellar juntas o formar una junta por si mismo. Se mantiene flexible, es resistente al solvente y llena imperfecciones en la superficie. La diferencia entre un sellador anaerobio y un sellador tipo RTV es como se seca. El RTV se seca cuando se expone al aire, mientras un sellador anaerobio se seca solamente en la ausencia de aire.

Sellador para rosca y pipa es usado para sellar conexiones hidráulicas, neumáticas y líneas de vacío. Es hecho por lo general de compuesto de teflón, y viene en un atomizador, pintura liquida y como una forma de cinta.

Productos químicos

Compuesto contra el atoramiento de las roscas previene de que se atoren las roscas por oxido, frío y corrosión. Este tipo de compuesto para temperaturas altas, por lo general está compuesto de cobre y lubricante de grafito, es usado en sistemas de escape y pernos en el múltiple del escape.

Compuesto anaerobio para las roscas se usan para mantener las tuercas en su lugar para que se aflojan bajo vibraciones y se seca después de que se instala, en ausencia de aire. Compuesto de media fuerza se usa para tuercas pequeñas, pernos y tornillos que se podrán remover más adelante. Compuesto de una fuerza más grande se usa en tuercas más grande, pernos y espárragos que no se remueven regularmente.

Aditivos para el aceite son catalogados debido a sus propiedades químicas que ayudan a reducir las fricciones interna del motor. Se debe mencionar que las mayorías de los fabricantes de aceite recomiendan no usar ningún tipo de aditivo con sus aceites.

Aditivos para la gasolina ejecutan varias funciones, dependiendo en los compuestos químicos. Usualmente contienen solventes que ayudan a eliminar el barniz que se acumula encima del carburador, sistema de inyección y los puertos de entrada. Estos también ayudan a eliminar los depósitos de carbón que se depositan encima de la cámara de combustión. Algunos aditivos contienen lubricante para la parte de encima de los cilindros, para lubricar las válvulas y los anillos de los pistones, y otros contienen químicos para remover la condensación en el tanque de gasolina.

Misceláneas

Fluido de freno es un fluido hidráulica especialmente formulado, que puede sostener el calor y la presión que se encuentra en el sistema de frenos. Mucho cuidado se debe de tener de que este fluido no entre en contacto con las partes pintadas del vehículo o plástico. Un recipiente abierto siempre se debe de sellar para prevenir contaminación de agua o tierra.

Adhesivo para caucho se usa para pegar caucho alrededor de las puertas, ventanas y el maletero. También aveces se usa para pegar molduras.

Selladores para la parte de abajo del vehículo es una base de petróleo, diseñada para proteger las superficies de metales de la parte de abajo del vehículo de la corrosión. También actúa como un agente para dosificar el sonido insolando la parte de abajo del vehículo.

Ceras y pulidores se usan para ayudar a proteger la pintura y las partes plateadas de la interpedie. Diferente tipos de pinturas pueden requerir diferente tipos de ceras y pulidores. Algunos pulidores utilizan limpiadores químicos o abrasivos para ayudar a remover la capa de encima de oxidación de la pintura (sin lustre) en los vehículos más antiguos. En los años recientes muchos pulidores sin ceras que contienen una variedad de químicos tales como los que son basados en silicona se han introducido. Estos pulidores sin cera son por lo general más fáciles de aplicar y duran un tiempo más largo que las ceras y pulidores convencionales.

Factores de conversión

Largo (distancia)

Pulgadas	X	25.4	=	Milímetros (mm)	X 0.0394 =	Pulgada
Pies	X	0.305	=	Metros (m)	X 3.281 =	Pies
Millas	X	1.609	=	Kilómetros (km)	X 0.621 =	Millas

Volumen (capacidad)

Pulgadas cubicas	X	16.387	=	Centímetros cúbicos	X 0.061 =	Pulgadas
Pinta imperial	X	0.568	=	Litros	X 1.76 =	Pinta imperial
Cuarto imperial	X	1.137	=	Litros	X 0.88 =	Cuarto imperial
Cuarto imperial	X	1.201	=	Cuarto US	X 0.833 =	Cuarto imperial
Cuarto US	X	0.946	=	Litros	X 1.057 =	Cuarto US
Galón imperial	X	4.546	=	Litros	X 0.22 =	Galón imperial
Galón imperial	X	1.201	=	Galón US	X 0.833 =	Galón imperial
Galón US	X	3.785	=	Litros	X 0.264 =	Galón US

Masa (peso)

Onzas	X	28.35	=	Gramo	X 0.035 =	Onzas
Libras	X	0.454	=	kilogramo	X 2.205 =	Libras

Fuerza

Onzas de fuerza	X	0.278	=	Newton	X 3.6 =	Onzas de fuerza
Libras de fuerza	X	4.448	=	Newton	X 0.225 =	Fuerza de libras
Newton	X	0.1	=	Kilogramo de fuerza	X 9.81 =	Newton

Presión

Libras de fuerza por pulgadas cuadradas	X	0.070	=	Kilogramo de fuerza	X 14.223 =	Libras de fuerza por pulgada cuadrada
Libras de fuerza por pulgadas cuadradas	X	0.068	=	Atmósfera	X 14.696 =	Libras de fuerza por pulgada cuadrada
Libras de fuerza por pulgadas cuadradas	X	0.069	=	Bars	X 14.5 =	Libras de fuerza por pulgada cuadrada
Libras de fuerza por pulgadas cuadradas	X	6.895	=	Kilopascals	X 0.145 =	Libras de fuerza por pulgada cuadrada
Kilopascals	X	0.01	=	Centímetro cuadrado kilogramo de fuerza por	X 98.1 =	Kilopascals

Torsión (momento de fuerza)

Fuerza de libras por pulgadas	X	1.152	=	Kilogramo de fuerza por centímetro	X 0.868 =	Fuerza de libras por pulgadas
Fuerza de libras por pulgadas	X	0.113	=	Metros Newton	X 8.85 =	Fuerza de libras por pulgadas
Fuerza de libras por pulgadas	X	0.083	=	Fuerza de libras por pies	X 12 =	Fuerza de libras por pulgadas
Fuerza de libras por pulgadas	X	0.138	=	Kilogramo de fuerza por metro	X 7.233 =	Fuerza de libras por pies
Fuerza de libras por pulgadas	X	1.356	=	Metros Newton	X 0.738 =	Fuerza de libras por pies
Metros Newton	X	0.102	=	Kilogramo de fuerza por metro	X 9.804 =	Metros Newton

Poder

Caballo de fuerza	X	745.7	=	Watts	X 0.0013 =	Caballo de fuerza

Velocidad

Millas por horas	X	1.609	=	Kilometro por horas	X 0.621 =	Millas por horas

Consumo de combustible *

Millas por galón, Imperial	X	0.354	=	Kilometro por litro	X 2.825 =	Millas por galón, Imperial
Millas por galón, US	X	0.425	=	Kilometro por litro	X 2.352 =	Millas por galón, US

Temperatura

Grados Fahrenheit = (°C x 1.8) + 32   Grados en Celsius (grados en centígrados; °C) = (°F - 32) x 0.56

* Es una práctica muy común de convertir las millas por galón (Mpg) a litros/100 kilómetros (1/100), cuando Mpg (Imperial) x 1/100 km = 282 y Mpg (US) x 1/100 km = 235

¡Seguridad primero!

Sin importar que tan entusiástico usted esté con el trabajo que usted va a desempeñar, tome el tiempo para asegurarse de que su seguridad no esté a riesgo. Un momento que le falte la concentración puede resultar en un accidente, igual que fallar a observar ciertas precauciones simples de seguridad. La posibilidad de un accidente existirá siempre, y la lista siguiente no se debe considerar una lista comprensiva de todos los peligros. Más bien, están hechas con la intención de ponerlo en alerta de estos riesgos y de promocionar una seguridad en su conciencia en todo tipo de trabajo que realice en su vehículo.

Esenciales SI y NO

NO confíe en un gato cuando esté trabajando debajo del vehículo. Siempre use estantes aprobados para este tipo de trabajo, para soportar el peso del vehículo e instálelos debajo del lugar recomendado o los puntos de soportes.

NO atente zafar tuercas o tornillos que estén muy apretados (tuercas de las ruedas) mientras el vehículo está en el gato - se puede caer.

NO ponga el motor en marcha antes de asegurarse de que la transmisión está en neutral (o estacionamiento donde sea aplicable) y el freno de estacionamiento está aplicado.

NO remueva la tapa del radiador del sistema de enfriamiento cuando esté caliente - déjelo que se enfríe o cúbralo con un pedazo de trapo y permita que la presión se salga gradualmente.

NO atente drenar el aceite del motor hasta que usted esté seguro de que se ha enfriado hasta el punto de que no se va a quemar.

NO toque ninguna parte del motor o del sistema de escape hasta que se haya enfriado lo suficiente para prevenir quemaduras.

NO remueva líquidos en forma de sifón tales como gasolina, anticongelante y fluidos de freno con la boca o permita de que entren en contacto con su piel.

NO respire polvo de los frenos - es potencialmente dañino **(vea asbestos más abajo)**

NO deje aceite derramado ni grasa que permanezca en el piso - séquelo antes de que alguien se resbale.

NO use herramientas que queden flojas u otro tipo de herramientas que se puedan resbalar y causar una lesión.

NO empuje en las herramientas cuando esté zafando o apretando tuercas o pernos. Siempre trate de halar la herramienta contra usted. Si la situación requiere empujar la herramienta (separándola de usted), empújela con la mano abierta para prevenir de golpearse la parte de enfrente de los dedos en el caso de que se resbale.

NO atente levantar un componente muy pesado sólo - pídale a alguna persona que lo ayude.

NO se apresure ni tome caminos cortos para terminar un trabajo.

NO deje que niños ni animales anden alrededor del vehículo mientras usted está trabajando.

SI use protección en los ojos cuando este usando herramientas de fuerza tales como taladros, esmeriladoras de banco, etc. y cuando esté trabajando debajo del vehículo.

SI mantenga ropa y pelo suelto bien retirado de cualquier parte que se esté moviendo.

SI esté seguro de que cualquier tipo de elevador tenga una capacidad adecuada para el trabajo que se está desempeñando.

SI tenga a una persona que chequee en usted periódicamente cuando esté trabajando sólo en el vehículo.

SI haga el trabajo en una secuencia lógica y asegúrese de que todo está correctamente ensamblado y apretado.

SI mantenga químicos y fluidos con tapa seguramente sellados y que no lo puedan alcanzar los niños o los animales.

SI se debe recordar que la seguridad de su vehículo afectará a usted y a otros. Si está en duda en cualquier momento, tome consejo de un profesional.

Asbestos

Algunos tipos de fricciones, aisladores, selladores y otros productos - tales como zapatas de freno, bandas de freno, forro del embrague, juntas, etc. - contienen asbestos. Cuidado extensivo se debe de tomar para evitar respirar el polvo de estos productos, ya que es peligroso para su salud. Si está en duda, supóngase de que contienen asbestos.

Fuego

Recuerde todo el tiempo de que la gasolina es muy inflamable. Nunca fume o tenga ningún tipo de llamas alrededor cuando esté trabajando en un vehículo. Pero el riesgo no termina aquí. Una chispa causada por un corto circuito, por dos superficies de metal haciendo contacto una con la otra, o hasta electricidad estática acumulada en su cuerpo bajo ciertas condiciones, pueden encender los vapores de gasolina, quienes en un lugar reducido pueden explotar. **NUNCA**, bajo ninguna circunstancia, use gasolina para limpiar partes. Use un solvente aprobado que no sea peligroso y de seguridad aprobada.

Siempre desconecte el cable negativo de la batería (-) antes de trabajar en el sistema de combustible o de electricidad. Nunca arriesgue derramar combustible en un motor caliente o en los componentes del escape. Es muy fuertemente recomendado que un extinguidor de fuegos esté disponible siempre cerca para usarlo en caso de un fuego eléctrico o de gasolina. Nunca trate de extinguir un fuego eléctrico o de gasolina con agua.

Vapores

Ciertos tipos de vapores son altamente tóxicos y rápidamente pueden causar inconsciencia y hasta la muerte si se respira hasta cierto punto. Los vapores de gasolina entran adentro de esta categoría, igual que algunos vapores de unos solventes de limpieza. Cualquier drenaje de cualquiera de estos fluidos volátiles se debe de hacer en una área bien ventilada.

Cuando esté usando fluidos de limpieza y solventes, lea las instrucciones en el recipiente muy cuidadosamente. Nunca use materiales de un recipiente que no esté marcado.

Nunca deje el motor en marcha en un espacio cerrado, tal como un garaje. Los vapores del escape contienen Monóxido de Carbón, que es extremadamente venenoso. Si usted necesita tener el motor en marcha, siempre hágalo al aire abierto, o por lo menos tenga la parte de atrás del vehículo fuera del área de trabajo.

Si está lo suficiente afortunado de tener

un hoyo en el piso para hacer inspecciones, nunca desagüe o derrame gasolina y nunca mantenga el vehículo en marcha encima del hoyo de inspección. Los vapores, siendo más pesados que el aire, se concentrarán en el hoyo con resultados letales.

La batería

Nunca inicie una chispa o permita que una bombilla sin cubierta se acerque a una batería. Normalmente las baterías despiden cierta cantidad de gas de hidrógeno, que es muy explosivo.

Siempre desconecte el cable negativo (-) de la batería antes de comenzar a trabajar en el sistema de gasolina o eléctrico.

Si es posible, afloje las tapas por donde se llena, cuando esté cargando la batería con una fuente externa (esto no se aplica a baterías selladas o de mantenimiento libre). No cargue la batería a una velocidad muy rápida o se puede estallar.

Tome precaución cuando agregue agua a la batería de mantenimiento libre y cuando transporte una batería. El electrólito, hasta cuando está diluido, es muy corrosivo y no se debe permitir poner en contacto con la ropa o piel.

Siempre use protección para los ojos cuando limpie la batería para prevenir que los depósitos cáusticos entren en sus ojos.

Corriente del hogar

Cuando esté usando una herramienta de poder eléctrica, luz de inspección, etc., que opere con corriente del hogar, siempre asegúrese que la herramienta está correctamente conectada en su enchufe y que, esté apropiadamente conectada a tierra. No use este tipo de artículo en condiciones húmedas y, de nuevo, no cree una chispa o aplique calor excesivo en la vecindad de gasolina o vapores de gasolina.

Voltaje del sistema secundario de la ignición

Un choque eléctrico severo puede resultar tocando ciertas partes del sistema de ignición (tal como los alambres de las bujías) cuando el motor esté en marcha o se esté tratando de poner en marcha, particularmente si los componentes están húmedos o el aislamiento está defectuoso. En el caso de un sistema de ignición electrónica, el voltaje del sistema secundario es más alto y podría probar ser fatal.

Identificación y resolución de problemas

Contenidos

Esta Sección provee una guía de referencia fácil a los problemas más comunes que ocurrirán durante la operación de su camión. Estos problemas y posibles causas son agrupadas debajo de varios componentes o sistemas, tal como motor, sistema de enfriamiento, etc., y también se refiere a Capítulo(s) y/o Sección(es) que tratan con el problema.

Recuérdese que para resolver un problema satisfactoriamente no es un arte misterioso que es practicado solamente por mecánicos profesionales. Es solamente el resultado de un poco de conocimiento, combinado con inteligencia y un acercamiento sistemático al problema. Siempre trabaje bajo un proceso de eliminación, empezando con la solución más simple y trabajando hacia la más compleja y nunca sobre mire lo obvio. A cualquiera se le puede olvidar llenar el tanque de combustible o dejar las luces encendida toda la noche, así que no asuma que nada de esto no sucede .

Finalmente, siempre ponga claro en su mente porqué un problema a ocurrido y tome pasos para asegurar que no suceda de nuevo. Si el sistema eléctrico falla a causa de una conexión pobre, cheque todas las otras conexiones en el sistema para asegurarse que no fallen igualmente. Si un fusible en particular continúa quemándose, averigüe porque - no solamente reemplace el fusible. Recuerde, el fallo de un componente pequeño a menudo puede ser indicación de un fallo más grande o funcionamiento incorrecto de un componente más importante o sistema.

Motor y rendimiento del motor

1 El motor no gira cuando se trata de poner en marcha

1   Las conexiones de los terminales de la batería están sueltas o corroídas. Cheque los términos del cable a la batería. Apriete el cable o remueva la corrosión según sea necesario (vea Capítulo 1).
2   Batería descargada o defectuosa. Si las conexiones de los cables están limpias y firme en la batería, gire la llave en la posición de encendido (ON) y encienda los faro del automóvil y/o los limpia parabrisas. Si no funcionan, la batería está descargada.
3   La transmisión automática no está completamente en Parqueo/Neutral o el embrague no está completamente deprimido.
4   Instalación eléctrica rota, suelta o desconectada en el circuito de arranque. Inspeccione todas las conexiones eléctricas y conecte la batería, solenoide del motor de arranque y el interruptor de la ignición.
5   Piñón del motor de arranque trabado en el anillo del volante. Si está equipado con una transmisión manual, ponga la transmisión en guía y meza el camión para manualmente mover el motor. Remueva el motor de arranque e inspeccione el piñón y el volante a la

conveniencia más rápida (Capítulo 5).
6   Solenoide del motor de arranque defectuoso (Capítulo 5).
7   Motor de arranque defectuoso (Capítulo 5).
8   Interruptor de la ignición defectuoso (Capítulo 12).

2 El motor gira pero no comienza

1   Tanque del combustible vacío.
2   Problema en el carburador o sistema de inyección (Capítulo 4).
3   Los terminales de las conexiones de la batería sueltos o corroídos.
4   Carburador inundado y/o nivel del combustible en el carburador incorrecto. Esto usualmente se acompaña con un olor de combustible fuerte debajo del capó. Espere unos minutos, deprima el pedal del acelerador hasta el suelo e intente poner el motor en marcha.
5   Control del estrangulador no está operando (Capítulo 4).
6   El combustible no llega al carburador o los inyectores de combustible. Con la llave de la ignición en la posición abierta, abra el capo/cofre, remueva la parte de encima de la tapa de la asamblea del depurador de aire y observe la parte de encima del carburador (moviendo manualmente la mariposa del estrangulador). Tenga un ayudante disponible para que deprima el pedal del acelerador y cheque si el combustible sale del carburador. Si no, cheque el filtro del combustible (Capítulo 1), línea de combustible y bomba de combustible (Capítulo 4).
7   Los inyectores de combustible, carburador o bomba de combustible defectuosa (camiones con inyección de combustible) (Capítulo 4).
8   No poder eléctrico a la bomba del combustible (Capítulo 4).
9   Gastadas, defectuosas o incorrectamente ajustada la luz de las bujías (Capítulo 1).
10   Instalación eléctrica rota, suelta o desconectada en el circuito de arranque (Capítulo 5).
11   Distribuidor suelto, causando el tiempo de la ignición que cambie. Gire la asamblea del distribuidor completamente para poner el motor en marcha, entonces fije el tiempo de la ignición lo más rápido posible (Capítulo 1).
12   Alambres sueltos, desconectados o defectuoso en la bobina de la ignición (Capítulo 5).

3 El motor de arranque gira sin girar el motor

1   Piñón del motor de arranque se está pegando. Remueva el motor de arranque (Capítulo 5) e inspeccionelo.
2   Piñón del motor de arranque o dientes del volante gastados o rotos. Remueva la tapa trasera en el motor e inspeccionelo.

4 El motor es difícil de poner en marcha cuando está frío

1   Batería descargada o baja. Check as described in Chapter 1.
2   Control del estrangulador sin estar operando o fuera de ajuste (Capítulo 4).
3   Carburador inundado.
4   El suministro del combustible no llega al carburador.
5   Carburador o sistema de inyección de combustible en necesidad de reparación (Capítulo 4).
6   Carbón en el rotor del distribuidor y/o mecanismo mecánico de avance oxidado (Capítulo 5).
7   Sistema de inyección no funcionando apropiadamente (Capítulo 4).

5 El motor es difícil de poner en marcha cuando está caliente

1   Filtro del aire obstruido (Capítulo 1).
2   Combustible no llegando a los inyectores o al carburador.
3   Conexiones eléctricas en la batería corroídas (Capítulo 1).
4   Mala conexión a tierra (Capítulo 1).
5   Motor de arranque gastado (Capítulo 5).
6   Conexiones eléctricas en los inyectores de combustible corroídas (Capítulo 4).

6 Motor de arranque muy ruidoso o excesivamente áspero cuando hace contacto con el volante

1   Piñón o dientes del volante gastados o rotos. Remueva la tapa de inspección trasera del motor (si está equipada) e inspeccionelo.
2   Pernos para el montaje del motor de arranque sueltos o faltando.

7 El motor arranca pero se apaga inmediatamente

1   Conexiones eléctricas del distribuidor sueltas o defectuosas, bobina o alternador.
2   Insuficiente combustible llegando al carburador o inyector de combustible. Desconecte la línea de combustible. Ponga un recipiente debajo de la línea de combustible desconectada y observe el flujo del combustible de la línea. Si muy pequeño o ninguno en absoluto, cheque por obstáculo en las líneas y/o reemplace la bomba del combustible (Capítulo 4).
3   Fuga de vacío en la junta de la superficie del carburador o unidad de inyección del combustible. Asegúrese que todos los pernos y tuercas que aseguran el montaje, están apretados firmemente y que todas las mangueras de vacío están conectadas al carburador o unidad de inyección y el múltiple de admisión, que estén instaladas apropiadamente y en buenas condiciones.

8 El motor falla o funciona erráticamente en marcha mínima

1   Fuga de vacío. Chequee los pernos y tuercas de montaje en el carburador o unidad de inyección y el múltiple de admisión para estar seguro de que estén apretados. Asegúrese que todas las mangueras de vacío estén conectadas y en buenas condiciones. Use un estetoscopio o un pedazo de manguera de combustible puesto contra su oreja para escuchar por fuga de vacío mientras el motor está en marcha. Se oirá un sonido como un chiflido. Chequee la superficie de la junta del carburador/inyector de combustible y el múltiple de admisión.
2   Fuga de la válvula EGR (recirculación de los gases de escape) o válvula PCV (ventilación positiva del cárter) obstruida (vea Capítulos 1 y 6).
3   Filtro del aire obstruido (Capítulo 1).
4   Bomba del combustible no entrega suficiente combustible al carburador/inyector de combustible.
5   Carburador fuera de ajuste (Capítulo 4).
6   Fuga de la junta de la cabeza. Si se sospecha esto, lleve el camión a un taller de reparación o su concesionario donde el motor se pueda chequear con presión.
7   Cadena de tiempo y/o engranes gastados (Capítulo 2).
8   Lóbulos del árbol de levas gastados (Capítulo 2).

9 El motor falla en marcha mínima

1   Bujías gastadas o luz incorrecta (Capítulo 1).
2   Alambre de bujía defectuoso (Capítulo 1).
3   Estrangulador no operando apropiadamente (Capítulo 1).
4   Componentes del sistema de las emisiones pegándose o defectuosos (Capítulo 6).
5   Filtro de combustible obstruido y/o material extranjero en el combustible. Remueva el filtro de combustible (Capítulo 1) e inspeccione.
6   Fuga de vacío en el múltiple de admisión o en las conexiones de las mangueras.
7   Marcha mínima incorrecta o mezcla para la marcha mínima incorrecta (Capítulo 1).
8   Tiempo de la ignición incorrecto (Capítulo 1).
9   Compresión desigual o baja de los cilindros. Chequee la compresión como se describió en el Capítulo 1.

10 Velocidad excesiva de marcha mínima

1   La varilla del acelerador se está atorando (Capítulo 4).
2   El estrangulador abierto en exceso en la

marcha mínima (Capítulo 4).
3   La marcha mínima ajustada incorrectamente (Capítulo 1).
4   Franqueo de las válvulas incorrecto (Capítulo 1).
5   La válvula de control para la marcha mínima fuera de ajuste (Capítulo 6).

11 La batería no mantiene carga

1   Banda del alternador defectuosa o no está ajustada apropiadamente (Capítulo 1).
2   El nivel de electrólito bajo o la batería descargada (Capítulo 1).
3   Términales de la batería sueltos o corroídos (Capítulo 1).
4   El alternador no está cargando apropiadamente (Capítulo 5).
5   Instalación eléctrica suelta, rota o defectuosa en el circuito de carga (Capítulo 5).
6   Corto en la instalación eléctrica del camión causando un drenaje continuo en la batería.
7   Batería defectuosa internamente.

12 La luz del alternador se queda prendida

1   Un fallo en el alternador o circuito de carga (Capítulo 5).
2   Banda del alternador defectuosa o no ajustada apropiadamente (Capítulo 1).

13 La luz del alternador no se prende cuando la llave se encienda

1   La bombilla está mala (Capítulo 12).
2   Alternador defectuoso (Capítulo 12).
3   Un fallo en el circuito imprimido, alambrado del tablero sostenedor de la bombilla (Capítulo 12).

14 El motor falla en todas las revoluciones

1   Filtro de combustible obstruido y/o impurezas en el sistema del combustible (Capítulo 1). También cheque por el rendimiento del combustible al carburador/inyector de combustible.
2   Bujías defectuosas o luz incorrecta (Capítulo 1).
3   Tiempo de la ignición incorrecto (Capítulo 1).
4   Cheque por grietas en la tapa del distribuidor, alambre del distribuidor desconectado y componentes del distribuidor dañados (Capítulo 1).
5   Fuga en los alambres de bujías (Capítulo 1).
6   Componentes del sistema de las emi-

siones defectuosos (Capítulo 6).
7   Compresión en los cilindros baja o dispareja. Remueva las bujías y cheque la compresión con un manómetro (Capítulo 1).
8   Sistema de la ignición débil o defectuoso (Capítulo 5).
9   Fuga de vacío en el carburador/unidad de la inyección del combustible o mangueras de vacío.

15 Titubeo durante aceleración

1   Tiempo de la ignición incorrecto (Capítulo 1).
2   El sistema de ignición no está operando apropiadamente (Capítulo 5).
3   Suciedad en el carburador o sistema de combustible (Capítulo 5).
4   Presión baja de combustible. Cheque por operación apropiada de la bomba de combustible y por restricción en el filtro de combustible y líneas (Capítulo 4).
5   Carburador fuera de ajuste (Capítulo 4).

16 El motor se apaga

1   Velocidad mínima incorrecta (Capítulo 1).
2   Filtro del combustible obstruido y/o agua e impuridades en el sistema de combustible (Capítulo 1).
3   Estrangulador impropiamente ajustado o pegándose (Capítulo 1).
4   Componentes del distribuidor húmedos o dañados (Capítulo 5).
5   Componentes del sistema de las emisiones defectuosos (Capítulo 6).
6   Defectuosa o incorrecta luz de las bujías (Capítulo 1). También chequee los alambres de las bujías (Capítulo 1).
7   Fuga de vacío en el carburador/unidad de la inyección del combustible o mangueras de vacío.

17 Al motor le falta poder

1   Tiempo de la ignición incorrecto (Capítulo 1).
2   Excesivo juego en el eje del distribuidor. Al mismo tiempo, cheque por un rotor desgastado, tapa del distribuidor defectuosa, alambres, etc. (Capítulos 1 y 5).
3   Bujía defectuosa o luz incorrecta (Capítulo 1).
4   Unidad de la inyección del combustible no ajustada apropiadamente o excesivamente desgastada (Capítulo 4).
5   Bobina defectuosa (Capítulo 5).
6   Frenos pegándose (Capítulo 1).
7   Nivel del flúido de la transmisión automática incorrecto (Capítulo 1).
8   Embrague resbalando (Capítulo 8).
9   Filtro del combustible obstruido y/o impurezas en el sistema del combustible (Capítulo 1).
10   Sistema del control de las emisiones

que no estén funcionando apropiadamente (Capítulo 6).

11   Uso de combustible de baja calidad. Llene el tanque del combustible con el combustible del octano apropiado.

12   Compresión desigual o baja de los cilindros. Cheque la compresión como se describió en el Capítulo 1. Que detectará fugas de válvulas y/o junta de la cabeza rota.

18   El motor hace explosiones

1   Sistema de las emisiones no funcionando apropiadamente (Capítulo 6).

2   Tiempo de la ignición incorrecto (Capítulo 1).

3   Sistema secundario de la ignición defectuoso (grieta en el aislador de la bujía, alambres de las bujías defectuosos, tapa del distribuidor y/o rotor) (Capítulos 1 y 5).

4   Carburador/unidad de inyección del combustible en necesidad de ajuste o desgastado excesivamente (Capítulo 4).

5   Fuga de vacío en la unidad de inyección del combustible o mangueras de vacío.

6   Juego del ajuste de las válvulas incorrecto, y/o válvulas atorándose en las guías (Capítulo 2).

7   Alambres de las bujías cruzados (Capítulo 1).

19   El motor titubea cuando el acelerador se mantiene sin moverse

1   Fuga en el múltiple de admisión (Capítulo 8).

2   La bomba de combustible no está funcionando apropiadamente.

20   Sonidos de golpeteo o detonación del motor durante aceleración o subiendo una cuesta

1   Calidad incorrecta de combustible. Llene el tanque del combustible con el octanaje apropiado.

2   Tiempo de la ignición incorrecto (Capítulo 1).

3   Carburador/unidad de la inyección del combustible en necesidad de ajuste o reparación (Capítulo 4).

4   Bujías inapropiadas. Verifique el tipo de bujía con la etiqueta de Información de Control de las Emisiones localizada en el compartimiento del motor. También chequee las bujías y los alambres por daño (Capítulo 1).

5   Componentes del distribuidor dañados o desgastados (Capítulo 5).

6   Sistema de las emisiones defectuoso (Capítulo 6).

7   Fuga de vacío.

8   Depósitos de carbón arriba de los cilindros (Capítulo 2).

21   El motor continúa corriendo después que se apaga el interruptor

1   Marcha mínima demasiado alta (Capítulo 1).

2   Solenoide eléctrico al lado de carburador no está funcionando apropiadamente (no todos los modelos, vea Capítulo 4).

3   Tiempo de la ignición ajustado incorrectamente (Capítulo 1).

4   Válvula para controlar el aire caliente que entra al depurador de aire no está operando apropiadamente (Capítulo 6).

5   Excesiva temperatura de operación del motor. Causas probables de esto son termostato no funcionando correctamente, radiador bloqueado, bomba del agua defectuosa (Capítulo 3).

6   Calidad incorrecta de combustible. Llene el tanque de gasolina con el octanaje apropiado.

22   Presión de aceite baja

1   Grado de aceite inapropiado.

2   Pernos flojos o junta de la cacerola dañada (Capítulo 3).

3   Bomba del aceite desgastada o dañada (Capítulo 2).

4   Sobrecalentamiento del motor (refiérase a la Sección 27).

5   Filtro de aceite obstruido (Capítulo 1).

6   Parrilla para el aceite obstruida (Capítulo 2).

7   Reloj para la presión de aceite no está operando apropiadamente (Capítulo 2).

23   Consumo de aceite en exceso

1   Tapón para el drenaje del aceite flojo.

2   Pernos flojos o junta de la cacerola dañada (Capítulo 2).

3   Pernos flojos o junta de la tapa del tiempo dañada (Capítulo 2).

4   Sello delantero o trasero del cigüeñal con fugas (Capítulo 2).

5   Pernos flojos o junta de la tapa de las válvulas dañada (Capítulo 2).

6   Filtro de aceite flojo (Capítulo 1).

7   Flojo o dañado interruptor de la presión del aceite (Capítulo 2).

8   Desgaste en exceso de los pistones y los cilindros (Capítulo 2).

9   Anillos de los pistones no están instalados apropiadamente (Capítulo 2).

10   Desgastados o dañados anillos de los pistones (Capítulo 2).

11   Sellos de aceite de las válvulas desgastados o dañados (Capítulo 2).

12   Vástagos de las válvulas desgastados.

13   Guías de las válvulas gastadas o dañadas (Capítulo 2).

24   Consumo excesivo de combustible

1   Filtro del aire sucio o obstruido (Capítulo 1).

2   Tiempo de la ignición incorrecto (Capítulo 1).

3   Estrangulador pegándose o impropiamente ajustado (Capítulo 1).

4   Sistema de las emisiones no está funcionando apropiadamente (no todos los camiones, vea Capítulo 6).

5   Marcha mínima y/o mezcla no está ajustada apropiadamente (Capítulo 1).

6   Partes interiores del carburador/inyección de combustible excesivamente gastadas o dañadas (Capítulo 4).

7   Presión de los neumáticos baja o tamaño del neumático incorrecto (Capítulo 1).

25   Olor de combustible

1   Fuga de combustible. Cheque todas las conexiones, líneas y componentes en el sistema de combustible (Capítulo 4).

2   Tanque del combustible sobrelleno. Llénelo solamente hasta que el automático de la bomba se pare.

3   Filtro para el canasto de carbón del sistema de control de las emisiones obstruido (Capítulo 1).

4   Fugas de vapor por las líneas del sistema de control de las emisiones evaporativas (Capítulo 1).

26   Ruidos misceláneos del motor

1   Un sonido busco que se hace más rápido según el motor acelera, indica gastados o dañados los cojinetes del cigüeñal o un cigüeñal desgastado. Para determinar el lugar del problema, remueva el alambre de cada bujía a la ves y ponga el motor en marcha. Si el ruido se detiene, el cilindro con el alambre desconectado indica el área con el problema. Reemplace el cojinete y o suminístrele servicio o reemplace el cigüeñal (Capítulo 1).

2   Un sonido (un poquito más alto) similar del cigüeñal haciendo ruido descrito en el párrafo anterior, que se hace más rápido según el motor acelera, indica cojinetes de las bielas desgastados o dañados (Capítulo 1). El procedimiento para localizar el cilindro con el problema es el mismo de como se prescribió en el párrafo 1.

3   Un sonido metálico que se cruza e incrementa en intensidad según la velocidad del motor incrementa, pero disminuye según el motor se calienta indica desgaste anormal del cilindro y del pistón (Capítulo 2). Para localizar el cilindro con el problema, use el procedimiento descrito en el párrafo 1.

4   Un ruido de un tipo como clic que incrementa según el motor incrementa en velocidad indica un pasador del pistón desgastado

u orificio en el pistón para el pasador. Este sonido ocurrirá cada ves que el pistón llega al punto más alto o más bajo en su carrera (Capítulo 2). El procedimiento para localizar el cilindro con el problema es el mismo de como se prescribió en el párrafo 1.

5   Un ruido de un tipo como clic metálico que proviene de la bomba de agua indica desgastados o dañados baleros de la bomba. Reemplace la bomba de agua con una nueva (Capítulo 2).

6   Un sonido rápido o clic que se hace más rápido según la velocidad del motor incrementa "sonido de válvulas" o ajuste de las válvulas (franqueo de válvulas) ajustadas inadecuadamente. Esto se puede identificar sosteniendo un lado de una sección de manguera en su oído e instalando el otro lado en un lugar sobre la tapa de la válvula. El punto donde el sonido es más profundo indica la válvula con el problema. Ajuste la válvula (Capítulo 1).

7   Un sonido continuo metálico proveniente del área de la tapa de la cadena del tiempo indica una cadena o el ajustador desgastado o dañado. Suminístrele servicio o reemplace la cadena y los componentes relacionados (Capítulo 2).

Sistema de enfriamiento

27   Sobre calentamiento

1   Insuficiente anticongelante en el sistema (Capítulo 1).
2   Banda de la bomba de agua defectuosa o no está ajustada apropiadamente (Capítulo 1).
3   El núcleo del radiador está obstruido o las rejillas sucias y restringidas (Capítulo 3).
4   Termostato defectuoso (Capítulo 3).
5   Hojas del ventilador rotas o crujidas (Capítulo 3).
6   La tapa del radiador no mantiene la presión apropiada. Permita que un taller o una gasolinera chequee la presión de la tapa del radiador.
7   Tiempo de la ignición incorrecto (Capítulo 1).

28   Sobre enfriamiento

1   Termostato defectuoso (Capítulo 3).
2   Reloj de la temperatura fuera de calibración (Capítulo 12).

29   Fuga externa de anticongelante

1   Mangueras o grapas deterioradas o dañadas. Reemplace las mangueras y/o apriete las grapas (Capítulo 1).
2   Sellos de la bomba de agua defectuosos. Si este es el caso, el agua se fugará por el orificio en el cuerpo de la bomba del agua (Capítulo 1).

3   Fuga atraves del radiador o del núcleo del calentador. Esto requeriría que el radiador o el núcleo del calentador fuera reparado por un profesional (vea Capítulo 3 para procedimientos de como removerlo).
4   Fugas de los tapones de las chaquetas de enfriamiento del bloque o para el desagüe del motores (vea Capítulo 2).

30   Fuga interna del anticongelante

Nota: *Se pueden descubrir fugas interiores del anticongelantes usualmente examinando el aceite. Cheque la varilla y dentro de la tapa de la mecedora por depósitos de agua y una consistencia del aceite parecida a leche.*
1   Fuga de la junta de la cabeza de los cilindros. Ponga el sistema de enfriamiento bajo presión para poder probarlo.
2   Cilindro del bloque o cabeza agrietada. Desmantele el motor e inspeccione (Capítulo 2).

31   Perdida anormal de anticongelante

1   Sistema sobrelleno (Capítulo 2).
2   Anticongelante hirviendo debido al sobrecalentamiento (vea las causas en la Sección 27).
3   Fuga interna o externa (vea Sección 29 y 30).
4   Falla en la tapa del radiador. Lleve para que prueben la tapa bajo presión.
5   El sistema de enfriamiento a estado presionado por la compresión del motor. Esto puede suceder por una cabeza o bloque cuarteado o fuga(s) de la junta(s) de la cabeza.

32   Circulación pobre del anticongelante

1   Bomba del agua no opera. Una prueba rápida es de pellizcar la manguera del radiador de encima con su mano mientras el motor está en marcha mínima, entonces suéltela. Usted debe de sentir el anticongelante fluir si la bomba está trabajando apropiadamente (Capítulo 1).
2   Restricción en el sistema de enfriamiento. Desagüe, limpie y rellene el sistema (Capítulo 1). Si es necesario, remueva el radiador (Capítulo 3) y límpielo de la forma opuesta de como fluye.
3   Banda de la bomba del agua defectuosa o no ajustada apropiadamente (Capítulo 1).
4   Termostato atorándose (Capítulo 3).

33   Corrosión

1   Impuridades en exceso en el agua. Agua limpia y suave es recomendada. Agua de lluvia o destilada es satisfactoria.

2   Insuficiente solución de anticongelante (refiérase al Capítulo 1 para la ración apropiada de agua y anticongelante).
3   Insuficiente drenaje y limpieza del sistema. El drenaje del sistema de enfriamiento se debe de hacer a sus intervalos específicos como se describe en el Capítulo 1.

Embrague

Nota: *Todos los servicios relacionados con la información del embrague están localizados en el Capítulo 8, como único que se indique de otra forma.*

34   No desembraga (pedal deprimido hasta el piso - la palanca no se mueve libremente entrando o saliendo de Reversa)

1   El sistema hidráulico del embrague está bajo o tiene aire en el sistema y necesita ser purgado (Capítulo 8).
2   Tenedor del embrague fuera de la pelota con el espárrago.
3   Plato del embrague torcido o dañado (Capítulo 8).

35   El embrague resbala (la velocidad del motor aumenta sin incrementar la velocidad del camión)

1   Plato del embrague saturado con aceite o el forro gastado. Remueva el embrague (Capítulo 8) e inspecciónelo.
2   Plato del embrague no está sentado. Puede que tome 30 o 40 arrancadas para que uno nuevo se siente.
3   Plato de presión desgastado (Capítulo 8).

36   El embrague (vibra) tan pronto el embrague hace contacto

1   Aceite en el forro del plato del embrague. Remueva (Capítulo 8) e inspeccione. Corrija cualquier fuente de fuga.
2   Calzos del motor o de la transmisión gastados o sueltos. Estas unidades se mueven ligeramente cuando se desengancha. Inspeccione los calzos y los pernos.
3   Estrías gastadas en el plato del embrague. Remueva los componentes del embrague (Capítulo 8) e inspecciónelo.
4   Plato de presión o plato flexible torcido. Remueva los compohentes del embrague e inspecciónelo.

37   El embrague hace ruido con el pedal suelto

1   Ajuste impropio; ningún juego libre

(Capítulo 1).
2   Balero del desembrague atorándose en el retenedor. Remueva los componentes del embrague (Capítulo 8) y chequee el balero. Remueva cualquier rebarba o mella, limpie y lubrique antes de instalarlo.
3   Resorte de regresar la varilla débil. Reemplace el resorte.

38   El embrague hace ruido con el pedal deprimido

1   Gastado, defectuoso o roto el balero de desembrague (Capítulo 8).
2   Gastado o roto los resortes del plato de presión (o dedos del diafragma) (Capítulo 8).
3   Aire en la línea hidráulica (Capítulo 8).

39   El pedal del embrague se queda en el piso cuando se desengancha

1   Varilla o balero de desembrague atorándose. Inspeccione la unión o remueva los componentes del embrague según sea necesario.
2   Resortes de la varilla han sido sobre estirado. Ajuste la varilla hasta obtener el juego libre apropiado. Asegúrese que el parachoques del pedal está apropiadamente instalado.
3   Cilindro del embrague hidráulico defectuoso o hay aire en el sistema.

Transmisión manual
Nota: *Todas las referencias siguientes son al Capítulo 7, a menos que sea notado diferente.*

40   Ruido en Neutral con el motor funcionando

1   Eje de entrada desgastado.
2   Balero de la guía principal dañado.
3   Balero del contra eje desgastado.
4   Laminas para el ajuste del juego libre del contraeje desgasta o dañada.

41   Ruidos en todas las guías

1   Cualquier de las causas de encima, y/o:
2   Insuficiente lubrificante (vea procedimientos para chequear en el Capítulo 1).

42   Ruido en una guía en particular

1   Diente en esa guía particular roto, desgastado o dañado.

2   Sincronizador para esa guía en particular dañado o desgastado.

43   Se resbala fuera de la guía alta

1   Transmisión floja o cubierta del embrague.
2   Sello de la palanca de cambio duro.
3   Varilla de cambio se está atorando.
4   Roto o flojo retenedor para el balero de entrada.
5   Tierra entre la caja de la transmisión y el motor o transmisión fuera de alineación.
6   Varilla desgastada.
7   Bolas de chequeo gastadas o dañadas, ranura para la bola en el tenedor o resorte.
8   Balero del eje principal o contra eje desgastado.
9   Pernos del calzo del motor sueltos.
10   Juego excesivo de la guía.
11   Sincronizadores desgastados.

44   Fuga de aceite

1   Excesiva cantidad de lubrificante en la transmisión (vea Capítulo 1 para los procedimientos correcto). Drene el lubrificante según sea necesario.
2   Tapa del lado suelta o junta dañada.
3   Sello del aceite trasero o sello del velocímetro necesita reemplazarse.
4   Sistema hidráulico del embrague tiene fuga (Capítulo 7).

45   Difícil de ponerla en guía

1   El embrague no desengancha completamente (vea ajuste del embrague en el Capítulo 8).
2   Varilla de cambios suelta, dañada o fuera de ajuste. Haga una inspección completa, reemplace las partes que sean necesarias (Capítulo 8).

46   Ruido sucede mientras se cambian las guías

1   Chequee la operación apropiada del em-brague (Capítulo 8).
2   Asamblea de los sincronizadores están fallando. Mida la distancia (luz) entre el anillo y la guía o cualquier parte de la asamblea de sincronización.

Transmisión automática
Nota: *Debido a la complejidad de la transmisión automática, es difícil para el mecánico del hogar de apropiadamente diagnosticar y darle servicio a este componente. Para otros problemas que no sean los que siguen, el camión se debe de llevar a un concesionario o un mecánico con buena reputación.*

47   Fuga de flúido

1   Flúido de la transmisión automática es de un color rojo. No se deben confundir las fugas del flúido de la transmisión con el aceite del motor, que se puede soplar fácilmente por el aire hacia la transmisión.
2   Para poder distinguir exactamente donde hay una fuga, primero remueva todo tipo de suciedad de arriba y alrededor de la transmisión. Agentes para remover grasa y/o limpieza con vapor pueden hacer este trabajo. Con la parte de abajo limpia, maneje el camión a velocidades bajas, de esta forma el flujo de aire no soplará el flúido hacia la parte de atrás del camión. Levante el camión y determine de donde proviene la fuga. Áreas comunes de fugas son:
  a) *Cacerola: Apriete los pernos y/o reemplace la junta según sea necesario (vea Capítulos 1 y 7).*
  b) *Pipa para llenar: Reemplace el sello de caucho donde la tubería entra en la caja de la transmisión.*
  c) *Líneas de enfriamiento de la transmisión: Apriete las conexiones donde las líneas entran a la caja de la transmisión y/o reemplace las líneas.*
  d) *Tubo de ventilación: El nivel del flúido de la transmisión está muy alto y/o hay agua en el flúido (vea los procedimientos de como chequearlo, Capítulo 1).*
  e) *Conector del velocímetro: Reemplace el sello O donde el cable del velocímetro entra en caja de la transmisión (Capítulo 7).*

48   Problemas generales del mecanismo de cambio

1   El Capítulo 7 trata con el chequeo y el ajuste de la varilla de los cambios en las transmisiones automáticas. Problemas comunes que se atribuyen a los ajustes de las varillas son:
  a) *El motor se pone en marcha en cualquier velocidad/guía otra que no sea Parque o Neutral.*
  b) *El indicador apunta a otra guía que no es la que realmente se está usando.*
  c) *El camión se mueve cuando se pone en Parqueo.*
2   Refiérase al Capítulo 7 para ajustar la varilla.

49   La transmisión no baja de guía con el acelerador completamente deprimido hasta el suelo

El Capítulo 7 trata con los ajustes del cable de detén para permitir que la transmisión baje de guía apropiadamente.

50 El motor se pone en marcha en otra guía que no sea Estacionamiento o Neutral

El Capítulo 7 trata con los ajustes del interruptor de la ignición en Neutral localizado en la transmisión automática.

51 Transmisión patina/resbala, cambios ásperos, hace ruido o no entra en guía hacia el frente o hacia atrás

1   Hay muchas causas probables que pueden causar los problemas precedentes, pero el mecánico de hogar se debe concernir con solo una posibilidad - el nivel del flúido.
2   Antes de llevar el camión a un taller de reparación, chequee el nivel y la condición del flúido como se describió en el Capítulo 1. Corrija el nivel del flúido según sea necesario o cambie el flúido y el filtro si es necesario. Si el problema persiste, deje que un profesional diagnostique la causa probable.

Flecha/cardán

52 Fuga de aceite al frente de la flecha

Sello de aceite trasero de la transmisión defectuoso. Vea Capítulo 7 para los procedimientos de reemplazo. Mientras se hace esto, cheque la parte de la caja por donde salen las estrías por áreas con condiciones ásperas que puedan dañar el sello. Estas áreas se pueden remover usando lija fina o una piedra húmeda fina.

53 Golpetea cuando la transmisión está bajo carga inicial (tan pronto se pone la transmisión en guía)

1   Componentes de la suspensión trasera, desconectados o sueltos. Cheque todo los pernos que lo aguantan, tuercas y bujes (Capítulo 10).
2   Pernos de la flecha sueltos. Inspeccione todos los pernos, tuercas y apriételos al par de torsión especificado.
3   Estrías de la flecha en necesidad de lubricación (Capítulo 1).
4   Baleros de la junta universal desgastados o dañados. Cheque por desgaste (Capítulo 8).

54 Sonidos metálicos consistente con la velocidad del camión

Desgaste pronunciado en los baleros de

las uniones universales. Chequéelo como se describió en el Capítulo 8.

55 Vibración

Nota: *Antes de tomar la asunción que la flecha es el problema, esté seguro de que los neumáticos están perfectamente balanceados.*

1   Instale un tacómetro dentro del camión para chequear las r.p.m. del motor según se maneja el camión. Maneje el camión y note la velocidad del motor cuando la vibración es más pronunciada. Ahora cambie la transmisión a una guía diferente y traiga la velocidad del motor al mismo punto.
2   Si la vibración ocurre a la misma velocidad del motor (r.p.m.) sin importar en que velocidad la transmisión está, la flechas NO ES el problema ya que la velocidad de la flecha varía.
3   Si la vibración disminuye o se elimina cuando la transmisión está en diferente guía a la misma velocidad (RPM) del motor, refiérase a las causas posibles que siguen.
4   Flecha virada o aboyada. Inspeccione y reemplace según sea necesario (Capítulo 8).
5   Sellador para la parte de abajo de la carrocería o bodoques de tierra, etc. en la flecha. Limpie la flecha completamente y chequéela de nuevo.
6   Baleros desgastados de la unión universal. Remueva e inspeccione (Capítulo 8).
7   Flecha y/o parte acompañante fuera de balance. Chequee por pesas que falten en la flecha. Remueva la flecha (Capítulo 8) y reinstálela 180-grados de la posición original. Deje que la flecha sea balanceada profesionalmente si el problema persiste.

56 Sonido como raspando

Esté seguro de que la cubierta para el polvo no está rozando con la extensión de la transmisión.

57 Ruido como chiflido

Balero central defectuoso, si está equipado.

Eje trasero y diferencial

Nota: *Para información de servicio del diferencial, refiérase al Capítulo 8, como único de que sea especificado de otra forma.*

58 Ruido

1   Ruido del camino. No hay ningún procedimiento correctivo disponible.
2   Ruido del neumático. Inspeccione los neumático y las presiones de los neumáticos

(Capítulo 1).
3   Baleros de las ruedas traseras flojos, desgastados o dañados (Capítulo 10).

59 Sonido de golpeteo

Ajuste del diferencial incorrecto o defectuoso.

60 Ruido cuando gira

Diferencial defectuoso.

61 Vibración

Vea causas probables debajo de flechas. Proceda debajo de los procedimientos listados para la flecha. Si el problema persiste, cheque los baleros traseros de las ruedas levantando la parte trasera del camión y girando las ruedas con la mano. Escuche por evidencia de (ruidos) áspero de los baleros. Remueva e inspeccione (Capítulo 8).

62 Fuga de aceite

1   Sello del piñón dañado (Capítulo 8).
2   Sello de aceite del eje dañado (Capítulo 8).
3   Fuga en la cubierta para la inspección del diferencial. Apriete los pernos o reemplace la junta según sea necesario (Capítulo 8).

Caja de transferencia (modelos de cuatro tracción)

Nota: *Todas las informaciones para el servicio de la caja de transferencia está localizada en el Capítulo 7.*

63 Hace ruido o se sale del rango bajo de las cuatro tracciones

1   La caja del diferencial no está completamente en su guía. Detenga el camión, cambie a la guía neutral y póngala en 4 baja (4L).
2   Varilla de los cambios floja, gastada o atorándose. Apriétela, repárela o lubrique la varilla según sea necesario.
3   Tenedor de los cambios cuarteado, buje del tenedor gastado o atorándose en el carril. Desármelo y repárelo según sea necesario.

64 Difícil de cambiar la caja de transfiera al rango deseado

1   La velocidad pueda que sea muy rápida para permitir que entre en el engranaje. Detenga el camión y cambie al rango dese-

ado.

2   Varilla del cambio suelta, virada o doblada. Cheque la varilla por daño o desgaste y reemplace o lubrique según sea necesario (Capítulo 7).

3   Insuficiente o calidad incorrecta del lubricante. Drene y rellene la caja de transferencia con el lubricante especificado (Capítulo 1).

4   Componentes internos desgastados o dañados. Desensamble y reparación completa de la caja de transferencia puede que sea necesario (Capítulo 7).

65 Ruido

1   Insuficiente aceite en la caja de transferencia (Capítulo 1).

2   Ruido en 4H (alta) y 4L (baja), pero si no hace ruido en 2H (alta) indica que la causa del ruido es en el diferencial del frente o eje del frente.

3   Ruido en 2H (alta), 4H (alta) y 4L (baja) indica que la causa del ruido es en el diferencial trasero o eje trasero.

4   Ruido en 2H (alta), 4H (alta) pero no en 4L (baja), o en 4L (baja) solamente, indica desgaste o daño interno de la caja de transferencia.

Frenos

Nota: *Antes de asumir de que un problema de freno existe, asegúrese de que los neumáticos están en buena condiciones e inflados apropiadamente (vea Capítulo 1), que la alineación de la suspensión del frente esté correcta y que el camión no esté cargado de una manera desigual.*

66 El camión tira hacia un lado cuando se aplica el freno

1   Defectivas, dañadas o contaminadas con aceite las pastillas o las balatas en un lado. Inspecciónelo como se describió en el Capítulo 9.

2   Desgaste excesivo de la balatas o material de las pastilla o tambor/disco en un lado. Inspecciónelo y corríjalo según sea necesario.

3   Componentes de la suspensión delantera sueltos o desconectados. Inspecciónelo y apriete todos los pernos al par de torsión especificado (Capítulo 10).

4   Tambor de freno defectuoso o asamblea de la mordaza. Remueva el tambor o la mordaza e inspeccione por un pistón atorado u otro daño (Capítulo 9).

67 Ruido (chiflido alto con los frenos aplicados)

Pastillas de los frenos gastadas. El ruido

viene del sensor de uso que frota contra el rotor (no aplica a todo los camiones). Reemplace las pastillas con unas nuevas inmediatamente (Capítulo 9).

68 Juego excesivo del pedal del freno

1   Fallo del sistema de freno parcial. Inspeccione el sistema completo (Capítulo 9) y corrija según sea necesario.

2   Insuficiente flúido en el cilindro maestro. Chequee (Capítulo 1), agregue flúido y purgue el sistema si es necesario (Capítulo 9).

3   El freno no ajusta propiamente. Haga una serie de salidas y paradas con el camión en marcha atrás. Si esto no corrige la situación, remueva los tambores e inspeccione el ajustador automático (Capítulo 9).

69 El pedal del freno se siente esponjoso

1   Aire en las líneas hidráulicas. Sangre el sistema del freno (Capítulo 9).

2   Mangueras flexibles defectuosas. Inspeccione todas las mangueras del sistema y líneas. Reemplace las partes según sea necesario.

3   Pernos para el montaje del cilindro maestro sueltos.

4   Cilindro maestro defectuoso (Capítulo 9).

70 Esfuerzo excesivo requerido para detener el camión

1   El amplificador para el freno de poder no está operando apropiadamente (Capítulo 9).

2   Desgastados excesivamente los forros de las balatas o las pastilla. Inspeccione y reemplace según sea necesario (Capítulo 9).

3   Uno o más pistones de las mordazas o cilindros de las ruedas atorándose o pegándose. Inspecciónelo y reconstrullalo según sea necesario (Capítulo 9).

4   Forros de las balatas de los frenos o pastilla contaminados con aceite o grasa. Inspeccione y reemplace según sea necesario (Capítulo 9).

5   Pastillas o balatas nuevas instaladas y todavía no se han acentuado. Tomará un tiempo mientras el material nuevo se sienta contra el tambor (o rotor).

71 El pedal viaja hasta el suelo con pequeña resistencia

Poquito o ningún flúido en el depósito del cilindro maestro causado por fugas en el

cilindro(s) de la rueda(s), fuga en el pistón(s) de la mordaza(s), líneas del freno sueltas. Inspeccione el sistema entero y corríjalo según sea necesario.

72 El pedal del freno pulsa durante la aplicación del freno

1   Baleros de las ruedas no ajustados apropiadamente o en necesidad de reemplazo (Capítulo 1).

2   Mordaza no deslizándose apropiadamente debido a una instalación impropia u obstrucciones. Remueva e inspeccione (Capítulo 9).

3   Rotor o tambor defectuoso. Remueva el rotor o tambor (Capítulo 9) y cheque por excesivo juego lateral, fuera de redondez y paralelismo. Lleve el tambor o rotor a ser rectificado o reemplácelo con uno nuevo.

73 Los frenos se pegan (indicado por poco rendimiento del motor o las ruedas muy caliente después de conducir el camión)

1   Varilla de salida del pedal del freno fuera de ajuste.

2   Compensador del cilindro maestro obstruido. Desarme el cilindro maestro y límpielo.

3   El pistón adentro del cilindro maestro se pegó. Reconstruya el cilindro maestro.

4   Las asambleas de las mordazas necesitan reparación general.

5   Las pastillas o balatas desgastadas.

6   Las copas adentro del cilindro maestro o las mordazas deformadas. Reconstruya el cilindro maestro.

7   El disco no está bajo especificación (Sección 72).

8   La asamblea del freno de emergencia no se libera.

9   Líneas de los frenos obstruidas.

10   Los baleros de las ruedas fuera de ajuste (Capítulo 1).

11   Altura del pedal del freno inapropiadamente ajustada.

12   Cilindros de las ruedas necesitan reconstrucción.

13   Juego libre inapropiado entre el tambor y la zapata. Ajústelo según sea necesario.

74 Los frenos traseros se bloquean bajo aplicación liviana del pedal

1   La presión de los neumáticos está muy alta.

2   Las ruedas excesivamente desgastadas (Capítulo 1).

3   Válvula LSPB defectuosa.

75 Los frenos traseros se bloquean bajo aplicación pesada del pedal

1   La presión de los neumáticos está muy alta.
2   Las ruedas excesivamente desgastadas (Capítulo 1).
3   Pastillas de los frenos del frente contaminadas con aceite, fango o agua. Limpie o reemplace las pastillas.
4   Las pastillas del frente excesivamente desgastadas.
5   Cilindro maestro defectuoso o asamblea de las mordazas.

Suspensión y sistemas de la dirección

Nota: *Todos los procedimientos de servicio para el sistema de suspensión y dirección están incluidos en el Capítulo 10, como único de que se mencione de otra forma.*

76 El camión tira hacia un lado

1   Presiones del neumático desigual (Capítulo 1).
2   Neumático defectuoso (Capítulo 1).
3   Desgaste excesivo en la suspensión o componentes de la dirección (Capítulo 10).
4   La suspensión del frente en necesidad de alineación.
5   Freno del frente se arrastra. Inspeccione los frenos como se describió en el Capítulo 9.

77 Vibración

1   Neumático o rueda fuera de balance o fuera de redondo. Llévela para que la balanceen profesionalmente.
2   Baleros de las ruedas sueltos, desgastados o fuera de ajuste (Capítulos 1 y 8).
3   Amortiguadores y/o componentes de la suspensión gastados o dañados (Capítulo 10).

78 Ruido excesivo y/o sonido de rodamiento cuando se dobla en las esquinas o mientras se frena

1   Amortiguadores defectuosos. Reemplácelo en juego (Capítulo 10).
2   Resortes de la suspensión débiles o rotos y/o componentes de la suspensión. Inspecciónelo como se describió en el Capítulo 10.

79 Flotando o inestabilidad general

1   Presión de los neumáticos inapropiada.
2   Bujes de los brazos superiores o inferiores desgastados o los de tracción.
3   Alineación incorrecta de la dirección delantera.
4   Varillas de la dirección desgastadas o dañadas.
5   Guía de la dirección inapropiadamente ajustada.
6   Ruedas fuera de balance.
7   Tuercas de las ruedas flojas.
8   Amortiguadores traseros gastados.
9   Resortes de hojas traseros dañados o fatigados.

80 Dirección excesivamente dura

1   Falta de flúido en el depósito de flúido de la dirección (Capítulo 1).
2   Presiones de los neumáticos incorrectas (Capítulo 1).
3   Falta de lubricación en las junturas de la dirección (Capítulo 1).
4   Suspensión del frente fuera de alineación.

81 Juego excesivo en la dirección

1   Baleros de la rueda del frente sueltos (Capítulo 1).
2   Desgaste excesivo en la suspensión o componentes de la dirección (Capítulo 10).
3   Caja de engranes de la dirección fuera de ajuste (Capítulo 10).

82 Falta de asistencia de poder

1   Banda para la bomba de poder de la dirección defectuosa o no está ajustada apropiadamente (Capítulo 1).
2   Nivel del flúido bajo (Capítulo 1).
3   Restricción en las mangueras o líneas. Inspecciónelas y reemplace las partes según sea necesario.
4   Aire en el sistema de poder de la dirección. Purgue el sistema (Capítulo 10).

83 Volante de la dirección no regresa a la posición directa recta

1   Alineación de la dirección incorrecta.
2   Presión del aire de los neumáticos baja.
3   Engranes de la dirección inapropiadamente instalados.
4   Columna de la dirección fuera de alineamiento.
5   Rotula dañada o desgastada.
6   Varilla de la dirección dañada o desgastada.

7   Brazo loco de la dirección inapropiadamente lubricado.
8   Insuficiente aceite en la caja de la dirección.
9   Insuficiente flúido en la bomba de la dirección.

84 Esfuerzo del volante no es lo mismo en ambas direcciones (con asistencia de potencia)

1   Fuga en la caja de la dirección.
2   Pasaje de flúido en la caja de la dirección obstruido.

85 Bomba de la dirección con ruido

1   Insuficiente aceite en la bomba.
2   Obstrucción en la manguera o en el filtro de la bomba.
3   Polea floja.
4   Banda . inapropiadamente ajustada (Capítulo 1).
5   Bomba defectuosa.

86 Ruidos misceláneos

1   Presión de los neumáticos inadecuada.
2   Insuficiente lubricación en las rotulas o varillas de la dirección.
3   Floja o desgastadas engranes de la caja de la dirección, varillas de la dirección o componentes de la suspensión.
4   Amortiguador (es) defectuoso.
5   Baleros defectuoso.
6   Dañadas varillas superiores o inferiores.
7   Resorte dañado.
8   Tuercas de las ruedas flojas.
9   Dañado o desgastado estría del eje trasero.
10 Buje del amortiguador trasero dañado o desgastado.
11 Juego del eje trasero incorrecto.
12 Vea también causas de ruidos en el eje trasero y la flecha.
13 Uniones de los ejes de mando dañadas o desgastadas modelos de 4WD.

87 Desgaste excesivo de los neumático (no específico a una área)

1   Presiones de los neumático incorrectas (Capítulo 1).
2   Neumático fuera de balance. Llévelo a balancear profesionalmente.
3   Ruedas dañadas. Inspecciónelas y reemplácelas según sea necesario.
4   Suspensión o componentes de la direcciones excesivamente gastados (Capítulo 10).

88 Desgaste excesivo de los neumático en el borde de afuera

1   Presiones de la inflación de los neumáticos incorrecta (Capítulo 1).
2   Velocidad excesiva en la vueltas.
3   Alineación del frente de la dirección incorrecta (excesiva convergencia). Lleve el camión para que sea alineado profesionalmente.
4   Brazo de la suspensión doblado o torcido (Capítulo 10).

89 Desgaste excesivo de los neumático en el borde de adentro

1   Presiones de la inflación de los neumáticos incorrecta (Capítulo 1).
2   Alineación del frente de la dirección incorrecta (excesiva divergencia). Lleve el camión para que sea alineado profesionalmente.
3   Componentes de la direcciones sueltos o dañados (Capítulo 10).

90 La rodadura del neumático desgastado en un solo lugar

1   Neumático fuera de balance.
2   Rueda torcida o dañada, Inspeccione y reemplace según sea necesario.
3   Neumático defectuoso (Capítulo 1).

Capítulo 1
Afinación y mantenimiento rutinario

Contenidos

Especificaciones

Lubricantes y flúidos recomendados

Aceite de motor
  Tipo .... API SF o SG
  Viscosidad .... Vea el diagrama que acompaña
Flúido para la transmisión automática .... DEXRON II ATF (flúido de transmisión automática)
Aceite para la transmisión manual
  Tipo .... API GL-4
  Viscosidad .... Vea el diagrama que acompaña
Aceite para el diferencial
  Tipo .... API GL-5
  Viscosidad .... Vea el diagrama que acompaña para el aceite de la transmisión
manual
Aceite para la caja de transferencia (modelos de 4WD)
  Hasta el 1990 .... API GL-5
  1991 y más moderno .... DEXRON II ATF (flúido de transmisión automática)
Flúido para la dirección de poder .... DEXRON II ATF (flúido de transmisión automática)
Flúido para el freno .... DOT (departamento de transportación) 3
Flúido para el embrague .... Flúido de freno DOT (departamento de transportación) 3

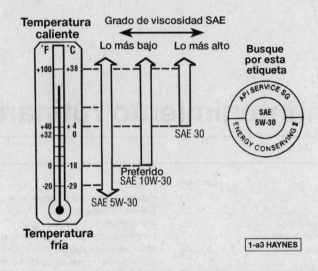

Lubricantes y flúidos recomendados (continuación)

Anticongelante.. Una mezcla de buena calidad basada de etileno glicol de anticongelante y agua, por lo menos una proporción de 50/50 (pero que no exceda una proporción de 70/30 de anticongelante para agua)

Aceite de la caja de la dirección manual .... API GL-4 (Vea el diagrama de aceite de transmisión manual para el peso correcto)

Componentes del chasis .... Grasa de chasis
Capó y bisagras de la puerta.. Aceite de motor
Ensamblaje del picaporte del capó
  Pivotes y resorte de anclaje .... Aceite de motor
  Retén de liberación .... Grasa de chasis
Cilindros de cierre.. Lubricante atomizador WD-40 o equivalente

Capacidades de los lubricantes y flúidos

Aceite de motor (capacidad aproximada)	Cuartos	Litros
1980		
Con filtro nuevo	4-1/2	4.3
Sin filtro nuevo	4	3.8
1981 y 1982		
Con filtro nuevo		
2WD	4-5/8	4.4
4WD	4-1/2	4.2
Sin filtro nuevo		
2WD	4-1/2	3.9
4WD	3-7/8	3.7
1983 al 1985		
Con filtro nuevo		
2WD	4-3/8	4.1
4WD	4-1/2	4.3
Sin filtro nuevo		
2WD	3-7/8	3.6
4WD	4	3.8
1986 en adelante		
Motor de cuatro cilindros		
2WD	4	3.8
4WD		
Hasta el 1990	4-1/2	4.1
1991 y más moderno	3-1/2	3.3
Motor V6		
2WD	4-1/4	4.1
4WD	3-5/8	4.0
Anticongelante (capacidad aproximada)		
1980	9-1/4	8.75
1981	10-1/2	9.9
1982	10	9.5

1983 al 1985
    Transmisión manual.. 10   9.5
    Transmisión automática... 10-3/4   10.2
1986 al 1990
    Motor de cuatro cilindros... 9-1/4   8.75
    Motor V6.. 11   10.4
1991 y más moderno
    Motor de cuatro cilindros
2WD.. 8-5/8   8.1
4WD.. 9-1/2   9.0
Motor V6
2WD.. 11-3/8   10.7
4WD.. 12-3/8   11.7
Transmisión (capacidad aproximada)
    1980 al 1983
      Transmisión manual
        Cuatro velocidades .... 3-5/8 pintas   1.7 litros
        Cinco velocidades .... 4-1/2 pintas   2.0 litros
      Transmisión automática... cuartos 5-7/8   5.5 litros
    1984 y 1985
      Transmisión manual.. 4-1/2 pintas   2.1 litros
      Transmisión automática... 5-7/8 pintas   5.5 litros
    1986 al 1989
      Motor de cuatro cilindros
        2WD
          Transmisión manual .... 4-1/4 pintas   2.0 litros
          Transmisión automática .... 7-3/8 cuartos   7.0 litros
        4WD
          Transmisión manual .... 5-1/8 pintas   2.4 litros
          Transmisión automática .... 7-3/8 cuartos   7.0 litros
      Motor V6
      2WD
        Transmisión manual .... 5-1/8 pintas   2.4 litros
        Transmisión automática .... 7-3/8 cuartos   7.0 litros
      4WD
        Transmisión manual .... 7-5/8 pintas   3.6 litros
        Transmisión automática .... 7-3/8 cuartos   7.0 litros
1990 en adelante
    Transmisión Manual FS5W71C
      2WD... 4.0 pintas   2.0 litros
      4WD... 8-1/2 pintas   4.0 litros
    Transmisión manual FS5R30A
      2WD... 5-1/8 pintas   2.4 litros
      4WD... 7-5/8 pintas   3.6 litros
    Transmisión automática
      2WD... 8-3/8 cuartos   7.9 litros
      4WD... 9 cuartos   8.5 litros
Aceite para la caja de transferencia
    1980 al 1985.. 1-1/2 cuartos   1.4 litros
    1986 en adelante.. 2-3/8 cuartos   2.2 litros
Aceite del diferencial trasero
    1980 al 1985
      US... 2-5/8 pintas   1.25 litros
      Canadá... 3-1/8 pintas   1.5 litros
      Modelos con doble ruedas .... 2-3/4 pintas   1.3 litros
Aceite del diferencial trasero (continuación)
    1986 en adelante
      H190... 3-1/8 pintas   1.5 litros
      C200... 2-3/4 pintas   1.3 litros
      Modelos con doble ruedas .... 5-7/8 pintas   2.8 litros
Aceite del diferencial delantero
    1980 al 1985... 2-1/8 pintas   1.0 litro
    1986 en adelante
      R180A... 2-3/4 pintas   1.3 litros
      R200A... 3-1/8 pintas   1.5 litros

Data de afinación

Tipo de bujía
    US (estándar) BP6ES-11
    Canadiense (estándar) y US (opcional)................. BP6ES

Data de afinación (continuación)

1981 al 1985
    Lado de admisión BPRS6ES
    Lado del escape BPRS5ES
1986 al 1989
    Motor de cuatro cilindros.. BPRS5ES
    Motor V6 .... BPRS5ES-11
1990 en adelante
    V6... BKR6EY
    KA24E ZFR5E-11
Espacio libre de la bujía
    1980 .... 0.039 a 0.043 pulgada(1.0 a 1.1 mm)
    1981 al 1989
    Motor de cuatro cilindros.. 0.031 a 0.035 pulgada (0.8 a 0.9 mm)
    Motor V6 .... 0.039 a 0.043 pulgada (1.0 a 1.1 mm)
    1990 en adelante
    Cuatro cilindro .... 0.040 (1.0 mm)
    V6... 0.031 - 035 (0.8 a 0.9 mm)

Franqueo de las válvulas

	Motor CALIENTE	Motor FRÍO
1980		
Admisión	0.010 pulgada (0.25 mm)	0.007 pulgada (0.17 mm)
Escape	0.012 pulgada (0.30 mm)	0.009 pulgada (0.24 mm)
1981 al 1989		
Admisión	0.012 pulgada (0.30 mm)	0.008 pulgada (0.21 mm)
Escape	0.012 pulgada (0.30 mm)	0.009 pulgada (0.24 mm)
1990 en adelante	Hidráulico	

Orden del encendido
    Motor de cuatro cilindros.. 1-3-4-2
    Motor V6.. 1-2-3-4-5-6

Regulación del tiempo de la ignición y velocidad de la marcha mínima
Nota: *Los modelos equipadòs con transmisión automática deben ser chequeados con la palanca del cambio en Marcha.*
1980
    US Federal y Cabina Canadiense/modelos del chasis................. 12 + - 2 grados BTDC (antes del punto muerto superior)
        600 + - 100 rpm

    California
        Modelos pesado.. 10 + - 2 BTDC/600 + - 100 RPM
        Todos los otros... 12 + - 2 BTDC/600 + - 100 RPM
    Canadiense (menos los modelos de chasis de cabina).............. 12 grados BTDC/600 rpm
Regulación del tiempo de la ignición y velocidad de la marcha mínima
1981
    Transmisión manual
        2WD.. 5 + - 2 grados BTDC/650 + - 100 RPM
        4WD.. 5 + - 2 grados BTDC/800 + - 100 RPM
    Transmisión automática... 5 + - 2 grados BTDC/650 + - 100 RPM
1982
    2WD (todo).. 3 + - 2 grados BTDC/650 + - 100 RPM
    4WD .... 3 + - 2 grados BTDC/800 + - 100 RPM
1983 en adelante... Refiérase a la etiqueta de información de control
        en el compartimiento del motor para las emisiones

Longitud de la terminal de carbón en la tapa del distribuidor
    1980 (todos) y 1981 4WD.. 0.470 pulgada (12 mm)
    Todos los otros .... 0.390 pulgada (10 mm)

La regulación del tiempo de la ignición debe ser chequeada con la manguera para el avance del encendido desconectada y tapada

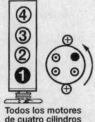

Todos los motores
de cuatro cilindros
con la excepción
de la serie Z

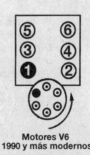

Motores V6
1990 y más modernos

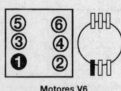

Motores V6
1989 y más antiguos

Ubicación de los cilindros y rotación del distribuidor

Deflección de la banda	Motor de cuatro cilindros	Motor V6
Alternador		
Hasta el 1990	3/8 a 7/16 pulgada	1/4 a 5/16 pulgada
1991 y más moderno	21/32 pulgada	15/32 pulgada
Bomba de la dirección de poder		
Hasta el 1990	25/64 a 15/32 pulgada	7/16 a 1/2 pulgada
1991 y más moderno	19/32 pulgada	21/32 pulgada
Compresor del aire acondicionado		
Hasta el 1990	7/32 a 25/64 pulgada	3/8 a 7/16 pulgada
1991 y más moderno	5/8 pulgada	5/8 pulgada

Calificación de la presión de la tapa del radiador .... 11 a 14 psi (libras por pulgadas cuadradas)

Pedal del embrague

Altura
1980 al 1983... 6.73 a 6.79 pulgada (171 a 172 mm)
1984 y 1985... 7.05 a 7.44 pulgada (179 a 189 mm)
1986 en adelante
  Motor de cuatro cilindros........................... 9.29 a 9.69 pulgada (236 a 246 mm)
  Motor V6... 8.94 a 9.33 pulgada (227 a 237 mm)
Juego libre
1980 al 1983... 0.040 a 0.200 pulgada (1 a 5 mm)
1984 y 1985... 0.040 a 0.120 pulgada (1 a 3 mm)
1986 en adelante... 0.039 a 0.059 pulgada (1 a 1.5 mm)

Pedal del freno

Altura
1980 al 1983... 6.61 a 6.85 pulgada (168 a 174 mm)
1984 y 1985... 6.93 a 7.32 pulgada (176 a 186 mm)
1986 en adelante
  Transmisión manual................................... 8.23 a 8.62 pulgada (209 a 219 mm)
  Transmisión automática............................. 8.35 a 8.74 pulgada (212 a 222 mm)
Juego libre
1980 al 1983... 0.040 a 0.200 pulgada (1 a 5 mm)
1984 y 1985... 0.012 a 0.039 pulgada (0.3 a 1.0 mm)
1986 en adelante... 0.039 a 0.118 pulgada (1.0 a 3.0 mm)
Altura presionada... 3-1/4 pulgada (82 mm) (4.72 pulgada/120 mm en los modelos 1986 y más modernos)

Frenos

Límite de desgaste de la pastilla del freno .... 5/64 pulgada (2 mm)
Límite de desgaste del forro de la balata trasera .... 1/16 pulgada (1.5 mm)

Especificaciones técnicas	Pies-libras
Pernos del cárter de la transmisión automática	4.3
Bujías	14 a 22
Tapón para el drenaje del aceite de motor	
Hasta el 1990	18
1991 y más moderno	22 a 29
Tuercas de los balancines	12 a 16
Contratuerca del pivote de los balancines	12 a 16
Transmisión manual	
Tapón para chequear/llenar	18 a 25
Tapón para drenar...	18 a 25
Diferencial	
Tapón para chequear/llenar	
Hasta el 1990	60
1991 y más moderno	43
Tapón para drenar	
Hasta el 1990	60
1991 y más moderno	
Delantero	29 a 43
Trasero	43 a 72
Tapones para chequear/llenar en la caja de transferencia..............	22
Tuercas de montaje del carburador	9 a 13
Tuercas de montaje para el cuerpo de aceleración (modelos con combustible inyectados)	
Hasta el 1992	9 a 13
1993 y mas moderno	
Paso 1	6.5 a 8.0
Paso 2	13 a 16

Especificaciones técnicas (continuación)

Pies-libras

Sensor de oxígeno
  Motor de cuatro cilindros
    Hasta el 1990 .... 13 a 17
    1991 y más moderno .... 30 a 37
  Motor V6 .... 30 a 37
Tuercas de las ruedas
  Ruedas de acero sencillas
    1980
      2WD 65
      4WD 97
    1981 y 1982 97
    1983 en adelante .... 87 a 108
  Ruedas de acero dobles (todas) .... 166 a 203
  Ruedas de aluminio
    1984 y 1985 .... 58 a 72
    1986 en adelante .... 87 a 108
Tuercas del cubo de la rueda delantera (2WD) ..... 25 a 29

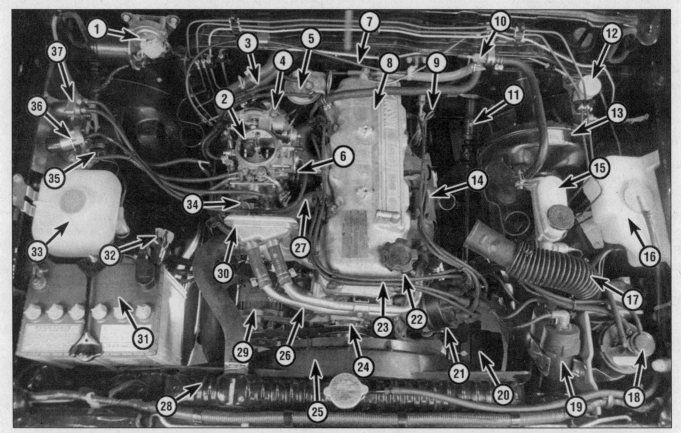

Componentes del compartimiento del motor - modelo 1981 y más moderno con motores de cuatro cilindros (típico)

1   Motor limpiador
2   Carburador
3   Manguera de la calefacción
4   Válvula EGR (recirculación de los gases de escape)
5   Válvula VVT (transductor del vacío de venturi)
6   Válvula PCV (ventilación positiva del cárter)
7   Cable del acelerador
8   Tapa de los balancines
9   Varilla graduada para medir el aceite de motor
10   Válvula unilateral para el amplificador de los frenos

11   Columna de la dirección
12   Cilindro maestro del embrague
13   Amplificador para los frenos
14   Múltiple de escape
15   Cilindro maestro para los frenos
16   Depósito del anticongelante
17   Conducto de aire (conectado al purificador de aire)
18   Canasto de carbón
19   Bobina para la ignición
20   Caja de la dirección
21   Distribuidor
22   Tapa para el abastecedor de aceite de motor
23   Alambres de las bujías

24   Polea de la bomba de agua y cigüeñal
25   Cubierta del ventilador
26   Tubos EAI (inducción de aire)
27   Múltiple de admisión
28   Radiador
29   Alternador
30   Albergue para la válvula de inducción de aire
31   Batería
32   Fusibles térmicos
33   Tanque del limpiador del parabrisas
34   Válvula AB (purga de aire)
35   Interruptor por vacío
36   Unidad de control de la amplificación
37   Compensador de altitud

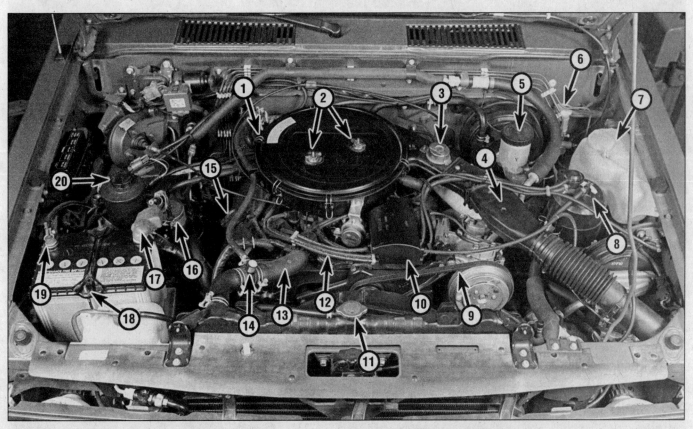

Componentes del compartimiento del motor - motores V6 (típico)

1   Resorte de retención para el albergue del purificador de aire
2   Tuercas de ala del albergue para el purificador de aire
3   Motor de vacío termostático para el purificador de aire
4   Tubo del conducto flexible de respiración del purificador de aire
5   Depósito del flúido de freno
6   Depósito del flúido del embrague
7   Depósito del flúido del limpiador del parabrisas
8   Canasto de carbón del sistema EEC (control electrónico del motor (computadora)

9   Banda del compresor del aire acondicionado
10 Distribuidor
11 Tapa del radiador
12 Alambres de las bujías
13 Manguera superior del radiador
14 Válvula de aire
15 Tapa del abastecedor de aceite del motor
16 Filtro de combustible
17 Cable positivo de la batería (+)
18 Abrazadera de afianzamiento de la batería
19 Cable negativo de la batería (-)
20 Varilla graduada para medir el flúido de la dirección

Vista inferior del motor/transmisión de cuatro cilindros - modelos 1981 y mas modernos 4WD (típico)

1 Brazo loco	19 Barra de torsión izquierda
2 Alternados	20 Pipa de escape delantera
3 Bomba de aceite	21 Eje propulsor delantero
4 Miembro transversal delantero para el diferencial	22 Tapón de drenaje para la transmisión manual
5 Polea del cigüeñal	23 Transmisión
6 Aislador del calzo para el diferencial delantero	24 Miembro transversal trasero para el diferencial
7 Barra estabilizadora	25 Barra de torsión derecha
8 Distribuidor	26 Cilindro para operar el embrague
9 Varilla transversal	27 Miembro transversal para la suspensión
10 Caja de la dirección	28 Eje propulsor derecho
11 Varilla de tensión izquierda	29 Eslabón inferior derecho
12 Aislador y soporte para el calzo del motor	30 Vástago
13 Varilla lateral	31 Brazo del vástago
14 Brazo del vástago de la dirección	32 varilla de tensión derecha
15 Vástago de la dirección	33 Varilla lateral
16 Eje propulsor izquierdo	34 Aislador y soporte para el calzo del motor
17 Varilla de acoplación izquierda	35 Cacerola del aceite
18 Diferencial delantero	

Vista inferior del motor/transmisión V6 - 4WD (típico)

1   Brazo loco de la dirección (copillas de grasa)
2   Manguera inferior del radiador
3   Banda
4   Copillas de grasa de la rótula de la dirección
5   Copillas de grasa de la rótula de la suspensión
6   Mordaza del freno
7   Manguera del freno

8   Fuelle del semieje
9   Tapón de drenaje del diferencial delantero
10   Acoplación U para el eje propulsor delantero
11   Acoplación del tubo de escape
12   Tapón de drenaje para la transmisión manual
13   Tapón de drenaje para el aceite del motor

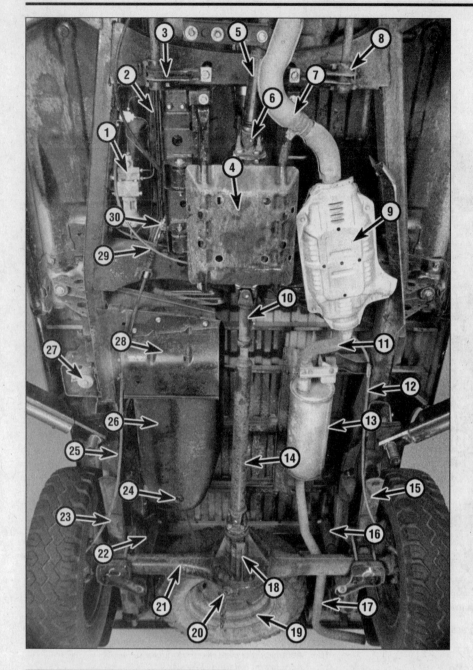

Vista inferior de los componentes en la parte trasera del vehículo - modelos 1981 y más moderno 4WD (típico)

1   Válvula detectora de la carga
2   Líneas de combustible y ventilación
3   Brazo de anclaje de la barra de torsión derecha
4   Protector para la caja de transferencia y contra piedras
5   Eje propulsor delantero
6   Acoplación universal del eje propulsor (crucetas)
7   Pipa de escape delantera
8   Brazo de anclaje de la barra de torsión izquierda
9   Convertidor catalítico
10 Yugo del eje propulsor
11 Tubo central
12 Cable izquierdo para el freno de estacionamiento
13 Silenciador
14 Eje propulsor trasero
15 Resorte de hojas trasero
16 Amortiguador izquierdo trasero
17 Cola de la pipa del escape
18 Diferencial trasero
19 Neumático de respuesto
20 Tapón de drenaje para el diferencial trasero
21 Eje trasero
22 Amortiguador trasero
23 Resorte de hojas derecho
24 Tapón de drenaje del tanque de combustible
25 Cable derecho trasero del freno de estacionamiento
26 Tanque de combustible
27 Bomba de combustible eléctrica
28 Protector para el tanque de combustible
29 Cable del espirómetro
30 Palanca equilibradora del freno de estacionamiento

1   Introducción

Este Capítulo está diseñado para ayudar al mecánico doméstico mantener la camioneta Nissan/Datsun y Pathfinder con las metas de rendimiento máximo, economía, seguridad y fiabilidad.

Incluido hay un mantenimiento de un programa maestro siga los procedimientos que sean específicamente para cada artículo de mantenimiento. Los chequeos visuales, ajustes, reemplazo de componente y otros artículos útiles son incluidos. Refiérase a las ilustraciones en el compartimiento del motor y debajo del lado lateral del vehículo para las ubicaciones de diversos componentes.

Rendirle servicio a su vehículo de acuerdo con el millaje planificado, o el pro-grama de mantenimiento de tiempo y los procedimientos graduales, deberían resultar en fiabilidad máxima y extiende la vida de su vehículo. Recuerde que es un mantenimiento comprensivo - manteniendo algunos artículos pero no los otros a los intervalos especificados no producirán los mismos resultados.

Según usted desempeña los procedimientos de mantenimiento rutinario, usted encontrará que muchos pueden y deberían, ser agrupados juntos a causa de la naturaleza de los procedimientos o a causa de la proximidad de dos componentes no relacionados.

Por ejemplo, si el vehículo se levanta para la lubricación del chasis, usted debería inspeccionar el escape, suspensión, dirección y sistema de combustible mientras usted está debajo del vehículo. Cuando usted rote los neumáticos, es un buen tiempo para chequear los frenos ya que las ruedas se removieron. Finalmente, supongamos que usted tiene que pedir o alquilar una llave torsiométrica. Aún cuando solamente tiene necesidad de ella para apretar las bujías, usted podría chequear también la torsión de muchas grapas y pernos críticos, según el tiempo lo permita.

El primer paso en este programa de mantenimiento prepararse usted para realizar el trabajo real. Lea a traves de todos los procedimientos que usted planifica hacer, entonces reúna todas las partes y las herramientas necesarias. Si ve que usted podría entrar en problemas durante un trabajo en particular, busque el consejo de un mecánico experimentado o alguien que haya hecho este trabajo anteriormente.

2 Programa de mantenimiento para las camionetas Nissan/Datsun y Pathfinder

Los intervalos de mantenimiento siguientes son con base en la suposición que el propietario del vehículo hará el mantenimiento o hará el trabajo del servicio, a diferencia de tener un departamento servicio de un concesionario que haga el trabajo. Aunque el tiempo y los intervalos de millas sean con base en las recomendaciones de fábrica, la mayoría se han acortado para asegurar, por ejemplo, que tales artículos como los lubrificantes y flúidos se chequeen/cambien a intervalos que promocionen que el motor tenga una vida de fuerza útil máxima. También, sujeto a la preferencia del propietario individual interesado en mantener el vehículo en su mejor condición en todo momento y con la reventa definitiva del vehículo en la mente, muchos de los procedimientos de mantenimiento pueden desempeñarse más frecuentemente que los recomendados en la planilla siguiente. Nosotros fomentamos tal iniciativa del propietario.

Cuando el vehículo es nuevo debe ser atendido inicialmente por el departamento de servicio de su concesionario autorizado para proteger la garantía de la fábrica. En muchos casos el chequeo inicial del mantenimiento es hecho a ningún costo al dueño - chequee con el departamento de servicio de su concesionario para más información.

Cada 250 millas o semanal, o cualquiera que ocurra primero

Chequee el nivel del aceite del motor (Sección 4)
Chequee el nivel del anticongelante (Sección 4)
Chequee el nivel del flúido del limpiaparabrisas (Sección 4)
Chequee los niveles del flúido del freno y del embrague (Sección 4)
Chequee el nivel del flúido para la transmisión automática (Sección 5)
Chequee el nivel del flúido de la dirección de poder (Sección 6)
Chequee los neumáticos y la presión del aire de los neumáticos (Sección 7)

Cada 7500 millas o 12 meses, o cualquiera que ocurra primero

Todos los artículos listado encima más:
Chequee y otórguele servicio a la batería (Sección 8)
Chequee el sistema de enfriamiento (Sección 9)
Inspeccione y si es necesario, reemplace los limpiaparabrisas (Sección 10)
Inspeccione y si es necesario, reemplace todas las mangueras debajo del capó (Sección 11)
Chequee/ajuste el pedal del freno (Sección 12)
Cambie el aceite y el filtro del motor (Sección 13)

Cada 15,000 millas o 12 meses, o cualquiera que ocurra primero

Todos los artículos listado encima más:
Haga que el departamento de servicio de su concesionario o taller de reparación chequee la proporción de la mezcla de aire combustible (modelos 1980 solamente)
Chequee y ajuste los franqueo de las válvulas (motor de cuatro-cilindros solamente) (Sección 14)
Lubrique los componentes del chasis (Sección 15)
Inspeccione los componentes de la suspensión y la dirección (Sección 16)*

Chequee el eje propulsor (s) (Sección 17)
Inspeccione el sistema del escape (Sección 18)
Chequee la altura del pedal del embrague y el juego libre (Sección 19)
Chequee el nivel del aceite de la transmisión manual (Sección 20)
Chequee el nivel del aceite de la caja de transferencia (Sección 21)*
Chequee el nivel del aceite del diferencial (Sección 22)*
Rote los neumáticos (Sección 23)
Chequee los frenos (Sección 24)
Chequee el sistema de combustible (Sección 25)
Chequee el termostato del purificador de aire (Sección 26)
Chequee y si es necesario, ajuste las bandas del motor (Sección 27)
Chequee los cinturones del asiento (Sección 28)
Reemplace las bujías (modelos 1980 solamente) (Sección 45)
Haga que la alineación delantera sea chequeada (especialmente si un desgaste anormal del neumático es evidente)

Cada 30,000 millas o 24 meses, o cualquiera que ocurra primero

Todos los artículos listado encima más:
Reemplace el purificador de aire y PCV (ventilación positiva del cárter) (Sección 29)
Reemplace el filtro del combustible (Sección 30)
Reemplace el purificador de aire de la válvula de inducción (Sección 31)
Reemplace el filtro de la bomba del aire (modelos 1980 solamente) (Sección 32)
Reemplace el filtro del canasto de carbón (Sección 33)
Chequee la operación del estrangulador del carburador (Sección 34)
Chequee el par de torsión de las tuercas del cuerpo de aceleración/carburador (Sección 35)
Chequee el pedal del acelerador y el cable (vehículos equipados con carburador solamente) (Sección 36)
Chequee y si es necesario, ajuste la velocidad de la marcha mínima del motor (Sección 37)

Cambie el aceite de la caja de transferencia (Sección 38)

Cambie el aceite para la transmisión manual (Sección 39)

Cambie el aceite del diferencial trasero (Sección 40)*

Cambie el flúido para la transmisión automática (Sección 41) **

Chequee y empaque los cojinetes de la rueda delantera (modelos de 2WD solamente) (Sección 42)

Otórguele servicio al sistema de enfriamiento (drene, limpie y rellene) (Sección 43)

Chequee y si es necesario, reemplace la válvula PCV (ventilación positiva del cárter) (Sección 44)

Reemplace las bujías (Sección 45)

Chequee/reemplace los alambres de las bujías (Sección 46)

Chequee/reemplace el rotor y la tapa del distribuidor (Sección 47)

Chequee y si es necesario, ajuste la regulación del tiempo de la ignición (Sección 48)

Reemplace el sensor de oxígeno (modelos 1985 de California solamente) (Sección 49)

Cada 50,000 millas o 24 meses, o cualquiera que ocurra primero

Reemplace el sensor de oxígeno (modelos 1985 de los 49 estados solamente) (Sección 49)

Cada 60,000 millas o 24 meses, o cualquiera que ocurra primero

Reemplace el sensor de oxígeno (todo los modelos 1986 y más modernos) (Sección 49)

Reemplace la banda del tiempo (motor V6 solamente) (Capítulo 2, Parte B)

*Este artículo es afectado por la operación de condición "severa" como está descrito mas abajo. Si su vehículo es operado bajo condiciones severas, realice todos los mantenimiento indicado con un **asterisco (*)** cada 3000 millas/intervalos de 3 mes. Las condiciones severas son **indicadas** si usted opera principalmente su vehículo bajo una o más de las siguientes condiciones:

Conducir en áreas polvorientas

Remolcar una casa remolque

Marcha mínima por un periodo de tiempo extendido y/o velocidad baja

Cuando las temperaturas exteriores permanecen bajo congelamiento y la mayoría de los viajes son menos de cuatro millas de distancia

**Si operó bajo una o más de las siguientes condiciones, cambie el flúido para la transmisión automática cada 15,000 millas:

En tráfico pesado de ciudad donde la temperatura exterior llega regularmente a 90 grados F (32 grados C) o más alto

Terrenos montuoso o montañoso

Remolcar casas remolques frecuentemente

3   Afinación - información general

El término afinación se usa en este manual para representar una combinación de operaciones individuales más bien que un procedimiento específico.

Si, desde el momento que el vehículo es nuevo, la planilla de mantenimiento rutinaria se sigue estrechamente y chequeos frecuentes se han hecho de los niveles de los flúidos y los artículos de alto desgaste, como sugerido a lo largo de este manual, el motor se mantendrá en una condición de marcha relativamente buena y la necesidad de trabajo adicional será minimizada.

Más probable que no, sin embargo, habrá veces cuando el motor corra pobremente debido a la falta de mantenimiento regular. Esto es aun más probable si se compra un vehículo usado, que no ha recibido los chequeos de mantenimiento frecuentemente y regulares. En tales casos, una afinación del motor se necesitará fuera de los intervalos regulares de mantenimiento rutinario.

El primer paso en cualquier afinación o procedimiento de diagnóstico para ayudar a corregir un motor que corre pobre es un chequéo de la compresión de los cilindro. Un chequeo de la compresión (vea Capítulo 2 Parte C) ayudará a determinar las condiciones de los componentes internos del motor y deberían usarse como una guía para la afinación y procedimientos de reparación. Si, por ejemplo, un chequeo de la compresión indica

desgaste serio interno del motor, una afinación corriente no mejorará el rendimiento del motor y sería un desgaste de tiempo y dinero. A causa de su importancia, el chequeo de la compresión debería ser hecha por alguien con el equipo adecuado y el conocimiento para usarlo adecuadamente.

Los procedimientos siguientes, son los más frecuentemente necesitados, para traer a un motor que generalmente corre pobre, de regreso a un estado apropiado de afinación.

Afinación menor

Chequee todos los flúidos relacionados con el motor

Limpie y chequee la batería (Sección 10)

Chequee y ajuste la bandas (Sección 16)

Reemplace las bujías (Sección 33)

Chequee la compresión de los cilindros (Capítulo 2)

Chequee la tapa del distribuidor y el rotor (Sección 35)

Chequee la bujía y el alambre de la bobina (Sección 34)

Reemplace el purificador de aire (Sección 30)

Chequee y ajuste la marcha mínima (Sección 17)

Chequee y ajuste el tiempo del encendido-(Sección 39)

Reemplace el filtro de combustible (Sección 40)

Chequee todas las mangueras debajo del capó (Sección 12)

Chequee la válvula PCV (ventilación positiva del cárter) (Sección 31)

Ajuste las luces de las válvulas (franqueo) (Sección 18)

Chequee y dele servicio al sistema de enfriamiento (Sección 11)

Afinación mayor

Todos los artículos mencionados debajo de afinación Menor más . . .

Chequee el sistema de la válvula EGR (recirculación de los gases de escape) (Capítulo 6)

Chequee el sistema de carga (Capítulo 5)

Chequee el sistema de la ignición (Capítulo 5)

Chequee el sistema de combustible (Sección 20 y Capítulo 4)

Reemplace los cable de las bujías, tapa del distribuidor y el rotor (Secciones 34 y 35)

4   Flúidos - chequeo de los niveles

Nota: *Los siguientes son chequeos de los niveles de los flúidos que se deben de hacer cada 250 millas o en base semanal. Los chequeos adicionales de los niveles de los flúidos pueden encontrarse en los procedimientos específicos de mantenimiento que siguen. Sin importar que tan frecuentemente los niveles de los flúidos se chequeen, observe por pozos debajo del vehículo - si fugas se notan, haga las reparaciones inmediatamente.*

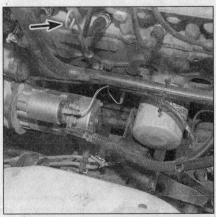

4.4a En los modelos 1980 de 2WD, la varilla graduada para medir el aceite del motor está localizada en el lado derecho (lado del pasajero) del motor (flecha), mientras . . .

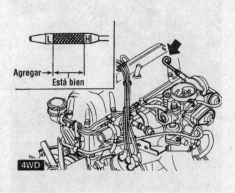

4.4b . . . que en los modelos de 4WD, está localizada en el lado izquierdo (lado del chófer)

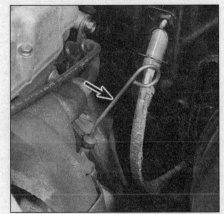

4.4c En los motores de cuatro cilindros con ocho bujías, la varilla graduada para medir el aceite está localizada en el lado izquierdo (lado del chófer), cerca de la parte trasera del motor

4.4d En los motores V6, la varilla graduada para medir el aceite está localizada hacia la parte trascra del compartimiento del motor, próximo al amplificador para los frenos

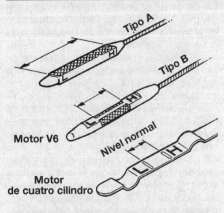

4.4e La varilla graduada para medir el aceite del motor pueda que esté marcada en una de varias maneras diferentes, pero el nivel correcto será obvio cuando la mire

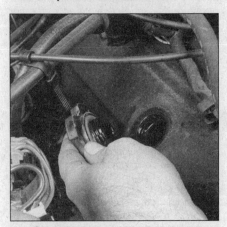

4.6 En los motores V6, la tapa del abastecedor de aceite está localizada en la tapa del balancín del lado derecho

1   Los flúidos son una parte imprescindible de la lubricación, enfriamiento, freno, embrague y sistemas de limpiaparabrisas. Porque los flúidos gradualmente llegan a ser agotados y/o contaminado durante la operación normal del vehículo, ellos deben periódicamente rellenarse. Vea flúidos y lubrificantes recomendados a principios de este Capítulo antes de agregar flúido a cualquiera de los componentes siguientes. **Nota:** *El vehículo debe estar en un suelo plano (nivelado) cuando los niveles de los flúidos se estén chequeando.*

Aceite del motor

Refiérase a las ilustraciones 4.4a, 4.4b, 4.4c, 4.4d, 4.4e y 4.6

2   El nivel del aceite del motor se chequea con una varilla que se extiende a través de un tubo en el cárter de aceite en la parte de abajo del motor.

3   El nivel de aceite debería chequearse antes de que el vehículo se haya conducido, o 15 minutos después de que el motor se

haya apagado. Si el aceite se chequea inmediatamente después de ser conducido el vehículo, algo del aceite permanecerá en los componentes superiores del motor, resultará en una lectura inadecuada en el nivel de la varilla.

4   Remueva la varilla fuera del tubo (vea las ilustraciones debajo del capó para los componentes al frente de este Capítulo) y limpie todo el aceite con una hoja de papel o un trapo limpio. Introduzca la varilla limpia completamente adentro del tubo, entonces remuévala nuevamente. Note el nivel del aceite al final de la varilla. Añada aceite según sea necesario para mantener el nivel entre la marca L (bajo) y la marca F (lleno) en la marca de nivel de la varilla **(vea ilustraciónes)**.

5   No sobre llene el motor agregando demasiado aceite ya que esto puede resultar en que el aceite suba a las bujías, fugas de aceite o fallas de los sellos de aceite.

6   El aceite se le añade al motor después de remover la tapa enroscada en la cubierta de las válvulas **(vea ilustración)**. Un embudo ayudará a reducir derrames.

7   Chequeando el nivel del aceite es un paso importante de mantenimiento preventivo. Un nivel de aceite coherentemente bajo indica fuga de aceite, sellos dañados, juntas defectuosas, guías de la válvula o anillos desgastados. Si el aceite se mira de color lechoso o tiene góticas de agua, la junta de la culata(s) puede estar rota, la cabeza(s) o el bloque pueden estar agrietado. El motor debería chequearse inmediatamente. La condición del aceite debería también ser chequeada. Cuando usted chequee el nivel del aceite, resbale su dedo índice y pulgar sobre la varilla antes de limpiar el aceite. Si usted ve partículas pequeñas de metal o suciedad que se agarran a la varilla, el aceite debería cambiarse (Sección 15).

Anticongelante del radiador

Refiérase a las ilustraciones 4.8

Peligro: *No permita que el anticongelante entre en contacto con su piel o la superficie de la pintura del vehículo. Enjuague el área que estuvo en contacto inmediatamente con suficiente agua. No guarde anticongelante*

4.8 El nivel del anticongelante se debe mantener entre las dos marcas en el lado del depósito - el anticongelante es agregado después de remover la tapa

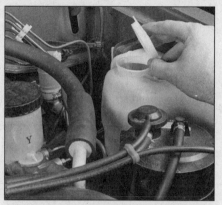

4.14 El nivel del flúido para el limpiador del parabrisas debe estar cerca de la cima del depósito - el flúido puede ser agregado después de remover la tapa (esté seguro de cerrarlo firmemente cuando haya terminado)

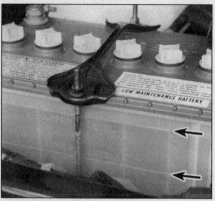

4.17 En las baterías de equipo original, el nivel del electrólito puede ser chequeado sin remover las tapas de la célula - se debe mantener entre las marcas en el casco (flechas)

nuevo o deje anticongelante viejo alrededor donde pueda ser fácilmente accesible por niños y animales domésticos - son atraídos por su sabor dulce. Ingestión, aunque sea de una pequeña cantidad puede ser fatal. Limpie el piso del garaje y la cacerola de goteo para derramamientos de anticongelante tan pronto ocurran. Guarde los recipientes del anticongelante cubiertos y repare cualquier fuga en su sistema de enfriamiento inmediatamente.

8   Todos los vehículo cubiertos por este manual se equipan con un sistema presurizado de recuperación de anticongelante. Un depósito de anticongelante plástico blanco ubicado en el compartimiento del motor es conectado por una manguera al orificio del llenador del radiador (vea ilustración). Si el motor se recalienta, el anticongelantes se fuga a través de una válvula en la tapa del radiador y viaja hasta el depósito a través de una manguera. Según el motor se enfría, el anticongelante se regresa automáticamente hacia el sistema de enfriamiento para mantener el nivel correcto.

9   El nivel del anticongelante en el depósito debería chequearse regularmente. **Peligro:** *No remueva la tapa del radiador para chequear el nivel del anticongelante cuando el motor esté caliente.* El nivel en el depósito varía con la temperatura del motor. Cuando el motor está frío, el nivel del anticongelante debería estar a, o, ligeramente arriba de la marca Baja (Low) en el depósito. Una vez que el motor se haya calentado completamente, el nivel debería estar a, o, cerca de la marca Llena (Full). Si no está, permita que el motor se enfríe, entonces remueva la tapa del depósito y añada una mezcla 50/50 de glicol de Etileno basado en anticongelante y agua.

10   Conduzca el vehículo y chequee nuevamente el nivel del anticongelante. Si solamente una pequeña cantidad de anticongelante se requiere para traer el sistema hasta el nivel apropiado, agua puede usarse. Sin embargo, repitiendo las adiciones de agua diluirán la solución de agua y anticongelante. A fin de mantener la relación apropiada de anticongelante y agua, siempre llene hasta arriba el nivel de anticongelante con la mez-

cla correcta. Un porrón o lejía de leche vacía de plástico es un recipiente óptimo para mezclar el anticongelante. No use inhibidores antióxido o aditivos.

11   Si los niveles del anticongelante se reducen coherentemente, puede haber una fuga en el sistema. Chequee el radiador, manguera, tapón de llenado, tapones de drenaje y la bomba de agua (vea Sección 11). Si ninguna fuga se nota, lleve para que chequeen la presión de la tapa del radiador en una estación de servicio.

12   Si usted tiene que remover la tapa del radiador, espere hasta que el motor se haya enfriado, entonces envuelva un paño grueso alrededor de la tapa y gírelo hasta la primera parada. Si hay fugas de vapor o de anticongelante, permita que el motor se enfríe por un tiempo más largo, entonces remueva la tapa.

13   Chequee la condición del anticongelante también. Debe de estar clara relativamente. Si está marrón o de color orín, el sistema debería vaciarse, limpiarse y ser rellenado. Aún cuando el anticongelante parece estar normal, los inhibidores de corrosión se desgastan, así que se deben de sustituirse a los intervalos especificados.

Flúido para el limpiaparabrisas

Refiérase a la ilustración 4.14

14   El flúido para el sistema del limpiaparabrisas se almacena en un depósito plástico ubicado cerca de la batería (vea ilustración). Si es necesario, refiérase a la ilustración de componente(s) debajo del capó a principios de este Capítulo para ubicar el depósito.

15   En climas más leves, agua solamente puede usarse en el depósito, pero no se debe mantener más de 2/3 partes lleno para permitir la expansión del agua cuando se congele. En climas más fríos, anticongelante especial para el sistema del limpiaparabrisas se debe de usar, disponible en cualquier refaccionaría para bajar el punto de congelación del flúido. Mezcle el anticongelante con agua según las instrucciones del fabricante en el recipiente. **Peligro:** *No use anticonge-*

lante del sistema de enfriamiento - dañará la pintura del vehículo.

16   Para ayudar a impedir la congelación en tiempo frío, caliente el parabrisas con el descongelador antes de usar el limpiaparabrisas.

Electrolito de la batería

Refiérase a la ilustración 4.17

17   Para chequear el nivel de electrólito en la batería, remueva todos los tapones de las celdas. Si el nivel está bajo, añada agua destilada hasta que esté encima de los platos. Las baterías originales son comúnmente translúcidas para que el nivel del electrólito pueda ser chequeado mirándolo por el lado lateral del albergue (vea ilustración). Las mayorías de las baterías de reemplazo tienen una división - anillo indicador en cada celda para ayudar a usted a juzgar cuando suficiente anticongelante se haya añadido - ¡no sobrellene las celdas!

Freno y embrague - flúido

Refiérase a las ilustraciones 4.19a y 4.19b

18   El cilindro maestro de los frenos se monta en la parte del frente de la unidad de amplificación de energía en el compartimiento del motor. El cilindro maestro para el embrague usado en la transmisión manual, se instala adyacente al cilindro maestro de los frenos en la pared para detener fuegos.

19   El flúido en el interior es fácilmente visible. El nivel debería estar entre las marcas MIN (mínimo) y MAX (máximo) en el depósitos (vea ilustraciones). Si un nivel bajo es indicado, esté seguro de limpiar la cubierta del depósito con un trapo limpio para impedir contaminación del flúido del freno y/o el sistema de embrague antes de remover la tapa.

20   Cuando tenga que añadir flúido, viértalo cuidadosamente en el depósito para evitar derrame en las superficies pintadas. Esté seguro que el flúido especificado se use, mezclando los tipos diferentes de flúidos de frenos pueden ocasionar daños al sistema. Vea flúidos y lubrificantes recomendados en el frente de este Capítulo o manual del propietario. **Peligro:** *Flúido de frenos puede*

4.19a El nivel del flúido del freno se debe mantener cerca de la marca superior en el depósito - es traslúcido así que la tapa no tiene que ser removida para chequear el nivel

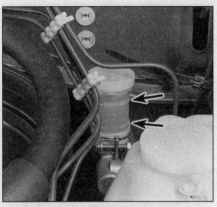

4.19b El nivel del flúido del embrague se debe mantener entre las marcas MIN y MAX en el depósito

dañar sus ojos y dañar las superficies de la pintura, tenga extremo cuidado cuando lo esté manejando o vertiéndolo. No use flúido de frenos que haya permanecido abierto o tiene más de un año de edad. El flúido de frenos absorbe humedad del aire. El exceso de humedad puede ocasionar una pérdida peligrosa de la eficiencia del freno.

21   En este momento el flúido y el cilindro maestro se pueden inspeccionar por contaminación. El sistema debería vaciarse y rellenarse si depósitos, partículas de suciedades o góticas de agua se ven en el flúido.

22   Después de llenar el depósito al nivel apropiado, asegúrese que la cubierta está bien apretada para impedir la fuga del flúido.

23   El nivel del flúido de frenos en el cilindro maestro se bajará ligeramente según las pastillas y las zapatas del freno en cada rueda se desgastan durante su operación normal. Si el cilindro maestro requiere adiciones repetidas de flúido para mantenerlo al nivel apropiado, es una indicación de fuga en el sistema de frenos, que debe corregirse inmediatamente. Chequee todas las líneas de freno y las acoplaciones (vea Sección 22 para más información).

24   Si, después de chequear el nivel del flúido del cilindro maestro, usted descubre uno o ambos depósitos vacíos o aproximadamente vacíos, el sistema de frenos debería sangrarse (Capítulo 9).

5   Transmisión automática - chequeo del nivel del flúido

Refiérase a las ilustraciones 5.3, 5.6a y 5.6b

1   El nivel del flúido de la transmisión automática debería ser cuidadosamente mantenido. El nivel bajo del flúido puede conducir a que se resbale o pérdida del accionamiento, mientras que el sobrellenar puede ocasionar espumas y pérdida del flúido.

2   Con el freno de estacionamiento puesto, ponga el motor en marcha, entonces mueva la palanca de cambios a través de todos los engranes, terminando en Estacio-

namiento. El nivel del flúido debe chequearse con el vehículo nivelado y el motor en marcha mínima. **Nota:** *Lecturas incorrectas del nivel del flúido resultarán si el vehículo se acaba de conducir a alta velocidad por un periodo de tiempo extendido, en tiempo caliente y en tránsito urbano, o si ha tirado un remolque. Si cualquiera de estas condiciones se aplican, espere hasta que el flúido se haya enfriado (alrededor de 30 minutos).*

3   Con la transmisión a la temperatura normal de operación, remueva la varilla de chequear el nivel del tubo. La varilla para chequear el nivel se ubica en la parte trasera del compartimiento del motor, comúnmente en el lado del conductor **(vea ilustración)**.

4   Cuidadosamente toque el flúido al final de la varilla para determinar si está frío (86 a 122 grados F) o caliente (123 a 176 grados F).

Limpie el flúido de la varilla con un trapo limpio y empujela adentro del tubo del llenador hasta que la tapa llegue a su asiento.

5   Remueva la varilla hacia fuera nuevamente y note el nivel del flúido.

6   Si el flúido se siente frío, el nivel debería estar dentro de la marca FRÍA (entre las ranuras) **(vea ilustraciones)**. Si el flúido está caliente, el nivel debería estar dentro de la escala CALIENTE.

7   Si se requiere flúido adicional, añádalo directamente en el tubo usando un embudo. Toma alrededor de una pinta para levantar el nivel desde la marca L (bajo) a la H (alto) con una transmisión caliente, así que añada el flúido un poco a la vez y mantenga chequeando el nivel hasta que esté correcto.

8   La condición del flúido debería también ser chequeada conjuntamente con el nivel. Si el flúido al final de la varilla es de un color obscuro rojizo - color marrón, o si se huele quemado, se debe cambiar. Si usted está en duda en la condición del flúido, compre flúido nuevo y compare los dos por color y olor.

6   Dirección de potencia - chequeo del nivel del flúido

Refiérase a ilustración 6.5

1   Diferente a la dirección manual, el sistema de dirección de poder confía en flúido, que a plazo de un tiempo, requiera ser rellenado.

2   El depósito del flúido para la bomba de servodirección en los motor V6 se ubica en la bomba en la parte del frente del motor. En un vehículo con motor de cuatro cilindros, el depósito está separado de la bomba y se

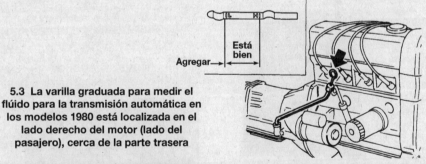

5.3 La varilla graduada para medir el flúido para la transmisión automática en los modelos 1980 está localizada en el lado derecho del motor (lado del pasajero), cerca de la parte trasera

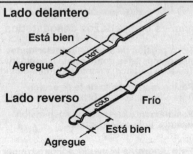

5.6a La varilla graduada para medir el nivel del flúido de la transmisión automática en los modelos 2WD está marcada como esta, mientras . . .

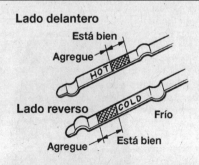

5.6b . . . que en los modelos de 4WD se parece a esta (típico)

6.5 Chequee el nivel del flúido de la dirección de poder en la varilla de medir el aceite después de torcer la tapa (se muestra un motor V6)

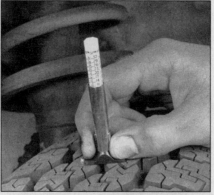

7.2 Un indicador para detectar la profundidad del rodamiento de los neumáticos se debe de usar para chequear el desgaste - están disponibles en los auto partes y las estaciones de servicio/gasolineras a un costo mínimo

7   Neumáticos y presión de los neumáticos - chequeo

Refiérase a las ilustraciones 7.2, 7.3, 7.4a, 7.4b y 7.8

1 Chequeo periódico de los neumáticos puede ahorrarle a usted la incomodidad de tener un neumático ponchado. Puede proveerle también a usted con información vital con problemas en el sistema de la suspensión y de la dirección antes de que el daño que ocurra sea más peligroso.

2 Los neumáticos originales en estos vehículos se equipan con barras indicadoras de desgaste, que aparecerán cuando la profundidad de los rodamientos alcancen un límite predeterminado, comúnmente 1/16-pulgada, pero ellos no aparecen hasta que los neumáticos se hayan desgastado. El desgaste de la superficie de los neumáticos puede chequearse con un dispositivo barato y simple, conocido como un indicador de profundidad (**vea ilustración**).

3 Anote cualquier desgaste anormal de la superficie de los neumáticos (**vea ilustración**). Las irregularidades de las bandas, tales como áreas planas y más desgastadas en un lado que en el otro, son indicaciones de problemas de alineación delantera y/o balanceo. Si cualquiera de estas condiciones se notan, lleve el vehículo a una estación de servicio o taller de reparar neumáticos para corregir el problema.

4 Mire cuidadosamente por cuarteaduras, perforaciones y clavos o tachuelas. A veces un neumático sostiene la presión de aire por un tiempo corto o se baja muy lentamente después de que un clavo haya penetrado. Si

monta en el guardabarros interior en el lado del conductor.

3 Para el chequeo, las ruedas delanteras deberían estar rectas y el motor debería estar apagado. El fluído de la dirección de poder y el motor deberían estar caliente en los modelos 1979 y 1980 (temperatura de operación normal). En 1981 y modelos más modernos el nivel puede chequearse con el fluído caliente (temperatura de operación normal) o frío. El fluído puede considerarse frío si el motor no ha sido conducido por lo menos cinco horas.

4 Use un trapo limpio para limpiar la tapa, la zona del depósito de afuera y sus alrededores. Esto ayudará e impedirá que cualquier material extranjero entre en el depósito durante el chequeo.

5 Remueva la tapa - tiene una varilla para chequear el nivel adyacente a la tapa (**vea ilustración**).

6 Limpie el fluído con un trapo limpio, instale la varilla para chequear el nivel, entonces retírela y note el nivel del fluído. El nivel debería estar dentro de la serie marcada en el nivel de la varilla. Nunca permita que el nivel del fluído baje más bajo de la marca inferior en la varilla.

7 Si fluído adicional se requiere, vierta el tipo especificado directamente en el depósito, use un embudo para impedir derrames.

8 Si el depósito requiere frecuentes adiciones de fluído, toda la dirección de poder, acoplaciones de las mangueras y la bomba de servodirección deberían cuidadosamente chequearse por fugas.

Poca presión de aire

Secciones con pedazos desgastados

- Poca presión de aire y/o irregularidades mecánicas tales como rueda o neumático fuera de balance, y llanta torcida o dañada.
- Posiblemente varilla de la dirección floja o desgastada o brazo loco.
- Posiblemente partes de la suspensión dañada, floja o desgastada.

7.3 Este diagrama le ayudará a determinar la condición de sus neumáticos, la causa(s) probable del desgaste anormal y la acción correctiva necesaria

Mucha presión de aire

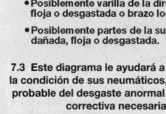

Convergencia/divergencia incorrecta o comba extrema

Desgaste en forma angular

7.4a Si el neumático continúa perdiendo la presión, chequee la válvula del neumático y asegúrese de que está apretada

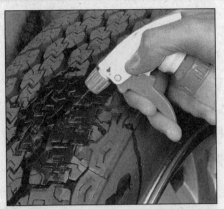

7.4b Si la válvula del neumático está apretada, eleve el lado del vehículo que tiene el neumático bajo de aire y rocíe el neumático con una solución de agua y jabón - fugas pequeñas de aire causarán que unas pequeñas burbujas aparezcan

7.8 Chequee la presión de los neumáticos por lo menos una ves por semana, con un medidor que esté bien calibrado (no se olvide del neumático de respuesto)

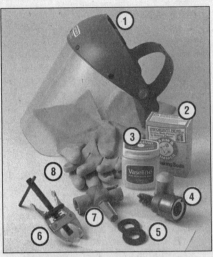

8.1 Herramientas y materiales para el mantenimiento de la batería, con postes normales encima

una fuga lenta persiste, chequee la válvula para asegurarse de que está apretada **(vea ilustración)**. Examine los rodamientos por objetos que se puedan haber penetrado por sí mismo en el neumático o por un "tapón" que pueda haber comenzado a tener fugas (las perforaciones para los neumáticos radiales se reparan con un tapón que se instala en la perforación). Si una perforación se sospecha, puede ser fácilmente chequeado con una solución de agua jabonosa en la zona de la perforación **(vea ilustración)**. La solución jabonosa burbujeará si hay una fuga. A menos que la perforación sea extraordinariamente grande, una estación de servicio o taller de neumático puede reparar el neumático.

5   Cuidadosamente inspeccione el interior del lado de cada neumático por evidencia de fuga de flúido de frenos. Si usted nota cualquier fuga, inspeccione los frenos inmediatamente.

6   La presión de aire correcta añade millas de vida a los neumáticos, mejor millaje y mejora la calidad del viaje. La presión de aire correcta no puede ser precisamente estimada solamente mirando los neumáticos, especialmente si son radiales. Un manómetro de aire para neumáticos es imprescindible. Mantenga un medidor preciso en el vehículo. Los manómetros para los neumáticas adjuntos a las mangueras de gasolineras son frecuentemente inadecuados.

7   Siempre chequee la presión de los neumáticos cuando los neumáticos estén fríos. Frío, en este caso, significa que el vehículo no se haya conducido más de una milla en las últimas tres horas que precedan un chequeo de la presión de los neumáticos. Que la presión se eleve de cuatro a ocho de libras es común una vez que los neumáticos se calienten.

8   Destornille la tapa que sale de la válvula de la rueda y empuje el medidor firmemente en la válvula **(vea ilustración)**. Note la lectura en el medidor y compare la figura con la presión recomendada mostrada en la puerta de la guantera. Esté seguro de reinstalar la tapa de la válvula para mantener la suciedad y la humedad fuera del mecanismo de la válvula.

Chequee todos los cuatro neumáticos y si es necesario, añada aire suficiente para traerlo a la presión recomendada.

9   No olvide mantener la presión del neumático de repuesto a la presión especificada (refiérase al manual del propietario o el lado del neumático).

8   Batería - chequeo y mantenimiento

Refiérase a ilustraciones 8.1, 8.6. 8.7a, 8.7b, 8.7c y 8.7d

Peligro: *Se deben seguir precauciones seguras y que están recomendadas cuando esté chequeando y dándole servicio a la batería. El gas de hidrógeno que está adentro de la batería, es muy inflamable, está presente siempre en las celdas de la batería, así que no fume o acerque la batería a llamas o chispas, mantenga estos objetos lejos de la batería. El electrólito adentro de la batería es ácido sulfúrico diluido, que causará lesión si se salpica en su piel o en sus ojos. Dañará también la ropa y las superficies de la pintura. Cuando*

1   *Protector para la cara* - *Cuando esté removiendo corrosión con una brocha o cepillo, las partículas de ácido fácilmente pueden caerle en el ojo*

2   *Bicarbonato* - *Una solución de bicarbonato y agua se puede usar para neutralizar la corrosión*

3   *Jalea de petróleo* - *Un filamento de esto aplicado a la batería ayudará a prevenir la corrosión*

4   *Limpiador para los postes y cables de la batería* - *Esta herramienta para limpiar es de alambre y removerá todo tipo de corrosión de los postes de la batería y de los cables*

5   *Arandela de fieltro curadas* - *Instalando una de estas arandelas en cada poste, directamente debajo de la grapa, ayudará a prevenir corrosión*

6   *Removedor* - *Muchas veces las grapas de los cables son difíciles de remover, aunque se hayan aflojado las tuercas y pernos completamente. Esta herramienta hala la grapa directamente hacia arriba sin dañar el poste*

7   *Limpiador de los postes y cables de la batería* - *Aquí hay unas herramientas para limpiar que son un poquito diferente que la de la versión numero 4 de encima, pero hace lo mismo*

8   *Guantes de caucho/goma* - *Otro equipo de seguridad que se debe considerar cuando le esté dando servicio a la batería; recuérdese que lo que está adentro de la batería es ácido*

remueva los cables de la batería, siempre desconecte el cable negativo primero y conéctelo por último.

Chequeo

1   El mantenimiento de la batería es un procedimiento importante que ayudará a asegurar que usted no se quede abandonado a causa de una batería muerta. Varias herramientas se requieren para este procedimiento **(vea ilustración)**.

8.6 Los pernos de la abrazadera del cable de la batería se deben mantener apretados para evitar problemas

8.7a La corrosión de las terminales de la batería usualmente aparecen como una cubierta de polvo de color blanco o verde

8.7b Remueva el cable del poste de la batería (el negativo primero) con una herramienta, algunas veces unas pinzas especiales para baterías son necesarias, si la corrosión a deteriorado las tuercas (siempre remueva el alambre negativo/tierra primero e instálelo de último)

2   El nivel del electrólito debería chequearse cada semana (vea Sección 4).

3   Periódicamente limpie la parte superior y lateral de la batería. Remueva toda la suciedad y humedad. Esto ayudará e impedirá corrosión y asegurará que la batería no llegue a ser parcialmente descargada por fuga de humedad y suciedad. Chequee el albergue por grietas y distorsión.

4   Chequee la seguridad de la retención del cable de la batería para asegurarse que sus acoplaciones eléctricas estén buenas. Chequee la longitud entera de cada cable, busque por aislamiento agrietado o rajado y conductores desgastados. La instalación y la remoción del cable de la batería se cubre en el Capítulo 5.

5   Si la corrosión, que comúnmente aparece como sedimentos esponjosos blancos, es evidente, remueva los cables desde los terminales, límpielos con un cepillo de batería y los reinstala. La corrosión puede mantenerse al mínimo aplicando una capa de jalea de petróleo a los terminales después de que los cables estén en su lugar.

6   Asegúrese que el dispositivo para sostener la batería está en buen estado y bien apretado. Si la batería se remueve, asegúrese que nada está en el fondo del dispositivo para sostener la batería antes de apretar las tuercas del afianzador **(vea ilustración)**.

7   El punto de congelación del electrolito depende de su viscosidad especifica. La congelación puede arruinar una batería, se debe guardar totalmente en estado de carga para protegerla contra congelación **(vea ilustraciones)**.

8   Si usted frecuentemente tiene que añadirle agua a la batería y el albergue se ha inspeccionado por grietas que puedan ocasionar fugas, pero nada se ha encontrado, la batería está siendo sobre cargada; el sistema de carga debería chequearse como está descrito en el Capítulo 5.

9   Si cualquier duda existe debido al estado de la carga de la batería, un hidrómetro debería ser usado para probar el electrolito de cada vaso, de uno en uno.

10   La viscosidad especifica del electrolito

a 80 grados F será aproximadamente 1.270 para una batería totalmente cargada. Por cada 10 grados F que la temperatura del electrolito está arriba de 80 grados F, añada 0.04 a la viscosidad especificada. Reste 0.04 si la temperatura está debajo de 80 grados F.

11   Una viscosidad especifica de 1.240 con una temperatura del electrolito de 80 grados F indica una batería media cargada.

12   Algunos de los fracasos comunes ocasionados por la batería son:

a) *Accesorios, especialmente faroles, dejados prendidos toda la noche o por varias horas.*

b) *Conducir a velocidades lentas o intervalos de viajes cortos.*

c) *La descarga eléctrica del vehículo siendo más alta que el rendimiento del alternador. Esto es muy común cuando varios accesorios de alta descarga están siendo usados simultáneamente (tal como radio/estéreo, aire acondicionado, desempañador para las ventanas, luces, etc.).*

d) *Problemas del sistema de carga tales como cortocircuitos, banda que se resbala, alternador defectuoso o regulador de voltaje defectuoso.*

e) *La batería abandonada, tal como terminales flojas, corroídas o dispositivos para sujetar la batería flojos.*

Cargando la batería

13   En el invierno cuando demandas pesadas se ponen en la batería, es una buena idea de ocasionalmente cargarla con una fuente externa.

14   Cuando cargue la batería, el cable negativo debería desconectarse. Los cables del cargador deberían conectarse a la batería antes de que el cargador se encienda. Si los cables se conectan a los bornes de la batería después de que el cargador está en marcha, ¡una chispa podría ocurrir y el gas de hidrógeno dado por la batería podría estallar!

15   La batería debería cargarse a un valor debajo de 4 a 6 amperios y debería dejarse por lo menos tres o cuatro horas. Un cargador de baja capacidad de 1.5 amperios puede

8.7c Sin importar el tipo de herramienta que usted use para limpiar los postes de la batería, una superficie limpia y brillante debe ser el resultado final

8.7d Cuando limpie las grapas de los terminales de las baterías, se debe quitar toda la corrosión (el interior de la grapa está hecha como un cono para que haga juego con la batería, así que no remueva mucho material)

SIEMPRE CHEQUE - las mangueras por si tienen áreas quemadas que puedan causar finalmente un malogro muy costoso.

MANGUERA SUAVE / BLANDA - indica deterioración interior. Esta deterioración puede contaminar el sistema de enfriamiento y las partículas pueden tapar al radiador.

MANGUERA DURA - una manguera dura puede fallar en cualquiera momento. Apretando la grapa que sella la conexión de la manguera no para la fug

MANGUERA HINCHADA - o las puntas empapadas de aceite indican un peligro y posiblemente un fracaso por el aceite o la contaminación de la grasa. Apriete la manguera con sus manos para localizar cualquier rajadura y rupturas que puedan causar fugas.

9.4 Las mangueras del sistema de enfriamiento deben de ser cuidadosamente inspeccionadas para prevenir problemas en la carretera, sin importar las condiciones de las mangueras en una buena idea de remplazarlas cada dos años

usarse si se va a cargar toda la noche.

16   Cargas especiales de impulso rápido que dicen que sirven para restaurar la energía de la batería en un tiempo corto, pueden ocasionar daño serio a las placas de la batería y debería únicamente ser usado en una situación de emergencia.

17   La batería debería dejarse en el cargador solamente hasta que la viscosidad especifica

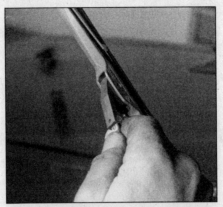

10.1 El limpiaparabrisas es removido presionando la proyección de liberación y halándola hacia fuera

del nivel normal se restablezca. ¡No sobre cargue la batería! **Nota:** *Algunos cargadores de baterías se desconectarán automáticamente después de que la batería se haya cargado totalmente, haciendo innecesario de mantener vigilancia por el estado de carga.*

18   Cuando esté desconectando el cargador, desconéctelo antes de desconectarlo de la batería.

9   Sistema de enfriamiento - chequeo

Refiérase a la ilustración 9.4

1   Muchos defectos importantes del motor pueden atribuirse al sistema de enfriamiento defectuoso. Si el vehículo se equipa con una transmisión automática, el sistema de enfriamiento también enfría el flúido de la transmisión, prolongando la vida de la transmisión.

2   El sistema de enfriamiento debería chequearse con el motor frío. Haga esto antes de que el vehículo se conduzca o después de que se haya apagado por lo menos tres horas.

3   Remueva la tapa del radiador girándola hacia la izquierda hasta que alcance la parada. Si usted oye un sonido como un silbido (indica que todavía hay presión en el sistema), espere hasta que se detenga. Ahora prense hacia abajo en la tapa con la palma de su mano y continúe girando hasta que pueda removerse. Completamente limpie la tapa, por dentro y por fuera, con agua limpia. También limpie el orificio para el llenado en el radiador. Todos los rasgos de corrosión deberían removerse. El anticongelante adentro del radiador debería estar relativamente transparente. Si está de color orín, el sistema debería vaciarse y ser rellenado (Sección 36). Si el nivel del anticongelante no está hasta encima, añada anticongelante adicional, mezcle el anticongelante con agua (vea Sección 4).

4   Cuidadosamente chequee la manguera superior e inferior del radiador conjuntamente con las mangueras de diámetro más pequeñas de la calefacción que salen del motor a la pared para detener fuegos. Chequee cada manguera a lo largo de su longitud entera, sustituyendo cualquier manguera que esté

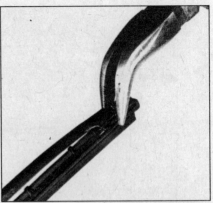

10.2 Si es necesario, el elemento del limpiaparabrisas puede ser removido apretando el clip retenedor con alicates

agrietada, hinchada o deteriorada. Las grietas pueden llegar a ser más evidente si la manguera se aprieta **(vea ilustración)**. Sin considerar su condición, es una buena idea de sustituir las mangueras con nuevas una vez cada dos años.

5   Asegúrese que todas las acoplaciones de las mangueras están apretadas. Una fuga en el sistema de enfriamiento se mostrará comúnmente como algo blanco o sedimentos de color orín en la zona donde está la fuga. Si grapas de alambre se usan en los extremos de las mangueras, puede que sea una buena idea de sustituirlas con grapas de tipo tornillo.

6   Use aire comprimido o una escobilla blanda para remover insectos, hojas, etc. desde la parte del frente del condensador del aire acondicionado o radiador. Tenga cuidado de no dañar las aletas delicadas de enfriamiento o que usted se baya a cortar con ellas.

7   Cada otro chequeo, o a la primera indicación de problemas del sistema de enfriamiento, pruebe la presión del sistema y la tapa. Si usted no tiene un comprobador de presión, la mayoría de las gasolineras y talleres de reparaciones pueden hacer esto por una carga mínima.

10   Limpiaparabrisas - inspección y reemplazo

Refiérase a las ilustraciones 10.1 y 10.2

1   El limpiaparabrisas es removido presionando la etiqueta de liberación en los fines del brazo limpiador **(vea ilustración)** y removiendo la hoja del brazo.

2   Si es necesario remover el elemento de caucho de la hoja, comprima los retenedores en los extremos de la hoja y deslice el elemento hacia fuera **(vea ilustración)**.

3   Si es necesario reemplazar el brazo limpiador, remueva la tapa y la tuerca reteniendo el brazo limpiador a la varilla y separe el brazo.

4   Cuando esté instalando el brazo limpiador, esté seguro de que está en fila con el otro brazo y está puesto correctamente en posición en el eje.

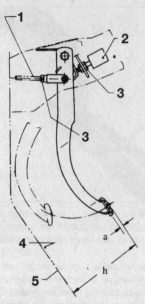

12.1 El pedal del freno se debe inspeccionar periódicamente por altura correcta (h) y juego libre (a)

1   *Varilla de entrada para el amplificador de los frenos.*
2   *Interruptor para la lampara de los freno.*
3   *Tuerca prisionera.*
4   *Aislador.*
5   *Piso.*

11   Mangueras debajo del capó - chequeo y reemplazo

General

1   **Peligro:** *El sistema de aire acondicionado está bajo alta presión.* **NO afloje** *ninguna de las mangueras, líneas, o remueva ningún componente hasta que el sistema se le haya removido la presión por un concesionario de vehículos, una estación de servicios o un taller especializado en aire acondicionados. Siempre use protección para sus ojos cuando esté desconectando las acoplaciones del aire acondicionado.*

2   Temperaturas altas en el compartimiento del motor pueden ocasionar deterioración de las gomas y las mangueras plásticas usadas en el motor, operación del sistemas de emisión y accesorio. Un chequeo periódico debería hacerse por grietas, afianzadores flojos, fugas y endurecimiento de los materiales. Las informaciones específicas de las mangueras del sistema de enfriamiento pueden encontrarse en la Sección 11.

3   Algunas, pero no todas, las mangueras se fijan a los acopladores con grapas. Donde se usen grapas, chequee para estar seguro que no hayan perdido su tensión, permitiendo que las mangueras tengan fugas. Si no se usan grapas, asegúrese que la manguera no se ha expandido y/o endurecido donde se desliza en el acoplador, permitiéndole que tenga fuga.

Mangueras de vacío

4   Es bastante común que las mangueras de vacío, especialmente esas en el sistema de emisiones, sean de color codificado o identificadas con franjas de colores moldeadas en ellas. Los diversos sistemas requieren mangueras con grosores de paredes diferentes, temperatura y resistencia de desplome. Cuando esté sustituyendo las mangueras, esté seguro que las nuevas sean hechas del mismo material.

5   Frecuentemente la única forma efectiva para chequear una manguera es de removerla completamente del vehículo. Si más de una de las mangueras se remueve, esté seguro de ponerle etiquetas a las mangueras y los acopladores para asegurar el montaje correcto.

6   Cuando las mangueas de vacío se chequeen, esté seguro de incluir en el chequeo cualquier acoplador T de plástico. Chequee los acopladores por grietas y la manguera donde se conecta a los acopladores por distorsión, que pueden ocasionar una fuga.

7   Un pedazo pequeño de manguera de vacío (1/4-pulgada de diámetro interior) puede usarse como un estetoscopio para detectar fugas de vacío. Sujete un extremo de la manguera a su oído y sonda alrededor las mangueras de vacío y los acopladores, escuchando por algo "silbando" característica de una fuga de vacío. **Peligro:** *Cuando esté sondeando con el estetoscopio de manguera de vacío, esté muy cuidadoso de no entrar en contacto con los componentes del motor que se estén moviendo, tales como las bandas y el ventilador.*

Manguera de combustible

Peligro: *Hay precauciones necesarias que se deben tomar cuando inspeccione o le otorgue servicio a los componentes del sistema del combustible. Trabaje en una área bien ventilada y que no hayan llamas abiertas como (cigarrillos, piloto del aparato del calentador de agua, etc.) o bombillas sin cubiertas (sin protección) que puedan alcanzar el área donde se está trabajando. Limpie ligeramente cualquier derramamiento de combustible inmediatamente y no guarde trapos empapados de combustible donde podrían calentarse y coger fuego. Vehículos equipados con inyección de combustible, el sistema del combustible está bajo presión, así que si cualquiera de las líneas del combustible se desconectan, se debe de remover la presión del sistema primero (vea Capítulo 4 para más información).*

8   Chequee todas las mangueras de combustible por deterioración. Chequee cuidadosamente por grietas en zonas donde la manguera se dobla y donde es acoplada a los acopladores.

9   Calidad alta para la línea de combustible, comúnmente identificada por palabras Fluroelastomer imprimida en la manguera, deberían usarse para el reemplazo de la línea de combustible. **Peligro:** *¡Nunca, debajo ninguna circunstancia, use línea de vacío sin*

refuerzo, tubería plástica clara o manguera de agua para línea de combustible!

10   Grapas de tipo resorte se usan generalmente en las líneas de combustible. Ellas frecuentemente pierden su tensión en un periodo de tiempo y pueden ser destruidas durante el desmontaje. Reemplace todas las grapas de tipo resorte con grapas de tipo roscas cuando una manguera se reemplace.

Tuberías metálicas

11   Secciones de tuberías metálicas se usan frecuentemente para la línea de combustible entre la bomba de combustible y la unidad de inyección de combustible o carburador. Chequee cuidadosamente para estar seguro de que la línea no se ha doblado o rizado y busque por grietas.

12   Si una sección de la línea de combustible de metal debe sustituirse, solamente tubería de acero debería usarse, debido ha que la tubería de aluminio y cobre no tienen la fuerza necesaria para resistir las vibraciones normales del motor.

13   Chequee las líneas de metal del freno donde entran en el cilindro maestro y la unidad de proporción del freno (si es usado) por grietas en las líneas y acopladores flojos. Cualquier señal de fuga del flúido de los frenos significa que un chequeo inmediato y completo debería hacerse del sistema de los frenos.

12   Pedal del freno - chequeo y ajuste

Refiérase a la ilustración 12.1

1   La altura de pedal del freno es la distancia que el pedal se asienta afuera del piso **(vea ilustración)**. La distancia debe ser como la especificada (vea especificaciones). Si la altura del pedal no está dentro de la distancia especificada, afloje la contratuerca en el interruptor para la luz del freno localizado en el soporte trasero del pedal del freno y gire el interruptor hacia adentro o hacia afuera hasta que la altura de pedal sea correcta. Apriete la contratuerca.

2   El juego libre es el juego del pedal o la distancia que el pedal se puede mover antes de que comience a tener cualquier efecto en los frenos (distancia A en la **ilustración 12.1**). Debe ser como está especificado. Si no es, afloje la contratuerca en la varilla de entrada del amplificador para los frenos, a donde el pedal del freno es conectado. Gire la varilla de entrada hasta que el juego libre sea corregido, entonces apriete la contratuerca.

13   Aceite del motor y filtro - cambio

Refiérase a las ilustraciones 13.3, 13.9, 13.11, 13.14 y 13.18

1   Cambios frecuentes de aceite son los procedimientos de mantenimientos preventivos más importante que pueden ser hechos por el mecánico doméstico. Según el aceite

del motor se envejece, llega a ser diluido y contaminado, que conduce al desgaste prematuro del motor.

2   Aunque algunas fuentes recomiendan que el filtro de aceite se cambie cada otro cambio de aceite, el costo mínimo de un filtro de aceite y el hecho que es fácil de instalar un filtro nuevo, indica que un filtro nuevo se instale cada vez que el aceite se cambie.

3   Reúna todos los materiales y herramientas necesarias antes de comenzar este procedimiento **(vea ilustración)**.

4   Usted debe tener una abundancia de periódicos y trapos limpios para limpiar cualquier derrame. El acceso a la parte de abajo del vehículo seria mejor si el vehículo puede levantarse en una planta, conducido sobre rampas o puesto encima de soportes. **Peligro:** *¡No trabaje debajo de un vehículo que esté soportado solamente por gatos de parachoques, hidráulicos o de tijeras!*

5   Si este es su primer cambio de aceite, métase debajo del vehículo y familiarícese usted mismo con las ubicaciones del tapón para el drenaje del aceite y el filtro de aceite. Los componentes del escape y el motor estarán caliente durante el trabajo actual, note como ellos se sitúan para evitar tocarlos cuando esté trabajando debajo del vehículo.

6   Caliente el motor a temperatura normal de operación. Si el aceite nuevo o cualquier herramientas se necesitan, use el periodo de calentamiento para obtener todo lo necesario para el trabajo. El aceite correcto para su aplicación puede encontrarse en los flúidos y lubricantes recomendados al principio de este Capítulo.

7   Con el aceite del motor caliente (aceite de motor caliente drenará más rápido y removerá mayor cantidad de partículas contaminantes), alce y ponga el vehículo sobre estantes. ¡Asegúrese de que está soportado firmemente!

8   Mueva todas las herramientas, trapos y periódicos necesarios debajo el vehículo. Coloque la cacerola para vaciar debajo del tapón de drenaje. Recuerde que el aceite fluirá inicialmente con fuerza desde la cacerola del aceite del motor; coloque la cacerola

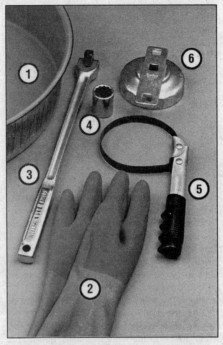

para colectar el drenaje de acuerdo con el chorro de aceite proveniente del motor.

9   Teniendo cuidado de no tocar ningunos de los componentes calientes del escape, use una herramienta para remover el tapón de drenaje cerca en el fondo del cárter de aceite **(vea ilustración)**. Depende de que tan caliente el aceite esté, usted debe de usar guantes mientras destornilla las últimas vueltas del tapón del aceite.

10   Permita que el aceite viejo drene en la cacerola. Puede ser necesario tener que mover la cacerola según el flujo de aceite disminuye a un goteo.

11   Después que todo el aceite se haya drenado, limpie el tapón de aceite con un trapo

13.3 Estas herramientas son necesarias cuando se le cambie el aceite y el filtro al motor

1   **Cacerola para drenar el aceite** - *Debe de ser llana en profundidad, pero ancha para prevenir derrame.*

2   **Guantes de caucho/goma** - *Cuando esté removiendo el tapón del drenaje y el filtro.*

3   **Palanca** - *Algunas veces el tapón del drenaje está bien apretado y una palanca larga es necesaria para aflojarlo.*

4   **Dado** - *Para ser usado con la palanca o la matraca (debe de ser del tamaño correcto del tapón - preferible de seis puntos).*

5   **Herramienta para el filtro** - *Esta es una herramienta con una banda de metal, que requiere suficiente espacio alrededor del filtro para que sea efectivo.*

6   **Herramienta para el filtro** - *Este tipo se pone debajo del filtro y se puede girar con una matraca o una palanca (hay diferente tipos de herramientas disponibles para diferente tipos de filtros).*

limpio. Las partículas pequeñas de metal pueden agarrarse al tapón y contaminar inmediatamente el aceite nuevo **(vea ilustración)**.

12   Limpie la zona alrededor del tapón de drenaje e instale el tapón. Apriete el tapón firmemente con la herramienta. Si una llave torsiométrica está disponible, úsela para apretar el tapón.

13   Mueva la cacerola de drenaje debajo del filtro de aceite.

14   Use la llave para aflojar el filtro de aceite para aflojar el filtro **(vea ilustración)**. Llaves de filtros de cadena o de metal pueden deformar el bote del filtro, pero esto no importa debido a que el filtro se desechará de cualquier manera.

13.11 ¡Esté seguro de limpiar el tapón de drenaje para remover cualquier partículas de metal que se adhieren a el!

13.9 Ubicaciones para el tapón de drenaje del aceite del motor (izquierdo - motor V6; derecho - motores de cuatro cilindros)

Gírelo contra las manillas del reloj para aflojarlo

Gírelo contra las manillas del reloj para aflojarlo

13.14 Ubicaciones del filtro de aceite (izquierdo - motor V6; derecho - motores de cuatro cilindros)

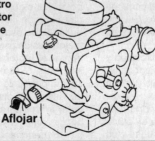

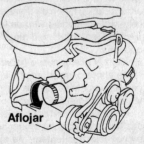

Aflojar

Aflojar

13.18 Lubrique la junta del filtro de aceite con aceite de motor limpio antes de instalar el filtro en el motor

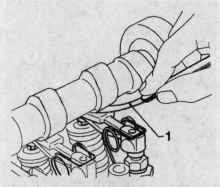

14.5 En los modelos 1980, mida el franqueo de las válvulas insertando un calibrador al tacto entre el talón del lóbulo de la leva y el balancín

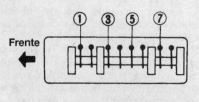

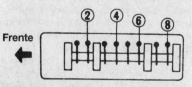

14.9 Con el lóbulo de la leva número uno apuntando hacia ENCIMA, las válvulas en la ilustración superior (1, 3, 5 y 7) pueden ser ajustadas, mientras que las válvulas en la ilustración inferior (2, 4, 6 y 8) pueden ser ajustadas cuando el lóbulo de la leva número uno esté apuntando hacia ABAJO (modelos 1980 solamente)

15   Completamente destornille el filtro viejo. Tenga cuidado; está lleno de aceite. Vacíe el aceite del interior del filtro en la cacerola de drenaje.

16   Compare el filtro viejo con el nuevo para asegurarse que son del mismo tipo.

17   Use un trapo limpio para remover todo el aceite, suciedad y fango desde la zona donde el filtro de aceite hace contacto con el motor. Chequee el filtro viejo para asegurarse que la junta de goma no se quedó en motor. Si la junta se quedó en el motor, remuévala.

18   Aplique una capa ligera de aceite limpio en la junta de goma en el filtro de aceite nuevo **(vea ilustración)**.

19   Instale el filtro nuevo al motor, siguiendo las instrucciones imprimidas en el filtro o en la caja del filtro. La mayoría de los fabricantes de filtros recomiendan que no se use una llave de filtros debido a la posibilidad de sobre apretar y dañar el sello.

20   Remueva todas las herramientas, trapos, etc. debajo del vehículo, teniendo cuidado de no derramar el aceite en la cacerola de drenaje, entonces baje el vehículo.

21   Muévase al compartimiento del motor y ubique la tapa por donde se llena el aceite.

22   Vierta el aceite nuevo a través de la apertura después que se remueva la tapa.

23   Vierta tres o cuatro cuartos de aceite nuevo en el motor. Espere unos minutos para permitir que el aceite llegue al cárter, entonces chequee el nivel en el indicador de aceite (vea Sección 4 si es necesario). Si el nivel del aceite está arriba de la marca L (bajo), ponga el motor en marcha y permita que el aceite nuevo circule.

24   Corra el motor aproximadamente un minuto y entonces apáguelo. Inmediatamente mire debajo del vehículo y chequee por fugas en el tapón de drenaje del cárter de aceite y alrededor del filtro de aceite. Si cualquiera de los dos tienen fugas, apriételo un poco más.

25   Con el aceite nuevo habido circulado y el filtro ahora completamente apretado, chequee nuevamente el nivel en la varilla y añada más aceite según sea necesario.

26   Durante los primeros viajes cortos después de un cambio de aceite, haga un punto de chequear frecuentemente por fugas y un

nivel de aceite correcto.

27   El aceite viejo drenado del motor no puede utilizarse nuevamente en su estado presente y usted debería deshacerce de el. Centros de reclamación de aceite, las gasolineras y talleres de reparaciones de vehículos, aceptarán normalmente el aceite, que puede refinarse y ser usado nuevamente. Después que el aceite se haya enfriado puede echarse en un recipiente (botellas o porrones plásticos tapados, cartones de leche, etc.) para transportarlo al sitio de reclamación.

14   Válvulas - ajuste del franqueo (motores de cuatro cilindros solamente)

1   Aunque las válvulas puedan ser ajustada con el motor frío, es mejor ajustarlas con el motor caliente. Si ellas son ajustadas en frío ellas se deben chequear completamente una vez que el motor se haya calentado y ajustadas nuevamente si es necesario en conforme a las especificaciones calientes del motor.

2   Ponga el motor en marcha y permita que alcance la temperatura normal de operación, entonces apague el motor.

3   Remueva la tapa de los balancines como está descrito en el Capítulo 2.

Modelos 1980

Refiérase a las ilustraciones 14.5, 14.9 y 14.11

4   Gire el cigüeñal hasta que el lóbulo del árbol de levas número uno (delantero) apunte recto hacia encima. Esto puede ser hecho con una matraca y un dado en el perno de la polea del cigüeñal en el frente del motor - gire el cigüeñal a la derecha. Remover las bujías hace esta operación más fácil. Otro método es de usar la llave de la ignición para operar el motor de arranque en pequeños intervalos. Si esto es hecho, el alambre de la bobina para la ignición se debe desconectar de la tapa del distribuidor y ponerlo a tierra en el motor para prevenir que el motor se ponga en marcha.

5   El franqueo de las válvulas es medido

insertando el calibrador de tacto del tamaño especificado entre el talón del lóbulo de la leva y el balancín **(vea ilustración)**. Usted debe sentir una cantidad leve de resistencia cuando el calibrador al tacto es movido de aquí para allá.

6   Si el espacio libre es demasiado grande o demasiado pequeño, afloje la contratuerca del pivote del balancín y gire el pivote de los balancines para obtener el espacio libre correcto.

7   Una vez que el espacio libre se haya alcanzado, detenga el pivote de los balancines en posición con una llave y apriete la contratuerca con la otra.

8   Chequee el franqueo de las válvulas. A veces cambiará levemente cuando la contratuerca del pivote es apretada. Si ese es el caso, ajústela de nuevo hasta que esté correcta.

9   Con el árbol de levas en esta posición las válvulas número 1, 3, 5 y 7 pueden ser ajustadas usando el procedimiento apenas descrito **(vea ilustración)**.

10   Gire el árbol de levas hasta que el lóbulo de la leva número uno esté apuntando directamente hacia abajo. En esta posición las válvulas número 2, 4, 6 y 8 pueden ser ajustadas de las mismas maneras.

11   Después de que las válvulas hayan sido ajustada, chequee el par de torsión en las contratuerca del pivote del balancín **(vea ilustración)**. Un adaptador especial, disponible en una refaccionaría importada, es requerido para este chequeo.

12   Después de que todas las válvulas hayan sido ajustadas, vuelva a instalar la tapa de los balancines.

Modelos 1981 y 1982

Refiérase a las ilustraciones 14.14 y 14.18

13   Gire el cigüeñal hasta que el lóbulo del árbol de levas número uno (delantero) esté recto hacia abajo. Esto puede ser hecho con una matraca y un dado en el perno del cigüeñal en el frente del motor. Gire el cigüeñal a la

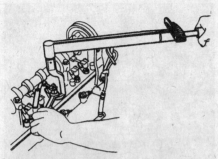

14.11 Como apretar correctamente la contratuerca del pivote para el balancín en los modelos 1980 requiere un adaptador especial (disponibles en el departamentos de partes de su concesionario o refaccionarías para vehículos importados)

derecha. Remover las bujías hará este procedimiento mas fácil. Otro método es de usar la llave de la ignición para operar el motor de arranque en intervalos cortos. Si esto es hecho, el alambre de la bobina para la ignición se debe de desconectar de la tapa del distribuidor y ponerlo a tierra en el motor para prevenir que el motor se ponga en marcha.

14 El franqueo de las válvulas es medido metiendo el calibrador al tacto del tamaño especificado entre el final del vástago de la válvula y el tornillo de ajuste (**vea ilustración**). Usted debe sentir una cantidad leve de resistencia cuando el calibrador al tacto es movido de aquí para allá.

15 Si el espacio libre es demasiado grande o demasiado pequeño, afloje la contratuerca y gire el tornillo de ajuste para obtener el espacio libre correcto.

16 Una vez que el espacio libre se haya logrado, detenga el tornillo en posición con un destornillador y apriete la contratuerca.

17 Chequee el franqueo de las válvulas. A veces cambiará levemente cuando la contratuerca es apretada. Si ese es el caso, ajústela hasta que esté correcta.

18 Con el árbol de levas en esta posición las válvulas número 1, 4, 6 y 7 pueden ser ajustadas usando el procedimiento descrito anteriormente (**vea ilustración**).

19 Gire el árbol de levas hasta que el lóbulo de la leva número uno esté apuntando directamente hacia encima. En esta posición las válvulas número 2, 3, 5 y 8 pueden ser ajustadas de la misma manera.

20 Después de que todas las válvulas hayan sido ajustadas, vuelva a instalar la tapa de los balancines.

Modelos 1983 y más modernos

Refiérase a la ilustración 14.22

21 Ponga el motor en marcha hasta que haya alcanzado la temperatura normal de operación. Remueva del motor la tapa de los balancines como está descrito en el Capítulo 2.

22 Posicione el pistón número uno en TDC (punto muerto superior) en la carrera de compresión (vea Capítulo 2). Los franqueos para

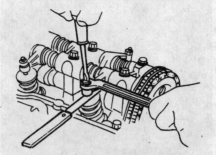

14.14 En los modelos 1981 y 1982, el franqueo de las válvulas es ajustado insertando un calibrador al tacto entre el tornillo de ajuste, el vástago de la válvula y girando el tornillo

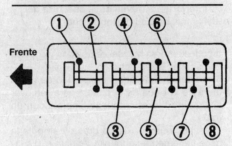

14.22 En los modelos 1983 y más modernos use este esquema para ubicar las válvulas

las válvulas 1, 2, 4 y 6 ahora pueden ser chequeados (**vea ilustración**).

23 Insercióne un calibrador al tacto de 0.012 pulgada (0.30 mm) entre el vástago de las válvulas y el tornillo de ajuste. Si los ataques del calibrador al tacto entre el vástago y el tornillo tienen una cantidad leve de resistencia, el espacio libre está correcto.

24 Si ajuste es requerido, afloje el tornillo de ajuste prisionero y afloje cuidadosamente o apriete el tornillo de ajuste hasta que usted sienta que una resistencia leve en el calibrador al tacto es notada cuando lo retire entre el vástago de las válvulas y el tornillo.

25 Detenga el tornillo de ajuste y apriete la contratuerca firmemente. Chequee el espa-

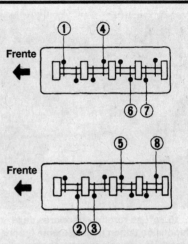

14.18 Cuando el lóbulo de la leva número uno está apuntando hacia ABAJO, las válvulas mostradas en la primera ilustración (1, 4, 6 y 7) pueden ser ajustadas; las válvulas mostradas en la ilustración inferior (2, 3, 5 y 8) pueden ser ajustadas cuando el lóbulo de la leva número uno esté apuntando hacia ENCIMA (modelos 1981 y 1982)

cio libre para asegurarse que no cambió.

26 Gire el cigüeñal una revolución completa (360 grados) a la derecha hasta que el pistón número cuatro esté en el TDC en la carrera de compresión. Chequee esto verificando donde el rotor del distribuidor está apuntando. Ajuste las válvulas número 3, 5, 7 y 8 (**vea ilustración 14.22**).

27 Instale la tapa de los balancines.

15 Chasis - lubricación

Refiérase a las ilustraciones 15.1, 15.3a, 15.3b, 15.3c, 15.3d y 15.3e

1 Una pistola de grasa y un cartucho lleno con la grasa recomendada son solamente los artículos requeridos para la lubricación del chasis, algunos trapos limpios y el equipo necesario para levantar y sostener el vehículo firmemente sobre soportes (**vea ilustración**).

15.1 Herramientas y materiales requeridos para la lubricación del chasis y la carrocería

1 **Aceite de motor** - *Aceite de motor fino en una lata como esta, se puede usar para lubricar las bisagras de las puertas y del cofre/capó*

2 **Rociador de grafito** - *Es usado para lubricar los cilindros de los seguros de las puertas.*

3 **Grasa** - *La grasa es disponible en una variedad de tipos y peso/espesor, son disponibles para usarlas en una pistola de grasa. Chequee las especificaciones que son requeridas para usted.*

4 **Pistola de grasa** - *Una pistola de grasa común, es mostrada aquí con una manguera removible, es necesaria para lubricar el chasis. Después que termine límpiela.*

15.3a Las rótulas superiores de la suspensión tienen generalmente tapones instalados en ves de copillas de grasa

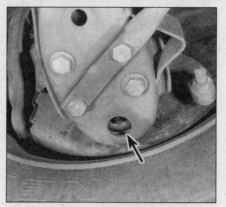

15.3b En algunos modelos más antiguos, el acceso a la copilla de grasa de la rótula inferior es a través de la abertura del brazo inferior (flecha)

15.3c Cada acoplación de la suspensión y la dirección está equipada con un tapón - un dado o llave para tuercas pequeñas se pueden usar para remover los tapones para que las copillas puedan ser instaladas

2   Hay varios puntos en la suspensión del vehículo, componentes de la dirección y línea de potencia que se deben lubricar periódicamente con grasa de uso múltiple basada en litio. Incluido son las rótulas superiores e inferiores de la suspensión, las acoplaciones de los pivotes en los acoplamientos de la dirección y en los modelos de 4WD, los ejes propulsores delanteros y traseros.

3   El punto para la grasa de cada rótula superior de la suspensión está encima de la rótula **(vea ilustración)** y es accesible removiendo la rueda delantera y el neumático. El acceso al punto inferior para la grasa de la rótula de la suspensión es el orificio en el fondo de la rótula inferior **(vea ilustración)**. Los acoplamiento de las varillas de la dirección están diseñados para ser lubricados **(vea ilustración)** y la horquilla del eje propulsor(es) y algunas acoplaciones universales requieren lubricación también **(vea ilustraciones)**.

4   Para acceso más fácil debajo del vehículo, levántelo con un gato y póngalo firmemente sobre estantes. ¡Asegúrese que el vehículo está firmemente sostenido sobre soportes!

5   Si las copillas no están ya instaladas, los

tapones tendrán que ser removidos y copillas enroscadas en su posición.

6   Fuerce una pequeña cantidad de grasa fuera de la boca de la pistola para remover cualquiera tierra, entonces límpiela con un trapo.

7   Limpie la copilla de grasa y empuje la boca firmemente sobre ella. Apriete el disparador en la engrasadora para forzar grasa en el componente. Ambas rótulas, acoplaciones y pivotes se deben lubricar hasta que el depósito de caucho esté firme al toque. No bombee mucha grasa en los acopladores o puede partir el depósito. Si la grasa se sale fuera alrededor de la boca de la engrasadora, la copilla está obstruida o la boca no está sentada completamente. Reasegure la boca de la pistola a la copilla y pruebe otra vez. Si es necesario, reemplace la copilla.

8   Limpie el exceso de grasa de los componentes y los acopladores.

9   Mientras usted está debajo del vehículo, limpie y lubrique el cable del freno de estacionamiento junto con las guías del cable y las palancas. Esto puede ser hecho poniendo parte de la grasa del chasis en el cable y sus partes relacionadas con sus dedos.

10   Baje el vehículo al piso para proceder a la lubricación del resto de la carrocería.

11   Abra el capó y la puerta elevadora trasera y ponga una cantidad pequeña de grasa de chasis en los mecanismos del picaporte. Haga que un ayudante hale la perilla de liberación adentro del vehículo según usted lubrica el cable en el picaporte.

12   Lubrique todas las bisagras (puertas, capó, picaportes) con unas pocas gotas de aceite de motor liviano para mantenerlos trabajando en el orden apropiado.

13   Los cilindros para las llaves pueden ser lubricados con atomizador de grafito, que están disponibles en las refaccionarías.

16   Suspensión y dirección - chequeo

1   Cuando el frente del vehículo se levante por cualquier razón, es una buena idea de visualmente chequear los componentes de la dirección y de la suspensión por desgaste.

2   Indicaciones de problemas de suspensión o dirección incluyen juego excesivo en el volante antes de que las ruedas delantera reaccionen, inclinación excesiva de la carrocería en la curvas o bamboleo excesivo en caminos rugosos y atoramiento en algunos puntos cuando el volante se gira.

3   Antes de levantar el vehículo para el chequeo, pruebe los amortiguadores empujando hacia abajo en cada esquina agresivamente. Si el vehículo no vuelve a una posición plana dentro de uno o dos rebotes, los amortiguadores están desgastados y deberían reemplazarse. Según se hace esto escuche por rechinamientos y otros ruidos provenientes de los componentes de la suspensión. La información sobre los componentes de la suspensión y amortiguadores pueden encontrarse en el Capítulo 10.

4   Levante el extremo delantero del vehículo y sopórtelo firmemente sobre soportes. ¡Asegúrese de que está soportado seguramente!

15.3d Algunos ejes propulsores tienen una copilla de grasa en la horquilla (flecha)

15.3e Algunas acoplaciones de juntas universales tienen un orificio para la copilla de grasa - use un destornillador para remover el tapón (flecha)

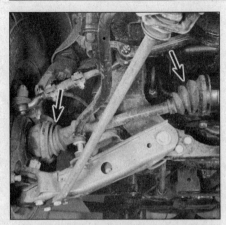

17.9 Daño a los fuelles del semieje delantero (flechas) pueden conducir rápidamente al fracaso de las acoplaciones CV (velocidad constante) (modelos de 4WD solamente)

5   Métase debajo del vehículo y chequee por pernos flojos, rotos o piezas desconectadas y guarniciones de caucho deterioradas en los componentes de la dirección y suspensión. Busque por grasa o flúido que se escape desde alrededor de los amortiguadores e instalaciones del mecanismo de la dirección. Si está equipado, chequee las acoplaciones y las mangueras de la dirección hidráulica por fugas. En los modelos 1986 y más modernos de 4WD, chequee el eje propulsor y guardapolvos de las rotulas por daño.

6   Los sellos de las rótulas deberían chequearse en este momento. Esto incluye no solamente las rótulas inferiores y superiores de la suspensión solamente, pero esas que conectan las varillas de la dirección también. Después de limpiar alrededor de las rotulas, inspeccione los sellos por grietas y daños. Chequee las rótulas en los vehículos de 2WD por desgaste.

7   Agarre la parte de encima y de abajo de cada rueda e intente de moverla hacia adentro y hacia afuera. No tomará mucho esfuerzo para ser capaz de sentir juego en los baleros de las ruedas. Si el juego es notable sería una buena idea de ajustarlo ahora mismo o podría confundir los chequeos adicionales.

8   Agarre cada lado de la rueda e intente moverla lateralmente. Presión constante, por supuesto, girará la dirección, pero presión de aquí para allá demostrará si hay una articulación de la dirección floja. Si algún juego se siente, sería más fácil de conseguir asistencia de una persona para que mueva la rueda lateralmente, para que la otra persona pueda mirar las articulaciones, bujes y acoplaciones en las varillas de la dirección.

9   Para chequear la caja de la dirección, primero asegúrese que los pernos que sostienen la caja de la dirección al chasis están apretados. Entonces consiga otra persona para que lo ayude a examinar el mecanismo. Uno debería mirar, o sujetar, el brazo que sale de la caja de la dirección mientras el otro

gira el volante de un lado al otro. La cantidad de movimiento perdido entre el volante y el brazo del engranaje indica el grado de desgaste en la caja de la dirección. Chequee el nivel de aceite de la caja de la dirección también. En los modelos de 2WD debe ser alrededor de 1-pulgada desde la parte de encima. En los modelos de 4WD debe ser alrededor de 1/2-pulgada desde la parte de encima. Refiérase a la sección recomendada de flúidos y lubricantes en las especificaciones si se necesita aceite.

10   Moviéndose al interior del vehículo, chequee el juego en el volante girándolo lentamente en ambas direcciones hasta que las ruedas se puedan sentir que giran. El juego libre del volante debería ser menos de 1-1/8 de pulgada. El juego excesivo es otra indicación de desgaste en el mecanismo de la dirección o varillaje.

11   Siguiendo el chequeo del frente, un chequeo similar debería hacerse de los componentes de la suspensión de las ruedas posteriores, nuevamente chequeando por pernos flojos, dañas o piezas desconectadas y bujes de cauchos deteriorados.

17   Eje propulsor - chequeo

Refiérase a la ilustración 17.9

1   Levante la parte trasera del vehículo y sopórtelo firmemente sobre estantes. Bloquee las ruedas delanteras. La transmisión debe estar en Neutral.

2   Arrástrese debajo del vehículo e inspeccione visualmente el eje propulsor. Busque por abolladuras y roturas en el tubo. Si alguno se encontró, el eje propulsor debe ser reemplazado (Capítulo 8).

3   Chequee por fuga de aceite en la parte delantera y trasera del eje propulsor. Fuga donde el eje propulsor entra a la transmisión indica un sello trasero defectuoso de la transmisión. Fuga donde el eje propulsor entra en el diferencial indica un sello defectuoso en el piñón. Para éstas operaciones de reparaciones refiérase a los Capítulos 7 y 8 respectivamente.

4   Mientras que está debajo del vehículo, haga que un ayudante gire la rueda trasera para girar el eje propulsor. Según esto se hace, chequee por obstrucción, ruido y juego excesivo en las universales U. En los modelos de Cama Larga y Cabina Grande, escuche por ruido del balero central, indicando que está desgastado o dañado. Refiérase al Capítulo 8 para corregir cualquier problema.

5   Las acoplaciones de las juntas universales también pueden ser chequeadas con el eje propulsor inmóvil, agarrando ambos lados de la acoplación y procure torcerla. Cualquier movimiento del todo en la coyuntura es un signo de desgaste considerable. Levantar hacia encima en el eje indicará también el movimiento en las acoplaciones de las juntas universales.

6   Chequee los pernos del calzo del eje propulsor en ambas puntas para asegurarse

que están apretados.

7   En los modelos de 4WD, el chequeo de encima para el eje propulsor debe ser repetido en todos los ejes propulsores. Además, chequee por fuga de grasa alrededor de la manga de la horquilla, que indica un fracaso del sello de la horquilla.

8   Chequee por fugas donde los ejes propulsores se conectan a la caja de transferencia.

9   Al mismo tiempo, chequee por juego en las acoplaciones de los semiejes delanteros. Chequee también los fuelles de las CV (velocidad constante) por daño, fugas y abrazaderas apretadas **(vea ilustración)**. Fuga de aceite en la acoplación del diferencial indica un sello de aceite lateral defectuoso. Fuga en el lado de la rueda indica un sello delantero del cubo defectuoso. Para otorgarle servicio a todos los componentes del sistema de 4WD, refiérase al Capítulo 9.

18   Sistema de escape - chequeo

1   Con el motor frío (por lo menos tres horas después que el vehículo no se haya conducido), chequee el sistema de escape desde el múltiple de escape hasta el extremo del tubo de cola. Tenga cuidado alrededor del convertidor catalítico, que puede ser que esté caliente hasta después de tres horas de haberse apagado el vehículo. El chequeo debería hacerse con el vehículo sobre una planta de elevar para tener acceso sin restricción. Si un elevador de vehículos no está disponible, levante el vehículo y póngalo firmemente sobre soportes.

2   Chequee los tubos de escape y las acoplaciones por señales de fuga y/o corrosión que indica un fracaso potencial. Asegúrese que todos los soportes y las perchas están en buenas condiciones y apretadas.

3   Inspeccione el lado de abajo de la carrocería por agujeros, corrosión, acoplaciones abiertas, etc. que puedan permitir que gases de escape entren en el departamento de los pasajeros. Selle todas las aperturas en la carrocería con silicona o sellador de fibra de plástico.

4   Rechinidos y otros ruidos pueden frecuentemente ser trazados al sistema de escape, especialmente las perchas, calzos y deflectores de calor. Intente de mover los tubos, silenciador y convertidor catalítico. Si los componentes pueden entrar en contacto con las partes de la suspensión o carrocería, asegure el sistema de escape con soportes y perchas nuevas.

19   Embrague - juego libre, chequeo y ajuste del pedal

Refiérase a la ilustración 19.2

1   En vehículos equipado con una transmisión manual, el juego libre y la altura del pedal del embrague debe ajustarse correctamente.

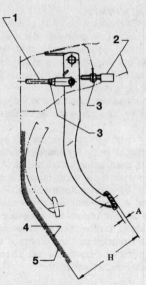

19.2 La altura (H) y el juego libre (A) del pedal del embrague es ajustado girando el interruptor del embrague y la varilla de empuje del cilindro maestro respectivamente

1   *Varilla de empuje del cilindro maestro*
2   *Interruptor del embrague*
3   *Tuerca prisionera*
4   *Aislador*
5   *Piso*

2   La altura del pedal del embrague es la distancia que el pedal está fuera del piso (mida desde el centro de la zapata de goma). La distancia debería ser como se especifica. Si la altura del pedal no está dentro de las especificaciones, afloje la contratuerca en el pedal y gire la varilla hacia fuera o hacia adentro hasta que la altura de pedal esté correcta. Apriete nuevamente la contratuerca **(vea ilustración)**.
3   El juego libre es el juego sin presión del pedal, o la distancia que el pedal puede apretarse antes de comenzar a tener cualquier efecto sobre el embrague. La distancia debería ser como se especifica. Si no es, afloje la contratuerca en la varilla de empuje en el cilindro maestro principal del embrague, gire la varilla de empuje hasta que el juego libre esté correcto, entonces apriete nuevamente la contratuerca

20   Transmisión manual - chequeo del nivel del aceite

Refiérase a la ilustración 20.1
1   Las transmisiones manuales no tienen una varilla para chequear el nivel del aceite. El nivel del aceite es chequeado removiendo un tapón en el lado lateral de la transmisión **(vea ilustración)**. Ubique el tapón, use un trapo para limpiar el tapón y el área alrededor del tapón. Si el vehículo se levanta para tener mejor acceso al tapón, esté seguro de ponerlo firmemente encima de soportes -

20.1 Los tapones de drenaje/relleno para la transmisión manual son accesible por debajo del vehículo - una extensión de 1/2 pulgada acoplará en el orificio cuadrado del tapón

¡NO se meta debajo del vehículo cuando esté soportado solamente por un gato!
2   Con la transmisión y el motor frío, remueva el tapón. Si lubricante inmediatamente comienza a escaparse, enrosque el tapón de regreso en la transmisión - el nivel está correcto. Si no, completamente remueva el tapón y ponga su dedo meñique adentro del agujero. El nivel debería estar uniforme con el fondo del tapón del agujero.
3   Si la transmisión necesita más lubricante, use una jeringa o bomba pequeña para añadirle a través del agujero del tapón.
4   Enrosque el tapón en la transmisión y apriételo firmemente. Conduzca el vehículo, entonces chequee por fugas alrededor el tapón.

21   Caja de transferencia - chequeo del nivel del aceite

Refiérase a la ilustración 21.1
1   El nivel del aceite de la caja de transferencia es chequeado removiendo un tapón en el lado lateral del albergue **(vea ilustración)**.

22.2 Ubicación de los tapones de chequear/llenar y drenaje del diferencial delantero (flechas)

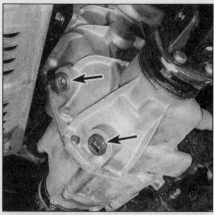

21.1 Remueva el protector de piedra de la caja de transferencia para tener acceso al tapón de chequear/llenar (superior) y el tapón de drenaje (inferior)

Remueva el protector para las piedras (si está equipado), entonces ubique el tapón y use un trapo para limpiar el tapón y el área alrededor del tapón. Si el vehículo se levanta para tener mejor acceso al tapón, esté seguro de ponerlo firmemente encima de soportes - ¡NO se meta debajo del vehículo cuando esté solamente soportado por un gato!
2   Con el motor y la caja de transferencia fría remueva el tapón. Si el lubricante inmediatamente comienza ha escaparse, enrosque el tapón en el albergue - el nivel del flúido está correcto. Si no, completamente remueva el tapón y meta su dedo meñique en el agujero. El nivel debería estar dentro de 3/16-pulgada del nivel del agujero donde se pone el tapón.
3   Si más aceite se necesita, use una jeringa o bomba pequeña para añadirle mediante la apertura.
4   Enrosque el tapón en el albergue y apriételo firmemente. Conduzca el vehículo, entonces chequee por fugas alrededor del tapón. Instale el protector para las piedras.

22   Diferencial - chequeo del nivel del aceite

Refiérase a la ilustración 22.2 y 22.3
1   El diferencial tiene un tapón que debe de ser removido para chequear el nivel de aceite. Si el vehículo se levanta para tener mejor acceso al tapón, esté seguro de ponerlo firmemente encima de soportes - ¡NO se meta debajo del vehículo cuando esté solamente soportado por un gato!
2   Remueva el tapón del aceite para chequear y llenar el diferencial **(vea ilustración)**.
3   El nivel de aceite debería estar al pie de la parte de abajo del tapón. Si no, use una jeringa para añadir el lubricante recomendado hasta que el aceite comience a salir a través de la apertura **(vea ilustración)**.
4   Instale el tapón y apriételo firmemente. Chequee por fugas después que conduzca unas pocas millas.

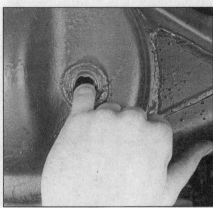

22.3 Use su dedo como una varilla graduada para estar seguro que el nivel del aceite está parejo con el fondo del orificio

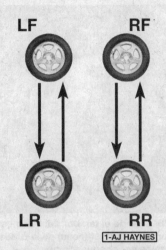

1-AJ HAYNES

23.2 Esquema de la rotación de los neumáticos

24.6 Las pastillas del freno de disco son visibles a través de las aberturas en las mordazas (flechas)

23   Ruedas - rotación

Refiérase a la ilustración 23.2

1   Los neumáticos deberían ser rotados a los intervalos especificados y cuando desgaste desigual se note. Debido a que el vehículo se levantará y los neumáticos se removerán, sería un tiempo ideal para chequear los frenos y lubricar los baleros de las ruedas también.

2   Refiérase a la ilustración acompañada para patrones preferidos de rotación de los neumáticos.

3   Refiérase a la información de elevar y remolcar en el frente de este manual para los procedimientos apropiados de seguir cuando esté levantando el vehículo y cambiando un neumático. Si los frenos van a ser chequeados, no aplique el freno de estacionamiento. Asegúrese que los neumáticos están obturados para impedir que el vehículo se ruede cuando se levante.

4   Preferentemente, el vehículo entero debería levantarse. Esto puede hacerse en un elevador o elevando cada esquina, entonces bajando el vehículo y colocándolo sobre estantes en el chasis. ¡Siempre use cuatro soportes y asegúrese que el vehículo está

24.12 Los tambores de los frenos traseros pueden ser removidos enroscando pernos en los orificios con roscas en cada tambor

soportado firmemente para que no vaya a producir ningún peligro!

5   Después de la rotación, chequee y ajuste la presión del aire de los neumáticos según sea necesario y esté seguro de chequear las tuercas para estar seguro de que están apretadas.

6   Para información adicional sobre las ruedas y los neumáticos, refiérase al Capítulo 10.

24   Frenos - chequeo

Refiérase a las ilustraciones 24.6, 24.12, 24.14 y 24.16
Nota: *Para fotografías detalladas del sistema de frenos, refiérase al Capítulo 10.*
Peligro: *El polvo del sistema de los frenos contiene asbesto, que es dañino a su salud. ¡Nunca lo sople con aire comprimido y no aspire ninguna de estas partículas. NO use gasolina o solventes para remover el polvo. Use alcohol desnaturalizado o un filtro especial para el sistema de frenos solamente!*

1   Además de los intervalos especificados, los frenos deberían inspeccionarse cada vez que las ruedas se remuevan.

2   Para chequear los frenos, el vehículo debe levantarse y ser puesto firmemente sobre soportes.

Frenos de disco

3   Los frenos de disco se usan en las ruedas delantera. Daño extensivo al rotor puede ocurrir si las pastillas se permiten que se desgasten más allá del límite especificado.

4   Levante el vehículo y sopórtelo firmemente sobre soportes, entonces remueva las cuatro ruedas (vea levantar/elevar y remolcar al frente de este manual si es necesario).

5   Las mordazas del freno de disco, que contienen las pastillas, son visibles con las ruedas removidas. Hay una almohadilla exterior y una almohadilla interior en cada mordaza. Todas las cuatro pastillas deberían inspeccionarse.

6   Cada mordaza tiene una apertura, que permitirá que usted pueda inspeccionar las

pastillas **(vea ilustración)**. Si el material de las pastillas se ha desgastado a un 1/8-pulgada o menos, las pastillas deberían reemplazarse.

7   Si usted está inseguro del grosor exacto del material del forro restante, remueva las pastillas para ser chequeadas adicionalmente o ser reemplazadas (refiérase al Capítulo 9).

8   Antes de instalar las ruedas, chequee por fuga y/o daño (grietas, rajaduras, etc.) alrededor de las acoplaciones del freno. Reemplace las mangueras o las conexiones según sea necesario, refiérase al Capítulo 9.

9   Chequee la condición del rotor. Busque por rayones profundos y manchas quemadas. Si estas condiciones existen, el cubo en el rotor debería removerse para ser rectificado.

Frenos de tambor

10   **Nota:** *En los modelos más modernos, el grosor del forro de las frenos puede chequearse sin remover el tambor - simplemente haciéndole palanca al tapón del orificio de inspección y removiéndolo fuera del plato de soporte (vea ilustración) y chequeando el forro a través del agujero. Un chequeo comprensivo requiere que se remueva el tambor de los frenos como se describe más adelante.* Remueva el tambor halándolo hacia afuera de su lugar de instalación en el eje y los frenos. Si está atorado, esté seguro que el freno de estacionamiento está suelto, entonces aplíquele aceite penetrante en la junta entre el cubo y el tambor. Permita que el aceite penetre antes de intentar de halar el tambor hacia fuera nuevamente.

11   Si el tambor todavía no puede removerse hacia fuera, las balatas del freno tendrán que ser ajustadas. Esto es hecho primero removiendo el guardapolvo del plato de soporte. Con la cubierta removida, use un destornillador pequeño para girar la rueda de estrella, que moverá las balatas de los freno lejos del tambor.

12   Como último recurso, enrosque un perno en cada uno de los agujeros en el tambor **(vea ilustración)** y apriete los pernos un poco a la vez para forzar el tambor hacia afuera.

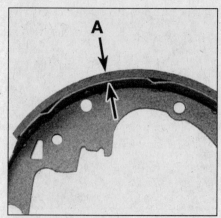

24.14 El espesor del forro de la balata trasero (A) es medido desde la superficie exterior del forro al metal de la balata

24.16 Cuando el tambor del freno esté fuera, el cilindro (flecha) de la rueda debe ser chequeado por fugas del flúido del freno

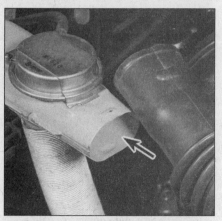

26.4 Remueva el conducto flexible del purificador del aire para que usted pueda observar directamente a través del tubo de respiración en la válvula para el control del aire

13   Con el tambor removido, tenga cuidado de no tocar nada del polvo de los frenos (vea **Peligro** al principio de esta Sección).

14   Note el grosor del material del forro en ambos frenos delanteros y traseros. Si el material se ha desgastado hasta un espesor de 1/16-pulgada del metal o de los remaches, los dos lados de las balatas deberían reemplazarse **(vea ilustración)**. Las balatas deberían también ser sustituidas si están cuarteadas, barnizadas (superficie lustrosa) o contaminadas con flúido de los frenos.

15   Asegúrese que todos los resortes para instalar los frenos están conectados y en buenas condiciones.

16   Chequee los componentes del freno por señales de fuga del flúido de los frenos. Cuidadosamente hágale palanca hacia atrás a los resguardos de goma sobre los cilindros de las ruedas ubicados encima de las balatas del freno con su dedo. Cualquier fuga es una indicación que los cilindros de la rueda deberían reconstruirse inmediatamente (Capítulo

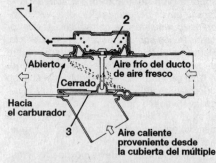

26.5 Cuando el motor está frío, la válvula para el control del aire debe moverse hacia la posición de encima y cerrar la abertura del tubo de respiración - según el motor se calienta, la válvula retrocederá hacia abajo para abrir el pasaje

1   Hacia el sensor de la temperatura del aire
2   Motor de vacío
3   Válvula para el control de aire

9). También chequee las acoplaciones y mangueras del freno por fuga **(vea ilustración)**.

17   Limpie el interior del tambor con un trapo de freno limpio y limpiador para frenos o alcohol desnaturalizado. Nuevamente, tenga cuidado de no inhalar el polvo de amianto (asbestos).

18   Chequee el interior del tambor por grietas, marcas de rayones profundos y manchas duras, que aparecerán como pequeños descolorimientos. Si las imperfecciones no pueden removerse con papel de esmeril fino, el tambor debe llevarse a un taller equipado con un torno para rectificar tambores.

19   Si todas las piezas están en estado de operación buenas, reinstale los tambores de los frenos.

20   Instale las ruedas y rebaje el vehículo.

Freno de estacionamiento

21   El freno de estacionamiento opera con una palanca de mano y bloquea los frenos traseros. La forma más fácil y quizás el método más obvio de periódicamente chequear la operación del freno de estacionamiento es de estacionar el vehículo en una colina con el freno de estacionamiento aplicado y la transmisión en Neutro. Si el freno de estacionamiento no puede impedir que el vehículo se ruede, está en necesidad de que se ajuste (vea Capítulo 9).

25   Sistema de combustible - chequeo

Peligro: La gasolina es sumamente inflamable, así que se deben tomar precauciones extras cuando esté trabajando en cualquier parte del sistema del combustible. No fume, deje llamas abiertas o bombillas sin cubierta cerca del área de trabajo. También, no trabaje en un garaje si un aparato de gas natural con un piloto encendido está presente. Debido a que la gasolina es dañina para su piel use guantes cuando haya una posibilidad de que

entre en contacto con su piel y si se le derrama cualquier cantidad en su piel límpiese inmediatamente con suficiente agua y jabón. Limpie cualquier derrame inmediatamente y no guarde trapos que estén húmedos con gasolina. El sistema de combustible de los modelos con inyección de combustible está bajo constante presión y si cualquiera de las líneas se van a desconectar, la presión en el sistema se debe de aliviar. Cuando usted conduzca cualquier tipo de trabajo en el sistema de combustible, use espejuelos de seguridad y tenga cerca un extintor de fuegos del tipo Clase B (vea Capítulo 4).

1   En la mayoría de los modelos el depósito de combustible principal se ubica en la parte trasera del vehículo.

2   El sistema de combustible debería chequearse con el vehículo levantado en un elevador de vehículos para que los componentes del vehículo sean fácilmente visibles y accesibles.

3   Si se nota un olor de gasolina mientras se está conduciendo el vehículo o después que el vehículo haya estado en el sol, el sistema debería completamente inspeccionarse inmediatamente.

4   Remueva la tapa del tanque del combustible y chequéela por daño, corrosión y si el sello en la junta está roto. Reemplace la tapa o junta con una nueva si es necesario.

5   Con el vehículo levantado, chequee el llenador y el cuello del tanque de gasolina por perforaciones, cuarteaduras y otros daños. La acoplación entre el cuello del llenador y el tanque es especialmente crítico. A veces la goma del cuello del llenador tiene fugas debido a grapas flojas o goma deteriorada, problemas que el mecánico doméstico puede rectificar comúnmente. **Peligro:** *Nunca, debajo ninguna circunstancia, trate de reparar los componentes de un tanque de combustible usted mismo (excepto los de goma). ¡Una soldadora o cualquier llama abierta puede ocasionar fácilmente que los vapores de combustible estallen si las precauciones apropiadas no son tomadas!*

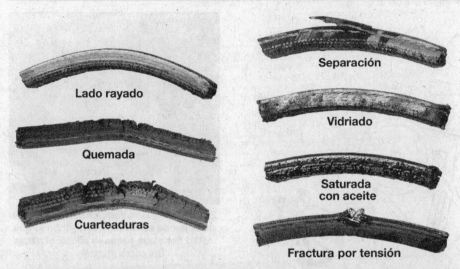

Lado rayado

Quemada

Cuarteaduras

Separación

Vidriado

Saturada con aceite

Fractura por tensión

27.3 Aquí se muestran algunos de los problemas más comunes asociados con las bandas (chequee las bandas muy cuidadosamente para prevenir una avería innecesaria)

6   Cuidadosamente chequee todas las mangueras de caucho y las tuberías metálicas que conducen el combustible desde el tanque. Busque por acoplaciones flojas, mangueras deterioradas, líneas rizadas y otros daños. Siga las líneas hasta el frente del vehículo, inspeccione cuidadosamente todas las mangueras. Repare o reemplace las secciones dañadas según sea necesario.

7   Si un olor de combustible es todavía evidente después del chequeo, refiérase al Capítulo 6 y chequee el sistema EVAP (Sistema de control de evaporación de las emisiones).

26   Aire termostático del depurador de aire - chequeo

Refiérase a las ilustraciones 26.4 y 26.5
1   Todos los modelos se equipan con un termostato para el purificador de aire controlado, que absorbe aire para el carburador desde ubicaciones diferentes dependiendo de la temperatura del motor.
2   Este es un chequeo visual simple. Sin embargo, si el acceso es difícil, un espejo pequeño puede que tenga que ser usado.
3   Abra el capó y encuentre la mariposa del aire (que abre y cierra la puerta) instalada en el purificador de aire. Se ubica en el lado interior de la tubería para la admisión del aire en la porción del purificador de aire.
4   Si hay un conducto de aire flexible adjunto al extremo de la tubería, desconéctelo lo suficiente para que usted pueda mirar hacia adentro en el extremo de la tubería y vea si se abre y se cierra la puerta interior **(vea ilustración)**. Un espejo puede necesitarse si usted no puede mirar adentro de la tubería.
5   El chequeo debería hacerse cuando el motor y el aire de afuera están fríos. Ponga el motor en marcha y mire que la puerta se abre y se cierra, que debe de moverse hacia arriba y cerrar el conducto de aire. Con la puerta cerrada, aire no puede entrar por la punta de la tubería, pero en vez entra en el purificador de aire mediante el conducto de aire caliente adjunto al colector de escape **(vea ilustración)**.
6   Según el motor se calienta a la temperatura de operación normal, la puerta se debe-

ría abrir para permitir que aire entre por el extremo de la tubería. Dependiendo de la temperatura de afuera del aire, esto puede tomar desde 10 a 15 minutos. Para acelerar el chequeo usted puede reconectar el conducto de la tubería de aire, conduzca el vehículo y entonces chequee la posición de la puerta.
7   Si el termostático para el purificador de aire no está operando adecuadamente, vea Capítulo 6 para más información.

27   Bandas - chequeo, ajuste y reemplazo

Refiérase a las ilustraciones 27.3, 27.4, 27.5a, 27.5b, 27.6a y 27.6b
1   Las bandas o bandas tipo V como se les llaman frecuentemente, se ubican en el frente del motor y juegan un papel importante en la operación general del motor y los accesorios. Debido a su función y su material de construcción, las bandas pueden fallar después de un periodo de tiempo corto y deberían inspeccionarse y ajustarse periódicamente para impedir daños mayores al motor.
2   El número de bandas usadas en un vehículo particular, depende de los accesorios instalados. Las bandas se usan para girar el alternador, bomba de aire, bomba de la servodirección, compresor del aire acondicionado y bomba de agua. Depende de la disposición de la polea, más de uno de los componentes pueden ser conducidos por una sola banda.
3   Con el motor apagado, localice las bandas al frente del motor. Use sus dedos (y una linterna eléctrica, si es necesario), mueva su dedo a lo largo de las bandas, para chequearlas por grietas y separación de las bandas. También chequee por desgaste y barniz, que le da a la banda un aspecto lustroso **(vea ilustración)**. Ambos lados de cada banda deberían inspeccionarse, esto significa que usted tendrá que torcer cada banda para chequear el lado inferior. Chequee las poleas por mellas, cuarteaduras, distorsión y corrosión.
4   Para chequear la tensión de cada banda según las recomendaciones de la fábrica, instale un medidor de tensión de banda. Mida la tensión según las instrucciones de medir la tensión y compare su medida de tensión con la de la banda especificada ya sea una banda usada o una banda nueva **(vea ilustración)**. **Nota:** *Una banda "nueva" se define como cualquier banda que no ha sido corrida; una banda "usada" es la que ha sido corrida por más de diez minutos.*
5   El medidor especial es la manera más precisa para chequear la tensión de la banda. Sin embargo, si usted no tiene un medidor y no puede pedir uno prestado, el siguiente método se recomienda como una alternativa. Coloque una regla recta a través del trecho libre más largo (la distancia entre las dos poleas) de la banda. Empuje hacia abajo firmemente sobre la banda en el medio y vea

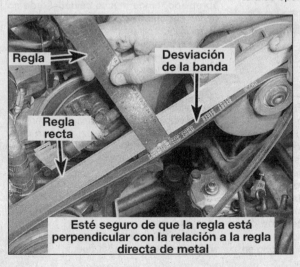

Regla

Desviación de la banda

Regla recta

27.4 Midiendo la deflección de la banda con dos reglas

Esté seguro de que la regla está perpendicular con la relación a la regla directa de metal

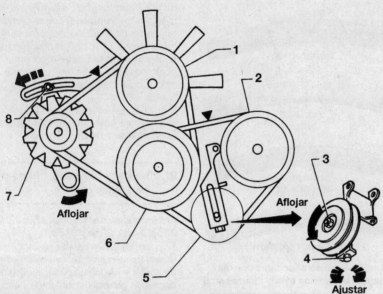

27.6a En algunos componentes, el ajuste de la banda es simplificado - todo lo que usted tiene que hacer es aflojar el perno del calzo (flecha) . . .

▼ : Chequeando el punto de la deflección de la banda

27.5a Modelo típico de los modelos más modernos para los puntos de ajuste de la banda en los motores de cuatro cilindros

1	Polea del ventilador	5	Polea loca
2	Polea del compresor	6	Polea del cigüeñal
3	Tuerca prisionera	7	Alternador
4	Perno de ajuste	8	Afloje para ajustar

27.5b Modelo típico para los puntos de ajuste de la banda en los motores V6

1 Polea para la bomba de la dirección
2 Polea para la bomba del agua
3 Polea para el compresor
4 Polea para el alternador
5 Polea para el cigüeñal

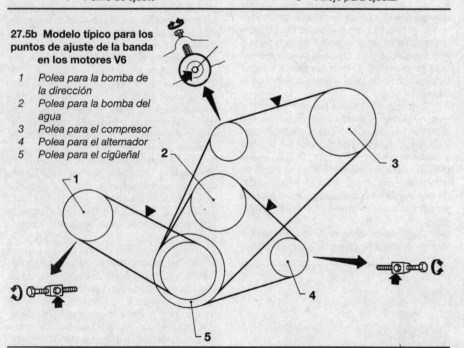

27.6b . . . y el perno de la cerradura (A), entonces gire el perno (B) de ajuste hasta que la presión de la banda sea corregida (se muestra un motor V6)

posición y chequee la tensión de banda. Si es correcto, apriete los dos pernos hasta que simplemente estén un poquito apretado, entonces chequee nuevamente la tensión. Si la tensión es correcta, apriete los pernos.

8   Usted puede que tenga que usar algún tipo de palanca o barra para mover el accesorio mientras la banda se ajusta. Si esto debe hacerse, para tener el apalancamiento apropiado, tenga mucho cuidadoso de no dañar el componente siendo movido o la pieza siendo palanqueada contra (especialmente la bomba de aire).

9   Para reemplazar una banda, siga los procedimientos de arriba para el ajuste de la banda pero deslice la banda fuera de las poleas y remuévalas. Debido a que las bandas tienden a desgastarse más o menos a la misma vez, es una buena idea de reemplazar todas ellas a la misma vez. Marque cada banda y la polea correspondiente para que cada banda pueda reemplazarse adecuadamente.

10   Lleve las bandas viejas con usted cuando compre nuevas, para poder hacer una comparación directa de la longitud, anchura y diseño.

11   Ajuste las bandas como se describió anteriormente en esta Sección.

cuánto se mueve la banda (desvío). Mida la flexión con una regla **(vea ilustraciones)**. La banda debería desviarse de 1/8 a 1/4-pulgada si la distancia desde el centro de la polea al centro de la otra polea es menos de 12 pulgadas; debería desviar desde 1/8 a 3/8-pulgada si la distancia desde el centro de la polea al centro de la otra polea es más de 12 pulgadas.

6   Si ajuste es necesario, para estirar la banda más o aflojarla más, se hace moviendo el accesorio que es movido por la banda en su pivote. Cada componente comúnmente tiene un perno regulador y un perno de pivote. Ambos pernos deben aflojarse ligeramente para permitir que usted pueda mover el componente. Algunos componentes tienen un perno regulador que puede girarse para cambiar la tensión de la banda después que el perno de cierre se afloje **(vea ilustraciones)**.

7   Después que los dos pernos se hayan aflojado, mueva el componente lejos del motor para apretar la banda o hacia el motor para aflojar la banda. Sujete el accesorio en

29.3 Desenganche los clips del resorte y remueva las tuercas de ala para separar el plato de la cima del purificador de aire

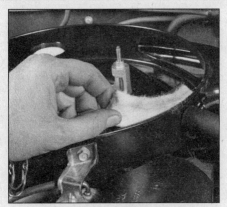

29.6 En los modelos que estén equipados, remueva el filtro de la válvula PCV (ventilación positiva del cárter) fuera del albergue adentro del purificador de aire

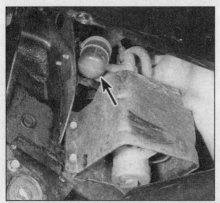

30.6 En los modelos que estén equipados con carburador con una bomba eléctrica de combustible, el filtro de combustible (flecha) está instalado en la cima del riel del chasis en el lado derecho, adyacente a la bomba de combustible

28   Cinturones de seguridad - chequeo

1   Chequee los cinturones del asiento, las hebillas, platos del picaporte y guías por cualquiera que sea el daño o signos obvios de desgaste.

2   Asegúrese de que la luz de recordatorio de los cinturones de seguridad se prendan en cuanto la llave sea prendida.

3   Los cinturones de los asientos están diseñados para bloquearse durante una parada o un impacto repentino, pero permite el movimiento libre durante el manejo normal. Los retractores deben detener el cinturón contra el pecho mientras está conduciendo y enrolla el cinturón cuando la hebilla sea liberada.

4   Si alguno de los chequeos de encima revela un problema con el sistema de los cinturones de seguridad, reemplace las partes según sea necesario.

29   Purificador de aire y PCV (ventilación positiva del cárter) - reemplazo

Refiérase a las ilustraciones 29.3 y 29.6

1   A los intervalos especificados, el purificador de aire debe ser reemplazado con uno nuevo. Un programa completo del mantenimiento preventivo llamaría también para que el filtro sea inspeccionado periódicamente entre cambios, especialmente si el vehículo es a menudo conducido en condiciones polvorientas.

2   El purificador de aire está localizado dentro del albergue del purificador de aire, que está instalado encima del cuerpo de aceleración o el carburador.

3   Remueva las tuercas de ala que retienen el plato superior al cuerpo del purificador de aire, libere los clips y levántelo hacia afuera **(vea ilustración)**.

4   Levante el purificador de aire hacia afuera del albergue. Si está cubierto con tierra, debe ser reemplazado.

5   Limpie el interior del albergue del purifi-

cador de aire con un trapo.

6   Remueva el filtro PCV viejo (si está equipado con uno) e instale el nuevo en el albergue **(vea ilustración)**.

7   Coloque el filtro viejo (si está en buena condición) o el filtro nuevo (si es necesario reemplazarlo) en el albergue del purificador de aire.

8   Vuelva a instalar el plato superior en el purificador de aire y apriete las tuercas de ala, entonces los clips en su posición.

30   Filtro de combustible - reemplazo

Peligro: La gasolina es extremadamente inflamable, razón por la cual se debe tener mucha precaución al trabajar en cualquier parte del sistema de combustible. No fume ni permita la presencia de llamas expuestas o bombillas sin protección cerca del área de trabajo y no trabaje en un taller donde haya artefactos de gas natural con un piloto (como calentadores de agua o secadores de ropa).

1   Este trabajo debe ser hecho con el motor frío (después de estar detenido por lo menos tres horas). Coloque un recipiente de metal, trapos o periódicos debajo del filtro para colectar el combustible rociado.

Modelos con carburador

Con bomba mecánica de combustible

2   El filtro de combustible está localizado en la esquina del lado delantero derecho del compartimiento del motor, adyacente a la batería. **Peligro:** *Antes de tratar de remover el filtro de combustible, desconecte el cable negativo de la batería y póngalo en posición fuera del camino para que no pueda entrar en contacto accidentalmente con el poste de la batería.*

3   Para reemplazar el filtro, afloje las abrazaderas y las desliza por debajo de las mangueras del radiador, a través de los acopladores en el filtro.

4   Tuerza cuidadosamente y hale las mangueras del radiador para separarlas del filtro. Si las mangueras del radiador están en mala forma, ahora sería un buen tiempo para reemplazarlas con nuevas.

5   Remueva el filtro del retenedor e instale uno nuevo, entonces instale las mangueras del radiador y apriete las abrazaderas firmemente. Ponga el motor en marcha y chequee cuidadosamente por fugas en las conexiones de la manguera del filtro.

Con bomba eléctrica de combustible

Refiérase a la ilustración 30.6

Peligro: *¡La bomba de combustible en estos modelos está instalada en el lado derecho del riel de chasis (lado del pasajero), encima del grillete del resorte delantero, cerca del tanque de combustible y es muy difícil de remover! Debido a que está instalada debajo del tanque, la gasolina se saldrá de las líneas de combustible cuando ellas sean desconectadas del filtro. Para prevenir esto, que es una situación muy peligrosa, absorba todo el combustible fuera del tanque o corra el vehículo hasta que el tanque esté seco antes de reemplazar el filtro.*

6   Después que el tanque se desagüe, note como el filtro está instalado, entonces hálelo hacia afuera del retenedor, afloje las abrazaderas y las desliza hacia abajo de las mangueras, pasando los acopladores en el filtro **(vea ilustración)**.

7   Tuerza cuidadosamente y hale en las mangueras para separarlas del filtro. Si las mangueras están en mala forma, ahora sería un buen tiempo para reemplazarlas con nuevas.

8   Conecte las mangueras al filtro nuevo e instálela en el retenedor. Asegúrese de que el filtro está apropiadamente orientado - el filtro de combustible tiene generalmente una flecha en el canasto que indica la dirección del flujo del combustible. Ponga el motor en marcha y chequee cuidadosamente por fugas en las conexiones de las mangueras del filtro.

30.10 Los modelos con combustible inyectados tienen un filtro de tipo canasto, localizado en el compartimiento del motor (se muestra un motor V6)

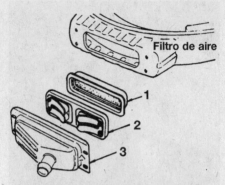

31.1 Esquema para los modelos mas antiguos con el filtro de la válvula de inducción y disposición de los componente de la válvula de aire de lengüeta

1   Filtro
2   Válvula
3   Albergue

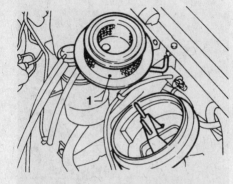

31.6a En los modelos más modernos, remueva la válvula inductora de aire de la carcaza remota del filtro para tener acceso al filtro (se muestra un motor de cuatro cilindros)

1   Filtro para la AIV (válvula de inyección de aire)

Modelos con combustible inyectado

Refiérase a la ilustración 30.10

9   Remuévale la presión del sistema de combustible (Capítulo 4).

10   Para reemplazar el filtro, afloje las abrazaderas y las desliza hacia abajo de las mangueras, pasando los acopladores en el filtro (vea ilustración).

11   Note como que el filtro está instalado (que extremo mira hacia encima) para que el filtro nuevo no sea instalado al revés. Tuerza cuidadosamente y hale las mangueras para separarlas del filtro. Si las mangueras están en malas condiciones, ahora sería un buen tiempo para reemplazarlas con nuevas.

12   Afloje el perno de la abrazadera y remueva el filtro.

13   Instale el filtro nuevo en la abrazadera y apriete el perno. Asegúrese de que el filtro está apropiadamente orientado - el filtro de combustible tiene generalmente una flecha en el canasto que indica la dirección del flujo del combustible.

14   Conecte las mangueras al filtro nuevo y apriete las abrazaderas firmemente.

15   Ponga el motor en marcha y chequee cuidadosamente por fugas en las conexiones de las mangueras del filtro.

31   Filtro de la válvula AIV (válvula de inyección de aire) - reemplazo

Modelos más antiguos

Refiérase a la ilustración 31.1

1   Remueva los tornillos que retienen el albergue de la AIV (válvula de inyección de aire) al albergue del purificador de aire (vea ilustración).

2   Uno de dos métodos que se pueden usar para obtener acceso al filtro: afloje las tuercas del tubo de inducción de aire en el múltiple de escape y soporte para el tubo, para que los tubos y el albergue se puedan separar del purificador de aire, o remueva el

albergue del purificador de aire.

3   Abra con una palanca el filtro viejo hacia afuera del albergue del purificador de aire.

4   Presione el filtro nuevo en su posición.

5   Vuelva a instalar el albergue de la válvula en el purificador de aire y apriete las tuercas del tubo de inducción de aire (si se aflojó).

Modelos más modernos

Refiérase a las ilustraciones 31.6a y 31.6b

6   Los modelos más modernos tienen un filtro AIV remoto localizado en un albergue separado. Remueva las tuercas de la tapa del albergue o pernos, levante la tapa hacia afuera y remueva el filtro (vea ilustraciones).

7   Instale el filtro nuevo y vuelva a instalar la tapa.

32   Filtro de la bomba de aire (modelos 1980 solamente) - reemplazo

Refiérase a la ilustración 32.1

1   Remueva la manguera de caucho del albergue del filtro de la bomba del aire (vea ilustración).

2   Desconecte el albergue del filtro del soporte.

3   El filtro es parte de la sección inferior del albergue. Separe las secciones del albergue y reemplace la sección del filtro del albergue con uno nuevo.

33   Filtro del canasto de carbón del sistema EEC (control electrónico del motor (computadora)) - reemplazo

1   La función del sistema de EEC es para extraer los vapores del combustible del tanque de combustible, almacenarlos en un canasto de carbón y quemarlos durante el proceso de operación normal del motor.

2   El filtro al fondo del canasto de carbón

debe ser reemplazado en los intervalos especificados. Si, sin embargo, un olor del combustible es detectado, el canasto, las mangueras de vacío del filtro y el sistema se deben inspeccionar inmediatamente (Capítulo 6).

3   Para reemplazar el filtro, localice el canasto en el compartimiento del motor. Tiene varias mangueras saliéndose por la parte de encima. Si es necesario, refiérase a las ilustraciones debajo del capó para los componentes al principio de éste Capítulo para localizar el canasto.

4   El canasto es sostenido a la carrocería por un resorte o abrazadera, asegurado alrededor del exterior del cuerpo del canasto. El canasto es removido levantándolo hacia afuera del montaje, libertándolo del resorte o la abrazadera.

5   Gire el canasto al revés y hale el filtro viejo del fondo del canasto.

6   Empuje el filtro nuevo en el fondo del canasto, asegúrese que está sentado.

7   Coloque el canasto otra vez adentro de su posición y hale el resorte alrededor para detenerlo.

8   El sistema EEC es explicado con más detalles en el Capítulo 6.

34   Estrangulador de aire - chequeo

Refiérase a la ilustración 34.3

1   El estrangulador opera solamente cuando el motor está frío, así que este chequeo debería desempeñarse antes de que el motor se haya comenzado por el día.

2   Abra el capó y remueva el plato de encima del purificador de aire. Se retiene en su lugar por una tuerca mariposa (o tuercas) en el centro y varios retenedores alrededor en el borde. Si cualquier manguera de vacío debe desconectarse, póngales etiquetas para marcarlas y asegurarse de la reinstalación correcta en sus posiciones iniciales.

3   Mire el centro del alojamiento del purificador de aire. Usted notará un plato plano en

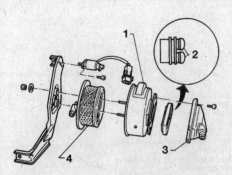

31.6b Detalles de la instalación del filtro de la válvula de inducción de aire para los motores V6

1   *Cubierta para el purificador del aire*
2   *Detenedor*
3   *Tapa para la válvula de lengüeta*
4   *Filtro para la AIV (válvula de inyección de aire) del purificador del aire*

---

la apertura del carburador **(vea ilustración)**.
4   Haga que un asistente deprima el pedal del acelerador al piso. El plato debería cerrarse completamente. Ponga el motor en marcha mientras usted mira en el plato del carburador. ¡No coloque su cara cerca del carburador, porque el motor podría hacer una contra explosión con llamas, ocasionándole quemaduras serias! Cuando comience el motor, el plato del estrangulador debería abrirse ligeramente.
5   Permita que el motor continúe corriendo en marcha mínima. Según el motor se calienta a temperatura normal de operación, el plato debería abrirse lentamente, permitiendo más aire que entre mediante la parte de encima del carburador.
6   Después de unos minutos, el plato del estrangulador debería completamente abrirse a la posición vertical. Péguele al acelerador para asegurarse que la leva de la marcha mínima rápida se desenganche.
7   Usted notará que la velocidad del motor corresponde con la apertura del plato. Con el plato cerrado, el motor debería correr a una marcha mínima rápida. Según el plato se abre y el acelerador se mueve para desenganchar la leva de la marcha mínima rápida, la velocidad del motor bajará.
8   Con el motor apagado y el acelerador abierto a la mitad, abra y cierre el estrangulador varias veces. Chequee la varillaje para ver si está conectada correctamente y asegúrese que no se atora.
9   Si el estrangulador o varillaje se traba o trabaja perezosamente, límpielo con limpiador para el depurador de estrangulador (rocío de aerosol están disponibles en los almacenes de auto partes). Si la condición persiste después de limpiarlo, reemplace las piezas problemáticas.
10   Visualmente inspeccione todas las mangueras de vacío para estar seguro que ellas están conectadas firmemente, busque por grietas y deterioración. Reemplácelas según sea necesario.

32.1 El filtro de la bomba de aire (flecha izquierda) está localizado anexo al canasto de carbón (flecha derecha) (modelos 1980 solamente)

11   Si el estrangulador falla de operar normalmente, pero ninguna causa mecánica puede encontrarse, refiérase al Capítulo 4.

---

35 Carburador/cuerpo de inyección de combustible - chequeo del par de torsión de las tuercas

1   La unidad del carburador o TBI (cuerpo de inyección de combustible) está conectada en la cima del múltiple de admisión con varios pernos o tuercas. Los afianzadores a veces se pueden aflojar por las vibraciones y cambio de temperatura durante la operación normal del motor y causan una fuga de vacío.
2   Si usted sospecha que una fuga de vacío existe en el fondo del cuerpo de aceleración o carburador, obtenga una longitud de dos pie de manguera de combustible. Ponga el motor en marcha y ponga un extremo de la manguera próximo a su oreja según usted tienta alrededor de la base con el otro extremo. Usted oirá un sonido que silba si un escape existe (tenga cuidado con los componentes del motor caliente o que se estén moviendo).
3   Remueva el ensamblaje del purificador de aire, marque cada manguera que se desconecta con un pedazo de cinta numerada para hacer la instalación de regreso más fácil.
4   Localice las tuercas o pernos de afianzamiento en la base del carburador o el cuerpo de aceleración. Decida qué herramientas o adaptadores especiales serán necesarios, si alguno, para apretar los afianzadores.
5   Apriete las tuercas o los pernos al par de torsión especificado. No los sobre.apriete, por que las roscas se podrían cruzar.
6   Si, después que las tuercas o los pernos son apropiadamente apretado, una fuga de vacío existe todavía, el cuerpo de aceleración o el carburador debe ser removido y una junta nueva instalada. Vea Capítulo 4 para más información.
7   Después que apriete los afianzadores,

34.3 Con el purificador de aire removido, el plato del estrangulador (flecha) es visible por encima del carburador

vuelva a instalar todas las mangueras del purificador de aire de regreso a las posiciones originales.

---

36 Pedal del acelerador y cable - chequeo y ajuste (modelos con carburador solamente)

Refiérase a las ilustraciones 36.2, 36.4a y 36.4b

1   Con el motor apagado, presione el pedal del acelerador varias veces para asegurarse que las varillas están operando suavemente. También, vea si el pedal se está regresando a su posición original cuando es liberado.
2   Chequee la altura (H) del pedal del acelerador **(vea ilustración)**. Debe estar acerca de 4-5/8 (118 mm) pulgada del piso. Si la altura no es correcta, afloje la contratuerca y gire el detenedor del pedal hasta que haga contacto, entonces apriete la contratuerca.

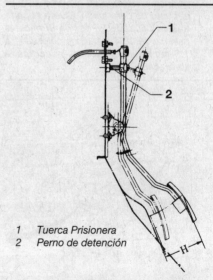

1   *Tuerca Prisionera*
2   *Perno de detención*

36.2 Ajuste del pedal es hecho girando el perno de detención en la parte de encima del eje

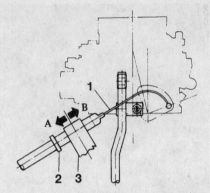

36.4a Puntos de ajuste para el cable en los modelos 1980

1   Alambre del acelerador
2   Dado
3   Abrazadera

3   Haga que un ayudante presione el pedal del acelerador completamente varias veces mientras usted observa el carburador para asegurarse que la válvula del acelerador se abre completamente cuando el pedal es presionado y se cierra completamente cuando el pedal es liberado.

4   Si el cable del acelerador debe ser ajustado use el siguiente procedimiento **(vea ilustraciones)**:

a) *Antes de ajustar, libere el mecanismo del estrangulador automático deteniendo el estrangulador abierto con sus dedos mientras usted hala la palanca del acelerador en el carburador hacia encima con la mano.*

b) *En los modelos 1980, ponga la palanca del acelerador en la posición completamente cerrada y afloje la abrazadera reteniendo el cable del acelerador. Hale lentamente el dado en el albergue del cable hacia afuera (A) de la dirección de la palanca del acelerador hasta que la palanca esté cerca de moverse. Este es el punto de cero juego. Mueva la parte trasera del dado (dirección B) hacia la palanca de 3/64 a 1/16 de pulgada (1 a 1.5 mm) del acelerador - y apriete la abrazadera.*

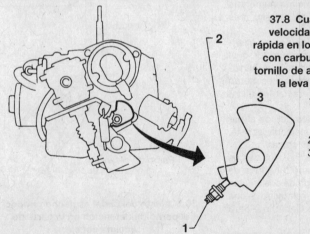

37.8 Cuando esté ajustando la velocidad de la marcha mínima rápida en los modelos más modernos con carburador, asegúrese que el tornillo de ajuste está en el paso 2 de la leva como está mostrado

1   Tornillo para el ajuste de la marcha mínima rápida
2   Segundo paso
3   Leva para la marcha mínima alta

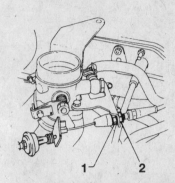

36.4b Modelos de vehículos más modernos equipados con cable para el acelerador del carburador

1   Tuerca prisionera
2   Tuerca de ajuste

c) *En los modelos 1981 y más modernos, afloje la contratuerca del cable del acelerador y asegúrese que la palanca del acelerador en el carburador está en la posición completamente cerrada. Apriete la tuerca de ajuste hasta que la palanca del acelerador esté acerca de moverse, que es el punto del juego de cero. De esta posición, destornille la tuerca que ajusta una a dos vueltas para que el juego del cable sea de 1/16 a 3/32-pulgada (1 a 2.5 mm).*

d) *Siguiendo el ajuste, repita los chequeos descritos en el paso 1.*

37   Velocidad de la marcha mínima - chequeo y ajuste

Refiérase a las ilustraciones 37.5, 37.8, 37.11a, 37.11b y 37.11c

1   La velocidad de la marcha mínima del motor es la velocidad en que el motor opera cuando ninguna presión del pedal del acelerador es aplicada. La velocidad de la marcha mínima es crítica para el rendimiento del mismo motor, también como muchos subsistemas del motor.

2   Un tacómetro sostenido a mano se

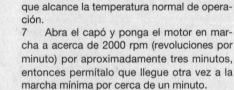

37.5 En los modelos 1986 más modernos, un arnés para el adaptador debe ser instalado como está mostrado antes de ajustar la velocidad de la marcha mínima

debe usar cuando esté ajustando la velocidad de la marcha mínima para obtener una lectura exacta. La conexión exacta para estos medidores varía con el fabricante, así que siga las instrucciones particulares incluidas.

3   Aplique el freno de estacionamiento y bloquee las ruedas. Esté seguro que la transmisión esté en Neutral (transmisión manual) o en Estacionamiento (transmisión automática).

4   Apague el aire acondicionado (si está equipado), las luces y cualquier otro accesorio durante este procedimiento.

5   En los modelos 1986 y más modernos, conecte un adaptador al cable del arnés (disponible en su concesionario - número de la herramienta especial EG11150000) entre los terminales primarios para la bobina de la ignición y el conector del arnés **(vea ilustración)**. Conecte un tacómetro al adaptador del arnés.

6   Ponga el motor en marcha y permítalo que alcance la temperatura normal de operación.

7   Abra el capó y ponga el motor en marcha a acerca de 2000 rpm (revoluciones por minuto) por aproximadamente tres minutos, entonces permítalo que llegue otra vez a la marcha mínima por cerca de un minuto.

8   En los modelos 1984 y más modernos, asegúrese que el brazo de la marcha mínima rápida del carburador está en el paso 2 de la leva para la marcha mínima alta **(vea ilustración)**.

9   En los vehículos equipados con transmisiones automáticas, haga que un ayudante cambie la palanca de cambio a Marcha mientras mantiene el pedal del freno firmemente deprimido. Coloque la palanca en Neutral en los vehículos equipados con transmisión manual.

10   Chequee la velocidad de la marcha mínima del motor con el tacómetro y compárela con la etiqueta VECI (etiqueta de información para el control de las emisiones del vehículo).

11   Si la velocidad de la marcha mínima no está correcta, gire el tornillo de ajuste para la velocidad de la marcha mínima (a la derecha

37.11a Ubicación típica para el tornillo de ajuste de la marcha mínima en los modelos más antiguos con carburador (flecha), (se muestra un modelo 1981)

para que vaya más rápido, a la izquierda para que vaya más lento) hasta que la velocidad de la marcha mínima sea corregida **(vea ilustraciones)**.

Modelos 1990 y más modernos

Refiérase a las ilustraciones 37.12a, 37.12b, 37.12c y 37.12d

12 En los vehículos 1990 y más modernos equipados con un sistema de MPFI (inyec-

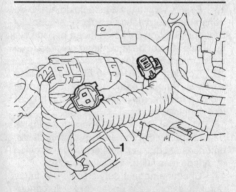

37.12a Desconecte el conector del arnés de la válvula AAC (control del aire auxiliar) antes de ajustar la velocidad de la marcha mínima

37.11b Ubicación para el ajuste de la velocidad de la marcha mínima para los motores de cuatro cilindros de 1986 y más modernos

ción de combustible con lumbreras), si la velocidad de la marcha mínima no está correcta, incapacite los componentes de la inyección de combustible que controla específicamente el sistema de la marcha mínima antes de proceder con el ajuste. Para más información con respecto al sistema de inyección de combustible, refiérase a los Capítulos 4 y 6.

a) *En los motores V6, desconecte el arnés eléctrico de la válvula AAC (control del aire auxiliar)* **(vea ilustración)**. *En los motores KA24E, desconecte el conector del arnés del sensor del acelerador* **(vea ilustración)**.
b) *Chequee la regulación del tiempo de la ignición (vea Sección 48).*
c) *Ajuste la velocidad de la marcha mínima del motor girando el tornillo de ajuste* **(vea ilustraciones)**.
d) *Conecte de nuevo la válvula AAC (motor V6) o el sensor del acelerador (motores KA24E) y ponga el motor en marcha a aproximadamente 2,000 rpm por unos cuantos minutos.*
e) *Si el motor todavía no marcha a la velocidad de la mínima apropiada, haga que la mezcla del CO (monóxido de carbono) sea chequeada por el departamento de servicio de su concesionario.*

13 Después del ajuste, cambie la transmisión automática a Estacionamiento y apague el motor.

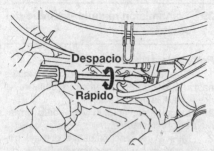

37.11c Ubicación del tornillo de ajuste para la velocidad de la marcha mínima en los motores V6

38 Caja de transferencia - cambio del aceite

1 Conduzca el vehículo por lo menos 15 minutos en 4WD (cuatro tracciones) para calentar el aceite en la caja.
2 Levante el vehículo y póngalo firmemente sobre estantes. Remueva el protector para las piedras (si está equipado).
3 Mueva una cacerola de drenaje, trapos, periódicos y una palanca o una matraca (para que entre en el agujero cuadrado en el tapón de drenaje en la caja de transferencia) debajo del vehículo.
4 Remueva el tapón de chequear y llenar **(vea ilustración 21.1)**.
5 Remueva el tapón de drenaje desde la parte inferior del albergue y permita que el aceite viejo se vacíe completamente.
6 Cuidadosamente limpie e instale el tapón de drenaje después que se vacíe la caja de transferencia completamente. Apriete el tapón firmemente.
7 Llene la caja de transferencia con el lubricante especificado hasta que llegue al nivel con el borde inferior del agujero del llenador.
8 Instale el tapón de chequeo, relleno y apriételo firmemente.
9 Instale el protector contra las piedras, entonces baje el vehículo.
10 Chequee cuidadosamente por fugas alrededor del tapón de drenaje después de pocas millas de conducirlo.

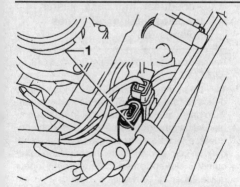

37.12b Desconecte el conector del arnés de sensor del acelerador antes de ajustar la velocidad de la marcha mínima

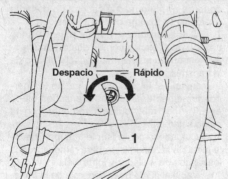

37.12c Ubicación del tornillo de ajuste para la marcha mínima en los motores V6

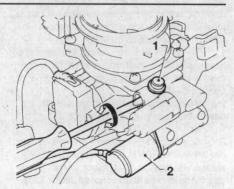

37.12d Ubicación del tornillo de ajuste para la marcha mínima en los motores KA24E

39   Transmisión manual - cambio del aceite

Refiérase a la ilustración 39.3

1   Conduzca el vehículo por unas millas hasta que completamente se caliente el aceite para la transmisión.
2   Levante el vehículo y póngalo firmemente sobre estantes.
3   Mueva una cacerola para el drenaje, trapos, periódicos y las herramienta debajo del vehículo. Con los periódicos y la cacerola para el drenaje en posición debajo de la transmisión, use la herramienta para remover el tapón de chequear/llenar en la parte lateral de la transmisión **(vea ilustración 25.1)**. Afloje el tapón de drenaje ubicado en el fondo de la transmisión manual **(vea ilustración)**.
4   Una vez aflojado, cuidadosamente destorníllelo con sus dedos hasta que usted pueda removerlo desde la transmisión. Permita que todo el aceite se vacíe en la cacerola. Si el tapón está demasiado caliente para tocarlo, use la herramienta para removerlo.
5   Si la transmisión se equipa con un tapón de drenaje magnético, mire si hay virutas de metal que se agarren a él. Si hay, es una señal de desgaste interno excesivo, indicando que la transmisión debería cuidadosamente inspeccionarse en el futuro próximo. Si la transmisión no está equipada con un tapón de drenaje magnético, permita que el aceite en la cacerola se enfríe, entonces con sus manos introducida en el fondo de la cacerola chequee por virutas.
6   Limpie el tapón de drenaje, entonces reinstálelo en la transmisión y apriételo firmemente.
7   Usando una bomba de mano o una jeringa, llene la transmisión con el grado correcto de aceite (vea las especificaciones), hasta que el nivel esté en la parte de abajo del orificio para llenar (vea Sección 25).
8   Instale el tapón para chequear, llenar y apriételo firmemente.

40   Diferencial - çambio del aceite

Nota: *El procedimiento siguiente puede usarse para el diferencial trasero así como también para el diferencial delantero en los vehículos de modelos de 4WD.*

1   Conduzca el vehículo por varias millas hasta calentar el aceite del diferencial, entonces levante el vehículo y póngalo firmemente sobre estantes.
2   Mueva una cacerola para drenar, trapos, periódicos y una herramienta debajo del vehículo.
3   Con la cacerola para el drenaje debajo del diferencial, use la herramienta para aflojar el tapón de drenaje. Es el tapón inferior de los dos tapones **(vea ilustraciones 22.2 y 22.3)**.
4   Una vez apretado, cuidadosamente destorníllelo con sus dedos hasta que usted pueda removerlo.
5   Permita que todo el aceite se vacíe en la

cacerola, entonces instale el tapón de drenaje y apriételo firmemente.
6   Sienta con sus manos en el fondo de la cacerola de drenaje por cualquier virutas de metal que puedan haber salido hacia fuera con el aceite. Si hay alguna, es una señal de desgaste excesivo, indicando que los componentes internos deberían cuidadosamente inspeccionarse pronto en el futuro.
7   Remueva el tapón para chequear y llenar. Usando una bomba de mano, jeringa o un embudo, llene el diferencial con el grado y cantidad correcta de aceite (vea las Especificaciones) hasta que el nivel esté en la parte de abajo del tapón de relleno.
8   Reinstale el tapón y apriételo firmemente.
9   Baje el vehículo. Chequee por fugas en el tapón de drenaje después de las primeras pocas millas de conducir.

41   Transmisión automática - cambio del flúido

1   A los intervalos especificados de tiempo, el flúido de la transmisión debería vaciarse, sustituirse y un filtro nuevo ser instalado. Debido a que el flúido debería estar caliente cuando se vacía, conduzca el vehículo por 15 o 20 minutos antes de proceder.
2   Antes de comenzar el trabajo, compre el flúido de transmisión especificado (vea flúidos y lubricantes recomendados al frente de este Capítulo).
3   Las otras herramientas necesarias para este trabajo incluyen soportes para soportar el peso del vehículo en una posición levantada, una cacerola para el drenaje capaz de sostener por lo menos ocho pintas, periódicos y trapos limpios.
4   Levante el vehículo y respáldelo firmemente sobre soportes.
5   Con una cacerola para drenaje en su lugar, remueva el tapón y permita que el flúido drene en la cacerola tenga cuidado de no quemarse usted mismo con nada - sería mejor usar guantes.
6   Remueva los pernos y separe la cacerola de la transmisión y el tubo de llenar. Deseche la junta. Si hay que hacerle palanca a la cacerola hacia fuera, ¡tenga mucho cuidado de no deformar la cacerola o dañar la superficie de la junta de la transmisión!
7   Cuidadosamente hágale palanca a los tubos para aflojarlos con un destornillador.
8   Remueva los pernos y separe el filtro de la transmisión.
9   Instale el filtro nuevo y apriete los pernos firmemente, entonces prense los tubos en su lugar muy cuidadosamente con la mano solamente.
10   Cuidadosamente limpie la superficie de la junta de la transmisión para remover todos los rasgos del sellador y junta vieja.
11   Vacíe el flúido de la cacerola de la transmisión, límpiela con solvente y séquela con aire a presión.
12   Aplique una capa delgada de sellador RTV (vulcanizador accionado a temperatura

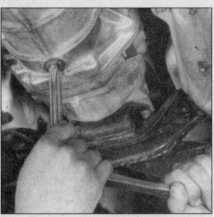

39.3 Use una matraca y una extensión para remover el tapón del drenaje de la transmisión manual

del ambiente) al lado lateral de la transmisión en la junta nueva.
13   Asegúrese que la superficie para la junta en la cacerola de la transmisión está limpia, entonces aplíquele una capa delgada de sellador RTV (vulcanizador accionado a temperatura del ambiente) y coloque la junta nueva sobre la cacerola. Ponga la cacerola en su lugar contra la transmisión, instale los pernos y trabajando alrededor de la cacerola, apriete cada perno un poco a la vez hasta que el torque final de torsión se alcance.
14   Baje el vehículo y añada flúido nuevo de transmisión automática mediante el tubo del llenador (Sección 5). La cantidad debería ser igual que el valor de la cantidad del flúido que se vació (usted no debe sobrellenarla).
15   Con la transmisión en Estacionamiento y con el freno de estacionamiento, corra el motor a marcha mínima alta, pero no lo acelere demasiado.
16   Mueva el selector del engranaje a través de cada guía y de regreso a Estacionamiento, entonces chequee el nivel del flúido (Sección 4). Añada más flúido según se requiera.
17   Chequee debajo del vehículo por fugas durante las primeras pocas millas de conducir.

42   Baleros de las ruedas delanteras - chequear, lubricar y ajustar, modelos de dos tracciones solamente

Refiérase a las ilustraciones 42.1, 42.6, 42.7, 42.11 y42.15

1   En la mayoría de los casos los baleros de las ruedas delanteras no necesitarán servicio hasta que las pastillas del freno se cambien. Sin embargo, los baleros deberían chequearse cuando se levante la parte del frente del vehículo por cualquier razón. Varios artículos, incluyendo una llave torsiométrica y grasa especial, se requieren para este procedimiento **(vea ilustración)**.
2   Con el vehículo firmemente sobre soportes, gire cada rueda y chequéela por ruido, resistencia de rodamiento y juego libre.

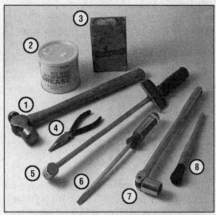

42.1 Herramientas y materiales necesario para el mantenimiento de los baleros del frente

1   **Martillo** - *Un martillo común será suficiente.*

2   **Grasa** - *Grasa de alta temperatura que tenga una formula especial para los baleros de las ruedas delantera.*

3   **Bloque de madera** - *Si usted tiene un pedazo de madera de 2x4, se puede usar para instalar el sello nuevo.*

4   **Pinzas con puntas finas** - *Se usan para remover el pasador de la rueda.*

5   **Un torquímetro** - *Este es un procedimiento muy importante; si el balero está muy apretado, la rueda no girará libremente - si está muy suelta, la rueda se tambaleará en el vástago/muñón.*

6   **Destornillador** - *Se usa para remover el sello (un destornillador largo es preferible).*

7   **Dado y palanca** - *Se necesita para aflojar la tuerca del vástago/muñón.*

8   **Cepillo** - *Junto con un poco de solvente, esto se usará para remover la grasa vieja.*

3   Agarre la parte superior de cada llanta con una mano y la parte de abajo con la otra. Mueva la rueda hacia adentro y hacia fuera sobre el eje. Si haya cualquier movimiento notable, los baleros deberían chequearse, entonces ser engrasados o sustituidos si es necesario.

4   Remueva la rueda(s).

5   Fabrique un bloque de madera para resbalarlo entre las pastillas del freno para mantenerlas separadas. Remueva la mordaza de freno (Capítulo 10) y cuélguela fuera del camino con un pedazo de alambre. Tenga cuidado de no rizar o estirar la manguera del freno.

6   Hágale palanca a la tapa fuera del cubo usando un destornillador o un martillo y un buril **(vea ilustración)**.

7   Enderece los extremos del pasador/chaveta, entonces remueva el pasador. Deseche el pasador y use uno nuevo durante el ensamble **(vea ilustración)**.

8   Remueva la tuerca prisionera, tuerca de regulación y la arandela de torsión desde el extremo del eje.

9   Tire el cubo hacia fuera ligeramente, entonces empújelo hacia adentro en su posición original. Esto debería forzar el balero

42.6 Hágale palanca a la tapa del polvo con un destornillador

exterior de la rueda hacia fuera del eje lo suficiente para que se pueda remover.

10   Hale el conjunto de cubo y disco fuera del eje.

11   Use un destornillador para hacerle palanca al sello fuera del cubo trasero **(vea ilustración)**. Según se hace esto, note como se instala el sello.

12   Remueva el balero interior de la rueda en el cubo.

13   Solvente se puede usar para remover todos los rastros de grasa vieja de los baleros, cubos y ejes. Una escobilla pequeña puede probar ser útil; pero esté seguro que ningún pelo de la escoba se quede impregnado en el balero.

14   Cuidadosamente inspeccione los baleros por grietas, descolorimiento por calor, baleros desgastados, etc. Chequee la pista interior del cubo del balero por desgaste y daño. Si las pistas de los baleros están defectuosas, los cubos deberían llevarse a un taller de torneo para que puedan remover las pistas viejas y prensar nuevas en su lugar. Note que los baleros y las pistas vienen juntas como un juego y los baleros viejos deberían nunca ser instalados sobre pistas nuevas.

15   Use grasa de alta temperatura para las ruedas delanteras para empacar los baleros. Trabaje la grasa para que entre completamente en los baleros, forzándola entre los rodillos, cono y jaula, desde el lado lateral **(vea ilustración)**.

42.11 Use un destornillador grande para hacerle palanca al sello de grasa desde la parte trasera del cubo

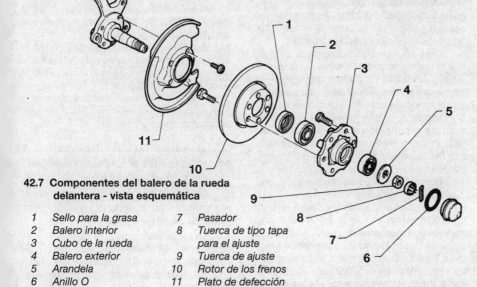

42.7 Componentes del balero de la rueda delantera - vista esquemática

1	Sello para la grasa	7	Pasador
2	Balero interior	8	Tuerca de tipo tapa
3	Cubo de la rueda		para el ajuste
4	Balero exterior	9	Tuerca de ajuste
5	Arandela	10	Rotor de los frenos
6	Anillo O	11	Plato de defección

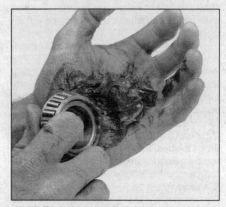

42.15 Trabaje grasa limpia en cada balero hasta que esté lleno

16   Aplique una capa delgada de grasa al eje y al asiento exterior de balero, al asiento interior del balero y al asiento del sello.

17   Ponga una cantidad pequeña de grasa detrás de cada pista del balero interior en el cubo. Use su dedo, forme un dique a estos puntos para proveer grasa extra y para mantener grasa delgada que fluya fuera del balero.

18   Coloque el balero interior empacado de grasa en la parte trasera del cubo y ponga un poco más de grasa en la parte de afuera del balero.

19   Instale un sello sobre el balero interior y golpe el sello igualmente en su lugar con un martillo y un bloque de madera hasta que esté raso con el cubo.

20   Cuidadosamente coloque e instale el cubo en el eje y empuje el balero empacado con grasa en la posición exterior.

21   Instale la arandela de torsión y la tuerca de regulación. Apriete la tuerca a la torsión inicial especificada.

22   Gire el cubo en dirección hacia el frente para asentar los baleros y remueva cualquier grasa o rebarbas que puedan ocasionar juego excesivo del balero después.

23   En los modelos 1979 hasta 1983, destornille la tuerca hasta que pueda ser girada a mano. Usando un dado solamente (no use una matraca o una barra de tipo ruptor), apriete la tuerca lo más posible con su mano. Usando un medidor de tensión de tipo resorte, chequee por la precarga especificada. Debe de ser entre 1.3 y 4.0 libras. Si la precarga es incorrecta, afloje o apriete la tuerca según sea necesario para obtener la precarga especificada. La tuerca no debería aflojarse en este punto más de media vuelta para instalar el pasador nuevo.

24   En los modelos 1984 y más antiguos, afloje la tuerca hasta que haya de 0.020 a 0.039 de pulgada de juego axial (hacia dentro y hacia fuera) en el cubo. Instale una escala de tipo resorte en uno de los pernos y mida la fuerza requerida para empezar que el cubo gire. Esta es la fricción del sello del aceite. Registre la medida. Apriete la tuerca hasta que la precarga sea de 1.3 a 4.0 pulgadas mayor que la fricción del sello del aceite. La precarga del balero es la fuerza requerida para comenzar a que gire el cubo (según se mide con la escala de tipo resorte). El juego axial del cubo debería ser menos de 0.002-pulgada.

25   Instale la tuerca retenedora y un pasador nuevo.

26   Doble los extremos del pasador hasta que ellos estén planos contra la tuerca. Corte cualquier longitud extra que pueda interferir con la tapa de polvo.

27   Instale la tapa de polvo. Golpéela en su lugar con un martillo.

28   Coloque la mordaza del freno cerca del rotor y cuidadosamente remueva el espaciador de madera. Instale la mordaza y apriétela (Capítulo 10).

29   Instale la rueda y apriete las tuercas de las ruedas.

30   Agarre la parte de encima y la parte de abajo de la llanta y chequee los baleros en la manera descrita anteriormente en esta Sección.

31   Baje el vehículo.

43   Sistema de enfriamiento - vaciar, limpiar y rellenar

Refiérase a las ilustraciones 43.4

Peligro: *No permita que el anticongelante entre en contacto con su piel o la superficie de la pintura del vehículo. Enjuague el área que estuvo en contacto inmediatamente con suficiente agua. No guarde anticongelante nuevo o deje anticongelante viejo alrededor donde pueda ser fácilmente accesible por niños y animales doméstico - son atraídos por su sabor dulce. Ingestión aunque sea de una pequeña cantidad puede ser fatal. Limpie el piso del garaje y la cacerola de goteo para derramamientos de anticongelante tan pronto ocurran. Guarde recipientes del anticongelante cubiertos y repare cualquier fuga en su sistema de enfriamiento inmediatamente.*

1   Periódicamente, el sistema de enfriamiento debería vaciarse, limpiarse y rellenarse para rellenar la mezcla de anticongelante e impedir formación de óxido y corrosión, que puede impedir el rendimiento del sistema de enfriamiento y causar daño al motor. Cuando el sistema de enfriamiento se le otorga servicio, todas las mangueras y la tapa del radiador deberían chequearse y sustituirse si es necesario.

2   Aplique el freno de estacionamiento y bloquee las ruedas. Si el vehículo acaba de ser conducido, espere varias horas para permitir que el motor se enfríe antes de comenzar este procedimiento.

3   Una vez que el motor se haya enfriado completamente, remueva la tapa del radiador. Coloque el control de la temperatura del calentador en la posición máxima de calentar.

4   Mueva un recipiente grande debajo del drenaje del radiador para colectar el anticongelante, entonces destornille el tapón del drenaje (un par de alicates pueda que se requiera para girarlo) **(vea ilustración)**.

5   Después que el anticongelante pare de fluir fuera del radiador, mueva el recipiente debajo del tapón de drenaje del bloque de los cilindros. Remueva el tapón(es) y permita que el anticongelante en el bloque se vacíe.

6   Mientras el anticongelante se drena, chequee la condición de las mangueras del radiador, mangueras del calentador y las grapas (refiérase a la Sección 11 si es necesario).

7   Reemplace cualquier manguera o grapas que estén dañadas.

8   Una vez que el sistema se haya vaciado completamente, enjuague el radiador con agua de una manguera de jardín hasta que el agua de desagüe que esté corriendo salga clara. La acción de cambiar el agua removerá los sedimentos del radiador pero no removerán el óxido y las escalas de las superficies

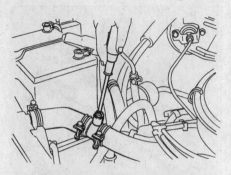

43.4 En los motores V6, abra la válvula de aire con un destornillador para facilitar drenar el anticongelante del radiador y el motor

de los tubos del radiador o del motor.

9   Estos sedimentos pueden removerse con un limpiador químico. Siga el procedimiento en el esquema en las instrucciones del fabricante. Si el radiador está corroído severamente, dañado o tiene fugas, se debe remover (Capítulo 3) y llévelo ha un taller de reparaciones para radiadores.

10   Remueva la manguera de rebose desde el depósito de recuperación para el anticongelante. Vacíe el depósito y enjuáguelo con agua limpia, entonces conecte la manguera nuevamente.

11   Reinstale y apriete el tapón de drenaje del radiador. Instale y apriete el tapón(es) de drenaje en el bloque.

12   Lentamente añada anticongelante nuevo (una mezcla de 50/50 de agua y anticongelante) al radiador hasta que esté lleno. Añada anticongelante al depósito de recuperación hasta la marca inferior.

13   Deje la tapa del radiador fuera y ponga el motor en marcha en una zona bien ventilada hasta que el termostato se abra (el anticongelante comenzará a fluir a través del radiador y la manguera superior del radiador se pondrá caliente).

14   Apague el motor y permítalo que se enfríe. Añada más refrigerante para traer la mezcla al nivel del labio hasta el cuello del llenador del radiador.

15   Apriete la manguera superior del radiador para expulsar el aire, entonces añada más anticongelante si es necesario. Reemplace la tapa del radiador.

16   Ponga el motor en marcha, permítalo que alcance su temperatura normal de operación y chequee por fugas.

44   Válvula PCV (ventilación positiva del cárter) - chequeo y reemplazo

Refiérase a la ilustración 44.1

1   En todos los modelos la válvula PCV se enrosca en el múltiple de admisión y es conectada por una manguera de caucho y un tubo de metal al cárter de cigüeñal **(vea ilustración)**.

44.1 La válvula de PCV (ventilación positiva del cárter) se enrosca en el múltiple de admisión (flecha) (se muestra un modelo 1982)

2   Cuando compre una válvula PCV de reemplazo, asegúrese que sea la correcta para su vehículo.
3   Remueva el purificador de aire.
4   Afloje la abrazadera que asegura la manguera a la válvula PCV y desconecte la manguera de la válvula.
5   Destornille la válvula del múltiple de admisión.
6   Compare la válvula vieja con la nueva y asegúrese que son la misma.
7   Enrosque la válvula nueva en el múltiple y conecte la manguera.
8   Más información relacionada con el sistema PCV puede ser encontrada en el Capítulo 6.

45 Bujías - reemplazo

Refiérase a las ilustraciones 45.2, 45.5a, 45.5b, 45.6 y 45.10
1   Reemplace las bujías con unas nuevas en los intervalos recomendados en el itinera-

rio de mantenimiento rutinario. Cuatro bujías son usadas en los motores 1980 de cuatro cilindros, mientras que los modelos más modernos de motores de cuatro cilindros requieren ocho bujías (dos por cilindro). Los motores V6, obviamente, tiene seis bujías.
2   En la mayoría de los casos, las herramientas necesarias para el reemplazo de las bujías incluyen un dado de bujía que se ajusta a una matraca (los dados para las bujías tienen almohadillas adentro para prevenir daño a los aisladores de porcelana en las bujías nuevas), varias extensiones y un medidor para chequear u ajustar el espacio libre **(vea ilustración)**. Una herramienta especial para remover el alambre de la bujía está disponible para separar las bujías de los fuelles de los alambres, pero no es absolutamente necesario. Una llave torsiométrica se debe usar para apretar las bujías nuevas.
3   El mejor enfoque cuando reemplace las bujías es de comprar las nuevas por adelantado, las ajusta al espacio libre apropiado y las reemplaza de una en una. Cuando compre las bujías nuevas, esté seguro de obtener el tipo correcto de bujía para su motor particular. Esta información se puede encontrar en la etiqueta de información para el control de las emisiones que está localizada debajo del capó y en el manual de fábrica para el propietario. Si diferencias existen entre las especificaciones para la bujía en la etiqueta de emisiones y en el manual del propietario, asuma que la etiqueta de emisiones está correcta.
4   Permita que el motor se enfríe completamente antes de procurar remover cualquiera de las bujías. Mientras está esperando que el motor se refresque, chequee las bujías nuevas por defectos y ajuste los espacios libres.
5   El espacio libre es chequeado metiendo el medidor del espesor apropiado entre los electrodos en el extremo de la bujía **(vea ilustración)**. El espacio libre entre los electrodos debe ser el mismo que el que se

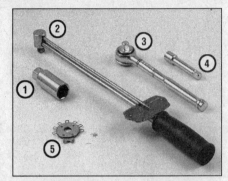

45.2 Herramientas requeridas para cambiar las bujías

1   **Dado para la bujía** - *Este dado tiene una esponja especial adentro para proteger la aislación de porcelana de la bujía.*
2   **Torquímetro** - *Aunque no es necesario, usando esta herramienta es la forma mas segura de apretar las bujías apropiadamente.*
3   **Matraca** - *Herramienta normal que se usa con el dado de bujía.*
4   **Extensión** - *Dependiendo del modelo y de los accesorios; pueda que usted necesite extensiones especiales y acoplaciones universales, para poder llegar a una o más de las bujías.*
5   **Calibrador de bujías** - *Este tipo de calibrador para chequear la luz de las bujías vienen en diferente tipos y estilos. Esté seguro que el calibrador tenga el diámetro que se necesita para su camión.*

especifica en la etiqueta de información de control de emisiones. El alambre debe deslizarse apenas entre los electrodos con una cantidad leve de resistencia. Si el espacio libre es incorrecto, use el ajustador en el cuerpo del medidor para doblar el electrodo curvo levemente hasta que el espacio libre apropiado sea obtenido **(vea ilustración)**. Si

45.5a Los fabricantes de bujía recomiendan usar un calibrador de alambre cuando esté chequeando la luz - Si el alambre no resbala entre los electrodos con una ligera fricción, se requiere ajuste

45.5b Para cambiar la luz de las bujías, vire el lado del electrodo lateral solamente, como se indica con las flechas y tenga mucho cuidado de no cuartear la porcelana que aísla el electrodo del centro

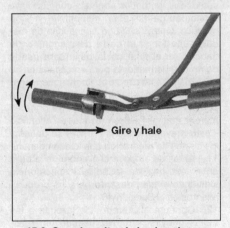
Gire y hale

45.6 Cuando quite el alambre de una bujía es importante de halar el cable de la bujía por la cubierta / bota (como se muestra en la figura del lado izquierdo) y no (como se muestra en el lado derecho) girando el cable un poco también ayuda

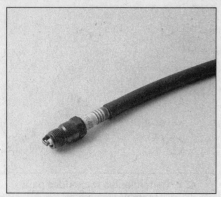

45.10 Una manguera de caucho de 3/16 de pulgadas de diámetro interno (ID) le ahorrará tiempo y prevendrá que la rosca se malogre

47.2 En los modelos más modernos, la tapa del distribuidor es afianzada en su posición por dos tornillos (flechas)

Insuficiente tensión del resorte

Punta del rotor corroída

Grietas

47.4 El rotor de la ignición se debe chequear por desgaste y corrosión como es indicado aquí (si está en duda acerca de su condición, compre uno nuevo)

el electrodo doblado no está exactamente en el electrodo central, dóblelo con el ajustador hasta que esté. Chequee por roturas en el aislador de porcelana (si se encontró alguna, la bujía no se debe usar).

6   Con el motor fresco, remueva el alambre de una bujía. Hale solamente en el fuelle a fines del alambre - no hale en el alambre. Una herramienta para remover el alambre de la bujía se debe usar si está disponible **(vea ilustración)**.

7   Si aire comprimido está disponible, úselo para soplar cualquier tierra o material extranjero hacia afuera del orificio de la bujía. Una bomba común de bicicleta trabajará también. La idea aquí es para eliminar la posibilidad de residuos que caigan en el cilindro según la bujía es removida.

8   Coloque el dado de la bujía en la bujía y remuévalo del motor girándolo en dirección a la izquierda.

9   Compare la bujía a esas mostradas en las fotos de color para obtener una indicación de la condición general del motor.

10   Enrosque una bujía nueva en el orificio hasta que usted no pueda girarla más con sus dedos, entonces apriétela con una llave torsiométrica (si está disponible) o una matraca. Quizás sea una buena idea de resbalar una longitud corta de manguera de caucho en el final de la bujía para usarla como una herramienta para enroscarla en su posición **(vea ilustración)**. La manguera agarrará la bujía lo suficiente para girarla, pero comenzará a resbalar si la bujía se pone en marcha con las roscas cruzadas en el orificio - esto prevendrá que las roscas se dañen y los costos de reparación que lo acompañan.

11   Antes de empujar el alambre de la bujía en el extremo de la bujía, inspecciónelo siguiendo el plan descrito para los procedimientos en la Sección 46.

12   Conecte el alambre de la bujía a las bujías nuevas, otra vez usando un movimiento de torcer en la tapa hasta que la bujía esté asentada.

13   Repita el procedimiento para el resto de las bujías, reemplazándolas de una en una para prevenir mezclar los alambres de las bujías.

46   Cables de las bujías - chequeo y reemplazo

1   Los alambres de las bujías deberían chequearse a los intervalos recomendados y cuando las bujías nuevas se instalen en el motor.

2   Los alambres deberían inspeccionarse de uno en uno para impedir que se mezcle el orden, que es imprescindible para la operación apropiada de motor.

3   Desconecte el cable de la bujía desde una bujía. Para hacer esto, agarre la cubierta de goma, tuerza ligeramente y hale el alambre para liberarlo. No hale el alambre en sí mismo, solamente sobre la cubierta de goma encima de la bujía **(vea ilustración 33.6)**.

4   Chequee adentro de la bota por corrosión, que se mirará como un polvo blanco. Empuje el alambre y la cubierta hacia adentro de la bujía. Debe de entrar ajustadamente en la bujía. Si no es, remueva el alambre y use un par de alicates para cuidadosamente apretar el conector de metal interior en la cubierta del alambre hasta que se ajuste firmemente sobre el extremo de la bujía.

5   Usando un trapo limpio, limpie la longitud entera del alambre para remover cualquier acumulación de suciedad y grasa. Una vez que el alambre esté limpio, chequee por agujeros, zonas quemadas, cuarteaduras y otros daños. No doble el alambre excesivamente o el conductor interior podría romperse.

6   Desconecte el alambre desde la tapa del distribuidor (y la bujía, si todavía está instalado). Nuevamente, hale solamente la cubierta de goma. Chequee por corrosión y un ajuste apretado en la misma manera como en el extremo de la bujía. Use un ohmímetro, chequee la resistencia del cable de la bujía y compárelo con las especificaciones. Si está encima de lo especificado, sustituya el alambre con uno nuevo (es una buena idea de reemplazar todos los alambres, aún cuando uno solamente está malo).

7   Chequee los alambres de las bujías restantes de uno en uno, asegurándose que ellos entran firmemente en el distribuidor y en

la bujía cuando el chequeo se haya acabado.

8   Si se necesitan alambres de bujías nuevos, compre un juego nuevo para su modelo específico de motor. Los juegos de alambre son disponibles ya cortados, con las cubiertas de goma ya montadas. Remueva y reemplace los alambres de uno en uno para evitar mezclarlos - en el orden de encendido. La ruta de los alambres es sumamente importante, así que esté seguro de notar exactamente como cada alambre se sitúa antes de removerlo.

47   Rotor y tapa del distribuidor - chequeo y reemplazo

Refiérase a las ilustraciones 47.2, 47.4, 47.5 y 47.8

Nota: *Es la práctica común de instalar un rotor nuevo y tapa de distribuidor cuando los alambres nuevos de las bujías son instalados.*

1   Aunque el distribuidor sin puntos usado en estos vehículos requieren mucho menos mantenimiento que un distribuidor convencional, las inspecciones periódicas se deben realizar en los intervalos especificados en el

47.5 Los rotores de los distribuidores mas modernos son retenidos por un perno (flecha) - ¡no trate de hacerle palanca al rotor hasta que el perno se haya aflojado!

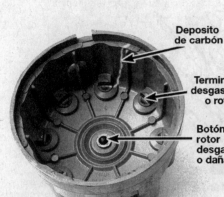

Deposito
de carbón

Terminales
desgastadas
o rotas

Botón del
rotor
desgastado
o dañado

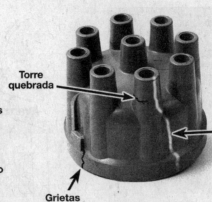

Torre
quebrada

47.8 Aquí se muestra algunos de los defectos comunes que se debe de buscar cuando esté inspeccionando la tapa del distribuidor (si está en duda acerca de su condición, instale una nueva)

Deposito
de carbón

Grietas

itinerario de mantenimiento rutinario y cuando cualquier trabajo sea realizado en el distribuidor.

2   Desconecte el alambre(s) de la bobina de la ignición, entonces desabroche los clips de resorte o afloje los tornillos que retienen la tapa al albergue del distribuidor **(vea ilustración)**. Separe la tapa del distribuidor y los alambres.

3   Coloque la tapa, con los alambres de la bujía y la bobina todavía conectada, fuera del camino. Use una longitud de alambre o lazo para asegurarlo, si es necesario.

4   El rotor es ahora visible en el final del eje del distribuidor. Chequee cuidadosamente por roturas y rastro de carbón. Asegúrese de que la tensión central de la terminal del resorte es adecuada (no todos los modelos), busque por corrosión y desgaste en la punta del rotor **(vea ilustración)**. Si está dudoso acerca de su condición, reemplácela con una nueva.

5   Si reemplazo es requerido, separe el rotor del eje e instale uno nuevo. En los modelos 1980, el rotor se puede remover simplemente fuera del eje. En los modelos más modernos, el rotor es retenido en el eje por un solo tornillo **(vea ilustración)**.

6   Chequee las conexiones del alambre en la unidad del ICM (módulo para el control de la ignición) (en los modelos 1980 esta es la unidad en el exterior del cuerpo del distribuidor, con un conector del alambrado conectado a el; en los modelos 1981 y más modernos, está dentro del distribuidor, con dos o tres alambres que van directamente a el). Asegúrese de que estén limpios y apretados. Chequee también los alambres para asegurarse que ellos no estén agrietados ni rotos.

7   Mientras la tapa del distribuidor está afuera, chequee el espacio libre del aire como está descrito en el Capítulo 5.

8   Chequee la tapa del distribuidor por rastro de carbón, roturas y otros daños. Examine de cerca las terminales en el interior de la tapa por corrosión y daños excesivos **(vea ilustración)**. Depósitos leves son normales. Otra vez, si está dudoso acerca de la condición de la tapa, reemplácela con una nueva.

9   Cuando reemplace la tapa, transfiera simplemente los alambres de las bujías y la bobina, de uno en uno, de la tapa vieja a la

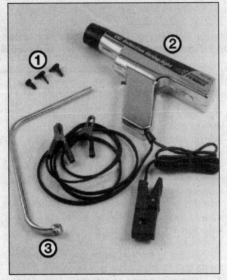

tapa nueva. ¡Tenga mucho cuidado de no mezclar los alambres!

10   Acople nuevamente la tapa al distribuidor, entonces apriete los tornillos o posicióne los clips de resorte para retenerlos en su posición.

48   Tiempo del encendido - chequeo y ajuste

Refiérase a las ilustraciones 48.1, 48.2 48.4 y 48.11

1   El ajuste apropiado del encendido para su vehículo está imprimido en la etiqueta VECI (etiqueta de información para el control de las emisiones del vehículo) ubicada en el lado de abajo del capó. Algunas herramientas especiales se requerirán para este procedimiento **(vea ilustración)**.

2   Ubique el plato de la tapa del tiempo en el frente del motor, cerca de la polea en el cigüeñal **(vea ilustración)**. La marca 0 es el TDC (punto muerto superior). Para ubicar la marcar en la polea que debe usarse para que la sincronización sea correcta, cuente desde la marca 0 el número de grados BTDC (antes del punto muerto superior) apuntado en la etiqueta VECI (etiqueta de información para el control de las emisiones del vehículo).

48.1 Herramientas necesarias para chequear y ajustar el tiempo

1   **Tapones de vacío** - *Algunas mangueras de vacío se tienen que desconectar algunas veces y ser bloqueadas, hay tapones moldeados en diferente tamaños disponibles para este tipo de trabajo.*

2   **Lámpara de tiempo inductible** - *Emite una luz clara, brillante y concentrada que se proporciona cuando la bujía numero uno dispara, conecte los alambres de acuerdo con las instrucciones suministradas con la luz.*

3   **Herramienta para el distribuidor** - *En algunos modelos, el tornillo que aguanta el distribuidor es difícil de alcanzar y girar con una herramienta o dado convencional. Una herramienta especial como esta se debe de usar.*

3   Ubique la marca de sincronización en la polea y márquela con un poco de pintura o tiza para que sea visible debajo de la luz estroboscópica. Para ubicar la marca puede que sea necesario de tener un asistente temporalmente girando la ignición de apagado a encendido para girar el cigüeñal. **Peligro:** *¡Esté libre de todos los componentes móviles del motor si el motor se gira de esta manera!*

48.2 Cuando esté ajustando la regulación del tiempo de la ignición, la mella en la polea del cigüeñal (marcado con pintura blanca) debe alinear con la mella o el punto especificado en el plato del tiempo (motores de cuatro cilindros)

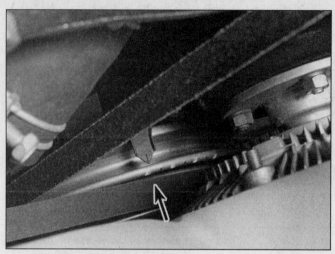

48.4 En el motor V6, las marcas para la regulación del tiempo están en el amortiguador de vibración y un indicador es conectado al motor

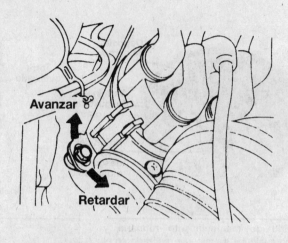

48.11 La regulación del tiempo de la ignición es ajustado girando el distribuidor levemente según sea necesario

4   Antes de intentar de chequear/ajustar la sincronización, asegúrese que la luz está correcta (vea Capítulo 5) **(vea ilustración)**.

5   Conecte un tacómetro según las instrucciones del fabricante y asegúrese que la marcha mínima está correcta. Ajústela si es necesario como se describió en la Sección 17.

6   Permita que el motor alcance su temperatura normal de operación. Esté seguro de que el aire acondicionado, si está equipado, esté apagado. En algunos modelos, como está notado en la etiqueta VECI (etiqueta de información para el control de las emisiones del vehículo), usted debe desconectar la manguera para la regulación del avance de vacío del distribuidor y bloquéela o conecte un alambre puente entre las terminales TE1 y E1 en el conector de chequeo.

7   Con el interruptor del encendido apagado, conecte el alambre de captación de la lámpara de tiempo al alambre en la bujía número. En los motores de cuatro cilindro, es el del frente. En los motores V6 es la primera bujía en el lado de la derecha cuando se mira desde el asiento del conductor. Use un alambre conductor entre los alambres y la bujía o un captador de tipo inductivo. No perfore el alambre o intente de introducir un alambre entre el alambre de la bujía y el aislador de la bujía. Conecte los alambres de energía eléctrica para la lámpara del tiempo según las instrucciones del fabricante.

8   Asegúrese que el cable para la lámpara del tiempo está libre de todos los componentes móviles del motor, entonces ponga el motor en marcha. Levante las revoluciones del motor dos o tres de veces, entonces permítalo que se mantenga a marcha mínima por un minuto.

9   Apunte la lámpara de tiempo a las marcas del tiempo, nuevamente teniendo cuidado de no entrar en contacto con piezas que se estén moviendo. Las marcas que usted marcó deberían aparecer estacionarias. Si las marcas están alineadas, la sincronización está correcta. Si las marcas no están alineadas, apague el motor.

10   Afloje la contratuerca del distribuidor hasta que el distribuidor pueda girarse.

11   Ponga el motor en marcha y lentamente gire el distribuidor hasta que las marcas del tiempo se alínee **(vea ilustración)**.

12   Apague el motor y apriete la contratuerca del distribuidor, teniendo cuidado de no mover el distribuidor.

13   Ponga nuevamente el motor en marcha y chequee nuevamente la sincronización para asegurarse que las marcas todavía están alineadas.

14   Desconecte la lámpara del tiempo.

15   Levante las revoluciones del motor dos o tres de veces, entonces permítalo correr a marcha mínima. Chequee nuevamente la marcha mínima con el tacómetro. Si ha cambiado desde el punto correcto ajústela.

16   Conduzca el vehículo y escuche por ruidos "golpeteo." Ellos serán perceptibles cuando el motor esté caliente y debajo de carga (ascendiendo una colina, acelerando desde un punto que esté parado). Si usted oye cascabeleo del motor, el tiempo del encendido está demasiado avanzado (antes del punto muerto superior). Reconecte la lámpara del tiempo y gire el distribuidor para mover la marca 1 grado o 2 grados en la dirección de retardo (a la derecha). Pruebe el vehículo nuevamente en la carretera para chequearlo por operación apropiada.

17   Para mantener el "golpeteo" a un mínimo y aún todavía permitirle usar el vehículo a su tiempo de sincronización especificado, use gasolina con el mismo octano todo el tiempo. Cambiando de marca de combustible, los niveles de octano pueden bajar el rendimiento, la economía y posiblemente dañar el motor.

49   Sensor de oxígeno - reemplazo

1   El sensor de oxígeno (para los gases del escape), usados en los modelos 1984 y mas modernos, deben ser remplazados a los intervalos especificados

2   El sensor está instalado enroscado en el múltiple de escape y puede ser identificado por los alambres conectados a el. El reemplazo consiste de desconectar el arnés de alambre y remover desenroscar el sensor del múltiple de escape. Apriete el sensor nuevo a la torsión especificada, entonces reconecte el arnés del alambre.

Capítulo 2 Parte A
Motores de cuatro cilindros

Contenidos

Especificaciones

Todos los motores

Números de los cilindros (del frente hacia atrás)	1-2-3-4
Orden de encendido	1-3-4-2
Desplazamiento	
L20B (1980)	1952 cc
Z20 (1984 y 1985)	1952 cc
Z22 (1981 al 1983)	2187 cc
Z24 (1984 y 1985)	2389 cc
Z24i (1986 en)	2389 cc
KA24E	2389 cc
Franqueo de las válvulas	Vea Capítulo 1

Motor L20B (1980)

Árbol de levas

Diámetro del muñón	1.8877 a 1.8883 pulgada (47.949 a 47.962 mm)
Diámetro interior del cojinete...	1.8898 a 1.8904 pulgada (48.000 a 48.016 mm)
Juego libre del cojinete para el aceite	0.0015 a 0.0026 pulgada (0.038 a 0.067 mm)
Límite de desviación	0.002 pulgada (0.05 mm)
Juego final	0.008 pulgada (0.2 mm)

Altura del lóbulo

Admisión	1.5866 a 1.5886 pulgadas (40.30 a 40.35 mm)
Escape	1.5866 a 1.5886 pulgadas (40.30 a 40.35 mm)

Bomba de aceite

Espacio libre de la punta del rotor

Estándar	Menos de 0.0047 pulgada (0.12 mm)
Límite..	0.0079 pulgada (0.20 mm)

Espacio libre exterior del rotor al albergue

Estándar	0.0059 a 0.0083 pulgada (0.15 a 0.21 mm)
Límite..	0.0197 pulgada (0.5 mm)
Juego final del rotor	Menos de 0.0024 pulgada (0.06 mm)
Espacio libre del albergue a la regla.......................................	Menos de 0.0012 pulgada (0.03 mm)

Especificaciones técnicas

	Pies-libras
Pernos de la cabeza de los cilindros.......................................	51 a 61
Pernos de la cabeza de los cilindros a la tapa delantera	3 a 6
Pernos de la tapa delantera al bloque	
6 mm	3 a 7
8 mm	7 a 12
Guía de la cadena y pernos del tensionador	4.3 a 7.2
Perno de la polea del cigüeñal	87 a 116
Pernos/tuercas del múltiple..	9 a 12
Perno para el engrane del árbol de levas	87 a 116
Pernos para el plato de impulso del árbol de levas..................	4.3 a 7.2
Pernos de la tapa de los balancines..	7 a 12
Pernos para el colador de aceite	7 a 12
Pernos de afianzamiento para la bomba de aceite	8 a 11
Pernos de la cacerola de aceite	4.3 a 7.2
Pernos del volante/plato flexible al cigüeñal	101 a 116

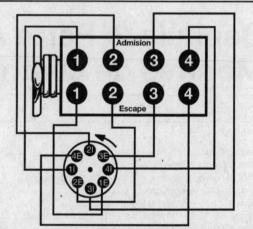

Orden del alambrado de las bujías para el motor Z24i de cuatro cilindros

Motor NAPS-Z (1981 en adelante)

Árbol de levas

Diámetro del muñón	1.2967 a 1.2974 pulgadas (32.935 a 32.955 mm)
Juego final	0.008 pulgada (0.2 mm)
Altura del lóbulo del árbol de levas	1.5148 a 1.5168 pulgadas (38.477 a 38.527 mm)
Límite de desgaste del lóbulo de la leva	0.0098 pulgada (0.25 mm)
Ovalación del árbol de levas (una mitad de la indicación	
total del indicador @ muñón central).....................................	0.008 pulgada (0.2 mm)
Diámetro interior del cojinete...	1.2992 a 1.3002 pulgadas (33.000 a 33.025 mm)
Juego libre del cojinete para el aceite	0.0018 a 0.0035 pulgada (0.045 a 0.090 mm)

Bomba de aceite

Espacio libre de la punta del rotor

Estándar	Menos de 0.0047 pulgada (0.12 mm)
Límite..	0.0079 pulgada (0.20 mm)

Espacio libre exterior del rotor al albergue

Estándar	0.0059 a 0.0083 pulgada (0.15 a 0.21 mm)
Límite..	0.0197 pulgada (0.50 mm)
Juego final del rotor	Menos de 0.0024 pulgada (0.06 mm)
Espacio libre del albergue a la regla.......................................	Menos de 0.0012 pulgada (0.03 mm)

Especificaciones técnicas

	Pies-libras
Perno para el engrane del árbol de levas	87 a 116 12 a 16
Guía de la cadena y pernos del tensionador	4.5 a 7
Perno de la polea del cigüeñal	87 a 116 12 a 16

Pernos de la cabeza de los cilindros

Motor Z22

1981 y 1982	51 a 58
1983	58 a 65

Pernos de la cabeza de los cilindros
   Motores Z20 y Z24
      Paso 1 22
      Paso 2 58
      Paso 3 .... Afloje todos los pernos
      Paso 4 22
      Paso 5 58
Pernos/tuercas del múltiple de escape .... 12 a 15
Pernos del volante/plato flexible al cigüeñal .... 101 a 116
Pernos de la tapa de los balancines............................ 0.7 a 2.2
Pernos de la tapa delantera al bloque
   6 mm .... 3 a 7
   8 mm .... 7 a 12
Pernos/tuerca del múltiple de admisión .... 12 a 15
Pernos de la cacerola de aceite .... 3.5 a 5
Pernos de afianzamiento para la bomba de aceite .... 8 a 11
Pernos de afianzamiento para la tapa de los balancines ...... 11 a 18

Todos los motores de cuatro cilindros excepto las series Z

Localidad de los cilindros y rotación del distribuidor

Motor KA24E (1990 en adelante)

Árbol de levas

Diámetro del muñón .... 1.2967 a 1.2974 pulgadas (32.935 a 32.955 mm)
Juego final .... 0.008 pulgada (0.2 mm)
Altura del lóbulo del árbol de levas .... 1.7653 a 1.7728 pulgadas (44.839 a 45.029 mm)
Límite de desgaste del lóbulo de la leva .... 0.0098 pulgada (0.25 mm)
Ovalación del árbol de levas (una mitad de la indicación
   total del indicador @ muñón central)............................ 0.0008 pulgada (0.02 mm)
Diámetro interior del cojinete... 1.2992 a 1.3002 pulgadas (33.000 a 33.025 mm)
Juego libre del cojinete para el aceite .... 0.0018 a 0.0035 pulgada (0.045 a 0.090 mm)

Bomba de aceite

Espacio libre de la punta del rotor
   Estándar .... Menos de 0.0047 pulgada (0.12 mm)
   Límite .... 0.0079 pulgada (0.20 mm)
Espacio libre exterior del rotor al albergue
   Estándar .... 0.0059 a 0.0083 pulgada (0.15 a 0.21 mm)
   Límite .... 0.0197 pulgada (0.50 mm)
Juego final del rotor.. Menos de 0.0024 pulgada (0.06 mm)
Espacio libre del albergue a la regla .... Menos de 0.0012 pulgada (0.03 mm)

Especificaciones técnicas

Pies-libras

Perno para el engrane del árbol de levas .... 87 a 116
Guía de la cadena y pernos del tensionador................... 5.1 a 9.0
Perno de la polea del cigüeñal .... 87 a 116
Pernos de la cabeza de los cilindros
   Paso 1 22
   Paso 2 58
   Paso 3 .... Afloje todos los pernos completamente
   Paso 4 22
   Paso 5 .... 54 a 61
Pernos/tuercas del múltiple de escape .... 12 a 15
Pernos del volante al cigüeñal .... 105 a 112
Pernos del plato flexible al cigüeñal .... 69 a 76
Pernos/tuercas de múltiple de admisión .... 12 a 15
Pernos de la cacerola de aceite .... 3.5 a 5.0
Pernos de afianzamiento para la bomba de aceite .... 8 a 11
Pernos de la tapa de los balancines.............................. 2.9 a 5.8
Pernos de afianzamiento para la tapa de los balancines ...... 27 a 30

1   Información general

Esta Parte del Capítulo 2 está dedicada a los procedimientos de reparación para los motores de cuatro cilindros adentro del vehículo. Toda la información con respecto a remover e instalar el motor y reconstrucción completa del bloque del motor y la cabeza de los cilindros puede ser encontrada en la Parte C de este Capítulo.

Los siguientes procedimientos de reparaciones están basados en la suposición que el motor está instalado en el vehículo. Si el motor ha sido removido del vehículo e instalado en un soporte, muchos de los pasos descritos en esta parte del Capítulo 2 no aplicarán.

Las especificaciones incluidas en esta parte del Capítulo 2 se aplican solamente a los procedimientos contenidos en esta Parte. La Parte C del Capítulo 2 contiene las especificaciones necesarias para reconstruir la cabeza de los cilindros y el bloque del motor.

En 1980, el primer año de los vehículos de Serie 720, el vehículo vino equipado con el motor L20B, remanente de la Serie 620. En 1981 el motor NAPS-Z fue introducido a la línea de los vehículos. Ambos tipos son motores en línea de cuatro cilindros OHC (árbol de levas sobre la cabeza).

El bloque del motor de hierro fundido contiene cuatro cilindros y actúa como un apoyo rígido para los cinco cojinetes principales del cigüeñal. Los cilindros están rodeados por camisas de agua para disipar el calor y controlar la temperatura de operación normal.

La cabeza de los cilindros es de aluminio e incorpora las cámara de combustión de tipo cuña. En los motores NAPS-Z, dos bujías son usadas por cada cilindro para quemar la mezcla de aire/combustible con mayor eficiencia.

Dos válvulas por cilindro son instaladas en un ángulo leve en la cabeza de los cilindros y son accionadas por un balancín en el árbol de levas que está en contacto directo. Doble resortes son instalados en cada válvula.

El árbol de levas es conducido por una cadena de rodillo en el frente del cigüeñal. La tensión de la cadena es controlada por un tensionador, que es operado por aceite y presión de resorte. El tensionador de tipo zapato de caucho controla la vibración y la tensión de la cadena.

Los pistones son una fundición especial de aluminio con puntales para controlar la expansión térmica. Hay dos anillos de compresión y un anillo de control de aceite. El pasador del pistón es un eje con orificio de acero que está flotando completamente en el pistón y está prensado en la biela. Los pistones son conectados al cigüeñal por bielas de acero forjado.

El distribuidor, que es instalado en el lado izquierdo del bloque del motor, es conducido por un engrane helicoidal instalado en

el frente del cigüeñal. La bomba de aceite, que está instalada debajo en el lado derecho del bloque está en una línea central común con el distribuidor y es conducida por el mismo engrane helicoidal.

El cigüeñal, que es hecho de acero forjado especial, tiene los pasajes internos de aceite para proporcionar la lubricación a los cojinetes principales y de biela. El aceite es entregado, vía el filtro y la válvula de liberación de presión, a la galería principal de aceite que pasa a través de los muñones de los cojinete principales y entonces a los muñones de los cojinetes de las bielas a través de orificios en el cigüeñal. El tiro del aceite fuera de los extremos inferiores de la biela, también como un orificio de esprea taladró en cada biela en el extremo inferior, proporciona la lubricación para los pistones y los extremos superiores de las bielas. Por encima del motor, galerías taladradas en el árbol de levas proporcionan aceite para los cinco cojinetes, mientras que un tubo que corre la longitud del árbol de levas, entrega aceite a cada superficie de la almohadilla de la leva, para proporcionar la lubricación para el balancín y el pivote.

2   Reparaciones posibles con el motor en el vehículo

Muchas operaciones importantes de reparaciones pueden hacerse sin remover el motor del vehículo.

Limpie el compartimiento del motor y el exterior del motor con algún tipo de limpiador a presión antes de hacer cualquier trabajo. Hará el trabajo más fácil y le ayuda a mantener la suciedad fuera de las áreas internas del motor.

Remueva el capó para tener mejor acceso al motor según se desempeñan las reparaciones (refiérase al Capítulo 12 si es necesario).

Si vacío, escape, lubricante o fugas de anticongelantes se desarrollan, indicando una necesidad del reemplazo de sello(s) o junta(s), las reparaciones pueden generalmente ser hechas con el motor en el vehículo. La junta del cárter de aceite, junta de la culata (cabeza), juntas del múltiple de escape y de admisión, juntas de la tapa de la cadena de distribución y los sellos para retener el aceite del cigüeñal son accesibles con el motor en su lugar.

Los componentes exteriores del motor, tal como la bomba de agua, el motor de arranque, el alternador, el distribuidor y los componentes del sistema de combustible, así como también los múltiples de admisión y escape, pueden removerse para ser reparados con el motor en su lugar.

Debido a que la cabeza de los cilindros pueden removerse sin remover el motor, el servicio de los componente de las válvulas y el árbol de levas pueden también ser hechos con el motor en el vehículo.

El reemplazo, reparaciones o chequeo

3.5a El pistón número uno está en el TDC (punto muerto superior) en la carrera de compresión cuando la mella en la polea del cigüeñal está alineada con el 0 en el plato de tiempo y el rotor está apuntando a la terminal de la bujía número uno en la tapa del distribuidor

de la cadena de distribución, los engranajes y la bomba de aceite son todos posibles con el motor en su lugar.

En casos extremos ocasionado por una falta de equipo, reparaciones o reemplazos necesarios de anillos de los pistones, los pistones y las bielas son posibles con el motor en el vehículo. Sin embargo, esta práctica no es recomendada a causa de la preparación y la limpieza que debe hacerse a los componentes involucrados.

3   TDC (punto muerto superior) - para la ubicación del pistón número uno

Refiérase a las ilustraciones 3.4, 3.5 y 3.6

1   TDC es el punto más alto en el cilindro que cada pistón alcanza cuando viaja hacia arriba y hacia abajo cuando el cigüeñal gira. Cada pistón alcanza el TDC en la carrera de compresión y nuevamente en la carrera de escape, pero el TDC generalmente se refiere al pistón cuando está en la carrera de compresión. Las marcas de distribución en la polea instaladas en el frente del cigüeñal es en referencia al pistón número uno en TDC en la carrera de compresión.

2   Colocando el pistón(es) a TDC es una parte imprescindible de muchos procedimientos tales como remover el árbol de levas, la cadena de distribución, los engranajes y el distribuidor.

3   A fin de traer cualquier pistón al TDC, el cigüeñal debe girarse usando uno de los métodos indicados más adelante. Cuando mire en el frente del motor, la rotación normal del cigüeñal es al favor de las saetas del reloj.

Peligro: *Antes de comenzar este procedimiento, esté seguro de colocar la transmisión en la guía de Neutro. También, remueva el cable desde el terminal de la bobina de la tapa del distribuidor y póngalo en el bloque* del motor a tierra.

a) El método preferido es de girar el cigüeñal con un dado grande y una matraca instalada en el perno de la polea en el frente del cigüeñal.

b) Un interruptor remoto para el motor de arranque, que puede ahorrar algo de tiempo, también se puede usar. Instale el interruptor a las terminales del solenoide. Una vez que el pistón esté cerca del TDC, use un dado y una matraca grande como está descrito en el párrafo anterior.

c) Si un asistente está disponible para girar el interruptor del encendido a la posición de arranque, usted puede llevar el pistón número uno cerca del TDC sin un interruptor remoto para el motor de arranque. Use un dado y una matraca como está descrito en el párrafo uno para completar el procedimiento.

4   Anote la posición de la terminal para el cable de la bujía número uno en la tapa del distribuidor. Use una pluma de fieltro o tiza para hacer una marca en el distribuidor directamente debajo de la terminal (vea ilustración). Remueva la tapa desde el distribuidor y colóquela a un lado.

5   Gire el cigüeñal (vea Párrafo 3 arriba) hasta que la ranura en la polea del cigüeñal se alinee con el 0 en la tapa de la cadena de distribución (ubicada al frente del motor) (vea ilustración).

6   Mire al rotor del distribuidor - debe de indicar directamente a la marca que usted hizo en el cuerpo del distribuidor (vea ilustración). Si el rotor indica a la terminal para la bujía número cuatro, el pistón número uno está a TDC en la carrera de escape.

7   Para llevar el pistón a TDC en la carrera de compresión, gire el cigüeñal una vuelta completa (360 grados) al favor de las saetas del reloj. El rotor ahora debería indicar a la marca en el distribuidor. Cuando el rotor indica al número uno en la terminal del alambre de la bujía en la tapa del distribuidor y las marcas del encendido se alineen, el pistón uno está a TDC en la carrera de compresión.

8   Después de que el pistón número uno se haya colocado a TDC en la carrera de compresión, el TDC para cualquiera de los pistones restantes pueden ser ubicados girando el cigüeñal 180 grados y siguiendo el orden del encendido.

4   Tapa de los balancines - remover e instalar

Refiérase a las ilustraciones 4.4 y 4.9

1   Remueva el purificador de aire (Capítulo 4).

2   Remueva los alambres de las bujías de todas las bujías y remueva los soportes de alambre de la tapa de los balancines. No desconecte los alambres de los soportes.

3   En los modelos 1981 y más modernos, desconecte la manguera de vacío del amplificador para los frenos y póngala fuera del camino.

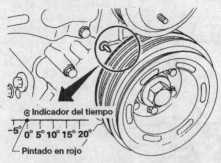

3.5b Marca para la regulación del tiempo en los motor KA24E

4   Remueva los pernos de la tapa de los balancines (vea ilustración).

5   Remueva la tapa de los balancines. Caución: Si la tapa está pegada a la cabeza, golpee el extremo con un bloque de madera y un martillo para tratar de aflojarla. Si esto no trabaja, pruebe resbalar un cuchillo flexible para masilla entre la cabeza y la tapa para romper el sello de la junta. No le haga palanca entre la cabeza y la tapa con una barra para removerla o daño a la superficie puede ocurrir, ocasionando fugas de aceite en el futuro.

6   Las superficies de acoplamiento de la cabeza y la tapa de los balancines debe estar perfectamente limpia cuando la tapa sea instalada. Use un raspador de junta para remover todos los rasgos de sellador y material de junta vieja, después limpie las superficies de acoplamiento con rebajador de pintura o acetona. Si hay sellador o aceite en las superficies de acoplamiento cuando la tapa sea instalada, fugas de aceite se pueden desarrollar.

7   Aplique una línea continua de sellador a la tapa y a la superficie de acoplamiento de la cabeza. Esté seguro de aplicarla en el interior de los orificios para los pernos.

8   Coloque la junta nueva en posición encima de la cabeza de los cilindros, entonces coloque la tapa de los balancines en la junta. Mientras que el sellador está todavía mojado, instale los pernos y apriételo al par de torsión especificado.

9   Complete la instalación invirtiendo el procedimiento de remover (vea ilustración).

5   Ensamblaje de los balancines (modelos 1980) - remover e instalar

Refiérase a las ilustraciones 5.3, 5.4a y 5.4b

1   Remueva la tapa de los balancines como está descrito en la Sección 4.

2   El cigüeñal se debe girar hasta que el lóbulo de la leva haga contacto con el balancín que va a ser removido esté apuntando directamente hacia encima. Esto puede ser hecho operando el motor de arranque en pequeños intervalos o girando el perno grande en el frente del cigüeñal con un dado conectado a una barra ruptora.

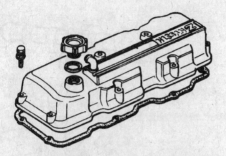

4.4 Tapa para los balancines y los componentes relacionados - vista esquemática

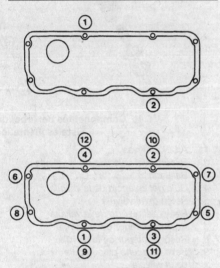

4.9 En los motores KA24E, apriete los pernos 1 y 2 a 2.2 pies-libras como está mostrado en el Paso 1, entonces apriete TODOS los otros pernos de 5.1 a 7.2 pies-libras en el orden mostrado en el Paso 2

3   Remueva el resorte de los balancines de la válvula (vea ilustración).

4   Afloje la contratuerca del pivote del balancín (vea ilustración). Después use un destornillador para presionar el resorte de las válvulas para que el balancín pueda ser

5.3 Removiendo los resorte de los balancines (motor L20B)

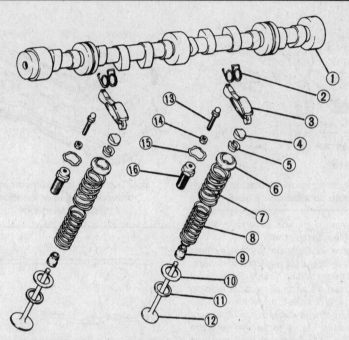

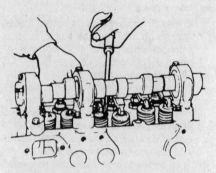

5.4a Componentes del árbol de levas y el tren de las válvulas - vista esquemática del motor (L20B)

1	Árbol de levas
2	Resorte del balancín de la válvula
3	Balancín
4	Guía del balancín de la válvula
5	Retén de la válvula
6	Retén del resorte de la válvula
7	Resorte exterior de la válvula
8	Resorte interior de la válvula
9	Sello de aceite para la guía de la válvula
10	Asiento exterior del resorte de la válvula
11	Asiento interior del resorte de la válvula
12	Válvula
13	Pivote del balancín de la válvula
14	Contratuerca del pivote del balancín
15	Retenedor del resorte del balancín
16	Buje pivote del balancín

5.4b Para remover los balancines en los modelos 1980 con motor (L20B), un destornillador puesto en posición como se muestra puede ser usado como es mostrado aquí para presionar el resorte de cada una de las válvulas

levantado **(vea ilustración)**. **Caución:** *No le haga palanca con el destornillador contra las superficies rectificadas de los lóbulos de la leva.*

5   Si más de un balancín va a ser removido, esté seguro de mantenerlos en orden para que ellos puedan ser reinstalados en sus posiciones originales en la cabeza de los cilindros.

6   Las guías de los balancines de las válvulas pueden ser levantadas de las válvulas, pero esté seguro de mantenerlas en orden.

7   Inspeccione las superficies de contacto de los balancines, las guías de los balancines, los pivotes de los balancines por daño y desgaste excesivo. Reemplace según sea necesario.

8   Para reemplazar el pivote de los balancines, afloje la contratuerca del pivote y destornille el pivote del buje **(vea ilustración 5.4a)**. No remueva la cabeza de los cilindros del buje pivote.

9   Antes de la instalación, aplique una cantidad pequeña de grasa a las superficies de contacto de los balancines, las guías de los balancines y los pivotes de los balancines.

10   La instalación se hace en el orden inverso al procedimiento de desensamble. Ajuste el franqueo de las válvulas primero según las especificaciones Frías y entonces las especificaciones Calientes como está detallado en el Capítulo 1.

6   Ensamblaje de los balancines de las válvulas (modelos 1981 y más modernos) - remover e instalar

1   Remueva la tapa de los balancines como está descrito en la Sección 4.

2   El ensamblaje de los balancines de las válvulas es sostenido en la cabeza de los cilindros por diez pernos de retención. Los pernos se deben aflojar 1/4 de vuelta a la vez, trabajando hacia el centro de ambas puntas. Afloje los pernos hasta que ellos estén libres de la cabeza de los cilindros, pero no los remueva del ensamblaje del balancín de las válvulas.

3   Una vez que todos los pernos de retención estén flojos, levante el ensamblaje de los balancines de las válvulas de la cabeza de los cilindros.

4   Si el ensamblaje de los balancines de las válvulas se debe remover para inspeccionar o reemplazar las partes, refiérase a la Sección 7. Si el ensamblaje de los balancines de las válvulas no se va a desarmar, no remueva los cuatro pernos en el extremo del ensamblaje (se desarmará si los pernos son removidos).

5   Cuando esté instalando el ensamblaje de los balancines de la válvula, primero apriete los pernos con los dedos, trabajando

en ambos extremos. Continúe apretándolos 1/4 de vuelta a la vez hasta que todos los pernos estén apretados al par de torsión especificado.

7   Ensamblaje de los balancines de las válvulas (modelos 1981 y más modernos) - desarmar y ensamblar

Refiérase a las ilustraciones 7.5a, 7.5b, 7.5c, 7.5d y 7.6

1   Si no hecho previamente, remueva todos los pernos del ensamblaje de los balancines de las válvulas menos los dos en el extremo final.

2   Mientras manteniendo el ensamblaje junto, remueva cuidadosamente los dos pernos de una punta del ensamblaje y permita que los resortes se expandan.

3   Remueva los componentes de los ejes, notando el orden de instalación. No mezcle los balancines; ellos deben estar instalados en sus lugares originales.

4   Si los ejes de ensamblaje de los balancines de las válvulas están excesivamente desgastado, dañados o rayados, ellos deben ser reemplazados con unos nuevos.

5   Para volver a instalar el ensamblaje de los balancines, detenga uno de los soportes finales y meta ambos ejes en el. Alinee los orificios para los pernos e inserción los dos pernos extremos. El eje de admisión tiene una ranura en la superficie delantera para identificarlo, mientras que el eje de escape no tiene marca de identificación. Ambos ejes de los balancines se deben armar para que las dos marcas del punzón en el frente queden hacia encima **(vea ilustraciones)**. También, esté seguro que los soportes están en sus lugares originales. Para asegurar esto, marcas de identificación son proporcionadas en las cabezas de los cilindros, también como en cada soporte **(vea ilustraciones)**.

6   Instale los componentes de los ensamblajes de los balancines de las válvulas en los ejes en el orden correcto, comprima los resortes lo necesario hasta que el extremo

del soporte pueda ser instalado con los dos pernos de afianzamiento. Por conveniencia el resto de los pernos pueden también ser instalados **(vea ilustración)**.

8 Árbol de levas - remover e instalar

Modelos 1980 con motor (L20B)

Refiérase a las ilustraciones 8.4, 8.6 y 8.13

1 Remueva la tapa de los balancines como está descrito en la Sección 4.

2 Remueva los balancines como está descrito en la Sección 5.

3 Traiga el pistón número uno al TDC (punto muerto superior) refiriéndose a la Sección 3, si es necesario.

4 ¡Si usted intenta remover el árbol de levas solamente, sin remover la cabeza de los cilindros, no altere la posición del engrane de tiempo en relación a la cadena del tiempo! Marque ambas, las cadena de tiempo y el engrane del árbol de levas para preservar la posición instalada original de los dos **(vea ilustración)**. La cadena debe ser reinstalada en el engrane del árbol de levas en exacta la misma relación. Si una reconstrucción completa mayor se está haciendo, entonces la relación del engrane/cadena no se tiene que mantener.

5 Antes de remover el engrane del árbol de levas, corte un pedazo de madera de 10 pulgadas de largo, 3/4 pulgada de grueso, 1-1/2 pulgadas de ancho y aproximadamente 1 pulgada de ancho en el fondo.

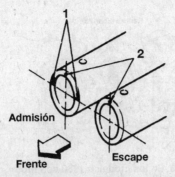

7.5a Cuando esté instalado, el eje de los balancines las ranuras deben estar en el lado de admisión y las marcas del punzón en ambos ejes deben estar en la posición 12 del reloj (encima) (se muestra un motor NAPS-Z)

1 Ranuras
2 Marcas hechas con el punzón

6 Ahora remueva el perno para el engrane del árbol de levas y la leva para accionar la bomba de combustible, si está equipado **(vea ilustración)**. Una varilla se puede posicionar en el árbol de levas para mantenerlo que no gire mientras el perno sea aflojado.

7 Inserciónе un pedazo de madera en el albergue del tiempo (el final pequeño hacia abajo) hasta que esté acuñado entre los dos

7.5b Para asegurarse que los soportes del ensamblaje del balancín de las válvulas estén instalados en sus posiciones correctas, marcas de identificación están proporcionadas en ambos soportes y la cabeza de los cilindros (se muestra un motor NAPS-Z)

lados de la cadena. Esté seguro que esté acuñado firmemente en su posición. La cadena del tiempo no se debe permitir que se separe del engrane del cigüeñal, porque se necesitaría remover la tapa delantera para volver a instalar la cadena del tiempo.

8 Remueva cuidadosamente el engrane del árbol de levas y trabaje la cadena hacia afuera hasta que el engrane pueda ser removido. La cadena se puede dejar descansando en el pedazo de madera.

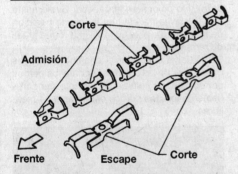

7.5c En los motores KA24E, esté seguro de instalar los retenedores con las ranuras mirando hacia afuera

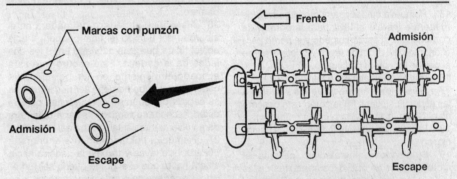

7.5d En los motores KA24E, las marcas del punzón mirarán hacia encima y hacia el frente

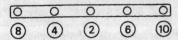

7.6 Apriete el ensamblaje de los balancines empezando desde adentro y trabajando hacia el exterior

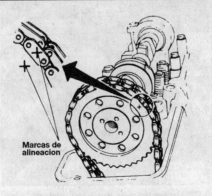

8.4 Antes de remover la cadena del tiempo del engrane del árbol de levas, marcas deben ser hechas para asegurarse que la instalación sea correcta

8.6 En los modelos equipados con una bomba de combustible mecánica, una leva es instalada en el engrane del árbol de levas

9 Remueva los pernos y separe el plato para el impulso del árbol de levas.

10 Note la posición de la clavija fija pequeña en el final del árbol de levas, entonces remueva la clavija. Remueva el árbol de levas cuidadosamente de las torres de la leva. Sosténgalo para que las superficies de los lóbulos no se rayen o mellen los cojinetes. **Caución: ¡NO afloje los pernos de afianzamiento de la torre del cojinete de la leva! Ellos están alineados y calibrados después de la instalación y se deben dejar en su posición.**

11 Las instrucciones de inspección del árbol de levas, balancines y cojinetes de la leva pueden ser encontrados en la Sección 9.

12 Antes de instalar el árbol de levas, aplique una capa de grasa de base moly o lubricación para el motor y las superficies para los cojinetes del árbol de levas, entonces instale cuidadosamente el árbol de levas en la cabeza. Gírelo hasta que la clavija fija esté puesta en posición correctamente.

13 Vuelva a instalar el plato para el impulso con la ranura rectangular mirando hacia el frente del motor **(vea ilustración)**.

14 Con el pedazo de madera todavía en su posición, trabaje cuidadosamente la cadena de tiempo en el engrane del árbol de levas y conecte el engrane en el final del árbol de levas con la clavija de la leva localizada en el orificio número uno del engrane. Esté seguro que las marcas hechas en la cadena y el engrane durante el proceso de remover forman una fila.

15 Remueva cuidadosamente el pedazo de madera e instale la leva para la bomba de combustible, si está equipado y el perno para el engrane del árbol de levas. Apriete el perno al par de torsión especificado.

16 Vuelva a instalar los balancines.

17 Ajuste los franqueos de las válvulas a las especificaciones Frías como está descrito en el Capítulo 1.

18 Instale nuevamente la tapa de los balancines.

19 Siguiendo la instalación, caliente el motor y ajuste de nuevo los franqueos de las válvulas a las especificaciones Calientes como está descrito en el Capítulo 1.

Modelos 1981 y más modernos (motores NAPS-Z y motores KA24E)

Refiérase a las ilustraciones 8.25, 8.27 y 8.31

20 Remueva la tapa de los balancines como está descrito en la Sección 4.

21 Remueva todas las bujías.

22 Traiga el pistón número uno al TDC refiriéndose a la Sección 3, si es necesario.

23 ¡Si usted intenta remover el árbol de levas solamente, sin remover la cabeza de los cilindros, NO altere la posición del engrane de tiempo en relación a la cadena del tiempo! Marque ambos la cadena de tiempo y el engrane del árbol de levas para preservar la posición instalada original de los dos. La cadena debe ser reinstalada en el engrane del árbol de levas en la misma relación exacta. Si una reconstrucción completa

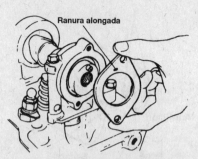

8.13 En los modelos 1980 con motor (L20B), el plato para el impulso de engrane del árbol de levas debe estar instalado con la ranura hacia encima y mirando hacia afuera

mayor es hecho, entonces la relación del engrane/cadena no se tiene que mantener.

24 Antes de remover el engrane del árbol de levas, corte un pedazo de madera de 10 pulgadas de largo, 3/4 de pulgada de grueso, 1-1/2 pulgadas de ancho y aproximadamente 1 pulgada de ancho en el fondo.

25 Ahora remueva el perno para el engrane del árbol de levas y la leva para la bomba de combustible, si está equipado. Una varilla puede ser insertada en el engrane del árbol de levas para mantenerlo que no gire mientras el perno es aflojado **(vea ilustración)**. En orden de remover el perno, el tapón de caucho localizado en el frente debe ser removido primero.

26 Insercióne el pedazo de madera en el albergue del tiempo (el final pequeño hacia abajo) hasta que esté acuñado entre los dos lados de la cadena. Esté seguro que está acuñado firmemente en su posición. La cadena del tiempo no debe ser permitida que se separe del engrane del cigüeñal, porque usted necesitaría remover la tapa delantera para volver a instalar la cadena del tiempo.

27 Remueva cuidadosamente el engrane del árbol de levas y trabaje la cadena hacia afuera hasta que el engrañe pueda ser removido. La cadena se puede dejar descansar en

8.27 Un pedazo de madera, cortado a las dimensiones listadas en el texto, debe ser usado para detener en su posición la cadena del tiempo mientras el engrane del árbol de levas está fuera

8.25 Detenga el árbol de levas para que no gire, insertando una barra a través de uno de los orificios del engrane para el árbol de levas, apoyando la barra contra el pedestal para el eje de los brazos de los balancines

el pedazo de madera **(vea ilustración)**.

28 Remueva el ensamblaje de los balancines de las válvulas como está descrito en la Sección 6.

29 Note la posición de la clavija pequeña fija en el final del árbol de levas, entonces levante hacia afuera la leva.

30 El árbol de levas, los balancines e instrucciones de como inspeccionar los cojinetes del árbol de levas pueden ser encontrados en la Sección 9.

31 Cuando esté instalando el árbol de levas, lubrique las superficies para los cojinetes con grasa de base moly o lubricación para el ensamblaje del motor **(vea ilustración)** y lo coloca en la cabeza. Gírelo hasta que la clavija fija esté en la misma posición de manera que esté en la misma forma antes de removerlo.

32 Vuelva a instalar el ensamblaje de los balancines de las válvulas. Apriete los pernos con los dedos solamente. Apriete temporariamente los dos pernos centrales a 14 pies-libras.

8.31 Las superficies de los cojinetes del árbol de levas se deben lubricar antes de la instalación del árbol de levas

33 Con el pedazo de madera todavía en su posición, trabaje cuidadosamente la cadena de tiempo en el engrane del árbol de levas y conecte el engrane al final del árbol de levas, con la clavija de la leva fija localizada en el orificio número dos del engrane. Esté seguro que las marcas hechas en la cadena y el engrane durante el proceso de remover están en línea.
34 Remueva cuidadosamente el pedazo de madera, después instale la leva para la bomba de combustible (si está equipado) y el perno para el engrane del árbol de levas. Apriete el perno al par de torsión especificado. Aplique sellador al tapón de caucho y lo vuelve a instalar en la cabeza de los cilindros.
35 Apriete los pernos de ensamblaje del balancín de las válvulas al par de torsión especificado.
36 Ajuste los franqueos de las válvulas a las especificaciones Frías como está descrito en el Capítulo 1.
37 Vuelva a instalar la tapa de los balancines y bujías.
38 Siguiendo la instalación, caliente el motor y ajuste de nuevo los franqueos de las válvulas Calientes a las especificaciones como está descrito en el Capítulo 1.

9 Árbol de levas, cojinetes y balancines - inspección

El árbol de levas, las superficies de los cojinetes y los procedimientos de inspección de los balancines son idéntico a los procedimientos para los componentes equivalente en el motor V6, así que refiérase al Capítulo 2, Parte B, Sección 15, para las instrucciones e ilustraciones. Esté seguro de referirse a las especificaciones aquí en la Parte A. Note que los Párrafos desde el 5 al 8 pueden ser ignorados, debido a que los motores de cuatro cilindros no tienen buzos.

10 Resortes de las válvulas y los sellos - reemplazo en el vehículo

Refiérase a las ilustraciones 10.4 y 10.7
Nota: *Resortes de las válvulas rotos y sellos de las guías de las válvulas con fugas/desgaste se pueden reemplazar sin tener que remover la cabeza de los cilindros. Dos tipos de herramientas especiales y una fuente de aire comprimido son requerido normalmente para realizar esta operación, así que lea a través de esta Sección cuidadosamente y alquile o compre las herramientas antes de comenzar el trabajo. Si el aire comprimido no está disponible, un pedazo de soga de nilón se puede usar para no permitir que las válvulas se caigan hacia adentro del cilindro durante éste procedimiento.*
1 Refiérase a la Sección 3 y remueva la tapa de los balancines. En los modelos 1980, remueva el árbol de levas (Sección 8). En los modelos 1981 y más modernos, remueva los ensamblajes de los balancines (Sección 6).

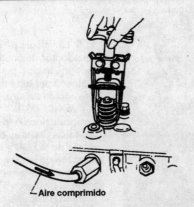

10.4 Aire comprimido se puede usar para detener las válvulas cerradas según los resortes son comprimidos . . .

2 Remueva la bujía del cilindro con el componente defectuoso. Si todos los sellos de los vástagos de las válvulas se van a reemplazar, toda las bujías deben ser removidas. En los motores con dos bujías por cilindro, remueva una de las bujías de cada cilindro.
3 Gire el cigüeñal hasta que el pistón en el cilindro afectado esté en el punto muerto superior en la carrera de compresión (refiérase a la Sección 3 para las instrucciones). Si usted está reemplazando todos los sellos de los vástagos de las válvulas, comience con el cilindro número uno y trabaje en las válvulas un cilindro a la vez. Muévase de cilindro a cilindro siguiendo la secuencia (1-3-4-2 del orden de encendido).
4 Enrosque un adaptador en el orificio de la bujía y conecte una manguera de aire a una fuente de aire comprimido (vea ilustración). La mayoría de las refaccionarías pueden suministrar el adaptador para la manguera de aire. **Nota:** *Muchos medidores de compresión para los cilindros utilizan un acoplador que puede trabajar con el acoplador de desconección rápida en la manguera de aire.*
5 Aplique aire comprimido al cilindro. Las válvulas deben ser sostenidas en su posición por la presión de aire. Si las caras de las válvulas o los asientos están en condiciones pobres, fugas pueden prevenir que la presión de aire detenga las válvulas - refiérase al procedimiento alternativo abajo.
6 Si usted no tiene acceso a aire comprimido, un método alternativo se puede usar. Posicione el pistón en un punto apenas antes del TDC (punto muerto superior) en la carrera de compresión, entonces suministre un pedazo largo de cuerda de nilón a través del orificio de la bujía hasta que llene la cámara de combustión. Esté seguro de dejar un pedazo de cuerda que cuelgue fuera del motor para que usted pueda removerlo fácilmente. Use una barra ruptora grande y un dado para que gire el cigüeñal en la dirección normal de rotación hasta que se sienta una resistencia leve.
7 Ponga trapos de taller en los orificios de la cabeza de los cilindros para prevenir que las partes y las herramientas no caigan aden-

10.7 . . . y los guardianes son removidos (flecha)

tro del motor, después use un compresor de resorte para comprimir los resorte de las válvulas. Remueva los guardianes con alicates de nariz de aguja pequeños o un imán (vea ilustración).
8 Remueva los retenedores del resorte y los resortes de la válvula, entonces remueva el sello de la guía de tipo paragua. **Nota:** *Si presión de aire falla en retener la válvula en la posición cerrada durante esta operación, la cara de la válvula o el asiento está probablemente dañado. Si ése es el caso, la cabeza de los cilindros tendrá que ser removida para operaciones adicionales de reparación.*
9 Envuelva una liga o cinta alrededor de la cima del vástago de la válvula para que la válvula no se caiga adentro de la cámara de combustión, entonces libere la presión de aire. **Nota:** *Si una cuerda se usó en vez de presión de aire, gire el cigüeñal levemente en la dirección de rotación normal opuesta.*
10 Inspeccione el vástago de las válvulas por daño. Gire la válvula en la guía y chequee el extremo por movimiento excéntrico, que indicaría que la válvula está doblada.
11 Mueva la válvula hacia encima y hacia abajo en la guía y asegúrese que no se atore. Si el vástago de la válvula se atora, la válvula está doblada o la guía está dañada. En cualquier caso, la cabeza tendrá que ser removida para la reparación.
12 Aplique presión de aire al cilindro para retener la válvula en la posición cerrada, entonces remueva la cinta o la liga del vástago de la válvula. Si una cuerda se usó en vez de presión de aire, gire el cigüeñal en la dirección normal de rotación hasta que se sienta una resistencia leve.
13 Lubrique el vástago de la válvula con aceite de motor e instale un sello nuevo de aceite en la guía de la válvula. Una herramienta especial es necesitada para los sellos de admisión - refiérase a la Sección 11 en la Parte C.
14 Instale los resortes en posición encima de la válvula. Asegúrese que el final estrecho del resorte exterior está contra la cabeza de los cilindros.
15 Instale el retén del resorte de la válvula. Comprima los resortes de la válvula y posicione los guardianes en la ranura. Aplique

11.9 La válvula BPT (transductor de contra presión), la pipa para la galería del tubo de la inyección de aire, la válvula EGR (recirculación de los gases de escape), el pasaje de la EGR y la ubicación de la válvula AB (purga de aire) (desde la izquierda a la derecha) (modelos 1980 solamente)

11.18 Ubicación del tubo EGR (recirculación de los gases de escape) (flecha), puesto en posición debajo del múltiple de admisión en los modelos 1980

una pequeña cantidad de grasa al interior de cada guardián para tenerlo en su posición si es necesario. Remueva la presión de la herramienta del resorte y asegúrese que los guardianes están sentados.

16   Desconecte la manguera de aire y remueva el adaptador del orificio de la bujía. Si una cuerda se usó en posición envés de presión de aire, hálela hacia fuera de los cilindros.

17   Instale el árbol de levas (modelos 1980) o el ensamblaje de los balancines de las válvulas (modelos 1981 y más modernos).

18   Instale la bujía(s) e instale el alambre(s).

19   Refiérase a la Sección 4 e instale la tapa de los balancines.

20   Ponga el motor en marcha y permítalo que corra, entonces chequee por fugas de aceite y sonidos extraños que provengan del área de la tapa de los balancines.

11   Múltiple de admisión - remover e instalar

Modelos 1980 con motor (L20B)

Refiérase a las ilustraciones 11.9 y 11.18
Nota: *Los múltiples de admisión y de escape en este motor comparten comúnmente una junta. Para prevenir fugas de aire y daño posible a las válvulas, la junta debe ser reemplazada cuando cualquier múltiple sea removido - los múltiples deben ser removidos e instalados juntos. El motor debe de estar completamente fresco cuando este procedimiento sea hecho.*

1   Desconecte el cable negativo de la terminal de la batería.

2   Drene el sistema de enfriamiento.

3   Remueva el purificador de aire.

4   Desconecte las líneas de vacío y de combustible del carburador. Tape las líneas de combustible para prevenir inmediatamente la fuga de combustible y para prevenir que tierra entre en las líneas. Marque todas las líneas y mangueras antes de removerla para asegurar una instalación correcta.

5   Desconecte todas las mangueras del múltiple de admisión.

6   Remueva todos los conector de alambre que se dirigen al carburador.

7   Desconecte la manguera para el amplificador de los frenos del múltiple de admisión.

8   Desconecte las mangueras de vacío/combustible de la válvula electrónica conectada en el frente de la cabeza de los cilindros. Entonces remueva los pernos de afianzamiento y separe el ensamblaje. **Nota:** *Las mangueras del radiador se deben tapar después de desconectarla.*

9   Desconecte la manguera de vacío de la EGR (recirculación de los gases de escape) y la válvula BPT (transductor de contra presión) **(vea ilustración)**.

10   Remueva la válvula del BPT y el soporte.

11   Desconecte la manguera que conecta los tubos de inyección de aire de la galería.

12   Remueva el soporte trasero para levantar el motor.

13   Remueva la válvula EGR, junto con el pasaje conectado a la EGR.

14   Remueva la válvula y el soporte AB (anti explosión) localizados atrás del carburador.

15   Remueva el conducto que corre entre el múltiple de escape y el purificador de aire.

16   Levante el frente del vehículo y sosténgalo firmemente sobre estantes.

17   Desconecte el tubo de escape delantero del múltiple de escape.

18   Remueva el tubo EGR **(vea ilustración)**.

19   Remueva del múltiple de escape el protector contra el calor.

20   Remueva los pernos de afianzamiento, separe del motor el múltiple completamente con el carburador y los otros componentes conectados. Si el múltiple debe ser reemplazado, los componentes pueden ser transferidos directamente al múltiple nuevo antes de la instalación.

21   Remueva el múltiple de escape, completo con los tubos e inyectores para la inyección de aire. Si el múltiple debe ser reemplazado, transfiéralo directamente al múltiple nuevo antes de la instalación.

22   Remueva la junta del múltiple.

23   Antes de instalar los múltiples, limpie

con trapos libre de pelusa los puertos del motor, remueva todos los rasgos de la junta vieja y sellador con un raspador. Limpie las superficies de acoplamiento con rebajador de pintura o acetona.

24   Comience la instalación poniendo la junta nueva en posición en el motor y vuelva a instalar el múltiple de escape. Esté seguro que el lado de la cara biselada de cada arandela mire al motor y apriete los pernos solamente hasta que ellos sostengan el múltiple. ¡Los pernos que son común a ambos múltiples deben ser apretados con los dedos solamente!

25   Coloque el múltiple de admisión en posición contra la cabeza de los cilindros e instale los pernos de retención, otra vez apriételos lo suficiente solamente para sostener el múltiple.

26   Una vez que ambos múltiples hayan sido instalados, los pernos de afianzamiento pueden ser apretados al par de torsión especificado (trabaje desde el centro hacia las puntas y apriételos hasta el punto final en tres o cuatro pasos).

27   El resto de la instalación se hace en el orden inverso al procedimiento de desensamble.

28   Llene el radiador con anticongelante, ponga el motor en marcha y chequee por fugas. Chequee también y ajuste la velocidad de la marcha mínima y el control de la mariposa como está descrito en el Capítulo 1.

Modelos 1981 y más modernos (motores NAPS-Z y motores KA24E)

Refiérase a la ilustración 11.36

29   Desconecte el cable negativo de la terminal de la batería.

30   Drene el sistema de enfriamiento.

31   Remueva el purificador de aire.

32   Desconecte donde se junta de manguera de vacío al amplificador para los frenos en el tubo de metal.

33   Desconecte todas las líneas de vacío del cuerpo de aceleración o del carburador y

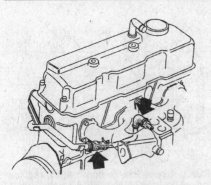

11.36 Ubicación de los tubos PCV (ventilación positiva del cárter) en los modelos 1981 y más modernos

12.4 Ubicación de los tubos para la inducción de aire (izquierdo) y el tubo EGR (recirculación de los gases de escape) (derecho) en el múltiple de escape (modelos 1981 y más modernos) (se muestra un motor NAPS-Z)

el múltiple de admisión. Márquelas antes de removerlas para asegurar una instalación correcta.

34 Desconecte las mangueras de combustible de caucho donde ellas se conectan a las líneas de metal debajo del múltiple de admisión. **Peligro:** *¡En los vehículos con combustible inyectado, la presión del sistema de combustible se debe aliviar antes de aflojar cualquier acoplación o desconectar cualquier línea! Refiérase al Capítulo 4 para las instrucciones.*

35 Desconecte las líneas de vacío que se dirigen al VVT (transductor del vacío de venturi) y los tubos EGR.

36 Desconecte el tubo de escape EGR de la válvula EGR y el tubo PCV (ventilación positiva del cárter) de la válvula PCV **(vea ilustración).**

37 Desconecte el cable del acelerador del cuerpo de aceleración o del carburador.

38 Desconecte cualquier alambre que se dirija al cuerpo de aceleración o al carburador y al múltiple de admisión.

39 Remueva la manguera superior del radiador.

40 Desconecte el cable de conexión a tierra de la batería del perno inferior del albergue del termostato.

41 Desconecte la manguera de la calefacción de la parte inferior del múltiple de admisión.

42 Desconecte la manguera de la válvula PCV.

43 Remueva los pernos del múltiple de admisión y separe del motor completamente el múltiple de admisión con el cuerpo de aceleración/carburador, válvula EGR y otros componentes. Si el múltiple debe ser reemplazado, los componentes pueden ser transferidos directamente al múltiple nuevo antes de la instalación.

44 Antes de instalar el múltiple, límpielo con unos trapos libre de pelusa en los puertos del motor y remueva todos los rasgos de la junta vieja y el sellador con un raspador. Limpie las superficies con rebajador de pintura o acetona.

45 Coloque una junta nueva en posición en el múltiple de admisión e instale los pernos y las arandelas inferiores del múltiple flojamente. Esté seguro que cada cara de las

arandelas biseladas miran hacia el motor. Coloque el múltiple en posición contra la cabeza de los cilindros e instale los pernos de retención que quedan.

46 Apriete los pernos en tres o cuatro pasos al par de torsión especificado. Trabaje desde el centro hacia afuera.

47 El resto de la instalación se hace en el orden inverso al procedimiento de desensamble.

48 Llene el radiador con anticongelante, ponga el motor en marcha y chequee por fugas. Chequee también y ajuste la velocidad de la marcha mínima como está descrito en el Capítulo 1.

12 Múltiple de escape - remover e instalar

Modelos 1980 con motor (L20B)

Debido a que el múltiple de escape comparte comúnmente una junta con el múltiple de admisión, la junta debe ser reemplazada cuando cualquier múltiple sea removido, ambos múltiples siempre deben ser removidos junto. Refiérase a la Sección 11 para el procedimiento.

Modelos 1981 y más modernos (motores NAPS-Z y motores KA24E)

Refiérase a la ilustración 12.4

1 Remueva los tubos de inducción de aire y albergue de la válvula, si está equipado.

2 Remueva el conducto que corre entre el múltiple de escape y el purificador de aire.

3 Remueva el protector contra el calor.

4 Desconecte el tubo EGR (recirculación de los gases de escape) de la parte trasera del múltiple de escape **(vea ilustración).**

5 Levante el frente del vehículo y sopórtelo firmemente sobre estantes.

6 Desconecte el tubo de escape delantero del múltiple de escape.

7 Remueva los alambres de las bujías de las bujías del lado del escape para tener acceso a los pernos/tuercas del múltiple de escape.

8 Remueva los pernos y las tuercas que retienen el múltiple de escape a la cabeza de los cilindros.

9 Separe el múltiple de escape.

10 Antes de instalar el múltiple, remueva todos los rasgos de la junta vieja con un raspador. Limpie las superficies de acoplamiento con rebajador de pintura o acetona.

11 Coloque una junta del múltiple de escape nueva en posición en la cabeza de los cilindros, entonces ponga el múltiple en su posición y apriete los pernos/tuercas con los dedos.

12 Apriete los pernos/tuercas, en tres o cuatro pasos, al par de torsión especificado. Trabaje desde el centro hacia afuera de los extremos del múltiple para prevenir la distorsión del múltiple.

13 Instale los componentes que quedan. El resto de la instalación se hace en el orden inverso al procedimiento de desensamble.

14 Ponga el motor en marcha y chequee por fugas de escape entre el múltiple y la cabeza y entre el múltiple y la pipa de escape.

13 Cabeza de los cilindros - remover

Modelos 1980 con motor (L20B)

Refiérase a la ilustración 13.10

1 Remueva los múltiples de admisión y de escape como está descrito en la Sección 11.

2 Remueva la manguera superior del radiador.

3 Remueva el albergue de termostato.

4 Desconecte la manguera de la calefacción de la acoplación en la esquina trasera derecha en la cabeza de los cilindros.

5 Desconecte los alambres de las bujías de las bujías y póngalos en posición fuera del camino, entonces remueva las bujías.

6 Remueva la bomba de combustible.

7 Remueva el perno que retiene el cable de conexión a tierra de la batería y soporte para levantar en el frente del motor, en la cabeza de los cilindros.

8 Remueva la tapa de los balancines.

9 Traiga el pistón número uno al TDC (punto muerto superior) (vea Sección 3) y remueva el engrane del árbol de levas - esté seguro de seguir el procedimiento en la Sección 8.

10 Usando una junta para la cabeza nueva, marque el patrón de los cilindros y los orificios para los pernos en un pedazo de cartón, esté seguro de indicar el frente para la referencia del motor. Hágale orificios en los lugares de los pernos. Afloje los diez pernos en la cabeza de los cilindros en incrementos de 1/4 de vuelta hasta que puedan ser removidos a

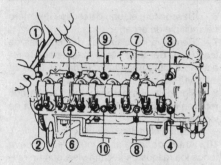

13.10 Secuencia de como AFLOJAR los pernos de la cabeza de los cilindros (motor 1980 L20B) - un dado Allen de 10 mm para la cabeza se necesitará para aflojar/apretar los pernos

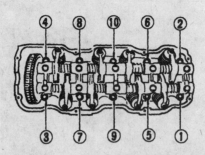

13.26a Secuencia de como AFLOJAR los pernos de la cabeza de los cilindros (modelos 1981 y más modernos)

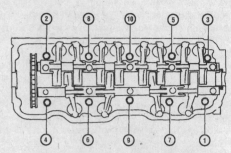

13.26b Secuencia de como AFLOJAR los pernos de la cabeza de los cilindros (se muestra un motor KA24E)

14.2 Vista esquemática de un motor KA24E

1   Tapa de los balancines
2   Ensamblaje del eje para los brazos de los balancines
3   Cabeza de los cilindros
4   Junta para la cabeza de los cilindros
5   Perno de la cabeza
6   Árbol de levas
7   Asiento de la válvula
8   Guía de la válvula
9   Asiento del resorte
10   Sello para el aceite
11   Retén de la válvula
12   Retenedores del resorte
13   Válvula y resorte
14   Junta para tapa de los balancines

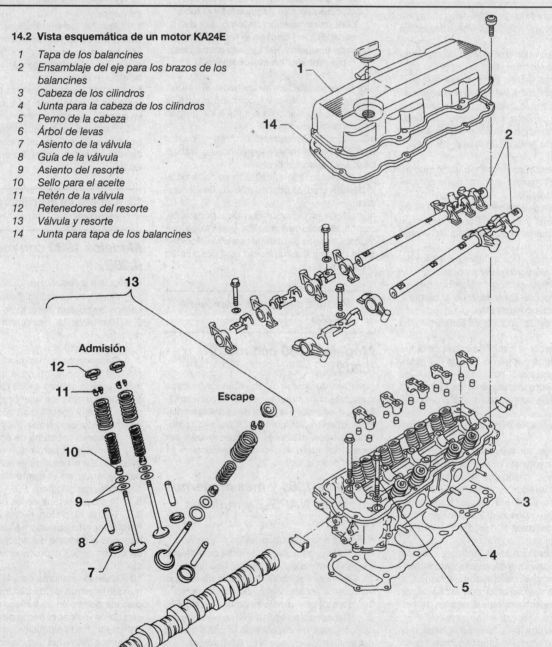

mano. Esté seguro de seguir la secuencia recomendada (vea ilustración). Almacene los pernos en el poseedor de cartón según ellos son removidos - esto asegurará que ellos sean reinstalados en sus lugares originales.

11 Remueva los pernos pequeños que conectan la cabeza de los cilindros a la tapa delantera.

12 Remueva la cabeza del motor. ¡Si está pegada, no le haga palanca entre la cabeza y el bloque - daño a las superficies de acoplamiento resultará! Para remover la cabeza, posicione un bloque de madera contra ella y golpee el bloque de madera con un martillo. La cadena del tiempo se debe dejar en su posición, descansando en la cuña de madera.

13 Remueva la junta de la cabeza de los cilindros. Coloque la cabeza en un bloque de madera para prevenir dañarla.

14 Refiérase a la Parte C para los procedimientos de inspección de la cabeza de los cilindros.

Modelos 1981 y más modernos (motores NAPS-Z y motores KA24E)

Refiérase a las ilustraciones 13.26a y 13.26b

15 Drene el sistema de enfriamiento. Refiérase al Capítulo 1, si es necesario.

16 Remueva el purificador de aire y si está equipado, la bomba de la dirección de poder y la polea loca.

17 Desconecte los alambres de las bujías de las bujías y remueva los soportes de la tapa de los balancines. Los alambres de las bujías no tienen que ser removidos de los soportes.

18 Remueva la pipa de inducción del aire y el albergue de la válvula, si está equipado.

19 Remueva el múltiple de admisión como se describe en la Sección 11.

20 Remueva la válvula del VVT (transductor del vacío de venturi) y el soporte de la pared contrafuego en el compartimiento del motor. Si está equipado.

21 Si está equipado, remueva el tubo EGR que corre atrás de la cabeza de los cilindros.

22 Remueva la bomba mecánica de combustible de la esquina del lado derecho delantero de la cabeza de los cilindros, si está equipado.

23 Separe del múltiple de escape la cabeza de los cilindros.

24 Remueva la tapa de los balancines.

25 Traiga el pistón número uno al TDC (vea Sección 3) y remueva el engrane del árbol de levas. Esté seguro de usar el procedimiento descrito en la Sección 8.

26 Usando una junta nueva para la cabeza, marque el patrón de los cilindros y los perno en un pedazo de cartón, esto de seguro indicara la referencia delantera del motor. Con un punzón haga orificios en los lugares para los pernos. Afloje los diez pernos de la cabeza de los cilindros en incrementos de 1/4 de vuelta hasta que puedan ser removidos con la mano. Esté seguro de seguir la secuencia recomendada (vea ilustraciones). Haga varios pasos en secuencia para liberar

lentamente la tensión. Almacene los pernos en el poseedor de cartón según ellos son removidos - esto asegurará que ellos sean reinstalados en sus lugares originales.

27 Remueva los pernos pequeños que conectan la cabeza de los cilindros a la tapa delantera.

28 Remueva la cabeza del motor. ¡Si está pegada, no le haga palanca entre la cabeza y el bloque - daños a las superficies de acoplamiento resultará! Para remover la cabeza, posicione un bloque de madera contra ella y golpee el bloque de madera con un martillo. La cadena de tiempo se debe dejar en su posición, descansando en la cuña de madera.

29 Remueva la junta para la cabeza de los cilindros. Coloque la cabeza en un bloque de madera para prevenir daño.

30 Refiérase a la Parte C para los procedimientos de inspección de la cabeza de los cilindros.

14 Cabeza de los cilindros - instalación

Refiérase a las ilustraciones 14.2, 14.5, 14.6a y 14.6b

1 Las superficies de acoplamiento de la cabeza en los cilindros y el bloque se deben limpiar perfectamente cuando la cabeza sea instalada. Use un raspador de junta para remover todos los rastros de carbón y material de junta vieja, después limpie las superficies de acoplamiento con rebajador de pintura o acetona. Si hay aceite en las superficies de acoplamiento cuando la cabeza sea instalada, la junta no podrá sellar correctamente y fugas podrían desarrollarse. Cuando esté trabajando en el bloque, llene los cilindros con trapos de taller limpios para que no entren residuos. Use una aspiradora para remover cualquier residuo que caiga adentro de los cilindros.

2 Chequee por mellas en el bloque y las superficies de acoplamiento de la cabeza, rayones y otros daños profundos (vea ilustración). Si el daño es leve, puede ser removido con una lima; si es excesivo, rectificación a máquina puede ser solamente la única alternativa.

3 Use una terraja macho del tamaño correcto para seguir las roscas para los pernos de la cabeza. Instale cada perno en una prensa y corra una terraja hembra en las roscas para remover la corrosión y rectificar las roscas. La tierra, la corrosión, el sellador y las roscas dañadas afectarán las lecturas del par de torsión.

4 Coloque la junta en su posición en las clavijas fijas del bloque del motor. Asegúrese que el pistón número uno está todavía en TDC (punto muerto superior), entonces baje cuidadosamente la cabeza de los cilindros en el motor, sobre las clavijas fija y la junta. Tenga cuidado de no mover la junta.

5 Instale los pernos de la cabeza de los cilindros. Note que los pernos en los modelos 1980 son de dos longitudes diferentes - asegúrese que son instalados en las roscas

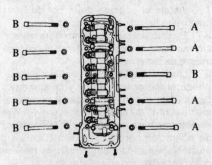

14.5 En los modelos 1980, dos pernos de la cabeza de diferentes longitudes son usados - esté seguro de que ellos están instalados en los orificios correcto

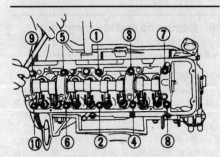

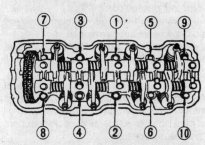

14.6a Secuencia de como APRETAR los pernos de la cabeza (encima - modelos 1980; debajo - modelos 1981 y más modernos)

correctamente (vea ilustración).

6 Apriete los pernos en incrementos de 1/4 de vuelta, siguiendo la secuencia recomendada (vea ilustraciones), hasta que el par de torsión especificado sea alcanzado. En los motores 1984 y más modernos, siga los cinco pasos para el procedimiento especifico del par de torsión.

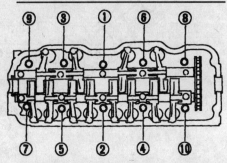

14.6b Secuencia de como APRETAR los pernos de la cabeza para los motores KA24E

7   Instale el engrane del árbol de levas como está descrito en la Sección 8.

8   El resto del procedimiento de la instalación se hace en el orden inverso al procedimiento de desensamble.

9   Llene el radiador con anticongelante, ponga el motor en marcha y chequee por fugas. Esté seguro de chequear completamente el nivel del anticongelante una vez que el motor se haya calentado a la temperatura de operación normal. También chequee y ajuste la velocidad de la marcha mínima como está descrito en el Capítulo 1.

10   Ajuste el franqueo de las válvulas a las especificaciones Calientes como está descrito en el Capítulo 1.

15   Bomba de aceite - remover e instalar

Refiérase a la ilustración 15.10

1   Posicione el pistón número uno en TDC (punto muerto superior) en la carrera de compresión. Refiérase a la Sección 3 si es necesario.

2   Remueva la tapa del distribuidor y marque la posición del rotor con relación al cuerpo del distribuidor.

3   Levante el frente del vehículo y sosténgalo firmemente sobre estantes.

4   Remueva los protectores de la parte inferior del compartimiento del motor.

5   Drene el aceite del motor.

6   En los modelos de 4WD, sostenga el diferencial delantero con un gato. Entonces remueva el miembro transversal del diferencial para obtener suficiente espacio libre para la bomba del aceite.

7   Remueva los pernos de la tapa de la bomba y remueva la bomba de aceite/ensamblaje del eje.

8   Si la bomba de aceite se debe inspeccionar o debe ser reconstruida, refiérase a la Sección 16.

9   Antes de la instalación, asegúrese que el pistón número uno está todavía en el TDC.

10   Llene el cuerpo de la bomba con aceite de motor para cargarla y alínee las marcas del punzón en el eje con el orificio de aceite debajo del engranaje de impulsión **(vea ilustración)**.

11   Instale una junta nueva e insercióne la bomba adentro de la depresión de la tapa delantera del motor.

12   Apriete los pernos de la bomba de aceite y chequee que el rotor esté todavía alineado con la marca hecha en el cuerpo del distribuidor. Si no está, repita el procedimiento de la instalación de la bomba de aceite.

13   Llene el motor con la cantidad y el grado apropiado de aceite de motor (refiérase al Capítulo 1, si es necesario).

14   Finalmente, chequee la regulación del tiempo de la ignición como está descrito en el Capítulo 1.

16   Bomba de aceite - inspección

Refiérase a las ilustraciones 16.1 y 16.4

1   Remueva la bomba, entonces destornille la tapa y remueva los rotores del interior y el exterior **(vea ilustración)**.

2   Remueva la tapa de la válvula del regulador de presión, arandela y extraiga el resorte y la válvula.

3   Limpie los componentes de la bomba con solvente y seque los componentes de la bomba con aire comprimido, si está disponible.

4   Chequee todos los componentes por desgaste excesivo y marcas de arañazos. Insercióne los rotores en el cuerpo de la bomba con los extremos marcados mirando hacia ADENTRO y chequee el juego del rotor en la siguiente manera **(vea ilustración)**:

a)   Chequee el juego libre entre los lóbulos en los rotores interiores y exteriores (1 en la ilustración 16.4).

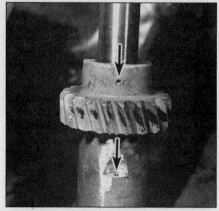

15.10 Cuando esté instalando la bomba de aceite, la marca del punzón en el lado del vástago debe estar alineada con el orificio en la bomba (flechas)

b)   Chequee el juego libre entre el rotor exterior y el cuerpo (2 en la **ilustración 16.4**).

c)   Chequee el juego final del rotor con una regla y un calibrador al tacto (3 en la **ilustración 16.4**).

d)   Otra vez, usando la regla colocada en el cuerpo, chequee el juego libre entre el cuerpo y la regla (4 en la **ilustración 16.4**).

5   Si los juegos libres no son como se especifica, reemplace la bomba. Los rotores del interior y el exterior son suministrados en

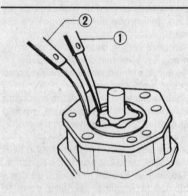

16.1 Componentes de la bomba de aceite - vista esquemática (típica)

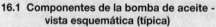

1   Eje ejecutor
2   Junta
3   Cuerpo de la bomba
4   Junta
5   Rotor
6   Cubierta de la bomba
7   Juego regulador para la válvula
8   Tapa
9   Arandela
10   Resorte
11   Válvula reguladora

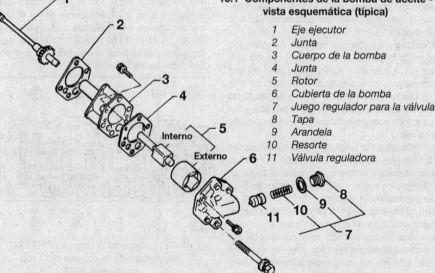

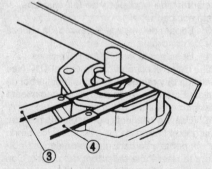

16.4 Los calibradores al tacto son usados para chequear el espacio libre del extremo exterior del rotor (1) extremo exterior del rotor al juego libre del cuerpo (2) espacio libre del rotor (3) y el espacio libre desde el cuerpo a la regla (4)

conjuntos como un juego solamente. Si el cuerpo de la bomba de aceite se ha desgastado o dañado, reemplace el ensamblaje de la bomba completa.

6   Chequee la condición de la válvula del regulador de presión y el resorte. La superficie donde se desliza la válvula no debe estar dañada o gastada. Reemplácela si es necesario.

17   Polea del cigüeñal - remover e instalar

Refiérase a la ilustración 17.6

1   Desconecte el cable negativo de la batería en la batería.
2   Remueva el radiador y la cubierta para el ventilador (Capítulo 3).
3   Afloje el protector para la salpicadura (si está equipado).
4   Remueva las bandas (Capítulo 1).
5   En los modelos equipados con transmisiones manuales, ponga la transmisión en el engranaje Alto y aplique el freno de estacionamiento. En las transmisiones automáticas, use una herramienta con una cadena para que no gire el cigüeñal. Remueva el tornillo de sujeción para la polea. Ellos están comúnmente muy apretados, use un dado de seis puntos y una barra de tipo ruptor de 1/2-pulgada.
6   Use un extractor para remover la polea desde el cigüeñal **(vea ilustración)**. NO USE un extractor que le aplique fuerza al borde exterior de la polea!
7   La instalación se hace en el orden inverso al procedimiento de desensamble. Esté seguro de aplicar grasa moly o aceite de motor limpio a la superficie de contacto del sello de la polea antes de instalar la polea en el cigüeñal. También, esté seguro de alinear la boca llave en el cubo de la polea con la llave en el cigüeñal o la polea no se deslizará en su lugar.
8   Apriete el perno de la polea al par de torsión especificado.

18   Sello delantero para el aceite del cigüeñal - reemplazo

Refiérase a las ilustraciones 18.2 y 18.3

1   Remueva la polea (Sección 17).
2   Cuidadosamente hágale palanca al sello fuera de la tapa de la cadena de distribución **(vea ilustración)** con un destornillador o herramienta de remover sello. No arañe la tapa o dañe el cigüeñal en el proceso (si el cigüeñal se daña el sello nuevo acabará teniendo fugas).
3   Limpie el orificio en la tapa y cubra el borde exterior del sello nuevo con aceite de motor o grasa de uso múltiple. Use un dado con el diámetro externo ligeramente menor que el diámetro de afuera del sello, cuidadosamente conduzca el sello nuevo en su lugar con un martillo **(vea ilustración)**. Si un dado no está disponible, una sección corta de un tubo de diámetro grande trabajará. Chequee

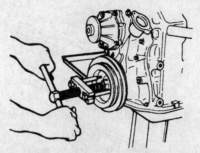

17.6 Un extractor tal como el que está mostrado aquí quizás tenga que ser usado para remover la polea del cigüeñal

el sello después de la instalación para estar seguro que el resorte no se salió fuera de su lugar.
4   Instale nuevamente la polea.
5   Las partes removidas para obtener acceso a la polea pueden ahora ser reinstaladas.
6   Ponga el motor en marcha y chequee por fugas.

19   Tapa delantera - remover e instalar

Refiérase a las ilustraciones 19.14a, 19.14b y 19.16

1   Drene el anticongelante del motor y el radiador (Capítulo 1).
2   Remueva el ventilador y el radiador como está descrito en el Capítulo 3.
3   Drene el aceite del motor.
4   Remueva el distribuidor como está descrito en el Capítulo 5.
5   Remueva la bomba de aceite como está descrito en la Sección 15.
6   Remueva la bomba de agua como está descrito en el Capítulo 3.
7   Remueva el perno superior de ajuste para el alternador. Entonces remueva los pernos que conectan el brazo del alternador para el ajusta a la tapa delantera y separe el brazo de ajuste.
8   Desconecte las mangueras de combustible/ensamblaje del tubo de vacío de la tapa delantera, entonces remueva el ensamblaje del tubo.
9   Si está equipado, desconecte el compresor del aire acondicionado del soporte y lo pone en posición fuera del camino. Remueva el soporte del compresor y la polea loca. **Peligro:** ¡No desconecte las mangueras del compresor a menos que el sistema haya sido evacuado!
10   Si está equipado con dirección de poder, remueva la bomba del soporte y la pone en posición fuera del camino. Las mangueras hidráulicas no se deben desconectar de la bomba.
11   Remueva la admisión de la bomba del agua del lado derecho de la tapa delantera.
12   Debido a que la tapa delantera está como un emparedado entre la cabeza de los cilindros y la cacerola de aceite, la cacerola de aceite debe ser removida para remover en

18.2 Después que remueva la polea del cigüeñal, hágale palanca cuidadosamente al sello (flecha) hacia afuera de la tapa delantera - ¡no raye o melle el cigüeñal o fugas de aceite se desarrollarán!

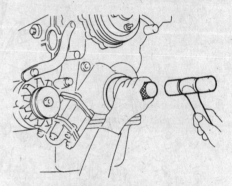

18.3 Instale el sello nuevo con un dado grande o sección de tubo y un martillo

orden la tapa delantera. Refiérase a la Sección 21 para este procedimiento.
13   Remueva la polea del cigüeñal (Sección 17).
14   Remueva los pernos que conectan la tapa delantera al bloque y la cabeza de los cilindros y separe la tapa delantera. Si no se suelta fácilmente, pegándole con cuidado con un martillo de cara suave le ayudará **(vea ilustraciones)**.

19.14a Cuando remueva la tapa delantera, tenga cuidado de no doblar ni dañar la parte delantera de la junta para la cabeza de los cilindros (flecha)

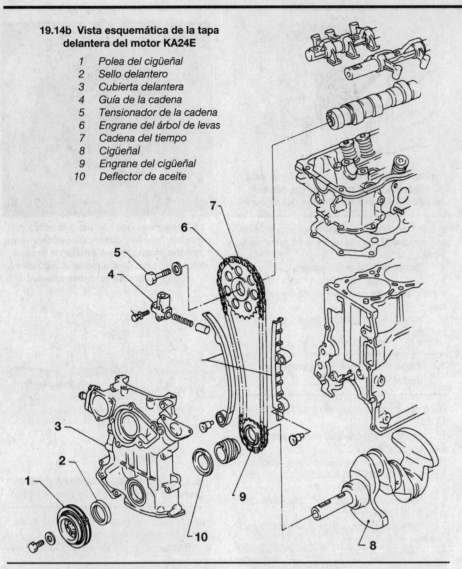

19.14b Vista esquemática de la tapa delantera del motor KA24E

1   *Polea del cigüeñal*
2   *Sello delantero*
3   *Cubierta delantera*
4   *Guía de la cadena*
5   *Tensionador de la cadena*
6   *Engrane del árbol de levas*
7   *Cadena del tiempo*
8   *Cigüeñal*
9   *Engrane del cigüeñal*
10   *Deflector de aceite*

Aplique sellador a las puntas

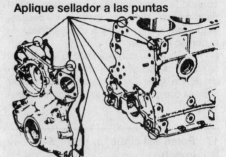

19.16 Antes de instalar la tapa delantera y la junta, sellador RTV (vulcanizador accionado a temperatura ambiente) debe ser aplicado en los puntos mostrados aquí

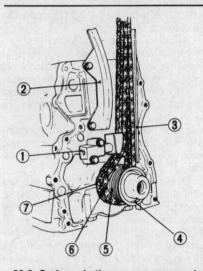

20.2 Cadena de tiempo y componentes relacionados

1   *Tensionador de la cadena*
2   *Guía del lado flojo de la cadena*
3   *Guía del lado de tensión de la cadena*
4   *Deflector del aceite*
5   *Engranaje de mando para la bomba de aceite*
6   *Engrane del cigüeñal*
7   *Cadena del tiempo*

15   Instale un sello nuevo en la tapa delantera refiriéndose a la Sección 18.

16   Coloque las juntas nuevas en posición en la tapa, entonces aplica sellador RTV (vulcanizador accionado a temperatura ambiente) a los puntos mostrados en la ilustración que acompaña.

17   Aplique una cantidad de grasa pequeña al labio del sello de aceite, entonces coloque los pernos de la tapa delantera en posición en el bloque e instale la instalación. Apriételos en varios pasos hasta el par de torsión especificado.

18   El resto de la instalación se hace en el orden inverso al procedimiento de desensamble.

20   Cadena del tiempo y los engranes - remover e instalar

Refiérase a las ilustraciones 20.2 y 20.5

Remover

1   Remueva la tapa delantera (Sección 19)
2   Remueva los pernos que conectan el tensionador de la cadena y las guías de la cadena al bloque, entonces remuévalos **(vea ilustración)**.

3   Remueva el perno para el engrane del árbol de levas y separe el engrane (vea Sección 8 si es necesario).

4   Remueva la banda del tiempo de los engranes del árbol de levas y el cigüeñal.

5   Remueva el deflector de aceite, el engranaje de impulsión de la bomba de aceite y el engrane de la cadena del tiempo del final del cigüeñal. El engrane muy probable pueda que requiera el uso de un extractor **(vea ilustración)**. Note que tres llaves Woodruff sean usadas para estos componentes.

6   Examine los dientes en ambos el engrane del cigüeñal y el engrane del árbol de levas por desgaste. Cada engrane forma una V invertida. Si está desgastado, el lado de cada engrane debajo de tensión estará levemente concavo en forma cuando se pueda comparar con el otro lado del engrane (i.e. en un lado de la V invertida estará concavo cuando se pueda comparar con el otro).
Si los dientes aparecen estar desgastados, los engranes deben ser reemplazados con unos nuevos.

7   La cadena debe ser reemplazada con

20.5 Un extractor tal como el que está mostrado aquí será necesario para remover el engrane del cigüeñal

20.12 Antes de instalar la cadena del tiempo, asegúrese que la llave Woodruff está apuntando hacia encima y la marca de tiempo en el engrane del cigüeñal está visible (flechas)

20.14a En los modelos 1980 con un motor (L20B), el eslabón brillante en la cadena del tiempo debe ser alineado con la marca para la regulación del tiempo número uno

20.14b En los modelos 1981 y más modernos, el eslabón brillante debe ser alineado con la marca número dos y la clavija fija del árbol de levas debe estar en el orificio número dos (flechas) (se muestra un motor NAPS-Z)

una nueva si los engranes están desgastados o si la cadena está floja. Es una buena idea de reemplazar la cadena cerca de 30,000 millas (48,000 km) y en kilometraje inferior si el motor es desarmado para una reconstrucción completa. Los rodillos en una cadena muy desgastada pueden estar acanalados levemente. Para evitar dificultad en el futuro, si hay cualquier duda del todo acerca de la condición de la cadena, reemplácela con una nueva.

8   Acople nuevamente el engrane del árbol de levas al árbol de levas y chequee el juego final con un indicador de tipo reloj. El juego final no debe exceder 0.008 pulgada (0.2 mm).

9   Examine los componentes de tensión de la cadena y las guías. Reemplace cualquier artículo que esté desgastado o dañado.

Instalar

Refiérase a las ilustraciones 20.12, 20.14a, 20.14b, 20.14c, 20.14d, 20.15a, 20.15b, 20.16a y 20.16b

10   Para poner en marcha la instalación, gire el árbol de levas hasta que las válvulas (delantera) del cilindro número uno estén cerradas (equivalente al pistón número uno en el TDC (punto muerto superior), entonces gire el cigüeñal hasta que el pistón número uno esté en el TDC.

11   Atornille ambas guías de la cadena del tiempo al bloque.

12   Instale el engrane, la bomba de aceite/engranaje del distribuidor y el deflector de aceite en el frente del cigüeñal. Asegúrese que las marcas de la regulación del tiempo en el engrane están visibles en el frente **(vea ilustración)**.

13   **Nota:** *No gire el cigüeñal o árbol de levas hasta que la cadena del tiempo esté instalada, de otro modo las válvulas harán contacto con la corona del pistón.*

14   Enganche el engrane del árbol de levas en el circulo superior de la cadena de la sincronización del tiempo, entonces comprometa la cadena con los dientes del engrane del cigüeñal y atornille el engrane del árbol de levas al árbol de levas. Note lo siguiente:

a) *La bocallave en el engrane del cigüeñal debe estar encima.*
b) *Las marcas de la regulación del tiempo (eslabones brillantes) en la cadena deben alinearse con las marcas en los dos engranes y puesta en posición en el lado derecho cuando se mire desde el frente* **(vea ilustraciones)**.
c) *La clavija fija en el frente del árbol de levas debe estar en el orificio número uno del engrane en los modelos 1980. En los modelos 1981 y más modernos, debe estar en el orificio del engrane número dos en el árbol de levas.*

15   Cuando vuelva a instalar la cadena usada en los modelos 1980, debe ser chequeada por desgaste excesivo como sigue.

a) *Con el en el pistón número uno en TDC (punto muerto superior) en la carrera de compresión, si la mella en el engrane del árbol de levas (con la cadena comprometida correctamente) aparece a la izquierda de la línea grabada en el plato para el impulso* **(vea ilustración)**. *Si está, desengrane el engrane del árbol de levas de la cadena y mueva el engrane alrededor para que cuando esté remachado con la cadena localice la clavija*

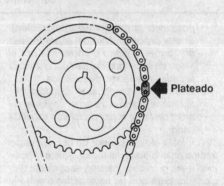

20.14c En los motores KA24E, alínee el eslabón de plata con la marca en el engrane del árbol de levas

fija con el árbol de levas en el orificio número dos. Si este ajuste no corrige el de la cadena, repita la operación con el engrane número tres en la ranura del árbol de levas comprometido con la clavija fija. Si el orificio número dos o tres del engrane se deben usar, entonces la marca número dos o tres de la regulación del tiempo se deben usar para

20.14d En todos los modelos, el eslabón brillante inferior de la cadena debe ser alineado con la marca de tiempo en el engrane del cigüeñal

20.15a Ubicación de la ranura en el plato para impulso y mella del engrane del árbol de levas usado para juzgar el desgaste de la cadena del tiempo (flecha)

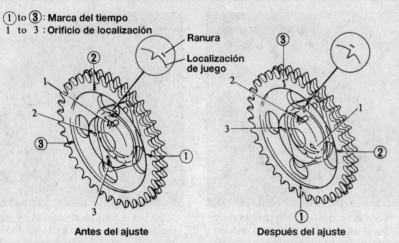

20.16a Cuando esté instalando la cadena del tiempo, el lado flojo de la guía para la cadena del tiempo debe estar hacia adentro lo más posible

Antes del ajuste   Después del ajuste

20.15b En los modelos 1980 con motor (L20B), si la mella del engrane del árbol de levas está a la izquierda del plato para el impulso, la cadena del tiempo está estirada y el próximo orificio del engrane y la marca de combinación para la regulación del tiempo se debe usar

posicionar la cadena (**vea ilustración**). *Si este procedimiento del ajuste todavía no corrige el juego o compensa por el juego en la cadena del tiempo, entonces la cadena debe ser reemplazada.*

b) Cuando el tiempo esté satisfactorio, apriete el perno para en el engrane del árbol de levas al par de torsión especificado.

16   Instale el tensionador de la cadena del tiempo en el bloque del motor. Ajuste la posición de la guía de la cadena encima del tensionador para que no haya espacio entre el cuerpo de tensión y la unidad del embolo del tensionador (**vea ilustraciones**).

17   Vuelva a instalar la tapa delantera, refiriéndose a la Sección 19 según sea necesario.

21   Cacerola del aceite - remover e instalar

1   Drene el aceite del motor.
2   Levante el frente del vehículo y sopórtelo firmemente sobre estantes colocados debajo del chasis.
3   Remueva el protector, si está equipado.
4   En los modelos de 2WD, remueva el miembro transversal delantero.
5   En los modelos de 4WD, remueva el diferencial delantero como está descrito en el Capítulo 9. Entonces desconecte los calzos del motor, la transmisión y levante el motor levemente con un elevador para motores.
Peligro: *¡No coloque ninguna parte de su cuerpo debajo del motor/transmisión cuando esté separado de los calzos!* Ponga bloques de madera debajo de los calzos para ayudar a apoyar el motor.
6   En los modelos 1980 de 2WD, remueva los pernos del brazo loco, baje el brazo loco y la varilla de cruce para proporcionar el espacio libre necesario para la cacerola del aceite.
7   Remueva los pernos y separe la cacerola del aceite. No le haga palanca con una

barra entre el bloque y la cacerola o puede resultar en un daño en la superficie del sellado y podría desarrollarse una fuga. Use un bloque de madera y un martillo para aflojar la cacerola si está pegada.
8   Use un raspador para remover todos los rasgos del material de la junta vieja y sellador del bloque y de la cacerola de aceite. Limpie las superficies para la junta con rebajador de pintura o acetona y asegúrese de que las roscas para los pernos en el bloque están limpios.
9   Chequee la distorsión de la pestaña del cárter de aceite, particularmente alrededor de las roscas para los pernos. Si es necesario, coloque la cacerola en un bloque de madera y use un martillo para aplastar y restaurar la superficie de la junta.
10   Antes de instalar la cacerola de aceite, aplique una capa delgada de sellador RTV (vulcanizador accionado a temperatura ambiente) a la pestaña. Conecte la junta nueva a la cacerola (asegúrese que los orificios para los pernos están alineados).
11   Posicione la cacerola del aceite contra el bloque del motor e instale los pernos de instalación. Apriételos al par de torsión especificado en un patrón cruzado.
12   Espere por lo menos 30 minutos antes de llenar el motor con aceite, entonces ponga el motor en marcha y chequee la cacerola por fugas.

22   Volante/plato flexible - remover e instalar

Refiérase a las ilustraciones 22.2 y 22.4
1   Si el motor está en el vehículo, remueva la cubierta del embrague y el disco del embrague como está descrito en el Capítulo 8, o la transmisión automática como está descrito en el Capítulo 7.
2   Aplaste las lengüetas en el plato de cierre (si es usado) y remueva los pernos que aseguran el volante/plato flexible en la pes-

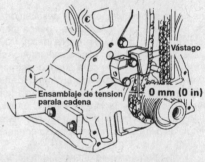

20.16b Con una cadena nueva y la guía de la cadena instalada apropiadamente, no debe haber espacio libre entre el cuerpo de tensión de la cadena y el embolo

taña trasera del cigüeñal. Tenga cuidado, el volante es muy pesado y no debe ser dejado caer. Si el cigüeñal gira según los pernos son aflojados, acuñe un destornillador en los dientes entre la corona dentada del motor de arranque (**vea ilustración**).
3   Separe el volante/plato flexible de la pestaña del cigüeñal.
4   Destornille y remueva el plato trasero del motor (**vea ilustración**). Ahora es un buen tiempo para chequear el tapón trasero del bloque del motor por fuga.
5   Si los dientes en la corona dentada del motor de arranque del volante/plato flexible están gravemente desgastados, o si algunos están omitidos, instale un volante o plato flexible nuevo.
6   Refiérase al Capítulo 8 para el procedimiento de inspección del volante.
7   Antes de instalar el volante/plato flexible, limpie las superficies de acoplamiento.
8   Si removió, vuelva a instalar el plato trasero.
9   Posicione el volante/plato flexible contra el cigüeñal, usando un espaciador nuevo, si está equipado e inserción los pernos de afianzamiento. Use Loctite en los pernos.
10   Apriete los pernos en un patrón cruzado al par de torsión especificado.
11   La instalación se hace en el orden inverso al procedimiento de desensamble.

23 Sello trasero del cigüeñal para el aceite - reemplazo

1 El sello trasero del aceite de cigüeñal puede ser reemplazado sin remover la cacerola del aceite o el cigüeñal.
2 Remueva la transmisión (Capítulo 7).
3 Si está equipado con una transmisión manual, remueva el plato de presión y el disco del embrague (Capítulo 8).
4 Remueva el volante o el plato flexible (Sección 22).
5 Usando una herramienta para remover sellos o un destornillador grande, hágale palanca cuidadosamente al sello hacia afuera del bloque. ¡No lo raye o melle el cigüeñal en el proceso!
6 Limpie los cilindros en el bloque y las superficies de contacto en el bloque para el sello en el cigüeñal. Chequee la superficie del cigüeñal por rayones y mellas que podrían dañar el labio nuevo del sello y causar fugas de aceite. Si el cigüeñal está dañado, la única alternativa es un cigüeñal nuevo o diferente.
7 Aplique una capa delgada de aceite de motor o grasa de propósito múltiple al exterior de la orilla del sello nuevo. Lubrique el labio del sello con grasa de base moly.
8 El labio del sello debe mirar hacia el frente del motor. Trabaje cuidadosamente el labio del sello en el extremo del cigüeñal, péguele al sello con un martillo y un punzón hasta que esté sentado en el cilindro.
9 Instale el volante o el plato flexible.
10 Si está equipado con una transmisión manual, vuelva a instalar el disco del embrague y el plato de presión.
11 Vuelva a instalar la transmisión como está descrito en el Capítulo 7.

24 Calzos de los motores - reemplazo

Refiérase a las ilustraciones 24.3, 24.6a y 24.6b

Peligro: *¡No posicione ninguna parte de su cuerpo debajo del motor cuando los calzos del motor estén destornillados!*
1 Los calzos del motor no son ajustables y requieren servicio rara vez. Periódicamente ellos deben ser inspeccionados por endurecimiento, roturas en el caucho y separación del caucho del metal de respaldo.
2 Para reemplazar los calzos del motor con el motor en posición, en el vehículo, use el siguiente procedimiento.
3 Afloje las tuercas y los pernos que retienen el aislador delantero al soporte del motor y el chasis. Haga esto en ambos lados (vea ilustración).
4 Después, el peso del motor se debe remover de los calzos del motor. Esto puede ser hecho usando un gato por debajo y un bloque de madera puesto en posición debajo de la cacerola de aceite después que remueva el miembro transversal (2WD) o el diferencial delantero (4WD), o desde encima

22.2 Para detener el volante inmóvil mientras los pernos de afianzamiento son aflojados, insercióne un destornillador a través de la abertura para el motor de arranque y comprométalo con los dientes del volante

removiendo el purificador de aire y usando un soporte para levantar el motor conectado a los dos soportes del motor. El motor debe ser levantado lentamente y cuidadosamente, mientras mantiene un chequeo constante alrededor de los espacios libres del motor para prevenir una obstrucción o ruptura. Pegue atención particular a las áreas tal como el ventilador, alambres de la bobina para la ignición, líneas de vacío que se dirigen al motor, mangueras de caucho y conductos.
5 Levante el motor apenas lo suficiente para proporcionar el espacio adecuado para remover el aislador.
6 Remueva las tuercas y los pernos reteniendo el aislador, entonces remuévalo hacia afuera, note como está instalado (vea ilustraciones).

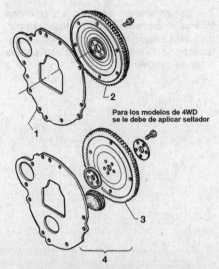

22.4 Vista esquemática de los componentes del volante/plato flexible

1 Plato trasero
2 Volante
3 Plato flexible
4 Para A/T (transmisión automática)

24.3 Ubicación de la tuerca y los pernos (flechas) conectando el calzo del motor al soporte y al chasis

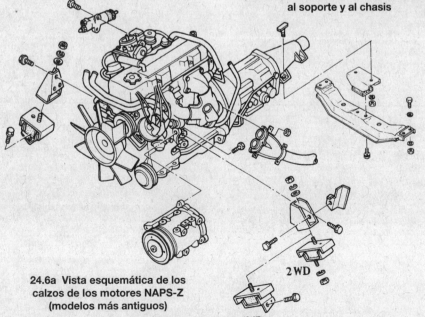

24.6a Vista esquemática de los calzos de los motores NAPS-Z (modelos más antiguos)

7   La instalación se hace en el orden inverso al procedimiento de desensamble, pero esté seguro que el aislador está instalado en la misma posición como estaba antes de removerlo.

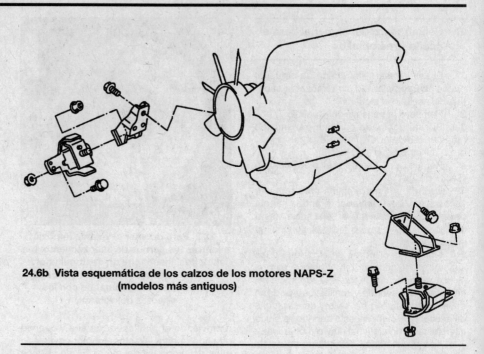

24.6b Vista esquemática de los calzos de los motores NAPS-Z (modelos más antiguos)

Capítulo 2 Parte B   Motor V6

Contenidos

Especificaciones

General

Desplazamiento	181 pulgadas cubicas (2960 cc)
Proporción de la compresión	9.0: 1
Orden del encendido	1-2-3-4-5-6
Números de los cilindros (desde el frente hacia atrás)	
Lado derecho (pasajero)	1-3-5
Lado izquierdo (chofer)..	2-4-6

Localidad de los cilindros y rotación del distribuidor

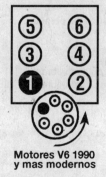

Motores V6 1990
y mas modernos

Motores V6 1989
y mas antiguos

Árbol de levas y componentes relacionados

Buzos
Diámetro exterior	0.6278 a 0.6282 pulgada (15.947 a 15.957 mm)
Guía del diámetro interior de los cilindros	0.6299 a 0.6304 pulgada (16.000 a 16.013 mm)
Espacio del buzo a la guía del buzo	0.0017 a 0.0026 pulgada (0.043 a 0.066 mm)
Límite de movimiento del buzo	0.040 pulgada (1.0 mm)

Balancines y ejes
Diámetro exterior del eje	0.7078 a 0.7087 pulgada (17.979 a 18.000 mm)
Diámetro interior para los cilindros de los balancines	0.7089 a 0.7098 pulgada (18.007 a 18.028 mm)
Espacio libre del balancín al eje	0.0003 a 0.0019 pulgada (0.007 a 0.049 mm)

Árbol de levas
Diámetro interior del cojinete	
Cojinete al frente	1.8898 a 1.8907 pulgadas (48.000 a 48.025 mm)
Cojinete trasero	1.6732 a 1.6742 pulgadas (42.500 a 42.525 mm)
Todos los otros	1.8504 a 1.8512 pulgadas (47.000 a 47.025 mm)
Diámetro exterior del muñón del árbol de levas	
Muñón delantero	1.8866 a 1.8874 pulgadas (47.920 a 47.940 mm)
Muñón trasero	1.6701 a 1.6709 pulgadas (42.420 a 42.440 mm)
Todos los otros	1.8472 a 1.8480 pulgadas (46.920 a 46.940 mm)
Juego libre del cojinete para el aceite (espacio libre del cojinete al muñón)	
Estándar	0.0018 a 0.0035 pulgada (0.045 a 0.090 mm)
Límite	0.0059 pulgada (0.15 mm)
Límite del desviación axial del árbol de levas (lectura total del indicador)	0.004 pulgada (0.10 mm)
Juego libre del árbol de levas	0.0012 a 0.0024 pulgada (0.03 a 0.06 mm)
Altura del lóbulo	1.5566 a 1.5641 pulgadas (39.537 a 39.727 mm)
Límite de desgaste del lóbulo	0.0059 pulgada (0.15 mm)

Bomba de aceite
Espacio libre del cuerpo al engrane exterior	0.0043 a 0.0079 pulgada (0.11 a 0.20 mm)
Espacio libre del engrane interior al creciente	0.0047 a 0.0091 pulgada (0.12 a 0.23 mm)
Espacio libre del engrane exterior al creciente	0.0083 a 0.0126 pulgada (0.21 a 0.32 mm)
Espacio libre del albergue al engrane interior	0.0020 a 0.0035 pulgada (0.05 a 0.09 mm)
Espacio libre del albergue al engrane exterior	0.0020 a 0.0043 pulgada (0.05 a 0.11 mm)

Especificaciones técnicas
Pies-libras (a menos que sea indicado de otra manera)

Tornillos para las tapas de los balancines	8.4 a 26.4 pulgada-libras
Pernos del eje de los balancines	13 a 16
Pernos del múltiple de admisión	
Paso 1	2.2 a 3.6
Paso 2	12 a 14
Tuercas del múltiple de admisión	
Paso 1	2.2 a 3.6
Paso 2	17 a 20
Tuercas de retención del múltiple de escape	13 a 16
Tuercas/pernos para la pipa del múltiple de escape	20 a 27
Perno de retención del amortiguador de vibraciones	90 a 98
Perno de la polea del árbol de levas	58 a 65
Tuerca de retención del tensionador de la banda del tiempo	32 a 43
Perno de retención del árbol de levas	58 a 65
Pernos de la cabeza de los cilindros	
Paso 1	22
Paso 2	43
Paso 3	Afloje todos los pernos
Paso 4	22
Paso 5	40 a 47
Pernos de retención del volante/plato flexible*	72 a 80
Pernos de retención de la cacerola de aceite	61 a 70 pulgada-libras
Pernos de retención de la bomba de aceite	61 a 70 pulgada-libras
Tapa para el regulador de la bomba de aceite	29 a 51
Pernos del colador a la bomba de aceite	12 a 15
Pernos de soporte para el colador de la bomba de aceite	3 a 6

Aplica Loctite a las roscas antes de la instalación

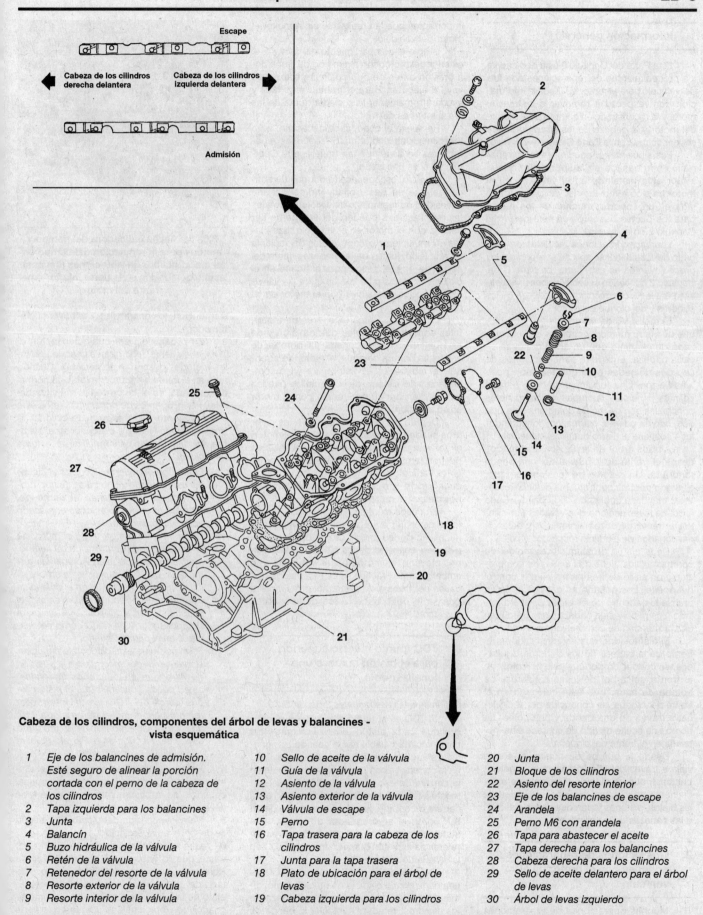

Escape

Cabeza de los cilindros derecha delantera

Cabeza de los cilindros izquierda delantera

Admisión

Cabeza de los cilindros, componentes del árbol de levas y balancines - vista esquemática

1 Eje de los balancines de admisión. Esté seguro de alinear la porción cortada con el perno de la cabeza de los cilindros
2 Tapa izquierda para los balancines
3 Junta
4 Balancín
5 Buzo hidráulica de la válvula
6 Retén de la válvula
7 Retenedor del resorte de la válvula
8 Resorte exterior de la válvula
9 Resorte interior de la válvula

10 Sello de aceite de la válvula
11 Guía de la válvula
12 Asiento de la válvula
13 Asiento exterior de la válvula
14 Válvula de escape
15 Perno
16 Tapa trasera para la cabeza de los cilindros
17 Junta para la tapa trasera
18 Plato de ubicación para el árbol de levas
19 Cabeza izquierda para los cilindros

20 Junta
21 Bloque de los cilindros
22 Asiento del resorte interior
23 Eje de los balancines de escape
24 Arandela
25 Perno M6 con arandela
26 Tapa para abastecer el aceite
27 Tapa derecha para los balancines
28 Cabeza derecha para los cilindros
29 Sello de aceite delantero para el árbol de levas
30 Árbol de levas izquierdo

1   Información general

Esta Parte del Capítulo 2 está dedicada a los procedimientos de reparaciones adentro del vehículo para el motor V6. Toda la información con respecto a remover e instalar el motor y la reconstrucción completa del bloque del motor y la cabeza de los cilindros puede ser encontrada en la Parte C de este Capítulo.

Los siguientes procedimientos de reparación son basado en la suposición que el motor está instalado en el vehículo. Si el motor ha sido removido del vehículo e instalado en un soporte, muchos de los pasos para los planes descritos en esta parte del Capítulo 2 no aplicarán.

Las especificaciones incluidas en esta parte del Capítulo 2 se aplican solamente a los procedimientos en esta parte. La parte C del Capítulo 2 contienen especificaciones necesarias para la reconstrucción de la cabeza de los cilindros y del bloque del motor.

El motor V6 de 60 grados tiene un bloque de hierro fundido y cabezas de flujo cruzado de aluminio con un árbol de levas en cada cabeza. El bloque tiene secciones de paredes delgadas para que tenga un peso más liviano. Una fundición de cuna para el cojinete principal - las tapas de los cojinetes principales son de molde como una sola unidad, con un puente, o armazón, conectándolos - sostiene el hierro dúctil del cigüeñal.

Ambos árbol de levas son accionados desde el frente del cigüeñal por una banda ranurada. Un resorte de tensión cargado, ajustado por una contratuerca de tipo excéntrica, mantiene la presión de la banda. Cada árbol de levas acciona dos válvulas por cilindro a través de buzos hidráulicos y balancines forjados de aluminio montados en ejes.

Cada pistón de aluminio es moldeado con tres anillos, tiene dos anillos de compresión y un anillo de tres partes para el control del aceite. Los pasadores del pistón están prensados adentro de las bielas de acero forjado. Los pistones de cabeza plana producen una proporción de compresión de 9.0:1.

El distribuidor, que está instalado en el frente de la cabeza de los cilindros izquierdos, es conducido por una guía helicoidal en el frente del árbol de levas izquierdo. La bomba de agua, que está colocada en el frente del bloque, es conducida por el cigüeñal a través de una banda y una polea. La bomba de aceite de tipo de engrane está instalada en el frente del cigüeñal.

Desde la bomba de aceite, el aceite viaja a través del filtro de aceite a la galería principal, que es dirigido directamente a los cojinetes principales, cigüeñal, cojinetes de las bielas, pistones y paredes de los pistones o las cabezas de los cilindros.

2   Operaciones de reparaciones posibles con el motor en el vehículo

Muchas operaciones de reparaciones importantes pueden realizarse sin remover el motor del vehículo.

Limpie el compartimiento del motor y el exterior del motor con algún tipo de limpiador a presión antes de que cualquier trabajo se vaya a ejecutar. Hará el trabajo más fácil y ayudará a mantener la suciedad fuera de las áreas internas del motor.

Remueva el capó, si es necesario, para tener mejor acceso al motor según las reparaciones se desempeñan (refiérase al Capítulo 12 si es necesario).

Si vacío, escape, aceite o fugas de anticongelante se desarrollan, indicando una necesidad de reemplazo de sello(s) o junta(s), las reparaciones pueden generalmente ser hechas con el motor en el vehículo. Las juntas del múltiple de escape, juntas del múltiple de admisión, juntas de las cabezas, junta del cárter de aceite, sellos para el aceite en el cigüeñal y juntas para las tapas de las válvulas son todos accesibles con el motor en su posición.

Los componentes exteriores de motor, tales como los múltiples de admisión y de escape, el cárter de aceite (la bomba de aceite), la bomba de agua, el motor de arranque, el alternador, el distribuidor y los componentes del sistema de combustible pueden removerse para su reparación con el motor en su posición.

Debido a que las cabezas de los cilindros pueden removerse sin remover el motor, el servicio de componentes de las válvulas pueden también ser realizados con el motor en el vehículo. Reemplazo de la banda de distribución y los engranajes es también posible con el motor en el vehículo.

En casos extremos ocasionado por una falta de equipo, reparación o reemplazo necesario de los anillos de los pistones, los pistones, cojinetes de las bielas y bielas son posible con el motor en el vehículo. Sin embargo, esta práctica no es recomendada a causa del trabajo de preparación y limpieza que se le debe hacer a los componentes involucrados.

3   TDC (punto muerto superior) para el pistón número uno - localizándolo

Refiérase a las ilustraciones 3.6a, 3.6b y 3.7

1   El TDC es el punto más alto en el cilindro que cada pistón alcanza según viaja hacia encima y hacia abajo cuando el cigüeñal da vueltas. Cada pistón alcanza el TDC en la carrera de compresión y nuevamente en la carrera de escape, pero el TDC generalmente se refiere a la localidad del pistón en la carrera de compresión. Las marcas de distribución en el amortiguador de vibraciones instaladas en el frente del cigüeñal es en referencia al pistón número uno en el TDC en la carrera de compresión.

2   Colocando el pistón(es) en el TDC es una parte imprescindible de muchos procedimientos, tales como remover la cabeza de los cilindros, remover e instalar la banda de

3.6a La flecha indicadora del tiempo y marcas para la regulación del tiempo en el amortiguador de vibraciones (flechas) están localizadas en la parte inferior en el frente del motor

distribución, los engranajes y remover el distribuidor.

3   En orden de traer cualquier pistón al TDC, el cigüeñal debe girarse usando uno de los métodos descrito más adelante. Cuando mire en el frente del motor, la rotación normal del cigüeñal es al favor de las manillas del reloj. **Peligro:** *Antes de poner en marcha este procedimiento, esté seguro de colocar la transmisión en Neutro y desconectar el alambre del distribuidor para inutilizar el sistema de ignición.*

a) *El método preferido es de girar el cigüeñal con un dado y una barra de tipo ruptor grande instalada en el perno del amortiguador de vibraciones enroscado en el frente del cigüeñal.*

b) *Un interruptor remoto para el motor de arranque, puede ahorrar algo de tiempo, también se puede usar. Adjunte las terminales del interruptor al alambre S (interruptor) y B (batería) en el solenoide del motor de arranque. Una vez que el pistón esté cerca del TDC, use una barra de tipo ruptor y un dado como se describió en el párrafo anterior.*

c) *Si un asistente está disponible para girar el interruptor del encendido a la posición de Arranque en pequeños intervalos, usted puede conseguir que el pistón llegue cerca del TDC sin un interruptor remoto para el motor de arranque. Use una barra de tipo ruptor y un dado según se describe en el Párrafo (a) para completar el procedimiento.*

4   Haga una marca en el albergue del distribuidor directamente debajo de la terminal del cable de la bujía número uno en la tapa del distribuidor.

5   Remueva la tapa del distribuidor según se describe en el Capítulo 1.

6   Gire el cigüeñal (vea Párrafo 3 encima) hasta que la línea en el amortiguador de vibraciones se alínee con la marca cero en la tapa del distribuidor **(vea ilustraciones)**. El plato de la banda de distribución y el amortiguador de vibraciones se ubican en la parte

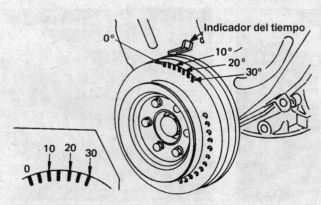

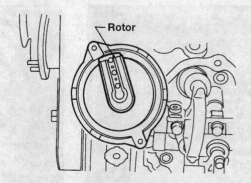

3.6b Cuando el 0 (cero) en el amortiguador de vibraciones esté alineado con la flecha del indicador del tiempo . . .

3.7 . . . y el rotor está apuntando a la marca en el albergue del distribuidor, el pistón número uno está en el TDC (punto muerto superior) en la carrera de compresión

baja en el frente del motor, combinado con la polea que gira las bandas.

7   El rotor debería indicar ahora directamente a la marca en el albergue del distribuidor **(vea ilustración)**. Si no está, el pistón está en el TDC en la carrera de escape.

8   Para llevar el pistón al TDC en la carrera de compresión, gire el cigüeñal una vuelta completa (360 grados) al favor de las manillas del reloj. El rotor debería indicar ahora a la marca. Cuando el rotor indique a la terminal del alambre número uno de la bujía en la tapa del distribuidor (que está indicado por la marca en la tapa) y las marcas de distribución del encendido se alíneen, el pistón número uno está en el TDC en la carrera de compresión.

9   Después que el pistón número uno se haya colocado en el TDC en la carrera de compresión, el TDC para cualquiera de los cilindros restantes puede ser ubicado girando el cigüeñal 120 grados a la vez y siguiendo el orden del encendido (refiérase a especificaciones).

4   Tapas de los balancines - remover e instalar

Refiérase a las ilustraciones 4.3 y 4.8

1   Alivie la presión del sistema de combustible (Capítulo 4).

2   Desconecte el cable negativo de la terminal negativa de la batería.

Remover

Tapa derecha

3   Remueva la manguera para PCV (ventilación positiva del cárter) deslizando la parte trasera de la abrazadera de la manguera y hale la manguera hacia afuera de la acoplación en la tapa de los balancines **(vea ilustración)**.

4   Remueva los alambres de las bujías número 1, 3 y 5 de las bujías. Márquelos claramente con pedazos de cinta para prevenir confusión durante la instalación.

5   Remueva los alambres y las mangueras de combustible conectadas a la tapa de los balancines.

6   Remueva los nueve tornillos y arandelas en la tapa de los balancines.

7   Separe la tapa de los balancines. **Caución:** *Si la tapa está pegada a la cabeza, golpee una punta con un bloque de madera y un martillo para aflojarla. Si esto no trabaja, pruebe resbalar un cuchillo flexible para masilla entre la cabeza y la tapa para romper el sello de la junta. No le haga palanca con una barra para remover la acoplación de la tapa y la cabeza porque daño puede ocurrir en la superficie de sellar (conduciendo a una fuga de aceite en el futuro).*

Tapa izquierda

8   Remueva la manguera de respiración de la tapa **(vea ilustración)**.

9   Póngale etiqueta y separe los alambres de las bujías.

10   Desabroche los soportes del alambrado de la tapa.

11   Remueva los nueve tornillos de la tapa de los balancines y levante la tapa de los balancines. Lea la **Caución** en el Paso 7.

Instalar

12   Las superficies de acoplamiento de cada cabeza para los cilindros y la tapa para los balancines deben estar perfectamente limpias cuando las tapas sean instaladas. Use un raspador de junta para remover todos los rasgos de sellador y material de junta vieja, después

limpie las superficies de acoplamiento con rebajador de pintura o acetona. Si hay sellador o aceite en las superficies de acoplamiento cuando la tapa sea instalada, fugas de aceite pueden desarrollarse.

13   Limpie las roscas de los tornillos con una terraja hembra para remover corrosión y reparar cualquier rosca dañada. Asegúrese que las roscas en la cabeza están limpias - corra una terraja macho en las roscas para remover corrosión y reparar las roscas dañadas.

14   Las juntas debe ser puestas contra las tapas antes de que las tapas sean instaladas. Aplique una capa ligera de sellador RTV (vulcanizador accionado a temperatura ambiente) a la ranura de la tapa, entonces posicióne la junta dentro de la tapa y permita que el sellador se adhiera a la junta y a la tapa. Si el sellador no es permitido que se asiente, la junta puede caerse de la tapa según es instalada en el motor.

15   Posicione cuidadosamente la tapa en la cabeza e instale los tornillos.

16   Apriete los tornillos en tres o cuatro pasos al par de torsión especificado.

17   La instalación se hace en el orden inverso al procedimiento de desensamble.

18   Ponga el motor en marcha y chequee cuidadosamente por fugas de aceite cuando el motor esté caliente.

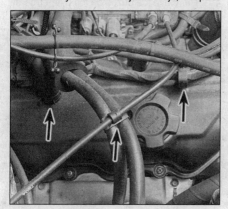

4.3 Artículos que se deben separar para remover la tapa derecha del balancín incluyen la manguera de PCV (ventilación positiva del cárter), arnés del alambrado y mangueras de combustible (flechas)

4.8 Remueva la manguera de respiración y el arnés del alambrado (flechas) para separar la tapa izquierda de los balancines

5.2 Para remover los ensamblajes de los ejes de los balancines, afloje los pernos un poquito a la vez para evitar doblar el eje

5.3 Los pernos de afianzamiento para el eje de los balancines, son de longitudes diferentes, deben ser reinstalados en sus lugares originales - una caja de cartón con orificios mantendrá los pernos en orden

5.4 Remueva los balancines y los ejes como un ensamblaje y mantenga todas las partes juntas

5   Componentes de los balancines - remover e instalar

Refiérase a las ilustraciones 5.2, 5.3 y 5.4

1   Remueva la tapa de los balancines (Sección 4).

2   Afloje los pernos de retención del eje de los balancines **(vea ilustración)** en dos o tres etapas, trabajando desde sus extremos hacia el centro del eje. **Caución:** *Algunas de las válvulas estarán abierta cuando usted afloje los pernos del eje de los balancines y el eje de los balancines estará bajo una cierta cantidad de presión del resorte de la válvula. Por lo tanto, los pernos se deben aflojar gradualmente. Aflojar un perno completamente de repente cerca de un balancín bajo presión del resorte podría doblar el eje de los balancines.*

3   Remueva los pernos reteniendo el eje de los balancines. Los pernos se deben mantener en orden para que ellos puedan ser instalados en sus lugares originales. Una caja del cartón con 12 orificios se puede usar para almacenar los pernos en orden. Esté seguro de marcar·el frente, el lado izquierdo y derecho de la caja de cartón **(vea ilustración)**.

4   Levante los ensamblajes del eje de los balancines de uno en uno y colóquelos encima de un banco de trabajo en la misma relación a cada uno como estaba instalado **(vea ilustra-**

ción). Ellos deben ser reinstalados en la misma cabeza de los cilindros. Refiérase a la ilustración de la vista esquemática en la página 91 si es necesario. Refiérase a la Sección 15 para los procedimientos de inspección.

5   La instalación se hace en el orden inverso al procedimiento de desensamble. Apriete los pernos reteniendo el eje de los balancines al par de torsión especificado en varios pasos. Trabaje los ejes desde los extremos hacia el centro.

6   Buzos - remover e instalar

Refiérase a las ilustraciones 6.2, 6.3 y 6.5

1   Remueva la tapa de los balancines (Sección 4) y los ensamblajes del eje de los balancines (Sección 5).

2   Asegure los buzos levantándolos levemente y envolviendo una goma alrededor de cada uno para prevenirlos que se caigan de las guías **(vea ilustración)**. **Nota:** *Si un buzo se cae de la guía, inmediatamente póngalo de regreso en su ubicación original.*

3   Remueva el ensamblaje hidráulico de la guía del buzo **(vea ilustración)**.

4   Remueva los buzos de los diámetros de los cilindros de uno en uno. Manténgalos en

orden. Cada buzo debe ser reinstalado en su orifico original. **Caución:** *Trate de evadir de tener que voltear los buzos al revés. Si usted voltea un buzo al revés, aire puede llegar a ser atrapado adentro del buzo y tendrá que ser purgado como sigue.*

5   Con el buzo en su orificio, empuje hacia abajo en el **(vea ilustración)**. Si se mueve más de 0.040 pulgada (1 mm), aire puede estar atrapado adentro del buzo.

6   Si usted piensa que aire está atrapado adentro de un buzo, vuelva a instalar los ensamblajes del eje de los balancines y la tapa de los balancines.

7   Purgue el aire de los buzos poniendo el motor en marcha a 1,000 rpm sin ninguna carga por cerca de 10 minutos.

8   Remueva la tapa de los balancines y los ensamblajes del eje de los balancines otra vez. Repita el procedimiento en el paso 5 una vez más. Si todavía hay aire en el buzo, reemplácelo con uno nuevo.

9   Mientras que los buzos están fuera del motor, inspecciónelos por desgaste. Refiérase a la Sección 15 para el procedimientos de inspección.

10   La instalación se hace en el orden inverso al procedimiento de desensamble. Esté seguro de lubricar cada buzo con cantidades liberales de aceite de motor limpio antes de la instalación.

6.2 Envuelva cada buzo con una liga para que no se puedan caer de la guía para los buzos

6.3 Con los buzos retenidos por ligas, el ensamblaje de la guía del buzo puede ser removido de la cabeza de los cilindros

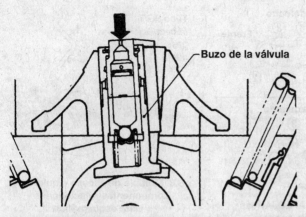

6.5 Presione el buzo a mano para ver que tanto se mueve

Buzo de la válvula

7.9 La polea loca para el aire acondicionador está sostenida en su posición con tres pernos (flechas)

7 Múltiple de admisión - remover e instalar

Remover

Refiérase a las ilustraciones 7.9 y 7.16

1 Libere la presión del sistema de combustible (Capítulo 4).

2 Desconecte el cable negativo de la terminal negativa de la batería.

3 Drene el sistema de enfriamiento (Capítulo 1).

4 Remueva el purificador de aire (Capítulo 4).

5 Remueva el cuerpo de aceleración (Capítulo 4).

6 Remueva la tapa del distribuidor y los alambres de las bujías. Esté seguro de marcar los alambres de las bujías para instalarlos apropiadamente.

7 Desconecte la válvula EGR (recirculación de los gases de escape) (Capítulo 6).

8 Remueva la banda del compresor del aire acondicionado (Capítulo 1).

9 Remueva los pernos que aseguran el soporte para la polea loca del aire acondicionado **(vea ilustración)** y separe el soporte.

10 Afloje la abrazadera de la manguera de desvío y remueva la manguera del albergue del termostato.

11 Asegúrese de remover el perno de la tapa para la banda del tiempo al albergue del termostato.

12 Remueva la manguera superior del radiador del albergue del termostato.

13 Desconecte las mangueras de vacío y los alambres después de marcarlos para la reinstalación.

14 Remueva cualquiera de las mangueras que queden, alambres y cables conectados al múltiple o sus componentes.

15 Desconecte las mangueras de la calefacción de la parte trasera del múltiple.

16 Afloje los pernos/tuercas del múltiple en incrementos de 1/4 de vuelta a la vez hasta que puedan ser removido a mano. Siga la secuencia recomendada **(vea ilustración)**.

17 El múltiple probablemente estará pegado a las cabezas de los cilindros y fuerza se puede requerir para romper el sello de la junta. **Caución:** *No haga palanca con una barra entre el múltiple y las cabezas o daño a las superficies del sellado de la junta puede ocurrir, conduciendo a fugas de vacío.*

Instalar

Refiérase a la ilustración 7.23

Nota: *Las superficies de acoplamiento en las cabezas de los cilindros y el múltiple de admisión se deben limpiar perfectamente cuando el múltiple sea instalado. Solventes en botes de aerosol para remover las juntas están disponibles en casi todas las refaccionarías y pueden ser útil cuando remueva los materiales de una junta vieja que estén pegadas a las cabezas y el múltiple (debido a que ellos son hechos de aluminio, raspar agresivamente puede causar daño). Esté seguro de seguir las direcciones impresas en el recipiente.*

18 Use un raspador de junta para remover todos los rasgos de sellador y material de junta vieja, después limpie las superficies de acoplamiento con rebajador de pintura o acetona. Si hay sellador o aceite en las superficies de acoplamiento cuando el múltiple viejo es instalado, aceite o fugas de vacío pueden desarrollarse. Use una aspiradora para remover cualquier cosa que caiga en los puertos de admisión en las cabezas.

19 Use una terraja macho del tamaño correcto para rectificar las roscas en los orificios para los pernos, después use aire comprimido (si está disponible) remueva los residuos de las roscas. **Peligro:** *¡Use lentes de seguridad o un protector de cara para proteger sus ojos cuando use aire comprimido!*

20 Posicione las juntas en las cabezas de los cilindros. Ningún sellador es requerido; sin embargo, siga las instrucciones incluidas con las juntas nuevas.

21 Asegúrese que todas las aberturas para los puertos de admisión, pasajes de anticongelante y orificios para los pernos están alineados correctamente.

22 Ponga cuidadosamente el múltiple en su posición. **Caución:** *No perturbe las juntas.*

23 Instale los pernos/tuercas y apriételo al par de torsión especificado siguiendo la secuencia recomendada **(vea ilustración)**. Llegue al par de torsión final en dos pasos.

24 La instalación se hace en el orden inverso al procedimiento de desensamble. Ponga el motor en marcha y chequee cuidadosamente por fugas de aceite y de anticongelante en las acoplaciones del múltiple de admisión.

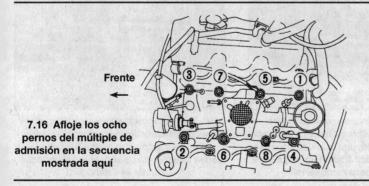

Frente

7.16 Afloje los ocho pernos del múltiple de admisión en la secuencia mostrada aquí

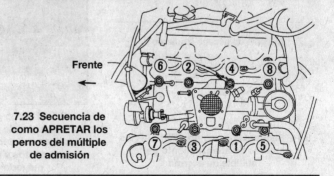

Frente

7.23 Secuencia de como APRETAR los pernos del múltiple de admisión

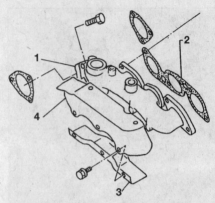

8.5 Múltiple de escape derecho y componentes relacionados - vista esquemática

1 Múltiple de escape derecho
2 Junta
3 Protector para el calor del múltiple de escape derecho
4 Protector para el calor del múltiple de escape izquierdo

8 Múltiples de escape - remover e instalar

1 Remueva el purificador de aire (Capítulo 4).
2 Desconecte el cable negativo de la terminal negativa de la batería.
3 Levante el vehículo y sopórtelo firmemente sobre estantes.
4 Trabajando debajo del vehículo, destornille el sistema del escape del múltiple(s) (Capítulo 4).

Remover

Lado derecho

Refiérase a las ilustraciones 8.5 y 8.6

5 Remueva los pernos de retención para el protector contra el calor de las dos mitades del protector contra el calor a la derecha del múltiple de escape **(vea ilustración)**.
6 Remueva las tuercas de retención del múltiple de escape en la secuencia recomendada **(vea ilustración)**.

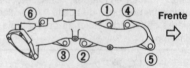

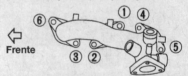

8.14 Secuencia de como APRETAR las tuercas de afianzamiento del múltiple de escape

8.6 Secuencia de como AFLOJAR las tuercas del múltiple de escape

7 Separe el múltiple de escape levantándolo hacia encima en la parte trasera, entonces levante el múltiple hacia afuera del compartimiento del motor.

Lado izquierdo

Refiérase a la ilustración 8.8

8 Remueva los pernos que aseguran el protector contra el calor al múltiple de escape izquierdo **(vea ilustración)**.
9 Desconecte el tubo EGR (recirculación de los gases de escape) del múltiple.
10 Trabajando por encima - y por debajo, cuando sea necesario - remueva las tuercas del múltiple de escape, tres encima y tres por debajo, en la secuencia apropiada **(vea ilustración 8.6)**.
11 Levante el múltiple fuera del compartimiento del motor.

Instalar

Refiérase a la ilustración 8.14

12 Antes de la instalación de cualquier múltiple, limpie todas las superficies de acoplamiento para la junta.
13 Instale una junta nueva en los espárragos reteniendo el múltiple a la cabeza.
14 Instale el múltiple y apriete las tuercas en la secuencia apropiada al par de torsión especificado **(vea ilustración)**.
15 La instalación de los componentes se

9.5 El perno grande reteniendo el amortiguador de vibración en su posición está bien apretado, ¡así que use un dado de seis puntos y una barra ruptora de 1/2 pulgada para removerlo!

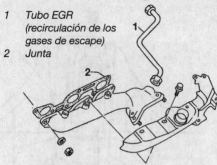

1 Tubo EGR (recirculación de los gases de escape)
2 Junta

8.8 Múltiple de escape izquierdo y componentes relacionados - vista esquemática

hace en el orden inverso al procedimiento de desensamble.

9 Amortiguador de vibraciones - remover e instalar

Refiérase a las ilustraciones 9.5 y 9.6

1 Desconecte el cable negativo de la terminal negativa de la batería.
2 Remueva el protector para el ventilador y el ventilador (Capítulo 3).
3 Remueva las bandas (Capítulo 1).
4 Remueva los pernos de retención de la polea y separe las poleas. **Caución:** *Antes de remover las poleas, marque la ubicación de cada una en relación con el amortiguador de vibraciones en orden de apropiadamente retener la orientación de la marca del tiempo durante la instalación.*
5 Remueva los pernos del motor de arranque y empuje el motor de arranque fuera del engranaje del volante. Ponga una cuña entre los dientes del volante/plato flexible para impedir que el cigüeñal gire mientras usted está aflojando el perno grande del amortiguador de vibraciones **(vea ilustración)**.
6 Deje el perno del amortiguador en su posición para proveerle al extractor algo para empujar contra. Use un extractor para remover el amortiguador **(vea ilustración)**. **Caución:** *No use un extractor con mordazas que*

9.6 Use el extractor recomendado para remover el amortiguador de vibraciones - si un extractor que aplica fuerza a la orilla exterior es usado, el amortiguador puede ser dañado

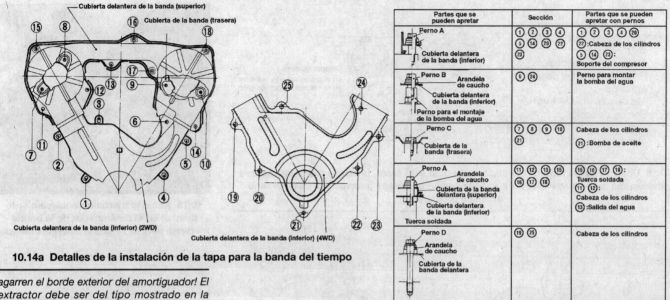

10.14a Detalles de la instalación de la tapa para la banda del tiempo

Partes que se pueden apretar	Sección	Partes que se pueden apretar con pernos
Perno A / Cubierta delantera de la banda (inferior)	① ② ③ ④ ⑤ ⑭ ⑳ ㉒ ㉓	① ② ③ ④ ⑳ ㉒:Cabeza de los cilindros ⑤ ⑭ ㉓: Soporte del compresor
Perno B / Arandela de caucho / Cubierta delantera de la banda (inferior) / Perno para el montaje de la bomba del agua	⑥ ㉔	Perno para montar la bomba del agua
Perno C / Cubierta de la banda (trasera)	⑦ ⑧ ⑨ ⑩ ㉑	Cabeza de los cilindros ㉑:Bomba de aceite
Perno A / Arandela de caucho / Cubierta de la banda delantera (superior) / Cubierta delantera de la banda (inferior) / Tuerca soldada	⑪ ⑫ ⑬ ⑮ ⑯ ⑰ ⑱	⑮ ⑯ ⑰ ⑱: Tuerca soldada ⑪ ⑫: Cabeza de los cilindros ⑬:Salida del agua
Perno D / Arandela de caucho / Cubierta de la banda delantera	⑲ ㉕	Cabeza de los cilindros

agarren el borde exterior del amortiguador! El extractor debe ser del tipo mostrado en la ilustración, que utiliza pernos para aplicar presión al cubo del amortiguador de vibraciones solamente.

7 Para instalar el amortiguador, colóquelo en la nariz del cigüeñal, alínee la chaveta e instale el perno. Apriete el perno a la torsión especificada.

8 Los pasos restantes para la instalación son los procedimientos opuestos de como se removió.

10 Banda del tiempo - chequear, remover, instalar y ajustar

Refiérase a las ilustraciones 10.14a, 10.14b, 10.15, 10.16, 10.17, 10.18, 10.20a y 10.20b

1 Alivie la presión del combustible (Capítulo 4).

2 Desconecte el cable negativo de la terminal negativa de la batería.

3 Drene el sistema de enfriamiento (Capítulo 1).

4 Posicione el pistón número uno en el TDC (punto muerto superior) en la carrera de compresión (Sección 3).

5 Remueva el ensamblaje del purificador de aire (Capítulo 4).

6 Remueva las tapas de los balancines (Sección 4).

7 Afloje los pernos de retención para el eje de los balancines (Sección 5).

8 Remueva todas las bandas (Capítulo 1).

9 Remueva el protector para el ventilador y el ventilador (Capítulo 3).

10 Remueva la polea loca del compresor del aire acondicionado, si está equipado (Capítulo 3).

11 Remueva el amortiguador de vibración (Sección 9). **Nota:** *No permita que el cigüeñal gire durante el proceso de remover el amortiguador de vibraciones. Si el cigüeñal se mueve, el pistón número uno no estará en el TDC.*

12 Desconecte la manguera inferior del radiador del tubo de metal y afloje la abrazadera de la manguera en el otro extremo del tubo de metal.

13 Remueva el perno que conecta el tubo de metal al soporte del motor y separe el tubo.

14 Remueva los pernos que retienen la tapa superior e inferior de la banda del tiempo **(vea ilustraciones)**. Note que varios

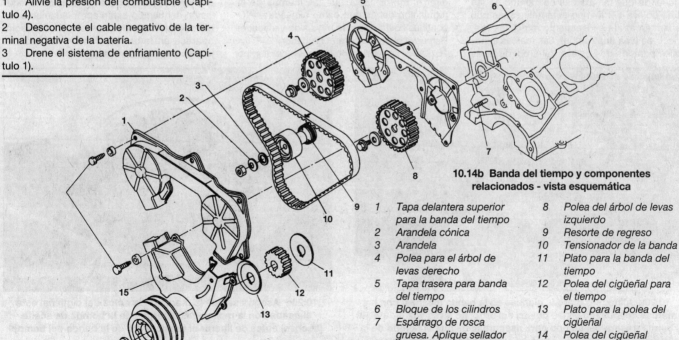

10.14b Banda del tiempo y componentes relacionados - vista esquemática

1 Tapa delantera superior para la banda del tiempo
2 Arandela cónica
3 Arandela
4 Polea para el árbol de levas derecho
5 Tapa trasera para banda del tiempo
6 Bloque de los cilindros
7 Espárrago de rosca gruesa. Aplique sellador a las roscas gruesas del espárrago
8 Polea del árbol de levas izquierdo
9 Resorte de regreso
10 Tensionador de la banda
11 Plato para la banda del tiempo
12 Polea del cigüeñal para el tiempo
13 Plato para la polea del cigüeñal
14 Polea del cigüeñal
15 Tapa delantera inferior para la banda del tiempo

1   Marcas de alineamiento
2   Tapa trasera para la banda
    del tiempo
3   Marcas de alineamiento
4   Polea para el árbol de levas
    izquierdo
5   Marcas de alineamiento
6   Bomba de aceite
7   Polea para el tiempo del cigüeñal
8   Polea para el árbol de levas derecho

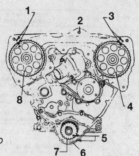

Cilindro número 1
en el punto muerto superior
en la carrera de compresión

10.15 Una vez que la tapa de la banda del tiempo esté fuera, chequee todas las marcas del tiempo para las válvulas para una alineación correcta - ¡alíneelas si es necesario antes de proceder!

10.16 Afloje la tuerca de enclavamiento (flecha) en el tensionador de la banda mediana para la sincronización del tiempo

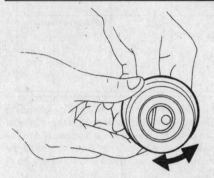

10.17 Chequee el tensionador de la banda y el resorte por desgaste y daño - la polea debe girar suavemente

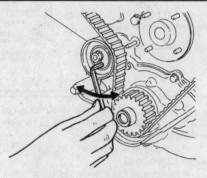

10.18 Gire el tensionador con una herramienta Allen para variar la tensión de la banda del tiempo

tipos y tamaños de pernos son usados. Ellos deben ser reinstaladas en sus lugares originales. En cada perno marque o haga un dibujo para ayudar a recordarle donde ellos van.

15   Confirme que el pistón número uno está en el TDC en la carrera de compresión chequeando que las marcas del tiempo en las tres poleas del tiempo estén alineadas con sus marcas de alineamiento inmóviles respectivas (**vea ilustración**). Las marcas inmóviles para las dos poleas del árbol de levas

son mellas en la tapa de la banda del tiempo. La marca inmóvil para la polea del cigüeñal es una mella en el albergue de la bomba de aceite. Si las marcas no forman fila, instale el perno de retención para el amortiguador de vibraciones del cigüeñal y use una llave para girar el motor hasta que las marcas de la regulación del tiempo estén alineadas. ¡NO continúe hasta que esto haya sido verificado! Remueva el perno del amortiguador.

16   Alivie la tensión de la banda del tiempo

aflojando la tuerca en el tensionador de la banda mediana de la sincronización del tiempo (**vea ilustración**).

17   Remueva la banda de la regulación del tiempo de la polea deslizándola hacia adelante. Chequee la tensión (**vea ilustración**). **Nota:** *Si la banda está agrietada, desgastada o contaminada con aceite o anticongelante, reemplácela con una nueva.*

18   Prepárese para instalar la banda para la regulación del tiempo girando el tensionador a la derecha con una herramienta Allen y apretando temporalmente la tuerca prisionera (**vea ilustración**).

19   Instale la banda para la regulación del tiempo con la flecha direccional apuntando hacia adelante.

20   Alínee las líneas blancas de fábrica en la banda del tiempo con la marca de punzón marcada en cada una de las poleas del árbol de levas y la polea del cigüeñal. Asegúrese que los tres juegos de las marcas de la regulación del tiempo están apropiadamente alineadas (**vea ilustraciones**). Si una flecha aparece en la banda, debe mirar hacia el frente de la tapa para la banda.

10.20a Alínee las marcas blancas en la banda (flechas) con las marcas del punzón en las poleas del árbol de levas y la tapa de la banda trasera del tiempo para asegurase de que el tiempo de la válvula esté correcto - ¡esto es extremadamente importante - no continúe con la instalación de la banda hasta que esté seguro que esté correcto!

10.20b Asegúrese que la marca de la polea del cigüeñal está alineada con la mella en el albergue de la bomba de aceite (flechas) antes de liberar el tensionador de la banda del tiempo

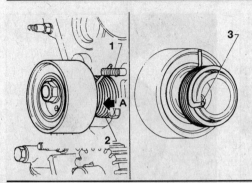

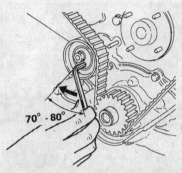

10.21 Detalles de la instalación del resorte del tensionador de la banda (si el espárrago es removido, use Loctite en las roscas durante la instalación)

1 Espárrago
2 Resorte de retorno
3 Resorte de retorno de tipo gancho

10.22 Use una herramienta Allen para girar la polea de tensión de 70 a 80 grados en una dirección al favor de las manecillas del reloj

Ajustar

Refiérase a las ilustraciones 10.21, 10.22, 10.26, 10.27 y 10.31

21 Si el tensionador fue removido, vuelva a instalarlo y asegúrese que el resorte esté puesto en posición apropiadamente **(vea ilustración)**. Mantenga el tensionador estabilizado con la herramienta Allen y afloje la tuerca prisionera.

22 Usando la herramienta Allen, hágale columpio al tensionador de 70 a 80 grados en una dirección al favor de las manecillas

del reloj y apriete temporariamente la tuerca prisionera **(vea ilustración)**.

23 Instale todas las bujías.

24 Lentamente gire el cigüeñal al favor de las manecillas del reloj dos o tres revoluciones completas, entonces regrese el pistón número uno al TDC en la carrera de compresión. **Caución:** *Si se siente resistencia mientras está girando el cigüeñal, es una indicación que los pistones están entrando en contacto con las válvulas. Vaya de regreso sobre el procedimiento para corregir la situación antes de proceder.*

25 Afloje la tuerca prisionera del tensionador mientras mantiene el tensionador estabilizado con la herramienta Allen.

26 Coloque un calibrador al tacto de 0.0138 pulgada de espesor adyacente al tensionador de la polea **(vea ilustración)**.

27 Lentamente gire el cigüeñal a la derecha hasta que el calibrador al tacto esté entre la banda y la polea del tensionador **(vea ilustración)**.

28 Apriete la tuerca prisionera del tensionador, mantenga el tensionador estabilizado con la herramienta Allen.

29 Gire el cigüeñal para remover el calibrador al tacto.

30 Lentamente gire el cigüeñal dos o tres revoluciones y regrese el pistón número uno al TDC.

31 Chequee la deflección de la banda para la sincronización del tiempo aplicando 22

libras de fuerza a medio camino entre las poleas del árbol de levas **(vea ilustración)**. La banda debe desviarse de 0.512 a 0.571 pulgada (13 a 14.5 mm). Ajuste de nuevo la banda si es necesario.

32 Instale los varios componentes removidos durante el proceso de desarmar, refiérase a las Secciones apropiadas en este Capítulo.

11 Sello delantero del cigüeñal para el aceite - reemplazo

Refiérase a las ilustraciones 11.3, 11.4, 11.6, 11.7, 11.8a y 11.8b

1 Desconecte el cable negativo de la terminal negativa de la batería.

2 Remueva el protector para el ventilador y el ensamblaje del ventilador (Capítulo 3), las bandas (Capítulo 1), las poleas (Sección 9), el amortiguador de vibración (Sección 9) y la banda del tiempo (Sección 10).

3 Insercióne dos destornilladores como cuñas atrás de la polea del cigüeñal **(vea ilustración)**. Cuidadosamente hágale palanca a la polea del cigüeñal hacia fuera. Algunas poleas de la banda del tiempo se le pueden hacer palanca fácilmente con destornilladores. Otras son más difíciles de remover porque la corrosión las funde con la nariz del

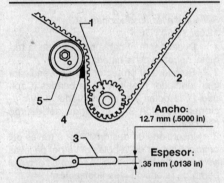

10.26 Posicióne el calibrador de tacto entre el tensionador de la polea y la banda como está mostrado aquí . . .

1 Cigüeñal
2 Banda del tiempo
3 Espesor del calibrador
4 Espesor del calibrador
5 Polea de aplicar tensión

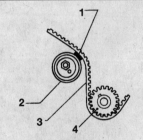

10.27 . . . entonces gire el cigüeñal para mover el calibrador al tacto al grado mostrado aquí (debe ser exacto, así que trabaje cuidadosamente)

1 Espesor del calibrador
2 Espesor del calibrador
3 Banda del tiempo
4 Cigüeñal

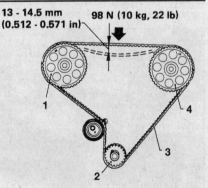

10.31 La deflección de la banda para la sincronización del tiempo es chequeada exactamente a la mitad entre las dos poleas del árbol de levas

1 Árbol de levas derecho
2 Árbol de levas izquierdo
3 banda del tiempo

11.3 Use dos destornilladores para hacerle palanca a la polea del cigüeñal y removerla . . .

11.4 . . . hasta que las mandíbulas del extractor encajen por detrás - esté seguro de instalar el perno para que el tornillo del extractor, no dañe las roscas en la nariz del cigüeñal

11.6 Remueva el sello haciéndole palanca al sello hacia afuera muy cuidadosamente con un destornillador - ¡si el cigüeñal es mellado o de otro modo dañado, el sello nuevo tendrá fugas!

11.7 Aplique grasa de base moly o lubricante de ensamblar motor al labio del sello nuevo antes de instalarlo (si usted aplica una cantidad de grasa pequeña a la orilla exterior, será más fácil de empujarla adentro del orificio)

cigüeñal. Si la polea en su motor es difícil de hacerle palanca para removerla, no trate de removerla completamente hacia afuera con destornilladores. En lugar, deslícela apenas lo suficiente hacia adelante para agarrarla con un extractor.

4   Una vez que haya suficiente espacio entre la polea y el albergue de la bomba de aceite para instalar un extractor de engrane pequeño, enrosque el perno del amortiguador de vibración en la nariz del cigüeñal e instale el extractor. El perno proporciona algo sólido para que el tornillo del extractor pueda empujar contra y para proteger las roscas del cigüeñal **(vea ilustración)**.

5   Gire el perno del extractor hasta que se salga la polea hacia afuera. Remueva el plato para la banda de la regulación del tiempo **(vea ilustración 10.14b)**.

6   Hágale palanca cuidadosamente al sello de aceite hacia afuera con un destornillador **(vea ilustración)**. ¡No raye o melle en el proceso el cigüeñal!

7   Antes de la instalación, aplique una capa delgada de lubricante de ensamblar al interior del sello **(vea ilustración)**.

8   Fabrique una herramienta para instalar sellos de una longitud corta de tubo del diámetro exterior igual o levemente más pequeña que el mismo sello. Lime el extremo del tubo que se cortó y hará contacto con el sello hasta que las orillas estén libres de puntas agudas. Usted necesitará también una arandela grande, levemente más grande que el diámetro del tubo, donde la cabeza del perno se pueda sentar **(vea ilustración)**. Instale el sello de aceite apretándolo en posición con la herramienta para la instalación del sello **(vea ilustración)**. Cuando usted sienta y vea que el sello se detiene, no gire el perno más o usted dañará el sello.

9   Deslice el plato para la banda del tiempo encima de la nariz del cigüeñal.

10   Asegúrese que la llave Woodruff está en su posición en el cigüeñal.

11   Aplique una capa delgada de lubricante de ensamblar motor en el interior de la polea del cigüeñal y la desliza hacia el cigüeñal.

12   La instalación del resto de los componentes se hace en el orden inverso al procedimiento de desensamble. Apriete todos los pernos al par de torsión especificado.

12   Sello de aceite para el árbol de levas - reemplazo

Refiérase a las ilustraciones 12.3, 12.4, 12.5a, 12.5b y 12.6

1   Desconecte el cable negativo de la terminal negativa de la batería.

2   Remueva el protector para el ventilador y el ventilador (Capítulo 3), la bandas (Capítulo 1), la polea y el amortiguador de vibraciones (Sección 9) y la banda del tiempo (Sección 10).

3   Insercióne un destornillador a través del orificio superior de la polea del árbol de levas para cerrarlo en su posición mientras afloja el perno de retención **(vea ilustración)**.

4   Una vez que el perno esté fuera, la polea puede ser removida con la mano. **Nota:** *Cada polea es marcada con una R o L* **(vea ilustración)**. *Si usted está removiendo ambas poleas de ambos árboles de levas, no las mezcle. Ellas deben ser instaladas en la misma leva que ellas fueron removidas.*

5   Remueva cuidadosamente el sello viejo

11.8a Fabrique una herramienta para instalar sellos de un pedazo de tubo y una arandela grande . . .

11.8b . . . para empujar el sello adentro del orificio - el tubo se debe soportar contra la orilla exterior del sello según el perno es apretado

12.3 Insercióne un destornillador a través de la polea del árbol de levas para detenerlo mientras afloja el perno de la polea

12.4 Cuando esté instalando las poleas de la banda del tiempo del árbol de levas, note las marcas R y L que designan las cabezas del lado derecho y del lado izquierdo de los cilindros - ¡no mezcle las poleas!

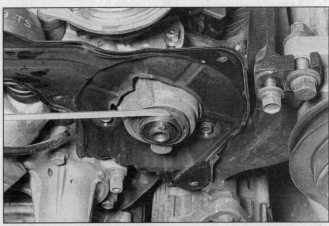

12.5a Hágale palanca al sello hacia afuera muy cuidadosamente con un destornillador (¡si el árbol de levas es mellado o rasguñado, el sello nuevo tendrá fugas!)

de aceite con un destornillador. No melle o rasguñe el árbol de levas en el proceso (vea ilustraciones). Refiérase a los Pasos 6, 7 y 8 en la Sección 11. La mismo herramienta usada para instalar el sello del cigüeñal se puede usar para los sellos de ambos árboles de levas (vea ilustración 11.8a).

6   Instale la polea. ¡Asegúrese que la marca R o L mira hacia fuera! El lado de la polea con el receso debe mirar hacia el motor, que significa que el receso superficial debe mirar hacia afuera (vea ilustración).

7   Insercióne un destornillador a través del orificio superior de la polea en el árbol de levas para detenerla en su posición mientras usted aprieta el perno.

8   La instalación de los componentes que quedan se hace en el orden inverso al procedimiento de desensamble.

13   Cabezas de los cilindros - remover e instalar

Refiérase a la ilustración 13.8

Nota: Permita que el motor se enfríe completamente antes de empezar este procedi-

miento.

1   Alivie la presión del combustible (Capítulo 4).

2   Desconecte el cable negativo de la terminal negativa de la batería.

3   Drene el anticongelante del motor (Capítulo 1).

4   Remueva la banda para la regulación del tiempo (Sección 10).

5   Remueva el cuerpo de aceleración (Capítulo 4).

6   Remueva el múltiple de admisión (Sección 7).

7   Remueva la polea de la leva(s) (Sección 12).

8   Separe la tapa trasera del tiempo removiendo los cuatro pernos (vea ilustración).

Remover

Refiérase a las ilustraciones 13.15a, 13.15b y 13.16

Cabeza izquierda de los cilindros

9   Remueva el compresor del aire acondicionado del soporte y póngalo a un lado. Pueda que sea ventajoso asegurar el compresor con alambre para estar seguro de que no se mueve (Capítulo 3). ¡NO desconecte ninguna de las líneas de refrigerante del compresor!

12.5b La misma herramienta que usted fabricó para la instalación del sello del frente del cigüeñal se puede usar para instalar los sellos del árbol de levas

10   Remueva el distribuidor (Capítulo 5).

11   Remueva el alternador y lo asegura fuera del camino (Capítulo 5).

12   Remueva los pernos que conectan el soporte del aire acondicionado/alternador al motor y remueva el soporte.

13   Remueva las tuercas del múltiple de escape en el lado izquierdo y deslice el múltiple hacia afuera de la cabeza de los cilindros (Sección 8).

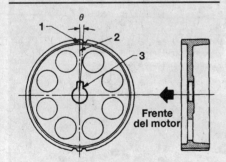

12.6 ¡Asegúrese que la polea del árbol de levas está instalada con la cara marcada hacia el lado de FUERA!

1   Marca de alineación
2   Marca de identificación estampada
3   Bocallave

13.8 Remueva los cuatro pernos de retención para separar la tapa trasera de la banda del tiempo

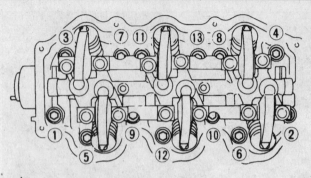

Frente del motor   Afloje numéricamente en orden

13.15a Secuencia de como AFLOJAR los pernos de la cabeza de los cilindros (afloje los pernos 1/4 de vuelta a la vez hasta que ellos puedan ser removidos a mano)

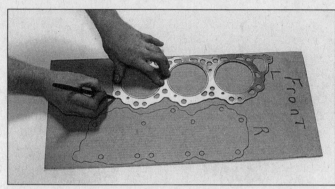

13.15b Para evitar mezclar los pernos de la cabeza, use una junta nueva para transferir el patrón de los orificio a un pedazo de cartón, haga orificios con un punzón para aceptar los pernos y empuje cada perno a través de cada orificio de referencia en el cartón

14 Remueva los componentes de los balancines (Sección 5).

15 Afloje los pernos de la cabeza de los cilindros en incrementos de 1/4 de vuelta hasta que ellos puedan ser removidos con la mano. Esté seguro de seguir la secuencia numérica apropiada **(vea ilustración)**. Los pernos de la cabeza deben ser reinstalados en sus posiciones originales. Para prevenir que no se mezclen, almacénelos en poseedores de cartón marcados para indicar el patrón de los pernos. Esté seguro de marcar los poseedores L y R e indique el frente del motor **(vea ilustración)**.

16 Remueva el perno pequeño, localizado en el frente inferior de la cabeza, asegurando la cabeza al bloque **(vea ilustración)**.

17 Levante la cabeza del bloque. Si se siente resistencia, afloje la cabeza golpeándola con un bloque de madera y un martillo. ¡Si hacerle palanca es requerido, tenga mucho cuidado de no dañar la cabeza ni el bloque!

Cabeza derecha de los cilindros

18 En los vehículos que estén equipados, destornille la bomba de la dirección de poder y hágale columpio para apartarla sin desconectar las mangueras hidráulicas.

19 Remueva el múltiple de escape (Sección 8).

20 Remueva los componentes de los balancines (Sección 5).

21 Remueva los pernos de la cabeza de los cilindros y manténgalos en orden como está descrito en el Paso 15.

22 Remueva el perno pequeño, localizado en la parte trasera de la cabeza, que asegura la cabeza de los cilindros al bloque del motor.

23 Levante la cabeza del motor.

24 Si se siente resistencia, afloje la cabeza golpeándolo con un bloque de madera y un martillo. ¡Si hacerle palanca es requerido, tenga mucho cuidado de no dañar la cabeza ni el bloque!

Instalar

Refiérase a las ilustraciones 13.29, 13.31a y 13.31b

25 Las superficies de acoplamiento de las cabezas de los cilindros y el bloque deben estar perfectamente limpias cuando las cabezas sean instaladas.

26 Use un raspador de junta para remover todos los rasgos de carbón y material de la junta vieja, después limpie las superficies de acoplamiento con rebajador de pintura o acetona. Si hay aceite en las superficies de acoplamiento cuando las cabezas sean instaladas, las juntas no podrán sellar correctamente y fugas pueden desarrollarse. Use una aspiradora para remover cualquier residuo que caiga adentro de los cilindros.

27 Chequee por mellas en el bloque y las superficies de acoplamiento de la cabeza, rayones y otros daños profundos. Si el daño es leve, puede ser removido con una lima - si es excesivo, rectificación a máquina puede ser solamente el único alternativo.

28 Use una terraja macho del tamaño correcto para seguir las roscas de los pernos en la cabeza. Ponga cada perno en una prensa y corra una terraja hembra en las roscas para remover la corrosión y rectificar las roscas. La tierra, corrosión, sellador y las roscas dañadas afectarán las lecturas técnicas.

29 Posicione las juntas nuevas en las clavijas fija del bloque **(vea ilustración)**.

30 Posicione cuidadosamente en el bloque las cabezas sin perturbador las juntas.

31 Instale los pernos en sus lugares originales y apriételo con los dedos. Asegúrese que las arandelas están en posición en los pernos - el lado del radius de la arandela debe estar contra la cabeza del perno, que

13.16 Remueva el perno pequeño delantero (flecha) antes de procurar separar la cabeza del lado derecho - la cabeza izquierda tiene un perno similar en la parte trasera

13.29 Cuando esté instalando la junta nueva, asegúrese que se emparejan apropiadamente con las clavijas de alineación (flechas)

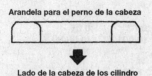

Arandela para el perno de la cabeza

Lado de la cabeza de los cilindro

13.31a Las arandelas en los pernos de la cabeza deben ser instaladas con el lado del radius contra la cabeza del perno

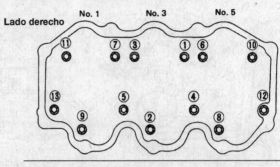

Lado derecho

No. 1   No. 3   No. 5

13.31b Secuencia de como APRETAR los pernos de la cabeza de los cilindros (note que los pernos 4, 5, 12 y 13 en la secuencia son más largo que el resto)

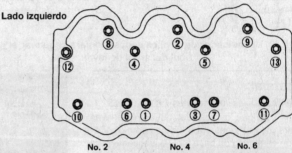

Lado izquierdo

No. 2   No. 4   No. 6

significa que el lado plano debe estar contra la superficie de la cabeza de los cilindros **(vea ilustración)**. Siga la secuencia reco-mendada y apriete los pernos en cinco pasos al par de torsión especificado **(vea ilustra-ción)**. **Caución:** *¡Los pernos 4, 5, 12 y 13 en la secuencia son más largo que los otros - esté seguro que todos los pernos están insta-lados en sus lugares originales!*

32   La instalación se hace en el orden inverso al procedimiento de desensamble.

33   Cambie el aceite y filtro del motor (Capí-tulo 1), entonces ponga el motor en marcha y chequee cuidadosamente por fugas de aceite y de anticongelante.

14   Árbol de levas - remover e instalar

Remover

Refiérase a las ilustraciones 14.4, 14.5a, 14.5b, 14.6 y 14.7

1   Remueva del motor la cabeza de los cilindros (Sección 13).

2   Remueva los buzos de las válvulas y la guía del buzo (Sección 6).

3   Remueva los ejes de los balancines (Sección 5).

4   Remueva los pernos y suavemente hágale palanca al plato de la tapa del árbol de levas **(vea ilustración)**.

5   Use la agarradera **(vea ilustración)** para asegurar el árbol de levas con una llave y aflo-jar el perno de retención **(vea ilustración)**. Remueva el perno y el plato de localización.

6   Hágale palanca cuidadosamente al sello

14.4 Remueva los tres pernos del plato de la tapa del árbol de levas

14.5a Detenga el árbol de levas en la agarradera (flecha) con una llave grande . . .

de aceite del árbol de levas hacia afuera de la cabeza con un destornillador pequeño **(vea ilustración)**. ¡No raye o melle el árbol de levas en el proceso!

7   Remueva el árbol de levas cuidadosa-mente hacia el frente de la cabeza usando un

movimiento de rotación **(vea ilustración)**. **Caución:** *No raye las superficies para los cojinetes con los lóbulos de la leva. Inspec-ción del árbol de levas y los cojinetes está cubierto en la Sección 15.*

14.5b . . . mientras afloja el perno de retención del árbol de levas

14.6 Hágale palanca cuidadosamente al sello de aceite del árbol de levas hacia afuera con un destornillador pequeño

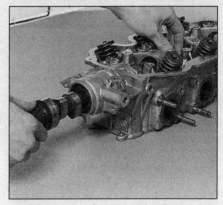

14.7 Remueva el árbol de levas por el frente de la cabeza, usando ambas manos para sostenerlo y evitar dañar las superficies de los cojinetes de la cabeza

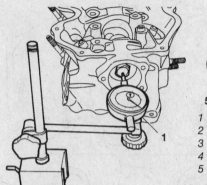

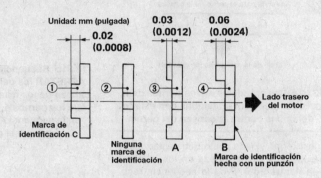

1 Indicador de tipo reloj
2 Juego final
3 Perno
4 Plato de ubicación
5 Árbol de levas

Unidad: mm (pulgada)
0.02 (0.0008)
0.03 (0.0012)
0.06 (0.0024)

Marca de identificación C
Ninguna marca de identificación
A
B
Marca de identificación hecha con un punzón
Lado trasero del motor

14.10 Un indicador de reloj es necesario para chequear el juego final del árbol de levas

14.13 El plato para el impulso del árbol de levas está disponible en diferentes espesores

Instalar

Refiérase a las ilustraciones 14.10 y 14.13

8   Lubrique los cojinetes del árbol de levas para los muñones y los lóbulos con lubricación con grasa de base moly o lubricante para ensamblar motor, después instale cuidadosamente la cabeza. ¡No raye las superficies para los cojinetes con los lóbulos de la leva!

9   Instale el perno de retención del árbol de levas y apriételo al par de torsión especificado.

10   El con el árbol de levas instalado en la cabeza, instale un indicador de tipo reloj para chequear el juego final **(vea ilustración)**.

11   Mueva el árbol de levas hacia atrás de la cabeza lo más posible que se pueda.

12   Ponga a cero el indicador de reloj. Mueva la leva hacia adelante lo mas que sea posible. El indicador debe leer entre 0.0012 a 0.0024 pulgada (0.03 a 0.06 mm).

13   El juego excesivo fuera de la distancia especificada requiere reemplazo del plato para el impulso. Mida el plato viejo **(vea ilustración)** y obtenga uno nuevo en su concesionario que produzca un juego libre lo más cerca como sea posible a 0.0020 pulgada (0.05 mm).

15   Árbol de levas, buzos, balancines, ejes y superficie de los cojinetes - inspección

Refiérase a las ilustraciones 15.1, 15.2, 15.3, 15.4, 15.5, 15.6, 15.7, 15.10 y 15.11

1   Chequee visualmente las superficies para los cojinetes del árbol de levas por orificios pequeños, marcas de rayones, abrasión y desgaste anormal. Si las superficies para los cojinetes están dañadas, la cabeza tendrá que ser reemplazada **(vea ilustración)**.

2   Mida el diámetro exterior de cada muñón del árbol de levas y registre sus medidas **(vea ilustración)**. Compárelas con los diámetros exteriores especificados para el muñón, entonces mida cada diámetro interior del cojinete que corresponde con el árbol de levas y registre las medidas. Compare las especificaciones con el diámetro interior del cojinete del árbol de levas. Reste cada diámetro exterior

15.1 Inspeccione las superficies para los cojinetes de la leva en cada cabeza por hoyos, marcas de rayones y desgaste anormal - si desgaste o daño es notado, la cabeza debe ser reemplazada

del muñón de la leva de su cojinete respectivo de la leva del diámetro interior para determinar el juego libre para el aceite de cada cojinete. Compare el resultado con el al espacio libre especificado del muñón al cojinete. Si alguna de las medidas están fuera de los límite de desgaste especificado, o el árbol de levas o la cabeza, o ambos, deben ser reemplazados.

3   Chequee la desviación axial del árbol de

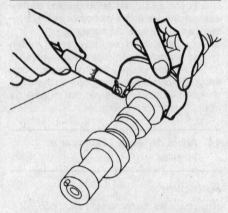

15.2 Mida el diámetro de cada muñón exterior del árbol de levas y el diámetro interior de cada cojinete para determinar los espacios libres

levas poniendo el árbol de levas entre dos bloques en forma de V y ponga un indicador de reloj en el muñón central **(vea ilustración)**. Ponga a cero el indicador de reloj. Gire el árbol de levas lentamente y note las lecturas del indicador de reloj. Registre sus lecturas y compárelas con la desviación especificada. Si la desviación medida excede la desviación especificada, reemplace el árbol de levas.

15.3 Un indicador de reloj y bloques V son necesitados para chequear la desviación axial del árbol de levas

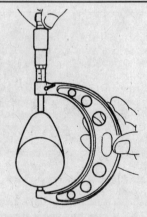

15.4 Midiendo la altura del lóbulo del árbol de levas con un micrómetro

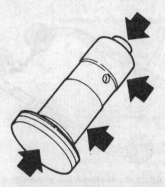

15.5 Chequee el contacto y las superficies deslizantes de cada buzo (flechas) por desgaste y daño

Diámetro externo:

15.947 - 15.957 mm
(0.6278 - 0.6282 pulgada)

15.6 Mida el diámetro exterior de cada buzo con un micrómetro . . .

15.7 . . . y el diámetro interior de cada buzo, entonces reste el diámetro del buzo para determinar el espacio libre entre el buzo y la guía (compare el resultado con las especificaciones)

4   Chequee la altura del lóbulo del árbol de levas midiendo cada lóbulo con un micrómetro **(vea ilustración)**. Compare la medida con la altura del lóbulo del árbol de levas especificado. Entonces reste la altura medida del lóbulo del árbol de levas de la altura especificada para computar el desgaste en los lóbulos de la leva. Compárelo al límite de desgaste especificado. Si es más que el límite de desgaste especificado, reemplace el árbol de levas.

5   Inspeccione las superficies de contacto y de deslizamiento de cada buzo por desgaste y rayones **(vea ilustración)**. **Nota:** *Si la almohadilla del buzo se ha desgastado, es una buena idea de chequear el lóbulo del árbol de levas correspondiente, porque está también probablemente desgastado.* **Caución:** *No gire los buzos al revés - aire puede entrar y puede llegar a ser atrapado adentro (vea Sección 6).*

6   Mida el diámetro exterior de cada buzo con un micrómetro **(vea ilustración)** y lo compara a las especificaciones. Si algún buzo está desgastado más allá del límite especificado, reemplácelo.

7   Chequee cada diámetro interior de los cilindros para el buzo en el ensamblaje de la guía de buzo **(vea ilustración)** y compare el resultado con las especificaciones. Si el diámetro del cilindro de algún buzo se a desgastado más allá del límite especificado, el ensamblaje de la guía del buzo debe ser reemplazado.

8   Reste el diámetro exterior de cada buzo del diámetro interior del cilindro para el buzo y compare la diferencia al espacio libre especificado. Si ambos el buzo y el diámetro de los cilindros están dentro de los límites aceptables, esta medida debe entrar en la tolerancia. Sin embargo, si usted compra un juego nuevo de buzos solamente, o un ensamblaje de guía para los buzos por sí mismo, usted puede encontrar que este espacio libre ya no cae adentro de los límites especificados.

9   Chequee los balancines y los ejes por desgaste anormal, orificios, abrasión, marcas de rayones y áreas ásperas. No atente de restaurar los balancines atentando de esmerilar las superficies de la almohadilla.

10   Mida el diámetro exterior del eje de los balancines en cada muñón del balancín **(vea ilustración)**. Compare las medidas exteriores

con el diámetro especificado de los balancines.

11   Mida el diámetro interior de cada balancín con un micrómetro interior o un calibrador de tipo esfera **(vea ilustración)**. Compare las medidas especificadas al diámetro interior de los cilindros de los balancines.

12   Reste el diámetro exterior del muñón de cada balancín del diámetro del eje interior de los cilindros correspondiente del balancín para computar el espacio libre entre el eje de los balancines y los balancines. Compare las medidas al espacio libre especificado. Si alguna de ellas caen fuera de los límites especificados, reemplace los balancines, el eje, o ambos.

16   Cacerola de aceite - remover e instalar

Refiérase a las ilustraciones 16.19, 16.20 y 16.21

1   Desconecte el cable negativo de la terminal negativa de la batería.
2   Levante el vehículo y supórtelo firmemente sobre estantes.
3   Remueva la parte inferior (cacerola de vientre).
4   Drene el aceite del motor (Capítulo 1).
5   Remueva el motor de arranque (Capítulo 5).
6   Remueva los refuerzos que unen el motor a la campana.
7   Remueva el brazo loco (Capítulo 11).
8   Remueva los pernos del soporte de la barra estabilizadora (Capítulo 11) (modelos de 2WD solamente).
9   Remueva el miembro transversal delantero de la suspensión debajo de la cacerola de aceite (modelos de 2WD solamente).
10   Remueva el portador del diferencial delantero y los calzos de soporte (Capítulo 9) (modelos de 4WD solamente).
11   Destornille los calzos de la transmisión del miembro transversal.
12   Destornille los tubos de escape de los múltiples (Capítulo 4).
13   Sostenga el motor/la transmisión firmemente con un elevador de motores encima o con un gato debajo de la campana. Proteja la

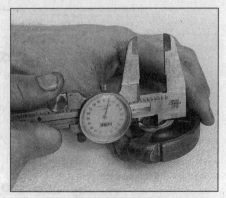

15.10 Mida el diámetro del eje de los balancines en cada muñón donde un balancín corre en el eje

campana poniendo un bloque de madera en la almohadilla del gato. **Peligro:** *¡Esté absolutamente cierto que el motor/la transmisión están seguramente sostenidos! NO coloque ninguna parte de su cuerpo debajo del motor/la transmisión - ¡lo podría aplastar si el gato o el elevador de motores fallan!*
14   Destornille los calzos del motor del chasis.
15   Levante cuidadosamente el motor para

15.11 Mida el diámetro interior de cada balancín, reste el diámetro correspondiente del eje de los balancines para obtener el espacio libre y comparar el resultado a las especificaciones

proporcionar un poquito de espacio libre para remover la cacerola de aceite. Si usted encuentra cualquier resistencia, pare inmediatamente y vea que es lo que lo está deteniendo.

16   Remueva los pernos y separe la cacerola de aceite. No le haga palanca con una barra entre la cacerola y el bloque para removerla o puede resultar en un daño a la superficie y fugas podrían desarrollarse. Si la cacerola está pegada, aflójela con un bloque de madera y un martillo.

17   Use un raspador de junta para remover todos los rasgos de material de la junta vieja, sellador de la cacerola y el bloque. Limpie las superficies de acoplamiento con rebajador de pintura o acetona.

18   Asegúrese que las roscas en el bloque están limpias (use una terraja macho para remover el sellador o la corrosión en cualquiera de las roscas).

19   Aplique una cantidad del sellador RTV (vulcanizador accionado a temperatura ambiente) pequeña a las superficies de acoplación de la bomba de aceite al bloque y del retenedor del sello trasero al bloque **(vea ilustración)**.

20   Aplique sellador a los mismos cuatro puntos en la junta nueva. Esté seguro y alínee la superficie superior e inferior **(vea ilustración)**.

21   Conecte la junta nueva a la cacerola, entonces posicióne la cacerola contra el bloque e instale los pernos. Apriete los pernos en tres o cuatro pasos, siguiendo la secuencia recomendada **(vea ilustración)**.

22   La instalación se hace en el órden inverso al procedimiento de desensamble.

17   Bomba de aceite - remover, inspeccionar e instalar

Refiérase a las ilustraciones 17.3, 17.4, 17.7, 17.10a, 17.10b y 17.13

Remover

1   Remueva la banda para la regulación del tiempo y la polea del cigüeñal (Secciones

16.19 Aplique sellador RTV (vulcanizador accionado a temperatura ambiente) al bloque del motor en la bomba de aceite y las acoplaciones del retenedor del sello principal de aceite trasero (flechas)

10 y 11). Remueva la cacerola del aceite (Sección 16).

2   Remueva los pernos y separe el colador de la bomba de aceite.

3   Remueva los pernos de la bomba de aceite al bloque del motor en el frente del motor **(vea ilustración)**.

4   Use un bloque de madera y un martillo para romper el sello de la junta de la bomba de aceite **(vea ilustración)**.

5   Hale hacia adelante en la bomba de aceite para removerla del bloque del motor.

6   Use un raspador para remover el material de la junta vieja y sellador de las superficies de acoplamiento para la bomba de aceite y el bloque del motor. Limpie las superficies de acoplamiento con rebajador de pintura o acetona.

Inspeccionar

7   Use un destornillador de estrella grande para remover los siete tornillos reteniendo las mitades delanteras y traseras de la bomba de aceite **(vea ilustración)**.

8   Limpie todos los componentes con solvente, entonces los inspecciona por desgaste y daño.

9   Remueva la tapa del regulador de pre-

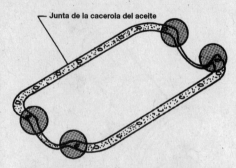

16.20 Aplique sellador a las superficies de la junta superior e inferior de la cacerola del aceite en las áreas con sombra antes de la instalación

sión del aceite, la arandela, el resorte y la válvula. Chequee la superficie deslizante de la válvula del regulador de presión del aceite y el resorte de las válvulas. Si el resorte o la válvula está dañado, ellos deben ser reemplazados como un juego.

10   Chequee los siguientes espacios libres con un calibrador al tacto **(vea ilustraciones)** y compare las medidas a los espacios libres especificados:

> *Cuerpo al engrane exterior*
> *Engrane interior a la cresta*
> *Engrane exterior a la cresta*
> *Albergue al engrane interior*
> *Albergue al engrane exterior*

Si cualquiera de los espacios libres son excesivo, reemplace el conjunto completo de engranes o el ensamblaje de la bomba de aceite completa.

11   **Nota:** *Empaque la bomba de aceite con jalea de petróleo para cargarla.* Arme la bomba de aceite y apriete los tornillos firmemente. Instale la válvula del regulador de presión del aceite, el resorte y la arandela, entonces apriete la tapa de los balancines del regulador de presión del aceite.

Instalar

12   Aplique sellador RTV (vulcanizador accionado a temperatura ambiente) a las superficies de montaje de la bomba de aceite.

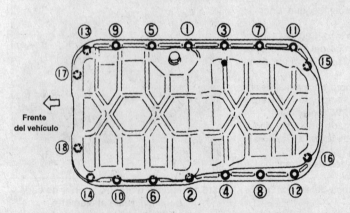

16.21 Secuencia de como apretar los pernos de la cacerola del aceite

17.3 Remueva los pernos de retención de la bomba de aceite (flechas) y separe la bomba del motor

17.4 Use un bloque de madera y un martillo para romper suavemente el sello de la junta de la bomba de aceite - ¡no golpée el albergue de la bomba con un martillo de acero!

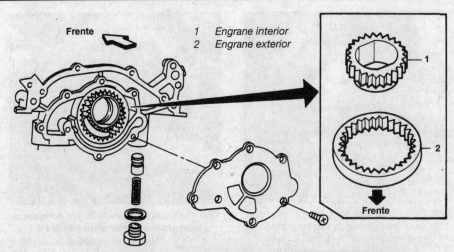

Frente

1 Engrane interior
2 Engrane exterior

Frente

17.7 Componentes de la bomba de aceite - vista esquemática

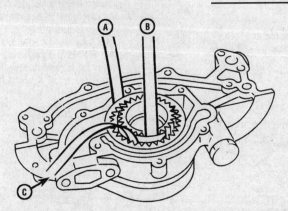

17.10a Use un calibrador al tacto para chequear el espacio libre del albergue al exterior del engrane (A), el espacio libre entre el engrane interior y el creciente (B) y el espacio libre entre el engrane exterior y el creciente (C)

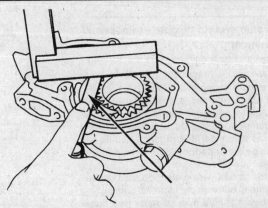

17.10b Chequee el espacio libre del albergue de la bomba de aceite al engrane interior y del albergue al engrane exterior con una regla de precisión y un calibrador al tacto (flecha)

13   Use juntas nuevas en todas las partes desarmadas e invierta el procedimiento de remover para la instalación. Apriete todos los afianzadores firmemente. **Nota:** *Antes de instalar el colador de la bomba de aceite, reemplace el anillo sellador de caucho de tipo O* **(vea ilustración).**

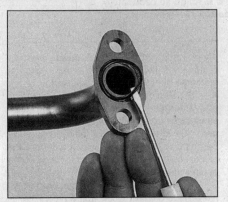

17.13 Antes de instalar el colador de aceite, reemplace el anillo sellador de tipo O de caucho

18   Sello trasero para el aceite del cigüeñal - reemplazo

Refiérase a las ilustraciones 18.3 y 18.6

1   Remueva la transmisión (vea Capítulo 7A para transmisión manual, Capítulo 7B para automática).

18.3 Remueva el sello hacia afuera muy cuidadosamente con una palanca o con un destornillador - ¡si el cigüeñal es dañado, el sello nuevo tendrá fugas!

2   Remueva el volante/plato flexible (Sección 19).

3   Insercióne un destornillador entre el sello del aceite y el cigüeñal, entonces remueva el sello hacia afuera del retenedor con una palanca **(vea ilustración).** ¡Tenga mucho cuidado de no mellar o rayar el cigüeñal en el proceso!

4   Aplique una capa de grasa de base moly a la orilla exterior y al labio del sello nuevo.

5   Empuje el sello hacia el cigüeñal y suavemente péguele para que entre adentro del orificio con un martillo de cara suave.

6   Una vez que la cara del sello esté plana con el retenedor del sello y la pestaña del cigüeñal, accione cuidadosamente el resto del sello en el retenedor con el extremo de un punzón. Un punzón de bronce es mejor **(vea ilustración). Caución:** *Sea extremadamente cuidadoso. Tómese su tiempo y accione el sello suavemente y uniformemente en su posición. Dañar el sello nuevo resultará en una fuga de aceite.*

7   El resto de la instalación se hace en el orden inverso al procedimiento de desensamble.

18.6 Una vez que el sello esté al nivel con la cara del retenedor, use un punzón (preferiblemente de bronce) para accionar cuidadosamente el resto del sello hacia adentro

19.3 Para asegurar un balance apropiado, marque el volante/plato flexible en relación al cigüeñal

19.4 Los pernos del volante/plato flexible están muy apretados, así que use un dado de seis puntos y una barra ruptora de 1/2 pulgada para aflojarlos

19   Volante/plato flexible - remover e instalar

Refiérase a las ilustraciones 19.3 y 19.4

1   Levante el vehículo y sopórtelo firmemente sobre estantes, entonces refiérase al Capítulo 7 y remueva la transmisión.

2   Remueva el plato de presión del embrague y el disco del embrague (Capítulo 8) (vehículos equipados con transmisión manual).

3   Use pintura para pintar una línea desde el volante al extremo del cigüeñal para instalarlo correctamente más adelante **(vea ilustración)**.

4   Remueva los pernos que retienen el volante a la brida trasera del cigüeñal **(vea ilustración)**. Si se encuentra dificultad para remover los pernos debido al movimiento del cigüeñal, use un destornillador como cuña a través de la apertura del motor de arranque para permitir que no gire el volante.

5   Remueva el volante/plato flexible desde la brida del cigüeñal.

6   Limpie cualquier grasa o aceite en el volante. Inspeccione la superficie del volante por ranuras hechas por los remaches, zonas quemadas y marcas de rayones. Rayones pequeños pueden removerse con tela de esmeril. Chequee por dentaduras agrietadas o rotas. Coloque el volante en una superficie nivelada y use una regla recta para chequear por combadura.

7   Limpie las superficies de contacto del volante/plato flexible y el cigüeñal.

8   Coloque el volante/plato flexible contra el cigüeñal, alínee las marcas que hizo cuando lo removió. Antes de instalar los pernos, aplíquele Loc-Tite a las roscas.

9   Con un destornillador hágale cuña entre el motor de arranque y la abertura para permitir que no gire el volante. Apriete los pernos a la torsión especificada en dos o tres pasos. Siga la secuencia recomendada

10   Los pasos restantes para la instalación se hacen en el orden inverso al procedimiento de desensamble.

20.2 Calzos del motor - vista esquemática

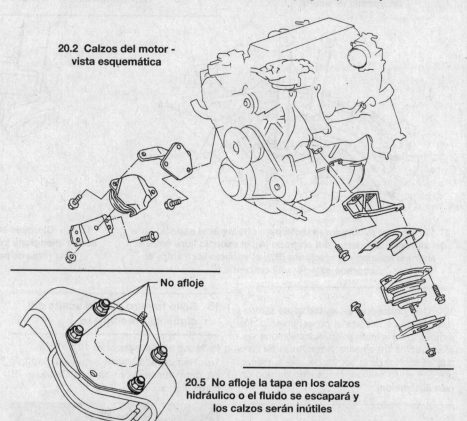

No afloje

20.5 No afloje la tapa en los calzos hidráulico o el fluido se escapará y los calzos serán inútiles

20   Soportes del motor - chequeo y reemplazo

Refiérase a las ilustraciones 20.2 y 20.5

1   Los soportes del motor deberían inspeccionarse periódicamente por cuarteaduras de la goma y separación de la goma desdе el soporte del metal.

2   Reemplace los calzos delanteros aflojando las tuercas y los pernos que los retienen al bloque del motor y al chasis en ambos lados del motor **(vea ilustración)**.

3   Remueva el peso del motor de los calzos con un gato y un bloque de madera entre el cárter de aceite y el gato. Cuidadosamente

levante el motor lo suficiente para permitir remover los calzos. Cuidado extremo debería ejercerse durante este procedimiento.

4   Si usted determina usar los calzos viejos nuevamente, márquelos claramente para asegurarse que ellos se instalan en el mismo lado que antes. Remueva las tuercas y los pernos que retienen los calzos y separe los calzos, notando la posición correcta de como están instalados.

5   No afloje la tapa en los calzos de tipo hidráulicos o fluido se escapará **(vea ilustración)**.

6   Los pasos restantes para la instalación se hacen en el orden inverso al procedimiento de desensamble.

Capítulo 2 Parte C
Procedimientos generales para la reconstrucción de motores

Contenidos

Especificaciones

Motor (1980) de cuatro cilindros L20B

General

Presión de aceite .... 50 a 60 psi (libras por pulgadas cuadradas) @ 3000 rpm
Presión de la compresión (@ 350 rpm)
  Estándar .... 171 psi
  Mínimo .... 128 psi

Árbol de levas .... Vea Capítulo 2, Parte A

Cabeza de los cilindros

Límite de la combadura .... 0.004 pulgada (0.1 mm)

Válvulas

Diámetro del vástago de las válvulas
  Admisión .... 0.3136 a 0.3142 pulgada (7.965 a 7.980 mm)
  Escape .... 0.3128 a 0.3134 pulgada (7.945 a 7.960 mm)
Longitud libre del resorte de las válvulas (admisión y escape)
  Interior .... 1.766 pulgadas (44.85 mm)
  Exterior .... 1.968 pulgadas (49.98 mm)
Altura de la guía de la válvula desde la superficie de la cabeza de los cilindros .... 0.417 pulgada (10.6 mm)
Diámetro interno de la guía de la válvula .... 0.3150 a 0.3154 pulgada (8.000 a 8.018 mm)
Espacio libre del vástago de la válvula a la guía de la válvula
  Admisión .... 0.0008 a 0.0021 pulgada (0.101 a 0.053 mm)
  Escape .... 0.0016 a 0.0029 pulgada (0.040 a 0.073 mm)
Límite de deflexión del vástago de la válvula .... 0.008 pulgada (0.2 mm)

Motor (1980) de cuatro cilindros L20B (continuación)

Bloque del motor

Límite de distorsión de la parte superior	0.004 pulgada (0.1 mm)
Diámetro interior de los cilindros	3.3465 a 3.3484 pulgadas (85.000 a 85.050 mm)
Conicidad de los cilindros/desviación radial	Menos de 0.0006 pulgada (0.015 mm)
Espacio libre del pistón al cilindro	0.0010 a 0.0018 pulgada (0.025 a 0.045 mm)

Pistones y anillos

Diámetro de los pistones	
Estándar	3.3459 a 3.3478 pulgadas (84.985 a 85.035 mm)
Primer tamaño sobre medida...	3.3648 a 3.3667 pulgadas (85.465 a 85.515 mm)
Segundo tamaño sobre medida..	3.3844 a 3.3864 pulgadas (85.965 a 86.015 mm)
Espacio libre lateral del anillo del pistón	
Anillo de compresión superior	0.0016 a 0.0029 pulgada (0.040 a 0.073 mm)
Segundo anillo de compresión	0.0012 a 0.0025 pulgada (0.030 a 0.063 mm)
Brecha del extremo del anillo del pistón	
Anillo de compresión superior	0.0098 a 0.0157 pulgada (0.25 a 0.040 mm)
Segundo anillo de compresión	0.0059 a 0.0118 pulgada (0.15 a 0.30 mm)
Anillo de aceite	0.0118 a 0.0354 pulgada (0.30 a 0.90 mm)

Cigüeñal, bielas y cojinetes principales

Juego final de la biela (espacio lateral)...	0.0079 a 0.118 pulgada (0.20 a 0.30 mm)
Juego final del cigüeñal	
Estándar	0.0020 a 0.0071 pulgada (0.05 a 0.18 mm)
Límite..	0.0118 pulgada (0.3 mm)
Diámetro del muñón principal	2.1631 a 2.1636 pulgadas (54.942 a 54.955 mm)
Diámetro del muñón de la biela	1.9670 a 1.9675 pulgadas (49.961 a 49.974 mm)
Conicidad del muñón/límite del desviación radial.............................	0.0004 pulgada (0.01 mm)
Juego libre del aceite para el cojinete principal	
Estándar	0.008 a 0.0024 pulgada)0.020 a 0.062 mm)
Límite..	0.0047 pulgada (0.12 mm)
Juego libre de la biela para el aceite	0.0010 a 0.0022 pulgada (0.025 a 0.055 mm)
Límite de la desviación radial del cigüeñal	0.0020 pulgada (0.05 mm)

Especificaciones técnicas*

	Pies-libras
Tuercas de las bielas	40
Pernos de la tapa para los cojinetes principales.............................	40
Pernos de la transmisión al motor..	35
Pernos del plato flexible al convertidor de torsión	35
Pernos del embrague al volante	15
Pernos de afianzamiento del volante/plato flexible..........................	110

Nota: Refiérase a la Parte A para las especificaciones técnicas adicionales.

Motores Z20, Z22 y Z24 (NAPS-Z) (1981 en adelante)

General

Presión del aceite	
En marcha mínima...	10.7 psi
A 3000 rpm)..	47 a 67 psi
Presión de la compresión	
Estándar	171 psi
Mínimo..	128 psi

Árbol de levas y los balancines... | Vea Capítulo 2, parte A

Cabeza de los cilindros

Límite de la combadura	0.004 pulgada (0.1 mm)

Válvulas

Diámetro del vástago de las válvulas	
Admisión	0.3136 a 0.3142 pulgada (7.965 a 7.980 mm)
Escape...	0.3128 a 0.3134 pulgada (7.945 a 7.960 mm)
Ángulo de la cara de la válvula...	45 grados
Anchura del margen de la válvula	
Admisión	
Estándar..	0.051 pulgada (1.3 mm)
Límite	0.020 pulgada (0.5 mm)

Escape
    Estándar.. 0.059 pulgada (1.5 mm)
    Límite .... 0.020 pulgada (0.05 mm)
Límite de rectificación de los vástagos de las válvulas..................... 0.020 pulgada (0.5 mm)
Longitud libre del resorte de las válvulas
    Resorte exterior... 1.9594 pulgadas (49.77 mm)
    Resorte interior.. 1.7362 pulgadas (44.10 mm)
Altura instalada del resorte de las válvulas
    Resorte exterior
        Estándar .... 1.575 pulgadas @ 50.7 libras (40.0 mm @ 23.0 kg)
        Límite.. 1.575 pulgadas @ 42.6 libras (40.0 mm @ 19.3 kg)
Resorte interior
    Estándar .... 1.378 pulgadas @ 24.3 libras (35.0 mm @ 11.0 kg)
    Límite.. 1.378 pulgadas @ 19.6 libras (35.0 mm @ 8.9 kg)
Resorte de las válvulas fuera del límite cuadrado
    Resorte exterior... 0.087 pulgada (2.2 mm)
    Resorte interior.. 0.075 pulgada (1.9 mm)
Diámetro interno de la guía de la válvula....................................... 0.3150 a 0.3157 pulgada (8.000 a 8.018 mm)
Espacio libre del vástago de la válvula a la guía de la válvula
    Admisión .... 0.0008 a 0.0021 pulgada (0.020 a 0.053 mm)
    Escape.. 0.0016 a 0.0029 pulgada (0.040 a 0.073 mm)
Límite de deflección del vástago de la válvula .... 0.008 pulgada (0.2 mm)
Asiento de la válvula
    Ángulo .... 45 grados
    Anchura
        Admisión... 0.071 a 0.094 pulgada (1.8 a 2.4 mm)
        Escape .... 0.059 a 0.075 pulgada (1.5 a 1.9 mm)

Bloque del motor
Límite de distorsión de la parte superior .... 0.004 pulgada (0.1 mm)
Diámetro interior de los cilindros
    Todos los motores Z22 .... 3.4252 a 3.4272 pulgadas (87.000 a 87.050 mm)
    Motor Z20
        1984 .... 3.3465 a 3.3484 pulgadas (85.000 a 85.050 mm)
        1985
        Estándar (1 grado) .... 3.3465 a 3.3468 pulgadas (85.000 a 85.010 mm)
        Grado 2 .... 3.3468 a 3.3472 pulgadas (85.010 a 85.020 mm)
        Grado 3 .... 3.3472 a 3.3476 pulgadas (85.020 a 85.030 mm)
        Grado 4 .... 3.3476 a 3.3480 pulgadas (85.030 a 85.040 mm)
        Grado 5 .... 3.3480 a 3.3484 pulgadas (85.040 a 85.050 mm)
    Todos los motores Z24
        Grado 1 .... 3.5039 a 3.5043 pulgadas (89.000 a 89.010 mm)
        Grado 2 .... 3.5043 a 3.5047 pulgadas (89.010 a 89.020 mm)
        Grado 3 .... 3.5047 a 3.5051 pulgadas (89.020 a 89.030 mm)
        Grado 4 .... 3.5051 a 3.5055 pulgadas (89.030 a 89.040 mm)
        Grado 5 .... 3.5055 a 3.5059 pulgadas (89.040 a 89.050 mm)
Conicidad de los cilindros/desviación radial .... Menos de 0.0006 pulgada (0.015 mm)
Espacio libre del pistón al cilindro .... 0.0010 a 0.0018 pulgada (0.025 a 0.045 mm)

Pistones y anillos
Diámetro
    Todos los motores Z22
        Estándar.. 3.4246 a 3.4266 pulgadas (86.985 a 87.035 mm)
        Primer tamaño sobre medida .... 3.4435 a 3.4455 pulgadas (87.465 a 87.515 mm)
        Segundo tamaño sobre medida .... 3.4632 a 3.4652 pulgadas (87.965 a 88.015 mm)
    Motor Z20
        1984
        Estándar.. 3.3451 a 3.3470 pulgadas (84.965 a 85.015 mm)
        Primer tamaño sobre medida .... 3.3459 a 3.3478 pulgadas (84.985 a 85.035 mm)
        Segundo tamaño sobre medida .... 3.3648 a 3.3667 pulgadas (85.465 a 85.515 mm)
        3rd demasiado grande.. 3.3844 a 3.3864 pulgadas (85.965 a 86.015 mm)
        1985
        Estándar (1 grado) .... 3.3451 a 3.3455 pulgadas (84.965 a 84.975 mm)
        Grado 2 .... 3.3455 a 3.3459 pulgadas (84.975 a 84.985 mm)
        Grado 3 .... 3.3459 a 3.3463 pulgadas (84.985 a 84.995 mm)
        Grado 4 .... 3.3463 a 3.3466 pulgadas (84.995 a 85.005 mm)
        Grado 5... 3.3466 a 3.3470 pulgadas (85.005 a 85.015 mm)

Motores Z20, Z22 y Z24 (NAPS-Z) (1981 en adelante) (continuación)

Motor Z24
    1984 y 1988 solamente

Estándar	3.5026 a 3.5045 pulgadas (88.965 a 89.015 mm)
Primer tamaño sobre medida	3.5033 a 3.5053 pulgadas (88.985 a 89.035 mm)
Segundo tamaño sobre medida	3.5222 a 3.5242 pulgadas (89.465 a 89.515 mm)
3rd demasiado grande	3.5419 a 3.5439 pulgadas (89.965 a 90.015 mm)

    1985 al 1987

Estándar (1 grado)	3.5026 a 3.5029 pulgadas (88.965 a 88.975 mm)
Grado 2	3.5029 a 3.5033 pulgadas (88.975 a 88.985 mm)
Grado 3	3.5033 a 3.5037 pulgadas (88.985 a 88.995 mm)
Grado 4	3.5037 a 3.5041 pulgadas (88.995 a 89.005 mm)
Grado 5	3.5041 a 3.5045 pulgadas (89.005 a 89.015 mm)

Brecha del extremo del anillo del pistón

Anillo de compresión superior	0.0098 a 0.0157 pulgada (0.25 a 0.40 mm)
Segundo anillo de compresión	0.0059 a 0.0118 pulgada (0.15 a 0.30 mm)
Anillo de aceite	0.0118 a 0.0354 pulgada (0.30 a 0.90 mm)

Espacio libre lateral del anillo del pistón

Anillo de compresión superior	0.0016 a 0.0029 pulgada (0.040 a 0.073 mm)
Segundo anillo de compresión	0.0012 a 0.0025 pulgada (0.030 a 0.063 mm)

Cigüeñal, bielas y cojinetes principales

Juego final de la biela (espacio lateral)

Estándar	0.008 a 0.012 pulgada (0.2 a 0.3 mm)
Límite	0.024 pulgada (0.6 mm)

Juego final del cigüeñal

Estándar	0.0020 a 0.0071 pulgada (0.05 a 0.18 mm)
Límite	0.012 pulgada (0.3 mm)
Diámetro principal del muñón del cojinete	2.1631 a 2.1636 pulgadas (54.942 a 54.955 mm)
Diámetro del muñón de la biela	1.9670 a 1.9675 pulgadas (49.961 a 49.974 mm)

Conicidad del muñón/desviación radial

Estándar	Menos de 0.0004 pulgada (0.01 mm)
Límite	0.0012 pulgada (0.03 mm)

Juego libre del aceite para el cojinete principal

Estándar	0.0008 a 0.0024 pulgada (0.020 a 0.062 mm)
Límite	0.0047 pulgada (0.12 mm)

Juego libre de la biela para el aceite

Estándar	0.0010 a 0.0022 pulgada (0.025 a 0.055 mm)
Límite	0.0047 pulgada (0.12 mm)
Límite de desviación del volante	0.0059 pulgada (0.15 mm)

Especificaciones técnicas*

Pies-libras

Pernos de la tapa para los cojinetes principales	36
Tuercas de la tapa para los cojinete de las bielas	36

*Nota: *Refiérase a la Parte A para las especificaciones técnicas adicionales.*

Motor V6

General

Presión del aceite

En marcha mínima	9 psi (libras por pulgadas cuadradas)
A 3200 rpm	53 a 67 psi

Presión de la compresión a 300 rpm

Estándar	173 psi
Mínimo	128 psi
Diferencia máxima entre cilindros	14 psi

Árbol de levas, componentes de los buzos y los balancines

	Vea Capítulo 2, Parte B

Cabeza de los cilindros

Combadura
    Estándar

Hasta 1990	Menos de 0.002 pulgada (0.05 mm)
1991 y más moderno	Menos de 0.0012 pulgada (0.03 mm)
Límite	0.004 pulgada (0.10 mm)
Altura (nominal)	4.213 + 0.008 pulgada (107 + 0.2 mm)

Válvulas y asientos

Límite de deflección de la válvula.. 0.0079 pulgada (0.20 mm)
Diámetro del vástago de las válvulas
   Admisión .... 0.2742 a 0.2748 pulgada (6.965 a 6.980 mm)
   Escape .... 0.3136 a 0.3138 pulgada (7.965 a 7.970 mm)
Diámetro interno de la guía de la válvula
   Admisión .... 0.2756 a 0.2763 pulgada (7.000 a 7.018 mm)
   Escape .... 0.3157 a 0.3154 pulgada (8.000 a 8.018 mm)
Espacio libre del vástago de la válvula a la guía de la válvula
   Estándar
     Admisión .... 0.0008 a 0.0021 pulgada (0.020 a 0.053 mm)
     Escape .... 0.0016 a 0.0029 pulgada (0.040 a 0.073 mm)
     Límite (admisión y escape) .... 0.0039 pulgada (0.10 mm)
Límite del margen de la válvula .... 0.020 pulgada (0.5 mm)
Longitud de la válvula
   Admisión .... 4.933 a 4.957 pulgadas (125.3 a 125.9 mm)
   Escape .... 4.890 a 4.913 pulgadas (124.2 a 124.8 mm)
Límite de rectificación de los vástagos de las válvulas .... 0.008 pulgada (0.20 mm)
Longitud libre del resorte de las válvulas
   Interior .... 1.736 pulgadas (44.10 mm)
   Exterior .... 2.016 pulgadas (51.20 mm)
Presión del resorte de la válvula/altura
   Interior .... 0.984 pulgada @ 57.3 libras (25.0 mm @ 26 Kg)
   Exterior .... 1.181 pulgadas @ 117.7 libras (30.0 mm @ 53.4 Kg)
Resorte de las válvulas fuera del límite cuadrado
   Interior .... 0.075 pulgada (1.9 mm)
   Exterior .... 0.087 pulgada (2.2 mm)
Altura instalada del resorte de las válvulas
   Interior .... 1.378 pulgadas (35.0 mm)
   Exterior .... 1.575 pulgadas (40.0 mm)
Asiento de la válvula
   Ángulo (admisión y escape) 45-grados
   Anchura
     Admisión .... 0.0689 pulgada (1.75 mm)
     Escape .... 0.067 pulgada (1.7 mm)

Bloque del motor

Distorsión de la parte superior del bloque
   Estándar .... Menos de 0.0012 pulgada (0.03 mm)
   Límite .... 0.0039 pulgada (0.10 mm)
Diámetro de los cilindros
   Diámetro (estándar)
     Grado no. 1 .... 3.4252 a 3.4256 pulgadas (87.000 a 87.010 mm)
     Grado no. 2 .... 3.4256 a 3.4260 pulgadas (87.010 a 87.020 mm)
     Grado no. 3 .... 3.4260 a 3.4264 pulgadas (87.020 a 87.030 mm)
     Grado no. 4 .... 3.4264 a 3.4268 pulgadas (87.030 a 87.040 mm)
     Grado no. 5 .... 3.4268 a 3.4272 pulgadas (87.040 a 87.050 mm)
   Límite de desgaste .... 0.0079 pulgada (0.20 mm)
   Conicidad/desviación radial .... Menos de 0.0006 pulgada (0.015 mm)

Pistones y anillos

Diámetro de los pistones (A en la **ilustración 17.11**)
   Grado no. 1 .... 3.4238 a 3.4242 pulgadas (86.965 a 86.975 mm)
   Grado no. 2 .... 3.4242 a 3.4246 pulgadas (86.975 a 86.985 mm)
   Grado no. 3 .... 3.4246 a 3.4250 pulgadas (86.985 a 86.995 mm)
   Grado no. 4 .... 3.4250 a 3.4254 pulgadas (86.995 a 87.005 mm)
   Grado no. 5 .... 3.4254 a 3.4258 pulgadas (87.005 a 87.015 mm)
Espacio libre del pistón al cilindro
   Hasta 1990 .... 0.0010 a 0.0018 pulgada (0.025 a 0.045 mm)
   1991 y más moderno .... 0.0006 a 0.0014 pulgada (0.015 a 0.035 mm)
Fuerza requerida para halar 0.0016 pulgada (0.04 mm) de espesor
   calibrador al tacto pasado a través del cilindro del pistón .... 0.4 a 3.3 libras (0.2 a 1.5 Kg)
Espacio libre lateral del anillo del pistón
   Anillo de compresión superior
     Estándar.. 0.0016 a 0.0029 pulgada (0.040 a 0.073 mm)
     Límite .... 0.004 pulgada (0.1 mm)
   Segundo anillo de compresión
     Estándar.. 0.0012 a 0.0025 pulgada (0.030 a 0.063 mm)
     Límite .... 0.004 pulgada (0.1 mm)
   Anillo de control para el aceite... 0.0006 a 0.0075 pulgada (0.015 a 0.190 mm)

Motor V6 (continuación)

Brecha del extremo del anillo del pistón
    Anillo de compresión superior
        Estándar...0.0083 a 0.0173 pulgada (0.21 a 0.44 mm)
        Límite ....0.039 pulgada (1.0 mm)
    Segundo anillo de compresión
        Estándar...0.0071 a 0.0173 pulgada (0.18 a 0.44 mm)
        Límite ....0.039 pulgada (1.0 mm)
    Anillo de control para el aceite......................................0.0079 a 0.0299 pulgada (0.20 a 0.76 mm)
Cigüeñal y bielas
Juego final de la biela (espacio lateral)
    Estándar ....0.0079 a 0.0138 pulgada (0.20 a 0.35 mm)
    Límite ....0.0157 pulgada (0.40 mm)
Juego final del cigüeñal
    Estándar ....0.0020 a 0.0067 pulgada (0.05 a 0.17 mm)
    Límite ....0.0118 pulgada (0.30 mm)
Diámetro del muñón principal
    Grado no. 0 ....2.4790 a 2.4793 pulgadas (62.967 a 62.975 mm)
    Grado no. 1 ....2.4787 a 2.4790 pulgadas (62.959 a 62.967 mm)
    Grado no. 2 ....2.4784 a 2.4787 pulgadas (62.951 a 62.959 mm)
Diámetro del muñón de la biela....................................1.9667 a 1.9675 pulgadas (49.955 a 49.974 mm)
Conicidad del muñón/desviación radial ....Menos de 0.0002 pulgada (0.005 mm)
Desviación radial del cigüeñal ....Menos de 0.0039 pulgada (0.10 mm)
Juego libre del aceite para el cojinete principal
    Estándar ....0.0011 a 0.0022 pulgada (0.028 a 0.055 mm)
    Límite ....0.0035 pulgada (0.090 mm)
Juego libre de la biela para el aceite
    Estándar ....0.0006 a 0.0021 pulgada (0.014 a 0.054 mm)
    Límite ....0.0035 pulgada (0.090 mm)
Cojinetes principales ....**Color de identificación**
    Grado no. 0 ....Negro
    Grado no. 1 ....Marrón
    Grado no. 2 ....Verde
    Grado no. 3 ....Amarillo
    Grado no. 4 ....Azul

Especificaciones técnicas*

Pies-libras

Pernos de la tapa para los cojinetes principales.....................67 a 74
Tuercas de la tapa para los cojinete de las bielas
    Paso 1 ....10 a 12
    Paso 2
        Con la llave torsiométrica convencional ....28 a 33
        Con la llave torsiométrica de indicar de ángulo..........Gire 60 a 65 grados adicionales
Pernos retenedores del sello de aceite trasero ....4.3 a 5.1

*__Nota:__ *Refiérase a la Parte B para las especificaciones técnicas adicionales.*

Motores KA24E (1990 en adelante)

General

Presión del aceite
    En marcha mínima..10.7 psi
    A 3000 rpm)..47 a 67 psi
Presión de la compresión
    Estándar ....192 psi
    Mínimo...142 psi

Árbol de levas y los balancines................................Vea Capítulo 2, Parte A

Cabeza de los cilindros

Límite de la combadura..0.004 pulgada (0.1 mm)

Válvulas

Diámetro del vástago de las válvulas
    Admisión ....0.2742 a 0.2748 pulgada (6.965 a 6.980 mm)
    Escape...0.3129 a 0.3134 pulgada (7.948 a 7.960 mm)
Ángulo de la cara de la válvula..45 grados 30 minutos

Anchura del margen de la válvula
    Admisión
        Estándar.. 0.0453 a 0.0571 pulgada (1.15 a 1.45 mm)
        Límite .... 0.020 pulgada (0.5 mm)
    Escape
        Estándar.. 0.0531 a 0.0650 pulgada (1.35 a 1.65 mm)
        Límite .... 0.020 pulgada (0.5 mm)
Límite de rectificación de los vástagos de las válvulas........................ 0.020 pulgada (0.5 mm)
Longitud libre del resorte de las válvulas
    Admisión
        Resorte exterior .... 2.2614 pulgadas (57.44 mm)
        Resorte interior .... 2.1000 pulgadas (53.34 mm)
    Escape
        Resorte exterior .... 2.0949 pulgadas (53.21 mm)
        Resorte interior .... 1.8878 pulgadas (47.95 mm)
Altura instalada del resorte de las válvulas
    Admisión - resorte exterior
        Estándar.. 1.480 pulgadas @ 135.8 libras (37.6 mm @ 61.6 kg)
        Límite .... 1.480 pulgadas @ 127.7 libras (37.6 mm @ 57.9 kg)
    Admisión - resorte interior
        Estándar.. 1.283 pulgadas @ 63.9 libras (32.6 mm @ 29.0 kg)
        Límite .... 1.283 pulgadas @ 60.0 libras (32.6 mm @ 27.2 kg)
    Escape - resorte exterior
        Estándar.. 1.343 pulgadas @ 144.0 libras (34.1 mm @ 65.3 kg)
        Límite .... 1.343 pulgadas @ 139.6 libras (34.1 mm @ 63.3 kg)
    Escape - resorte interior
        Estándar.. 1.146 pulgadas @ 73.9 libras (29.1 mm @ 33.5 kg)
        Límite .... 1.146 pulgadas @ 71.7 libras (29.1 mm @ 32.5 kg)
Resorte de las válvulas fuera del límite cuadrado
    Admisión
        Resorte exterior .... 0.098 pulgada (2.5 mm)
        Resorte interior .... 0.091 pulgada (2.3 mm)
    Escape
        Resorte exterior .... 0.091 pulgada (2.3 mm)
        Resorte interior .... 0.083 pulgada (2.1 mm)
Diámetro interno de la guía de la válvula
    Admisión .... 0.2756 a 0.2763 pulgadas (7.000 a 7.018 mm)
    Escape... 0.3150 a 0.3157 pulgada (8.000 a 8.018 mm)
Espacio libre del vástago de la válvula a la guía de la válvula
    Admisión .... 0.0008 a 0.0021 pulgada (0.020 a 0.053 mm)
    Escape... 0.0016 a 0.0028 pulgada (0.040 a 0.070 mm)
Límite de deflección del vástago de la válvula .... 0.008 pulgada (0.2 mm)
Asiento de la válvula
    Ángulo .... 45 grados
    Anchura
        Admisión .... 0.063 a 0.067 pulgada (1.6 a 1.7 mm)
        Escape .... 0.067 a 0.083 pulgada (1.7 a 2.1 mm)

Bloque del motor
Límite de distorsión de la parte superior .... 0.008 pulgada (0.2 mm)
Diámetro interior de los cilindros
    Grado 1 .... 3.5039 a 3.5043 pulgadas (89.000 a 89.010 mm)
    Grado 2 .... 3.5043 a 3.5047 pulgadas (89.010 a 89.020 mm)
    Grado 3 .... 3.5047 a 3.5051 pulgadas (89.020 a 89.030 mm)
Conicidad de los cilindros/desviación radial .... Menos de 0.0006 pulgada (0.015 mm)
Espacio libre del pistón al cilindro... 0.0008 a 0.0016 pulgada (0.020 a 0.040 mm)

Pistones y anillos
Diámetro
    Estándar
        Grado 1 .... 3.5027 a 3.5031 pulgadas (88.970 a 88.980 mm)
        Grado 2 .... 3.5031 a 3.5035 pulgadas (88.980 a 88.990 mm)
        Grado 3 .... 3.5035 a 3.5039 pulgadas (88.990 a 89.000 mm)
        Primer tamaño sobre medida (0.20 pulgada) .... 3.5224 a 3.5236 pulgadas (89.470 a 89.500 mm)
        Segundo tamaño sobre medida (0.39 pulgada) .... 3.5421 a 3.5433 pulgadas (89.970 a 90.000 mm)
Brecha del extremo del anillo del pistón
    Anillo de compresión superior .... 0.0110 a 0.0205 pulgada (0.28 a 0.52 mm)
    Segundo anillo de compresión .... 0.0177 a 0.0272 pulgada (0.45 a 0.69 mm)
    Anillo de aceite.. 0.0079 a 0.0272 pulgada (0.20 a 0.69 mm)

Motores KA24E (1990 en adelante) (continuación)

Espacio libre lateral del anillo del pistón
    Anillo de compresión superior .... 0.0016 a 0.0031 pulgada (0.040 a 0.080 mm)
    Segundo anillo de compresión .... 0.0012 a 0.0028 pulgada (0.030 a 0.070 mm)
    Anillo de aceite .... 0.0026 a 0.0053 pulgada (0.065 a 0.135 mm)

Cigüeñal, bielas y cojinetes principales

Juego final de la biela (espacio lateral)
    Estándar .... 0.008 a 0.016 pulgada (0.2 a 0.4 mm)
    Límite .... 0.024 pulgada (0.6 mm)
Juego final del cigüeñal
    Estándar .... 0.0020 a 0.0071 pulgada (0.05 a 0.18 mm)
    Límite .... 0.012 pulgada (0.3 mm)
Diámetro principal del muñón del cojinete
    Grado 0 .... 2.5057 a 3.5060 pulgadas (63.645 a 63.652 mm)
    Grado 1 .... 2.5060 a 2.5064 pulgadas (63.652 a 63.663 mm)
    Grado 2 .... 2.5064 a 3.5068 pulgadas (63.663 a 63.672 mm)
Diámetro del muñón de la biela .... 2.3603 a 2.3612 pulgadas (59.951 a 59.975 mm)
Conicidad del muñón/desviación radial
    Estándar
        Hasta 1990 .... Menos de 0.0004 pulgada (0.01 mm)
        1991 y más moderno .... 0 pulgada (0 mm)
    Límite
        Hasta 1990 .... 0.0012 pulgada (0.03 mm)
        1991 y más moderno .... 0.0004 pulgada (0.01 mm)
Juego libre del aceite para el cojinete principal
    Estándar .... 0.0008 a 0.0019 pulgada (0.020 a 0.047 mm)
    Límite .... 0.004 pulgada (0.1 mm)
Juego libre de la biela para el aceite
    Estándar .... 0.0004 a 0.0014 pulgada (0.010 a 0.035 mm)
    Límite .... 0.0035 pulgada (0.09 mm)
Límite desviación del volante/plato flexible .... 0.004 pulgada (0.1 mm)

Especificaciones técnicas*   Pies-libras

Pernos de la tapa para los cojinetes principales 36
Tuercas de la tapa para los cojinete de las bielas
    Primer paso .... 10 a 12
    Segundo paso .... 60 a 65 grados (28 a 33 pies libras)

*Nota: *Refiérase a la Parte A para las especificaciones técnicas adicionales.*

---

1   Información general

Incluida en esta porción del Capítulo 2 están los procedimientos generales de rectificación completa para la cabeza(s) de los cilindros y componentes internos del motor.

La información se extiende desde consejo que concierne a la preparación para una rectificación completa del motor y detalles para las partes de remplazo y paso por paso de los procedimientos que cubren remover e instalar los componentes internos del motor y chequeos de las piezas.

Las Secciones siguientes se han escrito con la suposición que el motor se ha removido desde el vehículo. Para información en lo que concierne a la reparación del motor en el vehículo, así como también remover e instalar los componentes externos necesarios para la rectificación completa, vea parte A o B de este Capítulo y Sección 7 de esta parte.

Especificaciones incluidas aquí en la parte C son solamente esas necesarias para los procedimientos de rectificación completa y chequeo que siguen. Refiérase a la Parte A y B para Especificaciones adicionales.

2   Compresión de los cilindros - chequeo

Refiérase a la ilustración 2.4

1   Un chequeo de compresión le dirá a usted en qué condición mecánica el extremo superior de su motor está (pistones, anillos, válvulas, junta de la cabeza(s). Específicamente, puede decirle a usted si la compresión está baja debido a la fuga ocasionada por anillos de los pistones desgastados, válvulas defectuosas y asiento o una junta de la cabeza quemada. **Nota:** *El motor debe estar a temperatura normal de operación y la batería debe estar totalmente cargada para este chequeo. También, si el motor se equipa con un carburador, el acelerador debe estar completamente abierto de tal manera para adquirir una lectura de compresión precisa (si el motor está cálido, el estrangulador debería estar abierto).*

2   Comience limpiando la zona alrededor las bujías antes que usted las remueva (aire comprimido debe usarse, si está disponible, de otra manera una brocha pequeña o una bomba para neumáticos de bicicleta traba-

jará también). La idea es de impedir que suciedad entre en los cilindros cuando esté chequeando la compresión de los cilindros. Remueva todas las bujías del motor (Capítulo 1).

3   Bloquee el acelerador completamente abierto. Remueva el alambre de la bobina desde la tapa del distribuidor e instálelo en el bloque de los cilindros. Use un caimán para sujetar el cable en ambos extremos para asegurar una tierra buena.

4   Con el manómetro de compresión en el orificio para la bujía número uno **(vea ilustración)**, apriete el pedal del acelerador completamente hacia el piso para abrir el acelerador. Gire el motor por lo menos cuatro carreras de compresión y mire el manómetro. La compresión debería subir hacia encima rápidamente en un motor que esté en buenas condiciones. Compresión baja en la primera carrera de compresión, seguida por presión gradualmente creciente en cada carrera de compresión consecutivas, indica anillos del pistón desgastados. Una compresión de lectura baja en la primera carrera de compresión, que no incrementa durante las carreras de compresión consecutivas, indican fugas

2.4 Un manómetro de compresión con un acoplador con roscas para el orificio de la bujía es preferido al tipo que requiere presión de mano para mantener el sello - ¡esté seguro de abrir el acelerador y el estrangulador lo más que sea posible durante el proceso de chequear la compresión!

en las válvulas o una junta de la cabeza quemada (una cabeza agrietada podría también ser la causa). Registre la lectura más alta obtenida en el medidor.

5   Repita el procedimiento para los cilindros restantes y compare los resultados con las especificaciones.

6   Añada algo de aceite de motor (alrededor de tres cucharadas adentro de los cilindros) al cilindro, atravéz del orificio para la bujía y repita la prueba.

7   Si un aumento en la compresión después de añadir el aceite se obtiene, los anillos del pistón están definitivamente desgastados. Si la compresión no aumenta significativamente, la fuga ocurre en las válvulas o la junta de la cabeza. Las fugas a través de las válvulas pueden ser ocasionadas por asientos de las válvulas quemados y/o las caras abaleadas, válvulas agrietadas o válvulas dobladas.

8   Si dos cilindros adyacentes tienen compresión igualmente baja, hay una posibilidad grande que la junta de la cabeza entre los dos cilindros esté quemada. La presencia de anticongelante en las cámaras de combustión o en el cárter del cigüeñal verificará esta condición.

9   Si la compresión está extraordinariamente alta, las cámaras de combustión están probablemente cubiertas con sedimentos de carbón. Si este es el caso, la cabeza de los cilindros debería removerse y ser descarbonizada.

10   Si la compresión está sumamente baja o varía mucho entre cilindros, sería una buena idea permitir que un taller de reparaciones automotriz conduzca una prueba de fuga. Esta prueba demostrará exactamente donde la fuga ocurre y que tan severa es.

3   Remover el motor - métodos y precauciones

Si usted ha decidido que el motor debe removerse para una rectificación completa o trabajo mayor de reparación, los varios pasos preliminares deberían tomarse.

Ubicar un lugar apropiado para trabajar es sumamente importante. El espacio adecuado para trabajar, conjuntamente con el espacio para almacenar el vehículo, es necesario. Si un taller o un garaje no está disponible, por lo menos un lugar plano, nivelado, con una superficie limpia y nivelada hecha de concreto o asfalto se requiere.

Limpiar el compartimiento del motor y el motor antes de poner en marcha el procedimiento de remover el motor le ayudará a mantener las herramientas limpias y organizadas.

Un elevador de motor o una base en forma de A también será necesario. Asegúrese que el equipo pueda sostener el exceso del peso combinado del motor y los accesorios. La seguridad es de importancia primaria, considerando los peligros potenciales involucrados en levantar el motor fuera del vehículo.

Si el motor está siendo removido por un novato, un ayudante debería estar disponible. El consejo y la asistencia de alguien más experimentado también sería útil. Hay muchas veces cuando una persona no puede desempeñar simultáneamente todas las operaciones requeridas cuando se está levantando el motor fuera del vehículo.

Planee la operación antes de tiempo. Arregle para obtener todas las herramientas y equipo que usted necesitará con anterioridad antes de poner en marcha el trabajo. Algunos de los equipos necesarios para desempeñar la instalación y remover el motor sin riesgo y con relativa facilidad son (además de un elevador de motor) un gato de piso pesado, un juego completo de herramientas y dados como esta descrito en el frente de este manual, bloques de madera, abundancia de trapos y solvente para limpiar cualquier derrame de aceite, anticongelante o gasolina derramada. Si el elevador de motores debe alquilarse, asegúrese que usted arregla esto por adelantado y desempeñe de antemano todas las operaciones posibles sin el elevador. Esto le ahorrará dinero y tiempo a usted.

Planee para que el vehículo esté fuera de uso por un buen tiempo. Un taller de rectificaciones se requerirá para que desempeñe algo del trabajo que el mecánico del hogar no podrá realizar por el mismo sin el equipo especial. Estos talleres frecuentemente están bien ocupados, sería una buena idea de consultar con ellos antes de remover el motor con el final de precisamente estimar la cantidad de tiempo requerido para la reconstrucción o reparación de los componentes que puedan necesitar trabajo.

Siempre esté sumamente cuidadoso cuando esté removiendo e instalando el motor. Daño serio puede resultar si se toman

acciones negligentes. Planifique hacia el futuro, tómese su tiempo y un trabajo de esta naturaleza, aunque sea mayor, puede realizarse exitosamente.

4   Motor - remover e instalar

Refiérase a la ilustración 4.40

Peligro: *El motor es muy pesado, así que el equipo diseñado específicamente para levantar motores se debe usar. ¡Nunca posicione ninguna parte de su cuerpo debajo del motor cuando esté sostenido por un elevador - podría moverse o podría caerse y podría causar una lesión grave o la muerte! También, el sistema del aire acondicionado está bajo alta presión; aflojando las acoplaciones causará una descarga repentina del refrigerante, que podría causarle una lesión grave. Haga que el sistema sea descargado por una estación de servicio antes de que cualquiera de las mangueras o líneas sean desconectadas.*

1   Lea a través de la Sección completa nombrada Remover el Motor - los métodos y las precauciones antes de comenzar cualquier trabajo. En los modelos de 2WD, la transmisión puede ser removida con el motor. En los modelos de 4WD, el motor se debe separar de la transmisión y la transmisión dejada en su posición en el vehículo (asegúrese que la transmisión está firmemente sostenida).

2   Remueva el capó (vea Capítulo 12 para el procedimiento correcto). Almacénelo en un lugar seguro donde no será dañado.

3   Remueva el ensamblaje del purificador de aire (vea Capítulo 4).

4   Desconecte el cable negativo de la terminal negativa de la batería (negativo primero, entonces el positivo).

5   Drene el anticongelante del radiador y del bloque del motor (refiérase al Capítulo 1 si es necesario).

6   Drene el aceite del motor.

7   Drene el aceite de la transmisión. Refiérase al Capítulo 1, si es necesario.

8   Remueva la manguera superior e inferior del radiador.

9   Desconecte todos los alambres y las mangueras de vacío entre el motor y los componentes conectados a la carrocería. **Nota:** *Antes de desconectar los alambres o remover las mangueras, márquelos con pedazos de cinta para identificar sus ubicaciones de instalación. Esto eliminará problemas y posibles confusiones durante el procedimiento de la instalación.*

10   Desconecte las mangueras de combustible de la bomba mecánica del combustible, si está equipado con una y la tapa para prevenir fuga de combustible y entrada de tierra.

11   En los modelos 1981 y más modernos, desconecte las mangueras de combustible donde ellas se conectan a las líneas de metal debajo del múltiple de admisión.

12   Si está equipado con aire acondicionado, remueva el compresor A/C (aire acondicionado) del soporte y lo asegura fuera del

camino. **Caución:** *No desconecte la manguera del compresor a menos que el sistema se haya descargado.*

13   Si está equipado con dirección de poder, remueva la bomba de la dirección de poder y la asegura fuera del camino. Deje la manguera conectada a la bomba.

14   Desconecte el alambre(s) de la bobina para la ignición de la tapa del distribuidor.

15   Separe el cable del acelerador cuerpo de aceleración o el carburador (vea Capítulo 4).

16   Desconecte la manguera de vacío del amplificador para los frenos y póngala fuera del camino.

17   Desconecte las mangueras de la calefacción donde ellas se conectan al motor.

18   Remueva la válvula VVT (transductor del vacío de venturi) y el soporte, si está equipado con una, de la pared contrafuego (vea Capítulo 6).

19   Levante el frente del vehículo y sosténgalo firmemente encima de soportes. Aplique el freno de estacionamiento y bloquee las ruedas traseras.

20   Desconecte los alambres del alternador y del motor de arranque. En vehículos con un motor V6, remueva el motor de arranque (Capítulo 5).

21   Si está equipado con una transmisión automática, desconecte las mangueras del enfriador de aceite del enfriador de aceite localizado en la base del radiador. Permita que el fluido drene en un recipiente.

22   Remueva el radiador y la tapa. Refiérase al Capítulo 3, si es necesario.

23   En los modelos de 2WD, separe el cable del velocímetro de la transmisión. Desconecte todos los alambres conectados a la transmisión.

24   En los modelos de 4WD, remueva los ejes impulsores primarios y delantero como está descrito en el Capítulo 9.

25   En los modelos de 4WD, remueva los cuatro pernos que conectan el diferencial delantero al miembro transversal, entonces remueva el perno de afianzamiento delantero y baje el diferencial delantero para que descanse en el miembro transversal.

26   En los modelos de 2WD, remueva el eje impulsor como está descrito en el Capítulo 8.

27   Desconecte el tubo de escape delantero del múltiple de escape.

28   Si está equipado con un embrague hidráulico, remueva el cilindro que opera el embrague de la transmisión. Refiérase al Capítulo 8 si es necesario.

29   Desconecte el cable del freno de estacionamiento y lo pone en posición fuera del camino.

30   Desconecte cualquier líneas que queden, mangueras o alambres que se dirijan al motor. Márquelos primero para evitar confusión durante la instalación.

31   En los modelos de 2WD, refiérase al Capítulo 7 y haga todo lo descrito para remover la transmisión menos remover el soporte y los pernos del motor a la transmisión.

32   En los modelos de 4WD, destornille la transmisión del motor (Capítulo 7).

33   En los modelos de 4WD con una transmisión automática, destornille el convertidor de torsión del plato flexible (Capítulo 7).

34   Conecte un elevador de motor a los dos soportes instalados en el motor. Ellos están localizados en los rincones de la cabeza. Asegúrese que la cadena está conectada firmemente con ganchos o tuercas de alta calidad, pernos y arandelas. El gancho en el elevador de motor debe estar en el centro del motor con las dos longitudes de la cadena a la misma longitud para que el motor pueda ser levantado directamente hacia encima.

35   Levante el motor apenas hasta que todo el juego flojo se haya removido de las cadenas.

36   En los modelos de 4WD, remueva los pernos que conectan el miembro trasero del diferencial delantero al chasis.

37   En los modelos de 2WD, remueva los pernos del brazo loco, baje el brazo loco y la varilla de cruce para proporcionar espacio libre adicional para la cacerola del aceite.

38   En los modelos de 2WD, remueva los pernos que conectan la transmisión al soporte de la carrocería. Entonces remueva los pernos que conectan el soporte a la transmisión. Remueva el amortiguador, si está equipado.

39   Remueva los pernos que conectan los calzos delantero al bloque del motor. **Caución:** *No afloje las tuercas de la tapa del aislador (modelos más modernos). Remover la cubierta resultará en la pérdida del fluido, que rendirá los calzos inútil.*

40   En los modelos de 4WD, levante el motor levemente, entonces lo mueve hacia adelante para separarlo de la transmisión. Chequee cuidadosamente para asegurarse que todo se ha desconectado. En los modelos de 2WD, incline el motor/ensamblaje de transmisión hacia abajo en la parte trasera para liberar el soporte del radiador según usted lo levante hacia encima y hacia fuera del compartimiento del motor **(vea ilustración)**.

41   Para separar el motor de una transmisión automática en los modelos de 2WD:

a) *Remueva la tapa de polvo de la mitad inferior del albergue del convertidor de torsión.*

b) *Remueva los pernos del convertidor de torsión del plato flexible. Acceso a los pernos se puede ganar (de uno en uno), girando el cigüeñal hasta que cada perno se vea a través de la mitad inferior del albergue del convertidor.*

c) *Remueva la transmisión automática, deje el plato flexible empernado a la pestaña trasera del cigüeñal.*

42   Para separar el motor de una transmisión manual en los modelos de 2WD:

a) *Remueva los pernos que aseguran la campana del embrague al bloque del motor.*

b) *Hale la transmisión recta hacia atrás para que su peso no cuelgue en el eje de entrada, mientras está todavía comprometida en el plato del embrague.*

4.40 Esté seguro que la cadena esté firmemente conectada a los soportes del motor y al elevador antes de elevar el motor

43   La instalación se hace en el orden inverso al procedimiento de desensamble. **Nota:** *En los modelos de 4WD, sellador se debe usar entre el motor y la transmisión (vea Capítulo 7).*

44   Apriete todos los afianzadores al par de torsión especificado.

45   Antes de poner el motor en marcha, asegúrese que el aceite y el nivel del anticongelante estén correcto.

46   Ponga el motor en marcha, chequee por fugas y operación apropiada de todos los accesorios, después instale el capó y pruebe el vehículo en la carretera.

5   Rectificación completa del motor - información general

Refiérase a la ilustración 5.4

No es siempre fácil determinar cuando, o si, un motor debería rectificarse completamente, debido a que varios números de factores se deben de considerar.

El millaje alto no es necesariamente una indicación que una rectificación completa se necesita, el millaje mientras bajo no excluye la necesidad de una rectificación completa. La frecuencia de servicio es probablemente la consideración más importante. Un motor que tenga regulares cambios de aceite y de filtros, así como también otros mantenimientos requeridos, muy probable otorgue muchas millas de servicio confiable. Viceversa, un motor abandonado puede requerir una rectificación completa muy temprano en su vida.

El consumo excesivo de aceite es una indicación de que los anillos de los pistones, sellos de las válvulas y/o guías de las válvulas están en la necesidad de atención. Asegúrese que fugas de aceite no son responsables antes de decidir que los anillos y/o las guías están malas. Haga que un chequeo de la compresión de los cilindros o chequeo de fugas sea desempeñado por un mecánico

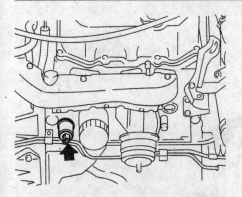

5.4 La presión del aceite puede ser chequeada removiendo la unidad emisora para la presión de aceite e instalar un medidor de presión en el orificio (se muestra un motor V6)

con experiencia para determinar la cantidad de trabajo requerido.

Si el motor hace golpeteo obvio o ruidos, los cojinetes de las bielas y/o cojinetes principales pueden que sean el problema. Chequee la presión del aceite con un medidor instalado en el lugar del pulmón para la presión de aceite **(vea ilustración)** y compare la presión con las especificaciones. Si está sumamente bajo de presión, los cojinetes y/o la bomba de aceite están probablemente desgastados.

La pérdida de potencia, marcha rugosa, ruido excesivo del tren de las válvulas y alto consumo de combustible pueden indicar también que una rectificación completa se necesita, especialmente si todos ellos están presente a la misma vez. Si una afinación completa no remedia la situación, trabajo mayor mecánico es la única solución.

Una rectificación completa del motor involucra restauración de las partes internas a las especificaciones de un motor nuevo. Durante una rectificación completa, los anillos de los pistones se sustituyen y las paredes de los cilindros se reparan nuevamente (rectificadas y/o esmeriladas). Si una rectificación de las paredes de los cilindros es hecha, pistones nuevos son requeridos. Los cojinetes principales y de bielas se sustituyen generalmente con nuevos y si es necesario, el cigüeñal puede ser rectificado para restaurar los muñones. Generalmente, las válvulas se rectifican también, debido a que ellas están comúnmente en menos que perfecta condiciones a este punto. Mientras el motor está siendo rectificado, otros componentes, tales como el distribuidor, motor de arranque y el alternador, pueden ser rectificado también. El resultado debería ser como un motor nuevo que otorgue muchas millas libre de problemas. **Nota:** *Los componentes críticos del sistema de enfriamiento tales como las mangueras, bandas, termostato y la bomba de agua DEBEN substituirse con partes nuevas cuando un motor se rectifique. El radiador debería chequearse cuidadosamente para asegurarse que no está obstruido o tiene*

fugas; si está en duda, sustitúyalo con uno nuevo. También, nosotros no recomendamos chequear la bomba de aceite - siempre instale una nueva cuando un motor sea rectificado.

Antes de poner en marcha la rectificación completa del motor, lea el procedimiento entero para que se familiarice usted mismo con el alcance y requerimientos del trabajo. La rectificación completa de un motor no es difícil, pero consume tiempo. Planee de antemano que el vehículo estará fuera de servicio por un mínimo de dos semanas, especialmente si las partes deben llevarse a un taller de rectificaciones automotriz para la reparación o rectificación completa. Chequee por la disponibilidad de partes y asegúrese que cualquier equipo o herramientas especiales necesarias se obtengan por adelantado. La mayoría del trabajo puede hacerse con herramientas típicas manuales, aunque un número de herramientas para medir de precisión se requieren para inspeccionar las partes para determinar si ellas deben sustituirse. Frecuentemente un taller de rectificaciones automotriz hará el chequeo y le ofrecerá consejo si las partes que conciernen necesitan ser rectificadas o reemplazadas. **Nota:** *Siempre espere hasta que el motor se halla desarmado completamente y todos los componentes, especialmente del bloque de los cilindros, se haya inspeccionado antes de decidir qué servicio y operaciones de reparación deben ser desempeñadas por un taller de rectificaciones automotriz.* Debido a que la condición del bloque será el factor más importante para considerar si el motor se rectificará o se comprará uno rectificado, nunca compre partes o haga trabajo mecánico en los otros componentes hasta que el bloque se haya inspeccionado completamente. Por regla general, el tiempo es el costo primario de una rectificación completa, tanto que no paga instalar partes desgastadas o que no estén en buenas condiciones.

Como una nota final, para asegurar una vida máxima y problema mínimo de un motor reconstruido, todo debe ensamblarse con cuidado en un lugar completamente limpio.

6 Alternativas para la reconstrucción completa del motor

La persona que hace el trabajo por si mismo se encontrará con un número de opciones cuando esté desempeñando una rectificación completa del motor. La decisión para sustituir el bloque de los cilindros, pistones, bielas y cigüeñal depende de un número de factores, con el número uno siendo la consideración de la condición del bloque. Las otras consideraciones son el costo, acceso a un taller de rectificaciones, partes disponibles, tiempo requerido para completar el proyecto y la experiencia de parte de la persona que irá ha ejecutar el trabajo.

Algunas de las alternativas para la reconstrucción incluyen:

Partes individuales - Si los procedimientos de chequeo dan a conocer que el bloque de los cilindros y la mayoría de los componentes del motor están en condiciones para usarlos nuevamente, comprando partes individuales puede ser la alternativa más económica. El bloque, cigüeñal, pistones y bielas deberían todos ser inspeccionados cuidadosamente. Aún cuando el bloque muestra poco desgaste, el cilindro debería ser superficialmente esmerilado.

Juego de partes para el cigüeñal - Estos paquetes de reconstrucción consiste de un cigüeñal rectificado y un juego completo de pistones y bielas. Los pistones ya vienen instalados en las bielas. Anillos de los pistones y los cojinetes necesarios se incluirán en el juego. Estos juegos están usualmente disponibles para cilindros de tamaño normal, así como también para bloques de cilindros que han sido rectificados a dimensiones más grandes.

Bloque corto - Un bloque corto consiste de un bloque de cilindros con un cigüeñal, los pistones y bielas ya instaladas. Se incorporan todos los cojinetes nuevos y todos los espacios serán corregidos. Las cabezas de los cilindros existente y las partes externas pueden ser instaladas al bloque corto con poco o ningún trabajo necesario de un taller de rectificaciones.

Bloque largo - Un bloque largo consiste de un bloque corto, más una bomba de aceite, cárter de aceite, cabeza(s) de cilindros, tapa para los balancines, árbol de levas y componentes del tren de las válvulas, cadena y engranajes o banda de sincronización del tiempo. Todos los componentes se instalan con cojinetes nuevos, sellos y juntas necesarias. La instalación de los múltiples y las partes externas es todo lo que es necesario.

Piense cuidadosamente que alternativa es mejor para que usted y discuta la situación con unos talleres de rectificaciones automotrices locales, concesionarios de partes y reconstructores con experiencia antes de ordenar o comprar partes de remplazo.

7 Rectificación completa del motor - secuencia desarmar

Refiérase a las ilustraciones 7.5a, 7.5b, 7.5c, 7.5d y 7.5e

1   Es más fácil desarmar y trabajar en el motor si se instala en un caballete portátil de motor. Un caballete puede frecuentemente ser alquilado con bastante economía en un lugar donde retan equipos para jardín. Antes de que el motor se instale en un caballete, el volante/plato flexible debería removerse desde el motor.

2   Si un caballete no está disponible, es posible desarmar el motor encima de bloques, en un banco de trabajo o en el piso. Tenga extra cuidado para no tumbar el motor

7.5a Componentes externos del motor de cuatro cilindros - vista esquemática (típica)

1 Tubo EGR (recirculación de los gases de escape)
2 Cable de alta tensión
3 Tubo EAI (inyección de aire para el escape)
4 Ensamblaje del tubo de vacío
5 Múltiple de escape
6 Bomba de agua
7 Ventilador
8 Polea del cigüeñal
9 Soporte del alternador
10 Banda del ventilador
11 Barra para el ajuste del ventilador
12 Alternador
13 Válvula PCV (ventilación positiva del cárter)
14 Emisor de la presión de aceite
15 Tubo PCV
16 Cubierta
17 Soporte del distribuidor
18 Distribuidor
19 Refuerzo
20 Eje impulsor de la bomba de aceite
21 Bomba de aceite
22 Soporte de montaje del motor
23 Filtro de aceite
24 Varilla para medir el aceite
25 Entrada del agua
26 Termostato
27 Salida del agua
28 Múltiple de admisión
29 Bomba de combustible
30 Bujía
31 Carburador

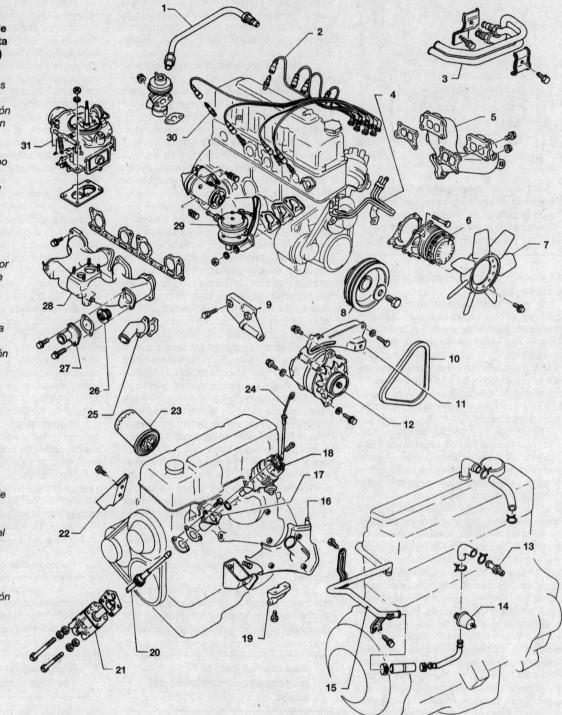

cuando esté trabajando sin un caballete.

3   Si usted va a obtener un motor de intercambio, todos los componentes externos deben de removerse primero, para ser transferido al motor de reemplazo, así como si usted estuviera haciendo una rectificación completa del motor usted mismo. Estos incluyen:

Alternador y soportes
Compresor A/C y soportes
Bomba de servodirección y soportes
Componentes de control de emisiones
Distribuidor, cables de las bujías y bujías
Termostato y tapa del termostato
Bomba de agua
Componentes del sistema de inyección de combustible o carburador
Múltiples de admisión y de escape
Filtro de aceite
Calzos del motor
Embrague y volante/plato flexible

Nota: *Cuando esté removiendo los compo-*

nentes externos del motor, preste suma atención a los detalles que puedan ser útiles o importantes durante el ensamblaje. Note la posición de la instalación de las juntas, sellos, espaciadores, clavijas, soportes, arandelas y otros artículos pequeños.

4   Si usted obtiene un bloque corto, que consiste del bloque de los cilindros, el cigüeñal, pistones y bielas conectadas, entonces la cabeza(s) de los cilindros, cárter de aceite y la bomba de aceite tendrán que ser removi-

7.5b Componentes internos del motor de cuatro cilindros - vista esquemática (típica)

1   Tapa para los balancines
2   Balancines y eje
3   Árbol de levas
4   Tapón de caucho
5   Retenedor de válvula
6   Retenedor del resorte
7   Sello de aceite
8   Asiento del resorte
9   Retenedor del anillo
10 Guía de la válvula
11 Asiento de la válvula
12 Perno de la cabeza de los cilindros
13 Cabeza de los cilindros
14 Camisa del cilindro
15 Bloque del cilindro
16 Volante
17 Plato trasero
18 Cigüeñal
19 Plato flexible
20 Sello de aceite trasero
21 Buje piloto
22 Tapa de los cojinetes principales
23 Tapón de drenaje para el aceite
24 Cacerola del aceite
25 Plato deflector y malla
26 Colador de aceite
27 Cojinete principal
28 Deflector de aceite
29 Engrane de mando para la bomba de aceite
30 Engrane del cigüeñal
31 Cojinetes de la biela
32 Sello de aceite delantero
33 Cubierta delantera
34 Tensionador de la cadena
35 Guía de la cadena
36 Leva para la bomba de combustible
37 Engrane del árbol de levas
38 Cadena del tiempo

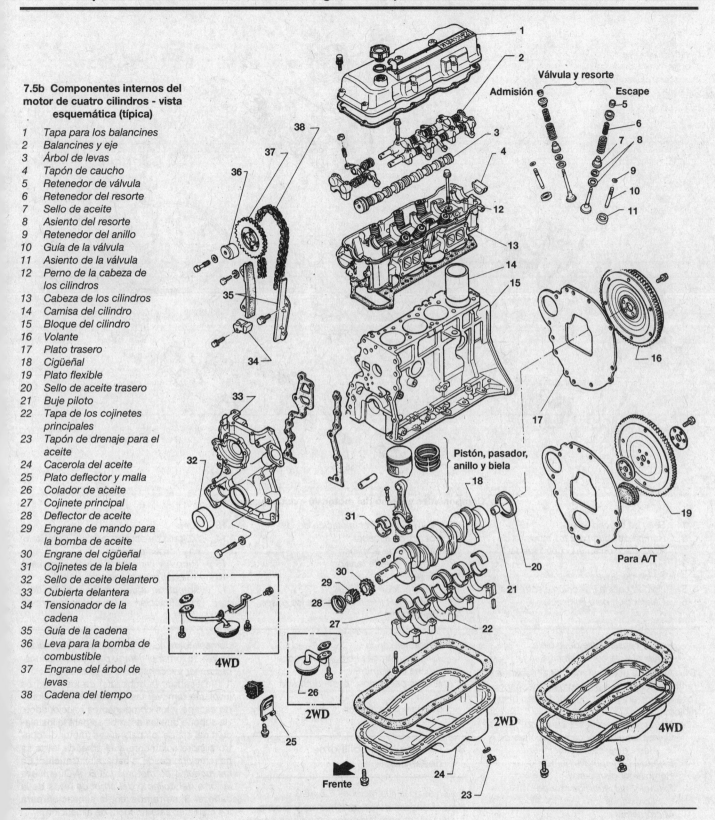

das también. Vea rectificación completa del motor y alternativas para información adicional con respecto a las diferentes posibilidades que deben de ser consideradas.

5   Si usted planea una rectificación general completa, el motor debe desarmarse y los componentes internos removidos en el orden siguiente (**vea ilustraciones**):

Tapa de los balancines
Múltiples de escape y de admisión
Tapa para la banda de distribución (Motor V6)
Tapa para la cadena de distribución

(Motores de cuatro cilindros)
Los componentes para el mecanismo de distribución (cadena o banda y engranajes)
Cabeza de los cilindros
Cárter de aceite
Bomba de aceite

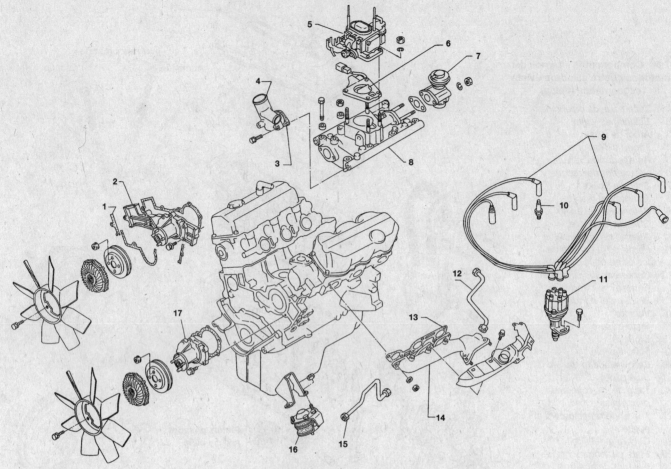

7.5c Componentes externo del motor V6 - vista esquemática

1	Sello de caucho	7	Válvula EGR (recirculación de los gases de escape)	13	Junta
2	Bomba de agua para los modelos de 4WD (tracción en las cuatro ruedas)	8	Múltiple de admisión	14	Múltiple de escape, aflójelo y apriételo en el orden correcto
3	Junta	9	Cables de alta tensión	15	Tubo AIV (válvula de inyección de aire)
4	Salida del agua	10	Bujía	16	Aislador para el calzo del motor
5	Unidad para la inyección electrónica	11	Distribuidor	17	Bomba de agua para los modelos de 2WD (tracción en las ruedas traseras)
6	Calefacción para la mezcla	12	Tubo EGR (recirculación de los gases de escape)		

Pistón y ensamblaje de la biela
Cigüeñal y cojinetes principales

6   Antes de poner en marcha el desarme y rectificación de los procedimientos, asegúrese que los artículos siguientes están disponibles:

Herramientas comunes de mano
Cajas pequeñas de cartón o bolsas de plástico para almacenar piezas
Espátula para remover juntas
Removedor de rebarba
Extractor del amortiguador de vibraciones
Micrómetros
Medidores telescópicos
Juego de indicador tipo reloj
Compresor para el resorte de las válvulas
Piedra para esmerilar cilindros
Herramienta para limpiar las ranuras de los anillos del pistón

Taladro eléctrico
Juego de terrajas hembras y macho
Brocha de alambre
Brocha para limpiar el conducto de aceite
Solvente para limpiar

8   Cabeza de los cilindros - desarmar

Refiérase a las ilustraciones 8.2 y 8.3
Nota: *Cabezas de cilindro nuevas y reconstruidas están comúnmente disponibles para la mayoría de los motores en los concesionarios y almacenes de partes. Debido a que algunas herramientas especializadas son necesarias para los procedimientos de chequeo, desarme y las partes de intercambio no están fácilmente disponibles, puede ser más práctico y económico para el mecánico*

doméstico de comprar cabezas de reemplazo en vez de tomar el tiempo para desarmar, inspeccionar y reconstruir la original(es).

1   Desarmar la cabeza(s) de los cilindros involucra remover las válvulas de admisión y de escape y los componentes relacionados. Se supone que las asambleas para la instalación del eje de los balancines (motor de cuatro cilindro solamente) y el árbol de levas se ha removido desde la cabeza(s). **Caución:** *En los modelos de motores L20B, ¡NO remueva la torre del cojinete del árbol de levas de la cabeza! Si se remueven, la alineación para los cojinetes estarán fuera de alineación.*

2   Antes de que las válvulas se remuevan, tome acción para ponerle etiquetas y las almacena, conjuntamente con sus componentes relacionados, para que se puedan guardar separadas y ser instaladas en las mismas guías de las válvulas desde donde ellas se removieron. También, mida la altura

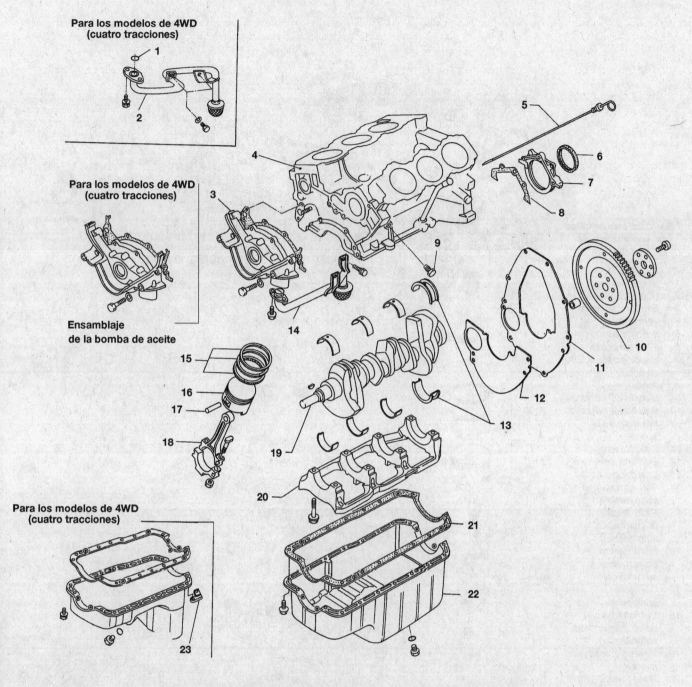

7.5d Componentes internos e inferiores del motor V6 - vista esquemática

1	Anillo O	
2	Colador de aceite	
3	Ensamblaje de la bomba de aceite (modelos de 2WD (tracción en las ruedas traseras)	
4	Bloque del motor	
5	Varilla para medir el aceite	
6	Sello de aceite	
7	Retenedor del sello de aceite trasero	
8	Junta	
9	Tapón para el drenaje del aceite	

10	Volante o plato flexible
11	Plato trasero para los modelos de 4WD (tracción en las cuatro ruedas) sellador se debe de usar
12	Cubierta del plato trasero
13	Cojinete principal, seleccione el espesor adecuado del cojinete principal
14	Colador de aceite para los modelos de 2WD

15	Anillos del pistón
16	Pistón
17	Pasador del pistón
18	Biela
19	Cigüeñal
20	Tapa para el cojinete principal
21	Junta
22	Cacerola del aceite para los modelos de 2WD
23	Sello de caucho

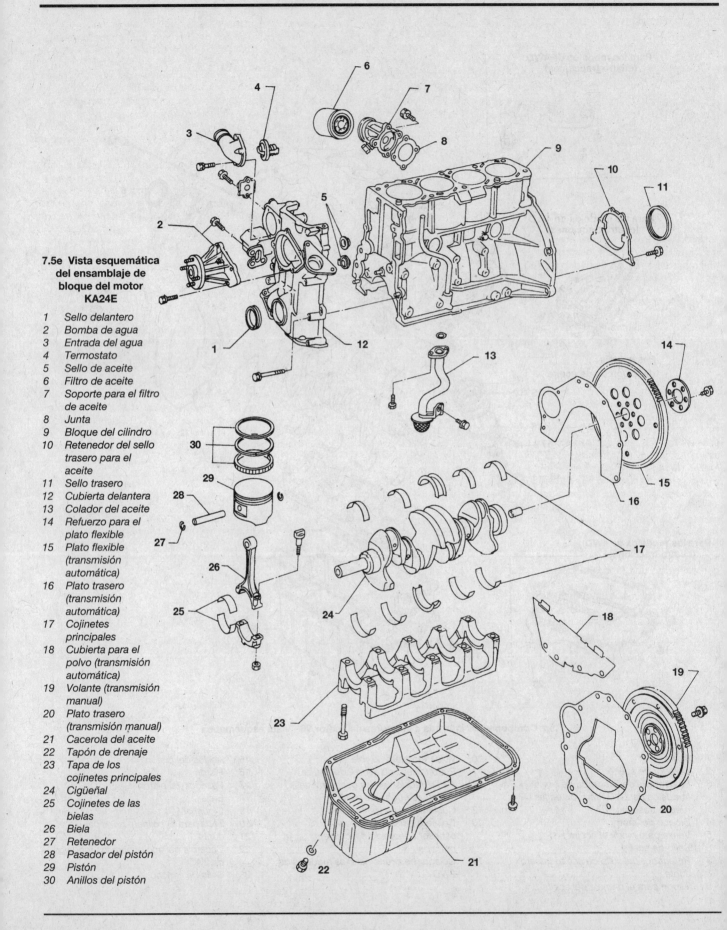

7.5e Vista esquemática del ensamblaje de bloque del motor KA24E

1   Sello delantero
2   Bomba de agua
3   Entrada del agua
4   Termostato
5   Sello de aceite
6   Filtro de aceite
7   Soporte para el filtro de aceite
8   Junta
9   Bloque del cilindro
10   Retenedor del sello trasero para el aceite
11   Sello trasero
12   Cubierta delantera
13   Colador del aceite
14   Refuerzo para el plato flexible
15   Plato flexible (transmisión automática)
16   Plato trasero (transmisión automática)
17   Cojinetes principales
18   Cubierta para el polvo (transmisión automática)
19   Volante (transmisión manual)
20   Plato trasero (transmisión manual)
21   Cacerola del aceite
22   Tapón de drenaje
23   Tapa de los cojinetes principales
24   Cigüeñal
25   Cojinetes de las bielas
26   Biela
27   Retenedor
28   Pasador del pistón
29   Pistón
30   Anillos del pistón

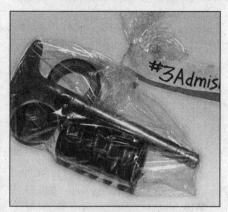

8.2 Una bolsa de plástico pequeña con una etiqueta apropiada se puede usar para guardar la válvula y los componentes del resorte para que se puedan reinstalar en la guía correcta

instalada para cada válvula y compárela con las especificaciones **(vea ilustración)**. Si las válvulas y los asientos son rectificados, los resortes puedan que tengan que utilizar laminillas de ajuste durante el ensamblaje para restaurar la altura de la instalación.

3 Comprima el resorte en la primera válvula con un compresor de resorte y remueva los guardianes **(vea ilustración)**. Cuidadosamente libere el compresor de resorte de la válvula y remueva el retenedor, los resortes y el asiento de los resortes. **Caución:** *Si usted está trabajando en un motor V6, ¡tenga mucho cuidado de no mellar o dañar el buzo cuando esté comprimiendo los resortes de la válvula!* Después, remueva el anillo para retener el aceite desde la guía, entonces hale la válvula hacia fuera de la cabeza. Si la válvula se atora en la guía (no sale), empújela hacia adentro en la cabeza y remueva la rebarba de la zona alrededor de la ranura alrededor del guardián con una lima fina o una piedra mojada.

4 Repita el procedimiento para las válvulas restantes. Recuerde mantener todas las partes para cada válvula juntas para que ellas

puedan reinstalarse en las mismas ubicaciones.

5 Una vez que las válvulas y los componentes relacionados se hayan removido y almacenados en una manera organizada, la cabeza debería completamente limpiarse y ser inspeccionada. Si una rectificación completa del motor se está haciendo, termine los procedimientos de desarmar el motor antes de poner en marcha el proceso de limpiar y chequear la cabeza(s) de los cilindros.

9 Cabeza de los cilindros - limpieza y chequeo

Refiérase a las ilustraciones 9.12, 9.14, 9.17, 9.18 y 9.19

1 Limpieza completa de la cabeza(s) de los cilindros y los componentes relacionados del tren de las válvulas, seguidos por un chequeo detallado, permitirá que usted pueda decidir cuánto trabajo de válvula debe hacerse durante la rectificación completa del motor.

Limpieza

2 Remueva todos los rasgos de juntas viejas y compuesto de sellador desde las superficies de contacto de las cabeza(s), múltiple de admisión y múltiple de escape. Tenga mucho cuidado de no acanalar la cabeza de los cilindros. Solventes especiales de suavizar y remover juntas, que hacen el trabajo de remover las juntas más fácil están disponibles en los almacenes de partes para el vehículo.

3 Remueva todas las escalas que se hayan acumulado en los pasajes del anticongelante.

4 Corra una brocha de alambre rígido en los diversos orificios para remover sedimentos que puedan haberse formado en ellos.

5 Corra una terraja del tamaño apropiado en cada unos de los orificios con roscas para remover sellador de las roscas y corrosión que puedan estar presente. Si aire compri-

mido está disponible, úselo para limpiar los orificios de los desechos producido por esta operación. **Peligro:** *¡Use protector para sus ojos cuando use aire comprimido!*

6 Limpie las roscas para los espárragos de los múltiples de admisión y de escape con una brocha de alambre o una terraja hembra.

7 Limpie la cabeza(s) de los cilindros con solvente y séquela completamente. El aire comprimido apurará el proceso de secar y asegurará que todos los orificios y las zonas rebajadas estén limpias. **Nota:** *Químicos para descarbonizar están disponibles y pueden ser muy útiles cuando se limpie la cabeza de los cilindros y los componentes del tren de las válvulas. Ellos son muy cáusticos y deben usarse con cuidado. Esté seguro de seguir las instrucciones en el recipiente.*

8 Limpie los balancines con solvente y séquelos (no los mezcle durante el proceso de limpieza). Aire comprimido apresurará el proceso de secar y se puede usar para limpiar los pasajes de aceite

9 Limpie todos los resortes de las válvulas, guardianes y retenedores con solvente y séquelos completamente. Haga los componentes de una válvula a la vez para evitar mezclar las piezas.

10 Remueva cualquier sedimentos pesados que puedan haberse formado en las válvulas, entonces use una brocha de alambre motorizado para remover sedimentos desde la cabeza de las válvulas y de los vástagos. Nuevamente, asegúrese que las válvulas no se mezclen.

Chequeo
Cabeza de los cilindros

11 Inspeccione la cabeza cuidadosamente por cuarteaduras, evidencia de fuga de anticongelante y otros daños. Si se encuentran grietas, una cabeza nueva de cilindro debería obtenerse.

12 Usando una regla de precisión recta y un calibrador al tacto, chequee la superficie de la junta de la cabeza por combadura **(vea ilustración)**. Si la combadura excede el límite

8.3 Use un compresor para resorte de válvulas para comprimir los resortes, entonces remueva los guardianes del vástago de la válvula con un imán pequeño (se muestra un motor V6)

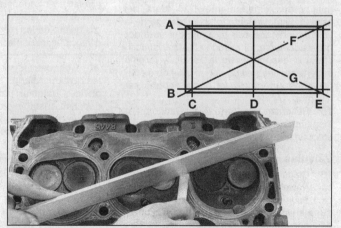

9.12 Chequee la superficie de la junta de la cabeza para ver si está plana, tratando de resbalar un calibrador palpador debajo de la regla recta (vea las especificaciones máximas permisibles y use un calibrador palpador de esa medida)

9.14 Un calibrador de reloj se puede usar para determinar la distancia libre entre el vástago de la válvula y la guía (mueva el vástago de la válvula como se indica en las flechas)

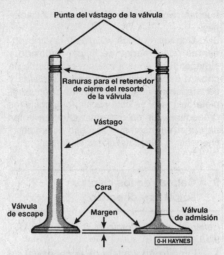

9.17 La anchura del margen de cada válvula debe ser como se especifica (si no existe ningún margen, la válvula no se puede ser empleada de regreso)

9.18 Mida la distancia libre de cada resorte de válvula (sin ser comprimido) y compárelo con las especificaciones

9.19 Chequee cada resorte de válvula para estar seguro de que están cuadrados

especificado, la cabeza puede ser rectificada en un taller de rectificaciones automotriz. **Nota:** *Si las cabezas de los motores V6 son rectificadas, los puertos del múltiple de admisión pueda que se tengan que rectificar. Si la cabeza de los cilindros es rectificada, asegúrese que el árbol de levas gire libremente con su mano. Si resistencia se siente cuando se gire el árbol levas, reemplace la cabeza con una nueva.*

13 Chequee los asientos de las válvulas en cada cámara de combustión. Si ellos tienen pequeños orificios, grietas o están quemados, la cabeza requerirá que se le otorgue servicio de válvula, que está más allá del alcance del mecánico doméstico.

14 Chequee el paralelismo del vástago de la válvula al balancín con un indicador de tipo reloj adjunto firmemente en la cabeza (**vea ilustración**). **Nota:** *Esto puede resultar muy difícil en cabezas de motores V6. Si es, permita que un taller de rectificaciones automotriz mida las válvulas y las guías para determinar el juego libre.* La válvula debe estar en la guía y aproximadamente 1/16 fuera del asiento. El movimiento total del vástago de la válvula indicado por la aguja del medidor debe apuntarse. Si excede el límite especificado, el espacio entre la válvula y la guía debería ser chequeado por un taller de rectificaciones automotriz (el costo debería ser mínimo).

15 Refiérase a la Parte B del Capítulo 2 e inspeccione las superficies de soporte del árbol de levas en la cabeza de los cilindros.

Válvulas

16 Cuidadosamente inspeccione la cara de cada válvula por desgaste desigual, deformación, fisura, orificios y zonas quemadas. Chequee el vástago de la válvula por rayones, pequeños orificios y grietas en el cuello. Gire la válvula y chequee por cualquier indicación obvia de que se haya doblado. Busque por pequeños orificios y desgaste excesivo en el extremo del vástago. La presencia de cual-

quiera de estas condiciones indica la necesidad de que la válvula se le otorgue servicio por un taller de rectificaciones automotriz.

17 Mida la anchura del margen en cada válvula (**vea ilustración**). Cualquier válvula con un margen más estrecho que 1/32 pulgada tendrá que ser substituida con una nueva.

Componentes de la válvula

18 Chequee cada resorte de válvula por desgaste (en los extremos) y pequeños orificios. Mida el largo libre y compárelo con especificaciones (**vea ilustración**). Cualquier resorte que esté más corto que lo especificado se ha vencido y no deben utilizarse. La tensión de todos los resortes debería chequearse con una herramienta especial antes de decidir que ellos son apropiados para el uso en una reconstrucción de motor (lleve los resortes a un taller de rectificación automotriz para este chequeo).

19 Ponga cada resorte en una superficie nivelada y chequéelo para estar seguro de que están cuadrados (**vea ilustración**). Si cualquiera de los resortes están deformados o vencidos, reemplace todos los resortes con partes nuevas.

20 Chequee los retenedores de los resortes, los guardianes por grietas y desgaste obvio. Cualquier parte que esté en duda deberían sustituirse con una nueva, debido ha que daño extenso ocurrirá si ellas fracasan durante la operación del motor.

Balancines y componentes

21 Refiérase a la Sección 15 en la Parte B del Capítulo 2 e inspeccione los balancines y componentes relacionados.

22 Si el proceso de chequeo indica que los componentes de las válvulas están en condiciones generalmente pobres y desgastados más allá de los límites especificados, que es comúnmente el caso en un motor que se esté chequeando, ensamble las válvulas en la

cabeza de los cilindros y refiérase a la Sección 10 para recomendaciones de servicio de las válvulas.

23 Si el resultado de la inspección indica que no hay partes excesivamente desgastadas y si las caras de las válvulas y los asientos están en buenas condiciones, los componentes del tren de válvula pueden ser reinstalados en la cabeza de los cilindros sin otorgarle servicio mayor. Refiérase a la Sección apropiada para el procedimiento de ensamblar la cabeza de los cilindros.

10 Válvulas - servicio

1 A causa de la naturaleza compleja del trabajo, las herramientas especiales y el equipo necesario, el servicio de las válvulas, los asientos de las válvulas y las guías de las válvulas, usualmente conocido como un trabajo de válvula, es mejor dejárselo a un profesional.

2 El mecánico doméstico puede remover y desarmar cada cabeza, hacer chequeo y limpieza inicial, entonces reensamblar y entregar la cabeza a un departamento de servicio de un concesionario o un taller de rectificaciones automotriz para el servicio actual de las válvulas.

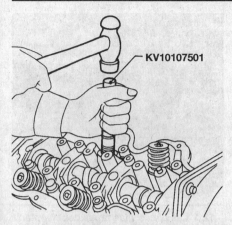

11.4 Los sellos de aceite requieren una herramienta especial para instalarlos (aunque un dado hondo se pueda usar si la herramienta no está disponible) - ¡no martille en los sellos una vez que ellos estén sentados!

11.5 Chequee la distancia de la cima del asiento del resorte a la cara inferior del retenedor, para determinar la altura instalada de los resortes de las válvulas

11.6 Asegúrese que cada resorte de las válvulas (derecho) sea instalado con el extremo estrecho (flecha) contra la cabeza de los cilindros

11.7 Aplique una pequeña cantidad de grasa a cada retenedor como se muestra aquí antes de instalarlos - los mantendrá en su lugar en la válvula hasta que se afloje el resorte

3   El departamento de servicio de su concesionario, o el taller de rectificaciones automotriz, removerá las válvulas y los resortes, recondicionará nuevamente o remplazará las válvulas y los asientos de las válvulas, recondicionará nuevamente o remplazará las guías de las válvulas, chequean y sustituyen los resortes de las válvulas, retenedores de los resortes y los guardianes (si es necesario) y aseguran que la altura instalada del resorte sea correcta. La superficie para la junta de la cabeza también será rectificada si está alabeada.

4   Después que el trabajo de válvula haya sido desempeñado por un profesional, la cabeza estará en una condición como nueva. Cuando la cabeza se regrese, esté seguro de limpiarla nuevamente antes de instalarla en el motor para remover cualquier partículas de metal y la arenilla abrasiva que puede estar presente todavía en la válvula después de las operaciones de rectificación de la cabeza. Aire comprimido debe usarse, si está disponible, para soplar todos los orificios para el aceite y los pasajes.

11   Cabeza de los cilindros - ensamblar

Refiérase a las ilustraciones 11.4, 11.5, 11.6, 11.7 y 11.8

1   A pesar de si o no la cabeza fue enviada a un taller de reparación automotriz para otorgarle servicio a las válvulas, asegúrese de que está limpia antes de comenzar a ensamblarla.

2   Si la cabeza fue enviada para otorgarle servicio a las válvulas, las válvulas y los componentes relacionados estarán ya en su posición. Comience el procedimiento de ensamble con el Paso 8.

3   Instale los asientos de los resortes de las válvulas (donde sea aplicable) antes de la instalación de los sellos de las válvulas.

4   Instale sellos nuevos en cada una de las guías de las válvulas. Los sellos de la válvula

de admisión requieren una herramienta especial (parte Nissan número KV10107501) o un dado hondo del tamaño apropiado. Gentilmente péguele a cada sello para ponerlo en su posición hasta que esté sentado en la guía **(vea ilustración)**. **Caución:** *No martille en los sellos de las válvulas de admisión una vez que ellos estén asentado o usted los puede dañar. No tuerza o atore los sellos durante la instalación o ellos no sellarán apropiadamente en los vástagos de las válvulas.*

5   Aplique grasa de base moly o lubricante para el ensamblaje del motor a la primera válvula e instálela en la cabeza. No dañe el sello de aceite nuevo con la guía de la válvula. Ponga el retenedor y los guardianes en su posición. Chequee la altura instalada del resorte levantando hacia encima el retenedor hasta que la válvula esté sentada. Mida la distancia entre el asiento(s) de la cima del resorte y la cara inferior del retenedor **(vea ilustración)**. Compare su medida a la altura instalada especificada. Agregue láminas para ajustes, si es necesario para obtener la altura especificada.

6   Una vez que la altura correcta esté establecida, remueva los guardianes, el retenedor e instala los resortes de la válvula. **Nota:** *El resorte exterior tiene un contorno graduado. Instálelo con el final del contorno estrecho contra la cabeza de los cilindros* **(vea ilustración)**.

7   Comprima los resortes y el retenedor con un compresor de resortes para las válvulas y resbale los guardianes en su posición. Libere el compresor y asegúrese que los guardianes están asentado apropiadamente en la ranura del vástago de las válvulas. Si es necesario, grasa se puede usar para detener los guardianes en su posición según el compresor es liberado **(vea ilustración)**.

8   Chequee nuevamente la altura instalada de los resortes de las válvulas para cada una de las válvulas y la compara con la altura instalada especificada **(vea ilustración)**. Si estaba correcto antes de instalarlo, todavía debe estar dentro de los límites especificados. Si no estaba, usted debe de instalar más láminas hasta que esté correcto. **Caución:**

¡Nunca, bajo ninguna circunstancia ponga laminas para ajustes de los resortes al grado donde la altura instalada sea menor que la especificada!

9   Instale el árbol de levas, componentes de los balancines y buzos (motor V6 solamente) como está descrito en la Parte A o B.

10   En los motores de cuatro cilindros, las válvulas deben ser ajustadas en frío (Capítulo 1).

11   Almacene la cabeza en una bolsa plástica limpia hasta que usted esté listo para instalarla.

11.8 Chequee dos veces la altura con los resortes de la válvula instalado (haga esto para cada una de las válvulas)

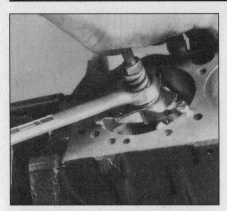

12.1 Use un removedor de rebarba para remover la rebarba de la parte de encima del cilindro antes de atentar de remover el pistón

12.3 Use un calibrador palpador para chequear el juego libre lateral de las bielas

12.4 Las bielas y las tapas deben estar marcadas para indicar en cuál cilindro ellas están instaladas - si ellas no están, ellas deben de ser marcadas con un punzón para evitar confusión dur;ante el proceso de instalar

12 Asamblea del pistón y la biela - remover

Refiérase a las ilustraciones 12.1, 12.3, 12.4, 12.5a y 12.5b

Nota: *Con anterioridad a remover el pistón/biela, remueva la cabeza de los cilindros, el cárter de aceite y la bomba de aceite refiriéndose a las Secciones apropiadas en el Capítulo 2, Parte A o B.*

1 Completamente remueva la rebarba en la parte de encima de cada cilindro con una herramienta para remover rebarba **(vea ilustración)**. Siga las instrucciones del fabricante de la herramienta. Si no se remueva la rebarba antes de atentar de remover el pistón y la asamblea de la biela pueden resultar en rotura del pistón.

2 Después de que las rebarbas de los cilindros se hayan removido, gire el motor hasta que el cigüeñal esté observando hacia encima.

3 Antes de que las bielas se remuevan, chequee el juego axial con calibradores de diferentes espesores. Los resbala entre la biela y las cigüeñas en el cigüeñal hasta que el juego se remueva **(vea ilustración)**. El juego axial es el valor del grosor del calibrador al tacto. Si el juego axial excede el límite de servicio, bielas nuevas se requerirán. Si las bielas nuevas (o un cigüeñal nuevo) es instalado, el juego axial puede caer debajo de la especificación mínima (si cae, las bielas tendrán que ser rectificadas - consulte con un taller de rectificaciones automotriz por consejo si es necesario). Repita el procedimiento para las bielas restantes.

4 Chequee las bielas y las tapas por marcas de identificación. Si no están marcados, simplemente use un punzón de centrar pequeño para hacer el número apropiado de identificación en cada biela y la tapa (1, 4 o 6, dependiendo de los cilindros y el tipo de motor que estén asociados) **(vea ilustración)**.

5 Afloje cada una de las tuercas de la tapa de la biela 1/2 vuelta a la vez hasta que ellas puedan ser removidas con la mano. Remueva la tapa del cojinete número uno y el cojinete de la biela. No tumbe el cojinete.

Deslice una longitud corta de manguera de plástico o tubo de caucho en cada tornillo de la biela para proteger el cigüeñal y la pared de los cilindros según el pistón se remueve **(vea ilustración)**. Empuje la biela y la asamblea del pistón por la parte de encima del bloque fuera del motor **(vea ilustración)**. Use el cabo de un martillo de madera para empujar el cojinete superior en la biela. Si se siente resistencia, chequee nuevamente para asegurarse que toda la rebarba de los cilindros se removió.

6 Repita el procedimiento para los cilindros restantes. Después de remover, reensamble las tapas de las bielas y los cojinetes en sus bielas respectivas e instale las tuercas de las tapas apretadas con sus dedos. Dejando los cojinetes viejos en su posición hasta que se ensamble ayudará e impedirá que las superficies de las bielas se mellen accidentalmente.

13 Cigüeñal - remover

Refiérase a las ilustraciones 13.1, 13.3 y 13.4
Nota: *El cigüeñal puede removerse solamente después de que el motor se haya removido fuera del vehículo. Se presume que el volante o plato flexible, amortiguador de*

vibraciones, cadena de distribución o banda, cárter de aceite, tubo captador de aceite y colador, bomba de aceite, la tapa de cubrir la cadena de distribución (motores de cuatro cilindros), los pistones y las bielas ya se han removido. El sello principal trasero para retener el aceite también debe ser destornillado y separado del bloque antes de proceder con el procedimiento de remover el cigüeñal.

1 Antes de que el cigüeñal se remueva, chequee el juego axial. Instale un indicador de tipo reloj en el vástago en conformidad con la línea recta del cigüeñal y simplemente tocando una de las cigüeñas en el cigüeñal **(vea ilustración)**.

2 Empuje el cigüeñal completamente hacia atrás y ponga el indicador de tipo reloj ha cero. Próximamente, hágale palanca al cigüeñal hacia el frente lo más fuera posible y chequee la lectura en el indicador de tipo reloj. La distancia que se mueve es el jugo axial. Si es mayor de lo especificado, chequee las superficies de empuje del cigüeñal por desgaste. Si ningún desgaste es evidente, arandelas de fricción nuevas deberían corregir el juego axial.

12.5a Para prevenir daño al muñón del cigüeñal y el cilindro, deslice pedazos de secciones de manguera en los pernos de la biela, . . .

12.5b . . . entonces cuidadosamente empuje el ensamblaje del pistón/biela hacia afuera por la parte de encima del motor con el mango de madera de un martillo

13.1 Chequeando el juego final del cigüeñal con un indicador de tipo reloj

13.3 Use un calibrador palpador para chequear el juego final de cigüeñal

13.4 Afloje los pernos de las bielas principales de las tapas principales en esta sucesión númerica (motores de cuatro cilindros solamente)

3   Si un indicador de tipo reloj no está disponible, los calibradores palpadores pueden usarse. Suavemente hágale palanca o empuje el cigüeñal completamente hacia el frente del motor. Los calibradores de espesores se pueden deslizar entre el cigüeñal y la cara delantera del cojinete principal de empuje para determinar el espacio **(vea ilustración)**. El cojinete de torsión principal en los motores de cuatro cilindros es el número tres (central), mientras que en los motores V6 es el número dos.

4   En los motores de cuatro cilindros, chequee el cojinete principal para ver si ellos están marcados para indicar sus ubicaciones. Ellos deberían numerarse consecutivamente desde el frente del motor hasta atrás. Si ellos no están, márquelos con números de tipo timbre o con una punta de centrar. Las tapas de los cojinete principales generalmente tienen una flecha como marca, que indica el frente del motor. Afloje las tapas de los cojinetes principales 1/4 de vuelta a la vez en la secuencia recomendada **(vea ilustración)**, hasta que ellos puedan ser removidos ha mano.

5   Suavemente golpe las tapas con un martillo nominal blando, entonces los separa desde el bloque de los cilindros. Si es necesario, úselos como palancas para remover las tapas. Trate de no tumbar los cojinetes si están fuera de las tapas. Las tapas de los cojinetes principales en los motores V6 son una asamblea de una sola pieza, que puede tener que ser cuidadosamente palanqueada fuera del bloque.

6   Remueva el cigüeñal fuera del motor. Con el cojinete introducido en el bloque de los cilindros y las tapas de los cojinetes principales o ensamblaje de las tapas, instale las tapas en el bloque de los cilindros y apriete los pernos con sus dedos.

14 Bloque de los cilindros - limpieza

Refiérase a las ilustraciones 14.1, 14.7 y 14.9
Nota: *Los tapones del bloque (también conocidos como tapones de congelación o tapones blandos) pueden ser difíciles o imposibles de recuperar si ellos se meten adentro de los pasajes del anticongelante del bloque.*

1   Perfore un orificio pequeño en el centro

14.1 Use un remover de juntas para remover todos los pedazos de la junta vieja y el sellador de la superficie del bloque (solventes para remover juntas están disponibles y preden remover las juntas que están bien difícil de remover mas fácil)

de cada bujía y los hala hacia fuera con un extractor para remover las abolladuras de la carrocería **(vea ilustración)**. Remueva todos los tapones con rosca desde el bloque.

2   Usando un removedor de junta, remueva todos los rasgos de material de junta desde el bloque de los cilindros. Tenga mucho cuidado para no mellar o acanalar las superficies donde sella la junta.

3   Remueva la tapa del cojinete principal o la asamblea de la tapa y separe el cojinete introducido desde las tapas y el bloque de los cilindros. Póngale etiquetas a los cojinetes, indicando de que cilindros ellos se removieron y si estaban en las tapas o en el bloque, entonces los coloca en un lado.

4   Si el motor está sumamente sucio se debe llevar a un taller de rectificaciones automotriz para ser limpiado con vapor o un tanque caliente.

5   Después de que se regrese el bloque, limpie todos los orificios y conductos de aceite una vez más. Brochas específicamente diseñadas para este trabajo están disponibles en las mayorías de los almacenes para partes de vehículos. Enjuague los pasajes con agua cálida hasta que el agua que sale se vea clara, seque el bloque completamente y aplíquele una pequeña película de aceite para prevenir la oxidación. Si usted

14.7 Todo los orificios del bloque - particularmente los de la tapa para los cojinetes principales y los de la cabeza - se deben limpiar y restaurar con una terraja macho (esté seguro de remover cualquier suciedad de los agujeros después de que haya terminado este procedimiento)

tiene acceso a aire comprimido, úselo para apurar el proceso de secar y para soplar todos los orificios y galerías de aceite. **Peligro:** *¡Use protector para sus ojos cuando use aire comprimido!*

6   Si el bloque no está extremadamente sucio o lleno de fango, usted puede hacer un trabajo adecuado limpiándolo con agua jabonosa caliente y una brocha rígida. Tome suficiente tiempo y haga un trabajo completo. Sin considerar el método usado para limpiar, esté seguro de limpiar todos los orificios, galerías de aceite completamente, seque el bloque completamente y aplíquele una pequeña capa de aceite a todas las superficies.

7   Los orificios con roscas en el bloque deben ser limpiados para asegurarse que lecturas precisas de torsión durante el ensamblaje se obtengan. Corra el tamaño apropiado de la terraja en cada uno de los orificios para remover cualquier óxido, corrosión, fango o sellador de las roscas y para restaurar las roscas dañadas **(vea ilustración)**. Si es posible, use aire comprimido para limpiar los orificios del desecho producido por esta operación. Ahora es un buen

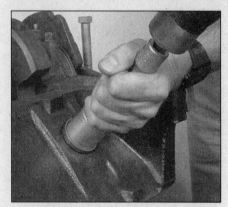

14.9 Un dado grande en una extensión se puede usar para instalar el tapón nuevo para el anticongelante adentro del orificio

tiempo para limpiar las roscas en los pernos de la cabeza y los de las tapas principales también.

8   Reinstale las tapas de los cojinetes principales y apriete los pernos con los dedos.

9   Después de aplicarle sellador RTV (vulcanizador accionado a temperatura del ambiente) a las superficies de los tapones nuevos del bloque del motor, instálelos en el bloque de los cilindros **(vea ilustración)**. Asegúrese que ellos se conducen rectos y asentados adecuadamente o fugas pueden resultar. Herramientas especiales están disponibles para este final, pero resultados igualmente buenos pueden obtenerse usando un dado grande, con el diámetro externo que se deslice encima del tapón, una extensión de 1/2 pulgada y un martillo.

10   Si el motor no va a ser ensamblado ahora mismo, cúbralo con un cartucho para basura de plástico grande para mantenerlo limpio.

15   Bloque de los cilindros - chequeo

Refiérase a las ilustraciones 15.4a, 15.4b, 15.4c, 15.6 y 15.7

1   Antes de que el bloque se inspeccione,

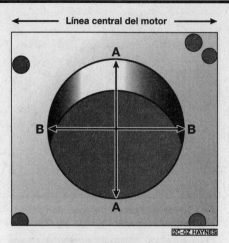

15.4a Mida el diámetro de cada cilindro debajo del borde de desgaste (A), en el centro (B) y al fondo (C)

se debe limpiar según se describe en la Sección 14. Chequee nuevamente para asegurarse que la rebarba en la parte de encima de cada cilindro se haya removido completamente.

2   Visualmente chequee el bloque por grietas, óxido y corrosión. Busque por roscas cruzadas. Es también una buena idea de llevar el bloque a un taller de rectificaciones automotriz que tiene el equipo especial para chequear por grietas para que hagan este tipo de trabajo. Si defectos se encuentran, haga que se repare el bloque, si es posible, o substitúyalo.

3   Chequee el cilindro para ver si está arañado o tiene rayones.

4   Mida el diámetro en la parte superior de cada cilindro (simplemente debajo de la zona de la rebarba), centro y el fondo de los cilindros, compárelo al axis del cigüeñal **(vea ilustraciones)**. Después, mida el diámetro de cada cilindro en las mismas tres ubicaciones hasta el axis del cigüeñal. Compare los resultados con las especificaciones. Si las paredes de los cilindros están bien arañadas o ralladas, o si están fuera de la ronda (ovaladas) o en forma de campana más allá de los

límites otorgados en las especificaciones, haga que el bloque de los cilindros sea rectificado nuevamente por un taller de rectificaciones automotriz. Si una rectificación del bloque donde los cilindros se harán más grande, pistones y anillos de sobremedida se requerirán.

5   Si los cilindros están en condiciones razonablemente buenas y no están desgastados fuera de los límites y si el espacio del pistón al cilindro pueden mantenerse adecuadamente, entonces ellos no tienen que tener los cilindros rectificados nuevamente. Pulírlo es todo lo que es necesario (Sección 16).

6   Usando una regla de precisión recta y calibradores de diferentes espesores, chequee la superficie del bloque (la superficie que hace contacto con la cabeza de los cilindros) por distorsión **(vea ilustración)**. Si la distorsión está más allá del límite especificado, puede ser rectificado por un taller de rectificaciones automotriz.

7   Si el bloque es reemplazado con uno nuevo, pistones y anillos nuevos que emparejen con los números de grado estampados en el bloque encima de cada cilindro **(vea ilustración)** debe ser también usado.

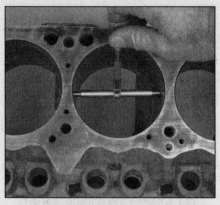

15.4b La habilidad de sentir cuando el medidor telescópico está en el punto correcto lo desarrollará con tiempo, así que trabaje despacio y repita el chequeo hasta que esté satisfecho de que la medida del cilindro es correcta

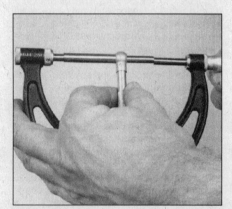

15.4c Mida el medidor telescópico con un micrómetro para determinar el tamaño del cilindro

15.6 Chequee la superficie del bloque (en ambos lados en el motor V6) por distorsión con una regla de la precisión y un calibrador al tacto

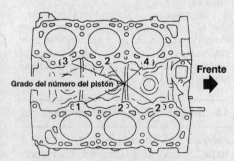

15.7 Coloque la regla de precisión recta a través del bloque, diagonalmente y desde un extremo al otro extremo cuando esté haciendo el chequeo

16 Herramienta de pulir los cilindros

Refiérase a las ilustraciones 16.3a y 16.3b

1 Con anterioridad al ensamblaje del motor, el cilindro debe esmerilarse para que los anillos nuevos del pistón se asienten correctamente y provean el mejor sello posible en la cámara de combustión. **Nota:** *Si usted no tiene las herramientas o no quiere hacer la operación de esmerilarlo, la mayoría de los talleres de rectificaciones automotrices lo harán por un costo razonable.*

2 Antes de esmerilar los cilindros, instale las tapas de los cojinete principales (sin los cojinetes) y los aprieta a la torsión especificada.

3 Dos tipos de herramientas de pulir los cilindros están usualmente disponibles - la de piedra flexible de esmerilar o "botella" y la de revestimiento más tradicional con piedras de esmerilar de resorte. Ambos harán el trabajo, pero para el mecánico menos experimentado la de "botella" será probablemente más fácil de usar. Usted necesitará también de una abundancia de aceite liviano o aceite para esmerilar, algunos trapos y un taladro de motor eléctrico. Proceda como se indica a continuación:

a) Instale el esmerilador en el taladro, comprima las piedras y deslícelas en el cilindro primero **(vea ilustración)**. *Esté seguro de usar gafas protectoras dé seguridad o un blindaje para cubrir su cara!*

b) *Lubrique el cilindro con abundante aceite, ponga en marcha el taladro y mueva la esmeriladora hacia encima y hacia abajo en el cilindro a una marcha que produzca un patrón cruzado en las paredes de los cilindros. Idealmente, las líneas del patrón cruzado se deberían cruzar aproximadamente ha un ángulo de 60 grados* **(vea ilustración)**. *Esté seguro de usar abundante lubricante y no remueva más material de lo que sea absolutamente necesario para producir el acabado deseado.* **Nota:** *Los fabricantes de anillos de pistones pueden especificar un patrón de ángulo cruzado menor que los de 60 grados tradicionales - lea y siga cualquier instrucción incluida con los anillos nuevos.*

c) *No retire la piedra de esmerilar desde los cilindros mientras está en marcha. En vez, desconecte el taladro y continúe moviendo la piedra de esmerilar hacia encima y hacia abajo en el cilindro hasta que se pare por si misma, entonces comprima las piedras y retire el taladro de esmerilar. Si usted usa una pulidora "de tipo botella," para el taladro, entonces gire la piedra en el sentido de rotación normal mientras remueva la piedra de esmeril desde los cilindros.*

d) *Limpie el aceite fuera de los cilindros y repita el procedimiento para los cilindros restantes.*

4 Después que el trabajo de esmerilar se haya completado, chaflane los bordes supe-

16.3a Una piedra de pulir de tipo botella, producirá mejor resultados si usted nunca a pulido un cilindro anteriormente

riores de los cilindros con una lima pequeña para que los anillos no se rayen cuando los pistones se instalen. Tenga mucho cuidado para no mellar las paredes de los cilindros con el extremo de la lima!

5 El bloque de los cilindros entero debe nuevamente lavarse completamente con agua cálida y jabonosa para remover todos los rasgos de arenilla abrasiva producida durante operación de esmerilar. **Nota:** *Se considera limpio cuando un paño blanco - húmedo con aceite de motor limpio - usado para limpiar no colecta nada más de residuo esmerilado, que se mostrará como zonas grises en el paño. Esté seguro de correr una brocha en todos los orificios, galerías de aceite y los enjuaga con el agua corriente.*

6 Después de enjuagarlo, seque el bloque y aplique una capa de aceite ligera para prevenir óxido a todas las superficies rectificadas. Envuelva el bloque en una bolsa de basura plástica para mantenerlo limpio y póngalo hacia un lado hasta que se vaya a ensamblar.

17 Asamblea de la biela y el pistón - inspección

Refiérase a las ilustraciones 17.4a, 17.4b, 17.5, 17.10 y 17.11

1 Antes de que el proceso de chequeo pueda efectuarse, el pistón/biela deben limpiarse y los anillos originales del pistón removerse desde los pistones. **Nota:** *Siempre use anillos nuevos de pistón cuando el motor se ensamble nuevamente.*

2 Usando una herramienta de instalar anillos de pistón, cuidadosamente remueva los anillos desde los pistones. Tenga cuidado de no mellar o acanalar los pistones en el proceso.

3 Raspe todos los rasgos de carbón desde la parte de encima del pistón. Una brocha de alambre de mano o un pedazo de tela de esmeril fina pueden usarse una vez que la mayoría de los sedimentos se hayan removido. Nunca, debajo ninguna circunstancia, use una brocha de alambre instalado en un taladro de motor para remover sedimentos desde los pistones. El material del

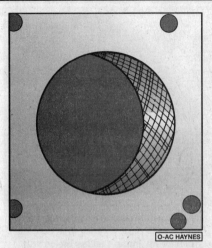

16.3b La pulida del cilindro debe de dejar un patrón donde las líneas se crucen aproximádamente a 60 grados

pistón es blando y puede desgastarse por brocha de alambre.

4 Use una herramienta de limpiar ranuras de pistón para limpiar la ranura del anillo de sedimentos de carbón en las ranuras del pistón. Si una herramienta no está disponible, un pedazo roto de anillo viejo hará el trabajo. Tenga mucho cuidado de remover solamente los sedimentos de carbón - no remueva ningún metal y no melle o rasguñe los lados de las ranuras del pistón **(vea ilustraciones)**.

17.4a Las ranuras del pistón para los anillos se puede limpiar con una herramienta especial, según se de muestra aquí . . .

17.4b . . . o una sección de un anillo roto

17.5 Asegúrese que el orificio para el aceite en la parte inferior final de cada biela está limpio - ¡si las bielas son separadas de los pistones, asegúrese que el orificio de aceite está en el lado derecho cuando ellos sean vueltos a instalar!

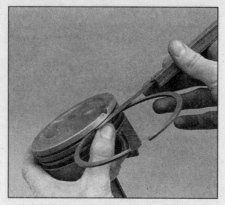

17.10 Con el anillo cuadrado en el cilindro, mida el espacio del anillo con un calibrador palpador

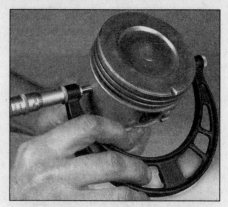

17.11 Mida el diámetro del pistón a un ángulo de 90 grados del pasador del pistón, acerca de 13/16 pulgada encima de la orilla inferior

5   Una vez que los sedimentos se hayan removido, limpie las asambleas del pistón/biela con solvente y séquelos con aire comprimido (si está disponible). Asegúrese que los orificios de retorno de aceite en los orificios de los canales del anillo y el orificio de lubricación en el extremo inferior de cada biela están limpios **(vea ilustración)**.

6   Si los pistones y las paredes de los cilindros no están dañados o desgastados excesivamente y si el bloque de los cilindros no se va ha rectificar, pistones nuevos no serán necesarios. El desgaste normal del pistón se muestra como desgaste vertical uniforme en la parte de empuje del pistón y un poco flojo en la parte superior de los anillos en su ranura. Anillos nuevos de pistón, por otra parte, deberían siempre usarse cuando un motor es rectificado.

7   Cuidadosamente inspeccione cada pistón por grietas alrededor de la falda, el pasador y las áreas para el anillo.

8   Busque por partes arañadas y rayones en las caras de empuje de las faldas, orificios en la parte superior del pistón y zonas quemadas al borde de la corona. Si la falda está rayada o arañada, el motor puede haber sufrido de un recalentamiento y/o combustión anormal, que ocasionó temperaturas de operaciones excesivamente altas. Los sistemas de enfriamiento y de lubricación deberían chequearse completamente. Un orificio en la corona superior del pistón es una indicación que la combustión anormal (pre encendido) ocurrió. Las zonas quemadas al borde de la cara superior del pistón son comúnmente evidencia de golpe de chispa (detonación). Si cualquiera de los problemas de encima existen, el problema debe corregirse o daño ocurrirá nuevamente.

9   Corrosión del pistón, en forma de orificios pequeños, indica que escape del anticongelante está entrando en la cámara de combustión y/o el cárter del cigüeñal. Nuevamente, la causa debe corregirse o el problema puede persistir en el motor reconstruido.

10   Mida el espacio lateral del anillo del pistón colocando un anillo de pistón nuevo en cada ranura del pistón y deslizando un calibrador al tacto en su lado **(vea ilustración)**. Chequee el espacio a tres o cuatro ubicaciones alrededor de cada ranura. Esté seguro de usar el anillo correcto para cada ranura; son diferentes. Si el espacio lateral es mayor de lo especificado, pistones nuevos tendrán que ser usados.

11   Chequee el espacio libre entre el pistón y el cilindro (Sección 15) midiendo el pistón y el cilindro. Asegúrese de que los pistones son los correctos para los cilindros. Mida el pistón en la falda, a un ángulo de 90 grados en el pasador del pistón, la distancia especificada desde la parte de encima del pistón al centro del pasador **(vea ilustración)**. Reste el diámetro del pistón desde el diámetro de los cilindros para obtener el espacio. Si es mayor de lo especificado, el bloque tendrá que ser rectificado y pistones y anillos nuevos ser instalados.

12   Chequee el espacio libre entre el pistón y la biela torciendo el pistón y la biela en direcciones opuestas. Cualquier juego perceptible indica desgaste excesivo, que debe corregirse. La asamblea del pistón/biela deberían llevarse a un taller de rectificaciones automotriz para rectificar los pistones, las bielas y pasadores nuevos instalados.

13   Si los pistones deben removerse desde las bielas por cualquier razón, ellos deberían llevarse a un taller de rectificaciones automotriz. Mientras ellos están en el taller haga que chequeen las bielas para chequear si están viradas o torcidas, debido a que los talleres de rectificaciones automotrices tienen equipos especiales para este chequeo. **Nota:** *A menos que pistones nuevos y/o las bielas sean instalados, no desarme los pistones y las bielas.*

14   Chequee las bielas por grietas y otros daños. Remueva los cojinetes viejos, limpie las superficies de los cojinetes y las tapas e inspecciónelas por mellas, rayones y arañazos. Después de chequear las bielas, reemplace los cojinetes viejos, deslice las tapas en su posición y apriete las tuercas con sus dedos.

18   Cigüeñal - chequeo

Refiérase a la ilustración 18.2

1   Limpie el cigüeñal con solvente y séquelo con aire comprimido (si está disponible). Esté seguro de limpiar los orificios de aceite con una brocha dura y los enjuaga con solvente. Chequee los muñones para la biela y el cojinete principal por desgaste desigual, arañado, pequeños orificios y grietas. Chequee el resto del cigüeñal por grietas y otros daños.

2   Usando un micrómetro, mida el diámetro de los muñones principales, las bielas y compare los resultados con las especificaciones **(vea ilustración)**. Midiendo el diámetro en un punto alrededor de la circunferencia de cada muñón, usted será capaz determinar si o no el muñón está fuera de la ronda (fuera de circunferencia). Tome la medida a cada extremo del muñón, cerca de la cigüeña, para determinar si el muñón está en forma de campana.

3   La excentricidad del cigüeñal debería chequearse también, pero bloques en tipo V grandes y un indicador de tipo reloj se necesitan para hacerlo correctamente. Si usted no tiene acceso a ellos, un taller de rectificaciones automotriz lo hará.

18.2 Mida el diámetro de cada muñón del cigüeñal en varios puntos para detectar las condiciones de conicidad y fuera de circunferencia

4   Si los muñones del cigüeñal se dañan, en forma de campana, fuera de la ronda (fuera de circunferencia) o desgastado más allá de los límites otorgados en las especificaciones, lleve el cigüeñal ha ser rectificado por un taller de rectificaciones automotriz. Esté seguro de usar el tamaño correcto de cojinetes si el cigüeñal se rectifica.

5   Chequee las superficies de contacto del sello para retener el aceite en ambos extremos del cigüeñal. Si ellos se rasguñan, mellan o de otra manera se dañan, los sellos para retener el aceite pueden tener fugas cuando el motor se ensamble nuevamente. La reparación puede ser posible (pregunte en un taller de rectificaciones automotriz), pero un cigüeñal nuevo pueda que se requiera.

6   Refiérase a la Sección 19 y chequee los cojinetes principales y de bielas.

19   Cojinetes principales y de bielas - inspección y selección de los cojinetes principales

Chequeo

1   Aunque los cojinetes principales y de bielas deberían substituirse con nuevos durante una rectificación completa del motor, los cojinetes viejos deberían retenerse para un chequeo más cerca, porque ellos pueden dar a conocer información valiosa acerca de la condición del motor.

2   Fracaso de los cojinetes ocurre a causa de la falta de lubricación, la presencia de suciedad u otras partículas extranjeras, sobre carga del motor y corrosión. Sin importar la causa del fracaso del cojinete, este problema se debe corregirse antes de que el motor se ensamble nuevamente para impedir que suceda nuevamente.

3   Cuando esté chequeando los cojinetes, remuévalos del bloque de los cilindros, la tapa de los cojinetes principales, las bielas y las tapas de las bielas y póngalo fuera en una superficie limpia en la misma posición general como estaban ubicados en el motor. Esto permitirá que usted pueda saber en que muñón del cigüeñal corresponde el cojinete con problemas.

4   Suciedad y otras partículas extranjeras entran en el motor en una variedad de mane-

ras. Pueden dejarse en el motor durante el ensamblaje, o puede pasar a través de los filtros o el sistema PCV (ventilación positiva del cárter). Puede entrar en el aceite y desde allí a los cojinetes. Astilla de metal de las operaciones de rectificación y el desgaste normal del motor están frecuentemente presente. Loa abrasivos son a veces dejados en los componentes del motor después de una rectificación completa, especialmente cuando las partes no son limpiadas completamente usando los métodos de limpiezas apropiados. Cualquiera que sea la fuente, estos objetos extranjeros frecuentemente acaban impregnado en las áreas blandas de los cojinetes y se reconocen fácilmente. Las partículas grandes no se incrustan en el cojinete, arañarán o acanalarán el cojinete o el muñón. La mejor prevención para esta causa de fallo de los cojinetes es limpiar todas las partes completamente para mantener todo limpio durante el ensamblaje del motor. Cambios regulares y frecuente del aceite del motor y el filtro se recomiendan también.

5   Falta de lubricación (o lubricación inadecuada) tiene un número de causas correlacionadas. El calor excesivo (que adelgaza el aceite), exceso de carga (que aprieta el aceite hacia fuera desde la superficie de contacto) y fugas de aceite o tirado (por luz excesiva en los cojinetes, bomba de aceite desgastada o velocidades altas del motor) todos contribuyen a la separación de la lubricación. Los pasajes obturados de aceite, que comúnmente son el resultado de orificios de lubricación fuera de alineación en el cojinete, también le carecerá aceite al cojinete y lo destruirá. Cuando la falta de lubricación es la causa del fracaso del cojinete, el material del cojinete se enjuaga o extrae desde el acero que respalda el cojinete. Las temperaturas pueden aumentar al punto que el acero de respaldo se vuelve azul debido al calentamiento.

6   Hábitos de marcha pueden tener un efecto definitivo en la vida del cojinete. Abertura completa del acelerador, operación de baja velocidad (con carga en el motor) pone cargas muy altas en los cojinetes, que tienden a apretar la película de aceite hacia afuera. Estas cargas ocasionan que los cojinetes se doblen, que producen grietas finas en la superficie de contacto (fracaso por fatiga). Eventualmente el material del cojinete

se desprenderá en pedazos y se separará del acero de respaldando. Viajes cortos conducen a la corrosión de los cojinetes porque insuficiente calor del motor se produce para remover el agua condensada y los gases corrosivos fuera del motor. Estos productos se coleccionan en el aceite del motor, formando ácido y fango. Según el aceite llega a los cojinetes del motor, los ácidos atacan y corroen el material del cojinete.

7   La instalación incorrecta del cojinete durante la instalación del motor conducirá a fracaso del cojinete también. Los cojinetes apretados también dejan poco espacio e insuficiente lubricante puede fluir y el resultado será que el cojinete se quede sin aceite. La suciedad o las partículas extranjeras atrapadas detrás de los cojinetes resultará en manchas altas en el cojinete que llevarán al fracaso del cojinete.

Selección (cojinetes principales solamente)

Refiérase a las ilustraciones 19.9a, 19.9b, 19.10a, 19.10b, 19.10c, 19.11 y 19.12

8   Si los cojinetes principales originales están desgastados o dañados, o si los espacios libres para el aceite están incorrectos (Sección 22), el procedimiento siguiente debería usarse para seleccionar los cojinetes nuevos correctos para el ensamblaje del motor. Sin embargo, si el cigüeñal ha sido rectificado, cojinetes nuevos de tamaño mayor (comúnmente llamados menor por la relación al cigüeñal) deben instalarse, el procedimiento siguiente no debería usarse si cojinetes de tamaño bajo se requieren. El taller de rectificaciones automotriz que rectifica el cigüeñal proveerá o ayudará ha usted a seleccionar los cojinetes del tamaño correctos. Sin importar como se determinan los tamaños de los cojinetes, use la luz para el aceite, medido con un Plastigage (hilachas de plástico) (Sección 22), como una guía para asegurarse que los cojinetes son del tamaño correcto.

9   Ubique el grado del muñón principal del cigüeñal, timbrado en la superficie de contacto para la cacerola del aceite en el bloque del motor (**vea ilustraciones**). **Nota:** *Los motores más modernos KA24E usan solamente un sistema de número para los grados de los cojinetes principales.*

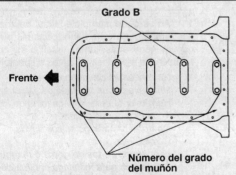

19.9a Ubicación de los números de grado del muñón del cojinete principal - motores de cuatro cilindros

Grado B

Frente

Número del grado del muñón

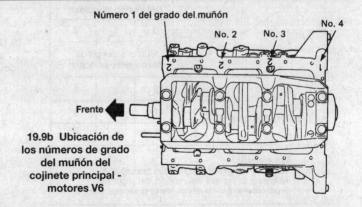

Número 1 del grado del muñón

No. 2   No. 3   No. 4

Frente

19.9b Ubicación de los números de grado del muñón del cojinete principal - motores V6

Grado del número del muñón 1, 3, & 5	0	Seleccione el grado del cojinete A
	1	Seleccione el grado del cojinete B
Para los muñones número 2 & 4 seleccione el grado del cojinete B		

19.10a Diagrama de selección de los cojinetes principales para los motores de cuatro cilindros

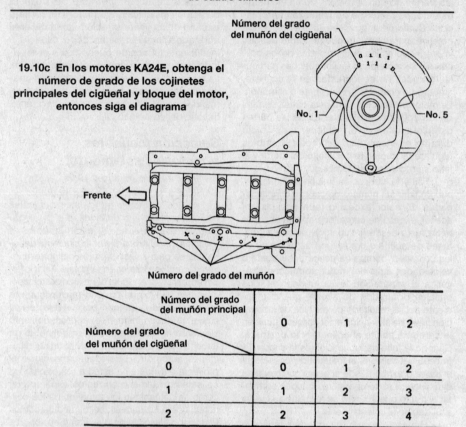

19.10c En los motores KA24E, obtenga el número de grado de los cojinetes principales del cigüeñal y bloque del motor, entonces siga el diagrama

Número del grado del muñón del cigüeñal

No. 1   No. 5

Frente

Número del grado del muñón

	Número del grado del muñón principal		
Número del grado del muñón del cigüeñal	0	1	2
0	0	1	2
1	1	2	3
2	2	3	4

10   Si usted está trabajando en un motor de cuatro cilindros, esté consciente que los muñones 2 y 4 siempre requieren un cojinete del grado B (como único, que el cigüeñal haya sido rectificado) Los muñones 1, 3 y 5 requieren diferentes grados (A o B) dependiendo en el número del grado en el bloque **(vea ilustraciones)**.

11   Si usted está trabajando en un motor V6, ubique el número del grado del muñón en el cigüeñal **(vea ilustración)**.

12   Use los diagramas que se acompañan

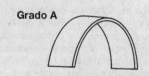

Grado A

Marca de color azul   Grado B

19.10b Los cojinetes de grado A no están marcados, mientras que los cojinetes de grado B están marcados con pintura azul en el lado

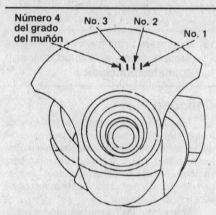

Número 4 del grado del muñón   No. 3   No. 2   No. 1

19.11 El cigüeñal del motor V6 tiene también las marcas del grado para cada muñón de los cojinetes principales (el número 1 está en el frente, el número 4 está en la parte trasera)

para determinar los cojinetes correctos para cada muñón **(vea ilustración)**.

13   Recuerde, el espacio para el aceite es el juez final cuando esté seleccionando los cojinetes de tamaños nuevos. Si usted tiene cualquier pregunta o no está seguro que cojinetes debe usar, obtenga la ayuda de un concesionario de partes Nissan o un departamento de servicio.

20 Rectificación completa del motor - secuencia del ensamble

1   Antes del ensamblaje inicial del motor, asegúrese que usted tiene todas las piezas nuevas necesarias, juntas y sellos así como también los artículos siguientes disponible:

Herramientas de mano comunes
Una llave dinamométrica de 1/2 pulgada
Herramienta para la instalación de los anillos de los pistones
Compresor para los anillos de los pistones
Longitudes cortas de goma o manguera plástica para instalarla encima de los pernos de las bielas
Plastigage (hilachas de plástico)
Calibradores palpadores

	Número del grado del muñón principal:		
	0	1	2
	Número del grado del cojinete principal		
Número del grado del muñón del cigüeñal	0	0	1	2

Número del grado del muñón del cigüeñal	0	0	1	2
	1	1	2	3
	2	2	3	4

19.12 Diagrama para la selección de los cojinetes principales de los motor V6

Por ejemplo:
Número del grado del muñón principal: 1
Número del grado del muñón del cigüeñal: 2
Número del grado del cojinete principal = 1 + 2

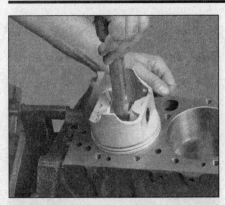

21.3 Cuando esté chequeando la luz en el final de los anillos, el anillo debe de estar perfectamente cuadrado en el cilindro (esto se hace empujando el anillo hacia abajo con la parte de encima del pistón según se demuestra)

Una lima con dientes finos
Aceite de motor nuevo
Lubricante para el ensamblaje del motor o grasa de base moly
RTV (vulcanizador accionado a temperatura del ambiente) - sellador de junta
Compuesto para el enclavamiento de las roscas

2 A final de ahorrar tiempo y evitar problemas, el ensamblaje del motor debe hacerse en el orden general siguiente:

Motores de cuatro cilindros

Anillos del pistón (Parte C)
Cigüeñal y cojinetes principales (Parte C)
Pistón/biela (Parte C)
Sello principal trasero para retener el aceite 1(Parte C)
Árbol de levas (Parte A)
Cabeza de los cilindros y balancines (Parte A)
Cadena de distribución y engranaje (Parte A)
Tapa de la cadena de distribución (Parte A)
Colador de aceite (Parte A)
Bomba de aceite (Parte A)
Cárter de aceite (Parte A)

Múltiples de escape y de admisión (Parte A)
Tapa para los balancines (Parte A)
Volante/plato flexible (Parte A)

Motor V6

Anillos del pistón (Parte C)
Cojinetes principales del cigüeñal (Parte C)
Pistón/biela (Parte C)
Retenedor para el sello del aceite trasero (Parte C)
Bomba de aceite (Parte B)
Cárter de aceite (Parte B)
Cabeza de los cilindros (Parte B)
Árboles de levas y buzos (Parte B)
Banda de distribución del tiempo y los engranes (Parte B)
Tapa para la banda de distribución del tiempo (Parte B)
Múltiples de admisión y de escape (Parte B)
Tapas de los balancines (Parte B)
Volante/plato flexible (Parte B)

21 Anillos del pistón - instalación

Refiérase a las ilustraciones 21.3, 21.4, 21.9a, 21.9b y 21.12
1 Antes de instalar los anillos nuevos del pistón, las separaciones de las terminales de los anillo deben chequearse. Se presume que el espacio lateral del anillo del pistón se ha chequeado y verificado que está correcto (Sección 17).
2 Ponga afuera el ensamblaje del pistón/biela y el juego de anillos nuevos para que el juego de anillos se comparen con el mismo pistón y el cilindro durante el momento de chequear el juego final de los anillos y el ensamblaje del motor.
3 Introduzca el anillo de encima (número uno) en el primer cilindro y póngalo cuadrado con las paredes de los cilindros empujándolo con la parte de encima del pistón (vea ilustración). El anillo debería estar cerca del fondo de los cilindros, al límite inferior del viaje del anillo.
4 Para medir la separación final del extremo, deslice calibradores de diferentes

espesores entre las puntas de los extremos del anillo hasta que un medidor del espesor de la anchura de la separación se encuentre (vea ilustración). El calibrador al tacto debería resbalar entre las terminales del anillo con una cantidad pequeña de fricción. Compare la medida a las especificaciones. Si la separación es mayor o menor que la especificada, chequee nuevamente para asegurarse que usted tiene los anillos correctos antes de proceder.
5 Si la separación es demasiado pequeña, reemplace los anillos - NUNCA lije los extremos para aumentar el espacio.
6 El exceso de la separación de los extremos no es crítico a menos que sea mayor de 0.040 pulgada. Nuevamente chequee para asegurarse que usted tiene los anillos correctos para su motor.
7 Repita el procedimiento para que cada anillo que se instalará en el primer cilindro y para cada anillo en los cilindros restantes. Recuerde mantenga los anillos, pistones y los cilindros en un mismo juego.
8 Una vez que las separaciones de las terminales de los anillos se han chequeado o corregido, los anillos pueden instalarse en los pistones.
9 El anillo de control de aceite (el inferior en el pistón) se instala primero. En la mayoría de los modelos está compuesto de tres componentes separados. Deslice el espaciador/expandor en la ranura (vea ilustración). Si una pestaña previene la rotación, asegúrese que se introduzca en el orificio perforado en la ranura del pistón. Después, instale el lado del carril inferior. No use una herramienta de instalar anillos de pistón en los carriles laterales del anillo de aceite, porque ellos pueden dañarse. En vez, coloque uno en el extremo del carril lateral en la ranura entre el espaciador/expandor y el anillo, sujételo firmemente en su posición y resbale su dedo alrededor del pistón mientras empuja el carril en la ranura (vea ilustración). Después, instale el carril lateral superior de la misma manera.
10 Después de que los tres componentes de los anillos de aceite se han instalado, chequee para asegurarse que ambos de los carriles laterales superiores e inferiores pueden girarse suavemente en la ranura del pistón.

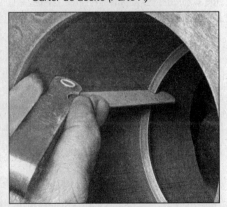

21.4 Con el anillo cuadrado en el cilindro, mida el boquete del anillo con un calibrador palpador

21.9a Instale el espaciador/ampliador en la ranura para el anillo del control de aceite

21.9b NO USE una herramienta para instalar anillos cuando esté instalando el anillo de aceite

21.12 Instalando los anillos de la compresión con un ensanchador del anillo

22.2 Asegúrese que el plato deflector y la parrilla de acero están en su posición en los motores de cuatro cilindros antes de que el cigüeñal sea instalado

22.5 Los cojinetes con la ranura de aceite (flecha) deben ser instalados en el bloque

11 El anillo número dos (medio) se instala después. Tiene una marca que debe estar boca encima, hacia la parte de encima del pistón. **Nota:** *Siempre siga las instrucciones imprimidas en el paquete del anillo o caja - los diferentes fabricantes pueden requerir diferentes formas. No mezcle los anillos de encima y los anillos del medio, ellos tienen diferentes secciones transversales.*

12 Use una herramienta para instalar anillos de pistón y asegúrese que la marca de identificación está en la parte de encima del pistón, entonces deslice el anillo en la ranura del medio en el pistón **(vea ilustración)**. No expanda el anillo más de lo que es necesario para resbalarlo en el pistón.

13 Instale el anillo número uno (superior) de la misma manera. Asegúrese que la marca está hacia encima. Tenga cuidado de no confundir los anillos número uno y número dos.

14 Repita el procedimiento para los anillos y los pistones restantes.

22 Cigüeñal - instalación y chequeo de la luz para el aceite de los cojinetes

Refiérase a las ilustraciones 22.2, 22.5, 22.10, 22.12a, 22.12b, 22.14, 22.19 y 22.24

1 Instalación del cigüeñal es el paso primero mayor en el ensamblaje del motor. Se presume a este punto que el bloque de los cilindros y el cigüeñal se ha limpiado, inspeccionado, reparado o rectificado.

2 Coloque el motor con la parte inferior observando hacia encima. En los motores de cuatro cilindros, esté seguro de que la red de acero y el plato deflector están en su lugar en el cigüeñal **(vea ilustración)**.

3 Remueva los pernos de las tapas principales y levante hacia afuera la tapa o la asamblea de las tapas. Coloque las tapas hacia afuera en el orden apropiado para asegurarse de que la instalación sea correcta.

4 Si todavía están en su posición, remueva el cojinete viejo desde el bloque y las tapas de los cojinetes principales. Limpie las superficies de los cojinetes principal del bloque y las tapas con un trapo limpio, paño

libre de hilachas. Ellos deben de mantenerse completamente limpios!

5 Limpie las partes traseras de los cojinetes principales nuevos y coloque las mitades de los cojinetes principales con el orificio para el aceite en el bloque. Coloque la otra mitad del cojinete en cada cojinete colocado en la tapa principal correspondiente. Asegúrese que la patilla en cada cojinete o bloque entre correctamente en la ranura del bloque o la tapa. También, los orificios de lubricación en el bloque deben alinearse con los orificios de lubricación en el cojinete **(vea ilustración)**. **Caución:** *No martille los cojinetes en su posición y no melle o acanale las caras de los cojinetes. Ninguna lubricación debería usarse en este momento.*

6 Si usted está trabajando en un motor V6, el cojinete de torsión debe instalarse en la tapa trasera y el asiento. En los motores de cuatro cilindros, los cojinetes de torsión (las arandelas) deben instalarse en la tapa número tres (central).

7 Limpie las caras para los cojinetes en el bloque y los muñones para el cojinete en el cigüeñal con un trapo limpio, paño libre de hilachas. Chequee o limpie los orificios de lubricación en el cigüeñal, cualquier suciedad aquí solamente puede ir ha un solo lugar - directamente al los cojinetes nuevos.

8 Una vez que usted esté seguro de que el cigüeñal está limpio, cuidadosamente colóquelo en su posición encima de los cojinetes principales.

9 Antes de que el cigüeñal pueda permanentemente instalarse, el espacio libre para la lubricación del cojinete principal **debe** chequearse.

10 Corte varios pedazos del tamaño apropiado de Plastigage (hilachas de plástico) (deben de ser ligeramente un poco más corto que la anchura de los cojinetes principales) y coloque un pedazo en cada muñón del cojinete del cigüeñal, paralelamente con el axis del muñón **(vea ilustración)**.

11 Limpie las caras de los cojinetes con las tapas e instale las tapas en sus posiciones respectivas (no las mezcle) con los ejes impulsores que indiquen hacia el frente del

22.10 Ponga los pedazos de Plastigage (hilachas para chequear la luz para el aceite en el cigüeñal) en los muñones para los cojinetes principales, paralelamente con la línea central del cigüeñal

motor. Si usted está trabajando en un motor V6, cuidadosamente coloque la tapa del cojinete principal en su lugar. No perturbe el Plastigage. Aplique una capa delgada de aceite a las roscas del perno y la parte debajo de las cabezas de los pernos, entonces los instala.

12 Siguiendo la secuencia recomendada **(vea ilustraciones)**, apretando las tapas de los cojinetes principales, en tres pasos, a la

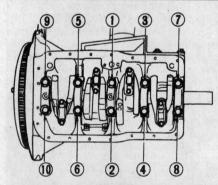

22.12a Secuencia de como APRETAR los pernos de la tapa de los cojinete - motores de cuatro cilindros

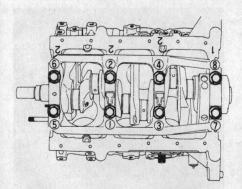

22.12b Secuencia de como APRETAR los pernos de la tapa de los cojinete - motores V6

22.14 Compare la anchura del Plastigage aplastado contra la escala suministrada para determinar la luz para el aceite (siempre tome la medida en el punto más ancho del Plastigage); esté seguro de usar la escala correcta - estándar y métricas son incluidas

Bloque del cilindro — Tapa para el cojinete del cilindro principal

20 - 25 (0.79 - 0.98)

25 - 30 (0.98 - 1.18)

Puntos donde se debe de aplicar sellador
Unidad: mm (pulgada)

22.19 Aplique una cantidad pequeña de sellador RTV (vulcanizador accionado a temperatura ambiente) a cada lado de la tapa trasera del cojinete principal y el bloque como está mostrado aquí (motores de cuatro cilindros solamente)

22.24 En los motores de cuatro cilindros, instale los sellos laterales en las ranuras de la tapa trasera del cojinete principal, después de cubrirlos con una capa pequeña de sellador RTV (vulcanizador accionado a temperatura ambiente)

torsión especificada. No gire el cigüeñal del todo durante esta operación!

13 Remueva los pernos cuidadosamente, levante hacia afuera las tapas de los cojinetes principales o las asambleas de las tapas. Manténgalas en orden. No perturbe el Plastigage o gire el cigüeñal. Si cualquiera de las tapas de los cojinetes principales son difíciles de remover, golpéelas suavemente desde el lado con un martillo de cara suave para aflojarlas.

14 Compare la anchura del Plastigage aplastado en cada muñón con la escala imprimida en el Plastigage para obtener el espacio de lubricación del cojinete principal **(vea ilustración)**. Chequee las especificaciones para asegurar que esté correcto.

15 Si el espacio no es como se especifica, los cojinetes pueden ser del tamaño equivocado (que significa que cojinetes diferentes se necesitarán - vea la Sección 19). Antes de decidir que cojinetes diferentes se necesitarán, asegúrese que ninguna suciedad o aceite esté entre los cojinetes y las tapas o el bloque cuando el espacio se esté midiendo. Si el Plastigage no notablemente más ancho en un extremo que en el otro, el muñón puede estar en forma de campana (Sección 10).

16 Cuidadosamente raspe todos los rasgos del material del Plastigage fuera de los muñones de los cojinetes principales y/o las caras de los cojinetes. No melle o rasguñe las caras de los cojinetes.

17 Cuidadosamente levante el cigüeñal fuera del motor. Limpie las caras de los cojinetes en el bloque, entonces aplique una capa uniforme delgada limpia de grasa de base moly o lubricante para ensamblar motor en cada una de las superficies de los cojinetes. Apliquele lubricante a las arandelas de torsión también.

18 Lubrique la superficie del cigüeñal que hace contacto con el sello de retener el aceite con grasa de base moly o lubricante para el ensamblaje del motor o aceite de motor limpio.

19 Asegúrese que los muñones del cigüeñal están limpios, entonces coloque el cigüeñal en su posición en el bloque. Limpie las caras de los cojinetes en las tapas, entonces apliquele lubricante. Instale las tapas en sus

posiciones respectivas con las flechas indicando hacia el frente del motor. **Nota:** *En los motores de cuatro cilindros la tapa trasera debe de tener sellador RTV (vulcanizador accionado a temperatura ambiente)* **(vea ilustración)**. Instale los pernos

20 Apriete nuevamente todos los pernos de las tapas principales a la torsión especificada, siguiendo la secuencia recomendada.

21 En modelos equipados con transmisiones manuales, instale un cojinete piloto nuevo en el extremo del cigüeñal (vea Capítulo 8).

22 Gire el cigüeñal varios números de veces con la mano para chequear si se está atorando.

23 Chequee el juego final del cigüeñal con un calibrador al tacto o un indicador de tipo reloj como se describió en la Sección 13. El juego final debería ser corregido si las caras de torsión de empuje del cigüeñal no están desgastadas o dañadas y las arandelas de torsión nuevas se han instalado.

24 Instale un sello principal trasero nuevo para retener el aceite en la tapa trasera después de cubrirlo con sellador RTV (vulcanizador accionado a temperatura ambiente) **(vea ilustración)**. No aplique mucho sellador.

23 Sello trasero principal para el aceite - instalación

Motores de cuatro cilindros

1 Limpie el cilindro en el bloque y la tapa trasera del cojinete principal en el bloque y la superficie de contacto del sello en el cigüeñal. Chequee las superficies del cigüeñal por rayones y mellas que podrían dañar el labio del sello nuevo y fugas de aceite podrían ocurrir. Si el cigüeñal está dañado, la única alternativa es un cigüeñal nuevo o diferente.

2 Aplique un capa delgada de aceite de motor o grasa de propósito múltiple a la orilla del sello exterior nuevo. Lubrique el labio del

sello con grasa de base moly.

3 Péguele cuidadosamente al sello nuevo en su posición con una herramienta Nissan número KV10105500 o J-25640-01 (si está disponible). El lado abierto (resorte) del sello debe mirar hacia el frente del motor. Si la herramienta especial no está disponible, trabaje cuidadosamente el labio del sello en el extremo del cigüeñal y péguele al sello con un martillo y un punzón para instalarlo hasta que esté sentado en el diámetro de los cilindros.

Motor V6

Refiérase a las ilustraciones 23.6, 23.8, 23.9a y 23.9b

4 El cigüeñal debe ser instalado primero y la tapa del cojinete principal atornillado en su ubicación, entonces el sello nuevo debe ser instalado en el retenedor y el retenedor atornillado al bloque.

5 Chequee la superficie de contacto del sello en el cigüeñal muy cuidadosamente por rayones y las mellas que podrían dañar el labio del sello nuevo y causar fugas de aceite. Si el cigüeñal está dañado, la única alternativa es un cigüeñal nuevo o diferente.

23.6 Después de remover el retenedor del bloque, sosténgalo entre dos bloques de madera y expulse el sello viejo con un punzón y un martillo

6   El sello viejo puede ser removido del retenedor accionándolo hacia afuera a través de la parte trasera con un martillo y un punzón **(vea ilustración)**. Esté seguro de notar que tan adentro está en el orificio de receso antes de removerlo; el sello nuevo tendrá que ser puesto en su receso una cantidad igual. Tenga mucho cuidado de no rasguñar ni de otro modo dañar el cilindro en el retenedor o fugas de aceite podrían desarrollarse.

7   Asegúrese que el retenedor esté limpio, entonces aplica una capa delgada de aceite de motor al exterior de la orilla del sello nuevo. El sello se debe prensar directamente dentro del orificio, así que martillarlo en su posición no es recomendado. Si usted no tiene acceso a una prensa, haga un emparedado del albergue y el sello entre dos pedazos lisos de madera y apriete el sello en su posición con las mandíbulas de una prensa grande. Los pedazos de madera deben ser lo suficiente grueso para distribuir la fuerza uniformemente alrededor de la circunferencia entera del sello. Trabaje lentamente y asegúrese que el sello entra en el diámetro del cilindro directamente.

23.9b . . . y cubra la superficie de la junta de acoplamiento del bloque del motor con sellador antes de instalar el sello/ensamblaje de retención

23.8 Accione el sello nuevo hacia adentro del retenedor con un bloque de madera o una sección de tubo, si usted tiene una sección de tubo lo suficiente grande - asegúrese que usted no atora el sello en el calibre del retenedor

8   En último caso, el sello puede ser instalado en el retenedor con un martillo. Use un bloque de madera para distribuir la fuerza uniformemente y asegúrese que el sello es empujado directamente **(vea ilustración)**.

9   Los labio del sello se deben lubricar con aceite de motor limpio o grasa de base moly antes de que el sello/retenedor sea resbalado en el cigüeñal y atornillado al bloque **(vea ilustración)**. Use una junta nueva, sellador y asegúrese que las clavijas fijas están en su posición antes de instalar el retenedor **(vea ilustración)**.

10   Apriete los pernos un poco a la vez hasta que todos ellos estén al par de torsión especificado.

24   Ensamblaje del pistón/biela - instalación y chequeo del juego libre para el aceite del cojinete de la biela

Refiérase a las ilustraciones 24.3, 24.5a, 25.5b, 24.6, 24.8a, 24.8b, 24.9, 24.11 y 24.13

1   Antes de instalar los ensamblajes de los pistones/bielas, las paredes de los cilindros deben ser limpiadas perfectamente, la orilla superior de cada cilindro debe estar biselada y el cigüeñal debe estar en posición.

2   Remueva la tapa para el cojinete de la biela número uno. Remueva los cojinetes viejos y limpie las superficies para los cojinetes de las bielas y la tapa con un trapo limpio libre de pelusa. Ellos deben ser mantenidos inmaculadamente limpios.

3   Limpie el lado de la mitad trasera superior del cojinete nuevo, entonces colóquelo adentro de su lugar en la biela. Asegúrese que la lengüeta en el cojinete se acopla adentro de la depresión de la biela **(vea ilustración)**. No martille el cojinete en su posición y tenga mucho cuidado de no mellar la cara del cojinete. No lubrique el cojinete en este tiempo.

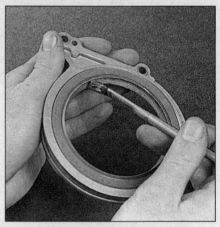

23.9a Aplique grasa de base moly o aceite limpio de motor a los labios del sello . . .

4   Limpie el lado de la parte trasera del cojinete e instálelo en la tapa de la biela. Otra vez, asegúrese de que la lengüeta en el cojinete se acopla adentro de la depresión de la tapa y no aplique lubricante. Es críticamente importante que las superficies de acoplamiento del cojinete y la biela estén perfectamente limpias y libre de aceite cuando ellas sean armadas.

5   Posicione los espacios libres para el anillo en el pistón en posiciones de diferentes intervalos alrededor del pistón **(vea ilustraciones)**, entonces resbale una Sección de manguera de plástico o caucho en cada perno de la tapa para el cojinete de la biela.

6   Lubrique con aceite de motor limpio el pistón, los anillos y conecte un compresor de anillos de pistón al pistón. Permita que la falda se quede afuera para guiar el pistón en el cilindro. Los anillos deben ser comprimido hasta que ellos estén a nivel con el pistón **(vea ilustración)**.

7   Gire el cigüeñal hasta que el muñón de la biela número uno esté en el BDC (punto muerto inferior) y aplique una capa de aceite de motor a las paredes de los cilindros.

8   Con la marca F. en el lado del pistón

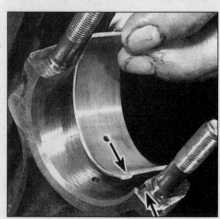

24.3 La lengüeta en cada cojinete debe insertarse en el receso de la biela o la tapa y los orificios del aceite deben de alinearse (flechas)

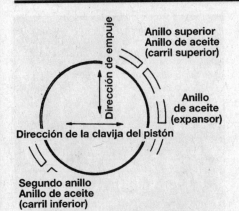

Dirección de empuje

**Anillo superior
Anillo de aceite
(carril superior)**

**Anillo de aceite
(expansor)**

Dirección de la clavija del pistón

**Segundo anillo
Anillo de aceite
(carril inferior)**

**24.5a Ponga las brechas de los extremos
de los anillos del pistón en forma de
escalones como está mostrado aquí antes
de instalar los pistones/ensamblajes de
las bielas en el motor**

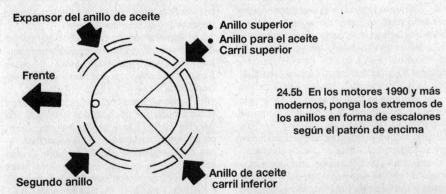

Expansor del anillo de aceite

Frente

Anillo superior
**Anillo para el aceite
Carril superior**

Segundo anillo

**Anillo de aceite
carril inferior**

**24.5b En los motores 1990 y más
modernos, ponga los extremos de
los anillos en forma de escalones
según el patrón de encima**

(motores de cuatro cilindros) o el hoyuelo encima del pistón (motores V6) **(vea ilustraciones)** mirando hacia el frente del motor, meta suavemente el ensamblaje del pistón/biela en el cilindro número uno y descanse la orilla del fondo del compresor de anillos en el bloque del motor. Utilice la primera orilla del compresor de anillos para asegurarse que está en contacto en la circunferencia completa alrededor del bloque.

9   Cuidadosamente péguele en la parte de encima del pistón con el mango de madera de un martillo **(vea ilustración)** mientras que guía el extremo final de la biela en su posición en el muñón del cigüeñal. Los anillos del pistón pueden tratar de salirse hacia afuera del compresor de anillos apenas antes de entrar en el cilindro, así que mantenga alguna presión hacia abajo en el compresor del anillos. Trabaje lentamente y si alguna resistencia es detectada según el pistón entra en el cilindro, pare inmediatamente. Averigüe qué se está atorando y repárelo antes de proceder. ¡Por ninguna razón, fuerce el pistón en el cilindro, porque usted quizás pueda romper un anillo y/o el pistón!

**24.6 Deslice seccione de pedazos de
manguera de caucho en los pernos de las
bielas, entonces comprima los anillos con
un compresor de anillo - deje la parte
inferior del pistón sobresaliéndose para
que se resbale en el cilindro**

10   Una vez que el ensamblaje del pistón/biela esté instalado, el juego de acoplación libre para el aceite del cojinete de la biela debe ser chequeado antes de que la tapa de la biela sea permanentemente puesta en su posición.

11   Corte un pedazo de Plastigage (hilo de calibración de plástico) del tamaño apropiado levemente más corto que la anchura del cojinete de la biela y colóquelo adentro del muñón de la biela número uno, paralelo

**24.8a La marca F en el lado de cada
pistón (motores de cuatro cilindros) . . .**

con el axis del muñón **(vea ilustración)**.

12   Limpie la cara de la tapa del cojinete para el cojinete de la biela, remueva las mangueras protectoras de los pernos de la biela e instale la tapa de la biela. Asegúrese que las marcas de acoplamiento en la tapa están en el mismo lado que la marcada en la biela. Instale las tuercas y apriételas al par de torsión especificado. **Nota:** *Use un dado de pared delgada para evitar lecturas técnicas erróneas que puedan resultar si el dado es acuñado entre la tapa de la biela y la tuerca. ¡No gire el cigüeñal durante esta operación!*

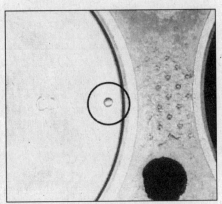

**24.8b . . . o hendidura en la cima de cada
pistón (motor V6) debe mirar hacia el
frente del motor según los pistones
son instalados**

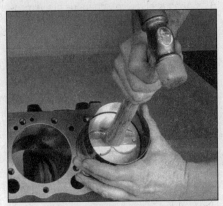

**24.9 Cada pistón puede ser suavemente
empujado en el cilindro con el extremo del
mango de madera de un martillo**

**24.11 Ponga los pedazos de Plastigage
(hilo de calibración de plástico) en el
muñón para la biela de cada cojinete,
paralelamente en línea central con el
cigüeñal**

13   Remueva la tapa de la biela, con mucho cuidado para no perturbar el calibrador de plástico. Compare la anchura del calibrador de plástico aplastado a la escala impresa en el recipiente del calibrador de plástico para obtener el juego libre para el aceite **(vea ilustración)**. Compárelo a las especificaciones para asegurarse que el espacio libre está correcto. Si el juego libre no está como se especifica, los cojinetes pueden ser del tamaño incorrecto (que significa que diferentes se requerirán). Antes de decidir si diferentes cojinetes son necesarios, asegúrese que ninguna tierra ni aceite estaban entre los cojinetes y la biela o la tapa cuando el espacio libre era medido. También chequee el diámetro del muñón. Si el calibrador de plástico está más ancho en una punta que en la otra, el muñón puede estar cónico (refiérase a la Sección 18).

14   Raspe cuidadosamente todos los indicios de material del calibrador de plástico del muñón, cara de la biela y/o cojinete. Tenga mucho cuidado de no rasguñar el cojinete con la uña o una tarjeta de crédito. Asegúrese que las caras de los cojinetes están perfectamente limpias, entonces aplique una capa uniforme de grasa de base moly o lubricante para ensamblar motor a ambos de ellos. Usted tendrá que empujar el pistón en el cilindro para exponer la cara del cojinete en la biela - esté seguro de resbalar las mangueras protectoras en los pernos de la biela primero.

15   Deslice la biela otra vez dentro de su lugar en el muñón, remueva las mangueras protectoras de los pernos de la tapa de la biela, instale la tapa de la biela y apriete las tuercas al par de torsión especificado.

16   Repita el procedimiento completo para el resto de los pistones/ensamblajes de las bielas. Mantenga los lados de la parte trasera de los cojinetes y el interior de la biela perfectamente limpios cuando usted los esté armando. Asegúrese que usted tiene el pistón correcto para el cilindro y que la marca en el pistón miran hacia el frente del motor cuando el pistón esté instalado. Recuerde, uso abundancia de aceite para lubricar el pistón antes de instalar el compresor de anillos. También, cuando esté instalando las tapas de las bielas

por vez final, esté seguro de lubricar las caras de los cojinetes adecuadamente.

17   Después que los pistones/ensamblajes de las bielas hayan sido apropiadamente instalados, gire el cigüeñal un número de veces a mano para chequear por cualquier obstrucción obvia.

18   Como un paso final, el juego del final de la biela debe ser chequeado. Refiérase a la Sección 12 para este procedimiento. Compare el juego final medido a las especificaciones para asegurarse que es correcto. Si está correcto antes de remover el cigüeñal y las bielas original fueron reinstaladas, todavía deben de estar bien. Si bielas nuevas o un cigüeñal nuevo fueron instalados, el juego final puede ser demasiado pequeño. Si ése es el caso, las bielas tendrán que ser removidas y tendrán que ser llevadas a un taller automovilístico de rectificación para reedificar el tamaño nuevamente.

25   Comienzo y desgaste inicial - después de la rectificación completa general

1   Una vez que el motor se haya instalado en el vehículo, chequee nuevamente el aceite del motor y el nivel del anticongelante.

2   Con las bujías fuera del motor y el sistema de ignición incapacitado (Sección 3), gire el motor hasta que la presión de aceite se registre en el medidor.

3   Instale las bujías, instale los alambres de las bujías y restaure el sistema de marcha de la ignición (Sección 2).

4   Ponga el motor en marcha. Pueda que tome unos minutos para que la gasolina llegue al carburador o los inyectores, pero el motor debería poner en marcha sin mucho esfuerzo.

5   Después de que comience el motor, se debe permitir calentar a la temperatura normal de operación. Mientras el motor se calienta a la temperatura normal de operación. Haga un chequeo completo por fugas de aceite y anticongelante.

6   Apague el motor y chequee nuevamente el aceite del motor y el nivel del anticonge-

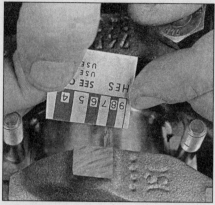

24.13 Mida la anchura del Plastigage (hilo de calibración de plástico) para determinar el juego de conectando libre para el aceite del cojinete de la biela (esté seguro de usar la escala correcta - escalas de pulgada y métricas están incluidas)

lante.

7   Conduzca el vehículo a una zona con tránsito mínimo, abra el acelerador completamente desde 30 hasta que llegue a 50 mph, entonces permita que el vehículo baje su velocidad hasta 30 mph con el acelerador completamente cerrado. Repita el procedimiento 10 o 12 veces. Esto carga los anillos del pistón y los causa que se asienten adecuadamente contra las paredes de los cilindros. Chequee nuevamente por fugas de aceite y anticongelante.

8   Conduzca el vehículo suavemente por las primeras 500 millas (no mantenga altas velocidades) y mantenga un chequeo constante en el nivel del aceite. Es común que un motor use aceite durante el periodo de desgaste inicial.

9   Aproximadamente entre 500 y 600 millas, cambie el aceite y el filtro.

10   Por las próximas cientos de millas, conduzca el vehículo normalmente. No lo trate como un niño pequeño pero tampoco lo abuse.

11   Después de 2000 millas, cambie el aceite y el filtro nuevamente y considere que el motor tuvo su desgaste inicial.

Capítulo 3   Sistemas de calefacción, enfriamiento y aire acondicionado

Contenidos

Especificaciones

General

Capacidad del anticongelante................................	Vea Capítulo 1
Calificación para la presión de la tapa del radiador	Vea Capítulo 1
Temperatura de la abertura del termostato	
Motores de cuatro cilindros	170 grados F
Motores V6	155 grados F
1990 y más moderno (todos los motores)	170 grados F

Aceite para el refrigerante

Tipo..	SUNISO 5GS o equivalente
Capacidad	
1980 al 1982...	5.3 onzas/150 milímetros
1983	
Compresor York..	6.3 onzas/180 milímetros
Compresor Hitachi....................................	5.3 onzas/150 milímetros
1984	8.8 onzas/250 milímetro
1985 en adelante......................................	7.0 onzas/200 milímetros

Especificaciones técnicas

Pernos de la bomba de agua	**Pies-libras** (a menos que sea indicado de otra manera)
Motores de cuatro cilindros	
Pernos de 6 mm..	35 a 86 pulgada-libras
Pernos de 8 mm..	7 a 12
Motor V6...	12 a 15
Pernos del albergue del termostato	12 a 15
Pernos de la admisión del agua (motores V6)............................	12 a 15
Pernos de la salida del agua..	12 a 15
Pernos de retención del radiador	26 a 35 pulgada-libras
Pernos del ventilador a la bomba de agua.................................	52 a 87 pulgada-libras
Pernos del ventilador al embrague..	52 a 87 pulgada-libras
Pernos para el soporte del compresor del aire acondicionado	
1980 al 1984..	33 a 40
1985 en adelante	
Motores de cuatro cilindros...	51 a 58
Motores V6..	27 a 37
Pernos del compresor del aire acondicionado a los pernos del soporte	
1980 al 1984..	33 a 40
1985 en adelante..	27 a 37

1   Sistema de enfriamiento - información general

Refiérase a la ilustración 1.2

Los componentes del sistema de enfriamiento son el radiador, manguera superior e inferior del radiador, la bomba de agua, el termostato, la tapa del radiador con la válvula para la liberación de la presión y las mangueras de la calefacción.

El principio del sistema es que el anticongelante en el fondo del radiador circula hacia encima a través de la manguera inferior del radiador a la bomba de agua, donde la de bomba empuja el anticongelante alrededor del bloque y las cabezas a través de varios pasajes para enfriar los cilindros, superficies de la combustión y asientos de las válvulas **(vea ilustración)**. Cuando suficiente calor ha sido absorbido por el anticongelante y el motor ha alcanzado la temperatura de operación normal, el anticongelante se mueve de la cabeza de los cilindros pasando a través del termostato que está ahora abierto, por la manguera al radiador y a la parte superior del radiador. El anticongelante entonces viaja hacia abajo de los tubos del radiador donde es rápidamente refrescado por el flujo natural de aire según el vehículo se mueve a través del camino. Un ventilador de hojas múltiples, instalado en la polea de la bomba de agua, ayuda a la acción de enfriar. El anticongelante ahora llega al fondo del radiador y el ciclo es repetido.

Cuando el motor está frío el termostato permanece cerrado hasta que el anticongelante llegue a una temperatura predeterminada (vea especificaciones). Esto ayuda a que se caliente rápido.

El sistema es presurizado por una tapa con presión de resorte en el abastecedor del radiador, que previene que hierva prematuramente y aumenta el punto de ebullición del anticongelante. Si la temperatura del anticongelante sube encima de este punto de ebullición, la presión extra en el sistema fuerza el resorte interno en la tapa del radiador fuera

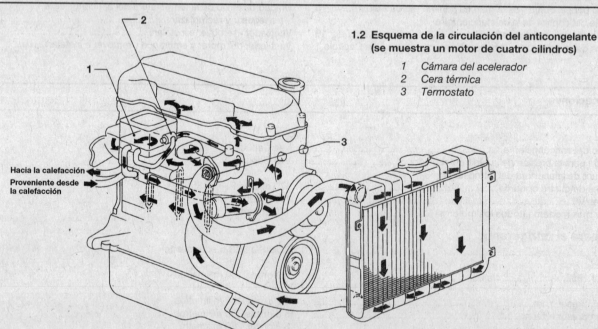

1.2 Esquema de la circulación del anticongelante (se muestra un motor de cuatro cilindros)

1   *Cámara del acelerador*
2   *Cera térmica*
3   *Termostato*

Hacia la calefacción
Proveniente desde la calefacción

3.5a Instalación de la posición correcta del termostato (modelos 1980 solamente)

3.5b Instalación de la posición correcta del termostato (modelos 1981 y más modernos de cuatro cilindros)

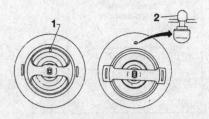

3.9 El termostato debe ser instalado con la válvula de purga de aire o válvula de meneo puesta en posición hacia encima (modelos 1981 y más modernos de cuatro cilindros)

1   Purga de aire
2   Válvula de meneo

de su asiento y se expone a la manguera de la capacidad excesiva, para que se fugue el anticongelante hacia el depósito de recuperación del anticongelante.

El sistema para la recuperación del anticongelante se compone de un depósito plástico en que la capacidad excesiva del anticongelante fluye desde el radiador cuando el motor está caliente. Cuando el motor se refresca, el anticongelante es absorbido otra vez adentro del radiador desde el depósito y mantiene el sistema de la capacidad repleta.2

Aparte de enfriar el motor durante su operación, el sistema de enfriamiento proporciona también el calor para la calefacción interior del vehículo y calienta el múltiple de admisión. En los vehículos equipados con una transmisión automática, el flúido de la transmisión es refrescado por un enfriador conectado a la base del radiador.

En los vehículos equipados con un sistema de aire acondicionado, un condensador es colocado adelante del radiador.

El ventilador para enfriar el radiador se incorpora con un acoplamiento de flúido o un acoplamiento controlado por temperatura. El dispositivo posterior consiste de un embrague operado con aceite y un termostato bimetálico enrollado que funciona para permitir que el ventilador se resbale cuando el motor esté bajo de la temperatura de operación normal y no requiere el flujo suplementario de aire proporcionado por el ventilador a la velocidad de marcha normal. A temperaturas más altas de operación del motor, el ventilador es acoplado y gira a la velocidad de la polea de la bomba de agua. El acoplamiento del ventilador es una unidad sellada y no requiere mantenimiento periódico.

Peligro: *La tapa del radiador no debe ser removida mientras el motor está caliente. La manera apropiada para remover la tapa es de envolver una tela gruesa alrededor de ella, gire la tapa lentamente a la izquierda hasta la detención y permita que una cantidad de presión residual se escape. No apriete la tapa hacia abajo hasta que todo el silbido haya parado, entonces empuje hacia abajo y gírela hacia afuera.*

2   Anticongelante - información general

1   Es recomendado que el sistema de enfriamiento sea llenado con una mezcla de agua/entilenoglicol basada en anticongelante que dará la protección baja a por lo menos 20 grados F. Esto proporciona protección contra la corrosión y aumenta el punto de ebullición del anticongelante. Cuando esté manejando el anticongelante, tenga cuidado que no sea rociado en la pintura del vehículo, porque le causará daño si no se remueve inmediatamente.

2   El sistema de enfriamiento se debe drenar, debe ser limpiado y debe ser rellenado por lo menos cada otra Primavera. El uso de soluciones de anticongelante por períodos más largos que dos años es probable que cause daño y ayude a la formación de la oxidación y escala debido a que los anticorrosivos gradualmente pierden su eficiencia.

3   La mezcla exacta del anticongelante con agua que usted debe usar depende en las condiciones relativas del tiempo. La mezcla debe contener por lo menos un 50 por ciento de anticongelante, pero bajo ninguna circunstancia debe la mezcla contener más del 70 por ciento de anticongelante.

3   Termostato - remover e instalar

1   El termostato es una válvula de restricción que es accionado por un elemento sensible al calor. Es instalado adentro de un albergue en el lado izquierdo del motor (modelos 1980), al frente del múltiple de admisión en los modelos 1981 y más modernos de cuatro cilindros y en los modelos V6 está en el lado delantero del motor en el lado derecho y está diseñado para abrir y cerrar a temperaturas predeterminadas para permitir que el anticongelante se caliente o se enfríe.

2   Para remover el termostato, comience drenando el sistema de enfriamiento (refiérase al Capítulo 1).

Modelos de cuatro cilindros

Refiérase a las ilustraciones 3.5a, 3.5b y 3.9

3   Remueva el purificador de aire y manguera superior del radiador.

4   Remueva los pernos que retiene la tapa del termostato.

5   Levante la tapa junto con la junta y el termostato. Note como el termostato está puesto en posición en el receso, porque debe ser reemplazado en la misma posición **(vea ilustraciones).**

6   Antes de la instalación, use un raspador de junta o cuchillo para masilla para remover cuidadosamente el rastro de la junta vieja en el albergue del termostato y la tapa.

7   Coloque una cantidad delgada de sellador de tipo silicona alrededor de la superficie del sello en la tapa del termostato.

8   Coloque una junta nueva en posición en el albergue (modelos 1980) o en la tapa (modelos 1981 y más modernos).

9   Coloque el termostato en posición en el albergue. En los modelos 1981 y más modernos, asegúrese que la válvula para la purga del aire está mirando hacia encima **(vea ilustración).** Entonces coloque la tapa encima del termostato y el albergue e instale los pernos. Apriételos al par de torsión especificado. En algunos modelos 1981 y más modernos, recuerde que el cable de conexión a tierra de la batería debe ser conectado al perno inferior de la tapa del termostato.

10   Vuelva a instalar la manguera superior del radiador.

11   Rellene el radiador con la mezcla apropiada de anticongelante y agua. Refiérase al Capítulo 1 si es necesario.

12   Con la tapa del radiador removida, ponga el motor en marcha y córralo hasta que la manguera superior del radiador llegue a estar caliente. En este punto, el termostato estará en la posición abierta. Chequee el nivel del anticongelante y agregue anticongelante según sea necesario.

13   Vuelva a instalar la tapa del radiador.

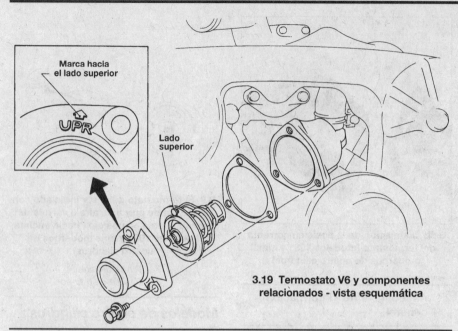

3.19 Termostato V6 y componentes relacionados - vista esquemática

inverso al procedimiento de desensamble, instale abrazaderas nuevas de mangueras si es necesario.

28 Rellene el sistema de enfriamiento, ponga el motor en marcha, chequee por fugas y una operación apropiada del termostato.

4   Radiador - remover e instalar

Refiérase a la ilustración 4.7

1   Con el motor frío, remueva la batería. Siempre desconecte el cable negativo primero, seguido por el cable positivo.

2   Remueva la cacerola inferior.

3   Abra la válvula del drenaje en la parte inferior del radiador y drene el anticongelante del radiador en un recipiente (vea Capítulo 1).

4   Remueva ambas mangueras del radiador superior e inferior.

5   Desconecte la manguera del depósito del cuello de reabastecimiento del radiador.

6   Remueva los tornillos que conectan la cubierta para el ventilador del radiador y deslícela hacia el motor.

7   Si está equipado con una transmisión automática, desconecte las mangueras de enfriamiento del radiador **(vea ilustración)**. Coloque una cacerola de goteo para colectar el flúido.

8   Remueva los pernos que conectan el radiador a la carrocería.

9   Levante hacia fuera el radiador.

10 Con el radiador removido, puede ser inspeccionado por fugas o daños. Si reparaciones son necesarias, haga que un taller profesional de radiadores o el concesionario realice el trabajo debido a que técnicas especiales son requeridas.

Modelos V6

Refiérase a las ilustraciones 3.19 y 3.25

14 Remueva el ventilador y la tapa.

15 Remueva las bandas, refiérase al Capítulo 1.

16 Alce el vehículo y sopórtelo firmemente sobre estantes.

17 Remueva la manguera inferior del radiador del tubo de succión de metal del agua, aflojando las abrazaderas de la manguera y los pernos del soporte de apoyo.

18 Afloje lo que queda de la abrazadera de la manguera y remueva el tubo de succión de agua del vehículo.

19 Remueva los tres pernos reteniendo el albergue del termostato **(vea ilustración)**.

20 Remueva el albergue del motor. Si es necesario, use un martillo de cara suave para romper el sello de la junta del albergue.

21 Remueva el termostato de la cavidad, cuidadosamente notando que lado mira hacia encima.

22 Raspe hacia afuera todos los residuos de junta y sellador de la superficie para la junta.

23 Insercióne el termostato nuevo en el albergue con el lado del resorte en el bloque. El termostato debe sentarse en la cavidad. El purgador para el aire debe estar mirando hacia encima **(vea ilustración 3.9)**.

24 Aplique junta de sellador a ambos lados de la junta nueva e instale la junta en el albergue del termostato.

25 Instale el albergue del termostato en el bloque, asegúrese que la flecha en la tapa está apuntando hacia encima **(vea ilustración)**.

26 Apriete los pernos del albergue al par de torsión apropiado.

27 La instalación se hace en el orden

3.25 Note la flecha en el albergue del termostato - debe señalar hacia encima durante la instalación (motor V6)

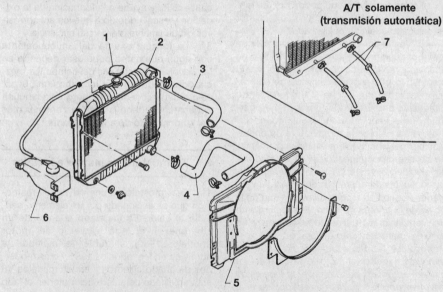

4.7 Vista esquemática de las conexiones para el enfriador de la transmisión y componentes del radiador (modelos 1980 al 1985)

1	Tapa del radiador	4	Manguera inferior del radiador
2	Radiador	5	Cubierta para el ventilador del radiador
3	Manguera superior del radiador	6	Depósito

11   Los bichos y la tierra se pueden limpiar del radiador con aire comprimido y una brocha suave. No doble las aletas de enfriamiento mientras se está haciendo esto.
12   La instalación se hace en el orden inverso al procedimiento de desensamble.
13   Después de la instalación, llene el sistema de enfriamiento con la mezcla apropiada de anticongelante y agua. Refiérase al Capítulo 1 si es necesario.
14   Ponga el motor en marcha y chequee por fugas. Permita que el motor alcance la temperatura normal de operación, indicado por la manguera caliente superior del radiador. Chequee el nivel del anticongelante y agregue más si es requerido.
15   En los modelos equipados con transmisión automática, chequee y agregue flúido según sea necesario.

5   Ventilador del motor y embrague - remover e instalar

Refiérase a las ilustraciones 5.1a, 5.1b y 5.4
1   En los modelos de cuatro cilindros, el embrague del ventilador es íntegro con la bomba de agua (vea ilustración). Para reemplazar el embrague del ventilador, vea Sección 8. En los motores V6, el embrague es separado (vea ilustración).
2   Remueva el radiador como dice en la Sección 4.
3   Remueva la tapa del radiador.
4   Remueva los pernos que retienen el ventilador al embrague y levante el ventilador (vea ilustración).
5   En los motores V6, el embrague del ventilador ahora se puede destornillar de la bomba de agua.

6   Depósito del anticongelante - remover e instalar

Refiérase a la ilustración 6.2
1   Desconecte la manguera del depósito en el cuello del radiador.

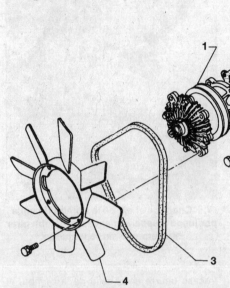
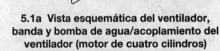

5.1a Vista esquemática del ventilador, banda y bomba de agua/acoplamiento del ventilador (motor de cuatro cilindros)
1   Bomba de agua con acoplador
2   Junta de la bomba
3   Banda
4   Ventilador

2   Destornille y levante el depósito hacia encima, entonces remueva el conector del alambrado (vea ilustración).
3   Remueva del compartimiento del motor el depósito.
4   Drene el anticongelante en un recipiente. Si el depósito va a ser reemplazado, desconecte la manguera de encima.
5   La instalación se hace en el orden inverso al procedimiento de desensamble.
6   Rellene el depósito con la mezcla apropiada de anticongelante y agua. Refiérase al Capítulo 1 si es necesario.

7   Bomba de agua - chequear

Refiérase a las ilustraciones 7.4 y 7.5
1   Un fracaso en la bomba de agua puede causar daño grave al motor debido al sobrecalentamiento.
2   Hay tres maneras de chequear la operación de la bomba de agua mientras está instalada en el motor. Si la bomba está sospe-

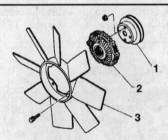

5.1b Vista esquemática de los componentes del ventilador para el motor V6
1   Polea del ventilador
2   Acoplador del ventilador
3   Ventilador

chosa, debe ser reemplazada con una nueva o con una unidad reconstruida.
3   Con el motor en marcha y calentado a la temperatura normal de operación, apriete la manguera superior del radiador. Si la bomba de agua está trabajando apropiadamente,

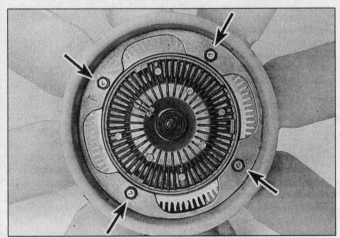

5.4 Si el acoplamiento del ventilador debe ser reemplazado, remueva los cuatro pernos que conectan el ventilador y el acoplamiento (flechas)

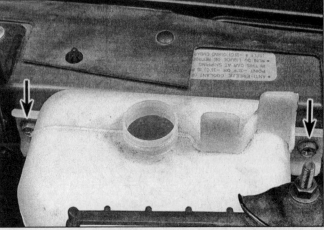

6.2 Pernos de afianzamiento para el depósito del anticongelante en los motores V6 (flechas)

7.4 Si el anticongelante está fugándose fuera del orificio, el sello de la bomba de agua está desgastado o dañado y la bomba tendrá que ser reemplazada

7.5 Chequee el eje de la bomba de agua por juego y aspereza excesiva - debe girar suavemente sin tener juego

8.10a Los pernos pequeños de la bomba de agua solamente tienen que ser aflojados lo suficiente para remover la bomba de agua (motores de cuatro cilindros)

una oleada de presión debe sentirse según la manguera es liberada.

4   Las bombas de agua están equipadas con orificios de drenaje o respiraderos. Si un

8.10b Remueva los seis pernos (flechas) reteniendo la bomba de agua al bloque del motor (motor V6)

fracaso ocurre en el sello de la bomba, el anticongelante se saldrá a través de este orificio. En la mayoría de los casos será necesario usar una linterna para encontrar el orificio en la bomba de agua mirando a través del espacio apenas debajo de la bomba por evidencia de fuga **(vea ilustración)**.

5   Si los baleros del eje de la bomba del agua fracasan puede hacer un sonido de chillido en el frente del motor mientras está en marcha. Desgaste del eje puede ser detectado si la polea de la bomba de agua es mecida hacia encima y hacia abajo **(vea ilustración)**. No confunda el resbalamiento de la banda, que también causa un sonido como chillido, con el fracaso de la bomba de agua.

8   Bomba de agua - remover e instalar

Refiérase a las ilustraciones 8.10a, 8.10b y 8.12

1   Desconecte el cable negativo de la ter-

minal negativa de la batería. Coloque el cable fuera del camino para que no pueda entrar accidentalmente en contacto con el terminal negativo de la batería, porque esto permitirá que una vez el poder entre en el sistema eléctrico del vehículo.

2   Alce el vehículo y sosténgalo firmemente encima de soportes.

3   Drene el sistema de enfriamiento (Capítulo 1).

4   Refiérase a las Secciones 4 y 5 para remover el ventilador y la cubierta para el ventilador del radiador.

5   Refiérase al Capítulo 1 y remueva las bandas.

6   Si su vehículo tiene un motor de cuatro cilindros, salte los Pasos 7, 8 y 9.

7   Remueva la polea de la bomba de agua (motor V6).

8   Refiérase al Capítulo 2B y remueva el amortiguador de vibraciones del cigüeñal.

9   Remueva la tapa superior e inferior de la banda del tiempo (refiérase al Capítulo 2B).

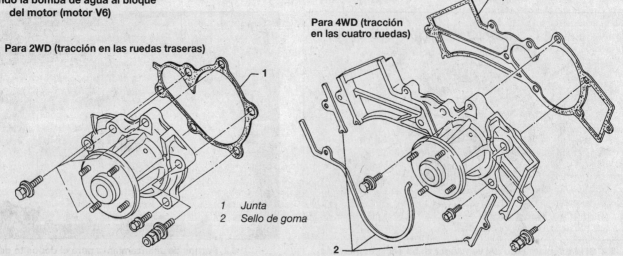

Para 2WD (tracción en las ruedas traseras)

Para 4WD (tracción en las cuatro ruedas)

1   Junta
2   Sello de goma

8.12 Bomba de agua y componentes relacionados - vista esquemática (motor V6)

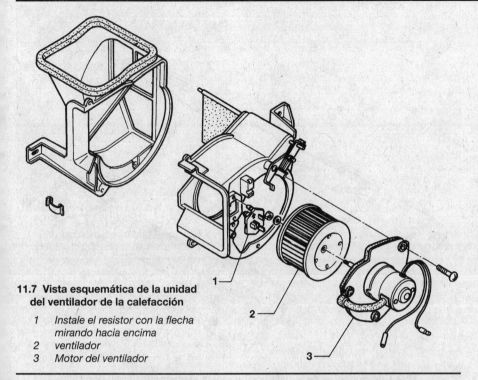

11.7 Vista esquemática de la unidad del ventilador de la calefacción

1   *Instale el resistor con la flecha mirando hacia encima*
2   *ventilador*
3   *Motor del ventilador*

10   Sistema de la calefacción - información general

Los componentes principales del sistema de calefacción incluyen la unidad de la calefacción (que contiene el núcleo de la calefacción y las válvulas operadas por cable) el motor para el ventilador, el ensamblaje del control (instalado en el tablero) y el conducto de aire que entrega el aire a varios lugares de la salida.

Aire exterior o aire interior (reciclado) (dependiendo de las instalaciones) es absorbido en el sistema para la unidad del ventilador. De allí el motor para el ventilador fuerza el aire adentro de la unidad de la calefacción.

Los ajustes de la palanca en el ensamblaje de control operan las válvulas en la unidad de la calefacción, que determina la mezcla del aire calentado y el de afuera regulando cuánto aire es pasado a través del núcleo de la calefacción. Mientras más caliente el ajuste la mayor cantidad de aire que pasa a través del núcleo.

El conducto del aire lleva el aire calentado de la unidad de la calefacción a la ubicación deseada. Otra vez, válvulas adentro del sistema de conducto regula donde el aire en el vehículo será entregado.

El núcleo de la calefacción es calentado por anticongelante del motor que pasa a través de él. La manguera de la calefacción lleva el anticongelante del motor al núcleo de la calefacción y entonces de regreso otra vez.

10   Remueva los pernos de la bomba de agua **(vea ilustraciones)**.

11   Remueva la bomba de agua del bloque del motor, raspe toda la junta y sellador de las superficies de montaje.

12   Cuando esté ejecutando la instalación, aplique sellador en ambos lados de la junta nueva e instale la bomba de agua en el bloque del motor **(vea ilustración)**. Note que los modelos de 2WD y 4WD se difieren en la junta usada para la bomba de agua.

13   Apriete todos los pernos de la bomba de agua, un poco a la vez, al par de torsión especificado.

14   El resto de la instalación se hace en el orden inverso al procedimiento de desensamble.

15   Ajuste la banda a la tensión apropiada. Refiérase al Capítulo 1 si es necesario.

16   Llene el sistema de enfriamiento con la mezcla apropiada del anticongelante y agua, otra vez refiérase al Capítulo 1 si es necesario. Entonces ponga el motor en marcha y permítalo que corra en marcha mínima hasta que llegue a la temperatura normal de operación. Esto es indicado por la manguera superior del radiador que se pone caliente. Chequee alrededor de la bomba de agua y el radiador por cualquier fugas.

17   Chequee el nivel del anticongelante y agregue más si es necesario.

9   Unidad de envío de la temperatura del anticongelante - chequear y reemplazar

Chequear

1   La unidad de envío de la temperatura del anticongelante proporciona una conexión eléctrica a tierra variable para el medidor de la temperatura del anticongelante.

2   La unidad de envío de la temperatura del anticongelante está localizada cerca de la esquina del lado delantero derecho del múltiple de admisión.

3   Si el medidor no registra, chequee los fusibles eléctricos. Entonces remueva el conector del alambrado de la unidad de envío para la temperatura del anticongelante y conecte un puente de alambre entre el y una conexión eléctrica limpia a tierra. Prenda la ignición brevemente y el medidor debe subir a la escala completa (caliente).

4   Si el medidor subió hasta Caliente, la unidad de envío está defectuosa; reemplácela.

5   Si el medidor no se movió, los circuitos del medidor o conexiones están probablemente defectuoso.

6   La unidad de envío se puede chequear con un ohmímetro puesto en una cacerola de agua y calentándolo. A 140 grados F, la resistencia debe ser aproximadamente entre 70 a 90 ohms y a 212 grados F, entre 21 a 24 ohms.

Reemplazo

7   Permita que el motor se enfríe completamente.

8   Drene el anticongelante (Capítulo 1).

9   Remueva el conector del alambrado de la unidad de envío.

10   Usando un dado hondo del tamaño apropiado o llave para tuerca de tubería, destornille la unidad de envío del múltiple de admisión.

11   Instale la unidad nueva y apriétela firmemente. No use sellador de rosca porque puede aislar eléctricamente la unidad emisora.

11   Ventilador - remover e instalar

1   Desconecte el cable negativo de la terminal negativa de la batería.

2   Remueva la bandeja de la parte inferior del tablero (si está equipado).

Modelos 1980 al 1985

Refiérase a la ilustración 11.7

3   En los modelos que no estén equipados con aire acondicionado, remueva el conducto de la calefacción.

4   Desconecte el conector del alambrado que se dirige al resistor.

5   Desconecte el cable de la puerta para el control de la admisión de aire de la unidad del ventilador.

6   Remueva los tornillos de la unidad del ventilador y levante la unidad hacia afuera.

7   Si la unidad del ventilador se debe remover, refiérase a la **ilustración que acompaña**.

8   La instalación se hace en el orden inverso al procedimiento de desensamble. **Nota:** *Antes de conectar de nuevo el cable de control para la puerta de admisión del aire, debe ser ajustado refiriéndose a la Sección 19.*

Modelos 1986 y más modernos

Refiérase a la ilustración 11.9

9   Remueva el conector eléctrico de la unidad del ventilador **(vea ilustración)**.

10   Desconecte la manguera de la unidad del ventilador.

11.9 En los modelos 1986 y más modernos, la unidad del ventilador para la calefacción está instalada debajo del compartimiento para los guantes en la esquina derecha

1   Conector eléctrico
2   Pernos de afianzamiento
3   Manguera

12.2 Las mangueras de la calefacción son conectadas a los acopladores del núcleo de la calefacción en la parte trasera del motor en la pared contrafuego (flechas)

11   Remueva los tres pernos de afianzamiento.
12   Baje la unidad del ventilador hacia afuera del albergue.
13   La instalación se hace en el orden inverso al procedimiento de desensamble.

---

12   Núcleo de la calefacción - remover e instalar

Refiérase a las ilustraciones 12.2, 12.3, 12.6a, 12.6b, 12.7 y 12.9
1   Drene el anticongelante en un recipiente limpio (vea Capítulo 1).
2   En los modelos equipados con aire acondicionado, desconecte las mangueras de la calefacción en la pared contrafuego **(vea ilustración)**.
3   En los modelos que no estén equipados con aire acondicionado, remueva el conducto de la calefacción **(vea ilustración)**.

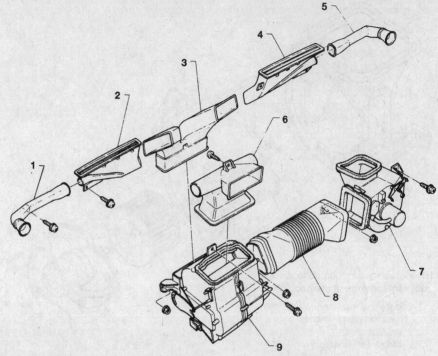

12.3 Componentes de la calefacción - vista esquemática (modelos 1980 al 1985 sin aire acondicionado)

1   Ducto lateral para el descongelador
2   Ducto para el descongelador
3   Ducto central para el descongelador
4   Ducto para el descongelador
5   Ducto lateral para el descongelador
6   Ducto central de ventilación
7   Unidad del ventilador
8   Ducto para la calefacción
9   Unidad de la calefacción

12.6a Componentes de la calefacción y del aire acondicionado - vista esquemática (modelos 1980 al 1985)

1   Ducto lateral del ventilador
2   Ducto lateral del descongelador
3   Ducto del descongelador
4   Ducto central del descongelador
5   Ducto del descongelador
6   Ducto lateral del descongelador
7   Ducto lateral del ventilador
8   Ducto central del ventilador
9   Unidad del ventilador
10   Unidad de enfriamiento
11   Unidad de la calefacción

**12.6b Componentes de la calefacción y del aire acondicionado
- vista esquemática (modelos 1986 y más modernos)**

1 Ducto del descongelador
2 Ducto lateral del descongelador
3 Unidad de la calefacción
4 Ubicación de los pernos de afianzamiento
5 Unidad de enfriamiento (aire acondicionado)
6 Ubicación de los pernos de afianzamiento
7 Ducto lateral del descongelador
8 Ducto de la calefacción (calefacción)
9 Caja de admisión
10 Ducto lateral del ventilador
11 Ducto de la calefacción (estándar)
12 Ducto inferior del
    ventilador (aire
    acondicionado)
13 Ducto lateral
    del ventilador

**12.7 Ubicación de los tornillos
para la unidad de la calefacción
(modelos 1980 al 1985)**

Entonces desconecte las mangueras de la calefacción de la unidad de la calefacción en el punto donde ellas entran al interior del vehículo en la pared contrafuego en el compartimiento del motor.

4   Trabajando en el interior, remueva la caja de la consola si está equipada. Para tener espacio libre adicional, remueva la bandeja inferior del tablero (modelos 1980 al 1985).

5   Desconecte el cable para el control de la admisión de aire de la unidad del ventilador.

6   En los modelos equipados con aire acondicionado, remueva la unidad del ventilador como se indica en la Sección 11. Entonces remueva las tuercas y los pernos de la unidad de enfriamiento (vea ilustraciones).

7   Remueva los tornillos de afianzamiento para la unidad de la calefacción y levante la

unidad hacia afuera (vea ilustración).

8   Una vez que se haya removido, la unidad de control de la calefacción/aire acondicionado se puede separar (vea Sección 19).

9   Si la unidad de la calefacción se debe remover para alcanzar el núcleo de la calefacción, desconecte la palanca de la puerta de combinación de aire del control de la

**12.9 Vista esquemática del núcleo de la calefacción (modelos 1980 al 1985 -
los modelos más modernos son similares)**

1 Puerta para el descongelador en el piso
2 Puerta para el ventilador
3 Núcleo de la calefacción
4 Puerta para la mezcla del aire
5 Grifo para el agua

mezcla, palanca de la puerta del piso, la palanca de la puerta del ventilador y remueva los afianzadores que conectan juntamente las mitades del albergue de la unidad de la calefacción (vea ilustración). Nota: Durante el proceso de ensamblar la varilla de control debe ser ajustada como se describe en la Sección 19.

13   Sistema del aire acondicionado - información general

Refiérase a las ilustraciones 13.3a y 13.3b

Nota: *El sistema de aire acondicionado en los modelos 1993 y más modernos usan el refrigerante que no reduce la ozona, referido como R-134a. El refrigerante R-134a y su aceite que lo lubrica no son compatible con el refrigerante del sistema R-12 y debajo de ninguna circunstancia los dos tipos diferentes de refrigerantes y aceite para la lubricación deben ser entremezclados. Si se mezclan, podría resultar en el fracaso caro del compresor debido a la lubricación impropia.*

El sistema de aire acondicionado usado en las camionetas Datsun/Nissan mantienen la temperatura apropiada para ciclar el compresor ha apagado y ha encendido según la presión adentro del sistema y manteniendo una mezcla de aire frío, aire exterior y aire calentado, usando el mismo ventilador, el núcleo de la calefacción y el sistema del conducto de salida que el sistema de la calefacción usa.

Un dispositivo para el control de la marcha mínima rápida regula la velocidad de la marcha mínima del motor cuando el aire acondicionado está operando.

Los componentes principales del sistema incluyen una banda impulsando el compresor, un condensador (instalado en el frente del radiador), un acumulador y un evaporador **(vea ilustraciones)**.

El sistema opera por aire (de afuera o reciclado) entrando en el núcleo del evaporador por la acción del ventilador, donde recibe enfriamiento máximo si los controles son puestos para enfriar. Cuando el aire sale del evaporador, entra en el ensamblaje del conducto del aire acondicionado/calefacción y por medio de un deflector de control manual, pasa a través o desvía el núcleo de la calefacción en las proporciones correctas para proporcionar la temperatura deseada del vehículo.

La distribución de este aire en el vehículo es entonces regulada por un deflector manualmente operado y es dirigido a los respiraderos del piso, respiraderos del tablero o respiraderos del descongelador según las instalaciones. **Peligro:** *En vista de la naturaleza tóxica de los productos químicos y gases empleados en el sistema, ninguna parte del sistema debe ser desconectada por el mecánico del hogar. Debido a la necesidad especializada para descargar y el equipo de cargar, tal trabajo debe ser dejado al departamento de servicio de su concesionario o un taller automotriz de aire acondicionado.*

14   Sistema del aire acondicionado - chequeo y mantenimiento

Refiérase a la ilustración 14.3

1   Los siguientes pasos de mantenimiento se deben realizar en una base regular para asegurar que el aire acondicionado continúe

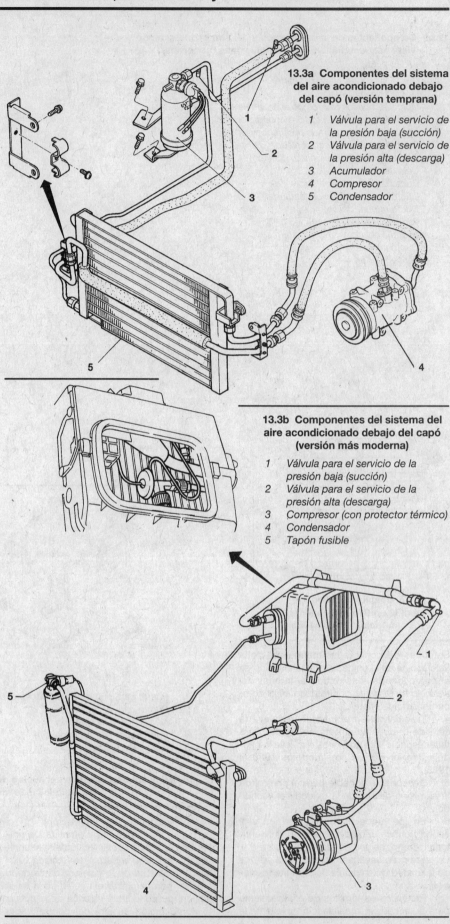

13.3a Componentes del sistema del aire acondicionado debajo del capó (versión temprana)

1   *Válvula para el servicio de la presión baja (succión)*
2   *Válvula para el servicio de la presión alta (descarga)*
3   *Acumulador*
4   *Compresor*
5   *Condensador*

13.3b Componentes del sistema del aire acondicionado debajo del capó (versión más moderna)

1   *Válvula para el servicio de la presión baja (succión)*
2   *Válvula para el servicio de la presión alta (descarga)*
3   *Compresor (con protector térmico)*
4   *Condensador*
5   *Tapón fusible*

14.3 Panorama superior del acumulador mostrando el vidrio de inspección (flecha)

operando a su máxima eficiencia.

a) Chequee la presión de la banda del compresor del aire acondicionado y ajústela si es necesario (refiérase al Capítulo 1).

b) Inspeccione visualmente la condición de las mangueras del radiador, buscando por cualquier roturas, endurecidas y otra deterioración. **Nota:** No remueva ninguna manguera hasta que el sistema se haya descargado.

c) Asegúrese que las aletas del condensador no están cubiertas con material extranjero, tal como hojas o bichos. Una brocha suave y aire comprimido suave se pueden usar para removerlos.

d) Esté seguro de que el drenaje para el evaporador está abierto deslizando un alambre ocasionalmente en el tubo de drenaje.

2   El compresor del aire acondicionado se debe correr acerca de 10 minutos por lo menos una vez cada mes. Esto es especialmente importante de recordarse durante los meses de invierno porque es un largo plazo que no se usa y puede causar que los sellos se endurezcan.

3   Debido a la complejidad del sistema de aire acondicionado y el equipo especial requerido para efectivamente trabajar en el, la identificación y resolución de problemas y las reparaciones exactas del sistema no pueden ser hechas por un mecánico de hogar y deben ser dejado a un profesional. De todos modos, debido a la naturaleza tóxica del refrigerante, antes de desconectar cualquier parte del sistema, el vehículo debe ser llevado a un concesionario de Nissan o un taller de reparaciones para hacer que el sistema sea descargado. Si el sistema pierde su acción de enfriamiento, algunas causas puede ser diagnosticadas por el mecánico del hogar. Busque por otros síntomas de problemas tales como ésos en la siguiente lista. En todos los casos, es una buena idea que el servicio sea otorgado por un profesional.

a) Si burbujas aparecen en el vidrio de inspección (localizado encima del acumulador (vea ilustración), esto es una indicación de una fuga pequeña de refrigerante o aire en el refrigerante. Si aire está en el refrigerante, el acumulador es la

sospechosa y debe ser reemplazado.

b) Si el vidrio de inspección toma una apariencia como niebla o muestra muchas burbujas, esto indica un escape grande del refrigerante. En tal caso, no opere el compresor del todo hasta que el defecto se haya corregido.

c) Sudar o cubrirse con escarcha en la válvula de expansión indica que la válvula de expansión está obstruida o defectuosa. Se debe limpiar o debe ser reemplazada según sea necesario.

d) Sudar o cubrirse con escarcha en la línea de succión (que corre entre la válvula de succión y el compresor) indica que la válvula de expansión está obstruida abierta o defectuosa. Se debe corregir o debe ser reemplazada según sea necesario.

e) Escarcha en el evaporador indica una válvula de succión defectuosa, que requiere reemplazo de la válvula.

f) Escarcha en la línea de líquido de presión alta (que corre entre el condensador, el acumulador y la válvula de expansión) indica que el secador o la línea de presión alta está restringida. La línea se tendrá que limpiar o el acumulador ser reemplazado.

g) La combinación de burbujas en el vidrio de inspección, una línea de succión muy caliente y posiblemente, sobrecalentamiento del motor es una indicación que el condensador no está operando apropiadamente o está sobre cargado de refrigerante. Chequee la presión de la banda y ajústela si es necesario (Capítulo 1). Chequee por partículas extranjeras en las aletas del condensador y límpielo si es necesario. También chequee por una operación apropiada del sistema de enfriamiento. Si ningún defecto puede ser encontrado en estos chequeos, el condensador quizás tenga que ser reemplazado.

15 Dispositivo para el control de la marcha mínima rápida - ajuste

1   Ponga el motor en marcha y permítalo que corra en marcha mínima hasta que llegue a la temperatura normal de operación.

2   Con el aire acondicionado apagado chequee que la velocidad de la marcha mínima esté correcta y ajústela si es necesario refiriéndose al Capítulo 1.

3   Gire el aire acondicionado a encendido y chequee la velocidad de la marcha mínima (en los modelos con transmisión automática se debe colocar en la posición N).

Modelos con carburador

Refiérase a las ilustraciones 15.4a y 15.4b

4   Los modelos de 2WD deben de estar en marcha mínima a 800 rpm (revoluciones por minuto) y los modelos de 4WD deben estar en marcha mínima a 950 rpm. Si esto no es el caso, el dispositivo de control para la marcha mínima rápida debe ser ajustado girando el tornillo localizado en la palanca del acelerador

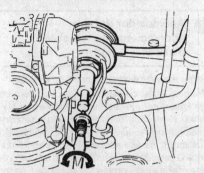

15.4a Ubicación del tornillo para el ajuste de la marcha mínima rápida (modelos 1980)

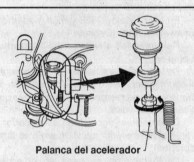

Palanca del acelerador

15.4b Ubicación del tornillo de ajuste para el dispositivo del control de la marcha mínima rápida (modelos 1981 y más modernos con carburador)

15.5 Dispositivo para el control de la marcha mínima rápida - modelos con combustible inyectado

1   Tornillo de ajuste FICD (dispositivo para el control de la marcha mínima rápida)

2   Válvula solenoide FICD

(vea ilustraciones). No cambie la posición del tornillo de la velocidad de la marcha mínima.

Modelos con combustible inyectado

Refiérase a la ilustración 15.5

5   Gire el tornillo de ajuste (vea ilustración) hasta que una velocidad de marcha mínima de 850 a 950 rpm sea obtenida.

6   Siguiendo el ajuste, presione y libere el pedal del acelerador varias veces para asegurarse que la velocidad del motor regresa a su ajuste apropiado con el aire acondicionado encendido y apagado.

16   Acumulador del aire acondicionado - remover e instalar

Refiérase a las ilustraciones 16.5a y 16.5b
Peligro: *Antes de desconectar cualquiera de las líneas del aire acondicionado en el sistema, el vehículo debe ser llevado a su concesionario Nissan o un taller de reparación automotriz de aire acondicionado para removerle la presión al sistema. Debido a la naturaleza tóxica de los productos químicos y gases usados en el sistema, esto no es un trabajo para el mecánico del hogar.*
1   Desconecte el cable negativo de la terminal negativa de la batería.
2   En los modelos 1986 y más modernos, remueva la parrilla (Capítulo 11).
3   Remueva los alambres del interruptor de presión.
4   Desconecte las líneas de refrigerante del acumulador. Use una llave para tuerca de tubería y una de respaldo para mantener que no se tuerza la línea.
5   Destornille el soporte de acumulador y levante el acumulador hacia afuera **(vea ilustraciones)**.
6   La instalación se hace en el orden inverso al procedimiento de desensamble. Cuando conecte de nuevo las mangueras, esté seguro que anillos O nuevos son usados y que ellos están instalados apropiadamente.
7   Una vez que todas las líneas de aire acondicionado se hayan conectado firmemente al vehículo debe ser llevado una vez más a un concesionario Nissan o un taller de reparación para hacer que el sistema sea cargado.

17   Compresor del aire acondicionado - remover e instalar

Refiérase a las ilustraciones 17.5, 17.7 y 17.9
Peligro: *Antes de desconectar cualquiera de las líneas del aire acondicionado en el sistema, el vehículo debe ser llevado a su concesionario Nissan o un taller de reparación automotriz de aire acondicionado para removerle la presión al sistema. Debido a la naturaleza tóxica de los productos químicos y gases usados en el sistema, este no es un trabajo para el mecánico del hogar.*
1   Opere el compresor, si es posible, acerca de diez minutos en velocidad de marcha mínima.
2   Los controles del aire acondicionado deben ser movidos a enfriamiento máximo y a la velocidad alta del ventilador, con todas las ventanas abiertas. Esto circulará el aceite adentro del sistema en el compresor.
3   Desconecte el cable negativo de la terminal negativa de la batería.
4   En los modelos 1981 y más modernos, remueva el distribuidor para tener espacio libre. Si es necesario, refiérase al Capítulo 5.
5   Afloje el perno en el centro de la polea loca del compresor y gire el perno de ajuste

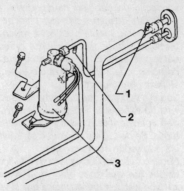

16.5a El acumulador del aire acondicionado en los modelos 1980 al 1985 está localizado en el interior del guardafango derecho

1   Válvula para el servicio de la presión baja (succión)
2   Válvula para el servicio de la presión alta (descarga)
3   Acumulador

para aflojar la banda del compresor del aire acondicionado **(vea ilustración)**.
6   Remueva la banda del compresor.
7   Desconecte ambas líneas en el compresor **(vea ilustración)**.
8   Desconecte todos los alambres conectados al compresor.
9   Remueva los pernos que retiene el compresor al soporte y separe el compresor **(vea ilustración)**.
10   Remueva del compartimiento del motor el compresor. **Nota:** *El compresor no se debe dejar en su lado ni al revés por intervalos de más de 10 minutos a la vez, porque el aceite del compresor podría entrar a las cámaras de baja presión y causar daño interno. Si esto acontece, el aceite se puede expulsar de las cámaras posicionando el compresor boca encima y girándolo con la mano varias veces.*
11   La instalación se hace en el orden inverso al procedimiento de desensamble. Cuando conecte de nuevo las líneas al compresor esté seguro de usar anillos de tipo O nuevos en cada conexión.
12   Una vez que el compresor y todas las líneas del aire acondicionado se hayan

17.7 Las líneas del compresor del aire acondicionado en el motor V6 se pueden separar después de remover los pernos (flechas)

16.5b Panorama superior del acumulador (modelos 1986 y más modernos)

1   Línea desde el condensador
2   Línea de salida
3   Interruptor de presión
4   Perno de pellizco del soporte

17.5 Polea loca para ajustar la banda del aire acondicionado en los motores V6 (afloje el A antes de girar el ajustador B)

conectado firmemente, el vehículo debe ser llevado una vez más a un concesionario de Nissan o un taller del aire acondicionado para hacer que el sistema sea cargado.

18   Condensador del aire acondicionado - remover e instalar

Peligro: *Antes de desconectar cualquiera de las líneas del aire acondicionado en el sistema, el vehículo debe ser llevado a su con-*

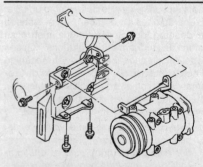

17.9 Arreglo del compresor del aire acondicionado y el soporte (típico)

19.3 Hale las perillas de control recta hacia afuera - interruptor del aire acondicionado (flecha) hale directamente hacia afuera (modelos 1986 y más modernos)

cesionario Nissan o un taller de reparación automotriz de aire acondicionado para removerle la presión al sistema. Debido a la naturaleza tóxica de los productos químicos y gases usados en el sistema, este no es un trabajo para el mecánico del hogar.

1   Remueva la parrilla como está descrito en el Capítulo ·11 y el guardia opcional de la parrilla si está equipado con uno.

2   Remueva el radiador como está descrito en la Sección 4.

3   Remueva el ensamblaje izquierdo de la luz.

4   Desconecte todos los tubos y mangueras del aire acondicionado de caucho del condensador.

5   Remueva los pernos que retienen el condensador a la carrocería y levante hacia afuera el condensador.

6   Si las aletas del condensador o pasajes del aire están obstruidos con materiales extranjeros, tales como tierra, insectos o hojas, use aire comprimido y una brocha suave para limpiar el condensador. Si el condensador está en necesidad de otras reparaciones, haga que un taller profesional de radiadores o su concesionario Nissan haga el trabajo.

7   La instalación se hace en el orden inverso al procedimiento de desensamble.

19.4b Remueva los tornillos (flechas) para remover el ensamblaje del control (modelos 1986 y más modernos)

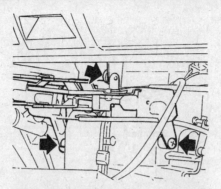

19.4a Ubicación de los tornillos para la calefacción/unidad para el control del aire acondicionado (modelos 1980 al 1985)

Cuando conecte las mangueras, esté seguro de instalar anillos de tipo O nuevos y esté seguro de que están instalados correctamente.

8   Una vez que todas las líneas del aire acondicionado se hayan conectado firmemente, el vehículo debe ser llevado una vez más a un concesionario Nissan o un taller del aire acondicionado para hacer que el sistema sea cargado.

19   Ensamblaje del control de la calefacción/aire acondicionado - remover e instalar

Remover e instalar

Refiérase a las ilustraciones 19.3, 19.4a y 19.4b

1   Desconecte el cable negativo de la terminal negativa de la batería y remueva la bandeja inferior del tablero (si está equipado).

2   Desconecte los cables del control de la unidad de la calefacción y la unidad del ventilador. **Nota:** *La puerta para mezclar el aire/cable para la válvula del agua en los modelos equipados con aire acondicionados es fácilmente desconectado con el conjunto de la palanca de control de la temperatura en la posición Fría.*

3   Separe las perillas de las palancas de control (**vea ilustración**) y remueva el panel

19.8 Procedimiento para ajustar la puerta de mezclar el aire/cable del grifo de agua

de la unidad del control.

4   Remueva los tornillos de la unidad del control de la calefacción/aire acondicionado (**vea ilustraciones**). Baje la unidad del tablero y desconecte cualquier arnés del alambrado que se dirija a la unidad.

5   El interruptor del ventilador puede ser chequeado refiriéndose al Capítulo 13, si es necesario. Para reemplazarlo, se debe separar del descanso de la unidad de control.

6   La instalación se hace en el orden inverso al procedimiento de desensamble. **Nota:** *Antes de conectar de nuevo los cables del control a las unidades de la calefacción y el ventilador, ellos deben ser ajustados como sigue.*

Ajuste

Modelos 1980 al 1985

Refiérase a las ilustraciones 19.8, 19.9a y 19.9b

7   Para ajustar la varilla para la puerta de la mezcla del aire, empuje primero la palanca de la puerta para mezclar el aire hasta que la puerta para mezclar el aire sea inclinada hacia el núcleo de la calefacción lo más posible. Con la palanca sostenida en esa posición, conecte la varilla de control. El grifo de agua debe ser cerrado.

8   Para instalar la puerta para mezclar el aire/cable del grifo de agua, empuje la palanca del control de la temperatura a la izquierda, empuje el albergue del cable hacia la pared contrafuego y detenga la parte trasera de la varilla (**vea ilustración**). De un golpe ponga la abrazadera de retención en su posición.

9   Para ajustar la puerta del piso y el control de la puerta del ventilador, levante primero el eslabón lateral completamente en la dirección mostrada en la ilustración que acompaña. Mientras detiene el eslabón lateral en esta posición, cierre ambas puertas del piso, la puerta del ventilador y conecte las varillas respectivas del control a las palancas (**vea ilustraciones**).

10   Para instalar el cable para la admisión del aire, empuje la palanca de control a la izquierda, empuje el albergue del cable y la palanca de la puerta completamente a la derecha e instale la abrazadera en el cable.

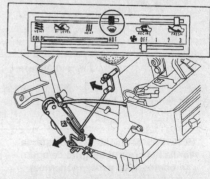

19.9a Procedimiento para ajustar la puerta del piso/cable de la puerta del ventilador

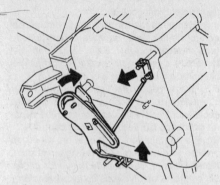

19.9b El eslabón lateral debe ser sostenido en la posición mostrada con la puerta del piso y la puerta del ventilador cerrada antes de conectar las varillas del control

Modelos 1986 y más modernos

Refiérase a las ilustraciones 19.12, 19.13, 19.14, 19.15, 19.16 y 19.17

11   Cuando esté ajustando la varilla de la puerta del ventilador y la varilla de la puerta del descongelador, desconecte el cable de control del eslabón lateral del aire primero y entonces ajuste la varilla de la puerta. Conecte de nuevo el cable del control del aire y lo ajusta de nuevo.

12   Para instalar la varilla del control de la puerta del ventilador, mueva el eslabón lateral en la dirección a la flecha (**vea ilustración**). Con las palancas superiores e inferiores de la puerta del ventilador sostenidas en la dirección de la flecha, conecte las varillas 1 y 2 a sus palancas corresponde para la puerta del ventilador en ese orden.

13   Para ajustar la varilla para el control de la puerta del descongelador, mueva el eslabón lateral en la dirección de la flecha (**vea ilustración**). Conecte la varilla al eslabón lateral, empuje la palanca de la puerta del descongelador en la dirección de la flecha.

14   Para ajustar el cable para el control del aire, empuje el forro exterior del cable y el eslabón lateral en la dirección de la flecha y la abrazadera del cable (**vea ilustración**).

15   Para ajustar la varilla para el control del

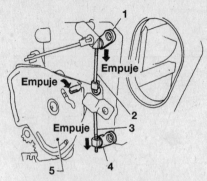

19.12 Procedimiento para ajustar la varilla del control de la puerta del ventilador (modelos 1986 y más modernos)

1   Palanca para la puerta (superior)
2   Varilla para la puerta 2
3   Varilla para la puerta 1
4   Palanca para la puerta (inferior)
5   Varilla lateral

grifo de agua, desconecte primero la palanca de la puerta de mezcla del aire del cable de control de la temperatura y entonces instale la varilla del control. Conecte de nuevo el cable de control de la temperatura y lo ajusta de nuevo. Empuje la palanca para la puerta de la mezcla del aire en la dirección de la flecha (**vea ilustración**). Hale la varilla del control del grifo de agua en la dirección de la flecha para proporcionar un espacio libre acerca de 0.08 pulgada entre las puntas de la palanca de la varilla, el eslabón y conecte la varilla a la palanca de la puerta.

16   Para instalar el cable del control de la temperatura, empuje el control a la izquierda (**vea ilustración**), empuje el cable exterior y palanca de la puerta para la mezcla del aire en la dirección de las flechas y la abrazadera al cable en su posición.

17   Para instalar el cable del control de la puerta de admisión, empuje el control a la izquierda (**vea ilustración**), empuje el albergue exterior del cable y la palanca de la puerta de admisión en la dirección de la fle-

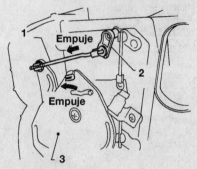

19.13 Procedimiento para ajustar la varilla del control de la puerta del descongelador (modelos 1986 y más modernos)

1   Varilla para la puerta
2   Planca para la puerta del descongelador
3   Varilla lateral

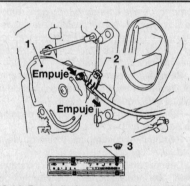

19.14 Procedimiento para ajustar el cable para el control del aire (modelos 1986 y más modernos)

1   Varilla para la puerta
2   Presilla
3   Posición

cha y la abrazadera del cable en posición.

18   Chequee la operación de todos los controles y complete la instalación invirtiendo la secuencia de remover.

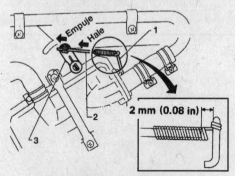

19.15 Procedimiento para ajustar la varilla del control del grifo de agua (modelos 1986 y más modernos)

1   Palanca
2   Varilla de control
3   Palance para la puerta de mezcla

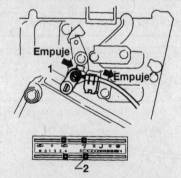

19.16 Procedimiento para ajustar el control del cable de la temperatura (modelos 1986 y más modernos)

1   Palanca para la puerta de mezcla
2   Posición para el máximo de enfriamiento

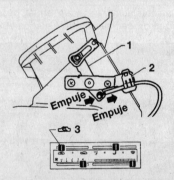

19.17 Procedimiento para ajustar el cable de control de la puerta de admisión (modelos 1986 y más modernos)

1   Palanca para la puerta admisión
2   Presilla
3   Posición

Capítulo 4
Sistemas de combustible y escape

Contenidos

Especificaciones

Carburador

Modelos
Modelos 1980	DCH340*
Modelos 1981 al 1983	DCR342*

Modelos 1984 (motores Z24)
California
Estándar	DFP384-3
Pesado	DFP384-12
4WD	DFP383-3

Los otros 49 estados
Estándar	DCR384-3
Pesado	DCR384-11A
4WD	DCR384-21A

Canadá
Estándar	DCR384-5
Pesado	DCR384-15
4WD	DCR384-25

Carburador

Modelos (continuación)
Modelos 1984 (con motores Z20 - todos)... DCR342-8
Modelos 1985 (con motores Z20)
California
2WD - con transmisión manual DFP384-5
2WD - con transmisión automática....................................... DFP384-6
4WD.. DFP384-5
Los otros 49 estados
2WD - con transmisión manual DFP384-7
2WD - con transmisión automática....................................... DFP384-8
4WD.. DFP384-7

Este es el número general del modelo. Carburadores levemente diferentes son usados, dependiendo del tipo de vehículo y ubicación geográfica. El número del modelo específico de su carburador está estampado en el carburador.

Modelos
Modelos 1985 (con motores Z20)
Canadá
2WD - con transmisión manual DCR384-7
2WD - con transmisión automática....................................... DCR384-8
4WD.. DCR384-26
Modelos 1985 (con motores Z20 - todos)................................. DFP342-11
Resistencia de la unidad de la calefacción del
estrangulador automático .... 3.7 a 8.9 ohm
Ajustes para el nivel del combustible
De la cima del flotador a la cima interior de la cámara del flotador... 0.283 pulgada (7.2 mm)
Asiento del flotador a la distancia de la válvula de tipo aguja .... 0.051 a 0.067 pulgada (1.3 a 1.7 mm)
Ajuste del ruptor por vacío
Modelos 1980 US.. 0.0969 a 0.1205 pulgada (2.46 a 3.06 mm)
Modelos 1980 del Canadá... 0.102 a 0.126 pulgada (2.6 a 3.2 mm)
Modelos 1981 al 1983 de California... 0.1228 a 0.1465 pulgada (3.12 a 3.72 mm)
Modelos 1981 al 1983 de los otros 49 estados .... 0.1031 a 0.1268 pulgada (2.62 a 3.22 mm)
Modelos 1984
California .... 0.1220 a 0.1457 pulgada (3.10 a 3.70 mm)
Los otros 49 estados
Motor Z24 .... 0.0965 a 0.1201 pulgada (2.45 a 3.0 mm)
Motor Z20 .... 0.1031 a 0.1268 pulgada (2.61 a 3.22 mm)
Canadá
Estándar 2WD .... 0.0913 a 0.1150 pulgada (2.32 a 2.92 mm)
4WD y de trabajo pesado.. 0.0965 a 0.1201 pulgada (2.45 a 3.0 mm)
Modelos 1985
USA
Motor Z24 .... 0.1339 ± 0.0118 pulgada (3.40 ± 0.30 mm)
Motor Z20 .... 0.1346 ± 0.0118 pulgada (3.42 ± 0.30 mm)
Canadá
Estándar 2WD .... 0.1031 ± 0.0118 pulgada (2.62 ± 0.30 mm)
4WD y de trabajo pesado.. 0.1083 ± 0.0118 pulgada (2.75 ± 0.30 mm)
Descargador del estrangulador
Modelos 1980 al 1983.. 0.0807 a 0.1122 pulgada (2.05 a 2.85 mm)
Modelos 1984 y 1985.. 0.0965 ± 0.0157 pulgada (2.45 ± 0.4 mm)
Ajuste del amortiguador para la velocidad
Modelos 1980 - transmisión automática....................................... 1650 a 1850 rpm
Modelos 1980 del Canadá - transmisión manual .... 1900 a 2100 rpm
Modelos 1981 al 1983 - transmisión automática............................ 1400 a 1600 rpm
Modelos 1984 y 1985
Transmisión manual... 1800 ± 200 rpm
Transmisión automática.. 1500 ± 200 rpm
Ajuste de la abertura de la válvula de entre cierre
Modelos 1980 al 1983... 0.2906 a 0.3299 pulgada (7.38 a 8.38 mm)
Modelos 1984 y 1985
Motor Z24 .... 0.3295 ± 0.0197 pulgada (8.37 ± 0.5 mm)
Motor Z20 .... 0.3102 ± 0.0197 pulgada (7.88 ± 0.5 mm)
Ajuste de la marcha mínima rápida
Transmisión manual (todos los modelos)....................................... 0.0319 a 0.0374 pulgada (0.81 a 0.95 mm)
Transmisión automática
Modelos 1980 .... 0.0402 a 0.0457 pulgada (1.02 a 1.16 mm)
Modelos 1981 al 1985
California .... 0.0386 a 0.0441 pulgada (0.98 a 1.12 mm)
Los otros 49 estados.. 0.0394 a 0.0433 pulgada (1.00 a 1.10 mm)

Sistema de inyección de combustible

Inspección de la marcha mínima rápida y ajuste (sistemas con TBI {cuerpo de inyección de combustible})	
Espacio libre G	0.020 a 0.118 pulgada (0.5 a 3.0 mm)
Espacio libre G ajustable	0.031 a 0.047 pulgada (0.8 a 1.2 mm)
Inspección de la marcha mínima rápida y ajuste	
(sistemas de MPFI {inyección de combustible con lumbreras}) motores (KA24E)	
Transmisión manual	0.091 pulgada (2.3 mm)
Transmisión automática	0.083 pulgada (2.1 mm)
Inspección de FICD (dispositivo para el control de la marcha mínima rápida) y ajuste	
Velocidad de la marcha mínima (aire acondicionado encendido)	
Transmisión manual	
Cuatro cilindros	900 $\pm$ 50 rpm
V6	800 $\pm$ 50 rpm
Transmisión automática	
Cuatro cilindros	650 $\pm$ 50 rpm
V6	700 $\pm$ 50 rpm
Velocidad de la marcha mínima (aire acondicionado encendido)	900 $\pm$ 50 rpm con la transmisión en Neutral
Velocidad para el amortiguador de velocidad	
Cuatro cilindros	1600 a 2000 rpm
V6	1300 a 1500 rpm

Bomba de combustible

Presión de la bomba mecánica	3.0 a 3.8 psi (libras por pulgadas cuadradas)
Volumen de la bomba mecánica (cantidad por minuto a 1000 rpm (revoluciones por minuto)	
Modelos 1980	33.8 onzas de flúido (1000 milímetros) (35.2 onzas de flúido)
Modelos 1981	57.5 onzas de flúido (1700 milímetros) (59.8 onzas de flúido)
Modelos 1982	50.7 onzas de flúido (1500 milímetros) (52.8 onzas de flúido)
Presión de la bomba eléctrica	
Carburador	
Modelos hasta el 1983	3.1 a 3.8 psi
Modelos 1984 y 1985	2.7 a 3.4 psi
Inyección de combustible (sistemas con TBI)	36.3 psi
Inyección de combustible (sistemas de MPFI)	
Motores V6	
Con vacío	34 psi
Sin vacío	43 psi
KA24E	
Con vacío	33 psi
Sin vacío	43 psi
Volumen de la bomba eléctrica - carburador solamente	47.3 onzas de flúido (1400 milímetros) (49.3 onzas de flúido) por minuto

Especificaciones técnicas

	Pies-libras
Tuercas para el afianzamiento del cuerpo de aceleración	
Hasta el 1992	9 a 13
1993	
Paso 1	6.5 a 8.0
Paso 2	13 a 16
Pernos de afianzamiento para la válvula de tipo solenoide	
Anti diesel (solenoide para detener que el motor	
continúe en marcha)	19
Tapón para el drenaje del tanque de combustible	40
Pernos para el soporte trasero del tanque de combustible	38
Pernos para el soporte del tanque de combustible	
Hasta el 1990	7
1991 y más moderno	20 a 26
Pernos de afianzamiento para el convertidor catalítico	
Hasta el 1990	27
1991 y más moderno	
Todos menos el V6 Pathfinder	23 a 31
V6 Pathfinder	32 a 41
Pernos de la pipa de escape delantera a los pernos del múltiple de escape	
Hasta el 1990	16
1991 y más moderno	
Todos menos el V6 Pathfinder	20 a 27
V6 Pathfinder solamente	30 a 35

1   Sistema de combustible - información general

Vehículos con carburador

Las versiones con carburador de este vehículo usan un sistema de combustible del diseño convencional. Puesto simplemente, el combustible es bombeado del tanque de combustible, a través de las líneas de combustible y el filtro de combustible en el carburador, donde es mezclado con aire para la combustión. El sistema de combustible, también como el sistema del escape, está correlacionado y trabajan en conjunto con los varios sistemas del control de emisiones cubiertos en el Capítulo 6. Así, que algunos elementos que se relacionan directamente a las funciones del sistema de combustible y el carburador son cubiertos en este Capítulo.

Todos los carburadores son de succión hacia abajo, del tipo de dos barriles. La información específica para el carburador puede ser encontrada en la Sección 9.

Dos tipos de bomba de combustible son usadas. Un tipo de diafragma convencional, bomba mecánica, es conectada al lado derecho delantero de la cabeza de los cilindros en los modelos más antiguos. El brazo de operación de la bomba se extiende hacia adentro de la cabeza de los cilindros donde es accionado por una leva excéntrica instalada en el frente del árbol de levas. Esta leva excéntrica, cuando gira, mueve el brazo de operación de aquí para allá, proporcionando la acción de la bomba.

Una bomba eléctrica es usada en los modelos más modernos. Es instalada en el riel del chasis en la cara inferior derecha del vehículo.

El tanque de combustible está localizado debajo de la cama en la parte trasera del vehículo. Además de la línea de suplemento de combustible que se dirige al filtro de combustible y a la bomba, el tanque también tiene una manguera de respiración para las emisiones hacia el canasto de carbón, una línea de ventilación de aire se conecta hacia adentro de la manguera de combustible y una manguera de regreso de combustible para dirigir el exceso de combustible hacia la parte trasera del tanque.

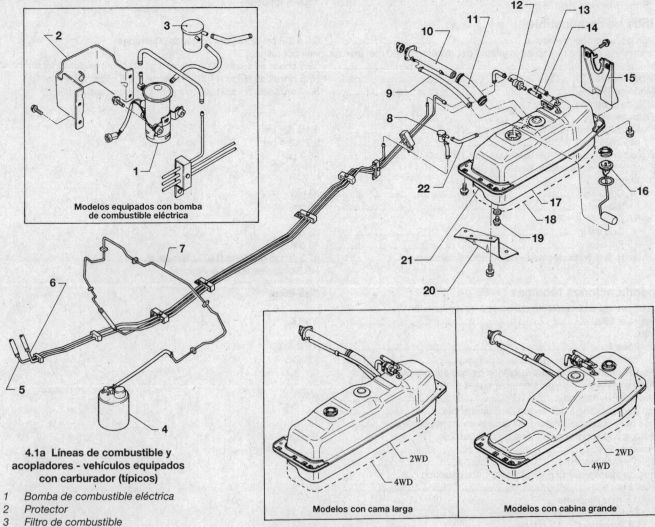

Modelos equipados con bomba de combustible eléctrica

4.1a Líneas de combustible y acopladores - vehículos equipados con carburador (típicos)

Modelos con cama larga

Modelos con cabina grande

1   Bomba de combustible eléctrica
2   Protector
3   Filtro de combustible
4   Canasto
5   Tubo de regreso del combustible
6   Tubo de suministro del combustible
7   Tubo de evaporación
8   Filtro de combustible
9   Manguera de ventilación para el aire
10 Tubo para llenar el tanque de combustible

11 Manguera para llenar el tanque de combustible
12 Válvula unilateral para el combustible
13 Manguera de respiración
14 Manguera de regreso
15 Soporte trasero del tanque
16 Unida emisora del nivel del combustible en el tanque

17 2WD (tracción en las ruedas traseras)
18 4WD (tracción en las cuatro ruedas)
19 Tapón de drenaje
20 Protector para el tanque de combustible 2WD
21 Tanque de combustible (modelos de cama regular)
22 Manguera de salida del combustible

Vehículos con combustible inyectado

Los vehículos más nuevos son de combustible inyectado. En estos modelos, el combustible es bombeado del tanque de combustible por una bomba de combustible eléctrica en el tanque de combustible a través de la línea de metal y un filtro de combustible a un par de inyectores de combustible localizados encima del cuerpo de inyección instalado en el múltiple de admisión. Para más información de vehículos con inyección de combustible, vea Sección 13. **Peligro:** *Siempre alivie la presión del combustible (vea Sección 15) antes de atentar de otorgarle servicio a los componentes en un vehículo con inyección de combustible.*

2   Filtro de combustible - reemplazo

Porque reemplazo del filtro de combustible es parte del itinerario de mantenimiento rutinario, refiérase al Capítulo 1 para este procedimiento.

3   Velocidad de la marcha mínima - chequeo y ajuste

Debido a que el ajuste de la velocidad de la marcha mínima es una parte íntegra de la operación de afinación, información acerca de este procedimiento está incluida en el Capítulo 1.

4   Líneas de combustible - reparación y reemplazo

Refiérase a las ilustraciones 4.1a y 4.1b
Peligro: *En los vehículos con inyección de combustible, la presión del sistema de combustible se debe aliviar antes de desconectar las líneas de combustible y los acopladores (vea Sección 15). La gasolina es extremadamente inflamable, así que precauciones extras se deben tomar cuando esté trabajando en el cualquier parte del sistema de combustible. No fume ni permita llamas abiertas ni bombillas sin protectores cerca del área de trabajo. También, no trabaje en un garaje donde un aparato de gas natural tal como una calefacción de agua o secadora de ropa esté presente. Finalmente, antes de cualquier operación en que una línea de combustible sea desconectada, remueva el cable negativo de la batería para eliminar la posibilidad de que chispas ocurran mientras los vapores de combustible están presente.*

1   Si una sección de la línea de combustible de metal debe ser reemplazada, debe usar una de acero sin costuras solamente, porque tuberías de cobre o de aluminio no tienen suficiente durabilidad para resistir las vibraciones normales del motor **(vea ilustraciones)**.

2   Si solamente una sección de una línea de combustible de metal está dañada, puede ser recortada y reemplazada con un pedazo de manguera de caucho. La manguera de caucho se debe cortar cuatro pulgadas (100 mm) más larga que la sección que va a ser reemplazada, así que haya acerca de dos pulgadas de superposición entre la tubería de caucho y el metal en cualquier extremo. Abrazaderas de manguera se deben usar para asegurar ambas puntas de la sección reparada.

3   Si una sección de la línea de metal es más larga que seis pulgadas, debe ser removida, use una combinación de tubería de metal y manguera de caucho para que las longitudes de la manguera no sean más largas que 10 pulgadas. **Peligro:** *¡Nunca use manguera de caucho adentro de cuatro pulgadas de cualquier parte del sistema de escape!*

4   Siempre reemplace los anillos selladores de tipo O y las abrazaderas de las mangueras.

5   No doble ni tuerza las mangueras del radiador o los tubos cuando los esté instalando.

6   Para evitar daño a las mangueras del radiador, no aprieta las abrazaderas de la manguera excesivamente.

7   Siempre ponga el motor en marcha y chequee por fugas de combustible antes de poner el vehículo en marcha después que las líneas se hayan reparado.

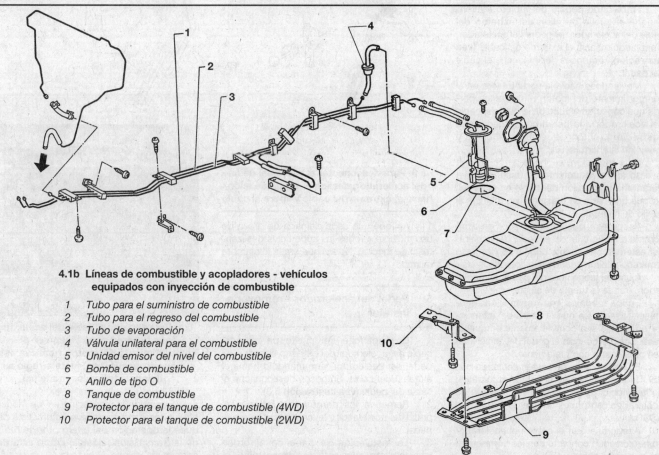

4.1b   Líneas de combustible y acopladores - vehículos equipados con inyección de combustible

1   *Tubo para el suministro de combustible*
2   *Tubo para el regreso del combustible*
3   *Tubo de evaporación*
4   *Válvula unilateral para el combustible*
5   *Unidad emisor del nivel del combustible*
6   *Bomba de combustible*
7   *Anillo de tipo O*
8   *Tanque de combustible*
9   *Protector para el tanque de combustible (4WD)*
10   *Protector para el tanque de combustible (2WD)*

5.2a Para separar el cable de acelerador o el cable del control de crucero del cuerpo de inyección, afloje la contratuerca(s) (flechas) y levante el ensamblaje del cable afuera del soporte del cable, entonces deslice el acoplador(es) en el final del cable(s) afuera de la leva en el eje del acelerador

5   Cable del acelerador - remover e instalar

Refiérase a las ilustraciones 5.2a, 5.2b, 5.3 y 5.4

1   Remueva el purificador de aire.

2   Desconecte el cable de acelerador del carburador/cuerpo de aceleración **(vea ilustraciones)**.

3   Trabajando debajo del tablero, desenganche el cuello de nilón del extremo del cable del acelerador del pedal del acelerador, empujándolo hacia el extremo del cable **(vea ilustración)**. Entonces desenganche el cable del pedal.

4   Moviéndose hacia la parte trasera en el compartimiento del motor, remueva los pernos que conectan el tubo de la guía del cable del acelerador a la pared contrafuego **(vea ilustración)**, entonces remueva el cable a través de la abertura.

5   La instalación se hace en el orden inverso al procedimiento de desensamble. Durante la instalación del cable en el pedal, aplique una capa de grasa de uso múltiple al cuello de nilón.

6   Asegúrese que el acelerador se abre completamente cuando el pedal del acelerador esté completamente deprimido y regrese a marcha mínima cuando sea liberado.

7   Ajuste el juego libre del pedal del acelerador girando la tuerca de ajuste.

8   En los modelos con transmisión automática, asegúrese que la varilla del interruptor de rebase sea completamente empujada hacia adentro cuando el pedal del acelerador sea presionado completamente.

9   En los modelos que estén equipado con ASCD (dispositivo para el control automático de la velocidad), ajuste primero el cable de acelerador, entonces ajuste el cable del ASCD.

10   Asegúrese que el cable del acelerador no hace ningún contacto con los componentes que estén cerca.

5.2b Componentes del pedal del acelerador y el cable - vehículos equipados con carburador (típicos)

1   Palanca del acelerador
2   Tuerca de ajuste
3   Tuerca prisionera
4   Soporte para el cable del acelerador
5   Abrazadera para el cable del acelerador
6   Palanca del acelerador
7   Tubo de guía
8   Collar de nilón
9   Tuerca prisionera
10   Soporte para el pedal del acelerador y resorte de retorno
11   Pedal del acelerador
12   Brazo del pedal
13   Cable del control

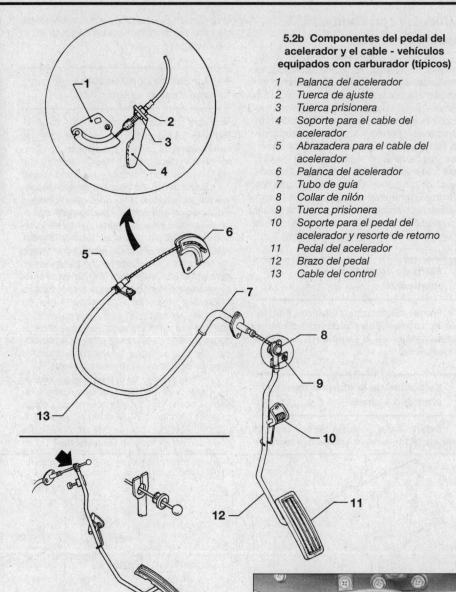

5.3 Para desconectar el cable del pedal del acelerador, deslice el cuello de nilón hacia el extremo del cable y libere el cable

11   Aplique una capa delgada de grasa de uso múltiple a todas las superficies deslizantes o de fricción. No aplique grasa al alambre mismo.

6   Pedal del acelerador - remover e instalar

1   Desenganche del cuello de nilón el cable del acelerador del extremo superior del pedal del acelerador, empujándolo hacia el extremo del cable. Entonces desenganche el cable del pedal **(vea ilustración 5.3)**.

2   Remueva los pernos que retienen el pedal del acelerador y levante hacia afuera el pedal.

3   La instalación se hace en el orden inverso al procedimiento de desensamble.

5.4 Para separar el cable del acelerador de la pared contrafuego en el compartimiento del motor, remueva estos dos pernos (flechas) (este arreglo es típico de todos los modelos)

4   Siguiendo la instalación en los modelos equipados con transmisión automática, chequee la operación del interruptor de rebase de la transmisión, ajústelo como está descrito en el Capítulo 7.

7 Bomba de combustible - chequear

Peligro: *La gasolina es sumamente inflamable, así que se deben tomar precauciones extras cuando esté trabajando en cualquier parte del sistema del combustible. No fume, deje llamas abiertas o bombillas sin cubierta cerca del área de trabajo. También, no trabaje en un garaje si un aparato de gas natural con un piloto encendido está presente. Debido a que la gasolina es dañina para su piel use guantes cuando halla una posibilidad de que entre en contacto con su piel y si se le derrama cualquier cantidad en su piel límpiese inmediatamente con suficiente agua y jabón. Limpie cualquier derrame inmediatamente y no guarde trapos que estén húmedos con gasolina. El sistema de combustible de los modelos con inyección de combustible están bajo constante presión y si cualquiera de las líneas se van a desconectar, la presión en el sistema se debe de aliviar. Cuando usted conduzca cualquier tipo de trabajo en el sistema de combustible, use espejuelos de seguridad y tenga cerca un extintor de fuegos del tipo Clase B.*

Vehículos con carburador

Bomba mecánica

1   Chequee que haya el combustible adecuado en el tanque de combustible.

2   Con el motor en marcha, chequee completamente todas las líneas de combustible entre el tanque de combustible y la bomba de combustible por fugas, conexiones flojas, dobladas o mangueras de caucho aplastadas. Haga esto rápidamente, antes de que el motor se caliente. Fugas de aire encima de la bomba de combustible pueden afectar gravemente el rendimiento de la bomba.

3   Chequee la pestaña del diafragma de la bomba por fugas.

4   Desconecte la línea de combustible en el carburador. Desconecte el alambre de la bobina de la ignición y la conexión a tierra del bloque en el motor (use un alambre puente para prevenir chispas) para que el motor se pueda girar sin ponerlo en marcha. Coloque un recipiente limpio tal como un bote de café en el extremo de la línea de combustible y gire el motor por varios segundos. Debe haber un chorro fuerte de gasolina de la línea en cada segunda revolución.

5   Si una pequeña cantidad o ninguna gasolina surge de la línea durante el proceso de poner en marcha el motor, entonces la línea está obstruida o la bomba de combustible no está trabajando apropiadamente. Desconecte la línea de combustible de la bomba y sople en la línea para estar seguro que está clara. Si la línea está limpia, entonces la bomba está sospechosa y se necesitará ser reemplazada con una nueva.

6   Un método más exacto de la capacidad del flujo de la bomba de combustible es realizando la prueba previa usando un recipiente de medir y un reloj. A 1000 rpm por un minuto, la bomba debe ser capaz de bombear las siguientes cantidades:

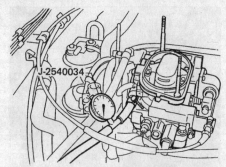

7.17a Para chequear la presión del combustible en los vehículos con inyección de combustible, separe la manguera de suministro del cuerpo de aceleración e instale un manómetro de presión entre la manguera y el cuerpo de aceleración - esté seguro que las abrazaderas de la manguera están apretadas lo suficiente para prevenir fugas de combustible

	Onzas de flúido
Modelos 1980	33.8
Modelos 1981	57.5
Modelos 1982	50.7

Bomba eléctrica

7   Desconecte la manguera de salida de combustible del acoplador de la bomba.

8   Conecte una manguera de caucho al acoplador (aproximadamente 1/4 pulgada/6 mm del diámetro interior), lo suficientemente largo para que alcance adentro del recipiente del medir localizado en una posición más alta que la bomba. **Nota:** *Una manguera con un diámetro más pequeño dará un resultado de prueba falsa.*

9   Desconecte el alambre secundario de la bobina para la ignición para prevenir que el motor se ponga en marcha. Use un puente de alambre para poner a tierra el alambre al bloque del motor.

10   Gire el interruptor de la ignición a la posición de marcha y opere la bomba por un minuto, en intervalos de 15 segundos.

11   Una bomba operando normalmente entregará 47.3 onzas de flúido (1400 milímetros, 49.3 onzas de flúido imperiales) adentro del recipiente en un minuto.

12   Si una pequeña cantidad o ningún combustible surge de la manguera, o el filtro de combustible o la línea está obstruida o la bomba está defectuosa. Remueva el filtro de combustible y sople aire a través de ambas líneas de combustible para asegurarse que ellas no están obstruidos. También, reemplace el filtro de combustible si no lo ha hecho ya. Si esto no mejora el resultado de la prueba, la bomba debe ser reemplazada con una nueva.

Vehículos con combustible inyectado

Refiérase a la ilustración 7.17a, 7.17b y 7.17c

13   Con el motor en marchar, chequee todas las líneas de metal y mangueras de

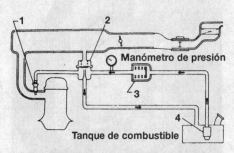

7.17b En los motores KA24E, instale el manómetro de presión entre el regulador de presión y el filtro de combustible. Esté seguro de registrar los valores del regulador de presión ENCENDIDO y APAGADO

1   Inyector
2   Regulador de presión
3   Filtro de combustible
4   Bomba de combustible y amortiguador

Milímetros	Onzas de flúido imperial
1000	35.2
1700	59.8
1500	52.8

caucho entre el tanque de combustible (bomba de gasolina eléctrica instalada adentro del tanque) y el cuerpo de aceleración para asegurarse que no hayan fugas. Apague el motor.

14   Alivie la presión del combustible (vea Sección 15).

15   Separe el cable del terminal negativo de la batería.

16   Desconecte la manguera de admisión de combustible en el cuerpo de aceleración.

17   Instale un medidor de presión en la línea de combustible entre la manguera de admisión de combustible y el cuerpo de aceleración **(vea ilustraciones)**.

18   Acople nuevamente el cable al terminal negativo de la batería.

19   Ponga el motor en marcha y chequee la línea de combustible por fuga de combustible.

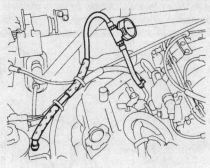

7.17c En los motores MPFI (inyección de combustible con lumbreras) V6, instale el manómetro de presión entre el filtro de combustible y el tubo de combustible (lado del motor). Esté seguro de registrar los valores del regulador de presión ENCENDIDO y APAGADO

8.1 En algunos vehículos con carburador, una bomba de combustible mecánica está localizada en el lado derecho de la cabeza de los cilindros

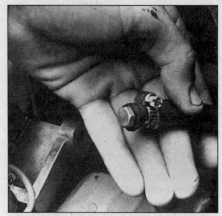

8.2 Para tapar las mangueras de caucho efectivamente, meta un perno en la abertura y lo asegura con una abrazadera para la manguera pequeña

8.7a En los otros vehículos con carburador, una bomba de combustible eléctrica es conectada al riel del chasis debajo del lado derecho del vehículo

20   Note la lectura indicada de la presión del combustible. Debe estar dentro de las especificaciones.
21   Libere la presión del combustible otra vez (vea Sección 15).
22   Separe el cable del terminal negativo de la batería.
23   Remueva el medidor para la presión de la línea de combustible.
24   Conecte de nuevo la manguera de admisión de combustible.
25   Conecte el cable al terminal negativo de la batería.

8   Bomba de combustible - remover e instalar

Refiérase a las ilustraciones 8.1, 8.2, 8.7a, 8.7b y 8.16
Peligro: *La gasolina es sumamente inflamable, así que se deben tomar precauciones extras cuando esté trabajando en cualquier parte del sistema del combustible. No fume, deje llamas abiertas o bombillas sin cubierta cerca del área de trabajo. También, no trabaje en un garaje si un aparato de gas natural con un piloto encendido está presente. Debido a que la gasolina es dañina para su piel use guantes cuando*

halla una posibilidad de que entre en contacto con su piel y si se le derrama cualquier cantidad en su piel límpiese inmediatamente con suficiente agua y jabón. Limpie cualquier derrame inmediatamente y no guarde trapos que estén húmedos con gasolina. El sistema de combustible de los modelos con inyección de combustible están bajo constante presión y si cualquiera de las líneas se van a desconectar, la presión en el sistema se debe de aliviar. Cuando usted conduzca cualquier tipo de trabajo en el sistema de combustible, use espejuelos de seguridad y tenga cerca un extintor de fuegos del tipo Clase B.*

Vehículos con carburador
Bomba mecánica
1   Localice la bomba de combustible en el lado delantero de la cabeza de los cilindros **(vea ilustración)**. Ponga trapos debajo de la bomba para colectar cualquier combustible rociado.
2   Desconecte las líneas de combustible de la bomba. Tápelas inmediatamente para prevenir fugas de combustible y la entrada de tierra **(vea ilustración)**.
3   Remueva las dos tuercas que conectan la bomba de combustible a la cabeza de los cilindros. **Nota:** *En algunos modelos, el*

soporte para elevar el motor tendrá que ser removido para obtener espacio libre.
4   Levante la bomba de la cabeza de los cilindros.
5   La instalación se hace en el orden inverso al procedimiento de desensamble.

Bomba eléctrica
Nota: *Si falta de combustible está ocurriendo, el filtro de la bomba de combustible puede estar obstruido. Vea el Paso 12 abajo.*
6   Si es necesario de obtener espacio libre, levanta la esquina trasera derecha del vehículo y lo sostiene encima de estantes.
7   Localice la bomba de combustible en riel del chasis, debajo del lado derecho del vehículo **(vea ilustraciones)**. Remueva el protector de la bomba de combustible.
8   Ponga trapos o un recipiente adecuado debajo de la bomba para colectar cualquier combustible. Entonces desconecte las líneas de combustible de la bomba y tápelas inmediatamente.
9   Desconecte el conector del alambrado que se dirige a la bomba.
10   Remueva los pernos que conectan la bomba a su soporte y levante la bomba hacia afuera.
11   La instalación se hace en el orden inverso al procedimiento de desensamble.
12   Porque no es una porción del itinerario de mantenimiento rutinario, el siguiente procedimiento no está en el Capítulo 1. Pero se debe notar que la bomba de combustible eléctrica en los vehículos con carburador tienen un filtro reemplazable que se debe inspeccionar en el primer signo de cualquier problema de falta de combustible o cuando la bomba de combustible sea removida.
13   Desconecte el cable negativo de la terminal negativa de la batería.
14   Desconecte y tape la línea del suplemento de combustible en la bomba de combustible.
15   Desconecte el alambre de conexión a tierra conectado a la bomba, entonces remueva la tapa de la bomba de combustible, tenga cuidado de no perder el imán de la

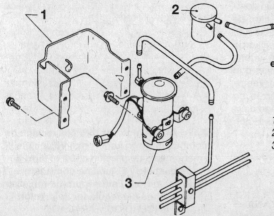

8.7b Una vista esquemática del ensamblaje típico de la bomba de combustible eléctrica en los modelos más modernos con carburador

1   *Protector*
2   *Filtro de combustible*
3   *Bomba de combustible eléctrica*

8.16 Una vista esquemática de la bomba de combustible eléctrica usada en los vehículos con carburador

1   Cilindro del émbolo
2   Albergue
3   Émbolo
4   Resorte de regreso
5   Válvula de admisión
6   Anillo de tipo O
7   Arandela
8   Retenedor del resorte
9   Junta
10 Filtro
11 Junta de la cubierta
12 Magneto
13 Cubierta
14 Alambre de tierra

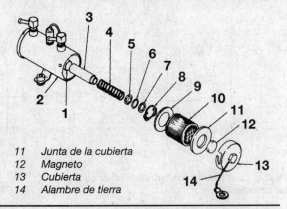

tapa ni la junta de la tapa, que están adentro de la tapa.

16   Deslice el filtro fuera del albergue de la bomba (vea ilustración) y lo inspecciona por daño.

17   Vuelva a instalar el filtro viejo, o uno nuevo si la inspección indica una necesidad.

18   Limpie el cuerpo del imán completamente y lo vuelve a instalar en la tapa, con una junta para la tapa nueva. Conecte el alambre de conexión a tierra y conecte la manguera de suplemento de combustible. Después de conectar de nuevo el cable negativo de la batería, ponga el motor en marcha y chequee por fugas alrededor de la bomba de combustible.

Vehículos con combustible inyectado

19   En los vehículos con combustible inyectados, la bomba de combustible eléctrica está instalada en el tanque de combustible.

20   Alivie la presión del combustible (vea Sección 14).

21   Desconecte el cable del terminal negativo de la batería.

22   Levante el vehículo y colóquelo firmemente sobre estantes.

23   Remueva el tanque de combustible (vea Sección 20).

24   Remueva la bomba de combustible/enviador de la unidad emisora de combustible usando un punzón de bronce y un martillo para girarlo a la derecha. **Peligro:** *Chispa causada por el uso de un destornillador o un punzón hecho de otro material que de bronce podría causar una explosión.*

25   Levante la bomba de combustible/ensamblaje de la unidad emisora del tanque.

26   Separe la bomba de combustible de la unidad emisora.

27   La instalación se hace en el orden inverso al procedimiento de desensamble.

9   Carburador - información general

El carburador es del tipo de absorción hacia abajo, de dos barriles. La mariposa primaria es operada mecánicamente mientras que la secundaria es operada por vacío por una unidad de diafragma que es accionada por vacío de venturi del carburador.

Un estrangulador automático de tipo bimetal eléctrico es incorporado. Este opera una mariposa que cierra uno de los barriles de venturi y es sincronizado con el plato del acelerador primario (el posterior se abre para proporcionar una mezcla suficientemente rica y una velocidad de marcha mínima aumentada para facilitar el arranque).

Para marcha mínima y marcha lenta, el combustible pasa a través de la esprea de marcha lenta, la purga de aire primaria lenta y la purga lenta del aire secundario. El combustible es finalmente expulsado de la desviación y los orificios de marcha mínima. Una válvula de tipo solenoide Anti diesel (solenoide para detener que el motor continúe en marcha) es incorporada para asegurar que el suministro del combustible se corte cuando la ignición sea apagada, así previniendo que el motor continúe en marcha.

La bomba aceleradora es sincronizada con la mariposa del acelerador. Durante los períodos de aceleración pesada, la bomba, que es de construcción de un solo pistón y una válvula, proporciona una cantidad medida adicional de combustible para enriquecer la mezcla normal.

El sistema secundario proporciona una mezcla para condiciones impulsoras normales por medio de una esprea principal y purga de aire. En algunos carburadores, un circuito adicional de alta velocidad es incorporado. Se compone de una esprea más rica, purga de aire más rica, garganta más rica y permite que el combustible adicional sea absorbido en el barril secundario según la velocidad de aire aumenta.

Un dispositivo BCDD (dispositivo para el control de la presión en desaceleración) es incorporado en algunos modelos para reducir los hidrocarburos emitidos (que tiende a ocurrir en exceso durante periodos de sobre corrida del motor) cuando la mezcla de aire/combustible en la cámara de combustión está muy pobre para permitir una combustión completa. El sistema BCDD se compone de una válvula solenoide de control de vacío y un interruptor que detecta la velocidad y un amplificador (transmisión manual) o un interruptor inhibidor (transmisión automática). Más información sobre el BCDD está proporcionado en el Capítulo 6.

En los carburadores usados en los modelos de transmisión automática (y algu-nos modelos de transmisión manual) un sistema de amortiguador es incorporado para reducir el valor en que la mariposa primaria del acelerador se cierra cuando se libere repentinamente. Esto reduce cualquier tendencia que el motor se atasque, particularmente cuando está frío.

Carburadores usados en ciertos modelos usan un compensador de altitud para corregir una mezcla de otro modo demasiado rica que puede ocurrir en altitudes.

La cámara del flotador está alimentada con una bomba de combustible por la bomba operada mecánicamente en el cárter del cigüeñal o la bomba eléctrica (ciertos modelos). El nivel en la cámara es crítico y debe ser mantenido siempre como está especificado.

El tornillo para la proporción de la mezcla del aire/combustible en todos los modelos 1981 y 1982 están en receso en el carburador. El tornillo para la proporción de la mezcla en los modelos 1980 es accesible. Este ajuste debe ser chequeado periódicamente. Ajuste apropiado debe ser hecho mientras está usando el equipo especial de detección de emisiones, haciéndolo un poco no muy práctico para el mecánico del hogar. Para hacer que la mezcla de la marcha mínima sea chequeada o ajustada, lleve su vehículo a un concesionario Nissan u otro taller mecánico calificado con el equipo apropiado.

10   Estrangulador automático - probar

Refiérase a las ilustraciones 10.6 y 10.10

Mecanismo del estrangulador automático

1   Con el motor frío, presione completamente el pedal del acelerador para cerrar la mariposa del estrangulador.

2   Remueva el purificador de aire y empuje la mariposa del estrangulador hacia adentro para chequear si se atora.

3   En los modelos 1980, chequee que la marca índice de la tapa bimetal esté correctamente ajustada al centro de la marca índice en el albergue del estrangulador. La marca índice de la tapa bimetal no se debe poner en ninguna otra posición.

4   Asegúrese que el alambrado del conector que se dirige al mecanismo del estrangulador esté firmemente conectado. Entonces ponga el motor en marcha y permita que se caliente a la temperatura de operación normal. En este punto la mariposa del estrangulador debe estar abierta completamente.

5   Si el ensamblaje del estrangulador no opera como está descrito, realice los otros chequeos descritos en la siguiente sub secciones. Si estos chequean bien, entonces la tapa bimetal (en los modelos 1980) o el ensamblaje de la cámara del estrangulador (en los modelos 1981 y 1982) deben ser reemplazados.

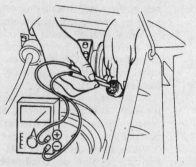

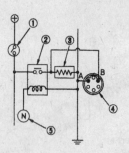

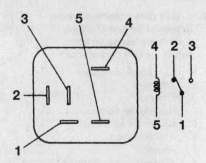

10.6 Identificación de las terminales A y B para el chequeo de la continuidad del circuito de calentamiento del estrangulador

1   Interruptor de la ignición
2   Relé del estrangulador automático
3   Estrangulador automático de la calefacción
4   Conector para la prueba
5   Alternador

10.10 Identificación de las terminales para el relé del estrangulador

1   Desde la posición IG
2   Al calentador del estrangulador automático
3   No es usado
4   Desde el alternador
5   Desde el interruptor de la ignición

Circuito del estrangulador automático por calefacción

6   Con el motor apagado, desconecte el conector del alambrado del estrangulador automático y conecte los alambres de un probador de continuidad a las terminales A y B **(vea ilustración)**. No los conecte a ninguna otras terminales. Si continuidad existe, el circuito está funcionando apropiadamente. Si ninguna continuidad existe, chequee por un alambre desconectado o roto. Un circuito abierto en la unidad de la calefacción podría ser también el problema y debe ser chequeado como está descrito en la siguiente sub sección.

7   Después, ponga el motor en marcha y conecte los alambres de un voltímetro a las terminales A y B. Una lectura en el voltímetro de 12 voltios debe ser indicada. Si el voltímetro lee cero, chequee por un alambre desconectado o roto, un circuito abierto o el relé del estrangulador defectuoso.

Unidad de la calefacción del estrangulador automático

8   Con el conector del alambrado del estrangulador automático desconectado, conecte un alambre de un ohmímetro al conector y el otro alambre al cuerpo del carburador. Una resistencia de 3.7 a 8.9 ohm se debe indicar. Si no, el ensamblaje de la cámara del estrangulador debe ser reemplazado.

Relé del estrangulador automático

9   Remueva el relé del estrangulador, que está instalado próximo a la manija del freno de estacionamiento debajo del tablero.
10   Conecte los alambre de un probador de continuidad a las terminales 4 y 5 **(vea ilustración)**. Continuidad debe existir.
11   Después, conecte los alambres de las terminales 1 y 2. Otra vez, continuidad debe existir.
12   Conecte los alambres a las terminales 1 y 3. Esta vez no debe indicar continuidad.
13   Ahora, use alambres puente para conec-

tar las terminales 4 y 5 a las terminales de una batería de 12 voltios y otra vez chequee por continuidad entre las terminales 1 y 2 y después las terminales 1 y 3. Con el poder aplicado, ninguna continuidad debe existir entre las terminales 1 y 2, mientras que continuidad debe existir entre las terminales 1 y 3.
14   Si la prueba no resulta como está descrito encima, reemplace el relé con uno nuevo.

11   Carburador - ajustes

Proporción de la mezcla del aire/combustible

1   Aunque el tornillo de la proporción de la mezcla de ajuste es accesible en los modelos 1980, el procedimiento es crítico y equipo especial es necesario para hacerlo. En los modelos 1981 y 1982, el tornillo de ajuste de la proporción de la mezcla para la marcha mínima es ajustado en la fábrica y entonces sellado con un tapón de acero. En los vehículos 1984 y 1985, la proporción de aire/combustible es ajustada automáticamente por un solenoide instalado en el cuerpo del carburador. Así que, ningún tornillo de mezcla de aire/combustible es incorporado. Por estas razones, nosotros recomendamos que cualquier ajuste de la proporción de la mezcla que sea necesario (debido a la reconstrucción completa del carburador, etc.) sea hecho por un concesionario Nissan o un taller de reparaciones.

Nivel del combustible

Refiérase a las ilustraciones 11.2 y 11.6

2   Con el motor en marcha mínima, chequee el nivel del combustible en la cámara del flotador observando la ventana en el frente del carburador **(vea ilustración)**. El nivel del combustible debe estar en el punto indicado (punto pequeño) en el centro de la ventana.
3   Si el nivel del combustible está encima o debajo de este punto, el flotador debe ser ajustado, que requiere que se remueva el carburador.
4   Desconecte la línea de combustible del

carburador y ponga el motor en marcha hasta que se detenga por falta de combustible.
5   Refiérase a la Sección 12 y remueva del motor el carburador, entonces remueva la tapa de la cámara del flotador del carburador.
6   Gire el carburador al revés para que el flotador entre en contacto con la válvula de aguja. Mida la dimensión H **(vea ilustración)**. Si esta medida es de 0.283 pulgada (7.2 mm), la posición superior del flotador está correcta. Si no, doble el asiento del flotador para traerlo al ajuste apropiado.
7   Después, levante completamente el flotador y mida la dimensión H en la figura que acompaña, entre el asiento del flotador y el vástago de la válvula de aguja. El ajuste apropiado es de 0.051 a 0.067 pulgada (1.3 a 1.7 mm). Si es necesario, doble el detenedor del flotador para traerlo al ajuste apropiado.
8   Vuelva a instalar la tapa de la cámara del flotador y el carburador. Con el motor en marcha mínima, otra vez chequee el nivel del combustible en el punto del indicador en la ventana.

11.2 La ventana para la inspección del nivel del combustible está localizada en el frente del carburador - si el nivel del combustible está correcto, estará en el punto indicado (el punto pequeño) en el centro de la ventana

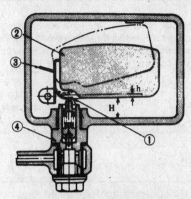

11.6 El nivel del combustible del carburador es ajustado ajustando las dimensiones H de la instalación h encima de las especificaciones apropiadas

1   Asiento del flotador
2   Flotador
3   Detenedor del flotador
4   Válvula de tipo aguja

Ruptor por vacío

Refiérase a la ilustración 11.11

9   Este mecanismo abre el plato del estrangulador después que el motor se haya comenzado para proporcionar la proporción de la mezcla correcta de aire/combustible bajo las condiciones predominantes de la operación del motor.

10   El ajuste correcto debe ser chequeado y cualquier ajuste ser ejecutado en la siguiente manera. Cierre el plato del estrangulador completamente con los dedos y retenga el plato de la válvula en esta posición usando una goma conectada entre la palanca del interruptor de vacío y el cuerpo del carburador.

11   Con un par de alicates, agarre el extremo de la varilla de operación del diafragma de la cápsula de vacío y retírelo hacia afuera lo más que se pueda sin ser forzado. Ahora doble la varilla (si es necesario) para

proporcionar un espacio libre entre la orilla del plato del estrangulador y el cuerpo del carburador (distancia B) según se otorgan en las especificaciones **(vea ilustración).**

Descargador del estrangulador

12   Cierre el plato de la mariposa del estrangulador completamente con los dedos y retenga el plato de la válvula en esta posición usando una goma conectada entre la palanca de interrupción de vacío y el cuerpo del carburador.

13   Hale la palanca del acelerador hasta que se abra completamente y doble la lengua del descargador (si es necesario) para proporcionar un espacio libre entre el estrangulador y el cuerpo del carburador como es indicado en las especificaciones.

Ajuste del amortiguador

14   Ponga el motor en marcha a la temperatura normal de operación y chequee que el ajuste para la velocidad de la marcha mínima (Capítulo 1) sea correcto. También, el aire acondicionado debe estar apagado.

15   Libere la contratuerca del amortiguador y entonces ajuste la posición del amortiguador hasta que acabe de tocar en el plato de parada cuando el motor esté en marcha en la velocidad indicada en las especificaciones.

16   Apriete la contratuerca sin mover el amortiguador.

17   Levante la velocidad del motor acerca de 2000 rpm y libere repentinamente el acelerador. La velocidad del motor debe ser reducida a 1000 rpm en aproximadamente tres segundos, de otro modo el ajuste se llevó a cabo incorrectamente o el amortiguador está defectuoso.

Abertura de entrecierre de las válvulas del acelerador

Refiérase a la ilustración 11.18

18   Chequee que cuando el plato primario del acelerador esté abierto a 50 grados, el plato de ajuste del acelerador esté en contacto con el plato de regreso en el punto A **(vea ilustración)**. Abra el plato del acelerador adicionalmente y chequee que el brazo de enclavamiento esté separado del brazo secundario del acelerador, para permitir que el sistema secundario funcione. Doble la palanca de conexión, si es necesario, para obtener la distancia especificada entre el plato del acelerador y la pared interior de la cámara del acelerador.

Marcha mínima rápida

Modelos 1980 al 1983

Refiérase a las ilustraciones 11.20 y 11.21

19   Remueva del motor el carburador, como se indica en la Sección 12.

20   Use un medidor de alambre (o una broca) para medir el espacio libre A **(vea ilustración)** entre la mariposa del acelerador y los barriles del carburador, mientras el lado superior del tornillo de marcha mínima rápida está en el segundo paso de la leva para la velocidad de la marcha mínima rápida. Refiérase a las especificaciones para el espacio libre apropiado.

21   Si el juego libre no está como se especifica, gire el tornillo de la marcha mínima rápida hasta que el espacio libre esté ajustado correctamente **(vea ilustración)**.

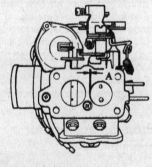

Pasos para la leva de la marcha mínima rápida

4th
3rd
2nd
1st

11.20 Para ajustar la marcha mínima rápida, establezca la dimensión del espacio libre A con la marcha mínima rápida puesta en la segunda parada de la leva para la velocidad de la marcha mínima rápida (1980 al 1983)

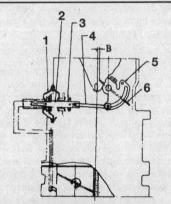

11.11 Para ajustar el interruptor de vacío, establezca la dimensión B

1   Cubierta del diafragma
2   Pistón de ruptura por vacío
3   Resorte del estrangulador
4   Varilla del ruptor por vacío
5   Palanca del ruptor por vacío
6   Estrangulador

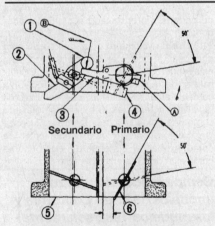

Secundario   Primario

11.18 Cuando esté ajustando la abertura de enganche de la mariposa del acelerador, el espacio libre entre la mariposa del acelerador y la pared de la cámara debe ser ajustada a las especificaciones apropiadas

1   Rodillo
2   Palanca de conexión
3   Plato de regreso
4   Plato ajustable
5   Cámara del acelerador
6   Mariposa del acelerador

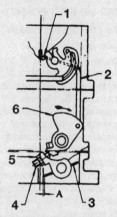

11.21 Si el juego libre no está como se especifica, gire el tornillo de la marcha mínima rápida hasta que el espacio libre esté correcto (1980 al 1983)

1   *Estrangulador*
2   *Varilla para el estrangulador*
3   *Mariposa del acelerador*
4   *Tornillo para la marcha rápida*
5   *Tuerca*
6   *Leva para la marcha mínima rápida*

Modelos 1984 y 1985

Refiérase a la ilustración 11.23

22   Caliente el motor y chequee que las rpm (revoluciones por minuto) y la regulación del tiempo de la ignición estén ajustados apropiadamente.
23   Ponga el brazo de la marcha mínima rápida en el paso 2 de la leva para la velocidad de la marcha mínima rápida **(vea ilustración)**.
24   Conecte un tacómetro al motor siguiendo las instrucciones del fabricante.
25   Chequee que las rpm de la marcha mínima rápida esté como se especifica en la Sección de las Especificaciones al frente de este Capítulo.
26   Si ajuste es requerido, gire el tornillo de ajuste de la marcha mínima rápida.

Bomba del acelerador

Refiérase a la ilustración 11.27

27   Realice un chequeo visual de la bomba del acelerador por cualquier signo de fuga de combustible **(vea ilustración)**. Si cualquiera es encontrado, la junta debe ser reempla-

11.27 Ubicación de la bomba aceleradora

zada con una nueva.
28   Al observar hacia abajo del barril de carburador, gire la mariposa del acelerador a mano y asegúrese que el combustible está inyectando en la garganta. Una linterna puede ser útil en verificar esto. Si esto no ocurre, el carburador se tendrá que remover para corregir el problema. Refiérase a la Sección 12.

Válvula de tipo solenoide Anti diesel (solenoide para detener que el motor continúe en marcha)

29   Esta válvula debe ser chequeada si el motor continúa corriendo después que el interruptor de la ignición se haya apagado, o si el motor no continua en marcha mientras está en marcha mínima.
30   Según el motor está en marcha mínima, desconecte el alambre que se dirige al solenoide de Anti diesel (solenoide para detener que el motor continúe en marcha). Si el motor no para de correr, realice el siguiente chequeo.
31   Use un voltímetro o luz de prueba para chequear el conector del alambrado para estar seguro que hay voltaje cuando el interruptor de la ignición esté Encendido. Si la corriente alcanza la válvula, el ensamblaje de la válvula solenoide debe ser reemplazado como una unidad. Si la corriente no alcanza la válvula, refiérase a los procedimientos de como probar el sistema de combustible como está descrito en el Capítulo 6.

Compensador de altitud (modelos 1981 de California y los modelos 1982 solamente)

32   El compensador de la altitud está diseñado para operar encima de una altitud de 1969 pies (600 m). No es ajustable y si está defectuoso debe ser reemplazado con uno nuevo. Las mangueras son codificadas con colores, según los acopladores están conectados en la unidad.
33   Si el compensador está operando en altitudes bajas, los siguientes síntomas se deben de notar: titubeo y tropiezo cuando se ponga en marcha, oleada mientras está en crucero acerca de 50 mph (80 km.), tambaleo cuando se acelere de 50 a 70 mph (80 a 112

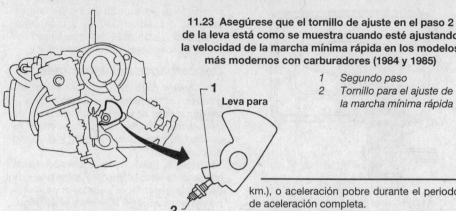

11.23 Asegúrese que el tornillo de ajuste en el paso 2 de la leva está como se muestra cuando esté ajustando la velocidad de la marcha mínima rápida en los modelos más modernos con carburadores (1984 y 1985)

1   *Segundo paso*
2   *Tornillo para el ajuste de la marcha mínima rápida*

km.), o aceleración pobre durante el periodo de aceleración completa.
34   Si el compensador no está trabajando en altitudes más altas, los siguientes síntomas se pueden experimentar: la velocidad del motor no aumenta en respuesta correcta a la depresión del acelerador, titubeo o oleadas cuando se comienza, aceleración pobre con la mariposa completamente abierta o corriendo suavemente con el acelerador parcialmente abierto. Éstos dependen en la altitud del vehículo.
35   El compensador es chequeado desconectando las mangueras de vacío de entrada y de salida y soplando aire a través de ellos. Si esto es hecho a una altitud baja y el aire fluye suavemente, la unidad está defectuosa y debe ser reemplazada. Si la prueba es realizada en una altitud alta y el aire no fluye suavemente, la unidad debe ser reemplazada con una nueva.

12   Carburador - remover, reconstrucción completa e instalar

Refiérase a las ilustraciones 12.7 y 12.11
Peligro: *La gasolina es sumamente inflamable, así que se deben tomar precauciones extras cuando esté trabajando en cualquier parte del sistema del combustible. No fume, deje llamas abiertas o bombillas sin cubierta cerca del área de trabajo. También, no trabaje en un garaje si un aparato de gas natural con un piloto encendido está presente. Debido a que la gasolina es dañina para su piel use guantes cuando halla una posibilidad de que entre en contacto con su piel y si se le derrama cualquier cantidad en su piel límpiese inmediatamente con suficiente agua y jabón. Limpie cualquier derrame inmediatamente y no guarde trapos que estén húmedos con gasolina. El sistema de combustible de los modelos con inyección de combustible están bajo constante presión y si cualquiera de las líneas se van a desconectar, la presión en el sistema se debe de aliviar. Cuando usted conduzca cualquier tipo de trabajo en el sistema de combustible, use espejuelos de seguridad y tenga cerca un extintor de fuegos del tipo Clase B.*

Modelos 1980 al 1983

1   Remueva el purificador de aire.
2   Desconecte las líneas de combustible y de vacío del carburador, estando seguro de

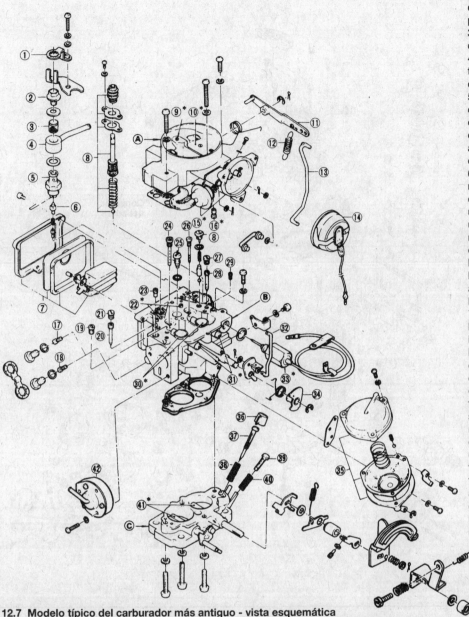

marcarlas en cuanto a sus lugares de instalación. Tape inmediatamente todas las líneas para prevenir la entrada de tierra.

3   Desconecte el cable del acelerador del carburador.

4   Desconecte todos los alambres conectados al carburador, note otra vez notando donde ellos se conectan.

5   Remueva las tuercas que conectan el carburador al múltiple de admisión y remueva el carburador. Esté seguro que usted no deja caer ninguna parte adentro del múltiple de admisión, porque el múltiple quizás tenga que ser removido.

6   Una vez que se determine que el carburador necesita ajuste o una reconstrucción completa, varias opciones son disponible. Si usted va a tratar de reconstruir el carburador usted mismo, obtenga primero un juego de reconstrucción para carburador de buena calidad (que incluirá todas las juntas necesarias, las partes internas, las instrucciones y una lista de las partes). Usted necesitará también algún solvente especial y un medio de soplar los pasajes internos del carburador con aire.

7   Porque los vehículos cubiertos por este libro son principalmente de combustible inyectado (todos los vehículos Canadienses y los modelos 1984 US están equipados con carburadores) y debido a que los diseños de carburadores son constantemente modificados por el fabricante en orden de reunir todas las regulaciones cada vez más rigurosas de las emisiones, no es posible para nosotros hacer un paso a paso de cada tipo de reconstrucción completa. Usted recibirá un juego bien ilustrado detallado de las instrucciones con cualquier juego de reconstrucción completa de carburador; ellos se aplicarán en una manera más específica al carburador en su vehículo. Una vista esquemática de los carburadores más típicos está incluida aquí **(vea ilustracion)**.

12.7 Modelo típico del carburador más antiguo - vista esquemática

1 Palanca de cerradura	18 Esprea principal secundaria	35 Partes de la cámara del diafragma
2 Tornillo para el Filtro	19 Purga de aire secundaria lenta	36 Tapa para el límite de la marcha mínima
3 Filtro de combustible	20 Esprea lenta secundaria	
4 Tetilla para el combustible	21 Tapón	37 Tornillo para el ajuste de la marcha mínima
5 Cuerpo para la aguja de la válvula	22* Purga de aire	
6 Válvula de tipo aguja	23 Esprea que costear	38 Resorte para el ajuste del tornillo de la marcha mínima
7 Partes de la cámara del combustible	24 Purga principal de aire secundario	
8 Partes de la bomba del acelerador	25 Válvula de poder	39 Tornillo para el ajuste de la marcha mínima
9* Enriquecedor de alta velocidad purga de aire	26 Purga de aire principal primario	
10* Mariposa del estrangulador	27 Tapón	40 Resorte para el tornillo de ajuste de la marcha mínima
11 Palanca de la bomba del acelerador	28 Esprea lenta primaria	
12 Resorte de retorno de la mariposa del carburador	29 Purga de aire lenta primaria	41* Mariposas del acelerador primaria y secundaria
13 Varilla de la bomba del acelerador	30* Venturi primaria y secundaria pequeña	
14 Tapa del estrangulador automático	31* Tornillo del tapón del venturi	42 Unidad para el control del aire de desviación
15* Cuerpo de estrangulador automático y diafragma ruptor por vacío	32 Varilla del estrangulador	A Cámara del estrangulador
	33 Válvula del solenoide Anti diesel (solenoide para detener que el motor continúe en marcha)	B Cuerpo central
16* Esprea de enriquecimiento		C Cámara para la mariposa del acelerador
17 Esprea principal primaria	34 Leva para la velocidad de la marcha mínima rápida	*No remueva

12.11 Modelos 1984 y 1985 con carburador - vista esquemática

1 Plato de cerradura
2 Tornillo para el filtro
3 Tetilla para el combustible
4 Filtro de combustible
5 Cuerpo de la válvula de Aguja
6 Válvula de aguja
7 Esprea principal primaria
8 Purga del aire principal secundaria
9 Purga del aire principal primaria
10 B. C. D. D. (dispositivo para el control de la presión en desaceleración)
11 Purga lenta de aire secundaria
12 Esprea principal secundaria
13 Tapón
14 Esprea lenta secundaria
15 Compensador de la marcha mínima
16 Partes de la bomba de aceleración
17 Tapón para el mecanismo de aceleración
18 Tapón
19 Resorte
20 Esprea lenta primaria
21 Venturi primaria y secundaria pequeña
22 Tornillo de ajuste la mariposa del acelerador
23 Resorte para el tornillo de ajuste del acelerador
24 Palanca de la bomba de aceleración
25 Válvula solenoide Anti diesel (solenoide para detener que el motor continúe en marcha)
26 Tapón ciego
27 Tornillo de ajuste para la marcha mínima
28 Resorte para el tornillo de ajuste de la marcha mínima
29 Varilla del estrangulador
30 Partes de la cámara del diafragma
31 Interruptor del acelerador
32 Plano
33 Solenoide para la proporción del aire combustible
34 Tapa de ventilación del aire
35 Amortiguador para la velocidad

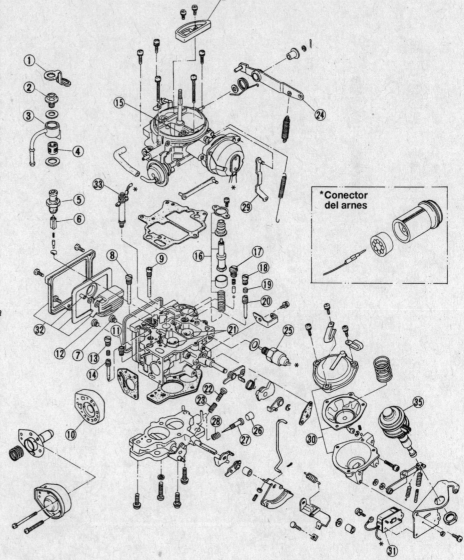

*Conector del arnes

8   Otra alternativa es de obtener un carburador nuevo o reconstruido. Ellos están disponible en los concesionarios y refaccionarías. Esté absolutamente seguro que el carburador de intercambio es idéntico al original. Una etiqueta es generalmente conectada al carburador. Ayudará a determinar el tipo exacto de carburador que usted tiene. Cuando obtenga un carburador reconstruido o un juego de reconstrucción, tómese el tiempo para asegurarse que el juego o el carburador son exactamente para su aplicación. Las diferencias aparentemente insignificantes pueden hacer una diferencia grande en el desempeño de su motor.

9   Si usted escoge reconstruir su propio carburador, permita suficiente tiempo para remover el carburador cuidadosamente, empape las partes necesarias en solvente de limpiar (generalmente por lo menos un medio día o según las instrucciones listadas en el

limpiador de carburador) y vuelva a ensamblarlo, que tomará generalmente mucho más tiempo que desarmarlo. Cuando remueva el carburador, empareje cada parte con la ilustración en el juego del carburador y coloque cada parte en orden en una superficie de trabajo limpia. Las reconstrucciones por mecánicos sin experiencia pueden resultar en un motor que marcha mal o marcha en lo absoluto. Para evitar esto, tenga cuidado y paciencia cuando remueva el carburador para que usted lo pueda volver a instalar correctamente.

10   La instalación se hace en el orden inverso al procedimiento de desensamble.

Modelos 1984 y 1985

11   Solamente cambios insignificante han sido hechos a los carburadores de modelos más modernos y por lo tanto la mayor parte de la información de encima aplicará. Una

vista esquemática del carburador 1984/1985 ha sido incluida aquí para su conveniencia **(vea ilustración)**.

---

13   Sistema EFI (inyección de combustible electrónica) - información general

Refiérase a las ilustraciones 13.1a y 13.1b
Nota: *Los esquemas muestran los componentes típico de los modelos 1990 y más modernos. Cuando realice los procedimientos en este Capítulo, refiérase a la fotografía apropiada para la ubicación de los componentes.*

Los motores en los vehículos más modernos usan un sistema EFI (inyección de combustible electrónica). Ellos están equipados con TBI (cuerpo de inyección de com-

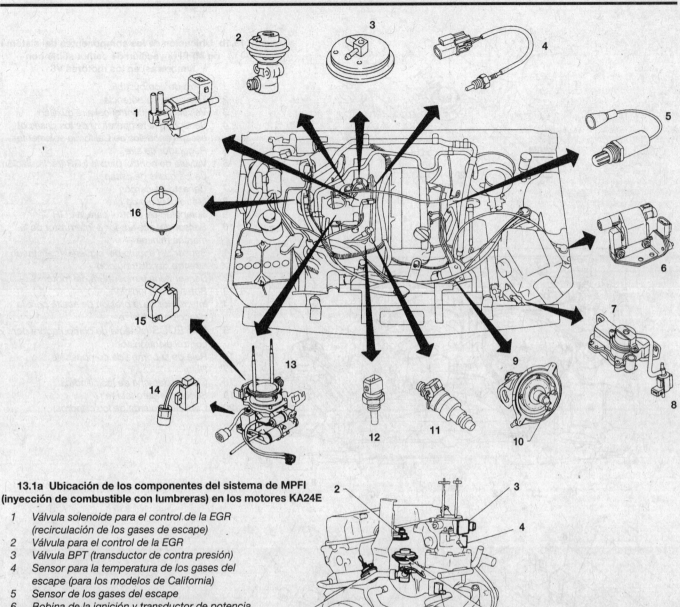

13.1a Ubicación de los componentes del sistema de MPFI (inyección de combustible con lumbreras) en los motores KA24E

1   *Válvula solenoide para el control de la EGR (recirculación de los gases de escape)*
2   *Válvula para el control de la EGR*
3   *Válvula BPT (transductor de contra presión)*
4   *Sensor para la temperatura de los gases del escape (para los modelos de California)*
5   *Sensor de los gases del escape*
6   *Bobina de la ignición y transductor de potencia*
7   *Albergue de la AIV (válvula de inyección de aire)*
8   *Válvula solenoide para el control de la AIV*
9   *Distribuidor*
10 *Sensor del ángulo del cigüeñal*
11 *Inyector*
12 *Sensor de la temperatura del motor*
13 *Cámara del acelerador*
14 *Sensor del acelerador*
15 *Metro para el flujo de aire*
16 *Filtro de combustible*

bustible) o MPFI (inyección de combustible con lumbreras). La inyección de combustible electrónica proporciona una mezcla óptima y esto, junto con las características inmediatas de respuesta de la inyección de combustible, permite que el motor corra en la mezcla posiblemente más pobre de aire/combustible. Esto reduce vastamente la emisión tóxica de los gases del escape. El sistema de combustible es correlacionado con y trabaja en conjunto con los controles de emisiones y sistemas de escape cubiertos en el Capítulo 6.

Así, algunos elementos que se relacionan directamente al sistema de combustible son cubiertos en este Capítulo.

El sistema de EFI (inyección de combustible electrónica) se compone de tres subsistemas: El sistema del flujo de combustible, el flujo del sistema de aire y el sistema eléctrico de señales. Los varios componentes que componen el sistema completo del sistema EFI son detallados en la Sección 13.

El combustible del tanque es entregado bajo presión por una bomba de combustible

eléctrica. La cantidad del combustible para ser inyectado es determinado por la duración del pulso del inyector también como por una diferencia de presión entre la presión del combustible y la presión de vacío del múltiple de admisión. La unidad de control ECCS (sistema de computadora por control electrónico) controla solamente la duración del pulso del inyector. Por esta razón, la diferencia de presión entre la presión del combustible y la presión de vacío del múltiple de admisión se debe mantener en un nivel cons-

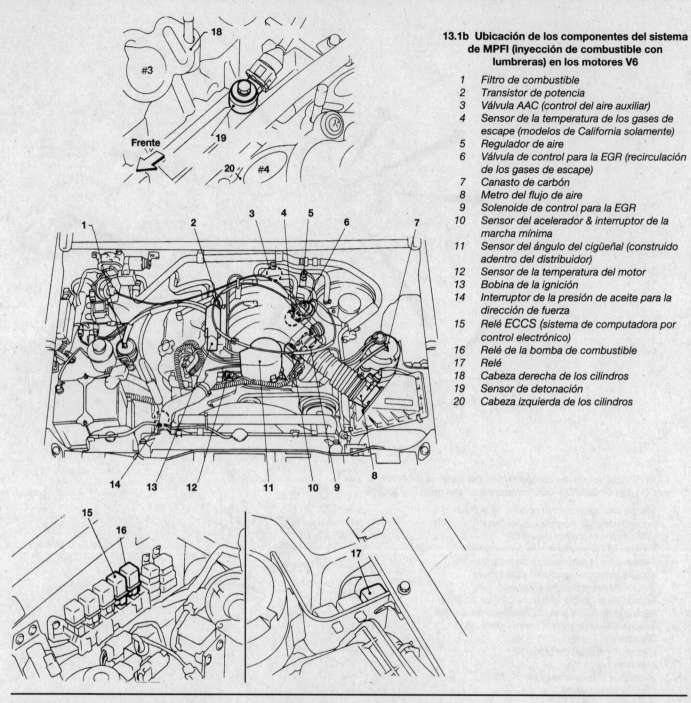

13.1b Ubicación de los componentes del sistema de MPFI (inyección de combustible con lumbreras) en los motores V6

1   Filtro de combustible
2   Transistor de potencia
3   Válvula AAC (control del aire auxiliar)
4   Sensor de la temperatura de los gases de escape (modelos de California solamente)
5   Regulador de aire
6   Válvula de control para la EGR (recirculación de los gases de escape)
7   Canasto de carbón
8   Metro del flujo de aire
9   Solenoide de control para la EGR
10 Sensor del acelerador & interruptor de la marcha mínima
11 Sensor del ángulo del cigüeñal (construido adentro del distribuidor)
12 Sensor de la temperatura del motor
13 Bobina de la ignición
14 Interruptor de la presión de aceite para la dirección de fuerza
15 Relé ECCS (sistema de computadora por control electrónico)
16 Relé de la bomba de combustible
17 Relé
18 Cabeza derecha de los cilindros
19 Sensor de detonación
20 Cabeza izquierda de los cilindros

tante. Debido a que la presión de vacío del múltiple de admisión varía con las condiciones de operación del motor, un regulador de presión es colocado en la línea de combustible para regular la presión del combustible en respuesta a los cambios en la presión del múltiple de admisión. Donde las condiciones del múltiple son tales que la presión del combustible puede estar más allá de la especificada, el regulador de presión de combustible regresa al tanque el exceso de combustible.

Una inyección de combustible ocurre una vez cada rotación del motor. Porque la señal de la inyección proviene de la unidad de control, todos los inyectores operan simultáneamente e independiente de la carrera del motor (MPFI solamente). Cada inyección suministra la mitad de la cantidad del combustible requerido por el cilindro y la longitud del período de inyección es determinado por la información suministrada a la unidad del control por varios sensores incluidos en el sistema.

Los elementos que afectan la duración de la inyección incluyen: rpm del motor, la cantidad y la temperatura del aire de admisión, abertura de la mariposa del acelerador, la temperatura del anticongelante del motor, la presión del vacío del múltiple de admisión y la cantidad de oxígeno en los gases del escape.

Porque el sistema EFI (inyección de combustible electrónica) opera en presión alta de combustible, cualquier escape puede afectar la eficiencia del sistema y presentar un riesgo grave de fuego. También, debido a que el flujo del aire de admisión es crítico a la operación del sistema, todavía un escape de aire leve causará una mezcla inexacta de aire/combustible. **Nota:** Ciertas precauciones se deben observar cuando esté trabajando en el sistema de EFI (inyección de combustible electrónica):

a) *No desconecte ningún cable de la batería mientras el motor está en marcha.*

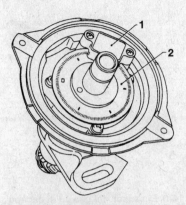

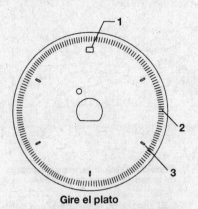

Gire el plato

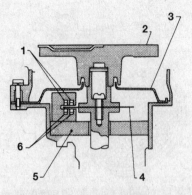

14.2a El sensor del ángulo del cigüeñal es el sensor principal de señales para el ECCS (sistema de computadora por control electrónico)

1   *Sensor del ángulo del cigüeñal*
2   *Plato rotor*

14.2b El plato rotor tiene 360 ranuras para indicar la velocidad del motor y seis aberturas para la señal del ángulo del cigüeñal

1   *Ranuras para la señal de 120 grados para el cilindro número 1*
2   *Ranura de señal de un grado*
3   *Ranuras para la señal de 120 grados*

14.2c La luz pasa a través de las ranuras en el plato del rotor, enviando señales en forma de pulsos a la unidad de control

1   *Diodo emisor de luz*
2   *Cabeza del rotor*
3   *Cubierta sellada*
4   *Rotor de tipo plato*
5   *Circuito formando hondas*
6   *Diodo fotográfico*

b) *Antes de cualquier operación en que la línea de combustible sea desconectada, la presión alta en el sistema se debe eliminar primero. Este procedimiento es descrito en la Sección 4. Desconecte el cable negativo de la terminal negativa de la batería para eliminar la posibilidad de que chispas ocurran mientras el combustible está presente.*

c) *Antes de remover cualquier componente del sistema EFI (inyección de combustible electrónica), esté seguro que el interruptor de la ignición esté Apagado y el cable negativo de la batería esté desconectado.*

d) *El conjunto del alambrado/arnés del sistema EFI (inyección de combustible electrónica) se debe mantener por lo menos cuatro pulgadas (10 mm) fuera de los arneses adyacentes. Esto incluye un cable de suministro para la antena de un radio CB (banda civil). Esto es para prevenir que los pulsos eléctricos en otros sistemas sean entrometidos con la operación del sistema EFI (inyección de combustible electrónica).*

e) *Esté seguro que todas las conexiones del alambrado del sistema EFI (inyección de combustible electrónica) están apretadas, limpias y seguras, porque una conexión pobre puede causar oleadas extremadamente altas de voltaje en la bobina para la ignición que podría drenar el circuito IC (control de la ignición).*

f) *El acelerador No se debe presionar antes de poner en marcha el motor. Inmediatamente después de haber comenzado, no eleve las revoluciones del motor innecesariamente.*

Los relevos usados en la bomba de combustible eléctrica, localizados en el compartimiento del motor, para que si el motor se para (causando que se detenga el alternador y la presión de aceite que se caiga), la bomba de combustible cesará de operar.

Algunos chequeos básicos de los componentes del sistema EFI (inyección de combustible electrónica) están incluidos en este Capítulo. Sin embargo, la complejidad del sistema previene que muchos problemas sean diagnosticados exactamente por el mecánico del hogar. Si un problema se desarrolla en el sistema que no puede ser localizado con toda precisión por los chequeos listados aquí, es mejor llevar el vehículo al departamento de servicio de su concesionario para localizar el defecto.

14   Componentes del ECCS (sistema de computadora por control electrónico) - información general

Sistema MPFI (inyección de combustible con lumbreras)

Refiérase a las ilustraciones 14.2a, 14.2b, 14.2c, 14.3, 14.4, 14.5, 14.6, 14.8, 14.9, 14.10, 14.11, 14.12, 14.14, 14.15, 14.16, 14.17, 14.18, 14.19, 14.20, 14.21 y 14.22.

Unidad de control ECCS (sistema de computadora por control electrónico)

1   La unidad ECCS, también conocida como ECU (unidad de control electrónica), es una micro computadora con conectores eléctricos para recibir la entrada/las señales de rendimiento y suministro de poder, luces de inspección y un selector de diagnóstico de modo. La unidad del control regula la cantidad del combustible que es inyectado, también como la regulación del tiempo de la ignición, velocidad de la marcha mínima, operación de la bomba de combustible y la retroalimentación de la proporción de la mezcla.

Sensor del ángulo del cigüeñal

2   El sensor del ángulo del cigüeñal se podría considerar como la mano derecha de la unidad de control ECCS, porque es la señal básica del sensor para el sistema completo del ECCS. Revisa la velocidad del motor, la posición del pistón y manda las señales a la unidad del control del ECCS para el control de la inyección de combustible, la regulación del tiempo de la ignición, la velocidad de la marcha mínima, la operación de la bomba de combustible y la función de la EGR (recirculación de los gases de escape) **(vea ilustraciones)**.

El sensor del ángulo del cigüeñal tiene un plato rotor y un circuito de formar ondas. El ensamblaje se compone de un plato rotor con 360 ranuras representando señales de un 1 grado (señal de la velocidad del motor) y seis aberturas para señales de 120 grados (señal del ángulo del cigüeñal). LED (diodos emisores de luz) y diodos fotográficos son construidos en el circuito de formar ondas.

En operación, el plato rotor de la señal pasa a través del espacio entre el LED y el diodo de fotografía y las aberturas en el plato del rotor de la señal corta intermitentemente la luz enviada al diodo de fotografía del LED. Esto causa un voltaje que alterna y es convertido en un pulso del circuito encendido/apagado en forma de onda. La señal de encendido/apagado es enviada a la unidad de control para procesar.

Medidor del flujo de aire

3   El medidor del flujo de aire mide la velocidad de la masa del aire admitido. El circuito del control emite una señal eléctrica de rendimiento que varía con relación a la cantidad de calor disipado de un alambre caliente colocado en el paso de aire de admisión **(vea ilustración)**.

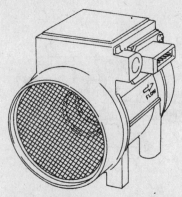

14.3 El medidor del flujo de aire mide el valor de la masa del aire de admisión

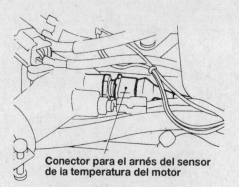

Conector para el arnés del sensor de la temperatura del motor

14.4 El sensor de la temperatura del motor está localizado en el albergue de admisión en la cabeza de los cilindros

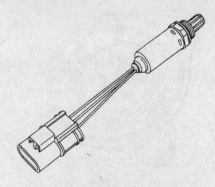

14.5 El sensor del gas en el escape chequea la calidad de oxígeno en el gas de escape

Sensor de la temperatura del motor

4   El sensor de la temperatura del motor detecta los cambios en la temperatura del anticongelante y envía la señal a la unidad del control del ECCS (sistema de computadora por control electrónico) (**vea ilustración**).

Sensor de los gases del escape

5   Instalado en el múltiple de escape, el sensor del gas de escape chequea la cantidad de oxígeno en los gases del escape (**vea ilustración**).

Interruptora del acelerador

6   El interruptor del acelerador está conectado en el exterior de la cámara del acelerador y acciona en respuesta al movimiento del pedal del acelerador. El interruptor está equipado con dos contactos, uno para la marcha mínima y el otro para el contacto con el acelerador completamente abierto. El contacto para la marcha mínima se cierra cuando la mariposa del acelerador está en la posesión de marcha mínima y se abre cuando está en cualquier otra posición. El contacto del acelerador completamente abierto es usado para las transmisiones automáticas controladas electrónicamente solamente (**vea ilustración**).

Sensor de la velocidad del vehículo

7   El sensor de la velocidad del vehículo proporciona una señal de velocidad a la unidad de control del ECCS (sistema de computadora por control electrónico). Dos tipos de sensores de velocidad son empleados, dependiendo en el tipo del velocímetro instalado. Los modelos con velocímetro del tipo de aguja utilizan un interruptor de lamina, que está instalado en la unidad del velocímetro y se transforma a velocidad del vehículo en una señal de pulso que es enviada a la unidad del control. El velocímetro de tipo digital se compone de un LED (diodo emisor de luz), diodo de foto, obturador y un circuito de formar ondas.

Sensor de la temperatura de los gases de escape (modelos de California solamente)

8   El sensor de la temperatura del gas del escape chequea la temperatura del gas de

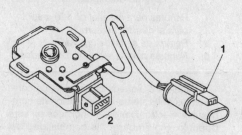

14.6 El interruptor de la apertura del acelerador informa a la unidad de control cuando el acelerador está en marcha mínima y en los modelos equipados con transmisiones controladas eléctricamente informa a la unidad de control cuando el acelerador está completamente abierto

1   Conector para el sensor del acelerador
2   Conector para el interruptor de la marcha mínima

escape y envía la información a la ECU (unidad de control electrónica). La información es usada para controlar la mezcla del aire y el combustible (**vea ilustración**).

Sensor de detonación

9   Conectado en el bloque de los cilindros, el sensor de detonación es capaz de detectar condiciones de detonación en el motor. Cualquier vibración de detonación del bloque de los cilindros es aplicado al elemento eléctrico. Esta presión es entonces convertida en una señal de voltaje que es entregada como señal de rendimiento a la unidad del control (**vea ilustración**).

Inyector de combustible

10   El inyector del combustible suministra combustible a cada cilindro. El inyector es una válvula solenoide pequeña de precisión. Según la unidad de control ECCS envía una señal de inyección a cada inyector de combustible, la bobina construida en la parte interna del inyector hala la aguja hacia atrás y el combustible es atomizado adentro del múltiple de admisión. La cantidad de combustible inyectado es controlado por la uni-

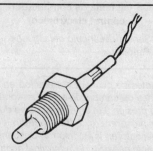

14.8 El sensor de la temperatura del gas en el escape permite que el módulo de control ECCS (sistema de computadora por control electrónico) sepa la temperatura del escape

dad ECCS, que controla la duración del pulso de la inyección (**vea ilustración**).

Transistor de potencia

11   La señal de la ignición de la unidad de control del ECCS es amplificada por el transistor de poder, que conecta y desconecta el circuito primario de la bobina para inducir el voltaje alto apropiado en el circuito secundario (**vea ilustración**).

Bobina para la ignición

12   La bobina de tipo moldeada para la ignición proporciona la chispa para el proceso de la combustión (**vea ilustración**).

Válvula AAC (control del aire auxiliar)

13   La válvula AAC está conectada al colector de admisión. La unidad del control ECCS acciona la válvula AAC por pulsos de apagado/encendido. Lo más largo que la señal esté encendida, la mayor cantidad de aire que será permitido fluir a través de la válvula AAC.

Unidad IAA (ajustador para la marcha mínima)

14   La unidad IAA está compuesta de la válvula AAC y el tornillo de ajuste para la marcha mínima. Recibe la señal de la ECU (unidad de control electrónica) y controla la velocidad de la marcha mínima fija a un valor predeterminado (**vea ilustración**).

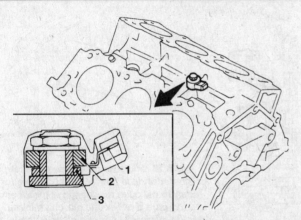

14.9 Un sensor de detonación está instalado en el bloque del motor en los modelos más modernos para detectar las condiciones de detonación del motor

1 Terminal
2 Peso
3 Elemento Piezoeléctrico

14.10 El inyector del combustible recibe una señal de la unidad del control y la válvula de aguja para abrir el inyector de combustible en el múltiple de admisión - la cantidad del combustible inyectado es determinado por la duración del pulso

1 Tobera
2 Terminal
3 Bobina
4 Válvula de aguja

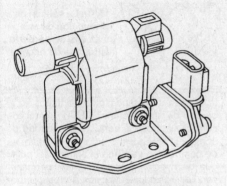

14.11 La señal de la ignición es amplificada por el transistor de poder, que dispara el voltaje apropiado alto en el circuito secundario

Bobina de la ignición

14.12 Bobina para la ignición

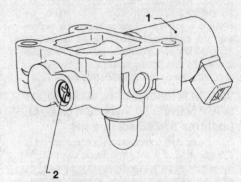

14.14 La unidad de IAA (ajustador para la marcha mínima) es una combinación de la válvula para el AAC (control del aire auxiliar) y el tornillo de ajuste para la marcha mínima. Esta unidad se puede fijar para controlar la velocidad de la marcha mínima

1 Válvula para el AAC
2 Tornillo para el ajuste de la marcha mínima

Válvula de control EGR (recirculación de los gases de escape)

15 La válvula del control EGR controla la cantidad de gas de escape circulado en el múltiple de admisión moviendo la válvula cónica conectada al diafragma, a la cual se le aplica vacío en respuesta a la abertura de la mariposa del acelerador. **Nota:** *Cuando esté instalando el tubo de guía de la EGR, tenga cuidado de su dirección. Las caras de salida miran hacia la parte trasera del motor. De otro modo la eficiencia de distribución del gas de escape será reducida* (**vea ilustración**).

Válvula solenoide para el control de la válvula EGR (recirculación de los gases de escape)

16 La válvula solenoide para el control de la válvula EGR corta la señal de vacío del múltiple de admisión para controlar la EGR. La válvula solenoide acciona en respuesta de encendido/apagado a la señal de la unidad de control del ECCS (sistema de computadora por control electrónico). Cuando el sole-

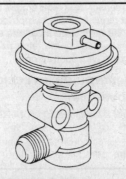

14.15 La válvula EGR (recirculación de los gases de escape) controla la cantidad de los gases de escape para ser circulado adentro del múltiple de admisión

noide está apagado, una señal de vacío del múltiple de admisión es alimentada a la válvula para el control de la EGR. Según la unidad de control envía una señal de encendido, entonces la bobina hala el embolo hacia abajo y corta la señal de vacío (**vea ilustración**).

Bomba de combustible

17 La bomba de combustible, que está localizada en el tanque de combustible, es

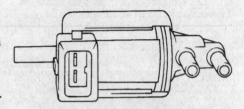

14.16 La válvula solenoide para el control de la válvula EGR (recirculación de los gases de escape) controla el vacío para la válvula EGR

una bomba del tipo mojada donde los rodillos de venas están directamente acoplados a un motor que está lleno con combustible (**vea ilustración**).

Regulador de aire

18　El regulador de aire otorga una desviación de aire cuando el motor está frío para permitir la marcha mínima rápida durante el periodo de calentamiento. Una calefacción bimetal y obturador rotatorio son construidos en el regulador de aire. Cuando la temperatura del bimetal está baja, el poste para la desviación de aire está abierto. Según se pone el motor en marcha y corriente eléctrica fluye a través de la calefacción, el bimetal comienza a girar en el obturador para cerrar el puerto de desviación. El pasaje de aire permanece cerrado hasta que el motor sea detenido y la temperatura del bimetal se caiga **(vea ilustración)**.

AIV (válvula de inyección de aire) (motores KA24E solamente)

19　La válvula de inyección de aire manda aire secundario al múltiple de escape a través de un vacío causado por la pulsación del escape en el múltiple de escape. Cuando la presión del escape está debajo de la presión atmosférica (vacío), aire secundario es enviado al múltiple de escape. Cuando la presión del escape está encima de la presión atmosférica, la caña de la válvula prevendrá que el aire secundario sea enviado de regreso al purificador de aire **(vea ilustración)**.

Válvula solenoide para el control de la AIV (válvula de inyección de aire) (motores KA24E solamente)

20　La válvula solenoide para el control de la AIV controla una señal de vacío de múltiple de admisión para la válvula de inducción de aire. La válvula solenoide acciona en respuesta a una señal de encendido/apagado en la unidad de control del ECCS. Cuando el solenoide está Apagado la señal de vacío del múltiple de admisión es cortado. Cuando esto acontece los rendimientos de la unidad del control de salida envía una señal de Encendido y la bobina hala el embolo hacia abajo, alimentando la señal de vacío a la válvula de control para el AIV **(vea ilustración)**.

Interruptor de la presión del aceite de la dirección de poder

21　El interruptor de la presión del aceite de la dirección de poder es conectado al tubo de

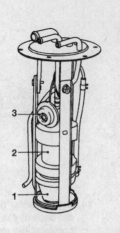
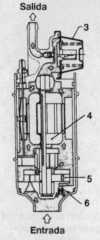

14.17　La bomba de combustible es una bomba del tipo mojada, donde los rodillos de las venas están directamente acoplados a un motor eléctrico que es sumergido en el combustible

1　Filtro
2　Bomba de combustible
3　Amortiguador del combustible
4　Motor
5　Bomba
6　Válvula de liberación

la dirección de poder de alta presión, detecta la carga de la dirección de poder y envía la señal de la carga a la ECU (unidad de control electrónica). La información es usada para controlar el sistema de la marcha mínima baja varias condiciones **(vea ilustración)**.

Sensor de la temperatura del aire

22　El sensor de la temperatura del aire controla la regulación del tiempo de la ignición cuando la temperatura del aire de admisión está extremadamente alta para prevenir detonación **(vea ilustración)**.

TBI (cuerpo de inyección de combustible)

Refiérase a las ilustraciones 14.23a, 14.23b y 14.23c

23　El sistema TBI es un sistema electrónicamente controlado con uno o con dos

14.18　El regulador de aire desvía el aire alrededor de la mariposa del acelerador adentro del colector cuando el motor está frío para proveer una marcha mínima rápida durante el periodo de calentamiento

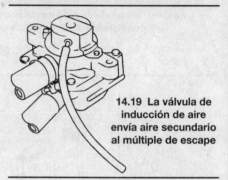

14.19　La válvula de inducción de aire envía aire secundario al múltiple de escape

inyectores de combustibles montados en el cuerpo de aceleración. La ECU (unidad de control electrónica) controla la cantidad de combustible que es inyectado en la cámara de combustión variando el tiempo del pulso que los inyectores de combustible permanecen "energizados." Muchos de los componentes del sistema con TBI son similares a los componentes equipado con el sistema MPFI (inyección de combustible con lumbreras) **(vea ilustraciones)**.

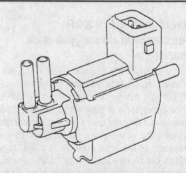

14.20　La válvula solenoide de control AIV (válvula de inyección de aire) controla la señal de vacío del múltiple de admisión a la válvula de inducción de aire

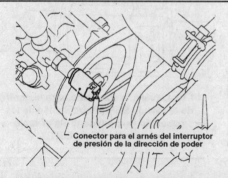

14.21　El interruptor para la presión del aceite de la dirección de poder envía la información a la ECU (unidad de control electrónica) para controlar la marcha mínima en varias condiciones

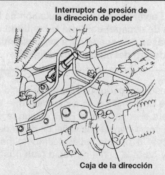

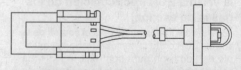

14.22　El sensor de la temperatura del aire controla el tiempo de la ignición cuando la temperatura del aire está muy alta

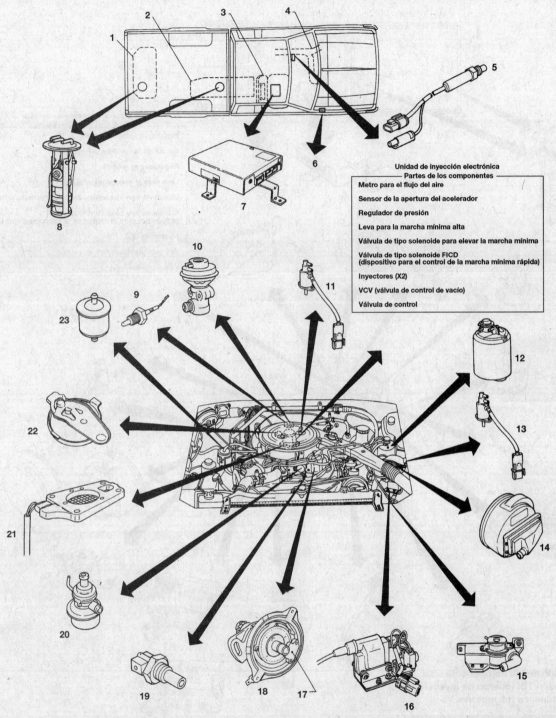

Unidad de inyección electrónica
— Partes de los componentes —
Metro para el flujo del aire
Sensor de la apertura del acelerador
Regulador de presión
Leva para la marcha mínima alta
Válvula de tipo solenoide para elevar la marcha mínima
Válvula de tipo solenoide FICD
(dispositivo para el control de la marcha mínima rápida)
Inyectores (X2)
VCV (válvula de control de vacío)
Válvula de control

14.23a Ubicación de los componentes del sistema de inyección TBI (cuerpo de inyección de combustible) en los motores de cuatro cilindros

1	Tanque de combustible (para las furgonetas)	9	Sensor de la temperatura de los gases del escape (modelos de California solamente)
2	Tanque de combustible (para las camionetas)	10	Válvula para el control EGR (recirculación de los gases de escape)
3	Asiento de asistencia	11	Válvula solenoide para el control de la EGR
4	Tubo de escape	12	Canasto
5	Sensor para los gases del escape	13	Válvula solenoide para el control del AIV (válvula de inyección de aire)
6	Relee de seguridad	14	Caja AIV (para el AIV caliente)
7	Unidad de control ECCS (sistema de computadora por control electrónico)		
8	Bomba de combustible		

15	Albergue AIV (para el AIV frío)
16	Bobina de la ignición y transistor de potencia
17	Sensor del ángulo del cigüeñal
18	Distribuidor
19	Sensor de la temperatura del sensor de la cabeza
20	Válvula AB (purga de aire)
21	Calefacción para la mezcla
22	Sensor para la temperatura del aire
23	Filtro de combustible

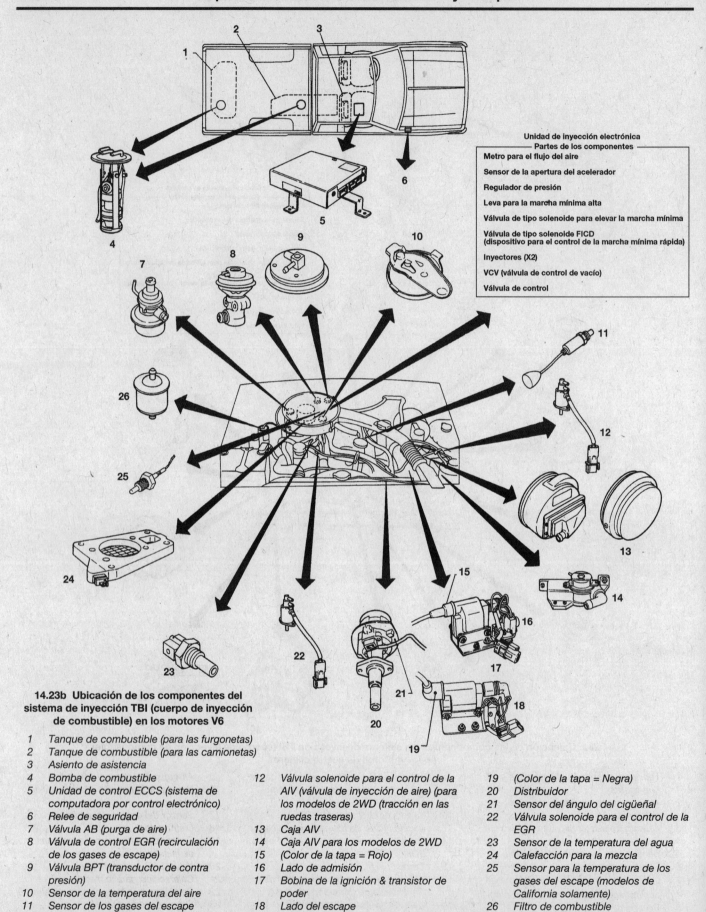

Unidad de inyección electrónica
— Partes de los componentes —

Metro para el flujo del aire

Sensor de la apertura del acelerador

Regulador de presión

Leva para la marcha mínima alta

Válvula de tipo solenoide para elevar la marcha mínima

Válvula de tipo solenoide FICD
(dispositivo para el control de la marcha mínima rápida)

Inyectores (X2)

VCV (válvula de control de vacío)

Válvula de control

14.23b Ubicación de los componentes del sistema de inyección TBI (cuerpo de inyección de combustible) en los motores V6

1   Tanque de combustible (para las furgonetas)
2   Tanque de combustible (para las camionetas)
3   Asiento de asistencia
4   Bomba de combustible
5   Unidad de control ECCS (sistema de computadora por control electrónico)
6   Relee de seguridad
7   Válvula AB (purga de aire)
8   Válvula de control EGR (recirculación de los gases de escape)
9   Válvula BPT (transductor de contra presión)
10 Sensor de la temperatura del aire
11 Sensor de los gases del escape

12 Válvula solenoide para el control de la AIV (válvula de inyección de aire) (para los modelos de 2WD (tracción en las ruedas traseras)
13 Caja AIV
14 Caja AIV para los modelos de 2WD
15 (Color de la tapa = Rojo)
16 Lado de admisión
17 Bobina de la ignición & transistor de poder
18 Lado del escape

19 (Color de la tapa = Negra)
20 Distribuidor
21 Sensor del ángulo del cigüeñal
22 Válvula solenoide para el control de la EGR
23 Sensor de la temperatura del agua
24 Calefacción para la mezcla
25 Sensor para la temperatura de los gases del escape (modelos de California solamente)
26 Filtro de combustible

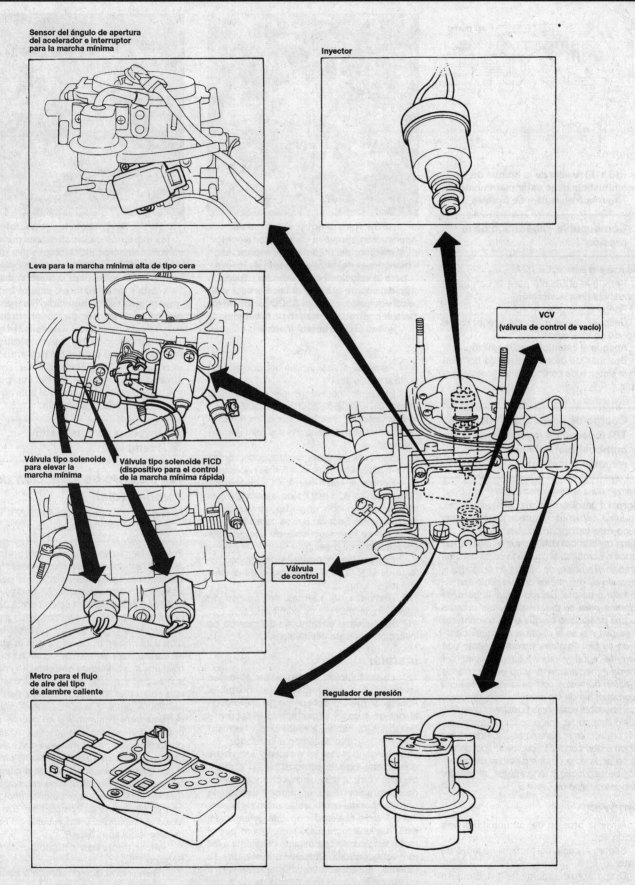

Sensor del ángulo de apertura del acelerador e interruptor para la marcha mínima

Inyector

Leva para la marcha mínima alta de tipo cera

VCV (válvula de control de vacío)

Válvula tipo solenoide para elevar la marcha mínima

Válvula tipo solenoide FICD (dispositivo para el control de la marcha mínima rápida)

Válvula de control

Metro para el flujo de aire del tipo de alambre caliente

Regulador de presión

14.23c Detalles del cuerpo de aceleración (1985 al 1989)

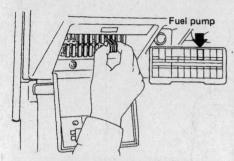

15.1 El fusible de la bomba de combustible debe estar claramente marcado en la caja de fusibles

15   Combustible - liberación de la presión

Refiérase a la ilustración 15.1

1   Remueva el fusible para la bomba de combustible (vea ilustración).
2   Ponga el motor en marcha.
3   Después que el motor se apaga, gire el motor dos o tres veces.
4   Apague el interruptor de la ignición.
5   Después de otorgarle servicio completado al sistema de combustible, reemplace el fusible.

16   Cuerpo de aceleración (sistemas TBI (cuerpo de inyección de combustible) solamente) - remover e instalar

Refiérase a las ilustraciones 16.5a y 16.5b
Peligro: *La gasolina es sumamente inflamable, así que se deben tomar precauciones extras cuando esté trabajando en cualquier parte del sistema del combustible. No fume, deje llamas abiertas o bombillas sin cubierta cerca del área de trabajo. También, no trabaje en un garaje si un aparato de gas natural con un piloto encendido está presente. Debido a que la gasolina es dañina para su piel use guantes cuando halla una posibilidad de que entre en contacto con su piel y si se le derrama cualquier cantidad en su piel límpiese inmediatamente con suficiente agua y jabón. Limpie cualquier derrame inmediatamente y no guarde trapos que estén húmedos con gasolina. El sistema de combustible de los modelos con inyección de combustible están bajo constante presión y si cualquiera de las líneas se van a desconectar, la presión en el sistema se debe de aliviar. Cuando usted conduzca cualquier tipo de trabajo en el sistema de combustible, use espejuelos de seguridad y tenga cerca un extintor de fuegos del tipo de Clase B.*

Remover

1   Alivie la presión del combustible (vea Sección 15).
2   Separe el cable del terminal negativo de la batería.
3   Drene aproximadamente 1-1/8 cuarto de galón de anticongelante del motor (vea Capítulo 1).

16.5a Para remover el cuerpo de aceleración, remueva el conector eléctrico al medidor del flujo de aire, separe las mangueras del anticongelante de la leva para la velocidad de la marcha mínima rápida, separe el cable del acelerador y si está equipado, el cable ASCD (dispositivo para el control automático de la velocidad) (control de crucero) (flechas), . . .

4   Remueva el ensamblaje del albergue del purificador de aire.
5   Separe los conectores eléctricos para el sensor del ángulo de apertura del acelerador, el interruptor de marcha mínima, los inyectores y el medidor del flujo del aire (vea ilustraciones).
6   Separe el cable del acelerador del control de la mariposa (vea Sección 5 si es necesario).
7   Separe el cable del ASCD (dispositivo para el control automático de la velocidad), si está equipado con uno, del control de la mariposa (vea Sección 5 si es necesario).
8   Separe las mangueras de combustible del regulador de presión.
9   Separe las mangueras de anticongelante de la leva para la velocidad de la marcha mínima rápida.
10   Remueva las tuercas del cuerpo de inyección del múltiple de admisión.
11   Remueva el ensamblaje del cuerpo de inyección y la junta del múltiple.

Instalar

12   La instalación se hace en el orden inverso al procedimiento de desensamble. Apriete las tuercas del cuerpo de aceleración al par de torsión especificado. Asegúrese que todos los cables, los alambres y las mangueras están apropiadamente instaladas.
13   Ponga el motor en marcha y asegúrese que no hay fuga de combustible en el espacio libre entre la tapa de inyector y el cuerpo de aceleración. Pare el motor y asegúrese que el vapor del combustible atomizado en la mariposa del acelerador no está goteando (si está, hay una fuga). Esté bien seguro que el motor está en marcha mínima constante a las rpm especificadas. Después que el motor se calentó, agregue aproximadamente 1-1/8 cuarto de galón de anticongelante de motor (vea Capítulo 1 si es necesario).

16.5b . . . desconecte los conectores en los extremos de los alambres para la válvula solenoide FICD (dispositivo para el control de la marcha mínima rápida), la válvula solenoide para la marcha mínima alta y los inyectores, separe las mangueras del combustible (flechas) del regulador de presión (la manguera inferior no está mostrada), desconecte el conector eléctrico (no está mostrado - en la parte trasera) sensor del acelerador y el interruptor de la marcha mínima, remueva todas las cuatro tuercas del cuerpo de aceleración y levante el cuerpo de aceleración

17   Inyector de combustible - reemplazo

TBI (cuerpo de inyección de combustible)

Refiérase a las ilustraciones 17.3, 17.4, 17.5a, 17.5b, 17.6, 17.7a, 17.7b, 17.7c, 17.9a, 17.9b, 17.9c, 17.12 y 17.14
Peligro: *La gasolina es sumamente inflamable, así que se deben tomar precauciones extras cuando esté trabajando en cualquier parte del sistema del combustible. No fume, deje llamas abiertas o bombillas sin cubierta cerca del área de trabajo. También, no trabaje en un garaje si un aparato de gas natural con un piloto encendido está presente. Debido a que la gasolina es dañina para su piel use guantes cuando halla una posibilidad de que entre en contacto con su piel y si se le derrama cualquier cantidad en su piel límpiese inmediatamente con suficiente agua y jabón. Limpie cualquier derrame inmediatamente y no guarde trapos que estén húmedos con gasolina. El sistema de combustible de los modelos con inyección de combustible están bajo constante presión y si cualquiera de las líneas se van a desconectar, la presión en el sistema se debe de aliviar. Cuando usted conduzca cualquier tipo de trabajo en el sistema de combustible, use espejuelos de seguridad y tenga cerca un extintor de fuegos del tipo Clase B.*

1   Alivie la presión del combustible (vea Sección 15).
2   Remueva el cuerpo de aceleración (vea Sección 16).
3   Remueva el sello de caucho y la hembri-

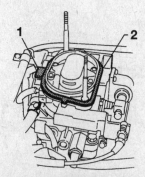

17.3 Remueva el sello de caucho y el del cuerpo de inyección de la hembrilla del arnés del inyector

1   Hembrilla para el arnés del inyector
2   Sello de caucho

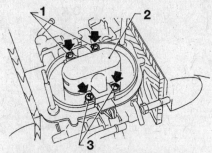

17.4 Remueva los tornillos de la tapa del inyector (flechas) y separe la tapa del inyector

1   Afloje estos tornillos
2   Cubierta del inyector
3   Afloje estos tornillos

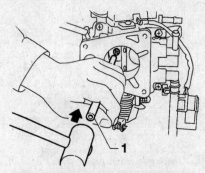

17.5a Con la mariposa del acelerador completamente abierta, péguele gentilmente en el fondo del inyector con una barra hueca como está mostrado

1   Barra hueca

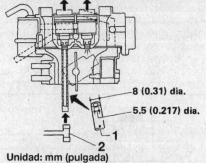

8 (0.31) dia.
5.5 (0.217) dia.
Unidad: mm (pulgada)

17.5b Asegúrese que la barra hueca tenga un diámetro interior de por lo menos 0.217 pulgada (para que no dañe la tobera del inyector)

1   Barra hueca
2   Martillo de plástico

1   Anillo O (grande)
2   Anillo O (pequeño)
3   Anillo de caucho

17.6 Cada vez que usted remueva los inyectores, reemplace los anillo de tipo O grandes, pequeños y los anillos de caucho con unos nuevos - esté seguro de aplicar algo de silicona a los anillo selladores de tipo O cuando los esté instalando

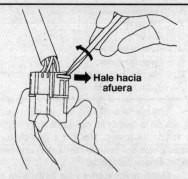

Hale hacia afuera

17.7a Antes de remover la terminal del conector del arnés, remueva el retenedor - la mejor manera de remover el retenedor hacia afuera es de hacerle palanca para aflojarlo con un destornillador pequeño, un punzón o un marcador

lla del arnés del inyector del cuerpo de inyección **(vea ilustración)**.
4   Remueva la tapa del inyector **(vea ilustración)**.
5   Con la mariposa del acelerador mantenida completamente abierta, péguele cuida-

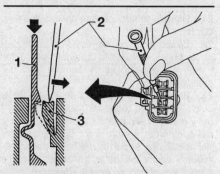

17.7b Para remover una terminal fuera del conector, incline la cerradura de la lengua con un destornillador pequeño, ralle como está mostrado y simultáneamente empuje hacia afuera la terminal

1   Terminal
2   Destornillador
3   Lengua de retención

dosamente al fondo del inyector de combustible con una barra hueca **(vea ilustración)**. **Nota:** La barra hueca debe tener un diámetro interior de no menos de 0.217 pulgada **(vea ilustración)**. Tenga cuidado de no dañar la punta de la tobera del inyector. Si la punta es deformada por la barra durante el proceso de remover, el inyector debe ser reemplazado.
6   Si usted simplemente está removiendo un inyector que tiene fuga, que de otro modo

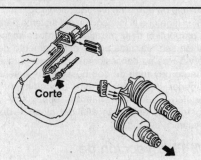

Corte

17.7c Para separar el arnés de un inyector malo fuera del arnés principal de los inyectores de combustible, corte los dos alambres en los fuelles como está mostrado (flechas) entonces hale los alambres del tubo del arnés, hembrilla y deseche el inyector

está bueno, remueva los anillos selladores de tipo O viejos, grande y pequeño y el anillo de caucho **(vea ilustración)** e instale unos nuevos. Esté seguro de aplicar algún tipo de aceite de silicona a ambos anillos selladores de tipo O nuevos cuando los esté instalando en el inyector. Entonces proceda al Paso 12.
7   Si usted está reemplazando un inyector defectuoso, desconecte el arnés del inyector malo del conector del arnés y remuévalo como sigue:

a) Remueva el retenedor de la terminal **(vea ilustración)**.
b) Con un destornillador pequeño, incline la lengua de cerradura y al mismo tiempo, empuje hacia afuera la terminal **(vea ilustración)**. **Caución:** Cuando extraiga una terminal, no hale los arneses del alambre. Siempre empuje la punta de la terminal. Tenga cuidado de no dañar ni rocíe gasolina en la tapa del sello a menos que usted intente reemplazarlo con uno nuevo.
c) Corte los fuelles del alambre como está indicado **(vea ilustración)**. **Caución:** Antes de cortar cualquier alambre, esté seguro que usted corta los alambres para el inyector que usted intenta reemplazar refiriéndose al diagrama que acompaña en el Paso 9.

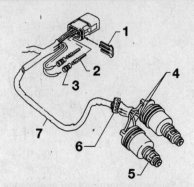

17.9a Para conectar un inyector nuevo a los arneses, enrosque los dos alambres a través de la hembrilla y el tubo, entonces exprima los fuelles y las terminales en su posición en las puntas de los alambres

1   *Retenedor de la terminal*
2   *Terminal*
3   *Fuelle*
4   *Arnés del inyector*
5   *Inyector nuevo*
6   *Hembrilla para el arnés del inyector*
7   *Tubo del arnés*

8·   Empuje el arnés en el inyector nuevo a través de la hembrilla del arnés del inyector y el tubo del arnés. **Nota:** *La hembrilla del arnés debe ser reemplazada con una nueva cada vez sea removida.*

9   Conecte los fuelles y las terminales a los arneses con alicates para terminales, entonces, refiriéndose al diagrama que acompaña, taponé las terminales del arnés en el conector **(vea ilustraciones). Caución:** Sea extremadamente cuidadoso cuando esté conectando las terminales al conector. Preste atención a los colores del arnés y números y a las posiciones de las terminales. De otro modo, el inyector(es) será dañado.

10   Empuje el retenedor de la terminal otra vez dentro del conector.

11   Instale anillo selladores de tipo O nuevos, grandes y pequeños y un anillo nuevo de caucho en el inyector (vea Paso 6 encima).

12   Coloque el ensamblaje del inyector en el cuerpo del inyección **(vea ilustración)**.

13   Empuje los inyectores en el cuerpo de aceleración a mano hasta que los anillo selladores de tipo O estén completamente sentados. Invierta el cuerpo de inyección y asegúrese que las puntas del inyector están apropiadamente asentados.

14   Aplique algo de silicona a la hembrilla del arnés del inyector **(vea ilustración)**.

15   Instale la tapa de inyector. Esté seguro de usar sellador de enclavamiento en las roscas del tornillo. Apriete los tornillos en un patrón cruzado para asegurarse que se asienta apropiadamente en el inyector y la tapa.

16   Conecte el sello de caucho a la cara superior del cuerpo de inyección con pegador de silicona. **Caución:** Esté seguro de aplicar algo de silicona al fondo del sello de caucho para que el caucho se adhiera al cuerpo de aceleración. No vuelva a instalar el ensamblaje del albergue del purificador de aire hasta que

O.K.

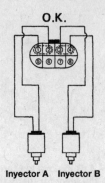

Inyector A   Inyector B

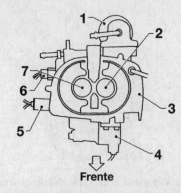

Frente

Actuador		Numero de la terminal	Color del arnés
Inyector A $\oplus$		①	G
Inyector A $\ominus$		②	W
Inyector B $\oplus$		③	B
Inyector B $\ominus$		④	R
Válvula solenoide FICD (dispositivo para el control de la marcha mínima rápida)	$\oplus$	⑤	B
Válvula solenoide FICD (dispositivo para el control de la marcha mínima rápida)	$\ominus$	⑥	B
Válvula solenoide para elevar la marcha mínima	$\oplus$	⑦	B/W
Válvula solenoide para elevar la marcha mínima	$\ominus$	⑧	B/W

Color del arnés para las partes de servicio (inyector)
Inyector $\oplus$: G/W
  Inyector A: Conéctelo a la terminal numero 1
  Inyector B: Conéctelo a la terminal numero 3
Inyector $\ominus$: Y/W
  Inyector A: Conéctelo a la terminal numero 2
  Inyector B: Conéctelo a la terminal numero 4

①	②	③	④
⑤	⑥	⑦	⑧

17.9b Refiérase al diagrama de encima cuando esté instalando un inyector nuevo en un motor V6 (VG30i) y los motores 1987 de cuatro cilindros (Z24i) más modernos para asegurarse que usted no mezcla los números de los terminales y los colores de los alambres - los esquemas en el centro y en el fondo están proporcionados para que usted no confunda ni el número del inyector ni el alambre a la conexión de las terminales

1   *Regulador de presión*
2   *Inyector B*
3   *Cuerpo del inyector*
4   *Elemento térmico*
5   *Válvula solenoide FICD (dispositivo para el control de la marcha mínima rápida)*
6   *Válvula solenoide para elevar la marcha mínima*
7   *Inyector A*

la silicona esté bien endurecida.

17   Instale el cuerpo de aceleración en el múltiple de admisión (vea Sección 15).

18   Haga que la inspección del sistema para la proporción de la mezcla de la retroalimentación sea realizada por el departamento de servicio de su concesionario para asegúrese que no hay fuga de combustible en el sello superior del inyector (este procedimiento requiere varias herramientas especiales y costosas y está más allá del alcance del mecánico de hogar).

MPFI (inyección de combustible con lumbreras)

Refiérase a las ilustraciones 17.22, 17.25 y 17.27.

19   Alivie la presión del combustible (vea Sección 15).

20   Desconecte el cable negativo de la terminal negativa de la batería.

21   Drene el anticongelante del sistema (vea Capítulo 1).

22   Desconecte los alambres de las bujías en las bujías, remueva la tapa del distribuidor y mueva el ensamblaje de alambre fuera del área de trabajo.

23   En el frente del colector de aire, marque cuidadosamente todas las líneas y mangueras y remueva el cable del acelerador, sensor del acelerador e interruptor de la mariposa del acelerador, soportes del cable del acelerador y todas las otras líneas de vacío y conectores eléctricos **(vea ilustración)**.

24   En todos los motores V6, remueva los pernos y levante el colector del aire del múltiple.

25   Remueva la manguera del suplemento de combustible y la manguera de regreso del ensamblaje del tubo de combustible del inyector.

26   Remueva los conectores del arnés del inyector **(vea ilustración)**.

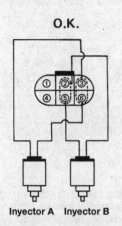

O.K.

Inyector A   Inyector B

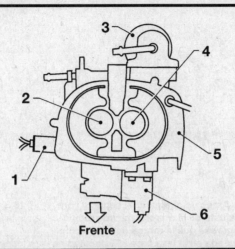

3

4

2

1

5

6

Frente

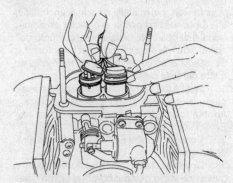

17.12 Después que el inyector nuevo sea apropiadamente conectado a los arneses, coloque los inyectores en el cuerpo de aceleración como está mostrado

Actuador	Numero de la terminal	Color del arnés
Inyector A ⊕	③	W
Inyector A ⊖	⑥	G
Inyector B ⊕	②	R
Inyector B ⊖	⑤	L
Válvula solenoide FICD (dispositivo para el control de la marcha mínima rápida) ⊕	①	B/W
Válvula solenoide FICD (dispositivo para el control de la marcha mínima rápida) ⊖	④	B

Color del arnés para las partes de servicio (inyector)

Inyector ⊕ : G/W   Conéctelo a la terminal numero 2 or 3

Inyector ⊖ : Y/W   Conéctelo a la terminal numero 5 or 6

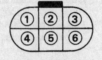

① ② ③
④ ⑤ ⑥

17.9c Refiérase al diagrama de encima cuando esté instalando un inyector nuevo en un motor 1986 y más antiguo de cuatro cilindros (Z24i) para asegurarse que usted no mezcle los números de las terminales y los colores de los alambres - los esquemas en el centro y en la parte inferior son proporcionados para que usted no confunda ni el número del inyector ni el alambre con las conexiones de las terminales

1 *Válvula solenoide FICD (dispositivo para el control de la marcha mínima rápida)*
2 *Inyector A*
3 *Regulador de presión*
4 *Inyector B*
5 *Cuerpo del inyector*
6 *Elemento térmico*

27 Remueva el ensamblaje del tubo de combustible del inyector. **Nota:** *Cuando desconecte las líneas de combustible coloque un trapo alrededor de la conexión para colectar*

cualquier combustible que se fugue.
28 Remueva cada uno de los pernos reteniendo el inyector y levante el ensamblaje del inyector.

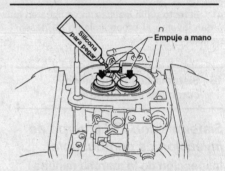

17.14 Aplique sellador de silicona a la hembrilla del arnés del inyector, entonces empuje la hembrilla en su posición

29 Si alguno de los inyectores individuales van a ser reemplazados, determine el inyector que va a ser reemplazado y remuévelo cuidadosamente del tubo de combustible.
30 Para instalar el inyector nuevo, moje los anillo selladores de tipo O nuevos con gasolina y apriete el ensamblaje del inyector en el ensamblaje del tubo de combustible.
31 Instale el ensamblaje del tubo.
32 Instale y apriete los pernos de retención para cada inyector.
33 Conecte todos los conectores eléctricos del inyector.
34 Limpie todos los rasgos del material de

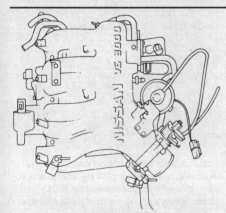

17.22 Colector del aire de admisión en el motor V6

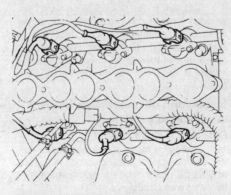

17.25 Desconecte el conector eléctrico de los inyectores (se muestra un motor V6)

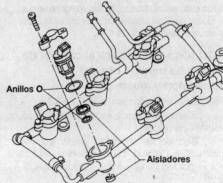

Anillos O

Aisladores

17.27 Cada inyector es atornillado a un ensamblaje del tubo de combustible

1 *Anillo O*   2 *Aislador*

la junta vieja y el múltiple de admisión. Instale una junta nueva y ponga el colector de admisión en su posición, dirigiendo el conjunto del alambrado trasero alrededor del colector.

35   Dirija el conjunto del alambrado/arnés al frente del lado del colector.

36   Instale los pernos de la cabeza que aseguran el colector al múltiple de admisión. Apriete los pernos al torque listado en las Especificaciones de éste Capítulo.

37   Conecte el tubo EGR al colector de aire de admisión.

38   Conecte todos los conectores y mangueras de vacío/combustible que fueron desconectados durante el proceso de remover.

39   Conecte todas las bandas de los arnés del alambrado al colector.

40   Instale el regulador de aire (vea Sección 12).

41   El resto de la instalación se hace en el orden inverso al procedimiento de desensamble.

18   Sistema de inyección de combustible - ajustes

Sistemas con TBI (cuerpo de inyección de combustible)

Inspección de la marcha mínima rápida y ajuste

Refiérase a las ilustraciones 18.2 y 18.3

1   Caliente el motor a su temperatura normal de operación.

2   Asegúrese que la marca de la alineación estampada en la leva para la velocidad de la marcha mínima rápida se reúne con el centro del rodillo instalado en la palanca del seguidor de la leva. Si no lo hace, corrija la ubicación de la leva para la velocidad de la marcha mínima rápida girando el tornillo de ajuste S1 **(vea ilustración)**. Si no puede ser ajustado apropiadamente, reemplace el elemento térmico.

3   Chequee el espacio libre "G" entre el rodillo y la leva para la velocidad de la marcha mínima rápida **(vea ilustración)** y compare su lectura con el espacio libre especificado. Si está fuera de ajuste, corríjalo girando el tornillo de ajuste S2 hasta que el espacio libre esté como está especificado. **Nota:** *Asegúrese que el motor se haya calentado cuando esté ajustando el espacio libre "G."*

FICD (dispositivo para el control de la marcha mínima rápida) inspección y ajuste

Refiérase a las ilustraciones 18.7 y 18.8

4   Caliente el motor a su temperatura normal de operación.

5   Chequee la velocidad de la marcha mínima (vea Capítulo 1) y compare su lectura a la velocidad de la marcha mínima especificada.

6   Gire el aire acondicionado a prendido y chequee la velocidad de la marcha mínima otra vez. Compare su lectura a la velocidad de la marcha mínima especifica con el aire

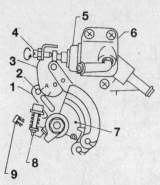

18.2 Antes de chequear el espacio libre del ajuste de la marcha mínima rápida, asegúrese que la marca de alineación estampada en la leva para la velocidad de la marcha mínima rápida está en el centro del rodillo instalado en la palanca de seguir la leva - si no, ajuste la leva para la velocidad de la marcha mínima rápida girando el tornillo de ajuste S1 (si no puede ser traído al ajuste apropiado, reemplace el elemento térmico)

1   *Palanca seguidora de la leva*
2   *Rodillo*
3   *Leva para la marcha mínima rápida*
4   *Tornillo de ajuste (S1)*
5   *Elemento térmico*
6   *Albergue térmico*
7   *Palanca del acelerador*
8   *Tornillo de ajuste (S2)*
9   *Tornillo para el ajuste de la mariposa del acelerador*

acondicionado prendido.

7   Si la velocidad de la marcha mínima está fuera de ajuste, ajústela girando el tornillo de ajuste **(vea ilustración)**.

8   Si la válvula del solenoide FICD no trabaja, chequee los arneses y la válvula del solenoide **(vea ilustración)** como sigue:

a)   *Desconecte el conector de 8 clavijas.*
b)   *Chequee el suministro de poder a los arneses con el interruptor de la ignición encendido y el aire acondicionado prendido.*
c)   *Chequee la continuidad eléctrica de la válvula solenoide.*

9   Si la válvula del solenoide no tiene continuidad a pesar de un suministro de poder apropiado, reemplácela con una nueva. **Nota:** *Esté seguro de usar una arandela nueva con la válvula de solenoide nueva y apriete la válvula al par de torsión especificado.*

Inspección del amortiguador para la velocidad y ajuste

Refiérase a la ilustración 18.11

10   Caliente el motor a su temperatura normal de operación. La velocidad de la marcha mínima del motor debe ser ajustada apropiadamente (vea Capítulo 1).

11   Gire la mariposa del acelerador a mano y lea la velocidad del motor cuando el amortiguador apenas toca el tornillo de ajuste **(vea ilustración)**. Compare su lectura a la veloci-

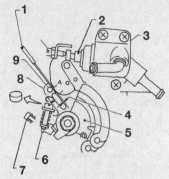

18.3 Si el espacio libre G entre el rodillo y la leva para la velocidad de la marcha mínima rápida no está como se especifica, corríjalo girando el tornillo de ajuste S2 (asegúrese que el motor se haya calentado lo suficientemente antes de hacer el ajuste)

1   *Espesor del calibrador del tornillo de ajuste (S1)*
2   *Elemento térmico*
3   *Albergue térmico*
4   *Espacio libre G*
5   *Palanca del acelerador*
6   *Tornillo de ajuste (S2)*
7   *Tornillo de ajuste para la mariposa del acelerador*
8   *Palanca para seguir la leva*
9   *Rodillo*

dad especificada de toque del amortiguador.

12   Si la velocidad del toque está fuera de la especificación, ajústela girando el tornillo de ajuste.

Inspección de la válvula solenoide para elevar la marcha mínima

Refiérase a la ilustración 18.13

13   Desconecte el conector de 8 clavijas **(vea ilustración)** y chequee por continuidad.

14   Si no hay continuidad, reemplace la válvula con una nueva. Esté seguro de usar una arandela nueva con la válvula nueva y apriete la válvula nueva al par de torsión especificado.

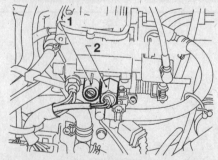

18.7 Ajuste la velocidad de la marcha mínima girando el tornillo de ajuste anexo a la válvula del solenoide FICD (dispositivo para el control de la marcha mínima rápida)

1   *Tornillo de ajuste*
2   *Válvula solenoide FICD*

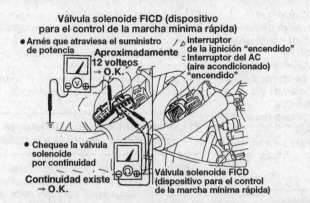

Válvula solenoide FICD (dispositivo para el control de la marcha mínima rápida)

- Arnés que atraviesa el suministro de potencia
- Chequee la válvula solenoide por continuidad

Aproximadamente 12 volteos → O.K.

Interruptor de la ignición "encendido"
Interruptor del AC (aire acondicionado) "encendido"

Continuidad existe → O.K.

Válvula solenoide FICD (dispositivo para el control de la marcha mínima rápida)

Válvula solenoide FICD (dispositivo para el control de la marcha mínima rápida)

- Chequee la válvula solenoide por continuidad

Conector superior

Continuidad existe → O.K.

- El suplemento de electricidad pasa

Tierra de la carrocería

Conector inferior

Aproximadamente 12 volteos → O.K.

18.8 Para chequear la válvula solenoide FICD (dispositivo para el control de la marcha mínima rápida) (A es un V6, B es el de cuatro) por continuidad, remueva el conector de 8 clavijas y chequee el suministro de poder a través del arnés de la ignición y prenda el aire acondicionado, entonces chequee la continuidad eléctrica en la válvula misma

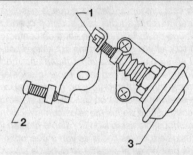

18.11 Ajuste el amortiguador para la velocidad girando el tornillo de ajuste

1   Tornillo para el ajuste del amortiguador para la velocidad
2   Tornillo de ajuste para el acelerador
3   Amortiguador para la velocidad

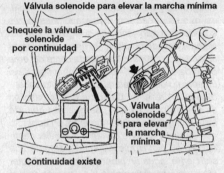

Válvula solenoide para elevar la marcha mínima

Chequee la válvula solenoide por continuidad

Válvula solenoide para elevar la marcha mínima

Continuidad existe

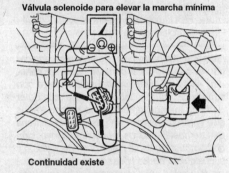

Válvula solenoide para elevar la marcha mínima

Continuidad existe

18.13 Para chequear la válvula solenoide para elevar la marcha mínima, desconecte el conector de 8 clavijas y chequee la válvula por continuidad como está mostrado (A es un motor V6, B es un motor de cuatro cilindros)

MPFI (inyección de combustible con lumbreras)

Inspección de la marcha mínima rápida y ajuste (motores KA24E)

Refiérase a las ilustraciones 18.17, 18.18, 18.19 y 18.20

15   Ponga el motor en marcha y caliéntelo hasta que alcance la temperatura normal de operación.

16   Detenga el motor y remueva el purificador de aire.

17   Asegúrese que la marca (Q) en la leva para la velocidad de la marcha mínima rápida está apuntando al centro del rodillo (**vea ilustración**).

18   Ajuste el tornillo de la marcha mínima (**vea ilustración**) hasta que la cima de la leva mire el centro del rodillo de la palanca.

19   Mida el espacio libre (G) entre el rodillo y la cima de la leva para la velocidad de la marcha mínima rápida (**vea ilustración**). Refiérase a las especificaciones listadas en este Capítulo.

20   Si el juego libre está incorrecto, ajuste el espacio libre usando el tornillo de ajuste (B) (**vea ilustración**) hasta que el espacio libre especificado sea obtenido.

19   Sistema de combustible - limpiar

Peligro: *La gasolina es sumamente inflamable, así que se deben tomar precauciones extras cuando esté trabajando en cualquier parte del sistema del combustible. No fume, deje llamas abiertas o bombillas sin cubierta cerca del área de trabajo. También, no trabaje en un garaje si un aparato de gas natural con un piloto encendido está presente. Debido a que la gasolina es dañina para su piel use guantes cuando*

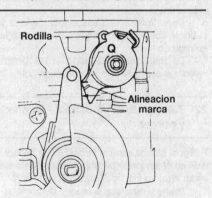

Rodilla

Q

Alineacion marca

18.17 Esté seguro de medir la punta (Q) de la leva para la velocidad de la marcha mínima rápida al rodillo. NO use la marca de alineación

1   Rodillo
2   Marca de alineación

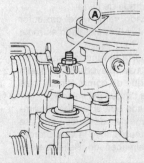

A

18.18 Afloje la tuerca de enclavamiento y el tornillo de ajuste (A) para mover la leva para la marcha mínima rápida

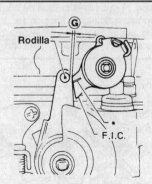

G

Rodilla

F.I.C.

18.19 Mida la medida del espacio libre G desde el rodillo a la punta de la leva para la marcha mínima rápida

1   Rodillo
2   FIC (dispositivo para el control de la marcha mínima rápida)

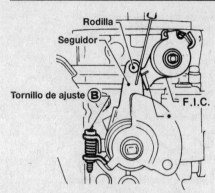

*: La marca nu tiene relacional ajuste

18.20 Ajuste la mariposa del acelerador girando el tornillo de ajuste B

1   Seguidor de la planca
2   Rodillo
3   FICD (dispositivo para el control de la marcha mínima rápida)

halla una posibilidad de que entre en contacto con su piel y si se le derrama cualquier cantidad en su piel límpiese inmediatamente con suficiente agua y jabón. Limpie cualquier derrame inmediatamente y no guarde trapos que estén húmedos con gasolina. El sistema de combustible de los modelos con inyección de combustible están bajo constante presión y si cualquiera de las líneas se van a desconectar, la presión en el sistema se debe de aliviar. Cuando usted conduzca cualquier tipo de trabajo en el sistema de combustible, use espejuelos de seguridad y tenga cerca un extintor de fuegos del tipo Clase B.

1   Con tiempo es probable que sedimento se reunirá en el fondo del tanque de combustible. La condensación, resultado en oxidación y otras impurezas, serán generalmente encontradas en el tanque de combustible de cualquier vehículo más de tres o cuatro años de viejos. El siguiente procedimiento se debe realizar para eliminar el material extranjero o el combustible contaminado del sistema de combustible.

2   Desconecte el cable negativo de la terminal negativa de la batería.

3   Drene y remueva el tanque de combustible como se indica en la Sección 19.

4   Remueva el filtro de combustible como está descrito en el Capítulo 1. Si el filtro está

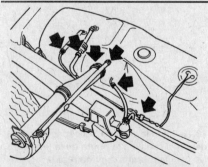

20.3 Ubicaciones de la manguera del tanque y conexiones del alambrado en un tanque de combustible típico (flechas)

obstruido, reemplácelo con uno nuevo.

5   Remueva la unidad emisora del tanque de combustible del tanque de combustible como se indica en la Sección 20.

6   Desconecte la línea del suministro de combustible en la bomba de combustible y limpie la línea aplicando presión de aire en la dirección del flujo del combustible.

7   Use presión de aire baja para limpiar los tubos en la unidad del tanque.

8   Refiérase a la Sección 21 para información adicional con respecto a limpiar el tanque de combustible.

20   Tanque de combustible - remover e instalar

Refiérase a la ilustración 20.3

Peligro: La gasolina es sumamente inflamable, así que se deben tomar precauciones extras cuando esté trabajando en cualquier parte del sistema del combustible. No fume, deje llamas abiertas o bombillas sin cubierta cerca del área de trabajo. También, no trabaje en un garaje si un aparato de gas natural con un piloto encendido está presente. Debido a que la gasolina es dañina para su piel use guantes cuando halla una posibilidad de que entre en contacto con su piel y si se le derrama cualquier cantidad en su piel límpiese inmediatamente con suficiente agua y jabón. Limpie cualquier derrame inmediatamente y no guarde trapos que estén húmedos con gasolina. El sistema de combustible de los modelos con inyección de combustible están bajo constante presión y si cualquiera de las líneas se van a desconectar, la presión en el sistema se debe de aliviar. Cuando usted conduzca cualquier tipo de trabajo en el sistema de combustible, use espejuelos de seguridad y tenga cerca un extintor de fuegos del tipo Clase B.

1   Desconecte el cable negativo de la terminal negativa de la batería.

2   Remueva el tapón de drenaje del fondo del tanque de combustible **(vea ilustraciones 4.1a y 4.1b)** y drene el combustible en un recipiente de gasolina aprobado.

3   De la cima del tanque de combustible, desconecte la manguera del filtro de combustible, la manguera de salida del combustible, manguera para la ventilación del aire, la manguera de respiración, manguera de regreso del combustible y el conector del alambrado que se dirige a la unidad emisora del tanque de combustible **(vea ilustración)**. Tape inmediatamente todas las aberturas para prevenir la entrada de tierra.

4   Si está equipado, remueva el protector del tanque de combustible instalado enfrente del tanque.

5   Mientras soporta el tanque usando un gato o con la ayuda de un ayudante, remueva los pernos del tanque de combustible y baje cuidadosamente el tanque del vehículo.

6   Es recomendado que el tanque sea limpiado inmediatamente después que se remueva, especialmente si se le va a otorgar trabajo o va a ser almacenado. Refiérase a la Sección 21.

7   Antes de instalar el tanque asegúrese que todos los indicios de tierra y corrosión son limpiado de el. Si el tanque está internamente oxidado, debe ser reemplazado con uno nuevo.

8   La instalación se hace en el orden inverso al procedimiento de desensamble.

21   Unidad emisora en el tanque de combustible - remover e instalar

Peligro: La gasolina es sumamente inflamable, así que se deben tomar precauciones extras cuando esté trabajando en cualquier parte del sistema del combustible. No fume, deje llamas abiertas o bombillas sin cubierta cerca del área de trabajo. También, no trabaje en un garaje si un aparato de gas natural con un piloto encendido está presente. Debido a que la gasolina es dañina para su piel use guantes cuando halla una posibilidad de que entre en contacto con su piel y si se le derrama cualquier cantidad en su piel límpiese inmediatamente con suficiente agua y jabón. Limpie cualquier derrame inmediatamente y no guarde trapos que estén húmedos con gasolina. El sistema de combustible de los modelos con inyección de combustible están bajo constante presión y si cualquiera de las líneas se van a desconectar, la presión en el sistema se debe de aliviar. Cuando usted conduzca cualquier tipo de trabajo en el sistema de combustible, use espejuelos de seguridad y tenga cerca un extintor de fuegos del tipo Clase B.

1   Desconecte el cable negativo de la terminal negativa de la batería.

2   Desconecte los alambres que se dirigen a la unidad emisora del tanque de combustible.

3   Remueva el tanque de combustible como se indica en la Sección 20.

4   Remueva el plato de cierre de la unidad emisora usando un punzón de bronce y un martillo para girarlo a la derecha. **Peligro:** No use un destornillador o un punzón hecho de otro material que no sea de bronce. ¡Ellos podrían causar chispas y podrían causar una explosión!

5   Levante la unidad emisora del tanque y cubra la abertura del tanque para prevenir la entrada de tierra.

6   La instalación se hace en el orden inverso al procedimiento de desensamble.

22   Tanque de combustible - limpiar y purgar

Peligro: Nunca realice trabajo de la reparación en el tanque implicando calor o llama sin hacer primero los siguientes procedimiento.

1   Drene y remueva el tanque de combustible como se indica en la Sección 19.

2   Remueva la unidad emisora del tanque de combustible como se indica en la Sección 20.

3   Invierta el tanque y vacíe cualquier cantidad de combustible que quede.

4   Si los trabajos de reparaciones necesa-

rias para el tanque de combustible no implican ningún calor ni llama, el tanque puede ser limpiado satisfactoriamente corriendo agua caliente adentro de el y permitiéndolo que se rebase hacia afuera de la cima por menos cinco minutos. Este método, sin embargo, no remueve los vapores del gas.

5   Si el trabajo de la reparación necesaria implica calor o llama, déjelo que sea hecho por un profesional experimentado. Lo siguiente, un procedimientos más completo se debe usar para remover el combustible y los vapores del tanque para el almacenamiento o el transporte a una facilidad de reparación.

6   Llene el tanque completamente con agua del chorro, agítelo vigórosamente y drénelo.

7   Agregue un agente para emulsionar la gasolina al tanque según las instrucciones del fabricante, rellénelo con agua, agítelo aproximadamente por 10 minutos y drénelo.

8   Limpie el rebase una vez más con agua por varios minutos y drénelo.

23   Sistema de escape - información general

El sistema del escape se compone del silenciador, el convertidor catalítico y los tubos de escape, e incluye cuatro pedazos principales; el tubo delantero de escape que se conecta al múltiple de escape, el convertidor catalítico, el tubo central y el silenciador/ensamblaje de tubo de cola. **Nota:** *Los modelos 1980 del Canadá usan un sistema de escape que consiste de dos pedazos solamente, el tubo de escape delantero y el silenciador/ensamblaje del tubo de cola.*

El convertidor catalítico es conectado a ambos el tubo de escape delantero y el tubo central por pernos de afianzamiento. El silenciador es conectado al tubo central por una abrazadera y es soldado al tubo de cola.

El interior del convertidor catalítico es un diseño de panal que es revestido con platino y rodium. Cuando estos elementos actúan recíprocamente con el HC (hidrocarburos), el CO (monóxido de carbono) y el NOX (óxido de nitrógeno) en el escape, causan que reacciones ocurran y esto se convierte en CO a CO_2 (dióxido de carbono), el HC a CO y H_2O (agua) y reduce el NOX.

Debido a que fósforo y aditivos en la gasolina pueden envenenar los elementos del convertidor catalítico, así rindiéndolo ineficaz en alterar los elementos tóxicos de los gases, solamente combustible sin plomo se debe usar en el vehículo.

El mantenimiento periódico del convertidor no es requerido, pero tiene una vida de trabajo limitada, después debe ser reemplazado.

En orden para chequear exactamente el funcionamiento del convertidor, un probador de CO es necesario. Por esta razón, nosotros recomendamos que usted lleve el vehículo a un concesionario Nissan u otro taller calificado para hacer que el convertidor sea chequeado.

Si hay daño físico, el uso de combustible con plomo o porque sus elementos activos se han reducido, el convertidor catalítico es rendido ineficaz, debe ser reemplazado como una unidad.

Caución: Se debe notar que desde que las conversiones químicas internas ocurren entre los 600 grados y 1200 grados F, el convertidor opera a una temperatura muy alta. Antes de realizar cualquier trabajo en o cerca del convertidor esté seguro que se haya refrescado lo suficientemente para evitar quemaduras graves.

Cuando reemplace cualquier partes del sistema de escape, esté seguro que usted permite suficiente espacio libre entre todos los puntos de la carrocería para evitar sobrecalentar la cacerola del piso y posiblemente dañar la alfombra y el aislamiento del interior.

El sistema completo del escape es conectado a la carrocería con ganchos de caucho y soportes. Si cualquiera de las partes es instalada inapropiadamente, exceso de ruido y vibración será transmitido a la carrocería.

Inspección regular del sistema del escape debe ser hecho para mantenerlo en eficiencia máxima. Busque por partes desgastadas o dañadas, costuras abiertas, orificios, conexiones flojas, corrosión excesiva u otros defectos que podrían permitir que los vapores del escape entraran en el vehículo.

24   Escape - chequeo del sistema

Porque la inspección del sistema del escape es parte del itinerario de mantenimiento rutinario, refiérase al Capítulo 1 para este procedimiento.

25   Tubo de escape delantero - remover e instalar

Refiérase a las ilustraciones 25.2a y 25.2b

1   Levante el frente del vehículo y sosténgalo firmemente encima de soportes.

2   Remueva el protector inferior del convertidor catalítico y el protector superior (si está equipado) **(vea ilustraciones)**.

3   Usando un pedazo de alambre grueso, asegure el convertidor catalítico a la parte

25.5a Sistema de escape típico usado en vehículos equipado con carburador (abajo - modelos 1980 Canadienses; encima - todos los otros)

1   *Convertidor catalítico*
2   *Silenciador*
3   *Tubo de escape delantero*
4   *Silenciador*

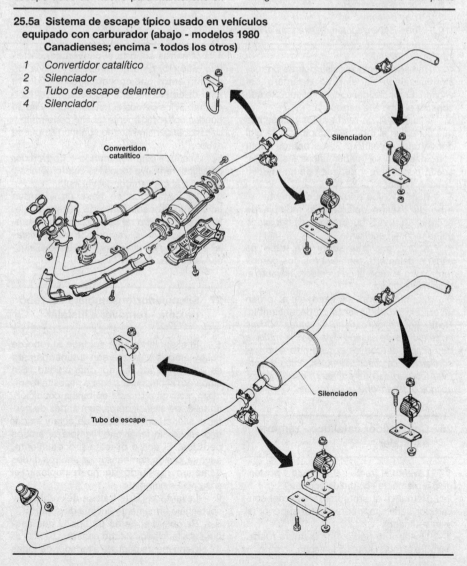

Convertidon catalítico

Silenciadon

Silenciadon

Tubo de escape

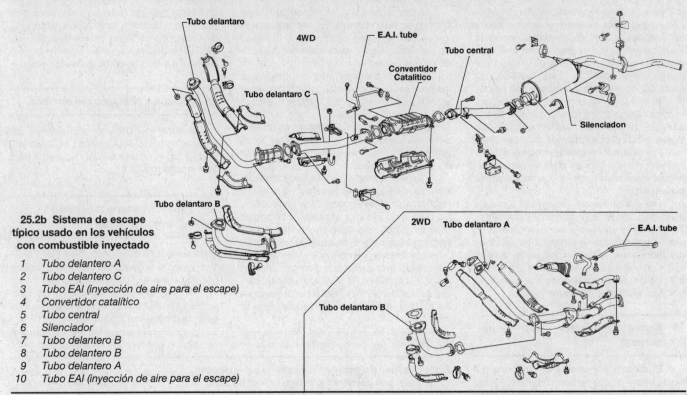

25.2b Sistema de escape
típico usado en los vehículos
con combustible inyectado

1   Tubo delantero A
2   Tubo delantero C
3   Tubo EAI (inyección de aire para el escape)
4   Convertidor catalítico
5   Tubo central
6   Silenciador
7   Tubo delantero B
8   Tubo delantero B
9   Tubo delantero A
10 Tubo EAI (inyección de aire para el escape)

inferior del vehículo.

4   Remueva cualquier aislación de protección instalada en el tubo delantero del escape. Entonces desconecte el soporte que conecta el tubo a la carrocería.

5   Afloje, pero no remueva los dos pernos que conectan el tubo de escape delantero al convertidor catalítico. Si los pernos están corroídos y no se pueden aflojar fácilmente, aceite penetrante y pegarle con un martillo pueden ayudar.

6   Remueva los pernos que conectan el tubo de escape delantero al múltiple de escape. Otra vez, pueda que sea necesario utilizar aceite penetrante.

7   Ahora, mientras soporta el tubo de escape delantero, remueva los dos pernos reteniendo el tubo al convertidor y levante el tubo hacia afuera.

8   La instalación se hace en el orden inverso al procedimiento de desensamble.
Nota: *Esté seguro de usar juntas nuevas entre el tubo de escape delantero, el múltiple de escape, el tubo de escape delantero y el convertidor catalítico. También, antes de instalar los pernos que conectan estas partes, aplique atascamiento a las roscas.*

26   Convertidor catalítico - remover e instalar

1   Levante el frente del vehículo y sosténgalo firmemente encima de soportes.

2   Remueva el protector inferior del convertidor catalítico y el protector superior (si está equipado).

3   Usando un pedazo de alambre fuerte, asegure el tubo central a la flecha.

4   Mientras soporta el convertidor catalítico, aflójelo, pero no remueva todavía los cuatro pernos que conecta el convertidor al tubo delantero del tubo de escape y el tubo central. Si los pernos están corroídos y no se pueden soltar fácilmente, aceite penetrante y pegándole gentilmente con un martillo puede ayudar.

5   Mientras está soportando el convertidor catalítico, remueva todos los cuatro pernos y remueva el convertidor del vehículo.

6   La instalación se hace en el orden inverso al procedimiento de desensamble.
Nota: *Esté seguro de usar durante la instalación juntas nuevas. También, antes de instalar los pernos de afianzamiento, aplique atascamiento a las roscas.*

27   Silenciador/ensamblaje del tubo de cola - remover e instalar

1   El silenciador está soldado al tubo de cola y ambos pedazos son diseñados para ser reemplazados como una unidad. Sin embargo, si cualquier pedazo necesita reemplazo, pero el otro está en buena condición, un taller de silenciadores será capaz de cortar el silenciador o el tubo de cola y soldar uno nuevo sin tener que reemplazar ambos pedazos. El costo de este procedimiento, aunque, puede compensar los ahorros dados como un resultado de no reemplazar el ensamblaje completo.

2   Levante la parte trasera del vehículo y sosténgalo firmemente encima de soportes.

3   Remueva el perno de tipo U que asegura el silenciador al tubo central.

4   Gentilmente péguele alrededor de todas las conexiones con un martillo para separar el sellador interno.

5   Con un martillo de cara suave, gentilmente péguele en el final delantero del silenciador para empujarlo hacia atrás hasta que el tubo del silenciador esté desenganchado del centro.

6   Remueva los pernos que conectan el soporte del tubo de cola al chasis y levante el ensamblaje hacia afuera.

7   La instalación se hace en el orden inverso al procedimiento de desensamble.
Nota: *Para asegurarse que ninguna fuga de escape ocurre desde el silenciador a la conexión del tubo central, un sellador de escape se debe usar durante la instalación. Siga las direcciones suministradas con el sellador.*

28   Tubo de escape central - remover e instalar

1   Remueva el silenciador/ensamblaje de tubo de cola como se indica en la Sección 27. Remueva las tuercas que conectan el soporte central del tubo de escape al chasis.

3   Remueva los pernos que conectan el tubo central al convertidor catalítico. Si ellos son difíciles de aflojar, use aceite penetrante y pegándole gentilmente con un martillo puede ayudar. El tubo central entonces se puede levantar hacia afuera.

4   La instalación se hace en el orden inverso al procedimiento de desensamble.
Nota: *Esté seguro de usar una junta nueva entre la instalación del tubo central y el convertidor catalítico. También, antes de instalar los pernos de afianzamiento, aplique atascamiento a las roscas.*

Capítulo 5
Sistemas eléctricos del motor

Contenidos

Especificaciones

Sistema de ignición

Distribuidor
Dirección de la rotación	A la izquierda
Espacio libre (modelos 1980 al 1985)	0.3 a 0.5 mm (0.012 a 0.020 pulgada)

Bobina para la ignición
Voltaje primario	12 voltios
Resistencia primaria a 68 grados F (20 grados C)	
1980	0.84 a 1.02 ohm
1981 al 1983	1.04 a 1.27 ohm
1984 y 1985	
Motor Z24	1.05 a 1.27 ohm
Motor Z20	0.84 a 1.02 ohm
1986 en adelante	0.8 a 1.0 ohm
Resistencia secundaria a 68 grados F (20 grados C)	
1980	8.2 a 12.4 ohm K
1981 al 1983	7.3 a 11.0 ohm K
1984 y 1985	
Motor Z24	8.4 a 12.6 ohm K
Motor Z20	8.3 a 12.6 ohm K
1986 en adelante	7.6 a 11.4 ohm
Resistencia del aislamiento de la tapa del distribuidor (1986 en adelante)	Sobre 50,000 ohm
Bujías	Vea Capítulo 1

Sistema de arranque

Motor de arranque
Longitud mínima de la brocha	
US	12 mm (0.470 pulgada)
Canadá	11 mm (0.430 pulgada)

Sistema de carga

Alternador

Rendimiento del regulador de voltaje.. 14.4 a 15.0 Voltios

Longitud mínima de la brocha

    1980 .... 7.5 mm (0.290 pulgada)

    1981 al 1985... 7.0 mm (0.280 pulgada)

    1986 en adelante.. Sobre 6.0 mm (0.240 pulgada)

1   Sistema de la ignición - información general

Para que el motor corra correctamente, es necesario de una chispa eléctrica para prender la mezcla de aire/combustible en la cámara de combustión exactamente en el momento correcto con relación a la velocidad del motor y la carga. El sistema de ignición es basado en un sistema de alimentación de bajo voltaje de la batería a la bobina, donde es convertido a alto voltaje. El alto voltaje es lo suficiente poderoso para saltar el espacio libre de la bujía en los cilindros muchas veces por segundo bajo presiones altas de compresión, proveyendo que el sistema esté en buena condición y que todos los ajustes estén correcto.

El sistema de la ignición está dividido en dos circuitos; el circuito de bajo voltaje y el circuito de alto voltaje.

El circuito de bajo voltaje (a veces conocido como circuito primario) se compone del interruptor de la ignición, ignición y relé de los accesorios, el embobinado primario de la bobina(s) para la ignición, la unidad de la ignición con transistor IC (control de la ignición), el ensamblaje captador en el distribuidor y todos los alambres de conexión.

El circuito de alto voltaje se compone del embobinado secundario de la bobina(s) para la ignición, el alambre grueso del centro de la bobina de la ignición a la tapa del distribuidor, el rotor, los alambres de las bujías y las bujías.

El distribuidor usado en los vehículos 1980 al 1985 es uno de tipo disparador de pulso, controlado por un transistor, la unidad inductiva de descarga para los platinos de un distribuidor convencional son reemplazados por un módulo de control y un ensamblaje magnético de captación.

El sistema funciona de la siguiente manera. El voltaje bajo suministrado a las bobinas es cambiado en alto voltaje por el captador magnético en el distribuidor. Cuando el interruptor de la ignición es prendido, la corriente fluye al circuito primario. Un reluctor en el eje del distribuidor es alineado con el elemento magnético del estator del ensamblaje del captador adentro del albergue del distribuidor y cuando lo gira induce un voltaje bajo en la bobina de captación. Cuando los dientes en el reluctor y los imanes en el estator forman una fila, una señal pasa a la unidad de la ignición IC (control de la ignición) que abre el circuito primario de la bobina. Cuando el circuito primario es abierto por la unidad del transistor, el campo primario magnético construido en el embobi-

nado se desploma e induce un voltaje alto en el embobinado secundario. La corriente alta del voltaje entonces fluye de la bobina, por el alambre grueso de la ignición, a la brocha de carbón en la tapa del distribuidor. De la brocha de carbón, la corriente fluye al rotor del distribuidor que distribuye la corriente a una de las terminales en la tapa del distribuidor. La chispa ocurre mientras el alto voltaje salta el espacio libre en la bujía. Este proceso es repetido para cada carrera de fuerza del motor.

El sistema tiene una duración larga de la chispa y el período del dwell automáticamente aumenta con la velocidad del motor. Esto es deseable para quemar las mezclas pobres proporcionadas por los sistemas de controles de emisiones.

La unidad de la ignición IC usada en los modelos 1981 al 1983 está localizada adentro del distribuidor, mientras que la unidad IC usada en los modelos 1980 está conectada al exterior del albergue del distribuidor.

Porque el motor de cuatro cilindros usado en los modelos 1981 y más modernos usan dos bujías para cada cilindro, el sistema de ignición utiliza dos bobinas para la ignición. Ambas están localizadas en el lado izquierdo del compartimiento del motor. La bobina superior trabaja en conjunto con las bujías del escape, mientras que la inferior trabaja con las bujías de admisión. Los modelos 1980 usan un juego convencional con una bujía por cilindro y una bobina para la ignición.

El distribuidor usado en todos los modelos está equipado con ambos avances del encendido regulado mecánicamente y por vacío del múltiple. El mecanismo mecánico del gobernador comprime dos pesas que se mueven hacia afuera del eje del distribuidor debido a la fuerza centrífuga cuando el motor aumenta de velocidad. Las pesas son sostenidas en posición por dos resortes livianos y es la presión de los resortes que es responsable por el avance correcto de la chispa.

El control de vacío se compone de un diafragma, un lado es conectado vía un pequeño orificio de un tubo a una fuente del vacío y el otro lado al ensamblaje magnético del captador. El vacío en el múltiple de admisión, que varía con la velocidad del motor y la abertura del acelerador, causa que el diafragma se mueva, que, en cambio, mueve el ensamblaje magnético captador, avanzando o retardando la chispa. El avance del encendido del distribuidor regulado por vacío del múltiple es controlado por el sistema de control de tiempo de la chispa y es explicado con todo detalle en el Capítulo 6.

Porque los vehículos fabricados después del 1986 están equipados con ECCS (sistema de computadora por control electrónico) (vea Capítulo 6), el distribuidor usado en estos modelos difiere en el diseño y la función de los distribuidores más antiguos. Un sensor del ángulo del cigüeñal adentro del distribuidor en todos los motores de cuatro cilindros (Z24i), motores KA24E y el V6 (VG30i) chequea la velocidad del motor y la posición del pistón, entonces manda una señal a la unidad del control al ECCS o ECU (unidad de control electrónica). La ECU usa esta señal para determinar la regulación del tiempo de la ignición, la duración del inyector de combustible y otras funciones. El ensamblaje del sensor del ángulo del cigüeñal se compone de un plato rotor, un circuito "formando una onda," un LED diodo electroluminiscente y un diodo de foto.

El plato rotor, que es conectado al eje del distribuidor, está en la base del albergue del distribuidor. Hay 360 aberturas rectificadas en la orilla exterior del plato de rotor. Estas aberturas corresponden a cada grado de rotación del cigüeñal. Adentro de esta fila exterior de aberturas hay una serie de cuatro o seis aberturas levemente más grande correspondiendo a cada cilindro en los motores de cuatro cilindros o los motores V6, respectivamente. En el distribuidor para los motores de cuatro cilindros, estas aberturas son espaciadas a 180 grados; en el distribuidor V6, ellas están espaciadas a 120 grados. En ambos los distribuidores de cuatro cilindros y V6, la abertura para el cilindro uno número es levemente más grande que las aberturas para los otros cilindros.

El circuito de formar ondas es puesto en posición debajo del plato del rotor. Un albergue pequeño conectado a un lado del circuito de formar ondas encierra las orillas superiores e inferiores exteriores del plato del rotor. Un LED (diodo electroluminiscente) es localizado en la mitad superior y un diodo de foto es localizado en la mitad inferior del albergue pequeño. Cuando el motor está en marcha, el LED emite un rayo continuo directamente al diodo de foto. Cuando la orilla exterior del plato del rotor pasa el albergue, las aberturas permiten que el rayo pase al diodo de foto, pero en los espacios sólidos entre las aberturas bloquean la luz del rayo. Esta interrupción constante genera pulsos que son convertidos en señales por el circuito de formar ondas y enviados al ECU (unidad de control electrónica). La ECU usa la señal de la fila exterior de aberturas para determinar la velocidad del motor y la posición del cigüeñal. Usa la señal generada por las aberturas interiores y más grandes para determinar cuando disparar cada cilindro. Esta información es entonces revelada a la bobina que construye el voltaje secundario y lo envía a la tapa del distribuidor en manera convencional, donde es distribuido por el rotor al cilindro apropiado.

Peligro: *A causa del voltaje alto generado por el sistema de la ignición electrónica, extrema caución se debe tomar cuando una operación sea realizada de los componentes implicando la ignición. Esto no sólo incluye el distribuidor, la bobina, el módulo de control y los alambres de la ignición, pero artículos relacionados que están conectados al sistema también, tales como las conexiones de las bujías, el tacómetro y cualquier equipo de prueba. Consecuentemente, antes de que cualquier trabajo sea conducido, tal como reemplazar los componentes de la ignición o hasta conectando los equipos de prueba, la ignición se debe apagar o el cable de conexión a tierra de la batería ser desconectado. Nunca desconecte ningún alambre de la ignición de alto voltaje cuando el motor esté en marcha o la unidad del transistor de la ignición será permanentemente dañada.*

---

2   Sistema de la ignición - chequeo

Refiérase a las ilustraciones 2.7a, 2.7b, 2.8a, 2.8b, 2.9a, 2.9b, 2.11a, 2.11b, 2.11c, 2.12a, 2.12b, 2.12c, 2.13, 2.14 y 2.15

Peligro: *Nunca toque los alambres de las bujías ni los alambres de la bobina con su mano sin aislamiento mientras el motor está en marcha o se está tratando de poner en marcha. Hasta las partes todavía aislada pueden causar un golpe de chispa si ellas están húmedas. Use guantes aislados secos o envuelva la parte en tela seca antes de tocarlas.*

1   Si el motor gira pero no se pone en marcha, el primer chequeo del sistema de la ignición debe ser visualmente la condición de las bujías, los alambres de las bujías, el rotor y tapa del distribuidor como está descrito en el Capítulo 1. Chequee también el espacio libre de aire en el distribuidor según se indica en la Sección 3.

2   Si todos éstos están en buenas condiciones y los alambres de las bujías están seguros en sus conexiones, el próximo chequeo debe ser si la corriente está fluyendo a través del circuito de alto voltaje y causando una chispa en las bujías.

a) Gire el interruptor de la ignición a Apagado.

b) Desconecte el conector del alambrado que dirige el conector de la válvula del solenoide Anti diesel (solenoide para detener que el motor continúe en marcha) para cortarle el combustible al motor.

c) Desconecte el alambre de la bobina para la ignición de la tapa del distribuidor y lo detiene aproximadamente 3/16 a 1/4 de pulgada (4 a 5 mm) en un área limpia de metal en el motor. Tenga a un

ayudante para que gire el motor y chequee si una chispa ocurre entre el alambre de la bobina y el motor. En sistemas con dos bobinas para la ignición, chequee ambos alambres de la bobina en esta manera.

d) Si una chispa ocurre, el sistema de la ignición está bueno y el problema está en otra parte del sistema. Si ninguna chispa ocurre, o ocurre intermitentemente, proceda con las pruebas adicionales del sistema de la ignición.

3   Para diagnosticar exactamente los problemas en el sistema de la ignición, un voltímetro que mida entre 0 a 20 voltios DC y 0 a 10 voltios AC y un ohmímetro que mide entre la escala de 0 a 1000 ohm y 0 a 5000 ohm es necesitado.

4   Si es posible, ponga el motor en marcha y permítalo que corra acerca de 5 a 15 minutos con el capó cerrado para traer todos los componentes a la temperatura normal de operación. Apague el motor.

5   Chequeando el voltaje de la batería sin carga:

a) Con la ignición puesta en la posición de apagado, conecte el alambre positivo de un voltímetro en la terminal positiva de la batería y el alambre negativo en la terminal negativa de la batería.

b) Note la lectura en el voltímetro. Si la lectura está entre 11.5 voltios y 12.5 voltios, la batería está buena y usted debe proceder al Paso 7.

c) Si la lectura está abajo de 11.5 voltios, la batería está insuficientemente cargada. Debe ser llevada a una carga completa poniendo el motor en marcha o usando un cargador de batería. Si el vehículo se ha usado en una base regular y no hay una causa obvia para la descarga de la batería (tal como dejando las luces encendidas), entonces la condición de la batería, sistema de carga y sistema de arranque debe ser chequeado como está descrito en este Capítulo o el Capítulo 1.

6   Chequeando el voltaje de la batería mientras el motor está arrancando:

2.7a La resistencia del alambre de la bujía es chequeado conectando el alambre del ohmímetro en el extremo del alambre de la bujía y la otra terminal a la parte correspondiente de la terminal interior de la tapa

a) Deje el voltímetro conectado a la batería como en la prueba anterior.

b) Desconecte el alambre(s) de la bobina para la ignición de la tapa del distribuidor y conéctelo a tierra del motor.

c) Haga que un ayudante gire el motor por cerca de 15 segundos y note la lectura en el voltímetro.

d) Si el voltaje es más de 9.6 voltios, la batería está buena y usted debe proceder al Paso 8. Si el voltaje está debajo de 9.6 voltios, la batería está insuficientemente cargada. Refiérase al Paso 6.

7   Chequee la tapa del distribuidor y los alambres secundarios (de las bujías):

a) Desconecte los alambres de las bujías en el lado de las bujías.

b) Desconecte el alambre(s) de la bobina para la bobina(s) de la ignición.

c) Remueva la tapa del distribuidor, con los alambres de las bujías y la bobina todavía conectada.

d) Conecte un ohmímetro para que un alambre sea insertado en el extremo de los alambres de las bujías y el otro extremo esté en contacto a la terminal interior de la tapa del distribuidor donde el alambre es conectado **vea ilustración).**

e) Si la lectura en el ohmímetro es de menos de 30,000 ohm, la terminal de la tapa y el alambre están bueno.

f) Si la lectura es más de 30,000 ohm, la resistencia es demasiado alta. Chequee la tapa y el alambre individualmente y reemplace la parte apropiada.

g) Repita esta prueba en cada alambre de bujía y la bobina.

h) Chequee la tapa y el rotor por polvo, depósitos de carbón y roturas. En los modelos 1986 al 1988, mida la resistencia de aislamiento entre los electrodos en las torres de la bobina y la bujía **(vea ilustración).** Si la lectura está debajo de la especificación, reemplace la tapa.

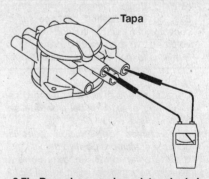

2.7b Para chequear la resistencia de la tapa del distribuidor en los modelos 1986 y más modernos, conecte un alambre del ohmímetro a la terminal de la bobina y el otro alambre a la terminal para cada alambre de la bujía (desde que hay dos bujías por cada cilindro en los motores de cuatro cilindros, esté seguro de chequear ambas terminales)

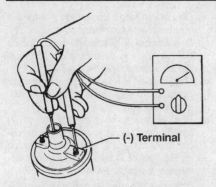

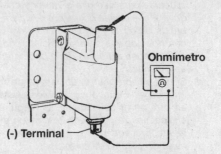

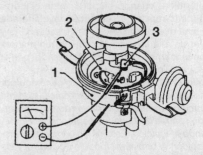

2.8a Coloque un alambre del ohmímetro adentro de la terminal de alto voltaje de la bobina y toque la otra terminal (-) para chequear la resistencia secundaria de la bobina en los modelos 1980 al 1985

2.8b Para chequear la resistencia secundaria de la bobina en los modelos 1986 y más modernos, coloque un alambre del ohmímetro adentro de la terminal de alto voltaje de la bobina y toque la otro terminal (-)

2.9a El circuito de suministro de poder en los modelos 1980 al 1985 con un sistema de ignición doble es chequeado conectando el alambre positivo del voltímetro a la terminal B en la unidad de la ignición IC (control de la ignición) en el distribuidor y poniendo a tierra el alambre negativo en el exterior del albergue del distribuidor

1   Albergue
2   Unidad de la ignición IC (control de la ignición)
3   Terminal "B" (suplemento de energía)

8   Chequeando el circuito secundario de la bobina de la ignición:

a) *Con la ignición puesta en la posición de apagado, conecte el ohmímetro para que un alambre esté haciendo contacto con el conector central del alambre de alto voltaje y el otro alambre sea contado a la terminal negativa de la bobina* **(vea ilustraciones)**.

b) *Si la lectura está dentro de la distancia especificada, los embobinados secundarios de la bobina están buenos.*

c) *Si la lectura del ohmímetro no está dentro de las especificación, reemplace la bobina para la ignición (en sistemas con bobinas dobles para la ignición esté seguro de chequear cada bobina).*

9   Chequee el circuito del suministro de poder en el distribuidor (modelos 1980 al 1985):

a) *En sistemas de doble ignición, conecte el alambre positivo del voltímetro a la terminal B en la unidad de la ignición IC (control de la ignición) en el distribuidor* **(vea ilustración)**. *Nota: Cuando realice este o cualquiera de las siguientes pruebas, no es necesario desconectar el conector del alambre cuando instale un voltímetro u ohmímetro, proveyendo que ellos tengan dos alambres que puedan ser insertados en el conector trasero.*

b) *Conecte a tierra el alambre negativo del voltímetro al exterior del albergue del distribuidor.*

c) *En sistemas de ignición sencilla, conecte el alambre positivo del voltímetro a la conexión B. Ponga a tierra el alambre negativo del voltímetro al distribuidor como está mostrado* **(vea ilustración)**.

d) *Gire la llave de la ignición a la posición de Encendido y note la lectura del voltímetro.*

e) *Si la lectura está entre 11.5 y 12.5 voltios, el circuito de suministro de poder está bueno. Si la lectura está bajo de 11.5 voltios, inspeccione el alambrado*

entre el interruptor de la ignición y la unidad IC por daño o conexiones flojas o sucias.

10   Chequeando el circuito primario de la bobina de la ignición (modelos 1980 al 1985):

a) *Conecte a tierra el alambre(s) secundario de la bobina al motor.*

b) *Conecte el voltímetro como en el Paso 9.*

c) *Haga que un ayudante gire el motor alrededor de 15 segundos y note la lectura en el voltímetro.*

d) *Si la lectura es menos de un voltio debajo del voltaje de arranque de la batería (medido en el Paso 6) y es más de 8.6 voltios, el circuito está bueno.*

e) *Si la lectura es más de un voltio debajo del voltaje de arranque de la batería y/o está debajo de 8.6 voltios, inspeccione el alambrado entre el interruptor de la ignición y la unidad IC por daño o conexiones flojas o sucias.*

11   Chequeando el circuito primario de la ignición (modelos 1980 al 1985):

a) *En los sistema de ignición sencilla, conecte el alambre del voltímetro positivo para que el alambre de là terminal C en la unidad IC (control de la ignición) y*

el alambre negativo haga contacto con el distribuidor como está mostrado (vea ilustración). Gire la llave de la ignición a la posición de Encendido y note la lectura del voltímetro. Si la lectura está entre 11.5 y 12.5 voltios, el circuito está bueno. Proceda al Paso 13. Si es menos de 11.5 voltios, proceda al Paso 12.

b) En el sistema de doble ignición, conecte el alambre positivo del voltímetro para que haga contacto con la terminal I en la unidad IC y el alambre negativo que haga contacto con el exterior del albergue del distribuidor **(vea ilustración)**. Gire la llave de la ignición a la posición de Encendido y note la lectura del voltímetro. Si los voltios mostrados son menos de 11.5, proceda al Paso 12. Si se muestra entre 11.5 y 12.5 voltios, conecte de nuevo el alambre positivo del voltímetro a la terminal E en la uni-

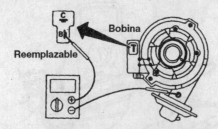

2.9b Para chequear el circuito del suministro de poder en los modelos 1980 al 1985 con un solo sistema de ignición, conecte el alambre positivo del voltímetro a la conexión B y la conexión a tierra del alambre negativo del voltímetro al exterior del albergue del distribuidor

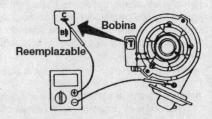

2.11a Conecte el alambre positivo del voltímetro a la terminal C en la unidad IC (control de la ignición) y conecte a tierra el alambre negativo del exterior del albergue del distribuidor para chequear el circuito primario en los modelos 1980 al 1985 con un sistema de ignición sencillo

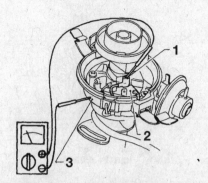

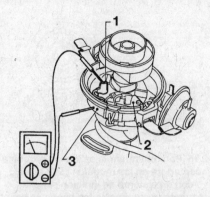

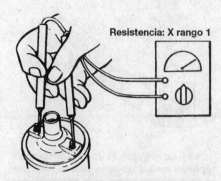

Resistencia: X rango 1

2.11b Para chequear el circuito primario de la ignición en los modelos 1980 al 1985 con sistema de doble ignición, conecte el alambre positivo del voltímetro a la terminal en la unidad del IC (control de la ignición) y conecte a tierra el alambre negativo al exterior del albergue del distribuidor . . .

1 Terminal "I"
2 Unidad de la ignición IC (control de la ignición)
3 Albergue

2.11c . . . y si su lectura es entre 11.5 y 12.5 voltios, conecte de nuevo el alambre positivo del voltímetro a la terminal E en la unidad IC (control de la ignición) y tome otra lectura

1 Terminal "E"
2 Unidad de la ignición IC (control de la ignición)
3 Albergue

2.12a Para chequear la bobina de la ignición chequee la resistencia primaria del circuito en los modelos 1980 al 1985, conecte los alambres del ohmímetro a las terminales positivas y negativas de la bobina como está mostrado (esté seguro de poner el ohmímetro en la escala de 1X)

dad IC **(vea ilustración)** y con la llave de la ignición todavía Encendida, tome la lectura del voltímetro. Si se muestra entre 11.5 y 12.5 voltios, el circuito está bueno. Proceda al Paso 13. Si se muestra 11.5 voltios o menos en esta lectura, proceda al Paso 12.

12 Chequeando el circuito primario de la bobina para la ignición:

a) Con la llave de la ignición puesta en la posición de apagado y el alambre de la bobina para la ignición removido de la bobina, conecte un ohmímetro (póngalo en la escala de X 1) entre la terminal positiva y negativa en la bobina de la ignición (vea ilustraciones).
b) Si el ohmímetro lee adentro del rango

especificado la bobina está buena. En los modelos 1980 al 1985 el interruptor de la ignición y el alambrado entre el interruptor de la ignición, la bobina y la unidad de IC deben ser chequeados por daño, o conexiones flojas o sucias.
c) Si el ohmímetro no lee adentro de estas especificaciones, la bobina para la ignición debe ser reemplazada.

Nota: En sistemas de doble ignición, esté seguro de chequear ambas bobinas para la ignición.

13 Chequeando el circuito de conexión a tierra de la unidad IC (modelos 1980 al 1985):

a) Remueva el alambre(s) para la bobina de la ignición de la tapa del distribuidor y conéctelo a tierra en el motor.
b) Conecte un alambre negativo del voltímetro a la terminal negativa de la batería

y al alambre positivo del distribuidor como está mostrado **(vea ilustración)**.
c) Haga que un ayudante gire el motor por cerca de 15 segundos y note la lectura del voltímetro.
d) Si más de 0.5 voltios es mostrado, chequee la tierra del distribuidor, el alambrado entre la batería y la conexión a tierra del chasis y la conexión del cable negativo de la batería.
e) Si la lectura muestra 0.5 voltios o menos en el sistema de doble ignición, la unidad IC debe ser reemplazada.
f) Si 0.5 voltios o menos es mostrado en un sistema de ignición sencilla, chequeos adicionales son necesarios. Proceda al Paso 14.

14 Chequeando la resistencia de la bobina de captación (modelos 1980 al 1985):

a) Para este chequeo el motor debe estar a la temperatura normal de operación.
b) Con el interruptor de la ignición en la posición de Apagado, conecte un ohmí-

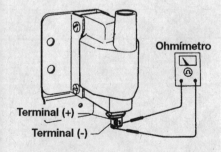

Ohmímetro
Terminal (+)
Terminal (-)

2.12b Para chequear la resistencia primaria de la bobina para la ignición en los modelos 1986 y más modernos, conecte los alambres del ohmímetro a las terminales positivas y negativas de la bobina como está mostrado (esté seguro de poner el ohmímetro en la escala de 1X)

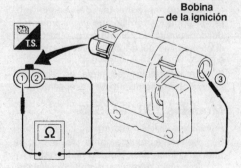

Bobina de la ignición

2.12c En las bobinas 1990 y 1991, chequee el valor de la resistencia entre las terminales 1 y 2. Debe ser entre 0.7 a 1.0 ohm. Entonces chequee la resistencia entre las terminales 1 y 3. Debe ser 10,000 ohm

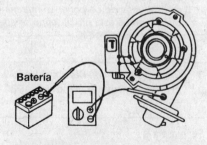

Batería

2.13 Para chequear el circuito de conexión a tierra de la unidad IC (control de la ignición) en los modelos 1980 al 1985, conecte un alambre del voltímetro a la terminal negativa de la batería y el alambre positivo al exterior del albergue del distribuidor como está mostrado

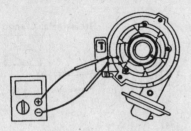

2.14 La resistencia de la bobina del captador en los modelos 1980 al 1985 con un solo sistema de ignición es chequeado conectando un voltímetro (en la escala de 100X) entre los puntos indicados

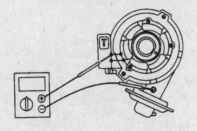

2.15 Para chequear la salida de la bobina captadora en los modelos 1980 al 1985 con un sistema de ignición sencillo, conecte un voltímetro (en la escala baja de volteos AC) entre los puntos indicados

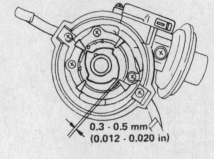

0.3 - 0.5 mm (0.012 - 0.020 in)

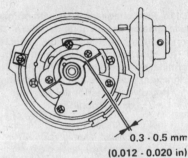

0.3 - 0.5 mm (0.012 - 0.020 in)

metro (en la escala de 100x) como está mostrado **(vea ilustración)** y note la lectura.

c) Si la lectura está substancialmente por encima de o por debajo de 400 ohm, inspeccione la bobina de captación y su alambrado por daño, o conexiones flojas o sucias.

15   Chequee el rendimiento de la bobina de captación (modelos 1980 al 1985):

a) El motor debe estar a la temperatura normal de operación.

b) Conecte un voltímetro (puesto en la escala baja del voltaje AC) entre los puntos indicados **(vea ilustración)**.

c) Desconecte el alambre de la bobina para la ignición de la tapa del distribuidor y usando un alambre para puente, conéctelo a tierra al motor. Haga que un ayudante gire el motor por cerca de 15 segundos y observe el movimiento de la aguja del voltímetro.

d) Si la aguja está estabiliza, chequee la condición física de la bobina de captación y reluctor por daño. Chequee también el alambrado entre la bobina de captación y la unidad de IC (control de la ignición) por daño, o conexiones flojas o sucias.

e) Si la aguja se mueve mientras el motor se está tratando de poner en marcha y todavía no se está produciendo chispa, reemplace la unidad IC.

---

3   Espacio libre del distribuidor - chequeo y ajuste (modelos 1980 al 1985)

Refiérase a la ilustración 3.4
Nota: *Para asegurarse que el sistema de la ignición funciona correctamente, el espacio libre de aire (la distancia entre la bobina de captación y el reluctor) debe estar como está especificado. Para hacer esto, proceda como sigue:*

1   Desengrane los dos clips reteniendo el resorte y remueva la tapa del distribuidor.
2   Remueva el rotor del final del eje del distribuidor.

3   Posicione uno de los segmentos levantados del reluctor directamente en el frente del polo de la bobina de captación. Esto es llevado a cabo mejor removiendo las bujías (para aliviar la compresión) y gire el cigüeñal usando una matraca y un dado en el perno del cigüeñal en el frente del motor.
4   Usando un calibrador al tacto, mida el espacio libre entre el alambre y el segmento del reluctor **(vea ilustración)**. Debe de estar entre 0.3 a 0.5 mm (0.012 a 0.020 pulgada). Si el espacio libre del aire requiere ajuste, afloje los tornillos reteniendo la bobina de captación y mueva la bobina en la dirección requerida.
5   Cuando el espacio libre correcto se ha obtenido, apriete los tornillos reteniendo la bobina de captación e instale el rotor y la tapa del distribuidor.

---

4   Unidad de la ignición IC (control de la ignición) - remover e instalar (modelos 1980 al 1985)

Modelos 1980

1   La unidad de la ignición IC usada en estos modelos está localizada en el exterior del albergue del distribuidor y es removida removiendo el conector del alambrado, removiendo los tornillos de afianzamiento y desconectando los alambres que se dirigen al ensamblaje del captador **(vea ilustración 8.5)**.
2   La instalación se hace en el orden inverso al procedimiento de desensamble.

Modelos 1981 al 1985

Refiérase a las ilustraciones 4.6 y 4.7
3   Remueva los alambres de la bobina para la ignición de la tapa del distribuidor.
4   Remueva la tapa del distribuidor del distribuidor y póngala fuera del camino.
5   Remueva el perno en el lado del rotor y remueva el rotor del eje del distribuidor.
6   Usando dos destornilladores, hágale palanca al reluctor hacia afuera del eje del distribuidor **(vea ilustración)**. Tenga cuidado de no dañar los dientes del reluctor.

3.4 Para chequear el espacio libre del aire en el distribuidor, ponga en posición uno de los segmentos levantados del reluctor directamente frente al imán del estator (el pedazo del polo) saliendo de la bobina de captación y usando un calibrador al tacto, mida el espacio libre entre ellos (modelo 1980 - encima; modelos 1981 al 1985 - en la parte inferior)

---

7   Remueva los tres alambres de la unidad de la ignición IC **(vea ilustración)**.
8   Remueva los dos tornillos reteniendo la unidad de la ignición IC al distribuidor y lo eleva hacia afuera.
9   La instalación se hace en el orden inverso al procedimiento de desensamble. **Nota:** *El reluctor puede ser instalado pren-*

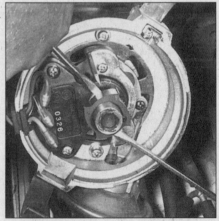

4.6 Para remover el reluctor del distribuidor en los modelos 1981 al 1985, hágale palanca para removerlo con un par de destornilladores (tenga cuidado de no dañar los dientes del reluctor)

4.7 Para remover la unidad IC (control de la ignición) del distribuidor en los modelos 1981 al 1985, remueva ambos tornillos (A), separe los tres alambres y remueva la unidad IC - para remover el estator y el imán (ensamblaje captador), remueva los tornillos (B) y los levanta hacia afuera

6.3 Antes de remover el distribuidor, esté seguro de marcar la relación del rotor al albergue del distribuidor para asegurar que los dos componentes están alineados correctamente cuando sea reinstalado (un distribuidor más antiguo es mostrado)

6.6a Antes de remover el distribuidor, esté seguro de marcar el perno de ajuste para asegurarse que el distribuidor sea instalado en el mismo lugar

6.6b Para remover el distribuidor en los modelos 1981 al 1985, destornille los dos pernos (flechas) pero no afloje los pernos de ajuste

sándolo en el eje del distribuidor. La clavija en el reluctor debe ser alineada con la línea plana en el eje del distribuidor.

---

5 Estator e imán (ensamblaje del captador) - remover e instalar (modelos 1980 al 1985)

Modelos 1980

1   Desconecte el alambre de la bobina para la ignición de la cima de la tapa del distribuidor.
2   Remueva la tapa del distribuidor del distribuidor y póngala fuera del camino.
3   Hale el rotor del eje del distribuidor.
4   Usando dos destornilladores (uno en cada lado del reluctor), hágale palanca cuidadocamonto al reluctor en el eje del distribuidor. Tenga cuidado de no dañar los dientes en el reluctor **(vea ilustración 8.5).**
5   Remueva los tornillos reteniendo el estator y el imán a la placa del ruptor del distribuidor y levántelo hacia afuera.
6   Desconecte el conjunto del alambrado/arnés del distribuidor y levante hacia afuera el ensamblaje de la bobina de captación.
7   La instalación se hace en el orden inverso al procedimiento de desensamble. Cuando esté instalando el reluctor, esté seguro que la clavija está en línea con el lado plano del eje del distribuidor. También, antes de apretar el estator, chequee y ajuste el espacio libre de aire como es indicado en la Sección 3.

Modelos 1981 al 1985

8   Remueva los alambres de la bobina para la ignición de la tapa del distribuidor.
9   Remueva la tapa del distribuidor del distribuidor y póngala fuera del camino.

10   Remueva el perno en el lado del rotor y remueva el rotor del eje del distribuidor.
11   Usando dos destornilladores (uno en cada lado del reluctor), hágale palanca al reluctor en el eje del distribuidor. Tenga cuidado de no dañar los dientes del reluctor **(vea ilustración 4.6).**
12   Remueva los tornillos reteniendo el estator y el imán a la placa del ruptor y elévelo hacia afuera **(vea ilustración 4.7).**
13   La instalación se hace en el orden inverso al procedimiento de desensamble. **Nota:** *El reluctor puede ser instalado prensándolo en el eje del distribuidor, pero esté seguro que la clavija en el reluctor está alineada con el lado plano en el eje del distribuidor. También, antes de apretar el estator, chequee y ajuste el espacio libre del aire según se indica en la Sección 3.*

---

6 Distribuidor - remover

Refiérase a las ilustraciones 6.3, 6.6a y 6.6b
1   Remueva el alambre(s) para la bobina de la ignición que se dirigen al distribuidor desde la bobina(s).
2   Remueva la tapa del distribuidor del distribuidor y póngala fuera del camino.
3   Marque el rotor en relación al albergue del distribuidor **(vea ilustración).**
4   Desconecte los alambres o el conector del alambrado que va a la unidad de la ignición IC (modelos 1980 al 1985) o el sensor del ángulo del cigüeñal (modelos 1986 al 1988).
5   Remueva la línea de vacío del canasto de avance del encendido regulado por vacío del múltiple (modelos 1980 al 1985 solamente).
6   Marque la posición del perno de ajuste para el distribuidor **(vea ilustración),** remueva los dos pernos para el afianzamiento del distribuidor **(vea ilustración)** y

levante hacia afuera el distribuidor. **Nota:** *No afloje los pernos para el ajuste del distribuidor en los modelos 1981 al 1985.*

---

7 Distribuidor - instalación

Refiérase a la ilustración 7.9

Si el cigüeñal no se giró después que se removió

1   Posicione el rotor exactamente como estaba cuando el distribuidor fue removido.
2   Baje el distribuidor hacia abajo en el motor. Para engranarlo en la ranura en el fondo del eje del distribuidor con el engrane (que gira el eje del distribuidor), pueda que sea necesario girar el rotor levemente.
3   Con la base del distribuidor completamente hacia abajo contra el bloque del motor y los orificios para el tornillo de afianzamiento en línea, el rotor debe estar apuntando a la marca hecha en el albergue del distribuidor

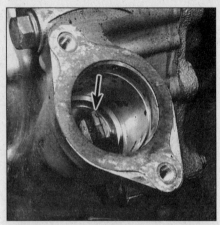

7.9 Si el pistón número uno está en el TDC (punto muerto superior), el engrane saliente del diente (flecha) del engrane del distribuidor debe estar casi vertical (inclinado levemente a la dirección contra las manecillas del reloj) y desviado hacia el frente del motor

durante el proceso de remover. Si el rotor no está en alineación con la marca, repita el Paso previo.

4   Instale el perno(s) de retención del distribuidor y apriételo firmemente.

5   Conecte la línea del vacío al canasto para el avance del encendido regulado por vacío del múltiple (si está equipado).

6   Conecte de nuevo los alambres a la unidad de IC (modelos 1980 al 1985) o sensor del ángulo del cigüeñal (modelos 1986 al 1988).

7   Vuelva a instalar la tapa del distribuidor y conecte el alambre(s) a la bobina para la ignición.

8   Chequee la regulación del tiempo de la ignición como está descrito en el Capítulo 1.

Si el cigüeñal se giró después que se removió

9   Posicione el pistón número uno en el TDC (punto muerto superior), refiriéndose al Capítulo 2, si es necesario. En los modelos 1980 al 1985 chequee que el pistón número uno esté en la carrera de compresión notando la posición del vástago del engrane del distribuidor. El engrane saliente debe estar casi vertical (inclinado levemente a la dirección izquierda) y desviándose hacia el frente del motor **(vea ilustración)**.

10   Instale temporariamente la tapa del distribuidor en el distribuidor. Note donde la terminal de la bujía número uno está localizada adentro de la tapa en relación al albergue del distribuidor y haga una marcada en el exterior del cuerpo en este punto.

11   Remueva la tapa del distribuidor otra vez. Gire el rotor hasta que se alinee con la marca. En esta posición debe estar apuntando a la bujía número uno.

12   Proceda con la instalación como está descrito en el Pasos 2 al 8. No le ponga atención a la marca de referencia del rotor en el Paso 3.

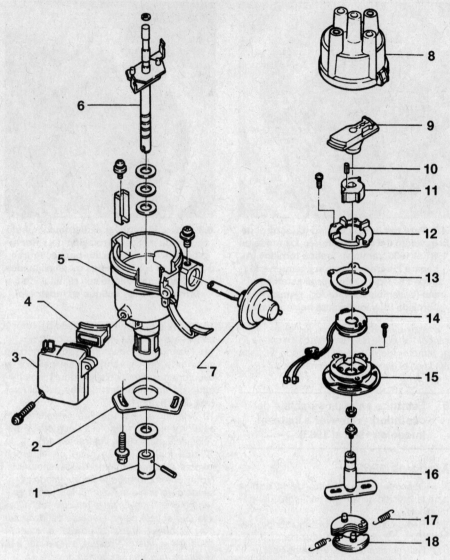

8.5 Vista esquemática del distribuidor usado en los modelos 1980

1	Collar	6	Ensamblaje del eje	13	Magneto
2	Plato de fijación	7	Controlador del vacío	14	Bobina captadora
3	Unidad de la ignición IC (control de la ignición)	8	Tapa	15	Plato ruptor
		9	Rotor	16	Eje del rotor
4	Hembrilla	10	Clavija de tipo rodillo	17	Resorte del gobernador
5	Albergue	11	Reluctor		
		12	Estator	18	Peso del gobernador

8   Distribuidor - remover y volver a instalar

Modelos 1980

Refiérase a la ilustración 8.5

1   Remueva el distribuidor del vehículo según se indica en la Sección 6.

2   Remueva la tapa del distribuidor.

3   Hale hacia afuera el rotor.

4   Desconecte el conector del alambrado que se dirige a la unidad IC.

5   Remueva los tornillos **(vea ilustración)** y levante hacia afuera el ensamblaje del estator y el imán.

6   Remueva los tornillos reteniendo el canasto de vacío y levántelo hacia afuera.

7   Usando dos destornilladores, uno en cada lado del reluctor, hágale palanca cuidadosamente al eje del distribuidor. Tenga cuidado de no dañar los dientes de reluctor.

8   Accione la clavija de rollo fuera del reluctor.

9   Remueva el ensamblaje de la bobina de captación.

10   Remueva los tornillos del conjunto de la placa ruptora y levante hacia afuera el ensamblaje de la placa del ruptor.

11   Usando un punzón adecuado, remueva la clavija del collar y hale hacia afuera el collar.

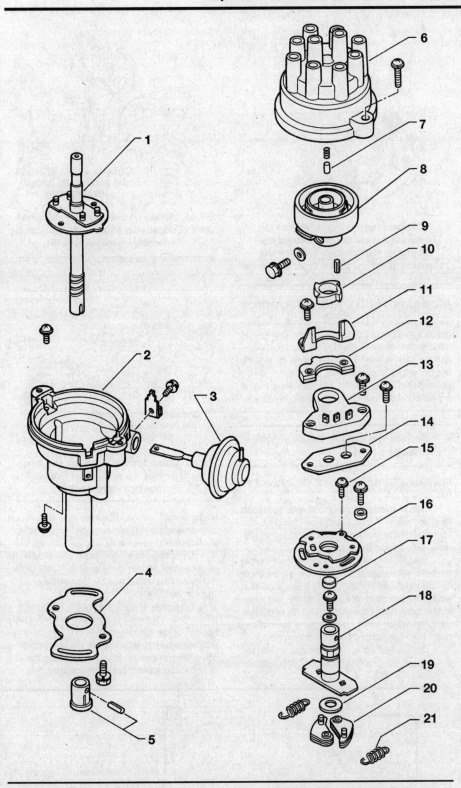

8.20 Vista esquemática del distribuidor usado en los modelos 1981 al 1985

1   Ensamblaje del eje
2   Albergue
3   Controlador de vacío
4   Plato de fijación
5   Collar de fijación
6   Tapa
7   Punto de carbón
8   Rotor
9   Clavija de rodillo
10   Reluctor
11   Estator
12   Magneto
13   Unidad de la ignición IC (control de la ignición)
14   Unidad de establecimiento
15   Tornillo de conexión para el controlador de vacío
16   Ensamblaje del plato ruptor
17   Empaque
18   Ensamblaje del eje del rotor
19   Arandela contra la fricción
20   peso del gobernador
21   Resorte del gobernador

al procedimiento de desensamble con las siguientes notas:

a) Esté seguro de alinear correctamente todas las marcas que se hicieron durante el periodo de remover para que todas las partes sean ensambladas en sus posiciones originales.

b) Cuando instale el reluctor en el eje, empuje la clavija de rollo en el reluctor para que su abertura sea puesta en posición hacia el extremo final del eje. Siempre use una clavija de tipo rollo nueva.

c) Antes de instalar la unidad de IC en el albergue del distribuidor, asegúrese que las superficies de acoplamiento de ambas unidades IC y el distribuidor están limpias y libre de tierra o humedad. Esto es muy importante.

d) Antes de apretar el plato del estator, ajuste el espacio libre de aire según se indica en la Sección 3.

Modelos 1981 al 1985

Refiérase a las ilustraciones 8.20, 8.25 y 8.28

18   Remueva el distribuidor del motor según se indica en la Sección 6.

19   Remueva la tapa del distribuidor.

20   Remueva el perno **(vea ilustración)** y levante el rotor.

21   Usando dos destornilladores, uno en cada lado del reluctor, hágale palanca cuidadosamente al eje del distribuidor. Tenga cuidado de no dañar los dientes del reluctor.

22   Remueva el tornillo reteniendo la unidad del IC y levante hacia afuera la unidad de IC y

---

12   Hale el ensamblaje del rotor y el eje de mando hacia fuera a través de la parte de encima del distribuidor.

13   Marque la posición relativa del eje y el rotor. Remueva el empaque en la parte de encima del eje del rotor, remueva el tornillo del eje del rotor y separe los dos ejes.

14   Marque la relación de uno de los resortes de gobernación a su soporte. Marque

también la relación de una de las pesas del gobernador a sus clavijas pivote.

15   Desenganche cuidadosamente y remueva los resortes del gobernador.

16   Remueva las pesas del gobernador. Una cantidad pequeña de grasa debe ser aplicada a las pesas después de ser removidas.

17   El ensamble se hace en el orden inverso

8.25 Antes de remover el ensamblaje de la placa ruptora, marque la relación del plato de fijación al albergue del distribuidor

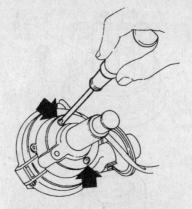

8.28 Para remover el retenedor del cojinete del eje del distribuidor del albergue, remueva los tornillos del retenedor (flechas) y levante el retenedor

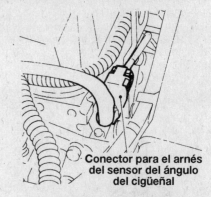

Conector para el arnés del sensor del ángulo del cigüeñal

9.4a Ubicación del conector del arnés para el sensor del ángulo del cigüeñal (se muestra un motor KA24E)

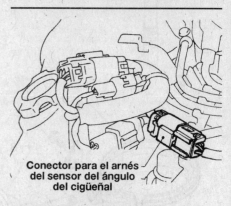

Conector para el arnés del sensor del ángulo del cigüeñal

9.4b Ubicación del conector del arnés para el sensor del ángulo del cigüeñal (se muestra un motor V6)

la unidad de fijación.

23   Remueva los tornillos que conectan el estator y eleve hacia afuera el estator y el imán.

24   Remueva los tornillos que retienen el canasto de vacío y levántelo hacia afuera.

25   Marque la relación del plato fijo al albergue del distribuidor **(vea ilustración)**, entonces remueva el ensamblaje de la placa ruptora.

26   Remueva el plato de fijación.

27   Usando un punzón adecuado, accione la clavija del collar y hale hacia afuera el collar.

28   Remueva los tornillos que conectan el retenedor del cojinete al albergue **(vea ilustración)** y levante el retenedor hacia afuera.

29   Hale el ensamblaje del eje del rotor y la flecha hacia afuera por la parte de encima del distribuidor.

30   Marque la posición relativa del eje del rotor y el eje. Remueva el empaque de la parte superior del eje del rotor, remueva el tornillo de acoplamiento del eje del rotor y separe los dos ejes.

31   Marque la relación de uno de los resortes del gobernador a su soporte. Marque también la relación de una de las pesas del gobernador a sus clavijas pivote.

32   Desganche cuidadosamente y remueva los resortes del gobernador.

33   Remueva las pesas del gobernador. Una cantidad pequeña de grasa debe ser aplicada a las pesas después de ser removidas.

34   El ensamble se hace en el orden inverso al procedimiento de desensamble notas:

a) Esté seguro de alinear correctamente todas las marcas en posición hechas durante el proceso de remover para que todas las partes sean armadas en sus posiciones originales.

b) Cuando esté instalando el reluctor en el eje, accione la clavija de rollo en el reluctor para que su abertura esté puesta en posición hacia el extremo exterior del eje. Siempre use un clavija de rollo nueva.

c) Antes de apretar el plato del estator, ajuste el espacio libre de aire según se indica en la Sección 3.

Modelos 1986 y más modernos

35   El motor V6 D4P84-01 y los distribuidores del motor de cuatro cilindros D4P84-04 usados en los vehículos 1986 y más modernos no pueden ser reconstruidos. Si el sensor del ángulo del cigüeñal, plato rotor, el circuito de forma de onda, etc. funciona mal el ensamblaje completo debe ser reemplazado.

9   Sensor del ángulo del cigüeñal - chequeo

Refiérase a las ilustraciones 9.4a, 9.4b, 9.5 y 9.6

1   Use el modo de diagnóstico automático (vea Sección 14 en el Capítulo 6) localice con toda precisión cualquier problema en el sistema de combustible del vehículo.

2   Si la ECU (unidad de control electrónica) destella 1 luz roja y 1 luz verde entonces el circuito del sensor del ángulo del cigüeñal está funcionando mal. Continúe los chequeos como está descrito abajo. Si el código de diagnóstico no se despliega, el sensor/circuito está funcionando apropiadamente.

3   Dependiendo en el sistema, el sensor del ángulo del cigüeñal y su circuito relacio-

nado tienen varios artículos que deben ser chequeados para localizar con toda precisión en orden el problema exacto.

4   Desconecte el conector del arnés del alambre del sensor para el ángulo del cigüeñal **(vea ilustraciones)** y Encienda el interruptor de la ignición.

5   Chequee el voltaje entre la terminal A y la conexión a tierra **(vea ilustración)**. Debe haber voltaje de batería.

6   Apague el interruptor de la ignición y chequee por continuidad entre la terminal D y la conexión a tierra **(vea ilustración)**.

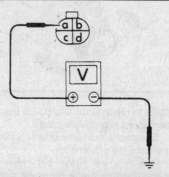

9.5 Chequee el voltaje en la terminal A con la llave de la ignición Encendida. Debe haber voltaje de batería

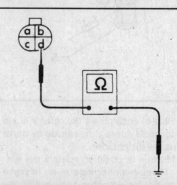

9.6 Chequee por continuidad en la terminal D con la llave de la ignición Apagada. Debe haber continuidad

7   Si las pruebas son correctas, haga que la ECU y el arnés sean chequeados por el departamento de servicio de su concesionario u otro taller de reparación profesional para vehículos.

10   Bobina para la ignición - remover e instalar

1   Remueva el alambre de la bobina proveniente de la tapa del distribuidor.
2   Remueva la tapa contra polvo.
3   Remueva las tuercas y separe los alambres primarios de la bobina.
4   Remueva los tornillos que retienen el soporte de la bobina al albergue y separe la bobina.
5   Si la bobina debe ser removida del soporte, afloje los tornillos del soporte hasta que la bobina pueda ser removida.
6   La instalación se hace en el orden inverso al procedimiento de desensamble.
Nota: *En los modelos pre 1986 con dos bobina para la ignición, el que tiene el tapón anaranjado controla las bujías en el lado de admisión, mientras que la bobina con el tapón negro controla las bujías en el lado del escape.*

11   Sistema de arranque - información general

La función del sistema de arranque es de girar el motor. Este sistema está compuesto de un motor de arranque, el solenoide y la batería. La batería suministra la energía eléctrica al solenoide, que entonces completa el circuito al motor de arranque que hace el trabajo verdadero de arrancar el motor.

Los modelos vendidos en los US usan un tipo de engrane en el motor de arranque sin reducción. En este motor de arranque, el solenoide está instalado en la parte superior del motor de arranque. Cuando el interruptor de la ignición es operado, la palanca del solenoide mueve el piñón del engrane del motor de arranque para que se comprometa con los dientes en el volante.

Los modelos vendidos en Canadá están equipados con un tipo de motor de arranque con reducción de engrane. Este motor de arranque opera en una manera similar al tipo descrito encima pero compensa por las temperaturas extremadamente bajas, aumentado el par de torsión para girar, es proporcionado a través de un engrane de reducción localizado entre la armadura y el engrane del piñón.

Un embrague de rueda libre es instalado en ambos tipos de motores de arranque para transmitir el par de torsión impulsor y para prevenir la armadura de invadir cuando el motor comience y se ponga en marcha.

El solenoide y el motor de arranque son instalados juntos en el lado trasero del motor. Ninguna lubricación ni mantenimiento periódico es requerido para los componentes del sistema del motor de arranque.

La red eléctrica de los circuitos del vehículo está arreglada para que el motor de arranque se pueda operar solamente con los modelos de transmisiones automáticas cuando la palanca está en P o N. **Caución:** *Nunca opere el motor de arranque por más de 30 segundos a la vez sin detener para permitir que se refresque por lo menos dos minutos. Periodos excesivos de arrancar pueden causar sobrecalentamiento, que puede dañar gravemente el motor de arranque.*

12   Sistema de arranque - chequeo

1   Si el motor de arranque no gira cuando el interruptor es operado en un modelo equipado con una transmisión automática, asegúrese que la palanca de cambio está en la posición P o N.
2   Chequee que la batería esté bien cargada y todos los cables, en la batería y las terminales del solenoide del motor de arranque, estén limpias, libre de corrosión y aseguradas.
3   Si el motor de arranque se puede oír girar pero el motor no gira, entonces el embrague de rueda libre en el motor de arranque está resbalándose y el ensamblaje debe ser removido del motor y ser reemplazado.
4   A menudo cuando el motor de arranque falla de operar, un sonido se puede oír provenir del solenoide del motor de arranque cuando el interruptor de la ignición es girado a la posición de Arranque. Si se oye, proceda al Paso 12.
5   Desconecte el alambre de la ignición del terminal de solenoide. Conecte una luz de prueba entre este alambre y la terminal negativa de la batería.
6   Haga que un ayudante gire la llave y note si la luz de prueba se ilumina o no. Si la luz se ilumina procede al Paso 12.
7   Si la luz de prueba no se ilumina, conecte un voltímetro (póngalo en la escala baja) entre la terminal positiva de la batería y el conector de bayoneta en el solenoide. El alambre de la ignición debe estar conectado.
8   Desconecte el alambre(s) de la bobina de la ignición en la tapa del distribuidor y póngalo a tierra en el motor, para que el motor no se ponga en marcha.
9   Haga que un ayudante atente de arrancar el motor y note la lectura en el voltímetro. Si menos de 1.5 voltios es mostrado, hay un circuito abierto en el motor de arranque y debe ser reemplazado con uno nuevo o con una unidad nueva reconstruida.
10   Si el voltímetro muestra más de 1.5 voltios, conecta un alambre puente entre el terminal positivo de la batería y la terminal S en el solenoide.
11   Gire el interruptor de la ignición a la posición de Arranque y escuche por un sonido del solenoide. Si todavía no hay un sonido y el motor de arranque no gira, ambos

el solenoide y el motor de arranque están defectuoso y deben ser reemplazados. Si un sonido se oye y el motor de arranque gira, entonces hay un circuito abierto en el interruptor de la ignición, interruptor inhibidor o relé (modelos equipados con transmisión automática) o en los alambres o conectores.
12   Si un sonido es oído mientras el interruptor de la ignición está girado a la posición de Arranque en el Paso 4, o si el motor de arranque gira del todo, entonces la corriente del motor de arranque se debe chequear. Desconecte el cable positivo de la batería en el motor de arranque.
13   Conecte un medidor para medir el amperaje (póngalo en la escala de 500A) entre este cable y su terminal en el motor de arranque.
14   Remueva los alambre(s) para la bobina de la ignición de la tapa del distribuidor para mantener que el motor no se ponga en marcha.
15   Haga que un ayudante atente de poner el motor en macha y note la lectura en el amperímetro y la velocidad en que el motor de arranque gira.
16   Si el amperímetro lee menos de lo especificado y la velocidad del motor de arranque no es normal, el motor de arranque está bueno y el problema está en otra parte.
17   Si la lectura es menos que lo que se especifica pero la velocidad del motor de arranque es lenta, proceda al Paso 22.
18   Si el amperímetro lee más que lo especificado, vuelva a instalar el alambre de la bobina para la ignición en la tapa del distribuidor.
19   Haga que un ayudante ponga el motor en marcha pero detenga la llave en la posición de Arranque para que el motor de arranque no deje de operar. Note que lee el amperímetro. (No permita el motor de arranque gire por más de 30 segundos a la vez).
20   Si el amperímetro lee menos que lo especificado y el motor de arranque gira rápido, entonces el problema es uno mecánico tal como un motor apretado. Asegúrese que el aceite del motor no es demasiado grueso y chequee por otras causas de la resistencia adentro del motor.
21   Si la lectura del amperímetro excede la carga de la corriente especificada sin carga el motor de arranque tiene un corto y debe ser reemplazado con uno nuevo.
22   Si la lectura en el amperímetro es menos que lo especificado en el Paso 15, pero el motor de arranque gira lentamente, pruebe por una caída de voltaje en el circuito positivo del motor de arranque.
23   Conecte un voltímetro (puesto en la escama baja) para que el alambre positivo esté en el poste positivo de la batería (o cable) y el alambre negativo sea conectado a la terminal del solenoide M (esta es la terminal con la banda de cobre instalada al motor de arranque).
24   Remueva el alambre(s) de la bobina para la ignición de la tapa del distribuidor y conéctelo a tierra en el motor.
25   Haga que un ayudante atente de poner

13.2 Ensamblaje típico del motor de arranque en un motor de modelo más antiguo de cuatro cilindros (pre 1986), instalado en el lado derecho trasero inferior del motor - esté seguro de separar todos los alambres de las terminales del solenoide antes de remover el motor de arranque

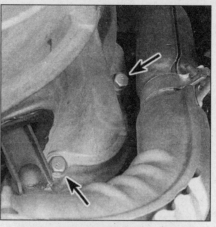

13.3 Pernos de afianzamiento para el motor de arranque en el motor V6 (flechas) - el motor de arranque está instalado en el lado derecho del motor (pasajero)

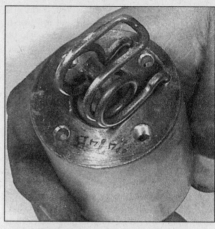

14.4 Ensamble el solenoide como está mostrado antes de instalarlo en el motor - asegúrese que el embolo está comprometido con la palanca del motor de arranque

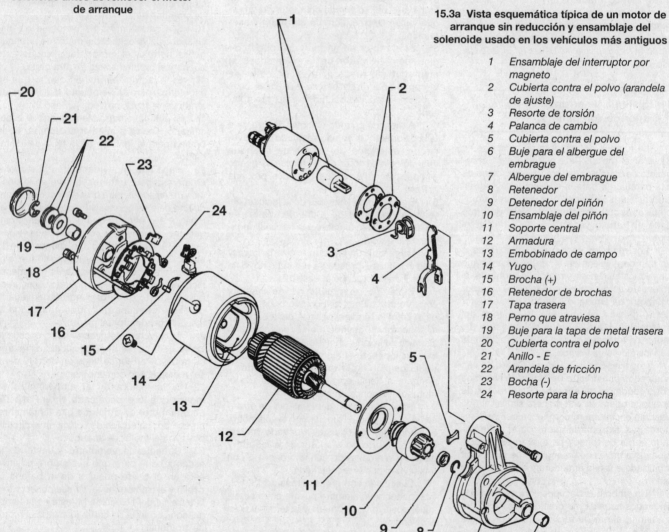

15.3a Vista esquemática típica de un motor de arranque sin reducción y ensamblaje del solenoide usado en los vehículos más antiguos

1   Ensamblaje del interruptor por magneto
2   Cubierta contra el polvo (arandela de ajuste)
3   Resorte de torsión
4   Palanca de cambio
5   Cubierta contra el polvo
6   Buje para el albergue del embrague
7   Albergue del embrague
8   Retenedor
9   Detenedor del piñón
10 Ensamblaje del piñón
11 Soporte central
12 Armadura
13 Embobinado de campo
14 Yugo
15 Brocha (+)
16 Retenedor de brochas
17 Tapa trasera
18 Perno que atraviesa
19 Buje para la tapa de metal trasera
20 Cubierta contra el polvo
21 Anillo - E
22 Arandela de fricción
23 Bocha (-)
24 Resorte para la brocha

en marcha el motor y note la lectura en el voltímetro. Si menos que un voltio es mostrado, proceda al Paso 28.

26   Si más que un voltio es mostrado, conecte el alambre negativo del voltímetro a la terminal del solenoide B (esta es la terminal que se conecta a la batería).

27   Haga que un ayudante gire el motor y note la lectura en el voltímetro. Si se muestra más de un voltio, entonces el problema es una conexión mala entre la batería y el solenoide para el motor de arranque. Chequee el cable positivo de la batería para estar seguro de que no está flojo o corroído. Si la lectura indica menos de un voltio, entonces el solenoide está defectuoso y debe ser reemplazado.

28   Si la prueba del voltímetro en el Paso 25 muestra una caída de menos de un voltio chequee por una caída de voltaje en el circuito de conexión a tierra del motor de arranque.

29   Conecte el alambre negativo del voltímetro (puesto en la escala baja) a la terminal negativa de la batería y detenga el alambre positivo del voltímetro en el albergue del motor de arranque. Esté seguro de hacer una buena conexión.

30   Haga que un ayudante gire el motor y note la lectura del voltímetro. Si la lectura muestra más de 0.5 voltios, entonces hay

una conexión a tierra mala. Chequee el cable negativo de la batería para estar seguro de que no está flojo o corroído. Chequee también las conexiones de conexión a tierra del motor de arranque y que tan apretado están los pernos del motor de arranque.

31   Si la lectura del voltímetro es menos de 0.5, regrese al Paso 7 y siga el plan general de procedimiento descrito allí.

13   Motor de arranque - remover e instalar

Refiérase a las ilustraciones 13.2 y 13.3

1   Desconecte el cable negativo de la terminal negativa de la batería. En los modelos equipados con un motor V6, levante el vehículo y sosténgalo firmemente encima de soportes.

2   Remueva los alambres del solenoide del motor de arranque (vea ilustración). Marque los alambres y las terminales para prevenir confusión durante la instalación.

3   Remueva los pernos de retención para el motor de arranque (vea ilustración).

4   Remueva el motor de arranque y el solenoide.

5   La instalación se hace en el orden inverso al procedimiento de desensamble.

14   Solenoide del motor de arranque - remover e instalar

Refiérase a la ilustración 14.4

1   Remueva el motor de arranque según se indica en la Sección 13.

2   Remueva la tuerca que retiene la banda de cobre al solenoide.

3   Remueva los dos tornillos de afianzamiento y separe el solenoide del motor de arranque.

4   La instalación se hace en el orden inverso al procedimiento de desensamble.
Nota: *Durante la instalación esté seguro de comprometer el embolo en el solenoide con la palanca del motor de arranque* (vea ilustración).

15   Motor de arranque - reemplazo de las brochas

Motor de arranque sin engrane de reducción

Refiérase a las ilustraciones 15.3a, 15.3b, 15.3c y 15.8

1   Remueva el motor de arranque (vea Sección 13).

2   Remueva el solenoide del motor de arranque (vea Sección 14).

3   Remueva la tapa trasera de polvo del motor de arranque (vea ilustraciones).

15.3b Vista esquemática típica de un motor de arranque sin reducción y ensamblaje del solenoide usado en los vehículos 1986 y más modernos de 2WD con un motor de cuatro cilindros

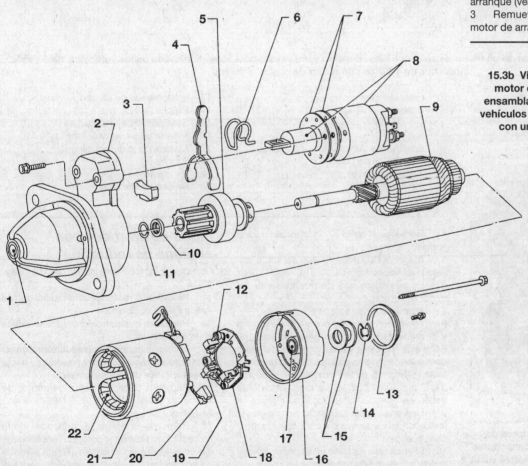

1	Buje de metal del albergue
2	Albergue
3	Cubierta contra el polvo
4	Palanca de cambio
5	Ensamblaje del piñón
6	Resorte de torsión
7	Palto de ajuste
8	Ensamblaje del interruptor magnético
9	Armadura
10	Detenedor del piñón
11	Anillo retenedor
12	Resorte de tipo brocha
13	Cubierta contra el polvo
14	Anillo E
15	Arandela contra el impulso
16	Cubierta trasera
17	Buje de metal para la cubierta trasera
18	Retenedor de las brochas
19	Brocha (-)
20	Brocha (+)
21	Yugo
22	Embobinado de campo

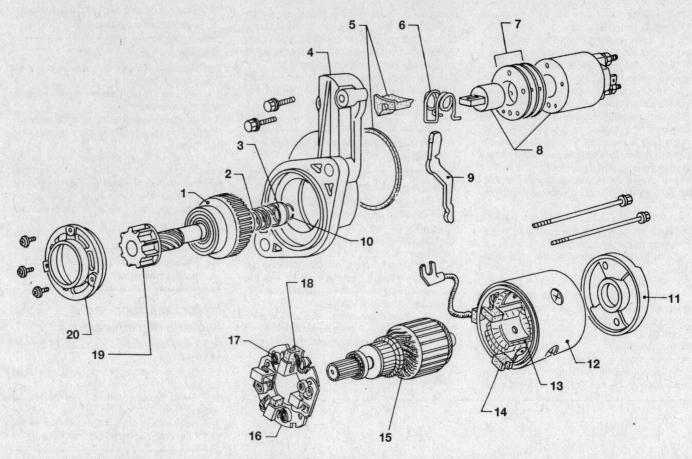

15.3c Vista esquemática típica de un motor de arranque sin reducción y ensamblaje del solenoide usado en los vehículos 1986 y más modernos de 4WD con un motor de cuatro cilindros

1 Ensamblaje del embrague	7 Plato de ajuste	13 Embobinado de campo
2 Resorte de retorno	Espesor del plato	14 Brocha (+)
3 Detenedor del piñón	0.5 (0.020)	15 Ensamblaje de la armadura
4 Albergue del engrane	0.8 (0.031)	16 Retenedor de las brochas
5 Cubierta contra el polvo	8 Ensamblaje del interruptor magnético	17 Resorte de las brochas
6 Resorte de torsión	9 Palanca de cambio	18 Brocha (+)
	10 Anillo detenedor	19 Eje del piñón
	11 Tapa trasera	20 Retenedor del balero
	12 Yugo	

15.8 Las brochas en los motores de arranque sin reducción están conectadas al poseedor de brochas por resortes y a la horquilla con acoplaciones de soldadura

4   Remueva el anillo E y la arandela para el impulso.

5   Remueva los dos tornillos del plato trasero poseedor de brocha.

6   Remueva los dos pernos traseros del motor de arranque.

7   Remueva la tapa trasera.

8   Levante el plato del poseedor de brocha y desconecte los resortes **(vea ilustración)**. Remueva cada una de las brochas del plato poseedor desengranándolos de sus resortes. Mida la longitud de las brochas. Si ellas son de 12 mm (0.47 pulgada) o más cortas ellas deben ser reemplazadas con unas nuevas.

9   Use una pistola de soldar para remover las brochas viejas y para conectar las brochas nuevas.

10   El ensamble se hace en el orden inverso al procedimiento de desensamble.

Motor de arranque con engrane de reducción

Refiérase a las ilustraciones 15.13a, 15.13b y 15.16

11   Remueva el motor de arranque según se indica en la Sección 13.

12   Remueva el solenoide según se indica en la Sección 14.

13   Remueva los pernos **(vea ilustraciones)** destornillándolos y extrayéndolos hacia afuera a través de la parte trasera.

14   Remueva la tapa trasera del motor de arranque. Tenga cuidado de no dañar el anillo sellador de tipo O.

15   Remueva la horquilla, poseedor de la armadura y brocha como un ensamblaje desde el albergue del centro. Tenga cuidado de no golpear las brochas, el conmutador ni la bobina contra ninguna parte adyacente.

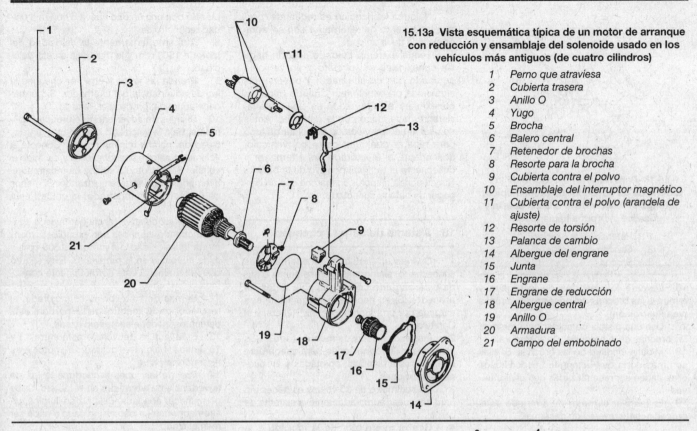

15.13a Vista esquemática típica de un motor de arranque con reducción y ensamblaje del solenoide usado en los vehículos más antiguos (de cuatro cilindros)

1	Perno que atraviesa
2	Cubierta trasera
3	Anillo O
4	Yugo
5	Brocha
6	Balero central
7	Retenedor de brochas
8	Resorte para la brocha
9	Cubierta contra el polvo
10	Ensamblaje del interruptor magnético
11	Cubierta contra el polvo (arandela de ajuste)
12	Resorte de torsión
13	Palanca de cambio
14	Albergue del engrane
15	Junta
16	Engrane
17	Engrane de reducción
18	Albergue central
19	Anillo O
20	Armadura
21	Campo del embobinado

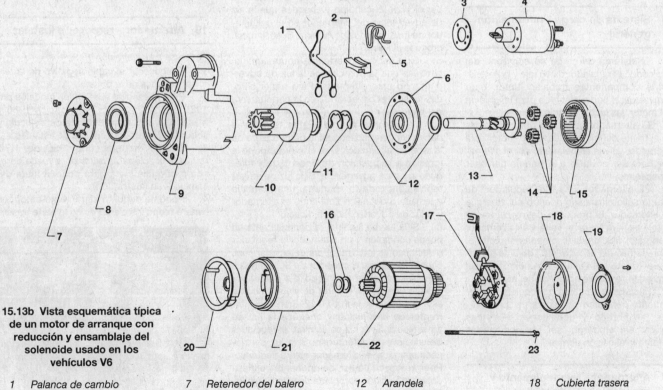

15.13b Vista esquemática típica de un motor de arranque con reducción y ensamblaje del solenoide usado en los vehículos V6

1	Palanca de cambio	7	Retenedor del balero	12	Arandela	18	Cubierta trasera
2	Cubierta contra el polvo	8	Balero de tipo que tiene bolas	13	Eje del piñón	19	Cubierta contra el polvo
3	Plato de ajuste			14	Engrane planetario	20	Soporte central (A)
4	Ensamblaje del interruptor magnético	9	Albergue del engrane	15	Engrane interno	21	Ensamblaje del yugo
		10	Ensamblaje del piñón	16	Arandela	22	Armadura
5	Resorte	11	Anillo E	17	Retenedor de las brochas	23	Perno que atraviesa
6	Soporte central (P)						

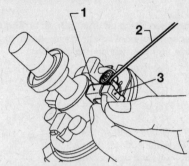

15.16 Para remover el resorte de la brocha de un poseedor de brocha típico, detenga el resorte de la brocha aparte y deslice la brocha hacia afuera

1 *Retenedor de brochas*
2 *Gancho de alambre*
3 *Brocha*

16   Levante los resortes de la brocha y remueva las brochas del poseedor de brocha **(vea ilustración)**.
17   Use una pistola de soldar para remover las brochas de la horquilla y la soldadura.
18   Mida la longitud de las brochas. Si ellas son más corta que la longitud especificada ellas deben ser reemplazadas con unas nuevas.
19   Ensamblar el motor de arranque es el procedimiento reverso de desarmar.

16   Sistema de carga - información general

El sistema de carga se compone del alternador, el regulador de voltaje y la batería. Estos componentes trabajan juntos para suministrar el poder eléctrico para la ignición del motor, las luces, el radio, etc.

El alternador es girado por una banda en el frente del motor. Cuando el motor está operando, voltaje es generado por el alternador para ser enviado a la batería para ser almacenado.

El alternador usa un regulador de estado sólido instalado adentro del albergue de alternador. El propósito del regulador de voltaje es para limitar el voltaje del alternador a un valor fijó, prevenir oleadas de voltaje, sobrecargas del circuito, etc., durante el rendimiento alto del voltaje. El rendimiento del regulador de voltaje no puede ser ajustado.

El sistema de carga no requiere mantenimiento periódico comúnmente. Las bandas, alambrado y conexiones eléctricas deben, sin embargo, ser inspeccionadas durante la afinación normal.

17   Alternador - mantenimiento y precauciones especiales

1   El mantenimiento del alternador se compone de ocasionalmente limpiar cualquier tierra o aceite que se pueda haber reunido en él.
2   Chequee la presión de la banda (refiérase al Capítulo 1).

3   Ninguna lubricación es requerida, porque los baleros del alternador son sellados por la vida de la unidad.
4   Tenga extremo cuidado cuando haga las conexiones del circuito a un vehículo equipado con un alternador y observe las siguientes precauciones: Cuando haga las conexiones al alternador de una batería, siempre haga juego con la polaridad. Antes de usar el equipo eléctrico de soldar de arco para reparar cualquier parte del vehículo, desconecte el alambrado del alternador y desconecte el terminal positivo de la batería. Nunca ponga el motor en marcha con un cargador de batería conectado.

18   Sistema de carga - chequeo

1   Cuando un problema del alternador es sospechado, siempre asegúrese que la batería está cargada completamente antes de proceder. Si es necesario, hágala que sea cargada por una fuente exterior. Refiérase al Capítulo 1.
2   Inspeccione visualmente todos los alambres y las conexiones para asegurarse que ellas están limpias, apretadas y en buenas condiciones.
3   Un voltímetro de 30 voltios es necesario para chequear apropiadamente el sistema de carga.
4   Gire el interruptor de la ignición a la posición de Encendido y chequee que la luz de advertencia del alternador en el aglutinador de instrumentos se ilumina. Si se ilumina, proceda al Paso 7.
5   Si la luz de advertencia no se ilumina, chequee que la bombilla de la luz de advertencia no esté quemada. Para hacer esto, desconecte el conector SL en la parte trasera del alternador y ponga a tierra el alambre L con un alambre puente. Estas terminales deben ser identificadas en la parte trasera de la tapa del alternador. Gire el interruptor de la ignición a la posición de Encendido y chequee la luz de advertencia. Si la luz de advertencia está todavía apagada, una bombilla quemada o conexión floja entre el alternador y la luz de advertencia es indicada.
6   Si la luz se ilumina, la bombilla está en buena condición y un alternador o regulador defectuoso es indicado. Para determinar cual, conecte de nuevo el conector de SL y ponga a tierra las brochas al cuerpo del alternador usando una Sección corta de alambre como está mostrado en la Fig. 20.12. Prenda el interruptor de la ignición y chequee la luz de advertencia. Si la luz se ilumina, el regulador de voltaje está defectuoso. Si la luz permanece apagada, el alternador está defectuoso. Reemplace cualquier componente refiriéndose a la Sección apropiada de este Capítulo.
7   Si la luz de advertencia se ilumina con el interruptor de la ignición en la posición de Encendido, ponga el motor en marcha y permítalo que corra en marcha mínima. La luz debe apagarse. Si permanece iluminada, aunque sea débilmente o como un destello, un alternador defectuoso es indicado. Reem-

plácelo con una unidad nueva o con una unidad reconstruida.
8   Aumente lentamente la velocidad del motor a 1500 rpm y lo mantiene en esa velocidad.
9   Prenda las luces y otra vez chequee la luz de advertencia del alternador. Si permanece apagada, proceda al Paso 11.
10   Si la luz de advertencia se prende débilmente, baje la velocidad del motor a la velocidad de marcha mínima normal. Conecte el voltímetro entre las terminales B y L y mida el voltaje. Si más de 0.5 voltios es mostrado el alternador debe ser reemplazando. Si menos de 0.5 voltios es mostrado, la unidad está buena.
11   Si la luz de advertencia permanece apagada cuando las luces son prendidas, mantenga la velocidad del motor a 1500 rpm y mida el voltaje en la terminal B. Esté seguro que la terminal S esté correctamente conectada.
12   Si más de 15.5 voltios es mostrado, el regulador de IC (control de la ignición) está defectuoso y debe ser reemplazado.
13   Si la lectura del voltaje está entre 13 y 15 voltios, baje la velocidad del motor a su nivel normal.
14   Prenda las luces y chequee la luz de advertencia de alternador en el tablero. Debe permanecer apagada. Si la luz se ilumina, un alternador defectuoso es indicado y debe ser reemplazado.

19   Alternador - remover e instalar

Refiérase a la ilustración 19.3
1   Desconecte el cable negativo de la terminal negativa de la batería.
2   Para el espacio libre en los modelos pre 1986 de 2WD y todos los modelos 1986 y más modernos, eleve el frente del vehículo y sopórtelo firmemente encima de estantes.
3   En los modelos pre 1986 de 4WD remueva la solapa de barro en la rueda derecha o póngale cinta para ponerla fuera del camino **(vea ilustración)**.
4   Póngale etiqueta claramente entonces separe todos los alambres de la parte trasera

19.3 Para obtener acceso al alternador en los vehículos pre 1984 de 4WD, póngale cinta a la solapa de caucho para detener el barro fuera del camino

20.2 Vista esquemática de un alternador típico usado en los modelos 1980

1   Cubierta delantera
2   Balero delantero
3   Rotor
4   Balero trasero
5   Estator
6   Tapa trasera
7   Regulador de voltaje IC (control de la ignición)
8   Ensamblaje de las brochas
9   Ensamblaje de los diodos (plato de afianzamiento)

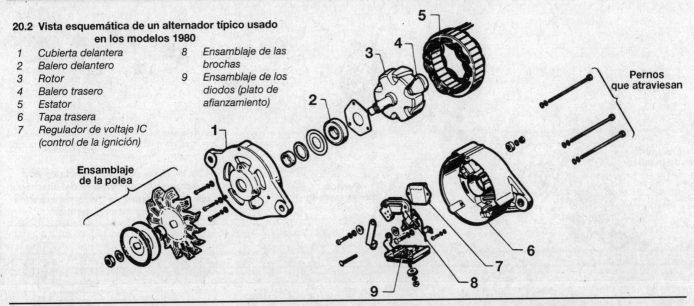

del alternador.

5   Refiérase al Capítulo 1 y remueva la banda.

6   Remueva los pernos de ajuste y de afianzamiento.

7   El alternador ahora se puede separar del motor. En los modelos pre 1986 de 2WD, se puede bajar hacia afuera por debajo, mientras que en los modelos pre 1986 de 4WD puede ser removida la rueda derecha. En los modelos 1986 y más modernos el alternador es removido por debajo.

8   La instalación se hace en el orden inverso al procedimiento de desensamble.

20   Regulador de voltaje del alternador y las brochas - reemplazo

Modelos 1980

Refiérase a las ilustraciones 20.2, 20.10 y 20.12

1   Remueva el alternador del vehículo según se indica en la Sección 19.

2   Remueva los cuatro pernos de la tapa trasera (**vea ilustración**).

3   Separe el ensamblaje de la tapa delantera/rotor de la tapa trasera/ensamblaje del estator pegándole ligeramente al soporte delantero con un martillo de cara suave.

4   Desconecte el alambre conectando el plato de los diodos a la brocha en la terminal de la brocha calentándola con una pistola de soldar.

5   Desconecte el plato del conjunto de diodo del lado de la cara de la tapa trasera.

6   Remueva la tuerca que asegura el perno del terminal de la batería.

7   Parcialmente levante el plato del conjunto de diodo junto con la bobina del estator de la tapa trasera. Remueva el tornillo conectando el conjunto de diodo al plato de la brocha.

8   Separe la tapa trasera, junto con la bobina del estator, el diodo, remueva la brocha y el regulador IC.

9   Chequee por movimiento libre de la brocha y asegúrese que el poseedor está limpio y sin daño.

10   Chequee por desgaste de la brocha o notando la línea del límite de desgaste de la brocha (**vea ilustración**) o midiendo la longitud de la brocha y comparándola con el límite de desgaste en las especificaciones al principio de éste Capítulo. Si la brocha se a desgastado más allá de cualquier límite, debe

ser reemplazada con una nueva.

11   Si el regulador de voltaje está defectuoso, el ensamblaje de la brocha debe ser reemplazado como una unidad.

12   El ensamble del alternador se hace en el orden inverso al procedimiento de desensamble, con las siguientes notas:

a) *Soldar los alambres de la bobina del estator al ensamblaje del diodo debe ser hecho lo más rápido como sea posible para prevenir que calor excesivo se acumule alrededor del ensamblaje del diodo.*

b) *Cuando esté instalando la terminal del diodo A, esté seguro de que el buje de protección está correctamente instalado.*

c) *Antes de unir las tapas delanteras y traseras empuje la brocha en la tapa trasera con sus dedos y deténgala allí (**vea ilustración**) metiendo un pedazo de alambre tieso a través del orificio en la brocha desde la parte de afuera. Después que la parte delantera y trasera se hayan unido, el alambre puede ser removido empujando el final del exterior hacia el centro del alternador y halarlo recto hacia afuera. Si el alambre no es removido de esta manera, la superficie de deslizamiento del anillo de tropiezo puede ser dañada.*

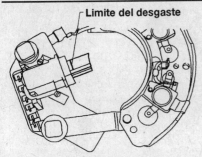

20.10 La manera más rápida de chequear el desgaste de la brocha es de notar que tanto la brocha ha llegado a la línea del límite

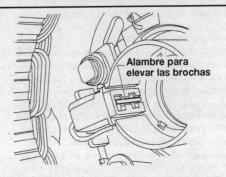

20.12 Durante el proceso de ensamblaje de la tapa delantera y trasera del alternador, las brochas deben ser retenidas por un alambre tieso insertado a través del orificio como está mostrado

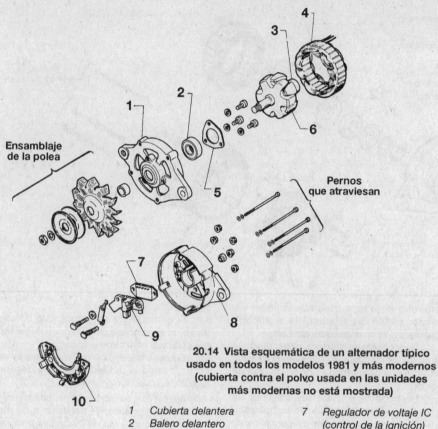

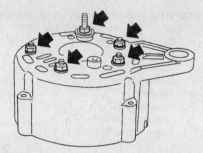

20.16 El ensamblaje del estator está conectado a la tapa trasera del alternador por cinco tuercas en todos los modelos 1981 y más modernos

20.14 Vista esquemática de un alternador típico usado en todos los modelos 1981 y más modernos (cubierta contra el polvo usada en las unidades más modernas no está mostrada)

1	Cubierta delantera	7	Regulador de voltaje IC (control de la ignición)
2	Balero delantero	8	Cubierta trasera
3	Balero trasero	9	Ensamblaje de las brochas
4	Estator	10	Ensamblaje de los diodos (plato de afianzamiento)
5	Retenedor del balero delantero		
6	Rotor		

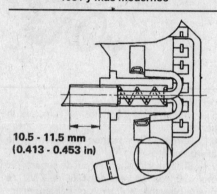

10.5 - 11.5 mm (0.413 - 0.453 in)

20.17a Antes de soldar la brocha nueva en el alternador, asegúrese que está puesta en posición como está mostrado

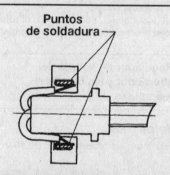

Puntos de soldadura

20.17b Soldando los alambres de la brocha del alternador que se dirigen al exterior de la terminal en los puntos indicados

Modelos 1981 y más modernos

Refiérase a las ilustraciones 20.14, 20.16, 20.17a, 20.17b y 20.18

13   Remueva el alternador del vehículo según se indica en la Sección 19.

14   Remueva los cuatro pernos que atraviesan la tapa trasera (**vea ilustración**).

15   Separe la tapa delantera/ensamblaje del rotor de la tapa trasera/del ensamblaje del estator pegándole suavemente al soporte delantero con un martillo de cara blanda. **Nota:** *Las tapas traseras en los alternadores 1986 y más modernos son protegidas por una tapa de polvo, conectada por un par de tornillos y una tuerca, que debe ser removida antes de desarmar el alternador.*

16   Remueva las cinco tuercas que retienen el ensamblaje del estator de la tapa trasera (**vea ilustración**), entonces levante hacia afuera el ensamblaje del estator.

17   Chequee la longitud y la operación de las brochas como está descrito en el Paso 9 y 10 y las reemplaza si es necesario. **Nota:** *Antes de soldar los alambres de las brochas, posicióne la brocha para que se extienda acerca de 7/16 (11 mm) pulgada del poseedor* **de brocha** (**vea ilustración**). Entonces enrolle el alambre 1-1/2 vuelta alrededor de la ranura terminal y suelde la parte exterior de la terminal (**vea ilustración**).

Tenga cuidado de no permitir que la soldadura se adhiera al tubo de aislación porque esto podría debilitar y poder agrietar el tubo.

18   Si el regulador de voltaje IC necesita ser reemplazado, usen el siguiente procedimiento: **Nota:** *No remueva el regulador a menos que baya a ser reemplazado con uno nuevo.*

a)   Desengrane el regulador del ensamblaje del diodo removiendo ambos el remacha y la soldadura (**vea ilustración**) que los conecta. Esto es hecho más fácil usando una pistola de soldar para desconectar los alambres del estator que provienen del ensamblaje del diodo.

b)   Para separar el regulador del poseedor de brocha, remueva la soldadura de la terminal y con un par de alicates, remueva los pernos que la conectan.

c)   Cuando esté instalando el regulador nuevo, colóquelo en el poseedor de brocha y prense los pernos en su posición usando una prensa de mano o cuidadosamente pegándole a ellos.

d)   Suelde nuevamente todas las conexiones e instale un remache nuevo. Estaque el remacha siguiendo la instalación.

19   El ensamble del alternador se hace en el orden inverso al procedimiento de desensamble, siguiendo las notas especiales listadas en el Paso 12.

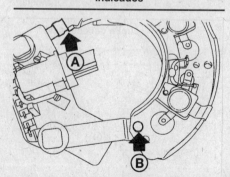

20.18 En los alternadores 1981 y más modernos, el regulador/ensamblaje de brocha es soldado (A) y remachado (B) al ensamblaje del diodo

Capítulo 6
Sistemas de control de emisiones

Contenidos

Especificaciones

General

Resistencia del regulador de aire	70 ohm
Resistencia del sensor del gas de escape	85.3 ± 8.5 Ohm K
Resistencia del sensor de la temperatura del motor (valores aproximados)	
A 68 grados F	2.3 a 2.7 ohm K
A 122 grados F	680 a 1000 ohm
A 176 grados F	300 a 330 ohm

Especificaciones técnicas

	Pies-libras
Tuerca de abocinamiento para la galería del aire	40
Tuerca para el tubo de escape EGR en la bomba de aire	29
Válvula de vacío térmica (máximo)	16

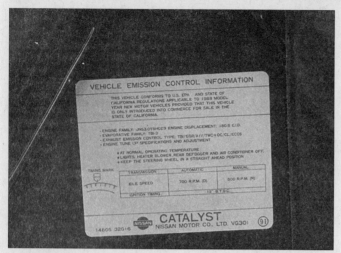

1.5a Si hay una discrepancia entre la información proporcionada en este Capítulo y los dispositivos verdaderos debajo del capó de su vehículo, la VECI (etiqueta de información para el control de las emisiones del vehículo), localizada en la parte inferior del capó, siempre se debe considerar la VECI la autoridad final

1.5b Si hay cualquier duda con respecto a la ruta de las mangueras de vacío proporcionadas en este Capítulo, la etiqueta de la ruta de las mangueras de vacío, localizada en la cara inferior del capó, le dará el esquemático de dirección más exacto para su vehículo

1   Información general

Refiérase a las ilustraciones 1.5a, 1.5b, y 1.5c

Debido a que los estándares del smog (humo) han llegado a ser más rigurosos, los sistemas del control de emisiones desarrollados para reunir estos requisitos no sólo han llegado a ser cada vez más diversos y complejos, son ahora diseñados como partes íntegra de la operación del motor. Antes los dispositivos anticontaminantes usados eran instalados como componentes periféricos "agregados," el trabajo de los sistemas presente trabajan de cerca con otros sistemas como el sistema de combustible, sistemas de ignición y del escape. Todas las operaciones esenciales del motor son controladas por el sistema de control de emisiones.

A causa de esta integración cercana de sistemas, desconectando o no manteniendo los sistemas de control de emisiones, además de ser ilegales, puede afectar adversamente el desempeño del motor y la vida, también como la economía del combustible.

Esto no quiere decir que los sistemas de emisiones son particularmente difíciles para el mecánico de hogar de mantener y otórgale servicios. Usted puede realizar chequeos operacionales generales y hacer la mayoría del mantenimiento regular fácilmente (si no todo) y rápidamente en casa con herramientas de afinación comunes y de mano. **Nota:** *La causa más frecuente de los problemas de emisiones es simplemente una manguera de vacío o alambre flojo o roto, así que siempre chequee las mangueras de vacío, los alambres y los conectores antes de ejecutar las reparaciones mayores.*

Mientras que el resultado final de los varios sistemas de emisiones es para reducir el rendimiento de contaminantes en el aire HC (hidrocarburos), CO (monóxido de carbono) y NOx (oxido de nitrógeno), la varias funciones de los sistemas independiente-

mente van hacia esta meta. Esta es la manera en que este Capítulo es dividido.

Nota: *Siempre refiérase a la etiqueta de Información VECI (etiqueta de información para el control de las emisiones del vehículo). Para información específica con respecto a* los componentes de emisiones en su vehículo. Semejantemente, siempre use el esquema para las mangueras de vacío (**vea ilustraciones**) como la palabra final con respecto a la dirección de las mangueras para su vehículo particular.

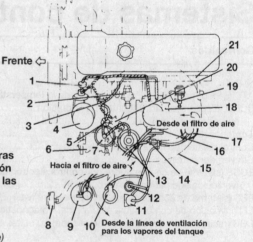

1.5c Ubicación típica de las mangueras de vacío y esquemática de la dirección para los componentes del sistema de las emisiones en los modelos 1980 de California

1   *Válvula de demora del vacío (transmisión automática solamente)*
2   *Válvula unilateral*
3   *Válvula de vacío térmica*
4   *Distribuidor*
5   *Válvula de demora del vacío (para la EGR (recirculación de los gases de escape)*
6   *Bomba de aire*
7   *Válvula BPT (transductor de contra presión)*
8   *Purificador de aire para la bomba de aire*
9   *Canasto*
10 *Válvula CAC (combinada para controlar el aire)*
11 *Unidad para el control de la amplificación*
12 *Interruptor de vacío*
13 *Válvula para el control de la EGR (recirculación de los gases de escape)*
14 *Hacia el múltiple de escape*
15 *Purificador de aire*
16 *Unidad de control para el desvío del aire*
17 *Válvula AB (purga de aire)*
18 *Carburador*
19 *Válvula amortiguadora para controlar la velocidad A/T (transmisión automática solamente)*
20 *Válvula para el intercambio M/T (transmisión manual solamente)*
21 *Galería de aire*

1.5d Ubicación típica de las mangueras de vacío y esquemática de la dirección para los componentes del sistema de las emisiones en los modelos 1980 (Federal - lado izquierdo; Canadá - lado derecho)

1 Válvula de vacío térmica
2 Distribuidor
3 Válvula BPT (transductor de contra presión)
4 Válvula EGR (recirculación de los gases de escape)
5 Canasto
6 Válvula para el control de la amplificación
7 Interruptor de vacío
8 Hacia el múltiple de escape
9 Válvula para la inducción de aire
10 Válvula AB (purga de aire)
11 Carburador
12 Válvula amortiguadora para controlar la velocidad A/T (transmisión automática)

1 Válvula unilateral
2 Válvula térmica de vacío
3 Distribuidor
4 Bomba de aire
5 Válvula BPT (transductor de contra presión)
6 Purificador de aire para la bomba de aire
7 Canasto
8 Válvula para el control de la EGR (recirculación de los gases de escape)

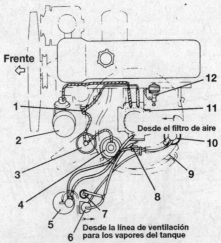
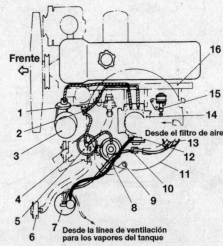

Vacío de puerto (distribuidor)
Vacío de puerto EGR (recirculación de los gases de escape)
Vacío de puerto
Vacío del múltiple

9 Válvula de relieve
10 Hacia el múltiple de admisión
11 Purificador de aire ATC (sensor para el control automático del acelerador)
12 BCDD (dispositivo para el control de la presión en desaceleración)

13 Válvula AB (purga de aire)
14 Carburador
15 Válvula amortiguadora para controlar la velocidad
16 Galería para el aire

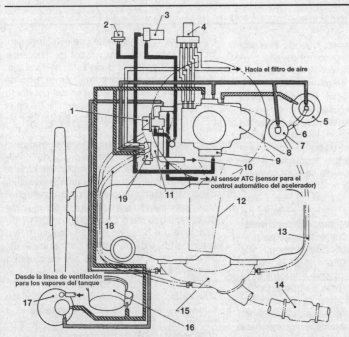
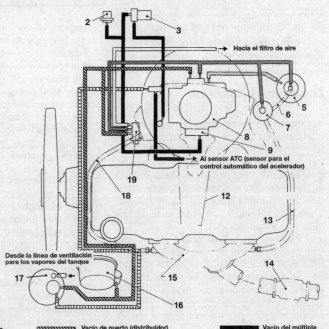

1.5e Ubicación típica de las mangueras de vacío y esquemática de la dirección para los componentes del sistema de las emisiones en los modelos 1981 al 1985 (California - lado izquierdo; Federal y Canadá - lado derecho)

Vacío de puerto (distribuidor)
Vacío de puerto EGR (recirculación de los gases de escape)
Vacío de venturi
Vacío del múltiple
Aire
Purga del canasto

1 Válvula AB (purga de aire)
2 Interruptor para el vacío
3 Unidad para el control de la amplificación
4 Compensador de la altitud
5 Válvula VVT (transductor del vacío de venturi)
6 Tubo BP (contra presión)
7 Válvula de control para la EGR (recirculación de los gases de escape)
8 Carburador
9 Unidad de control para el desvío del aire
10 Hacia el purificador de aire
11 Válvula para la inducción de aire y el albergue de la válvula
12 Purificador de aire controlado por la temperatura del aire
13 Tubo EGR (recirculación de los gases de escape)
14 Catalítico
15 Múltiple de admisión
16 Distribuidor
17 Canasto
18 Tubo EAI (inyección de aire para el escape)

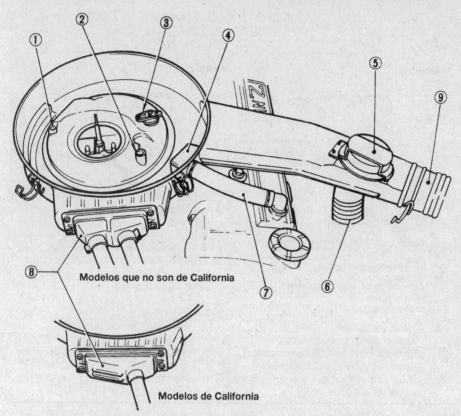

Modelos que no son de California

Modelos de California

2.2 Ensamblaje típico del purificador de aire equipado con un ATC (control para la temperatura del aire) usado en los modelos 1981 al 1985 (los modelos 1986 y más modernos son semejantes)

1   Manguera de aire para el TCS (sistema de chispa controlada por la transmisión) y el sistema de EGR (recirculación de los gases de escape)
2   Admisión de aire para la válvula de AB (purga de aire)
3   Sensor de la temperatura
4   Filtro para los gases que se escapan a través de los anillos
5   Motor de vacío
6   Conducto de aire caliente
7   Manguera para los gases de compresión que se escapan a través de los anillos hacia el cárter
8   Albergue para la válvula de inducción de aire
9   Conducto flexible para el aire

2   ATC (sensor para el control automático de la temperatura)

Refiérase a la ilustración 2.2

Descripción general

1   El sistema de ATC mejora la eficiencia del motor y reduce las emisiones de los hidrocarburos durante el período de calentamiento inicial del motor manteniendo un control de la temperatura del aire en el carburador. El control de la temperatura del aire entrante permite que las calibraciones más pobres del carburador y el estrangulador ayuden a prevenir la congelación del carburador en tiempo frío.

2   El sistema **(vea ilustración)** usa una válvula para el control del aire localizada en el tubo de respiración del albergue del purificador de aire para controlar la proporción de aire frío y caliente en el carburador. Esta válvula es controlada por un motor de vacío que es, en cambio, modulado por una válvula sensible a la temperatura de la purga de aire o sensor de temperatura en el purificador de aire. Esta válvula de purga de aire cierra cuando la admisión de la temperatura del aire está fría, así permitiendo que el vacío del múltiple de admisión alcance el motor de vacío. Cuando el aire está caliente, la válvula se abre, pero cerrándose al vacío del múltiple.

3   Es durante las primeras pocas millas de manejo (dependiendo de la temperatura exterior) que este sistema tiene su efecto más grande en el desempeño del motor y rendimiento de emisiones. Cuando el motor está frío, la válvula del control de aire bloquea el tubo de respiración de admisión para el purificador de aire, permitiendo solamente aire caliente del múltiple de escape para entrar en el carburador. Gradualmente, según el motor se calienta, la válvula de pasaje se abre al tubo de respiración, incrementando la cantidad de aire frío permitido que entre. Una vez que el motor llega a la temperatura normal de operación, la válvula se abre completamente, para permitir solamente aire frío y fresco que entre.

4   A causa de este funcionamiento del motor frío solamente, es importante de periódicamente chequear que este sistema prevenga el desempeño pobre del motor cuando está frío, o sobrecalentamiento de la mezcla del combustible una vez que el motor haya alcanzado las temperaturas de operación. Si la válvula de aire se atora en la posición "no calor," el motor no correrá bien, se detendrá y consumirá más combustible hasta que se haya calentado por sí mismo. Una válvula que está obstruida en la "posición de calor" causa que el motor corra como si estuviera fuera de afinación debido al flujo constante de aire caliente al carburador.

Chequeo

Sensor de la temperatura

5   Con el motor apagado, note la posición de la válvula de aire del control adentro del tubo de respiración del purificador de aire. Si el vehículo está equipado con un conducto de aire en el final del tubo de respiración, tendrá que ser removido antes de este chequeo. Si el acceso visual a la válvula es difícil, use un espejo. La válvula debe estar hacia abajo, significando que el aire fluirá en el tubo de respiración y ninguno a través del conducto de aire del múltiple de escape caliente en la parte inferior del albergue del purificador de aire.

6   Ahora haga que un ayudante ponga el motor en marcha y continúe vigilando la válvula adentro del tubo de respiración. Con el motor frío y en marcha mínima, la válvula debe cerrar todo el tubo de respiración, permitiendo aire calentado del múltiple de escape que entre en la admisión del purificador de aire. Cuando el motor se calienta a la temperatura de operación normal la válvula se debe mover, permitiendo aire de afuera a través del tubo de respiración que sea incluido en la mezcla. Eventualmente, la válvula debe moverse hacia abajo al punto donde la mayor parte del aire entrante es a través del tubo de respiración y no el conducto del múltiple de escape.

7   Si la válvula no cerró el conducto del tubo de aire de respiración cuando el motor se comenzó en frío primero, desconecte la manguera de vacío en el motor de vacío del tubo de respiración y coloque el dedo pulgar en el final de la manguera, chequeando por vacío. Si hay vacío dirigiéndose al motor, chequee que la válvula y el eslabón no estén atorados ni haya obstrucción en el tubo de respiración del purificador de aire. Reemplace el motor de vacío si la ruta de la manguera está correcta y la válvula se mueve libremente.

8   Si no había vacío dirigiéndose al motor en la prueba de encima, chequee las mangueras para asegurarse que ellas no están agrietadas, pellizcadas ni desconectadas. Si las mangueras están limpias y en buenas condiciones, reemplace el sensor de la temperatura adentro del albergue del purificador de aire.

Motor de vacío

9   Separe la manguera del vacío del motor de vacío y conecte un probador de vacío en su posición.
10   Aplique vacío al motor. A 10.0 - kPa (-75 mm Hg o - 2.95 pulgada Hg) la válvula debe de comenzar a abrirse. A 22.0 - kPa (-165 mm Hg o - 6.5 pulgada Hg) la válvula debe de estar abierta completamente.
11   Si el motor de vacío no trabaja como está descrito debe ser reemplazado.

Reemplazo de componentes

Sensor de la temperatura

12   Usando alicates, aplaste el retenedor que retiene la manguera del vacío al sensor.
13   Desconecte la manguera de vacío del sensor.
14   Note cuidadosamente la posición del sensor. El sensor nuevo debe ser instalado exactamente en la misma posición.
15   Remueva el retenedor del tubo del sensor y remueva el filtro de aire del sensor.
Nota: *La junta entre el sensor y el purificador de aire está pegada al purificador de aire y no debe ser removida.*
16   Instale el sensor nuevo con una junta nueva en la misma posición como la vieja.
17   Apriete el retenedor en el sensor. No dañe el mecanismo de control en el centro del sensor.
18   Conecte las mangueras de vacío e instale el purificador de aire en el motor.

Motor de vacío

19   Remueva los tornillos que conectan el retenedor del motor de vacío al purificador de aire.
20   Gire el motor de vacío para desengancharlo de la válvula del control de aire y levántelo hacia afuera.
21   La instalación se hace en el orden inverso al procedimiento de desensamble.

---

3   Compensador para la marcha mínima

Refiérase a las ilustraciones 3.7 y 3.8

Descripción general

1   El compensador para la marcha mínima es una válvula termostática bimetal que está diseñada para dirigir aire directamente al filtro de aire en el múltiple de admisión. Esto compensa el enriquecimiento anormal de la mezcla que puede ocurrir en temperaturas altas de aire exterior cuando está en marcha mínima. Los modelos 1980 usan una unidad de doble válvula, con cada una de las válvu-

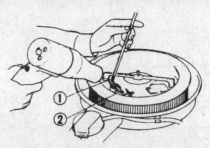

3.7 Para chequear la operación del compensador de la marcha mínima en los modelos 1980 al 1984, sostenga un termómetro anexo al compensador para dirigirle con una pistola de aire caliente a el - si el compensador está en buena condición, un sonido que silba se oirá cuando cada una de las válvulas llegan a su temperatura de abertura (modelo 1980, con las válvulas bi metal no. 1 y la bi metal no. 2, mostrado; modelos 1981 y más modernos tienen una válvula)

---

las calibradas para abrir (permitiendo que aire entre en el múltiple de admisión) en un rango de temperatura diferente. La válvula número 1 se abre entre 140 a 158 grados F (60 a 70 grados C) mientras que la válvula número 2 se abre entre 158 a 194 grados F (70 a 90 grados C). El compensador de la marcha mínima en estos modelos está localizado adentro del purificador de aire.
2   El compensador de la marcha mínima en los modelos 1981 al 1984 US y los modelos Canadienses 1981 al 1985 es una válvula de una sola unidad y está conectada directamente al carburador. La unidad se abre aproximádamente a 127 grados F (53 grados C).

Chequeo

(Modelo 1980 US y modelos Canadienses)

3   Un compensador de marcha mínima defectuoso es sospechado si la marcha mínima llega a ser irregular. Para chequearlo, asegúrese que el motor está frío y remueva la tapa del purificador de aire.
4   Desconecte la manguera que se dirige al compensador y atente de absorber aire a través de ella. Cuando el motor está frío, ningún aire debe pasar a través. Si pasa, reemplace el compensador de la marcha mínima.
Nota: *Chequee ambas válvulas individualmente deteniendo la otra cerrada con su dedo mientras la está chequeando.*
5   Después reemplace la tapa del purificador de aire, cierre el capó, entonces ponga el motor en marcha y permítalo que alcance la temperatura normal de operación.
6   Con el motor completamente caliente, abra el capó otra vez y remueva la tapa del purificador del aire.
7   Mientras detiene un termómetro anexo al compensador de la marcha mínima, apunte una pistola de aire caliente al compensador (**vea ilustración**). Si el compensador está en buena condición un sonido que silba será oído según cada válvula llega a su

3.8 En los modelos 1981 al 1984 US (y los modelos 1981 al 1985 Canadienses), el compensador de la marcha mínima y la válvula de control del desvío del aire (flechas) están localizados en el carburador

---

temperatura de abertura. Si ellas no se abren como está descrito, reemplace la unidad con una nueva.

Modelos US 1981 al 1984 y modelos 1981 al 1985 Canadienses

8   Porque el compensador de la marcha mínima en estos modelos es instalado íntegramente con el carburador (**vea ilustración**), el único método efectivo de chequearlo es de remover el carburador. Visualmente chequee que la válvula está en su posición cerrada cuando está fría. Entonces, mientras sostiene un termómetro en un costado, dirija una pistola de aire caliente para traerla a la temperatura de abertura. Observe para estar seguro que la válvula bimetal se abre a su temperatura correcta. Si no, reemplácela con una nueva.

Reemplazo

1980 US y modelos Canadienses

9   Remueva el plato superior del purificador de aire.
10   Desconecte la manguera de aire de la unidad.
11   Remueva los tornillos que retienen el purificador de aire y levántelo hacia afuera, junto con su junta.
12   La instalación se hace en el orden inverso al procedimiento de desensamble.
Nota: *Si está reemplazando el compensador, esté seguro que el nuevo tiene el mismo número de identificación como el viejo.*

Modelos 1981 al 1984 US y modelos 1981 al 1985 Canadienses

13   Remueva el purificador de aire.
14   Remueva los tornillos del compensador de la marcha mínima de la tapa del compensador y la tapa, entonces levante hacia afuera el compensador y la junta.
15   La instalación se hace en el orden inverso al procedimiento de desensamble.
Nota: *Si está reemplazando la unidad, esté seguro que la nueva tiene el mismo número de identificación que la vieja.*

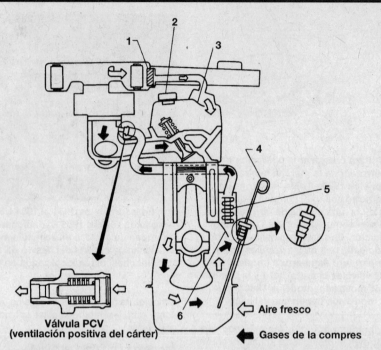

4.2 El sistema PCV (ventilación positiva del cárter) usado en los modelos 1981 al 1985

1 Filtro PCV	4 Medidor para el nivel del aceite sellado
2 Tapa para llenar sellada	5 Red de acero
3 Plato deflector	6 Plato deflector

Válvula PCV
(ventilación positiva del cárter)

⇦ Aire fresco

◀ Gases de la compres

4   PCV (ventilación positiva del cárter)

Refiérase a la ilustración 4.2

Descripción general

1   La ventilación positiva del cigüeñal, o sistema PCV, como es llamado comúnmente, reduce las emisiones de hidrocarburos circulando aire fresco en el cárter del cigüeñal. Este aire combinado con gases que pasan a través de los anillos del pistón durante la compresión y esta combinación es entonces absorbida en el múltiple de admisión para ser quemada nuevamente por el motor.

2   Este proceso es logrado usando un tubo de aire que corra de la tapa de los balancines hacia el purificador, una válvula unilateral PCV localizada en el lado del múltiple de admisión y un segundo tubo de aire que corre del cárter del cigüeñal a la válvula PCV **(vea ilustración)**.

3   Durante la operación parcial del acelerador, el vacío creado en el múltiple de admisión es magnífico para absorber bastante de los gases en el cárter del cigüeñal, a la válvula PCV y adentro del múltiple. La válvula PCV permite que los gases entren en el múltiple, pero no los permitirá entrar en la otra dirección.

4   El aire de ventilación es absorbido adentro del filtro de aire desde la tapa de los balancines y entonces adentro del cárter del cigüeñal.

5   Bajo operación del acelerador completamente abierto, el vacío en el múltiple de admisión no es suficiente para absorber los

gases hacia adentro. Bajo esta condición los gases de la compresión que se escapan a través de los anillos fluyen de regreso hacia la tapa de los balancines, a través del tubo de aire y adentro del purificador de aire, donde es dirigido hacia el múltiple de admisión adentro del flujo normal de aire.

Chequeo

6   El sistema PCV puede ser chequeado por una operación apropiada rápidamente y fácilmente. Este sistema debe ser chequeado regularmente porque carbón y depositados de mugre de los gases atascarán eventualmente las mangueras de vacío para la válvula PCV y/o sistema. Cuando el flujo del sistema PCV es reducido o detenido, los síntomas comunes son marcha mínima áspera o velocidad del motor reducida en marcha mínima.

7   Para chequear por el vacío apropiado en el sistema, desconecte la manguera de aire de caucho de donde sale del purificador de aire.

8   Con el motor en marcha mínima, coloque el dedo pulgar ligeramente en el final de la manguera. Usted debe sentir una leve succión de vacío. La succión se puede oír según su dedo pulgar es liberado. Esto indicará que el aire es absorbido completamente a través del sistema. Si un vacío es detectado, el sistema está funcionando apropiadamente.

9   Si hay muy poco vacío o ninguno del todo, en el final de la manguera, el sistema está obstruido y debe ser inspeccionado un poco más.

10   Con el motor todavía en marcha mínima, desconecte la manguera de caucho de la válvula PCV. Ahora ponga su dedo en el

final de la válvula y si sienta por una succión. Usted debe sentir un vacío relativamente fuerte en este punto. Esto indica que la válvula está buena.

11   Si ningún vacío es detectado en la válvula PCV, remueva la válvula del múltiple de admisión. Sacúdala y escuche por un sonido de cascabeleo. Esto es la matraca de la válvula aguja unilateral. Si la válvula no cascabelea libremente, reemplácela.

12   Si un vacío fuerte es detectado en la válvula PCV, pero no hay vacío durante el paso descrito en el Paso 8, entonces uno de los tubos de respiración del sistema está probablemente obstruido. Deben ser removidos y deben ser soplados con aire comprimido.

13   Si, después de limpiar los tubos de respiración, todavía no hay succión en el tubo de aire, hay un bloqueo en un pasaje interno, posiblemente en el plato deflector y red de acero adentro del cárter del cigüeñal. Esto requiere desarmar el motor para corregirlo.

14   Cuando compre una válvula PCV nueva, asegúrese que es la apropiada para su vehículo. Una válvula PCV inexacta puede extraer demasiado o muy poco vacío, posiblemente causando daño al motor.

5   EGR (recirculación de los gases de escape)

Refiérase a las ilustraciones 5.13, 5.18a, 5.18b, 5.19, 5.34 y 5.40

Descripción general
Vista general (todos los modelos)

1   Este sistema es usado para reducir el NOx (oxido de nitrógeno) emitido desde el escape. La formación de estos contaminantes suceden a temperaturas muy altas; consecuentemente, ocurren durante el período de la temperatura alta en el proceso de la combustión. Para reducir las temperaturas altas y así la formación de NOx, una cantidad pequeña del gas de escape es tomada del sistema de escape y reciclada en el ciclo de la combustión.

2   Diferentes sistemas EGR levemente diferentes son usados en los modelos de los años 1980.

3   Además, dentro de cada sistema varias válvulas EGR son usadas según la transmisión usada y la altitud que el vehículo sea destinado a operar. Para reemplazar, la válvula EGR puede ser identificada por el número de parte estampada en la porción superior de receso de la válvula.

4   Porque un sistema EGR funcionando mal puede afectar severamente el rendimiento del motor, es importante entender cómo cada sistema trabaja en orden de localizar las fallas exactamente. Los problemas comunes del motor asociados con el sistema de EGR son: marcha mínima áspera o atascamiento cuando está en marcha mínima, desempeño áspero del motor en la aplicación liviana del acelerador y atascamiento en deceleración.

5.13 Esquemática para el sistema EGR (recirculación de los gases de escape) usado en los modelos 1981 al 1984 (menos los vehículos 1984 de California)

1 Válvula de vacío térmica (de 3 puertos)
2 Venturi del carburador
3 Mariposa del acelerador
4 Puerto de vacío EGR (recirculación de los gases de escape)
5 Anticongelante del motor

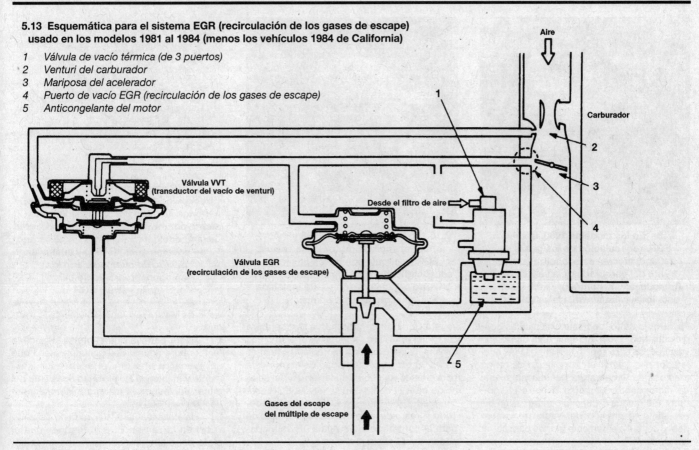

Modelos 1980

5   El sistema EGR usado en los modelos 1980 incorpora una válvula EGR, una válvula BPT (transductor de contra presión) y una válvula TVV (válvula térmica interruptora de vacío). Además, los modelos de California usan también una válvula de retraso del vacío instalada en la línea de vacío entre la válvula de BPT y la TVV.

6   El corazón de cualquier sistema EGR es la válvula EGR, que controla el flujo de los gases de escape en el múltiple de admisión para que se quemen nuevamente. Bajo las condicione normales la válvula EGR está cerrada, que previene el pasaje de los gases de escape en el múltiple de admisión. El tipo de válvula TVV bimetal y la válvula de BPT son incorporados en el sistema para controlar la abertura de la válvula para que abra solamente en el tiempo óptimo.

7   La señal directa del vacío que abre la mariposa del acelerador en el carburador. Esta señal de vacío es solamente para abrir la válvula EGR durante posiciones de medianas aperturas del acelerador. En la marcha mínima y cuando la aceleración es completa, la señal de vacío disminuye y la válvula EGR se cerrará otra vez.

8   La TVV está colocada en la línea de señal de vacío entre el carburador y la válvula EGR y está diseñada para no permitir que la señal de vacío alcance la válvula EGR hasta que la temperatura del anticongelante del motor llegue a 122 grados F (50 grados C), o la temperatura normal de operación. Esto

previene que el sistema EGR empobrezca la mezcla rica de aire/combustible necesitada durante la operación fría del motor.

9   La válvula BPT es instalada en la línea de la señal de vacío después de la TVV y permite una purga de aire que suceda en la línea hasta que esté cerrada. Esta purga de aire, cuando está presente, mantiene la presión de vacío baja, así previniendo la válvula EGR que se abra.

10   La válvula BPT es también conectada por una línea a la porción inferior de la válvula EGR, que se abre a la presión del escape en el múltiple de escape. Cuando esta presión llega a un punto predeterminado, vencerá el resorte del diafragma cargado en la válvula BPT y cerrará la válvula. Cerrando la válvula detiene la purga de aire en la línea de señal y así permite que la señal de vacío llegue y abra la válvula EGR.

11   La válvula de retraso de vacío, usada en los modelos de California, es una válvula diseñada de tal manera para prevenir una fuga brusca de vacío en la línea de la señal de vacío a la válvula TVV, así incrementando la longitud de operación de la válvula EGR. Permite que pase aire libremente hacia el múltiple de admisión pero limita severamente la cantidad permitida que pasa hacia la válvula EGR. El lado marrón de la válvula siempre debe estar hacia la TVV.

12   Las condiciones, entonces, para que la válvula EGR se abra en este sistema son: 1) el anticongelante de motor debe estar a 122 grados F (50 grados C o más alto), 2) la presión del gas en el múltiple de escape debe

ser magnificentemente suficiente para cerrar la válvula BPT y 3) el acelerador debe de estar a media posición.

Modelos 1981 al 1984 (menos los modelos de California 1984)

13   El sistema EGR usado en estos modelos (vea ilustración) es similar al descrito encima con un par de diferencias principales. La válvula TVV (válvula térmica interruptora de vacío) usada en este sistema está diseñada para permitir una purga de aire en la línea de la señal del vacío cuando se abre la EGR y por lo tanto debe ser cerrada antes de que la válvula EGR pueda abrirse. Esta TVV está calibrada para permanecer abierta hasta que el anticongelante del motor llegue a 140 grados F (60 grados C). En este punto el sensor de cera se ensanchará y sellará la fuga de aire.

14   Otra diferencia mayor es que una VVT (transductor del vacío de venturi) es usada en lugar de la válvula BPT (transductor de contra presión). Como la TVV, la válvula VVT permite también una purga de aire y por lo tanto debe ser cerrada antes de que la válvula EGR pueda abrirse. La válvula VVT puede ser cerrada por cualquiera de las dos maneras. Un método, como con la válvula BPT en el sistema 1980, es que si la contrapresión del gas de escape llega a ser lo suficiente grande, esta presión causará que la válvula se cierre. La válvula VVT tiene también una línea de señal del vacío de venturi del carburador. Un vacío suficientemente grande en este punto causará también que la válvula VVT se cierre.

5.18a En los modelos 1980, la válvula EGR (recirculación de los gases de escape) (flecha) está localizada en el frente del carburador y la válvula BPT (transductor de contra presión) (flecha) está localizada anexa a la válvula EGR

5.18b En los modelos 1986 y más modernos con un motor V6, la válvula EGR (recirculación de los gases de escape) (flecha) está localizada atrás del cuerpo de aceleración y está instalada en el múltiple de admisión

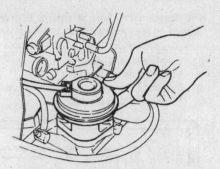

5.19 Para chequear la válvula EGR (recirculación de los gases de escape), ponga su dedo debajo de la válvula y sienta por movimiento libre del diafragma levantándolo hacia encima - esté seguro de ponerse guantes si hay cualquier peligro de quemarse con los componentes caliente cerca de la válvula EGR

15 Por lo tanto, con este sistema, las condiciones que se deben reunir para que la válvula EGR se abra son: 1) la mariposa del acelerador debe estar en la posición de rango medio, 2) la temperatura del anticongelante del motor debe estar por lo menos a 140 grados F (60 grados C), 3) o la contrapresión del escape o la presión del vacío de venturi deben ser suficientemente grande para cerrar la válvula VVT.

1984 California y todos los modelos 1985 y 1986 con motores de cuatro cilindros solamente

16 Aunque básicamente similar a los diseños previos, el sistema EGR en los modelos 1984 de California, todos los modelos de vehículos 1985 y 1986 con motores de cuatro cilindros están equipados con una válvula BPT en vez de un VVT. Este BPT, es idéntico en diseño y operación al BPT usado en los modelos 1980, contiene un diafragma activado por la presión del escape. Este diafragma, en cambio, regula la cantidad de vacío aplicado a la válvula del control EGR. Así, que la cantidad de gas recirculando del escape varía con la condición de operación del motor.

Modelos 1987 y 1988 de cuatro cilindros y 1986 y más modernos con motores V6

17 La última versión del sistema EGR está bajo del control de la unidad ECCS (sistema de computadora por control electrónico) ECU (unidad de control electrónica). Utilizando entradas del sensor del ángulo del cigüeñal, sensor de temperatura de la cabeza de los cilindros y el sensor del acelerador, la ECU computa la velocidad del motor, la temperatura del motor y la posición de la mariposa del acelerador, respectivamente. la ECU interpreta estos datos y manda una señal a la válvula del solenoide para el control de la válvula EGR, que controla la válvula EGR. Básicamente, en cualquier momento que el motor

vaya a ponerse en marcha, la temperatura del motor está baja, el motor está en marcha mínima, la velocidad del motor está alta (más de 3,200 rpm) o la velocidad del motor está baja (menos de 900 rpm), la válvula del solenoide para el control de la válvula EGR está "prendida" y el sistema EGR está apagado. Todo el resto de las otras veces, el solenoide para el control de la válvula EGR está apagado y la EGR está prendida.

Chequeo
Válvula EGR (recirculación de los gases de escape)

18 Localice la válvula EGR montada en el frente del múltiple de admisión en los modelos 1980, o en la parte trasera del múltiple de admisión en los modelos 1981 y más modernos **(vea ilustraciones)**.
19 Coloque su dedo debajo de la válvula EGR y levante el plato del diafragma **(vea ilustración)**. El diafragma debe moverse libremente de la posición cerrada a la posición abierta. Si no lo hace, reemplace la válvula EGR.
20 Ahora ponga el motor en marcha y córralo a la velocidad de marcha mínima. Mientras el motor está todavía apenas calentándose, otra vez levante el diafragma de la EGR con su dedo. Si la válvula o accesorios adyacentes están caliente, use guantes para prevenir quemarse sus dedo. Cuando el diafragma sea apretado (la válvula se abre para reciclar el escape), el motor debe bajar de velocidad, se tambalea o se para. Si el motor no cambia de velocidad, el tubo para el gas de escape que se dirige a la válvula EGR debe ser chequeado por obstrucción.
21 Si está equipado con una válvula BPT (transductor de contra presión), desvíela conectando una manguera directamente entre la TVV (válvula térmica interruptora de vacío) y la válvula EGR. Si está equipado con una válvula VVT (transductor del vacío de venturi), desconecte la línea de la señal del

vacío de la válvula y tape firmemente la manguera.
22 Ahora permita que el motor alcance la temperatura normal de operación. Haga que un ayudante presione el acelerador levemente y mantenga la velocidad constante del motor encima de la marcha mínima acerca de 2,000 a 2,500 rpm.
23 Hale hacia afuera la línea de la señal de vacío en la válvula EGR y chequee que el plato del diafragma se mueve hacia abajo, acompañado de un aumento en la velocidad del motor.
24 Vuelva a instalar la línea de la señal de vacío a la válvula y el plato del diafragma debe moverse hacia encima con una disminución en la velocidad del motor.
25 Si el diafragma no se mueve, asegúrese que el motor esté a la temperatura de operación normal. Repita la prueba si está dudoso.
26 Si el diafragma todavía no se mueve, el próximo chequeo sería que el vacío alcance la válvula EGR. Hale hacia afuera la manguera de vacío en la válvula y con el motor en marcha y el acelerador levemente apretado, chequee por vacío en el final de la manguera con su dedo pulgar. Si hay vacío en el, reemplace la válvula EGR con una nueva. Si no hay señal de vacío, siga la manguera de vacío a su fuente, inspeccionando por cualquier roturas, interrupciones o bloqueo en las líneas. También chequee que la TVV y la válvula de retraso del vacío (si está equipado) estén trabajando apropiadamente.

Válvula BPT (transductor de contra presión)

27 Desconecte ambas mangueras de vacío de la cima de la válvula.
28 Remueva del motor la válvula como está descrito en otra parte de esta sección.
29 Tape uno de los acopladores superiores y conecte una manguera a la otra.
30 Atente de absorber aire a través de la manguera. Si no se puede absorber aire a través de la manguera, la válvula está obstruida cerrada y debe ser reemplazada.

5.34 El VVT (transductor del vacío de venturi) (encima) y la válvula EGR (recirculación de los gases de escape) (abajo) están localizados atrás del carburador en los modelos 1981 y 1982

31 Después, conecte una bomba de aire de mano al fondo de la acoplación de la válvula.

32 Mientras está aplicando presión de aire a la válvula otra vez, atente de absorber aire. Si usted puede, la válvula está atorada en la posición cerrada y debe ser reemplazada. **Nota:** *Si una bomba de aire no está disponible, el mismo efecto puede ser logrado conectando una manguera al fondo de la acoplación y haga que ayudante sople aire adentro de la válvula en orden de cerrarla.*

33 Antes de conectar de nuevo la línea de

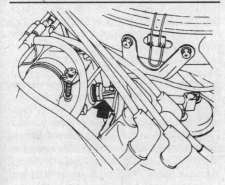

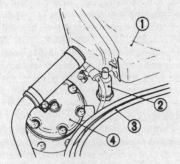

5.40 Ubicación de la válvula de vacío térmica encima - modelos 1980; abajo - modelos 1981 al 1985)

1   Purificador de aire
2   TV (válvula conectada al acelerador)
3   Alambres de las bujías
4   Bomba de combustible

presión del escape abajo de la válvula, asegúrese que la línea no está obstruida soplando aire a través de ella.

Válvula VVT (transductor del vacío de venturi)

34 Siga la manguera de la señal del vacío en el centro superior de la válvula y la desconecta en su primera acoplación **(vea ilustración).**

35 Atente absorber aire a través de la manguera. Si aire no se puede absorber a través de la manguera, la válvula está obstruida cerrada y debe ser reemplazada.

36 Desconecte la manguera de contrapresión del escape del fondo de la válvula y conecte una bomba de aire de mano a la acoplación. Mientras está aplicando presión de aire a la válvula, otra vez atente de absorber a través de la manguera para la señal del vacío. En este momento usted no debe ser capaz de absorber aire a través de ella. Si usted puede, la válvula está defectuosa y debe ser reemplazada. Si una bomba de aire no está disponible, el mismo efecto puede ser logrado conectando una manguera, del mismo diámetro como la que se removió, a la acoplación y haga que un ayudante sople a través de la válvula.

37 Antes de conectar de nuevo la manguera de la presión del escape al fondo de la válvula, asegúrese que la línea no está obstruida soplando aire adentro de ella.

38 Después, desconecte la manguera del vacío de venturi del lado superior de la válvula y conecte una bomba de vacío a la acoplación. Mientras está aplicando vacío a la válvula, una vez más atente de absorber aire a través de la manguera de la señal de vacío. Si usted es capaz de absorber aire a través, la válvula está obstruida abierta y debe ser reemplazada.

39 Antes de conectar de nuevo la manguera de vacío de venturi, asegúrese que no está obstruida soplando a través de ella. Entonces sígala a lo largo de su longitud completa chequeando que no haya roturas, ni otras fugas.

Válvula TVV (válvula térmica interruptora de vacío)

40 Para chequear la función apropiada de la válvula térmica de vacío, comience con un motor frío. En los modelos 1980, desconecte la línea de vacío de la válvula BPT, o de la válvula de retraso de vacío, si está equipado **(vea ilustración).** En los modelos 1981 y 1982, desconecte primero la manguera de vacío del centro superior de la válvula VVT y la tapa. Entonces desconecte la línea de la señal del vacío de la válvula EGR.

41 Ahora ponga el motor en marcha y con su dedo pulgar, sienta si algún vacío proviene a través de la línea. Si el vacío alcanza la válvula inmediatamente después de poner en marcha el motor, la TVV debe ser reemplazada.

42 Ahora espere que el motor alcance la temperatura normal de operación (encima de 122 grados F para modelos 1980 y encima

de 140 grados para los modelos 1981 y 1982) y otra vez, sienta por vacío en el final de la manguera. Si ningún vacío está presente en el final de la manguera, chequee primero que la manguera no esté obstruida. Entonces, si todas las líneas están limpias, reemplace la TVV con una nueva.

43 Otro método de probar que la TVV es con el motor apagado. Con el motor frío, remueva la TVV completa con las mangueras. En los modelos 1981 y 1982, cierre la manguera con una abrazadera conectada a la acoplación inferior de la válvula. Atente de absorber aire a través de la manguera de vacío conectada a la acoplación inferior (modelos 1980) o la acoplación del medio (modelos 1981 y 1982). Mientras que la válvula está fría (a temperatura de la habitación) la TVV en los modelos 1980 debe estar cerrada, previniéndole a usted que absorba aire a través. En los modelos 1981 y 1982 debe estar abierta, permitiendo que aire sea absorba a través. Si este no es el caso, reemplace la válvula.

44 Ahora ponga la válvula en una cacerola y la sumerge en agua. No permita que el agua entre en la manguera o el interior de la válvula. Caliente el agua hasta que su temperatura esté encima de 122 grados F (modelos 1980 o 140 grados F (modelos 1981 y 1982). Ahora atente de absorber aire como antes. En este punto la válvula en los modelos 1980 debe estar abierta, mientras que en los modelos 1981 y 1982, ahora debe estar cerrada. Si la válvula no funciona en esta manera y la manguera no está obstruida ni partida, reemplace la válvula con una nueva.

Válvula de retraso del vacío

45 Remueva la válvula, notando su dirección instalada. Sople a través de la válvula del lado de la válvula EGR. El flujo de aire debe fluir libremente a través de la válvula. Ahora sople en el otro lado (lado marrón). El flujo debe ser restringido. Si este no es el caso, reemplace la válvula.

Válvula solenoide para cortar el vacío de la EGR (modelos 1986 y modelos más modernos 1988 V6 y modelos 1987 y 1988 de cuatro cilindros)

46 Porque una porción de la prueba para una operación normal de la válvula solenoide para cortarle el vacío a la EGR (recirculación de los gases de escape) implica una prueba de circuito EGR y una prueba de rendimiento de entrada/salida de la ECU (unidad de control electrónica), ambos requieren equipo de diagnóstico especial, chequeando el solenoide está más allá del alcance del mecánico del hogar. Adicionalmente, todos los dispositivos para los sistemas del control de las emisiones por computadora son protegidos por una garantía extendida Federalmente puesta bajo mandato (chequee con su concesionario para averiguar los detalles del alcance en su vehículo) y molestar cualquiera de estos dispositivos sin autorización es ilegal o puede anular la garantía.

Reemplazo de componentes

Pasaje de la EGR (recirculación de los gases de escape) (modelos 1980)

47   Desconecte el tubo del escape de la EGR aflojando la tuerca de retención.
48   Desconecte todas las mangueras del pasaje de la EGR, note como ellas están instaladas.
49   Remueva los pernos para el afianzamiento del pasaje de la EGR y levántelo hacia afuera.
50   Limpie las superficies de acoplamiento del pasaje de la EGR y el múltiple de admisión, remueva todos los rasgos de material de la junta vieja.
51   La instalación se hace en el orden inverso al procedimiento de desensamble. **Nota:** *Esté seguro de usar una junta nueva.*

Válvula EGR (recirculación de los gases de escape) (modelos 1981 y más modernos)

52   En los modelos 1981 y más modernos desconecte el tubo del escape de la EGR aflojando la tuerca de retención.
53   Desconecte la manguera de vacío de la parte superior de la válvula.
54   Remueva las tuercas de la válvula EGR y levántela hacia afuera.
55   Limpie las superficies de acoplamiento del pasaje de la válvula EGR y el múltiple de admisión o EGR, remueva todos los rasgos de material de la junta vieja.
56   La instalación se hace en el orden inverso al procedimiento de desensamble. **Nota:** *Esté seguro de usar una junta nueva. También, cuando reemplace la válvula EGR, esté seguro que la nueva es del mismo tipo como la vieja.*

Válvula BPT (transductor de contra presión)

57   Desconecte las mangueras de la señal de vacío de la parte superior de la válvula BPT.
58   Remueva los tornillos que retienen la válvula al soporte y levante la válvula.
59   Desconecte la manguera de contrapresión del escape abajo de la válvula y remueva la válvula del compartimiento del motor.
60   La instalación se hace en el orden inverso al procedimiento de desensamble. **Nota:** *Cuando reemplace la válvula, esté seguro que la válvula nueva tiene el mismo número estampado como la válvula vieja.*

Válvula VVT (transductor del vacío de venturi)

61   Desconecte todas las mangueras de la válvula VVT. Esté seguro de marcarlas en cuanto a su ubicación.
62   Remueva los dos tornillos que retienen la válvula al soporte, entonces baje la válvula del soporte y remuévala del compartimiento del motor.
63   La instalación se hace en el orden inverso al procedimiento de desensamble.

Nota: *Cuando reemplace la válvula VVT esté seguro que la válvula nueva tiene el mismo número estampado como la válvula vieja.*

Válvula térmica del vacío

64   Drene acerca de un cuarto de galón de anticongelante del radiador.
65   Desconecte la mangueras de vacío del interruptor de vacío, notando sus posiciones para volver a instalarla.
66   Usando una llave, remueva el interruptor.
67   Cuando esté instalando el interruptor, aplique sellador de rosca a las roscas, tenga cuidado de no permitir que el sellador toque el fondo del sensor.
68   Instale el interruptor y apriételo al par de torsión especificado.

---

6   Inducción del aire - sistema

Refiérase a las ilustraciones 6.2, 6.7a. 6.7b, 6.10, 6.13 y 6.20

Descripción general

1   El propósito del sistema de aire de inducción es para reducir los hidrocarburos en el escape extrayendo aire fresco directamente en el múltiple de escape. El aire fresco, rico en oxígeno ayuda a completar la combustión de los hidrocarburos parcialmente quemados antes de que ellos sean expulsados como escape. Todo los modelos 1981 y 1982 están equipados con este sistema, también como los modelos 1980 US Federal y de Canadá de trabajo pesado.
2   Los componentes de este sistema sencillo incluye un filtro de aire y una válvula de lengüeta, ambos están localizados en un albergue conectado al purificador de aire, uno o dos (dependiendo en el modelo) los tubos EAI conectan el albergue de la válvula con el múltiple de escape y con una válvula de AB (anti explosión) en los sistemas de tipo A. Todos los modelos 1980, 1981 y 1982 de California usan el sistema de tipo A mientras los modelos 1981 y 1982 US Federal y de Canadá usan el sistema de tipo B, que no usan un sistema de válvula de AB. Los sistemas tipo A (California) y tipo B (Federal y Canadá) 1983 y 1984 en todos los vehículos usan una válvula de AB. Todos los vehículos 1985 al 1988 están equipados con sistemas idénticos con una válvula de AB. Los modelos 1986 y más modernos están equipados también con una válvula solenoide para cortar el vacío **(vea ilustración)**, que regula el vacío de acuerdo con las señales de la ECU (unidad de control electrónica).
3   La abertura y cerradura de las válvulas del escape crean pulsos de vacío que absorben el aire fresco en el ensamblaje del filtro y la válvula. La válvula de lengüeta admite solamente aire para ser absorbido en el múltiple y previene que la contrapresión del escape fuerce los gases que se retiren. En algunos sistemas, este aire fresco que entra en el múltiple de escape puede causar una contra explosión durante deceleración debido a una mezcla de combustible rica. La válvula de AB,

6.2 La AIV (válvula de inyección de aire) válvula solenoide para cortar el vacío (flecha) regula la señal de vacío al sistema AIV (válvula de inyección de aire) de acuerdo con una señal eléctrica de la ECU (unidad de control electrónica)

que es accionada por vacío del múltiple de admisión, corrige esto dirigiendo aire adicional (desde el filtro del aire) en el múltiple de admisión durante la deceleración.

Chequeo

4   La sencillez del sistema es uno muy seguro que causa rara vez problemas. Chequeos periódicos deben ser hechos, sin embargo, se debe chequear la condición de los componentes para estar seguro que no hay fugas ni roturas en el sistema. Siempre haga un chequeo visual de las mangueras y los tubos por conexiones malas, rizo, doblados o deterioración antes de chequear los componentes de la AIV (válvula de inyección de aire).
5   Dos pruebas funcionales sencillas se pueden realizar para asegurarse que el sistema está operando apropiadamente. Desconecte las mangueras de los tubos de metal EAI (inyección de aire para el escape). Para la primera prueba, atente de absorber aire a través de la manguera de caucho y entonces atente de soplar aire a través de la manguera. La válvula de lengüeta debe permitir que usted absorba aire a través de la manguera pero previene que usted sople de regreso. Si usted es capaz de soplar aire a través de la manguera entonces la válvula está defectuosa y debe ser reemplazada. Si usted no es capaz de absorber aire hacia adentro, entonces chequee por un filtro de aire o manguera obstruida. Si esto no es el caso, entonces reemplace la válvula.
6   Para la segunda prueba, ponga el motor en marcha y permítalo que corra en marcha mínima. Con el motor en marcha mínima sostenga su mano encima de los tubos de metal EAI (inyección de aire para el escape). Debe haber una corriente constante de aire que sea absorbido. Haga que un ayudante aplique el acelerador y según el motor aumenta las revoluciones la succión debe aumentar. Si esto no acontece, hay fugas o bloqueo en los tubos.

6.7a La válvula de AB (purga de aire) en los modelos 1981 y 1982 está localizada en frente del carburador

6.7b La válvula de AB (purga de aire) en los vehículos 1986 y más modernos está localizada en el múltiple de admisión enfrente del cuerpo de inyección

6.10 El albergue AIV (válvula de inyección de aire) para la válvula de lengüeta está aislado de la caja AIV para el filtro en los vehículos 1986 y más modernos - remueva la válvula de lengüeta, destornillando los tornillos de estrella, levante hacia encima la primera mitad del albergue y abra hacia afuera con una palanca la lengüeta; remuévala del albergue, separe la manguera de vacío, afloje las tuercas de afianzamiento y deslice los aisladores de caucho fuera de la hendidura de los soportes de afianzamiento

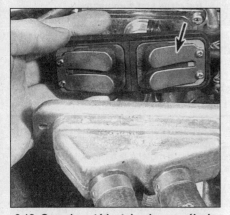

6.13 Cuando esté instalando una válvula de lengüeta nueva, asegúrese que las lengüetas miran hacia la dirección apropiada o el sistema no funcionará apropiadamente - asegúrese también que el "detenedor" (flecha) está atornillado apretadamente

6.20 Para remover la válvula AB (purga de aire) en los vehículos 1986 y más modernos, equipados con un motor V6, remueva el albergue del purificador de aire y separe el tubo en la cara inferior del purificador de aire de la manguera corta gorda conectada en la parte trasera de la válvula AB (flecha), entonces separe la línea de vacío (flecha) encima y la manguera de aire (flecha) abajo

7 Para chequear la válvula de AB (anti explosión), primero remueva el purificador de aire y desconecte la manguera de caucho de la válvula de AB (vea ilustraciones). Ponga el motor en marcha y permítalo que alcance la temperatura normal de operación. Cuando el motor esté completamente caliente, haga que un ayudante corra el motor acerca de 3,000 rpm mientras usted tiene un dedo cerca de la acoplación de salida de la válvula de AB. Haga que su ayudante libere bruscamente el acelerador para que el motor vuelva rápidamente a marcha mínima. Cuando esto acontece, usted debe sentir un halón o succión en la acoplación de válvula de AB. Si esto no es el caso, la válvula está funcionando normalmente. Si no, debe ser reemplazada con una nueva.

Reemplazo de componentes

Válvula de inducción de aire y filtro

8 Refiérase al Capítulo 1 para este procedimiento.

Albergue de la válvula de inducción de aire

9 La manguera(s) de caucho son prensada al albergue de la válvula. Solamente si el albergue de la válvula o manguera(s) necesitan ser reemplazada separada de las otras, corte la abrazaderas(s) que asegura las dos juntas y sepárelas.
10 Si usted tiene un vehículo pre 1986, remueva los cuatro tornillos que conectan el albergue de la válvula al albergue del filtro de aire. Los vehículos más modernos tienen un albergue para la AIV (válvula de inyección de aire) separado (vea ilustración) localizado en la esquina izquierda delantera en el compartimiento del motor. Para removerlo, márquelo claramente y separe todas las mangueras, entonces remueva todos pernos de afianzamiento.
11 Desconecte la manguera(s) de caucho del tubo(s) de metal para el aire.
12 Chequee la válvula de lengüeta por rotura, cuarteaduras o deformación. Chequee el "detenedor" para ver si está flojo y apriételo si es necesario. Hágale palanca a la

válvula de lengüeta para abrirla y reemplácela si es necesario.
13 La instalación se hace en el orden inverso al procedimiento de desensamble. Esté seguro que la válvula de lengüeta está instalado con la cara de la lengüeta mirando hacia la dirección apropiada (vea ilustración). Nota: Si la manguera(s) de caucho ha sido removida del albergue de la válvula, abrazaderas para las mangueras se deben usar para asegurarlas juntas.

Tubos EAI (inyección de aire para el escape)

14 Remueva los tornillos que conectan el albergue de la válvula al purificador de aire.
15 Destornille la tuerca que conecta cada tubo al múltiple de escape. Debido a la temperatura alta en esta área, estas tuercas pueden ser difíciles de aflojar. Aceite penetrante aplicado a las roscas de estas tuercas puede ayudar.
16 Remueva el perno que asegura el soporte en su tubo y levante el ensamblaje hacia afuera. El albergue de la válvula y las mangueras entonces pueden ser removidas de los tubos.
17 Antes de instalar, aplique una capa de atascamiento a las roscas de las tuercas grandes en los extremos.
18 La instalación se hace en el orden inverso al procedimiento de desensamble.

Válvula AB (anti explosión)

19 Remueva el purificador de aire.
20 Desconecte las mangueras y líneas de vacío de la válvula (vea ilustración) y remuévala.
21 La instalación se hace en el orden inverso al procedimiento de desensamble.

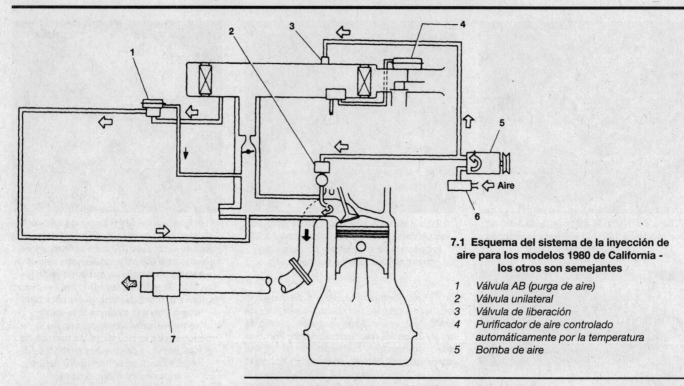

7.1 Esquema del sistema de la inyección de aire para los modelos 1980 de California - los otros son semejantes

1   Válvula AB (purga de aire)
2   Válvula unilateral
3   Válvula de liberación
4   Purificador de aire controlado automáticamente por la temperatura
5   Bomba de aire

7   Inyección de aire - sistema

Refiérase a las ilustraciones 7.1, 7.25, 7.34 y 7.37

Descripción general

1   Este es un método de inyectar aire (generado por un compresor externo) en el múltiple de escape para reducir los hidrocarburos y monóxido de carbono en el gas del escape proporcionando las condiciones favorables para que se queme en la combustión nuevamente. El sistema está compuesto de un purificador de aire, bomba de aire conducida por una banda, válvula unilateral, válvula para la antiexplosión, galería de aire y las mangueras relacionadas. Los modelos para el uso en California tienen también una válvula CAC (combinada para controlar el aire) con una válvula íntegra para aliviar la temperatura excesiva en el convertidor catalítico. Los modelos de Canadá usan una válvula más sencilla de relieve que realiza básicamente la misma función **(vea ilustración)**.
2   Aire absorbido por el purificador de aire de la bomba de aire y comprimido es dirigido a la válvula unilateral a la galería y las toberas de inyección de aire. Durante la operación de alta velocidad, la presión excesiva de la bomba es ventilada a la atmósfera a través de la válvula CAC o válvula de relieve.
3   La válvula unilateral es instalada en la línea de entrega en la galería de inyección. La función de esta válvula es para prevenir que cualquier escape de gas pase a la bomba de aire si la presión del múltiple es más que la presión de la bomba de inyección. Es diseñada para cerrar contra la presión del múltiple de escape si la bomba de aire falla como resultado, por ejemplo una banda rota.

4   Durante la deceleración, el vacío del múltiple de admisión abre la válvula antiexplosión para permitir el flujo fresco de aire en el múltiple de admisión. Esto asegura que el ciclo de la combustión sea más efectivo y reduzca la cantidad de los gases parcialmente quemados.
5   En los modelos de California, la válvula CAC se abre cuando la presión combinada de la bomba de aire y el vacío del múltiple de admisión alcanzan un nivel predeterminado según acontece durante las condiciones ligeramente cargadas. El aire desde la bomba de aire es purgado hacia el purificador de aire que significa que el sistema de inyección es menos efectivo, la temperatura del gas de escape es bajada y la temperatura del convertidor catalítico se puede mantener a la temperatura óptima de operación.
6   La válvula de liberación usada en los modelos de el Canadá purga el aire de la bomba de aire cuando hay una condición prolongada baja de succión del múltiple como acontece durante la operación continua de alta velocidad. Esto anula el sistema de inyección de aire, reduce la temperatura del gas de escape y previene que el convertidor catalítico se sobrecaliente.
7   El sistema de inyección de aire usado en los modelos de California de trabajo pesado es un sistema mucho más complejo, implicando componentes electrónicos. Por esta razón, otorgarle servicio a este sistema debe ser dejado a un concesionario u otro mecánico calificado.

Chequeo

8   Chequee todas las mangueras, galería de los tubos de aire y toberas por seguridad y condición.
9   Chequee y ajuste la tensión de la banda

de la bomba de aire como está descrito en el Capítulo 1.
10   Con el motor a la temperatura normal de operación, desconecte la manguera que se dirige a la válvula unilateral.
11   Ponga el motor en marcha a aproximádamente 2,000 rpm y entonces permita que la velocidad regrese a la marcha mínima, mientras vigila por fugas del gas de escape en la válvula. Dónde éstos son evidentes, reemplace la válvula.
12   Chequee la operación de la válvula de liberación de la bomba de aire desconectando primero las mangueras de vacío de la válvula de regreso y entonces remueva la válvula CAC del conector de la manguera. Tape el conector.
13   Ponga el motor en una marcha constante 3,000 rpm y coloque la mano en la salida de aire de la válvula de liberación en caso de emergencia (los modelos de California). Una presión de aire definida debe ser detectada. Si no es detectada, reemplace la válvula.
14   Ahora hale la válvula del control del aire de la manguera de vacío. Si la inyección de aire cesa de la salida de la tobera, la válvula está en buenas condiciones pero si persiste, reemplace la válvula (que debe estar defectuosa).
15   La válvula para la antiexplosión (atrapa la llama) puede ser chequeada, cuando el motor está a la temperatura normal de operación, desconectando la manguera del filtro de aire y poniendo su dedo en el final de la manguera. Ponga el motor en marcha a acerca de 3,000 rpm y entonces regréselo a marcha mínima. Durante esta acción, un efecto fuerte de succión debe ser detectado en la manguera, que indica que la válvula está trabajando apropiadamente.

7.25 Dos herramientas se deben usar para remover la válvula unilateral de inyección de aire del tubo de la galería del aire

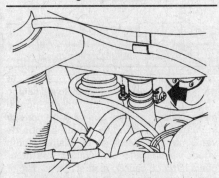

7.37 Ubicación de la válvula de liberación, instalada debajo del purificador de aire en los modelos de Canadá

Reemplazo de los componentes

Filtro de la bomba de aire

16   Refiérase al Capítulo 1.

Bomba de aire

17   Remueva las mangueras de la bomba de aire.
18   Remueva la banda de la bomba, refiérase al Capítulo 1, si es necesario.
19   Remueva todas las mangueras de la bomba.
20   Remueva el calzo y los pernos de ajuste y levante la bomba hacia afuera.
21   Si es necesario, remueva la polea de la bomba.
22   La instalación se hace en el orden inverso al procedimiento de desensamble.

Válvula unilateral

23   Remueva el purificador de aire.
24   Desconecte la manguera de aire de la válvula unilateral.
25   Remueva del tubo de la galería del aire la válvula unilateral, usando dos llaves (**vea ilustración**).
26   La instalación se hace en el orden inverso al procedimiento de desensamble.

Tubo de la galería de aire y toberas de inyección

27   A causa de la probabilidad de doblar o dañar los tubos durante el periodo de remover, los tubos no deben ser removidos a menos que ellos estén ya dañados y sea necesario reemplazarlos.

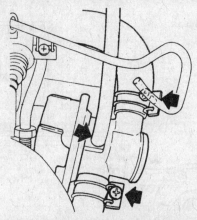

7.34 Para remover la válvula AB (purga de aire) en los modelos 1980, separe las líneas de vacío y las mangueras de aire

28   Remueva el purificador de aire.
29   Desconecte la manguera de la válvula unilateral.
30   Desconecte o remueva todas las líneas y mangueras que interfieren con remover el ensamblaje de la galería de aire.
31   Aplique aceite penetrante a las tuercas que conectan la galería de aire al múltiple de escape, entonces aflójelos hasta que la galería se pueda levantar hacia afuera.
32   Levante hacia afuera los inyectores con las aberturas con roscas en el múltiple de escape.
33   La instalación se hace en el orden inverso al procedimiento de desensamble. Esté seguro de apretar las tuercas de la galería de aire a sus especificaciones técnicas apropiadas.

Válvula AB (anti explosión)

34   Localice la válvula AB en el lado trasero del purificador de aire (**vea ilustración**). El purificador de aire quizás tenga que ser removido para tener acceso.
35   Remueva las mangueras de aire de la válvula y la levanta hacia afuera.
36   La instalación se hace en el orden inverso al procedimiento de desensamble.

Válvula de liberación

37   La válvula de liberación (**vea ilustración**) está instalada en la cara inferior del purificador de aire. Desconecte la manguera de aire de la válvula.
38   Remueva los tornillos que conectan la válvula de liberación al purificador de aire y lo separa. Si es necesario hacer esto, remueva el purificador de aire.
39   La instalación se hace en el orden inverso al procedimiento de desensamble.

Válvula CAC (combinada para controlar el aire)

40   La válvula CAC está localizada bajo el soporte del dispositivo de control.
41   Desconecte las mangueras del radiador y la válvula electrónica de aire de la válvula.
42   Remueva los tornillos que aseguran la válvula CAC y lo levanta hacia afuera.

43   La instalación se hace en el orden inverso al procedimiento de desensamble.

8   Control del tiempo de la chispa - sistema

Refiérase a las ilustraciones 8.10, 8.12 y 8.30

Descripción general

1   El sistema de control del tiempo de la chispa está diseñado para controlar el avance del encendido regulado por vacío del múltiple del distribuidor bajo variar condiciones, en orden de ayudar para reducir los HC (hidrocarburos) y las emisiones de NOx (oxido de nitrógeno), también asegurar una marcha mínima fija y economía buena del combustible.
2   Aunque la función básica del sistema es lo mismo en todos los modelos, el diseño del sistema es algo diferente, dependiendo en el año y el modelo del vehículo. Estas diferencias son notadas en los siguientes sub secciones. **Nota:** *Los modelos 1980 US Federal y los modelos de el Canadá no están equipados con este sistema.*

Modelos 1980 de California (con transmisión manual)

3   El sistema del control del tiempo de la chispa usado en estos modelos usa una válvula de cambio de vacío para controlar la actuación del avance del encendido regulado por vacío del múltiple del distribuidor.
4   Con este sistema, una línea de la señal de vacío corre de la mariposa del acelerador al mecanismo de avance del encendido regulado por vacío del múltiple para el distribuidor. Utilizado en esta línea hay una válvula de cambio de vacío. Cuando esta válvula se abre permite que haya una purga de aire, así eliminando la señal de vacío de la mariposa del acelerador y previniendo alcanzar el distribuidor. Cuando la válvula de cambio de vacío está cerrada, sella hacia afuera la purga de aire y la señal de vacío que afecta el mecanismo de avance.
5   Abrir y cerrar la válvula para el cambio de vacío es controlado eléctricamente por un interruptor en la transmisión llamado interruptor de engrane alto. Localizado en el lado derecho de la transmisión, este interruptor está Encendido (permitiendo que la corriente pase a través de el) solamente cuando la transmisión es cambiada a las posiciones de los engranes de 4ta o 5ta.
6   La válvula para el cambio de vacío está diseñada para que se abra menos cuando el interruptor de encima esté Encendido. Por lo tanto la única ves que la válvula de cambio está cerrada, así avanzando el distribuidor, es cuando la transmisión está en las posiciones de los engranes de 4ta o 5ta.

Modelos 1980 de California (con transmisión automática)

7   El sistema del control del tiempo de la chispa usado en estos modelos es uno extremadamente sencillo, uno que usa una válvula

8.10 Esquema del sistema del tiempo de la chispa para los modelos 1981 al 1985

1   Válvula para el control del vacío
2   Puerto para el vacío de venturi
3   Puerto de vacío
4   Carburador
5   Mariposa del acelerador
6   Múltiple de admisión
7   Válvula térmica de vacío
8   Distribuidor

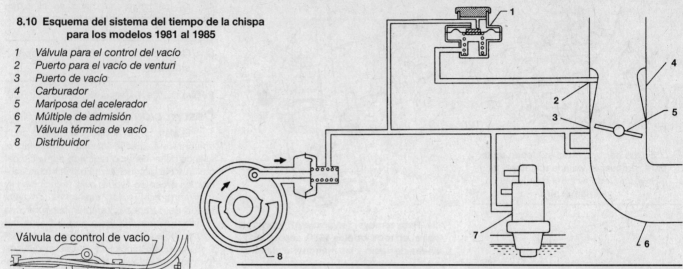

Válvula de control de vacío

8.12 La válvula de control de vacío usada en los sistemas más modernos de tiempo de control para la chispa está localizada en el múltiple de admisión en el frente del carburador

de retraso de vacío en la línea para la señal del vacío entre el carburador y el canasto de avance del encendido regulado por vacío del múltiple de distribuidor.

8   La válvula de retraso del vacío en la línea es esencialmente una válvula para restringir el flujo de aire hacia el carburador. Esto reduce el valor del cambio que alcanza el vacío al distribuidor durante los períodos de aceleración rápida, así le proporciona a la unidad de avance para el encendido regulado por vacío del múltiple alguna demora del tiempo para responder.

9   A causa del diseño unilateral de la válvula, una disminución de vacío en el carburador (en marcha mínima o acelerador completamente abierto) es pasado en una manera normal al distribuidor, así desactivando el mecanismo de avance.

Modelos 1981 al 1985

10   El sistema usado en los modelos 1981 al 1985 **(vea ilustración)** usan una válvula TVV (válvula térmica interruptora de vacío) de vacío para controlar la actuación del mecanismo de avance con relación a la temperatura del motor. Esta TVV es puesta en la línea de la señal de vacío entre la mariposa del acelerador y el distribuidor. Cuando la TVV está abierta permite una purga de aire en la línea de la señal de vacío que previene que el vacío avance el tiempo. Solamente cuando la TVV está cerrada, puede el vacío alcanzar el mecanismo de avance.

11   Abrir y cerrar la válvula es determinado por la temperatura del anticongelante del motor. La TVV usada en los modelos de California está calibrada para ser cerrada hasta que la temperatura del anticongelante llega a 59 grados F (15 grados C). Hasta este punto permanecerá abierta entre 59 grados y 140 grados F (60 grados C). Encima de 140 grados se cerrará otra vez. Por lo tanto, el distribuidor es avanzado mientras el motor está frío, en orden de calentar rápidamente el motor. Cuando el motor se calienta, la señal del vacío es cortada y el tiempo es retardado hasta que el motor llega a su temperatura normal de operación, cuando avanza otra vez. Además, desde que la señal del vacío es tomada de la mariposa del acelerador, en marcha mínima el vacío no es lo suficiente para avanzar el distribuidor, así que el sistema de control del tiempo de la chispa no opera del todo en marcha mínima.

12   Los sistemas de modelo más modernos del tiempo de la chispa están equipados también con una válvula para el control de vacío **(vea ilustración)** la cuál es instalada en la línea de vacío de venturi entre el carburador y el distribuidor. Cuando el vacío del venturi del carburador excede el valor fijó, el aire es purgado a la línea del vacío del distribuidor, retardando el tiempo de la chispa levemente.

Chequeo

Modelos 1980 de California (con transmisión manual)

13   Comience cualquier chequeo de este sistema inspeccionando todas las líneas y mangueras del radiador, para asegurarse que ellas están apropiadamente conectadas y que no hay fugas ni roturas.

14   Después el mecanismo de avance adentro del distribuidor debe ser chequeado para estar seguro que está operando correctamente. Para hacer esto, remueva primero la tapa del distribuidor para que la rotación del plato de la sincronización del tiempo pueda ser observada. Desconecte luego la línea de vacío del distribuidor y conecte una bomba de vacío a la acoplación. Aplique presión de

vacío al distribuidor y observe que el plato del tiempo gire adentro. Si el plato del tiempo no gira, entonces hay un defecto con el mecanismo de avance que se debe corregir (refiérase al Capítulo 5). Si una bomba de vacío no está cercana, el mismo efecto puede ser logrado conectando una manguera larga de caucho (con el mismo diámetro como la manguera de vacío removida) a la acoplación y absorba en la manguera.

15   Conecte de nuevo la línea del vacío al distribuidor y vuelva a instalar la tapa del distribuidor.

16   Ponga una luz de regulación (lámpara de tiempo) según las instrucciones del fabricante.

17   Haga que un ayudante ponga el motor en marcha y córralo acerca de 2,000 rpm. Mientras está chequeando la regulación del tiempo de la ignición con la luz de regulación (lámpara de tiempo), haga que un ayudante presione el embrague y entonces cambie la transmisión en cada uno de los engranes por unos pocos segundos a la vez. **Caución:** *Esté seguro que el freno de emergencia esté aplicado y las ruedas estén firmemente bloqueadas. Esté seguro que el embrague permanezca presionado completamente mientras la transmisión está en engrane para prevenir que el vehículo se mueva. El tiempo de la chispa debe avanzar completamente solamente cuando la transmisión es cambiada en el engrane de 4ta o 5ta. En cualquier otro engrane, el tiempo debe permanecer en su instalación original o solamente avanzar levemente.*

18   Si el tiempo no opera como está descrito encima, los componentes del sistema deben ser chequeados localizando individualmente el problema.

19   La válvula de cambio del vacío es fácilmente chequeado desconectando los alambres de ella. Entonces con la luz de regulación (lámpara de tiempo) enganchada encima como antes, corra el motor a cerca de 2,000 rpm mientras usted chequea el tiempo. Ahora use alambres puente para conectar los alambres de la válvula directamente a las terminales de la batería y con el motor otra vez a 2,000 rpm observe el tiempo. Ahora debe ser avanzado de su posición anterior. Si no, ase-

gúrese que todas las líneas de vacío están libres. Si está, entonces reemplace la válvula de cambio del vacío con una nueva.

20   Para chequear el interruptor del engrane de alta, localícelo en el lado derecho de la transmisión y desconecte el conector del alambrado. Conecte los alambres de un ohmímetro probador o de continuidad a los alambres del interruptor. Entonces haga que un ayudante cambia la transmisión a través de todos los engranes. El interruptor debe mostrar continuidad solamente cuando la transmisión esté en las posiciones de los engranes de 4ta o 5ta. Si no, reemplace el interruptor con uno nuevo.

21   Cuando un chequeo final de la electricidad está alcanzando la válvula de cambiar el vacío, desconecte los alambres de la válvula y conecte los alambres de un voltímetro o luz de prueba a ellos y repita la prueba de encima. Si voltaje no es indicado cuando la transmisión esté en las posiciones de los engranes de 4ta o 5ta, hay una conexión o interrupción floja en el alambrado.

Modelos 1980 de California (con transmisión automática)

22   Remueva la válvula de retraso de vacío que se dirige a la línea de señal de vacío del distribuidor.

23   Sople aire a la válvula en el lado del carburador. Si el aire fluye sin restricción, la válvula está normal. Si no, se necesita reemplazarla.

24   Después, atente de soplar aire en el lado del distribuidor (marrón). Si hay resistencia más grande que en el paso previo (algo de aire debe escapar al lado opuesto), la válvula está en buena condición. Si no, reemplácela. **Nota:** *Cuando esté instalando la válvula en la línea de vacío esté seguro de que el lado marrón está hacia el distribuidor.*

Modelos 1981 al 1985

25   Comience cualquier inspección del sistema examinando todas las mangueras y alambres para estar seguro de que ellos están apropiadamente conectados y en buena condición.

26   Después, el mecanismo de avance del

encendido regulado por vacío del múltiple adentro del distribuidor debe ser chequeado como está descrito en los Pasos 14 y 15.

27   Enganche una luz de regulación (lámpara de tiempo) según las instrucciones del fabricante. Con el motor frío, ponga el motor en marcha y haga que un ayudante aplique la mariposa del acelerador para mantener el motor en marcha alrededor de 2,000 rpm. Chequee inmediatamente el tiempo de la chispa con la luz de regulación (lámpara de tiempo). La aguja en el medidor de la temperatura del anticongelante debe estar en la posición Fría. Si la temperatura exterior está abajo de 59 grados F el tiempo debe comenzar a retardarse según el motor comienza a calentarse.

28   Continúe corriendo el motor a 2,000 rpm y observe el tiempo de la chispa mientras el motor se calienta. Usted puede que quiera ajustar el tornillo para la velocidad de la marcha mínima para mantener esta velocidad del motor. Si la temperatura exterior está abajo de 59 grados F el tiempo debe retardarse comenzando cuando el motor se caliente.

29   Una vez que el motor se acerque a la temperatura normal de operación (la aguja en el centro del medidor), el avance para la regulación del tiempo de la chispa debe de haber avanzado otra vez. Si esta secuencia no sucede, la TVV está sospechosa y debe ser reemplazada con una nueva.

30   Para chequear la válvula de control de vacío, separe la manguera de vacío del venturi debajo de la válvula de control de vacío. Conecte una bomba de vacío al tubo para esta manguera **(vea ilustración)** y aplique vacío a la válvula. Si el tiempo de la chispa se retarda, la válvula está funcionando bien; si no lo hace, la válvula está funcionando mal.

31   Separe la válvula del sistema y remuévala. Note si el lado del distribuidor de la válvula está abierto o cerrado procurando absorber aire a la válvula mientras esta le está aplicando vacío a la válvula de acuerdo con el siguiente vacío especificado. Debajo de 13.3 kPa (100 mm Hg, 3.94 pulgada Hg), el lado del distribuidor de la válvula debe estar cerrado; encima de estas figuras, debe estar abierto. Si la válvula falla de trabajar

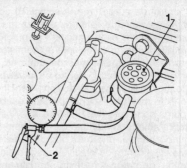

8.30 Para chequear la operación de la válvula de control de vacío, separe la línea de vacío debajo del venturi, conecte una bomba de vacío y aplíquele vacío - el tiempo se debe retardar

1   *Válvula de control de vacío*
2   *Bomba de vacío*

como está descrito, reemplácela.

Reemplazo del componente

32   El procedimientos para remover e instalar una TVV está descrito en la Sección 5.

33   Para reemplazar la válvula de control de vacío, márquela claramente y separe las líneas de vacío y destornille la válvula. La instalación se hace en el orden inverso al procedimiento de desensamble.

9   EEC (sistema de control de emisiones evaporativas)

Refiérase a las ilustraciones 9.2, 9.3a, 9.3b, 9.6 y 9.8

Descripción general

1   El EECS (sistema de control de emisiones evaporativas) está diseñado para prevenir la liberación de hidrocarburos en la forma de vapor de combustible al aire exterior.

2   Esto es logrado ventilando el vapor en el tanque de combustible a un canasto **(vea ilustración)** lleno con carbón activado, donde el vapor es almacenado cuando el motor no está en marcha.

3   Encima de este canasto hay una válvula

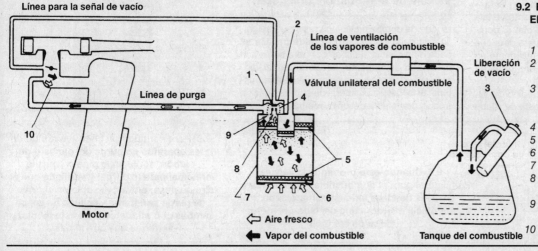

9.2 Esquema típico de un sistema EECS (sistema de control de emisiones evaporativas)

1   *Diafragma*
2   *Válvula de control para la purga*
3   *Tapa para el combustible con sello positivo con válvula para liberar la presión*
4   *Resorte del diafragma*
5   *Rejilla*
6   *Filtro*
7   *Canasto de carbón*
8   *Orificio para el control de la purga*
9   *Orificio constante para el control de la purga*
10   *Múltiple de admisión*

de control de purga **(vea ilustración)** con dos mangueras que salen de ella. La manguera más ancha es la manguera de purga y corre directamente al múltiple de admisión, mientras la manguera más pequeña es la línea de señal de vacío. Dentro de la válvula de control de la purga, hay dos orificios. Uno, un orificio muy pequeño, es llamado orificio de purga constante **(vea ilustración)** y está siempre abierto al múltiple de admisión. El segundo orificio, uno más grande directamente en el centro de la válvula, es el orificio principal de purga y no está normalmente cubierto por el diafragma de la válvula.

4   Cuando el motor es puesto en marcha y aire fresco es absorbido en el canasto en una abertura en el fondo. Este aire fresco recoge los vapores almacenados y los lleva al múltiple de admisión. En marcha mínima, hay suficiente succión en la línea para constantemente purgar una cantidad pequeña de esta mezcla de aire/vapor a través del orificio constante de purga. La válvula de control para la purga, sin embargo, permanece cerrada. Cuando el motor aumenta de velocidad, el vacío del múltiple llega a ser suficiente para abrir bastante el diafragma de la válvula de control de la purga, que permite que la mezcla de aire/vapor sea absorbida en una cantidad mayor hacia el múltiple de admisión.

5   La operación de este sistema depende de mantener un sistema de combustible sellado. Por lo tanto, una tapa de combustible sellada es usada, la cual bajo condiciones normales, proporciona solamente un respiradero pequeño de aire hacia afuera y se abrirá completamente solamente si la presión de vacío adentro del tanque de combustible llega a ser demasiado grande. Una válvula de liberación de vacío es construida en la tapa de gas.

6   Una válvula unilateral de combustible **(vea ilustración)** está localizada en la línea de respiración entre el tanque de combustible y el canasto. Cuando el motor está apagado, esta válvula permite que el vapor del combustible se purgue hacia afuera en el canasto cuando la presión en el tanque de combustible llega a un cierto nivel. Cuando el motor está en marcha, esta válvula permite que aire de afuera sea absorbido en el tanque del canasto. Esto efectivamente ventila el tanque de combustible para que el combustible sea absorbido hacia afuera para sea quemado y no cause eventualmente un vacío en el tanque y produzca una traba de vapor.

7   Otro que el reemplazo periódico del filtro de aire en el canasto como está detallado

9.3a Componentes típicos de la válvula de control para la purga del canasto

1   Cubierta
2   Diafragma
3   Retenedor
4   Resorte del diafragma

en el Capítulo 1, el sistema EEC no requiere normalmente atención periódica. Hay, sin embargo, unos pocos componentes que deben ser chequeados de vez en cuando para asegurarse de la operación apropiada del sistema.

Chequeo

Canasto de carbón

8   Para chequear el canasto de carbón **(vea ilustración)**, sople aire a través del tubo por el orificio principal de purga y chequee que ningún aire pueda atravesar. Entonces sople aire en la válvula de control de la purga y los tubos de la línea del respiradero de vapor y chequee si el aire atraviesa. Si el orificio principal de purga, la válvula de control de la purga o la línea del respiradero de vapor no pasan la prueba, reemplace el canasto (vea Capítulo 1).

Válvula para la liberación del vacío del tanque de combustible

9   Remueva la tapa del abastecedor del combustible. Limpie el albergue de la válvula. Trate de absorber aire en la tapa en el lado del tanque de combustible. Una resistencia leve acompañada con un sonido que "cascabelea" indica que la válvula está en una condición mecánica buena. La resistencia y los chasquidos, deben desaparecer según la absorción continúa. Si la válvula está obstruida o si ninguna resistencia es evidente, reemplace la tapa.

Válvula de combustible unilateral

10   Sople aire en el conector en el lado del tanque de combustible. Una resistencia significativa debe ser evidente y parte del aire se debe dirigir hacia el canasto. Ahora sople aire en el lado del canasto. El aire debe ser dirigido suavemente hacia el tanque de combustible. Si la válvula unilateral de combustible no trabaja como está descrito, reemplácela.

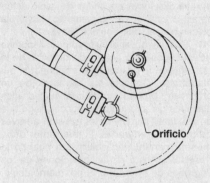

9.3b Ubicación del orificio de purga constante debajo de la válvula para el control de la purga

Reemplazo del componente

11   Compre un juego para el diafragma.
12   Remueva las tres mangueras de vacío de su acoplación encima del canasto.
13   Libere el resorte de retención alrededor del cuerpo del canasto y remuévalo hacia afuera del compartimiento del motor.
14   Hágale palanca a la tapa superior de la válvula de control de la purga.
15   Remueva el diafragma del interior de la tapa superior.
16   Instale un diafragma nuevo en la tapa superior, asegúrese que la orilla del diafragma está localizado en su ranura completamente alrededor de la tapa.
17   Reemplace el resorte del diafragma y el retenedor con uno nuevo suministrado con el juego del diafragma.
18   Con el resorte y el retenedor nuevo en su posición, ponga de regreso la tapa en el canasto.
19   Vuelva a instalar el canasto.
20   Conecte de nuevo las tres mangueras, asegúrese que ellas están en sus lugares apropiados.

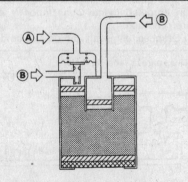

9.8 Para conducir un chequeo rápido de los aparatos de purga del canasto de carbón, sople en la pipa A (válvula principal para la purga) y verifique que el aire no pasa, entonces sople en el orificio de purga constante y la línea de vapor (ambas con etiquetas B en este dibujo) y verifique que aire si pasa

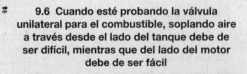

Lado del tanque de combustible

Lado del motor

⇦ Flujo del combustible evaporativo
⬅ Flujo del aire fresco

9.6 Cuando esté probando la válvula unilateral para el combustible, soplando aire a través desde el lado del tanque debe de ser difícil, mientras que del lado del motor debe de ser fácil

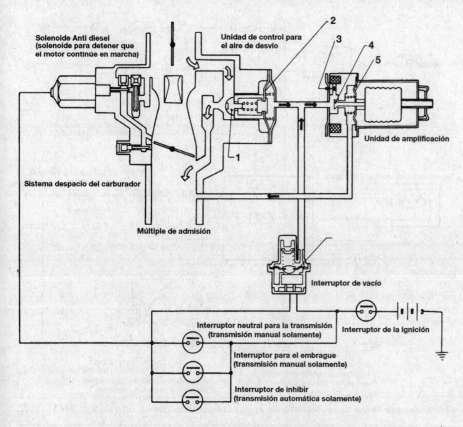

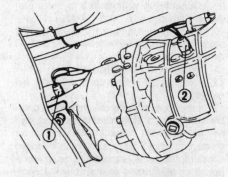

10.5a El interruptor de neutral para la transmisión manual está localizado en el lado izquierdo de la transmisión

1   Interruptor de neutral
2   Interruptor de retroceso

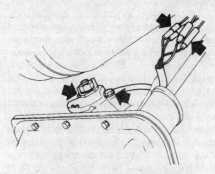

10.5b El interruptor inhibidor de la transmisión automática está localizado en el lado izquierdo de la transmisión

10.1 Esquema típico de un sistema de apagar el combustible en los modelos 1980 al 1983

1.   Válvula de control para el aire de desvío
2   Diafragma 2
3   Tobera de aire
4   Válvula de control de la sobre presión
5   Diafragma 1

10   Sistema para apagar el combustible

Refiérase a las ilustraciones 10.1, 10.5a, 10.5b, 10.6, 10.15 y 10.29

Descripción general

1   El sistema para apagar el combustible **(vea ilustración)** es usado en todos los modelos 1980 al 1985 menos los modelos 1980 de Canadá estándar. El propósito de este sistema es de reducir las emisiones de hidrocarburos y para aumentar la economía del combustible durante la deceleración. Esto es logrado accionando el solenoide anti diesel instalado en el carburador durante los períodos de deceleración, que apaga el flujo del combustible en el carburador lentamente.

2   La actuación del solenoide anti diesel es controlado por varios otros interruptores: el interruptor de vacío (en todos los modelos), el interruptor de la transmisión en neutral y el embrague (en los modelos de transmisión manual) y el interruptor inhibidor (en los modelos con transmisión automática). El solenoide anti diesel es accionado solamente cuando todos estos interruptores están Apagado al mismo tiempo. Si cualquiera de ellos

está Encendido, el sistema de apagar el combustible no está accionado.

3   El interruptor de vacío está localizado anexo al canasto de carbón en los modelos 1980 y en la esquina derecha del capó atrás del tanque para el limpia parabrisas en los modelos 1981 al 1984 (menos California). Este interruptor, que es conectado por una manguera de vacío a la válvula de amplificación (descrita en la Sección 11), está normalmente Encendida. Solamente durante deceleración, cuando hay vacío muy alto en el múltiple de admisión, la válvula de control de la amplificación transmite una señal de vacío a la válvula de vacío que la Apaga hasta que el vacío sea reducido otra vez.

4   El interruptor del embrague, usado en los modelos con transmisión manual, está instalado en un soporte en la parte superior del pedal del embrague. Solamente cuando el pedal del embrague es presionado el embrague se desconecta.

5   Un interruptor neutral **(vea ilustración)** es usado con los modelos de transmisión manual y está localizado en el lado izquierdo de la transmisión. El interruptor inhibidor **(vea ilustración)** es usado con los modelos de transmisión automática y está también localizado en el lado izquierdo. El interruptor de neutral está Encendido, (permitiendo que la

corriente pasar a través de el) solamente cuando los engranes están en la posición de Neutral. El interruptor inhibidor está Encendido solamente cuando los engranes están en Neutral o la posición de Estacionamiento. Por lo tanto, el solenoide anti diesel es accionado (apaga el flujo del sistema de combustible lentamente) solamente durante deceleración y cuando la transmisión está en engrane y el pedal del embrague es liberado.

6   El sistema de apagar el combustible en los modelos 1984 de California y los modelos 1985 está bajo el control de la ECU (unidad de control electrónica) **(vea ilustración)**. El interruptor de neutral y el interruptor del embrague (los modelos con transmisión manual) o interruptor inhibidor (los modelos con transmisiones automáticas) todavía funcionan semejantemente, pero su señales son enviadas a la ECU en vez de un interruptor de vacío al solenoide anti diesel. Y el solenoide anti diesel ha sido reemplazado por un solenoide de apagar el combustible (esencialmente el mismo dispositivo).

Chequeo
Modelos con transmisión manual

7   Corra el motor en marcha mínima.
8   Desconecte el ensamblaje de la válvula del solenoide anti diesel.

9   Conecte un voltímetro a la tierra y al lado del arneses.

10   Conecte el alambre de la válvula del solenoide anti diesel directamente al lado (+) de la batería.

11   Ponga el motor en marcha.

12   Desconecte el interruptor del pedal del embrague.

13   Empuje en el pedal del embrague, cambie el engrane a 4ta y levante las revoluciones del motor sin carga. Mantenga el motor en marcha entre 2,500 y 3,000 rpm, entonces cierre rápidamente la mariposa del acelerador. Si el alambrado está en buena condición, el voltímetro debe caerse desde 12 voltios a cero voltios instantáneamente. Si no lo hace, o el interruptor de Neutral o el interruptor de vacío para apagar el combustible están fuera de orden.

14   Conecte de nuevo el interruptor del pedal del embrague y desconecte el conector del interruptor de vacío para apagar el combustible.

15   Conecte un ohmímetro al interruptor de vacío **(vea ilustración)**. Aumente la velocidad del motor entre 2,500 y 3,000 rpm, entonces cierre rápidamente la mariposa del acelerador. Chequee la continuidad entre las terminales A y B y entre A y C. Si la operación de "Apagado y Encendido" no es normal, el interruptor de vacío de apagar el combustible está en buen orden de trabajo. **Nota:** *La polaridad entre A y B se debe invertir de esa de A y C. Conecte de nuevo el conector de vacío para el interruptor de apagar el combustible y repita el Paso 13. Si el voltímetro inmediatamente no se mueve de 12 voltios a cero voltios, reemplace el interruptor de Neutral.*

Modelos con transmisiones automáticas

16   Corra el motor en marcha mínima.

17   Desconecte el conector de la válvula del solenoide anti diesel. El motor se debe detener. Si no lo hace, reemplace el ensamblaje de la válvula solenoide anti diesel.

18   Conecte un voltímetro a la tierra y al lado del arnés.

19   Conecte el alambre de la válvula anti diesel de solenoide directamente al lado (+) de la batería.

20   Ponga la palanca de cambio en la posición P o N.

21   Ponga el motor en marcha entre 2,500 y 3,000 rpm, entonces apague la mariposa del acelerador rápidamente. Si el voltímetro de 12 voltios no se cae a cero voltios instantáneamente, el interruptor del inhibidor o el interruptor de vacío para apagar el combustible se necesitan reemplazar.

22   Conecte de nuevo los arneses a la válvula del solenoide anti diesel.

23   Desconecte los arneses a la válvula del solenoide anti diesel.

24   Ponga el motor en marcha entre 2,500 y 3,000 rpm y cierre rápidamente la mariposa del acelerador. Esta vez chequee la continuidad entre A y B y entre A y C. Si la operación de "Apagado y Encendido" es normal, el inte-

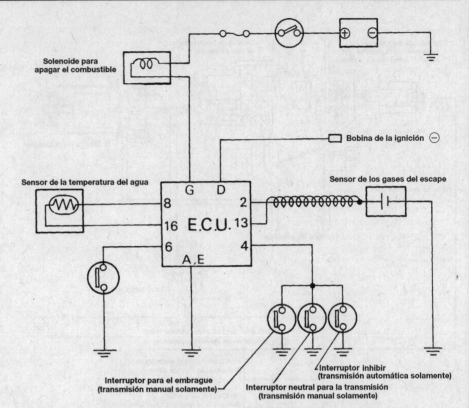

Solenoide para apagar el combustible

Bobina de la ignición ⊖

Sensor de la temperatura del agua

Sensor de los gases del escape

G   D
8   2
E.C.U.
16   13
6   4
A,E

Interruptor para el embrague (transmisión manual solamente)

Interruptor neutral para la transmisión (transmisión manual solamente)

Interruptor inhibir (transmisión automática solamente)

10.6 Esquema típico de un sistema de apagar el combustible en un vehículo 1984 o 1985

rruptor de vacío para apagar el combustible está trabajando en buena condición. **Nota:** *La polaridad entre A y B se debe invertir de la polaridad entre A y C. Conecte de nuevo el conector del interruptor de vacío para apagar el combustible y repita la prueba. Si la aguja del voltímetro no se mueve inmediatamente de 12 voltios a cero voltios, reemplace el interruptor inhibidor.*

25   Los interruptores del embrague, Neutral e interruptor inhibidor pueden ser probados individualmente desconectando los alambres y conectando un probador de continuidad a sus alambres. Con el motor apagado pero el interruptor de la ignición Encendido, haga que un ayudante cambie el selector de los engranes a través de todos los engranes. El interruptor de neutral debe mostrar continuidad solamente cuando la transmisión está en Neutral. El interruptor inhibidor debe mostrar continuidad solamente cuando la transmisión está en Estacionamiento (P) o Neutral (N). El interruptor del embrague debe mostrar continuidad solamente cuando el pedal es presionado. Si esto no es el caso, el interruptor debe ser reemplazado.

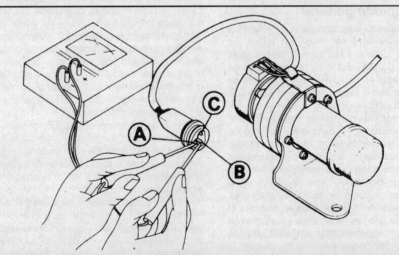

10.15 Refiérase a esta guía para la terminal del conector cuando esté chequeando la continuidad entre las terminales del interruptor de vacío en el sistema de apagar el combustible

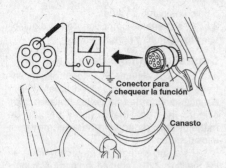

10.29 Para chequear la señal al interruptor de Neutral o inhibidor, localice el conector de chequear la función cerca del canasto de vapor, remuévalo e inserciónela sonda de un voltímetro en la terminal indicada

Modelos 1984 de California y todos los modelos de 1985

26   Antes de realizar la siguiente prueba, chequee visualmente el sistema de apagar el combustible. Si algún interruptor está roto, reemplácelo.

27   Si su vehículo está equipado con una transmisión manual, remueva el conector de Neutral en el arnés del interruptor; si su vehículo está equipado con una transmisión automática, remueva el conector del arnés del interruptor inhibidor.

28   Ponga el motor en marcha y caliéntelo hasta su temperatura normal de operación.

29   Para chequear la señal a cualquier interruptor, localice el conector de chequear la función cerca del canasto de vapor (vea ilustración) y conecte un voltímetro como está mostrado.

30   Levante la velocidad del motor encima de 2,000 rpm y chequee el voltaje del conector durante la deceleración. Encima de 1,800 rpm, debe haber cero voltaje; entre 1,500 y 1,800 rpm, debe haber 12 voltios; debajo de 1,500 rpm, debe haber cero voltaje.

31   Si el voltaje indicado en el conector no está como se especifica, chequeos eléctricos adicionales se deben realizar en el sistema de ECCS (sistema de computadora por control electrónico). Estas pruebas están más allá del alcance del mecánico de hogar. Lleve el vehículo al departamento de servicio de su concesionario.

11   Sistema para controlar el vacío del múltiple de admisión

Refiérase a las ilustraciones 11.9a, 11.9b y 11.14

Descripción general

1   El sistema de control de vacío del múltiple de admisión es usado en todos los modelos menos los modelos 1980 de el Canadá estándar.

2   Este sistema es diseñado para reducir el consumo de aceite del motor durante la

11.9a En los modelos 1980, la válvula para el control de amplificación e interruptor de vacío (flechas) están instaladas próximo al canasto de carbón

deceleración, cuando hay extremadamente un vacío alto en el múltiple de admisión. Dos componentes son usado en el sistema: la unidad del control de amplificación y la unidad de control para el desvío del aire.

3   La unidad del control de amplificación es instalada cerca del canasto de carbón en los modelos 1980 y en el borde derecho detrás del tanque para el limpia parabrisas en los modelos 1981 al 1984. Es diseñado para detectar el vacío del múltiple de admisión. Cuando el vacío sobrepasa un nivel predeterminado, la unidad abre, pasando la señal de vacío a la unidad de desvío del control del aire.

4   La unidad del control del aire de desvío está instalada en el carburador y se compone de un resorte y un diafragma. En su posición normal, está cerrado por presión del resorte, tapando un pasaje de aire encima del carburador. Cuando el vacío en el múltiple de admisión aumenta y la unidad de control de amplificación aumenta envía una señal de vacío en la unidad de desvío, el vacío hala hacia atrás el diafragma, venciendo la presión del resorte y la abertura del pasaje para la desviación del aire. Esto permite un mayor flujo de aire en el múltiple, así reduciendo la situación alta de vacío.

Chequeo

5   La unidad del control de amplificación es fácilmente chequeada desconectando la manguera de la señal de vacío donde se conecta a la válvula de control del desvío de aire y poniendo su dedo en el extremo de ella. Haga que un ayudante ponga el motor en marcha acerca de 2,000 a 3,000 rpm y entonces libere bruscamente el acelerador completamente. Mientras esto se hace, usted debe sentir un vacío a fines de la manguera de vacío.

6   Si ningún vacío es detectado, inspeccione todas las conexiones de las mangueras de vacío por fugas o malas conexiones. Entonces desconecte la manguera en la válvula del control de amplificación que se

11.9b En los modelos 1981 y más modernos, la válvula del control de amplificación, interruptor de vacío y sensor de altitud están instalados juntos en el compartimiento derecho en el lado del motor

dirige al múltiple de admisión y repita la prueba en esa. Si el vacío es detectado aquí, pero no en la primera prueba, la unidad del control de amplificación debe ser reemplazada con una nueva.

7   Chequee la unidad de desvío para el control del aire removiendo el carburador (como está más abajo). Conecte una manguera a la acoplación y entonces chupe en la manguera. La bomba de vacío de la válvula debe retractar la unidad cuando la succión es aplicada. Si no, la unidad debe ser reemplazada.

8   Aunque la unidad del control de amplificación es diseñada para ser ajustada, esto no es una operación rutinaria y se requerirá normalmente solamente cuando una unidad nueva sea instalada. A causa de la naturaleza crítica de esta operación, debe ser realizada por un departamento de servicio de su concesionario Nissan u otra facilidad calificada de reparación.

Reemplazo del componente

Unidad de control para la amplificación

9   Desconecte las mangueras de vacío de la unidad de vacío. Esté seguro de notar donde ellas están instaladas (vea ilustraciones).

10   Remueva los pernos de afianzamiento de la unidad y levántela hacia afuera de su soporte.

11   La instalación se hace en el orden inverso al procedimiento de desensamble. **Nota:** *Si está instalando una unidad nueva esté seguro que es el mismo número de modelo y marcas de identificación como la vieja.*

Válvula de control para el desvío del aire

12   Remueva el purificador de aire.

13   Desconecte la línea de vacío de la unidad.

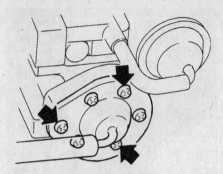

11.14 Ubicación de los tres tornillos para la válvula de control del desvío del aire

14   Remueva los tres tornillos (**vea ilustración**) que conectan la unidad al carburador y levántelo hacia afuera.
15   La instalación se hace en el orden inverso al procedimiento de desensamble.

12   BCDD (dispositivo para el control de la presión en desaceleración)

Descripción general

1   Este dispositivo, usado solamente en los modelos 1980 de Canadá (menos los de trabajo pesado), está diseñado para reducir la emisión de los hidrocarburos durante los períodos cuando el vehículo está costeando. La unidad está instalada en el carburador y suministra aire extra al múltiple de admisión para mantener el vacío del múltiple en orden en su presión de operación correcta.
2   La unidad incorpora dos diafragmas, uno para controlar el vacío del múltiple y abrir la válvula de control de vacío y el segundo opera la válvula del control de aire según la cantidad de vacío transmitido a la válvula de control de vacío.
3   Las presiones de operación varían debido a las diferencias de operación de altitud son tomadas en consideración.

Remover e instalar

4   El BCDD (dispositivo para el control de la presión en desaceleración) es fácilmente removido destornillando su tres tornillos de afianzamiento y levantándolo hacia afuera. El BCDD no está diseñado para ser desenganchado. Si está defectuoso, debe ser reemplazado como una unidad.
5   Aunque el BCDD está diseñado para ser ajustado, esto no es una operación rutinaria y se requerirá normalmente solamente cuando una unidad nueva sea instalada. A causa de la naturaleza crítica de esta operación, esto debe ser realizado por el departamento de servicio de su concesionario Nissan u otra facilidad calificada de reparación.

13   ECCS (sistema de control concentrado electrónico) (vehículos equipados con carburador)

Refiérase a las ilustraciones 13.7 y 13.8

En el 1984 las funciones del manejo de combustible e ignición en los vehículos de California fueron colocadas debajo del control de una micro computadora. En 1985 todos los vehículos fueron equipados con este sistema.

Descripción general

1   El ECCS es básicamente un sistema de monitores que alimentan información a una caja electrónica. El sistema entonces dirige un solenoide instalado en el carburador para controlar cuánto combustible es contenido en la mezcla de aire/combustible. De esta manera el motor operará en su desempeño óptimo/niveles de emisiones bajo todas las condiciones de manejo.
2   El único momento que este sistema no está en operación (condición de control del ciclo abierto), es cuando el motor está frío, cuando esté manejando en altas velocidades o bajo una carga pesada.
3   El sistema se compone de los siguientes subsistemas y componentes:

Control de cambio de la bujía

4   Este sub sistema ECC (control concentrado electrónico) es diseñado para recortar el encendiendo de una de las bujías a cada cilindro (hay dos) bajo cargas pesada de manejo. Esto reduce el ruido del motor en esos tiempos.
5   Este sub sistema no es incorporado en los motores Z20. También, no es operacional en ciertos de modelos para ser usado en altitudes altas.

Apagar el combustible

6   Este sub sistema apaga el suministro del combustible durante la deceleración, cuando el motor no requiere combustible. Este sistema no opera cuando el motor está frío o bajo ninguna condición de carga, donde atascamiento podría ocurrir.

Control del calentador para la mezcla

7   En orden de mejorar la maniobrabilidad del vehículo cuando está frío, una calefacción para la mezcla (**vea ilustración**) ha sido construida en el aislador del puerto primario en el carburador.

Unidad de control

8   La unidad de control ECC (**vea ilustración**) es una micro computadora montada debajo del asiento del conductor. Es el "cerebro" del sistema y controla la operación del sistema.

Solenoide para el control de la proporción del aire/combustible

9   Este solenoide es instalado en el cuerpo del carburador y controla el flujo del combustible en el carburador. Opera continuamente durante la operación del motor y obtiene sus mensajes de la unidad del control.

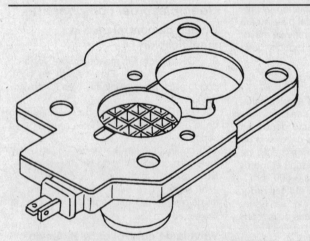

13.7 El calentador para la mezcla, localizado entre el carburador y el múltiple de admisión, es un dispositivo eléctricamente calentado que mejora la maniobrabilidad del vehículo cuando está frío y ayuda a evaporizar la mezcla

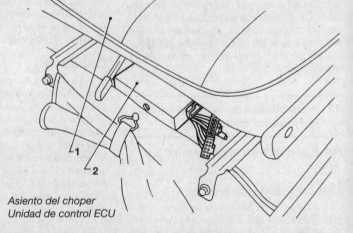

1   Asiento del choper
2   Unidad de control ECU

13.8 La unidad del sistema ECU (unidad de control electrónica) está localizada debajo del asiento del conductor donde está segura del calor, humedad, vibración, etc. pero es accesible para otorgarle servicio

Sensor para los gases de escape

10   Este sensor es instalado en el múltiple de escape y controla la cantidad de oxígeno en los gases del escape. Manda esta información a la unidad de control para ser procesada, últimamente altera la mezcla en el carburador para alcanzar la mezcla óptima. El sensor del gas del escape debe ser reemplazado periódicamente; la información de afinación y mantenimiento está en este suplemento.

Sensor de la temperatura del agua

11   Este sensor, construido en la chaqueta de agua en el múltiple de admisión, chequea los cambios en la temperatura del agua. Entonces manda esta información a la unidad de control.

Interruptores

12   Hay varios interruptores incorporados en el sistema de ECC que manda también información a la unidad de control.
13   El interruptor del acelerador está localizado en el carburador y acciona en respuesta al movimiento del pedal del acelerador. Este interruptor envía señales a la unidad de control para describir la marcha mínima, condiciones de la mariposa del acelerador abierta parcialmente o acelerador completamente abierto.
14   El inhibidor/interruptor de neutral detecta la posición del selector del engrane de la transmisión.
15   El interruptor del embrague manda una señal a la unidad de control para indicar la posición del embrague (presionado o liberado).
16   Un interruptor de vacío localizado en el múltiple de admisión detecta la mariposa del acelerador completamente abierto o condiciones pesadas de carga y manda una señal a la unidad de control describiendo éstas condiciones de vacío bajas.

Calentador para la mezcla

17   El calentador para la mezcla está situado en el lado primario del aislador del carburador y es eléctricamente operado. Como mencionado previamente, calienta la mezcla de aire/combustible bajo ciertas condiciones para obtener la combustión óptima.

Solenoide anti diesel (solenoide para detener que el motor continúe en marcha)

18   Este solenoide está localizado en el carburador y apaga el suministro del combustible bajo ciertas condiciones para prevenir que el motor continúe en marcha.

Sistema del sensor de detonación (motor Z20)

19   La función de este sistema es para detectar "la detonación" del motor o el golpe de chispa y entonces casi instantáneamente alterar la ignición para eliminar la condición.
20   El sistema se compone de un sensor de detonación conectado al bloque de cilindro, una unidad de control y el alambrado nece-

sario entre estos dos componentes y el distribuidor del sistema de ignición.
21   Si problemas con este sistema son sospechados (generalmente debido a la excesiva detonación del motor o condiciones de marcha pobre) haga que el sistema sea inspeccionado por un concesionario Nissan.

Chequeo

22   De otra manera que inspeccionar por problemas obvios, tales como mangueras o alambres desconectados, el sistema ECC debe ser chequeado por el departamento de servicio de su concesionario Nissan.

14   EFI (inyección de combustible electrónica) - diagnóstico general

Información general

El ECCS (sistema de computadora por control electrónico) controla el sistema de inyección de combustible, el sistema de avance de la chispa, el sistema de diagnóstico automático, el ventilador de enfriar, etc. por medios de la ECU (unidad de control electrónica).

El ECU recibe señales de varios sensores que controlan los cambios de las operaciones del motor tal como el volumen del aire de admisión, la temperatura del aire de admisión, la temperatura del anticongelante, rpm del motor, la aceleración/deceleración, la temperatura del escape etc. Estas señales son utilizadas por la ECU para determinar la duración correcta de la inyección y la regulación del tiempo de la ignición.

Las secciones en este Capítulo incluyen las descripciones generales y los procedimientos de chequeo, adentro del alcance del mecánico del hogar y los procedimientos para el reemplazo de los componentes (cuando sea posible). Antes de asumir que el combustible y el sistema de ignición están funcionando mal, chequee el sistema del control de emisiones completamente (vea Capítulo 6). El sistema de emisión y el sistema de combustible están de cerca ínterrelacionados pero pueden ser chequeados separadamente. El diagnóstico de algunos de los dispositivos de combustible y control de las emisiones requieren herramientas especializadas, equipo e instrucción. Si chequear y otorgarle servicio llega a ser demasiado difícil o si un procedimiento está más allá de su habilidad, consulte con el departamento de servicio de su concesionario. Recuerde, la causa más frecuente de los problemas de combustible y emisiones es simplemente una manguera de vacío o alambre flojo o roto, así que siempre chequee las conexiones de las mangueras y el alambrado primero.
Nota: A causa de una ley obligatoria extendida Federal que cubre los componentes del sistema del control de las emisiones, (y cualquier otro componente que tenga un propósito primario otro que los componentes de las

emisiones pero tienen un efecto significante en las emisiones), chequee con su concesionario acerca del alcance de la garantía antes de trabajar en cualquier sistema relacionado a las emisiones. Una vez que la garantía se haya expirado, usted puede realizar algunos de los chequeos de los componentes y los procedimientos de reemplazo en este Capítulo para ahorrar dinero.

Precauciones

a)   Siempre desconecte el poder girando la llave de la ignición a apagado o desconectando las terminal de la batería antes de desconectar los conectores del alambrado EFI (inyección de combustible electrónica).
b)   Cuando esté instalando una batería, tenga mucho cuidado para evitar invertir el cable positivo y el cable negativo.
c)   No someta la EFI ni los componentes relacionados con las emisiones ni el ECCS (sistema de computadora por control electrónico) a **impactos severos durante el periodo de r**emover o instalar.
d)   Tómese su tiempo durante el periodo de identificación y resolución de problemas. Hasta un contacto mínimo de la terminal aunque sea leve puede invalidar un procedimiento de chequeo e incluso dañar uno de los numerosos circuitos con transistores.
e)   Nunca atente de trabajar en la ECU ni abrir la tapa de la ECU. La ECU está protegida por una garantía extendida debido a un mandato del gobierno que será anulada si usted trabaja en la computadora.
f)   Si usted está inspeccionando los componentes electrónicos del sistema de control durante un tiempo lluvioso, asegúrese que ninguna agua entra en ninguna parte. Cuando lave el compartimiento del motor, no le eche agua a estas partes ni sus conectores.

Sistema de diagnóstico automático

Nota: Para tener acceso a los códigos de información en los modelos 1996, es necesario de usar un GST (herramienta exploradora genérica) o la herramienta exploradora CONSULT y el equipo de soporte para la prueba. Estas herramientas son muy caras y no son recomendadas para el uso del mecánico del hogar. La luz LED de destello verde y roja en la unidad de control ya no se usan en estos modelos. Si usted sospecha un problema con los componentes relacionados con las emisiones, haga que el sistema sea chequeado por el departamento de servicio de su concesionario u otro taller de reparación.

El diagnóstico automático es útil para diagnosticar los funcionamientos mayores de los defectos en los sensores y actuadores del sistema ECCS (sistema de computadora por control electrónico). Hay cinco modos en el sistema de diagnóstico automático.

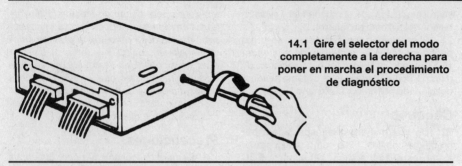

14.1 Gire el selector del modo completamente a la derecha para poner en marcha el procedimiento de diagnóstico

1   **Modo 1** - Monitor del sensor del gas de escape - Durante una condición de ciclo cerrado (cuando el motor está caliente), cuando la lámpara verde de inspección se PRENDE, indica una condición pobre o APAGADA para una condición rica. Durante una condición de ciclo abierto (cuando el motor está frío) la lámpara verde permanece PRENDIDA o APAGADA.

2   **Modo 2** - Monitor del control de la proporción de la mezcla de retroalimentación - Durante la operación de ciclo cerrado, la lámpara roja de inspección se PRENDE y se APAGA simultáneamente con la lámpara verde de inspección cuando la proporción de la mezcla es controlada adentro de los valores especificados. Durante la condición de ciclo abierto, la lámpara roja permanece PRENDIDA o APAGADA.

3   **Modo 3** - Diagnóstico automático - Este modo almacena todas las funciones malas de los artículos de diagnósticos en su memoria. Se almacenará en la memoria de la ECU (unidad de control electrónica) hasta que el motor de arranque se opere cincuenta vez, o hasta que el suministro de energía eléctrica a la ECU sea interrumpido.

4   **Modo 4** - Diagnóstico de APAGA-DO/PRENDIDO - Durante este modo, la lámpara de inspección controla la porción del interruptor de la mariposa del acelerador, El interruptor del motor de arranque, sensor para la velocidad del vehículo y otros interruptores con una condición de APA-GADO/PRENDIDO.

5   **Modo 5** - Diagnóstico en tiempo real - El momento que el funcionamiento defectuoso es detectado, el despliegue se presentará. Este es el modo en que el funcionamiento defectuoso se puede observar durante una prueba en el camino, cuando ocurre.

Cambio de los modos - sistemas MPFI (1990 al 1995)

Refiérase a la ilustración 14.1

Gire el interruptor de la ignición a la posición de Encendido. Gire el selector de diagnóstico de modo en la ECU completamente a la derecha **(vea ilustración)** y espere hasta que las luces de inspección empiecen a destellar. Cuente el número de destellos para encontrar en cuál modo usted está, entonces gire el selector de diagnóstico del modo completamente a la izquierda.

Cuando el interruptor de la ignición es apagado durante el diagnóstico, en cada modo y entonces prendido otra vez después que el poder a la ECU se haya dejado caer completamente, el diagnóstico volverá automáticamente al Modo 1.

La luz CHECK ENGINE en el tablero de instrumentos (modelos de California solamente) se ilumina cuando el interruptor de la ignición es prendió o en el Modo 1 cuando hay un funcionamiento defectuosos en el sistema de emisión (cuando el motor está en marcha).

Los malos funcionamientos relacionados a los sistemas de combustible y los sistemas de control de las emisiones se pueden diagnosticar usando los códigos de diagnóstico automático del Modo 3.

Para poner en marcha el procedimiento de diagnóstico, remueva la ECU debajo del asiento de pasajero. Ponga el motor en marcha y caliéntelo hasta que llegue a la temperatura normal de operación. Gire el selector de diagnóstico en la ECU completamente hacia la derecha **(vea ilustración 14.1)**. Después que las luces de inspección hayan destellado 3 veces, gire el selector de diagnóstico de modo completamente a la izquierda. La ECU ahora está en Modo 3. Chequee el diagrama de código de problema para el funcionamiento defectuoso particular.

Después que las pruebas se hayan realizado y las reparaciones se hayan completado, borre la memoria girando el selector de diagnóstico de modo en la ECU completamente a la derecha. Después que las luces de inspección hayan destellado 4 veces, gire el selector del modo completamente a la izquierda. Esto borrará cualquier señal que la ECU haya almacenado concerniendo cierto componente.

CÓDIGOS DE PROBLEMAS DEL SISTEMA DE AUTO DIAGNOSTICO (MODO 3)

Código	Funcionando malo del componente/circuito	Chequeo/procedimiento de reparación
Código 11 (1 destello rojo, 1 destello verde)	Ángulo del cigüeñal sensor/circuito	Refiérase al Capítulo 5 para el chequeo del sensor del ángulo del; cigüeñal y remplazo del componente or abierto.
Código 12 (1 destello rojo, 2 destellos verdes)	Metro del flujo de aire/circuito	Metro del flujo de aire or circuito(s) de tierra pueda que esté en corto Chequee el flujo del metro de aire
Código 13 (1 destello rojo, 3 destellos verdes)	Sensor de la temperatura del motor	La fuente del sensor o el circuito(s) de conexión a tierra puede estar a corto o abierto. Chequee el sensor de la temperatura/circuito(s) (Sección 15).
Código 14 (1 destello rojo, 4 destellos verdes)	Sensor de la velocidad del vehículo	El circuito de la señal del sensor de la velocidad del vehículo está abierto. Esta reparación debe ser realizada por el departamento de servicio de su concesionario.
Código 21 (2 destellos rojos, 1 el destello verde)	Señal de la ignición	La señal de la ignición en el circuito primario no está entrando durante el periodo que se está arrancando el motor o está en marcha. Esta reparación ser por el departamento de servicio de su concesionario
Código 31 (3 destellos rojos, 1 el destello verde)	Unidad de control ECU	La señal de entrada de la ECU está más allá del rango "normal." Esta reparación debe ser realizada por el departamento de servicio de su concesionario.

Código 32 (3 destellos rojos, 2 destellos verdes)	Función de la EGR	La válvula de control para la EGR no opera (vea Capítulo 6)
Código 33 (3 destellos rojos, 3 destellos verdes)	Sensor del gas de escape	El circuito del sensor del gas del escape está abierto (vea Sección 15)
Código 34 (3 destellos rojos, 4 destellos verdes)	Sensor de detonación	El circuito de detonación está abierto o tiene un corto. Esta reparación se debe realizar por el departamento de servicio de su concesionario.
Código 35 (3 destellos rojos, 5 destellos verdes)	Sensor de la temperatura del gas	El circuito del sensor del gas del escape está abierto (vea Sección 15) de escape
Código 41 (4 destellos rojos, 1 destello verde)	Sensor de la temperatura del aire	El circuito del sensor de la temperatura del aire está abierto o el circuito tiene un corto (motores KA24E solamente) (vea Sección 15)
Código 43 (4 destellos rojos, 3 destellos verdes)	Sensor del acelerador	El circuito del sensor de la mariposa del acelerador está abierto o tiene un corto. Esta reparación debe ser realizada por el departamento de servicio de su concesionario.
Código 45 (4 destellos rojos, 5 destellos verdes)	Fuga del inyector	El inyector(es) tiene fuga de combustible (vea Sección 17).
Código 51 (5 destellos rojos, 1 destello verde)	Circuito del inyector (Motor V6 solamente)	El circuito del inyector está abierto. Esta reparación debe ser realizada por el departamento de servicio de su concesionario.
Código 55 (5 destellos rojos, 5 destellos verdes)	ECCS Operación normal	

Modos de intercambio - sistemas con TBI (cuerpo de inyección de combustible)

Refiérase a la ilustración 14.5

Si la luz CHECK ENGINE se ilumina mientras el motor está en marcha (vehículos de California solamente), o si el vehículo comienza a correr repentinamente mal, pueda que indique que algo está mal con uno de los componentes de las emisiones del motor bajo el control de la ECU. Si esta situación ocurre, chequear estos dispositivos será imposible sin el equipo costoso y sofisticado. Vea a su concesionario y haga que el vehículo sea chequeado por un profesional.

Sin embargo, si usted desea determinar el área general en que un funcionamiento defectuoso está ocurriendo antes de consultar con su concesionario, usted lo puede hacer usted mismo.

Remueva la ECU debajo del asiento del pasajero. **Caución:** *No desconecte el conector del arneses de la ECU o usted borrará cualquier códigos de diagnóstico almacenado.*

Gire el interruptor de la ignición a Encendido. La luz roja y verde de inspección en la ECU deben iluminarse.

Prenda el selector del modo **(vea ilustración)**. La luz roja y verde de inspección deben destellar repetidas veces en la secuencia mostrada en el diagrama.

Note que hay cinco modos posibles. Usted solamente tiene que estar concernido con el Modo 3 (modo de diagnóstico automático).

Gire el selector del modo a apagado inmediatamente después que las luces de inspección destellen tres vez.

Ahora, cuente el número de veces que la luz de inspección destella. Primero, los

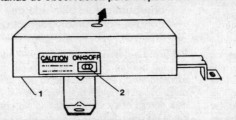

Vista superior   Vista lateral

Ventanas de observación para inspeccionar las luces

destellos rojos, entonces los destellos verdes. La luz roja denota las unidades de diez, la luz verde nota las unidades de uno. Por ejemplo, si el destello rojos es una vez y los destellos verdes son dos veces, la ECU está desplegando el número 12, que indica que el medidor del flujo de aire está funcionando mal.

Si el interruptor de la ignición está apagado durante cualquiera de la lectura de diagnóstico en cualquier modo, el diagnóstico volverá automáticamente al Modo 1 después que la ignición sea prendida otra vez.

La memoria o las memorias almacenadas se perderán si, por cualquier razón, el terminal de la batería es desconectado o si, después que el Modo 3 haya sido escogidos, el Modo 4 será escogido.

Para borrar la memoria después de que el Modo 3 de los código diagnóstico automático se hayan notado y haya sido registrado, gire el selector de diagnóstico de modo a Encendido. Después que las luces de inspección hayan destellado cuatro veces, gire el selector de diagnóstico de modo a Apagado.

Gire el interruptor de la ignición a Apagado.

14.5 Para activar la función diagnóstica en la ECU del vehículo, empuje el interruptor de modo a la izquierda - la luz roja y verde deben de comenzar a destellar (modelos hasta 1995)

1   Unidad de control
2   Selector del modo de diagnostico

15 Regulador de aire (motores V6 solamente) - remover, chequear e instalar

Refiérase a la ilustración 15.10
Nota: *El regulador de aire no está incorporado en el sistema de diagnóstico automático. Los problemas de maniobrabilidad y emisión pueden ser eliminados chequeando el regulador de aire por una operación apropiada.*

Remover

1   Separe la manguera del final del regulador de aire **(vea ilustración 13.1d** en el Capítulo 4).
2   Desconecte el regulador eléctrico del aire del conector.
3   Remueva los pernos y separe el regulador de aire del colector del aire del regulador.

Chequeo

4   Debido a la complejidad del sistema del regulador del control de aire, el mecánico de hogar está limitado a una inspección visual de operación de la válvula y chequear la resistencia y el voltaje, que puede ser hecho

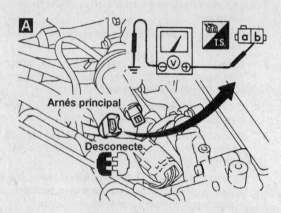

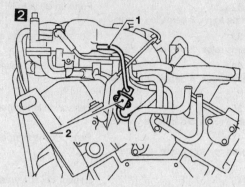

**16.10 Ubicación del regulador de presión del combustible
en el motor V6**

1   Manguera de vacío
2   Regulador de la presión de combustible

**15.10 Conecte el alambre positivo de un voltímetro a la terminal
A y conecte a tierra el alambre negativo del voltímetro**

con un multímetro. Si el voltaje está disponible al regulador de aire y la resistencia es correcta, pero la válvula no se cierra según se calienta el regulador, lleve el vehículo al departamento de servicio de su concesionario para el diagnóstico.

5   Mire en el final del regulador y note la posición del obturador. En una temperatura alrededor de 65 a 70 grados F, el obturador debe estar cubriendo acerca de una mitad del puerto. En temperaturas más frías, la abertura será más grande.

6   Use alambres puente para aplicar voltaje de la batería directamente a las terminales del regulador de aire. **Caución:** *Uno de los alambres puente debe tener un fusible en línea para evitar daño si las terminales de los alambres hacen contacto una con la otra.*

7   Cuando el regulador de aire se comienza a calentar por el voltaje aplicado, el obturador debe cerrar el puerto (esto debe ocurrir dentro de cinco minutos). Si lo hace, el regulador de aire está funcionando correctamente - proceda al paso 10.

8   Si el obturador toma mucho tiempo para cerrar el puerto, o si no se cierra suavemente, use un ohmímetro para chequear la resistencia del regulador de aire conectando los alambres del medidor a las terminales. La resistencia correcta está listada en las especificaciones de este Capítulo.

9   Si la resistencia está incorrecta, reemplace el regulador de aire.

10   Para chequear por electricidad en el regulador de aire, conecte un voltímetro al alambre positivo de la terminal A en el lado del arnés del conector y conecte a tierra el voltímetro del alambre negativo **(vea ilustración)**.

11   Prenda el interruptor de la ignición. El medidor debe indicar 12 voltios (después de 5 segundos el voltaje debe caer a cero). Si no se indican 12 voltios, los alambres del arnés pueden tener una apertura o un corto en algún lugar (tal como un alambre desconectado o roto).

12   Aunque el voltaje esté presente en la terminal A, el regulador de aire no operará a menos que esté a tierra en la ECU. Si el regulador está bueno y hay poder en el, chequee

el alambre de conexión a tierra del regulador a la ECU por una apertura o un corto.

Instalar

13   La instalación se hace en el orden inverso al procedimiento de desensamble, pero esté seguro de usar un anillo sellador de tipo O nuevo donde el regulador de aire se acopla con el colector del aire de admisión.

16   Regulador de la presión del combustible y solenoide de control - chequeo y reemplazo

Peligro: *La gasolina es sumamente inflamable, así que se deben tomar precauciones extras cuando esté trabajando en cualquier parte del sistema del combustible. No fume, deje llamas abiertas o bombillas sin cubierta cerca del área de trabajo. También, no trabaje en un garaje si un aparato de gas natural con un piloto encendido está presente. Debido a que la gasolina es dañina para su piel use guantes cuando halla una posibilidad de que entre en contacto con su piel y si se le derrama cualquier cantidad en su piel límpiese inmediatamente con suficiente agua y jabón. Limpie cualquier derrame inmediatamente y no guarde trapos que estén húmedos con gasolina. El sistema de combustible de los modelos con inyección de combustible están bajo constante presión y si cualquiera de las líneas se van a desconectar, la presión en el sistema se debe de aliviar. Cuando usted conduzca cualquier tipo de trabajo en el sistema de combustible, use espejuelos de seguridad y tenga cerca un extintor de fuegos del tipo de Clase B.*

Chequeo

1   El solenoide para el control del regulador de la presión de combustible corta la señal de vacío al regulador de presión durante condiciones calientes de comienzo, que aumentará la presión del combustible para mejorar el comienzo durante estas condiciones.

2   Si el regulador de presión del combusti-

ble funciona apropiadamente cuando una bomba de vacío es conectada pero no trabaja apropiadamente cuando la línea del control de vacío es conectada, chequee el solenoide para el control del regulador de presión como sigue.

3   Chequee la fuente de poder desconectando el conector eléctrico del solenoide y girando el interruptor de la ignición a la posición de Encendido. Chequee el voltaje entre las terminales y la tierra. El voltímetro debe leer el voltaje de la batería.

4   Desconecte la línea de vacío del regulador de presión del combustible y sople aire hacia adentro para que pase através de la válvula cuando no está con energía.

5   Si el solenoide para el control de la presión del combustible falla cualquiera de estas pruebas, reemplácelo.

Reemplazo

Solenoide para el control del regulador de presión del combustible

6   Desconecte las mangueras de vacío, remueva el conector eléctrico y destornille el solenoide.

7   La instalación se hace en el orden inverso al procedimiento de desensamble.

Regulador de presión del combustible

Refiérase a la ilustración 16.10

8   Alivie la presión del sistema de combustible (vea Capítulo 4).

9   Desconecte el cable negativo en la batería.

10   Afloje las abrazaderas de la manguera y separe las dos mangueras del combustible del regulador **(vea ilustración)**. Si hay cualquier duda en cuanto a cuál acoplación la manguera va a ser conectada, márquelas con pedazos de cinta.

11   Desconecte la línea de vacío y el conector eléctrico del sensor de temperatura de combustible (si está equipado).

12   Afloje la abrazadera de la manguera y desconecte la línea de combustible de regreso de la cara inferior del regulador.

17.6 La resistencia del sensor de la temperatura de la cabeza de los cilindros debe disminuir según el sensor es calentado

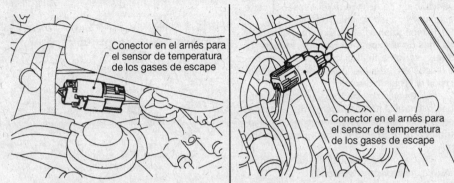

17.13 Ubicación del conector del arneses del sensor de temperatura del gas de escape en los motor V6 y KA24E

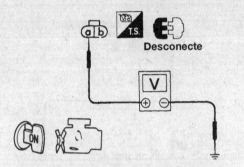

17.15 Chequee por voltaje con la llave de la ignición ENCENDIDA entre la terminal A y la tierra. Debe haber 5 voltios.

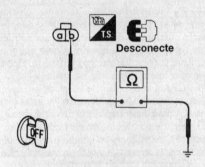

17.16 Chequee por continuidad entre las terminales B y la tierra con la ignición apagada

13 Remueva los pernos y remueva el regulador.

14 La instalación se hace en el orden inverso al procedimiento de desensamble. **Nota:** *Moje la parte interior de las líneas de combustible con gasolina para facilitar la instalación de la manguera.*

17 Sensores de información

Sensor de la temperatura del motor - chequeo y reemplazo

Refiérase a la ilustración 17 6

Chequeo

1 Use el modo de diagnóstico automático (vea Sección 14) localice con toda precisión cualquier problema en el sistema de combustible del vehículo.

2 Si la ECU (unidad de control electrónica) hace 1 destello rojo y 3 destellos verdes entonces el circuito del sensor de la temperatura del motor está funcionando mal. Continúe los chequeos como está descrlto más abajo. Si no se despliega el código de diagnóstico automático, el sensor/circuito está funcionando apropiadamente.

3 Dependiendo en el síntoma, el sensor de la temperatura del motor y su circuito relacionado tienen varios artículos que deben de ser chequeados en orden de señalar con precisión exacta.

4 Si el vehículo es imposible de poner en marcha y hay un sonido de combustión parcial, desconecte el sensor del conector y gire el motor. Si el vehículo todavía no se pone en marcha, chequee la resistencia del sensor.

5 Remueva el sensor de la temperatura de la cabeza de los cilindros para probarlo **(vea ilustración 14.4 en el Capítulo 4).**

6 Remueva el sensor y colóquelo en una cacerola de agua tibia. Use un termómetro para controlar la temperatura del agua. Use un ohmímetro para chequear el valor de la resistencia del sensor **(vea ilustración).**

7 Coloque la cacerola en una fuente del calor (plato caliente, estufa etc.) y eleve la temperatura del agua. Chequee cuidadosamente los valores de la resistencia según la temperatura del agua aumenta. Si los valores no son como está listado en las especificaciones de este Capítulo, reemplace el sensor.

8 Si los valores de la resistencia son aceptable, chequee el circuito del sensor de temperatura por continuidad en la cabeza de los cilindros con un ohmímetro.

9 La instalación se hace en el orden inverso al procedimiento de desensamble.

Sensor de la temperatura del gas de escape - chequeo

Refiérase a las ilustraciones 17.13, 17.15 y 17.16

10 Use el modo de diagnóstico automático (vea Sección 14) localice con toda precisión cualquier problema en el sistema de combustible del vehículo.

11 Si la ECU destella 3 destellos rojos y 5 destellos verdes entonces el circuito del sensor del gas de escape está funcionando mal. Continúe chequeando como está descrito más abajo. Si el código de diagnóstico automático no se despliega, el sensor/circuito está funcionando apropiadamente.

12 Dependiendo en el síntoma, el sensor del gas de escape y su circuito relacionado tienen varios artículos que deben ser chequeados para localizar con toda precisión en orden el problema exacto.

13 Si el vehículo se conduce mal y tiene oleadas mientras está en crucero, desconecte el sensor de la temperatura del gas de escape del conector eléctrico **(vea ilustración)** y conduzca el vehículo.

14 Si la maniobrabilidad del vehículo mejora, reemplace el sensor.

15 Si no se mejora, desconecte el conector del arneses del sensor de la temperatura del gas de escape con el interruptor de la ignición Encendido, chequee el voltaje entre la terminal A **(vea ilustración)** y la tierra. Debe ser 5 voltios.

16 Gire el interruptor de la ignición a apagado y chequee por continuidad entre la terminal B **(vea ilustración)** y la tierra del motor. El ohmímetro debe indicar continuidad.

17 Si el resultado de la prueba es incorrecto, reemplace el sensor de la temperatura del gas de escape.

Sensor del gas de escape - chequeo

Refiérase a las ilustraciones 17 21, 17.24 y 17.25

18 Use el modo de diagnóstico automático (vea Sección 14) para localizar con toda precisión cualquier problema en el sistema de combustible del vehículo.

19 Si la ECU destella 3 destellos rojos y 3 destellos verdes entonces el circuito del sensor del gas de escape está funcionando mal. Continúe chequeando como está descrito más abajo. Si el código de diagnóstico del

vehículo no se despliega, el sensor/circuito está funcionando apropiadamente.

20   Dependiendo en el síntoma, el sensor del gas de escape y su circuito relacionado tienen varios artículos que deben ser chequeados en orden de localizar con toda precisión el problema exacto.

21   Si el vehículo está trabajando mal y titubea mientras está en crucero, desconecte el sensor del gas de escape del conector eléctrico **(vea ilustración)** y conduzca el vehículo.

22   Si la maniobrabilidad del vehículo mejora, reemplace el sensor.

23   Si no mejora, corra el motor acerca de 2,000 rpm por cerca de 2 minutos (sin ninguna carga) y observe para asegúrese que la luz verde en la ECU parpadea ENCENDIDA y APAGADA.

24   En los motores V6 solamente, gire la llave de la ignición a ENCENDIDA y desconecte el conector del arneses del sensor del gas de escape y chequee el voltaje entre la terminal C **(vea ilustración)** y la tierra. Debe ser igual que el voltaje de la batería.

25   Gire el interruptor de la ignición a apagado y chequee por continuidad entre la terminal A **(vea ilustración)** y la tierra del motor. El ohmímetro debe indicar continuidad. **Nota:** *En los motores V6 chequee la continuidad entre la terminal A y la tierra mientras que en los motores KA24E, la continuidad es chequeada entre la terminal A y la terminal número 19 en la ECU.*

26   Si la prueba resulta ser incorrecta, reemplace el sensor del gas de escape.

Chequeo

27   Use el modo de diagnóstico automático (vea Sección 14) localice con toda precisión cualquier problema en el sistema de combustible del vehículo.

28   Si la ECU destella 4 destellos rojos y 1 destello verde entonces el circuito del sensor de la temperatura del aire está funcionando mal. Continúe chequeando como está descrito más abajo. Si no se despliega el código de diagnóstico automático, el sensor/circuito está funcionar apropiadamente.

29   Dependiendo en el síntoma, el sensor de la temperatura del combustible y su circuito relacionado tienen varios artículos que deben ser chequeados en orden para localizar con toda precisión el problema exacto.

30   Desconecte el conector del sensor de la temperatura del aire del arnés**(vea ilustración)** y con la llave de la ignición ENCENDIDA, chequee el voltaje entre las terminales B y la tierra **(vea ilustración)**. El voltaje debe ser de 5 voltios.

31   Si la prueba del voltaje es correcta, chequee la continuidad del circuito del sensor de la temperatura del combustible entre la terminal A y la tierra. Continuidad debe existir.

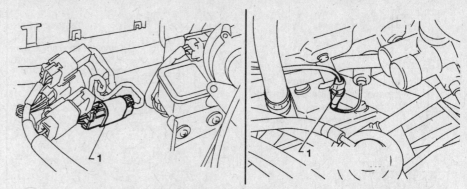

17.21 Ubicación de los arneses del sensor del gas de escape, conectores en los motores V6 y KA24E

1   Conector en el arnés para el sensor de temperatura de los gases de escape

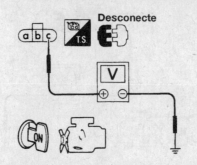

17.24 En los motores V6 solamente, con la ignición APAGADA, el voltímetro debe indicar voltaje de batería

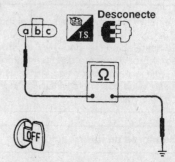

17.25 En los motores V6 solamente, con la ignición APAGADA, chequee por continuidad entre la terminal A y la tierra

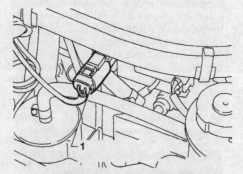

17.30a El conector del arneses del sensor de la temperatura del aire está localizado anexo al purificador de aire

1   Conector para el arnés del sensor de la temperatura del aire

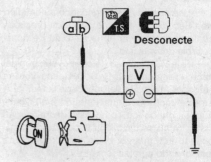

17.30b Chequee el voltaje en las terminales B y la tierra

32   Chequee la resistencia del sensor de la temperatura del aire en el conector del arnés. Cuando la temperatura del sensor esté bajo (68 grados F) la resistencia debe estar entre 2,100 a 2,900 ohm. Cuando la temperatura está caliente (176 grados F), la resistencia debe estar entre 270 a 380 ohm.

Reemplazo

33   Remueva el sensor de la temperatura del aire del albergue del purificador de aire.

34   La instalación se hace en el orden inverso al procedimiento de desensamble.

Capítulo 7 Parte A
Transmisión manual

Contenidos

Especificaciones

Transmisión de 4 velocidades F4W71B y F4W71C

Espacio libre del anillo Baulk/al engrane	
Medida estándar	0.0472 a 0.0630 pulgada (1.20 a 1.60 mm)
Límite de desgaste..	0.031 pulgada (0.787 mm)
Límite de servicio del engrane de juego libre	0.002 al 0.004 pulgada (0.05 a 0.10 mm)
Juego libre del engrane	
Primera velocidad	0.013 a 0.015 pulgada (0.32 a 0.39 mm)
Segunda velocidad...	0.005 a 0.007 pulgada (0.12 a 0.19 mm)
Tercera velocidad..	0.005 a 0.014 pulgada (0.13 a 0.37 mm)

Transmisión de 5 velocidades FS5W71B

Anillo Baulk/espacio libre del engrane	
Todos menos la 5ta velocidad	
Medida estándar..	0.0472 a 0.0551 pulgada (1.20 a 1.60 mm)
Límite de desgaste..	0.031 pulgada (0.787 mm)
5ta velocidad	
Medida estándar..	0.0394 a 0.551 pulgada (1.00 a 1.40 mm)
Límite de desgaste..	0.020 pulgada (0.51 mm)
Límite de servicio del juego del engrane	0.002 al 0.004 pulgada (0.050 a 0.10 mm)
Juego final del engrane	
Primera velocidad	0.0126 a 0.015 pulgada (o.32 a 0.39 mm)
Segunda velocidad...	0.0047 a 0.0075 pulgada (0.12 a 0.19 mm)
Tercera velocidad..	0.0051 a 0.0146 pulgada (0.13 a 0.37 mm)
Quinta velocidad...	0.0126 a 0.019 pulgada (0.32 a 0.50 mm)
Engrane de reversa loca..	0.002 a 0.020 pulgada (0.05 a 0.50 mm)

Transmisión de 5 velocidades FS5W71C

Anillo de Baulk/espacio libre del engrane
    Todo menos la 5ta velocidad

Medida estándar...	0.0472 a 0.0630 pulgada (1.20 a 1.60 mm)
Límite de desgaste...	0.031 pulgada (0.787 mm)

    Quinta velocidad (hasta 1987)

Medida estándar...	0.0394 a 0.0551 pulgada (1.00 a 1.40 mm)
Límite de desgaste...	0.020 pulgada (0.51 mm)

    Quinta velocidad (hasta 1988 en adelante)

Medida estándar...	0.0472 a 0.0630 pulgada (1.20 a 1.60 mm)
Límite de desgaste...	0.0315 pulgada (0.80 mm)
Engrane del multiplicador de velocidad (1990 a 1991)................	0.0472 a 0.630 pulgada (1.20 a 1.60 mm)

Juego final del engrane

Primera velocidad	0.0122 a 0.0161 pulgada (0.31 a 0.41 mm)
Segunda velocidad..	0.0043 a 0.0083 pulgada (0.11 a 0.21 mm)
Tercera velocidad..	0.0043 a 0.0083 pulgada (0.11 a 0.21 mm)

    Quinta velocidad

Hasta 1987...	0.0126 a 0.0154 pulgada (0.32 a 0.39 mm)
1988 en adelante	0.0094 a 0.0161 pulgada (0.24 a 0.41 mm)
Multiplicador de velocidad (1990 y 1991)...............................	0.0094 a 0.016 pulgada (0.24 a 0.41 mm)

Transmisión de 5 velocidades FS5R30A

Juego final del engrane

Todos menos el engrane principal de primera................................	0.0091 a 0.0130 pulgada (0.23 a 0.33 mm)
Engrane principal de reversa...	0.0130 a 0.0169 pulgada (0.33 a 0.43 mm)
Juego libre del eje loco de reversa	0.0118 a 0.0209 pulgada (0.30 a 0.53 mm)

Especificaciones técnicas   Pies-libras

Pernos de la transmisión al motor

1980 al 1985..	32 a 43

    1986 en adelante con motor de cuatro cilindros

Pernos superior..	29
Dos pernos inferiores...	18
Motor V6..	29
Bola de retención..	14 a 18
Cilindro para la operación del embrague	22 a 30
Perno del albergue delantero al albergue de la tapa de la transmisión ..	12 a 15

Extensión trasera al albergue de la transmisión

F4W71B/c y FS5W71B/C...	12 a 15
FS5R30A	23 a 31
Tuerca prisionera del eje principal (F4W71B/C y FS5W71B/C) ......`.......	101 a 123
Tuerca prisionera del contraeje (F4W71B/C y FS5W71B/C)..................	72 a 94

1   Información general

    Estos modelos están equipados con transmisiones de 4 y 5 velocidades, de dos diseños diferentes. El FS5W71B y FS4W71C de 5 velocidades y su variación de 4 velocidades, las F4W71B y F4W71C están disponibles en ambos modelos 720 y los D21 más modernos. La transmisión FS5R30A de 5 velocidades se introdujo en el 1986 en los modelos D21.

2   Sellos del aceite - reemplazo

Refiérase a las ilustraciones 2.3, 2.4 y 2.10

Sello delantero del aceite

1   Remueva la transmisión como se describe en la Sección 3.
2   Remueva el balero de liberación como está descrito en el Capítulo 8.
3   Remueva los pernos que retiene la tapa

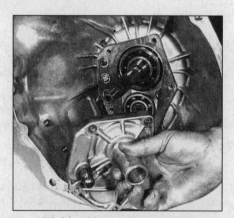

2.3 La cubierta delantera de la transmisión está localizada en la campana/albergue del embrague

delantera de la transmisión al albergue y levante la tapa **(vea ilustración)**.
4   Tenga cuidado de no mellar o dañar la tapa delantera, hágale palanca hacia afuera para remover el sello de aceite delantero de

2.4 El sello de aceite delantero de la transmisión está localizado en la cubierta delantera y puede ser removido haciéndole palanca hacia afuera con un destornillador

la tapa **(vea ilustración)**.
5   Instale el sello nuevo en posición en la tapa usando el dado del tamaño apropiado.

2.10 El sello de aceite trasero de la transmisión puede ser removido con la transmisión todavía en el vehículo haciéndole palanca hacia afuera con un destornillador

6   Aplique una capa delgada de aceite de engrane a los labio del sello y el eje impulsor, entonces vuelva a instalar la tapa delantera.

7   Vuelva a instalar los componentes en el orden inverso de como se removió.

Sello trasero del aceite

8   Remueva el eje impulsor como está descrito en el Capítulo 8 (2WD) o 9 (4WD).

9   En los modelos más modernos pueda que sea necesario remover la tapa del polvo para tener acceso al sello de aceite.

10   Tenga cuidado para no dañar el eje de salida del albergue de la transmisión, use un destornillador para hacerle palanca hacia afuera al sello viejo (**vea ilustración**).

11   Aplique una capa de aceite de engrane al labio del sello nuevo e instálelo en su posición usando un dado calibrado apropiado.

12   Vuelva a instalar el eje de mando.

---

3   Transmisión manual - remover e instalar

Refiérase a las ilustraciones 3.5a, 3.5b, 3.11 y 3.18

1   Desconecte el cable negativo de la terminal negativa de la batería.

2   Trabajando adentro del vehículo, desconecte el acoplamiento del acelerador.

3   Remueva la consola como está descrito en el Capítulo 13.

4   Remueva la tapa de caucho de la palanca de cambio.

5   Coloque la palanca de cambio en la posición de Neutral. Entonces remueva el anillo E, la clavija o anillo de retención y levante hacia afuera la palanca de cambio (**vea ilustraciones**).

6   Levante el vehículo y soporte su peso en bloques o encima de soportes. Esté seguro que el vehículo esté lo suficiente alto para que la transmisión pueda ser deslizada hacia afuera por debajo del vehículo después que sea removida.

7   Remueva el tubo de escape delantero.

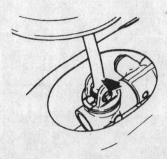

3.5a En los modelos más modernos la palanca de cambio es retenida con una clavija (flecha)

3.11 El engrane del espirómetro está localizado en la transmisión en los modelos de 2WD (tracción en las ruedas traseras)

8   En los modelos de 4WD (tracción en las cuatro ruedas), remueva el eje impulsor primario y delantero. Refiérase al Capítulo 9, si es necesario. Entonces sostenga el diferencial delantero con el gato y remueva el apoyo del miembro transversal trasero del diferencial delantero. Si se necesita espacio libre adicional para remover la transmisión, remueva el diferencial delantero como está descrito en el Capítulo 9.

9   Remueva el eje impulsor, como está descrito en el Capítulo 8. Mientras esto se hace, tape o cubra la abertura en la parte trasera de la transmisión para prevenir fuga de aceite.

10   Desconecte los alambres del interruptor para las luces de reversa, el interruptor de la primera velocidad, el interruptor de neutral y/o el interruptor del multiplicador de velocidad, según esté equipado.

11   Desconecte el cable del velocímetro (**vea ilustración**). En los modelos de 4WD, el cable del velocímetro está conectado en la caja de transferencia.

12   Drene el aceite de la transmisión.

13   Destornille y remueva el cilindro de operación del embrague y amárrelo afuera del camino. No hay necesidad de desconectar la línea hidráulica (información adicional puede ser encontrada en el Capítulo 8).

14   Sostenga el motor bajo la cacerola de aceite usando un gato adecuado y un bloque

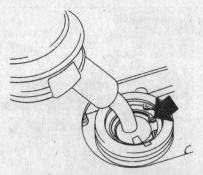

3.5b En los modelos más modernos un anillo de retención (flecha) retiene la palanca de cambio

3.18 Soporte la transmisión seguramente con bloques o un gato

de madera como un aislador.

15   Coloque un segundo gato bajo la transmisión.

16   Afloje y remueva las tuercas que aseguran el aislador a la transmisión, los pernos del calzo al chasis y entonces levante el calzo hacia afuera.

17   Remueva el motor de arranque de la campana.

18   Destornille y remueva los pernos que aseguran la campana del embrague al cárter del cigüeñal del motor (**vea ilustración**).

19   Baje cada uno de los dos gatos simultáneamente, hasta que la transmisión pueda ser retirada hacia atrás y ser removida por debajo del vehículo. No permita que el peso de la transmisión cuelgue en el eje de entrada mientras está comprometido con las estrías del plato de empuje del embrague.

20   Para los detalles de como reparar o reconstruir una transmisión manual, refiérase a la Sección 5 o 6 según sea apropiado.

21   La instalación se hace en el orden inverso al procedimiento de desensamble pero ponga un poco de grasa en las estrías del eje de entrada y en la partes que se mueven de la palanca del cambio y las varillas de cambio. También chequee si el disco del embrague ha sido alineado apropiadamente como está descrito en el Capítulo 8.

22   Chequee el juego libre del pedal del embrague y ajústelo si es necesario (Capítulo 1). Recuerde de llenar la transmisión con el grado y la cantidad correcta de aceite.

4.4 Interruptores eléctricos pueden ser removidos desde la transmisión destornillándolos

4.5 Remueva el perno y remueva el ensamblaje del engrane del espirómetro

4.6 Use un cincel para remover hacia afuera la guía de detención

4 Transmisión de 4 velocidades F4W71B/F4W71C - reconstrucción completa

Refiérase a las ilustraciones 4.4, 4.5, 4.6, 4.7, 4.8, 4.10, 4.18, 4.38, 4.56, 4.84, 4.85 y 4.106

Nota: *Este procedimiento se aplica a las transmisiones fabricadas antes del 1993 solamente. Debido a la complejidad de las transmisiones 1993 y más modernas, es recomendado que los procedimientos internos sean dejados al departamento de servicio de su concesionario o un taller de transmisiones.*

Desarme inicial

1   Con la transmisión removida, limpie completamente el exterior de los albergues.

2   Remueva la tapa de caucho a través de la apertura en la campana del embrague.

3   Remueva el balero de liberación y el cubo junto con la palanca retirada (Capítulo 8).

4   Remueva el interruptor para la luz de reversa, interruptor de neutral, interruptor del primer engrane y/o el interruptor del engrane para el multiplicador de velocidad, según esté equipado **(vea ilustración)**.

5   En los modelos de 2WD, remueva el tornillo que retiene el engrane del velocímetro al albergue de la extensión trasera y remueva el engrane **(vea ilustración)**.

6   Hágale palanca para remover el anillo E desde la clavija de retención y remueva la clavija **(vea ilustración)**.

7   Remueva el tapón del resorte de retorno, remueva el resorte de retorno y la bomba de vacío **(vea ilustración)**.

8   Remueva los dos tornillos que retienen la tapa de reversa al albergue y eleve hacia afuera la manga unilateral de reversa **(vea ilustración)**.

9   Destornille los pernos y separe el albergue trasero de la extensión del albergue principal de la transmisión, usando un martillo de cara blanda.

10   Destornille y remueva los pernos reteniendo la tapa delantera: remueva la tapa delantera, extraiga la lamina para los baleros del contraeje y el anillo de retención del balero del eje de entrada **(vea ilustración)**.

11   Remueva el pedazo de la

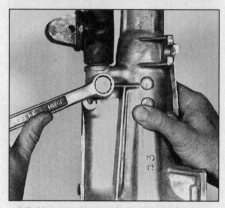

4.7 Use una herramienta para aflojar el tapón del resorte de regreso

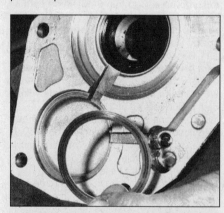

4.10 Esté seguro de capturar la lámina de ajuste para el balero del contraeje, el cual se caerá hacia afuera cuando la cubierta delantera sea removida

campana/transmisión de una sola pieza del plato adaptador.

12   Haga un plato adecuado y atorníllelo al plato del adaptador de la transmisión, entonces asegure el plato de apoyo en una mordaza.

13   Remueva las clavijas que aseguran cada uno de los retenedores de cambio, usando una deriva adecuada delgada.

14   Destornille y remueva los tres tapones de las bolas de retención.

15   Remueva las varillas de selección del plato adaptador.

4.8 Remueva los dos pernos y extraiga la camisa unilateral de reversa

16   Agarre los tenedores de cambio, extraiga las bolas y los resortes según las varillas del selector son removidas. Las cuatro bolas más pequeñas son las bolas de retención.

17   A este punto, inspeccione los engranes y los ejes por cualquier desgaste, astilla o grietas.

18   También, use un calibrador de hojas entre cada engrane del eje principal para determinar la cantidad del juego que existe en el final del engrane **(vea ilustración)**. El

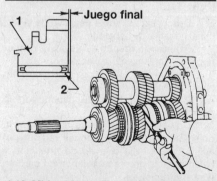

4.18 Mida el juego libre del engrane antes y después de desarmar la transmisión para chequear por desgaste y estar seguro del ensamblaje apropiado

1   *Engrane*
2   *Eje principal o buje*

juego final estándar está listado en las especificaciones.

19 Si el juego final del engrane no está dentro de las especificaciones o si los engranes o los ejes muestran desgaste o daño, los ensamblajes del engrane se deben remover y reemplazar las partes defectuosas.

20 Obstruya los engranes y extraiga el balero delantero del contraeje con un extractor de balero.

21 Extraiga el anillo de retención que ahora está expuesto del contraeje.

22 Remueva el engrane del contraeje junto con el eje de entrada. Tenga cuidado de no dejar caer las agujas del balero de rodillo que está localizado en el frente del eje principal.

23 Extraiga el anillo de retención del final delantero del eje principal, seguido por la arandela para el impulso.

24 Remueva la unidad del sincronizador para la 3ra/4ta seguido por el engrane de 3ra.

25 Ambas la tuerca del eje principal y las tuercas del contraeje son estacadas para prevenirlas que se aflojen. Use un martillo y un punzón para remover el área estacada.

26 Remueva el engrane de reversa y el espaciador.

27 Use un extractor de engrane para remover el engrane del multiplicador de velocidad del contraeje y el balero.

28 Remueva la tuerca del contraeje. Una vez removida, esta tuerca no debe ser vuelta a emplear.

29 Remueva el anillo de retención del eje loco de reversa y remueva el engrane loco de reversa.

30 Remueva el anillo de retención que retiene el engrane del velocímetro al eje principal, remueva el engrane del velocímetro y las bolas de acero.

31 Remueva los otros dos anillos de tipo empuje por detrás del engrane del velocímetro y remueva el balero del eje principal del multiplicador de velocidad.

32 Remueva hacia afuera la estaca en la tuerca del eje principal y remuévela. Una vez removido, esta tuerca no debe ser vuelta a emplear.

33 Remueva la arandela para el impulso, buje del engrane del multiplicador de velocidad, balero de aguja, engrane del multiplicador de velocidad, ensamblaje del sincronizador del multiplicador de velocidad y el retenedor de inserción, si está equipado.

34 Accione los ensamblajes del eje principal y contraeje simultáneamente del plato del adaptador, usando un martillo de cara blanda.

Eje principal

35 Examine cuidadosamente las estrías de los engranes y el eje por astilla de los dientes o desgaste y entonces desarme el tren del engrane, reemplazando cualquier artículo dañado o desgastado.

36 Examine el eje mismo por rayones o surcos, también las estrías por torsión, conicidad o desgaste general.

37 Examine por roturas las unidades sincrónicas o desgaste o flojedad general en el

ensamblaje y reemplácela si es evidente, particularmente si ha habido una historia de cambios ruidosos donde el sincrónico puede haber sido fácilmente golpeado.

38 Apriete el anillo Baulk contra el cono de sincrónico y mida el espacio libre entre los dos componentes. Si es menos que lo que se especifica, reemplace los componentes (refiérase a las Especificaciones e **ilustraciones que acompañan**).

39 Cuando vuelva a instalar la unidad del sincrónico, asegúrese que las puntas del anillo de retención en los lados opuestos de las unidades no se enganchan en las mismas hendiduras.

40 Comience el ensamblaje del eje principal instalando las agujas del balero de 2da velocidad, el engrane de 2da y el anillo Baulk seguidos por la unidad del sincrónico de 1ra/2da, notando cuidadosamente la dirección de la instalación.

41 Ahora instale el primer anillo del engrane Baulk, balero de aguja, bola de acero, arandela para el impulso, el buje y la primera velocidad. Esté seguro que la bola de acero está bien engrasada cuando la instale.

Contraeje

42 El balero del contraeje delantero fue removido cuando se desarmó la transmisión en unidades mayores.

43 El balero del contraeje trasero se dejó en posición en el plato del adaptador.

44 Remueva el engranaje del contraeje de impulsión y extraiga las dos llaves Woodruff.

45 Chequee todos los componentes por desgaste, especialmente los dientes del engrane y estrías del eje por astilla. Vuelva a instalar las llaves de Woodruff y el anillo de retención.

46 El ensamblaje se hace en el orden inverso al procedimiento de desensamble.

Eje de entrada (engranaje principal de impulsión)

47 Remueva el anillo de retención y el espaciador.

48 Remueva el balero usando un extractor de dos patas en una prensa. Una vez removido (por medio de su pista de rodamiento exterior), tire el balero.

49 Apriete el balero nuevo en el eje, aplicando la presión a la pista de rodamiento central solamente.

50 Vuelva a instalar la arandela.

51 Varios espesor de anillos de tipo empuje están disponible para el balero principal del eje de entrada, como está listado en las especificaciones. Seleccione un tamaño que elimine el juego final de balero.

Sellos de aceite

52 Remueva el sello de aceite hacia afuera con una palanca desde la extensión trasera e instale uno nuevo, con los labios del sello mirando hacia adentro.

53 Vuelva a instalar el sello de tipo O en la camisa del piñón del velocímetro.

54 Vuelva a instalar el sello de aceite en la tapa delantera haciéndole palanca hacia

4.38 Chequee el anillo baulk por desgaste acoplándolo con su engrane y midiendo el espacio libre con un calibrador de hojas

afuera al viejo e instalando el nuevo, con un dado del tamaño apropiado.

Extensión del albergue trasero

55 Afloje la tuerca en el extremo de la clavija de la varilla, hasta que sea la mitad de las roscas.

56 Usando la tuerca como una guía, empuje la clavija de retención desde la varilla con un punzón (vea ilustración).

57 Deslice la palanca de la varilla que se le pega y remueva la varilla desde la parte trasera del albergue.

58 Chequee la varilla y la palanca por daño o desgaste y reemplácela si es necesario. Reemplace el anillo sellador de tipo O en la varilla.

59 Inspeccione el buje en la parte trasera de la extensión del albergue. Si este buje se a desgastado o agrietado, la extensión del albergue trasero completo debe ser reemplazado.

60 Vuelva a instalar la varilla invirtiendo el procedimiento de remover.

Ensamblar

61 Antes de comenzar a volver a ensamblar la transmisión, el eje principal y los baleros del plato adaptador del contraeje deben ser removidos, deben ser examinados y deben ser reemplazados si están desgastados. Para hacer esto, destornille los seis tornillos que retienen el plato retenedor del balero al plato

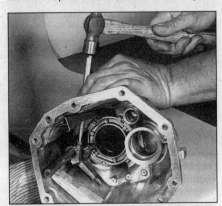

4.56 Use un martillo y un punzón largo para remover hacia afuera la clavija de retención de la varilla

del adaptador. El uso de un impulsor por impacto se requerirá probablemente para esta operación.

62   Con el plato del retenedor del balero removido, apriete el eje principal y los baleros del contraeje desde el plato adaptador. Aplique presión solamente a las pista de rodamiento exterior de los baleros.

63   Chequee los baleros por desgaste primero antes de lavarlos en solvente limpio y secarlo con aire de una bomba para neumático. Gírelos con los dedos y si ellos hacen ruido o tienen una operación floja, reemplácelos con unos nuevos.

64   Chequee que la clavija fija y el paso para el aceite estén correctamente puesto en posición en el plato adaptador.

65   Péguele suavemente al balero del eje principal ligeramente y cuadradamente en posición en el plato adaptador.

66   Instale el eje loco de reversa en el plato adaptador para que 2/3 de su longitud esté proyectada hacia atrás. Asegúrese que la moldura en el eje está puesta en posición para recibir la orilla del plato retenedor del balero.

67   Instale el plato retenedor del balero y apriete los tornillos al par de torsión especificado.

68   Estaque cada tornillo en dos ubicaciones para prevenirlos que se aflojen.

69   Péguele al balero del contraeje trasero en posición en el plato adaptador.

70   Apriete el ensamblaje del eje principal en posición en el plato adaptador del balero. Sostenga el centro trasero del balero durante esta operación.

71   Apriete el ensamblaje de contraeje en posición en el balero en el plato adaptador. Otra vez soporte el centro de la pista trasera del balero durante esta operación.

72   Instale el balero de aguja, engrane de 3ra, anillo Baulk y los sincrónicos para la 3ra/4ta en el frente del eje principal.

73   Instale la arandela de impulso y entonces seleccione un anillo de retención del tamaño listado en las especificaciones que aminorarán el juego final.

74   Inserciónele el balero piloto de agujas en su receso a fines del eje de entrada.

75   Acople el engrane de impulsión del contraeje con el engrane de 4ta en el eje de entrada. Empuje el engrane de mando y el eje de entrada en el contraeje y el eje principal simultáneamente, pero un pedazo de tubería se necesitará para prensar el engrane del contraeje en posición mientras soporta la parte trasera del contraeje.

76   Seleccione un anillo de retención de engrane para el contraeje del tamaño listado en las especificaciones, para que el juego final del engrane se disminuya.

77   Usando un dado del tamaño apropiado, presione el balero delantero en el contraeje.

78   Instale el espaciador del engrane del contraeje en el contraeje trasero.

79   Instale el anillo de retención, la arandela para el impulso, balero de aguja, engrane loco de reversa, arandela para el impulso de reversa y el anillo de retención en el eje loco de reversa.

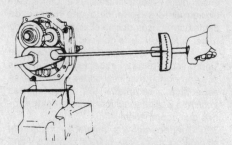

4.84 Atore el eje principal con un adaptador tal como el que se muestra aquí antes de apretar la tuerca prisionera con una llave torsiométrica

80   Hacia el lado trasero del eje principal, instale el retenedor de adición (si está equipado), ensamblaje del sincronizador, engrane de reversa, buje del engrane del multiplicador de velocidad, el balero de aguja y el anillo Baulk.

81   Instale el contraengrane en el contraeje.

82   Acople el engrane del multiplicador de velocidad con el contraengrane e instálelos en sus ejes respectivos con el engrane de sobre marcha en el eje principal y el engrane de contraeje en el contraeje.

83   Aplique grasa a la bola de acero e instálela y la arandela para el impulso en el eje principal trasero.

84   Instale una tuerca nueva de seguridad en el eje principal trasero y apriétela al par de torsión especificado. **Nota:** *En orden para apretar exactamente la tuerca a sus especificaciones técnicas, un adaptador de herramienta se debe usar como está mostrado en la ilustración que acompaña. Usado con el adaptador, la lectura del par de torsión en la llave no será correcta y debe ser convertida al torque correcto referido en el diagrama mostrado* **(vea ilustración).**

85   Instale el balero trasero en la parte trasera del contraeje en el contraeje **(vea ilustración).**

86   Instale la contratuerca del contraeje y apriétela al par de torsión a especificado.

87   Use un martillo y un punzón para estacar ambos el eje principal y las tuercas de la cerradura del contraeje para que ellos se comprometan en sus ejes respectivos.

88   Mida una vez más el juego final de engrane, como está descrito en el Párrafo 18.

89   Acople un anillo de retención en el eje principal y después instale el balero del eje principal para el multiplicador de velocidad.

90   Use un anillo de retención del tamaño listado en las especificaciones para eliminar el juego final del balero trasero del eje principal.

91   Instale el próximo anillo de retención, entonces engrase la bola de acero e instale la bola y el engrane de mando del velocímetro en el eje principal. Instale finalmente el último anillo de retención.

92   Localice el tenedor del cambio para la 1ra/2da en la unidad del sincronizador del multiplicador de velocidad, (el final largo del tenedor de cambio debe estar hacia el con-

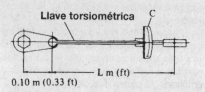

Llave torsiométrica

0.10 m (0.33 ft)

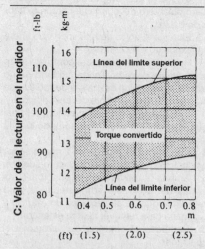

4.85 Cuando esté apretando la tuerca prisionera del eje principal, el torque verdadero puede ser encontrado comparando las lecturas de torque en la herramienta con el diagrama de encima

traeje). Ahora localice el tenedor del cambio para la 3ra/4ta en la unidad del sincronizador de 3ra/4ta, (el final largo del tenedor del cambio debe estar en el lado opuesto al tenedor del cambio para la 1ra/2da).

93   Localice el tenedor de cambio del multiplicador de velocidad en el sincronizador del multiplicador de velocidad para que el orificio superior de la varilla esté en la línea con el tenedor del cambio de 3ra/4ta.

94   Deslice la varilla del selector de 1ra/2da en el plato del adaptador y en el tenedor del cambio para la 1ra/2da; alinee el orificio en la varilla con el orificio en el tenedor y prense una clavija de retención nueva.

95   Alinee la mella en la varilla del selector para la 1ra/2da con el detenedor del diámetro de la bola (unilateral), después instale la bola de retención (unilateral), resorte y enrosque la bola en el tapón de retención. Aplique un poquito de sellador en la bola de retención.

96   Ahora invierta el ensamblaje del plato adaptador (detenga la 3ra/4ta y los tenedores de cambio de la OD (sobre marcha) y reversa) para que el ensamblaje del tapón de la bola de retención se ensamble como en el Párrafo 95, es la parte inferior. Deje caer dos bolas de entrecierre adentro del orificio de detención para la 3ra/4ta y usando una sonda delgada adecuada, empújelos hacia encima contra la varilla del selector de la 1ra/2da (si el plato del adaptador está correctamente puesto en posición, las bolas de entrecierre se dejarán caer en posición). Deslice la varilla del selector de 3ra/4ta en el orificio superior del tenedor de cambio de OD/reversa y el plato del adaptador, asegurándose que las bolas de cierre son

detenidas entre la varilla selectora y la varilla de selección para la 1ra/2da y dentro del tenedor de cambio de la 3ra/4a. Alinee los orificios en el tenedor de cambio y la varilla de selección y prense una clavija nueva. Ahora instale una bola de retención, resorte y tapón de retención (con sellador de rosca aplicado) al orificio para el tapón de la bola de retención para la 3ra/4ta. Asegúrese que la mella en la varilla del selector para la 3ra/4ta está alineada con el tapón de retención antes de ensamblar la bola de retención.

97 Deje caer dos bolas de entre cierre adentro del orificio para el tapón de la bola de retención, asegurando que ellas se localizan contra la varilla de selección de 3ra/4ta. Deslice el selector del multiplicador de velocidad/reversa a través del tenedor de cambio de la sobre marcha y adentro del plato adaptador. Asegúrese de que las dos bolas de entrecierre están en posición entre el selector de 3ra/4ta y la varilla para el multiplicador de velocidad/reversa, deslizando la varilla del selector para el multiplicador de velocidad/reversa adentro del plato adaptador hasta que la ranura en la varilla selectora alinee con el orificio del tapón de la bola de retención. Instale la bola de retención, resorte y tapón para la bola de retención como antes. Presione una clavija de retención nueva para retener el tenedor de cambio del multiplicador de velocidad/reversa a la varilla selectora para el multiplicador de velocidad/reversa.

98 Finalmente, apriete los tres tapones de las bolas de detención al par de torsión especificado.

99 Engrase completamente el ensamblaje y chequee para observar que las varillas de selección operan correctamente y suavemente.

100 Limpie las caras de acoplamiento del plato del adaptador, el albergue de la transmisión y aplique sellador a ambas superficies.

101 Péguele al albergue de la transmisión en posición en el plato del adaptador usando un martillo de cara blanda, teniendo cuidado de que acople correctamente con el balero del eje de entrada y el balero del contraeje delantero.

102 Acople el anillo de retención exterior al balero del eje de entrada.

103 Limpie las caras de acoplamiento del plato adaptador, la carcaza trasera de la extensión y aplique sellador de junta.

104 Arregle el tenedor de cambio en el modo de neutral y entonces baje el albergue trasero de la extensión en el plato del adaptador para que la palanca enganche correctamente con las varillas del selector.

105 Instale los pernos que acoplan las secciones de la transmisión y apriételo al par de torsión especificado.

106 Mida la cantidad que el balero del contraeje delantero sale de la cara delantera del albergue de la transmisión (**vea ilustración**). Use calibradores palpadores para esto y entonces seleccione las laminas de ajustes apropiadas después de referirse a la siguiente tabla:

Medidas

0.1150 a 0.1185 pulgada. (2.92 a 3.01 mm)
0.1189 a 0.1124 pulgada (3.02 a 3.11 mm)
0.1228 a 0.1264 pulgada (3.12 a 3.21 mm)
0.1268 a 0.1303 pulgada (3.22 a 3.31 mm)
0.1307 a 0.1343 pulgada (3.32 a 3.41 mm)
0.1346 a 0.1382 pulgada (3.42 a 3.51 mm)

Lamina (espesor)

0.0236 pulgada (0.6 mm)
0.0197 pulgada (0.5 mm)
0.0157 pulgada (0.4 mm)
0.0118 pulgada (0.3 mm)
0.0079 pulgada (0.2 mm)
0.0039 pulgada (0.1 mm)

107 Ponga la lámina para ajustes en posición usando un toque pequeño de grasa gruesa, entonces conecte la tapa delantera al albergue de la transmisión (dentro de la campana del embrague) completo con una junta nueva y tenga cuidado de no dañar el sello de aceite según pasa por encima de las estrías del eje de entrada.

108 Apriete los pernos de afianzamiento al par de torsión especificado, asegúrese que las roscas del perno están cubiertas con sellador de junta para prevenir fuga de aceite.

109 Complete el ensamble invirtiendo los pasos descrito en los Párrafos 1 al 8 de esta Sección.

5 Transmisión de 5 velocidades FS5W71B/FS5W71C - reconstrucción completa

1 El procedimiento de la reconstrucción completa para la transmisión de 4 velocidades es básicamente el mismo que para la transmisión de 5 velocidades. Las únicas diferencias son esas notadas abajo.

2 Los siguientes procedimientos se debe usar en posición en vez de los Pasos 17 al 34 de la Sección 4.

a) Inspeccione los engranes y los ejes por cualquier desgaste, astillas o grietas.
b) Use un calibrador de hojas entre cada engrane del eje principal para determinar la cantidad de juego final que existe en el engrane. El juego final estándar para cada engrane está listado en las especificaciones.
c) Si el juego final del engrane no está adentro de las especificaciones, o si los engranes o ejes muestran signos de uso o daño, los ensamblajes del engrane deben ser removidos y las partes defectuosas reemplazadas.
d) Cierre los engranes y usando un extractor de dos patas interno, extraiga el balero delantero del contraeje.
e) Extraiga el anillo de retención ahora que está expuesto del contraeje.
f) Remueva el engrane del contraeje junto con el eje de entrada. Tenga cuidado para no dejar caer los rodillos de aguja del balero que está localizado en el frente del eje principal.
g) Extraiga el anillo de retención del final delantero del eje principal, seguido por la arandela para el impulso.
h) Remueva la unidad del sincronizador de 3ra/4ta, seguido por el engrane de 3ra.
i) Libere la tuerca del eje principal y entonces aflójela.

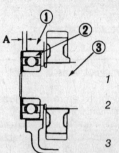

1 Albergue de la transmisión
2 Balero delantero para el contraengrane
3 Contraengrane

4.106 Mida la sección A para la selección del contraeje de la lámina de ajuste del balero delantero

j) Remueva la tuerca del eje principal, la arandela para el impulso y engrane de reversa.
k) Extraiga el final de atrás del anillo de retención del contraeje y remueva el contraengrane de reversa.
l) Presione el eje principal y el contraeje simultáneamente desde el plato adaptador, usando un martillo de cara blanda.

3 Los siguientes procedimientos se deben usar en posición en vez de los Pasos 78 al 91 de la Sección 4.

a) Hacia atrás del eje principal, instale el engrane de reversa, la arandela simple y atornille la tuerca, apretada con los dedos.
b) Instale el contraengrane de reversa en el contraeje y use un anillo de retención del espesor listado para obtener el final mínimo del juego.
c) Instale el engrane loco de reversa en el eje loco de reversa.
d) Apriete la tuerca del eje principal (después de obstruir los engranes) al par de torsión especificado.
e) Estaque el cuello de la tuerca en la ranura del eje principal.
f) Una vez más, mida el juego libre final del engrane, como está descrito en el Párrafo 2.

6 Transmisión de 5 velocidades FS5R30A - reconstrucción completa

Refiérase a las ilustraciones 6.5, 6.9, 6.16, 6.17, 6.35, 6.36, 6.37, 6.38, 6.39, 6.42, 6.43, 6.44 y 6.45

Remoción inicial

1 Con la transmisión removida (Sección 3), limpia completamente el exterior del albergue.

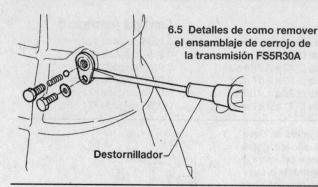

6.5 Detalles de como remover el ensamblaje de cerrojo de la transmisión FS5R30A

Destornillador

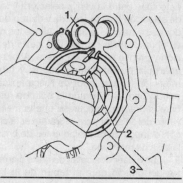

6.9 Remueva el anillo de retención y el anillo de retención para el balero de ejecución principal

1 Anillo de retención
2 Alicates para el anillo de retención
3 Anillo de retención para el balero de ejecución principal

2 Remueva el ensamblaje de la liberación del embrague.
3 Destornille los interruptores eléctricos del albergue de la transmisión.
4 Con la transmisión en Neutral, remueva el perno de la abrazadera y levante hacia afuera el piñón del velocímetro.
5 Remueva los pernos y use un destornillador para abrir el tapón de la bola de retención con una palanca, resorte y ensamblaje de cierre hacia afuera del albergue (vea ilustración).
6 Remueva el albergue del control del cambio, resorte de retorno y ensamblaje de bola de retención.
7 Use un martillo y un punzón para expulsar la clavija de tipo rodillo.
8 Remueva los pernos y use un martillo de cara blanda para pegarle al albergue para separar el albergue de la extensión o el engrane del multiplicador de velocidad.
9 Remueva los pernos y separe la tapa delantera del albergue. Remueva el anillo de retención y use un alicate de anillo de retención para remover el anillo de retención del balero principal (vea ilustración).

Plato adaptador y desarmar el eje principal

10 Coloque el albergue firmemente en una prensa, usando bloques de madera o tela para proteger la superficie.
11 Remueva el multiplicador de velocidad/varilla de cambio de reversa.
12 Remueva la clavija de tipo rollo de la palanca, usando un punzón y un martillo adecuado.
13 Remueva la varilla, palanca y ensamblaje de entrecierre del plato adaptador.
14 Remueva los tenedores de cambio de la 1ra/2da, 3ra/4ta y reversa.

15 Remueva el tenedor de cambio para el multiplicador de velocidad usando un punzón y un martillo adecuado y remueva el tenedor de la varilla de cambio.
16 Use un calibrador de hojas para medir el juego libre del engrane (vea ilustración). Compare las medidas finales del juego a las Especificaciones. Anillos de retención selectivos (disponible en su concesionario), son usados para corregir el juego exceso. Inspeccione las arandelas del eje principal por daño o desgaste.
17 Remueva la camisa de acoplación de reversa y los componentes del contraeje y el engrane impulsado principal del lado trasero (vea ilustración).
18 Remueva el eje trasero principal y los anillos de retención del contraengrane.
19 Use un martillo y el punzón adecuado para remover el poseedor del anillo C y los anillos del eje principal C.
20 Use una herramienta adecuada para extraer el balero del engrane del contraeje y entonces remueva el engrane loco de reversa y las arandela.
21 En los modelos de 2WD, use una herramienta extractora para remover el eje principal del balero trasero.
22 Remueva el engrane principal de reversa, el espaciador y el cubo de reversa del sincronizador, usando una herramienta extractora. Remueva las agujas de los baleros del engrane de reversa.
23 Use un extractor para remover el contraengrane de reversa, seguido por el sincronizador del multiplicador de velocidad.
24 Lleve el plato adaptador a un taller adecuado de rectificación para hacer que el eje principal y el engrane impulsado sean removidos del plato usando una prensa hidráulica y una herramienta adecuada adaptadora.

25 Remueva la arandela de la primera velocidad, bola de acero, primera velocidad y balero de aguja del eje principal.
26 Detenga la 2da velocidad, el buje de 1ra velocidad y sincronizador de 1ra/2da prensados en el eje principal.
27 Remueva el anillo de retención del eje principal delantero.
28 Haga que el engrane de la 3ra velocidad, el sincronizador de 3ra/4ta y las agujas del balero del engrane de la 3ra velocidad sean apretados afuera del eje principal.

Desensamble del contraeje y el engrane

29 Remueva el anillo de retención del subengrane.
30 Remueva el resorte del sub engrane, subengrane y la bola de acero del frente del contraeje. La instalación se hace en el orden inverso al procedimiento de desensamble.

Desensamble del eje de entrada y engrane

31 El eje de entrada y el ensamblaje del engrane es servido como una sola unidad y solamente el balero es reemplazado. Si es necesario de remplazar el balero, remueva el anillo de retención y el espaciador. Lleve el ensamblaje a un taller de rectificación equipado para que el balero viejo sea prensado hacia afuera y uno nuevo instalado.

Plato adaptador y ensamble del eje principal

32 Haga que el sincronizador del engrane de 3ra/4ta y el balero de agujas para la 3ra sean prensado en el eje con una prensa hidráulica. Instale el anillo de retención selec-

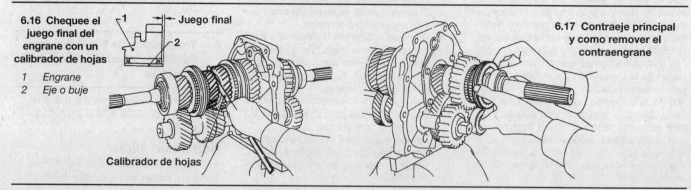

6.16 Chequee el juego final del engrane con un calibrador de hojas
Juego final
1 Engrane
2 Eje o buje
Calibrador de hojas

6.17 Contraeje principal y como remover el contraengrane

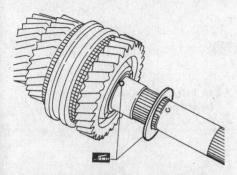

6.35 Lubrique el eje principal con grasa de propósito múltiple en los puntos que se muestra

tivo más grueso que ajuste en la ranura. Chequee el espacio libre del anillo con un calibrador de hojas y asegúrese que no exceda 0.004 (0.1 mm) de pulgada.

33 Haga que el sincronizador de 1ra/2da, el engrane de 2da y las agujas del balero sean prensadas en el eje principal con una prensa hidráulica.

34 Haga que el buje del primer engrane y la arandela sean prensados en una prensa hidráulica y después instale la primera velocidad y el balero de aguja.

35 Cubra la bola de acero y la arandela con jalea de petróleo o grasa de uso múltiple e instale el eje principal **(vea ilustración)**.

36 Arme el contraeje y lo instala en el plato adaptador **(vea ilustración)**.

37 Instale el plato adaptador en el plato de la transmisión usando 2 pernos. Instale un indicador de reloj, póngalo en cero y entonces levante y libere el engrane impulsado **(vea ilustración)**. Haga una nota de la lectura

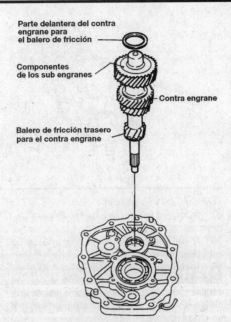

6.36 Detalles de la instalación del contraeje

y reste 0.0039 a 0.0098 pulgada (0.10 a 0.25 mm) para determinar la lamina del engrane impulsado del tamaño apropiado para la lamina de ajuste para el balero delantero que vaya a ser instalada.

38 Instale el engrane loco de reversa, balero de aguja, arandelas de empuje y el eje en la extensión del albergue (2WD) o albergue del multiplicador de velocidad de (4WD) **(vea ilustración)**.

39 Instale un indicador de reloj en el frente

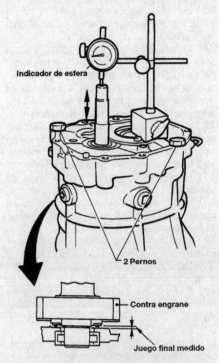

6.37 Use un indicador de tipo esfera para chequear el juego del contraengrane

del eje loco de reversa y use una regla de precisión **(vea ilustración)**. Ponga el indicador a cero, para levantar y liberar el eje del controlador de la marcha mínima y mida el juego final. El juego final debe estar entre 0.118 a 0.209 pulgada (0.30 a 0.35 mm). Si el juego final no está dentro de la especificación, reemplace la arandela trasera para el impulso con una nueva.

40 Destornille el albergue de la transmisión del plato adaptador y lo coloca firmemente en una prensa, usando un bloque de madera o tela para proteger la superficie.

41 Lubrique las superficies del balero trasero para el contraengrane con grasa de uso múltiple e instale el eje principal parcialmente en su balero delantero en el plato adaptador.

42 Instale el contraengrane en el balero trasero del contraengrane en el plato adaptador y después empújelo hacia arriba en los rodillos del balero, usando un destornillador para asentar el ensamblaje **(vea ilustración)**.

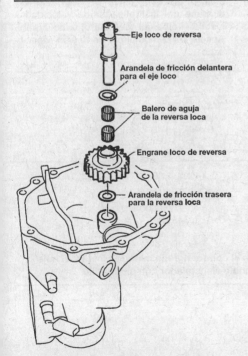

6.38 Despliegue de los componentes de la reversa loca

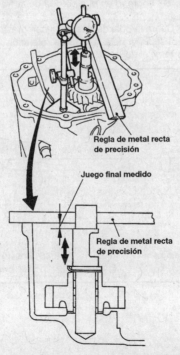

6.39 Chequeando el juego final del eje loco de reversa

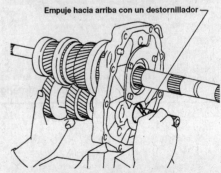

6.42 Use un destornillador para asentar el ensamblaje del contraengrane

43 Instale el eje de entrada con el balero piloto y el espaciador en el eje principal **(vea ilustración)**.

44 Instale la herramienta J-26349-3 en el plato adaptador con el anillo C y el retenedor del anillo C en el eje principal y después instale la herramienta J-34328. Extienda la herramienta para instalar el engrane del eje principal y el contraeje **(vea ilustración)**.

45 Instale el buje del engrane del multiplicador de velocidad pegándole en su posición con un martillo para empujar en la parte trasera del contraengrane **(vea ilustración)**.

46 Instale el engrane del multiplicador de velocidad.

47 Instale el plato del adaptador completo con el ensamblaje del engrane en el albergue de la transmisión.

48 Instale el balero de aguja del engrane multiplicador de velocidad seguido por el engrane impulsado del multiplicador de velocidad y el eje loco de reversa.

49 En modelos de 2WD, instale el buje de reversa del engrane con el engrane del velocímetro.

50 Instale el cono de reversa.

51 Instale el anillo bloqueador del multiplicador de velocidad en el engrane impulsado del multiplicador de velocidad.

52 Instale el contraengrane de reversa, balero de aguja, engrane principal de reversa, engrane loco de reversa y arandela para el impulso, seguido por el cubo de reversa.

53 En los modelos de 2WD, instale el espaciador del eje principal y el balero trasero.

54 Instale el balero trasero del engrane de contraeje.

55 Remueva el ensamblaje del plato de adaptador del albergue de la transmisión y lo instala en la prensa otra vez.

56 Instale un anillo C en el eje principal nuevo y el anillo de retención del engrane del contraeje. Con el anillo apropiado instalado, el espacio libre de la ranura no debe

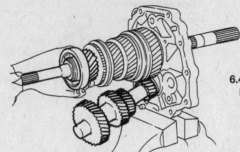

6.43 Instalando el eje de entrada y balero piloto en el eje principal

exceder 0.004 pulgada (0.1 mm).

57 Instale el ensamblaje de reversa del sincronizador.

58 Mida el juego libre del engrane como está descrito en el Paso 16.

59 Instale la varilla del multiplicador de velocidad y el tenedor de cambio, alinee las varillas y los orificios del tenedor e instale una clavija de rodillo nueva, usando un martillo y un cincel.

60 Instale los tenedores de cambio de 1ra/2da, 3ra/4ta y reversa en sus ranuras del sincronizador.

61 Instale la varilla para comprometer los tenedores de cambio, palanca y entrecierre. Alinee la varilla y orificios de la clavija en la palanca e instale una clavija nueva de rodillo, usando un martillo y un punzón adecuado.

Ensamblaje del albergue de la transmisión

62 Aplique el sellador adecuado a las superficies de contacto del albergue de la transmisión.

63 Instale el plato adaptador y el ensamblaje del engrane en el albergue de la transmisión

64 Cubra la bola de retención con grasa de uso múltiple y meta la bola de retención y el resorte en el detenedor.

65 Aplique sellador a las roscas del tapón, instale el tapón y lo aprieta al par de torsión especificado.

66 Instale el anillo de detención y lo asegura con un anillo de retención nuevo para el balero principal.

67 Instale la tapa delantera, usando una junta nueva. Cubra las roscas del fondo de los 3 pernos de la tapa con sellador e instale todos los pernos delanteros de la tapa. Apriete los pernos al par de torsión especificado.

68 Aplique el sellador adecuado a las superficies de contacto del plato adaptador.

69 Instale la extensión del albergue (2WD) o albergue del multiplicador de velocidad (4WD) al plato del adaptador con el brazo.

70 Alínee los orificios de las clavijas e instale una clavija de rollo nueva en el brazo, usando un martillo y el punzón del tamaño adecuado.

71 Instale la bola de control de retención del albergue y el resorte de retorno (refiérase a la **ilustración 6.6**).

72 Aplique sellador al albergue de la extensión o las superficies del albergue del engrane del multiplicador de velocidad e instale el albergue de control y los pernos. Apriete los pernos al par de torsión especificado.

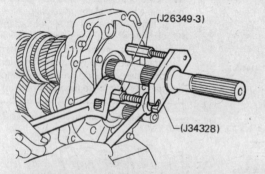

6.44 Herramientas especiales son requeridas para la instalación del contraengrane

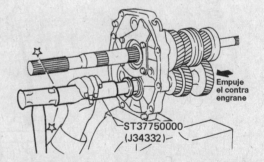

6.45 Empuje en el contraengrane mientras instala el buje pegándole al instalador con un martillo

Capítulo 7 Parte B
Transmisión automática

Contenidos

Especificaciones

Modelos

1980 al 1985	3N71B
1986 en adelante	
2WD con motor de cuatro-cilindros	L4N71B
2WD con motor V6	E4N71B
4WD	
1987	L3N71B
1988	RE4R01A o RL4R01A

General

Desviación máxima admisible del plato flexible	0.020 pulgada (0.5 mm)
Posición de la instalación del convertidor de torque A	
1980 al 1985	0.846 pulgada (21.5 mm)
1986 al 1990	1.38 pulgadas (35 mm)
1991 y más moderno	1.024 pulgadas (26.0 mm) o más
Flúido recomendado	Vea Capítulo 1
Capacidad del flúido	Vea Capítulo 1

Especificaciones técnicas — Pies-libras

Pernos del convertidor de torque al plato flexible	33
Pernos del albergue del convertidor de torque al motor	
Todos los modelos de cuatro cilindros y los modelos V6 hasta el 1990	33
1991 y los modelos más modernos V6	
Superior 4 pernos	33
Inferior 4 pernos	25
Pernos para instalar el interruptor inhibidor	4.3
Contratuerca de la varilla de cambio	
1980 al 1985	25
1986 en adelante	
2WD (tracción en las ruedas traseras) cambio en el piso	8
4WD (tracción en las cuatro ruedas) cambio en el piso	3.3 a 4.3
Cambio en la columna	8

1   Información general

La transmisión automática usada en los modelos fabricados entre el 1980 y 1985 es del tipo JATCO 3N71B, proporcionando tres velocidades hacia adelante y una de reversa. Los vehículos de modelos más modernos (1986 al 1988) usan una variedad de transmisiones de 4 velocidades automáticas, dependiendo en el motor usado y si es de 2WD o de 4WD. Cambio de la relación de las velocidades hacia adelante es completamente automático con relación a la velocidad del vehículo, rendimiento del torque del motor y depende en la presión del vacío en el múltiple y la velocidad del vehículo en el camino para accionar el engrane de cambio mecánico al tiempo preciso.

La transmisión automática usada en los modelos 1990 y 1991 es la RL4R01A o una RE4R01A. Estas transmisiones automáticas nuevas están equipadas con muchas características. Una unidad de multiplicación de velocidad está construida también en ella, como un convertidor de torque de enclavamiento para aumentar el millaje del combustible y la eficiencia. También, ellas están equipadas con un sistema de diagnóstico automático. Los códigos son accedidos a través del control de cambio y la llave de la ignición. Este sistema es bueno para los mecánicos entrenados, que pueden interpretar los datos para resolver los problemas en el cuerpo de válvula o circuitos del sensor.

La transmisión tiene un selector de siete posiciones:

P Posición de estacionamiento, que obstruye el eje de salida a la pared interior del albergue de la transmisión. Este es un dispositivo de seguridad para ser usado cuando el vehículo está estacionado en una inclinación. El motor se puede poner en marcha con la P seleccionada y esta posición siempre se debe seleccionar cuando se esté ajustando el motor en marcha. Nunca atente de poner el seleccionador en P cuando el vehículo se esté movimiento.

R Engrane de reversa.

N Neutral. Seleccione esta posición para poner el motor en marcha o cuando esté en marcha mínima en tráfico por períodos largos.

O Multiplicador de velocidad (si está equipado). El engrane de 4ta es seleccionado automáticamente una vez que el interruptor (cuatro-cilindros) del multiplicador de velocidad es prendido o el interruptor de cambio de poder (motor V6) esté en la posición Automática. Consulte con su manual de propietario para pautas del uso apropiado del multiplicador de velocidad.

D Marcha, es para todas las condiciones normales de manejo.

2 Retiene la transmisión en el segundo engrane para caminos de condiciones mojadas, subir una cuesta o descender. El motor puede que sobre pase sus revoluciones normales en esta posición.

1 La selección de esta velocidad

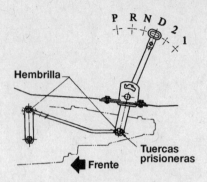

2.3 Para ajustar la varilla de acoplamiento manual para el cambio en los modelos pre 1986, coloque la palanca de cambio en el engrane, afloje las contratuercas, mueva la palanca de cambio para que alínee con la posición D, mueva la palanca del selector en la transmisión para que también alínee con la posición D y apriete las contratuercas

encima de 25 mph (40 kph) aproximadamente comprometerá el segundo engrane según la velocidad cae debajo de 25 mph (40 kph), la transmisión se comprometerá en el primer engrane. Proporcionando retardo máximo en una bajada bien inclinada.

Debido a la complejidad de la transmisión automática, cualquier ajuste interno u otorgarle servicio debe ser dejado a su concesionario Nissan, o a otro especialista de transmisiones calificado. La información otorgada en este Capítulo es por lo tanto limitada a esas operaciones que son consideradas dentro del alcance del mecánico de hogar. Una transmisión automática debe de dar muchos miles de millas de servicio proveyendo que el mantenimiento y los ajustes normales sean proporcionados a sus intervalos requeridos. Cuando la transmisión requiere finalmente una reconstrucción mayor completa, consideración debe ser dada a cambiar la transmisión vieja con una de fábrica reconstruida, remover e instalar está bien al alcance de las capacidades del mecánico de hogar como está descrito más adelante en este Capítulo.

El diagrama rutinario de mantenimiento en el Capítulo 1 indica que el flúido para la transmisión automática sea cambiado cada 30,000 millas. Este intervalo debe ser acortado a 15,000 millas si el vehículo es normalmente conducido bajo una o más de las siguientes condiciones: tráfico pesado de la ciudad, donde la temperatura exterior llega normalmente a 90°F o más alto; en áreas montañosas; o si un remolque es frecuentemente halado. Refiérase al Capítulo 1 para los procedimientos apropiados para chequear y cambiar el flúido de la transmisión automática y el filtro.

La transmisión automática usa un enfriador de aceite, localizado en el radiador, para prevenir las temperaturas excesivas adentro de la transmisión. Si el enfriador de aceite necesita ser limpiado u otorgarle servi-

2.10a Ubicación de la contratuerca de acoplamiento de cambio manual en los modelos 1986 y más modernos de 2WD (y los modelos 1986 y 1988 de 4WD) de cambio en el piso

cio, llévelo al concesionario o un especialista de radiadores.

Si cambios áspero u otros funcionamientos defectuosos ocurren en la transmisión automática, chequee los siguientes artículos primero antes de asumir que el defecto es adentro de la misma transmisión; nivel del flúido, ajuste del interruptor de rebase, ajuste de la varilla de cambio manual y afinación del motor. Todos estos elementos pueden afectar adversamente el desempeño de la transmisión.

Limpie periódicamente el exterior del albergue de la transmisión, según la acumulación de tierra y aceite es responsable por causar sobrecalentamiento de la transmisión bajo condiciones extremas.

2   Varilla de cambio - ajuste

Refiérase a las ilustraciones 2.3, 2.10a, 2.10b, 2.11, 2.13, 2.18 y 2.19

Modelos 1980 al 1985

1   Para chequear el ajuste de la varilla de acoplamiento de cambio manual, mueva la palanca de cambio completamente a través de todos los engranes. Usted debe ser capaz de sentir cuando se detiene en cada engrane. Si no se detecta cada engrane o si el eje propulsor no está alineado apropiadamente con la selección del engrane correcto, el acoplamiento de cambio debe ser ajustado de la siguiente manera.

2   Con el motor apagado, coloque la palanca de cambio en el engrane.

3   Trabajando debajo del vehículo, afloje las contratuercas **(vea ilustración)**.

4   Mueva la palanca de cambio para que se alínee correctamente con la posición D.

5   Mueva la palanca del selector en la transmisión para que esté también correctamente alineada en la posición D.

6   Apriete las contratuercas y chequee las palancas. No debe haber tendencia para que la varilla selectora empuje, ni hale una varilla contra la otra.

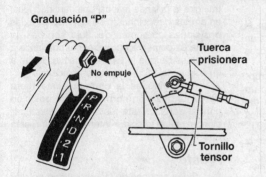

2.10b Ubicación de la contratuerca de acoplamiento de cambio manual en los modelos 1987 de 4WD con cambio en el piso

2.11 Para ajustar la varilla de cambio manual en los modelos 1986 y más modernos de 2WD (y los modelos 1986 y 1988 de 4WD) de cambio en el piso, coloque la palanca del selector en la posición "P," afloje las contratuercas, apriete la contratuerca X hasta que toque la cruceta, retroceda la contratuerca X de 1/4 a 1/2 vuelta y apriete la contratuerca Y al par de torsión especificado

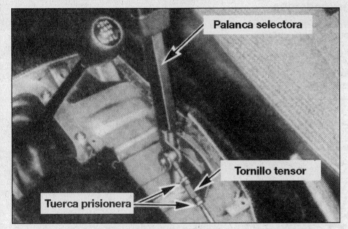

2.13 Para ajustar la varilla de cambio manual en los modelos 1987 de cambio en el piso en los modelos de 4WD, coloque la palanca del selector en la posición "P," afloje las contratuercas, apriete el tornillo tensor hasta que alínee con el cable interior, afloje el tornillo tensor una vuelta y apriete las contratuercas al par de torsión especificado

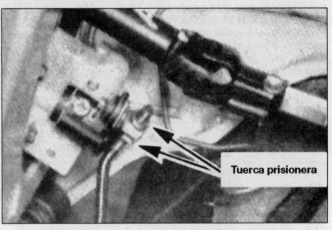

2.18 Ubicación de la contratuerca de acoplamiento para el cambio manual en los modelos 1986 al 1988 de cambio en la columna

7   Otra vez corra la palanca de cambio a través de todas las posiciones de los engranes. Si todavía hay problemas, las hembrillas que conectan la varilla del selector con las palancas pueden estar desgastadas o dañadas y deben ser reemplazadas.

Modelos 1986 y más modernos

Modelos con cambio en el piso

8   Mueva el selector desde la posición "P" a la posición "1." Usted debe ser capaz de sentir cuando se detiene en cada posición. Si la detención no puede ser sentida, ni la flecha que indica la posición está impropiamente alineada, la varilla tiene que ser ajustada.
9   Coloque la palanca del selector en la posición "P."
10   Afloje las contratuercas (**vea ilustraciones**).

Modelos de 2WD

11   Apriete la contratuerca X (**vea ilustración**) hasta que toque la cruceta de la palanca selectora hacia la posición "R" sin empujar el botón.

2.19 Para ajustar la varilla del cambio manual en los modelos 1986 al 1988 de cambio en la columna, coloque la palanca de cambio en la posición "P," afloje las contratuercas, apriete la contratuerca A hasta que toque la cruceta, afloje la contratuerca A dos vueltas y apriete la contratuerca B al par de torsión especificado

12   Afloje la contratuerca X 1/4 a 1/2 de vuelta y la aprieta al par de torsión especificado.

Modelos 1987 de 4WD y más modernos

13   Apriete el tornillo tensor (**vea ilustración**) hasta que se alínee con el cable interior, halando la palanca selectora hacia la posición "R" sin empujar el botón.
14   Afloje el tornillo tensor una vuelta y apriete las contratuercas al par de torsión especificado.
15   Mueva la palanca del selector desde la posición "P" a la posición "1." Asegúrese que la palanca selectora se mueve suavemente.

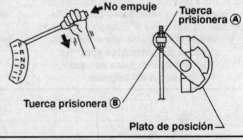

Modelos con cambio en la columna

16   Mueva la palanca de cambio desde la posición "P" a la posición "1." Usted debe ser capaz de sentir que se detiene en cada posición. Si la detención no puede ser detectada o la flecha que indica la posición está impropiamente alineada, la varilla tiene necesidades de ajuste.
17   Coloque la palanca de cambio en la posición "P."
18   Afloje las contratuercas (**vea ilustración**).
19   Apriete la contratuerca A (**vea ilustración**) hasta que toque con la cruceta, halando la palanca selectora hacia la posición "R" sin empujar el botón.

20 Afloje la contratuerca A dos vueltas y apriete la contratuerca B al par de torsión especificado.

21 Mueva la palanca de control desde la posición "P" a la posición "1." Asegúrese que la palanca de control puede moverse suavemente.

3 Interruptor inhibidor - chequeo y ajuste

Refiérase a las ilustraciones 3.6, 3.8a, 3.8b, 3.8c y 3.8d

Chequeo

1 El interruptor inhibidor realiza dos funciones. Proporciona la corriente a las luces de reserva cuando la transmisión está en la posición de Reversa. Previene también que el vehículo se ponga en marcha en cualquier posición de las velocidades menos Estacionamiento (P) o Neutral (N). Si las luces de reserva fallan de operar, o si el vehículo no comienza cuando la palanca de cambio está en el centro de la P o posición N, el interruptor inhibidor debe ser chequeado y si es necesario, ser ajustado.

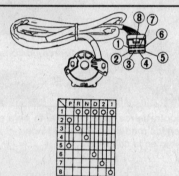

3.6 Para chequear la continuidad de los interruptores inhibidores 1986 y más modernos, remueva el conector del arnés y usando el diagrama que acompaña, chequee la continuidad entre las terminales indicadas en cada posición del engrane

Modelos 1980 al 1985

2 Localice el interruptor inhibidor en el lado derecho de la transmisión y conecte un probador de continuidad a los alambres negros y amarillos.

3 Con el motor apagado, pero el interruptor de la ignición Encendido, haga que un ayudante corra la palanca de cambio del engrane a través de las diferentes posiciones del engrane. El probador debe mostrar continuidad en el interruptor solamente cuando la palanca de cambio esté en la posición P o N.

4 Ahora conecte el probador de continuidad a los alambres rojos y negros. Con este arreglo el probador debe mostrar la continuidad en el interruptor solamente cuando la palanca de cambio esté en la posición de Reversa (R).

Modelos 1986 y más modernos

5 Desconecte los arneses del interruptor inhibidor en su conector eléctrico, entonces remueva el interruptor.

6 Chequee la continuidad en las terminales indicadas **(vea ilustración)** en cada posición. Con la palanca del selector sostenida en Neu-

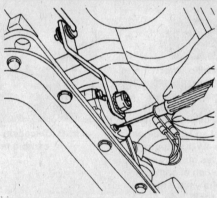

3.8a Para ajustar el interruptor inhibidor en cualquier modelo de 2WD, coloque la válvula manual en Neutral (posición vertical), remueva el tornillo del orificio de alineación (1987 e interruptores más modernos no tienen orificios para los tornillos de alineación) . . .

tral, gire la palanca manual una cantidad igual en ambas direcciones para determinar si las posiciones corrientes del flujo son casi la misma (la corriente normalmente comienza a fluir antes de que la palanca manual llegue a un ángulo de 1.5° en cualquier dirección).

7 Si el flujo de la corriente está fuera desde la posición normal, o si la posición normal del flujo está fuera de la especificación, ajuste el inhibidor interruptor como está descrito encima.

Ajuste

8 Si las pruebas de la continuidad no dieron el resultado descrito encima, el interruptor debe ser ajustado como sigue:

a) *Coloque la palanca del selector de la transmisión en la posición Neutral (vertical).*

b) *En todos los interruptores menos los modelos 1987 y 1988 de 4WD, remueva el tornillo (vea ilustración).*

c) *Afloje los pernos de conectar el interruptor inhibidor (vea ilustración).*

d) *Usando una varilla de alineación o un pedazo de alambre (vea ilustraciones) con un diámetro alrededor de 2 mm (0.079 pulgada), alínee el orificio del tornillo con el orificio en el rotor atrás del interruptor, moviendo el interruptor. Teniendo esta alineación, apriete nuevamente los pernos de conectar el interruptor inhibidor.*

e) *Remueva la varilla de alineación o el alambre e instale el tornillo.*

9 Con el interruptor ajustado, reexamínelo por continuidad repitiendo los Pasos 3 y 4. Si el interruptor todavía no funciona apropiadamente, reemplácelo con uno nuevo.

4 Interruptor de rebase - ajuste

Refiérase a la ilustración 4.3

1 El interruptor de rebase, acoplado con

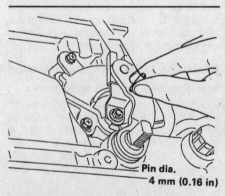

3.8d Cuando esté ajustando el interruptor inhibidor en los modelos 1987 y 1988 de 4WD usted debe ser capaz de meter una clavija, varilla o pedazo de alambre delgado a través de ambos el interruptor y la palanca de cambio manual de la transmisión automática (asegúrese que la palanca está lo más vertical que sea posible)

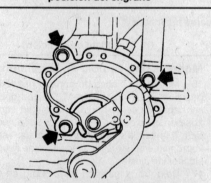

3.8b . . . afloje los pernos de retención para el interruptor inhibidor(flechas) - (se muestra el interruptor para los modelos 1987/1988 de 4WD - otros pernos para los interruptores son similares) . . .

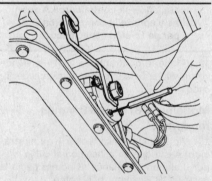

3.8c . . . y con una varilla de alineación o pedazo de alambre (2 mm o 0.079 pulgadas de diámetro), mueva el interruptor hasta que la clavija caiga en el orificio en el rotor y apriete los pernos y la acoplación igualmente

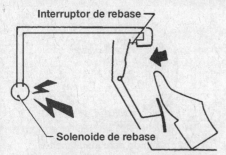

Interruptor de rebase

Solenoide de rebase

4.3 El interruptor del rebase para las transmisiones 1980 al 1985, localizado en el poste superior del pedal del acelerador, energiza el solenoide de rebase cuando el pedal del acelerador es completamente deprimido, proveyendo poder adicional para poder rebasar - para chequear el interruptor, prenda el interruptor de la ignición (con el motor apagado), presione el pedal del acelerador completamente y escuche cuidadosamente por un sonido apenas antes de que el pedal llegue al fondo

el solenoide de rebase, causa que la transmisión cambie a rebase cuando el pedal del acelerador es completamente deprimido. Esto proporciona el poder adicional para rebasar. Si la transmisión no cambia a rebase con el acelerador completamente abierto, el sistema debe ser inspeccionado.

2 Con el motor apagado, pero la ignición Encendida, presione el pedal del acelerador completamente y escuche por un sonido apenas antes de que el pedal llegue al fondo.

3 Si ningún sonido es oído, localice el interruptor de rebase en el poste superior del

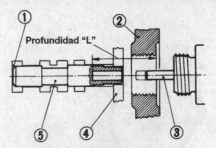

Profundidad "L"

5.4 Refiérase a esta ilustración cuando instale la varilla del diafragma

1 Note el cuerpo de válvula sellado
2 Pared del caso de la transmisión
3 Varilla del diafragma
4 Plato lateral del cuerpo de válvulas
5 Válvula para el acelerador de vacío

pedal del acelerador (vea ilustración). Afloje la contratuerca y con el pedal todavía presionado, extienda el interruptor hasta que haga contacto con el poste y haga un chasquido. El interruptor debe chasquear solamente cuando el pedal llega al fondo. Si chasquea demasiado pronto, causará que la transmisión cambie a rebase con el acelerador parcialmente abierto.

4 Apriete la contratuerca y chequee el ajuste.

5 Si el ajuste del interruptor de rebase está correcto pero la transmisión todavía no rebasa, chequee que le esté llegando corriente al interruptor y con un probador de continuidad, chequee que la corriente esté pasando a través del interruptor.

6 Si el interruptor chequea bien, pero el problema persiste, lleve el vehículo a un con-

cesionario y haga que el solenoide de rebase sea chequeado y reemplazado si es necesario. Probar los circuitos de rebase requiere equipos especializados y está más allá del alcance del mecánico del hogar.

5 Varilla para el diafragma de vacío - ajuste

Refiérase a la ilustración 5.4

1 El diafragma de vacío y la longitud de su varilla afectan los patrones de cambio de la transmisión. Si la transmisión no está cambiando precisamente en los puntos correctos, una varilla diferente del diafragma de vacío tendrá que ser instalada.

2 Desconecte la manguera de vacío del diafragma de vacío en el interior izquierdo de la transmisión.

3 Remueva el diafragma de vacío.

4 Esté seguro que el acelerador es empujado adentro del cuerpo de la válvula tan afuera como sea posible y mida la posición L (vea ilustración) con un medidor de la profundidad.

5 Una vez que esta medida sea tomada, use el diagrama de abajo para determinar la longitud correcta de la varilla del diafragma de vacío.

6 Sello trasero del aceite - reemplazo

Refiérase a las ilustraciones 6.2 y 6.3

1 Remueva el eje propulsor (Capítulo 8). En los modelos de 4WD remueva la caja de transferencia (Capítulo 9).

2 Tenga cuidado de no dañar el albergue del eje de salida ni la transmisión, use un destornillador para hacerle palanca hacia afuera al sello viejo (vea ilustración).

3 Aplique una capa de aceite de engrane al labio del sello nuevo y presiónelo en su posición usando un dado del tamaño apropiado (vea ilustración).

Medido de la profundidad L Mm (pulgada)	*Longitud de la varilla Mm (pulgada)*
Debajo 25.55 (1.0059)	29.0 (1.142)
25.65 a 26.05 (1.0098 a 1.0256)	29.5 (1.161)
26.15 a 26.55 (1.0295 a 1.0453)	30.0 (1.181)
26.65 a 27.05 (1.0492 a 1.0650)	30.5 (1.201)
Sobre 27.15 (1.0689)	31.0 (1.220)

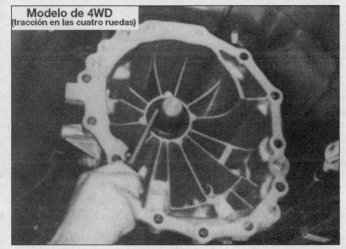

Modelo de 4WD (tracción en las cuatro ruedas)

6.2 Hágale palanca hacia afuera al sello de aceite viejo con un destornillador - tenga cuidado de no dañar el diámetro de los cilindros para el sello (se muestra un modelo de 4WD)

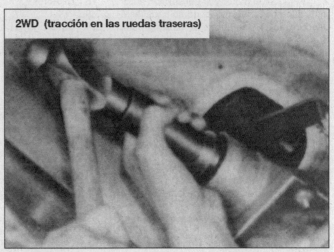

2WD (tracción en las ruedas traseras)

6.3 Para instalar el sello nuevo, cubra la orilla exterior y los labios del sello con aceite de engrane y presiónelo en su posición con un dado del tamaño apropiado

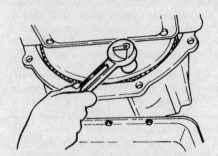

7.17 Para remover los pernos del plato flexible al convertidor de torque, gire el cigüeñal y remueva los pernos según ellos se observan en la parte inferior

4   Vuelva a instalar el eje propulsor (Capítulo 8) y en los modelos de 4WD, la caja de transferencia (Capítulo 9).

7   Transmisión automática - remover e instalar

Refiérase a las ilustraciones 7.17, 7.24, 7.25 y 7.27

Nota: *Debido a la complejidad de la transmisión automática y el equipo especial necesario para otorgarle servicio, una reconstrucción completa de la transmisión automática no es práctico que sea realizada por el mecánico de hogar. Sin embargo, considerable dinero se puede ahorrar usted, removiendo e instalando la transmisión usted mismo. Lea esta Sección para que usted se familiarice con los procedimientos y las herramientas necesarias para el trabajo. El vehículo debe ser elevado lo suficientemente alto para poder bajar la transmisión y deslizarla hacia afuera por debajo del vehículo.*

1   Antes de remover la transmisión, haga que el vehículo sea chequeado y diagnosticado por un especialista calificado en transmisiones, para que él pueda determinar la naturaleza y la causa del problema.
2   Remover el motor y la transmisión automática como una unidad combinada está descrito en el Capítulo 2 de este manual. Dónde sea decidido de remover la transmisión dejando el motor en posición en el vehículo, proceda como sigue:
3   Desconecte el cable negativo de la terminal negativa de la batería.
4   Drene el flúido de la transmisión (Capítulo 1).
5   Levante el vehículo a una altura de trabajo adecuada y sopórtelo firmemente sobre estantes.
6   Remueva el eje propulsor (vea Capítulo 8). Mientras esto se hace, tape o cubra la abertura en la parte trasera de la transmisión para prevenir fugas de aceite.
7   Remueva el tubo de escape delantero (vea Capítulo 4).
8   Remueva el conector eléctrico del interruptor inhibidor.
9   Remueva el conector eléctrico del solenoide de rebase.

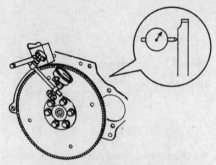

7.24 Si usted está reemplazando el convertidor de torque, o si es removido por cualquier razón, prepare un medidor de esfera y mida la medida de desviación del plato flexible - si la desviación excede el máximo admisible especificado, reemplace el plato flexible

10   Desconecte el tubo de vacío de la cápsula de vacío (si está equipado con uno) localizado apenas adelante del solenoide de rebase.
11   Separe la palanca del selector de acoplamiento afuera del selector.
12   Desconecte el cable del velocímetro del albergue de la extensión trasera.
13   Desconecte los tubos de enfriamiento para el flúido. Tape la abertura.
14   Desconecte los tubos de enfriamiento de la extensión trasera.
15   Sostenga la cacerola de aceite del motor con un gato y use un bloque de madera para prevenir dañar la superficie de la cacerola del aceite.
16   Remueva la tapa de la mitad inferior del albergue del convertidor de torque y el plato flexible y marque sus posiciones con relación el uno con el otro para el reemplazo exacto.
17   Destornille y remueva los cuatro pernos **(vea ilustración)** que aseguran el convertidor de torque al plato flexible. Acceso a cada uno de estos pernos es obtenido girando el motor lentamente, usando una herramienta en el perno de la polea del cigüeñal.
18   Destornille y remueva el motor de arranque.
19   Sostenga la transmisión con un gato (preferiblemente uno que se pueda rodar).
20   Remueva los pernos que aseguran los calzos del soporte de la transmisión en la transmisión.
21   Remueva los calzos de soporte de la transmisión de la carrocería.
22   Destornille y remueva los pernos que aseguran la transmisión al motor.
23   Baje los dos gatos lo suficientemente para permitir que la transmisión sea retirada por debajo y hacia la parte trasera del vehículo. Se requerirá probablemente la ayuda de un ayudante debido al peso de la transmisión automática. Si una transmisión automática está en la necesidad de reparación menor, llévela a su concesionario Nissan u otro especialista calificado en transmisiones. Si es necesario una reconstrucción completa, pueda que sea más económico reemplazar la transmisión vieja con una reconstruida.

7.25 Cuando esté instalando el convertidor de torque, esté seguro de alinear la mella en el convertidor con la pestaña en la bomba de aceite adentro de la transmisión

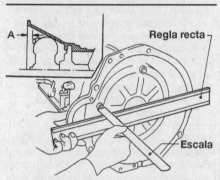

7.27 Después que instale el convertidor de torque, mida la distancia "A" y compare su medida con la distancia especificada para su transmisión

24   Si el convertidor de torque es removido, mida la desviación del plato flexible **(vea ilustración)**. Si la desviación excede el máximo admisible especificado, reemplace el plato flexible (vea Capítulo 2).
25   La instalación se hace en el orden inverso al procedimiento de desensamble pero si el convertidor de torque ha sido separado del ensamblaje principal, asegúrese que la mella en el convertidor está alineada correctamente con la bomba de aceite en la transmisión **(vea ilustración)**.
26   Cuando esté atornillando el convertidor de torque al plato flexible, esté seguro que las marcas hechas durante el periodo de remover están alineadas.
27   Después de instalar el convertidor de torque a la posición de la distancia medida "A" en la transmisión **(vea ilustración)** para chequear que el convertidor de torque esté correctamente instalado.
28   Apriete todos los pernos al par de torsión especificado.
29   Una vez que el convertidor esté instalado y los pernos estén apretados, gire el cigüeñal varias vueltas para asegurarse de que la transmisión gira libremente sin ninguna obstrucción.
30   Llene la transmisión con el grado correcto del flúido y la cantidad (vea Capítulo 1).
31   Después de volver a instalar la transmisión chequee la operación del interruptor inhibidor, el acoplamiento del selector y ajústelo según sea necesario.

Capítulo 8
Embrague y línea de transmisión

Contenidos

Especificaciones

Embrague

Desviación del disco..	0.040 pulgada (1.0 mm)
Disparejo máximo del plato de presión altura máxima para el resorte del diafragma.....................................	0.020 pulgada (0.5 mm)

Especificaciones técnicas — Pies-libras

Pernos del volante al plato de presión	
1980 al 1983...	12 a 15
1984 en adelante..	16 a 22
Pernos de afianzamiento del cilindro maestro del embrague	6 a 9
Pernos de afianzamiento del cilindro de liberación.........................	22 a 30
Pernos de afianzamiento para la cubierta del cilindro amortiguador......	3 a 4

Eje propulsor

Límite de desviación	0.024 pulgada (0.6 mm)
Límite axial del juego del muñón	0.008 pulgada (0.2 mm)

Anillo de tipo retención para la universal

Hasta 1990
0.0587 pulgada (1.49 mm)
0.0598 pulgada (1.52 mm)
0.0610 pulgada (1.55 mm)
0.0622 pulgada (1.58 mm)
0.0634 pulgada (1.61 mm)
0.0646 pulgada (1.64 mm)
0.0657 pulgada (1.67 mm)
0.0787 pulgada (2.00 mm)
0.0795 pulgada (2.02 mm)
0.0803 pulgada (2.04 mm)
0.0811 pulgada (2.06 mm)
0.0819 pulgada (2.08 mm)
0.0827 pulgada (2.10 mm)
0.0835 pulgada (2.12 mm)

1991 y más moderno
0.0783 pulgada (1.99 mm)
0.0795 pulgada (2.02 mm)
0.0807 pulgada (2.05 mm)
0.0819 pulgada (2.08 mm)
0.0831 pulgada (2.11 mm)
0.0843 pulgada (2.14 mm)
0.0854 pulgada (2.17 mm)
0.0866 pulgada (2.20 mm)

Especificaciones técnicas — Pies-libras

Pernos del eje propulsor al diferencial

2WD

1980 al 1985	17 a 24
1986 en adelante	29 a 33
4WD - eje propulsor trasero (ambas puntas)	58 a 65

Primer eje a los segundos pernos de la brida del eje

2WD	25 a 33
4WD	58 a 65

Contratuerca central del balero

1980 al 1985 (2 y 4 WD)

Tipo de la brida	181 a 217
Tipo de tuerca y arandela	145 a 174

1986 en adelante

2WD	181 a 217
4WD	174 a 203
Pernos del soporte central del balero al chasis	12 a 16

Diferencial y eje trasero

Precarga del piñón impulsor (con el sello instalado)

H190A	9.5 a 13.9 pulgada-libras (1.1 a 1.6 Nm)
C200	9.5 a 14.8 pulgada-libras (1.1 a 1.7 Nm)
H233B	4.3 a 8.7 pulgada-libras (0.5 a 1.0 Nm)

Juego libre del eje trasero

Modelos con frenos de tambor trasero	0.0008 a 0.0059 pulgada (0.02 a 0.15 mm)
Modelos con frenos de disco traseros	0 pulgada (0 mm)

Espesor de las láminas de ajuste del eje trasero
0.0020 pulgada (0.05 mm)
0.0028 pulgada (0.07 mm)
0.0039 pulgada (0.10 mm)
0.0059 pulgada (0.15 mm)
0.0079 pulgada (0.20 mm)
0.0197 pulgada (0.50 mm)
0.0394 pulgada (1.00 mm)

Juego libre del balero de la rueda (cubo) (con dobles neumáticos)	0.0031 pulgada (0.08 mm) el máximo.
Precarga del balero de la rueda (con sellos de grasa nuevos)	4.6 a 8.2 libras (20.6 a 36.6 N)

Especificaciones técnicas — Pies-libras

Tuerca del piñón impulsor

H190A y C200	94 a 217
H233B	145 a 181
Tuerca prisionera para el balero de la rueda (con dobles neumáticos)	123 a 145
Eje al cubo de la rueda (con dobles neumáticos)	42 a 55
Pernos de afianzamiento del diferencial	16

1 Embrague - información general

Peligro: *El polvo producido por el sistema de embrague puede contener asbesto que es dañino para la salud. Nunca lo sople con aire comprimido ni lo inhale. Cuando usted esté trabajando en el sistema de embrague usted debe utilizar una máscara filtrante aprobada. No utilice, bajo ninguna circunstancia, solventes derivados del petróleo para limpiar las partes del sistema del embrague. Utilice solamente limpiador para sistemas de embrague o alcohol desnaturalizado! Después que los componentes para el embrague sean enjuagados séquelo con un trapo, esté seguro de deshacerse de los trapos y el limpiador contaminado en un recipiente cubierto y marcado.*

El embrague está localizado entre el motor y la transmisión y sus componentes principales son el disco del embrague, ensamblaje del plato de presión, buje piloto y balero de liberación. Otros componentes que arman el sistema de operación hidráulica del embrague son el pedal del embrague, el cilindro maestro del embrague, el cilindro de liberación, amortiguador del embrague (modelos 1984 y más modernos) y la palanca de liberación.

El disco del embrague es instalado como un emparedado entre el volante y el plato de presión y tiene un cubo con ranuras que se compromete y gira el eje de entrada de la transmisión. Cuando está comprometido, el plato de presión es sostenido contra el disco del embrague por la presión de los dedos y el disco del embrague, en cambio, es sostenido contra el volante.

El pedal del embrague es conectado al cilindro maestro del embrague por una varilla de empuje corta. El cilindro maestro y el depósito hidráulico están instalado en la pared contrafuego enfrente del chófer en el lado del motor.

Presionando el pedal del embrague mueve el pistón del cilindro maestro hacia adelante y fuerza el flúido hidráulico del embrague a través del tubo hidráulico al cilindro de liberación.

El pistón en el cilindro de liberación se mueve y acciona la palanca de liberación del embrague por medio de una varilla de empuje corta.

El otro final de la palanca de la liberación, localizada adentro del albergue del embrague es en forma de un tenedor. Este tenedor compromete el balero de liberación del embrague y fuerza el cojinete contra los dedos de liberación del ensamblaje del plato de presión. Cuando los dedos reciben la presión del balero de liberación ellos se retiran de la superficie de acoplamiento del plato de presión del disco del embrague, que libera el ensamblaje del embrague del volante.

Cuando los forros de fricción en el disco del embrague se desgastan, el plato de presión se mueve automáticamente más cerca del disco para compensar y eliminar la necesidad para el ajuste. **Nota:** *Porque el acceso al componente del embrague es difícil, en cualquier momento de que el motor o la transmisión sean removidos, el disco del embrague, ensamblaje del plato de presión y el balero de liberación se deben inspeccionar cuidadosamente y si es necesario, reemplazarlos. Debido a que el disco del embrague se desgasta más, debe ser reemplazado automaticamente si hay alguna duda acerca de su condición.*

2 Pedal del embrague - remover, instalación y ajuste

Refiérase a las ilustraciones 2.3a, 2.3b y 2.6

Remover

1   Desconecte la varilla de empuje del cilindro maestro del pedal haciéndole palanca a la clavija y removiendo la abrazadera que la retiene.
2   Remueva el perno de detención o interruptor del embrague de su soporte.
3   Hágale palanca al anillo E de la clavija del fulcro (modelos más antiguos). La clavija del fulcro en los modelos más modernos es asegurada con una tuerca y una arandela **(vea ilustraciones)**.
4   Remueva el pedal del embrague y el resorte de retorno.
5   Limpie las partes en solvente y reemplace cualquiera que esté dañada o excesivamente desgastada. El buje en el pedal es prensado y si está defectuoso, el pedal completo debe ser reemplazado con uno nuevo.

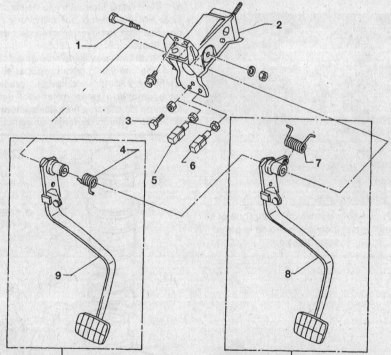

Sin resorte asistente para el embrague   Con resorte asistente para el embrague

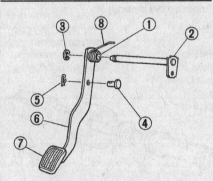

2.3a Detalles de como montar el pedal del embrague - modelos más antiguos

1   *Buje del pedal*
2   *Clavija del fulcro*
3   *Anillo E*
4   *Abrazadera de la clavija*
5   *Pasador de retención*
6   *Pedal del embrague*
7   *Almohadilla del pedal*
8   *Resorte de retorno*

2.3b Detalles de como montar el pedal del embrague - modelos más modernos (izquierdo - motor de cuatro-cilindros; derecho - motor V6)

1   *Clavija del fulcro*
2   *Soporte del pedal*
3   *Retenedor del pedal*
4   *Resorte de retorno*
5   *Interruptor del embrague*
6   *Interruptor para el control automático de la velocidad*
7   *Resorte de asistencia*
8   *Pedal del embrague*
9   *Pedal del embrague*

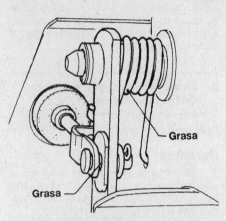

2.6 Grasa debe ser aplicada en los puntos mostrados durante la instalación del pedal del embrague

Instalación

6   La instalación se hace en el orden inverso al procedimiento de desensamble. **Nota:** *Durante la instalación, aplique grasa de uso múltiple al buje del pedal, clavija del resorte de retorno y el fulcro. También, cuando esté conectando la varilla de empuje del cilindro maestro al pedal, aplique una cantidad pequeña de grasa en la clavija* **(vea ilustración).**

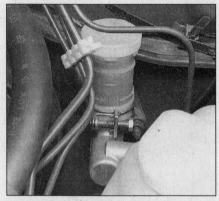

3.3 El cilindro maestro del embrague está conectado al lado izquierdo de la pared contrafuego

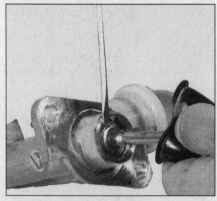

3.5 El anillo de detención puede ser removido con un destornillador estrecho

Ajuste

7   Siguiendo la instalación, chequee la altura y el juego libre del pedal del embrague y haga los ajustes necesarios como está descrito en el Capítulo 1.

---

3   Cilindro maestro del embrague - remover, chequeo e instalación

---

Refiérase a las ilustraciones 3.3, 3.5, 3.7 y 3.13
Caución: *El flúido de los frenos puede dañar sus ojos y dañar la superficie de la pintura, tenga extremo cuidado cuando lo esté manejando o vertiéndolo. No use flúido de frenos que haya permanecido abierto o tenga más de un año de edad. El flúido de frenos absorbe humedad del aire. El exceso de humedad puede ocasionar una pérdida peligrosa de la eficiencia del freno.*
1   Desconecte la varilla de empuje del cilindro maestro en el pedal del embrague.
2   Desconecte la línea de líquido del cilindro maestro y drene el flúido en un recipiente.
3   Remueva los pernos de afianzamiento de la brida del cilindro maestro y retírelo de la unidad en el compartimiento del motor **(vea ilustración).**
4   Drene todo el flúido del depósito y limpie toda la suciedad externa del cilindro.
5   Hale hacia atrás el fuelle de caucho flexible en el extremo del cilindro y hágale palanca para remover el anillo de retención **(vea ilustración).**
6   Remueva la varilla de empuje del cilindro.
7   Use una varilla para presionar el pistón adentro del cilindro y deténgalo presionado para remover el perno retenedor desde el fondo de los cilindros **(vea ilustración).**
8   Con el perno de retención removido, el

ensamblaje del pistón y el resorte pueden ser removidos. **Nota:** El pistón no está diseñado para ser desarmado.
9   A menos que esté dañado, no lo separe del depósito del cuerpo del cilindro, porque uno nuevo tendrá que ser instalado si el viejo es removido.
10   Examine la superficie interior del diámetro interior del cilindro. Si está rayado o exhibe áreas brillantes de desgaste, el cilindro maestro completo debe ser reemplazado.
11   Si el cilindro está en buena condición, obtenga un juego de reconstrucción para el cilindro maestro del embrague, que contiene todas las partes necesarias de reemplazo.
12   Antes de instalar cualquier parte, primero sumérjalas en flúido de freno para lubricarlas. **Nota:** No use otros solventes o lubricantes.
13   Si los sellos del pistón no están ya instalados en el pistón nuevo suministrado con el juego de reconstrucción, use sus dedos para manipularlos en sus ranuras. Esté seguro que el labio de la cara mira hacia la dirección apropiada **(vea ilustración).**
14   La instalación de las partes en el cilindro es el procedimiento reverso de como se removió.
15   La instalación del cilindro maestro es el procedimiento reverso de como se removió, pero chequee la altura del pedal y el juego libre como está descrito en el Capítulo 1 y purgue el sistema hidráulico (Sección 6).

---

4   Cilindro para operar el embrague - remover, chequeo e instalación

---

Refiérase a las ilustraciones 4.5, 4.6 y 4.11

Remover

1   Para prevenir la pérdida excesiva del flúido hidráulico, cuando la manguera del

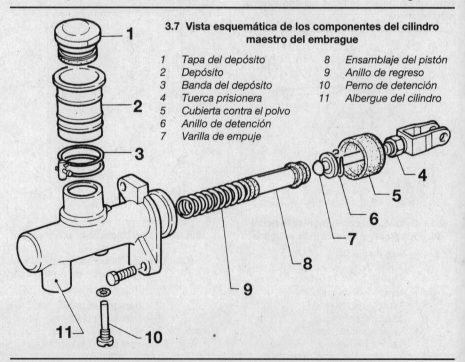

3.7 Vista esquemática de los componentes del cilindro maestro del embrague

1	Tapa del depósito	8	Ensamblaje del pistón
2	Depósito	9	Anillo de regreso
3	Banda del depósito	10	Perno de detención
4	Tuerca prisionera	11	Albergue del cilindro
5	Cubierta contra el polvo		
6	Anillo de detención		
7	Varilla de empuje		

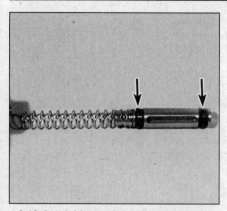

3.13 Los labios en los sellos del pistón (flechas) deben mirar en la dirección mostrada

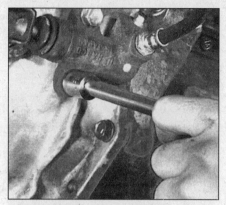

4.5 El cilindro de liberación del embrague está localizado en el lado derecho de la campana de la transmisión

11   Instale el sello nuevo usando solamente sus dedo para manipularlo en su posición. Esté seguro que la cara del labio mira en la dirección apropiada (**vea ilustración**).

12   Moje el ensamblaje del pistón en fluído de freno limpio antes de instalarlo y antes de instalar el resorte en el cilindro.

13   Vuelva a instalar el tornillo de purgar.

14   Complete el ensamble instalando la varilla de empuje y la tapa de polvo. Esté seguro que la tapa para el polvo esté asegurada en el albergue de los cilindros.

Instalación

15   La instalación se hace en el orden inverso al procedimiento de desensamble pero purgue el sistema hidráulico como está descrito en la Sección 6.

cilindro de liberación es desconectada, remueva la tapa del depósito y coloque un pedazo de plástico en el depósito abierto. Entonces enrosque la tapa de regreso. Esto creará un vacío que detendrá que el fluído corra hacia afuera de la manguera abierta.

2   Afloje la tuerca de la línea del embrague

en el soporte instalado en la parte lateral del cilindro.

3   Remueva el clip de enclavamiento del soporte y afloje la manguera.

4   Remueva la manguera del embrague del cilindro de liberación.

5   Remueva los dos pernos que aseguran el cilindro de liberación al albergue del embrague (**vea ilustración**). El cilindro de liberación ahora puede ser removido.

Chequeo

6   Hale hacia afuera la tapa contra polvo y la varilla de empuje, entonces péguele suavemente al cilindro con un bloque de madera para extraer el pistón y el resorte (**vea ilustración**).

7   Remueva el tornillo de purgar.

8   Examine las superficies del pistón y el cilindro por rayones o áreas brillantes de desgaste. Si alguno es encontrado, tire el cilindro y compre uno nuevo.

9   Si los componentes están en buenas condiciones, lávelos en fluído de freno limpio, remueva el sello y tírelo, notando cuidadosamente de que manera el labio del sello mira.

10   Obtenga un juego de reparación que contiene todos los artículos nuevos necesarios.

5   Amortiguador del embrague - remover, chequeo e instalación

Refiérase a las ilustraciones 5.1, 5.3a y 5.3b

Remover

1   Usando una llave para tuerca de tubería, desconecte las dos líneas hidráulicas del amortiguador (**vea ilustración**). Tenga abundante trapos disponibles para limpiar el derramamiento y taponé las líneas después de desconectarlas.

2   Remueva los dos tornillos y separe el amortiguador.

Chequeo

Nota: *Compre un juego de reconstrucción, que contenga todas las partes necesarias de reemplazo.*

3   Remueva los pernos y separe la tapa. Remueva las partes restantes, usando los dibujos que acompañan como referencia (**vea ilustraciones**).

4   Limpie todas las partes con fluído de

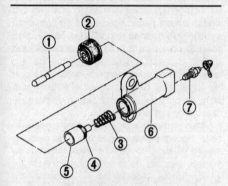

4.6 Vista esquemática del cilindro de liberación del embrague

1   Varilla de empuje
2   Tapa contra el polvo
3   Resorte del pistón
4   Pistón
5   Copilla del pistón
6   Cilindro de liberación
7   Tornillo de purgar

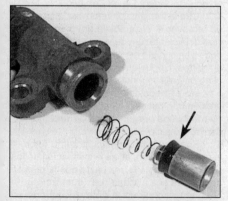

4.11 El labio en el pistón del cilindro de liberación (flecha) debe mirar en la dirección mostrada

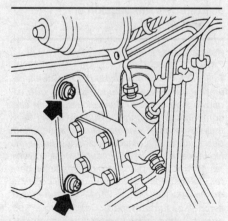

5.1 El amortiguador del embrague está conectado a la pared contrafuego con dos tornillos (flechas)

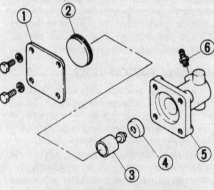

5.3a Vista esquemática del amortiguador del embrague (estilo más antiguo)

1   La tapa del amortiguador
2   Caucho del amortiguador
3   Pistón
4   Copilla del pistón
5   Cilindro
6   Tornillo de purgar

freno limpio o alcohol desnaturalizado. No use solventes basados en petróleo.

5   Chequee el cilindro y el pistón por marcas de arañazos u oxidación. Si alguno es encontrado, el amortiguador tendrá que ser reemplazado con uno nuevo.

6   Chequee que el juego libre entre el cilindro y el pistón. Si es más de 0.0059 pulgada (0.15 mm), el pistón o el amortiguador tendrán que ser reemplazados con partes nuevas para obtener el espacio libre apropiado.

7   Durante el periodo de ensamblaje, moje la copilla del pistón nuevo, el pistón y el cilindro con flúido de freno limpio. Use las partes nuevas que vinieron con el juego de reconstrucción y ponga atención a la dirección instalada de todas las partes de caucho.

Instalación

8   Instale el amortiguador en el orden inverso de como se removió.

9   Purgue el sistema del embrague como está descrito en la Sección 6.

10   Ajuste la altura del pedal del embrague y el juego libre del pedal, refiriéndose a los procedimientos en el Capítulo 1.

---

6   Embrague, sistema hidráulico - purgar

Caución: *El flúido de los frenos puede dañar sus ojos y dañar la superficie de la pintura, tenga extremo cuidado cuando lo esté manejando o vertiéndolo. No use flúido de frenos que haya permanecido abierto o tengan más de un año de edad. El flúido de frenos absorbe humedad del aire. El exceso de humedad puede ocasionar una pérdida peligrosa de la eficiencia del freno.*

1   Purgar será requerido siempre que el sistema hidráulico se haya desarmado y haya sido ensamblado y aire haya entrado en el sistema.

2   Llene primero el depósito de flúido con flúido de freno limpio que haya estado almacenado en un recipiente hermético. Nunca use flúido que se haya drenado del sistema ni se haya purgado en una ocasión previa, puede contener granos de suciedad.

Modelos 1980 al 1983

3   Ponga un pedazo de caucho o tubo plástico en el tornillo de purgar en el cilindro de liberación y sumerja el extremo abierto del tubo en un recipiente de vidrio conteniendo una o dos pulgadas de flúido de freno.

4   Abra el tornillo de purgar acerca de media vuelta y haga que un ayudante presione rápidamente el pedal del embrague completamente. Apriete el tornillo de purgar y entonces libere lentamente el pedal del embrague hasta que el pedal esté completamente removido. Repita esta secuencia de operaciones hasta que las burbujas de aire no sean expulsadas más del final del tubo abierto en el frasco del flúido.

5   Después de dos o tres carreras del pedal, chequee que el nivel del flúido en el

depósito no se haya bajado demasiado. Manténgalo lleno de flúido fresco, de otro modo aire otra vez será absorbido en el sistema.

6   Apriete el tornillo de purgar hacia abajo (no lo sobre apriete), remueva el tubo de caucho y el frasco, llene el depósito hasta el máximo e instale la tapa.

7   Si la ayuda de un ayudante no está disponible, la alternativa de una operación de "un hombre" puede ser conducida usando un tubo de purga acoplado con una válvula unilateral o un juego de purgar con presión, ambos deben ser usados de acuerdo con las instrucciones del fabricante.

Modelos 1984 y más modernos

8   Siga el procedimiento de encima, pero antes de purgar el cilindro de liberación el amortiguador del embrague debe ser purgado.

---

7   Componentes del embrague - remover, inspección e instalación

---

Refiérase a las ilustraciones 7.6, 7.7, 7.9 y 7.15

Peligro: *El polvo producido por el sistema de embrague puede contener asbesto que es dañino para la salud. Nunca lo sople con aire comprimido ni lo inhale. Cuando usted esté trabajando en el sistema de embrague usted debe utilizar una máscara filtrante aprobada. No utilice, bajo ninguna circunstancia, solventes derivados de petróleo para limpiar las partes del sistema del embrague. Utilice solamente limpiador para sistemas de embrague o alcohol desnaturalizado! Después que los componentes del embrague sean enjuagados séquelo con un trapo, esté seguro de deshacerse de los trapos y el limpiador contaminado en un recipiente cubierto y marcado.*

5.3b Vista esquemática del amortiguador del embrague (estilo más moderno)

1   *Cubierta para amortiguador*
2   *Junta*
3   *Cuerpo del cilindro*
4   *Tornillo para la purga*
5   *Superficie de fricción para el ensamblaje del pistón*
6   *Resorte*
7   *Copilla del pistón*
8   *Ensamblaje del pistón*
9   *Superficie de contacto para el ensamblaje del pistón*
10   *Caucho de amortiguación*

1   Debido a las calidades de desgaste despacio del embrague, no es fácil de decidir cuando hacer el trabajo de remover la transmisión para chequear el desgaste del forro de fricción. La única indicación positiva que algo debe ser hecho es cuando se comienza a resbalar o cuando ruidos en el proceso de acoplación indica que los forros de fricción se han desgastado hasta el remache. En tales casos se puede esperar solamente que las superficies de fricción en el volante y el plato de presión no hayan sido muy desgastadas ni hayan sido rayadas.

2   Un embrague se desgasta de acuerdo de la manera se haya usado. Mucho resbalamiento intencional del embrague mientras se maneja - en vez de la selección correcta de los engranes - acelerará el desgaste. Es seguro de asumir, sin embargo, que el disco del embrague necesitará reemplazo alrededor de 40,000 millas (64,000 km).

3   A causa de la ubicación del embrague entre el motor y la transmisión, el embrague no puede ser trabajado sin remover el motor o la transmisión. Si las reparaciones que requieren remover el motor es necesario, la manera más rápida de obtener acceso al embrague es removiendo la transmisión, como está descrito en el Capítulo 7.

4   Con la transmisión removida, pero antes de remover el ensamblaje del plato de presión del volante, chequee que ninguno de los dedos en el plato de presión estén torcidos o doblados. Si cualquier daño es evidente, el plato de presión tendrá que ser reemplazado.

5   No es necesario de marcar el plato de presión con relación al volante, porque solamente puede ser instalado de una manera debido a las clavijas de posición.

6   En un patrón diagonal, para no retorcer el plato de presión, afloje la instalación de los pernos un poco a la vez hasta que la presión del resorte sea aliviada **(vea ilustración)**. Si el volante comienza a girar, inserción un destornillador a través de la abertura del motor de arranque y lo compromete con los dientes del volante.

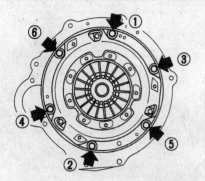

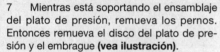

7.6 Los pernos de afianzamiento del plato de presión deben ser aflojados y deben ser apretados en un patrón cruzado, un poco a la vez, para evitar abalear el plato de presión

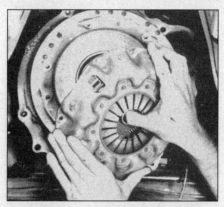

7.7 Después de remover los pernos, separe el disco del plato de presión y el embrague

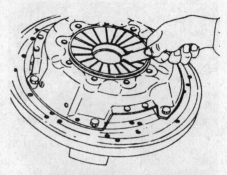

7.9 Use un calibrador al tacto para chequear que tan disparejo están los dedos del resorte del diafragma del embrague

7   Mientras está soportando el ensamblaje del plato de presión, remueva los pernos. Entonces remueva el disco del plato de presión y el embrague **(vea ilustración)**.

8   Limpie el plato de presión, superficie de acoplamiento del volante y la superficie exterior del retenedor del balero para remover cualquier aceite y grasa.

9   Examine la superficie del plato de presión donde hace contacto con el disco del embrague. Esta superficie debe estar lisa, sin rayones, arañazos o alabeo. Chequee la tapa del plato de presión y los dedos por daño. Use un calibrador al tacto para medir el disparejo del resorte del diafragma a su altura y chequee que esté adentro del límite, como está mostrado en las especificaciones **(vea ilustración)**. Si algún defecto es encontrado con el ensamblaje del plato de presión, debe ser reemplazado con una unidad completa.

10   Inspeccione el disco del embrague por desgaste del forro. Chequee por remaches o resortes flojos o rotos. A causa de la dificultad de alcanzar el embrague, si el forro del plato de fricción no tiene por lo menos 1/32 pulgada (0.8 mm) encima del remache, el disco debe ser reemplazado con uno nuevo. Si el material del forro muestra signos de separación o áreas negras donde la contaminación de grasa ha ocurrido, deben ser reemplazados también. Si hay cualquier duda, reemplácelo.

11   Inspeccione la superficie del volante por ranuras del remache, áreas quemadas o rayones. Si el daño es leve, el volante puede ser removido y rectificado usando un torno. Si el daño es profundo, el volante debe ser reemplazado. Chequee que los dientes de la corona dentada no estén rotos, agrietados ni gravemente quemados. Refiérase al Capítulo 2 para el procedimiento de remover el volante.

12   Si algunos indicios de aceite son detectado en los componentes del embrague la fuente se debe encontrar y debe ser eliminada. Si aceite está proviniendo desde el centro del volante, esto indica un fracaso en el sello de aceite trasero del cigüeñal (Capítulo 2). Aceite en el ensamblaje trasero del embrague puede indicar la necesidad de reemplazar el sello del eje de entrada de la transmisión (Capítulo 7).

13   Mientras le esté otorgando servicios a estos componentes del embrague, es también una buena idea de reemplazar el balero de liberación al mismo tiempo. Refiérase a la Sección 8. Chequee también el buje piloto por rayones y desgaste en general, reemplácelo si es necesario (Sección 9).

14   Antes de la instalación, aplique una capa delgada de grasa de base moly a las estrías del eje de entrada de la transmisión. Remueva cualquier exceso de grasa.

15   Para instalar el embrague, detenga el disco y el plato de presión juntos contra el volante y meta una herramienta de alineación en el centro entre ellos. Debido a que el eje de entrada de la transmisión debe pasar a través del centro de estos componentes, ellos deben ser alineados apropiadamente durante la instalación de la transmisión. Si una herramienta de alineación no está disponible en un tamaño apropiado, un dado en una extensión de una matraca trabaja también **(vea ilustración)**.

16   Localice el plato de presión del embrague para que la tapa acople con las clavijas e instale los pernos de afianzamiento. Apriételos en varios pasos, siguiendo un patrón de cruce, hasta que ellos estén todos al par de torsión especificado **(vea ilustración 7.6)**.

17   Instale la transmisión.

8   Balero de liberación - reemplazo

Refiérase a las ilustraciones 8.4, 8.6, 8.7, 8.9 y 8.11

1   El balero de liberación sellado, aunque es diseñado para una vida larga, vale reemplazarlo al mismo tiempo que los otros componentes del embrague van a ser reemplazados o servicio otorgado.

2   La deterioración del balero de liberación se debe sospechar cuando hay signos de fuga de grasa o la unidad está ruidosa cuando se gira con los dedos.

3   Remueva la tapa de caucho contra el polvo que rodea la palanca de liberación en la abertura de la campana.

4   Usando un destornillador, desganche y separe el resorte retenedor del pivote de bola

7.15 Antes de apretar los pernos del plato de presión debe de ser centrado con una herramienta de alineación (disponible en la mayoría de las refaccionarías) o una extensión y un dado como está mostrado

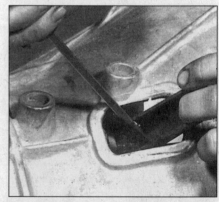

8.4 Un destornillador se puede usar para liberar el resorte en la palanca de liberación del pivote de bola

en la campana **(vea ilustración)**.

5   Remueva la palanca.

6   El balero de liberación del embrague y el ensamblaje del cubo ahora pueden ser removidos **(vea ilustración)**. **Nota:** *Chequee que la palanca no se ha agrietado ni doblado. Gire lentamente la cara delantera del balero de liberación, asegúrese que gira libremente y sin ningún ruido. El balero de liberación está prelubricado y no debe ser lavado en solvente. Cuando un embrague nuevo es insta-*

8.6 El balero de liberación y el cubo son removidos del eje de entrada como un ensamblaje

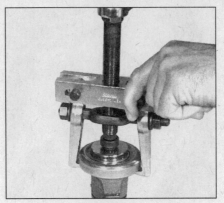

8.7 Un extractor es necesario para separar el balero de liberación del cubo

8.11 Cuando está apropiadamente instalada, la palanca de liberación se debe comprometer con el resorte del balero de liberación

lado, un balero de liberación nuevo debe siempre ser usado.

7   Si es necesario, remueva el balero de liberación del cubo con un extractor de dos o tres mandíbulas **(vea ilustración)**.

8   Prense en el balero nuevo, pero aplique presión solamente a la pista de rodamiento central.

9   El ensamblaje se hace en el orden inverso al procedimiento de desensamble. Aplique grasa de alta temperatura al receso interno del cubo del balero de liberación **(vea ilustración)**.

10   Aplique también grasa similar a los puntos del pivote de la palanca del embrague, la superficie que se desliza de la manga del cojinete y las estrías en el engranaje principal de impulsión de la transmisión. **Nota:** *Aplique solamente una capa delgada de grasa a estos puntos, porque mucha grasa se correrá al forro de fricción cuando esté caliente, causando daño a las superficies del disco del embrague.*

11   Cuando esté instalando la palanca de liberación del balero, asegúrese que los resortes de retención del balero de liberación están enganchados en las puntas de la palanca de liberación **(vea ilustración)**.

9.9 . . . o usted puede empacar el receso atrás del cojinete con grasa gruesa y lo fuerza hacia afuera hidráulicamente con una varilla de acero levemente más pequeña que el diámetro del buje piloto - cuando el martillo golpee la varilla, el buje se saldrá hacia afuera del cigüeñal

9   Buje piloto - reemplazo

Refiérase a las ilustraciones 9.5, 9.9 y 9.10

1   El buje piloto del embrague es un cojinete impregnado con aceite que es prensado en la parte trasera del cigüeñal. Su propósito primario es de sostener el frente del eje de entrada de la transmisión. El buje piloto se debe inspeccionar cuando los componentes del embrague son removidos del motor. Debido a su inaccesibilidad, si usted está dudoso acerca de su condición, reemplácelo con uno nuevo. **Nota:** *Si el motor ha sido removido del vehículo, ignore los siguientes pasos que no aplican.*

2   Remueva la transmisión (refiérase al Capítulo 7 Parte A).

3   Remueva los componentes del embrague (Sección 3).

4   Usando un trapo limpio, limpie el cojinete e inspecciónelo por cualquier desgaste excesivo, rayones o daños obvios. Una linterna será útil para dirigir la luz en el receso.

5   Remoción puede ser hecho con un extractor especial **(vea ilustración)**, pero un método alternativo trabaja también muy bien.

6   Encuentre una barra sólida de acero que sea levemente más pequeña en diámetro que el cojinete. Las alternativas a una barra sólida serían una clavija de madera o un dado con un perno fijado en su posición para hacerlo sólido.

7   Chequee el ataque de la barra - debe de apenas resbalarse en el cojinete con muy poquito espacio libre.

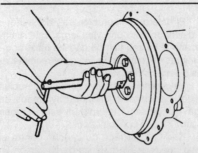

9.5 Un extractor especial es disponible para remover el buje piloto del final del cigüeñal . . .

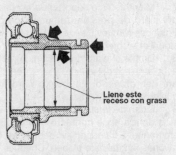

Llene este receso con grasa

8.9 Empaque el receso del balero de liberación con grasa y aplique una capa ligera de grasa a los puntos indicados por las flechas

8   Empaque el cojinete y el área atrás de él (receso en el cigüeñal) con grasa gruesa. Empáquelo apretadamente para eliminar la mayor cantidad de aire como sea posible.

9   Insercióne la barra en el orificio para el cojinete y martille en la barra, que forzará la grasa en la parte trasera del cojinete y empújela hacia afuera **(vea ilustración)**. Remueva el cojinete y limpie toda la grasa del receso del cigüeñal.

10   Usando un dado del tamaño apropiado o un pedazo de tubo, presione el cojinete nuevo en el orificio hasta que el final exterior del cojinete sea 0.157 pulgada (4.0 mm) de la superficie exterior de la brida del cigüeñal **(vea ilustración)**.

11   Vuelva a instalar el ensamblaje del embrague y la transmisión.

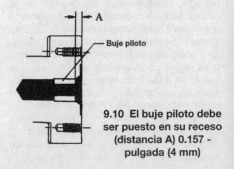

A — Buje piloto

9.10 El buje piloto debe ser puesto en su receso (distancia A) 0.157 - pulgada (4 mm)

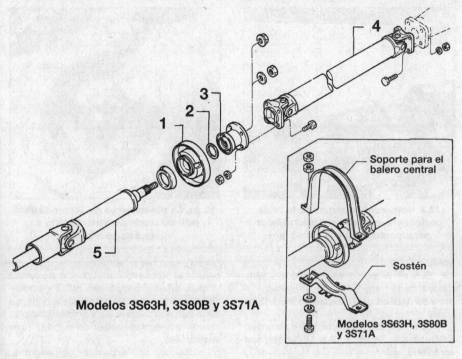

Modelos 3S63H, 3S80B y 3S71A

Soporte para el balero central

Sostén

Modelos 3S63H, 3S80B y 3S71A

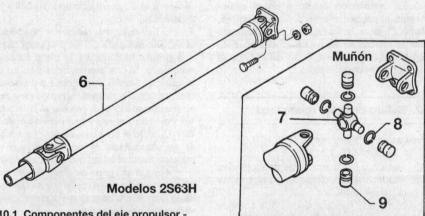

Modelos 2S63H

Muñón

10.1 Componentes del eje propulsor - vista esquemática (típica)

1 Balero central
2 Arandela
3 Acompañante de la brida
4 Segundo tubo del eje propulsor

5 Primer tubo del eje propulsor
6 Ensamblaje del eje propulsor
7 Cruceta
8 Resorte de retención
9 balero

11.2 Brida trasera del eje propulsor y la brida del piñón del diferencial se deben marcar antes de separarlos

11.3 Un destornillador colocado en la junta universal detendrá que el eje propulsor gire mientras remueve los pernos

10   Eje propulsor, diferencial y eje trasero - información general

Refiérase a la ilustración 10.1
Nota: *La información del eje propulsor, diferencial y eje trasero en este Capítulo cubren los componentes usados en las camionetas de modelo de 2WD, el eje trasero y eje propulsor en los modelos de 4WD. Para información en los otros componentes usados en los modelos de 4WD, refiérase al Capítulo 9.*

Dos ejes propulsores diferentes son usados, dependiendo en el modelo. Los modelos de camas regulares que usan una transmisión manual, usan un eje propulsor de una pieza, que incorporan dos juntas universales, una en cada extremo del eje **(vea ilustración)**.

Todos los otros modelos usan ejes propulsores de dos piezas, que incorporan un cojinete central en la parte trasera del primer eje. Este eje propulsor usa tres juntas universales; una en el extremo de la transmisión, una atrás del balero central y una en la brida del diferencial. Todas las juntas universales son del tipo sólido y pueden ser reemplazadas separadamente del eje propulsor.

El eje propulsor es finamente balanceado durante la fabricación y cuando es removido o desarmado, debe ser vuelto a ensamblar y ser reinstalado en exacta la misma manera y posición como estaba originalmente, para evitar vibración excesiva.

El eje trasero es de un tipo semiflotante, teniendo una carcaza de diseño que parece un "banjo," que es sostenido en alineación apropiada por la suspensión trasera.

Instalado en el centro del eje trasero está el diferencial que transfiere la fuerza giratoria del eje propulsor a los ejes traseros, en que las ruedas traseras están instaladas.

Los ejes tienen estrías en sus extremos interiores para que entren en las estrías en los engranes laterales del diferencial; apoyo exterior para el eje es obtenido por el balero trasero de la rueda.

A causa de la complejidad y la naturaleza crítica de los ajustes del diferencial, también como el equipo especial necesario para realizar las operaciones, nosotros recomendamos que cualquier desensamble del diferencial sea hecho por el departamento de servicio de su concesionario Nissan o un taller de reparación calificado.

11   Eje propulsor - remover e instalar

Refiérase a las ilustraciones 11.2 y 11.3
1   Levante la parte trasera del vehículo y sosténgalo sobre estantes.
2   Marque las orillas de la brida trasera del eje propulsor y la brida del piñón del diferencial para que ellas puedan ser alineados durante la instalación **(vea ilustración)**.
3   Usando un destornillador colocado en la junta universal trasera para detener de que el eje gire, remueva los cuatro pernos que conectan la brida trasera con la brida del piñón **(vea ilustración)**.

**12.2 La parte delantera del eje propulsor
y la brida de acompañamiento se deben
marcar (flecha) antes de separarlas**

**12.3 Remueva los pernos de la brida
compañera, usando un destornillador
para mantener que el eje no gire**

**12.5a La contratuerca del balero central
está estacada para mantenerla de
que no se afloje**

4   En los ejes propulsores de tipo de dos piezas, mientras soporta el eje propulsor, remueva los dos pernos que conectan el soporte central del balero de apoyo a la carrocería.

5   Empuje el eje hacia adelante desconectando levemente las bridas traseras. Entonces baje el eje y cuidadosamente hálelo hacia atrás hasta que el extremo delantero finalmente se salga de la parte trasera de la transmisión.

6   Mientras el eje propulsor es removido, el eje trasero de la transmisión se debe cubrir o debe ser tapado para prevenir la pérdida de

aceite.

7   Si el eje propulsor es removido, la parte trasera de la transmisión se debe cubrir o debe ser tapada para prevenir la pérdida de aceite.

8   Si el eje propulsor se debe remover, refiérase a la Sección 12 o 13, según sea apropiado.

9   La instalación se hace en el orden inverso al procedimiento de desensamble. **Nota:** *Durante la instalación asegúrese de que las marcas en las bridas se alinean. Esté seguro de apretar las tuercas de la brida al par de torsión especificado.*

12   Balero central - reemplazo

Refiérase a las ilustraciones 12.2, 12.3, 12.5a, 12.5b, 12.6 y 12.11

1   Remueva las tuercas que aseguran las dos mitades del soporte de apoyo junto y las separa del eje propulsor.

2   Marque la relación de la brida compañera a la sección delantera del eje propulsor **(vea ilustración).**

3   Usando un destornillador largo colocado en la junta universal central para mantener el eje que no gire, remueva los cuatro pernos que conectan el eje propulsor a la brida compañera **(vea ilustración).**

4   Marque la brida compañera con relación a la hendidura en el eje roscado.

5   La tuerca central es estacada para prevenirla que se afloje **(vea ilustración).** Para removerla, use primero un punzón para golpear la estaca hacia afuera y la destornilla del eje. Para mantener la brida que no gire

obtenga una herramienta especial diseñada para este propósito o una puede ser hecha usando una barra de acero plana y pernos viejos insertados en las roscas de la brida. La barra se debe taladrar para emparejar por lo menos dos de las roscas de la brida **(vea ilustración).**

6   Usando un extractor de engrane, remueva la brida de acompañamiento **(vea ilustración).**

7   El balero central puede ser removido de la sección delantera del eje propulsor usando una prensa hidráulica y el plato de apoyo apropiado. Si una prensa hidráulica no está disponible, lleve el ensamblaje a un taller de rectificación o al departamento de servicio de su concesionario para prensar el balero central viejo hacia afuera y uno nuevo instalado.

8   Cuando el balero nuevo es prensado en el eje, asegúrese de que la carta F está mirando hacia el frente del vehículo.

9   Aplique una capa de grasa de uso múltiple a la cara del balero central y ambos lados de la arandela, entonces meta la arandela en el final del balero central.

10   Alínee la marca en la brida compañera con la hendidura en el eje e instale la brida.

11   Instale la contratuerca y la aprieta al par de torsión especificado **(vea ilustración).** Estaque la tuerca para que se comprometa con la ranura del eje como antes.

12   Alínee las marcas en la brida compañera y la brida central e instale los pernos que la conectan.

13   El resto del ensamblaje es lo inverso del procedimiento de remover. **Nota:** *Esté seguro que la acoplación en el caucho central del balero está mirando hacia encima cuando el soporte de apoyo esté instalado.*

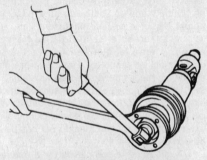

**12.5b Cuando esté removiendo la
contratuerca del balero central, una
herramienta se debe fabricar para
mantener el eje propulsor que no gire**

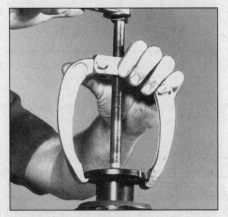

**12.6 Un extractor es necesitado para
separar la brida compañera del primer eje**

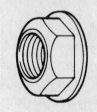
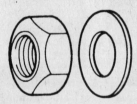

**12.11 Los dos tipos de
contratuercas para el balero central
usadas en los ejes propulsores de
dos piezas son del tipo de brida
(izquierdo) y el tipo de tuerca y
arandela (derecha) y (cada una tiene
un valor de torque diferente)**

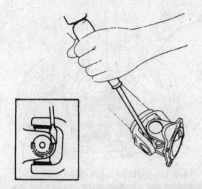

13.2 Remueva los anillos de tipo empuje de los baleros de acoplación U pegándole gentilmente hacia afuera con un destornillador y un martillo

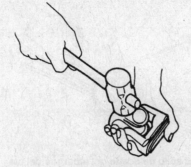

13.3 Con los anillos de tipo empuje removidos, los cojinetes pueden ser removidos utilizando la horquilla con un martillo

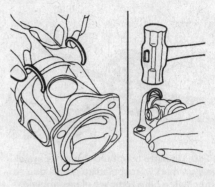

13.6 Anillos de tipo empuje nuevos son instalados cuidadosamente pegándole gentilmente en su posición

13 Juntas universales - reemplazo

Refiérase a las ilustraciones 13.2, 13.3 y 13.6
Caución: *Las juntas universales en ciertos modelos no son reemplazables. Consulte a su suministrador de partes para la disponibilidad de las partes antes de remover el eje propulsor.*
Nota: *Anillos de tipo empuje selectivos son usados para retener las juntas universales en las horquillas. En orden de mantener el eje propulsor balanceado, usted debe usar anillos de tipo empuje de reemplazo del mismo*

tamaño como el originalmente usado. Anillo de tipo empuje selectivos están listados en las especificaciones.

1   Marque la relación de todos los componentes para que todos ellos puedan ser instalados en sus posiciones originales.
2   Limpie hacia afuera toda la tierra de los extremos de los cojinetes en las horquillas para que los anillo de tipo empuje puedan ser removidos con un destornillador pequeño **(vea ilustración)**. Si ellos están muy apretados, utilice el final del cojinete (adentro del anillos de tipo empuje) con un punzón y un martillo para aliviar la presión.
3   Una vez que los anillos de tipo empuje son removidos péguueles suavemente a las juntas universales en la horquilla con un martillo de cara suave; los cojinetes se saldrán

del albergue y podrán ser removidos fácilmente **(vea ilustración)**.
4   Una vez que los cojinetes son removidos de cada horquilla del muñón opuesto, el muñón se puede liberar fácilmente.
5   En caso de extremo desgaste o negligencia, es posible que el albergue de los baleros en el eje propulsor, manga o brida estén tan desgastados que los cojinetes acoplen muy flojo. En tal caso, será también necesario reemplazar el componente desgastado.
6   La instalación se hace en el órden inverso al procedimiento de desensamble.
Nota: *Esté seguro de engrasar la superficie interior de los baleros antes de instalarlo. También esté seguro de instalar el anillo apropiado de tipo empuje en posición como está notado en el principio de esta Sección* **(vea ilustración)**. *La diferencia en el espesor del anillo de tipo empuje en las puntas opuestas no debe ser más de 0.0024 pulgada (0.06 mm).*

14 Eje, balero trasero de la rueda y sello del aceite - remover e instalar

Modelos con un solo neumático

Refiérase a las ilustraciones 14.6a, 14.6b, 14.7, 14.9, 14.10, 14.13, 14.16, 14.22 y 14.23

Remover

1   Levante la parte trasera del vehículo y sosténgalo firmemente encima de soportes.
2   Remueva la rueda y el neumático.
3   Remueva el tambor de freno. Refiérase al Capítulo 10, si es necesario.
4   Desconecte el cable del freno de estacionamiento y freno de atrás de la línea de freno. Refiérase al Capítulo 10, si es necesario.
5   Remueva las tuercas de afianzamiento de la placa de apoyo del freno.
6   El eje, completo con el ensamblaje de freno, ahora puede ser removido del eje trasero **(vea ilustraciones)**. Si el eje no sale a mano, un martillo resbaladizo puede ser

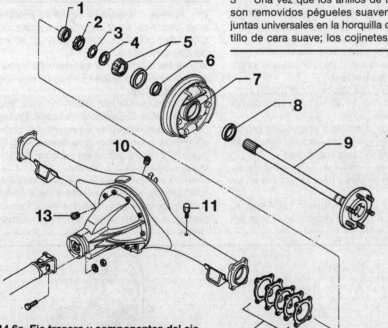

14.6a Eje trasero y componentes del eje - solos los modelos con un solo neumático

1   Sello de aceite
2   Tuerca prisionera para el balero de la rueda
3   Arandela de la tuerca prisionera para el balero de la rueda
4   Arandela plana
5   Balero de la rueda
6   Espaciador

7   Jaula para el balero de la rueda
8   Sello de grasa para el balero de la rueda
9   Eje
10   Tapón de llenar
11   Respirador
12   Láminas de ajuste para el albergue del eje
13   Tapón de drenaje

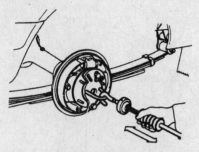

14.6b Un plato adaptador trasero para el eje y un martillo resbaladizo pueda que se necesiten para remover el ensamblaje del eje trasero

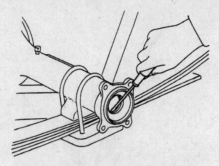

14.7 El sello de aceite del albergue del eje debe ser reemplazado cuando el eje es removido

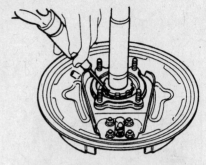

14.9 Un punzón o un destornillador pueden ser usados para enderezar las lengüetas de la arandela de seguridad para la tuerca de retención del balero

conectado a los espárragos de la rueda usando un plato adaptador.

7   Hágale palanca hacia afuera al sello de aceite viejo del final del albergue del eje **(vea ilustración)**. Éste siempre debe ser reemplazado cuando el eje es removido. Un sello nuevo puede ser instalado cuidadosamente utilizarlo un dado del tamaño apropiado.

8   Debido a que el balero de la rueda es prensado en el eje, removerlo e instalarlo requerirá el uso de herramientas especiales y o un extractor especial o una prensa hidráulica. Si el equipo necesario no está disponible, esta operación debe ser dejada a su concesionario o taller de reparación. Si el equipo está disponible, proceda según sigue.

9   Use un destornillador para enderezar las lengüetas de la arandela de seguridad de la tuerca del balero **(vea ilustración)**. La arandela siempre debe ser reemplazada, una vez que sea removida.

10   Usando una llave para tuerca de tipo anillo, remueva la contratuerca del balero **(vea ilustración)**. El eje necesitará ser asegurado en una prensa para remover la tuerca. Use protectores de mandíbula o bloques de madera para prevenir dañar el eje.

11   Usando un extractor diseñado especial para este propósito o una prensa hidráulica equipada con los apoyos necesarios, prense el eje hacia afuera del ensamblaje del freno y la jaula del balero.

12   Usando un punzón de deriva o un destornillador, remueva el sello de aceite del

albergue del balero. Una vez removido, este sello de aceite debe ser reemplazado con uno nuevo.

13   Si la pista de rodamiento exterior del balero necesita ser reemplazada (porque tiene pequeños orificios o rayones), puede ser removida de la jaula del balero usando un punzón de bronce **(vea ilustración)**. La pista de rodamiento exterior debe ser reemplazada cuando un balero nuevo es instalado.

Instalar

14   Comience la instalación instalando un sello de aceite nuevo en el albergue del balero usando un dado del tamaño apropiado. Después de la instalación del sello, aplique una capa pequeña de grasa entre los labio del sello.

15   Utilice cuidadosamente una pista de rodamiento exterior nueva en su posición, otra vez usando un punzón de bronce.

16   Instale el espaciador en el eje con el lado chafado del espaciador hacia la brida del eje **(vea ilustración)**.

17   Péguele cuidadosamente al balero principal para instalarlo en su lugar usando un punzón de bronce.

18   Instale la arandela y la arandela prisionera. Después instale la tuerca del balero con el lado encarado hacia la arandela.

19   Doble las lengüetas de la arandela de seguridad en la tuerca para asegurarla en su posición.

20   Aplique grasa de balero de rueda al balero de la rueda y al receso en el final del albergue del eje.

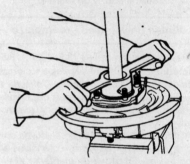

14.10 Una llave para anillo es necesaria para remover la contratuerca del balero de la rueda

21   Aplique una capa de aceite de engrane a las estrías del eje y una capa de grasa del balero de rueda a los labio del sello de aceite del albergue del eje.

22   Antes de instalar el eje, reemplace cualquier lámina para ajustes removida en el eje **(vea ilustración)**.

23   Si ambos ejes han sido removidos, instale el primero (izquierdo o derecho). Entonces conecte un medidor de esfera al final del eje y mida el juego libre **(vea ilustración)**. El juego libre para el primer eje debe ser 0.012 a 0.035 pulgada (0.3 a 0.9 mm). Si no lo es, remueva el eje otra vez y agregue o remueva láminas para ajustes hasta obtener el juego libre apropiado. Los tamaños de la lámina para ajustes están listados en las especificaciones.

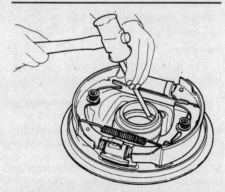

14.13 Extraiga la pista de rodamiento exterior de la jaula con un punzón de bronce

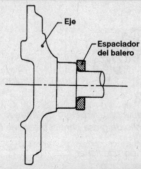

Eje

Espaciador del balero

14.16 El diámetro interior chafado del espaciador del balero debe mirar la brida del eje

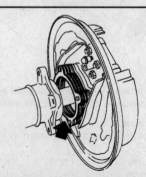

14.22 Láminas para ajustes son colocadas entre el albergue del eje y el retenedor del balero para ajustar el juego libre del eje

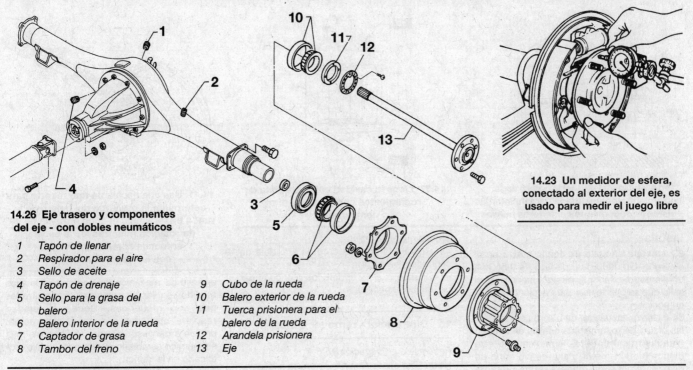

14.26 Eje trasero y componentes del eje - con dobles neumáticos

1   Tapón de llenar
2   Respirador para el aire
3   Sello de aceite
4   Tapón de drenaje
5   Sello para la grasa del balero
6   Balero interior de la rueda
7   Captador de grasa
8   Tambor del freno
9   Cubo de la rueda
10 Balero exterior de la rueda
11 Tuerca prisionera para el balero de la rueda
12 Arandela prisionera
13 Eje

14.23 Un medidor de esfera, conectado al exterior del eje, es usado para medir el juego libre

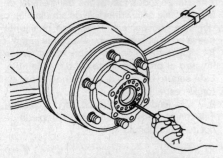

14.27 La arandela de seguridad es retenida por un tornillo

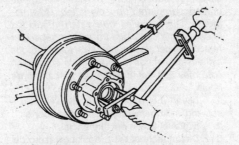

14.28 Remueva la contratuerca del balero de la rueda. Si esta herramienta especial no se puede obtener, usted puede fabricar una de dos clavijas de acero atornillada a través de una barra de metal plana. Para propósitos de la instalación, taladre y hágale rosca a un orificio entre las dos clavijas e instale un perno grande. La herramienta ahora puede aceptar una llave torsiométrica

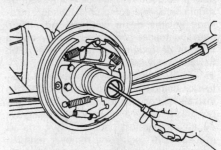

14.30 El sello de aceite del eje puede ser removido hacia afuera del albergue del eje con una palanca y un destornillador

24   Si solamente un eje fue removido o cuando esté instalando el segundo eje, el juego libre debe ser como está listado en las especificaciones.

25   El resto del procedimiento de la instalación se hace en el orden inverso al procedimiento de desensamble.

Modelos con dobles neumáticos

Refiérase a las ilustraciones 14.26, 14.27, 14.28, 14.30, 14.32, 14.34, 14.37, 14.41 y 14.42

Remover

26   Remueva los seis pernos reteniendo el eje al cubo y remueva el eje del albergue **(vea ilustración)**.

27   Remueva el tornillo reteniendo la arandela de seguridad y la arandela de seguridad **(vea ilustración)**.

28   Remueva la contratuerca del balero de rueda. Una llave especial (herramienta Nissan No. KV40105400) es requerida para aflojar esta tuerca **(vea ilustración)**.

29   Hale el ensamblaje del cubo y tambor hacia afuera del albergue. Tenga cuidado de no permitir que el balero exterior se caiga del cubo.

30   Usando un destornillador, remueva el sello de aceite haciéndole palanca hacia afuera del albergue **(vea ilustración)**.

31   Ponga el ensamblaje del cubo boca abajo en la mesa de trabajo y hágale palanca al sello de grasa hacia afuera del cubo usando un destornillador grande. El balero interior ahora puede ser removido.

32   Inspeccione los baleros de las ruedas y las pistas de rodamientos por roturas, jaulas dobladas, orificios pequeños, asperesa u otros signos de desgastes. Si los baleros van a ser reemplazados, será necesario golpear

Barra de bronce

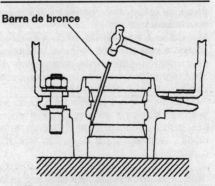

14.32 Remueva las pistas de rodamiento exteriores del cubo con una barra de bronce y un martillo

las pista de rodamientos exteriores hacia afuera del cubo, porque los baleros/pistas de rodamientos vienen en juegos. Usando un punzón de bronce y un martillo, remueva las pista de rodamiento para el balero **(vea ilustración)**.

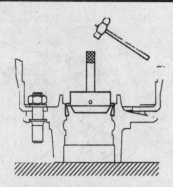

14.34 Un instalador de balero es la herramienta recomendada para instalar las pistas de rodamientos exteriores nuevas

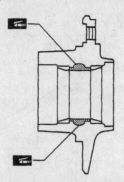

14.37 Llene la cavidad entre las pista de rodamientos con grasa de alta temperatura

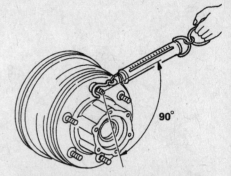

14.41 Use una escala de tipo resorte para determinar la precarga del balero de la rueda trasera; hale el cubo a través de 90° de rotación mientras lee la escala, entonces compare la medida con las especificaciones

Instalar

33   Instale un sello de aceite nuevo en el albergue. Un dado o un pedazo de tubo con un diámetro exterior levemente menor que el sello que se puede usar para accionar el sello en posición.

34   Use un instalador de balero para instalar las pistas de rodamientos nuevas en el cubo **(vea ilustración)**. Si tal herramienta no está disponible, un método alternativo sería de usar un bloque de madera y una pista de rodamiento vieja como un instalador, colocada encima de la pista de rodamiento nueva, entonces péguele cuidadosamente a la pista de rodamiento nueva en el cubo hasta que esté sentada.

35   Si los baleros se van a volver a usar, lávelos completamente con solvente. Seque los baleros con aire comprimido, si está disponible, entonces empáquelos con una grasa de alta temperatura para los baleros de las ruedas. Esté seguro de remover también todos los rasgos de grasa vieja del cubo.

36   Baleros nuevos se deben empacar también con grasa de alta temperatura para los baleros de las ruedas.

37   Empaque el interior del cubo y cubra las pistas de rodamientos con la misma grasa **(vea ilustración)**.

38   Coloque el balero interior de la rueda en el cubo e instale el sello de grasa. Un bloque de madera se puede usar para prensar el sello uniformemente. Aplique una capa pequeña de grasa al labio del sello.

39   Instale el balero exterior de la rueda en el cubo y deslice el ensamblaje en el albergue. Instale la contratuerca del balero de la rueda y la aprieta al par de torsión especificado.

40   Gire el cubo varias veces en ambas direcciones entonces apriete nuevamente la contratuerca.

41   Chequee la precarga del balero de la rueda con una escala de tipo resorte **(vea ilustración)**. Afloje o apriete la contratuerca hasta que la precarga deseada listada en las especificaciones, sea alcanzada.

42   Usando un indicador de reloj, mida el juego axial final del cubo **(vea ilustración)**. No debe exceder el final especificado del juego como está listado en las especificaciones. Si hay exceso en el juego final, repita el

procedimiento de ajuste.

43   Instale la contratuerca, la arandela de seguridad y el tornillo.

44   Instale el eje y apriete los pernos al par de torsión especificado.

15 Diferencial - remover e instalar

Refiérase a la ilustración 15.5

Nota: *Este procedimiento se aplica a diferenciales que pueden ser removidos como una unidad completa "tipo de calabaza" solamente. Diferenciales que están instalados íntegramente con el eje trasero no deben ser removidos del albergue, porque realizar todos los ajustes críticos después de la instalación está más allá del alcance del mecánico de hogar.*

1   Levante la parte trasera del vehículo y sosténgalo firmemente encima de soportes.

2   Drene el aceite del diferencial.

3   Desconecte el eje propulsor trasero del diferencial como se indica en la Sección 11 y póngalo en posición fuera del camino.

4   Parcialmente retire ambos ejes como se indica en la Sección 14, según ellos son desenganchados del diferencial.

5   Destornille las tuercas de afianzamiento del albergue del diferencial uniformemente y en un patrón cruzado **(vea ilustración)** y levante el diferencial hacia afuera del eje trasero.

6   La reconstrucción completa del eje trasero del diferencial no está dentro del

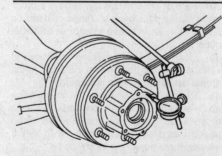

14.42 Posicione un indicador de tipo reloj en la superficie del cubo y mueva el cubo hacia adentro y hacia afuera, notando la lectura total del juego libre

alcance del mecánico del hogar, debido a los medidores y las herramientas especializadas que son requeridas. Dónde la unidad requiere otorgarle servicio o reparación, debido a desgaste o ruido excesivo, es más económico cambiarlo por un ensamblaje rectificado en la fábrica.

7   Raspe todos los rasgos del material de la junta vieja de la superficie de acoplamiento del albergue del eje. Posicione una junta nueva en el albergue (use sellador de junta).

8   La instalación se hace en el orden inverso al procedimiento de desensamble. Esté seguro de apretar los pernos al par de torsión especificado.

9   Siguiendo la instalación, llene el diferencial con el grado y la cantidad apropiada de aceite (vea Capítulo 1).

16 Sello delantero de aceite para el piñón del diferencial - reemplazo

Refiérase a las ilustraciones 16.5 y 16.6

1   Coloque un recipiente debajo del diferencial, entonces remueva el tapón de drenaje y permita que el aceite drene fuera de la

15.5 Los pernos de afianzamiento del diferencial deben de ser aflojados y apretados un poquito a la vez en un patrón de tipo de cruce

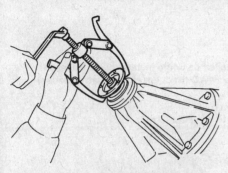

16.5 Un extractor de dos mandíbulas trabaja bien para remover la brida del piñón

unidad. Instale el tapón de drenaje.

2   Levante la parte trasera del vehículo para obtener acceso a la unidad, sostenga el chasis y el albergue del diferencial firmemente sobre estantes o bloques.

3   Desconecte la parte trasera del eje propulsor como se indica en la Sección 11 y mueva el eje propulsor a un lado.

4   Sostenga la brida del piñón poniendo pernos de dos pulgadas (50 mm) de largo a través de los dos orificios opuestos. Apretán-

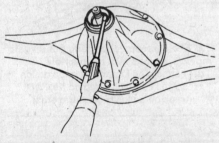

16.6 Hágale palanca y remueva el sello viejo del piñón desde el albergue - tenga cuidado de no dañar el eje del piñón

dolos, remueva la tuerca de enclavamiento con un destornillador grande o palanca para neumático entre los dos pernos y la palanca.

5   Usando un extractor, retire la brida del piñón de la unidad del diferencial (vea ilustración).

6   Remueva el sello de aceite defectuoso haciéndole palanca hacia afuera (vea ilustración).

7   Instale el sello de aceite nuevo después de engrasar las superficies de acoplamiento del sello y el albergue del eje. El labio del sello de aceite debe mirar hacia adentro. Usando un dado grande, prense cuidadosamente el sello de aceite nuevo en el receso hasta que la cara del sello esté plana con el albergue. Asegúrese que el final del piñón no se ha movido durante esta operación.

8   Instale la brida del piñón, la arandela para el impulso y la tuerca.

9   Otra vez reteniendo la brida del piñón para que no se mueva con el destornillador o palanca para neumático, apriete la tuerca del piñón hasta que no haya juego axial.

10   Una vez que la tuerca del piñón esté apretada, use la llave para tuerca para girar el eje del piñón en ambas direcciones varias veces, para asentar los rodillos del balero. Entonces acople una llave torsiométrica de pulgada libra en la tuerca del piñón y gire lentamente el eje del piñón, note la cantidad del par de torsión necesitado para girar el eje. Esto es la precarga del piñón y debe ser como está especificado. Si la preçarga está debajo de lo normal, apriete la tuerca del piñón un poquito a la vez hasta que la precarga apropiada sea obtenida. **Nota:** *Esta precarga es obtenida usando un espaciador que se desploma adentro del diferencial. Si la pre carga está encima de las especificaciones recomendada el diferencial tendrá que*

ser removido y el espaciador reemplazado.

11   El resto de la instalación se hace en el orden inverso al procedimiento de desensamble.

12   Siguiendo la instalación, rellene el diferencial con el grado y la cantidad apropiada de aceite (vea Capítulo 1).

17 Ensamblaje del eje trasero - remover e instalar

Refiérase a las ilustraciones 17.7a, 17.7b, 17.8 y 17.10

Remover

1   Levante la parte trasera del vehículo y sosténgalo firmemente encima de soportes debajo de los miembros de la carrocería.

2   Sostenga el ensamblaje del eje bajo del diferencial con un gato movible del tipo de garaje.

3   Remueva las ruedas y los neumáticos.

4   Desconecte el eje propulsor trasero del diferencial como está descrito en la Sección 11 y póngalo en posición afuera del camino.

5   Desconecte los cables del freno de estacionamiento y líneas de frenos de los frenos traseros, como está descrito en el Capítulo 10. Tape las líneas de freno para prevenir que entre tierra.

6   Remueva la tuerca de afianzamiento inferior para el amortiguador desde ambos amortiguadores y comprima los amortiguadores.

Suspensión de resorte de hoja

7   Remueva los pernos de tipo U y los soportes inferiores para los pernos de tipo U alrededor del eje y resortes traseros de hojas (vea ilustraciones).

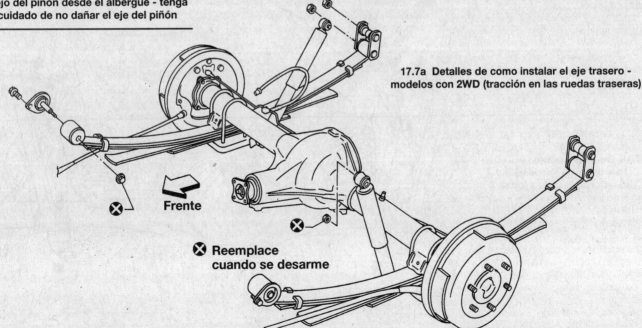

17.7a Detalles de como instalar el eje trasero - modelos con 2WD (tracción en las ruedas traseras)

Frente

⊗ **Reemplace cuando se desarme**

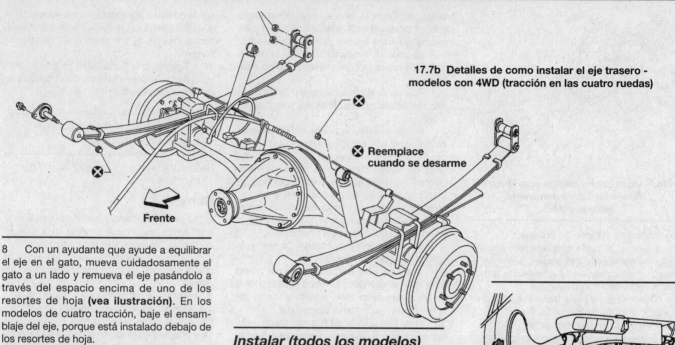

17.7b Detalles de como instalar el eje trasero - modelos con 4WD (tracción en las cuatro ruedas)

⊗ **Reemplace cuando se desarme**

Frente

8   Con un ayudante que ayude a equilibrar el eje en el gato, mueva cuidadosamente el gato a un lado y remueva el eje pasándolo a través del espacio encima de uno de los resortes de hoja **(vea ilustración)**. En los modelos de cuatro tracción, baje el ensamblaje del eje, porque está instalado debajo de los resortes de hoja.

Suspensión de resorte espiral

9   Desconecte los eslabones de la barra estabilizadora de la carrocería (vea Capítulo 11).
10   Destornille los eslabones superiores e inferiores del chasis **(vea ilustración)**.
11   Destornille la barra inferior del albergue del eje (vea Capítulo 11).
12   Baje lentamente el ensamblaje del eje y remueva los resortes espirales. Cuando lo esté instalando, refiérase al Capítulo 11 para el procedimiento correcto de la instalación de resorte espiral.

Instalar (todos los modelos)

13   Si el albergue trasero del eje debe ser reemplazado, remueva los ensamblajes traseros del freno, los ejes, los componentes relacionados, el diferencial y los transfiere al eje nuevo.
14   La instalación se hace en el orden inverso al procedimiento de desensamble. Refiérase a los Capítulos y las Secciones apropiadas para la instalación de los componentes individual.
15   Purgue el sistema de frenos como está descrito en el Capítulo 10.

17.8 El eje trasero, soportado por un gato movible, es más fácil removerlo a través del espacio en la parte encima de los resortes de hojas (modelo de 2WD (tracción en las ruedas traseras)

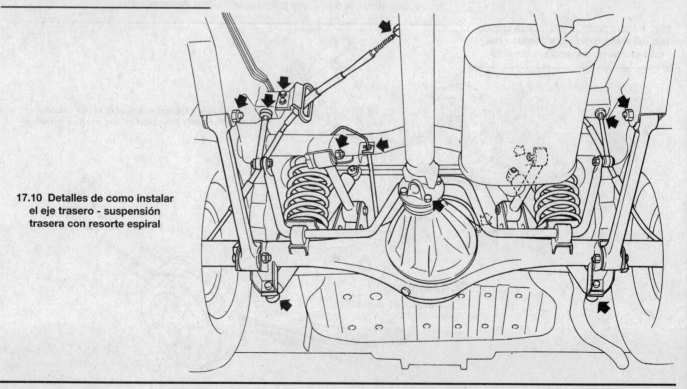

17.10 Detalles de como instalar el eje trasero - suspensión trasera con resorte espiral

Capítulo 9
Sistemas de cuatro tracciones

Contenidos

Especificaciones

Ensamblaje del cubo delantero

Precarga del balero de la rueda	
1980 al 1983..	0.5 a 2.2 pies-libras (0.7 a 3.0 Nm)
1984 en adelante..	1.59 a 4.72 pies-libras (2.15 a 6.4 Nm)
Juego final del semieje	0.004 a 0.012 pulgada (0.1 a 0.3 mm)
Espesores de los anillos de retención final del semieje	0.043 pulgada (1.1 mm)
	0.051 pulgada (1.3 mm)
	0.059 pulgada (1.5 mm)
	0.067 pulgada (1.7 mm)
	0.075 pulgada (1.9 mm)
	0.083 pulgada (2.1 mm)
Longitud instalada para el fuelle del semieje	
Acoplación interior	
Hasta 1990..	4.06 pulgadas (103 mm)
1991 y más moderno	3.70 pulgadas (94 mm)
Acoplación exterior	
1980 al 1983..	4.65 pulgadas (118 mm)
1984 al 1990..	3.82 pulgadas (97 mm)
1991 y más moderno	3.82 pulgadas (97 mm)
Cantidad de grasa para la acoplación del semieje	
1980 al 1983	
Acoplación interior	5.64 onzas (160 g)
Acoplación exterior	8.46 onzas (240 g)
1984 y 1985	
Acoplación interior	5.46 onzas (160 g)
Acoplación exterior	3.53 onzas (100 g)
1986 en adelante	
Acoplación interior	7.76 onzas (220 g)
Acoplación exterior	5.64 onzas (160 g)

Ensamblaje del cubo delantero (continuación)

Espesores del collar del balero de la rueda

Número	Espesor
0	1.0996 pulgadas (27.93 mm)
1	1.1016 pulgadas (27.98 mm)
2	1.1035 pulgadas (28.03 mm)
3	1.1055 pulgadas (28.08 mm)
4	1.1075 pulgadas (28.13 mm)
5	1.1094 pulgadas (28.18 mm)
6	1.1114 pulgadas (28.23 mm)
7	1.1134 pulgadas (28.28 mm)
8	1.1154 pulgadas (28.33 mm)
9	1.1173 pulgadas (28.38 mm)
A	1.1193 pulgadas (28.43 mm)
B	1.1213 pulgadas (28.48 mm)
C	1.1232 pulgadas (28.53 mm)
D	1.1252 pulgadas (28.58 mm)

Eje propulsor

Límite de desviación del eje propulsor	0.024 pulgada (0.6 mm)
Límite del juego axial del muñón	Menos de 0.0008 pulgada (0.02 mm)

Caja de transferencia (1980 al 1985 solamente)

Juego final del engrane

Engrane de Alta	0.0039 a 0.0079 pulgada (0.10 a 0.20 mm)
Engrane de Baja	0.0039 a 0.0079 pulgada (0.10 a 0.20 mm)
Cubo de la camisa de acoplamiento	0 a 0.0079 pulgada (0 a 0.20 mm)

Espesor de la selección del anillo de cierre del cubo de la camisa del acoplamiento

0.051 pulgada (1.3 mm)
0.055 pulgada (1.4 mm)
0.059 pulgada (1.5 mm)
0.063 pulgada (1.6 mm)
0.067 pulgada (1.7 mm)

Selección de la lámina para ajustes del engrane principal de la guía delantera

Resultado de A + C - E	Espesor de lámina para ajustes
0.0024 a 0.0059 pulgada (0.06 a 0.15 mm)	Ninguno
0.0063 a 0.0098 pulgada (0.16 a 0.25 mm)	0.0039 pulgada (0.10 mm)
0.0102 a 0.0138 pulgada (0.26 a 0.35 mm)	0.0079 pulgada (0.20 mm)
0.0142 a 0.0177 pulgada (0.36 a 0.45 mm)	0.0118 pulgada (0.30 mm)
0.0181 a 0.0217 pulgada (0.46 a 0.55 mm)	0.0157 pulgada (0.40 mm)

Selección de lámina para ajustes de la caja de transferencia delantera

Resultado de B + D - F	Espesor de lámina para ajustes
0 a 0.0051 pulgada (0 a 0.13 mm)	Ninguno
0.0055 a 0.0091 pulgada (0.14 a 0.23 mm)	0.0039 pulgada (0.10 mm)
0.0094 a 0.0130 pulgada (0.24 a 0.33 mm)	0.0079 pulgada (0.20 mm)
0.0134 a 0.0169 pulgada (0.34 a 0.43 mm)	0.0118 pulgada (0.30 mm)
0.0173 a 0.0209 pulgada (0.44 a 0.53 mm)	0.0157 pulgada (0.40 mm)
0.0213 a 0.0248 pulgada (0.54 a 0.63 mm)	0.0197 pulgada (0.50 mm)

Diferencial delantero

Precarga del piñón (con el sello de aceite)

Motor de cuatro cilindros	7.8 a 14.8 pulgada-libras (0.9 a 1.7 Nm)
Motor V6	10.0 a 15.2 pulgada-libras (1.13 a 1.72 Nm

Especificaciones técnicas

	Pies-libras	Nm
Tuerca prisionera del balero de la rueda		
1980 al 1983	108 a 145	147 a 196
1984 en adelante	58 a 72	78 a 98
Pernos de acoplación para el cubo libre	18 a 25	25 a 34
Pernos de la rótula superior a la acoplación superior	12 a 15	16 a 21
Pernos de la rótula inferior a la acoplación inferior	28 a 38	38 a 52
Perno del brazo del vástago de la dirección al perno del vástago de la dirección	53 a 72	72 a 97
Mordaza de los frenos al soportes (o clavija deslizante)	16 a 23	22 a 31
Mordaza del frene al vástago	53 a 72	72 a 97
Pernos del semieje al diferencial		
1980 al 1985	20 a 27	27 a 37
1986 en adelante	25 a 33	34 a 44

Pernos del eje propulsor al diferencial

1980 al 1985	25 a 33	34 a 44
1986 en adelante	58 a 65	78 a 88

Pernos del eje propulsor a la caja de transferencia

1980 al 1985	25 a 33	34 a 44
1986 en adelante	58 a 65	78 a 88

Tuerca delantera del piñón del diferencial

Motor de cuatro cilindros	123 a 145	167 a 196
Motor V6	137 a 217	186 a 294
Tapón de la bola unilateral	16	22

Tuercas de la pestaña de acompañamiento de la caja de transferencia

1980 al 1985	87 a 101	118 a 137
1986 en adelante	166 a 239	226 a 324
Caja de transferencia al pernos de la transmisión	22 a 30	31 a 41
Tuercas de las ruedas	Vea Capítulo 1	

1 Información general

Refiérase a las ilustraciones 1.1a y 1.1b

El sistema usado para enviar la fuerza a las cuatro ruedas en los modelos de 4WD (tracción en las cuatro ruedas) es un sistema agregado que trabaja en conjunto con los componentes estándar de 2WD (tracción en las ruedas traseras) **(vea ilustraciones)**.

En los modelos 1985 y más antiguos un eje propulsor primario corto sale de la parte trasera de la transmisión manual y se conecta a la caja de transferencia, que está instalada en la sección central del vehículo. Los vehículos 1986 y más modernos están equipados con una caja de transferencia que se atornilla directamente en la parte trasera de la transmisión, eliminando la necesidad de un eje propulsor primario. La caja de transferencia transmite el poder a ambos diferenciales delanteros y traseros a través de dos otros ejes propulsores (ejes propulsores delanteros y traseros).

El diferencial delantero es instalado debajo de la cacerola de aceite del motor.

Dos semiejes conectan las ruedas delanteras que giran las ruedas cuando el vehículo está en el modo de 4WD.

Los cubos que giran libres son usados cuando están sin enclavar (en la posición libre) permiten que las ruedas delanteras giren mientras el vehículo está en el modo de 2WD sin girar los semiejes y así reduciendo el desgaste del diferencial delantero o sus componentes. Cuando el vehículo es cambiado al modo de 4WD, los cubos entonces se deben enclavar para comprometer las ruedas con los semiejes. Los modelos 1984 y más

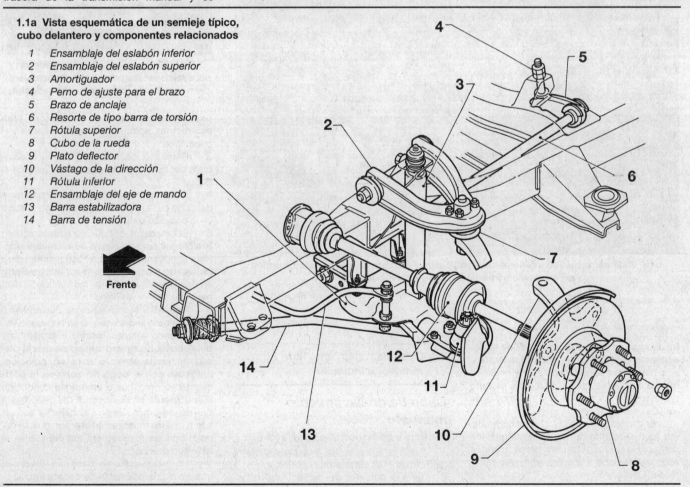

1.1a Vista esquemática de un semieje típico, cubo delantero y componentes relacionados

1   Ensamblaje del eslabón inferior
2   Ensamblaje del eslabón superior
3   Amortiguador
4   Perno de ajuste para el brazo
5   Brazo de anclaje
6   Resorte de tipo barra de torsión
7   Rótula superior
8   Cubo de la rueda
9   Plato deflector
10   Vástago de la dirección
11   Rótula inferior
12   Ensamblaje del eje de mando
13   Barra estabilizadora
14   Barra de tensión

Frente

1.1b Vista esquemática inferior de la transmisión y sistema de 4WD (tracción en las cuatro ruedas) (modelos 1986 y más modernos)

1	Semieje	4	Eje propulsor delantero
2	Diferencial delantero	5	Caja de transferencia
3	Transmisión	6	Eje propulsor trasero

modernos son ofrecidos con cubos de enclavamiento automático en la parte delantera, eliminando la necesidad de salir y enclavar manualmente los cubos cuando la caja de transferencia es colocada en el modo de 4WD.

El diferencial trasero y el ensamblaje del eje son exactamente los mismos que los componentes de 2WD. Para procedimientos relacionados con estos componentes refiérase al Capítulo 8.

2   Cubo de rodamiento libre - remover e instalar

Cubo de enclavamiento manual

Refiérase a las ilustraciones 2.2, 2.3 y 2.5

1   Levante el frente del vehículo y sosténgalo firmemente encima de soportes.
2   Gire la cubierta de plástico del cubo

2.2 La cubierta para el cubo de rodamiento libre es removida desenganchándola de las tuercas de la rueda

2.3 Una herramienta Torx es necesaria para remover los pernos de afianzamiento para el cubo de rodamiento libre (flechas)

para desengancharlo de las tuercas (**vea ilustración**), entonces remueva la rueda y el neumático.
3   Remueva los seis tornillos del ensamblaje del cubo (**vea ilustración**) y levante el cubo.
4   Si es necesario desarmar el ensamblaje del cubo para ser desarmado, ponga el cubo en la posición de Cerrado.
5   El embrague conducido es retenido en el albergue por una clavija de enclavamiento. Para remover el embrague, use un imán para removerlo hacia afuera (**vea ilustración**), entonces gírelo al favor de las saetas del reloj para liberarlo y removerlo.
6   Remueva la clavija de enclavamiento para el albergue del cubo, si es necesario.
7   Cuando vuelva a instalar el ensamblaje del cubo, esté primero seguro de que la clavija de enclavamiento está en posición. Entonces con el juego del cubo en la posición Libre, enrosque el embrague conducido a la izquierda en el albergue del cubo hasta que no vaya más. Gírelo a la derecha apenas hasta que las muescas en el embrague se alineen con las roscas para los pernos en el albergue del cubo.
8   La instalación se hace en el orden inverso al procedimiento de desensamble.

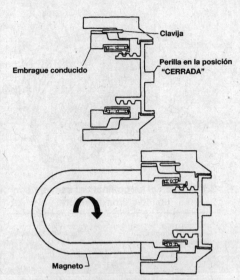

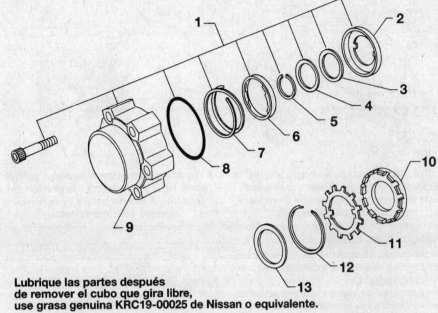

2.5 Para remover el embrague conducido del cubo de rodamiento libre, use un imán para halarlo hacia afuera y lo gira a la derecha

Lubrique las partes después de remover el cubo que gira libre, use grasa genuina KRC19-00025 de Nissan o equivalente.

2.11 Vista esquemática del ensamblaje del cubo de rodamiento libre de enclavamiento automático

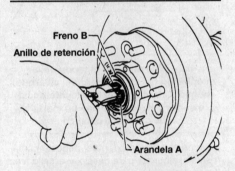

1	Cubo de rodamiento libre de enclavamiento automático	9	Subensamblaje del cubo de rodamiento libre de enclavamiento automático
2	Freno "B"		
3	Arandela "A"	10	Tuerca prisionera del balero de la rueda
4	Arandela "B"		
5	Anillo de presión	11	Arandela prisionera
6	Freno "A"	12	Anillo de retención
7	Resorte	13	Arandela
8	Anillo O		

2.12 Después de remover el anillo de retención, los componentes que quedan del cubo pueden ser removidos

Cubo de enclavamiento automático

Refiérase a las ilustraciones 2.11, 2.12 y 2.13

9   Remueva el fuelle de la rueda y la rueda.
10 Usando una herramienta Torx, remueva los seis pernos.
11 Hale cuidadosamente el cubo hacia afuera. El anillo sellador de tipo O, resorte y freno "A" **(vea ilustración)**, se soltará también. Asegúrese que todas las partes son mantenidas en el mismo orden según ellas son removidas para ayudar en el proceso de instalar.
12 Remueva el anillo de retención, las varias arandelas y el freno "B" **(vea ilustración)**.
13 Mida el espesor del freno "A" y "B" **(vea ilustración)**. Si el espesor es menor que el límite especificado, los frenos deben ser reemplazado como un juego.
14 La instalación se hace en el orden inverso al procedimiento de desensamble. Durante el periodo de ensamblar, **refiérase a la ilustración 2.11** y lubrique las partes designadas con la grasa recomendada.

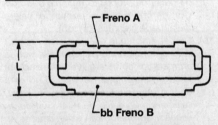

2.13 Coloque el freno A adentro del freno B y mida el espesor del ensamblaje - si la dimensión es menos que lo especificado, reemplace el freno A y B como un conjunto

3   Semiejes - remover e instalar

Refiérase a las ilustraciones 3.6, 3.15, 3.17a y 3.17b

Remover

1   Levante el frente del vehículo y sosténgalo firmemente encima de soportes.
2   Remueva la rueda y el neumático.
3   Remueva el ensamblaje del cubo de la rueda que gira libre (Sección 2).
4   Remueva el anillo de retención del extremo del vástago del semieje.
5   Deslice del embrague el engrane (cubos

3.6 Ponga marcas de alineamiento en el resbaladero del albergue de la acoplación del semieje y la pestaña del eje lateral del diferencial, entonces remueva los pernos

de enclavamiento manuales) o la arandela y el freno "B" (cubos de enclavamiento automático).
6   Remueva los pernos que conectan el semieje al diferencial delantero **(vea ilustración)**.
7   Remueva el perno de afianzamiento inferior del amortiguador.

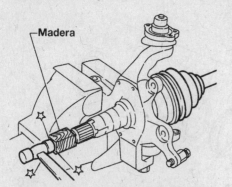

3.15 Con el vástago agarrado en una prensa, péguele gentilmente al semieje hacia afuera usando un bloque de madera para almohadillar el impacto

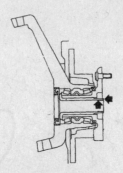

3.17a Antes de instalar el semieje, aplique grasa (ejes propulsores) a la porción de apoyo de cobre del balero de la rueda, adentro del cubo delantero

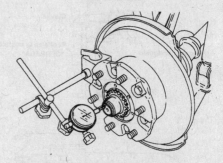

3.17b Mida el juego final del semieje con un indicador de esfera

Modelos 1980 al 1985

8   Remueva los cauchos de rebote de los parachoques delanteros, localizados encima del eslabón inferior.

9   Remueva los pernos que conectan la barra estabilizadora al eslabón inferior, junto con las hembrillas de caucho, las arandelas y los espaciadores. Mantenga los componentes en su orden apropiado.

10   Si está removiendo el semieje izquierdo, gire el volante completamente a la izquierda. Si está removiendo el semieje derecho, gire la dirección a la derecha.

11   Desconecte la acoplación del albergue de resbalamiento desde la pestaña del semieje del diferencial del eje lateral, entonces hálelo hacia afuera del cubo delantero. Usted quizás tenga que pegarle suavemente al extremo del eje con un martillo y un bloque de madera para libertarlo de las estrías del cubo.

Modelos 1986 y más modernos

12   Remueva la mordaza del freno y la cuelga fuera del camino con un pedazo de alambre (vea Capítulo 10).

13   Desconecte el extremo de la barra de acoplamiento del vástago para la dirección (vea Capítulo 11).

14   Sostenga el eslabón inferior con un gato y levántelo levemente. Remueva los pernos y las tuercas que aseguran las rótulas superiores e inferiores a los eslabones superiores e inferiores, entonces remueva cuidadosamente el vástago de la dirección y el semieje como un ensamblaje.

15   Instale el vástago de la dirección para la dirección en una prensa y péguele gentilmente con un martillo y un bloque de madera al semieje para removerlo hacia afuera del vástago de la dirección **(vea ilustración)**.

Todos los modelos

16   Si algún defecto existe en el eje, fuelles de caucho o acoplaciones, refiérase a la Sección 4 para desarmarlo.

Instalar

17   La instalación se hace en el orden inverso al procedimiento de desensamble

4.3a Doble las lengüetas del albergue resbaladero de la acoplación del tapón, después mueva el tapón con el sello (semiejes de estilo temprano)

con las siguientes notas.

a)   *Antes de la instalación, aplique una capa de grasa de propósito múltiple a la porción de cobre para el apoyo del balero de la rueda* **(vea ilustración)**.

b)   *Con el embrague de ejecución reinstalado en el extremo del semieje, ponga un medidor de esfera* **(vea ilustración)** *mida el juego final del eje. Si no está dentro de los límites especificados, seleccione un anillo de retención de un espesor apropiado (de esos listados en las especificaciones) eso producirá el juego final correcto.*

4   Semiejes - reemplazo del cubo, desarmar y ensamblar

Refiérase a las ilustraciones 4.3a, 4.3b, 4.4a, 4.4b, 4.9, 4.12 y 4.15
Nota: *Una prensa hidráulica es necesaria para esta operación.*

1   Remueva el semieje como se indica en la Sección 3.

2   Asegure el semieje en una prensa usando bloques de madera para prevenir dañar el eje.

3   Trabajando en el lado del eje del diferencial, enderece las etiquetas que aseguran el tapón y lo levanta hacia afuera junto con el sello de tapón (modelos más antiguos). En

4.3b Para remover el tapón de la acoplación del resbaladero del albergue, péguele alrededor de la circunferencia exterior del albergue con un martillo de caucho o plástico

los modelos más modernos, péguele gentilmente al albergue para desalojar el sello **(vea ilustraciones)**.

4   Remueva ambas bandas del fuelle **(vea ilustraciones)**.

5   Mueva ambos el fuelle y la acoplación del albergue resbaladizo hacia el lado de la rueda del eje.

6   Marque la posición instalada del ensamblaje cruceta en el eje.

7   Usando una prensa y un apoyo, prense el eje fuera de la cruceta.

8   Remueva el fuelle y la acoplación del albergue resbaladizo de los ejes.

9   La acoplación exterior (lado de la rueda) en los modelos más antiguos (1980 al 1983) no es movible. Si el fuelle del lado de la rueda debe ser removido, remueva las bandas del fuelle y deslice el fuelle del extremo interior del eje. La acoplación exterior en los modelos más modernos (1984 en adelante) puede ser removida del semieje suavemente pegándole gentilmente **(vea ilustración)**. Esté seguro de marcar la relación de la acoplación al semieje antes de removerlo. Después que la acoplación haya sido removida, remueva el clip redondo del eje.

10   Limpie todas las partes en solvente, inspecciónela por daño y desgaste excesivo. El sub ensamblaje/eje propulsor (modelos más antiguos), acoplación exterior (modelos más modernos) y el ensamblaje de la cruceta no

4.4a Vista esquemática de los componentes del ensamblaje del semieje (modelos 1980 al 1985)

1   Subensamblaje del eje propulsor
2   Fuelle
3   Banda para el fuelle
4   Banda para el fuelle
5   Fuelle
6   Albergue de la acoplación deslizante
7   Ensamblaje de las crucetas
8   Sello del tapón
9   Tapón

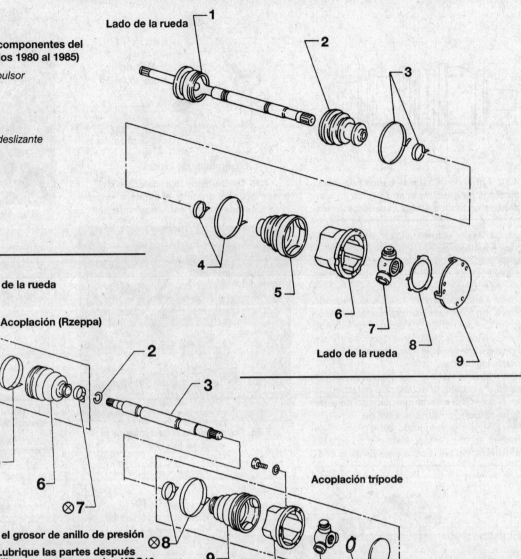

Lado de la rueda

Acoplación (Rzeppa)

* **El axial final es ajustado por el grosor de anillo de presión**

Grasa de la junta universal: Lubrique las partes después de remover el cubo que gira libre, use grasa genuina KRC19-00025 de Nissan o equivalente.

Tenga cuidado de no dañar el fuelle: Use un protector adecuado o trapo durante el periodo de remover e instalar

⊗ Reemplace cuando esté desensamblando

Acoplación trípode

Lado portador del diferencial

4.4b Vista esquemática de los componentes del ensamblaje del semieje (modelos 1986 y modelos de cuatro cilindros más modernos, los modelos V6 son similares)

1 Anillo de retención	5 Banda para el fuelle (grande)	10 Albergue de la acoplación deslizante
2 Anillo de presión	6 Fuelle (lado de la rueda)	11 Ensamblaje de cruceta
3 Eje propulsor	7 Banda para el fuelle (pequeña)	12 Anillo de retención
4 Ensamblaje de acoplación (lado de la rueda)	8 Banda del fuelle	13 Sello del tapón
	9 Fuelle	

son diseñados para ser desarmados y si están defectuosos deben ser reemplazados como una unidad.

11   Comience el ensamblaje empacando el subensamblaje del semieje (acoplación exterior) con la cantidad especificada de grasa de alta calidad de propósito múltiple.

12   Envuelva cinta alrededor de las estrías del eje, deslice el fuelle en el eje y lo instala en el subensamblaje (modelos más antiguos). Asegure el fuelle con una banda nueva

4.9 Los modelos 1984 y más modernos emplean una acoplación CV (velocidad constante) exterior removible que puede ser removida pegándole hacia afuera del eje

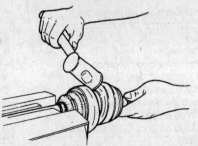

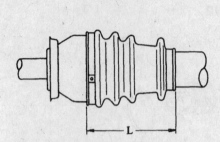

4.12 Antes de instalar la banda pequeña, ajuste la longitud de la acoplación (L) a la dimensión listada en las especificaciones

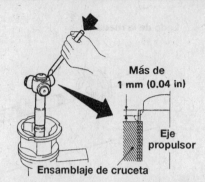

4.15 Después de la instalación del ensamblaje de cruceta, el semieje se debe estacar como está mostrado

5.6a Pernos de la rótula superior al eslabón superior

grande. Ajuste el fuelle a la longitud especificada **(vea ilustración)**. Iguale la presión en el fuelle metiendo una hoja destornillador bajo el fuelle (tenga cuidado para no dañar el fuelle). Asegúrese que no está torcida ni hinchada y entonces instale una banda pequeña nueva. En los modelos más modernos, deslice el fuelle en el eje, instale un clip redondo nuevo, llene la acoplación exterior con grasa y péguele gentilmente a la acoplación del eje. Instale las bandas.

13 Instale el fuelle lateral del diferencial, las bandas y deslice la acoplación del albergue en el eje. Otra vez tenga cuidado para no dañar el fuelle en las estrías del eje.

14 Con el eje asegurado entre bloques de madera en una prensa, instale la cruceta en el extremo del eje, con la cara dentada cha-

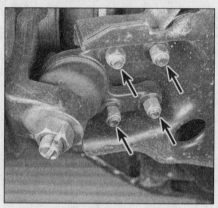

5.6b Pernos de la rótula inferior al eslabón inferior

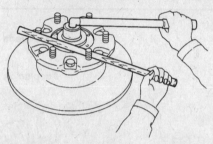

6.3 Cuando remueva la tuerca prisionera de la rueda delantera, posicione una barra entre los espárragos de la rueda para detener que gire el cubo

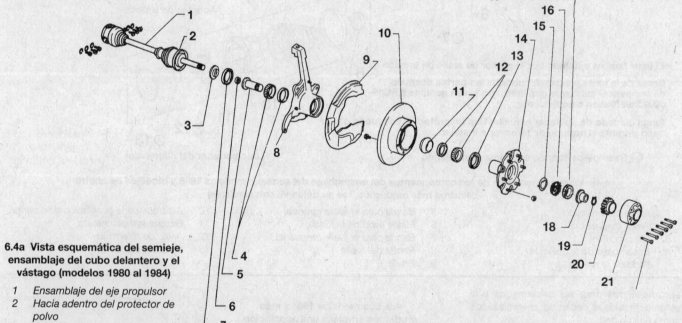

6.4a Vista esquemática del semieje, ensamblaje del cubo delantero y el vástago (modelos 1980 al 1984)

1   Ensamblaje del eje propulsor
2   Hacia adentro del protector de polvo
3   Espaciador
4   Balero interior de la rueda
5   Soporte del balero de la rueda en la porción de cobre
6   Balero del eje propulsor
7   Sello de grasa
8   Vástago en la cavidad entre los baleros

9   Plato deflector
10   Rotor
11   Collar del balero de la rueda
12   Balero exterior de la rueda
13   Sello de grasa
14   Cubo de la rueda
15   Arandela especial

16   Plato de obstrucción
17   Tuerca prisionera
18   Embrague ejecutor
19   Anillo de retención
20   Embrague conducido
21   Ensamblaje del cubo de rodamiento libre

6.4b Vista esquemática del semieje, ensamblaje del cubo delantero y el vástago (modelos 1985 y más modernos)

1   Ensamblaje del cubo de rodamiento libre de enclavamiento automático
2   Anillo de retención
3   Ensamblaje del cubo de rodamiento libre de enclavamiento manual
4   Anillo de retención
5   Embrague conducido
6   Plato de enclavamiento
7   Tuerca prisionera del balero de la rueda
8   Balero exterior
9   Cubo de la rueda
10 Balero interior
11 Sello de grasa "A"
12 Disco del rotor
13 Plato deflector
14 Sello de grasa
15 Vástago
16 Balero de tipo aguja
17 Espaciador
18 Sello de grasa
19 Ensamblaje del eje propulsor

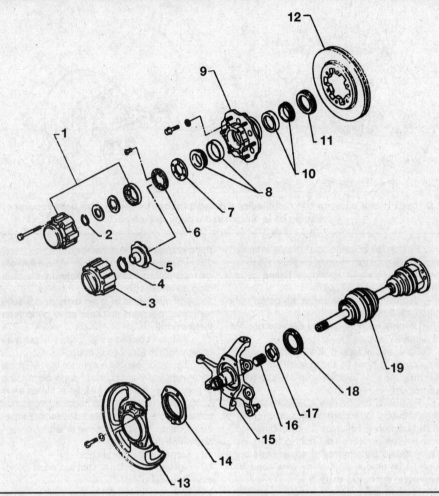

fada hacia el eje. **Nota:** *Si la cruceta usada va a ser instalada nuevamente esté seguro que las marcas hechas durante el proceso de remover forman una fila. Si una cruceta nueva es instalada, debe ser alineada lo más posible a la del extremo de la rueda.*

15   Con el ensamblaje de la cruceta instalado, use un punzón o un cincel para estacar los dientes en el extremo del eje para asegurar la cruceta. El procedimiento debe ser hecho en dos puntos que no hayan sido ya hundido y deben ser más de 1 mm de profundidad (**vea ilustración**).
16   Deslice el albergue resbaladizo y fuelle en posición sobre la cruceta y empáquela con una cantidad especificada de grasa de alta calidad de propósito múltiple.
17   Asegure el fuelle con una banda nueva grande.
18   Aplique una capa de grasa al sello del tapón e instale el tapón. Asegúrelos al albergue temporariamente con tres pernos, tuercas y asegure el tapón estacándolo en tres lugares.
19   Ponga el fuelle a la longitud especificada (**vea ilustración 4.12**) entonces iguale la presión en el fuelle. Instale una banda pequeña nueva.

5   Cubo y muñón delantero - remover e instalar

Refiérase a las ilustraciones 5.6a y 5.6b
1   Levante el frente del vehículo y sosténgalo firmemente encima de soportes.
2   Remueva la rueda y el neumático.
3   Remueva el ensamblaje de la mordaza de los frenos como está descrito en el Capítulo 10. La mordaza se puede sostener con alambres fuera del camino en el chasis u otro

componente, sin desconectar la manguera del freno, eliminando la necesidad de purgar los frenos más tarde.
4   Remueva el semieje como se indica en la Sección 3.
5   Afloje, pero no remueva, el extremo de la barra de acoplamiento a la tuerca del brazo del vástago de la dirección. Usando un extractor, separe el extremo de la barra de acoplamiento del brazo del vástago de la dirección (vea Capítulo 11).
6   El vástago de la dirección es fácilmente removido con las rótulas superiores e inferiores conectadas. Coloque un gato bajo el eslabón inferior para sostener la presión del resorte de la barra de torsión. El gato debe permanecer abajo del eslabón inferior durante el procedimiento completo. Remueva los pernos que conectan ambas rótulas a los eslabones (**vea ilustraciones**).
7   Las rótulas ahora se deben de separar de los eslabones, del ensamblaje del vástago y el cubo debe ser elevado hacia fuera. Si el vástago de la dirección debe ser reemplazado, entonces las rótulas deben ser removidas. Esto es hecho aflojando, pero no removiendo, las tuercas de las rótulas para que ellas se puedan extender en el extremo del espárrago. Use un extractor o herramienta para separar o liberar las rótulas del vástago de la dirección. La tuerca se debe dejar en el espárrago para prevenir que la acoplación

superior o inferior se separe violentamente del espárrago de la rótula.
8   La instalación se hace en el orden inverso al procedimiento de desensamble. Cuando vuelva a instalar el semieje, esté seguro de ajustar el juego final del eje como se indica en la Sección 3.

6   Balero de la rueda delantera y sello de grasa - remover, instalar y instalar

Refiérase a las ilustraciones 6.3, 6.4a, 6.4b, 6.6, 6.8, 6.14, 6.16 y 6.18

Remover

1   Remueva el ensamblaje del cubo delantero y el vástago como se indica en la Sección 5.
2   Usando un destornillador, enderece las lengüetas de los platos de cierre alrededor de la tuerca prisionera (modelos más antiguos). En los modelos más modernos remueva el tornillo reteniendo el plato de retención.
3   Remueva la tuerca prisionera. Para mantener que el cubo no gire, coloque una palanca ruptora entre los espárragos de la rueda (**vea ilustración**).
4   Remueva el plato de obstrucción y la arandela especial (**vea ilustraciones**).

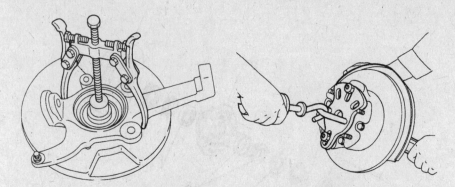

6.6 Un extractor o un martillo resbaladizo y un adaptador se pueden usar para separar el vástago de la dirección del cubo delantero

6.8 La pista de rodamiento interior del balero puede ser removida del vástago de la dirección accionándola hacia afuera con una barra de bronce y un martillo

5   Remueva el sello de grasa interior haciéndole palanca hacia afuera con un destornillador. Empuje el apoyo del balero de la rueda hacia afuera del cubo.

6   Separe el vástago de la dirección del cubo **(vea ilustración)**.

7   Levante hacia afuera el collar del balero de la rueda.

8   Remueva el balero interior de la rueda expulsando la pista de rodamiento del balero con una barra de bronce y un martillo **(vea ilustración)**.

9   Remueva los pernos que conectan el rotor, el cubo y los separa. Si ellos no se separarán fácilmente, refiérase al procedimiento para remover el rotor en el Capítulo 10.

10   Péguele gentilmente al ensamblaje del cubo en un bloque de madera para cambiar la posición del balero exterior.

11   Usando una prensa y apoyos, prense el balero exterior hacia afuera del cubo. Remueva también el sello de grasa.

12   Remueva el balero del semieje del soporte del balero de la rueda, usando una barra de bronce, si es necesario.

13   Limpie todas las partes con solvente.

Instalar

14   Comience la instalación cubriendo el balero del semieje con grasa de propósito múltiple y lo instala en el apoyo del balero de la rueda, usando un punzón de deriva o un dado grande **(vea ilustración)**.

15   Usando un dado grande, instale la pista de rodamiento exterior del balero en el vástago de la dirección.

16   Aplique grasa al labio exterior del sello de grasa, después instálelo en el cubo **(vea ilustración)**.

17   Instale el balero de la rueda y la pista de rodamiento exterior en el cubo.

18   Empaque el balero exterior con la grasa recomendada y aplique una capa de grasa a la pista de rodamiento. Instálelos juntos en el cubo. Aplique fuerza solamente a la pista de rodamiento cuando la esté instalando. Empaque el centro del cubo con la grasa recomendada **(vea ilustración)**.

19   Conecte el rotor al cubo.

20   Vuelva a instalar el vástago de la dirección en el cubo.

21   Instale el collar del balero. Si el collar va ser reemplazado, instale un collar del mismo espesor como el viejo (el número estampado en los collares será el mismo).

22   Empaque el balero interior con grasa y aplique una capa de grasa a la pista de rodamiento interior, entonces, usando una prensa, instale las dos juntas en el vástago de la dirección. Aplique la fuerza solamente a la pista de rodamiento cuando esté instalando el balero.

23   Instale la arandela especial y el plato de obstrucción. **Nota:** *Siempre use un plato de*

obstrucción nuevo *(modelos más antiguos solamente)*.

24   Instale la tuerca prisionera y la aprieta al par de torsión especificado.

25   Gire el cubo en ambas direcciones varias veces para sentar apropiadamente el balero de la rueda.

26   Empaque los labio del sello interior de grasa nuevo con grasa y lo instala en el vástago de la dirección, esté seguro que las caras del labio están en la dirección apropiada.

Ajuste

Modelos 1980 al 1983

27   Chequee la instalación de la precarga del balero de la rueda con una llave torsiométrica en la tuerca prisionera y gire lentamente el cubo a la derecha, notando a que par de torsión el cubo comienza a girar. Compare esta precarga del balero de la rueda listado en las especificaciones. Si la precarga no está dentro del rango, el collar del balero debe ser reemplazado con otro de un espesor diferente, como está listado en las especificaciones. **Nota:** *Si la medida de la precarga es mayor que lo especificado, un collar más ancho debe ser instalado (indicado por un número estampado más alto), mientras que si la precarga está más baja que lo especificado, reemplácela con un collar más delgado (indicado por un número inferior estampado. Cambie el espesor del collar solamente*

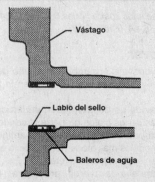

6.14 Empaque el balero del semieje con grasa y lo empuja en el cubo con el sello en el lado interior del vástago de la dirección

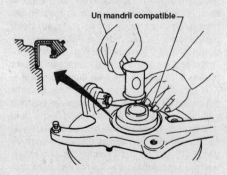

6.16 Use un impulsor de sello o un dado grande para sentar el sello interior en el cubo - el lado abierto del sello debe mirar boca abajo

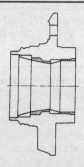

6.18 Empaque el centro del cubo (área con sombra) con grasa

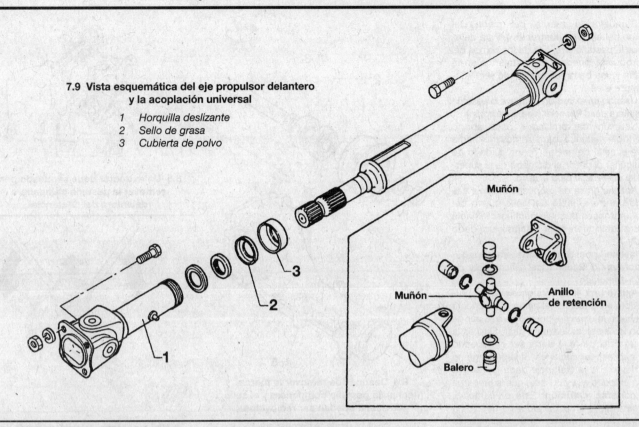

7.9 Vista esquemática del eje propulsor delantero y la acoplación universal

1   Horquilla deslizante
2   Sello de grasa
3   Cubierta de polvo

Muñón

Muñón

Anillo de retención

Balero

un número en cualquier dirección a la vez.

28   Una vez que la precarga apropiada haya sido obtenida, doble las lengüetas en el plato de enclavamiento hacia adentro de las ranuras de la tuerca prisionera.

Modelos 1984 y más modernos

Nota: Una herramienta especial es requerida para aflojar y apretar la tuerca prisionera del balero de la rueda. No lo atente sin la herramienta especial. Refiérase al Capítulo 8 para las instrucciones de fabricar una herramienta alternativa si la herramienta recomendada no está disponible.

29   Usando una llave torsiométrica y la herramienta especial, apriete la tuerca prisionera al par de torsión recomendado.

30   Ahora afloje la tuerca prisionera y chequee el juego final, que debe ser cero.

31   Gire la rueda varias veces en ambas direcciones.

32   Conecte una escala de tipo resorte al espárrago superior de la rueda y mida la fuerza necesaria para poner en movimiento el cubo de la rueda. Anote este número, designándolo con la letra A, para referencia más adelante.

33   Gire la tuerca prisionera del balero de la rueda 15 a 30 grados y ataque el plato de cerradura en la tuerca prisionera.

34   Gire el cubo de la rueda varias veces en ambas direcciones para sentar apropiadamente los baleros de las ruedas.

35   Enganche la escala de tipo resorte otra vez y mida la fuerza para empezar ahora. Anote este número, designándolo con la letra B.

36   La precarga del balero de la rueda es B

menos A en el chequeo hecho encima.

37   Repita el procedimiento hasta que la precarga apropiada sea obtenida.

38   Instale el anillo de retención en la ranura de la tuerca prisionera.

39   Instale los componentes que quedan en el orden inverso de como se removió.

7   Ejes propulsores - remover e instalar

Refiérase a la ilustración 7.9

Eje propulsor primario

1   Levante el frente del vehículo y sosténgalo firmemente encima de soportes. Si es necesario para obtener espacio libre, remueva el eje propulsor delantero como está descrito en la próxima sub sección.

2   Marque la posición de la pestaña trasera del eje propulsor y la pestaña de la caja de transferencia para asegurarse de que ellas sean reinstaladas en la misma manera.

3   Remueva los pernos de la pestaña y separe el eje propulsor de la caja de transferencia.

4   Remueva la caja de transferencia como está indicado en la Sección 11.

5   Remueva el eje propulsor primario hacia afuera de la parte trasera de la transmisión y tape inmediatamente el extremo de la transmisión para prevenir la pérdida de aceite.

6   La instalación se hace en el orden inverso al procedimiento de desensamble, pero esté seguro que las marcas hechas en las pestañas durante el proceso de remover están alineadas.

Ejes propulsores delanteros y traseros

Nota: Para los modelos 1986 y más modernos remueva e instale el eje propulsor trasero, refiérase al Capítulo 8.

7   Marque las posiciones de las pestañas del eje propulsor en ambos el diferencial y la caja de transferencia.

8   Remueva los pernos de afianzamiento en ambos extremos y baje el eje propulsor del vehículo.

9   Si es necesario, la camisa de la horquilla se puede separar del eje propulsor y el sello de grasa ser reemplazado (vea ilustración).

10   La instalación se hace en el orden inverso al procedimiento de desensamble, pero esté seguro que las marcas hechas en la pestaña durante el proceso de remover están alineadas.

8   Sellos para el aceite del diferencial delantero - reemplazo

Sello trasero del aceite

Refiérase a las ilustraciones 8.4 y 8.5

1   Remueva el tapón de drenaje del diferencial delantero y drene el aceite en un recipiente.

2   Levante el frente del vehículo y sosténgalo firmemente encima de soportes. Esté seguro que el freno de estacionamiento está aplicado.

3   Desconecte el eje propulsor delantero de la pestaña del piñón del diferencial. Refiérase a la Sección 7, si es necesario.

4   Remueva la tuerca del piñón del extremo del eje (**vea ilustración**). Para detener que la pestaña gire, dos de los pernos del eje propulsor pueden ser instalados en la pestaña y una barra ruptora puede ser instalada entre ellos.

5   Usando un extractor, remueva la pestaña compañera del diferencial (**vea ilustración**).

6   Use un destornillador para abrirlo haciéndole palanca para removerlo hacia afuera el sello de aceite. Tenga cuidado de no rasguñar ni dañar el diámetro de la superficie del diferencial para el sello.

7   Aplique grasa de propósito múltiple a la cavidad entre el labio del sello nuevo del aceite, entonces péguele gentilmente hacia adentro del diferencial usando un dado grande.

8   Instale la pestaña compañera y asegúrela apretando la tuerca del piñón al par de torsión apropiado.

9   Ajuste una llave torsiométrica de pulgada libra en la tuerca del piñón y lentamente gírela hacia la derecha, notando a que par de torsión los ejes comienzan a girar. Esto es la precarga del piñón y debe ser chequeado contra las especificaciones. Si la precarga no está dentro de la distancia dada, apriete la tuerca un poco a la vez hasta que la precarga esté correcta. **Caución:** *Esta precarga es lograda usando un espaciador de desplome adentro del diferencial. Si la precarga es puesta encima de la especificación recomendada, el diferencial tendrá que ser desarmado y el espaciador reemplazado.*

10   El resto del procedimiento de la instalación se hace en el orden inverso al procedimiento de desensamble. Refiérase al Capítulo 1 si es necesario para llenar el diferencial con aceite.

Sello lateral del aceite

Refiérase a las ilustración 8.12

Lado izquierdo (todos los años) y lado derecho hasta los modelos 1985

11   Remueva el semieje como se describe en la Sección 3.

12   Remueva la pestaña lateral haciéndole palanca hacia afuera con dos barras (**vea ilustración**).

13   Remueva el sello de aceite lateral.

14   Instale el sello nuevo en el diferencial con un dado grande.

15   Aplique grasa a la cavidad entre los labios del sello.

16   Vuelva a instalar la pestaña lateral y el semieje.

Lado derecho (modelos 1986 y más modernos)

Refiérase a las ilustraciones 8.17, 8.19 y 8.21

17   Remueva los cuatro pernos de retención del tubo de extensión y hale el eje lateral del diferencial del tubo de extensión (**vea ilustración**).

18   Instale el eje en una prensa. Coloque un bloque de madera en ambos lados del eje para prevenir daño y un bloque de madera

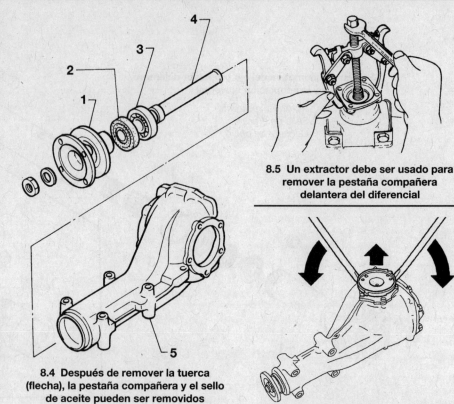

8.4 Después de remover la tuerca (flecha), la pestaña compañera y el sello de aceite pueden ser removidos

1	Pestaña compañera
2	Sello de aceite
3	Balero piloto
4	Espaciador para el balero

8.5 Un extractor debe ser usado para remover la pestaña compañera delantera del diferencial

8.12 La pestaña delantera lateral del diferencial es removida haciéndole palanca hacia afuera con dos barras posicionadas como está mostrado

debajo del eje para sostenerlo.

19   Usando un cincel frío, corte el collar del balero hacia afuera del eje (**vea ilustración**).

20   Remueva los cuatro pernos de los tubos de extensión al portador del diferencial y separe el tubo de extensión del portador.

21   Vuelva a instalar el eje lateral y el retenedor en el tubo de extensión e instale los pernos. Usando un extractor de dos mandíbulas, empuje el eje lateral hacia afuera del retene-

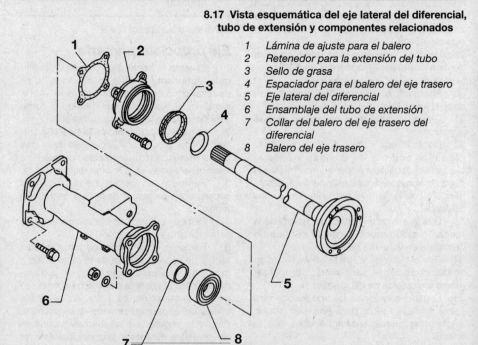

8.17 Vista esquemática del eje lateral del diferencial, tubo de extensión y componentes relacionados

1	Lámina de ajuste para el balero
2	Retenedor para la extensión del tubo
3	Sello de grasa
4	Espaciador para el balero del eje trasero
5	Eje lateral del diferencial
6	Ensamblaje del tubo de extensión
7	Collar del balero del eje trasero del diferencial
8	Balero del eje trasero

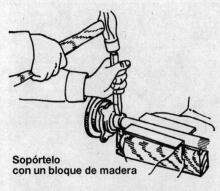

Sopórtelo
con un bloque de madera

8.19 Cuando esté usando el cincel para remover el collar del balero hacia afuera, tenga mucho cuidado para no dañar el eje

dor y el balero (**vea ilustración**).

22 Usando un destornillador grande, hágale palanca para removerlo hacia afuera con una palanca al sello del retenedor. El sello nuevo puede ser prensado en el retenedor con un bloque de madera o un dado con el mismo diámetro exterior como el sello.

23 Destornille el retenedor del tubo de extensión y lo coloca en el eje lateral. Deslice el balero en el eje, seguido por un collar nuevo. Éstos se deben apretar en posición. Si el acceso a una prensa hidráulica no está disponible, lleve el ensamblaje a un taller de rectificación o su concesionario Nissan.

24 El resto del procedimiento de la instalación se hace en el orden inverso al procedimiento de desensamble.

---

9   Diferencial delantero - remover e instalar

Refiérase a las ilustraciones 9.6a, 9.6b y 9.10

1   Levante el frente del vehículo y sosténgalo firmemente encima de soportes. Aplique el freno de estacionamiento o bloquee las ruedas de atrás.

2   Remueva el tapón del drenaje y drene el aceite del diferencial en un recipiente.

3   Desconecte el eje propulsor delantero del diferencial trasero, refiriéndose a la Sección 7, si es necesario.

4   Remueva los pernos que conectan los semiejes al diferencial y los pone en posición fuera del camino, colgándolos con pedazos de alambres para evitar dañar las acoplaciones CV (velocidad constante) exteriores.

5   Posicione un gato debajo del diferencial para sostenerlo cuando los pernos de afianzamientos sean removidos.

6   Remueva los pernos de afianzamiento del diferencial en el frente (**vea ilustraciones**).

Modelos 1980 al 1985

7   Remueva los pernos de afianzamiento de la parte trasera del diferencial.

8   Remueva los pernos que conectan el miembro transversal, directamente debajo del diferencial, al chasis y levántelo hacia afuera del miembro transversal.

Modelos 1986 y más modernos

9   Remueva los pernos de afianzamiento del motor y levante el motor con una grúa o un gato y un bloque de madera debajo de la cacerola de aceite.

10   Remueva los pernos de afianzamiento del miembro del diferencial al chasis (**vea ilustración**). El miembro de afianzamiento será removido junto con el diferencial.

8.21 Reensamble el eje lateral en el tubo de la extensión y prense el eje hacia afuera del balero con un extractor

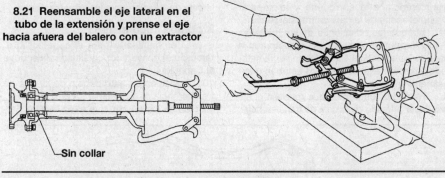

Sin collar

9.6b Pernos de afianzamiento para la ubicación del diferencial delantero (flechas) - modelos 1986 y más modernos

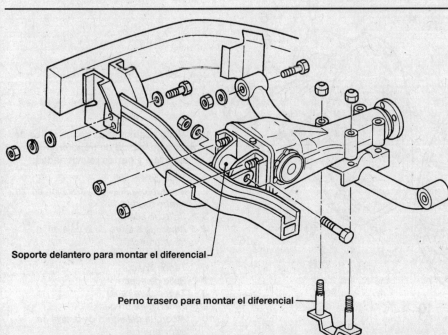

Soporte delantero para montar el diferencial

Perno trasero para montar el diferencial

9.6a Detalles de como está montado el diferencial delantero (modelos 1980 al 1985)

9.10 Remueva los pernos de afianzamiento del miembro del diferencial al chasis (el perno derecho está mostrado aquí)

10   Sellos de aceite de la caja de transferencia - reemplazo

Refiérase a las ilustraciones 10.2 y 10.5

1   Levante el vehículo y sosténgalo firmemente encima de soportes. Remueva el protector para las piedras de la caja de transferencia y drene el aceite.
2   Marque la posición apropiada de la pestaña del eje propulsor con relación a la pestaña de la caja de transferencia **(vea ilustración)**. Remueva los pernos y desconecte el eje propulsor.
3   Remueva la tuerca prisionera de la pestaña compañera a la caja de transferencia. Para mantener de que la pestaña no gire, vuelva a instalar dos de los pernos del eje propulsor y comprometa una barra ruptora entre ellos.
4   Usando un extractor, remueva la pestaña compañera.
5   Hágale palanca cuidadosamente al sello de aceite hacia afuera con un destornillador, esté seguro de no rasguñar ni dañar el diámetro de los cilindros del sello en el albergue **(vea ilustración)**. Un bloque de madera colocado entre el destornillador y el albergue puede proporcionar apalancamiento adicional.
6   Lubrique el labio del sello con aceite de engrane y lo instala en su posición con un dado o un bloque de madera.
7   Coloque la pestaña compañera en su posición. Instale la tuerca prisionera y la aprieta al par de torsión especificado.
8   Vuelva a instalar el eje propulsor, esté seguro que las marcas que se hicieron en las

pestañas durante el proceso de remover están alineadas.
9   Rellene la caja de transferencia con aceite, refiérase al Capítulo 1 si es necesario.
10 Vuelva a instalar el protector contra las piedras y baje el vehículo al piso.

Todos los modelos

11 Baje cuidadosamente el gato, entonces retire el diferencial por debajo del vehículo.
12 La instalación se hace en el orden inverso al procedimiento de desensamble.

11   Caja de transferencia - remover e instalar

Refiérase a las ilustraciones 11.7, 11.8, 11.11, 11.17 y 11.18

Remover

1   Desconecte el cable negativo de la batería que viene de la batería.
2   Levante la parte trasera del vehículo y sosténgalo firmemente encima de soportes. Bloquee las ruedas delanteras.
3   Remueva los pernos que retienen el protector contra las piedras de la caja de transferencia a la carrocería y lo separa. Drene el aceite de la caja de transferencia.
4   Marque las posiciones de las pestañas del eje propulsor que está en contacto con la caja de transferencia. Ellos deben ser reinstalados exactamente según ellos estaban originalmente instalados.
5   Remueva los pernos que retienen el eje propulsor primario de la caja de transferencia.

10.2 Marque la relación del eje propulsor a la pestaña compañera en la caja de transferencia antes de remover los pernos (esto asegurará un alineamiento correcto durante la instalación del eje)

6   Remueva los ejes propulsores delanteros y traseros.
7   Desconecte el alambre que se dirige al interruptor de 4WD (tracción en las cuatro ruedas) **(vea ilustración)**.
8   Desconecte el cable del velocímetro de la caja de transferencia **(vea ilustración)**.

Modelos 1980 al 1985

9   Si es necesario para el espacio libre, remueva el convertidor catalítico refiriéndose al Capítulo 4.
10 Posicione un gato debajo de la caja de transferencia para sostener su peso.
11 Afloje los pernos que aseguran los cal-

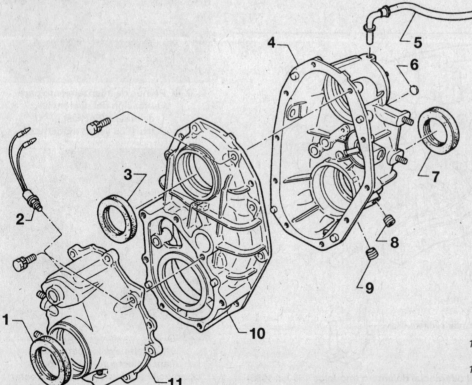

10.5 Vista esquemática de los sellos de aceite de la caja de transferencia, albergue y partes relacionadas

1   *Sello de aceite*
2   *Interruptor para 4WD (tracción en las cuatro ruedas)*
3   *Sello de aceite*
4   *Albergue trasero de la caja de transferencia*
5   *Tubo de respiración*
6   *Tapón Welch*
7   *Sello de aceite*
8   *Tapón para llenar*
9   *Tapón para drenar*
10 *Albergue delantero de la caja de transferencia*
11 *Cubierta delantera para el albergue delantero de la caja de transferencia*

11.7 Remueva todos los conectores (flechas) eléctricos conectados a los alambres que se dirigen a la caja de transferencia

11.8 El cable del velocímetro se conecta en la parte derecha trasera de la caja de transferencia (flecha)

zos aisladores a la caja de transferencia **(vea ilustración)**.

12 Moviéndose al interior, remueva el fuelle de caucho de alrededor de la palanca de cambio de la caja de transferencia.

13 Remueva los pernos que conectan los calzos aisladores al chasis y baje cuidadosamente la caja de transferencia del vehículo.

14 Deslice la caja de transferencia hacia afuera y si es necesario, remueva los calzos aisladores desde ella.

Modelos 1986 y más modernos

15 Remueva la barra de torsión (vea Capítulo 11).

16 Sostenga la transmisión con un gato y un bloque de madera, entonces remueva el miembro transversal inferior de la caja de transferencia.

17 Remueva la palanca de control de transferencia a la tuerca de la palanca exterior de cambio, entonces deslice la varilla hacia afuera del espárrago **(vea ilustración)**.

18 Sostenga la caja de transferencia con un gato de piso. Remueva los pernos de la caja de transferencia a la transmisión **(vea ilustración)** y deslice la caja de transferencia hacia atrás, desenganchándola de la transmisión. Bajándola cuidadosamente al piso.

19 Antes de instalar la caja de transferencia, aplique una capa de sellador Nissan No. KP610-00250 o equivalente a la superficie de acoplamiento de la caja de transferencia (modelos equipados con transmisión manual solamente).

Instalar

20 La instalación se hace en el orden inverso al procedimiento de desensamble, pero esté seguro que las marcas de la pestaña del eje propulsor hechas durante el proceso de remover están alineadas. Si es necesario, refiérase al Capítulo 1 para rellenar la caja de transferencia con aceite.

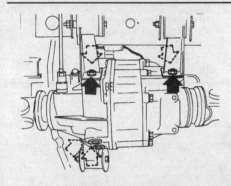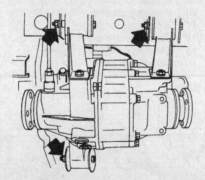

11.11 Pernos de afianzamiento para la ubicación de la caja de transferencia (izquierda) y los pernos del soporte al chasis (derecha) (modelos 1980 al 1985)

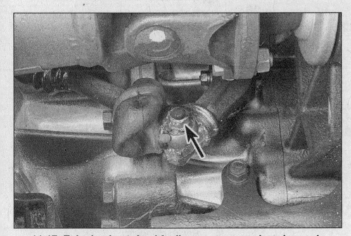

11.17 Eche hacia atrás el fuelle para exponer la palanca de control de transferencia a la tuerca para la palanca de cambiar (flecha), remueva la tuerca y deslice la varilla hacia afuera del espárrago

11.18 Los pernos de la caja de transferencia a la transmisión en los modelos 1986 y más modernos deben ser instalados en los mismos orificios - los tres pernos inferiores son más largos que los otros (no todo puede ser observado desde este ángulo)

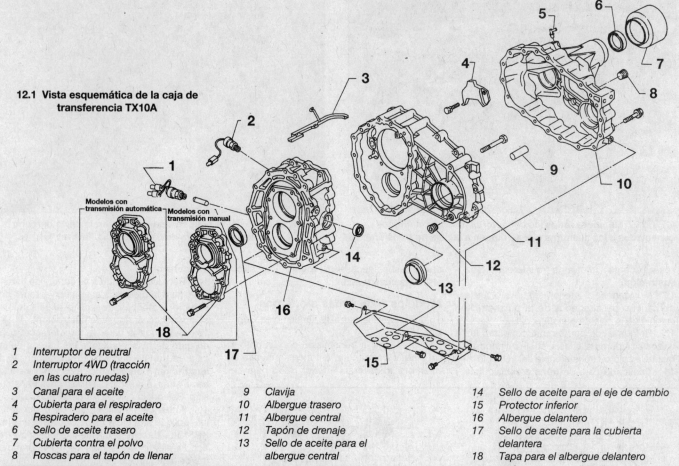

12.1 Vista esquemática de la caja de transferencia TX10A

1   Interruptor de neutral
2   Interruptor 4WD (tracción en las cuatro ruedas)
3   Canal para el aceite
4   Cubierta para el respiradero
5   Respiradero para el aceite
6   Sello de aceite trasero
7   Cubierta contra el polvo
8   Roscas para el tapón de llenar

9   Clavija
10 Albergue trasero
11 Albergue central
12 Tapón de drenaje
13 Sello de aceite para el albergue central

14 Sello de aceite para el eje de cambio
15 Protector inferior
16 Albergue delantero
17 Sello de aceite para la cubierta delantera
18 Tapa para el albergue delantero

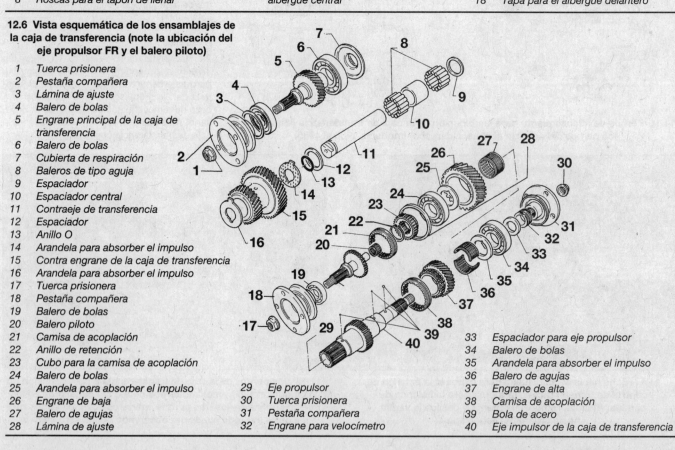

12.6 Vista esquemática de los ensamblajes de la caja de transferencia (note la ubicación del eje propulsor FR y el balero piloto)

1   Tuerca prisionera
2   Pestaña compañera
3   Lámina de ajuste
4   Balero de bolas
5   Engrane principal de la caja de transferencia
6   Balero de bolas
7   Cubierta de respiración
8   Baleros de tipo aguja
9   Espaciador
10 Espaciador central
11 Contraeje de transferencia
12 Espaciador
13 Anillo O
14 Arandela para absorber el impulso
15 Contra engrane de la caja de transferencia
16 Arandela para absorber el impulso
17 Tuerca prisionera
18 Pestaña compañera
19 Balero de bolas
20 Balero piloto
21 Camisa de acoplación
22 Anillo de retención
23 Cubo para la camisa de acoplación
24 Balero de bolas
25 Arandela para absorber el impulso
26 Engrane de baja
27 Balero de agujas
28 Lámina de ajuste

29 Eje propulsor
30 Tuerca prisionera
31 Pestaña compañera
32 Engrane para velocímetro

33 Espaciador para eje propulsor
34 Balero de bolas
35 Arandela para absorber el impulso
36 Balero de agujas
37 Engrane de alta
38 Camisa de acoplación
39 Bola de acero
40 Eje impulsor de la caja de transferencia

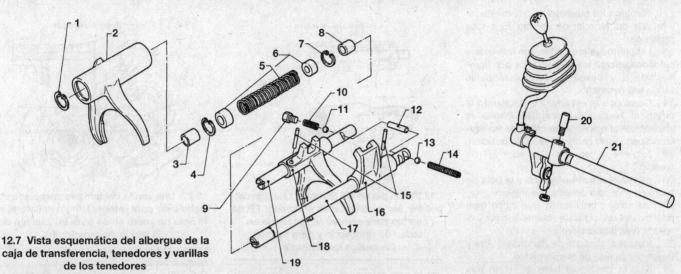

12.7 Vista esquemática del albergue de la caja de transferencia, tenedores y varillas de los tenedores

1	Anillo de retención	
2	Tenedor de cambio FR	
3	Espaciador	
4	Anillo de retención	
5	Resorte para el tenedor de cambio	
6	Buje para retener el resorte	
7	Anillo de retención	

8	Espaciador
9	Tapón para la bola unilateral
10	Resorte unilateral
11	Bola unilateral
12	Embolo de enclavamiento
13	Bola unilateral
14	Resorte unilateral

15	Clavija de retención
16	Soporte para la varilla del tenedor FR
17	Varilla del tenedor FR
18	Tenedor de cambio para la alta y la primera
19	Varilla para el tenedor de cambio para la alta y la primera

12   Caja de transferencia - reconstrucción completa

Refiérase a las ilustraciones 12.1 12.6, 12.7, 12.14, 12.21, 12.27, 12.45, 12.59, 12.63, 12.80a y 12.80b

Nota 1: *Este procedimiento se aplica a los vehículos fabricados desde el 1980 al 1985 solamente. Debido a la complejidad de los modelos 1986 y la caja de transferencia más moderna y las herramientas especiales requeridas, es recomendado que estos procedimientos de reparación interna sean dejados al departamento de servicio de su concesionario o un taller de reparación. El acceso a una prensa hidráulica es necesario para algunos pasos en el siguiente procedimiento.*

Nota 2: *Los modelos 1990 y 1991 están equipados con un caja de transferencia pesada (modelo TX10A). Esta unidad de tres pedazos* **(vea ilustración)** *incorpora engranes más grandes que requieren espacios libres diferentes. Es recomendado que las reparaciones internas sean dejadas al departamento de servicio de su concesionario u otro taller de reparación profesional.*

Tenedores y varillas para los tenedor

1   Con la caja de transferencia removida del vehículo, remueva toda la tierra y la grasa de las superficies exteriores.

2   Cambie la caja de transferencia a la posición de 4L y a la posición de 2H, entonces remueva las tuercas prisioneras de las tres pestañas de acompañamiento. Para mantener de que la pestaña no gire, vuelva a instalar los dos pernos de los ejes propulso-

res en el calzo y comprometa una barra ruptora entre ellos.

3   Usando un extractor, remueva las pestañas de acompañamiento.

4   Remueva el interruptor para la 4WD.

5   Remueva los pernos de la tapa delantera y entonces remueva la tapa delantera utilizándolo un martillo con cara suave. Si la tapa del balero delantero debe ser reemplazada refiérase al Paso 88.

6   Remueva el eje propulsor FR y el balero piloto **(vea ilustración)**.

7   Remueva el anillo de retención que retiene el tenedor del cambio FR **(vea ilustración)**. Remueva el ensamblaje del tenedor de cambio y el espaciador, junto con la camisa de acoplamiento.

8   Remueva el anillo de retención que retiene los cubos de la camisa de acoplamiento.

9   Extraiga el cubo de la camisa de acoplamiento.

10   Remueva los pernos de afianzamiento para el albergue delantero y entonces remueva el albergue delantero pegándole gentilmente con un martillo de cara suave.

11   Remueva la tuerca de la clavija. Péguele gentilmente a la clavija hacia afuera con un martillo.

12   Remueva el eje de cambio de cruz.

13   Remueva la palanca de cambio con la palanca del diferencial.

14   Remueva el tapón de la bola unilateral localizado en el exterior del albergue y remueva el resorte unilateral y la bola **(vea ilustración)**.

15   Usando un punzón, péguele hacia afuera a la clavija de retención para el tenedor de Alta y Baja.

16   Péguele gentilmente al ensamblaje del

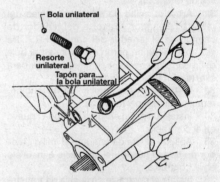

12.14 Ubicación del tapón de bola unilateral

eje propulsor trasero de la caja de transferencia, remuévalo con el tenedor de cambio y el ensamblaje del contra engrane de alta y baja. Tenga cuidado de no dejar caer las agujas de los baleros.

17   Remueva el ensamblaje del engrane principal.

18   Remueva la lámina para ajustes de la caja de transferencia delantera.

19   Remueva las varillas de los tenedores de Alta, Baja y FR, pulmón de entrecierre, bola de acero y el resorte unilateral.

20   Asegure la varilla del tenedor FR en una prensa y remueva la clavija de retención. El soporte de la varilla del tenedor FR entonces puede ser removido.

21   Insercióne un perno de 8 mm y la tuerca del tenedor del cambio de FR. Apriete la tuerca para eliminar la tensión del resorte del tenedor de cambio, entonces remueva el anillo de retención con alicates para anillos de cierre **(vea ilustración)**.

22   Remueva los bujes del resorte retenedor y resorte del tenedor de cambio. Entonces sepárelos.

23   Limpie todas las partes con solvente y cuidadosamente las inspecciona por rayones, daño y desgaste, reemplazándolas según sea necesario.

24   Comience el ensamblaje instalando la tapa del respirador, después instale el ensamblaje principal del engrane de transferencia pegándole gentilmente en su posición.

25   Expulse el tapón del tenedor FR de cambio.

26   Instale el resorte unilateral y la bola de acero en el orificio del albergue trasero.

27   Inserciône una varilla que calce bien adentro del orificio para retener la bola y el resorte **(vea ilustración)**.

28   Instale el tenedor de cambio de Alta y Baja en la camisa de acoplamiento.

29   Con la varilla del tenedor FR en una prensa, péguele gentilmente a la clavija de retención en su posición.

30   Instale la varilla del tenedor FR, empujando la varilla usada para retener la bola y el resorte hacia afuera de su posición. Después instale la clavija de retención.

31   Conecte el soporte de la varilla del tenedor FR a la varilla del tenedor FR con la clavija de retención.

32   Arme el anillo de retención, bujes del resorte retenedor y resorte del tenedor de cambio en el tenedor del cambio FR. Otra vez, inserciône un perno de 8 mm en el buje del resorte retenedor y apriete la tuerca para eliminar la tensión del resorte.

33   Instale el otro anillo de retención, remueva el perno y la tuerca.

34   Instale un anillo sellador de tipo O nuevo en el contraeje.

35   Aplique aceite de engrane al anillo sellador de tipo O nuevo del contraeje e instálelo en el contraeje.

36   Instale el contraeje en la caja de transferencia.

37   Con la arandela para absorber el impulso del contra engrane instalada en su posición, instale el ensamblaje del contra engrane.

38   Levante el ensamblaje del contra engrane levemente e instale el ensamblaje del eje propulsor, acoplándolos uno con el otro.

39   Instale la pestaña de acompañamiento en el lado trasero del eje propulsor y apriete la tuerca con los dedos.

40   Péguele gentilmente al extremo delantero del ensamblaje del eje propulsor y lo instala en el albergue trasero.

41   Instale la varilla del tenedor de Alta y Baja y la asegura con la clavija de retención.

42   Aplique sellador al orificio y vuelva a instalar el tapón.

43   Instale la bola unilateral y el resorte unilateral.

44   Aplique sellador a las roscas del tapón de la bola unilateral y lo instala en su posición.

45   Instale la camisa de acoplación del cubo y mida el juego final **(vea ilustración)**. Un anillo de retención del espesor apropiado (como está listado en las especificaciones) debe ser

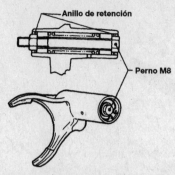

12.21 Un perno M8 (8 mm) y una tuerca pueden ser insertados en el tenedor FR de cambio para comprimir el resorte en orden de removerlo y para instalar los anillos de retención

usado para retener el cubo de la camisa de acoplamiento, así que el juego final será de 0 a 0.0079 pulgada (0 a 0.20 mm).

46   Instale la palanca de cambio con la palanca diferencial.

47   Instale el eje de cambio de cruz.

48   Aplique grasa a la arandela para absorber el impulso, el engrane delantero principal y láminas de ajustes delanteras para la caja de transferencia y colóquelas en sus posiciones.

49   Esté seguro que la superficie de acoplamiento del albergue delantero está limpia y aplique sellador en una capa continua alrededor de el.

50   Instale el albergue delantero pegándole gentilmente en su posición.

51   Instale el espaciador, ensamblaje del tenedor de cambio FR con la camisa de acoplamiento, otro espaciador y asegúrelos con un anillo de retención.

52   Aplique aceite de engrane al balero piloto y lo instala en su posición.

53   Conecte el eje propulsor FR al eje propulsor de la caja de transferencia.

54   Esté seguro que las superficies de acoplamiento delanteras del albergue y la cubierta delantera están limpias, entonces aplique una capa de sellador continua a la parte delantera del albergue.

55   Conecte la tapa delantera a la parte delantera del albergue e instale los pernos de

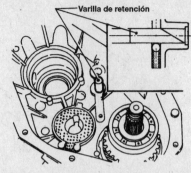

12.27 Una varilla del tamaño apropiada se debe usar para retener la bola unilateral y la bola de acero antes de la instalación de la varilla del tenedor FR

afianzamiento.

56   Instale las pestañas de acompañamiento y asegúrelas con tuercas prisioneras nuevas.

57   Instale el interruptor para el 4WD.

Engranes y ejes

58   Remueva el ensamblaje del eje propulsor de la caja de transferencia, ensamblaje del contra engrane, tenedores y varillas de los tenedores como está descrito en la sub sección previa.

59   Remueva el engrane de transferencia principal y la cubierta del respirador de la parte trasera del albergue. Antes de desarmar, el ensamblaje del engranado debe de ser medido para el juego libre usando un calibrador al tacto **(vea ilustración)**. Compare estas medidas con las especificaciones, indicarán la cantidad de desgaste.

60   Apriete el balero del engrane de transferencia principal para el eje delantero.

61   Apriete el balero del engrane de transferencia principal del eje trasero.

62   Remueva los baleros de aguja, espaciador central y el espaciador del contra engrane.

63   Usando un extractor, remueva el balero delantero del ensamblaje del engrane de Baja **(vea ilustración)**.

64   Remueva la arandela para absorber el impulso y la bola de acero.

65   Remueva el engrane de Baja y el balero de aguja.

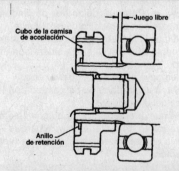

12.45 El juego final del cubo de la camisa de acoplamiento debe ser medido en el punto mostrado

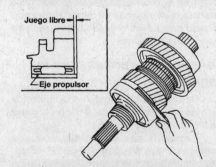

12.59 El juego final del engrane del eje propulsor de la caja de transferencia debe ser medido antes y después de removerlo

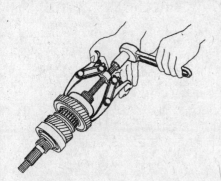

12.63 Un extractor se puede usar para remover los baleros delanteros y traseros del eje propulsor

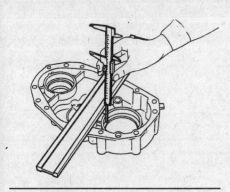

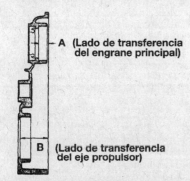

A **(Lado de transferencia del engrane principal)**

B **(Lado de transferencia del eje propulsor)**

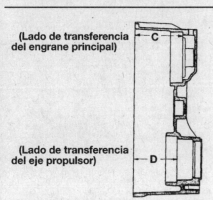

(Lado de transferencia del engrane principal)   C

(Lado de transferencia del eje propulsor)   D

12.80a Para el ajuste apropiado de las láminas, las medidas mostradas encima deben ser hechas para ambos albergues delanteros y traseros

66   Prense el engrane gusano del ensamblaje del velocímetro hacia afuera del engrane de Alta.

67   Remueva el espaciador y la bola de acero.

68   Usando un extractor, remueva el balero trasero del ensamblaje del engrane de Alta.

69   Remueva la arandela para absorber el impulso y la bola de acero.

70   Remueva el engrane de Alta, baleros de aguja y camisas de acoplamiento.

71   Limpie todas las partes en solvente e inspeccione todos los engranes por desgaste excesivo, astillas, roturas o cualquier otros daños y reemplácelas según sea necesario.

72   Comience el ensamblaje del engrane de Alta aplicando primero aceite de engrane a los baleros de aguja. Instálelos y el engrane de Alta en el eje propulsor de la caja de transferencia.

73   Aplique grasa a la bola de acero, la arandela para absorber el impulso y las conecta al engrane de Alta.

74   Prense el balero del eje propulsor trasero, esté seguro de detener el engrane de Alta con su mano para evitar dejar caer la arandela de impulso.

75   Instale el espaciador del eje propulsor.

76   Aplique grasa a la bola de acero e instale la bola y el engrane gusano del velocímetro.

77   Comience el ensamblaje del engrane de baja aplicándole aceite de engrane al balero de aguja, después instale el balero de aguja, camisa de acoplamiento y engrane de Baja en el eje propulsor.

78   Aplique grasa a la bola de acero, a la arandela para absorber el impulso y las conecta al engrane de baja.

79   Prense el balero del eje propulsor delantero en el eje, esté seguro de detener el engrane de baja con su mano para evitar dejar caer la arandela para absorber el impulso. Otra vez, mida el juego final del engrane para estar completamente seguro de instalarlo apropiadamente.

80   En cualquier momento que la arandela para absorber el impulso, cualquier balero de bolas, eje propulsor, engrane principal de la caja de transferencia o el albergue delantero o trasero son reemplazado con partes nuevas, la caja de transferencia debe ser ajustada con láminas de ajuste como está descrito más abajo:

a)   *Mida la distancia entre la parte exterior de ambos diámetros de los cilindros de los baleros y la orilla delantera del albergue, refiérase a esas dimensiones como A y B* (vea ilustración) *y escriba las medidas.*

b)   *Mida las mismas distancias en el albergue trasero (refiérase a estas medidas como C y D y anótelas también. Cuando mida la C, esté seguro que la tapa del respirador está instalada en su posición normal.*

c)   *Mida la distancia entre las orillas exteriores de los baleros en el ensamblaje del engrane de transferencia principal. Marque esta medida E* (vea ilustración).

d)   *Mida la distancia entre las orillas exteriores de los baleros del eje de transferencia y marque esta medida F.*

e)   *La lámina correcta para ajustes del engrane principal delantero es determinado agregando las medidas A y C y entonces restando la E del total. Anote el resultado y refiérase a las especificaciones para el espesor apropiado de las láminas para ajustes.*

f)   *La lámina para ajuste correcta para la caja de transferencia delantera es encontrada igualmente agregando las medidas B y D y entonces restando la F del total. Refiérase a las especificaciones para encontrar el espesor apropiado de la lámina de ajustes que se debe usar.*

g)   *Una vez que los espesores correctos de las láminas para ajustes sean encontrado, instálelas en posicione.*

81   Comience el ensamblaje del engrane de transferencia principal y contra engrane prensando el engrane de transferencia principal del balero delantero en el eje.

82   Prense el balero trasero del engrane principal en el eje.

83   Instale la tapa del respirador, si no lo ha hecho ya y después instale el engrane principal de la caja de transferencia.

84   Aplique grasa a todos los baleros de aguja y los espaciadores.

85   Instale el espaciador central en el contra engrane, entonces ensamble los baleros de aguja y los espaciadores en el contra engrane. Después de instalar los baleros de aguja, aplique una capa gruesa de grasa para detenerlas en su lugar.

86   Instale el ensamblaje del eje propulsor de la caja de transferencia, tenedores y varillas de los tenedores, refiriéndose a la sub sección previa.

Tapa delantera del balero

87   Remueva la tapa delantera refiriéndose a la sub sección de tenedores y varillas de tenedores.

88   Hágale palanca hacia afuera del sello de aceite de la tapa delantera.

89   Remueva el anillo de retención que retiene el balero.

90   Prense el balero hacia afuera de la tapa.

91   La instalación se hace en el orden inverso al procedimiento de desensamble.

12.80b Midiendo la distancia entre ambas orillas exteriores del ensamblaje del balero para el engrane principal (E) y el eje propulsor (F)

Notas

Capítulo 10   Frenos

Contenidos

Especificaciones

Frenos de disco
Desviación máxima del rotor
- 1980 al 1983 ... 0.0059 en (0.15 mm)
- 1984 en adelante ... 0.0028 pulgada (0.07 mm)

Variación (paralelismo) máximo del espesor del rotor
- 1980 al 1983 ... 0.0028 pulgada (0.07 mm)
- 1984 ... 0.0012 pulgada (0.03 mm)
- 1985 en adelante ... 0.0008 pulgada (0.02 mm)

Espesor mínimo del rotor
- 1980 al 1983 ... 0.413 pulgada (10.5 mm)
- 1984 y 1985 ... 0.787 pulgada (20.0 mm)
- 1986 en adelante
  - CL25VA (modelos de 2WD de 4 cilindros) ... 0.787 pulgada (20.0 mm)
  - CL25VD (todo los modelos V6 de 4WD) ... 0.945 pulgada (24.0 mm)
  - AD14VB (rotor trasero del freno de disco) ... 0.630 pulgada (16.0 mm)

Frenos de tambor
Diámetro interior máximo del tambor (fundido en el tambor)
- 1980 al 1983 ... 10.06 pulgadas (255.5 mm)
- 1984 en adelante
  - LT26B (2WD de trabajo livianos) ... 10.30 pulgadas (261.5 mm)
  - DS25B, DS25C, DS25D (HD 2WD y 4WD) ... 10.06 pulgadas (255.5 mm)
  - DS22 (modelos con dobles neumáticos) ... 8.72 pulgadas (221.5 mm)
  - LT30A (1991 y los modelos más modernos) ... 11.67 pulgadas (296.5 mm)

Límite de desviación radial del tambor
- 1980 al 1983 ... 0.0047 pulgada (0.12 mm)
- 1984 ... 0.0012 pulgada (0.03 mm)
- 1985 en adelante ... 0.002 pulgada (0.05 mm)

Fuera del límite de lo redondo del tambor
- 1980 al 1983 ... 0.0006 pulgada (0.015 mm)
- 1984 ... 0.002 pulgada (0.05 mm)
- 1985 en adelante ... 0.0012 pulgada (0.03 mm)

Conicidad máxima del tambor
- 1980 al 1983 ... 0.0008 pulgada (0.02 mm)
- 1984 en adelante ... 0.0016 pulgada (0.04 mm)

Amplificador para los frenos

Longitud de la varilla de rendimiento
1980 al 1983...	0.384 a 0.394 pulgada (9.75 a 10.0 mm)
1984 y 1985..	No es ajustable
1986 en adelante...	0.4045 a 0.4144 pulgada (10.275 a 10.525 mm)

Longitud de la varilla de entrada
1980	7.09 pulgada (180 mm)
1981 al 1983...	10.83 pulgadas (275 mm)
1984 y 1985..	10.10 pulgadas (256.5 mm)
1986 en adelante...	No es ajustable

Especificaciones técnicas

	Pies-libras
Pernos de afianzamiento de la mordaza (1980 al 1983)....................	53 a 72
Pernos de la horquilla al cuerpo del cilindro (1980 al 1983)....................	12 a 15
Pernos de la clavija de la mordaza al resbaladero (1984 en adelante)....	16 a 23
Pernos del miembro de torque al vástago (1984 en adelante)..............	53 a 72
Clavijas (1988) traseras de la guía de la mordaza del freno...................	16 a 23
Miembro de torque al albergue del eje trasero (1988).........................	40 a 47
Pernos del rotor al cubo	
1980 al 1983...	33
1984 en adelante...	36 a 51
Perno de la manguera del freno a la acoplación de a la mordaza	12 a 14
Tuerca de la clavija del fulcro del pedal del freno	
Hasta el 1990	6 a 8
1991 y más moderno	12 a 16
Amplificador de los frenos a la pared para detener el fuego	
Hasta el 1990	6 a 8
1991 y más moderno	9 a 12
Tuercas de afianzamiento del cilindro maestro...........................	6 a 8
Plato de apoyando de los frenos al eje trasero	
Modelos con un solo neumático	39 a 46
Modelos con dobles neumáticos.......................	62 a 80
Tuercas de afianzamiento de los cilindros de las ruedas	
1980 al 1983...	11 a 13
1984 al 1990...	3.9 a 5.4
1991 y más moderno	4.3 a 8.0
Pérnos de afianzamientos para la válvula de detección de la carga	
Hasta el 1990	5.8 a 8.0
1991 y más moderno	12 a 15

1   Información general

El sistema de frenos en los vehículos cubiertos por este manual son de un diseño de sistema separado. Incorporan dos circuitos separados; uno para los frenos delanteros y uno para los frenos traseros. Con este sistema, si un circuito falla, el otro circuito todavía funcionará.

El cilindro maestro es diseñado para el sistema separado e incorpora un pistón primario para un circuito y un pistón secundario para el otro.

Una unidad de amplificación de vacío es usada para absorber el vacío del múltiple de admisión para aumentar la asistencia de poder a la presión normal del freno.

La válvula de detección de la carga Nissan (NLSV) es diseñada para prevenir que las ruedas traseras se obstruyan en condiciones de frenado severo. La válvula opera cambiando la distribución de la presión del flúido del freno delantero y trasero en respuesta a la carga del vehículo.

Las ruedas delanteras están equipadas con frenos de disco. Éstos se componen de una parte plana, semejante a un rotor o un disco que es conectado al eje y la rueda. Alrededor de una sección del rotor es instalado un ensamblaje inmóvil de la mordaza que alberga las dos pastillas hidráulicamente operadas para el freno de disco. En los modelos más antiguos la pastilla interior es instalada con una cara mirando hacia la superficie interior del pistón del rotor, mientras que la pastilla exterior es instalada en una horquilla y las caras de las superficies exteriores del rotor. Los modelos más modernos tienen un arreglo sencillo o de mordaza de pistón deslizante doble. Cuando el pedal del freno es aplicado, la presión del flúido de freno fuerza ambas pastillas contra el rotor. La presión y la fricción resultante en el rotor es lo qué lentamente detiene la rueda.

Los frenos traseros en algunos modelos usan los frenos de tambor convencional de tipo de amplificador de doble servo. Otros modelos emplean una acción sencilla, de balata directriz/balata portante con un punto pivote en el fondo de cada balata. Con cual-

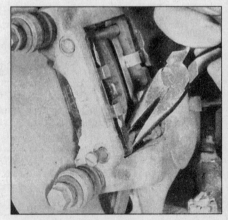

2.2a Use un destornillador para remover la clavija de retención para la pastilla hacia afuera

quiera de estos diseños, la presión del flúido del cilindro maestro fuerza los pistones traseros de los cilindros de las rueda hacia el exterior, que en cambio fuerza las balatas del freno contra el tambor que está girando del

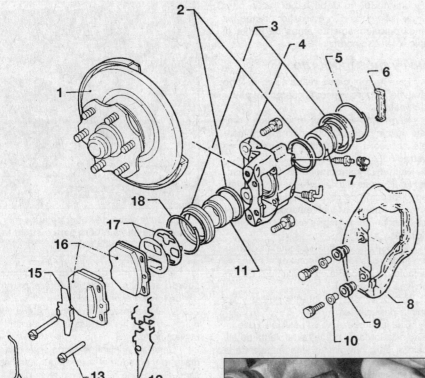

2.2b Vista esquemática del sistema de frenos de discos delanteros (1980 al 1983)

1   Rotor
2   Sello del pistón
3   Sello contra el polvo
4   Cuerpo del cilindro
5   Anillo de retención
6   Retenedor de la horquilla
7   Pistón interno
8   Horquilla
9   Agarradero
10 Collar
11 Pistón exterior
12 Resorte
13 Clavija de la pastilla
14 Retenedor
15 Lámina de ajuste
16 Pastilla
17 Lámina de ajuste
18 Anillo de retención

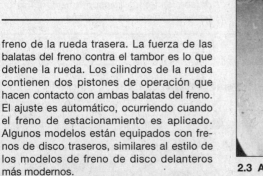

2.3 Alicates se pueden usar para remover las clavijas de las pastillas

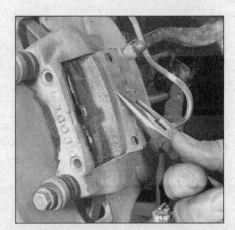

2.4 Alicates se pueden usar para remover las pastillas de las mordazas

freno de la rueda trasera. La fuerza de las balatas del freno contra el tambor es lo que detiene la rueda. Los cilindros de la rueda contienen dos pistones de operación que hacen contacto con ambas balatas del freno. El ajuste es automático, ocurriendo cuando el freno de estacionamiento es aplicado. Algunos modelos están equipados con frenos de disco traseros, similares al estilo de los modelos de freno de disco delanteros más modernos.

El freno de estacionamiento (freno de mano) es operado por un cable de manija instalada en el tablero y a las ruedas traseras.

Después de completar cualquier operación que implique el desarme de cualquier parte del sistema de frenos, siempre conduzca el vehículo para chequear por un desempeño apropiado del frenado antes de reasumir el manejo normal. Cuando esté probando los frenos, realice las pruebas en una superficie limpia, seca y plana. Condiciones otras que no sean éstas pueden llevar a un resultado inexacto de la prueba. Pruebe los frenos a varias velocidades con ambas presión del pedal ligera y pesada. El vehículo debe frenar uniformemente sin moverse de un lado al otro. Evite enclavamiento de los frenos, porque esto resbala los neumáticos, disminuye la eficiencia del frenado y el control.

Los neumáticos, la carga y la alineación de la suspensión delantera son los factores que afectan también el desempeño del frenar.

2   Pastillas de los frenos de disco - reemplazo

Refiérase a las ilustraciones 2.2a, 2.2b, 2.3, 2.4, 2.8, 2.14a, 2.14b, 2.14c, 2.15, 2.17, 2.19 y 2.20
Nota: *La siguiente información se aplica a ambos los frenos delanteros y traseros de disco (en los vehículos que estén equipados con discos de frenos traseros).*
Peligro: *Las pastillas de los frenos tienen que ser reemplazadas en las dos ruedas delanteras o traseras a la vez - nunca reemplace las pastillas en una sola rueda. También, el polvo creado por el sistema de los frenos contiene asbesto, el cual es muy dañoso para su salud. Nunca sople este polvo con un compresor de aire y no inhálelo tampoco. Al trabajar con los frenos, usted debe de usar una máscara de tipo filtro, la cual haya sido oficialmente aprobada. Bajo ninguna circunstancia utilice sol-*

ventes a base de petróleo para limpiar las piezas de los frenos. Solamente utilice solventes para frenos o alcohol desnaturalizado! Al otorgarles servicio a los frenos de disco, utilice solamente pastillas de calidad alta, de marca reconocida nacionalmente.
1   Afloje las tuercas de la rueda, levante el frente del vehículo y sopórtelo firmemente sobre estantes. Remueva la rueda.

1980 a 1983

2   Remueva el retenedor de la pastilla **(vea ilustraciones)**.
3   Mientras retiene los resortes en posición, remueva las dos clavijas de las pastillas. Remueva los resortes **(vea ilustración)**.
4   Levante hacia afuera las pastillas del freno y cualquier lámina para ajustes **(vea ilustración)**. **Nota:** *Después de remover las pastillas, no presione el pedal del freno, porque esto forzará el pistón hacia afuera del cilindro.*

5   Si las pastillas están barnizadas, dañadas, llenas de aceite o grasa, o desgastadas más allá de su límite (vea las especificaciones, Capítulo 1), ellas deben ser reemplazadas con unas nuevas. **Nota:** *Siempre reemplace las cuatro pastillas en el eje (dos en cada ensamblaje del freno) al mismo tiempo y no mezcle las pastilla de diferentes materiales.*

6   Remueva la tapa en el cilindro maestro del freno y absorba hacia afuera un poquito del flúido en el depósito.

7   Use un destornillador grande para forzar cuidadosamente el pistón otra vez adentro de la mordaza. No lo empuje demasiado hacia adentro, porque daño resultará. Deslice la pastilla interior nueva en su posición.

8   Ahora use un destornillador para deslizar la horquilla hacia el exterior para hacer lugar para la pastilla exterior nueva **(vea ilustración).**

9   Aplique una capa ligera de grasa a las clavijas de las pastillas.

10   Mientras retiene los resortes en su posición, instale las clavijas de las pastillas. Tenga cuidado para no ponerle grasa en los lados de fricción de las pastillas.

11   Instale el retenedor de las pastillas.

12   Vuelva a instalar la rueda, baje el vehículo y apriete las tuercas al par de torsión especificado.

13   Chequee el nivel del flúido en el cilindro maestro y agregue el flúido según sea necesario. Si ninguna manguera de flúido se ha

desconectado, no debe haber razón para purgar los frenos. Sin embargo, pruebe los frenos cuidadosamente antes de poner el vehículo en uso normal.

1984 y más moderno

14   Remueva el perno resbaladizo de tipo clavija del cilindro inferior al cuerpo **(vea ilustraciones).**

15   Hágale columpio al ensamblaje completo de la mordaza hacia encima, permitiéndole acceso a las pastillas del freno **(vea ilustración).**

16   Remueva los retenedores de las pastillas, las láminas para ajustes y las pastillas. Pegue atención cerca a la posición de cada láminas para ajustes y el retenedor, para que ellas puedan ser reinstaladas en sus lugares originales.

17   Aplique una cantidad pequeña de grasa para frenos basada en silicona a las áreas de contacto de la pastilla en el miembro de torque **(vea ilustración).**

18   Instale la pastilla interior nueva y las láminas para ajustes.

19   Gire la mordaza en su posición y use un destornillador largo o una herramienta de alineación para remover el ensamblaje de la mordaza del lado exterior **(vea ilustración).**

20   Levante la mordaza e instale la pastilla y las láminas para ajustes exteriores, seguido por los retenedores de las pastillas **(vea ilustración).**

21   Baje la mordaza en su posición e instale

2.8 Se le debe de hacer palanca a la horquilla hacia afuera para instalar la pastilla exterior

los pernos inferior de deslizamiento para el cuerpo de los cilindros. Apriete el perno al par de torsión especificado.

22   Vuelva a instalar la rueda, baje el vehículo y apriete las tuercas al par de torsión especificado.

23   Chequee el nivel del flúido en el cilindro maestro y agregue el flúido según sea necesario. Si ninguna de las mangueras del flúido se han desconectado, no debe haber la razón para purgar los frenos. Sin embargo, pruebe los frenos cuidadosamente antes de poner el vehículo en uso normal.

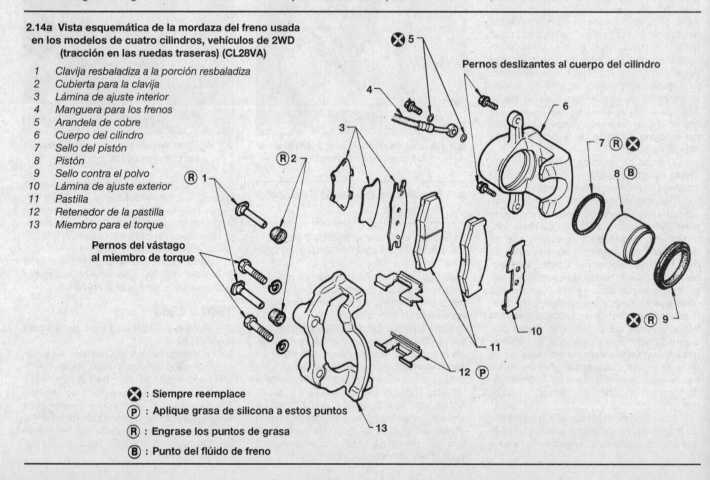

2.14a Vista esquemática de la mordaza del freno usada en los modelos de cuatro cilindros, vehículos de 2WD (tracción en las ruedas traseras) (CL28VA)

1   *Clavija resbaladiza a la porción resbaladiza*
2   *Cubierta para la clavija*
3   *Lámina de ajuste interior*
4   *Manguera para los frenos*
5   *Arandela de cobre*
6   *Cuerpo del cilindro*
7   *Sello del pistón*
8   *Pistón*
9   *Sello contra el polvo*
10   *Lámina de ajuste exterior*
11   *Pastilla*
12   *Retenedor de la pastilla*
13   *Miembro para el torque*

Pernos deslizantes al cuerpo del cilindro

Pernos del vástago al miembro de torque

✖ : Siempre reemplace
Ⓟ : Aplique grasa de silicona a estos puntos
Ⓡ : Engrase los puntos de grasa
Ⓑ : Punto del flúido de freno

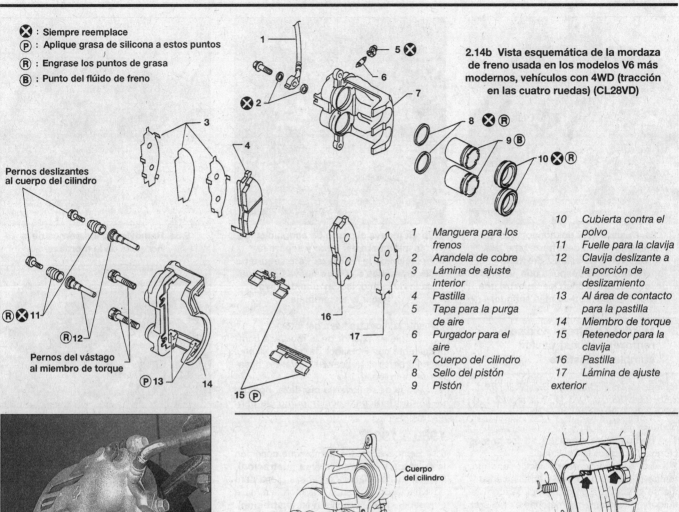

- ✕ : Siempre reemplace
- Ⓟ : Aplique grasa de silicona a estos puntos
- Ⓡ : Engrase los puntos de grasa
- Ⓑ : Punto del flúido de freno

2.14b Vista esquemática de la mordaza de freno usada en los modelos V6 más modernos, vehículos con 4WD (tracción en las cuatro ruedas) (CL28VD)

Pernos deslizantes al cuerpo del cilindro

Pernos del vástago al miembro de torque

1 Manguera para los frenos
2 Arandela de cobre
3 Lámina de ajuste interior
4 Pastilla
5 Tapa para la purga de aire
6 Purgador para el aire
7 Cuerpo del cilindro
8 Sello del pistón
9 Pistón
10 Cubierta contra el polvo
11 Fuelle para la clavija
12 Clavija deslizante a la porción de deslizamiento
13 Al área de contacto para la pastilla
14 Miembro de torque
15 Retenedor para la clavija
16 Pastilla
17 Lámina de ajuste exterior

2.14c Remueva el perno de tipo resbaladizo a la parte inferior del cuerpo del cilindro . . .

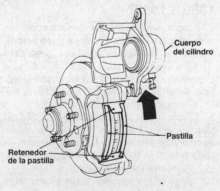

2.15 . . . entonces hágale columpio a la mordaza hasta obtener acceso a las pastillas del freno

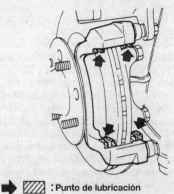

2.17 Aplique grasa basada en silicona a estos cuatros puntos

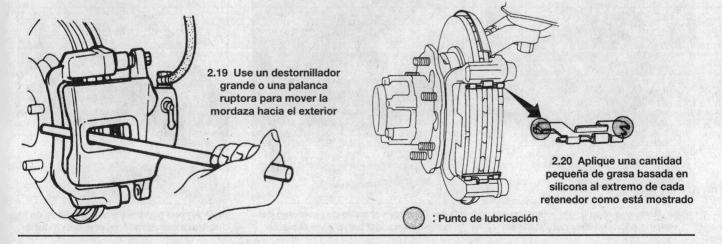

2.19 Use un destornillador grande o una palanca ruptora para mover la mordaza hacia el exterior

2.20 Aplique una cantidad pequeña de grasa basada en silicona al extremo de cada retenedor como está mostrado

: Punto de lubricación

3.2a Cuando esté desconectando las líneas del freno delantero, tape las aberturas de la línea del freno inmediatamente después que se haya desconectado la línea (se muestra una mordaza de modelo más antiguo)

3 Mordaza del freno de disco - remover, reconstrucción completa e instalar

Refiérase a las ilustraciones 3.2a, 3.2b, 3.6a, 3.6b, 3.8a, 3.8b, 3.10, 3.11, 3.20 al 3.27, 3.29, 3.33, 3.35 y 3.36
Remover

1　Remueva las pastillas de los frenos como se indica en la Sección 5.
2　En las mordazas de estilo antiguo, remueva el tubo del freno y tape inmediatamente la abertura para prevenir la fuga del flúido y para mantener materias extranjeras que entren en la línea **(vea ilustración)**. En las mordazas de estilo más modernos, remueva el perno de tipo copilla de la manguera del freno **(vea ilustración)**, desconecte la manguera de la mordaza y envuelva una bolsa plástica apretadamente alrededor de la manguera para prevenir la pérdida excesiva o contaminación del líquido.
3　Remueva los dos pernos de retención para la mordaza (estilo más antiguo) o los pernos de los cilindros superiores al cuerpo del miembro de torque (estilo más moderno)

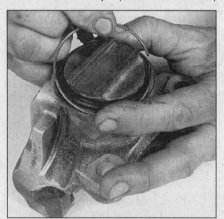

3.8a Remueva el anillo de retención del sello de polvo interior para el pistón

3.2b Remueva el perno de acoplación de la manguera del freno y separe la acoplación de la mordaza. Esté seguro de usar arandelas de cobre nuevas en cada lado de la acoplación cuando vaya a hacer el ensamblaje

y levante la mordaza fuera del rotor.
4　Limpie el exterior de la mordaza completamente con limpiador de freno o alcohol desnaturalizado. Nunca use solventes basados en petróleo.
5　Antes de remover la mordaza, compre un juego de reconstrucción completa para las mordazas.

1980 a 1983

6　Remueva los dos pernos que conectan la mordaza a la horquilla **(vea ilustración)**. Use un destornillador de cabeza plana para abrir haciéndole palanca a la mordaza hacia el exterior de la horquilla **(vea ilustración)**. Esto desenganchará el pistón de la horquilla.
7　Remueva la mordaza de la horquilla.
8　Remueva el poseedor de la horquilla del pistón interior, entonces remueva los anillos de retención del sello de polvo localizados en cada lado de la mordaza **(vea ilustraciones)**.
9　Remueva los sellos de polvo.
10　Empuje los pistones hacia afuera de la mordaza del lado de la pastilla **(vea ilustración)**.
11　Usando una clavija de madera o plástica, remueva los sellos del pistón del interior

3.8b Remueva el anillo de retención del sello exterior del polvo para el pistón

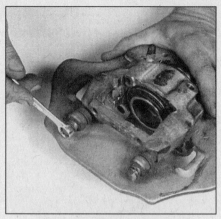

3.6a Removiendo los pernos de la horquilla de la mordaza

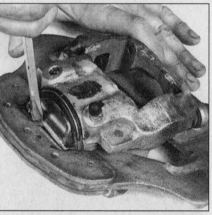

3.6b Use un destornillador para hacerle palanca al poseedor de la horquilla en la horquilla

del diámetro del cilindro de la mordaza **(vea ilustración)**.
12　Limpie todas las partes de metal en el flúido de freno o alcohol desnaturalizado. **Nota:** *Nunca use solventes basados en mineral, porque esto puede causar que los sellos de caucho se hinchen y posiblemente fallen.*
13　Chequee el interior de la superficie de los cilindros por cualquier rayón, oxidación, mellas u otros daños. Si rayones leves o

3.10 Ambos pistones son removidos de la mordaza empujando en el pistón exterior

3.11 Remueva el sello del pistón del cilindro de la mordaza. El uso de una herramienta de metal no es recomendado, porque puede rasguñar o rayar el cilindro

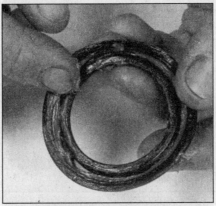

3.20 Aplique grasa basada en silicona (generalmente suministrada con el juego de reconstrucción) al interior del sello de polvo antes de la instalación

3.21 Instalando el sello exterior de polvo para el pistón

3.22 Instale el anillo de retención en el sello para el polvo exterior del pistón. Asegúrese que se asienta uniformemente alrededor de la circunferencia completa

pequeña oxidación está presente puede ser removido con una tela de esmeril de grado 600. Si el daño es profundo, el cuerpo completo tendrá que ser reemplazado.

14 Chequee por roturas de la horquilla, desgastes u otros daños excesivos y reemplace si es necesario.

15 Inspeccione el pistón por rayones, oxi-

dación, mellas u otros daños. La superficie donde el pistón se desliza es cromado y no puede ser pulido con papel de esmeril. Si cualquier desperfecto es encontrado, el pistón debe ser reemplazado. Si grasa para caucho es suministrada con el juego de reconstrucción completa, úsela para lubricar los cilindros del pistón. Flúido de freno se puede usar también para este propósito.

16 Instale los dos sellos de caucho en las ranuras en los cilindros para el pistón de la mordaza. Lubrique los sellos con grasa de caucho o flúido de freno.

17 Lubrique la superficies exterior de ambos pistones con o la grasa para caucho suministrada con el juego de reconstrucción completa o flúido de freno.

18 Insercióne cuidadosamente cada pistón en el cilindro respectivo. Tenga cuidado de no perturbar los sellos de caucho adentro de los cilindros.

19 Apriete el pistón exterior hacia adentro del cilindro para que la ranura del sello del pistón esté en línea con la orilla interior de las ranuras del sello de la mordaza.

20 Si una grasa anaranjada es suministrada con el juego de reconstrucción completa, la usa para llenar el interior de la superficie del sello exterior para el polvo (vea ilustración). Si ninguna grasa anaranjada es suministrado,

use una grasa aprobada de base de silicona.
21 Instale el sello de polvo para que ajuste correctamente en ambas ranuras del sello del pistón y la ranura del sello de la mordaza (vea ilustración).

22 Instale el anillo de retención firmemente alrededor del sello de polvo (vea ilustración).

23 Repita el mismo procedimiento con el pistón interior y el sello interior para el polvo.

24 Apriete el poseedor de la horquilla en su ranura en la cara interior del pistón (vea ilustración).

25 Insercióne la mordaza en posición adentro de la horquilla, asegurándose que el pistón exterior con el poseedor de la horquilla está alineado apropiadamente con la horquilla. Coloque este ensamblaje en una superficie nivelada para que el pistón exterior mire hacia abajo y aplique presión al pistón interior para apretar el poseedor de la horquilla en la horquilla (vea ilustración). Esto puede ser también hecho con una prensa hidráulica si una está disponible.

26 Una vez que el poseedor de la horquilla es apretado en la horquilla, instale los dos pernos de retención al albergue de la horquilla de la mordaza. Nota: Antes de instalar estos pernos chequee la condición de los fuelles de caucho, bujes y si ellos están desgastados o dañados, reemplácelos (vea ilustración). Apriete estos pernos al par de torsión especificado.

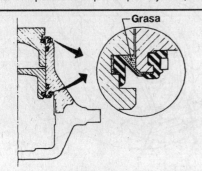

3.23 Los pistones del freno de disco se deben posicionar como está mostrado cuando sean instalados los sellos contra el polvo (aplique grasa a las ranuras del sello antes de instalarlas)

3.24 Coloque el poseedor de la horquilla en posición en el pistón interior

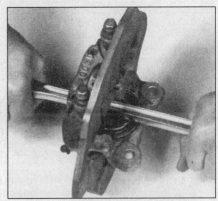

3.25 Para asentar el poseedor de la horquilla en la horquilla, se debe aplicar presión hacia abajo al pistón interior

3.26 Antes de instalar los pernos de la horquilla a la mordaza, inspeccione los bujes y los fuelles de caucho. Lubrique los bujes con grasa basada en silicona

1984 y más modernos

Nota: *Aunque este procedimiento muestre una sola reconstrucción completa de la mordaza de un solo pistón, también se aplica a la mordaza de doble pistón.*

27   Posicione un bloque de madera o bastantes trapos de taller en la mordaza como un cojín, después use aire comprimido para remover el pistón de la mordaza **(vea ilustración)**. Use solamente suficiente presión de aire para remover el pistón fuera del cilindro. Si el pistón es expulsado rápidamente, aun con el cojín en su posición, el pistón todavía puede ser dañado. **Peligro:** *Nunca coloque sus dedos enfrente del pistón en un atento de capturarlo o protegerlo cuando aplique aire comprimido, porque lesión grave podría ocurrir.*

28   Hágale palanca cuidadosamente a la tapa contra polvo hacia afuera del cilindro de la mordaza.

29   Usando una madera o herramienta plástica, remueva el sello del pistón de la ranura en el cilindro de la mordaza **(vea ilustración)**. Las herramientas de metal pueden causar daños a los cilindros.

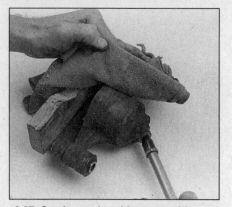

3.27 Con la mordaza bien protegida con trapos para colectar el pistón, use aire comprimido para forzar el pistón hacia afuera del cilindro. Asegúrese que las manos o los dedos no estén entre el pistón y la mordaza

30   Remueva la válvula de purga en la mordaza, entonces remueva las clavijas del resbaladero y la cubiertas desde el miembro de torque de la mordaza (todavía conectado al vástago de la dirección). Deseche todas las partes de caucho.

31   Limpie las partes que quedan con limpiador de freno o alcohol desnaturalizado éntonces sóplelas con aire comprimido para secarlas.

32   Examine cuidadosamente el pistón por mellas, rebarbas y pérdida del cromo. Si defectos en la superficie están presente, las partes deben ser reemplazadas. Chequee el cilindro de la mordaza en una manera similar. Pulido liviano con tela de esmeril es permisible para remover la corrosión y las mancha ligeras. Deseche los pernos de afianzamiento si están corroídos o dañados.

33   Cuando esté ensamblando, lubrique los cilindros del pistón y el sello con flúido de freno limpio. Posicione el sello en los cilindros de la mordaza **(vea ilustración)**.

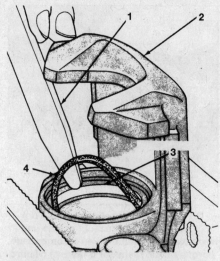

3.29 El sello del pistón debe ser removido con un plástico o herramienta de madera para evitar dañar el cilindro y la ranura del sello

1   Varilla de plástico
2   Mordaza
3   Ranura para el sello del pistón
4   Sello del pistón

34   Lubrique el pistón con flúido de freno limpio, entonces instale una tapa nueva en la ranura del pistón con los dóbleces hacia el extremo abierto del pistón.

35   Insericóne el pistón directamente en el cilindro de la mordaza, entonces aplique fuerza hasta llevar el pistón hasta el fondo del cilindro **(vea ilustración)**.

36   Posicione la tapa contra polvo en el orificio escariado de la mordaza. Asegúrese que los fuelles se asientan en la tapa de los cilindros apropiadamente **(vea ilustración)**.

37   Instale la válvula de purga.

38   Lubrique las clavijas de resbalamiento con grasa basada en silicona y las instala en el miembro de torque junto con las tapas nuevas de la clavija.

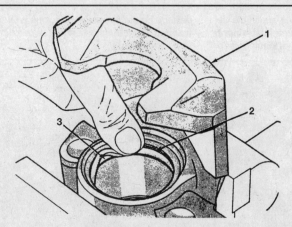

3.33 Comience el sello nuevo en la ranura del pistón y lo empuja con sus dedos (asegúrese que no está torcido)

3.35 Instale el pistón y la tapa a mano solamente

1   Mordaza   3   Ranura del pistón   1   Fuelle   3   Mordaza
2   Sello del pistón   2   Pistón

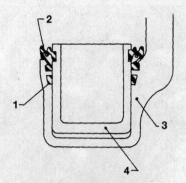

3.36 La tapa (fuelle) para el polvo se debe sentar directamente en la ranura de retención

1   *Sello del pistón*
2   *Cubierta contra el polvo*
3   *Cuerpo del cilindro*
4   *Pistón*

39   Cuando esté conectando los acopladores de las mangueras del freno a la mordaza, instale arandelas de cobre nuevas en cada lado de las acoplaciones.

Todos los modelos

40   La instalación se hace en el orden inverso al procedimiento de desensamble. Esté seguro de purgar las mordazas como se indica en la Sección 13.

4   Disco de freno (rotor) delantero - inspección, remover e instalar

Refiérase a las ilustraciones 4.3, 4.4a, 4.4b, 4.5a, 4.5b, 4.13a y 4.13b
Nota: *Para remover el disco de freno/cubo en los vehículos de 4WD, refiérase al Capítulo 9.*

Inspección

1   Afloje las tuercas de la rueda, levante el vehículo y sosténgalo firmemente encima de soportes. Remueva las ruedas.
2   Remueva la mordaza del freno como está descrito en la Sección 3. No es necesario desconectar la manguera del freno. Después de remover los pernos de la mordaza,

4.3 Chequee la superficie del rotor por ranuras y marcas de arañazos profundos (esté seguro de inspeccionar ambos lados)

suspenda la mordaza fuera del camino con un pedazo de alambre, entonces remueva los pernos del miembro de torque al vástago de la dirección (modelos más modernos).
3   Inspeccione visualmente la superficie del rotor por rayones o daños. Los rayones ligeros y ranuras superficiales son normales después del uso y no siempre pueden ser perjudicial a la operación del frenado, pero rayones profundo - encima de 0.015 pulgada (0.38 mm) - requieren remover el rotor y que sea rectificado por un taller de rectificaciones automotriz. Esté seguro de chequear ambos lados del rotor **(vea ilustración)**. Si pulsación se ha notado durante la aplicación de los frenos, sospeche desviación lateral del rotor.
4   Para chequear la desviación lateral del rotor, coloque un indicador de reloj en el centro de la superficie de contacto de la pastilla **(vea ilustracións)**. Ponga el indicador a cero y gire el rotor. La lectura del indicador no debe exceder el límite admisible especificado de desviación. Si lo hace, el rotor debe ser rectificado por un taller de rectificación automotriz.
Nota: *Los profesionales recomiendan rectificar el disco de freno a pesar de la lectura indicada por el reloj (para producir una superficie lisa y plana que eliminará la pulsación del pedal del freno y otros síntomas indeseables relacionados con los discos). Por lo menos, si usted elige de no rectificar los discos, remueva*

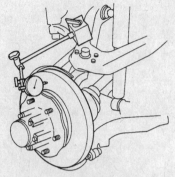

4.4a Para chequear la desviación del rotor, un indicador de reloj es conectado a la mordaza con el indicador tocando el centro del área de contacto del rotor. Gire el rotor una revolución completa y note la lectura del indicador

el brillo con una tela de esmeril de grados mediano (use un movimiento espiral para asegurar un acabado sin dirección).
5   Es absolutamente crítico que el rotor no sea rectificado a un espesor debajo del espesor admisible del rotor, mínimo y especificado. El espesor mínimo está estampado en el interior del rotor **(vea ilustración)**. El espesor del rotor puede ser chequeado con un micrómetro **(vea ilustración)**.

Remover

6   Use un destornillador para hacerle palanca hacia afuera a la tapa de polvo en el cubo.
7   Remueva la chaveta.
8   Remueva la tapa de ajuste.
9   Remueva la tuerca del balero de la rueda y la arandela.
10   Remueva el balero exterior de la rueda.
11   Remueva el ensamblaje del cubo y el rotor.
12   Si necesita rectificación a máquina para el rotor, remueva el sello del balero interior de la rueda y el balero.
13   Si el rotor necesita ser reemplazando se debe separar del cubo. Primero, remueva los pernos que aseguran el rotor al cubo **(vea ilustración)**. Después use un martillo plástico

4.4b Usando un movimiento que sea espiral, remueva el vitrificado del rotor con papel de lija de grado medio

Marcas para el espesor mínimo

XX.XX mm

4.5a El disco puede ser rectificado si el espesor mínimo no será excedido

4.5b Un micrómetro es usado para medir el espesor del rotor. Tome las medidas en varios puntos alrededor del rotor

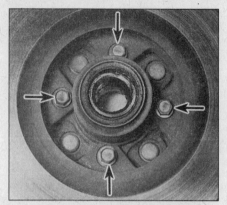

4.13a Para separar el rotor del cubo, remueva los cuatro pernos que conectan los dos componentes . . .

4.13b . . . entonces levante el cubo del rotor. Pueda que sea necesario pegarle gentilmente al rotor para removerlo del cubo

5.4 El tambor del freno se puede forzar del cubo enroscando los pernos del tamaño apropiado en las roscas proporcionadas para este propósito

5.6 El resorte y el retenedor antirrechinante pueden ser removidos presionándolos y girándolos 90°

para pegarle a la orilla exterior del cubo hasta que el cubo pueda ser removido del rotor **(vea ilustración)**. Una vez que el cubo se haya separado levemente, dos destornilladores de cabeza plana (uno en cada lado) pueden ser usados para hacerle palanca y separar los dos pedazos aparte. Si el cubo y el rotor no se separan fácilmente, aplique aceite penetrante donde los dos se reúnen.

Instalación

14   Cuando conecte el rotor al cubo, póngalo en posición en el cubo y flojamente instale los pernos.
15   Apriete los pernos en un patrón cruzado un poco a la vez hasta que ellos estén apretados al par de torsión de las especificaciones.

16   Para completar el procedimiento de la instalación, referirse al Capítulo 11 para empacar los baleros de las ruedas e instalar el ensamblaje del cubo y el rotor en el vástago.

5   Frenos traseros de tambor - reemplazo de las balatas

Refiérase a las ilustraciones 5.4, 5.6, 5.7a al 5.7g, 5.8, 5.15 y 5.16
1   Levante la parte trasera del vehículo y sosténgalo firmemente encima de soportes. Esté seguro que el freno de estacionamiento esté liberado.

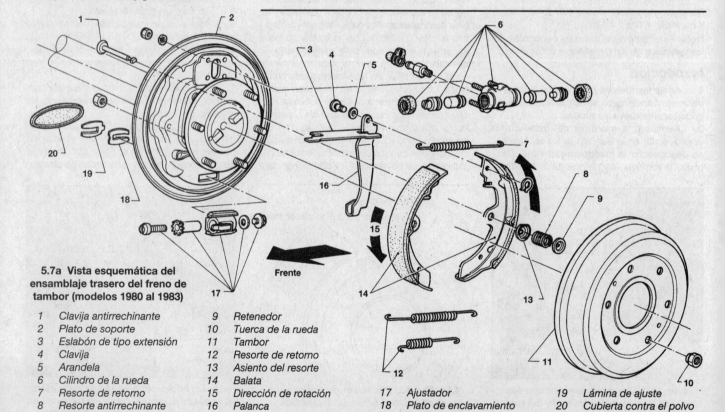

5.7a Vista esquemática del ensamblaje trasero del freno de tambor (modelos 1980 al 1983)

1 Clavija antirrechinante	9 Retenedor	17 Ajustador	19 Lámina de ajuste
2 Plato de soporte	10 Tuerca de la rueda	18 Plato de enclavamiento	20 Cubierta contra el polvo
3 Eslabón de tipo extensión	11 Tambor		
4 Clavija	12 Resorte de retorno		
5 Arandela	13 Asiento del resorte		
6 Cilindro de la rueda	14 Balata		
7 Resorte de retorno	15 Dirección de rotación		
8 Resorte antirrechinante	16 Palanca		

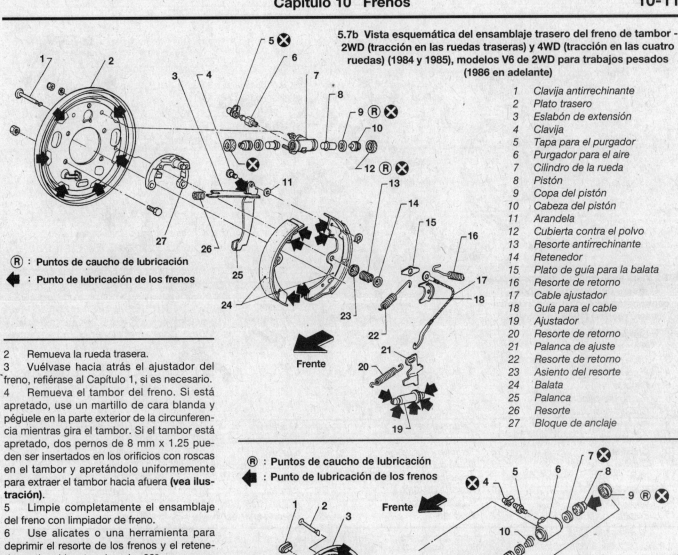

5.7b Vista esquemática del ensamblaje trasero del freno de tambor - 2WD (tracción en las ruedas traseras) y 4WD (tracción en las cuatro ruedas) (1984 y 1985), modelos V6 de 2WD para trabajos pesados (1986 en adelante)

1   Clavija antirrechinante
2   Plato trasero
3   Eslabón de extensión
4   Clavija
5   Tapa para el purgador
6   Purgador para el aire
7   Cilindro de la rueda
8   Pistón
9   Copa del pistón
10 Cabeza del pistón
11 Arandela
12 Cubierta contra el polvo
13 Resorte antirrechinante
14 Retenedor
15 Plato de guía para la balata
16 Resorte de retorno
17 Cable ajustador
18 Guía para el cable
19 Ajustador
20 Resorte de retorno
21 Palanca de ajuste
22 Resorte de retorno
23 Asiento del resorte
24 Balata
25 Palanca
26 Resorte
27 Bloque de anclaje

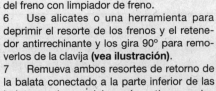

(R) : Puntos de caucho de lubricación
◄ : Punto de lubricación de los frenos

2   Remueva la rueda trasera.
3   Vuélvase hacia atrás el ajustador del freno, refiérase al Capítulo 1, si es necesario.
4   Remueva el tambor del freno. Si está apretado, use un martillo de cara blanda y péguele en la parte exterior de la circunferencia mientras gira el tambor. Si el tambor está apretado, dos pernos de 8 mm x 1.25 pueden ser insertados en los orificios con roscas en el tambor y apretándolo uniformemente para extraer el tambor hacia afuera (vea ilustración).
5   Limpie completamente el ensamblaje del freno con limpiador de freno.
6   Use alicates o una herramienta para deprimir el resorte de los frenos y el retenedor antirrechinante y los gira 90° para removerlos de la clavija (vea ilustración).
7   Remueva ambos resortes de retorno de la balata conectado a la parte inferior de las balatas en los modelos más antiguos, o los resortes superiores de retorno en los modelos más modernos (vea ilustraciones). No mezcle los resortes.

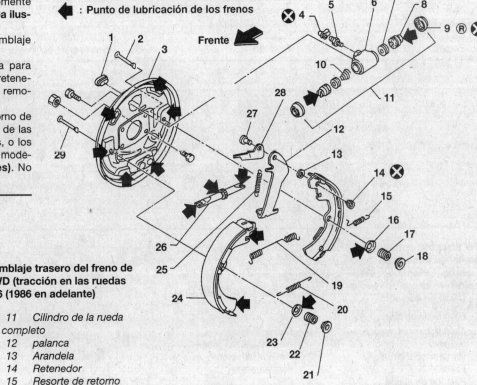

5.7c Vista esquemática del ensamblaje trasero del freno de tambor - cuatro-cilindros de 2WD (tracción en las ruedas traseras) y camionetas V6 (1986 en adelante)

1   Tapón
2   Clavija antirrechinante
3   Plato trasero
4   Tapa para el purgador del aire
5   Purgador para el aire
6   Cilindro
7   Copa del pistón
8   Pistón
9   Cubierta del pistón
10 Resorte
11 Cilindro de la rueda completo
12 palanca
13 Arandela
14 Retenedor
15 Resorte de retorno
16 Asiento para el resorte
17 Resorte antirrechinante
18 Retenedor
19 Resorte de retorno
20 Resorte de retorno
21 Retenedor
22 Resorte antirrechinante
23 Asiento para el resorte
24 Balata
25 Resorte de retorno
26 Ajustador
27 Clavija
28 Palanca de ajuste
29 Clavija antirrechinante

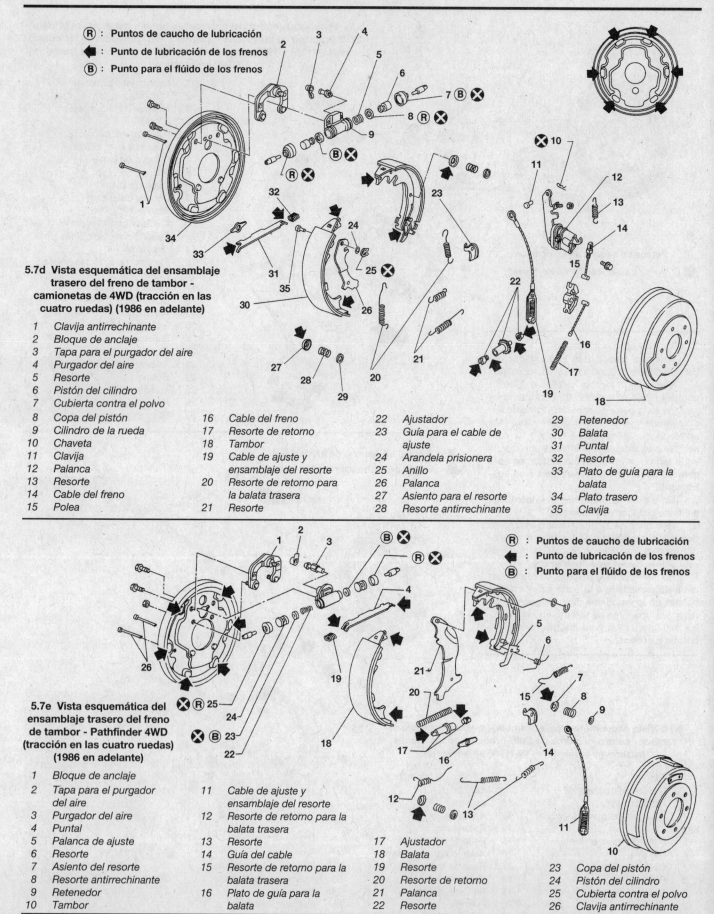

R : Puntos de caucho de lubricación

◀ : Punto de lubricación de los frenos

B : Punto para el flúido de los frenos

5.7d Vista esquemática del ensamblaje trasero del freno de tambor - camionetas de 4WD (tracción en las cuatro ruedas) (1986 en adelante)

1	Clavija antirrechinante
2	Bloque de anclaje
3	Tapa para el purgador del aire
4	Purgador del aire
5	Resorte
6	Pistón del cilindro
7	Cubierta contra el polvo

8	Copa del pistón	16	Cable del freno	22	Ajustador	29	Retenedor
9	Cilindro de la rueda	17	Resorte de retorno	23	Guía para el cable de ajuste	30	Balata
10	Chaveta	18	Tambor			31	Puntal
11	Clavija	19	Cable de ajuste y ensamblaje del resorte	24	Arandela prisionera	32	Resorte
12	Palanca	20	Resorte de retorno para la balata trasera	25	Anillo	33	Plato de guía para la balata
13	Resorte			26	Palanca	34	Plato trasero
14	Cable del freno	21	Resorte	27	Asiento para el resorte	35	Clavija
15	Polea			28	Resorte antirrechinante		

R : Puntos de caucho de lubricación

◀ : Punto de lubricación de los frenos

B : Punto para el flúido de los frenos

5.7e Vista esquemática del ensamblaje trasero del freno de tambor - Pathfinder 4WD (tracción en las cuatro ruedas) (1986 en adelante)

1	Bloque de anclaje
2	Tapa para el purgador del aire
3	Purgador del aire
4	Puntal
5	Palanca de ajuste
6	Resorte
7	Asiento del resorte
8	Resorte antirrechinante
9	Retenedor
10	Tambor

11	Cable de ajuste y ensamblaje del resorte	17	Ajustador		
12	Resorte de retorno para la balata trasera	18	Balata		
13	Resorte	19	Resorte	23	Copa del pistón
14	Guía del cable	20	Resorte de retorno	24	Pistón del cilindro
15	Resorte de retorno para la balata trasera	21	Palanca	25	Cubierta contra el polvo
16	Plato de guía para la balata	22	Resorte	26	Clavija antirrechinante

5.7f Ubicación de los resortes inferiores de retorno para la balata (no los mezcle con los resortes superiores)

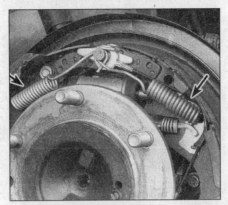

5.7g Ubicación de los resortes superiores de retorno para la balata, plato de guía y cable ajustador

5.8 Con las balatas de los freno separada, el puntal puede ser removido hacia afuera o instalado

8   Separe las balatas levemente y remueva el resorte de retorno superior (modelos más antiguos) y el eslabón de extensión **(vea ilustración)**.

9   Hágale palanca cuidadosamente a las balatas para separarlas otra vez y las remueva de las hendiduras en el ajustador y los pistones del cilindro de la rueda. Note que la balata portante (secundaria) se debe separar de la palanca removiendo la clavija (modelos más antiguos). Si los pistones de los cilindros de las ruedas se pueden preve-

nir que se salgan, usando ligas de caucho o cinta adhesiva para detenerlas en su posición, no será necesario purgar los frenos después que se terminen.

10   Desconecte el cable del freno de estacionamiento de la palanca.

11   No presione el pedal del freno mientras las balatas están afuera, de otro modo los pistones se forzarán afuera de los cilindros.

12   Chequee que los pistones estén libres para moverse adentro del cilindro, que las tapas contra el polvo de caucho no estén

dañadas, estén en posición y no hayan fugas de flúido hidráulico. **Nota:** *Si hay signos de fuga de flúido o los cilindros de las ruedas van a ser reconstruido por cualquier razón, realice esta operación ahora, antes de que los forros nuevos de las balatas sean instalados. Refiérase a la Sección 10.*

13   Aplique una pequeña cantidad de grasa para frenos a las roscas del ajustador.

14   Antes del ensamble, aplique una capa pequeña de grasa para frenos en los lugares de las plataformas y ubicación de las balatas en el cilindro y el ajustador. No permita que ninguna grasa entre en contacto con los forros o partes de caucho.

15   Cuando esté instalando las balatas, instale los resortes superiores e inferiores, entonces posicione el final inferior de la balata trasera en la hendidura del ajustador seguido por el final inferior de la balata delantera. Las balatas entonces se pueden esparcir y ser ranurado adentro del cilindro de la rueda. Entonces las partes que quedan pueden ser instaladas **(vea ilustración)**.

16   Instale el tambor de freno y la rueda.

17   Ajuste el freno y baje el vehículo al piso. En los modelos más modernos los ajustes se llevan a cabo operando el freno de estacionamiento unas varias veces. Si hay cualquier chance de que aire haya entrado en el sistema, es esencial que sea purgado, como se indica en la Sección 3.

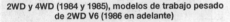

2WD y 4WD (1984 y 1985), modelos de trabajo pesado de 2WD V6 (1986 en adelante)

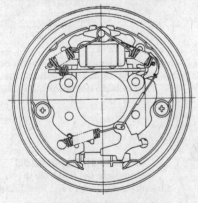

Camionetas de 4WD (1986 en adelante)

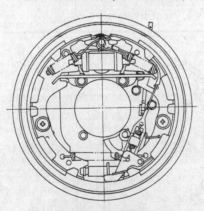

Pathfinder de 4WD (1986 en adelante)

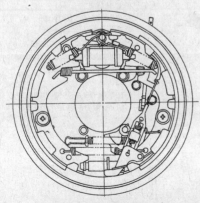

Camionetas de 2WD de cuatro cilindros y V6 (1986 en adelante)

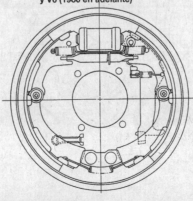

5.15 Detalles de la instalación de los componentes del freno de tambor (se muestra la rueda izquierda)

5.16 El diámetro máximo del tambor está estampado en cada tambor

6   Cilindro trasero de la rueda - remover, reconstrucción completa e instalar

Refiérase a las ilustraciones 6.4 y 6.6

1   Obtenga un juego de reconstrucción para los cilindros de las ruedas.
2   Remueva el tambor del freno y las balatas como se indica en la Sección 5.
3   Coloque un trapo o bandeja de drenaje debajo del plato de soporte para colectar cualquier flúido hidráulico que se pueda expulsar de la línea del freno o del cilindro de la rueda.
4   Limpie la conexión de la línea del freno en la parte trasera de los cilindros de la rueda

6.4   Una llave para tuerca de tubería es recomendada cuando afloje la línea hidráulica (flecha) del cilindro de la rueda

y destornille el perno del conector (modelos más antiguos). Remueva las dos arandelas hacia afuera, una a cada lado del conector. En los modelos más modernos destornille la tuerca del tubo del cilindro de la rueda **(vea ilustración)**.
5   Afloje y remueva las cuatro arandelas de las tuercas y el resorte que asegura el cilindro de la rueda al plato de soporte. Remueva el cilindro de la rueda.
6   Para remover el cilindro de la rueda, remueva primero los dos fuelles de polvo **(vea ilustración)**. Retire las dos cabezas del

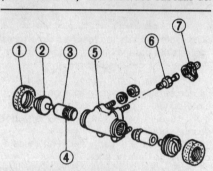

6.6   Vista esquemática del cilindro de la rueda trasera

1   Tapa contra el polvo
2   Cabeza del pistón
3   Pistón
4   Copa del pistón
5   Cilindro de la rueda
6   Tornillo de purgar
7   Tapa de purga

pistón y entonces los pistones. Remueva el sello de cada pistón y note de que manera está instalado.
7   Inspeccione los cilindros interiores por marcas de rayones causados por impurezas en el flúido hidráulico. **Nota:** *Si el cilindro de la rueda debe ser reemplazado, siempre asegúrese que el reemplazo es exactamente idéntico al que se removió.*
8   Si el cilindro está en buena condición, límpielo completamente con flúido hidráulico limpio.
9   Aplíquele a los sellos nuevos de caucho flúido hidráulico e instale los pistones, asegúrese que los labios miran hacia adentro cuando se ensamble.

7.4   Cuando arme el ajustador del freno trasero, grasa debe ser aplicada en las áreas indicadas por las flechas

7.5   Cuando esté instalando el ajustador, la grasa debe ser aplicada a la hendidura en el plato deflector

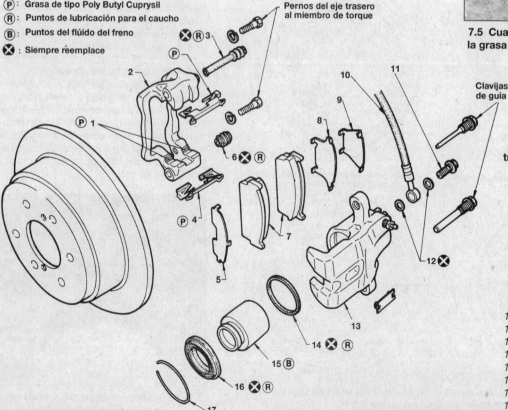

(P) :   Grasa de tipo Poly Butyl Cuprysil
(R) :   Puntos de lubricación para el caucho
(B) :   Puntos del flúido del freno
(X) :   Siempre reemplace

Pernos del eje trasero al miembro de torque

Clavijas de guía

8.2   Vista esquemática del ensamblaje del freno de disco trasero - modelos 1988 Pathfinder

1   A las áreas de contacto para la pastilla
2   Miembro de torque
3   Fuelle de la clavija
4   Retenedor de la pastilla
5   Lámina de ajuste exterior
6   Fuelle de la clavija
7   Pastilla
8   Lámina de ajuste interior
9   Cubierta de la lámina de ajuste
10   Manguera de los frenos
11   Perno de tipo ojo
12   Arandelas de cobre
13   Cuerpo del cilindro
14   Sello del pistón
15   Pistón
16   Sello contra el polvo
17   Retenedor

10   Inserciòne con cuidado los pistones hacia adentro para no arrollar el labio del sello. Instale las dos cabezas de los pistones y entonces las tapas contra el polvo.

11   La instalación de los cilindros de las ruedas se hacen en el orden inverso al procedimiento de desensamble. Será necesario purgar el sistema hidráulico, como se indica en la Sección 13.

7   Ajustador del freno de tambor (modelos 1980 al 1983) - remover, inspeccionar e instalar

Refiérase a las ilustraciones 7.4 y 7.5

1   Remueva el tambor del freno y las bala-

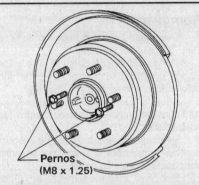

Pernos (M8 x 1.25)

8.3 El disco de freno se puede forzar de la pestaña del eje, enroscando los pernos del tamaño apropiado en las roscas proporcionadas para este propósito

tas como se indica en la Sección 5.

2   Apriete el ajustador firmemente contra el plato del soporte del freno, remueva la tapa de caucho, el resorte, plato de cierre y lámina para ajustes del plato de soporte.

3   Examine las partes por daño, corrosión y distorsión, reemplácelas con partes nuevas según sea necesario.

4   Ensamble el ajustador usando una pequeña cantidad de grasa para frenos en todas las partes moviéndose **(vea ilustración)**.

5   La instalación se hace en el orden inverso al procedimiento de desensamble, pero aplique una capa de grasa pequeña para frenos en las superficies que frotan del ajustador y en la hendidura del plato de soporte **(vea ilustración)**.

8   Disco de freno trasero (rotor) - inspección, remover e instalar

Refiérase a las ilustraciones 8.2 y 8.3

1   Inspeccione el rotor como se indica en la Sección 4 de este Capítulo. Antes de chequear la desviación del rotor con un indicador de tipo reloj, sin embargo, vuelva a instalar dos tuercas para retener el rotor contra la pestaña del eje.

2   Remueva la mordaza como se indica en la Sección 3, entonces remueva los dos pernos del miembros de torque al albergue del eje **(vea ilustración)**.

3   Hale el rotor hacia afuera de la pestaña

del eje. Si el rotor está obstruido y no se libera, aplique aceite penetrante alrededor de los espárragos de la rueda y permita que se empape por unos pocos minutos. Inserciòne dos pernos en los orificios roscados en el centro del rotor y apriételo uniformemente, extraiga el rotor del eje **(vea ilustración)**.

4   La instalación se hace en el orden inverso al procedimiento de desensamble. Esté seguro de apretar los pernos del miembro de torque y las clavijas de guía al par de torsión especificado.

9   Balatas del freno de estacionamiento (modelos con discos de frenos traseros) - remover e instalar

Refiérase a las ilustraciones 9.2, 9.3, 9.7 y 9.14

Peligro: *El polvo producido por el sistema de frenos puede contener asbesto que es dañino para la salud. Nunca lo sople con aire comprimido ni lo inhale. Cuando usted esté trabajando en los frenos usted debe utilizar una máscara filtrante aprobada. No utilice, bajo ninguna circunstancia, solventes derivados del petróleo para limpiar las partes del sistema de freno. Utilice solamente limpiador para sistemas de frenos o alcohol desnaturalizado! Después que los componentes para los frenos sean enjugados séquelo con un trapo, esté seguro de deshacerse de los trapos y el limpiador contaminado en un recipiente cubierto y marcado.*

Remover

1   Remueva el disco de freno siguiendo el procedimiento del plan general en la Sección 8.

2   Usando un par de alicates, empuje hacia abajo en el retenedor, gírelo 90° para desengancharlo de la clavija antirrechinante entonces remueva el asiento antirrechinante del resorte y resorte **(vea ilustración)**. Repita este paso en el otro retenedor y el resorte.

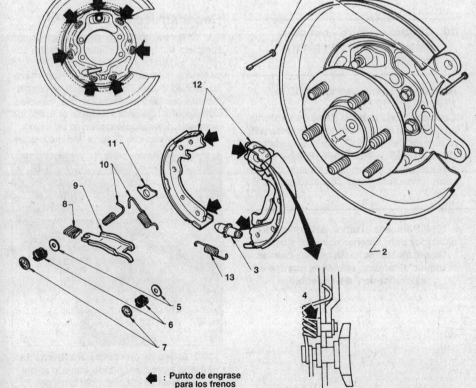

9.2 Vista esquemática del ensamblaje trasero del freno de estacionamiento - modelos con freno de disco trasero

1   Clavija antirrechinante
2   Plato deflector
3   Ajustador
4   Superficies de acoplamiento
5   Asiento del resorte
6   Resorte antirrechinante
7   Retenedor
8   Resorte
9   Puntal
10   Resorte de retorno
11   Plato de guía
12   Balata
13   Tornillo resorte para el ajuste

◄ : **Punto de engrase para los frenos**

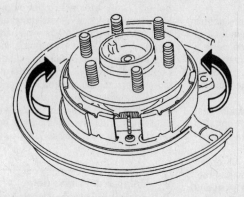

9.3 Después que los retenedores y el resorte sean removidos, meza las balatas hacia afuera y remueva los resortes de retorno

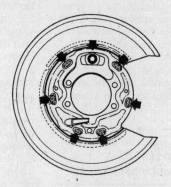

9.7 Aplique una capa de grasa ligera a los puntos indicados (flechas)

3   Meza las balatas hacia afuera del plato deflector (**vea ilustración**) y remueva los dos resortes de retorno, plato de guía y puntal.

4   Separe las balatas en la parte superior y las hala hacia afuera en la pestaña del eje, entonces desconecte el cable del freno de estacionamiento de la palanca.

5   Remueva el resorte del tornillo ajustes y el ajustador. Limpie el ajustador con solvente y lubrique las roscas con grasa de uso múltiple.

6   Si está reemplazando las balatas, transfiera la palanca del freno de estacionamiento a la balata portante nueva.

Instalación

7   Conecte el resorte del tornillo de ajuste para las balatas e instale el ajustador entre el área nivelada al fondo de cada balata. Asegúrese que el final de cada hendidura del ajustador está apropiadamente comprometida con las balatas.

8   Aplique una capa delgada de grasa de uso múltiple a las áreas de contacto de la balata en el plato deflector (**vea ilustración**).

9   Conecte el cable del freno de estacionamiento a la palanca.

10   Separe las balatas y las pone en posición contra el plato deflector. Coloque el puntal del freno de estacionamiento entre las dos balatas con las puntas del puntal en las mellas apropiadas.

11   Instale las clavijas antirrechinante, los asientos del resorte, resortes y retenedores.

12   Instale el plato de la guía y resortes de retorno.

13   Coloque el rotor en la pestaña del eje e instale dos tuercas para detener el rotor en su posición durante el procedimiento de ajuste. Instale el miembro de torque y la mordaza.

Ajuste

14   Chequee que el freno de estacionamiento esté completamente liberado. Remueva el tapón del orificio para el ajustador en el plato deflector y usando un destornillador, gire la rueda del ajustador hasta que las balatas toquen el tambor del freno (**vea ilustración**).

15   Regrese la rueda de ajuste 7 o 8 chasquidos, gire el tambor y asegúrese que no hay resistencia entre las balatas y el tambor.

16   Instale el tapón para el orificio del ajustador.

---

10   Cilindro maestro - remover, reconstrucción completa e instalar

Refiérase a las ilustraciones 10.3, 10.9a, 10.9b, 10.9c y 10.19

Caución: *Tenga cuidado de no derramar ningún flúido de freno en la superficie pintada de la pintura del vehículo, porque la dañará. Cubra los guardafangos para proteger la pintura y limpie cualquier flúido rociado o derramado inmediatamente con abundancia de agua.*

Remover

1   Desconecte el cable negativo de la terminal negativa de la batería.

2   Ponga periódicos en su lugar o trapos bajo el cilindro maestro para colectar cualquier flúido de freno que se fugue.

3   Afloje las tuercas del tubo que aseguran las líneas del freno al cilindro maestro (**vea ilustración**).

4   Remueva las dos tuercas que aseguran el cilindro maestro a la unidad del amplificador para los frenos de poder.

5   Remueva cuidadosamente el cilindro afuera de los espárragos, remueva las líneas de los cilindros de los frenos e inmediatamente coloque su dedo en la línea para prevenir la fuga del flúido. Levante el cilindro hacia afuera del compartimiento del motor.

6   Tape las líneas del flúido para prevenir fuga adicional del flúido.

Reconstrucción completa

7   Obtenga un juego de reconstrucción completa para el cilindro maestro. **Nota:** *Los vehículos cubiertos por este manual usan uno de las dos marcas diferentes de cilindro maestro, un Nabco o un Tokico. Porque no hay partes intercambiables entre los dos modelos, esté seguro que usted obtiene el juego de reconstrucción apropiado para su vehículo.*

8   Limpie siempre la tierra externa, enton-

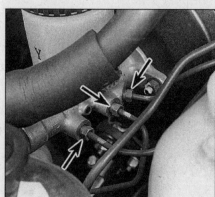

10.3 El uso de una llave para tuerca de tubería es recomendado cuando afloje las tuercas (flechas) del tubo del cilindro maestro

9.14 Remueva el tapón del orificio del ajustador para obtener acezo al ajustador. Gire el ajustador hasta que las balatas toquen el tambor, entonces regrese el ajustador de 7 a 8 chasquidos

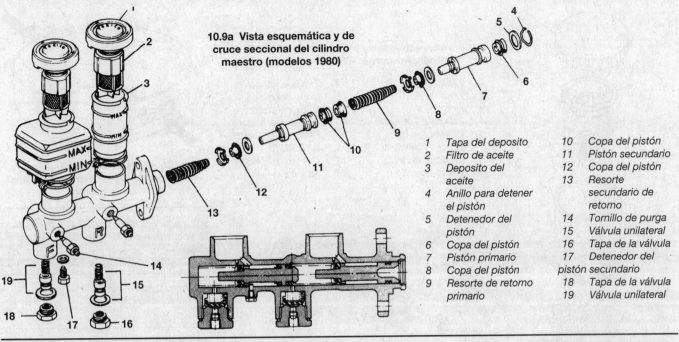

10.9a Vista esquemática y de cruce seccional del cilindro maestro (modelos 1980)

1	Tapa del deposito	10	Copa del pistón
2	Filtro de aceite	11	Pistón secundario
3	Deposito del aceite	12	Copa del pistón
4	Anillo para detener el pistón	13	Resorte secundario de retorno
5	Detenedor del pistón	14	Tornillo de purga
6	Copa del pistón	15	Válvula unilateral
7	Pistón primario	16	Tapa de la válvula
8	Copa del pistón	17	Detenedor del pistón secundario
9	Resorte de retorno primario	18	Tapa de la válvula
		19	Válvula unilateral

ces remueva las tapas del depósito, los filtros y vacíe hacia afuera el flúido.

9   Desde el extremo del cilindro maestro, hágale palanca hacia afuera al anillo retenedor (modelos más antiguos) o hágale palanca hacia afuera a la tapa de detención (modelos más modernos). Entonces remueva la arandela de detención (si está equipado), el pistón primario y el resorte **(vea ilustraciones)**.

10   Insercióne una varilla para presionar el pistón secundario y entonces destornille el tornillo de parada del cilindro maestro (modelos más antiguos). Libere la varilla y retire el pistón secundario. En los modelos más modernos, invierta el cilindro y lo coloca en un bloque de madera para expulsar el ensamblaje secundario de pistón.

11   Los ensamblajes de la válvula pueden ser removidos destornillando los tapones de la válvula unilateral (modelos más antiguos).

12   En esta etapa, inspeccione las superficies de los pistones y los cilindros por rayones, áreas desgastadas o "brillante." Si éstos son evidente, reemplace el cilindro maestro completo con uno nuevo o con una unidad reconstruida.

13   Desmonte los ensamblajes del pistón, resorte y remueva todas las copas del pistón. **Nota:** *El pistón primario en los modelos 1981 y más modernos no es diseñado para ser desarmado.*

14   Lave todos los componentes en flúido hidráulico limpio o alcohol solamente.

15   No separe los depósitos a menos que sea absolutamente necesario.

16   Comience el ensamble manipulando los sellos nuevos en posición usando los dedos solamente. Esté seguro que los labio del sello miran en las direcciones apropiadas.

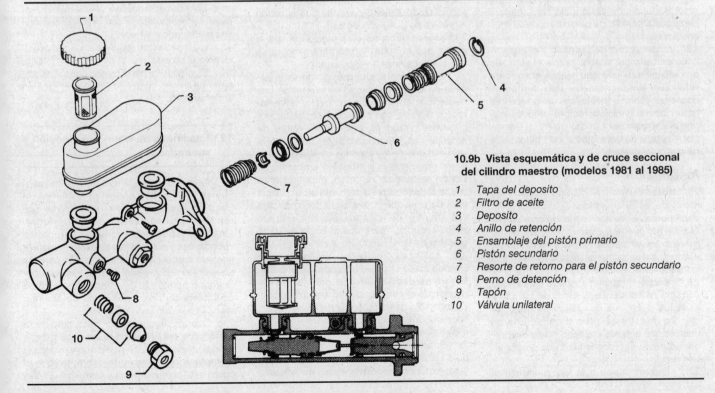

10.9b Vista esquemática y de cruce seccional del cilindro maestro (modelos 1981 al 1985)

1   Tapa del deposito
2   Filtro de aceite
3   Deposito
4   Anillo de retención
5   Ensamblaje del pistón primario
6   Pistón secundario
7   Resorte de retorno para el pistón secundario
8   Perno de detención
9   Tapón
10   Válvula unilateral

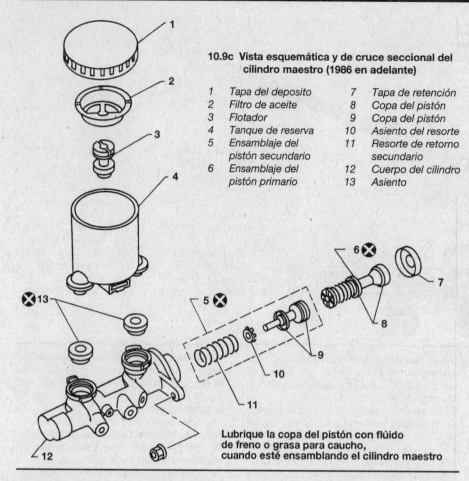

10.9c Vista esquemática y de cruce seccional del cilindro maestro (1986 en adelante)

1	Tapa del deposito	7	Tapa de retención
2	Filtro de aceite	8	Copa del pistón
3	Flotador	9	Copa del pistón
4	Tanque de reserva	10	Asiento del resorte
5	Ensamblaje del pistón secundario	11	Resorte de retorno secundario
6	Ensamblaje del pistón primario	12	Cuerpo del cilindro
		13	Asiento

Lubrique la copa del pistón con flúido
de freno o grasa para caucho,
cuando esté ensamblando el cilindro maestro

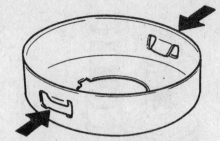

10.19 Antes de instalar la tapa del retenedor, doble las espigas (pestaña) hacia adentro

solamente hasta la cima del divisor del depósito para prevenir derrame cuando la tapa sea instalada.
27 Instale cuidadosamente el cilindro maestro invirtiendo los pasos para remover, entonces purgue los frenos en las válvulas de purgar en la rueda.

11 Válvula detección de la carga - remover e instalar

Refiérase a las ilustraciones 11.2a y 11.2b
1   Desconecte todas las líneas de freno de la válvula y tape inmediatamente cada una para prevenir la fuga del flúido y tierra que entre en el sistema.
2   Remueva los pernos que conectan la válvula y el soporte de la válvula al chasis y los remueve **(vea ilustraciones)**.
3   Si la válvula va ser reemplazada con una nueva, remuévala de su soporte. **Nota:** *La válvula de detección de carga no está diseñada para ser desarmada y si está defectuosa debe ser reemplazada con una nueva o con una unidad reconstruida.*
4   La instalación se hace en el orden inverso al procedimiento de desensamble.
5   Siguiendo la instalación, purgue el sistema de frenos completo como se indica en la Sección 13.

12 Las líneas de freno - inspección y reemplazo

1   Alrededor de cada seis meses, las mangueras flexible que conectan las líneas de freno de acero se deben inspeccionar por roturas, cuarteaduras exteriores, fugas, ampollas y otros daños. Éstos son partes importantes y vulnerables del sistema de frenos y la inspección debe ser completa. Una luz y un espejo probará ser útil para un chequeo completo. Si una manguera exhibe cualquiera de las condiciones de encima, reemplácela con una nueva.
2   Cuando llegue a ser necesario para reemplazar las líneas de acero, use tubería solamente de acero de pared doble. Nunca la reemplace con tubería de cobre, porque el cobre está sujeto a fatiga y corrosión. El diá-

17   Sumerja todos los componentes internos en flúido hidráulico limpio antes del ensamblaje.
18   Instale el ensamblaje secundario del resorte y el pistón. Deténgalo presionado y enrosque el tornillo de parada (modelos más antiguos).
19   Instale el resorte primario y el ensamblaje primario del pistón. Instale la arandela de detención (si está equipado) y el anillo de retención. En los modelos más modernos doble las espigas (pestañas) de la tapa del tapón interno **(vea ilustración)** después instale el extremo del cilindro maestro. Reemplace la tapa de detención si está deformada de cualquier manera.

Instalación

20   **Nota:** *Cuando el cilindro maestro es removido, el sistema hidráulico completo se debe purgar. El tiempo requerido para purgar el sistema, puede ser reducido si el cilindro maestro es llenado con flúido y sangrado en el banco antes de que el cilindro maestro sea instalado en el vehículo.*
21   Insercióne tapones roscado del tamaño correcto en las roscas de salida del cilindro y llene los depósitos con flúido de freno. El cilindro maestro se debe soportado de tal manera que el flúido de freno no se desbordará durante el procedimiento de purgar en una banca.
22   Afloje un tapón a la vez y empuje el

ensamblaje del pistón para forzar hacia afuera el aire del cilindro maestro. Para prevenir que el aire sea absorbido otra vez adentro del cilindro, el tapón apropiado debe ser reemplazado antes de permitir que el pistón regrese a su posición original.
23   Mueva hacia adentro y hacia afuera el pistón tres o cuatro veces para asegurarse que todo el aire se ha expulsado.
24   Debido a que alta presión no es implicada en el procedimiento de purgar en una banca, una alternativa a remover y reemplazar los tapones con cada carrera del ensamblaje del pistón es disponible. Antes de empujar en el ensamblaje del pistón, remueva uno de los tapones completamente. Antes de liberar el pistón, sin embargo, en vez de reemplazar el tapón, ponga simplemente su dedo apretadamente en el orificio para detener que el aire sea absorbido otra vez adentro del cilindro maestro. Espere varios segundos para que el flúido de freno sea absorbido del depósito al cilindro del pistón, entonces repita el procedimiento. Cuando usted empuje hacia adentro el pistón forzará su dedo afuera del orificio, permitiendo que el aire de adentro sea expulsado. Cuando solamente flúido de freno sea expulsado del orificio, reemplace el tapón y pase al otro puerto.
25   Rellene los depósitos del cilindro maestro e instale el ensamblaje del diafragma y la tapa. **Nota:** *Los depósitos deben ser llenados*

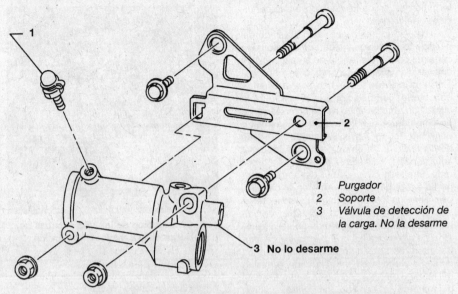

1 Purgador
2 Soporte
3 Válvula de detección de
   la carga. No la desarme

3 No lo desarme

11.2a Detalles del montaje de la válvula de detección de la carga (tipo A)

metro exterior de la tubería es usado para las dimensiones.

3 Algunas refaccionarías o casas de suministro para partes de freno tienen varias longitudes prefabricadas de líneas de freno. Dependiendo del tipo de tubería usada, estas secciones pueden o ser dobladas a mano en la forma deseada o deben ser doblado en un doblador de tubería.

4 Si longitudes prefabricadas no están disponibles, obtenga la tubería recomendada de acero y la acoplación de acero para emparejarla con la línea que va ser reemplazada. Determine la longitud correcta

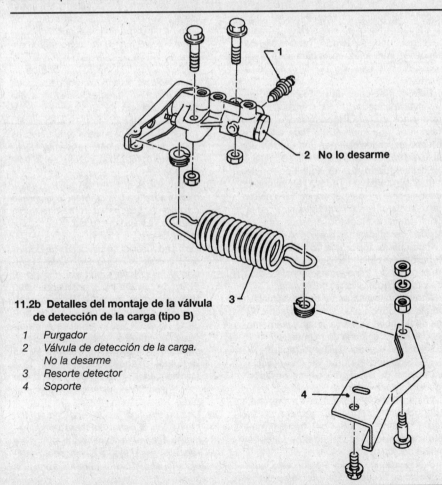

2 No lo desarme

11.2b Detalles del montaje de la válvula de detección de la carga (tipo B)

1 Purgador
2 Válvula de detección de la carga.
   No la desarme
3 Resorte detector
4 Soporte

midiendo la sección vieja de la línea de freno y corte la tubería nueva para instalarla, deje acerca de 1/2-pulgada de exceso para el abocamiento de las puntas.

5 Instale los acopladores en el corte de la tubería y abocine las puntas usando una herramienta para abocamiento ISO.

6 Usando un doblador de tubería, doble la tubería para emparejar la forma de la línea de freno vieja.

7 Abocamiento del tubo y doblar generalmente pueden ser hecho por una refaccionaría local con el equipo apropiado mencionado si los equipos en los párrafos 5 y 6 no están disponibles.

8 Cuando esté instalando la línea de freno, deje por lo menos 3/4 pulgada (19 mm) de espacio libre entre la línea y cualquier parte movible o vibrante.

13 Sistema de freno hidráulico - purgar

Refiérase a la ilustración 13.6
Caución 1: *Tenga cuidado de no derramar ningún flúido de freno en la superficie pintada de la pintura del vehículo, porque la dañará. Cubra los guardafangos para proteger la pintura y limpie cualquier flúido rociado o derramado inmediatamente con abundancia de agua.*
Caución 2: *En los modelos equipados con frenos ABS (frenos antibloqueantes), Desconecte el cable negativo de la batería antes de purgar los frenos.*

1 En cualquier momento que cualquier parte del sistema de frenos sea desmontado o desarrolle una fuga, o cuando el flúido en el depósito del cilindro maestro se baje hasta el punto de absorber aire, aire entrará en el sistema y causará una disminución del desempeño del frenado. Para eliminar este aire en los frenos, se debe purgar usando el procedimiento descrito en esta Sección.

2 Si aire ha entrado en el sistema porque el cilindro maestro se ha desconectada, o el flúido en el depósito del cilindro maestro se ha bajado mucho, o si un cambio completo del flúido del sistema es necesario, los frenos de las cuatro ruedas se deben purgar. Si una línea de freno se ha desconectado solamente, entonces solamente ese freno tiene que ser purgado. Igualmente, si cualquier línea es desconectado dondequiera que sea en el sistema, el freno sirviendo esa línea debe ser purgada.

3 Antes de comenzar, tenga a un ayudante a la mano, también como un suministro amplio de flúido de freno nuevo, un recipiente claro vacío tal como un frasco de vidrio, una longitud de manguera de plástico de 3/16-pulgada, tubería de caucho o vinilo para instalarla en la válvula de purga y una llave para tuerca de tubería para abrir y cerrar la válvula de purgar. El vehículo quizás tenga que ser levantado y quizás tenga que ser colocado encima de estantes para tener espacio libre.

4   Si el vehículo es equipe con frenos de potencia, remueva la reserva de vacío en el sistema aplicando los frenos varias veces.

5   Chequee que el depósito del cilindro maestro esté lleno de flúido y esté seguro de mantenerlo por lo menos medio lleno durante la operación completa. Si, en cualquier punto, el depósito corre bajo del flúido, el procedimiento completo de purgar se debe repetir. **Nota:** *No mezcle los tipos diferentes de flúidos de freno y no vuelva a usar ningún flúido viejo, porque este podría deteriorar los componentes del sistema de frenos.*

6   En los modelos que estén equipado, comience en una de las válvulas de purgar localizada en el cilindro maestro. En los modelos donde el cilindro maestro no tiene válvulas de purga, comience con la válvula de detección de la carga, conectada a la derecha del riel del chasis, enfrente del tanque de combustible **(vea ilustración)**. Afloje la válvula de purga para que esté levemente floja entonces la aprieta a un punto donde sea cómodo pero pueda ser aflojada todavía rápidamente y fácilmente.

7   Coloque una punta de la tubería en la válvula de purga y sumerja el otro extremo en el flúido de freno en el recipiente.

8   Con su ayudante sentado en el asiento del conductor, hágalo que bombee los frenos unas cuantas vez para obtener presión en el sistema. En la última bombeada hágalo que detenga el pedal firmemente presionado.

9   Mientras el pedal está sostenido presionado, abra la válvula del respirador apenas lo suficiente para permitir que bastante flujo del flúido pueda salir de la válvula. Observe por burbujas de aire saliendo del final sumergido del tubo. Cuando el flúido fluye lento después de un par de segundos, cierre la válvula otra vez y haga que su ayudante libere el pedal. Si él libera el pedal antes de que la válvula sea cerrado otra vez aire puede ser absorbido adentro del sistema.

10   Repita los Pasos 8 y 9 hasta que más aire no sea observado en el flúido saliendo del tubo. Entonces apriete completamente la válvula de purga y proceda a la otra válvula del cilindro maestro, la válvula de detección de carga (si es necesario), la rueda trasera derecha, la rueda trasera izquierda, la rueda delantera izquierda y la rueda del frente del lado derecho, en ese orden y realice la misma operación. Esté seguro de chequear el flúido en el depósito del cilindro maestro frecuentemente.

11   Rellene el cilindro maestro con flúido al final de la operación.

---

14   Amplificador para los frenos - información general y prueba

---

1   Una unidad de amplificación para los frenos de poder es instalada en el circuito hidráulico del freno en serie con el cilindro maestro, para proporcionar ayuda al chófer cuando el pedal del freno es presionado. Esto reduce el esfuerzo requerido por el chó-fer para operar los frenos bajo todas condiciones del frenado.

2   La unidad opera por vacío obtenido del múltiple de admisión y está compuesta básicamente por un diafragma de amplificación y una válvula unilateral. La unidad de amplificación y el cilindro hidráulico maestro están conectados juntos para que la varilla de la unidad de amplificación actúe como la varilla de empuje del cilindro maestro. El esfuerzo del freno del chófer es transmitido a través de otra varilla de empuje en la unidad del amplificador y su sistema de control incorporado. El pistón de la unidad del amplificador no se acopla apretadamente en el cilindro, pero tiene un diafragma fuerte para mantener sus orillas en constante contacto con la pared del cilindro, asegurando un sello apretado de aire entre las dos partes. La cámara delantera es sostenido debajo condiciones de vacío creadas en el múltiple de admisión del motor y durante períodos cuando el pedal del freno no está en uso, los controles abren un pasaje a la cámara trasera para proveer vacío también bajo estas condiciones. Cuando el pedal del freno es presionado, el pasaje del vacío a la cámara trasera es cortada y la cámara se abre a la presión atmosférica. El flujo de aire llega al pistón del amplificador en la cámara de vacío y opera la varilla de empuje principal al cilindro maestro.

3   Los controles son diseñados para que ayuden debajo de todas las condiciones y cuando los frenos no son requeridos, el vacío en la cámara trasera es establecido cuando el pedal del freno es liberado. Todo el aire de la atmósfera que entra en la cámara trasera es pasado a través de un filtro de aire pequeño.

4   Bajo operaciones de condiciones normales el amplificador de los frenos es muy seguro y no requiere reconstrucción completa amenos en kilometraje muy alto. En este caso es mejor obtener una unidad de cambio, en vez de reparar la unidad original.

5   Es acentuado que el amplificador de potencia participa en reducir el esfuerzo requerido por el pie del pedal y en caso de un fracaso, el sistema de freno hidráulico es en ninguna manera afectado amenos que la necesidad de aplicar más presión al pedal.

6   Para chequear por una operación satisfactoria del amplificador de potencia, presione el pedal del freno varias veces. La distancia que el pedal viaja no debe variar.

7   Ahora detenga el pedal completamente deprimido y ponga el motor en marcha. El pedal debe moverse hacia abajo levemente cuando el motor se pone en marcha.

8   Presione el pedal del freno, apague el motor deteniendo el pedal del freno hacia abajo acerca de 30 segundos. La posición del pedal no debe cambiar.

9   Vuelva a poner el motor en marcha, córralo por un minuto o dos y entonces lo apaga. Presione el pedal del freno firmemente varias veces. El viaje del pedal debe disminuir con cada aplicación.

10   Si la unidad no acciona como está indicado, localice la fuente del problema reali-

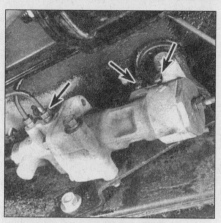

13.6 Ubicación de las tres válvulas de purga en la válvula de detección de la carga (flechas)

zando las siguientes pruebas:

a)   *Primero, inspeccione cuidadosamente la condición de las conexiones de las mangueras de vacío al amplificador con la válvula unilateral, la válvula unilateral con el múltiple de admisión y la válvula unilateral con sus otras conexiones. Si cualquier orificio, roturas u otros daños es encontrado reemplace las mangueras de vacío defectuosa.*

b)   *Después, remueva la válvula unilateral de la línea de vacío. Si una bomba de vacío está disponible, aplique 7.87 pulgada Hg (26.7 kPa) de vacío a la abertura de la válvula que se dirige a la unidad del amplificador. Si una bomba de vacío no está disponible, ponga su boca en la abertura y atente de chupar aire a través de la válvula. Si la presión en la bomba se cae más de 0.39 pulgada Hg (1.3 kPa) en 15 segundos, o si usted es capaz de chupar aire en la válvula, la válvula está defectuosa y debe ser reemplazada.*

c)   *Ahora sople aire en la válvula en la misma abertura como antes. Si la válvula no permite que usted sople aire hacia adentro, está defectuosa y debe ser reemplazada.*

d)   *Para chequear el amplificador de potencia, conecte un vacuómetro entre la unidad y la válvula unilateral. Ponga el motor en marcha y aumente lentamente la velocidad del motor. Apague el motor cuando el vacío que llega a 19.69 pulgada Hg (66.7 kPa) y observa el medidor. Si la lectura se cae más de 0.98 pulgada Hg 1/4 93.3 kPa) adentro de 15 segundos después que el motor haya sido apagado, la unidad del amplificador está defectuosa y debe ser reemplazada.*

e)   *Una prueba final es de repetir la prueba previa con el pedal del freno completamente deprimido. Otra vez, si la fuga de vacío es más que lo especificado, reemplace el amplificador para los frenos de poder.*

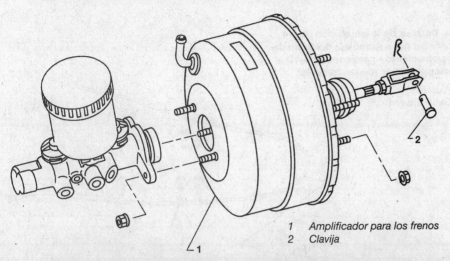

1   Amplificador para los frenos
2   Clavija

15.3 Detalles de la instalación del amplificador para los frenos de poder

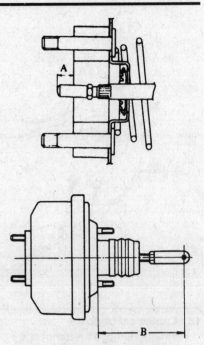

15.5 La longitud de la varilla de rendimiento (A) y/o la longitud (B) de la varilla de entrada del amplificador para los frenos, deben ser ajustadas (dependiendo del modelo del año) a las medidas listadas en las especificaciones

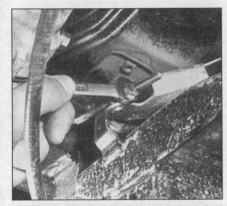

16.4a El ajustador para el freno de estacionamiento está ubicado en la parte derecha del camión enfrente del tanque de combustible (se muestra un modelo más antiguo de 4WD (tracción en las cuatro ruedas)

16.4b El freno de estacionamiento en los modelos más modernos es ajustado girando la tuerca del cable (flecha)

necesita ajuste.

3   Para el espacio libre, levante la parte trasera del vehículo y sosténgalo firmemente encima de soportes.

4   Afloje la contratuerca en el ajustador del cable del freno de estacionamiento (vea ilustraciones).

5   Gire la tuerca de ajuste hasta que la palanca del freno de estacionamiento, cuando se estire, se mueve la distancia apropiada.

6   Apriete nuevamente la tuerca prisionera.

7   Antes de bajar el vehículo, chequee que ambas ruedas traseras giren libremente con el freno de estacionamiento liberado y que no haya fricción de las balatas del freno.

17   Manija de control para el freno de estacionamiento - remover e instalar

1   Desconecte el conector del alambre que se dirige a la manija del freno de estacionamiento.

2   Desconecte el cable del freno de estacionamiento del ensamblaje de la manija removiéndolo de la clavija.

3   Remueva los pernos de afianzamiento y tornillos que conectan el soporte del control a la pared contrafuego o los pernos que afianzan el ensamblaje de la manija al piso.

4   Remueva el retenedor de resorte del lado del compartimiento del motor.

5   Remueva el ensamblaje de la manija de control.

6   La instalación se hace en el orden inverso al procedimiento de desensamble.

15   Amplificador para los frenos - remover e instalar

Refiérase a las ilustraciones 15.3 y 15.5

1   Remueva el cilindro maestro como se indica en la Sección 12.

2   Desconecte la línea de vacío de la unidad del amplificador.

3   Trabajando debajo del tablero, desconecte la varilla de empuje del amplificador del pedal del freno removiendo la clavija (vea ilustración).

4   Remueva las cuatro tuercas de retención de los espárragos para la unidad del amplificador. Regrese al compartimiento del motor y retire la unidad del vehículo.

5   La instalación se hace en el orden inverso al procedimiento de desensamble. **Nota:** *Siguiendo la instalación, mida la longitud de la varilla de empuje de la unidad y/o la varilla de operación (dependiendo del año)* (vea ilustración) antes de instalar el cilindro maestro. Si ellas no están como se especifica, ajústela. Si la cantidad del ajuste de la varilla de rendimiento excede 0.020 pulgada

(0.5 mm), reemplace el ensamblaje completo del amplificador para los frenos, porque se ha desgastado más allá de sus límites de servicio.

6   Purgue el sistema de frenos completo como se indica en la Sección 13.

7   Chequee la altura del pedal del freno, juego libre y ajústelo si es necesario como está descrito en el Capítulo 1.

16   Freno de estacionamiento - ajuste

Refiérase a las ilustraciones 16.4a y 16.4b

1   El freno de estacionamiento no necesita mantenimiento rutinario, pero el cable pueda que se estire durante un período de tiempo y necesite ajuste. También, el freno de estacionamiento debe ser chequeado por ajuste apropiado cuando los cables traseros del freno se hayan desconectado.

2   Mientras está sentado en el asiento del conductor, hale para atrás el cable del freno de estacionamiento con una fuerza de halar grande. Cuando esté correctamente ajustado, la palanca debe removerse de 6 a 10 chasquidos. Si el movimiento de la palanca es más corta o más largo que esto, el cable

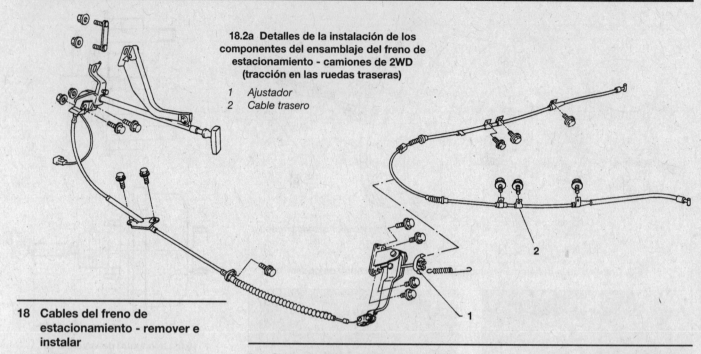

18.2a Detalles de la instalación de los componentes del ensamblaje del freno de estacionamiento - camiones de 2WD (tracción en las ruedas traseras)

1   Ajustador
2   Cable trasero

18   Cables del freno de estacionamiento - remover e instalar

Refiérase a las ilustraciones 18.2a, 18.2b y 18.2c

Cable delantero

1   Esté seguro que el freno de estacionamiento está completamente liberado.
2   Desconecte el cable de la manija del control removiendo la clavija **(vea ilustraciones).**

3   Si es necesario, levante la parte trasera del vehículo y sosténgalo firmemente encima de soportes.
4   Remueva la tuerca de ajuste del freno de estacionamiento y desconecte el cable opuesto trasero de la palanca de balance 4WD, o en los modelos de 2WD, desganche el cable trasero del ajustador.
5   Desconecte el cable trasero izquierdo del cable delantero.

6   Remueva los pernos de la palanca del compensador.
7   Separe todas las abrazaderas del cable y remueva la palanca al frente del cable y el compensador.
8   La instalación se hace en el orden inverso al procedimiento de desensamble. Aplique un poquito de grasa de propósito general a todos los puntos de las superficies y el pivote que se desliza.

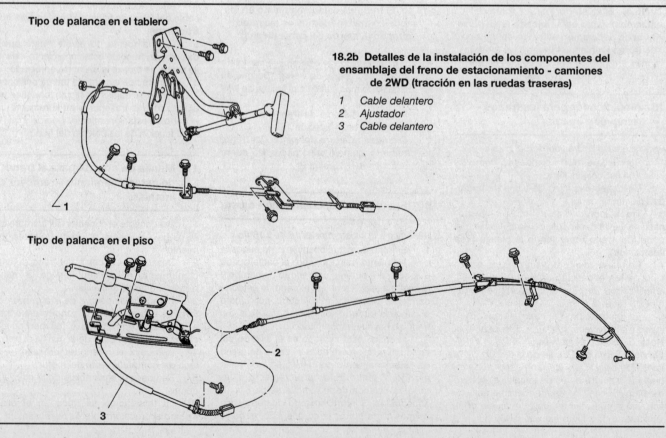

Tipo de palanca en el tablero

18.2b Detalles de la instalación de los componentes del ensamblaje del freno de estacionamiento - camiones de 2WD (tracción en las ruedas traseras)

1   Cable delantero
2   Ajustador
3   Cable delantero

Tipo de palanca en el piso

18.2c Detalles de la instalación de los componentes del ensamblaje del freno de estacionamiento - Pathfinder

1   Cable delantero
2   Ajustador
3   Cable trasero

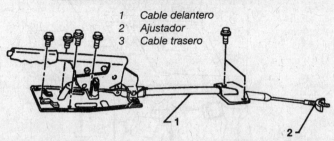
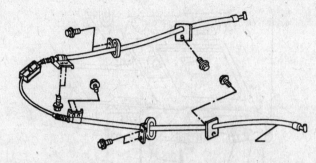

Cable trasero

9   Esté seguro que el freno de estacionamiento está completamente liberado.

10   Remueva la tuerca de ajuste del freno de estacionamiento y desconecte el cable trasero derecho de la palanca 4WD, o en los modelos 2WD desganche el cable trasero del ajustador.

11   Desconecte el cable trasero izquierdo del cable delantero.

12   Remueva ambos tambores del freno trasero, refiriéndose a la Sección 5, si es necesario.

13   Desconecte el cable trasero de la palanca en cada freno trasero.

14   Remueva ambos frenos traseros de atrás de los cables y los hala hacia afuera de atrás de la placa de apoyo.

15   Separe los cables de cualquier abrazadera que los retengan y remueva los cables.

16   La instalación se hace en el orden inverso al procedimiento de desensamble.

Aplique una pequeña cantidad de grasa de propósito general a todos los puntos de las superficies y el pivote que se desliza.

19   Interruptor para la luz del freno - remover e instalar

1   El interruptor de la luz del freno está instalado en la chaqueta del pedal del freno apenas en la parte trasera del pedal del freno.

2   Desconecte los alambres que se dirigen al interruptor.

3   Afloje la contratuerca.

4   Destornille el interruptor del soporte.

5   La instalación se hace en el orden inverso al procedimiento de desensamble. Note que el interruptor de la luz del freno controla la altura del pedal del freno. Instale el interruptor para que la altura del pedal del freno como está descrito para el ajuste en el Capítulo 1.

20   ABS (frenos antibloqueantes) - información general y acceso a los códigos

Descripción

El sistema de frenos antibloqueantes usados en estos vehículos controla las ruedas traseras solamente. Es diseñado para mantener la maniobrabilidad del vehículo, la estabilidad direccional y la deceleración óptima bajo condiciones severas de frenado en la mayoría de las superficies del camino. Hace esto controlando la velocidad giratoria de las ruedas traseras y el control de la presión del freno durante el frenado. Esto previene que las ruedas se enclaven.

Componentes

Refiérase a la ilustración 20.2

Ensamblaje del actuador

El ensamblaje del actuador, que está instalado en el riel del chasis, se compone de un aislamiento y una válvula de descarga. Las válvulas operan cambiando la presión del flúido de freno en respuesta a las señales de la unidad del control **(vea ilustración)**.

Unidad de control

La unidad del control está localizado debajo del tablero en el lado derecho. La función de la unidad del control es para aceptar y procesar información recibida del sensor de velocidad y el interruptor de la luz del freno para controlar la presión hidráulica de la línea, evitando el enclavamiento de la rueda. La unidad del control también controla constantemente el sistema, todavía bajo condiciones de manejo normales, para encontrar los defectos dentro del sistema.

Si un problema se desarrolla adentro del sistema, la luz de advertencia de ANTI-LOCK o ABS en el tablero se iluminará. Un código de diagnóstico se almacenará que se puede recuperar usando el procedimiento listado debajo para el Acezo a los códigos de problemas más abajo.

Sensor trasero

El sensor trasero, que es instalado en el frente del ensamblaje del diferencial, directamente atrás de la pestaña compañera, monitorea la velocidad giratoria de las ruedas

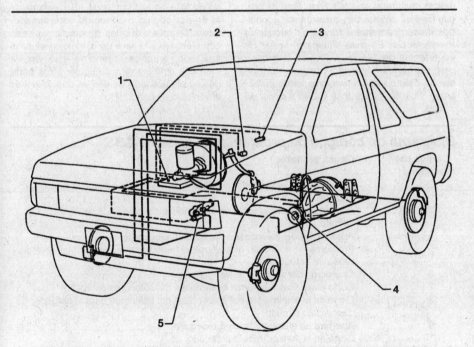

20.2 Ubicación de los componentes del sistema ABS (frenos antibloqueantes)

1   Modulo para la unidad de control ABS   3   Luz de advertencia
    (frenos antibloqueantes)   4   Sensor trasero
2   Interruptor para los frenos   5   Actuador

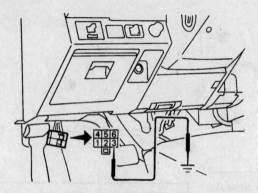

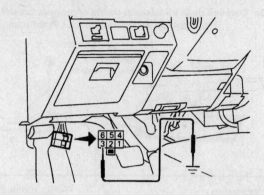

20.10a Para extraer los códigos de problemas de la unidad de control para el ABS (frenos antibloqueantes), ponga a tierra la Terminal número 3 del conector de chequeo con el motor en marcha (se muestra un modelo desde el 1991 al 1993)

20.10b En los modelos 1992, la terminal número 3 está en una ubicación diferente en el conector de chequeo

traseras, enviando esta información a la unidad de control. La unidad de control opera el ensamblaje del actuador para aliviar la presión del sistema de frenos cuando presiente cambios repentinos y dramáticos en la rueda trasera de la velocidad giratoria cuando el pedal del freno es aplicado.

Interruptor para la luz del freno

Además de su función en el circuíto de la luz del freno, el interruptor de la luz del freno es usado como parte del sistema de ABS (frenos antibloqueantes) para enviar una señal al módulo de control, indicando cuando el chófer está presionando el pedal del freno. Sin esta señal, el sistema de ABS no se activará.

Diagnóstico y reparación

Si la luz de advertencia de ANTI-LOCK o ABS se ilumina en el tablero y permanece iluminada, asegúrese que no hay problemas con el sistema del freno hidráulico. Si eso no es la causa, el sistema antibloqueante está probablemente funcionando mal. Aunque los procedimientos especiales de la prueba son necesario para diagnosticar apropiadamente el sistema, el mecánico de hogar puede realizar unos cuantos chequeos preliminares antes de llevar el vehículo al departamento de servicio de su concesionario.

a) *Asegúrese de que los frenos, los cilindros de las mordazas y de las ruedas están en buenas condiciones.*
b) *Chequee los conectores eléctricos en la unidad de control.*
c) *Chequee los fusibles.*
d) *Siga el conjunto del alambrado/arnés al sensor de velocidad, el interruptor de la luz del freno y asegúrese que todas las conexiones están segura y el alambrado no está dañado.*

Si los chequeos preliminares de encima no rectifican el problema, primero trate de identificar el área del problema usando los códigos para los problemas listados más abajo, entonces lleve el vehículo al departamento de servicio de su concesionario.

Accediendo los códigos de los problemas

Refiérase a las ilustraciones 20.10a y 20.10b

Si la luz de advertencia ANTI-LOCK o ABS se ilumina en el tablero y permanece iluminada, hay una buena posibilidad que el módulo de control haya almacenado un código de problema que puede ayudar al técnico de encontrar el área del problema en el sistema. **Caución:** *Si el vehículo es de 4WD, las ruedas traseras se obstruirán si las ruedas delanteras se obstruyen. Esto es porque los ejes delanteros y traseros son acoplados mecánicamente a través de la caja de transferencia. En esta situación, la luz de advertencia de "ANTI-LOCK" se iluminará, pero los frenos funcionarán todavía normalmente. Este no es un funcionamiento defectuoso. Cuando el motor se vuelve a poner en marcha, el ABS se reactiva y la luz de advertencia se apagará.*

Para tener acezo a un código de problema, conduzca el vehículo a 25 mph por lo menos un minuto (en 2WD si el vehículo es un modelo de 4WD). Permita que el motor esté en marcha, entonces encuentre el conector de "Chequear" debajo del tablero en el lado de chófer y ponga a tierra la Terminal número 3 del conector **(vea ilustraciones)**.

La luz de advertencia destellará para indicar el problema del código (1 destello para el código 1, 2 destellos para el código 2, 3 destellos para el código 3, etc.) Refiérase al diagrama que acompaña para determinar el problema indicado por el código. Si hay más de un fallo en el sistema de ABS, solamente el primer código reconocido será almacenado. Después que las reparaciones sean completadas y la llave de la ignición se haya apagado, entonces prendida otra vez, la memoria está limpia y cualquier otros códigos se almacenará, de uno en uno, mientras el vehículo es conducido.

Diagrama de códigos de problema del sistema ABS

Código del problema	Causa probable
2	Apertura en el aislamiento de ensamblaje del solenoide de actuación o circuito
3	Apertura en el aislamiento de ensamblaje del solenoide de descarga o circuito
4	Aislamiento del solenoide de actuación bloqueado
5	Problema en el circuito hidráulico del freno trasero o ensamblaje defectuoso de actuador
6	Operación del sensor trasero irregular
7	Corto en el aislamiento del ensamblaje del solenoide o circuito
8	Corto en el aislamiento del ensamblaje del solenoide para el actuador de descarga o circuito
9	Apertura en el sensor trasero o circuito
10	Corto en el sensor trasero o circuito
13, 14 o 15 .	Funcionamiento defectuoso en la unidad de control o circuito

Capítulo 11
Sistemas de dirección y suspensión

Contenidos

Especificaciones

Suspensión delantera

Instalación inicial del brazo de anclaje
  1980 al 1983 (dimensión A) .... 0.28 a 0.67 pulgada (7 a 17 mm)
  1984 (dimensión G)
    Lado izquierdo .... 4.33 a 4.72 pulgadas (110 a 120 mm)
    Lado derecho .... 5.12 a 5.51 pulgadas (130 a 140 mm)
  1985
    2WD (dimensión A) .... 1.46 pulgadas (37 mm)
    4WD (dimensión G)
      Lado izquierdo .... 3.74 pulgadas (95 mm)
      lado derecho .... 4.33 pulgadas (110 mm)
  1986 en adelante (dimensión G)
    2WD .... 0.24 a 0.71 pulgada (6 a 18 mm)
    4WD .... 1.97 a 2.36 pulgadas (50 a 60 mm)
Ajuste secundario del perno del brazo de anclaje (dimensión L)
  1980 al 1983 .... 2.36 a 2.76 pulgadas (60 a 70 mm)
  1984
    Lado izquierdo .... 2.72 pulgadas (69 mm)
    Lado derecho .... 2.83 pulgadas (72 mm)
  1985
    2WD .... 2.36 a 2.76 pulgadas (60 a 70 mm)
    4WD
      Lado izquierdo .... 3.50 pulgadas (89 mm)
      Lado derecho .... 3.86 pulgadas (98 mm)
  1986 en adelante
    HD 2WD, Cabina & Chasis y los modelos estándar .... 1.38 pulgadas (35 mm)
    todos los otros modelos de 2WD .... 1.93 pulgadas (49 mm)
    4WD .... 3.03 pulgadas (77 mm)

Altura del chasis del vehículo (dimensión H)
  1980 al 1983
    2WD .... 4.88 a 5.08 pulgadas (124 a 129 mm)
    4WD .... 5.28 a 5.47 pulgadas (134 a 139 mm)
  1984
    2WD
      Cabina grande .... 4.45 a 4.61 pulgadas (113 a 117 mm)
      Cabina regular .... 4.65 a 4.80 pulgadas (118 a 122 mm)
    4WD
      Cabina grande .... 1.54 a 1.69 pulgadas (39 a 43 mm)
      Cabina regular .... 1.73 a 1.89 pulgadas (44 a 48 mm)
Altura del chasis del vehículo (dimensión H)
  1985
    2WD .... 5.04 a 5.20 pulgadas (128 a 132 mm)
    4WD .... 2.09 a 2.24 pulgadas (53 a 57 mm)
  1986 en adelante
    2WD .... 4.25 a 4.65 pulgadas (108 a 118 mm)
    4WD .... 1.61 a 2.01 pulgadas (41 a 51 mm)
Posición del vástago superior
  Dimensión A
    1980 al 1983 .... 5.34 a 5.42 pulgadas (135.6 a 137.6 mm)
    1984 y 1985
      2WD .... 5.34 a 5.42 pulgadas (135.6 a 137.6 mm)
      4WD .... 4.33 pulgadas (110 mm)
    1986 en adelante .... 4.33 pulgadas (110 mm)
  Dimensión B
    1980 al 1983 .... 1.114 pulgadas (28.3 mm)
    1984 y 1985
      2WD .... 1.114 pulgadas (28.3 mm)
      4WD .... 0.98 pulgada (25 mm)
    1986 en adelante .... 1.26 pulgadas (32 mm)

Especificaciones técnicas   **Pies-libras**

Rótula del vástago superior de la dirección
  1980 al 1983 .... 58 a 72
  1984 y 1985
    2WD .... 58 a 72
    4WD .... 58 a 108
  1986 en adelante (todos) .... 58 a 108
Rótula superior al brazo de control superior .... 12 a 15
Vástago superior al brazo de control superior .... 52 a 76
Vástago superior a la acoplación del chasis .... 80 a 108
Brazo de control inferior al chasis .... 80 a 108
Rótula inferior al brazo de control inferior
  1980 al 1985 .... 28 a 38
  1986 en adelante .... 35 a 45
Rótula inferior al vástago de la dirección
  1980 al 1984 2WD y todos los 1985 .... 87 a 123
  1980 al 1983 4WD .... 43 a 72
  1986 en adelante .... 87 a 141
Brazo de torsión al brazo de control inferior
  1980 al 1983
    Interior .... 26 a 33
    Exterior .... 20 a 27
  1984 y 1985
    2WD
      Interior .... 26 a 33
      Exterior .... 20 a 27
    4WD .... 66 a 87
  1986 en adelante
    2WD .... 37 a 50
    4WD
      Interior .... 33 a 44
      Exterior .... 66 a 87
Varilla de tensión para el brazo de control inferior
  1980 al 1985 .... 33 a 44
  1986 en adelante .... 36 a 47
Varilla de tensión al chasis (todos) .... 87 a 116
Varilla de compresión al brazo de control inferior .... 87 a 108
Varilla de compresión al chasis .... 87 a 116

Suspensión trasera
Especificaciones técnicas   Pies-libras
Tuerca de la clavija delantera para el resorte de hojas
    1980 al 1985... 37 a 50
    1986 en adelante... 58 a 72
Tuercas al grillete del resorte
    1980 al 1985... 37 a 50
    1986 en adelante... 58 a 72
Pernos de brazo de control superiores e inferiores (resortes espirales) . 80 a 108
Pernos de afianzamiento para varilla de Panhard
    Lado izquierdo
        Hasta el 1990... 36 a 51
        1991 y más modernos .... 94 a 123
    Lado derecho .... 80 a 108

Sistema de dirección
Caja de la dirección manual
Juego final del eje sector.. 0.0004 a 0.0012 pulgada (0.01 a 0.03 mm)
Lamillas de ajustes para el eje sector..................................... 0.0620 t0 0.0630 pulgada (1.575 a 1.600 mm)
                                                    0.0610 a 0.0620 pulgada (1.550 a 1.575 mm)
     0.0600 a 0.0610 pulgada (1.525 a 1.550 mm)
     0.0591 a 0.0600 pulgada (1.500 a 1.525 mm)
     0.0581 a 0.0591 pulgada (1.475 a 1.500 mm)
     0.0571 a 0.0581 pulgada (1.450 a 1.475 mm)
     0.0768 pulgada (1.95 mm)
     0.0787 pulgada (2.00 mm)
     0.0807 pulgada (2.05 mm)
Precarga para el balero del sinfín
    1980 al 1983... 3.5 a 5.2 pulgada-libra (0.39 a 0.59 Nm)
    1984 en adelante... 1.7 a 5.2 pulgada-libra (0.20 a 0.59 Nm)
Precarga para la caja de la dirección (todos los años)
    Partes nuevas.. 7.4 a 10.9 pulgada-libra (0.83 a 1.23 Nm)
    Partes usadas.. 5.2 a 8.7 pulgada-libra (0.59 a 0.98 Nm)
Varilla de la dirección
Longitud estándar de la varilla lateral
    2WD
        1980 al 1985... 13.07 pulgadas (332 mm)
        1986 en adelante .... 13.54 pulgadas (344 mm)
    4WD
        1980 al 1983... 10.83 pulgadas (275 mm)
        1984 y 1985 .... 11.54 pulgadas (293 mm)
        1986 y más modernos .... 11.06 pulgadas (281 mm)

Especificaciones técnicas   Pies-libras
Tuerca del volante
    1980 al 1985... 29 a 36
    1986 en adelante... 22 a 29
Soporte del tubo de la camisa al panel del tablero
    1980 al 1985... 2.2 a 3.2
    1986 en adelante... 6.5 a 10.1
Eje sinfín al acoplamiento
    1980 al 1983... 29 a 36
    1984 y 1985 .... 11 a 16
    1986 en adelante... 17 a 22
Tuercas del espárrago de la bola (todos) .... 40 a 72
Tuercas de la abrazadera de la varilla lateral
Hasta el 1985 .... 8 a 12
    1986 al 1990... 10 a 14
    1991 y más modernos... 8 a 10
Contratuerca de la varilla lateral (1984 y más modernos) .... 58 a 72
Pernos del brazo loco al chasis
    Hasta el 1990 .... 36 a 51
    1991 y más modernos... 40 a 51
Tuerca del brazo loco .... 40 a 51
Pernos de la caja de la dirección al chasis........................... 62 a 71
Pernos del brazo del engrane de la dirección (brazo Pitman) a la tuerca del eje
    Dirección manual
        Hasta el 1990 .... 94 a 108
        1991 y más modernos.. 174 a 195
    Dirección de poder .... 101 a 130

1.1 Componentes de la suspensión y la dirección delantera

1   Vástago de la dirección
2   Rótula superior
3   Brazo de control superior
4   Varilla lateral
5   Brazo loco
6   Barra estabilizadora
7   Cruce la varilla
8   Brazo de la caja de la dirección (Brazo Pitman)
9   Rótula inferior
10 Brazo de control inferior
11 Amortiguador
12 Varilla de compresión
13 Barra de torsión

1 Sistema de suspensión - información general

Refiérase a las ilustraciones 1.1, 1.2a, 1.2b, 1.3 y 1.4

El sistema de suspensión delantera es de un tipo independiente usando barras de torsión. Los componentes principales son los brazos de control superiores e inferiores, el muñón del vástago, los amortiguadores, las varillas de tensión, la barra estabilizadora y las barras de torsión **(vea ilustración)**.

Ambas acoplaciones de tipo pivote en el chasis del extremo interior y están conectados a las rótulas del vástago de la dirección en el extremo exterior. El muñón del vástago de la dirección está conectado directamente al cubo delantero.

El extremo delantero de la barra de torsión está conectado a un brazo de torsión

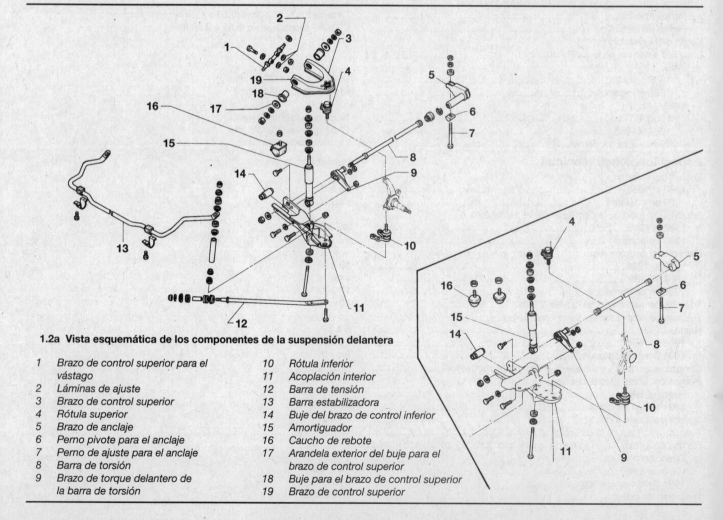

1.2a Vista esquemática de los componentes de la suspensión delantera

1   Brazo de control superior para el vástago
2   Láminas de ajuste
3   Brazo de control superior
4   Rótula superior
5   Brazo de anclaje
6   Perno pivote para el anclaje
7   Perno de ajuste para el anclaje
8   Barra de torsión
9   Brazo de torque delantero de la barra de torsión
10 Rótula inferior
11 Acoplación interior
12 Barra de tensión
13 Barra estabilizadora
14 Buje del brazo de control inferior
15 Amortiguador
16 Caucho de rebote
17 Arandela exterior del buje para el brazo de control superior
18 Buje para el brazo de control superior
19 Brazo de control superior

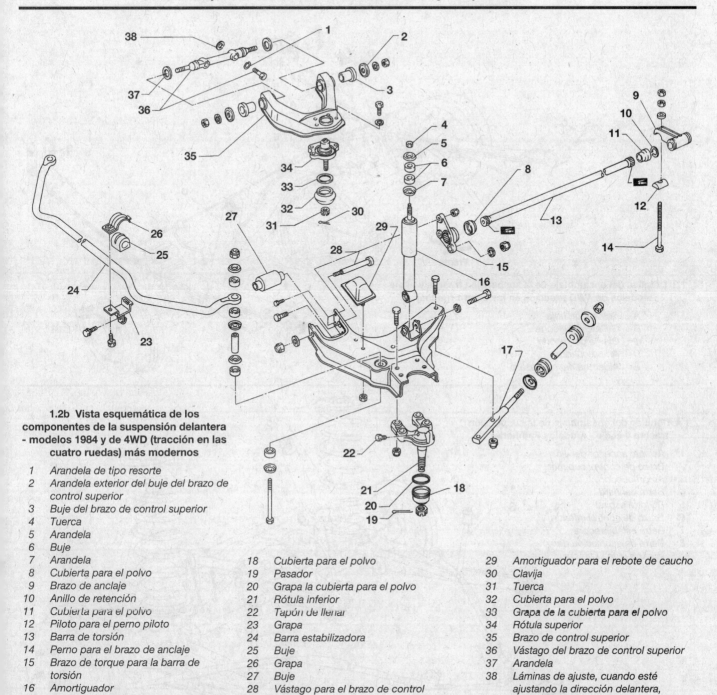

1.2b Vista esquemática de los componentes de la suspensión delantera - modelos 1984 y de 4WD (tracción en las cuatro ruedas) más modernos

1   Arandela de tipo resorte
2   Arandela exterior del buje del brazo de control superior
3   Buje del brazo de control superior
4   Tuerca
5   Arandela
6   Buje
7   Arandela
8   Cubierta para el polvo
9   Brazo de anclaje
10   Anillo de retención
11   Cubierta para el polvo
12   Piloto para el perno piloto
13   Barra de torsión
14   Perno para el brazo de anclaje
15   Brazo de torque para la barra de torsión
16   Amortiguador
17   Barra de compresión

18   Cubierta para el polvo
19   Pasador
20   Grapa la cubierta para el polvo
21   Rótula inferior
22   Tapón de llenar
23   Grapa
24   Barra estabilizadora
25   Buje
26   Grapa
27   Buje
28   Vástago para el brazo de control inferior

29   Amortiguador para el rebote de caucho
30   Clavija
31   Tuerca
32   Cubierta para el polvo
33   Grapa de la cubierta para el polvo
34   Rótula superior
35   Brazo de control superior
36   Vástago del brazo de control superior
37   Arandela
38   Láminas de ajuste, cuando esté ajustando la dirección delantera, selecciónela

que está instalado al brazo de control inferior. El diferencial trasero está conectado a un brazo de anclaje instalado directamente al chasis. Es a causa de este arreglo que las acoplaciones (la rueda y el neumático) son regresados a sus posiciones originales después de un bache. El ajuste de la barra de torsión es hecho por los pernos de ajuste del brazo de anclaje.

Los amortiguadores son unidades convencionales hidráulicas selladas, conectadas en el extremo superior a un soporte o al chasis y en el extremo inferior al brazo de control inferior. El amortiguador de doble acción amortigua el movimiento inicial hacia arriba,

la fuerza de un choque y la fuerza de rebote. Algunos modelos usan amortiguadores ajustables, controlados eléctricamente desde el compartimiento del chófer.

Las fuerzas delanteras y traseras son controladas por varillas de tensión (varillas de compresión en los modelos 1984 y más modernos de 4WD (tracción en las cuatro ruedas) y una barra delantera estabilizadora es instalada para controlar que la carrocería no se ruede en las curvas.

La suspensión trasera en algunos modelos usan resortes elípticos de hojas, instalados en los extremos del chasis y en el centro del eje trasero por pernos de tipo U

(vea ilustración). En otros modelos resortes espirales son usado, localizados en el chasis a través de los brazos de control superiores e inferiores y una varilla de panhard. Una barra trasera estabilizadora es también usada en estos modelos (vea ilustración). Los amortiguadores traseros son instalados entre el eje y el chasis. Igual que los amortiguadores delanteros, las unidades traseras no son ajustables, no se pueden llenar nuevamente y no se pueden desarmar.

Nunca trate de calentar ni enderezar ninguna parte de la suspensión, porque esto puede debilitar el metal o de otra manera dañar la parte.

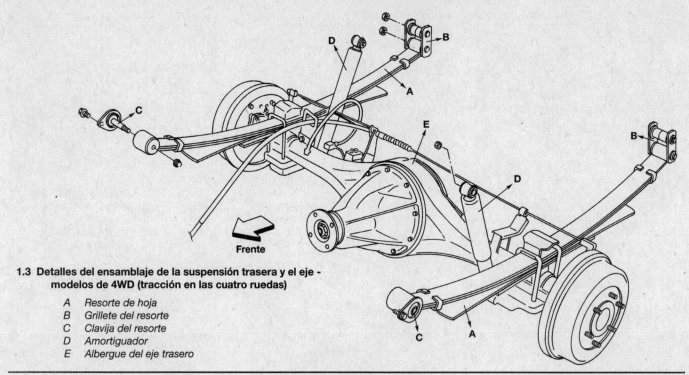

**1.3 Detalles del ensamblaje de la suspensión trasera y el eje -
modelos de 4WD (tracción en las cuatro ruedas)**

   A   Resorte de hoja
   B   Grillete del resorte
   C   Clavija del resorte
   D   Amortiguador
   E   Albergue del eje trasero

**1.4 Detalles del ensamblaje de la suspensión
trasera y el eje - modelos Pathfinder**

   1   Asiento superior del eje
   2   Brazo de control superior
   3   Amortiguador
   4   Barra panhard
   5   Resorte espiral
   6   Brazo de control inferior
   7   Barra estabilizadora
   *8   Barra de acoplación de
         la barra estabilizadora*

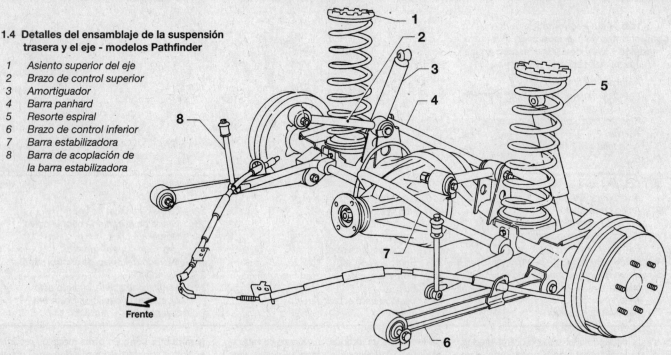

2   Espárrago de la rueda - reemplazo

1   Levante el vehículo y sopórtelo firmemente encima de estantes.
2   Remueva la rueda.
3   Remueva la mordaza del freno como
está descrito en el Capítulo 10.
4   Remueva el rotor como está descrito en
el Capítulo 10.
5   En las ruedas delanteras, el cubo se
tendrá que separar del rotor como está descrito en el Capítulo 10.
6   Posicione el espárrago para ser reemplazado en la posición de 5 o 7 en el reloj.
Instale una tuerca en el extremo del espárrago y usando un removedor de espárrago
apropiado para las ruedas, prense el espárrago hacia afuera de su asiento.
7   Remueva la tuerca del espárrago y
entonces el espárrago.
8   Con el orificio del espárrago a las 5 o 7
en la posición del reloj, meta el espárrago
nuevo en el orificio, asegúrese que las serra-
ciones están alineadas con ésas hechas por
el perno original.
9   Coloque cuatro arandelas planas en el
extremo exterior del espárrago y entonces
enrosque una tuerca al espárrago.
10   Apriete la tuerca hasta que el asiento de
la cabeza del espárrago se asiente con la
parte trasera del cubo. Entonces remueva la
tuerca y las arandelas.
11   Vuelva a instalar los componentes en el
orden reverso a como ellos fueron removidos.
12   Instale la rueda y baje el vehículo al piso.

3.3 Antes de remover la tuerca (flecha) de la varilla de la barra estabilizadora, anote como los bujes, las arandelas y el espaciador están instalados

3.5 Después de remover los pernos (flecha) de soporte de la barra estabilizadora, la barra puede ser removida del vehículo

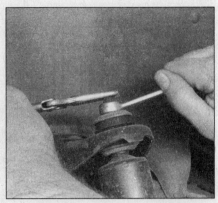

4.2 Detenga la varilla del amortiguador con un par de alicates de enclavamiento para aflojar la tuerca con una llave

4.3 El extremo inferior del amortiguador es atornillado a un soporte en el brazo de control inferior

4.6 El extremo inferior del amortiguador trasero es conectado a la almohadilla del resorte por una tuerca (flecha)

4.7 El extremo superior del amortiguador trasero es conectado al espárrago del chasis por una tuerca (flecha)

3   Barra estabilizadora - remover e instalar

Refiérase a las ilustraciones 3.3 y 3.5

Remover

1   Levante la parte delantera del vehículo y póngalo firmemente encima de estantes.

2   Remueva el protector.

3   Remueva las tuercas superiores de ambas varillas estabilizadoras localizadas en cada extremo de la barra estabilizadora (**vea ilustración**).

4   Remueva las varillas de la barra y las varillas inferiores, estando seguro de mantener los bujes, arandelas y espaciadores en el orden de instalación.

5   Remueva los pernos que conectan los soportes de la barra estabilizadora al chasis y levante la barra (**vea ilustración**).

6   Si los bujes de la barra estabilizadora necesitan ser reemplazados, simplemente sepárelos y los desliza de la barra.

7   Inspeccione los bujes de la varilla estabilizadora por grietas o cualquier otros daños y reemplácelo según sea necesario.

Instalar

8   La instalación se hace en el orden inverso al procedimiento de desensamble,

con las siguientes notas:

a)   *La barra debe ser instalada para que las marcas blancas pintadas en la barra cerca de los bujes se puedan ver en ambos lados del vehículo.*

b)   *Los componentes de la varilla de acoplación deben ser instalado en su orden original y posiciones.*

c)   *Los pernos de afianzamiento de la barra estabilizadora no deben de ser completamente apretados hasta que el vehículo haya sido bajado al piso y el peso completo esté en las ruedas.*

4   Amortiguadores - remover e instalar

Refiérase a las ilustraciones 4.2, 4.3, 4.6 y 4.7

Delantero

1   Gire la rueda delantera hacia afuera para permitir acceso al amortiguador. Para espacio libre adicional, remueva la rueda.

2   Mientras detiene la varilla de amortiguación del amortiguador para prevenirla que gire, remueva la tuerca, arandela y el buje de caucho (**vea ilustración**).

3   Remueva el perno que atraviesa en el extremo inferior del amortiguador (**vea ilustración**).

4   La instalación se hace en el orden inverso al procedimiento de desensamble. Asegúrese que el perno en el extremo inferior está instalado con su cabeza mirando hacia el frente del vehículo.

Trasero

5   Chequee las ruedas delanteras, entonces levante la parte trasera del vehículo lo más alto como sea posible para que sea sostenido en el tubo del eje. Esté seguro de que apoyo adecuado sea proporcionado antes de empezar el trabajo.

6   Mientras sostiene la parte inferior del vástago del amortiguador para prevenirlo que gire, remueva las tuercas, arandelas y el buje de caucho (estilo más antiguo). En los modelos más modernos, remueva la tuerca del espárrago en la almohadilla inferior del resorte (**vea ilustración**).

7   Remueva la tuerca del calzo en el extremo superior y remueva el amortiguador (**vea ilustración**).

8   La instalación se hace en el orden inverso al procedimiento de desensamble. Esté seguro que el peso esté en las ruedas antes de apretar las ruedas.

5.2a Ubicación de los pernos del anclaje de la barra de torsión - modelos 1980 al 1983

5.2b Ubicación de la tuerca del perno de ajuste de la barra de torsión (flecha) - modelos 1984 y de 4WD más modernos

5   Barra de torsión - remover e instalar

Refiérase a las ilustraciones 5.2a, 5.2b, 5.3, 5.6, 5.7, 5.11, 5.12, 5.13, 5.15, 5.16a y 5.16b

Remover

1   Levante la parte delantera del vehículo y póngalo firmemente encima de estantes.
2   Remueva las tuercas de ajuste del perno de anclaje de la barra de torsión y remueva el perno de anclaje **(vea ilustraciones)**.
3   Remueva la tapa de polvo y separe el anillo de presión del brazo de anclaje **(vea ilustración)**.
4   Hale el brazo de anclaje hacia afuera de la parte trasera del vehículo (modelos de 2WD).
5   Retire la barra de torsión hacia la parte trasera del vehículo (modelos de 2WD).
6   Remueva el brazo de torque desde el brazo de control inferior (modelos de 2WD) **(vea ilustración)**.
7   En los modelos de 4WD, destornille el brazo de torque al brazo de control inferior **(vea ilustración)** entonces remueva el brazo de la barra de torsión y el brazo de torque

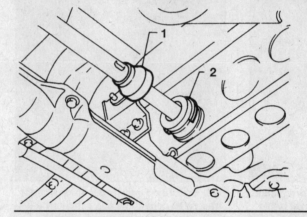

5.3 Deslice la tapa para el polvo hacia adelante en la barra de torsión para obtener acceso al anillo de cierre en el brazo del anclaje

1   *Cubierta para el polvo*
2   *Anillo de retención*

hacia el frente del vehículo.
8   Chequee la barra de torsión por desgaste excesivo, torcida, dobles u otros daños. Chequee también cada parte dentada para asegurarse que ellas están en buenas condiciones.

Instalar

9   Comience la instalación volviendo a instalar el brazo de torque al brazo de control inferior (modelos de 2WD). Apriete los pernos de retención al par de torsión especificado.

10   Aplique una capa de grasa a las cuarteaduras en la barra de torsión y después instale la barra de torsión en el brazo de torque (modelos de 2WD). En los modelos de 4WD, instale la barra de torsión y el brazo de torque al brazo de control inferior y apriete los pernos al par de torsión especificado. **Nota:** *Si ambas barras de torsión son removidas al mismo tiempo, asegúrese que cada una está instalada en el lado correcto del vehículo. Ellas están marcadas con una R (derecho) o L (izquierdo) en el extremo final de la barra.*

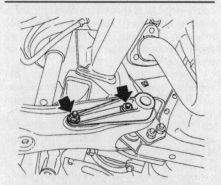

5.6 Ubicación de las tuercas de acoplación del brazo de torque en los modelos con brazo de control inferior (pre 1984 de 2WD - los otros son similares)

5.7 Ubicación de las tuercas de acoplación del brazo de torque inferior (flechas) - modelos más modernos de 4WD

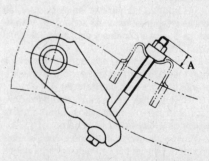

5.11 En los vehículos 1980 al 1983, mida la posición inicial del brazo de torque (A) y ajústelo a la dimensión listada en las especificaciones

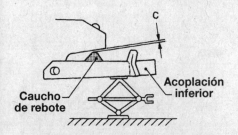

5.12 Antes de ajustar la regulación inicial del brazo de torque en los modelos 1984 y más modernos, levante el brazo de control inferior hasta que los parachoques de rebote apenas hagan contacto con el chasis

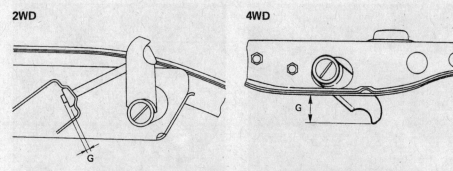

5.13 Instale el brazo de anclaje y ajústelo a su posición inicial (G) a las especificaciones listadas

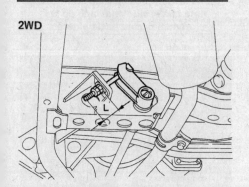

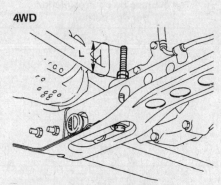

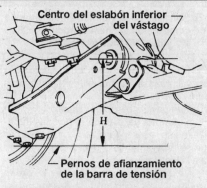

5.16a Cuando esté chequeando la altura del chasis del vehículo, la medida (H) se debe tomar en los puntos mostrados (modelos 1980 al 1983 de 4WD y todos los modelos de 2WD)

5.15 Gire la tuerca del brazo de anclaje hasta que la porción expuesta del perno de ajuste llegue a la longitud correcta, como se muestra en las especificaciones

11   Instale el brazo de anclaje en la barra de torsión trasera e instale el perno de ajuste del brazo de anclaje y las tuercas (1980 a 1983). La posición inicial correcta del brazo de anclaje debe ser puesto a la dimensión rendida en las especificaciones **(vea ilustración)**.

12   En los modelos 1984 y más modernos levante el brazo de control inferior hasta que no haya espacio libre entre los parachoques de rebote y el chasis **(vea ilustración)**.

13   Instale el brazo de anclaje y ajuste la instalación inicial del brazo de torque a la dimensión otorgada en las especificaciones **(vea ilustración)**.

14   Instale el anillo de retención en la ranura del brazo de anclaje y deslice la tapa del polvo en posición.

15   Gire la tuerca del brazo de anclaje hasta que el perno del brazo de anclaje salga de la longitud especificada **(vea ilustración)**.

16   Baje el vehículo al piso y empújelo hacia abajo varias veces para poner la suspensión en su posición. Mida la altura del chasis en los puntos indicados **(vea ilustraciones)**. Si la dimensión no está como se especifica, gire la tuerca de ajuste del perno de anclaje hasta que esté correcto.

17   Conduzca el vehículo a un taller de alineación y haga que la alineación sea chequeada y si es necesario ajustada.

6   Barra de tensión o compresión - remover e instalar

Refiérase a las ilustraciones 6.2a, 6.2b, 6.3 y 6.6

1   Levante la parte delantera del vehículo y póngalo firmemente encima de estantes para obtener espacio libre. Remueva el protector, si está equipado.

2   Remueva la tuerca grande del final de la barra de tensión o compresión y levante los bujes y arandelas **(vea ilustraciones)**.

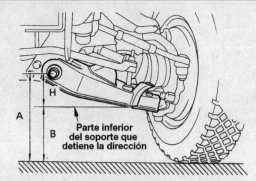

5.16b En los modelos 1984 y de 4WD más modernos, chequee la altura del chasis del vehículo en la distancia H y ajuste la barra de torsión según sea necesario

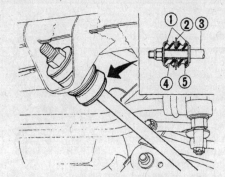

1   Arandela para el impulso
2   Chasis
3   Varilla de tensión
4   Buje
5   Collar

6.2a Varilla de tensión, detalles de como instalar el buje y la arandela (modelos 1980 al 1983 de 4WD y todos los modelos de 2WD)

6.2b Detalles de la instalación de la varilla de compresión al chasis (modelos 1984 y de 4WD más modernos)

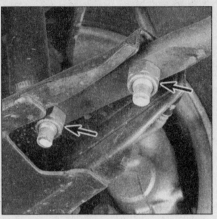

6.3 La varilla de compresión es sostenida en el brazo de control inferior por dos pernos

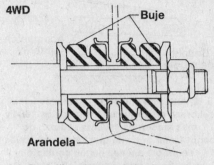

6.6 Posición correcta de los bujes de la varilla de compresión y las arandelas - note que el lado ondulado de las arandelas mira hacia afuera

3   Remueva los pernos que aseguran la barra al brazo de control inferior **(vea ilustración)**.
4   Remueva la barra del vehículo.
5   Si ambas barras son removidas inmediatamente, esté seguro de notar las marcas que se refieren al lado derecho e izquierdo para la instalación.
6   La instalación se hace en el orden inverso al procedimiento de desensamble. Esté seguro de instalar los bujes y arandelas en la dirección apropiada **(vea ilustración)**. **Nota:** *No apriete los pernos hasta que el vehículo haya sido bajado al piso y el peso completo esté en las ruedas.*

7   Brazo de control superior y rótula - remover e instalar

Refiérase a las ilustraciones 7.5a, 7.5b, 7.6a, 7.6b y 7.15

1   Levante la parte delantera del vehículo y póngalo firmemente encima de estantes.
2   Remueva la rueda.
3   Remueva la tuerca superior del amortiguador y comprima el amortiguador lo más posible.
4   Coloque un gato bajo el brazo de control inferior para tomar el peso del ensamblaje.
5   Afloje, pero no remueva, la tuerca superior de la rótula. Usando una herramienta adecuada, separe la rótula superior del muñón del vástago **(vea ilustraciones)**, entonces remueva la tuerca.
6   Remueva los pernos que conectan el vástago superior a la acoplación del chasis y levante hacia afuera el ensamblaje superior completo de la acoplación, incluyendo cualquier láminas para ajustes. Ponga atención cerca al número y la posición de todas las lámina para ajustes **(vea ilustraciones)**.
7   La rótula ahora puede ser removida del brazo de control superior removiendo las tuercas retenedoras. La rótula no se puede desarmar. Si está defectuosa, debe ser reemplazada con una nueva.

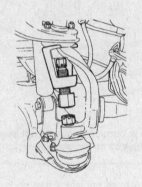

7.5a Un extractor especial se debe usar para liberar la rótula superior o inferior del muñón del vástago

8   Si los bujes de los brazos superiores están endurecidos o agrietados ellos deben ser reemplazados. Esto es hecho removiendo las tuercas superiores del eje para el brazo en ambos extremos del eje superior y prensándolo de la acoplación. Una prensa hidráulica pueda que sea necesaria para este procedimiento.

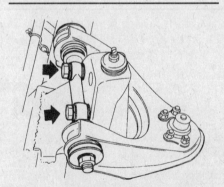

7.6a Ubicación de los pernos del vástago al brazo de control superior (modelos 1980 al 1984)

7.5b Una herramienta alternativa de separar rótulas se puede fabricar de un perno grande, tuerca, arandela y un dado, arreglado como está mostrado - cuando la tuerca es apretada contra el dado, la cabeza del perno (debe ser sostenida con una llave para prevenirla que gire) empujará en el espárrago de la rótula, aflojándolo del vástago de la dirección

7.6b Ubicación de los pernos del vástago al brazo de control superior (modelos 1985 y más modernos)

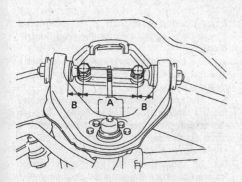

7.15 Chequee para estar seguro que la acoplación del vástago superior está apropiadamente centrado midiendo las dimensiones A y B - refiérase a las especificaciones para las medidas deseadas

9   Para instalar los bujes nuevos, aplique primero una solución de agua enjabonada a un buje. Entonces apriételo en el brazo hasta que la pestaña del buje esté encima contra el final del cuello en el brazo. Otra vez, una prensa hidráulica pueda que sea necesaria para este procedimiento.

10   Con un buje instalado, insercióne el eje en el brazo y las arandelas interiores. Posicione las arandelas con las orillas de las caras redondeadas mirando hacia adentro.

11   Presione el otro buje hacia adentro de la misma manera como el primero.

12   Instale las tuercas del eje y apriételas con los dedos.

13   Instale la rótula al brazo de control superior.

14   Conecte el ensamblaje del brazo superior al chasis volviendo a instalar el brazo superior de la acoplación instalando los pernos y láminas para ajustes. Esté seguro que las lámina para ajustes están en sus posiciones originales y apriete los pernos al par de torsión especificado.

15   Después de conectar el brazo de control superior al chasis, chequee las dimensiones A y B **(vea ilustración)** esté seguro que la acoplación está apropiadamente centrada. Compare sus medidas con las especificaciones y ajústelas según sea necesario.

16   El resto del procedimiento de la instalación se hace en el orden inverso al procedimiento de desensamble. **Nota:** *No apriete completamente las tuercas superiores del vástago de acoplación hasta que el vehículo sea bajado al piso. Siguiendo la instalación, conduzca el vehículo a un taller de alineación y haga que la alineación sea chequeada y si es necesario ajustada.*

8   Brazo de control inferior y rótula - remover e instalar

Refiérase a la ilustración 8.8

1   Levante la parte delantera del vehículo y póngalo firmemente encima de estantes.

2   Remueva la rueda.

3   Remueva la barra de torsión, como se indica en la Sección 5.

4   Desconecte el calzo inferior del amortiguador desde el brazo de control inferior.

5   Remueva la varilla de la barra estabilizadora al brazo de control inferior.

6   Afloje, pero no remueva, la tuerca inferior de la rótula y use una herramienta adecuada para separar el brazo de control inferior del muñón del vástago. Un extractor de dos mandíbulas trabajará en los vehículos de 1984 y 4WD más modernos. Todos los otros modelos deben usar una herramienta de separar rótulas.

7   Desconecte la varilla de tensión o de compresión del brazo de control inferior.

8   Remueva la tuerca inferior delantera de la acoplación del pivote **(vea ilustración)** y empuje el espárrago hacia afuera en la parte trasera.

9   Remueva el brazo de torque del brazo de control inferior y levante la acoplación hacia afuera del chasis.

10   La rótula puede ser removida de la acoplación removiendo los pernos de retención. La rótula no se puede desarmar. Si está defectuosa, debe ser reemplazada con una

nueva.

11   Si es necesario, el buje inferior de la acoplación puede ser removido del chasis utilizándolo un martillo y dado del tamaño adecuado.

12   La instalación se hace en el orden inverso al procedimiento de desensamble. Esté seguro de apretar todas las tuercas de la rótula al brazo de control inferior, las tuercas del espárrago de la rótula del muñón del vástago y la tuerca pivote inferior de la acoplación al par de torsión especificado.

13   Siguiendo la instalación, baje el vehículo al piso y chequee la altura del chasis (refiérase a la Sección 5).

14   Conduzca el vehículo a un taller de alineación y haga que la alineación sea chequeada y si es necesario ajustada.

9   Resorte trasero de hoja - remover e instalar

Refiérase a las ilustraciones 9.3, 9.6 y 9.7

1   Levante la parte trasera del vehículo y sopórtelo seguramente encima de estantes.

2   Posicione un gato debajo del diferencial para tomar el peso del eje trasero.

3   Remueva la tuerca inferior del amortiguador y desconecte el amortiguador del plato resorte. Remueva las tuercas del perno de tipo U, levante los pernos de tipo U y el plato **(vea ilustración)**.

4   En los modelos de 4WD, desconecte cualquier abrazadera del cable de freno trasero de estacionamiento desde el lado lateral del resorte de hoja que va ser removido.

5   En los modelos de 2WD, levante el eje trasero fuera del resorte de hoja. En los modelos de 4WD, el eje trasero se debe bajar del resorte. En cualquier caso, esté seguro que el eje esté adecuadamente equilibrado en el gato.

6   Remueva la tuerca inferior y afloje la tuerca del grillete superior del resorte de atrás **(vea ilustración)**. Expulse cuidadosamente el perno inferior para liberar el eje trasero del resorte.

8.8 Ubicación de la tuerca del brazo de control inferior (flecha)

9.3 Remueva la tuerca inferior del amortiguador (A) desde el plato del resorte, entonces remueva las cuatro tuercas del plato del resorte (B)

9.6 Afloje la tuerca superior del grillete y remueva la tuerca inferior, entonces remueva el perno inferior hacia afuera del grillete con un martillo y un punzón

7   Remueva la clavija en la parte del extremo delantero del resorte para permitir que el resorte sea removido **(vea ilustración)**.

8   Examine el resorte por hojas torcidas o rotas; si alguna se encuentra, un resorte de reemplazo se debe obtener. Si los bujes de caucho están desgastados, ellos pueden ser prensados hacia afuera con una deriva y un espaciador entre las mandíbulas de una prensa. Cubra los nuevos con una solución

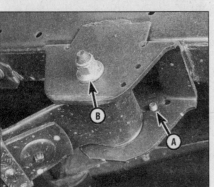

9.7 Para remover la clavija del resorte delantero, remueva el perno de localización (A) entonces la tuerca de la clavija (B) - empuje la clavija hacia afuera a través del buje

● Temporalmente apriete todas las acoplaciones, entonces ponga el vehículo en el piso. Después de menear la carrocería hacia arriba y hacia abajo dos o tres veces, apriete las acoplaciones firmemente.

● Cuando esté instalando pernos y tuercas de seguridad, esté seguro de seleccionar el tipo apropiado e instálelo correctamente.

del jabón y agua para simplificar la instalación.

9   La instalación del resorte se hace en el orden inverso al procedimiento de desensamble, pero asegúrese que el peso del vehículo está encima de las ruedas antes de que la tuerca delantera de la clavija, tuercas del grillete y los calzos del amortiguador sean apropiadamente apretados.

10   Resorte trasero espiral - remover e instalar

Refiérase a las ilustraciones 10.3 y 10.6

1   Levante la parte trasera del vehículo y sopórtelo firmemente en estantes colocados debajo de los rieles del chasis.

2   Sostenga el eje trasero con un gato de piso colocado debajo del diferencial.

3   Remueva las tuercas inferiores del amortiguador y deslice el amortiguador afuera de la clavija de montaje **(vea ilustración)**.

4   Baje el eje trasero lentamente, hasta que los resortes espirales estén completamente extendidos.

5   Remueva el resorte espiral y los asientos del resorte afuera del vehículo. Chequee los asientos por grietas, endurecimiento u otros signos de deterioración y reemplácelo según sea necesario.

6   La instalación se hace en el orden inverso al procedimiento de desensamble. Cuando esté instalando el resorte y el asiento inferior del resorte, asegúrese que la cara mira hacia la dirección de la parte trasera del vehículo **(vea ilustración)**. También, no apriete las tuercas del amortiguador inferior hasta que el vehículo sea bajado al piso.

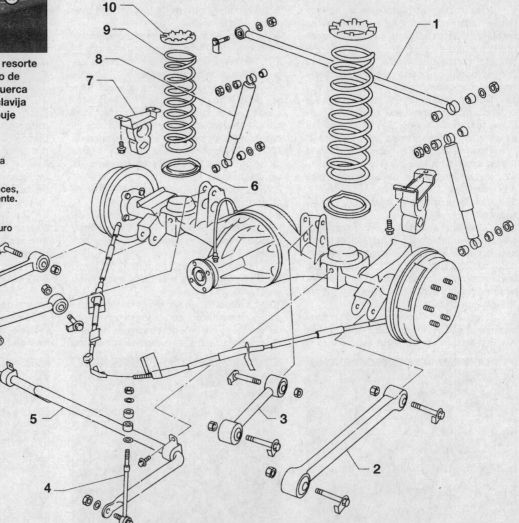

10.3 Ubicación de los componentes de acoplación de la suspensión trasera con resortes espirales - vista esquemática

1 Varilla panhard	6 Asiento inferior del resorte
2 Brazo de control inferior	7 Caucho para el rebote
3 Brazo de control superior	8 Amortiguador
4 Varilla de acoplación para la barra estabilizadora	9 Resorte espiral
5 Barra estabilizadora	10 Asiento superior del resorte

11 Ubicaciones de las acoplaciones de la suspensión trasera - remover e instalar

Nota: *Este procedimiento se aplica a los brazos de control superiores e inferiores y la varilla de panhard. Remueva solamente un eslabón a la vez a menos que vaya a remover el ensamblaje trasero completo del eje.*

1   Levante el vehículo y sopórtelo firmemente encima de estantes puestos en posición debajo de los rieles del chasis.

2   Sostenga el eje trasero con un gato de piso colocado debajo del diferencial.

3   Remueva las tuercas de los extremos a la acoplación, entonces expulse el perno del buje y el soporte, si es necesario. Remueva la acoplación del vehículo.

4   La instalación se hace en el orden inverso al procedimiento de desensamble. No apriete las tuercas de acoplación completamente hasta que el vehículo se haya bajado

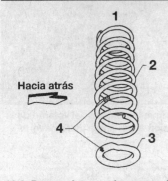

Hacia atrás

10.6 Ponga cinta en el resorte y la marca direccional en el asiento inferior del resorte deben mirar hacia la parte trasera del vehículo cuando esté instalado

1   Superior
2   Resorte espiral
3   Asiento inferior del resorte
4   Marcas de dirección

y esté descansando a la altura normal del chasis.

12 Barra estabilizadora trasera - remover e instalar

Refiérase a la ilustración 12.2

1   Levante la parte trasera del vehículo y sopórtelo seguramente encima de estantes.

2   Remueva las tuercas superiores de ambas varillas del estabilizador localizadas a cada extremo de la barra estabilizadora. Detenga la varilla con una llave pará mantenerla de que gire **(vea ilustración)**.

3   Remueva las varillas de los eslabones de la barra y el brazo de control inferior, esté seguro de retener los bujes, arandelas y espaciadores en su orden de instalación.

4   Remueva los pernos que conectan los soportes de la barra estabilizadora al albergue trasero del eje y baje la barra del vehículo.

5   Si los bujes de la barra estabilizadora

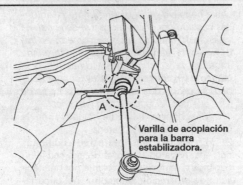

Varilla de acoplación para la barra estabilizadora.

12.2 Cuando esté removiendo la tuerca de la varilla de la barra estabilizadora, deténgala con una llave para evitar que gire

necesitan ser reemplazados, simplemente sepárelos y los desliza fuera de la barra.

6   Inspeccione los bujes de la barra estabilizadora por grietas o cualquier otros daños y los reemplaza según sea necesario.

7   La instalación se hace en el orden inverso al procedimiento de desensamble, con las siguientes notas:

a)   Los componentes de la varilla deben ser instalados en su orden original y sus posiciones originales.

b)   Los pernos de la barra estabilizadora no se deben apretar completamente hasta que el vehículo haya sido bajado al piso y el peso completo del vehículo esté en las ruedas.

13 Sistema de dirección - información general

Refiérase a las ilustraciones 13.1a y 13.1b

El sistema de dirección es de sinfín y bola de tipo circulante. Los componentes que compone el sistema manual son el volante, la columna de la dirección, la caja de la dirección y el ensamblaje de las varillas de acoplamiento de la dirección **(vea ilustraciones)**. Además estos sistemas de dirección de poder usan también una banda conduciendo una bomba de aceite con el tanque de depósito integrado que proporciona una presión hidráulica.

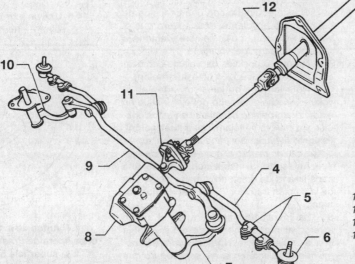

13.1a Componentes del sistema de dirección manual

1   Volante de la dirección
2   Cierre para el volante de la dirección
3   Tubo de la columna de la dirección
4   Varilla lateral
5   Grapa de la varilla lateral
6   Rótula
7   Brazo de la caja de la dirección
8   Caja de la dirección
9   Varilla de cruce
10   Brazo loco
11   Acoplamiento del caucho
12   Soporte de la camisa del tubo
13   Soporte para montar la columna de la dirección

13.1b Componentes del sistema de la dirección de poder

1 Mecanismo de inclinación	4 Bomba de aceite
2 Ensamblaje de la caja de	5 Tanque de aceite
la dirección	6 Columna de la dirección
3 Varilla de la dirección	7 Volante de la dirección

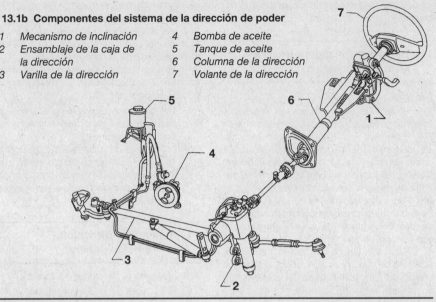

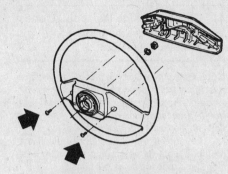

14.3 La almohadilla de la bocina en los modelos más modernos está retenida con dos tornillos

14.5 Marque la relación del volante de la dirección al eje antes de removerlo

En un sistema manual, el movimiento de girar el volante es transferido a la columna y al sinfín de la caja de la dirección. Instalado en el sinfín es una tuerca de bola de movimiento libre. Los dientes del engrane en la bola son acoplados con los dientes en el eje sector de la caja de la dirección, que está directamente conectado al acoplamiento. Es a través de esta bola y el eje sector que el movimiento circular del volante se obtiene desde la derecha y la izquierda de la varilla de acoplamiento y en cambio, hace girar las ruedas delanteras.

El sistema de dirección de poder opera esencialmente de la misma manera como el sistema manual con la excepción de que el ensamblaje de caja de la dirección de poder usa presión hidráulica para aumentar la fuerza manual de la dirección.

Si el sistema de dirección de poder pierde su presión hidráulica, todavía funcionará manualmente, pero con esfuerzo aumentado.

La columna de la dirección es desplegable, tipo de absorción de energía, diseñada para comprimir en caso de un choque extremo delantero para aminorar la lesión al chófer. La columna también alberga el interruptor de la ignición, la cerradura de la columna de la dirección, interruptor de las luces delanteras, el control de las direccionales, interruptor atenuador para las luces delanteras y control para el limpiador del parabrisas. En la mayoría de los modelos, la ignición y el volante pueden ambos ser cerrados mientras el vehículo está estacionado para prohibir el robo.

14   Volante de la dirección - remover e instalar

Refiérase a las ilustraciones 14.3, 14.5, 14.6 y 14.7
Peligro: *Los modelos 1996 están equipados con un bolsa de aire en el lado de chófer en el centro del volante. Siempre desconecte el*

cable negativo de la batería primero, entonces seguido por el cable positivo de la batería y espere 10 minutos antes de comenzar a trabajar en la vecindad de los sensores de impacto, la columna de la dirección o el tablero de instrumentos para evitar la posibilidad del despliegue accidental de la bolsa de aire, que podría causar lesión personal.

1   Desconecte el cable negativo de la batería que viene de la batería.

2   En los modelos que estén equipados con una, haga que la bolsa de aire sea incapacitada o removida del volante por una facilidad de reparación automotriz o el departamento de servicio de su concesionario.

3   Agarre la parte superior central del volante y lo hala hacia fuera del volante (modelos más antiguos) o remueva los dos tornillos de la parte trasera del volante (modelos más modernos antes del 1994) **(vea ilustración)**. En los modelos 1994, insercióne un destornillador de cabeza de estrella en el orificio del lado inferior y remueva el tornillo y la abrazadera, entonces levante la almohadilla de la bocina.

4   Si está equipado con una dirección de cerrojo para el volante, esté seguro que el volante está en la posición libre y entonces remueva la tuerca del volante.

5   Marque la posición del volante con relación al eje de la dirección **(vea ilustración)**.

6   Note los dos orificios roscados en el volante en cualquier lado del eje. Instale un extractor apropiado de volante en estos orificios y remueva el volante **(vea ilustración)**. **Peligro:** *¡Nunca, por ninguna razón, no le pegue con un martillo ni golpee el final del eje!*

7   Antes de la instalación, aplique una capa liviana de grasa en la parte deslizante de la porción trasera del volante **(vea ilustración)**.

8   La instalación se hace en el orden inverso al procedimiento de desensamble con la siguiente nota: **Nota:** *Cuando esté instalando el volante en el eje esté seguro que las marcas de alineamiento en el volante*

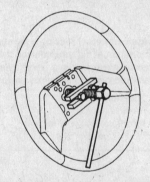

14.6 Use un extractor para remover el volante - no martille en el eje!

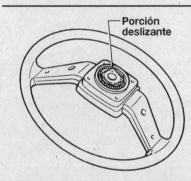

14.7 Antes de instalar el volante, una capa ligera de grasa debe de ser aplicada a la superficie que se desliza en el contacto de la bocina

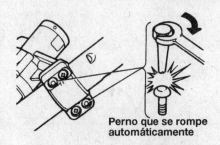

15.7 Los tornillos que se rompen automáticamente son usados en las posiciones mostradas para retener la cerradura de la dirección a la columna (estilo más antiguo) - los modelos más modernos usan solamente dos tornillos, ambos de ellos se rompen automáticamente

16.1 Acceso a la caja de la dirección es obtenido removiendo la rueda izquierda delantera y la solapa de caucho

16.2a Ubicación de los pernos de pellizco del acoplamiento flexible de la columna de la dirección (flechas) (modelos con dirección manual)

16.2b Ubicación del perno de pellizco del brazo de control inferior (flecha) de la caja de la dirección (modelos de dirección de poder)

acuerdan con el eje. Apriete la tuerca del volante al par de torsión apropiado y gire el volante para chequear la resistencia.

15 Cerrojo de la dirección - remover e instalar

Refiérase a la ilustración 15.7

Remover

1   Obtenga dos tornillos que se rompen automáticamente de su concesionario Nissan, necesitados para volver a instalar la cerradura de la dirección.
2   Remueva el volante como se indica en la Sección 14.
3   Remueva la tapa de la columna de la dirección.
4   La cerradura de la dirección es asegurada al eje de la dirección con dos tornillos regulares y dos tornillos que se rompen automáticamente. Remueva los tornillos que se rompen automáticamente, que implicará taladrar con mucho cuidado los tornillos. Comience por pegarle con un punzón en el centro del tornillo. Seleccione una broca que sea cerca del diámetro de la raíz de la rosca. Cuidadosamente, asegúrese que la broca esté cuadrada con el tornillo, taladre hacia afuera el centro del tornillo hasta que un extractor de tornillo se pueda usar para remover el tornillo.
5   Remueva los dos tornillos regulares que conectan y desacoplan la cerradura del eje de la dirección. Desconecte los alambres del interruptor de la ignición.

Instalar

6   Para instalar, alinee la superficie de acoplamiento de la cerradura de la dirección con el orificio en el tubo de la columna de la dirección. Entonces instale flojamente los dos tornillos regulares que se conectan. Una vez que la operación de la cerradura sea chequeada usando la llave, estos tornillos se pueden apretar.
7   Instale los dos tornillos que se rompen automáticamente, asegurándose que las par-

tes superiores se rompan (**vea ilustración**).
8   El resto de la instalación se hace en el orden inverso al procedimiento de desensamble.

16 Caja de la dirección - remover e instalar

Refiérase a las ilustraciones 16.1, 16.2a, 16.2b, 16.3 y 16.5

Remover

1   Para obtener espacio libre, remueva la rueda izquierda delantera y el neumático. Entonces o remueva la solapa de caucho del lado del compartimiento del motor o la remueve afuera del camino (**vea ilustración**).
2   Destornille y remueva el perno de pellizco del acoplamiento flexible (modelos más antiguos) o remueva el perno de pellizco del brazo de control inferior (modelos más modernos) (**vea ilustraciones**).
3   Marque la relación del brazo del engrane al eje sector de la caja de la dirección. Destornille la tuerca del fondo del eje sector de la dirección, remueva la arandela y entonces usando un extractor pesado, remueva el brazo del engrane (**vea ilustración**).
4   En los modelos con dirección de poder, coloque una bandeja de drenaje adecuada

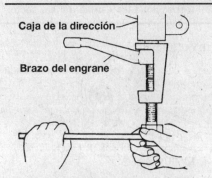

Caja de la dirección

Brazo del engrane

16.3 Un extractor se debe usar para separar el brazo de engrane del eje sector de la caja de la dirección

debajo de las conexiones de las mangueras de la caja de la dirección, desconecte las mangueras y permita que el aceite drene desde la dirección a la cacerola. Tape las puntas abiertas de las mangueras y los puertos abiertos en la caja de la dirección.
5   Remueva los pernos de retención de la caja de la dirección y retire el engrane a través del lado izquierdo (**vea ilustración**).

16.5 Las tuercas de los pernos de afianzamiento de la caja de la dirección (flechas) están localizados en el interior del riel izquierdo del chasis

Instalar

6   La instalación se hace en el orden inverso al procedimiento de desensamble pero observe los siguientes puntos:

a) *Antes de instalar el perno de pellizco que asegura el acoplamiento al eje sinfín, esté seguro que las ruedas delanteras están en la posición recta mirando hacia adelante. Esté también seguro que el volante esté apropiadamente puesto en posición. La ranura en el sinfín debe ser alineada con el orificio del perno de pellizco en el acoplamiento flexible y el perno de pellizco debe pasar fácilmente através. Apriete los pernos de montaje y los pernos de pellizco al par de torsión especificado.*

b) *Cuando esté instalando el brazo del engrane al eje sector, asegúrese que las cuatro estrías y las ranuras están alineadas. Apriete la tuerca al par de torsión especificado.*

c) *En los modelos de dirección de poder, cuando la instalación esté completa, rellene el depósito de la bomba de aceite con aceite nuevo del grado y la cantidad correcta. Purgue el aire del sistema como se indica en la Sección 20.*

17   Caja de la dirección (sistema manual) - reconstrucción completa

Refiérase a las ilustraciones 17.2, 17.5, 17.6, 17.18, 17.20, 17.22 y 17.27

1   Con la caja de la dirección removida del vehículo, destornille el tapón de llenar y drene el aceite.

2   Libere la contratuerca en el tornillo ajustador del eje sector y entonces extraiga los pernos que retienen la tapa del eje sector en posición **(vea ilustración)**.

3   Gire el tornillo ajustador a la derecha para destornillarlo fuera de la tapa y entonces remueva la tapa.

4   Retire el eje sector y desenganche el tornillo de ajuste.

5   Usando una herramienta especial disponible de su concesionario Nissan, remueva la contratuerca del tapón de ajuste **(vea ilustración)**.

6   Retire el ensamblaje de engrane sinfín, completamente con el tapón de ajuste **(vea ilustración)**. **Nota:** *No permita que la bola ruede hacia abajo de cualquier lado del sinfín o los extremos de la guía de la bola pueda que se dañen. Si está desgastado o dañado, la bola y el sinfín deben ser reemplazados como un ensamblaje.*

7   No procure remover los baleros de aguja del eje sector. Si ellos están desgastados, el albergue completo del engrane debe ser reemplazado.

8   Separe el tapón de ajuste del ensamblaje sinfín. Use una terraja macho para remover hacia afuera el sello de aceite desde el tapón de ajuste usando un dado del tamaño apropiado.

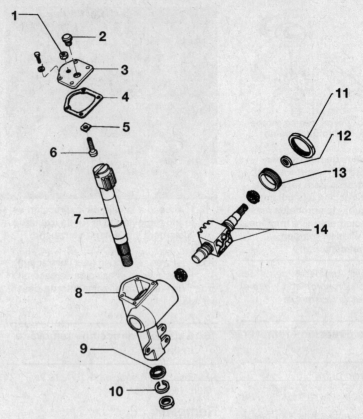

17.2 Componentes del ensamblaje de la caja de la dirección (sistema manual) - vista esquemática

1	*Tuerca prisionera*	8	*Albergue de la caja de la dirección*
2	*Tapón de llenar*	9	*Sello de aceite*
3	*Cubierta para el eje sector*	10	*Arandela de tipo resorte*
4	*Junta*	11	*Tuerca prisionera*
5	*Lámina de ajuste*	12	*Sello de aceite*
6	*Tornillo de ajuste para el eje sector*	13	*Tapón de ajuste*
7	*Eje sector*	14	*Ensamblaje del sinfín y la bola*

9   Hágale palanca hacia afuera al sello de aceite desde la parte inferior del albergue de la caja de la dirección.

10   Lave todas las partes en solvente limpio.

11   Inspeccione cuidadosamente los dientes del engrane en el eje sector por cualquier orificio pequeño, rebarbas, roturas u otros daños.

12   Inspeccione las estrías del eje sector por daño o distorsión, reemplace el eje sector si es necesario.

13   Inspeccione los dientes del engrane de la tuerca de bola y el ensamblaje del sinfín por orificios pequeños, rebarbas, desgastes u otros daños. Chequee también, que la bola gire libremente y suavemente en el engrane sinfín. Chequee por esto moviendo la bola hasta un extremo del sinfín. Detenga el engrane sinfín vertical hasta que la bola se

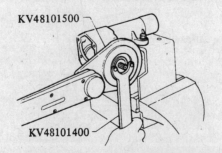

17.5 El tapón de ajuste y la tuerca son fácilmente removidos e instalados con las herramientas especiales Nissan

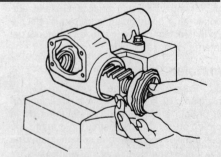

17.6 El engrane sinfín debe ser removido e instalado con la tapa de ajuste instalada en el eje

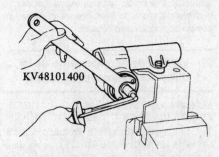

KV48101400

17.18 Midiendo y ajustando la precarga del balero del sinfín

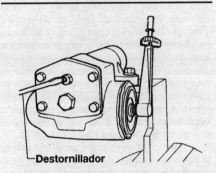

Destornillador

17.27 Gire el sinfín con una llave torsiométrica mientras gira el tornillo de ajuste con un destornillador - apriete la contratuerca cuando la fuerza requerida para girar el sinfín iguala la precarga deseada

mueva hacia abajo por su propio peso. Si la bola no se mueve libremente en la pista de rodamiento completa, reemplace el ensamblaje. **Nota:** *Tenga cuidado que usted no permita que la bola corra hasta el extremo del diente del engrane sinfín.*

14 Chequee que el balero sinfín se mueva libremente sin cualquier obstrucción o ruido. Si es necesario, reemplace el balero y la pista de rodamiento exterior como una sola unidad.

15 Durante la instalación, lubrique todas las partes con aceite antes de instalarlas. También, use todos los sellos de aceite nuevos, instalándolos para que las letras sean visibles cuando observadas desde afuera. Llene el espacio entre los labio del sello con grasa de propósito multi.

16 Instale un sello de aceite nuevo en el tapón de ajuste.

17 Instale el tapón de ajuste en el engrane del sinfín e instale el ensamblaje en el albergue. Comience el tapón de ajuste en sus roscas en el acoplamiento del albergue.

18 La precarga del balero del sinfín no se debe ajustar ahora. Para hacer esto, una herramienta de tapón de ajuste y una llave torsiométrica de pulgada-libra se necesitarán **(vea ilustración)**. Apriete el tapón de ajuste un poco a la vez hasta que el par de torsión requerido para poner en marcha el sinfín sea como está listado en las especificaciones. Para medir el par de torsión, gire primero el eje sinfín unas cuantas vueltas en cualquier

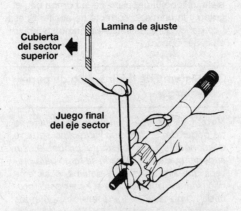

Lamina de ajuste

Cubierta del sector superior

Juego final del eje sector

17.20 Un calibrador al tacto se puede usar para medir el juego libre entre el tornillo de ajuste y el eje sector

dirección para asentar los baleros, después use la llave torsiométrica. Para obtener un buen agarre en las estrías del sinfín, alinee un dado del tamaño apropiado con un cartón delgado y lo instala encima del eje.

19 Siguiendo el ajuste de la precarga del balero sinfín, aplique un sellador de rosca a las roscas de la contratuerca que ajusta y la instala en el tapón de ajuste. Esté seguro que el tapón no gira mientras está apretando la contratuerca y chequee nuevamente después de la precarga del balero sinfín para asegurarse de que todavía está adentro de las especificaciones.

20 Inserciéne el tornillo de ajuste en la ranura formada T en el extremo del eje sector. Usando un calibrador al tacto, chequee el juego entre el fondo de la ranura y la cara inferior del tornillo de ajuste **(vea ilustración)**. Use láminas para ajustes si es necesario para proporcionar el juego final deseado listado en las especificaciones. Las láminas para ajustes están disponibles en varios espesores; vea las especificaciones.

21 Instale un sello de aceite nuevo en el fondo del albergue del sinfín.

22 Instale la tapa del sector en el eje sector girando el tornillo de ajuste a la izquierda **(vea ilustración)**. Entonces instale flojamente la contratuerca en el tornillo de ajuste.

23 Cubra ambos lados de una junta nueva de la tapa del sector con sellador de junta y lo coloca en posición en el interior de la tapa pasándolo encima del eje sector.

24 Gire el sinfín a mano hasta que la bola esté en el centro de su viaje, después instale el eje sector completo con el tornillo de ajuste. Asegúrese que el engrane central del eje sector se compromete con la ranura central de la tuerca. Tenga cuidado de no cortar ni dañar los labios de los sellos del aceite durante estas operaciones.

25 Instale los cuatro pernos de la tapa del sector y apriételo al par de torsión especificado.

26 Vierta la cantidad recomendada de aceite de engrane (vea Sección de Especificaciones) en la caja de la dirección, e instale el tapón de llenar.

Tornillo de ajuste

17.22 El tornillo de la tapa del sector de ajuste y la tuerca deben ser instalados en el eje sector antes de instalarlo en el albergue de la caja de la dirección

27 Usando una llave torsiométrica de pulgada-libra en el sinfín, como anteriormente, mida la precarga de la caja de la dirección y ajuste según sea necesario girando el tornillo de ajuste en la tapa del sector **(vea ilustración)**. El par de torsión apropiado para poner en marcha el eje sinfín debe ser como está listado en las especificaciones. Como anteriormente, cuando mida el par de torsión, gire primero el sinfín unas cuantas vueltas en ambas direcciones para asentar la caja de la dirección, entonces mida la precarga en la caja de la dirección mirando en la posición recta hacia adelante.

28 Cuando la precarga haya sido ajustada, apriete la contratuerca, asegúrese que el tornillo de ajuste no gira. Chequee la precarga una última vez para estar seguro que está todavía dentro de las especificaciones.

18 Sistema de la dirección de poder - mantenimiento y ajuste

1 Los componentes hidráulicos usados en el sistema de la dirección de poder incluyen una banda conduciendo la bomba de aceite con el tanque del depósito integrado, un ensamblaje de la caja de la dirección de poder y mangueras de conexión y líneas.

2 El mantenimiento normal del sistema de la dirección de poder consiste principalmente de chequeando periódicamente el nivel del fluído en el depósito, mantener la tensión correcta de la banda de la bomba y chequeando visualmente las mangueras por cualquier evidencia de fuga de flúido. Será también necesario, después que un componente del sistema haya sido removido, de purgar el sistema como se indica en la Sección 20.

3 Si las características operacionales del sistema aparecen ser sospechosas, el mantenimiento y el ajuste mencionados en esta la Sección está en orden, el vehículo debe ser llevado a su concesionario Nissan, que tendrá el equipo necesario para chequear la presión en el sistema y el par de torsión necesario para girar el volante. Estas dos operacio-

nes son consideradas más allá del alcance del mecánico del hogar, en vista de la alta presión de trabajo del sistema y las herramientas especiales requeridas.

4   Si los chequeos mencionados en el paso 2 prueban que el ensamblaje de la bomba de aceite o el ensamblaje de caja de la dirección están defectuosos, una bomba nueva o reconstruida o un ensamblaje de la caja de la dirección se tendrán que comprar porque no es posible reconstruirlos.

5   Si hay fugas de aceite en el ensamblaje de la caja de la dirección de poder, los sellos de aceite individuales pueden ser reemplazados sin reemplazar el ensamblaje completo. Pero, una vez más, debido a la naturaleza crítica del ensamblaje, este trabajo debe ser hecho por un concesionario Nissan u otro taller de reparación calificado.

6   La tensión de la banda es ajustada aflojando la contratuerca de la polea del controlador y girando el perno de ajuste según sea necesario. Refiérase al Capítulo 1 para el procedimiento apropiado.

7   Excluyendo la bomba de aceite, la caja de la dirección de poder y sus mangueras asociadas con la presión, el resto de los componentes del sistema de dirección son idénticos a esos usados en los modelos de la dirección manual. Otorgarle servicio a estos componentes es llevado a cabo siguiendo las operaciones descritas en las Secciones pertinentes en este Capítulo.

19   Bomba de la dirección de poder y depósito - remover e instalar

1   Si la bomba de aceite de la dirección de poder es encontrada estar defectuosa, ambos la bomba de aceite y el tanque del depósito deben ser reemplazados juntos.

2   Afloje la contratuerca en el controlador de la polea y gire el perno de ajuste de la banda a la izquierda para aflojar la banda.

3   Remueva la banda de la bomba de la dirección de poder.

4   Afloje, pero no remueva las mangueras donde ellas se conectan a la bomba.

5   Remueva los pernos de la bomba y el tanque de depósito y levante estos componentes hacia encima lo más que las mangueras lo permitan. Colóquelas en una bandeja de drenaje superficial y desconecte las mangueras, permita que el aceite drene en la cacerola.

6   Tape firmemente las puntas de las mangueras para prevenir la pérdida de aceite o que tierra entre en la manguera.

7   Si es necesario, la polea puede ser removida destornillando la tuerca de retención y usando un extractor estándar remueve la polea del eje.

8   El ensamblaje de la bomba de aceite se hace en el orden inverso al procedimiento de desensamble pero antes de apretar los pernos asegúrese que la tensión correcta de la banda existe, como está descrito en el Capítulo 1.

9   Una vez que la instalación esté com-

pleta, rellene el depósito de la bomba con el grado y la cantidad correcta de aceite. Si es necesario, purgue el sistema como se indica en la Sección 20.

20   Sistema de la dirección de poder - purgar

Note: *Cuando una manguera en el sistema de poder de la dirección hidráulico se haya desconectado, es bastante probable, sin importar que tanto cuidado se tomó para prevenir que aire entre en el sistema, el sistema necesita ser purgado. Para hacer esto, proceda como está descrito en los siguientes párrafos.*

1   Primero, asegúrese que el nivel del depósito está correcto; si es necesario, agregue el flúido para subir el nivel a la marca en la varilla de medir el aceite. Si es necesario, refiérase al Capítulo 1. Si el vehículo no ha sido apenas conducido, el flúido de la dirección de poder debe ser llevado a la temperatura de operación normal. Esto puede ser hecho poniendo el motor en marcha mínima y volteando el volante de la izquierda a la derecha alrededor de dos minutos.

2   Levante el extremo delantero del vehículo hasta que las ruedas delanteras estén libres del piso.

3   Gire rápidamente el volante completamente a la derecha hasta el tope y entonces hasta la izquierda hasta el tope. No permita que los topes de detención sean golpeados con presión. Trate de detectar el extremo del tope y toque solamente ligeramente los pernos que detienen el limite. Esta operación se debe repetir acerca de diez veces.

4   Ahora chequee el nivel del flúido en el depósito otra vez, como está detallado en el paso 1.

5   Ponga el motor en marcha y permítalo que corra en marcha mínima por un tiempo corto. Entonces párelo y chequee el flúido otra vez.

6   Ponga el motor en marcha otra vez de tres a cinco segundos, entonces lo detiene y chequee el nivel de flúido. Finalmente, gire el volante de extremo a extremo una vez más acerca de diez veces y chequee nuevamente el nivel del flúido.

7   Si la purga de aire es insuficiente, el depósito del aceite estará extremadamente espumoso y la bomba hará ruido. En este caso, permita que la espuma en el depósito se disperse, chequee el nivel otra vez y repita el proceso completo de purga.

8   Si llega a ser obvio, después de varias veces, que el sistema no se puede purgar satisfactoriamente, es bastante probable que haya un escape en el sistema. Haga que un ayudante gire el volante de tope a tope varias veces y entonces lo detiene acerca de cinco segundos en cada parada. **Nota:** *No detenga el volante en la posición extrema de un lado por más de quince segundos a la vez. Chequee visualmente las mangueras y sus conexiones por fugas. Si ninguna fuga es evidente, el problema podría estar en la caja de la*

dirección y la única solución es de hacer que el sistema sea completamente chequeado por un concesionario Nissan.

21   Varillas de acoplamiento de la dirección - remover e instalar

Refiérase a las ilustraciones 21.2, 21.4, 21.5, 21.8, 21.10 y 21.12

1   El acoplamiento de la dirección es básicamente un sistema de varillas que es diseñado para transmitir el movimiento del volante de la dirección en la caja de la dirección a las ruedas delanteras.

2   Incluido en este sistema hay una varilla de cruce, un brazo loco, un brazo de engrane y dos varillas laterales con rótulas interiores y exteriores. El brazo de engrane conecta la caja de la dirección a una punta de la varilla de cruce. El otro extremo de la varilla de cruce está conectado al brazo loco, que en cambio se acopla directamente a la carrocería. Cada extremo de la varilla de cruce está también conectado a las ruedas delanteras por las varillas laterales **(vea ilustración)**.

3   Los componentes del acoplamiento de la dirección pueden ser removidos completamente. Siguiendo cualquier desarme del acoplamiento de la dirección, la alineación delantera debe ser chequeada y ajustada, si es necesario **Nota:** *Para cada uno de los siguientes procedimientos, el frente del vehículo debe ser levantado y debe ser sostenido encima de estantes. Siguiendo la reinstalación de los componentes, todas las tuercas que están acopladas con bujes deben ser dejadas apretadas solamente con los dedos hasta después que el vehículo haya sido bajado al piso. Solamente cuando el peso completo esté en las ruedas deben estas tuercas ser apretadas al par de torsión especificado.*

Varilla lateral

4   Remueva las chavetas y las contratuercas en ambos extremos de la varilla lateral **(vea ilustración)**.

5   Usando una herramienta especial para separar **(vea ilustración)** o un extractor de dos mandíbulas, desacople la varilla lateral del brazo del vástago, varilla de cruce y la remueve hacia afuera.

6   Inspeccione las puntas de las rótula por juego o holgura excesiva y las reemplaza si es necesario.

7   Si es necesario de desmontar la varilla lateral, primero marque los puntos del ajuste aplicando un toque ligero de pintura blanca en las abrazaderas que acoplan y el tubo central. Entonces afloje los pernos de ajuste y destornille los extremos de las rótulas del tubo central.

8   Ensamblar e instalación se hace en el orden inverso al procedimiento de desensamble. Si la varilla lateral vieja se ha desmontado, esté seguro que el ajuste se restablece en las marcas hechas durante el proceso de remover. Si una varilla nueva lateral es instalada, antes de la instalación, ajuste la distancia entre los extremos de la rótula como está lis-

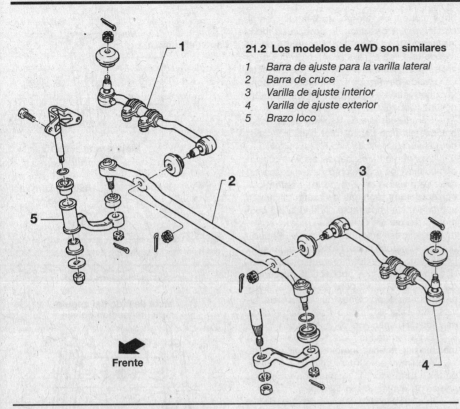

21.2 Los modelos de 4WD son similares

1 Barra de ajuste para la varilla lateral
2 Barra de cruce
3 Varilla de ajuste interior
4 Varilla de ajuste exterior
5 Brazo loco

Frente

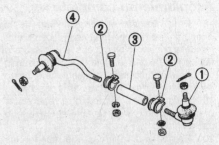

21.4 Vista esquemática de los componentes de la varilla lateral

1 Ensamblaje de la varilla de ajuste lateral exterior
2 Abrazadera de la varilla de ajuste lateral
3 Tubo del ajuste para la varilla de ajuste lateral
4 Ensamblaje de la varilla de ajuste lateral interior

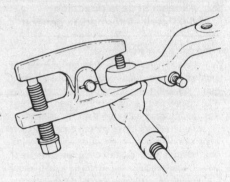

21.5 Una herramienta especial para separar se puede usar para separar el espárrago de bola del brazo del vástago - un extractor de dos mandíbulas trabajará también

tado en las especificaciones **(vea ilustración)**. Conduzca el vehículo a un taller de alineación para hacer que la alineación sea chequeada y si es necesario, ajustada.

Brazo loco

9 El juego en el ensamblaje del brazo loco puede ser remediado reemplazando los bujes.

10 Remueva los pernos que aseguran el brazo loco al chasis **(vea ilustración)**.

11 Hágale columpio al brazo loco alrededor en una posición accesible. Si es necesario remover el brazo loco, remueva la chaveta y la contratuerca que retienen la varilla de cruce. Entonces usando una herramienta apropiada para separar, desengrane el brazo loco de la varilla de cruce.

12 Si solamente los bujes en el brazo loco tienen que ser reemplazados, primero remueva la tuerca inferior y la arandela **(vea ilustración)**. Entonces levante el soporte del brazo loco hacia fuera y remueva los dos bujes. Instale unos nuevos. Ensamble el brazo loco.

13 La instalación se hace en el orden inverso al procedimiento de desensamble. Esté seguro de apretar todas las tuercas al par de torsión especificado.

Varilla de cruce

14 Remueva los cuatro juegos de chavetas y la contratuerca que retienen la varilla de cruce al brazo loco, brazo del engrane y ambas varillas laterales.

15 Usando una herramienta apropiada para separar, desengrane la varilla de cruce de cada uno de estos otros componentes y levante hacia afuera la varilla de cruce.

16 Inspeccione los bujes en cada extremo de la varilla por endurecimiento, grietas y los reemplaza si es necesario.

17 La instalación se hace en el orden inverso al procedimiento de desensamble.

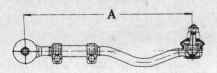

21.8 Ajuste estándar de las varillas de ajustes laterales. Refiérase a las especificaciones para la instalación correcta

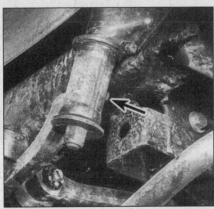

21.10 Ubicación del ensamblaje del brazo loco en el miembro derecho del lado del chasis

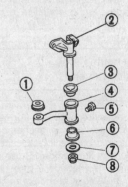

21.12 Componentes del ensamblaje del brazo loco

1 Remueva la tapa para el polvo
2 Soporte del brazo loco
3 Buje del brazo loco
4 Brazo loco
5 Tapón de llenar
6 Buje del brazo loco
7 Arandela
8 Tuerca

Acoplamiento completo

18 Para remover el acoplamiento de la dirección como un ensamblaje completo, remueva primero la tuerca que retiene el brazo del engrane a la caja de la dirección. Usando un extractor apropiado, desengrane el brazo del engrane del eje de la caja de la dirección.

19 Remueva los pernos que retienen el brazo loco al chasis y levante el brazo loco hacia afuera.

20 Remueva las tuercas que retienen las chavetas y las varillas de enclavamiento lateral a los brazos del vástago de la dirección. Entonces usando una herramienta apropiada para separar, desengrane las varillas laterales de los brazos del vástago.

21 El ensamblaje de acoplamiento completo de la dirección ahora se puede bajar del vehículo.

22 La instalación se hace en el orden inverso al procedimiento de desensamble.

22 Alineación de la dirección delantera - información general

Refiérase a la ilustración 22.1

1 Una alineación delantera se refiere a los ajustes hechos a las ruedas delanteras para que ellas estén en relación angular apropiada a la suspensión y la conexión al piso. Las ruedas delanteras que están fuera de alineación no solamente afectan el control de la dirección pero también aumentan el desgaste de los neumáticos. Los ajustes delanteros requeridos en los vehículos cubiertos en este manual son la comba, la inclinación del eje delantero y la convergencia **(vea ilustración)**.

2 Hacer la alineación apropiada de las ruedas delanteras es un proceso muy exacto y uno en el cual se requieren máquinas complicadas y costosas necesarias para realizar el trabajo apropiadamente. A causa de esto, es conveniente tener a un especialista con el equipo apropiado para que realice estas tareas.

23 Ruedas y neumáticos - información general

Refiérase a la ilustración 23.1

1 Todos los vehículos cubiertos por este manual están equipados con neumáticos radiales métricos de capas de fibras de acero o fibras de vidrio **(vea ilustración)**. El uso de otros tamaños de neumáticos u otro tipo pueden afectar el viaje y la maniobra del vehículo. No mezcle los tipos diferentes de neumáticos, tal como radiales y regulares, en el mismo vehículo porque puede afectar gravemente como conduce.

2 Es recomendado que los neumáticos sean reemplazados en pares en el mismo eje, pero si solamente un neumático va a ser reemplazado, esté seguro que es del mismo tamaño, estructura y diseño de rodamiento como los otros.

3 Porque la presión de aire de los neumá-

ticos tienen un efecto substancial en la maniobra y el desgaste, la presión en todos los neumáticos debe ser chequeada por lo menos una vez al mes o antes de cualquier viaje y ponerlos a la presión de aire correcta. La presión de aire de los neumáticos debe ser chequeada y ajustada con los neumáticos frío (Capítulo 1).

4 Para lograr la vida máxima de sus neumáticos ellos se deben rotar a los intervalos como está especificado en el Capítulo 1.

5 Los neumáticos deben ser reemplazados cuando los rodamientos estén desgastados. La presión de aire de los neumáticos correcta y las técnicas de conducir tienen una influencia importante en la vida del neumático. Tomar las curvas bien rápido, aceleración excesivamente rápida y frenado brusco aumentan el desgaste del neumático. Los neumáticos extremadamente desgastados no son sólo muy susceptible a que tengan una perforación pero es especialmente peligroso en condiciones de tiempos de lluvias. Refiérase al Capítulo 1 para los procedimientos de inspección del neumático.

6 El patrón de los rodamiento de los neumáticos pueden dar una buena indicación de los problemas en el mantenimiento o ajuste de los neumáticos, la suspensión y componentes de la suspensión delantera.

7 Las ruedas deben ser reemplazadas si ellas están torcidas, abolladas, aire se escapa, los pernos han alargado los orificios, están pesadamente oxidadas, fuera de simetría vertical o si las tuercas no permanecen apretadas. Reparación de la rueda que requiera soldadura u otro tipo de reparación no es recomendado, porque esto puede debilitar el metal.

8 El balanceo del neumático y la rueda es importante en la maniobra completa, frenado y el desempeño del vehículo. Las ruedas fueras de balance pueden afectar adversamente la maniobra y características del viaje también como la vida del neumático. Cuando un neumático es instalado en una rueda, el neumático y la rueda deben ser balanceados.

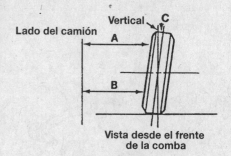

Vista desde el frente de la comba

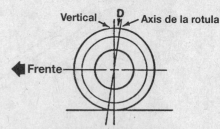

Vista de lado del ángulo de inclinación del eje

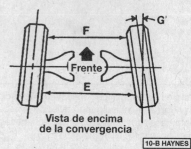

Vista de encima de la convergencia

10-B HAYNES

22.1 Los tres ajustes implicados en una alineación de la suspensión delantera son la comba (encima), la inclinación del eje delantero (en el centro) y la convergencia (en la parte inferior) - el ajuste actual de estos ángulos está más allá del alcance del mecánico del hogar y deben ser realizados por un taller de alineación o estación de servicio

TAMANOS DE NEUMÁTICOS MÉTRICOS

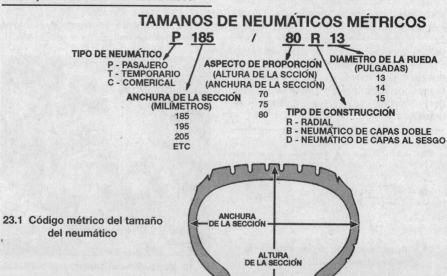

23.1 Código métrico del tamaño del neumático

Capítulo 12   Carrocería

Contenidos

Especificaciones

Especificaciones técnicas

	Pies-libras
Pernos para el soporte de la defensa	
Hasta el 1990	16
1991 y más modernos..	26 a 33
Pernos de la defensa a los soportes	
Hasta el 1990	16
1991 y más modernos..	9 a 12
Pernos de la bisagra del capó a la carrocería	
Hasta el 1990	3.2
1991 y más modernos..	4 a 5
Pernos de la bisagra de la puerta	14 a 20
Pernos para el asiento	14 a 20
Pernos para el ancla de los cinturones de seguridad	20 a 26
Pernos para la bisagra de la puerta de cargo trasera	
Hasta el 1990	14
1991 y más modernos..	15 a 20
Pernos de anclaje traseros de la cama	
Hasta el 1990	44
1991 y más modernos..	14 a 17
Tuercas de la puerta trasera elevadora del Pathfinder	15 a 20

1   Información general

Las camionetas Nissan de la serie 720 están disponibles en tres estilos básicos de carrocería: el modelo de cama regular (Li'l Hustler), modelo de cama grande (que usa la misma cabina con una cama extendida) y el modelo de Cabina grande (que usa la cama regular con una cabina extendida). Cada uno de estos modelos están disponibles en las versiones de 2WD o de 4WD. Además, varios equipos de molduras de lujo están disponibles con ciertos modelos, que incluyen el de lujo, GL y las versiones Deportivas.

Los estilos de la carrocería para el Nissan D21 y los Pathfinder son similares a la configuración de la serie 720 con la excepción de que el Pathfinder tiene una sección trasera de furgoneta fija.

La carrocería de la camioneta se compone de una cabina y la cama es separada, ambas son soldadas a un acero prensado, chasis en sección de tipo caja. La única diferencia principal del chasis entre los modelos de camionetas es la longitud de la cama regular y la cama larga en los modelos de Cabina grande.

Ciertos paneles de la carrocería que son particularmente vulnerable al daño de accidente pueden ser reemplazados destornillándolos e instalando artículos de reemplazo. Estos paneles incluyen los guardafangos, las faldas interiores de los guardafangos, la parrilla, falda delantera, los parachoques, el capó y la puerta de cargo trasera. Además, debido al daño o por razones de conversión, la cama trasera completa puede ser removida fácilmente del chasis.

2   Carrocería y chasis - mantenimiento

1   La condición de la carrocería de su vehículo es muy importante, porque es en esto que el valor principalmente dependerá. Es mucho más difícil de reparar una carrocería descuidada o dañada que es reparar componentes mecánicos. Las áreas escondidas de la carrocería, tal como los guardafangos, el chasis y el compartimiento del motor, son igualmente importante, aunque ellos obviamente no requieran la atención tan frecuente como el resto de la carrocería.

2   Una vez al año, o cada 12,000 millas, es una buena idea de limpiar la parte inferior de la carrocería y el chasis con vapor. Todos los indicios de tierra y aceite serán removidos y la parte inferior entonces se puede inspeccionar cuidadosamente por oxidación, líneas de freno dañadas, alambrado eléctrico frito, cables dañados y otros problemas. Los componentes de la suspensión delantera se deben engrasar después de la conclusión de este trabajo.

3   Al mismo tiempo, limpie el motor y el compartimiento del motor usando un limpiador de vapor o un removedor de grasa soluble con el agua.

4   Las partes interiores de los guardafangos se le deben pegar atención particular, porque la parte de protección inferior se puede pelar hacia afuera y piedras y tierra expulsada por los neumáticos pueden causar que la pintura se astille y se escame, permitiendo que la oxidación se asiente. Si oxidación es encontrada, limpie completamente hasta que llegue al metal virgen y aplique una pintura para prevenir la oxidación.

5   La carrocería se debe lavar según sea necesario. Moje el vehículo para ablandar completamente la tierra, entonces lo lava con una esponja suave y abundancia de agua limpia con jabón. Si el exceso de tierra no es lavado cuidadosamente, en tiempo desgastará la pintura.

6   Áreas de alquitrán o asfalto tirado por el camino deben ser removidas con una tela empapada en solvente.

7   Una vez cada seis meses, dele a la carrocería y al cromo una aplicación completa de cera. Si un limpiador de cromo es usado para remover la oxidación de cualquier parte cromada del vehículo, recuerde que el limpiador remueve también parte del cromo, así que úselo limitadamente.

3   Tapicería y alfombras - mantenimiento

1   Remueva cada tres meses las alfombras o esterillas y limpie el interior del vehículo (más frecuentemente si es necesario). Limpie con una aspiradora la tapicería y las alfombras para remover la tierra y el polvo flojo.

2   Si la tapicería está llena de aceite, aplique limpiador de tapicería con una esponja húmeda y lo limpia con un trapo limpio, tela seca.

4   Reparación de la carrocería - daño menor

Vea sección de fotografías

Reparación de rayones menores

1   Si la raya es superficial y no ha penetrado el metal de la carrocería, repararla es bastante sencillo. Ligeramente frote el área rayada con un solvente delicado para remover toda la pintura y la cera acumulada. Enjuague el área con agua limpia.

2   Aplique una pintura de retoque en la raya, usando una brocha pequeña. Continúe aplicando delgadas bases de pintura hasta que la superficie de la raya esté al mismo nivel que la pintura a su alrededor. Permita que la pintura se seque por lo menos dos semanas, después prosiga a pulir la pintura con un compuesto de pulir muy delicado. Finalmente, aplique una capa de cera al área rayada.

3   Si la raya ha penetrado la pintura y expone el metal de la carrocería, causando óxido en el metal, una técnica diferente de

reparación es necesaria. Remueva todo el óxido desde la parte más profunda de la raya con una navaja, prosiga aplicando una pintura anti - óxido para prevenir la formación de óxido en el futuro, cubra el área rayada con un relleno especial para este procedimiento. Si se necesita, el relleno se puede mezclar con un rebajador de pintura para crear una pasta fina, la cual es ideal para rellenar rayas delgadas. Antes de que el relleno se sequé, envuelva su dedo con un pedazo de paño de algodón suave. Empape el paño del rebajador de pintura y rápidamente frotó a lo largo de la superficie de la raya. Esto asegurará que la superficie del relleno sea un poco hundido. La raya ahora se puede cubrir con pintura como se describió en la Sección anterior.

Reparación de golpes

4   Cuando se reparen los golpes, lo primero que hay que hacer es remover el golpe hasta que el área afectada haya regresado lo más cerca posible a su forma original. No tiene sentido tratar de restaurar la forma original completamente ya que el metal en el área dañada se ha estirado por el impacto y no se puede regresar a su forma original. Es mejor tratar de que el golpe llegue a un nivel de 1/8 de pulgada por debajo del metal que lo rodea. En casos donde el golpe es muy pequeño, no vale la pena tratar de removerlo.

5   Si la parte de atrás del golpe es accesible, se puede martillar por detrás gentilmente usando un martillo con un lado suave. Mientras está haciendo esto, mantenga un bloque de madera firmemente en el lado opuesto del metal para absorber los golpes del martillo y prevenir que el metal se estire.

6   Si el golpe es en una sección de la carrocería que tiene doble banda, u otro factor que impida el acceso por detrás, otra técnica es necesaria. Taladre varios agujeros a través del área dañada, particularmente en las secciones de mayor profundidad. Atornille tornillos largos que se abren camino ellos mismos en los agujeros lo suficiente para obtener un control del metal. Ahora el golpe se puede remover halando de las cabezas sobresalientes de los tornillos con un alicate de presión.

7   La próxima etapa de la reparación es eliminar la pintura del área dañada y de una pulgada más o menos del metal del alrededor. Esto se hace fácilmente con un cepillo de alambre o con un taladro con un disco de lijar, aunque también se puede hacer eficazmente a mano con papel de lija. Para completar la preparación del relleno, marque la superficie del metal con un destornillador o con el filo de una lima o haga pequeños agujeros en el área afectada. Esto proveerá una buena base para el relleno. Para completar la reparación, vea la Sección de relleno y pintura.

Reparación de agujeros con óxido o rajadas

8   Remueva toda la pintura del área afectada y de una pulgada más o menos del metal del alrededor con un taladro y disco de

lijar o cepillo de alambre. Si no tiene ninguno de los dos, unos cuantos pliegues de papel de lija harán el trabajo eficazmente.

9   Con la pintura removida, usted podrá determinar la gravedad de la corrosión y decidir si es que tiene que remover todo el panel, si es posible, o reparar el área afectada. Nuevos paneles no son tan caros como la mayoría de las personas piensan y es muchas veces más rápido instalar un panel nuevo que reparar grandes áreas con óxido.

10   Remueva todos los pedazos de moldura del área afectada excepto aquellos que le servirán de guía para restaurar la forma original de la carrocería dañada, como las molduras de las luces del frente, etc. Usando tijeras de metal o una hoja de segueta, remueva todo el metal suelto y otro metal que éste muy dañado por el óxido. Martille los bordes del agujero hacia adentro para crear una pequeña depresión para el material de relleno.

11   Con un cepillo de alambre, cepille todo el óxido para remover todo el polvo de óxido de la superficie del metal. Si la parte de atrás del área óxidada es accesible, trátela con pintura anti-óxido.

12   Antes de terminar de rellenar, bloqueé el agujero de alguna manera. Esto se puede hacer con una hoja de metal remachada o atornillada en su lugar, o rellenando el agujero con una red de metal.

13   Una vez que el agujero a sido bloqueado, el área afectada puede ser rellenada y pintada. Vea la Sub-sección siguiente acerca de relleno y pintura.

Relleno y pintura

14   Muchos tipos de rellenos están disponibles, pero hablando generalmente, un estuche para reparación de carrocería que contenga pasta para rellenar y un tubo de endurecedor de resina es lo mejor para este tipo de trabajo de reparación. Un aplicador flexible y ancho o un aplicador de nilón será necesario para impartir un acabado perfecto a la superficie del material de relleno. Mezcle una pequeña cantidad de relleno en un pedazo de madera o cartón limpio (use el endurecedor de resina escasamente). Siga las instrucciones del fabricante en el paquete, de otra forma el relleno se secará incorrectamente.

15   Usando el aplicador, aplique la pasta de rellenar al área preparada. Mueva el aplicador a través de la superficie de relleno para obtener el contorno deseado y para nivelar la superficie del relleno. Tan pronto como consiga un contorno aproximado al original, deje de trabajar con la pasta. Si usted continua, la pasta se le pegará al aplicador. Continúe añadiendo capas de pasta delgadas cada 20 minutos hasta que el nivel del relleno sea un poquito más alto que el resto del metal.

16   Una vez que el relleno esté seco, el exceso se puede eliminar con una lima de carrocería. De ahí en adelante, debe usarse papel de lija fino progresivamente, empezando con un grano de 180 y terminando con papel de un grano 600 húmedo o seco. Siempre envuelva el papel de lija alrededor

de una goma recta o un bloque de madera, de otra forma la superficie de relleno no quedará completamente lisa. Mientras lija la superficie de relleno, el papel húmedo o seco debe ser enjuagado periódicamente con agua. Esto asegurará un acabado lizo al final.

17   A este punto, el área de reparación debe ser rodeada por un anillo de metal sin pintura que a su vez debe ser rodeado por una capa fina de buena pintura. Enjuague el área reparada con agua limpia hasta que todo el polvo producido al lijar se desaparezca.

18   Rocié el área entera con una ligera capa de pintura. Esto revelará cualquier imperfección en la superficie del relleno. Repare las imperfecciones con una pasta de relleno delgada y una vez más, iguale la superficie con papel de lija. Repita este procedimiento de reparación y rocío hasta que usted esté satisfecho de que la superficie del relleno y el borde de la base estén perfectos. Enjuague el área con agua limpia y permita que se seque completamente.

19   El área reparada está ya lista para pintar. Para pintar con una pistola de pulverización debe hacerse con una atmósfera caliente, seca y sin aire. Estas condiciones pueden ser creadas si usted tiene acceso a una área grande de trabajo totalmente cubierta, pero si usted está forzado a trabajar al aire libre, usted tendrá que escoger el día muy cuidadosamente. Si usted está trabajando en un área totalmente cubierta, rocié el piso donde va a trabajar con agua, esto le ayudará a reducir el polvo en el aire. Si el área de reparación está limitada a solo un panel, envuelva los paneles de alrededor con papel grueso. Esto le ayudará a minimizar los efectos de no tener el color de pintura perfecto. Los pedazos de molduras como pedazos de lámina de cromo, asas de las puertas, etc. también deben ser protegidas con papel grueso o deben ser removidas. Use cinta adhesiva y varias capas de papel de periódico como protección.

20   Antes de pintar con rociador o pintura en lata bajo presión, bata bien el bote de pintura, después rocié un área de prueba hasta que haya dominado la técnica de rociar pintura. Cubra el área de reparación con una capa gruesa de base para la pintura. El espesor de la base se aumenta con varias capas finas y no con una sola capa gruesa. Usando papel de lija de grano 600 húmedo o seco, frote la superficie de la pintura de base hasta que esté bien liza. Mientras hace esto, el área de trabajo debe ser enjuagada completamente con agua, así como el papel de lija húmedo o seco. Permita que la base se sequé antes de aplicar más manos.

21   Rocié la última mano de pintura, una vez más aumentando su espesor con varias capas finas. Empiece rociando el centro del área de reparación, usando un movimiento circular, vaya aumentando el circulo hasta que toda el área de reparación y aproximadamente dos pulgadas de la pintura original estén cubiertas. Remueva toda la cinta adhesiva y papel de 10 a 15 minutos después de haber rociado la última capa de pintura. Per-

mita que la pintura nueva se seque por lo menos dos semanas, después use un compuesto de pulidor suave para igualar los extremos de la pintura nueva con la pintura que existía. Finalmente aplique una capa de cera.

5   Reparación de la carrocería y el chasis - daño mayor

1   Daños mayores deben ser reparados por un taller de carrocería especializado en reparación de carrocería y chasis con el equipo necesario para soldar, al igual que equipo hidráulico.

2   Si el daño ha sido serio, es vital que la alineación del chasis del camión sea chequeada o las características en como el camión opera pueden ser adversamente afectadas. Otros problemas, como o el desgaste excesivo de las ruedas, desgaste en la línea de la flecha y en la suspensión pueden ocurrir.

3   Debido a que todos los componentes más importantes de la carrocería (capo, guardafangos, etc.) son separados y se pueden reemplazar, cualquier componente dañado seriamente debe de ser reemplazado antes de ser reparado. Algunas veces estos componentes pueden ser hallados en un rastro de camiones que se especializan en componentes de camiones usados, muchas veces a un ahorro considerable en comparación con la parte nueva.

6   Bisagras y cerraduras - mantenimiento

Cada 3000 millas o tres meses, las bisagras de la puerta, del capó y las cerraduras se deben lubricar con unas pocas gotas de aceite. Los platos percutores de la puerta se le deben aplicar también una capa delgada de grasa blanca basada en litio para reducir el desgaste y asegurar el movimiento libre.

7   Vidrio del parabrisas y vidrios fijos - reemplazo

1   Reemplazo del vidrio del parabrisas y los vidrios fijos requieren el uso de un adhesivo rápido especial para la instalación y de algunas herramientas especializadas. Es recomendado que estas operaciones sean dejadas a un concesionario o un taller que se especialice en el trabajo de vidrio.

8   Parachoques - remover e instalar

Refiérase a las ilustraciones 8.5a, 8.5b y 8.6

1   Desconecte el cable negativo de la batería que proviene desde la batería.

2   Desconecte cualquier alambrado que se dirige a los parachoques.

3   En los parachoques delanteros, remueva los pernos que conectan los lados laterales de los parachoques a los guardafangos.

Estas fotos ilustran un método de reparación de pequeñas abolladura. Son con la intención de suplementar la reparación de la Carrocería - daños pequeños en este Capítulo y no se deben usar como las únicas instrucciones para la reparación de la carrocería en estos camiones

Si usted no tiene acceso a la parte trasera del panel de la carrocería para remover la abolladura, hálelo con un martillo deslizante de extraer abolladuras. En las porciones más profundas de la abolladura o ha lo largo de la línea de la arruga, taladre o haga agujero(s) por lo menos cada una pulgada . . .

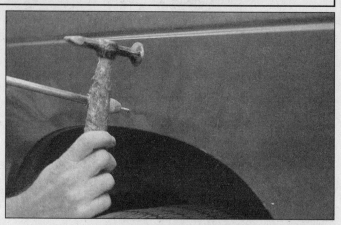

. . . entonces atornille el martillo deslizante adentro del agujero y opérelo. Péquele suavemente con un martillo cerca del borde de la abolladura para ayudar a que el metal regrese a su forma original. Cuando haya terminado, el área de la abolladura debe de estar cerca de su forma original y alrededor de 1/8-pulgada debajo de la superficie del metal del alrededor

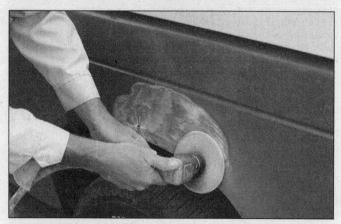

Usando papel de lija grueso, remueva completamente la pintura hasta que llegue al metal. Lijando a mano trabaja bien, pero la lijadora que se muestra aquí hace el trabajo más rápido. Use papel de lija más fino (alrededor de un espesor de 320) para mezclar la pintura por lo menos alrededor de una pulgada en el área de la abolladura

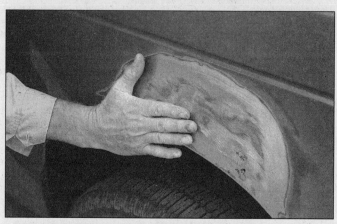

Cuando la pintura se haya removido, palpar probablemente ayudará más que mirar para notar si el metal está recto. Martille hacia abajo las partes altas o eleve las partes bajas según sea necesario. Limpie el área reparada con removedor de cerca y silicona

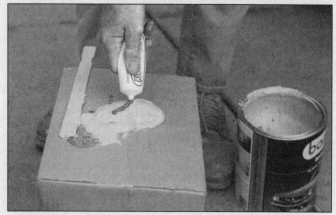

Siga las instrucciones de la etiqueta, mezcle un poco de llenador de plástico y endurecedor. La porción del llenador al endurecedor es critico, y , si usted lo mezcla incorrectamente, no se curará apropiadamente o se curará muy rápido (usted no tendrá tiempo de llenarlo y lijarlo a su molde)

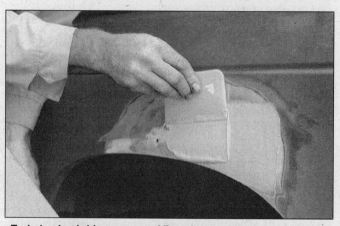

Trabajando rápido para que el llenador no se endurezca, use un aplicador de plástico para empujar el llenador de la carrocería firmemente adentro del metal, asegurando que se pegue completamente. Trabaje el llenador hasta que esté igual que la forma original y un poquito encima del metal del alrededor

Permita que el llenador se endurezca hasta que usted pueda abollarlo con las uñas de su dedo. Use una lija de carrocería o una herramienta Surform (la que se muestra aquí) para ásperamente darle molde al llenador

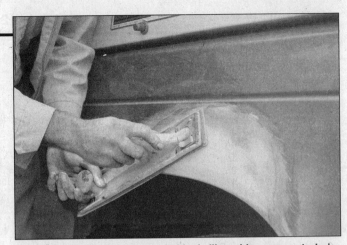

Use papel de lija grueso y una tabla de lijar o bloque para trabajar el llenador hacia abajo hasta que esté lizo y parejo. Baya bajando el espesor del papel de lija - siempre usando una tabla o bloque - terminando con un espesor de 360 o 400

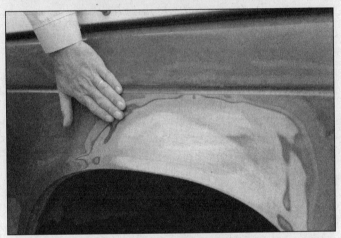

Usted podrá detectar cualquier reborde en la transición desde el llenador al metal o desde el metal a la pintura vieja. Tan pronto la reparación esté plana y uniforme, remueva el polvo y empapele los paneles adyacentes o pedazos de molduras

Aplique varias capas de sellador al área. No atomice el sellador muy grueso, porque se corre y esté seguro de que cada capa está seca antes de que aplique la próxima. Una pistola para atomizar de tipo profesional se usa en esta fotografía, atomizadores en lata de aerosol están disponibles en los almacenes de auto parte

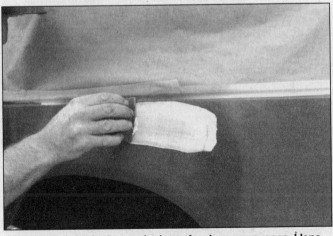

El sellador ayudará a revelar imperfecciones o rayones. Llene estos con compuesto especial para este tipo de rayones. Siga las instrucciones de la etiqueta y líjelo con papel de lija 360 o 400 hasta que esté suave. Repita aplicando el llenador especial, lijando y atomizando con el sellador hasta que el sellador revele una superficie perfectamente suave

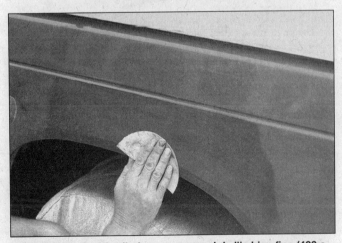

Termine de lijar el sellador con un papel de lija bien fino (400 o 600 de espesor) para remover la sobre atomización del sellador. Limpie el área con agua y permítala que se seque. Use un paño que tenga la capacidad de adherir para remover cualquier polvo, después aplique la capa final. No atente de limpiar o aplicarle cera al área reparada hasta que la pintura se haya secado completamente (por lo menos dos semanas)

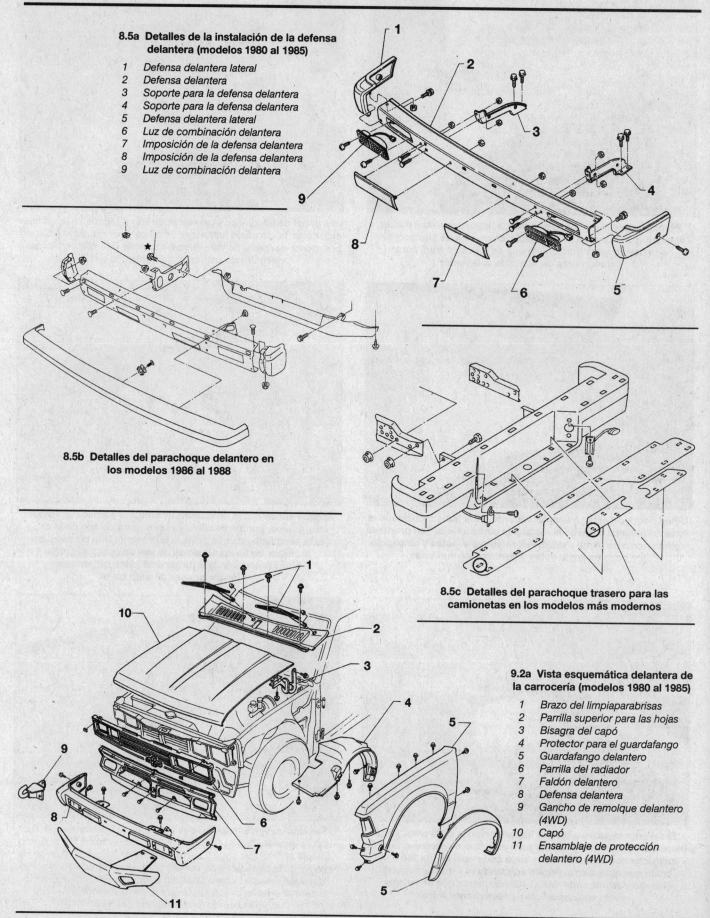

8.5a Detalles de la instalación de la defensa delantera (modelos 1980 al 1985)

1   Defensa delantera lateral
2   Defensa delantera
3   Soporte para la defensa delantera
4   Soporte para la defensa delantera
5   Defensa delantera lateral
6   Luz de combinación delantera
7   Imposición de la defensa delantera
8   Imposición de la defensa delantera
9   Luz de combinación delantera

8.5b Detalles del parachoque delantero en los modelos 1986 al 1988

8.5c Detalles del parachoque trasero para las camionetas en los modelos más modernos

9.2a Vista esquemática delantera de la carrocería (modelos 1980 al 1985)

1   Brazo del limpiaparabrisas
2   Parrilla superior para las hojas
3   Bisagra del capó
4   Protector para el guardafango
5   Guardafango delantero
6   Parrilla del radiador
7   Faldón delantero
8   Defensa delantera
9   Gancho de remolque delantero (4WD)
10 Capó
11 Ensamblaje de protección delantero (4WD)

4   El parachoque puede ser removido, removiendo las tuercas que retienen los parachoques a sus soportes, o removiendo los pernos que conectan los soportes de los parachoques a la carrocería.

5   En los parachoques delanteros, los parachoques laterales y las molduras, pueden ser removidos, si es necesario, removiendo simplemente los pernos o los aseguran a los parachoques **(vea ilustraciones)**.

6   En los parachoques traseros, desconecte cualquier alambrado, remueva los pernos y baje los parachoques **(vea ilustración)**.

7   La instalación se hace en el orden inverso al procedimiento de desensamble.

9   Parrilla - remover e instalar

Refiérase a las ilustraciones 9.2a, 9.2b y 9.3

1   Abra el capó.

2   La parrilla está asegurada a la carrocería por cuatro retenedores localizados en la parte superior. Con un destornillador, simplemente gire los retenedores hasta que los retenedores formen una fila con los orificios de montaje de la parrilla y hale la parte superior de la parrilla hacia encima para poderla liberar. Entonces hale la parrilla recta hacia encima y hacia afuera de sus orificios inferiores de ubicación **(vea ilustraciones)**.

3   Antes de instalar la parrilla, remueva los retenedores superiores de la carrocería e instálelos adentro de los orificios de alineación de la parrilla **(vea ilustración)**. Entonces simplemente insercióne las lengüetas inferiores de la parrilla en sus orificios y apriete los retenedores superiores en su posición hasta que ellos se cierren.

4   Cierre el capó.

10   Faldón delantero - remover e instalar

Refiérase a las ilustraciones 9.2a y 9.2b

1   Remueva los parachoques delanteros y la parrilla delantera como se describe previamente en las Secciones 8 y 9.

2   Remueva los pernos de retención y levante el faldón delantero.

3   La instalación se hace en el orden inverso al procedimiento de desensamble.

11   Parrilla del capó - remover e instalar

Refiérase a la ilustración 11.3

1   Remueva el capó como se describe en la Sección 14.

2   Remueva ambos brazos limpiadores del parabrisas. Refiérase al Capítulo 13, si es necesario.

3   Remueva los tornillos que retienen la parrilla del capó y levántelo hacia afuera **(vea ilustración)**.

4   La instalación se hace en el orden inverso al procedimiento de desensamble.

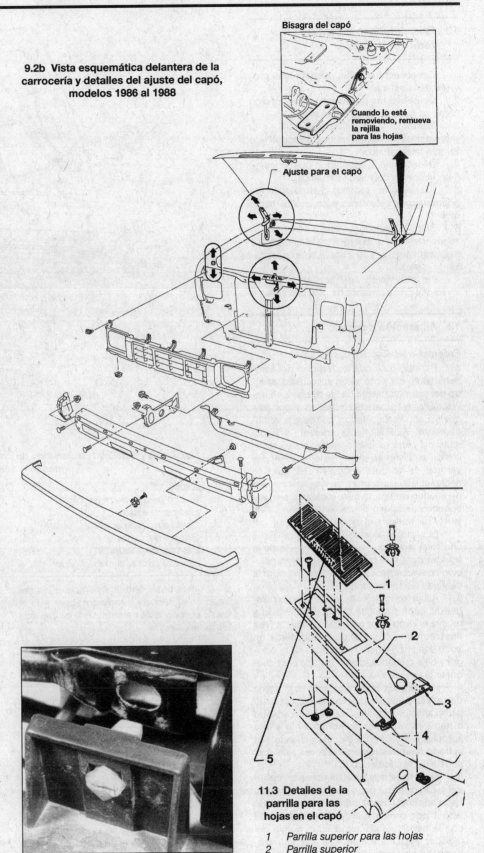

9.2b Vista esquemática delantera de la carrocería y detalles del ajuste del capó, modelos 1986 al 1988

Bisagra del capó

Cuando lo esté removiendo, remueva la rejilla para las hojas

Ajuste para el capó

9.3 Antes de la instalación, remueva los retenedores superiores de la carrocería e instálelos en la parrilla (se muestra un modelo 1980 al 1985)

11.3 Detalles de la parrilla para las hojas en el capó

1   *Parrilla superior para las hojas*
2   *Parrilla superior*
3   *Retén*
4   *Caucho sellador superior para la parrilla de las hojas superior*
5   *Cinta adhesiva de doble cara*

12 Guardafangos delanteros - remover e instalar

1   Desconecte el cable negativo que proviene de la batería.

2   Remueva los parachoques delanteros como se describe en la Sección 9.

3   Remueva los tornillos que retienen el protector delantero de los guardafangos y lo levanta hacia afuera.

4   Desconecte el alambrado que se dirige a las lámparas del marcador lateral.

5   Remueva los tornillos que retienen los guardafangos delanteros y los levante hacia afuera.

6   Si los guardafangos van a ser reemplazados, remueva el albergue de la lámpara del marcador lateral y lo instala en el guardafango nuevo.

7   La instalación se hace en el orden inverso al procedimiento de desensamble.

13 Alineación del capó

Refiérase a las ilustraciones 13.3 y 13.4

1   Para prevenir que los vapores del compartimiento del motor sean absorbidos adentro del compartimiento de los pasajeros a través de la rejilla para las hojas, es importante que el capó sea ajustado y que selle apropiadamente. Ajustes hacia adelante y hacia atrás del capó es hecho moviendo los tornillos de las bisagras en sus hendiduras. Ajuste vertical de la parte delantera del capó es hecho ajustando la altura de los parachoques de caucho de tipo tornillo, localizados en los rincones de apoyo del radiador y pernos de ajuste central para el picaporte del capó.

2   El capó es ajustado como sigue: Ralle una línea alrededor del plato completo de la bisagra para que pueda ser puesta en posición nuevamente. Esto le ayudará a juzgar la cantidad del movimiento.

3   Afloje los tornillos apropiados en la bisagra del capó para que pueda ser ajustado y mueva el capó en la alineación correcta **(vea ilustración)**. Mueva el capó solamente un poco a la vez. Apriete los tornillos de la bisagra y baje cuidadosamente el capó para chequear la posición.

4   Luego afloje la contratuerca en el perno del ensamblaje del picaporte de capó. El perno ahora se puede enroscar hacia adentro o hacia afuera para proporcionar la altura apropiada en el frente del capó cuando sea cerrado **(vea ilustración)**. Una vez ajustado, apriete la contratuerca.

5   Si es necesario, el ensamblaje completo del picaporte del capó puede ser ajustado hacia adelante y hacia atrás, también como de lado a lado para que alinee apropiadamente con la cerradura del capó en el apoyo del radiador. Para hacer esto, ralle una línea alrededor del picaporte del capó alrededor de los tornillos para proporcionar un punto de referencia. Entonces aflójelos y ponga en posición el ensamblaje del picaporte según sea necesario. Siguiendo el ajuste, apriete los pernos.

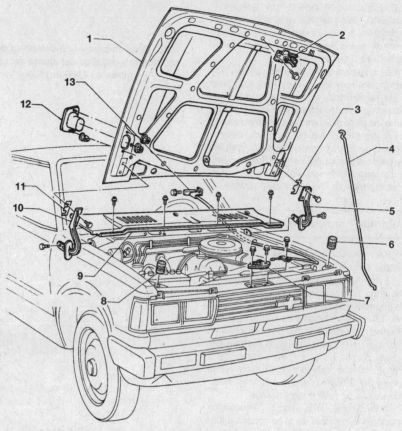

13.3 Capó y detalles relacionados de los componentes (se muestra un modelo desde el 1980 al 1985)

1	Capó	8	Caucho amortiguador
2	Macho para el cierre del capó	9	Parrilla superior para las hojas
3	Lámina de ajuste	10	Bisagra del capó
4	Varilla para retener el capó abierto	11	Lámina de ajuste
5	Bisagra del capó	12	Persianas del capó terminadas
6	Caucho amortiguador	13	Perilla de control para el cerrojo del capó
7	Hembra para el cierre del capó		

6   Ajuste finalmente los parachoques del capó en el apoyo de radiador, para que el capó, cuando esté cerrado, esté a nivel con los guardafangos.

7   El ensamblaje del picaporte del capó, también como las bisagras, se deben lubricar periódicamente para prevenir que se obstruyan o se peguen.

14 Capó - remover e instalar

1   Levante el capó.

2   Use colchas o las telas para cubrir el área de retención de las hojas en la carrocería y los guardafangos. Esto protegerá la carrocería y la pintura según el capó es removido hacia afuera.

3   Marque la posición del capó en sus bisagras alrededor del plato de la bisagra. Esto ayudará a la alineación cuando lo esté instalando.

4   Mientras un ayudante sostiene el capó, remueva los tornillos de la bisagra del capó en ambos lados y remueva hacia afuera las láminas para el ajuste de la bisagra.

5   Remueva el capó.

6   La instalación se hace en el orden inverso al procedimiento de desensamble.

7   Chequee la alineación del capó y ajústelo si es necesario como se describe en la Sección 10.

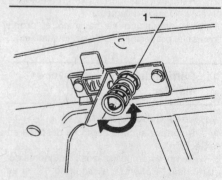

13.4 La altura del frente del capó es ajustada girando el perno en el ensamblaje del picaporte del capó (se muestra un modelo desde el 1980 al 1985)

1   Tuerca prisionera

15   Picaporte del capó - remover e instalar

Refiérase a la ilustración 15.2

1   El ensamblaje del picaporte del capó se compone de dos componentes: el ensamblaje del picaporte (macho) localizado en la cara inferior del capó y el ensamblaje de la cerradura (hembra) localizado en el apoyo del radiador. La cerradura del capó, al cual el cable de liberación del picaporte del capó es conectado, incorpora el mecanismo primario para la liberación del capó y no es ajustable. El ensamblaje del picaporte incorpora el mecanismo secundario de la liberación del capó y su posición puede ser ajustada para alinearlo con la cerradura del capó.

2   Para remover el ensamblaje del picaporte del capó, marque primero la posición de los pernos rayando un círculo alrededor de ellos. Esto simplificará la alineación durante la instalación. Entonces simplemente remueva los pernos de afianzamiento **(vea ilustración)**.

3   Para instalar el ensamblaje, invierta el procedimiento de remover, estando seguro de emparejar los tornillos con su posición original.

4   Para remover el ensamblaje de la cerradura del capó del apoyo del radiador, remueva primero la parrilla. Entonces remueva simplemente los tornillos, desconecte el cable de

liberación y lo levanta hacia afuera.

5   Ambos el picaporte del capó y los ensamblajes de la cerradura se deben lubricar periódicamente.

16   Cable de liberación para el picaporte del capó - remover e instalar

1   El cable para la liberación del picaporte del capó es un ensamblaje de un pedazo que incluye la manija, cable de control y carcaza flexible.

2   Para removerlo, levante el capó y libere el cable de la cerradura del capó en el apoyo del radiador. Tome precauciones para prevenir que el capó se caiga y se cierre mientras el cable está desconectado.

3   Desenganche el cable de cualquier clip que lo esté reteniendo a la carrocería.

4   Moviéndose al interior del vehículo, remueva los dos tornillos que retienen el soporte de la manija al panel lateral.

5   Retire cuidadosamente el cable de la pared contrafuego.

6   La instalación se hace en el orden inverso al procedimiento de desensamble. Cuando esté instalándolo, chequee que el anillo sellador de goma localizado donde el cable pasa atravéz de la pared contrafuego está en su posición.

15.2 Detalles de los pernos del capó para los modelos más modernos

17   Puerta trasera de cargo - remover e instalar

Refiérase a las ilustraciones 17.2a, 17.2b y 17.5

1   Abra la puerta trasera de cargo.

2   Remueva los pernos que conectan el retenedor de la puerta trasera de cargo a la puerta trasera de cargo **(vea ilustraciones)**.

3   Remueva los pernos que conectan las bisagras de la puerta trasera de cargo a la carrocería, remueva las láminas para ajustes de la bisagra y levante la puerta

17.2a Detalles de la instalación de la cama en las camionetas (modelos 1980 al 1985)

1   Marco de protección (opcional)
2   Marco delantero
3   Plato para el gancho de la soga
4   Gancho para la soga
5   Instale el gancho con su abertura mirando hacia abajo (± 30º)
6   Panel interior
7   Cerrojo de la puerta de la cama
8   Control remoto de la puerta de la cama
9   Precutor de la puerta de la cama
10 Cerrojo de la puerta de la cama
11 Retención de la puerta de la cama
12 Defensa trasera (opcional)
13 Gancho trasero de remolque
14 Lámina para esconder la manilla
15 Manilla para abrir la puerta trasera
16 Puerta de la cama
17 Retención de la puerta de la cama
18 Caucho de la defensa
19 Precutor de la puerta de la cama
20 Gancho para la soga
21 Carrocería trasera
22 Plato para el gancho de la soga
23 Perno con ojo

Encima del guardafango (4WD)

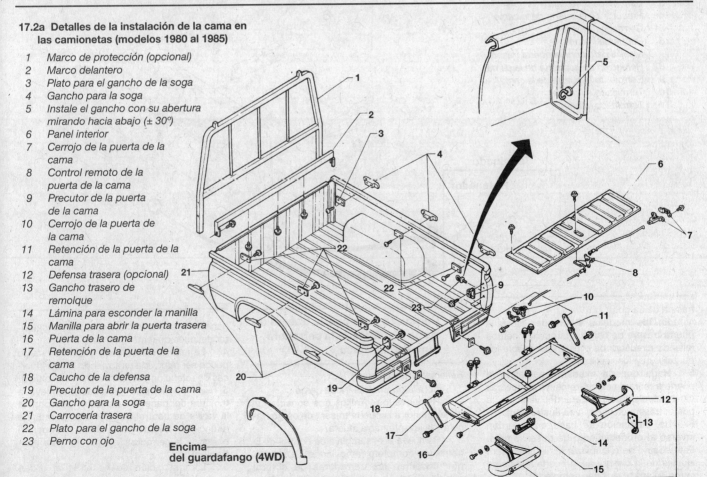

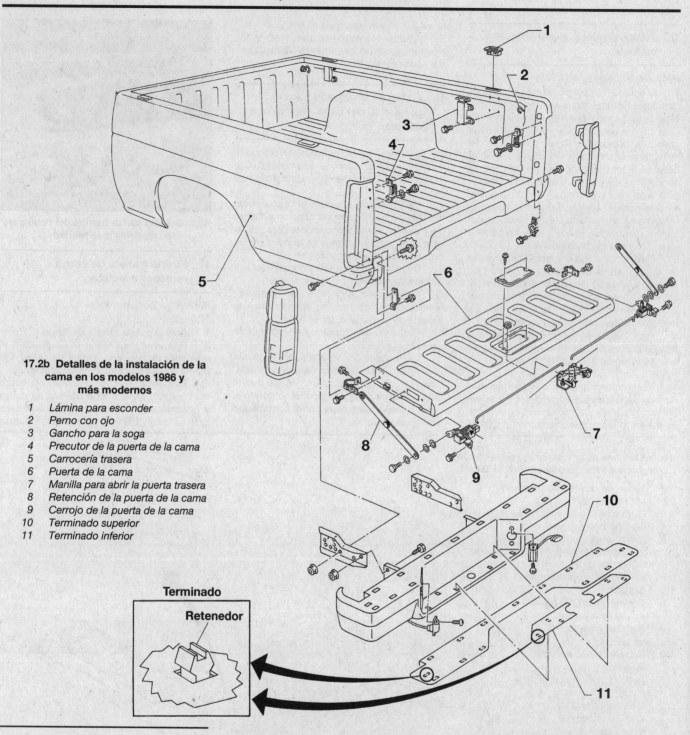

**17.2b Detalles de la instalación de la
cama en los modelos 1986 y
más modernos**

1   *Lámina para esconder*
2   *Perno con ojo*
3   *Gancho para la soga*
4   *Precutor de la puerta de la cama*
5   *Carrocería trasera*
6   *Puerta de la cama*
7   *Manilla para abrir la puerta trasera*
8   *Retención de la puerta de la cama*
9   *Cerrojo de la puerta de la cama*
10 *Terminado superior*
11 *Terminado inferior*

Terminado

Retenedor

---

trasera de cargo.
4   En los modelos Pathfinder, abra la
puerta trasera de cargo, marque los pernos
rallando alrededor de ellos y desconecte los
puntales que los sostienen.
5   Haga que un ayudante sostenga la
puerta trasera de cargo, remueva las tuercas
y remuévala hacia afuera del vehículo la
puerta trasera de cargo **(vea ilustración)**.
6   La instalación se hace en el orden
inverso al procedimiento de desensamble.
Esté seguro de reemplazar las láminas para
ajustes de la bisagra de la puerta trasera de
cargo en sus posiciones apropiadas.

**18   Cerradura de la puerta trasera de
cargo y control de la cerradura -
remover e instalar**

Refiérase a la ilustración 18.5
1   Abra la puerta trasera de cargo.
2   Remueva los tornillos que conectan el
panel interior a la puerta trasera de cargo trasera y la levante hacia afuera.
3   Remueva el ensamblaje de control de la
cerradura completo removiendo los pernos
que conectan las cerraduras de control
remoto y cerrojo de la puerta trasera. Si es

necesario, el ensamblaje se puede desmontar después de removerlo.
4   La manija de la puerta trasera de cargo
puede ser removida removiendo las dos tuercas de retención y levantándola hacia afuera.
5   En los modelos Pathfinder, remueva la
moldura del panel del elevador. Desconecte
la varilla de control, remueva los pernos de
retención y levante hacia afuera los ensamblajes de la cerradura y el control **(vea ilustración)**.
6   La instalación se hace en el orden
inverso al procedimiento de desensamble.

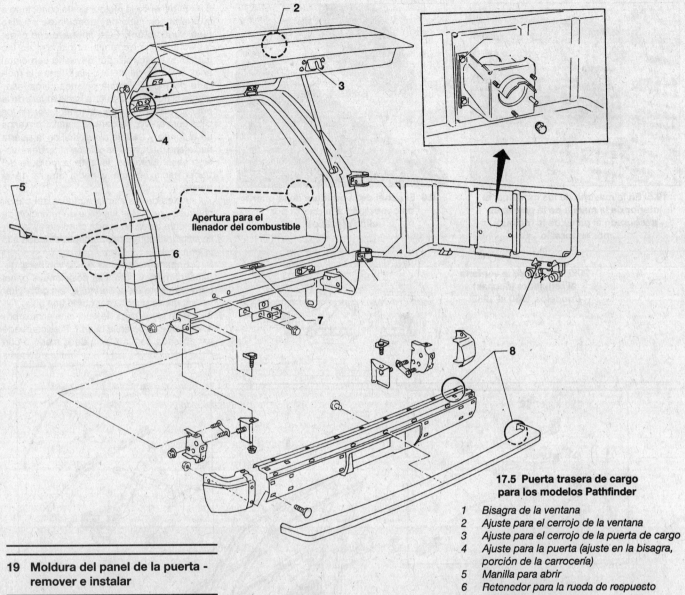

17.5 Puerta trasera de cargo para los modelos Pathfinder

1   Bisagra de la ventana
2   Ajuste para el cerrojo de la ventana
3   Ajuste para el cerrojo de la puerta de cargo
4   Ajuste para la puerta (ajuste en la bisagra, porción de la carrocería)
5   Manilla para abrir
6   Retenedor para la rueda de respuesto
7   Ajuste para el precutor
8   Terminado

19 Moldura del panel de la puerta - remover e instalar

Refiérase a las ilustraciones 19.5 y 19.6

1   Baje el vidrio de la puerta completamente.
2   Remueva los tornillos que retienen el descanso del brazo a la moldura del panel.
3   Remueva la manija de la manivela de la ventana. La manija de la manivela está sostenida en su eje por un retenedor de resorte, se requiere el uso de una herramienta de remover en figura de gancho pequeña. Puede ser fabricada de un pedazo de perchero. Con una mano, apriete la moldura del panel hacia adentro para exponer levemente el eje, el retenedor y con la otra mano meta la herramienta atrás de la manija de la manivela hasta que usted pueda enganchar el retenedor del resorte. Entonces, hale el retenedor hacia la perilla de la manija y remuévalo. Remueva la manija de la manivela y la arandela plástica.
4   Remueva la perilla de la cerradura de la puerta.
5   Remueva la manija de la puerta **(vea ilustración)**.

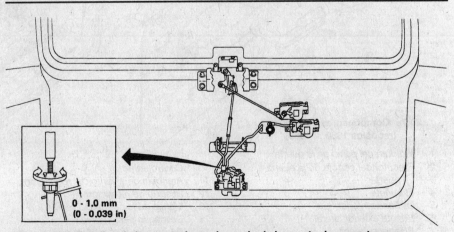

18.5 Detalles de los controles y el cerrojo de la puerta de cargo trasera, modelos Pathfinder

19.5 En la mayoría de los modelos, el interior de la manija de la puerta es asegurado al panel de la moldura por un tornillo

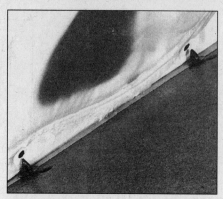

19.6 El panel de la moldura de la puerta es conectado a la puerta por clips plásticos

20.5 Pernos de la ventana al regulador (flechas) (modelos 1980 al 1985)

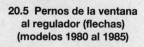

6　El panel de la moldura está conectado a la puerta con clips de retención de plástico **(vea ilustración)**. Para liberar estos clips, insercióne una herramienta plana y sin filo (como un destornillador envuelto con cinta) entre la lámina de metal de la puerta y la moldura del panel. Hágale palanca cuidadosamente al panel de la puerta hacia afuera de la puerta, mantenga la herramienta cerca de los clips para prevenirle daño al panel. Comience en el fondo y trabaje alrededor de la puerta hacia encima. Una vez que los clips de retención sean liberados, levante la moldura del panel hacia encima y hacia afuera de la puerta.

7　Antes de instalar la moldura del panel, chequee que todos los clips de retención de la moldura estén en buena condición y la rejilla selladora esté correctamente aplicada a la puerta.

8　Enganche la cima de la moldura del panel primero y entonces posicione el panel correctamente en la puerta. El eje para girar la ventana se puede usar como una guía.

9　Prense los clips de retención en sus orificios respectivos en la puerta. Presión puede ser aplicada con la palma de la mano o con

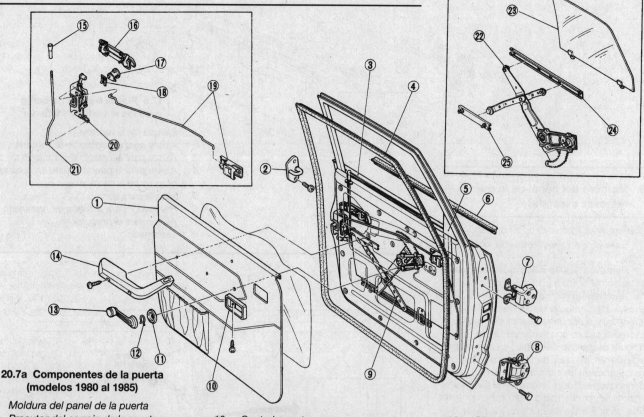

20.7a Componentes de la puerta (modelos 1980 al 1985)

1	Moldura del panel de la puerta	10	Control remoto	18	Clip de retención
2	Precutor del cerrojo de la puerta	11	Arandela de asiento del regulador	19	Ensamblaje del control remoto
3	La puerta	12	Resorte de retención	20	Ensamblaje del cerrojo de la puerta
4	El burlete	13	Manija de la puerta del regulador	21	Varilla para el cerrojo de la puerta
5	La banda inferior	14	Descanso para el brazo	22	Regulador
6	Burlete exterior lateral	15	Perilla para la cerradura de la puerta	23	Vidrio de la ventana
7	Bisagra superior	16	Manija del exterior	24	Guía del canal A
8	Bisagra inferior	17	Cilindro para el cerrojo de la puerta	25	Guía del canal B
9	Ensamblaje del regulador				

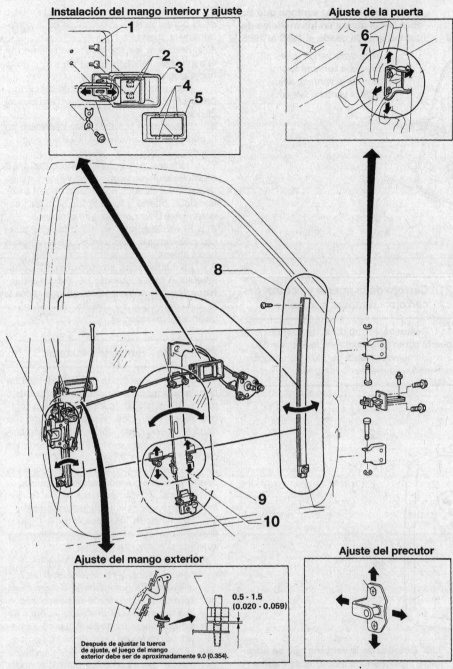

Instalación del mango interior y ajuste

Ajuste de la puerta

Ajuste del mango exterior

0.5 - 1.5
(0.020 - 0.059)

Después de ajustar la tuerca de ajuste, el juego del mango exterior debe ser de aproximadamente 9.0 (0.354).

Ajuste del precutor

20.7b Vista esquemática y ajuste de los componentes de la puerta, modelos 1986 y más modernos

1 Panel interior de la puerta	7 Ajuste
2 Retenedor	8 Ajuste de la faja
3 Asa interior	9 Ajuste del regulador
4 Cubierta	10 Ajuste del vidrio del regulador
5 Ajuste del asa interior	11 Gire la tuerca de ajuste
6 Bisagra	

un mazo de caucho limpio.

10   Complete la instalación invirtiendo el procedimiento de como se removió. Para instalar la manija de la manivela, instale primero el retenedor del resorte en su ranura en la manija con la cara hacia el final cerrado de la perilla de la manija, alinee la manija con la que está en la puerta opuesta y la empuja en su eje hasta que el clip del resorte entre en su lugar.

20 Ventana y regulador de la puerta - remover e instalar

Refiérase a las ilustraciones 20.5, 20.7a, 20.7b y 20.9

1   Remueva la moldura del panel de la puerta como se describe en la Sección 16.

2   Usando un destornillador de cabeza

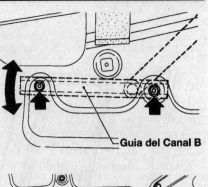

Guia del Canal B

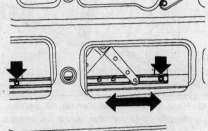

20.9 Ubicación de las tuercas y los pernos para la guía del canal (modelos 1980 al 1985)

Superior: Ajuste para la inclinación de la ventana
Inferior: Ajuste hacia adelante y hacia atrás de la ventana

plana, gire los clips del molde exterior de retención 90 grados, levante y remueva la moldura.

3   Remueva el plástico de la rejilla selladora.

4   Remueva la faja inferior.

5   Remueva los pernos que conectan la ventana al ensamblaje del regulador **(vea ilustración)**.

6   Remueva el vidrio de la puerta halándolo hacia encima y hacia afuera de la puerta.

7   Si es necesario, remueva los pernos del regulador y remueva el regulador del orificio grande de acceso **(vea ilustraciones)**.

8   Antes de instalar el regulador y guía del canal, aplique una capa delgada de grasa basada en litio a toda su superficie de deslizamiento.

9   La instalación se hace en el orden inverso al procedimiento de desensamble. Siguiendo la instalación de la ventana, levántela completamente hacia encima y use el siguiente procedimiento para ponerla en alineación correcta.

a) La inclinación de la ventana puede ser ajustada aflojando las tuercas que retienen el canal B y moviendo el vidrio para que su orilla superior esté paralela con la faja superior **(vea ilustración)**. Siguiendo el ajuste, apriete las tuercas de retención.

b) Para ajustar la ventana en las posiciones hacia adelante y hacia atrás, afloje los pernos que retiene el canal y el vidrio de la puerta. Entonces ajuste el vidrio para que su orilla y su esquina trasera superior sean sentadas firmemente en el caucho del marco de la puerta. Siguiendo el ajuste, apriete los pernos de retención.

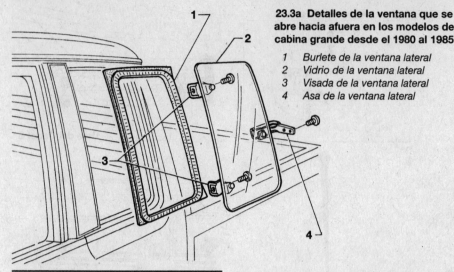

23.3a Detalles de la ventana que se abre hacia afuera en los modelos de cabina grande desde el 1980 al 1985

1   *Burlete de la ventana lateral*
2   *Vidrio de la ventana lateral*
3   *Visada de la ventana lateral*
4   *Asa de la ventana lateral*

c) Para ajustar la resistencia de desliza-miento de la ventana, afloje los pernos de retención de la faja delantera inferior del piso y deslice la banda hacia ade-lante o hacia atrás para que el vidrio pueda ser levantado o pueda ser bajado suavemente. Siguiendo el ajuste, apriete los pernos de retención.

21 Cerrojo de la puerta y control del cerrojo - remover e instalar

1   Remueva la moldura del panel de la puerta como se describe en la Sección 19.
2   Remueva la rejilla de plástico selladora, teniendo cuidado de no romperla.

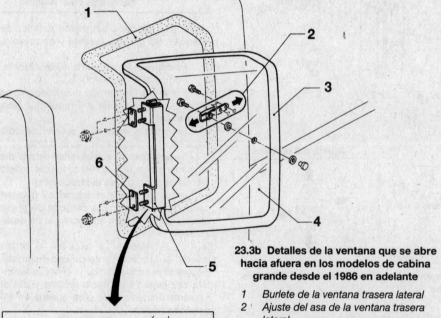

23.3b Detalles de la ventana que se abre hacia afuera en los modelos de cabina grande desde el 1986 en adelante

1   *Burlete de la ventana trasera lateral*
2   *Ajuste del asa de la ventana trasera lateral*
3   *Protector de la ventana trasera lateral*
4   *Ventana trasera lateral*
5   *Bisagra de la ventana trasera lateral*
6   *Caucho sellador*
7   *Protector de la ventana trasera lateral*
8   *Panel de la carrocería*
9   *Porción del agente adhesivo*
10 *Ventana trasera lateral*
11 *Bisagra*
12 *Perno soldado*
13 *caucho sellador*
14 *Refuerzo del ancla del cinturón del asiento*

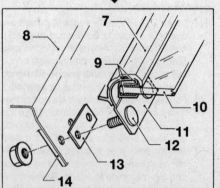

3   Desengrane la biela interior de la manija de la conexión en el ensamblaje de la cerra-dura de la puerta.
4   Remueva los tornillos que retienen el ensamblaje interior de la manija y lo levante hacia afuera.
5   Remueva el clip de retención del cilindro de la cerradura de la puerta y remueva el cilindro.
6   Desengrane la varilla de la cerradura de la puerta del ensamblaje de la cerradura de la puerta.
7   Remueva los tres tornillos del ensamblaje de la cerradura de la puerta poniendo tornillos de calzo, localizados en la parte trasera exte-rior de la puerta y levante hacia afuera del ensamblaje de la cerradura de la puerta.
8   Si es necesario, remueva las dos tuer-cas reteniendo la manija exterior y la remueve hacia afuera.
9   La instalación se hace en el orden inverso al procedimiento de desensamble.
Nota: *Durante la instalación, aplique grasa a la superficie que se desliza de todas las palancas y los resortes.*

22 Puerta - remover e instalar

1   Ponga un gato o un soporte debajo de la puerta o tenga a un ayudante a la mano para sostenerla cuando los pernos de la bisa-gra sean removidos. **Nota:** *Si un gato o soporte va ser usado, coloque un trapo entre el y la puerta para proteger las superficies pintadas de la puerta.*
2   Remueva los pernos de la bisagra de la puerta y levante cuidadosamente la puerta.
3   La instalación se hace en el orden inverso al procedimiento de desensamble.
4   Siguiendo la instalación de la puerta, chequee que esté alineada apropiadamente y ajustada si es necesario como sigue:

a) *Ajustes hacia encima y hacia abajo y hacia adelante y hacia atrás son hechos aflojando los pernos de la bisagra de la carrocería y moviendo la puerta según sea necesario. El protector interior de los guardafangos tendrá que ser remo-vido en orden de alcanzar estos pernos.*

b) *El precutor de la cerradura de la puerta puede ser ajustado también hacia encima y hacia abajo y de lado para pro-porcionar un acoplamiento positivo con el mecanismo de enclavamiento. Esto es fácilmente hecho aflojando los pernos de retención y moviendo el precutor según sea necesario.*

23 Ventana que abre hacia el lado de afuera - remover e instalar

Refiérase a las ilustraciones 23.3a, 23.3b y 23.3c
1   Remueva los dos tornillos reteniendo el soporte de la manija al pilar trasero.
2   Hágale palanca para removerla cuida-dosamente a las tapas de las bisagras (si

está equipado) usando un destornillador. Tenga cuidado de no dañar las superficies pintadas use un pedazo de trapo entre el destornillador y la tapa.

3   Remueva las tuercas de retención de la bisagra o los tornillos y remueva las ventanas laterales **(vea ilustraciones)**.

4   Si es necesario, remueva el burlete de alrededor de la abertura de la ventana.

5   La instalación se hace en el orden inverso al procedimiento de desensamble.

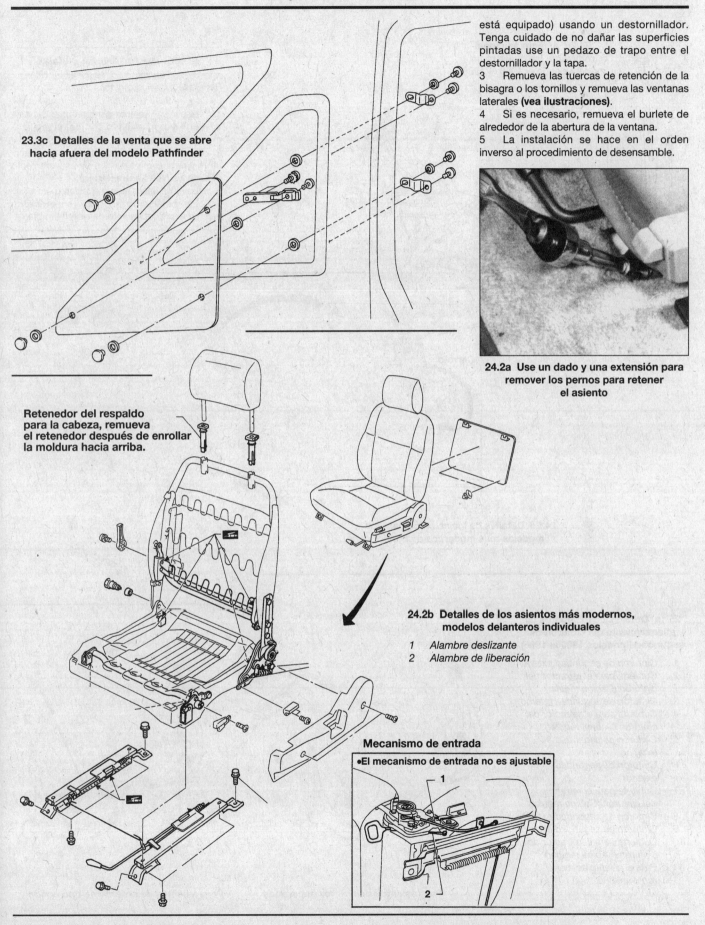

23.3c Detalles de la venta que se abre hacia afuera del modelo Pathfinder

24.2a Use un dado y una extensión para remover los pernos para retener el asiento

Retenedor del respaldo para la cabeza, remueva el retenedor después de enrollar la moldura hacia arriba.

24.2b Detalles de los asientos más modernos, modelos delanteros individuales

1   *Alambre deslizante*
2   *Alambre de liberación*

Mecanismo de entrada

●**El mecanismo de entrada no es ajustable**

1

2

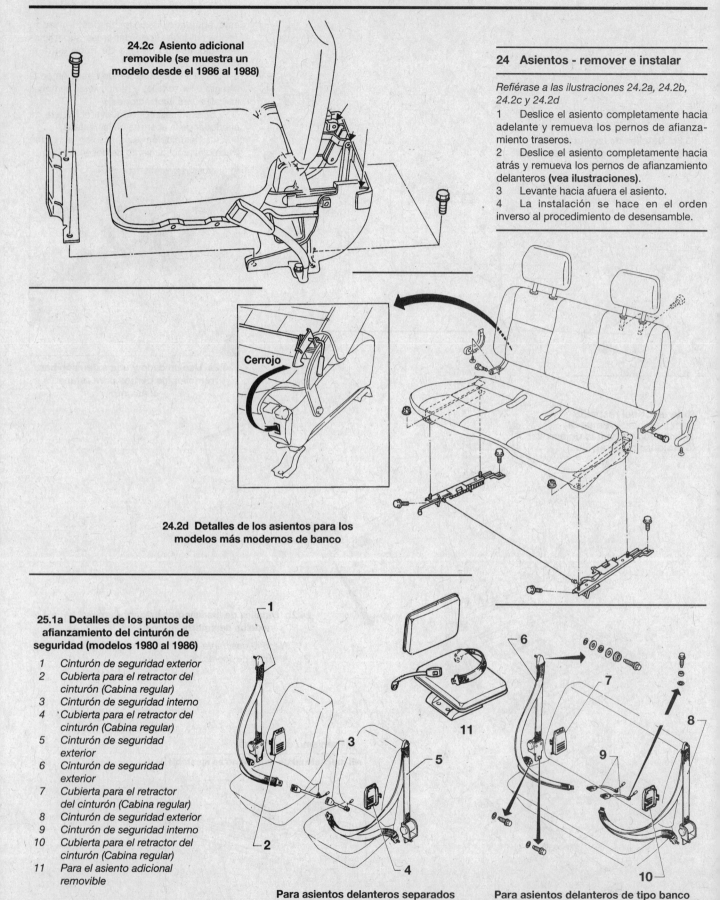

24.2c Asiento adicional removible (se muestra un modelo desde el 1986 al 1988)

24   Asientos - remover e instalar

Refiérase a las ilustraciones 24.2a, 24.2b, 24.2c y 24.2d

1   Deslice el asiento completamente hacia adelante y remueva los pernos de afianzamiento traseros.

2   Deslice el asiento completamente hacia atrás y remueva los pernos de afianzamiento delanteros **(vea ilustraciones)**.

3   Levante hacia afuera el asiento.

4   La instalación se hace en el orden inverso al procedimiento de desensamble.

Cerrojo

24.2d Detalles de los asientos para los modelos más modernos de banco

25.1a Detalles de los puntos de afianzamiento del cinturón de seguridad (modelos 1980 al 1986)

1   Cinturón de seguridad exterior
2   Cubierta para el retractor del cinturón (Cabina regular)
3   Cinturón de seguridad interno
4   Cubierta para el retractor del cinturón (Cabina regular)
5   Cinturón de seguridad exterior
6   Cinturón de seguridad exterior
7   Cubierta para el retractor del cinturón (Cabina regular)
8   Cinturón de seguridad exterior
9   Cinturón de seguridad interno
10   Cubierta para el retractor del cinturón (Cabina regular)
11   Para el asiento adicional removible

Para asientos delanteros separados

Para asientos delanteros de tipo banco

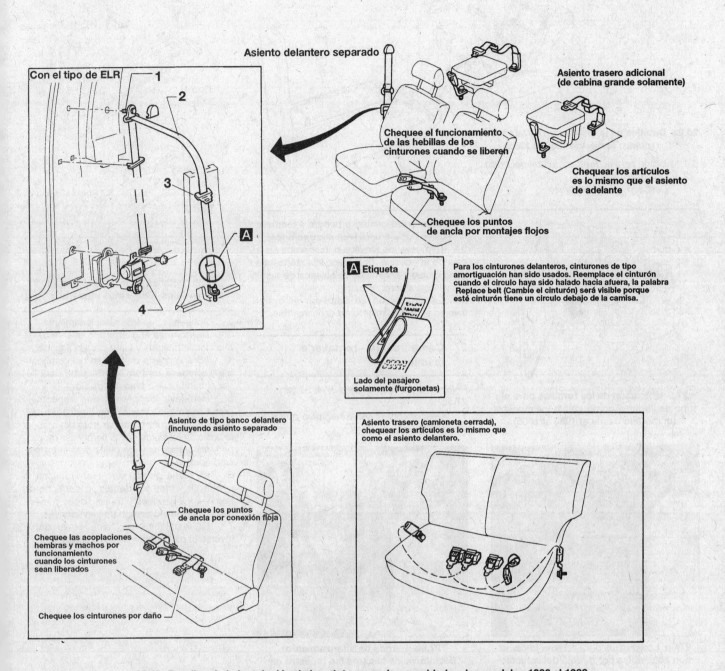

25.1b Detalles de la instalación de los cinturones de seguridad en los modelos 1986 al 1988

1 *Chequee los puntos de afianzamiento por montajes flojos*
2 *Chequee los cinturones por daño*
3 *Chequee las hebillas como se cierran y como se abren*
4 *Chequee el retractor por una operación suave*

25 Cinturones de seguridad - información general

Refiérase a las ilustraciones 25.1a y 25.1b
1   Las retenciones del cinturón de seguridad están mostradas en la figura que acompaña. Si cualquier componente de los cinturones tiene un defecto, el cinturón completo se debe de reemplazar (**vea ilustraciones**).

Lo mismo aplica si los cinturones son estirados en un accidente.
2   Para limpiar la costura del cinturón use solamente una brocha de cerda suave y una solución de jabón o detergente, entonces remueva el exceso y permítalo que se seque naturalmente. Nunca use blanqueador de ropa ni limpiadores químicos porque éstos pueden causar que la costura se deteriore.

26 Consola central - remover e instalar

Refiérase a las ilustraciones 26.2a y 26.2b
1   Levante la tapa de descanso del brazo central y remueva el tapón del fondo del compartimiento de almacenamiento (si está equipado).
2   Remueva los tornillos de la tapa de des-

26.2a Detalles de la instalación de la consola del centro (modelos 1980 al 1985)

1   Tapón para el descaso central del brazo
2   Consola
3   Descaso central del brazo

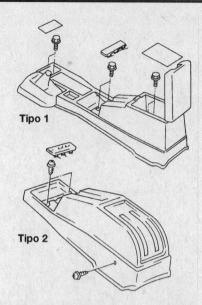

Tipo 1

Tipo 2

26.2b Detalles de la consola para los modelos 1986 y más modernos

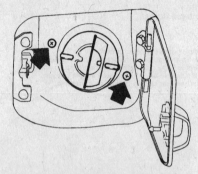

27.5 Ubicación de los tornillos para el tubo de llenar el combustible (se muestra un modelo desde el 1980 al 1985)

canso del brazo central o pernos y remueva la sección hacia afuera **(vea ilustraciones)**.
3   Remueva los tornillos o los pernos de la caja de la consola. Entonces, levante la caja de la consola encima de la palanca de cambio y hacia afuera.
4   La instalación se hace en el orden inverso al procedimiento de desensamble.

27   Cama trasera - remover e instalar

Refiérase a las ilustraciones 27.4, 27.5a y 27.5b
1   Desconecte el cable negativo que proviene de la batería.

2   Aplique el freno de estacionamiento.
3   Desconecte el alambrado que se dirige a las luces traseras y la luz para la licencia.
4   Abra la puerta de acceso del combustible y remueva los tornillos del tubo para llenar el combustible **(vea ilustración)**.
5   Remueva los pernos que conecta la cama trasera al chasis **(vea ilustraciones)**.
Nota: *Esté seguro de tomar nota del orden y la posición instalada de las hembrillas de caucho, las arandelas y los bujes para la instalación apropiada.*
6   La cama puede ser levantada con la ayuda de varios ayudantes, o conectando sogas a los ganchos para las sogas y levantándola hacia afuera con un elevador.
7   La instalación se hace en el orden inverso al procedimiento de desensamble.

27.6a Los pernos para retener la cama son accesibles por debajo del vehículo

27.6b Pernos de afianzamiento delanteros de la cama (se muestra un modelo desde el 1980 al 1985)

Capítulo 13
Sistema eléctrico del chasis

Contenidos

Especificaciones

Bombillas

Aplicación	Potencia en vatios	Tipo
Faros delanteros (sellados - 1980 al 1985)		
Interior - alto	50	4651
Exterior - alto/bajo	40/60	4652
Faros delanteros de halógeno (1980 al 1985)		
Interior - alto	50	H4651
Exterior (tipo 2) - alto/bajo	35/35	H4656
Faros delanteros (1986 en adelante)		
Faros sellados	65/55	H6052
Halógeno	65/35	H6054
Luces delanteras de combinación		
Direccionales	27	1156
Espacio libre (1980 y 1981)	5	-
Espacio libre (1982 en adelante)	8	-
Luz lateral de marcar (1980 y 1981)		
Delantera	8	-
Trasera	8	-

Bombillas (continuación)

Aplicación	Potencia en vatios	Tipo
Luz lateral de marcar (1982 en adelante)		
Delantera	5	-
Trasera	3.8	-
Luz trasera de combinación		
Freno/cola	27/8	1157
Direccionales...	27	1156
Reserva	27	1156
Luz de la licencia		
Luz delantera interior		
Menos con Cabina grande	5	-
Con Cabina grande..	10	-
Medidor de combinación		
Luz de iluminación (1980 y 1981).......................................	1.7	-
Luz de iluminación (1982 en adelante)...............................	3.4	-
Luz de advertencia...	3.4	158
Luz para iluminar el encendedor de cigarrillo	1.4	-
Luz para iluminar el medidor de la presión de aceite 4WD..............	3.4	158
Luz para iluminar el medidor del voltímetro 4WD	3.4	158
Luz indicadora de las 4WD	3.4	158
Luz para iluminar el panel de control para la		
calefacción y el aire acondicionado................................	3.4	158
Luz para iluminar el radio..	3.4	158
Luz para iluminar la palanca selectora (todos los		
modelos con transmisión automática).............................	3.4	158
Luz indicadora para el interruptor del eliminador		
de niebla de la ventana trasera......................................	1.4	-
Luz para iluminar el interruptor del eliminador de		
niebla de la ventana trasera...	3.4	158

Fusibles

1980

Circuito	Calificación de amperios
Faros delanteros...	20
Trasera, licencia, claras, marcador lateral, iluminación, luz interior	10
Frenos, advertencia	15
Bocina, reloj..	10
Radio, encendedor de cigarrillos	15
Limpiador del parabrisas, lavador, aire acondicionado, calefacción	15
Calefacción (con calefacción accionada alta)	20
Luces de advertencia, relojes, direccionales........................	15
Control del motor...	10

1981 en adelante

Circuito	Calificación de amperios
Faros delanteros	
Al 1990	10
1991 y más modernos..	15
Trasera, licencia, claras, marcador lateral, iluminación, luz interior	
Al 1990	15
1991 y más modernos..	10
Luces de los frenos	
Al 1990	15
1991 y más modernos..	10
Bocina	10
Reloj 10	
Radio, encendedor de cigarrillos	15
Limpiaparabrisas, lavador, aire acondicionado, calefacción	15
Calefacción	
Al 1990	20
1991 y más modernos..	15
Luz de advertencia, relojes, direccionales	
Al 1990	15
1991 y más modernos..	10
Eliminador de niebla trasero...	15
Control del motor	15
Bobina para la ignición...	10

Fusibles térmicos
1980

Circuito	Color
Circuitos del aire acondicionado	Verde
Todos los circuitos de carga	Rojo

1981 en adelante

Circuito	Color
Circuito de los faros delanteros	Verde
Suministro de poder (ignición/accesorio en la caja de fusible)	Verde
Suministro de poder (batería en la caja de fusible)	Negro

Codificación del color del arnés del alambrado

Circuito	Color base
Arranque y los sistemas de ignición	Negro (B)
Sistema de carga	Blanco (W)
Sistema de la iluminación	Rojo (R)
Direccionales y bocina	Verde (G)
Sistemas de instrumentos	Amarillo (Y)
Los otros	Azul (L), Marrón (Br) y Verde Pálido (Lg)
Sistema de tierra	Negro (B)

1 Información general

Este Capítulo cubre los procedimientos de reparación y servicio para varios componentes de iluminación y eléctricos que no son asociados con el motor, identificación y resolución de problemas, también como información general en los varios circuitos eléctricos. La información de la batería, generador, distribuidor y el motor de arranque pueden ser encontrado en el Capítulos 5.

El sistema eléctrico es del tipo negativo de 12 voltios de conexión a tierra con el suministro de poder otorgado por una batería de tipo plomo/ácido que es cargada por el alternador.

Los componentes eléctricos localizados en el tablero no usan alambres de conexión a tierra ni correas, pero envés usa unos circuitos de conexión a tierra que son integrados en el circuito impreso instalados en la parte trasera del aglutinador de instrumentos.

Debe ser notado que cuando se trabaje en las porciones del sistema eléctrico, el cable negativo de la batería se debe desconectar para prevenir cortos y/o fuegos eléctricos.

2 Identificación y resolución de problemas eléctricos - información general

Un circuito eléctrico típico se compone de un componente eléctrico, cualquier interruptor, relees, motores, etc. pertinente a ese componente, alambrado y a los conectores que conectan el componente a ambas la batería y el chasis. Para ayudar a localizar un problema en un circuito eléctrico, esquemas completos del alambrado están incluidos en el final de este Capítulo. También de beneficio para localizar los circuitos específicos en el vehículo son las ilustraciones del conector del alambrado que identifican todos los conectores usados en el vehículo. Éstos son encontrado también en el final de este Capítulo.

Antes de atacar cualquier circuito eléctrico molestoso, primero estudie completamente los esquemas apropiados para obtener una comprensión completa de lo que compone ese circuito individual. Áreas de problemas, por ejemplo, a menudo pueden ser reducidas notando si otro componente relacionado a ese circuito está operando apropiadamente o no.

Si varios componentes o circuitos fallan a la misma vez, pueda que el defecto esté en la conexión del fusible o conexión a tierra, porque varios circuitos a menudo son dirigidos en las mismas conexiones del fusible y conexión a tierra. Esto puede ser confirmado refiriéndose a la caja de fusible y esquemas de distribución de conexión a tierra en este Capítulo.

A menudo, los problemas eléctricos provienen de causas sencillas, tal como conexiones flojas o corroídas, un fusible quemado o un fusible térmico fundido. Antes de cualquier identificación y resolución de problema eléctrico, siempre chequee visualmente la condición del fusible, los alambres y las conexiones del circuito del problema.

Si instrumentos de probar van a ser utilizados, use los esquemas para planear adelante donde usted hará las conexiones necesarias en orden de poder localizar con toda precisión exactamente el lugar del problema.

Las herramientas básicas necesitadas para la identificación y resolución de problemas eléctricos incluyen un probador de circuito o voltímetro (una bombilla de 12 voltios y un juego de alambres de pruebas que se pueden usar también), un probador de continuidad (que incluye una bombilla, batería y juego de alambres de prueba) y un alambre puente, preferiblemente con un interruptor del circuito incorporado, que se puede usar para desviar componentes eléctricos.

Los chequeos de voltaje se deben realizar si un circuito no está funcionando apropiadamente. Conecte un alambre de un probador de circuito a la terminal negativa de la batería o una conexión buena a tierra.

Conecte el otro alambre a un conector en el circuito que va ser chequeado, preferiblemente más cerca a la batería o al fusible. Si la bombilla del probador se ilumina cuando voltaje es alcanzado, señala que la parte del circuito entre ese conector y la batería está libre de problemas. Continúe chequeando a lo largo del circuito mismo. Cuando usted alcance un punto donde no haya voltaje presente, el problemas está entre ahí y el último punto de prueba bueno. La mayor parte del tiempo el problema es debido a una conexión floja. Mantenga en mente que algunos circuitos reciben solamente voltaje cuando la llave de la ignición está en Accesorio o Posición de Marcha.

Un método de encontrar cortos en un circuito es de remover el fusible y conectar una luz de prueba o un voltímetro en su posición en las terminales del fusible. No debe haber carga en el circuito. Mueva el conjunto del alambrado/arnés de lado a lado y observe la luz de prueba. Si la bombilla se ilumina, hay un corto a la conexión a tierra en algún lugar en esa área, probablemente donde el aislamiento se ha removido de un alambre. La misma prueba se puede realizar en otros componentes del circuito, inclusive el interruptor.

Un chequeo de la conexión a tierra debe ser hecho si un componente es puesto a tierra apropiadamente. Desconecte la batería y conecte el alambre de una luz de prueba de continuidad con su propia batería a una buena conexión de tierra conocida. Conecte el otro alambre a la conexión del alambre o la conexión a tierra que va ser chequeada. Si la bombilla se ilumina, la conexión a tierra está buena. Si la bombilla no se ilumina, la conexión a tierra no está buena.

Un chequeo de la continuidad es realizado para ver si un circuito, sección de un circuito o componente individual está pasando electricidad apropiadamente. Desconecte la batería y conecte un alambre de luz de prueba que se energiza por si mismo, tal como un probador de continuidad a un extremo del circuito que se está probando y el otro alambre al extremo del circuito. Si la bombilla se ilumina, no hay continuidad, que quiere decir que el circuito está pasando

electricidad através de el apropiadamente. Los interruptores se pueden chequear en la misma forma.

Recuerde que todos los circuitos eléctricos están compuestos básicamente de la corriente eléctrica corriendo de la batería, através de los alambres, los interruptores, los relees, etc. al componente eléctrico (la bombilla, el motor, etc.). Desde allí corre a la carrocería (conexión a tierra) donde es pasada de regreso a la batería. Cualquier problema eléctrico es básicamente una interrupción en el flujo de corriente eléctrica desde la batería o de regreso.

3   Fusibles - información general

Refiérase a las ilustraciones 3.1a, 3.1b, 3.1c, 3.1d, 3.1e y 3.1f

Los circuitos eléctricos del vehículo están protegidos por una combinación de fusibles y fusibles térmicos (**vea ilustraciones**).

La caja del fusible está localizado en el panel lateral debajo del tablero o atrás de un panel en la tapa del tablero en el lado

izquierdo del vehículo. El acceso a los fusibles es logrado simplemente desabrochando la tapa para los fusibles.

Cada uno de los fusibles es diseñado para proteger un circuito específico, como está identificado en la tapa de fusible.

Si un componente eléctrico ha fallado, el primer chequeo debe ser el fusible. Un fusible que se ha "quemado" puede ser identificado rápidamente inspeccionando el elemento curvo de metal adentro del albergue plástico. Si este elemento está roto, el fusible está inoperable y debe ser reemplazado con uno nuevo.

Los fusibles son reemplazados simplemente removiendo el viejo y empujando el nuevo en su posición.

Es importante que el fusible correcto sea instalado. Los circuitos eléctricos diferentes necesitan cantidades variadas de protección, indicado por el valor de amperaje en el fusible. Un fusible con una calificación demasiado baja se quemará prematuramente, mientras que un fusible con una calificación demasiado alta no se puede quemar lo suficientemente rápido para evitar un daño grave.

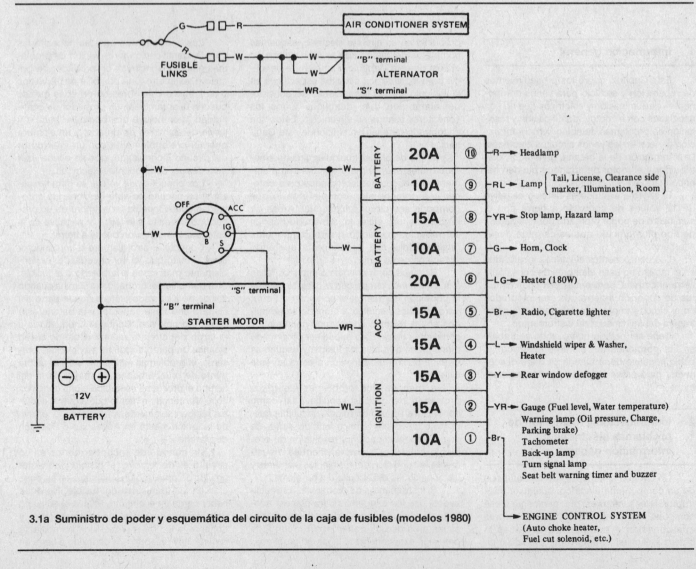

3.1a Suministro de poder y esquemática del circuito de la caja de fusibles (modelos 1980)

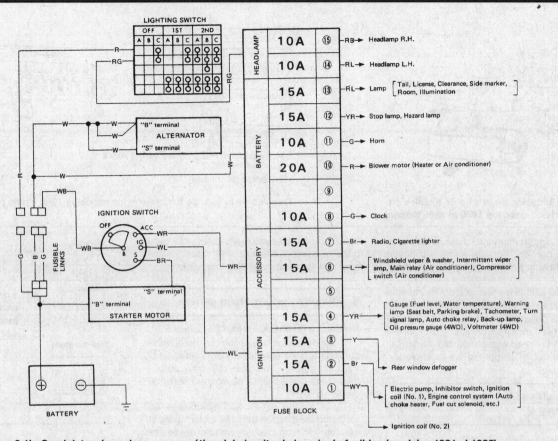

3.1b Suministro de poder y esquemática del circuito de la caja de fusibles (modelos 1981 al 1985)

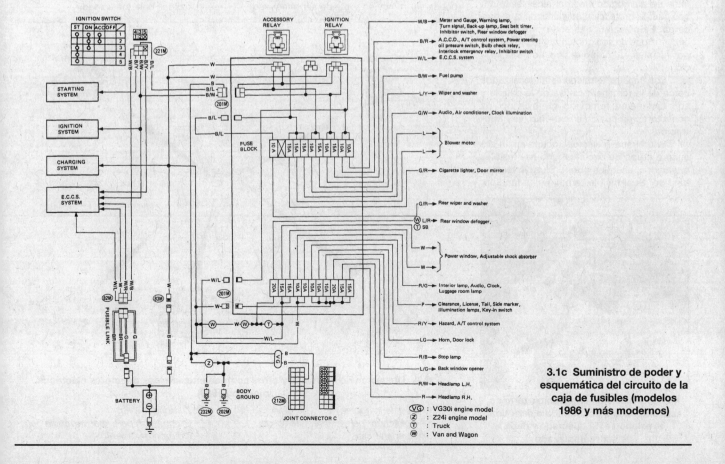

3.1c Suministro de poder y esquemática del circuito de la caja de fusibles (modelos 1986 y más modernos)

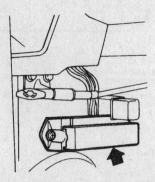

3.1d Ubicación de la caja de fusibles en los modelos desde el 1980 al 1985 (flecha)

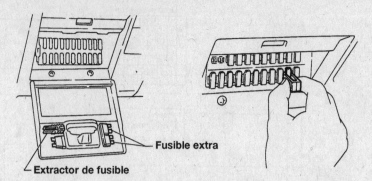

3.1e Detalles de la caja de fusibles en los modelos 1986 y más modernos

3.1f Los tipos de fusibles usados en estos modelos pueden ser chequeados

En ningún momento debe el fusible ser saltado con una hoja de metal o aluminio. Daño grave al sistema eléctrico podría resultar.

Si el fusible de reemplazo falla inmediatamente, no lo reemplace con otro hasta que la causa del problema sea aislada y corregida. En la mayoría de los casos esto será un corto circuito en el sistema del alambrado causado por un alambre roto o deteriorado.

4   Fusibles térmicos - información general

Refiérase a la ilustración 4.2

Además de los fusibles regulares, el sistema del alambrado incorpora fusibles térmicos para la protección adicional de la sobrecarga. Estos eslabones son usados en los circuitos que no son comúnmente protegidos por fusibles, tal como el circuito de la ignición.

Los fusibles térmicos están localizados cerca de la terminal positiva de la batería y son fácilmente removido removiendo los conectores en cualquier extremo **(vea ilustración)**.

Si un fracaso eléctrico ocurre en un circuito o grupo de circuitos y no hay fusibles quemados, chequee para un fusible térmico fundido. Si el fusible térmico está fundido,

debe ser reemplazado, pero solamente después que sea chequeado y el defecto eléctrico que lo causó, haya sido corregido.

5   Relees - información general

Refiérase a las ilustraciones 5.2a, 5.2b y 5.2c

Varios accesorios eléctricos en el vehículo usan relees para transmitir la señal eléctrica al componente. Si el relé está defectuoso, ese componente no operará apropiadamente.

Los varios relees son agrupados en varias ubicaciones debajo del tablero para la conveniencia en caso necesario del reemplazo **(vea ilustraciones)**.

Si un relé defectuoso es sospechado, puede ser removido y puede ser chequeado

por un concesionario Nissan u otro taller calificado. Los relees defectuosos deben ser reemplazados con una unidad.

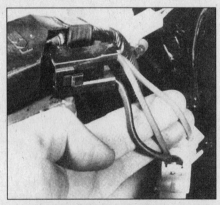

4.2 Si la aislación en el fusible térmico está ampollada, decolorada o derretida, el eslabón está quemado y debe de ser reemplazado

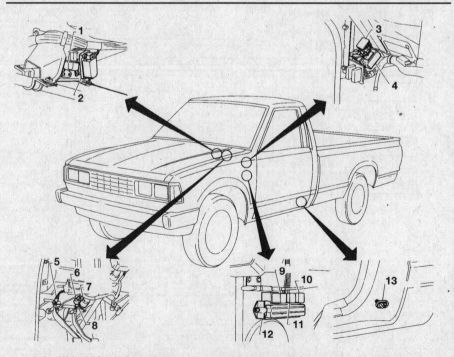

5.2a Ubicación de los relees y otros componentes de los conectores eléctricos (modelos 1980)

1	Relee de la bocina	3	Zumbador
2	Amplificador para el intermitente del limpiaparabrisas	4	Cronometro para la advertencia del cinturón del asiento

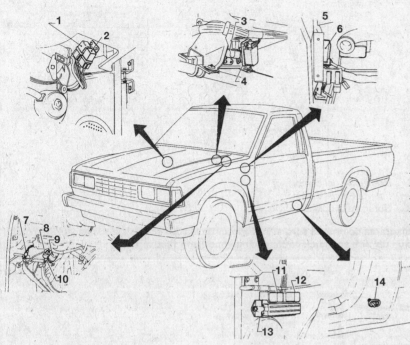

5.2b Ubicación de los relees y otros componentes de los conectores eléctricos (modelos 1981 al 1985)

1　Relee para estrangulador automático en el lado derecho del panel
2　Relee aislador
3　Relee de la bocina
4　Amplificador para el intermitente del limpiaparabrisas
5　Panel izquierdo lateral del tablero
6　Unidad de advertencia para el cinturón del asiento
7　Interruptor del embrague
8　Unidad de destello de advertencia
9　Unidad de destello para las direccionales
10　Interruptor para las luces de los frenos
11　Relee de la calefacción
12　Relee para las luces delanteras
13　Bloque de los fusibles
14　Interruptor de la puerta

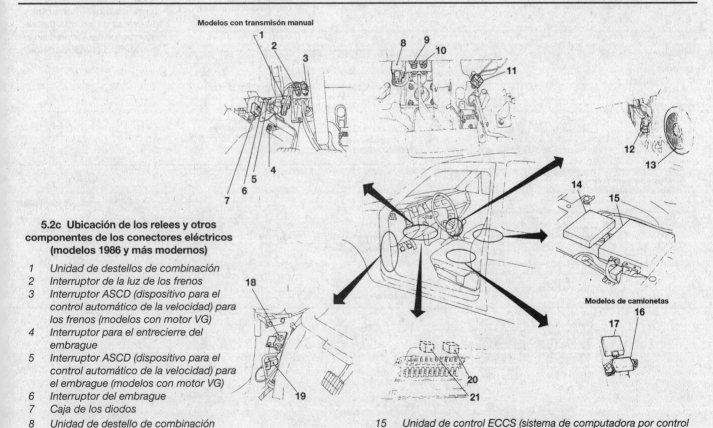

Modelos con transmisón manual

5.2c Ubicación de los relees y otros componentes de los conectores eléctricos (modelos 1986 y más modernos)

1　Unidad de destellos de combinación
2　Interruptor de la luz de los frenos
3　Interruptor ASCD (dispositivo para el control automático de la velocidad) para los frenos (modelos con motor VG)
4　Interruptor para el entrecierre del embrague
5　Interruptor ASCD (dispositivo para el control automático de la velocidad) para el embrague (modelos con motor VG)
6　Interruptor del embrague
7　Caja de los diodos
8　Unidad de destello de combinación
9　Interruptor para las luces de los frenos
10　Interruptor ASCD (dispositivo para el control automático de la velocidad) para los frenos (modelos con motor VG)
11　Interruptor para el rebase
12　Relee de seguridad (naranja)
13　Altavoz de la puerta del lado derecho
14　Unidad de control para las transmisiones automáticas (modelos de camionetas)

15　Unidad de control ECCS (sistema de computadora por control electrónico)
16　Cronometro para el cerrojo de la puerta
17　Unidad de control para el ASCD (dispositivo para el control automático de la velocidad)
18　Cronometro para el cinturón del asiento
19　Campaneo de advertencia
20　Relee de la ignición (azul)
21　Relee de los accesorios (azul)

Modelos de camionetas

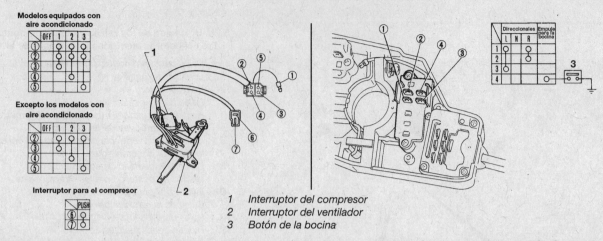

1 Interruptor del compresor
2 Interruptor del ventilador
3 Botón de la bocina

6.3a Identificación de las terminales del interruptor y diagrama de prueba para el interruptor de las direccionales/bocina y el interruptor para el ventilador de la calefacción del aire acondicionado (encima) (modelos 1980 al 1982)

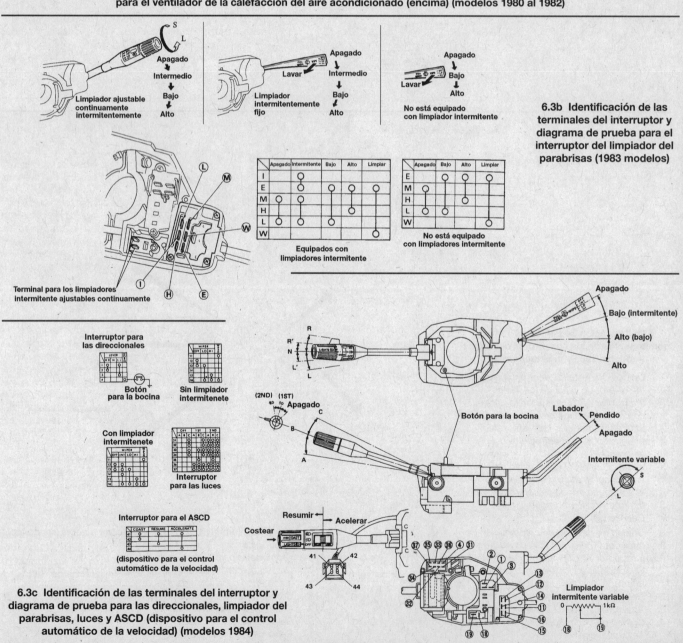

6.3b Identificación de las terminales del interruptor y diagrama de prueba para el interruptor del limpiador del parabrisas (1983 modelos)

6.3c Identificación de las terminales del interruptor y diagrama de prueba para las direccionales, limpiador del parabrisas, luces y ASCD (dispositivo para el control automático de la velocidad) (modelos 1984)

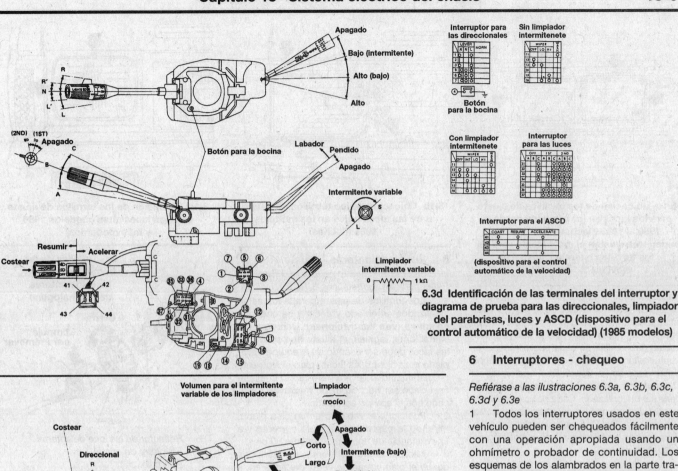

6.3d **Identificación de las terminales del interruptor y diagrama de prueba para las direccionales, limpiador del parabrisas, luces y ASCD (dispositivo para el control automático de la velocidad) (1985 modelos)**

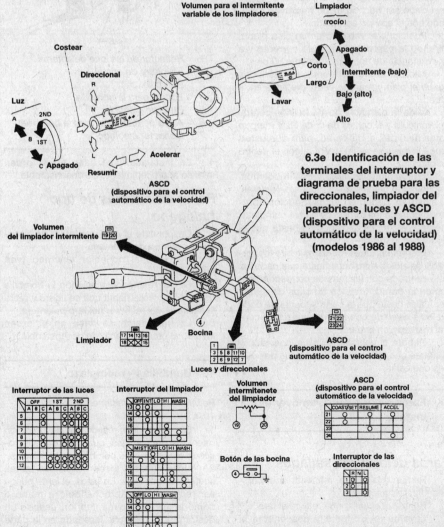

6.3e **Identificación de las terminales del interruptor y diagrama de prueba para las direccionales, limpiador del parabrisas, luces y ASCD (dispositivo para el control automático de la velocidad) (modelos 1986 al 1988)**

6 Interruptores - chequeo

Refiérase a las ilustraciones 6.3a, 6.3b, 6.3c, 6.3d y 6.3e

1   Todos los interruptores usados en este vehículo pueden ser chequeados fácilmente con una operación apropiada usando un ohmímetro o probador de continuidad. Los esquemas de los alambrados en la parte trasera de este Capítulo contienen toda la información necesaria para el chequeo de cada interruptor. Además, la figura que acompaña proporciona más información para chequear las direccionales/interruptor de la bocina y la calefacción/interruptor del ventilador del aire acondicionado.

2   Interruptores sencillos de apagado y encendido, tal como el interruptor del freno de estacionamiento, son más fácil de chequear. Esta clase de interruptor está normalmente cerrado o normalmente abierto. Identifique cuál tipo de interruptor usted está chequeando refiriéndose a las claves del esquema del alambrado. Entonces desconecte los alambres del interruptor y conecte los alambres del probador de continuidad o un ohmímetro a los alambres del interruptor. Opere el interruptor en ambas posiciones, apagado y encendido y note el resultado. Cuando el interruptor está cerrado, continuidad debe existir (indicado por la bombilla del probador iluminada o por la aguja del ohmímetro moviéndose hacia afuera de la marca O). Cuando el interruptor se abre, ninguna continuidad debe existir.

3   Interruptores que usan múltiple terminales de conectores requieren un procedimiento levemente diferente para probarlo. Cada interruptor en los esquemas del alambrado es acompañado con un esquema que identifica las terminales del conector del alambrado del interruptor (**vea ilustraciones**). Cada interruptor es también acompañado con un diagrama que muestra cuál terminal debe desplegar continuidad en cada posición del interruptor.

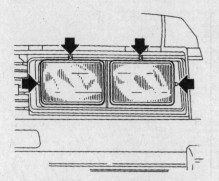

8.1a Ubicación de los tornillos de ajuste para las luces en los modelos desde el 1980 al 1985 (flechas); los tornillos superiores ajustan el movimiento vertical, los tornillos laterales ajustan el movimiento horizontal

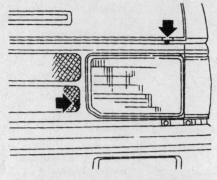

8.1b Ubicación de los tornillos de ajuste para las luces bajas en los modelos 1986 (flechas)

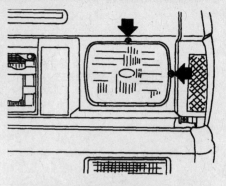

8.1c Ubicación de los tornillos de ajuste para las luces altas (modelos 1986 y más modernos)

Hacia abajo en el lado izquierdo del diagrama están las terminales del conector y hasta encima están las varias posiciones del interruptor. Las terminales entre la cuál la continuidad debe existir en cada posición del interruptor están indicadas por círculos pequeños conectados en las líneas. Si el interruptor no chequea como está mostrado en el diagrama, debe ser reemplazado. Cada posición del interruptor de iluminación está separado en las posiciones A, B y C. A es la posición superior, B es la posición inferior y C es la posición de halar hacia afuera.

7   Destelladores para las direccionales y de emergencia - información general

Las unidades destelladoras pequeñas de las luces intermitentes están incorporadas en los circuitos eléctricos para las luces direccionales y las señales de advertencia. Éstas están localizadas debajo del tablero y apenas encima de la columna de la dirección.

Cuando las unidades están funcionando apropiadamente, un sonido audible se puede oír con el circuito en operación. Si las direccionales fallan en un lado solamente y la unidad de destellos no se puede oír, es una indicación de una bombilla defectuosa. Si el destellador se puede oír, es una indicación de un corto en el alambrado.

Si las direccionales fallan en ambos lados, el defecto puede ser debido a un fusible quemado, la unidad defectuosa de luces intermitentes o interruptor, o una conexión a tierra floja. Si el fusible se ha quemado, chequee el alambrado por un corto antes de instalar un fusible nuevo.

Las luces de advertencia de peligro son chequeadas de la misma manera como en el Párrafo 3 de encima.

Cuando reemplace cualquiera de estos destelladores de luces intermitentes, es importante comprar un destellador de reemplazo de la misma capacidad. Chequee el destellador nuevo contra el viejo para asegurarse del reemplazo apropiado.

8   Luces delanteras - ajuste

Refiérase a las ilustraciones 8.1a, 8.1b y 8.1c

1   Los tornillos de ajuste para la luz están localizados en el lado y encima de cada luz delantera **(vea ilustraciones)**. Debido a las limitaciones legales, el ajuste apropiado de las luces debe ser usando en el equipo apropiado para ajustar las luces, pero el siguiente procedimiento lo llevará muy cerca. El ajuste final debe ser hecho por un mecánico calificado con el equipo apropiado.

2   Posicione el vehículo en un piso plano, mirando la pared en el ángulo correcto y a una distancia de aproximadamente 30 pies.

3   Mida la altura del centro de las luces desde el piso y marque estas medidas en la pared.

4   Mida la distancia desde la línea central del vehículo y el centro de cada luz y marque estas medidas en la pared, para que usted tenga líneas que se interceptan con el centro de cada luz.

5   En los modelos 1986 y más modernos, remueva los biseles de las luces delanteras. El ajuste es hecho en estos modelos apretando primero los tornillo de ajuste completamente y entonces aflojándolos hasta que el ajuste sea logrado.

6   Prenda las luces regulares y gire los tornillos de ajuste horizontal hasta que cada luz esté centrada con las marcas correspondientes en la pared. Gire los tornillos de ajuste verticales hasta que la parte superior de cada luz esté nivelada con la línea horizontal central marcada en la pared.

7   Rebote el vehículo en su suspensión y chequee que las luces vuelvan a sus posiciones originales.

9   Faros delanteros - remover e instalar

Refiérase a la ilustración 9.6

Faros delanteros sellados

1   Remueva la parrilla, refiriéndose al Capítulo 13, si es necesario.

2   Remueva el anillo que retiene el faro.

3   Levante la luz fuera y desconecte el conector del alambrado.

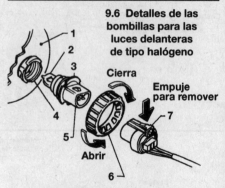

9.6 Detalles de las bombillas para las luces delanteras de tipo halógeno

1   Reflector de las luce delanteras
2   Envoltura de cristal
3   Bombilla
4   Zócalo para la bombilla
5   Base de plástico
6   Anillo de retención para la bombilla
7   Conector eléctrico

4   La instalación se hace en el orden inverso al procedimiento de desensamble.

Faros delanteros de tipo halógeno

5   Desconecte el cable negativo de la terminal negativa de la batería.

6   Remueva el conector eléctrico **(vea ilustración)**.

7   Gire el retenedor reteniendo la bombilla hacia la izquierda hasta que se libere y retire la bombilla del reflector del faro delantero.

8   La instalación se hace en el orden inverso al procedimiento de desensamble.

10   Bombillas - reemplazo

Refiérase a las ilustraciones 10.2a, 10.2b y 10.3

1   Los lentes de la mayoría de las luces son retenidos por tornillos, que hace que el proceso para llegar a las bombillas sean simples.

2   Unas cuantas luces tienen sus lentes sostenidos por clips. En éstos, el lente puede ser removido desabrochándolo a mano o como la luz de encima interior, usando un destornillador pequeño insertado en la parte trasera para abrirlo con una palanca hacia

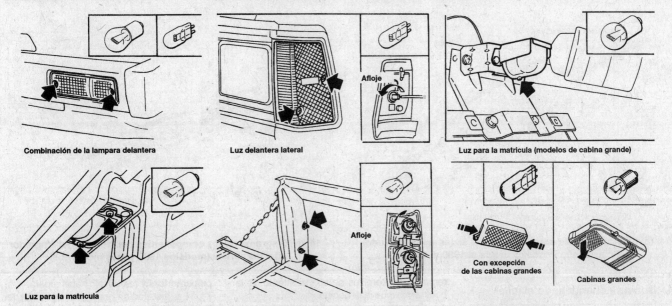

Combinación de la lampara delantera

Luz delantera lateral

Afloje

Luz para la matricula (modelos de cabina grande)

Luz para la matricula

Afloje

Con excepción
de las cabinas grandes

Cabinas grandes

10.2a Detalles del reemplazo de la bombilla en los modelos desde el 1980 al 1985

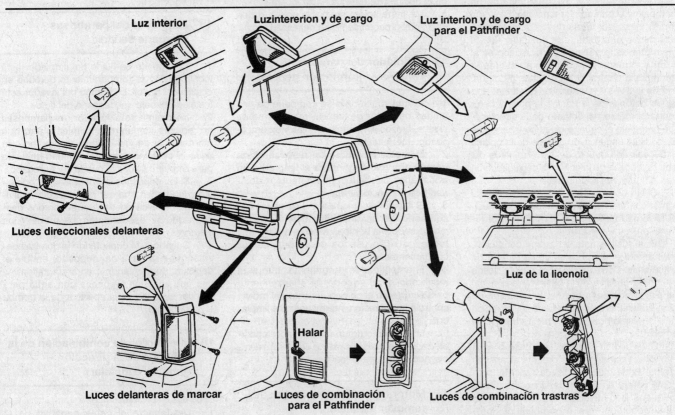

Luz interior

Luzintererion y de cargo

Luz interion y de cargo
para el Pathfinder

Luces direccionales delanteras

Luz de la licencia

Luces delanteras de marcar

Halar

Luces de combinación
para el Pathfinder

Luces de combinación trastras

10.2b Detalles del reemplazo de la bombilla en los modelos 1986 y más modernos

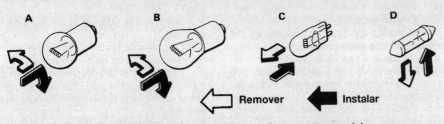

A   B   C   D

Remover   Instalar

10.3 Los cuatro tipos de bombillas usados en estos modelos

afuera (vea ilustraciones).

3   Cuatro tipos diferentes de bombillas son usadas (vea ilustración). Tipo A y B son removidas empujando hacia adentro y girándola a la izquierda. El tipo D simplemente se le remueve los clips de sus terminales y el Tipo C se remueve simplemente del receptáculo.

4   Para obtener acceso a las bombillas de iluminación del tablero de instrumentos, el medidor de combinación debe ser removido como dice en la Sección 18.

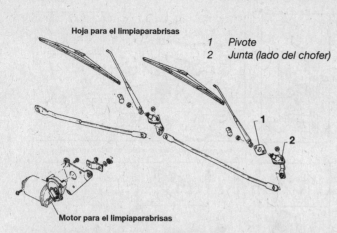

Hoja para el limpiaparabrisas

1   Pivote
2   Junta (lado del chofer)

Motor para el limpiaparabrisas

14.2a Diagrama de los componentes del sistema del limpiador del parabrisas (modelos desde el 1980 al 1985)

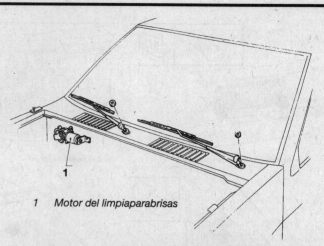

1   Motor del limpiaparabrisas

14.2b Diagrama de los componentes del sistema del limpiador del parabrisas (modelos 1986 y más modernos)

11   Bocina - chequeando el fallo

1   Dos bocinas son usadas, una con un tono bajo y la otra con un tono alto. Ellas son ambas instaladas atrás de los parachoques delanteros, una debajo de cualquier luz. El interruptor de la bocina está localizado en el volante y puede ser activado apretando la almohadilla central o, en algunos modelos, uno de los botones laterales. El apretar uno de los botones de la bocina la pone a tierra contra el marco del volante de la dirección, que completa el circuito eléctrico y hace que las bocinas hagan ruido. El relé de la bocina está localizado debajo del lado izquierdo del tablero, encima de la columna de la dirección (vea la figura que acompaña).
2   Si la bocina prueba estar inoperable, su primer chequeo debe ser el fusible. Un fusible quemado se puede identificar rápidamente en la caja de fusible.
3   Si el fusible está en buena condición, desconecte el alambre eléctrico en una de las bocinas. Corra un alambre puente desde el terminal positivo de la batería a la terminal del alambrado en la bocina. Si la bocina no toca, el defecto está en la tierra de la bocina o en la misma bocina. Pruebe la otra bocina también.
4   Si la bocina sonó en la prueba previa, esto indica que ninguna corriente alcanza la bocina. En la mayoría de los casos el problema estará en el relé de la bocina. Otros chequeos deben incluir los contactos de metal doblados en el ensamblaje del interruptor de la bocina, o alambres flojos o rotos en el sistema.

12   Bocina - remover e instalar

1   Desconecte el cable negativo de la batería que proviene desde la batería.
2   Remueva la luz de combinación delantera, localizada en la parte delantera de la bocina, desde el parachoques delantero.
3   Usando un destornillador insertado a través de la luz de combinación delantera,

remueva los tornillos de afianzamiento de la bocina y remueva la bocina.
4   Desconecte el conector del alambrado de la bocina y remuévala hacia afuera.
5   La instalación se hace en el orden inverso al procedimiento de desensamble.

13   Limpiador del parabrisas, sistema - información general

1   El limpiaparabrisas se compone de una unidad de motor de limpiar, mecanismo de enlace, brazos limpiadores, hojas y un amplificador intermitente.
2   El motor incorpora un dispositivo de parada automática y opera el limpiador en tres etapas diferentes: intermitente, velocidad baja y velocidad alta.
3   El lavador eléctrico para el parabrisas se compone de un depósito (con un motor incorporado y la bomba), toberas de limpiar y tubos de vinilo usados para conectar los componentes.
4   El amplificador intermitente, que está localizado en el soporte de afianzamiento para el releé en el compartimento del motor, controla la operación intermitente del limpiador.
5   En el evento de un fracaso, no es posible reparar el amplificador y debe ser reemplazado como una unidad.

14   Motor limpiador del parabrisas - remover e instalar

Refiérase a las ilustraciones 14.2a y 14.2b
1   Remueva el capó, refiriéndose al Capítulo 13, si es necesario.
2   Remueva los brazos limpiadores del parabrisas **(vea ilustraciones)**.
3   Remueva el capó (Capítulo 11).
4   Remueva el anillo de detención que retiene la varilla del limpiador al motor del limpiaparabrisas.
5   Desconecte el conector del alambrado del motor del limpiaparabrisas.
6   Remueva los tornillos del motor del lim-

piaparabrisas y remuévalo hacia afuera.
7   La instalación se hace en el orden inverso al procedimiento de desensamble.

15   Limpiador del parabrisas - otorgarle servicio

1   El depósito de flúido del limpiador está localizado en el compartimiento derecho en el lado del motor. La bomba del lavador está instalada debajo del depósito del fluido.
2   Normalmente el lavador del parabrisas no requiere ningún mantenimiento otro que mantener el depósito lleno al máximo con agua, al cual una pequeña cantidad de flúido para limpiar parabrisas puede ser agregado.
3   Si los depósitos del parabrisas o bomba eléctrica tienen que ser remplazados individualmente, ellos pueden ser separados después que se desconecten los tubos y los alambres.
4   Cuando esté conectando la bomba nuevamente a la base del depósito, entibie el depósito sumergiéndolo en agua caliente y use una solución jabonosa con agua para lubricar el cuello de la abertura de la bomba en el depósito.

16   Interruptor de combinación de la columna de la dirección - remover e instalar

Refiérase a la ilustración 16.5
1   Desconecte el cable negativo de la batería que proviene desde la batería.
2   Remueva el volante, refiérase al Capítulo 12 si es necesario.
3   Remueva la tapa de la columna de la dirección.
4   Desconecte los conectores del alambrado del interruptor de combinación.
5   Afloje los tornillos reteniendo el interruptor de combinación y deslice el interruptor desde la columna de la dirección **(vea ilustración)**.
6   La instalación se hace en el orden inverso al procedimiento de desensamble.

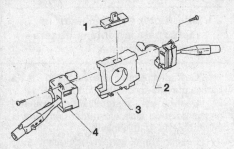

16.5 Detalles del interruptor de combinación más moderno típico

1 *Interruptor de emergencia*
2 *Interruptor para limpiador y lavador*
3 *Interruptor de base*
4 *Interruptor de iluminación, e interruptor ASCD (dispositivo para control automático de la velocidad)*

17 Interruptor de la ignición - remover e instalar

Refiérase a la ilustración 17.4

1 Desconecte el cable negativo de la batería que proviene desde la batería.
2 Remueva la tapa de la columna de la dirección de la columna de la dirección.
3 Desconecte el conector del alambrado del interruptor de la ignición.
4 El interruptor de la ignición ahora puede ser removido (**vea ilustración**). En los modelos equipados con una dirección de cerradura, el interruptor de la ignición es conectado a la cerradura por un tornillo retenedor en la parte trasera.
5 La instalación se hace en el orden inverso al procedimiento de desensamble.

18 Medidor de combinación - remover e instalar

Refiérase a las ilustraciones 18.2, 18.3 y 18.5

1 Desconecte el cable negativo de la batería que proviene desde la batería.
2 Remueva los tornillos que retienen el metro de combinación al tablero y remuévalo hacia afuera (**vea ilustración**).
3 Remueva los tornillos que retienen el medidor de combinación en el tablero (**vea ilustración**).

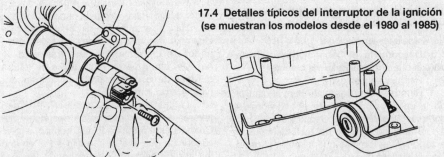

17.4 Detalles típicos del interruptor de la ignición (se muestran los modelos desde el 1980 al 1985)

Con cerrojo en la columna   Sin cerrojo en la columna

18.2 Detalles de afianzamiento para el medidor de combinación (modelos desde el 1980 al 1985)

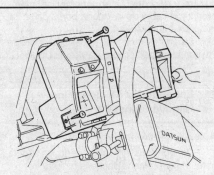

18.3 Ubicación de los tornillos de afianzamiento para el medidor de combinación (modelos desde el 1980 al 1985)

4 Cuidadosamente hale el medidor de combinación fuera del tablero lo suficiente para desconectar el alambrado y el velocímetro desde la parte trasera. Remueva el medidor de combinación del tablero.
5 El albergue del medidor de combinación se puede desarmar para permitir acceso a los relojes e indicadores encerrados, removiendo los tornillos de retención (**vea ilustra-**

ción). El circuito impreso puede ser removido removiendo los enchufes de las bombillas y entonces removiendo los tornillos o los clips que lo retienen. Tenga cuidado para que usted no rompa ni dañe la tabla del circuito impreso.
6 La instalación se hace en el orden inverso al procedimiento de desensamble.

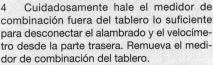

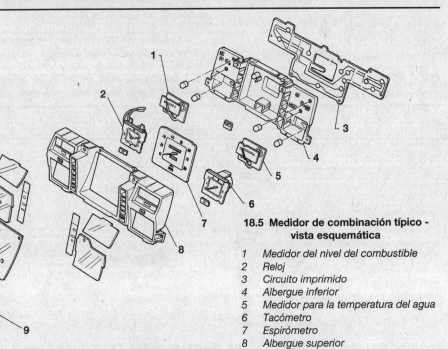

18.5 Medidor de combinación típico - vista esquemática

1 *Medidor del nivel del combustible*
2 *Reloj*
3 *Circuito imprimido*
4 *Albergue inferior*
5 *Medidor para la temperatura del agua*
6 *Tacómetro*
7 *Espirómetro*
8 *Albergue superior*
9 *Cubierta del aglutinador*

19 Radio - remover e instalar

Refiérase a las ilustraciones 19.4 y 19.5
1   Desconecte el cable negativo de la batería que proviene desde la batería.
2   Remueva el cenicero.
3   Remueva el ensamblaje para el control de la calefacción y el aire acondicionado como está descrito en el Capítulo 3.
4   Trabajando debajo del tablero, remueva el tapón y los tornillos que afianzan el radio **(vea ilustración)**.
5   Remueva el radio cuidadosamente del tablero y desconecte el conector del alambrado y el cable de la antena por la parte del radio **(vea ilustración)**.
6   La instalación se hace en el orden inverso al procedimiento de desensamble.

20 Encendedor de cigarrillos - remover e instalar

Refiérase a la ilustración 20.4
1   Desconecte el cable negativo de la batería que proviene desde la batería.
2   Desconecte los alambres que se dirigen al encendedor de cigarrillos.

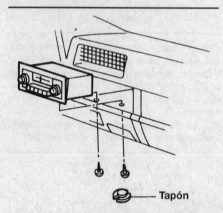

19.4 Detalles típicos de la instalación del radio

3   Remueva la tuerca que retiene el encendedor de cigarrillos desde la parte de atrás.
4   Hale el ensamblaje del encendedor de cigarrillos desde la parte delantera del aglutinador de instrumentos. Mientras esto se hace, el albergue de la bombilla se saldrá también de la parte trasera del aglutinador **(vea ilustración)**.
5   La instalación se hace en el orden inverso al procedimiento de desensamble. Cuando esté instalando los componentes, asegúrese que ellos están alineados en una fila apropiadamente enganchando las lengüetas en sus hendiduras de localizaciones respectivas.

21 Unidad de control para la iluminación - remover e instalar

1   Desconecte el cable negativo de la batería que proviene desde la batería.
2   Hale hacia afuera la perilla del interruptor.
3   Remueva la tuerca de tipo anillo.
4   Desconecte el conector del alambrado desde el interruptor.
5   El interruptor puede ser removido por la parte de atrás del tablero de instrumentos.
6   La instalación se hace en el orden inverso al procedimiento de desensamble.

22 Interruptor de advertencia de peligro - remover e instalar

1   Desconecte el cable negativo de la batería que proviene desde la batería.
2   Remueva la tapa de la columna de la dirección.
3   Desconecte el conector del alambrado de peligro del interruptor de advertencia de peligro.
4   Remueva los tornillos que retienen el interruptor de advertencia de peligro a la tapa y levante el interruptor.
5   La instalación se hace en el orden inverso al procedimiento de desensamble.

23 Interruptor del eliminador de niebla para la ventana trasera - remover e instalar

1   Desconecte el cable negativo de la batería que proviene desde la batería.
2   Usando un destornillador pequeño, hágale palanca hacia afuera para remover el interruptor de su ubicación.
3   Desconecte el conector del alambrado del interruptor y levántelo hacia afuera.
4   La instalación se hace en el orden inverso al procedimiento de desensamble.

24 Rejilla trasera para el eliminador de niebla - chequear y reparar

1   Esta opción se compone de una ventana trasera con varios elementos horizontales que son horneados en la superficie del vidrio durante la operación de formar el vidrio.
2   Interrupciones pequeñas en el sistema del elemento se pueden reparar exitosamente sin remover la ventana trasera.
3   Para chequear las rejillas por una operación apropiada, ponga el motor en marcha y prenda el sistema.
4   Conecte un alambre a tierra de una lámpara de prueba y toque ligeramente el otro alambre a cada línea de la reja.
5   El brillo de la luz de prueba debe aumentar según la sonda es movida a través del elemento desde la derecha a la izquierda. Si la luz de prueba resplandece brillantemente en ambas puntas de la línea de la rejilla, chequee por una conexión de un alambre a tierra para el sistema flojo. Todas las líneas de la rejilla deben ser chequeadas por lo menos en dos lugares.
6   Los materiales necesitados para reparar una línea de la rejilla que está rota incluyen un conducto de plata (disponible específicamente para este propósito), una pluma de dibujar, cinta eléctrica, alcohol y tela. Juegos completos de reparación se pueden obtener también.
7   Para reparar una interrupción, apague

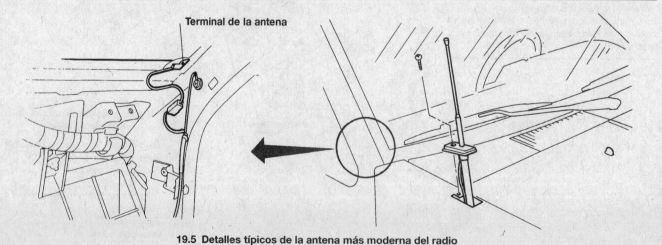

Terminal de la antena

19.5 Detalles típicos de la antena más moderna del radio

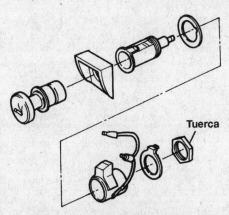

20.4 Detalles típicos de la instalación del encendedor de cigarrillos

primero el sistema y permítalo que pierda su energía por unos cuantos minutos.

8   Limpie ligeramente el área de la línea de la rejilla con una lana de acero fino y entonces limpie completamente el área con alcohol.

9   Use cinta de electricista en la parte superior e inferior debajo del área que va a ser reparada. El espacio entre los pedazos de la cinta debe ser de la misma anchura de la línea que existe en la rejilla. Esto puede ser chequeado desde la parte de afuera del vehículo. Apriete la cinta firmemente contra el vidrio para prevenir fuga.

10   Moje la pluma en la plata y aplíquela en la interrupción entre los pedazos de cinta, superponiendo el área dañada levemente para prevenir cualquier fuga.

11   Remueva cuidadosamente la cinta. Si una pistola de aire caliente está disponible, aplique una corriente constante de aire caliente directamente al área reparada. Una pistola de calor ajustada entre 500 a 700 grados Fahrenheit es recomendada. Mantenga la pistola acerca de una pulgada del vidrio desde uno a dos minutos.

12   Si la línea nueva de la rejilla aparece de otro color, tintura de yodo se puede usar para limpiar la reparación y traerla de regreso al color apropiado. La mezcla no debe permanecer en la reparación por más de 30 segundos.

13   Aunque el eliminador de niebla está ahora completamente operacional, el área reparada no se debe perturbar por lo menos 24 horas.

25   Bolsa de aire - información general

Los modelos 1996 están equipados con el SRS (sistema suplemental de restricción), más común conocido como una bolsa de aire. Este sistema es diseñado para proteger al chófer en caso de un choque de dos vehículo frontalmente hasta 30 grados de la línea central del vehículo. Se compone de un módulo inflador para la bolsa de aire en el centro del volante, un sensor en la zona de choque (modelos de 4WD), una unidad de sensor de diagnóstico y un cable espiral en la columna de la dirección.

En los modelos equipados con un bolsa de aire, **no remueva el volante** sin primero hacer que la bolsa de aire sea incapacitada o removida del volante por una facilidad de reparación automotriz o el departamento de servicio de su concesionario. El fracaso de hacer esto puede resultar en el despliegue accidental de la bolsa de aire y lesión física grava.

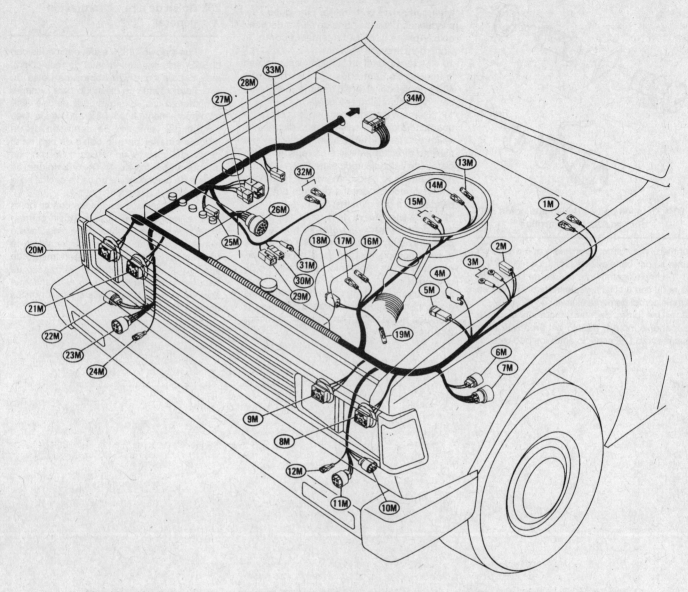

Identificación de los conectores del conjunto del alambrado/arnés en el compartimiento del motor (típico)

1M   Hacia la válvula de imán FICD (dispositivo para el control de la marcha mínima rápida)

2M   Hacia el condensador

3M   Hacia la bobina para la ignición

4M   Hacia la válvula de intercambio de vacío (modelos de California para trabajo pesado)

5M   Hacia la válvula del control del aire (modelos de California para trabajo pesado)

6M   Hacia el interruptor de vacío (modelos de los Estados Unidos)

7M   Conector de chequeo

8M   Hacia la luz delantera izquierda (Tipo 2)

9M   Hacia la luz delantera izquierda (Tipo 1)

10M   Hacia la luz delantera izquierda del marcador lateral

11M   Hacia la luz delantera izquierda de combinación

12M   Hacia la bocina baja

13M   Hacia el calentador automático del estrangulador

14M   Hacia el solenoide para cortar el combustible

15M   Hacia el solenoide para cortar el vacío (modelos de California)

16M   Hacia el transmisor térmico

17M   Hacia el punto de tierra del distribuidor

18M   Hacia el distribuidor

19M   Hacia el compresor del aire acondicionado

20M   Hacia la luz delantera derecha (Tipo 2)

21M   Hacia la luz delantera derecha (Tipo 1)

22M   Hacia la lámpara derecha del marcador lateral

23M   Hacia la lámpara de combinación delantera derecha

24M   Hacia la bocina alta

25M   Hacia el resistor (tacómetro)

26M   Hacia el arnés 1S de la transmisión

27M   Hacia el arnés 3S de la transmisión

28M   Hacia el arnés 2S de la transmisión

29M   Hacia el eslabón fusible (para el aire acondicionado)

30M   Hacia el eslabón fusible

31M   Hacia la conexión a tierra

32M   Hacia el interruptor de presión baja

33M   Hacia el motor del limpiaparabrisas

34M   Hacia el motor limpiador

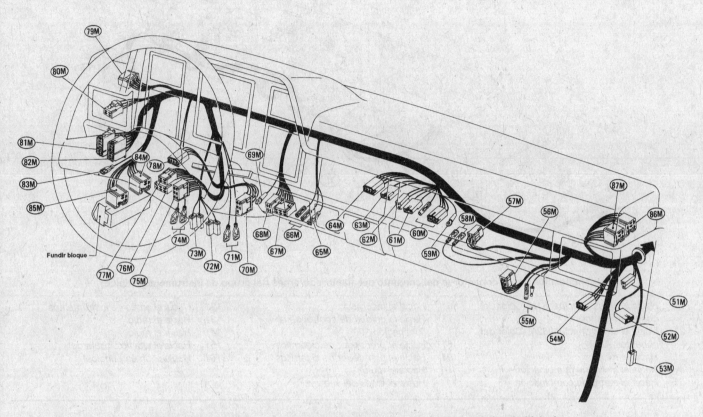

Identificación de los conectores interiores principales del alambrado/arnés (típico)

51M   Hacia el diodo (modelos con trans-
       misión automática)

52M   Hacia el cable de la luz del cuarto 1R

53M   Hacia el altavoz trasero derecho

54M   Conector opcional (para la calefac-
       ción)

55M   Hacia el motor del ventilador

56M   Hacia el resistor

57M   Hacia el relee del aire acondicionado

58M   Hacia el interruptor térmico

59M   Hacia la conexión a tierra

60M   Hacia el interruptor del ventilador

61M   Hacia la calefacción y la luz de ilumi-
       nación del panel de control del aire
       acondicionado

62M   Hacia el interruptor del compresor

63M   Hacia la luz de advertencia del aire
       acondicionado

64M   Hacia el arnés de la consola (para el
       medidor del voltímetro y la presión

del aceite) (4WD)

65M   Hacia el interruptor del freno de
       estacionamiento

66M   Hacia el interruptor de rebase (mod-
       elos con transmisión automática)

67M   Hacia el amplificador del limpiador
       intermitente

68M   Hacia el relee de la bocina

69M   Hacia la conexión a tierra

70M   Hacia el interruptor de la ignición

71M   Hacia el interruptor para la luz de los
       frenos

72M   Hacia la unidad de destellos de las
       luces de las señales intermitentes

73M   Hacia la unidad de destellos de las
       luces de las señales intermitentes de
       emergencia

74M   Hacia el interruptor del embrague

75M   Hacia el limpiador e interruptor de
       lavar

76M   Hacia el interruptor de las luces inte-
       riores

77M   Hacia el interruptor de las direc-
       cionales

78M   Hacia el interruptor de emergencia

79M   Hacia la unidad de advertencia de
       los cinturones de seguridad

80M   Conector opcional (para el descon-
       gelador de la ventana trasera 1D)

81M   Hacia el arneses de los instrumentos
       1 (Color del conector: blanco)

82M   Hacia el arneses de los instrumentos
       2 (Color del conector: Azul)

83M   Hacia el cerrojo

84M   Hacia el relee de las luces delanteras

85M   Hacia el relee de la calefacción

86M   Hacia el relee del estrangulador
       automático

87M   Hacia el relee de inhibidor (modelos
       con transmisión automática)

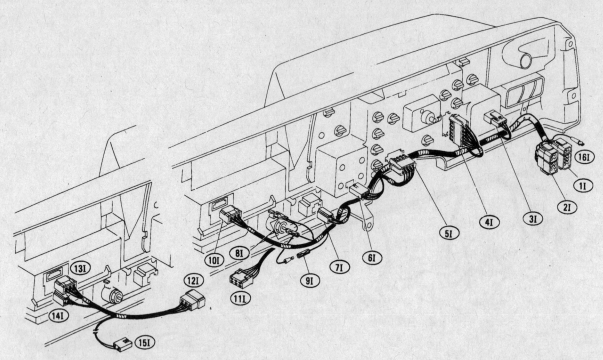

Identificación de los conectores del conjunto del alambrado/arnés del grupo de instrumentos (típico)

1I Hacia el arnés principal 81M (Color del conector: Blanco)	6I Hacia el tacómetro	12I Hacia el arnés de instrumentos
	7I Hacia la unidad de control de la iluminación	13I Hacia el radio
2I Hacia el arnés principal 82M (Color del conector: Azul)	8I Hacia el prendedor de cigarrillos	14I Hacia el radio
3I Hacia el reloj	9I Hacia el prendedor de cigarrillos	15I Hacia el alta voz izquierdo
4I Hacia el metro de combinación	10I Hacia el radio	16I Hacia el arnés principal
5I Hacia el metro de combinación	11I Hacia el arnés del alta voz	

Identificación de los conectores de conjunto del alambrado/arnés de chasis

1C Hacia el arnés principal 102M
2C Hacia la unidad emisora del tanque de combustible
3C Hacia el arnés de las luces traseras 1T
4C Hacia el interruptor de la caja de transferencia (4WD)
5C Hacia la bomba eléctrica de combustible

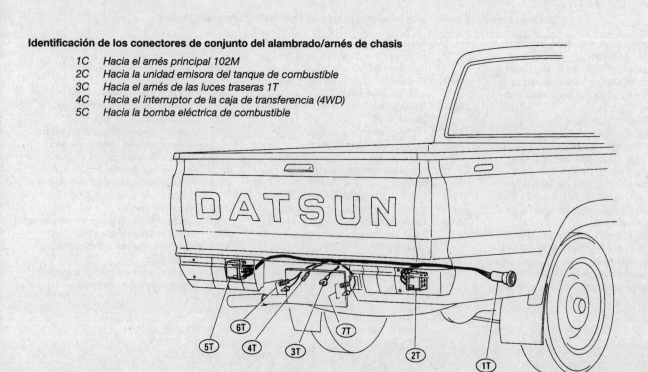

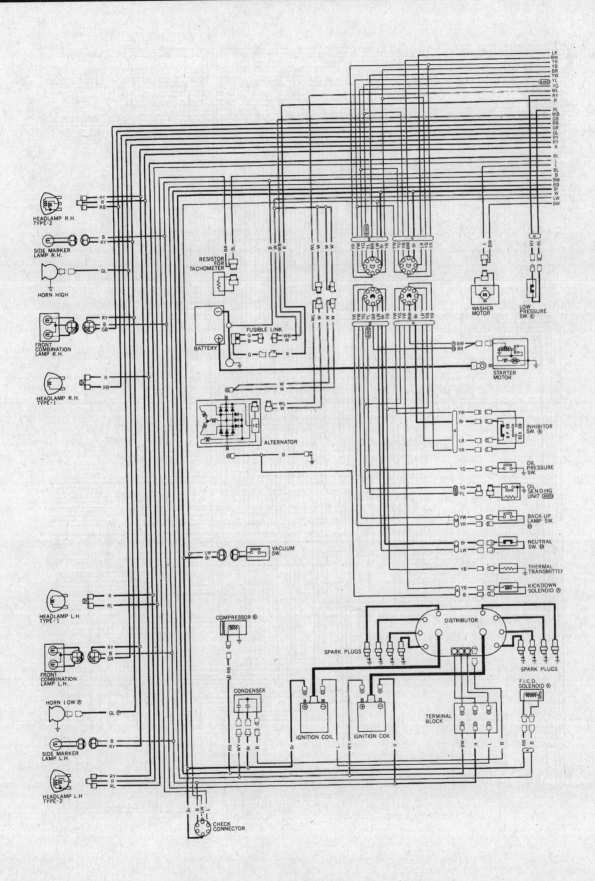

Esquema típico del alambrado del chasis (1 de 3)

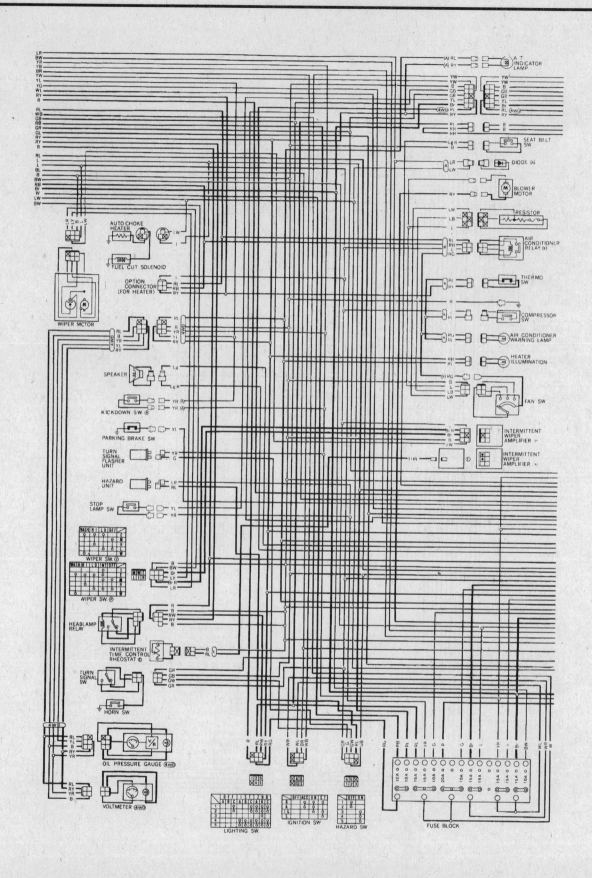

Esquema típico del alambrado del chasis (2 de 3)

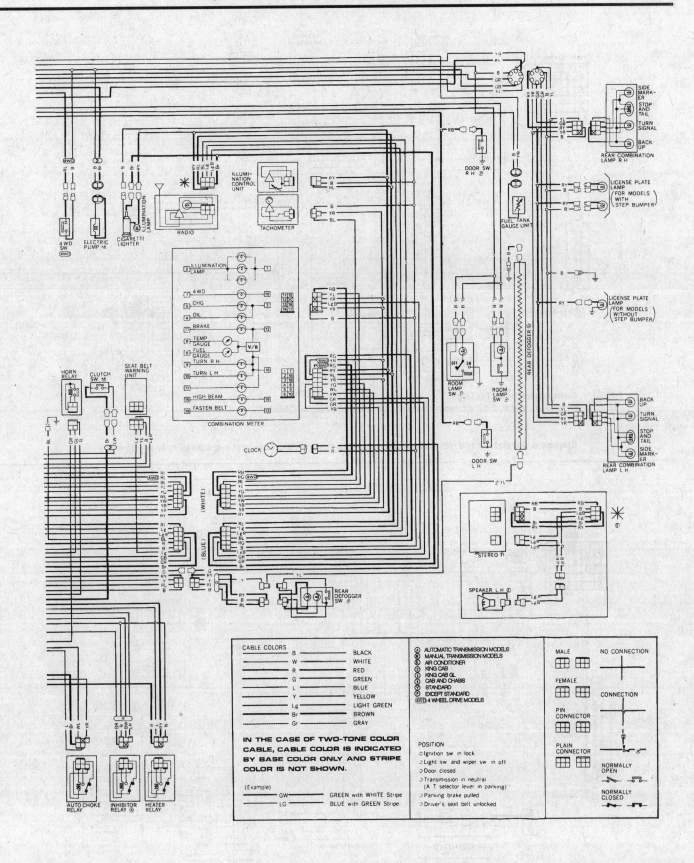

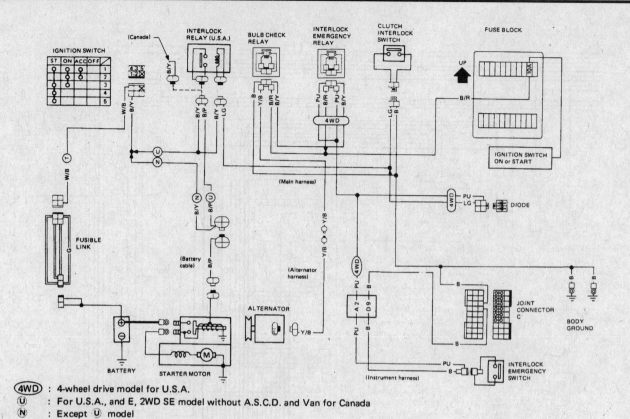

(4WD) : 4-wheel drive model for U.S.A.
(U) : For U.S.A., and E, 2WD SE model without A.S.C.D. and Van for Canada
(N) : Except (U) model

Esquema del alambrado del sistema de arranque (transmisión manual - modelos más modernos)

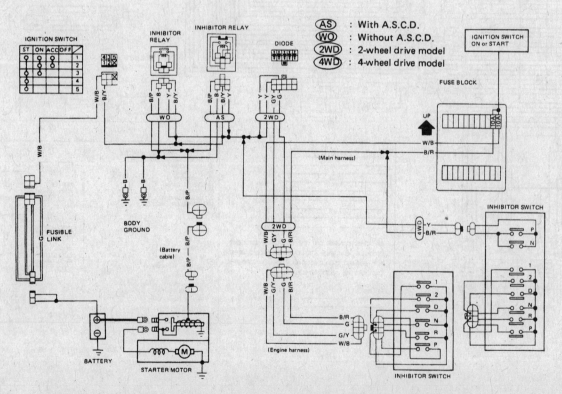

Esquema del alambrado del sistema de arranque (transmisión automática - modelos más modernos)

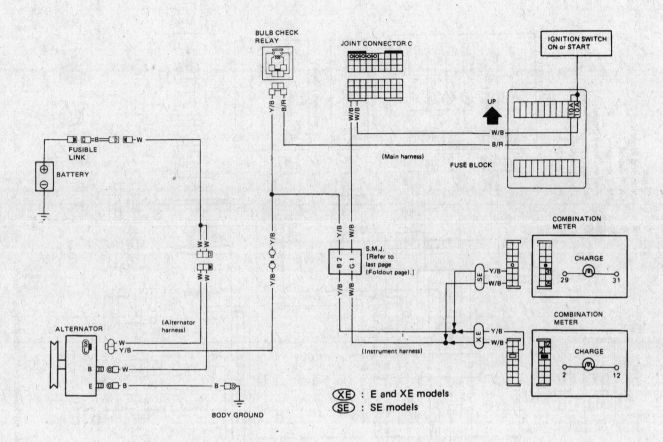

Esquema del alambrado del sistema de carga (modelos más modernos)

WIRE COLOR CODING

B	= Black	BR	= Brown
W	= White	OR	= Orange
R	= Red	P	= Pink
G	= Green	PU	= Purple
L	= Blue	GY	= Gray
Y	= Yellow	SB	= Sky Blue
LG	= Light Green		

When the wire color is striped, the base
color is given first, followed by the stripe
color as shown below:

Example: L/W = Blue with White Stripe

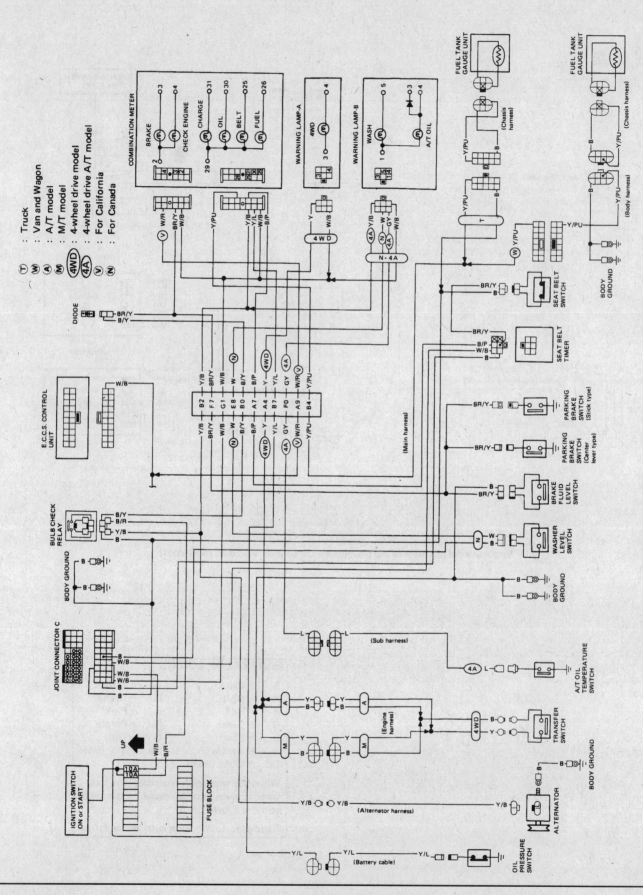

Luces de advertencia (modelos más modernos - típico)

Glosario

ABS	Frenos antibloqueantes	Choke	Estrangulador
A.I.R.	Regulador de la inyección de aire	Cigarette lighter	Encendedor de cigarros
Air conditioning	Aire acondicionado	Circ.	Circuito
AC	Aire acondicionado	Circuit breaker	Corta circuito
Acc	Accesorio	Clearance side	Marcador lateral
Accel	Acelerador	Clock	Reloj
Accessory	Accesorio	Close Loop	Ciclo cerrado
Accessory relay	Relé para los accesorios	Cluster	Agrupador de instrumentos
Adjustable	Ajustable	Clutch	Embrague
Advance	Avance	Code	Código
Air	Aire	Coil	Bobina
Air diverter valve	Válvula de desviación del aire	Colis	Bobinas
ALDL	Conector para extraer códigos	Cold	Frío
Alt	Alternador	Color	Color
Alternator	Alternador	Combination	Combinación
Amp	Amplificador	Comp	Compresor
Amplifier	Amplificador	Compresor	Compresor
Ann	Aniversario	Compresor switch	Interruptor del compresor
Antilock	Frenos antibloqueantes	Compt	Compartimiento
Ashtray	Cenicero	Computer	Computadora
AT	Transmisión automática	Cond	Condición
Auto	Automático	Conn	Conector
Auto choke	Estrangulador automático	Conns	Conectores
Aux	Auxiliar	Connector	Conector
AW	Ruedas de aleación	Contact	Contacto
AWD	Tracción en todas las ruedas	Control	Control
Back window opener	Abridor para la ventana trasera	Controller	Controlador
Backing	Retroceder	Conv	Convertible
Backup	Retroceso	Coolant	Anticongelante
Backup lamps	Luces de retroceso	Cooling fan	Ventilador de enfriamiento
Bat	Batería	Cooling SW	Interruptor para el ventilador de enfriamiento
Battery	Batería	Courtesy	Cortesía
Beam	Luz	CPE	Cupé
BK	Negro	Crash	Accidente
BK/O	Negro/Naranja	Cruise	Crucero
BK/W	Negro/Blanco	Ctrl	Control
Blk	Negro	Ctsy	Cortesia
Blower	Ventilador	Cut	Cortar
Blower motor	Motor del ventilador	Cutoff	Apagar
Blu	Azul	Cyl	Cilindros
Blwr	Ventilador	Dash panel	Tablero
Body ground	Tierra de la carrocería	Defog	Descongelador
Box	Caja	Detention	Detención
Brak	Freno	DFRS	Asientos traseros que se miran uno al otro
BRK	Freno	DG	Verde Oscuro
Brn	Café Obscuro	Diagnostic	Diagnosticar
Brn	Marrón	Diesel	Diesel
Bulb	Bombilla	Digital	Digital
Bumper	Defensa	Diode	Diodo
Buzzer	Zumbador	Dir	Direccionales
Bypass	Desvío	Direction	Dirección
Cab	Cabina	Dist.	Distribuidor
Canister purge	Purga del canasto de carbón	Distrib	Distribuidor
Carb	Carburador	Dk Blu	Azul Obscuro
Cargo	Cargo	Dk Grn	Verde Obscuro
Cass	Casete	DLX	De lujo
CC	Control de crucero	Dome light	Luz para el interior
Charge	Carga	Dome LP	Luz para el interior
Charging system	Sistema de carga	Door	Puerta
Check	Chequeo	Door locks	Cerrojos eléctricos
Check eng	Luz de Advertencia de la computadora	Door mirror	Retrovisores de la puerta
Chk	Chequear	Down	Baja

DR.	Puerta	Heavy	Pesado
Drive	Marcha/tracción	HEGO	Sensor de oxígeno para los gases de escape
Dsl	Diesel	HI Beam	Luces altas
Dual	Doble	HI/LO	Luces altas y bajas
EEC	Control electrónico del motor	High	Alto
ECCS system	Systema ECCS (sistema de control por	Horn	Corneta/bocina
	computadora para el motor)	Horns	Cornetas/bocinas
ECM	Modulo de control electrónico	HT, HDTP	Techo duro (techo sin el poste del centro)
EGR	Recirculación de los gases del escape	Htr Blo	Ventilador
Elect	Electrónico	Idle	Marcha mínima
Electric	Eléctrico	Ign	Ignición
Electric pump	Bomba eléctrica	Ignition	Ignición
Emission	Emisión	Ignition relay	Relé de la ignición
En.	Motor	Ignition sw.	Interruptor de la ignición/llave
Enable	Podrá	Ignition switch	Interruptor de la ignición/llave
Eng	Motor	Ignition system	Sistema de la ignición/llave
Engine	Motor	Inhibitor switch	Interruptor inhibidor
Engine control system	Sistema para el control del motor	Illum	Iluminación
Exc	Excelente	Illumination	Iluminación
Ext	Extendido	Immac	Inmaculado
Ext.	Exterior	In	En o adentro
Extended	Extendido	Ind	Indicador
Fac	Factoría	Indicator	Indicador
Fan	Ventilador	Inertia	Inercia
Fender	Guadafango	Injector	Inyector
FI	Inyección de combustible	Input	Entrada
Flasher	Intermitente	Inside	Adentro
Fluid	Fluido	Inst	Instrumento
Fog LT	Luces para la neblina	Instrument	Instrumento
Four	Cuatro	Inst cluster	Aglutinador de instrumentos
Frame	Chasis	Int	Interior
From	Desde	Interior	Interior
Front	Frente	Interlock	Trabar
Frt.	El frente	Internal	Interno
Fuel	Combustible	Intermittent	Intermitente
Fuel cut solenoide	Solenoide para el corte del combustible	Interval	Intervalos
Fuel level	Nivel del combustible	Ir. signal	Direccionales
Fuel pump	Bomba de combustible	Jamb	Jamba
Fus	Fusible	Joint	Acoplación
Fuse	Fusible	Jumper	Cable de empalme
Fuse block	Bloque de fusibles	Junction box	Caja de acoplamiento
Fuse panel	Panel de fusibles	Key	Llave
Fusible links	Eslabones térmicos	Kickdown	Rebase
FWD	Tracción en las cuatro ruedas	Kicker	Accionador
FWD	Tracción en las ruedas delanteras	L.H.	Lado izquierdo
Gauge	Reloj del tablero	Lamp	Luz/lampara
Gear	Engrane	LB	Azul Pálido
Gen	Generador	LB/PK	Azul Pálido/Rosado
Generator	Generador	LB/R	Azul Pálido/Rojo
Glove box	Guantera	Left	Izquierda
Glow	Iluminar	Level	Nivel
GLS RF	Techo de vidrio	Lever	Palanca
Gn	Verde	LG	Verde Pálido
Governor	Governador	LG/BK	Verde Pálido/Negro
Grd	Tierra	LG/R	Verde Pálido/Rojo
Green	Verde	LHD	Con volante a la mano izquierda
Grn	Verde	Lic	Placa/matricula
Gry	Gris	License	Placa/matricula
GY	Gris	Life	Vida
H SRRA	Páguete para la montaña	Light	Luz
Harn	Arnés	Lighter	Encendedor
Harness	Grupo de alambres	Lighting switch	Atenuador de las luces
Hazard	Peligro	Line	Línea
Hazard lamp	Luz de peligro	Link	Eslabon
Haz Flasher	Intermitente de emergencia	Located	Localisado
Head lamp	Faroles delanteros	Lock	Cerrado
Head lt	Faroles delanteros	Low	Baja
Headlamp	Luz delantera	Low Beam	Luces bajas
Heated	Calentado	LP	Azul Pálido
Heater	Calentador	LT	Luz

LTS	Luces		PS	Dirección de potencia
Lt Blu	Azul pálido		PU	Camioneta
Lt Brn	Marrón pálido		Pulse	Pulsación
Lt Grn	Verde pálido		Pump	Bomba
Lt Tan	Café pálido		PW	Ventanas eléctricas
LTHR	Piel (cuero)		Pwr	Fuerza
M/T	Transmisión manual		PWR	Voltaje
Main	Principal		R	Rojo
Main relay	Relé principal		R.H.	Lado derecho
Man	Manual		R/PK	Rojo/rosado
Magnetic	Magnetico		R/W	Rojo/Blanco
MAP	Presión absoluta del múltiple de admisión		R/Y	Rojo/Amarillo
Marker	Indicador		RABS	Frenos anti bloqueantes
Meter	Medidor		Radiator	Radiador
MI	Millaje		Radio	Radio
Mkr	Marcador		Rear	Atrás
Model	Modelo		Rear window defogger	Descongelador de la ventana trasera
Module	Modulo		Red	Rojo
Motor	Motor		Ref	Referencia
Multi-fuction SW	Interruptor de función múltiple		Regulator	Regulador
Neut	Neutral		Relay	Relé
Neutral	Neutral		Res	Resistencia
Neu.Sfty.Sw.	Interruptor de seguridad		Res	Resistor
Not used	No se usa		Resistor	Resistor
Off	Apagado		Right	Derecha
Oil	Aceite		Rly	Relé
Oil pressure	Presión de aceite		Rlys	Relees
Omitted	Omitido		Roof marker lps.	Luz para el techo
Only	Solamente		Room	Cuarto
Open Loop	Ciclo abierto		RSE	Paquete royal SE
Org	Naranja		Run	Correr
Orn	Naranja		Sac	Sacrificar
Output	Salida		Safety	Seguridad
Outside	Afuera		Seat belt	Cinturón de seguridad
Overdrive	Sobremarcha		Seat belt timer	Sincronizador de los cinturones de seguridad
OW	Ventana de opera		Seat belt warning	Advertencia de los cinturones de seguridad
OX	Oxigeno		Seat(s)	Capacidad para sentarse adicional
Oxygen	Oxigeno		SED	Sedan
Oxygen sensor	Sensor de oxigeno		Select	Seleccionar
P/B	Frenos de potencia		Send	Enviador
P/S	Dirección hidráulica		Sender	Enviador de señal
P/W	Morado/Blanco		Sens	Sensor
P/W	Ventanas eléctricas		Sensor	Sensor
Panel	Panel		Self-test output conn	Conector para la prueba de salida
Park	Estacionar		Servo	Servo
Parking	Estacionando		Shock absorber	Amortiguador
Parking brake	Frenos de estacionamiento		Shift	Cambio
PB	Frenos de potencia		Shut-off	Apagar
PCM	Módulo de control de la potencia del motor, (computadora)		Side	Lado
			Sig.	Indicador
PDL	Cierre de las puertas automáticos		Socket	Enchufe
PERF	Paquete de alto rendimiento		Sol.	Solenoide
Pick-up	Camioneta		Spark	Chispa
PK/LG	Rosado/Verde Pálido		Spd	Velocidades
PKG	Paquete		Speaker	Bocina
PLUG	Tapón		Spec	Especial
PM	Espejos eléctricos		Speed	Velocidad
Pnk	Rosado		Splice	Conector
Pos	Posición		Start	Arranque
POS	Positivo		Starter	Motor de arranque
Position	Posición		Starter motor	Motor de arranque
Power	Poder		Starter system	Sistema de arranque
Power antena	Antena eléctrica		Stop	Freno o limitador
Power door locks	Cierre de puertas eléctricos		Stop lamp	Luz del freno
Power seats	Asientos eléctricos		Strap	Correa
Power windows	Ventanas eléctricas		SW	Interruptor
Ppl	Morado		SWB	Distancia entre los dos ejes
Press	Presión		SWS	Interruptores
Pressure	Presión		Switch	Interruptor
Printed circuit	Circuito impreso		System	Sistema

T/LG	Café Pálido/Verde Pálido	Vehicle	Vehículo
Tachometer	Tacómetro	Volt Reg	Regulador de voltaje
Tail	Trasera	Voltage	Voltaje
Tail gate	Puerta trasera de cargo	Voltmeter	Voltímetro
Tan	Café Pálido	W	Con
Tank	Tanque	W/LB	Blanco/Azul Pálido
TCC	Embrague del par de torsión	W/O	Sin
Temp	Temperatura	W/S Washer	Bote para el limpiador del parabrisas
Term	Terminal	W/shield	Parabrisas
Terminal	Terminal	Warn	Peligro
Test	Prueba	Warning	Peligro
TFI	Pelicula integrada gruesa	Washer	Labador
Thermistor	Termistor	Water	Agua
Thermo	Termostato	Water temperature	Temperatura del agua
Throttle	Acelerador	WB	Distancia entre los ejes
Throttle pos sensor	Sensor de la posición del acelerador	WDO	Sin
Timer	Reloj	Wheel	Rueda
Timing	Tiempo	Whls	Ruedas
To sheet metal	A la carrocería	Wht	Blanco
Top	Arriba	Window	Ventana
Torque conv clutch	Embrague del par de torsión	Windshield	Parabrisas
Traffic	Tráfico	Windshield wiper	Windshield
Trailer	Remolque	Wiper	Limpia parabrisas
Trans	Transmisión	Wiper motor	Motor limpia parabrisas
Truck	Camión	Wire	Alambre
Turn signal lamps	Luces direccionales	Wiring	Alambrado
Two	Dos	With	Con
Unit	Unidad	Without	Sin
Used	Usado	Wrg.	Alambrado
Useful	Servible	Wrng	Peligro
Vac	Vacío	Y/LG	Amarillo/Verde Pálido
Vacuum	Vacío	Yel	Amarillo
Valve	Válvula		

CALIBRE DE LOS ALAMBRES Y COLOR DEL AISLAMIENTO

El calibre del alambre y el color del aislamiento están marcados en los esquemáticos para ayudar a identificar cada circuito. Cuando se marcan dos colores de aislamiento, el primero es el color general y el segundo es el color de la raya. Los alambres negros siempre son de tierra. El calibre de los alambres está dado en AWG (Calibre Americano de Alambres).

Colores para los alambres

Nota: *Cuando usted encuentre una combinación de letras, por ejemplo Ppl/Wht, las primeras letras (Ppl) indican el color del alambre, la línea que las separan quieren decir que el alambre tendrá una línea fina con un color (Wht), en este ejemplo el alambre sería de color Morado con una línea Blanca.*

B	Negro	Gry	Gris	Pk	Rosado
Bk	Negro	Gy	Gris	Pnk	Rosado
Blk	Negro	L	Pálido	Ppl	Morado
Blu	Azul	LBL	Azul pálido	R	Rojo
Brn	Café oscuro	Lg	Verde Pálido	Red	Rojo
D	Oscuro	Lt	Pálido	T	Café Pálido
DBL	Azul Oscuro	O	Naranja	Tan	Café Pálido
DG	Verde Oscuro	Or	Naranja	W	Blanco
G	Verde	Org	Naranja	Wht	Blanco
Gn	Verde	Orn	Naranja	Y	Amarillo
Grn	Verde	P	Morado	Yel	Amarillo

Índice

Manuales automotrices Haynes

NOTA: Si usted no puede encontrar su vehículo en esta lista, consulte con su distribuidor Haynes, para información de la producción más moderna.

ACURA
- 12020 Integra '86 thru '89 & Legend '86 thru '90
- 12021 Integra '90 thru '93 & Legend '91 thru '95
  Integra '94 thru '00 - see HONDA Civic (42025)
  MDX '01 thru '07 - see HONDA Pilot (42037)
- 12050 Acura TL all models '99 thru '08

AMC
  Jeep CJ - see JEEP (50020)
- 14020 Concord/Hornet/Gremlin/Spirit '70 thru '83
- 14025 (Renault) Alliance & Encore '83 thru '87

AUDI
- 15020 4000 all models '80 thru '87
- 15025 5000 all models '77 thru '83
- 15026 5000 all models '84 thru '88
  Audi A4 '96 thru '01 - see VW Passat (96023)
- 15030 Audi A4 '02 thru '08

AUSTIN
  Healey Sprite - see MG Midget (66015)

BMW
- 18020 3/5 Series '82 thru '92
- 18021 3 Series including Z3 models '92 thru '98
- 18022 3-Series incl. Z4 models '99 thru '05
- 18023 3-Series '06 thru '10
- 18025 320i all 4 cyl models '75 thru '83
- 18050 1500 thru 2002 except Turbo '59 thru '77

BUICK
- 19010 Buick Century '97 thru '05
  Century (front-wheel drive) - see GM (38005)
- 19020 Buick, Oldsmobile & Pontiac Full-size (Front wheel drive) '85 thru '05
- 19025 Buick, Oldsmobile & Pontiac Full-size (Rear wheel drive) '70 thru '90
- 19030 Mid-size Regal & Century '74 thru '87
  Regal - see GENERAL MOTORS (38010)
  Skyhawk - see GM (38030)
  Skylark - see GM (38020, 38025)
  Somerset - see GENERAL MOTORS (38025)

CADILLAC
- 21015 CTS & CTS-V '03 thru '12
- 21030 Cadillac Rear Wheel Drive '70 thru '93
  Cimarron, Eldorado & Seville - see GM (38015, 38030, 38031)

CHEVROLET
- 10305 Chevrolet Engine Overhaul Manual
- 24010 Astro & GMC Safari Mini-vans '85 thru '05
- 24015 Camaro V8 all models '70 thru '81
- 24016 Camaro all models '82 thru '92
  Cavalier - see GM (38015)
  Celebrity - see GM (38005)
- 24017 Camaro & Firebird '93 thru '02
- 24020 Chevelle, Malibu, El Camino '69 thru '87
- 24024 Chevette & Pontiac T1000 '76 thru '87
  Citation - see GENERAL MOTORS (38020)
- 24027 Colorado & GMC Canyon '04 thru '10
- 24032 Corsica/Beretta all models '87 thru '96
- 24040 Corvette all V8 models '68 thru '82
- 24041 Corvette all models '84 thru '96
- 24045 Full-size Sedans Caprice, Impala, Biscayne, Bel Air & Wagons '69 thru '90
- 24046 Impala SS & Caprice and Buick Roadmaster '91 thru '96
  Impala '00 thru '05 - see LUMINA (24048)
- 24047 Impala & Monte Carlo all models '06 thru '11
- 24048 Lumina '90 thru '94 - see GM (38010)
- 24048 Lumina & Monte Carlo '95 thru '05
  Lumina APV - see GM (38035)
- 24050 Luv Pick-up all 2WD & 4WD '72 thru '82
  Malibu - see GM (38026)
- 24055 Monte Carlo all models '70 thru '88
  Monte Carlo '95 thru '01 - see LUMINA
- 24059 Nova all V8 models '69 thru '79
- 24060 Nova/Geo Prizm '85 thru '92
- 24064 Pick-ups '67 thru '87 - Chevrolet & GMC
- 24065 Pick-ups '88 thru '98 - Chevrolet & GMC
- 24066 Pick-ups '99 thru '06 - Chevrolet & GMC
- 24067 Chevy Silverado & GMC Sierra '07 thru '12
- 24070 S-10 & GMC S-15 Pick-ups '82 thru '93
- 24071 S-10, Sonoma & Jimmy '94 thru '04
- 24072 Chevrolet TrailBlazer, GMC Envoy & Oldsmobile Bravada '02 thru '09
- 24075 Sprint '85 thru '88, Geo Metro '89 thru '01
- 24080 Vans - Chevrolet & GMC '68 thru '96
- 24081 Full-size Vans '96 thru '10

CHRYSLER
- 10310 Chrysler Engine Overhaul Manual
- 25015 Chrysler Cirrus, Dodge Stratus, Plymouth Breeze, '95 thru '00
- 25020 Full-size Front-Wheel Drive '88 thru '93
  K-Cars - see DODGE Aries (30008)
  Laser - see DODGE Daytona (30030)
- 25025 Chrysler LHS, Concorde & New Yorker, Dodge Intrepid, Eagle Vision, '93 thru '97
- 25026 Chrysler LHS, Concorde, 300M, Dodge Intrepid '98 thru '04
- 25027 Chrysler 300, Dodge Charger & Magnum '05 thru '09
- 25030 Chrysler/Plym. Mid-size '82 thru '95
  Rear-wheel Drive - see DODGE (30050)
- 25035 PT Cruiser all models '01 thru '10
- 25040 Chrysler Sebring '95 thru '06, Dodge Stratus '01 thru '06, Dodge Avenger '95 thru '00

DATSUN
- 28005 200SX all models '80 thru '83
- 28007 B-210 all models '73 thru '78
- 28009 210 all models '78 thru '82
- 28012 240Z, 260Z & 280Z Coupe '70 thru '78
- 28014 280ZX Coupe & 2+2 '79 thru '83
  300ZX - see NISSAN (72010)
- 28018 510 & PL521 Pick-up '68 thru '73
- 28020 510 all models '78 thru '81
- 28022 620 Series Pick-up all models '73 thru '79
  720 Series Pick-up - see NISSAN (72030)
- 28025 810/Maxima all gas models '77 thru '84

DODGE
  400 & 600 - see CHRYSLER (25030)
- 30008 Aries & Plymouth Reliant '81 thru '89
- 30010 Caravan & Ply. Voyager '84 thru '95
- 30011 Caravan & Ply. Voyager '96 thru '02
- 30012 Challenger/Plymouth Saporro '78 thru '83
  Challenger '67-'76 - see DART (30025)
- 30013 Caravan, Chrysler Voyager, Town & Country '03 thru '07
- 30016 Colt/Plymouth Champ '78 thru '87
- 30020 Dakota Pick-ups all models '87 thru '96
- 30021 Durango '98 thru '99, Dakota '97 thru '99
- 30022 Durango '00 thru '03, Dakota '00 thru '04
- 30023 Durango '04 thru '09, Dakota '05 thru '11
- 30025 Dart, Challenger/Plymouth Barracuda & Valiant 6 cyl models '67 thru '76
- 30030 Daytona & Chrysler Laser '84 thru '89
  Intrepid - see Chrysler (25025, 25026)
- 30034 Dodge & Plymouth Neon '95 thru '99
- 30035 Omni & Plymouth Horizon '78 thru '90
- 30036 Dodge and Plymouth Neon '00 thru '05
- 30040 Pick-ups all full-size models '74 thru '93
- 30041 Pick-ups all full-size models '94 thru '01
- 30042 Pick-ups full-size models '02 thru '08
- 30045 Ram 50/D50 Pick-ups & Raider and Plymouth Arrow Pick-ups '79 thru '93
- 30050 Dodge/Ply./Chrysler RWD '71 thru '89
- 30055 Shadow/Plymouth Sundance '87 thru '94
- 30060 Spirit & Plymouth Acclaim '89 thru '95
- 30065 Vans - Dodge & Plymouth '71 thru '03

EAGLE
  Talon - see MITSUBISHI (68030, 68031)
  Vision - see CHRYSLER (25025)

FIAT
- 34010 124 Sport Coupe & Spider '68 thru '78
- 34025 X1/9 all models '74 thru '80

FORD
- 10320 Ford Engine Overhaul Manual
- 10355 Ford Automatic Transmission Overhaul
- 11500 Mustang '64-1/2 thru '70 Restoration Guide
- 36004 Aerostar Mini-vans '86 thru '97
  Aspire - see FORD Festiva (36030)
- 36006 Contour/Mercury Mystique '95 thru '00
- 36008 Courier Pick-up all models '72 thru '82
- 36012 Crown Victoria & Mercury Grand Marquis '88 thru '10
- 36016 Escort/Mercury Lynx '81 thru '90
- 36020 Escort/Mercury Tracer '91 thru '02
  Expedition - see FORD Pick-up (36059)
- 36022 Escape & Mazda Tribute '01 thru '11
- 36024 Explorer & Mazda Navajo '91 thru '01
- 36025 Explorer/Mercury Mountaineer '02 thru '10
- 36028 Fairmont & Mercury Zephyr '78 thru '83
- 36030 Festiva & Aspire '88 thru '97
- 36032 Fiesta all models '77 thru '80
- 36034 Focus all models '00 thru '11
- 36036 Ford & Mercury Full-size '75 thru '87
- 36044 Ford & Mercury Mid-size '75 thru '86
- 36045 Ford Fusion & Mercury Milan '06 thru '10
- 36048 Mustang V8 all models '64-1/2 thru '73
- 36049 Mustang II 4 cyl & V8 '74 thru '78
- 36050 Mustang & Mercury Capri '79 thru '93
- 36051 Mustang all models '94 thru '04
- 36052 Mustang '05 thru '10
- 36054 Pick-ups and Bronco '73 thru '79
- 36058 Pick-ups and Bronco '80 thru '96
- 36059 Pick-ups & Expedition '97 thru '09
- 36060 Super Duty Pick-up, Excursion '99 thru '10
- 36061 F-150 full-size '04 thru '10
- 36062 Pinto & Mercury Bobcat '75 thru '80
- 36066 Probe all models '89 thru '92
  Probe '93 thru '97 - see MAZDA 626 (61042)
- 36070 Ranger/Bronco II gas models '83 thru '92
- 36071 Ford Ranger '93 thru '10 &
  Mazda Pick-ups '94 thru '09
- 36074 Taurus & Mercury Sable '86 thru '95
- 36075 Taurus & Mercury Sable '96 thru '01
- 36078 Tempo & Mercury Topaz '84 thru '94
- 36082 Thunderbird/Mercury Cougar '83 thru '88
- 36086 Thunderbird/Mercury Cougar '89 thru '97
- 36090 Vans all V8 Econoline models '69 thru '91
- 36094 Vans full size '92 thru '10
- 36097 Windstar Mini-van '95 thru '07

GENERAL MOTORS
- 10360 GM Automatic Transmission Overhaul
- 38005 Buick Century, Chevrolet Celebrity, Olds Cutlass Ciera & Pontiac 6000 '82 thru '96
- 38010 Buick Regal, Chevrolet Lumina, Oldsmobile Cutlass Supreme & Pontiac Grand Prix front wheel drive '88 thru '07
- 38015 Buick Skyhawk, Cadillac Cimarron, Chevrolet Cavalier, Oldsmobile Firenza Pontiac J-2000 & Sunbird '82 thru '94
- 38016 Chevrolet Cavalier/Pontiac Sunfire '95 thru '05
- 38017 Chevrolet Cobalt & Pontiac G5 '05 thru '11
- 38020 Buick Skylark, Chevrolet Citation, Olds Omega, Pontiac Phoenix '80 thru '85
- 38025 Buick Skylark & Somerset, Olds Achieva, Calais & Pontiac Grand Am '85 thru '98
- 38026 Chevrolet Malibu, Olds Alero & Cutlass, Pontiac Grand Am '97 thru '03
- 38027 Chevrolet Malibu '04 thru '10
- 38030 Cadillac Eldorado & Oldsmobile Toronado '71 thru '85, Seville '80 thru '85, Buick Riviera '79 thru '85
- 38031 Cadillac Eldorado & Seville '86 thru '91, DeVille & Buick Riviera '86 thru '93, Fleetwood & Olds Toronado '86 thru '92
- 38032 DeVille '94 thru '05, Seville '92 thru '04 Cadillac DTS '06 thru '10
- 38035 Chevrolet Lumina APV, Olds Silhouette & Pontiac Trans Sport '90 thru '96
- 38036 Chevrolet Venture, Olds Silhouette, Pontiac Trans Sport & Montana '97 thru '05
  GM Full-size RWD - see BUICK (19025)
- 38040 Chevrolet Equinox '05 thru '09 Pontiac Torrent '06 thru '09
- 38070 Chevrolet HHR '06 thru '11

GEO
  Metro - see CHEVROLET Sprint (24075)
  Prizm - see CHEVROLET (24060) or TOYOTA (92036)
- 40030 Storm all models '90 thru '93
  Tracker - see SUZUKI Samurai (90010)

GMC
  Vans & Pick-ups - see CHEVROLET

HONDA
- 42010 Accord CVCC all models '76 thru '83
- 42011 Accord all models '84 thru '89
- 42012 Accord all models '90 thru '93
- 42013 Accord all models '94 thru '97
- 42014 Accord all models '98 thru '02
- 42015 Accord '03 thru '07
- 42020 Civic 1200 all models '73 thru '79
- 42021 Civic 1300 & 1500 CVCC '80 thru '83
- 42022 Civic 1500 CVCC all models '75 thru '79
- 42023 Civic all models '84 thru '91
- 42024 Civic & del Sol '92 thru '95
- 42025 Civic '96 thru '00, CR-V '97 thru '01, Acura Integra '94 thru '00
- 42026 Civic '01 thru '10, CR-V '02 thru '09

HYUNDAI
- 43010 Elantra all models '96 thru '10
- 43015 Excel & Accent all models '86 thru '09
- 43050 Santa Fe all models '01 thru '06
- 43055 Sonata all models '99 thru '08

INFINITI
  G35 '03 thru '08 - see NISSAN 350Z (72011)

ISUZU
  Hombre - see CHEVROLET S-10 (24071)
- 47017 Rodeo, Amigo & Honda Passport '89 thru '02
- 47020 Trooper '84 thru '91, Pick-up '81 thru '93

JAGUAR
- 49010 XJ6 all 6 cyl models '68 thru '86
- 49011 XJ6 all models '88 thru '94
- 49015 XJ12 & XJS all 12 cyl models '72 thru '85

JEEP
- 50010 Cherokee, Comanche & Wagoneer Limited all models '84 thru '01
- 50020 CJ all models '49 thru '86
- 50025 Grand Cherokee all models '93 thru '04
- 50026 Grand Cherokee '05 thru '09
- 50029 Grand Wagoneer & Pick-up '72 thru '91
- 50030 Wrangler all models '87 thru '11
- 50035 Liberty '02 thru '07

KIA
- 54050 Optima '01 thru '10
- 54070 Sephia '94 thru '01, Spectra '00 thru '09, Sportage '05 thru '10

LEXUS
  ES 300/330 - see TOYOTA Camry (92007) (92006)
  RX 330 - see TOYOTA Highlander (92095)

LINCOLN
  Navigator - see FORD Pick-up (36059)
- 59010 Rear Wheel Drive all models '70 thru '10

MAZDA
- 61010 GLC (rear wheel drive) '77 thru '83
- 61011 GLC (front wheel drive) '81 thru '85
- 61012 Mazda3 '04 thru '11
- 61015 323 & Protegé '90 thru '03
- 61016 MX-5 Miata '90 thru '09
- 61020 MPV all models '89 thru '98
  Navajo - see Ford Explorer (36024)
- 61030 Pick-ups '72 thru '93
  Pick-ups '94 on - see Ford (36071)
- 61035 RX-7 all models '79 thru '85
- 61036 RX-7 all models '86 thru '91
- 61040 626 (rear wheel drive) '79 thru '82
- 61041 626 & MX-6 (front wheel drive) '83 thru '92
- 61042 626 '93 thru '01, & MX-6/Ford Probe '93 thru '02
- 61043 Mazda6 '03 thru '11

MERCEDES-BENZ
- 63012 123 Series Diesel '76 thru '85
- 63015 190 Series 4-cyl gas models, '84 thru '88
- 63020 230, 250 & 280 6 cyl sohc '68 thru '72
- 63025 280 123 Series gas models '77 thru '81
- 63030 350 & 450 all models '71 thru '80
- 63040 C-Class: C230/C240/C280/C320/C350 '01 thru '07

MERCURY
- 64200 Villager & Nissan Quest '93 thru '01
  All other titles, see FORD listing.

MG
- 66010 MGB Roadster & GT Coupe '62 thru '80
- 66015 MG Midget & Austin Healey Sprite Roadster '58 thru '80

MINI
- 67020 Mini '02 thru '11

MITSUBISHI
- 68020 Cordia, Tredia, Galant, Precis & Mirage '83 thru '93
- 68030 Eclipse, Eagle Talon & Plymouth Laser '90 thru '94
- 68031 Eclipse '95 thru '05, Eagle Talon '95 thru '98
- 68035 Galant '94 thru '10
- 68040 Pick-up '83 thru '96, Montero '83 thru '93

NISSAN
- 72010 300ZX all models incl. Turbo '84 thru '89
- 72011 350Z & Infiniti G35 all models '03 thru '08
- 72015 Altima all models '93 thru '06
- 72016 Altima '07 thru '10
- 72020 Maxima all models '85 thru '92
- 72021 Maxima all models '93 thru '01
- 72025 Murano '03 thru '10
- 72030 Pick-ups '80 thru '97, Pathfinder '87 thru '95
- 72031 Frontier Pick-up, Xterra, Pathfinder '96 thru '04
- 72032 Frontier & Xterra '05 thru '11
- 72040 Pulsar all models '83 thru '86
- 72050 Sentra all models '82 thru '94
- 72051 Sentra & 200SX all models '95 thru '06
- 72060 Stanza all models '82 thru '90
- 72070 Titan pick-ups '04 thru '10, Armada '05 thru '10

OLDSMOBILE
- 73015 Cutlass '74 thru '88
  For other OLDSMOBILE titles, see BUICK, CHEVROLET or GM listings.

PLYMOUTH
  For PLYMOUTH titles, see DODGE.

PONTIAC
- 79008 Fiero all models '84 thru '88
- 79018 Firebird V8 models except Turbo '70 thru '81
- 79019 Firebird all models '82 thru '92
- 79025 G6 all models '05 thru '09
- 79040 Mid-size Rear-wheel Drive '70 thru '87
  Vibe '03 thru '11 - see TOYOTA Matrix (92060)
  For other PONTIAC titles, see BUICK, CHEVROLET or GM listings.

PORSCHE
- 80020 911 Coupe & Targa models '65 thru '89
- 80025 914 all 4 cyl models '69 thru '76
- 80030 924 all models incl. Turbo '76 thru '82
- 80035 944 all models incl. Turbo '83 thru '89

RENAULT
  Alliance, Encore - see AMC (14020)

SAAB
- 84010 900 including Turbo '79 thru '88

SATURN
- 87010 Saturn all S-series models '91 thru '02
- 87011 Saturn Ion '03 thru '07
- 87020 Saturn all L-series models '00 thru '04
- 87040 Saturn VUE '02 thru '07

SUBARU
- 89002 1100, 1300, 1400 & 1600 '71 thru '79
- 89003 1600 & 1800 2WD & 4WD '80 thru '94
- 89100 Legacy models '90 thru '99
- 89101 Legacy & Forester '00 thru '06

SUZUKI
- 90010 Samurai/Sidekick/Geo Tracker '86 thru '01

TOYOTA
- 92005 Camry all models '83 thru '91
- 92006 Camry all models '92 thru '96
- 92007 Camry/Avalon/Solara/Lexus ES 300 '97 thru '01
- 92008 Toyota Camry, Avalon and Solara & Lexus ES 300/330 all models '02 thru '06
- 92009 Camry '07 thru '11
- 92015 Celica Rear Wheel Drive '71 thru '85
- 92020 Celica Front Wheel Drive '86 thru '99
- 92025 Celica Supra all models '79 thru '92
- 92030 Corolla all models '75 thru '79
- 92032 Corolla rear wheel drive models '80 thru '87
- 92035 Corolla front wheel drive models '84 thru '92
- 92036 Corolla & Geo Prizm '93 thru '02
- 92037 Corolla models '03 thru '11
- 92040 Corolla Tercel all models '80 thru '82
- 92045 Corona all models '74 thru '82
- 92050 Cressida all models '78 thru '82
- 92055 Land Cruiser FJ40/43/45/55 '68 thru '82
- 92056 Land Cruiser FJ60/62/80/FZJ80 '80 thru '96
- 92060 Matrix & Pontiac Vibe '03 thru '11
- 92065 MR2 all models '85 thru '87
- 92070 Pick-up all models '69 thru '78
- 92075 Pick-up all models '79 thru '95
- 92076 Tacoma, 4Runner & T100 '93 thru '04
- 92077 Tacoma all models '05 thru '09
- 92078 Tundra '00 thru '06, Sequoia '01 thru '07
- 92079 4Runner all models '03 thru '09
- 92080 Previa all models '91 thru '95
- 92081 Prius '01 thru '08
- 92082 RAV4 all models '96 thru '10
- 92085 Tercel all models '87 thru '94
- 92090 Sienna all models '98 thru '09
- 92095 Highlander & Lexus RX-330 '99 thru '07

TRIUMPH
- 94007 Spitfire all models '62 thru '81
- 94010 TR7 all models '75 thru '81

VW
- 96008 Beetle & Karmann Ghia '54 thru '79
- 96009 New Beetle '98 thru '11
- 96016 Rabbit, Jetta, Scirocco, & Pick-up gas models '75 thru '92 & Convertible '80 thru '92
- 96017 Golf, GTI & Jetta '93 thru '98, Cabrio '95 thru '02
- 96018 Golf, GTI & Jetta '99 thru '05
- 96019 Jetta, Rabbit, GTI & Golf '05 thru '11
- 96020 Rabbit, Jetta, Pick-up diesel '77 thru '84
- 96023 Passat '98 thru '05, Audi A4 '96 thru '01
- 96030 Transporter 1600 all models '68 thru '79
- 96035 Transporter 1700, 1800, 2000 '72 thru '79
- 96040 Type 3 1500 & 1600 '63 thru '73
- 96045 Vanagon air-cooled models '80 thru '83

VOLVO
- 97010 120, 130 Series & 1800 Sports '61 thru '73
- 97015 140 Series all models '66 thru '74
- 97020 240 Series all models '76 thru '93
- 97040 740 & 760 Series all models '82 thru '88

TECHBOOK MANUALS
- 10205 Automotive Computer Codes
- 10206 OBD-II & Electronic Engine Management
- 10210 Automotive Emissions Control Manual
- 10215 Fuel Injection Manual, '78 thru '85
- 10220 Fuel Injection Manual, '86 thru '99
- 10225 Holley Carburetor Manual
- 10230 Rochester Carburetor Manual
- 10240 Weber/Zenith/Stromberg/SU Carburetor
- 10305 Chevrolet Engine Overhaul Manual
- 10310 Chrysler Engine Overhaul Manual
- 10320 Ford Engine Overhaul Manual
- 10330 GM and Ford Diesel Engine Repair
- 10333 Engine Performance Manual
- 10340 Small Engine Repair Manual
- 10345 Suspension, Steering & Driveline
- 10355 Ford Automatic Transmission Overhaul
- 10360 GM Automatic Transmission Overhaul
- 10405 Automotive Body Repair & Painting
- 10410 Automotive Brake Manual
- 10415 Automotive Detailing Manual
- 10420 Automotive Electrical Manual
- 10425 Automotive Heating & Air Conditioning
- 10430 Automotive Reference Dictionary
- 10435 Automotive Tools Manual
- 10440 Used Car Buying Guide
- 10445 Welding Manual
- 10450 ATV Basics
- 10452 Scooters 50cc to 250cc

SPANISH MANUALS
- 98903 Reparación de Carrocería & Pintura
- 98904 Manual de Carburador Modelos Holley & Rochester
- 98905 Códigos Automotrices de la Computadora
- 98906 OBD-II & Sistemas de Control Electrónico del Motor
- 98910 Frenos Automotriz
- 98913 Electricidad Automotriz
- 98915 Inyección de Combustible '86 al '99
- 99040 Chevrolet & GMC Camionetas '67 al '87
- 99041 Chevrolet & GMC Camionetas '88 al '98
- 99042 Chevrolet Camionetas Cerradas '68 al '95
- 99043 Chevrolet/GMC Camionetas '94 al '04
- 99048 Chevrolet/GMC Camionetas '99 al '06
- 99055 Dodge Caravan/Ply. Voyager '84 al '95
- 99075 Ford Camionetas y Bronco '80 al '94
- 99076 Ford F-150 '97 al '09
- 99077 Ford Camionetas Cerradas '69 al '91
- 99088 Ford Modelos de Tamaño Mediano '75 al '86
- 99089 Ford Camionetas Ranger '93 al '10
- 99091 Ford Taurus & Mercury Sable '86 al '95
- 99095 GM Modelos de Tamaño Grande '70 al '90
- 99100 GM Modelos de Tamaño Mediano '70 al '88
- 99110 Jeep Cherokee, Wagoneer & Comanche '84 al '00
- 99110 Nissan Camionetas & Pathfinder '80 al '96
- 99118 Nissan Sentra '82 al '94
- 99125 Toyota Camionetas y 4-Runner '79 al '95

Sobre 100 manuales de motocicletas también están incluidos

7-12